to help with course and exam prep!

Online Learning Center (OLC). Please visit **www.mhhe.com/rwj**.

More

Links to McGraw-Hill/Irwin's exclusive free study tools such as *Corporate Finance Online* and *Finance Around the World* are also available on the OLC. Offering exercises and discussion questions on key corporate finance and global finance concepts, these programs are great practice to help master your course.

Standard & Poor's Educational Version of Market Insight

A free (with each new text purchased) exclusive partnership through McGraw-Hill/Irwin and the Institutional Market Services division of Standard & Poor's allows you to access this rich online database. Containing six years of fundamental financial data for over 1,000 companies, you can use this database to research and help answer the corresponding end-of-chapter S&P problems. For more details and to register, please see the bound-in card inside the front cover of this text or visit **www.mhhe.com/edumarketinsight**.

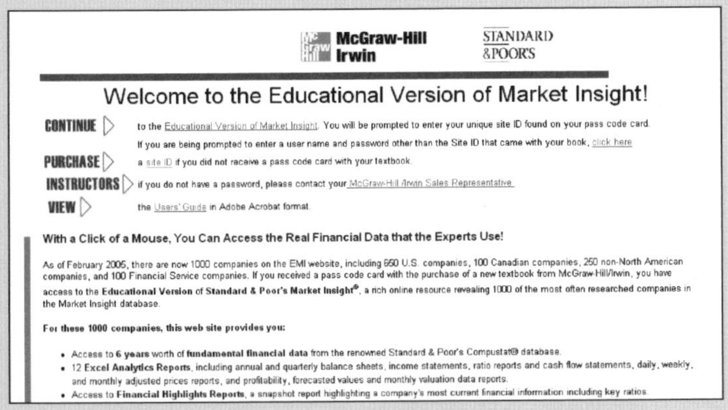

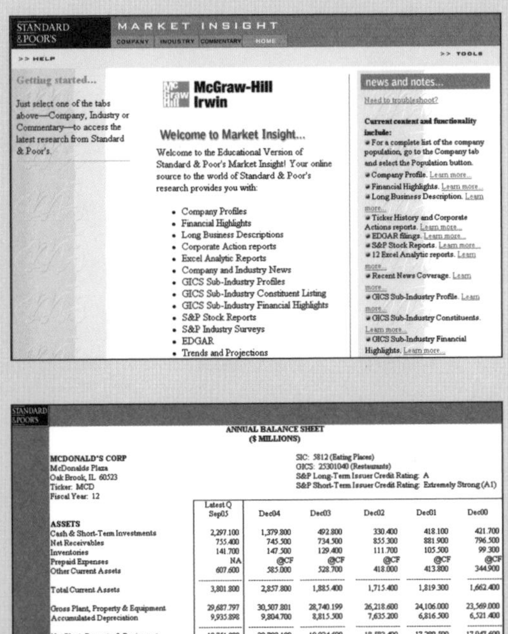

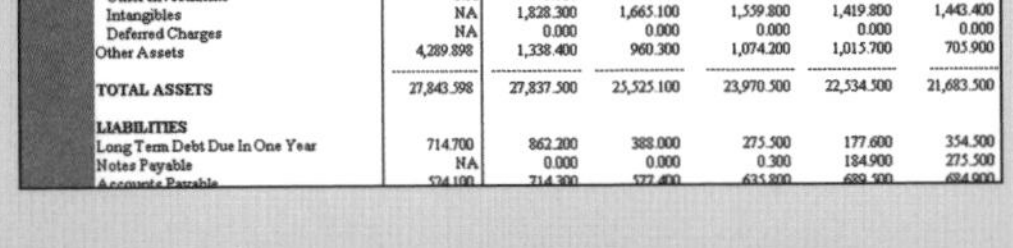
STANDARD &POOR'S

ANNUAL BALANCE SHEET
($ MILLIONS)

MCDONALD'S CORP
McDonalds Plaza
Oak Brook, IL 60523
Ticker: MCD
Fiscal Year: 12

SIC: 5812 (Eating Places)
GICS: 25301040 (Restaurants)
S&P Long-Term Issuer Credit Rating: A
S&P Short-Term Issuer Credit Rating: Extremely Strong (A1)

	Latest Q Sep05	Dec04	Dec03	Dec02	Dec01	Dec00
ASSETS						
Cash & Short-Term Investments	2,297.100	1,379.800	492.800	330.400	418.100	421.700
Net Receivables	755.400	745.500	734.500	855.300	881.900	796.500
Inventories	141.700	147.500	129.400	111.700	105.500	99.300
Prepaid Expenses	NA	@CF	@CF	@CF	@CF	@CF
Other Current Assets	607.600	585.000	528.700	418.000	413.800	344.900
Total Current Assets	3,801.800	2,857.800	1,885.400	1,715.400	1,819.300	1,662.400
Gross Plant, Property & Equipment	29,687.797	30,507.801	28,740.199	26,218.600	24,106.000	23,569.000
Accumulated Depreciation	9,935.898	9,804.700	8,815.500	7,635.200	6,816.500	6,521.400
Net Plant, Property & Equipment	19,751.898	20,703.100	19,924.699	18,583.400	17,289.500	17,047.600
Investments at Equity	NA	1,109.900	1,089.600	1,037.700	990.200	824.200
Other Investments	NA	0.000	0.000	0.000	0.000	0.000
Intangibles	NA	1,828.300	1,665.100	1,559.800	1,419.800	1,443.400
Deferred Charges	NA	0.000	0.000	0.000	0.000	0.000
Other Assets	4,289.898	1,338.400	960.300	1,074.200	1,015.700	705.900
TOTAL ASSETS	27,843.598	27,837.500	25,525.100	23,970.500	22,534.500	21,683.500
LIABILITIES						
Long Term Debt Due In One Year	714.700	862.200	388.000	275.500	177.600	354.500
Notes Payable	NA	0.000	0.000	0.300	184.900	275.500

CORPORATE FINANCE
CORE PRINCIPLES & APPLICATIONS

The McGraw-Hill/Irwin Series in Finance, Insurance, and Real Estate

Stephen A. Ross
Franco Modigliani Professor of Finance and Economics
Sloan School of Management
Massachusetts Institute of Technology
Consulting Editor

FINANCIAL MANAGEMENT

Adair
Excel Applications for Corporate Finance
First Edition

Benninga and Sarig
Corporate Finance: A Valuation Approach

Block and Hirt
Foundations of Financial Management
Eleventh Edition

Brealey, Myers, and Allen
Principles of Corporate Finance
Eighth Edition

Brealey, Myers, and Marcus
Fundamentals of Corporate Finance
Fifth Edition

Brooks
FinGame Online 4.0

Bruner
Case Studies in Finance: Managing for Corporate Value Creation
Fifth Edition

Chew
The New Corporate Finance: Where Theory Meets Practice
Third Edition

Chew and Gillan
Corporate Governance at the Crossroads: A Book of Readings
First Edition

DeMello
Cases in Finance
Second Edition

Grinblatt and Titman
Financial Markets and Corporate Strategy
Second Edition

Helfert
Techniques of Financial Analysis: A Guide to Value Creation
Eleventh Edition

Higgins
Analysis for Financial Management
Eighth Edition

Kester, Ruback, and Tufano
Case Problems in Finance
Twelfth Edition

Ross, Westerfield, and Jaffe
Corporate Finance
Seventh Edition

Ross, Westerfield, Jaffe, and Jordan
Corporate Finance: Core Principles and Applications
First Edition

Ross, Westerfield, and Jordan
Essentials of Corporate Finance
Fifth Edition

Ross,Westerfield, and Jordan
Fundamentals of Corporate Finance
Seventh Edition

Shefrin
Behavioral Corporate Finance: Decisions that Create Value
First Edition

Smith
The Modern Theory of Corporate Finance
Second Edition

White
Financial Analysis with an Electronic Calculator
Sixth Edition

INVESTMENTS

Bodie, Kane, and Marcus
Essentials of Investments
Sixth Edition

Bodie, Kane, and Marcus
Investments
Sixth Edition

Cohen, Zinbarg, and Zeikel
Investment Analysis and Portfolio Management
Fifth Edition

Corrado and Jordan
Fundamentals of Investments: Valuation and Management
Third Edition

Hirt and Block
Fundamentals of Investment Management
Eighth Edition

FINANCIAL INSTITUTIONS AND MARKETS

Cornett and Saunders
Fundamentals of Financial Institutions Management

Rose and Hudgins
Bank Management and Financial Services
Sixth Edition

Rose and Marquis
Money and Capital Markets: Financial Institutions and Instruments in a Global Marketplace
Ninth Edition

Santomero and Babbel
Financial Markets, Instruments, and Institutions
Second Edition

Saunders and Cornett
Financial Institutions Management: A Risk Management Approach
Fifth Edition

Saunders and Cornett
Financial Markets and Institutions: An Introduction to the Risk Management Approach
Third Edition

INTERNATIONAL FINANCE

Beim and Calomiris
Emerging Financial Markets

Eun and Resnick
International Financial Management
Fourth Edition

Kuemmerle
Case Studies in International Entrepreneurship: Managing and Financing Ventures in the Global Economy
First Edition

Levich
International Financial Markets: Prices and Policies
Second Edition

REAL ESTATE

Brueggeman and Fisher
Real Estate Finance and Investments
Twelfth Edition

Corgel, Ling, and Smith
Real Estate Perspectives: An Introduction to Real Estate
Fourth Edition

Ling and Archer
Real Estate Principles: A Value Approach
First Edition

FINANCIAL PLANNING AND INSURANCE

Allen, Melone, Rosenbloom, and Mahoney
Pension Planning: Pension, Profit-Sharing, and Other Deferred Compensation Plans
Ninth Edition

Altfest
Personal Financial Planning
First Edition

Crawford
Life and Health Insurance Law
Eighth Edition (LOMA)

Harrington and Niehaus
Risk Management and Insurance
Second Edition

Hirsch
Casualty Claim Practice
Sixth Edition

Kapoor, Dlabay, and Hughes
Focus on Personal Finance: An Active Approach to Help You Develop Successful Financial Skills
First Edition

Kapoor, Dlabay, and Hughes
Personal Finance
Eighth Edition

CORPORATE FINANCE
CORE PRINCIPLES & APPLICATIONS

Stephen A. Ross

Sloan School of Management
Massachusetts Institute of Technology

Randolph W. Westerfield

Marshall School of Business
University of Southern California

Jeffrey F. Jaffe

Wharton School of Business
University of Pennsylvania

Bradford D. Jordan

Gatton College of Business and Economics
University of Kentucky

Boston Burr Ridge, IL Dubuque, IA Madison, WI New York San Francisco St. Louis
Bangkok Bogotá Caracas Kuala Lumpur Lisbon London Madrid Mexico City
Milan Montreal New Delhi Santiago Seoul Singapore Sydney Taipei Toronto

CORPORATE FINANCE: CORE PRINCIPLES AND APPLICATIONS
Published by McGraw-Hill/Irwin, a business unit of The McGraw-Hill Companies, Inc., 1221 Avenue of the Americas, New York, NY, 10020.

Some ancillaries, including electronic and print components, may not be available to customers outside the United States.

This book is printed on acid-free paper.

1 2 3 4 5 6 7 8 9 0 VNH/VNH 0 9 8 7 6

ISBN-13: 978-0-07-353059-8
ISBN-10: 0-07-353059-X

Editorial director: *Brent Gordon*
Publisher: *Stephen M. Patterson*
Executive sponsoring editor: *Michele Janicek*
Developmental editor II: *Jennifer V. Rizzi*
Marketing manager: *Julie Phifer*
Media producer: *Jennifer Fisher*
Lead project manager: *Christine A. Vaughan*
Lead production supervisor: *Michael R. McCormick*
Senior designer: *Kami Carter*
Lead media project manager: *Becky Szura*
Cover image: © *Getty Images*
Typeface: *10/12 Baskerville Book*
Compositor: *Interactive Composition Corporation*
Printer: *Von Hoffmann Corporation*

Library of Congress Cataloging-in-Publication Data

Corporate finance: core principles & applications / Stephen A. Ross . . . [et al.].
p. cm. – (McGraw-Hill/Irwin series in finance, insurance, and real estate)
Includes index.
ISBN-13: 978-0-07-353059-8 (alk. paper)
ISBN-10: 0-07-353059-X (alk. paper)
1. Corporations–Finance. I. Ross, Stephen A.
HG4026.C643 2007
658.15–dc22

2005058384

www.mhhe.com

To our family and friends with love and gratitude.

S.A.R.   R.W.W.   J.F.J.   B.D.J.

ABOUT THE AUTHORS

Stephen A. Ross

SLOAN SCHOOL OF MANAGEMENT, MASSACHUSETTS INSTITUTE OF TECHNOLOGY

Stephen A. Ross is the Franco Modigliani Professor of Financial Economics at the Sloan School of Management, Massachusetts Institute of Technology. One of the most widely published authors in finance and economics, Professor Ross is recognized for his work in developing the Arbitrage Pricing Theory, as well as for having made substantial contributions to the discipline through his research in signaling, agency theory, option pricing, and the theory of the term structure of interest rates, among other topics. A past president of the American Finance Association, he currently serves as an associate editor of several academic and practitioner journals. He is a trustee of CalTech and Freddie Mac.

Randolph W. Westerfield

MARSHALL SCHOOL OF BUSINESS, UNIVERSITY OF SOUTHERN CALIFORNIA

Randolph W. Westerfield is Dean Emeritus of the University of Southern California's Marshall School of Business and is the Charles B. Thornton Professor in Finance.

Professor Westerfield came to USC from the Wharton School, University of Pennsylvania, where he was the chairman of the finance department and member of the finance faculty for 20 years. He is a member of several public company boards of directors including Health Management Associates, Inc., William Lyon Homes, and the Nicholas Applegate Growth Fund. His areas of expertise include corporate financial policy, investment management, and stock market price behavior.

Jeffrey F. Jaffe

WHARTON SCHOOL OF BUSINESS, UNIVERSITY OF PENNSYLVANIA

Jeffrey F. Jaffe has been a frequent contributor to finance and economic literature in such journals as the *Quarterly Economic Journal, The Journal of Finance, The Journal of Financial and Quantitative Analysis, The Journal of Financial Economics,* and *The Financial Analysts Journal.* His best known work concerns insider trading, where he showed both that corporate insiders earn abnormal profits from their trades and that regulation has little effect on these profits. He has also made contributions concerning initial public offerings, regulation of utilities, the behavior of market makers, the fluctuation of gold prices, the theoretical effect of inflation on the interest rate, the empirical effect of inflation on capital asset prices, the relationship between small capitalization stocks and the January effect, and the capital structure decision.

Bradford D. Jordan

GATTON COLLEGE OF BUSINESS AND ECONOMICS, UNIVERSITY OF KENTUCKY

Bradford D. Jordan is Professor of Finance and holder of the Richard W. and Janis H. Furst Endowed Chair in Finance at the University of Kentucky. He has a long-standing interest in both applied and theoretical issues in corporate finance and has extensive experience teaching all levels of corporate finance and financial management policy. Professor Jordan has published numerous articles in leading journals on issues such as initial public offerings, capital structure, and the behavior of security prices. He is a past president of the Southern Finance Association, and he is coauthor of *Fundamentals of Investments: Valuation and Management,* 4e, a leading investments text, also published by McGraw-Hill/Irwin.

PREFACE

It was probably inevitable that the four of us would collaborate on this new project. Over the last 15 or so years, we have been working as two separate "RWJ" teams. In that time, we have managed (much to our own amazement) to coauthor two widely adopted undergraduate texts and an equally successful graduate text, all in the corporate finance area. These three books have collectively totaled 17 editions (and counting), plus a variety of country-specific editions and international editions, and they have been translated into at least a dozen foreign languages.

Even so, we've known for some time that there was a hole in our lineup at the graduate (MBA) level. We've continued to see a need for a concise, up-to-date, and to-the-point product, the majority of which can be realistically covered in a typical single term or course. As we began to develop this book, we realized (with wry chuckles all around) that, between the four of us, we have been teaching and researching finance principles for well over a century. From our own very extensive experience with this material, we recognize that corporate finance introductory classes often have students with extremely diverse educational and professional backgrounds. We also recognize that this course is increasingly being delivered in alternative formats ranging from traditional semester-long classes to highly compressed modules to purely online courses, taught both synchronously and asynchronously.

To achieve our objective of reaching out to the many different types of students and the varying course environments, we worked to distill the subject of corporate finance down to its core, while maintaining a decidedly modern approach. We have always maintained that corporate finance can be viewed as the working of a few very powerful intuitions. We also know that understanding the "why" is just as important, if not more so, than understanding the "how." Throughout the development of this book, we continued to take a hard look at what is truly relevant and useful. In doing so, we have worked to downplay purely theoretical issues and minimize the use of extensive and elaborate calculations to illustrate points that are either intuitively obvious or of limited practical use.

Perhaps more than anything, this book gave us the chance to pool all that we have learned about what really works in a corporate finance text. We have received an enormous amount of feedback over the years. Based on that feedback, the two key ingredients that we worked to blend together here are the careful attention to pedagogy and readability that we have developed in our undergraduate books and the strong emphasis on current thinking and research that we have always stressed in our graduate book.

From the start, we knew we didn't want this text to be encyclopedic. Our goal instead was to focus on what students really need to carry away from a principles course. After much debate and consultation with colleagues who regularly teach this material, we settled on a total of 20 chapters. Chapter length is typically 30 pages, so most of the book (and, thus, most of the key concepts and applications) can be realistically covered in a single term or module. Writing a book that strictly focuses on core concepts and applications necessarily means some picking and choosing, with regard to both topics and depth of coverage. Throughout, we strike a balance by introducing and covering the essentials, while leaving more specialized topics to follow-up courses.

As in our other books, we treat net present value (NPV) as the underlying and unifying concept in corporate finance. Many texts stop well short of consistently integrating this basic principle. The simple, intuitive, and very powerful notion that NPV represents the excess of market value over cost often is lost in an overly mechanical approach that emphasizes computation at the expense of comprehension. In contrast, every subject we cover is firmly rooted in valuation, and care is taken throughout to explain how particular decisions have valuation effects.

Also, students shouldn't lose sight of the fact that financial management is about management. We emphasize the role of the financial manager as decision maker, and we stress the need for managerial input and judgment. We consciously avoid "black box" approaches to decisions, and where appropriate, the approximate, pragmatic nature of financial analysis is made explicit, possible pitfalls are described, and limitations are discussed.

In addition to providing a focused text, we have also worked with many talented and dedicated professionals to prepare support and enrichment materials that are unrivaled at the graduate level (details can be found later). Whether you use just the textbook, or the book in conjunction with other products, we believe you will find a combination that will meet your current as well as your changing needs.

Stephen A. Ross
Randolph W. Westerfield
Jeffrey F. Jaffe
Bradford D. Jordan

PEDAGOGY

Corporate Finance: Core Principles and Applications **is rich in valuable learning tools and support to help students succeed in learning the fundamentals of financial management.**

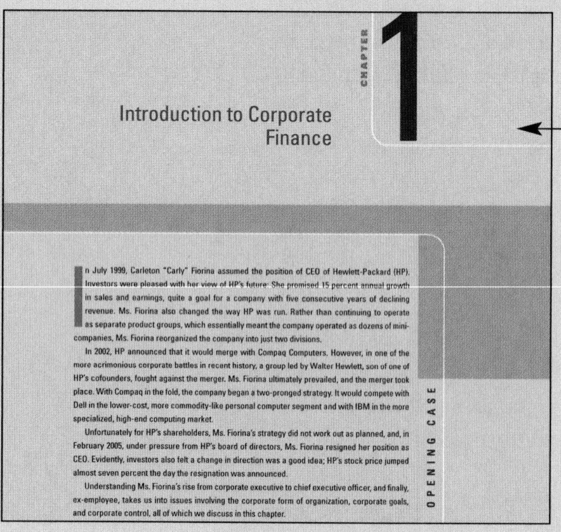

CHAPTER 1

Introduction to Corporate Finance

OPENING CASE

In July 1999, Carleton "Carly" Fiorina assumed the position of CEO of Hewlett-Packard (HP). Investors were pleased with her view of HP's future: She promised 15 percent annual growth in sales and earnings, quite a goal for a company with five consecutive years of declining revenue. Ms. Fiorina also changed the way HP was run. Rather than continuing to operate as separate product groups, which essentially meant the company operated as dozens of mini-companies, Ms. Fiorina reorganized the company into just two divisions.

In 2002, HP announced that it would merge with Compaq Computers. However, in one of the more acrimonious corporate battles in recent history, a group led by Walter Hewlett, son of one of HP's cofounders, fought against the merger. Ms. Fiorina ultimately prevailed, and the merger took place. With Compaq in the fold, the company began a two-pronged strategy. It would compete with Dell in the lower-cost, more commodity-like personal computer segment and with IBM in the more specialized, high-end computing market.

Unfortunately for HP's shareholders, Ms. Fiorina's strategy did not work out as planned, and, in February 2005, under pressure from HP's board of directors, Ms. Fiorina resigned her position as CEO. Evidently, investors also felt a change in direction was a good idea; HP's stock price jumped almost seven percent the day the resignation was announced.

Understanding Ms. Fiorina's rise from corporate executive to chief executive officer, and finally, ex-employee, takes us into issues involving the corporate form of organization, corporate goals, and corporate control, all of which we discuss in this chapter.

Chapter Opening Case

Each chapter begins with a recent real world event to introduce students to chapter concepts.

Explanatory Web Links

These Web links are provided in the margins of the text. They are specifically selected to accompany text material and provide students and instructors with a quick way to check for additional information using the Internet.

Treasurer

Controller

Cash Manager

Credit Manager

Tax Manager

Cost Accounting Manager

Capital Expenditures

Financial Planning

Financial Accounting Manager

Information Systems Manager

The Financial Manager

In large firms, the finance activity is usually associated with a top officer of the firm, such as the vice president and chief financial officer, and some lesser officers. Figure 1.3 depicts a general organizational structure emphasizing the finance activity within the firm. Reporting to the chief financial officer are the treasurer and the controller. The treasurer is responsible for handling cash flows, managing capital expenditure decisions, and

For current issues facings CFOs, see www.cfo.com.

Figures and Tables

This text makes extensive use of real data and presents them in various figures and tables. Explanations in the narrative, examples, and end-of-chapter problems will refer to many of these exhibits.

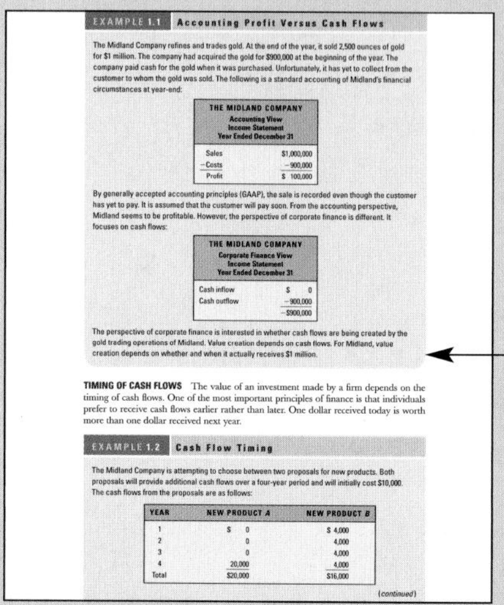

EXAMPLE 1.1 **Accounting Profit Versus Cash Flows**

The Midland Company refines and trades gold. At the end of the year, it sold 2,500 ounces of gold for $1 million. The company had acquired the gold for $900,000 at the beginning of the year. The company paid cash for the gold when it was purchased. Unfortunately, it has yet to collect from the customer to whom the gold was sold. The following is a standard accounting of Midland's financial circumstances at year-end:

THE MIDLAND COMPANY Accounting View Income Statement Year Ended December 31	
Sales	$1,000,000
−Costs	−900,000
Profit	$ 100,000

By generally accepted accounting principles (GAAP), the sale is recorded even though the customer has yet to pay. It is assumed that the customer will pay soon. From the accounting perspective, Midland seems to be profitable. However, the perspective of corporate finance is different. It focuses on cash flows:

THE MIDLAND COMPANY Corporate Finance View Income Statement Year Ended December 31	
Cash inflow	$ 0
Cash outflow	−900,000
	−$900,000

The perspective of corporate finance is interested in whether cash flows are being created by the gold trading operations of Midland. Value creation depends on cash flows. For Midland, value creation depends on whether and when it actually receives $1 million.

TIMING OF CASH FLOWS The value of an investment made by a firm depends on the timing of cash flows. One of the most important principles of finance is that individuals prefer to receive cash flows earlier rather than later. One dollar received today is worth more than one dollar received next year.

EXAMPLE 1.2 **Cash Flow Timing**

The Midland Company is attempting to choose between two proposals for new products. Both proposals will provide additional cash flows over a four-year period and will initially cost $10,000. The cash flows from the proposals are as follows:

YEAR	NEW PRODUCT *A*	NEW PRODUCT *B*
1	$ 0	$ 4,000
2	0	4,000
3	0	4,000
4	20,000	4,000
Total	$20,000	$16,000

(continued)

Examples

Separate numbered and titled examples are extensively integrated into the chapters. These examples provide detailed applications and illustrations of the text material in a step-by-step format. Each example is completely self-contained, so students don't have to search for additional information.

Highlighted Concepts

Throughout the text, important ideas are pulled out and presented in a highlighted box–signaling to students that this material is particularly relevant and critical for their understanding.

12 PART 1 Overview

late in some way to controlling risk. Unfortunately, these two types of goals are somewhat contradictory. The pursuit of profit normally involves some element of risk, so it isn't really possible to maximize both safety and profit. What we need, therefore, is a goal that encompasses both factors.

The Goal of Financial Management

The financial manager in a corporation makes decisions for the stockholders of the firm. Given this, instead of listing possible goals for the financial manager, we really need to answer a more fundamental question: From the stockholders' point of view, what is a good financial management decision?

If we assume that stockholders buy stock because they seek to gain financially, then the answer is obvious: Good decisions increase the value of the stock, and poor decisions decrease the value of the stock.

Given our observations, it follows that the financial manager acts in the shareholders' best interests by making decisions that increase the value of the stock. The appropriate goal for the financial manager can thus be stated quite easily:

The goal of financial management is to maximize the current value per share of the existing stock.

The goal of maximizing the value of the stock avoids the problems associated with the different goals we listed earlier. There is no ambiguity in the criterion, and there is no short-run versus long-run issue. We explicitly mean that our goal is to maximize the *current* stock value.

If this goal seems a little strong or one-dimensional to you, keep in mind that the stockholders in a firm are residual owners. By this we mean that they are only entitled to what is left after employees, suppliers, and creditors (and everyone else with legitimate claims) are paid their due. If any of these groups go unpaid, the stockholders get nothing. So, if the stockholders are winning in the sense that the leftover, residual portion is growing, it must be true that everyone else is winning also.

THE REAL WORLD

SARBANES-OXLEY

In response to corporate scandals at companies such as Enron, WorldCom, Tyco, and Adelphia, Congress enacted the Sarbanes-Oxley Act in 2002. The act, better known as "Sarbox," is intended to protect investors from corporate abuses. For example, one section of Sarbox prohibits personal loans from a company to its officers, such as the ones that were received by WorldCom CEO Bernie Ebbers.

One of the key sections of Sarbox took effect on November 15, 2004. Section 404 requires, among other things, that each company's annual report must have an assessment of the company's internal control structure and financial reporting. The auditor must then evaluate and attest to management's assessment of these issues.

Sarbox contains other key requirements. For example, the officers of the corporation must review and sign the annual reports. They must explicitly declare that the annual report does not contain any false statements or material omissions; that the financial statements fairly represent the financial results; and that they are responsible for all internal controls. Finally, the annual report must list any deficiencies in internal controls. In essence, Sarbox makes company management responsible for the accuracy of the company's financial statements.

Of course, as with any law, there are compliance costs, and Sarbox has increased the cost of corporate audits, sometimes dramatically. Estimates of the increase in company audit costs to comply with Sarbox range from $500,000 to over $5 million, which has led to some unintended consequences. For example, in 2003, 198 firms delisted their shares from exchanges, or "went dark." This was up from 30 delistings in 1999. For 2004, estimates of the number of companies that would go dark ranged from 134 to 250. Most of the companies that delisted stated that their reason was to avoid the cost of compliance with Sarbox. Some conservative estimates put the national Sarbox compliance tab at $35 billion in the first year alone, which is roughly 20 times the amount originally estimated by the SEC. For a large multibillion-dollar revenue company, the cost might be .05 percent of revenues, but it could be 3 percent or so for smaller companies, an enormous cost.

A company that goes dark does not have to file quarterly or annual reports. Annual audits by independent auditors are not required, and executives do not have to certify the accuracy of the financial statements, so the savings can be huge. Of course, there are costs. Stock prices typically fall when a company announces it is going dark. Further, such companies will typically have limited access to capital markets and usually will have a higher interest cost on bank loans.

Foreign companies have also been affected. Lastminute, a British online travel group, and Lion Bioscience, a German software company, have already initiated the process to withdraw from U.S. exchanges. And it is not just smaller foreign companies that are considering delisting from U.S. exchanges. German conglomerate Siemens AG, with worldwide sales approaching $100 billion, is considering delisting, and the London Stock Exchange has reported that several companies have discussed going public on that exchange rather than list on a U.S. exchange, to avoid the compliance costs of Sarbox.

The Real World Box

Exploring information found in recent publications and building upon concepts learned in each chapter, these boxes work through real world issues relevant to the surrounding text.

Spreadsheet Techniques

This feature either introduces students to Excel or helps them brush up on their Excel spreadsheet skills, particularly as they relate to corporate finance. This feature appears in self-contained sections and shows students how to set up spreadsheets to analyze common financial problems–a vital part of every business student's education.

Numbered Equations

Key equations are numbered within the text and listed on the back end sheets for easy reference.

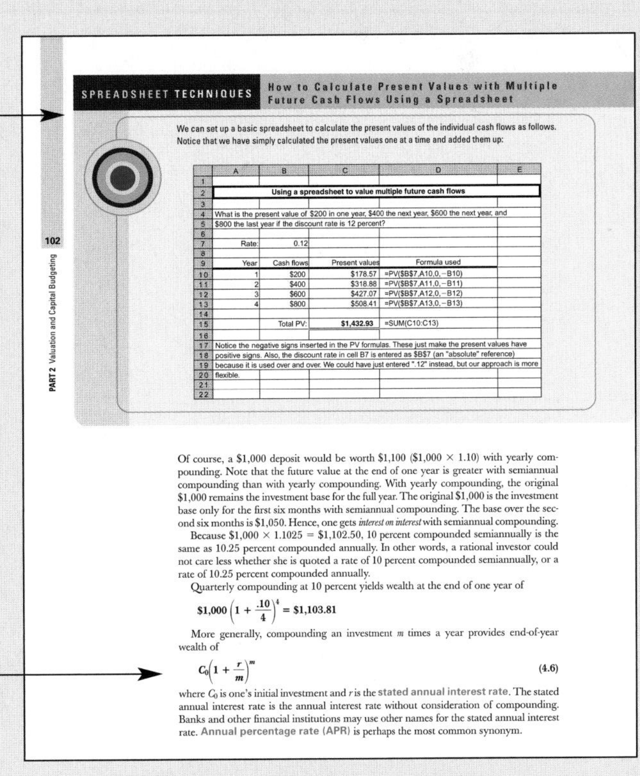

102 PART 2 Valuation and Capital Budgeting

SPREADSHEET TECHNIQUES **How to Calculate Present Values with Multiple Future Cash Flows Using a Spreadsheet**

We can set up a basic spreadsheet to calculate the present values of the individual cash flows as follows. Notice that we have simply calculated the present values one at a time and added them up:

	A	B	C	D	E
1					
2	**Using a spreadsheet to value multiple future cash flows**				
3					
4	What is the present value of $200 in one year, $400 the next year, $600 the next year, and				
5	$800 the last year if the discount rate is 12 percent?				
6					
7	Rate:	0.12			
8					
9	Year	Cash flows	Present values	Formula used	
10	1	$200	$178.57	=PV(B7,A10,0,−B10)	
11	2	$400	$318.88	=PV(B7,A11,0,−B11)	
12	3	$600	$427.07	=PV(B7,A12,0,−B12)	
13	4	$800	$508.41	=PV(B7,A13,0,−B13)	
14					
15		Total PV:	**$1,432.93**	=SUM(C10:C13)	
16					
17	Notice the negative signs inserted in the PV formulas. These just make the present values have				
18	positive signs. Also, the discount rate in cell B7 is entered as B7 (an "absolute" reference)				
19	because it is used over and over. We could have just entered ".12" instead, but our approach is more				
20	flexible.				
21					
22					

Of course, a $1,000 deposit would be worth $1,100 ($1,000 × 1.10) with yearly compounding. Note that the future value at the end of one year is greater with semiannual compounding than with yearly compounding. With yearly compounding, the original $1,000 remains the investment base for the full year. The original $1,000 is the investment base only for the first six months with semiannual compounding. The base over the second six months is $1,050. Hence, one gets *interest on interest* with semiannual compounding.

Because $1,000 × 1.1025 = $1,102.50, 10 percent compounded semiannually is the same as 10.25 percent compounded annually. In other words, a rational investor could not care less whether she is quoted a rate of 10 percent compounded semiannually, or a rate of 10.25 percent compounded annually.

Quarterly compounding at 10 percent yields wealth at the end of one year of

$$\$1{,}000\left(1 + \frac{.10}{4}\right)^4 = \$1{,}103.81$$

More generally, compounding an investment m times a year provides end-of-year wealth of

$$C_0\left(1 + \frac{r}{m}\right)^m \tag{4.6}$$

where C_0 is one's initial investment and r is the **stated annual interest rate**. The stated annual interest rate is the annual interest rate without consideration of compounding. Banks and other financial institutions may use other names for the stated annual interest rate. **Annual percentage rate (APR)** is perhaps the most common synonym.

END-OF-CHAPTER MATERIAL

The end-of-chapter material reflects and builds on the concepts learned from the chapter and study features.

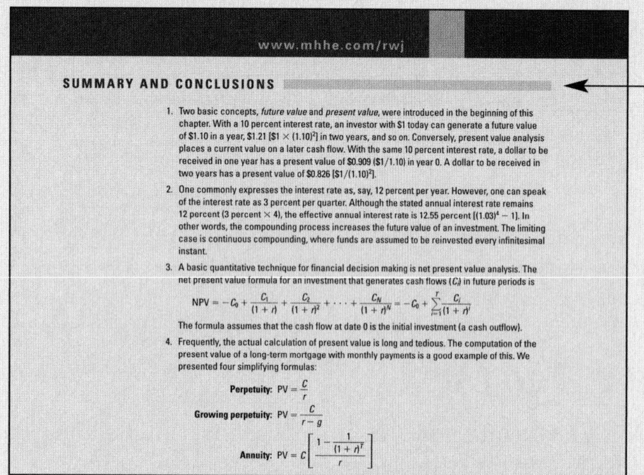

www.mhhe.com/rwj

SUMMARY AND CONCLUSIONS

1. Two basic concepts, *future value* and *present value*, were introduced in the beginning of this chapter. With a 10 percent interest rate, an investor with $1 today can generate a future value of $1.10 in a year, $1.21 [$\$1 \times (1.10)^2$] in two years, and so on. Conversely, present value analysis places a current value on a later cash flow. With the same 10 percent interest rate, a dollar to be received in one year has a present value of $0.909 ($1/1.10) in year 0. A dollar to be received in two years has a present value of $0.826 [$\$1/(1.10)^2$].
2. One commonly expresses the interest rate as, say, 12 percent per year. However, one can speak of the interest rate as 3 percent per quarter. Although the stated annual interest rate remains 12 percent (3 percent × 4), the effective annual interest rate is 12.55 percent [$(1.03)^4 - 1$]. In other words, the compounding process increases the future value of an investment. The limiting case is continuous compounding, where funds are assumed to be reinvested every infinitesimal instant.
3. A basic quantitative technique for financial decision making is net present value analysis. The net present value formula for an investment that generates cash flows (C_i) in future periods is

$$\text{NPV} = -C_0 + \frac{C_1}{(1+r)} + \frac{C_2}{(1+r)^2} + \cdots + \frac{C_N}{(1+r)^N} = -C_0 + \sum_{i=1}^{T} \frac{C_i}{(1+r)^i}$$

The formula assumes that the cash flow at date 0 is the initial investment (a cash outflow).
4. Frequently, the actual calculation of present value is long and tedious. The computation of the present value of a long-term mortgage with monthly payments is a good example of this. We presented four simplifying formulas:

Perpetuity: $\text{PV} = \frac{C}{r}$

Growing perpetuity: $\text{PV} = \frac{C}{r-g}$

Annuity: $\text{PV} = C\left[\frac{1 - \frac{1}{(1+r)^T}}{r}\right]$

Summary and Conclusions

Each chapter ends with a numbered, concise, but thorough, summary of the important ideas presented in the chapter–helping students review the key points and providing closure.

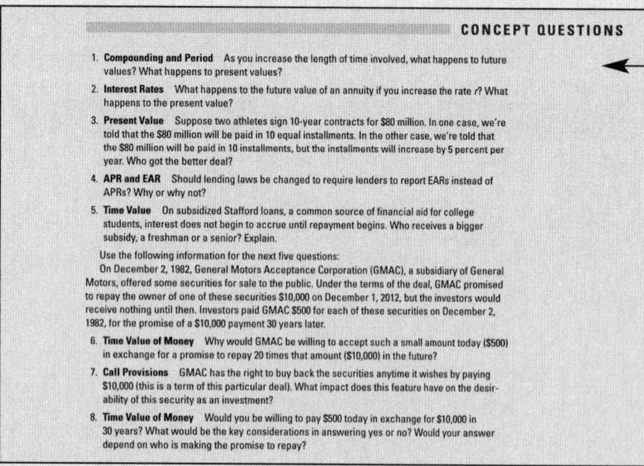

CONCEPT QUESTIONS

1. **Compounding and Period** As you increase the length of time involved, what happens to future values? What happens to present values?
2. **Interest Rates** What happens to the future value of an annuity if you increase the rate *r*? What happens to the present value?
3. **Present Value** Suppose two athletes sign 10-year contracts for $80 million. In one case, we're told that the $80 million will be paid in 10 equal installments. In the other case, we're told that the $80 million will be paid in 10 installments, but the installments will increase by 5 percent per year. Who got the better deal?
4. **APR and EAR** Should lending laws be changed to require lenders to report EARs instead of APRs? Why or why not?
5. **Time Value** On subsidized Stafford loans, a common source of financial aid for college students, interest does not begin to accrue until repayment begins. Who receives a bigger subsidy, a freshman or a senior? Explain.

Use the following information for the next five questions:

On December 2, 1982, General Motors Acceptance Corporation (GMAC), a subsidiary of General Motors, offered some securities for sale to the public. Under the terms of the deal, GMAC promised to repay the owner of one of these securities $10,000 on December 1, 2012, but the investors would receive nothing until then. Investors paid GMAC $500 for each of these securities on December 2, 1982, for the promise of a $10,000 payment 30 years later.

6. **Time Value of Money** Why would GMAC be willing to accept such a small amount today ($500) in exchange for a promise to repay 20 times that amount ($10,000) in the future?
7. **Call Provisions** GMAC has the right to buy back the securities anytime it wishes by paying $10,000 (this is a term of this particular deal). What impact does this feature have on the desirability of this security as an investment?
8. **Time Value of Money** Would you be willing to pay $500 today in exchange for $10,000 in 30 years? What would be the key considerations in answering yes or no? Would your answer depend on who is making the promise to repay?

Concept Questions

This end-of-chapter section facilitates your students' knowledge of key principles, as well as their intuitive understanding of the chapter concepts. A number of the questions relate to the chapter opening case–reinforcing students' critical-thinking skills and the review of chapter material.

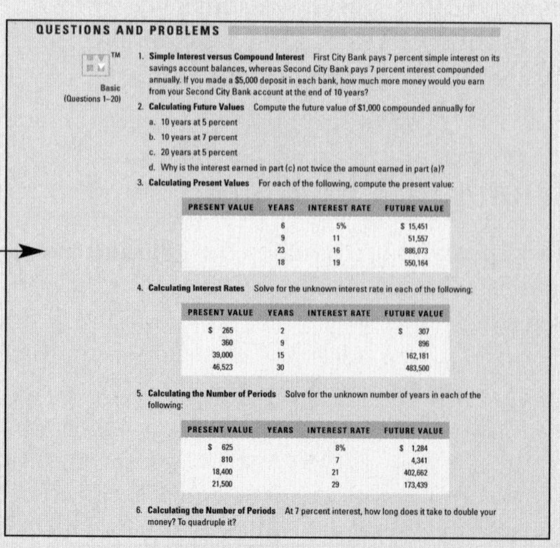

QUESTIONS AND PROBLEMS

Basic (Questions 1–20)

1. **Simple Interest versus Compound Interest** First City Bank pays 7 percent simple interest on its savings account balances, whereas Second City Bank pays 7 percent interest compounded annually. If you made a $5,000 deposit in each bank, how much more money would you earn from your Second City Bank account at the end of 10 years?
2. **Calculating Future Values** Compute the future value of $1,000 compounded annually for
   a. 10 years at 5 percent
   b. 10 years at 7 percent
   c. 20 years at 5 percent
   d. Why is the interest earned in part (c) not twice the amount earned in part (a)?
3. **Calculating Present Values** For each of the following, compute the present value:

PRESENT VALUE	YEARS	INTEREST RATE	FUTURE VALUE
	6	5%	$ 15,451
	9	11	51,557
	23	16	886,073
	18	19	550,164

4. **Calculating Interest Rates** Solve for the unknown interest rate in each of the following:

PRESENT VALUE	YEARS	INTEREST RATE	FUTURE VALUE
$ 265	2		$ 307
360	9		896
39,000	15		162,181
46,523	30		483,500

5. **Calculating the Number of Periods** Solve for the unknown number of years in each of the following:

PRESENT VALUE	YEARS	INTEREST RATE	FUTURE VALUE
$ 625		8%	$ 1,284
810		7	4,341
18,400		21	402,662
21,500		29	173,439

6. **Calculating the Number of Periods** At 7 percent interest, how long does it take to double your money? To quadruple it?

Questions & Problems

Because solving problems is so critical to students' learning, we provide extensive end-of-chapter questions and problems. The questions and problems are segregated into three learning levels: Basic, Intermediate, and Challenge. All problems are fully annotated so that students and instructors can readily identify particular types. Also, all problems are available in McGraw-Hill's Homework Manager–see the next section of this preface for more details.

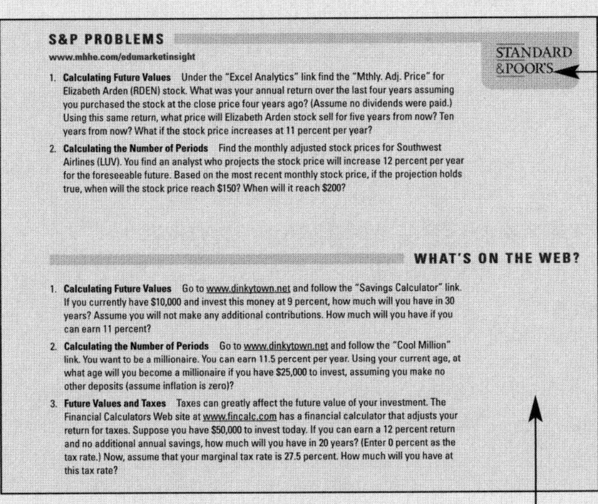

S&P PROBLEMS

www.mhhe.com/edumarketinsight

STANDARD & POOR'S

1. **Calculating Future Values** Under the "Excel Analytics" link find the "Mthly. Adj. Price" for Elizabeth Arden (RDEN) stock. What was your annual return over the last four years assuming you purchased the stock at the close price four years ago? (Assume no dividends were paid.) Using this same return, what price will Elizabeth Arden stock sell for five years from now? Ten years from now? What if the stock price increases at 11 percent per year?
2. **Calculating the Number of Periods** Find the monthly adjusted stock prices for Southwest Airlines (LUV). You find an analyst who projects the stock price will increase 12 percent per year for the foreseeable future. Based on the most recent monthly stock price, if the projection holds true, when will the stock price reach $150? When will it reach $200?

WHAT'S ON THE WEB?

1. **Calculating Future Values** Go to www.dinkytown.net and follow the "Savings Calculator" link. If you currently have $10,000 and invest this money at 9 percent, how much will you have in 30 years? Assume you will not make any additional contributions. How much will you have if you can earn 11 percent?
2. **Calculating the Number of Periods** Go to www.dinkytown.net and follow the "Cool Million" link. You want to be a millionaire. You can earn 11.5 percent per year. Using your current age, at what age will you become a millionaire if you have $25,000 to invest, assuming you make no other deposits (assume inflation is zero)?
3. **Future Values and Taxes** Taxes can greatly affect the future value of your investment. The Financial Calculators Web site at www.fincalc.com has a financial calculator that adjusts your return for taxes. Suppose you have $50,000 to invest today. If you can earn a 12 percent return and no additional annual savings, how much will you have in 20 years? (Enter 0 percent as the tax rate.) Now, assume that your marginal tax rate is 27.5 percent. How much will you have at this tax rate?

S&P Problems

Most chapters include two or three end-of-chapter problems that make use of the Educational Version of Market Insight, Standard & Poor's powerful and well-known Compustat database (free access–packaged with each new book). These problems provide an easy, online way for students to incorporate current, real world data into their learning.

What's On the Web?

These end-of-chapter activities show students how to use and learn from the vast amount of financial resources available on the Internet.

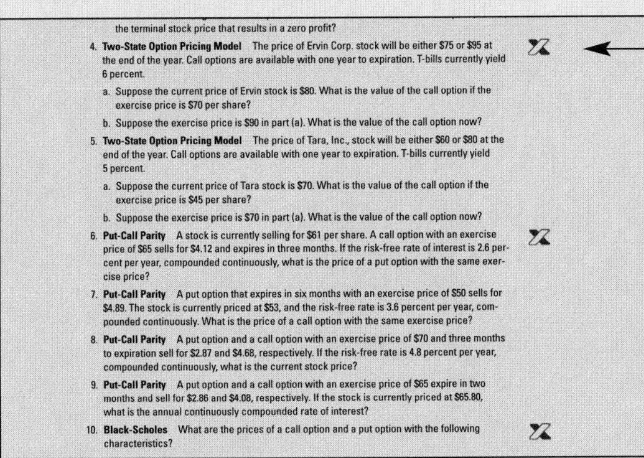

the terminal stock price that results in a zero profit?

4. **Two-State Option Pricing Model** The price of Ervin Corp. stock will be either $75 or $95 at the end of the year. Call options are available with one year to expiration. T-bills currently yield 6 percent.
   a. Suppose the current price of Ervin stock is $80. What is the value of the call option if the exercise price is $70 per share?
   b. Suppose the exercise price is $90 in part (a). What is the value of the call option now?
5. **Two-State Option Pricing Model** The price of Tara, Inc., stock will be either $60 or $80 at the end of the year. Call options are available with one year to expiration. T-bills currently yield 5 percent.
   a. Suppose the current price of Tara stock is $70. What is the value of the call option if the exercise price is $45 per share?
   b. Suppose the exercise price is $70 in part (a). What is the value of the call option now?
6. **Put-Call Parity** A stock is currently selling for $61 per share. A call option with an exercise price of $65 sells for $4.12 and expires in three months. If the risk-free rate of interest is 2.6 percent per year, compounded continuously, what is the price of a put option with the same exercise price?
7. **Put-Call Parity** A put option that expires in six months with an exercise price of $50 sells for $4.89. The stock is currently priced at $53, and the risk-free rate is 3.6 percent per year, compounded continuously. What is the price of a call option with the same exercise price?
8. **Put-Call Parity** A put option and a call option with an exercise price of $70 and three months to expiration sell for $2.87 and $4.68, respectively. If the risk-free rate is 4.8 percent per year, compounded continuously, what is the current stock price?
9. **Put-Call Parity** A put option and a call option with an exercise price of $65 expire in two months and sell for $2.86 and $4.08, respectively. If the stock is currently priced at $65.80, what is the annual continuously compounded rate of interest?
10. **Black-Scholes** What are the prices of a call option and a put option with the following characteristics?

Excel Problems

Indicated by the Excel icon in the margin, these problems are integrated in the Questions and Problems section of almost all chapters. Located on the book's Web site (see Online Resources), Excel templates have been created for each of these problems, where students can use the data in the problem to work out the solution using Excel skills.

End-of-Chapter Cases

Located at the end of each chapter, these mini-cases focus on common company situations that embody important corporate finance topics. Each case presents a new scenario, data, and a dilemma. Several questions at the end of each case require students to analyze and focus on all of the material they learned in that chapter.

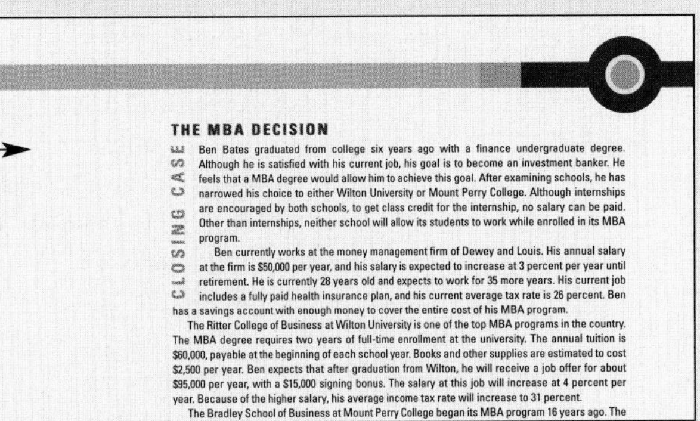

THE MBA DECISION

CLOSING CASE

Ben Bates graduated from college six years ago with a finance undergraduate degree. Although he is satisfied with his current job, his goal is to become an investment banker. He feels that a MBA degree would allow him to achieve this goal. After examining schools, he has narrowed his choice to either Wilton University or Mount Perry College. Although internships are encouraged by both schools, to get class credit for the internship, no salary can be paid. Other than internships, neither school will allow its students to work while enrolled in its MBA program.

Ben currently works at the money management firm of Dewey and Louis. His annual salary at the firm is $50,000 per year, and his salary is expected to increase at 3 percent per year until retirement. He is currently 28 years old and expects to work for 35 more years. His current job includes a fully paid health insurance plan, and his current average tax rate is 26 percent. Ben has a savings account with enough money to cover the entire cost of his MBA program.

The Ritter College of Business at Wilton University is one of the top MBA programs in the country. The MBA degree requires two years of full-time enrollment at the university. The annual tuition is $60,000, payable at the beginning of each school year. Books and other supplies are estimated to cost $2,500 per year. Ben expects that after graduation from Wilton, he will receive a job offer for about $95,000 per year, with a $15,000 signing bonus. The salary at this job will increase at 4 percent per year. Because of the higher salary, his average income tax rate will increase to 31 percent.

The Bradley School of Business at Mount Perry College began its MBA program 16 years ago. The

COMPREHENSIVE TEACHING

Corporate Finance: Core Concepts and Applications **has many options in terms of the textbook, instructor supplements, student supplements, and multimedia products. Mix and match to create a package that is perfect for your course.**

INSTRUCTOR SUPPLEMENTS

Instructor's CD-ROM ISBN 10: 0073207667/ISBN 13: 9780073207667

This CD contains all the necessary supplements–Instructor's Manual, Test Bank, Computerized Test Bank, and PowerPoint–all in one useful product in an electronic format.

- **Instructor's Manual**
  prepared by Steven Dolvin, Butler University and Joseph Smolira, Belmont University
  A great place to find new lecture ideas. The IM has three main sections. The first section contains a chapter outline and other lecture materials. The annotated outline for each chapter includes lecture tips, real world tips, ethics notes, suggested PowerPoint slides, and, when appropriate, a video synopsis. Detailed solutions for all end-of-chapter problems appear in section two.
- **Test Bank**
  prepared by Patricia Ryan, Colorado State University
  Great format for a better testing process. The Test Bank has 75–100 questions per chapter that closely link with the text material and provides a variety of question formats (multiple-choice questions/problems and essay questions) and levels of difficulty (basic, intermediate, and challenge) to meet every instructor's testing needs. Problems are detailed enough to make them intuitive for students and solutions are provided for the instructor.
- **Computerized Test Bank (Windows)**
  Create your own tests in a snap! These additional questions are found in a computerized test bank utilizing McGraw-Hill's EZ Test testing software to quickly create customized exams. This user-friendly program allows instructors to sort questions by format; edit existing questions or add new ones; and scramble questions for multiple versions of the same test.
- **PowerPoint Presentation System**
  prepared by Steven Dolvin, Butler University
  Customize our content for your course. This presentation has been thoroughly revised to include more lecture-oriented slides, as well as exhibits and examples both from the book and from outside sources. Applicable slides have Web links that take you directly to specific Internet sites, or a spreadsheet link to show an example in Excel. You can also go to the Notes Page function for more tips in presenting the slides. If you already have PowerPoint installed on your PC, you have the ability to edit, print, or rearrange the complete presentation to meet your specific needs.

AND LEARNING PACKAGE

Videos ISBN 10: 0073207691/ISBN 13: 9780073207698

Now available in DVD format. Current set of videos on hot topics! McGraw-Hill/Irwin has produced a series of finance videos that are 10-minute case studies on topics such as Financial Markets, Careers, Rightsizing, Capital Budgeting, EVA (Economic Value Added), Mergers and Acquisitions, and Foreign Exchange. Discussion questions for these videos, as well as video clips, are available in the Instructor's Center at www.mhhe.com/rwj.

DIGITAL SOLUTIONS

Online Learning Center (OLC): Online Support at www.mhhe.com/rwj

The Online Learning Center (OLC) contains FREE access to additional Web-based study and teaching aids created for this text, such as:

Student Support

- **Self-Study Software**
  With this self-study program, students can test their knowledge of one chapter or a number of chapters by using self-grading questions written specifically for this text. There are at least 100 questions per chapter. Students can set a timer function to simulate a test environment, or they can choose to have answers pop up as they finish each question. Questions were prepared by Kay Johnson, Penn State University–Erie.

- **Narrated PowerPoint Examples**
  Created by Kay Johnson, Penn State University–Erie, exclusively for students. Each chapter's slides follow the chapter topics and provide steps and explanations showing how to solve key problems. Knowing that each student learns differently, a quick click on each slide will "talk through" its contents with you!

- **Interactive FinSims**
  Created by Eric Sandburg, Interactive Media, each module highlights a key concept of the book and simulates how to solve its problems, asking the student to input certain variables. This hands-on approach guides students through difficult and important corporate finance topics.

- **Excel Templates**
  Corresponding to most end-of-chapter problems, each template allows the student to work through the problem using Excel. Each end-of-chapter problem with a template is indicated by an Excel icon in the margin beside it.

- **More**
  Be sure to check out the other helpful features found on the OLC including: key term flashcards, links to Corporate Finance Online study problems, and Finance Around the World.

Teaching Support

Along with having access to all of the same material your students can view on the book's OLC, you also have password-protected access to the Instructor's Manual, solutions to end-of-chapter problems, Instructor's PowerPoint, Excel Template Solutions, video clips, video projects and questions, and teaching notes to Corporate Finance Online.

OLCs can be delivered in multiple ways—through the textbook Web site (www.mhhe.com/rwj), through PageOut (see Packages below), or within a course management system like Blackboard, WebCT, TopClass, or eCollege. Ask your campus representative for more details.

Standard & Poor's Educational Version of Market Insight

McGraw-Hill/Irwin and the Institutional Market Services division of Standard & Poor's are pleased to announce an exclusive partnership that offers instructors and students FREE access to the educational version of Standard & Poor's Market Insight with each new textbook. The educational version of Market Insight is a rich online resource that provides six years of fundamental financial data for over 1,000 companies in the database. S&P-specific problems can be found at the end of almost all chapters in this text and ask students to solve a problem by using research found on this site. For more details, please see the bound-in card inside the front cover of this text or visit www.mhhe.com/edumarketinsight.

Corporate Finance Online

As part of the OLC, instructors and students will also have access to *Corporate Finance Online,* found on the opening page. Corporate Finance Online is an exclusive Web tool from McGraw-Hill/Irwin. The site provides over 54 exercises for 27 key corporate finance topics, allowing students to complete challenging exercises and discussion questions that draw on recent articles, company reports, government data, and other Web-based resources. For instructors, there are also password-protected teaching notes to assist with classroom integration of the material.

McGraw-Hill Investments Trader

Students receive free access to this Web-based portfolio simulation with a hypothetical $100,000 brokerage account to buy and sell stocks and mutual funds. Students can use the real data found at this site in conjunction with the chapters on investments. They can also compete against other students around the United States. Please click on the corresponding link found in the OLC for more details. This site is powered by Stock-Trak, the leading provider of investment simulation services to the academic community.

PageOut at www.pageout.net

FREE to adopters, this Web page generation software is designed to help you create your own course Web site, without all of the hassle. In just a few minutes, even the most novice computer user can have a functioning course Web site.

Simply type your material into the template provided and PageOut instantly converts it to HTML. Next, choose your favorite of three easy-to-navigate designs and your class Web home page is created, complete with online syllabus, lecture notes, and bookmarks. You can even include a separate instructor page and an assignment page.

PageOut offers enhanced point-and-click features, including a Syllabus Page that applies a real world link to original text material, an automatic grade book, and a discussion board where you and your students can exchange questions and post announcements. Ask your campus representative to show you a demo.

PACKAGE OPTIONS AVAILABLE FOR PURCHASE & PACKAGING

You may also package either version of the text with a variety of additional learning tools that are available for your students.

McGraw-Hill's Homework Manager and Homework Manager Plus

Are you looking for a way to spend less time grading and to have more flexibility with the problems you assign as homework and tests? McGraw-Hill's Homework Manager is an exciting new package option developed for this text. Homework Manager is a Web-based tool for instructors and students for delivering, answering, and grading end-of-chapter problems and tests and providing a limitless supply of self-graded practice for students.

All of the book's end-of-chapter Questions and Problems are loaded into Homework Manager, and instructors can choose to assign the exact problems as stated in the book, or algorithmic versions of them so each student has a unique set of variables for the problems. You create the assignments and control parameters, such as do you want your students to receive hints, is this a graded assignment or practice, and so on. The test bank is also available in Homework Manager, giving you the ability to use those questions for online tests. Both the problems and the tests are automatically graded and the results are stored in a private grade book, which is created when you set up your class. Detailed results let you see at a glance how each student does on an assignment or an individual problem–you can even see how many tries it took a student to solve it. If you order this special package, your students will receive a Homework Manager User's Guide and an access code packaged with their text.

There is also an enhanced version of McGraw-Hill's Homework Manager through the Homework Manager Plus option. If you order the text packaged with HM Plus, your students will receive Homework Manager as described above, but with an integrated online text included. When students are in Homework Manager and need more help to solve a problem, there will be a link that takes them to the section of the text online that explains the concept they are struggling with. All of McGraw-Hill's media assets, such as videos, narrated lectures, and additional online quizzing, are integrated at the appropriate places of the online text to provide students with a full learning experience. HM Plus also gives students access to PowerWeb for Corporate Finance–current events and articles pertaining to finance linked to appropriate chapters–all accessible with one access code. If you order this special package, students will receive the HM

Plus card packaged with their text, which will give them access to all of these products, as well as an online Homework Manager User's Guide.

McGraw-Hill's Homework Manager is powered by Brownstone.

Solutions Manual

(ISBN 10: 0073216836/ISBN 13: 9780073216836)

Prepared by Joseph Smolira, Belmont University, this manual contains detailed, worked-out solutions for all of the problems in the end-of-chapter material. It has also been reviewed for accuracy by multiple sources. The Solutions Manual is also available for purchase for your students.

The Wall Street Journal

If you order this package, your students can subscribe to *The Wall Street Journal*–both print and online versions–for 15 weeks at a specially priced rate of $20.00 in addition to the price of the text. Students will receive a "How to Use the *WSJ*" handbook plus a card explaining how to start the subscription to both versions.

BusinessWeek

Your students can subscribe to 15 weeks of *BusinessWeek* for a specially priced rate of $8.25 in addition to the price of the text. Students will receive a pass-code card shrink-wrapped with their new text. The card directs students to a Web site where they enter the code and then gain access to *BusinessWeek*'s registration page to enter address info and set up their print and online subscription.

Financial Times

Your students can subscribe to the *Financial Times* for 15 weeks at a specially priced rate of $10 in addition to the price of the text by ordering this special package. Students will receive a subscription card shrink wrapped with their new text to fill in and send to the *Financial Times* to start receiving their subscription. Instructors, once you order, make sure you contact your sales representative to receive a complimentary one-year subscription.

Excel Applications for Corporate Finance, by Troy Adair, University of Michigan–Ann Arbor, can be packaged with the text at a discounted price. This supplement teaches students how to build financial models in Excel, and shows students how to use these models to solve a variety of common corporate finance problems. For more information about this supplement, visit www.mhhe.com/adair1e.

FinGame Online 4.0, by LeRoy Brooks, John Carroll University
(ISBN 10: 0072922192/ISBN 13: 9780072922196)

Just $15.00 when packaged with this text. In this comprehensive simulation game, students control a hypothetical company over numerous periods of operation. The game is now tied to the text by exercises found on the Online Learning Center. As students make major financial and operating decisions for their company, they will develop and enhance skills in financial management and financial accounting statement analysis.

Financial Analysis with an Electronic Calculator, Sixth Edition

by Mark A. White, University of Virginia, McIntire School of Commerce
(ISBN 10: 0073217093/ISBN 13: 9780073217093)
The information and procedures in this supplementary text enable students to master the use of financial calculators and develop a working knowledge of financial mathematics and problem solving. Complete instructions are included for solving all major problem types on three popular models: HP 10-B and 12-C, TI BA II Plus, and TI-84. Hands-on problems with detailed solutions allow students to practice the skills outlined in the text and obtain instant reinforcement. *Financial Analysis with an Electronic Calculator* is a self-contained supplement to the introductory financial management course.

ACKNOWLEDGMENTS

To borrow a phrase, writing a finance textbook is easy—all you do is sit down at a word processor and open a vein. We never would have completed this book without the incredible amount of help and support we received from our colleagues, students, editors, family members, and friends. We would like to thank, without implicating, all of you.

Clearly, our greatest debt is to our many colleagues (and their students) who, like us, wanted to try an alternative to what they were using. Needless to say, without this support, we would not be publishing this text.

To the following reviewers, then, we are grateful for their many contributions:

Dean Baim, *Pepperdine University*
William Chittenden, *Texas State University*
Louis C. Gasper, *University of Dallas*
Louis Gingerella, *Rensselaer at Hartford*
Edward Harding, *Plymouth State University*
Brett A. King, *University of North Alabama*
Dr. Phillip T. Kolbe, *University of Memphis*
Yulong Ma, *California State University-Long Beach*
Edward Morris, *Lindenwood University*
Jeryl L. Nelson, *Wayne State College*
Srinivas Nippani, *Texas A&M University-Commerce*
Dr. Vivek Pandey, *University of Texas at Tyler*
Janet Payne, *Texas State University*
Wayne Price, *Golden Gate University-San Francisco*
William A. Reese, Jr., *Tulane University*
Mark Sunderman, *University of Wyoming*
Mahmoud Wahab, *University of Hartford*
Joseph Vu, *DePaul University*

We owe a special thanks to Steven Dolvin, Butler University. Steve worked on many of the supplements that accompany this book, including the Instructor's Manual and the Instructor PowerPoint Presentation.

We also thank Joseph Smolira of Belmont University for his work on this book. Joe worked closely with us to develop portions of the Instructor's Manual, along with the many vignettes and real-world examples. In addition, we would like to thank Kay Johnson, Penn State University–Erie, for creating the self-study questions on the OLC, as well as the Student PowerPoints.

We would also like to thank Charles Bebrowsky, University of Kentucky; Lei Wen, Buena Vista University; Linda De Angelo, Dennis Draper, Kim Dietrich, Harry De Angelo, Aris Protopapadakis, Suh-Pyng Ku, and Mark Westerfield, all of the Marshall School of Business at the University of Southern California; and Jordan Strauss Esq.; and Michael Griffin, University of Massachusetts–Dartmouth, for their contributions to this edition. We also owe a debt of gratitude to Edward I. Altman of New York University; Robert S. Hansen of Virginia Tech; and Jay Ritter of the University of Florida, who have provided many thoughtful comments and immeasurable help.

The following University of Kentucky doctoral students did outstanding work on this edition: Evgenia Dyshlyuk, Hinh Khieu, Jim Wolin, Jon Fulkerson, and Pankaj Maskara. To them fell the unenviable task of technical proofreading, and in particular, careful checking of each calculation throughout the text and Instructor's Manual.

Finally, in every phase of this project, we have been privileged to have had the complete and unwavering support of a great organization, McGraw-Hill/Irwin. We especially thank the McGraw-Hill/Irwin sales organization. The suggestions they provide, their professionalism in assisting potential adopters, and the service they provide have been a major factor in our success.

We are deeply grateful to the select group of professionals who served as our development team on this edition: Michele Janicek, Senior Sponsoring Editor; Jennifer Rizzi, Development Editor II; Rhonda Seelinger, Executive Marketing Manager; Julie Phifer, Marketing Manager; Christine Vaughan, Lead Project Manager; Kami Carter, Senior Designer; and Rose Hepburn, Lead Production Supervisor. Others at McGraw-Hill/Irwin, too numerous to list here, have improved the book in countless ways.

Finally, we wish to thank our families, Carol, Kate, Jon, Jan, Mark, Lynne, and Susan, for their forbearance and help.

Throughout the development of this edition, we have taken great care to discover and eliminate errors. Our goal is to provide the best textbook available on the subject. To ensure that future editions are error-free, we gladly offer $10 per arithmetic error to the first individual reporting it as a modest token of our appreciation. More than this, we would like to hear from instructors and students alike. Please write and tell us how to make this a better text. Forward your comments to: Dr. Brad Jordan, c/o Editorial–Finance, McGraw-Hill/Irwin, 1333 Burr Ridge Parkway, Burr Ridge, IL 60527 or visit us online at www.mhhe.com/rwj.

Stephen A. Ross
Randolph W. Westerfield
Jeffrey F. Jaffe
Bradford D. Jordan

BRIEF CONTENTS

PART ONE **Overview**

CHAPTER ONE — Introduction to Corporate Finance 1
CHAPTER TWO — Financial Statements and Cash Flow 22
CHAPTER THREE — Financial Statements Analysis and Long-Term Planning 45

PART TWO **Valuation and Capital Budgeting**

CHAPTER FOUR — Discounted Cash Flow Valuation 89
CHAPTER FIVE — Interest Rates and Bond Valuation 131
CHAPTER SIX — Stock Valuation 167
CHAPTER SEVEN — Net Present Value and Other Investment Rules 203
CHAPTER EIGHT — Making Capital Investment Decisions 240
CHAPTER NINE — Risk Analysis, Real Options, and Capital Budgeting 271

PART THREE **Risk and Return**

CHAPTER TEN — Risk and Return Lessons from Market History 297
CHAPTER ELEVEN — Return and Risk: *The Capital Asset Pricing Model (CAPM)* 322
CHAPTER TWELVE — Risk, Cost of Capital, and Capital Budgeting 365

PART FOUR **Capital Structure and Dividend Policy**

CHAPTER THIRTEEN — Corporate Financing Decisions and Efficient Capital Markets 390
CHAPTER FOURTEEN — Capital Structure: *Basic Concepts* 426
CHAPTER FIFTEEN — Capital Structure: *Limits to the Use of Debt* 455
CHAPTER SIXTEEN — Dividends and Other Payouts 487

PART FIVE **Special Topics**

CHAPTER SEVENTEEN — Options and Corporate Finance 523
CHAPTER EIGHTEEN — Short-Term Finance and Planning 565
CHAPTER NINETEEN — Mergers and Acquisitions 596
CHAPTER TWENTY — International Corporate Finance 625

APPENDIX A — Mathematical Tables 653
APPENDIX B — Solutions to Selected End-of-Chapter Problems 663
INDEX 667

CONTENTS

PART ONE Overview

CHAPTER ONE
Introduction to Corporate Finance 1

1.1 What Is Corporate Finance? 2

The Balance Sheet Model of the Firm 2

Capital Structure 3

The Financial Manager 4

Identification of Cash Flows 5

Timing of Cash Flows 6

Risk of Cash Flows 7

1.2 The Corporate Firm 7

The Sole Proprietorship 7

The Partnership 8

The Corporation 9

A Corporation by Another Name . . . 10

1.3 The Goal of Financial Management 11

Possible Goals 11

The Goal of Financial Management 12

A More General Goal 12

1.4 The Agency Problem and Control of the Corporation 13

Agency Relationships 13

Management Goals 13

Do Managers Act in the Stockholders' Interests? 14

Managerial Compensation 14

Control of the Firm 14

Conclusion 15

Stakeholders 15

1.5 Financial Markets 15

The Primary Market: New Issues 16

Secondary Markets 16

Dealer versus Auction Markets 16

Trading in Corporate Securities 16

Exchange Trading of Listed Stocks 17

Listing 18

Summary and Conclusions 19

Closing Case: The McGee Cake Company 21

CHAPTER TWO
Financial Statements and Cash Flow 22

2.1 The Balance Sheet 23

Accounting Liquidity 24

Debt versus Equity 24

Value versus Cost 24

2.2 The Income Statement 25

Generally Accepted Accounting Principles 26

Noncash Items 27

Time and Costs 27

2.3 Taxes 28

Corporate Tax Rates 28

Average versus Marginal Tax Rates 28

2.4 Net Working Capital 30

2.5 Financial Cash Flow 30

2.6 The Accounting Statement of Cash Flows 33

Cash Flow from Operating Activities 33

Cash Flow from Investing Activities 34

Cash Flow from Financing Activities 35

Summary and Conclusions 36

Closing Case: Cash Flows at Warf Computers, Inc. 43

CHAPTER THREE
Financial Statements Analysis and Long-Term Planning 45

3.1 Financial Statements Analysis 46

Standardizing Statements 46

Common-Size Balance Sheets 46

Common-Size Income Statements 48

3.2 Ratio Analysis 48
Short-Term Solvency or Liquidity Measures 49
Current Ratio 49
Quick (or Acid-Test) Ratio 50
Cash Ratio 51
Long-Term Solvency Measures 51
Total Debt Ratio 51
Times Interest Earned 51
Cash Coverage 52
Asset Management or Turnover Measures 52
Inventory Turnover and Days' Sales in Inventory 52
Receivables Turnover and Days' Sales in Receivables 53
Total Asset Turnover 53
Profitability Measures 54
Profit Margin 54
Return on Assets 54
Return on Equity 54
Market Value Measures 55
Price-Earnings Ratio 55
Market-to-Book Ratio 55
3.3 The Du Pont Identity 56
A Closer Look at ROE 56
An Expanded Du Pont Analysis 58
3.4 Using Financial Statement Information 59
Choosing a Benchmark 59
Time-Trend Analysis 60
Peer Group Analysis 61
Problems with Financial Statement Analysis 65
3.5 Long-Term Financial Planning 66
A Simple Financial Planning Model 66
The Percentage of Sales Approach 67
The Income Statement 67
The Balance Sheet 68
A Particular Scenario 70
3.6 External Financing and Growth 71
EFN and Growth 72
Financial Policy and Growth 74
The Internal Growth Rate 74
The Sustainable Growth Rate 75
Determinants of Growth 76
A Note on Sustainable Growth Rate Calculations 78
3.7 Some Caveats regarding Financial Planning Models 78
Summary and Conclusions 79
Closing Case: Ratios and Financial Planning at East Coast Yachts 86

PART TWO Valuation and Capital Budgeting

CHAPTER FOUR
Discounted Cash Flow Valuation 89

4.1 Valuation: The One-Period Case 90
4.2 The Multiperiod Case 93
Future Value and Compounding 93
The Power of Compounding: A Digression 96
Present Value and Discounting 97
The Algebraic Formula 101
4.3 Compounding Periods 101
Distinction between Stated Annual Interest Rate and Effective Annual Rate 103
Compounding over Many Years 105
Continuous Compounding 106
4.4 Simplifications 107
Perpetuity 107
Growing Perpetuity 108
Annuity 110
Trick 1: A Delayed Annuity 112
Trick 2: Annuity due 113
Trick 3: The Infrequent Annuity 114
Trick 4: Equating Present Value of Two Annuities 114
Growing Annuity 115
4.5 What Is a Firm Worth? 117
Summary and Conclusions 118
Closing Case: The MBA Decision 130

CHAPTER FIVE
Interest Rates and Bond Valuation 131

5.1 Bonds and Bond Valuation 132
Bond Features and Prices 132
Bond Values and Yields 132
Interest Rate Risk 135
Finding the Yield to Maturity: More Trial and Error 137
5.2 More on Bond Features 139
Is It Debt or Equity? 141
Long-Term Debt: The Basics 141

The Indenture *142*
Terms of a Bond 143
Security 143
Seniority 144
Repayment 144
The Call Provision 144
Protective Covenants 145
5.3 Bond Ratings 145
5.4 Some Different Types of Bonds 147
Government Bonds *147*
Zero Coupon Bonds *148*
Floating Rate Bonds *148*
Other Types of Bonds *149*
5.5 Bond Markets 150
How Bonds Are Bought and Sold *150*
Bond Price Reporting *151*
A Note on Bond Price Quotes *154*
5.6 Inflation and Interest Rates 154
Real versus Nominal Rates *154*
The Fisher Effect *155*
5.7 Determinants of Bond Yields 156
The Term Structure of Interest Rates *156*
Bond Yields and the Yield Curve: Putting It All Together *159*
Conclusion *160*
Summary and Conclusions 160
Closing Case: Financing East Coast Yachts's Expansion Plans with A Bond Issue 166

CHAPTER SIX
Stock Valuation 167

6.1 The Present Value of Common Stocks 168
Dividends versus Capital Gains *168*
Valuation of Different Types of Stocks *169*
Case 1 (Zero Growth) 170
Case 2 (Constant Growth) 170
Case 3 (Differential Growth) 171
6.2 Estimates of Parameters in the Dividend Discount Model 172
Where Does g *Come From?* *172*
Where Does R *Come From?* *173*
A Healthy Sense of Skepticism *175*
6.3 Growth Opportunities 175
Growth in Earnings and Dividends versus Growth Opportunities *178*
Dividends or Earnings: Which to Discount? *178*
The No-Dividend Firm *179*
6.4 The Dividend Growth Model and the NPVGO Model 179
The Dividend Growth Model *180*
The NPVGO Model *180*
Summation *181*
6.5 Price-Earnings Ratio 181
6.6 Some Features of Common and Preferred Stocks 183
Common Stock Features *183*
Shareholder Rights 183
Proxy Voting 185
Classes of Stock 185
Other Rights 185
Dividends 186
Preferred Stock Features *186*
Stated Value 186
Cumulative and Noncumulative Dividends 186
Is Preferred Stock Really Debt? 187
6.7 The Stock Markets 187
Dealers and Brokers *187*
Organization of the NYSE *188*
Members 188
Operations 189
Floor Activity 189
NASDAQ Operations *190*
NASDAQ Participants 191
Stock Market Reporting *193*
Summary and Conclusions 195
Closing Case: Stock Valuation at Ragan Thermal Systems 201

CHAPTER SEVEN
Net Present Value and Other Investment Rules 203

7.1 Why Use Net Present Value? 204
7.2 The Payback Period Method 206
Defining the Rule *206*
Problems with the Payback Method *207*
Problem 1: Timing of Cash Flows within the Payback Period 207
Problem 2: Payments after the Payback Period 207
Problem 3: Arbitrary Standard for Payback Period 208

Managerial Perspective 208
Summary of Payback 208
7.3 The Discounted Payback Period Method 209
7.4 The Average Accounting Return Method 209
Defining the Rule 209
Step 1: Determining Average Net Income 210
Step 2: Determining Average Investment 211
Step 3: Determining AAR 211
Analyzing the Average Accounting Return Method 211
7.5 The Internal Rate of Return 212
7.6 Problems with the IRR Approach 214
Definition of Independent and Mutually Exclusive Projects 214
Two General Problems Affecting Both Independent and Mutually Exclusive Projects 215
Problem 1: Investing or Financing? 216
Problem 2: Multiple Rates of Return 216
NPV Rule 217
Modified IRR 217
The Guarantee against Multiple IRRs 218
General Rules 218
Problems Specific to Mutually Exclusive Projects 219
The Scale Problem 219
The Timing Problem 221
Redeeming Qualities of IRR 223
A Test 223
7.7 The Profitability Index 224
Calculation of Profitability Index 224
Application of the Profitability Index 224
7.8 The Practice of Capital Budgeting 226
Summary and Conclusions 228
Closing Case: Bullock Gold Mining 238

CHAPTER EIGHT
Making Capital Investment Decisions 240

8.1 Incremental Cash Flows 241
Cash Flows—Not Accounting Income 241
Sunk Costs 241
Opportunity Costs 242
Side Effects 242
Allocated Costs 242
8.2 The Baldwin Company: An Example 243
An Analysis of the Project 244
Investments 244
Income and Taxes 245
Salvage Value 247
Cash Flow 247
Net Present Value 247
Which Set of Books? 247
A Note on Net Working Capital 248
A Note on Depreciation 248
Interest Expense 249
8.3 Inflation and Capital Budgeting 249
Discounting: Nominal or Real? 250
8.4 Alternative Definitions of Operating Cash Flow 252
The Bottom-Up Approach 253
The Top-Down Approach 253
The Tax Shield Approach 254
Conclusion 254
8.5 Investments of Unequal Lives: The Equivalent Annual Cost Method 254
The General Decision to Replace 256
Summary and Conclusions 258
Closing Case: Bethesda Mining Company 268

CHAPTER NINE
Risk Analysis, Real Options, and Capital Budgeting 271

9.1 Decision Trees 272
Warning 273
9.2 Sensitivity Analysis, Scenario Analysis, and Break-Even Analysis 274
Sensitivity Analysis and Scenario Analysis 275
Revenues 275
Costs 275
Break-Even Analysis 278
Accounting Profit 278
Present Value 279
9.3 Monte Carlo Simulation 280
Step 1: Specify the Basic Model 280
Step 2: Specify a Distribution for Each Variable in the Model 281
Step 3: The Computer Draws One Outcome 282
Step 4: Repeat the Procedure 283
Step 5: Calculate NPV 283
9.4 Real Options 284
The Option to Expand 284
The Option to Abandon 285
Timing Options 287
Summary and Conclusions 288
Closing Case: Bunyan Lumber, LLC 295

PART THREE Risk and Return

CHAPTER TEN
Risk and Return Lessons from Market History 297

10.1 Returns 298
Dollar Returns 298
Percentage Returns 299
10.2 Holding Period Returns 301
10.3 Return Statistics 305
10.4 Average Stock Returns and Risk-Free Returns 308
10.5 Risk Statistics 310
Variance 310
Normal Distribution and Its Implications for Standard Deviation 311
10.6 More on Average Returns 312
Arithmetic versus Geometric Averages 312
Calculating Geometric Average Returns 313
Arithmetic Average Return or Geometric Average Return? 314
Summary and Conclusions 315
Closing Case: A Job at East Coast Yachts 320

CHAPTER ELEVEN
Return and Risk: *The Capital Asset Pricing Model (CAPM)* 322

11.1 Individual Securities 323
11.2 Expected Return, Variance, and Covariance 323
Expected Return and Variance 323
Covariance and Correlation 324
11.3 The Return and Risk for Portfolios 327
The Example of Supertech and Slowpoke 327
The Expected Return on a Portfolio 327
Variance and Standard Deviation of a Portfolio 328
The Variance 328
Standard Deviation of a Portfolio 329
The Diversification Effect 329
An Extension to Many Assets 330
11.4 The Efficient Set 331
The Two Asset Case 331
The Efficient Set for Many Securities 335
11.5 Riskless Borrowing and Lending 336
The Optimal Portfolio 338
11.6 Announcements, Surprises, and Expected Returns 339
Expected and Unexpected Returns 339
Announcements and News 340
11.7 Risk: Systematic and Unsystematic 341
Systematic and Unsystematic Risk 342
Systematic and Unsystematic Components of Return 342
11.8 Diversification and Portfolio Risk 342
The Effect of Diversification: Another Lesson from Market History 343
The Principle of Diversification 343
Diversification and Unsystematic Risk 344
Diversification and Systematic Risk 345
11.9 Market Equilibrium 345
Definition of the Market Equilibrium Portfolio 345
Definition of Risk When Investors Hold the Market Portfolio 346
The Formula for Beta 349
A Test 349
11.10 Relationship between Risk and Expected Return (CAPM) 351
Expected Return on Market 351
Expected Return on Individual Security 351
Summary and Conclusions 354
Closing Case: A Job at East Coast Yachts, Part 2 363

CHAPTER TWELVE
Risk, Cost of Capital, and Capital Budgeting 365

12.1 The Cost of Equity Capital 366
12.2 Estimation of Beta 368
Real World Betas 369
Stability of Beta 370
Using an Industry Beta 371
12.3 Determinants of Beta 372
Cyclicality of Revenues 372
Operating Leverage 372
Financial Leverage and Beta 374
12.4 Extensions of the Basic Model 375
The Firm versus the Project: Vive la Différence 375
The Cost of Capital with Debt 376
12.5 Estimating Eastman Chemical's Cost of Capital 379
Eastman's Cost of Equity 379
Eastman's Cost of Debt 380
Eastman's WACC 381
Summary and Conclusions 384
Closing Case: The Cost of Capital for Goff Computer, Inc. 389

PART FOUR Capital Structure and Dividend Policy

CHAPTER THIRTEEN
Corporate Financing Decisions and Efficient Capital Markets 390

13.1 Can Financing Decisions Create Value? 391
13.2 A Description of Efficient Capital Markets 393
Foundations of Market Efficiency 394
Rationality 394
Independent Deviations from Rationality 394
Arbitrage 395
13.3 The Different Types of Efficiency 395
The Weak Form 396
The Semistrong and Strong Forms 396
Some Common Misconceptions about the Efficient Market Hypothesis 398
The Efficacy of Dart Throwing 398
Price Fluctuations 398
Stockholder Disinterest 398
13.4 The Evidence 399
The Weak Form 399
The Semistrong Form 401
Event Studies 401
The Record of Mutual Funds 403
The Strong Form 403
13.5 The Behavioral Challenge to Market Efficiency 404
Rationality 404
Independent Deviations from Rationality 404
Arbitrage 405
13.6 Empirical Challenges to Market Efficiency 405
13.7 Reviewing the Differences 411
Representativeness 411
Conservatism 411
13.8 Implications for Corporate Finance 412
1. Accounting Choices, Financial Choices, and Market Efficiency 412
2. The Timing Decision 413
3. Speculation and Efficient Markets 415
4. Information in Market Prices 416
Summary and Conclusions 418
Closing Case: Your 401(K) Account at East Coast Yachts 424

CHAPTER FOURTEEN
Capital Structure: *Basic Concepts* 426

14.1 The Capital Structure Question and the Pie Theory 427
14.2 Maximizing Firm Value versus Maximizing Stockholder Interests 427
14.3 Financial Leverage and Firm Value: An Example 429
Leverage and Returns to Shareholders 429
The Choice between Debt and Equity 431
A Key Assumption 433
14.4 Modigliani and Miller: Proposition II (No Taxes) 433
Risk to Equityholders Rises with Leverage 433
Proposition II: Required Return to Equityholders Rises with Leverage 434
MM: An Interpretation 439
14.5 Taxes 440
The Basic Insight 440
Present Value of the Tax Shield 442
Value of the Levered Firm 442
Expected Return and Leverage under Corporate Taxes 444
The Weighted Average Cost of Capital R_{WACC} and Corporate Taxes 445
Stock Price and Leverage under Corporate Taxes 445
Summary and Conclusions 447
Closing Case: Stephenson Real Estate Recapitalization 454

CHAPTER FIFTEEN
Capital Structure: *Limits to the Use of Debt* 455

15.1 Costs of Financial Distress 456
Direct Bankruptcy Costs 456
Indirect Bankruptcy Costs 456
Agency Costs 457
Summary of Selfish Strategies 459
15.2 Can Costs of Debt Be Reduced? 460
Protective Covenants 460
Consolidation of Debt 461
15.3 Integration of Tax Effects and Financial Distress Costs 461
Pie Again 463
15.4 Signaling 464
15.5 Shirking, Perquisites, and Bad Investments: A Note on Agency Cost of Equity 466
Effect of Agency Costs of Equity on Debt-Equity Financing 468
Free Cash Flow 468
15.6 The Pecking-Order Theory 468
Rules of the Pecking Order 470
Rule #1 Use Internal Financing 470
Rule #2 Issue Safe Securities First 470
Implications 470

15.7 Growth and the Debt-Equity Ratio 471

No Growth 471

Growth 472

15.8 How Firms Establish Capital Structure 473

15.9 A Quick Look at the Bankruptcy Process 478

Liquidation and Reorganization 478

Bankruptcy Liquidation 478

Bankruptcy Reorganization 479

Financial Management and the Bankruptcy Process 480

Agreements to Avoid Bankruptcy 481

Summary and Conclusions 481

Closing Case: McKenzie Corporation's Capital Budgeting 486

CHAPTER SIXTEEN
Dividends and Other Payouts 487

16.1 Different Types of Dividends 488

16.2 Standard Method of Cash Dividend Payment 488

16.3 The Benchmark Case: An Illustration of the Irrelevance of Dividend Policy 490

Current Policy: Dividends Set Equal to Cash Flow 490

Alternative Policy: Initial Dividend Is Greater than Cash Flow 491

The Indifference Proposition 491

Homemade Dividends 492

A Test 493

Dividends and Investment Policy 494

16.4 Repurchase of Stock 494

Dividend versus Repurchase: Conceptual Example 496

Dividends versus Repurchases: Real World Considerations 497

1. Flexibility 497

2. Executive Compensation 497

3. Offset to Dilution 497

4. Repurchase as Investment 497

5. Taxes 497

16.5 Personal Taxes, Issuance Costs, and Dividends 498

Firms without Sufficient Cash to Pay a Dividend 498

Firms with Sufficient Cash to Pay a Dividend 499

Summary on Personal Taxes 501

16.6 Real World Factors Favoring a High-Dividend Policy 501

Desire for Current Income 501

Behavioral Finance 501

Agency Costs 502

Information Content of Dividends and Dividend Signaling 503

Information Content 503

16.7 The Clientele Effect: A Resolution of Real World Factors? 504

16.8 What We Know and Do Not Know about Dividend Policy 505

Corporate Dividends Are Substantial 505

Corporations Smooth Dividends 506

Payouts Provide Information to the Market 508

A Sensible Payout Policy 508

Some Survey Evidence on Dividends 509

16.9 Stock Dividends and Stock Splits 510

Some Details on Stock Splits and Stock Dividends 510

Example of a Small Stock Dividend 510

Example of a Stock Split 511

Example of a Large Stock Dividend 511

Value of Stock Splits and Stock Dividends 511

The Benchmark Case 512

Popular Trading Range 512

Reverse Splits 512

Summary and Conclusions 513

Closing Case: Electronic Timing, Inc. 521

PART FIVE Special Topics

CHAPTER SEVENTEEN
Options and Corporate Finance 523

17.1 Options 524

17.2 Call Options 524

The Value of a Call Option at Expiration 524

17.3 Put Options 526

The Value of a Put Option at Expiration 526

17.4 Selling Options 527

17.5 Option Quotes 528

17.6 Combinations of Options 529

17.7 Valuing Options 532

Bounding the Value of a Call 532

Lower Bound 532

Upper Bound 533

The Factors Determining Call Option Values 533

Exercise Price 533

Expiration Date 534

Stock Price 534
The Key Factor: The Variability of the Underlying Asset 535
The Interest Rate 536
A Quick Discussion of Factors Determining Put Option Values 536
17.8 An Option Pricing Formula 536
A Two-State Option Model 537
Determining the Delta 538
Determining the Amount of Borrowing 538
Risk-Neutral Valuation 538
The Black-Scholes Model 539
17.9 Stocks and Bonds as Options 544
The Firm Expressed in Terms of Call Options 544
The Stockholders 544
The Bondholders 545
The Firm Expressed in Terms of Put Options 546
The Stockholders 546
The Bondholders 546
A Resolution of the Two Views 547
A Note on Loan Guarantees 548
17.10 Options and Corporate Decisions: Some Applications 549
Mergers and Diversification 549
Options and Capital Budgeting 550
17.11 Investment in Real Projects and Options 552
Summary and Conclusions 554
Closing Case: Exotic Cuisine Employee Stock Options 563

CHAPTER EIGHTEEN
Short-Term Finance and Planning 565

18.1 Tracing Cash and Net Working Capital 566
18.2 The Operating Cycle and the Cash Cycle 568
Defining the Operating and Cash Cycles 568
The Operating Cycle 568
The Cash Cycle 568
The Operating Cycle and the Firm's Organization Chart 571
Calculating the Operating and Cash Cycles 571
The Operating Cycle 572
The Cash Cycle 573
Interpreting the Cash Cycle 573
18.3 Some Aspects of Short-Term Financial Policy 574
The Size of the Firm's Investment in Current Assets 574
Alternative Financing Policies for Current Assets 577
An Ideal Case 577
Different Policies for Financing Current Assets 577
Which Financing Policy Is Best? 579
Current Assets and Liabilities in Practice 580
18.4 The Cash Budget 580
Sales and Cash Collections 580
Cash Outflows 581
The Cash Balance 582
18.5 Short-Term Borrowing 582
Unsecured Loans 583
Compensating Balances 583
Cost of a Compensating Balance 583
Letters of Credit 584
Secured Loans 584
Accounts Receivable Financing 584
Inventory Loans 585
Other Sources 585
18.6 A Short-Term Financial Plan 586
Summary and Conclusions 587
Closing Case: Keafer Manufacturing Working Capital Management 594

CHAPTER NINETEEN
Mergers and Acquisitions 596

19.1 The Legal Forms of Acquisitions 597
Merger or Consolidation 597
Acquisition of Stock 598
Acquisition of Assets 599
Acquisition Classifications 599
A Note on Takeovers 599
Alternatives to Merger 600
19.2 Taxes and Acquisitions 600
Determinants of Tax Status 600
Taxable versus Tax-Free Acquisitions 600
19.3 Accounting for Acquisitions 601
The Purchase Method 601
Pooling of Interests 602
More on Goodwill 602
19.4 Gains from Acquisition 603
Synergy 603
Revenue Enhancement 604
Marketing Gains 604

Strategic Benefits 604
Market Power 605
Cost Reductions 605
Economies of Scale 605
Economies of Vertical Integration 605
Complementary Resources 605
Lower Taxes 606
Net Operating Losses 606
Unused Debt Capacity 606
Surplus Funds 606
Asset Write-Ups 607
Reductions in Capital Needs 607
Avoiding Mistakes 607
A Note on Inefficient Management 608
19.5 Some Financial Side Effects of Acquisitions 608
EPS Growth 608
Diversification 609
19.6 The Cost of an Acquisition 609
Case I: Cash Acquisition 610
Case II: Stock Acquisition 610
Cash versus Common Stock 611
19.7 Defensive Tactics 612
The Corporate Charter 612
Repurchase and Standstill Agreements 612
Poison Pills and Share Rights Plans 612
Going Private and Leveraged Buyouts 613
Other Devices and Jargon of Corporate Takeovers 614
19.8 Some Evidence on Acquisitions: Does M&A Pay? 615
19.9 Divestitures and Restructurings 615
Summary and Conclusions 616
Closing Case: The Birdie Golf–Hybrid Golf Merger 623

CHAPTER TWENTY
International Corporate Finance 625

20.1 Terminology 626
20.2 Foreign Exchange Markets and Exchange Rates 627
Exchange Rates 628
Exchange Rate Quotations 628
Cross-Rates and Triangle Arbitrage 630
Types of Transactions 631
20.3 Purchasing Power Parity 632
Absolute Purchasing Power Parity 632
Relative Purchasing Power Parity 633
The Basic Idea 633
The Result 635
Currency Appreciation and Depreciation 636
20.4 Interest Rate Parity, Unbiased Forward Rates, and the International Fisher Effect 636
Covered Interest Arbitrage 636
Interest Rate Parity 637
Forward Rates and Future Spot Rates 638
Putting It All Together 639
Uncovered Interest Parity 639
The International Fisher Effect 639
20.5 International Capital Budgeting 640
Method 1: The Home Currency Approach 640
Method 2: The Foreign Currency Approach 641
Unremitted Cash Flows 642
20.6 Exchange Rate Risk 642
Short-Run Exposure 642
Long-Run Exposure 643
Translation Exposure 644
Managing Exchange Rate Risk 645
20.7 Political Risk 645
Summary and Conclusions 646
Closing Case: East Coast Yachts Goes International 651

APPENDIX A MATHEMATICAL TABLES 653

APPENDIX B SOLUTIONS TO SELECTED END-OF-CHAPTER PROBLEMS 663

INDEX 667

LIST OF BOXES

THE REAL WORLD BOXES

CHAPTER 1 Sarbanes-Oxley 18

CHAPTER 2 Putting a Spin on Cash Flows 34

CHAPTER 3 What's in a Ratio? 58

CHAPTER 4 Jackpot! 104

CHAPTER 5 Beauty is in the Eye of the Bondholder 150

CHAPTER 6 How Fast Is Too Fast? 176
The Wild, Wild West of Stock Trading 192

CHAPTER 9 When Things Go Wrong . . . 274

CHAPTER 11 Beta, Beta, Who's Got the Beta? 350

CHAPTER 12 The Cost of Oil 382

CHAPTER 13 Can Stock Market Investors Add and Subtract? 406

CHAPTER 16 Stock Buybacks: No End in Sight 500

CHAPTER 18 A Look at Operating and Cash Cycles 570

CHAPTER 20 McPricing 634

CHAPTER 1

Introduction to Corporate Finance

OPENING CASE

In July 1999, Carleton "Carly" Fiorina assumed the position of CEO of Hewlett-Packard (HP). Investors were pleased with her view of HP's future: She promised 15 percent annual growth in sales and earnings, quite a goal for a company with five consecutive years of declining revenue. Ms. Fiorina also changed the way HP was run. Rather than continuing to operate as separate product groups, which essentially meant the company operated as dozens of mini-companies, Ms. Fiorina reorganized the company into just two divisions.

In 2002, HP announced that it would merge with Compaq Computers. However, in one of the more acrimonious corporate battles in recent history, a group led by Walter Hewlett, son of one of HP's cofounders, fought against the merger. Ms. Fiorina ultimately prevailed, and the merger took place. With Compaq in the fold, the company began a two-pronged strategy. It would compete with Dell in the lower-cost, more commodity-like personal computer segment and with IBM in the more specialized, high-end computing market.

Unfortunately for HP's shareholders, Ms. Fiorina's strategy did not work out as planned, and, in February 2005, under pressure from HP's board of directors, Ms. Fiorina resigned her position as CEO. Evidently, investors also felt a change in direction was a good idea; HP's stock price jumped almost seven percent the day the resignation was announced.

Understanding Ms. Fiorina's rise from corporate executive to chief executive officer, and finally, ex-employee, takes us into issues involving the corporate form of organization, corporate goals, and corporate control, all of which we discuss in this chapter.

1.1 WHAT IS CORPORATE FINANCE?

Suppose you decide to start a firm to make tennis balls. To do this, you hire managers to buy raw materials, and you assemble a work force that will produce and sell finished tennis balls. In the language of finance, you make an investment in assets such as inventory, machinery, land, and labor. The amount of cash you invest in assets must be matched by an equal amount of cash raised by financing. When you begin to sell tennis balls, your firm will generate cash. This is the basis of value creation. The purpose of the firm is to create value for you, the owner. The value is reflected in the framework of the simple balance sheet model of the firm.

The Balance Sheet Model of the Firm

Suppose we take a financial snapshot of the firm and its activities at a single point in time. Figure 1.1 shows a graphic conceptualization of the balance sheet, and it will help introduce you to corporate finance.

The assets of the firm are on the left-hand side of the balance sheet. These assets can be thought of as current and fixed. *Fixed assets* are those that will last a long time, such as buildings. Some fixed assets are tangible, such as machinery and equipment. Other fixed assets are intangible, such as patents and trademarks. The other category of assets, *current assets,* comprises those that have short lives, such as inventory. The tennis balls that your firm has made, but has not yet sold, are part of its inventory. Unless you have overproduced, they will leave the firm shortly.

Before a company can invest in an asset, it must obtain financing, which means that it must raise the money to pay for the investment. The forms of financing are represented on the right-hand side of the balance sheet. A firm will issue (sell) pieces of paper called *debt* (loan agreements) or *equity shares* (stock certificates). Just as assets are classified as long-lived or short-lived, so too are liabilities. A short-term debt is called a *current liability.* Short-term debt represents loans and other obligations that must be repaid within one year. Long-term debt is debt that does not have to be repaid within one year. Shareholders' equity represents the difference between the value of the assets and the debt of the firm. In this sense, it is a residual claim on the firm's assets.

From the balance sheet model of the firm, it is easy to see why finance can be thought of as the study of the following three questions:

1. In what long-lived assets should the firm invest? This question concerns the left-hand side of the balance sheet. Of course, the types and proportions of assets the firm needs tend to be set by the nature of the business. We use the term **capital budgeting** to describe the process of making and managing expenditures on long-lived assets.
2. How can the firm raise cash for required capital expenditures? This question concerns the right-hand side of the balance sheet. The answer to this involves the firm's **capital structure**, which represents the proportions of the firm's financing from current and long-term debt and equity.
3. How should short-term operating cash flows be managed? This question concerns the upper portion of the balance sheet. There is often a mismatch between the timing of cash inflows and cash outflows during operating activities. Furthermore, the amount and timing of operating cash flows are not known with certainty. The financial managers must attempt to manage the gaps in cash flow. From a balance sheet perspective, short-term management of cash flow is associated with a firm's **net working capital**. Net working capital is defined as current assets minus current liabilities. From a financial perspective, the short-term cash flow problem comes from the mismatching of cash inflows and outflows. It is the subject of short-term finance.

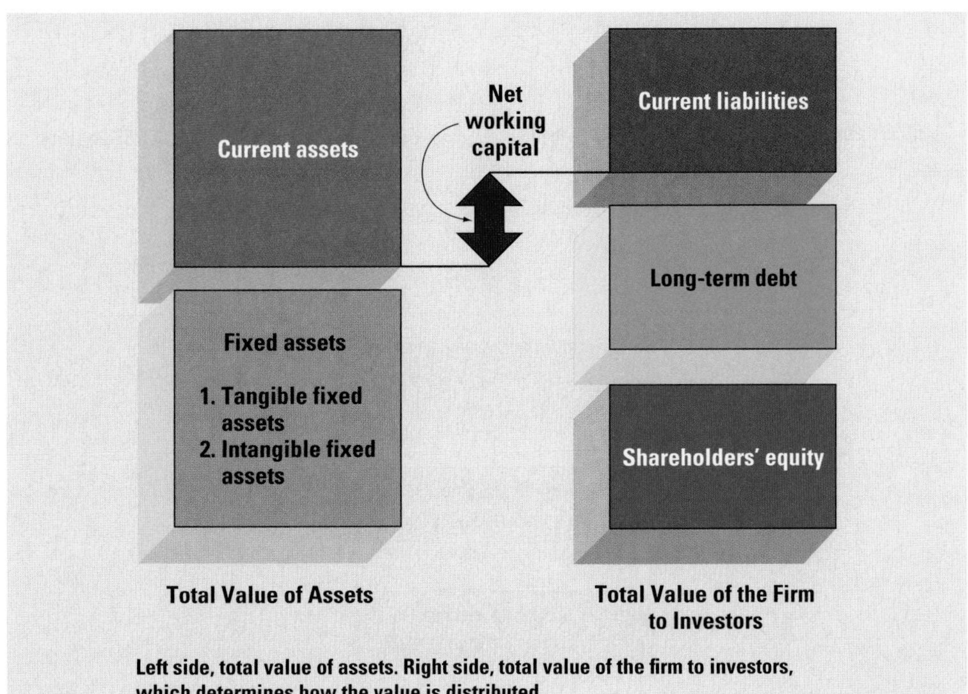

FIGURE 1.1
The Balance Sheet Model of the Firm

Capital Structure

Financing arrangements determine how the value of the firm is sliced up. The persons or institutions that buy debt from (i.e., loan money to) the firm are called *creditors.*[1] The holders of equity shares are called *shareholders.*

Sometimes it is useful to think of the firm as a pie. Initially, the size of the pie will depend on how well the firm has made its investment decisions. After a firm has made its investment decisions, it determines the value of its assets (e.g., its buildings, land, and inventories).

The firm can then determine its capital structure. The firm might initially have raised the cash to invest in its assets by issuing more debt than equity; now it can consider changing that mix by issuing more equity and using the proceeds to buy back (pay off) some of its debt. Financing decisions like this can be made independently of the original investment decisions. The decisions to issue debt and equity affect how the pie is sliced.

The pie we are thinking of is depicted in Figure 1.2. The size of the pie is the value of the firm in the financial markets. We can write the value of the firm, V, as

$$V = B + S$$

where B is the value of the debt and S is the value of the equity. The pie diagrams consider two ways of slicing the pie: 50 percent debt and 50 percent equity, and 25 percent debt and 75 percent equity. The way the pie is sliced could affect its value. If so, the goal of the financial manager will be to choose the ratio of debt to equity that makes the value of the pie–that is, the value of the firm, V–as large as it can be.

[1]We tend to use the words *creditors, debtholders,* and *bondholders* interchangeably. In later chapters we examine the differences among the kinds of creditors. In algebraic notation, we will usually refer to the firm's debt with the letter B (for bondholders).

FIGURE 1.2
Two Pie Models of the Firm

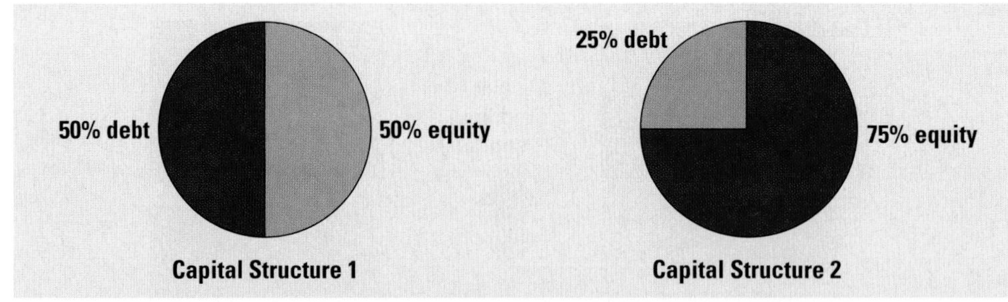

FIGURE 1.3
Hypothetical Organization Chart

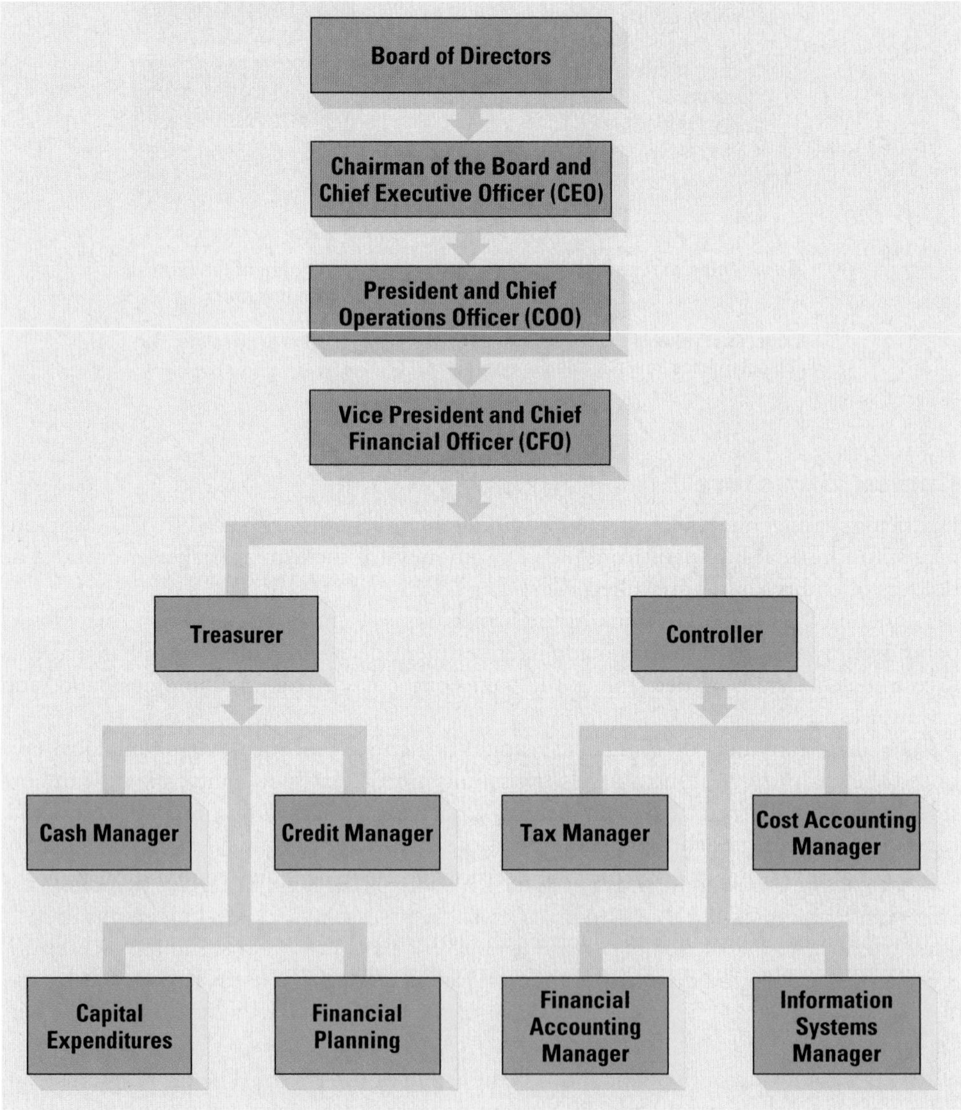

Board of Directors

Chairman of the Board and Chief Executive Officer (CEO)

President and Chief Operations Officer (COO)

Vice President and Chief Financial Officer (CFO)

Treasurer

Controller

Cash Manager

Credit Manager

Tax Manager

Cost Accounting Manager

Capital Expenditures

Financial Planning

Financial Accounting Manager

Information Systems Manager

The Financial Manager

In large firms, the finance activity is usually associated with a top officer of the firm, such as the vice president and chief financial officer, and some lesser officers. Figure 1.3 depicts a general organizational structure emphasizing the finance activity within the firm. Reporting to the chief financial officer are the treasurer and the controller. The treasurer is responsible for handling cash flows, managing capital expenditure decisions, and

For current issues facings CFOs, see www.cfo.com.

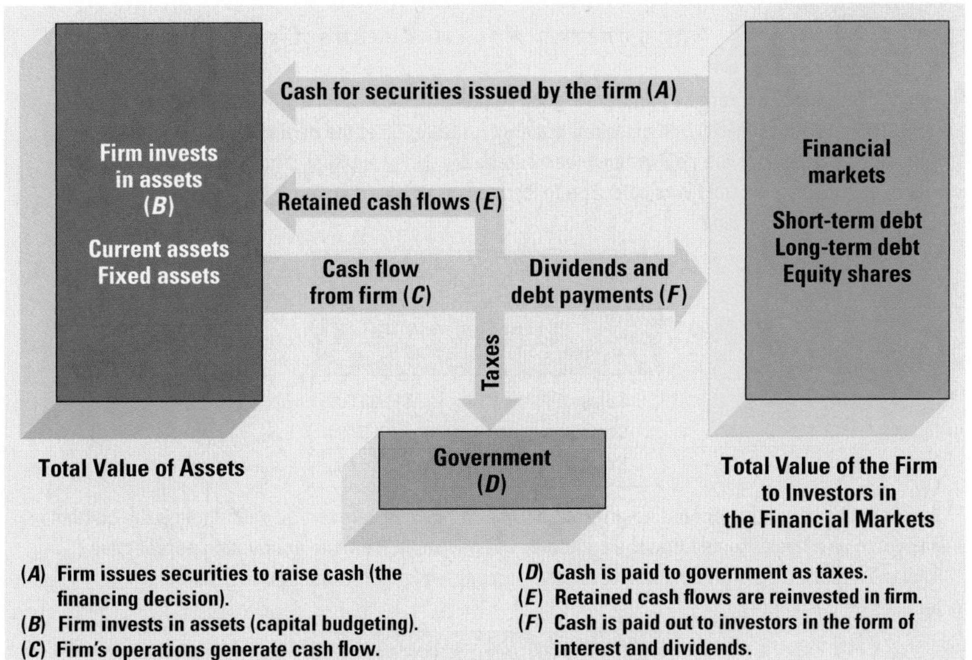

FIGURE 1.4
Cash Flows Between the Firm and the Financial Markets

making financial plans. The controller handles the accounting function, which includes taxes, cost and financial accounting, and information systems.

We think the most important job of a financial manager is to create value from the firm's capital budgeting, financing, and net working capital activities. How do financial managers create value? The answer is that the firm should:

1. Try to buy assets that generate more cash than they cost.
2. Sell bonds and stocks and other financial instruments that raise more cash than they cost.

Thus, the firm must create more cash flow than it uses. The cash flows paid to bondholders and stockholders of the firm should be greater than the cash flows put into the firm by the bondholders and stockholders. To see how this is done, we can trace the cash flows from the firm to the financial markets and back again.

The interplay of the firm's activities with the financial markets is illustrated in Figure 1.4. The arrows in Figure 1.4 trace cash flow from the firm to the financial markets and back again. Suppose we begin with the firm's financing activities. To raise money, the firm sells debt and equity shares to investors in the financial markets. This results in cash flows from the financial markets to the firm (A). This cash is invested in the investment activities (assets) of the firm (B) by the firm's management. The cash generated by the firm (C) is paid to shareholders and bondholders (F). The shareholders receive cash in the form of dividends; the bondholders who lent funds to the firm receive interest and, when the initial loan is repaid, principal. Not all of the firm's cash is paid out. Some is retained (E), and some is paid to the government as taxes (D).

Over time, if the cash paid to shareholders and bondholders (F) is greater than the cash raised in the financial markets (A), value will be created.

IDENTIFICATION OF CASH FLOWS Unfortunately, it is not all that easy to observe cash flows directly. Much of the information we obtain is in the form of accounting statements, and much of the work of financial analysis is to extract cash flow information from accounting statements. The following example illustrates how this is done.

EXAMPLE 1.1 Accounting Profit Versus Cash Flows

The Midland Company refines and trades gold. At the end of the year, it sold 2,500 ounces of gold for $1 million. The company had acquired the gold for $900,000 at the beginning of the year. The company paid cash for the gold when it was purchased. Unfortunately, it has yet to collect from the customer to whom the gold was sold. The following is a standard accounting of Midland's financial circumstances at year-end:

THE MIDLAND COMPANY Accounting View Income Statement Year Ended December 31	
Sales	$1,000,000
−Costs	−900,000
Profit	$ 100,000

By generally accepted accounting principles (GAAP), the sale is recorded even though the customer has yet to pay. It is assumed that the customer will pay soon. From the accounting perspective, Midland seems to be profitable. However, the perspective of corporate finance is different. It focuses on cash flows:

THE MIDLAND COMPANY Corporate Finance View Income Statement Year Ended December 31	
Cash inflow	$ 0
Cash outflow	−900,000
	−$900,000

The perspective of corporate finance is interested in whether cash flows are being created by the gold trading operations of Midland. Value creation depends on cash flows. For Midland, value creation depends on whether and when it actually receives $1 million.

TIMING OF CASH FLOWS The value of an investment made by a firm depends on the timing of cash flows. One of the most important principles of finance is that individuals prefer to receive cash flows earlier rather than later. One dollar received today is worth more than one dollar received next year.

EXAMPLE 1.2 Cash Flow Timing

The Midland Company is attempting to choose between two proposals for new products. Both proposals will provide additional cash flows over a four-year period and will initially cost $10,000. The cash flows from the proposals are as follows:

YEAR	NEW PRODUCT *A*	NEW PRODUCT *B*
1	$ 0	$ 4,000
2	0	4,000
3	0	4,000
4	20,000	4,000
Total	$20,000	$16,000

(continued)

At first it appears that new product *A* would be best. However, the cash flows from proposal *B* come earlier than those of *A*. Without more information, we cannot decide which set of cash flows would create the most value to the bondholders and shareholders. It depends on whether the value of getting cash from *B* up front outweighs the extra total cash from *A*. Bond and stock prices reflect this preference for earlier cash, and we will see how to use them to decide between *A* and *B*.

RISK OF CASH FLOWS The firm must consider risk. The amount and timing of cash flows are not usually known with certainty. Most investors have an aversion to risk.

EXAMPLE 1.3 Risk

The Midland Company is considering expanding operations overseas. It is evaluating Europe and Japan as possible sites. Europe is considered to be relatively safe, whereas operating in Japan is seen as very risky. In both cases, the company would close down operations after one year.

After doing a complete financial analysis, Midland has come up with the following cash flows of the alternative plans for expansion under three equally likely scenarios—pessimistic, most likely, and optimistic:

	PESSIMISTIC	MOST LIKELY	OPTIMISTIC
Europe	$75,000	$100,000	$125,000
Japan	0	150,000	200,000

If we ignore the pessimistic scenario, perhaps Japan is the best alternative. When we take the pessimistic scenario into account, the choice is unclear. Japan appears to be riskier, but it also offers a higher expected level of cash flow. What is risk and how can it be defined? We must try to answer this important question. Corporate finance cannot avoid coping with risky alternatives, and much of our book is devoted to developing methods for evaluating risky opportunities.

1.2 THE CORPORATE FIRM

The firm is a way of organizing the economic activity of many individuals. A basic problem of the firm is how to raise cash. The corporate form of business, that is, organizing the firm as a corporation, is the standard method for solving problems encountered in raising large amounts of cash. However, businesses can take other forms. In this section we consider the three basic legal forms of organizing firms, and we see how firms go about the task of raising large amounts of money under each form.

The Sole Proprietorship

A **sole proprietorship** is a business owned by one person. Suppose you decide to start a business to produce mousetraps. Going into business is simple: You announce to all who will listen, "Today, I am going to build a better mousetrap."

Most large cities require that you obtain a business license. Afterward, you can begin to hire as many people as you need and borrow whatever money you need. At year-end all the profits and the losses will be yours.

Here are some factors that are important in considering a sole proprietorship:

1. The sole proprietorship is the cheapest business to form. No formal charter is required, and few government regulations must be satisfied for most industries.

For more on small business organization, see the "Business and Human Resources" section at www.nolo.com.

2. A sole proprietorship pays no corporate income taxes. All profits of the business are taxed as individual income.
3. The sole proprietorship has unlimited liability for business debts and obligations. No distinction is made between personal and business assets.
4. The life of the sole proprietorship is limited by the life of the sole proprietor.
5. Because the only money invested in the firm is the proprietor's, the equity money that can be raised by the sole proprietor is limited to the proprietor's personal wealth.

The Partnership

Any two or more persons can get together and form a **partnership**. Partnerships fall into two categories: (1) general partnerships and (2) limited partnerships.

In a *general partnership,* all partners agree to provide some fraction of the work and cash and to share the profits and losses. Each partner is liable for all of the debts of the partnership. A partnership agreement specifies the nature of the arrangement. The partnership agreement may be an oral agreement or a formal document setting forth the understanding.

Limited partnerships permit the liability of some of the partners to be limited to the amount of cash each has contributed to the partnership. Limited partnerships usually require that (1) at least one partner be a general partner and (2) the limited partners do not participate in managing the business. Here are some things that are important when considering a partnership:

1. Partnerships are usually inexpensive and easy to form. Written documents are required in complicated arrangements, including general and limited partnerships. Business licenses and filing fees may be necessary.
2. General partners have unlimited liability for all debts. The liability of limited partners is usually limited to the contribution each has made to the partnership. If one general partner is unable to meet his or her commitment, the shortfall must be made up by the other general partners.
3. The general partnership is terminated when a general partner dies or withdraws (but this is not so for a limited partner). It is difficult for a partnership to transfer ownership without dissolving. Usually, all general partners must agree. However, limited partners may sell their interest in a business.
4. It is difficult for a partnership to raise large amounts of cash. Equity contributions are usually limited to a partner's ability and desire to contribute to the partnership. Many companies, such as Apple Computer, start life as a proprietorship or partnership, but at some point they choose to convert to corporate form.
5. Income from a partnership is taxed as personal income to the partners.
6. Management control resides with the general partners. Usually a majority vote is required on important matters, such as the amount of profit to be retained in the business.

It is very difficult for large business organizations to exist as sole proprietorships or partnerships. The main advantage to a sole proprietorship or partnership is the cost of getting started. Afterward, the disadvantages, which may become severe, are (1) unlimited liability, (2) limited life of the enterprise, and (3) difficulty of transferring ownership. These three disadvantages lead to (4) difficulty raising cash.

The Corporation

Of the many forms of business enterprises, the **corporation** is by far the most important. It is a distinct legal entity. As such, a corporation can have a name and enjoy many of the legal powers of natural persons. For example, corporations can acquire and exchange property. Corporations can enter into contracts and may sue and be sued. For jurisdictional purposes, the corporation is a citizen of its state of incorporation (it cannot vote, however).

Starting a corporation is more complicated than starting a proprietorship or partnership. The incorporators must prepare articles of incorporation and a set of bylaws. The articles of incorporation must include the following:

1. Name of the corporation.
2. Intended life of the corporation (it may be forever).
3. Business purpose.
4. Number of shares of stock that the corporation is authorized to issue, with a statement of limitations and rights of different classes of shares.
5. Nature of the rights granted to shareholders.
6. Number of members of the initial board of directors.

The bylaws are the rules to be used by the corporation to regulate its own existence, and they concern its shareholders, directors, and officers. Bylaws range from the briefest possible statement of rules for the corporation's management to hundreds of pages of text.

In its simplest form, the corporation comprises three sets of distinct interests: the shareholders (the owners), the directors, and the corporation officers (the top management). Traditionally, the shareholders control the corporation's direction, policies, and activities. The shareholders elect a board of directors, who in turn select top management. Members of top management serve as corporate officers and manage the operations of the corporation in the best interest of the shareholders. In closely held corporations with few shareholders, there may be a large overlap among the shareholders, the directors, and the top management. However, in larger corporations, the shareholders, directors, and the top management are likely to be distinct groups.

The potential separation of ownership from management gives the corporation several advantages over proprietorships and partnerships:

1. Because ownership in a corporation is represented by shares of stock, ownership can be readily transferred to new owners. Because the corporation exists independently of those who own its shares, there is no limit to the transferability of shares as there is in partnerships.
2. The corporation has unlimited life. Because the corporation is separate from its owners, the death or withdrawal of an owner does not affect its legal existence. The corporation can continue on after the original owners have withdrawn.
3. The shareholders' liability is limited to the amount invested in the ownership shares. For example, if a shareholder purchased $1,000 in shares of a corporation, the potential loss would be $1,000. In a partnership, a general partner with a $1,000 contribution could lose the $1,000 plus any other indebtedness of the partnership.

Limited liability, ease of ownership transfer, and perpetual succession are the major advantages of the corporation form of business organization. These give the corporation an enhanced ability to raise cash.

TABLE 1.1
A Comparison of Partnerships and Corporations

	CORPORATION	PARTNERSHIP
Liquidity and marketability	Shares can be exchanged without termination of the corporation. Common stock can be listed on stock exchange.	Units are subject to substantial restrictions on transferability. There is usually no established trading market for partnership units.
Voting rights	Usually each share of common stock entitles the holder to one vote per share on matters requiring a vote and on the election of the directors. Directors determine top management.	Some voting rights by limited partners. However, general partner has exclusive control and management of operations.
Taxation	Corporations have double taxation: Corporate income is taxable, and dividends to shareholders are also taxable.	Partnerships are not taxable. Partners pay personal taxes on partnership profits.
Reinvestment and dividend payout	Corporations have broad latitude on dividend payout decisions.	Partnerships are generally prohibited from reinvesting partnership profits. All profits are distributed to partners.
Liability	Shareholders are not personally liable for obligations of the corporation.	Limited partners are not liable for obligations of partnerships. General partners may have unlimited liability.
Continuity of existence	Corporations may have a perpetual life.	Partnerships have limited life.

There is, however, one great disadvantage to incorporation. The federal government taxes corporate income (the states do as well). This tax is in addition to the personal income tax that shareholders pay on dividend income they receive. This is double taxation for shareholders when compared to taxation on proprietorships and partnerships. Table 1.1 summarizes our discussion of partnerships and corporations.

Today, all 50 states have enacted laws allowing for the creation of a relatively new form of business organization, the limited liability company (LLC). The goal of this entity is to operate and be taxed like a partnership but retain limited liability for owners, so an LLC is essentially a hybrid of partnership and corporation. Although states have differing definitions for LLCs, the more important scorekeeper is the Internal Revenue Service (IRS). The IRS will consider an LLC a corporation, thereby subjecting it to double taxation, unless it meets certain specific criteria. In essence, an LLC cannot be too corporationlike, or it will be treated as one by the IRS. LLCs have become common. For example, Goldman, Sachs and Co., one of Wall Street's last remaining partnerships, decided to convert from a private partnership to an LLC (it later "went public," becoming a publicly held corporation). Large accounting firms and law firms by the score have converted to LLCs.

To find out more about LLCs, visit www.corporate.com.

A Corporation by Another Name . . .

The corporate form of organization has many variations around the world. The exact laws and regulations differ from country to country, of course, but the essential features of public ownership and limited liability remain. These firms are often called *joint stock companies, public limited companies,* or *limited liability companies,* depending on the specific nature of the firm and the country of origin.

Table 1.2 gives the names of a few well-known international corporations, their country of origin, and a translation of the abbreviation that follows the company name.

TABLE 1.2
International Corporations

COMPANY	COUNTRY OF ORIGIN	Type of Company: IN ORIGINAL LANGUAGE	Type of Company: TRANSLATED
Bayerische Moterenwerke (BMW) AG	Germany	Aktiengesellschaft	Corporation
Dornier GmBH	Germany	Gesellschaft mit Beschraenkter Haftung	Limited liability company
Rolls-Royce PLC	United Kingdom	Public limited company	Public limited company
Shell UK Ltd.	United Kingdom	Limited	Corporation
Unilever NV	Netherlands	Naamloze Vennootschap	Joint stock company
Fiat SpA	Italy	Societa per Azioni	Joint stock company
Volvo AB	Sweden	Aktiebolag	Joint stock company
Peugeot SA	France	Société Anonyme	Joint stock company

1.3 THE GOAL OF FINANCIAL MANAGEMENT

Assuming that we restrict ourselves to for-profit businesses, the goal of financial management is to make money or add value for the owners. This goal is a little vague, of course, so we examine some different ways of formulating it in order to come up with a more precise definition. Such a definition is important because it leads to an objective basis for making and evaluating financial decisions.

Possible Goals

If we were to consider possible financial goals, we might come up with some ideas like the following:

- Survive.
- Avoid financial distress and bankruptcy.
- Beat the competition.
- Maximize sales or market share.
- Minimize costs.
- Maximize profits.
- Maintain steady earnings growth.

These are only a few of the goals we could list. Furthermore, each of these possibilities presents problems as a goal for the financial manager.

For example, it's easy to increase market share or unit sales; all we have to do is lower our prices or relax our credit terms. Similarly, we can always cut costs simply by doing away with things such as research and development. We can avoid bankruptcy by never borrowing any money or never taking any risks, and so on. It's not clear that any of these actions are in the stockholders' best interests.

Profit maximization would probably be the most commonly cited goal, but even this is not a very precise objective. Do we mean profits this year? If so, then we should note that actions such as deferring maintenance, letting inventories run down, and taking other short-run cost-cutting measures will tend to increase profits now, but these activities aren't necessarily desirable.

The goal of maximizing profits may refer to some sort of "long-run" or "average" profits, but it's still unclear exactly what this means. First, do we mean something like accounting net income or earnings per share? As we will see in more detail in the next chapter, these accounting numbers may have little to do with what is good or bad for the firm. Second, what do we mean by the long run? As a famous economist once remarked, in the long run, we're all dead! More to the point, this goal doesn't tell us what the appropriate trade-off is between current and future profits.

The goals we've listed here are all different, but they do tend to fall into two classes. The first of these relates to profitability. The goals involving sales, market share, and cost control all relate, at least potentially, to different ways of earning or increasing profits. The goals in the second group, involving bankruptcy avoidance, stability, and safety, relate in some way to controlling risk. Unfortunately, these two types of goals are somewhat contradictory. The pursuit of profit normally involves some element of risk, so it isn't really possible to maximize both safety and profit. What we need, therefore, is a goal that encompasses both factors.

The Goal of Financial Management

The financial manager in a corporation makes decisions for the stockholders of the firm. Given this, instead of listing possible goals for the financial manager, we really need to answer a more fundamental question: From the stockholders' point of view, what is a good financial management decision?

If we assume that stockholders buy stock because they seek to gain financially, then the answer is obvious: Good decisions increase the value of the stock, and poor decisions decrease the value of the stock.

Given our observations, it follows that the financial manager acts in the shareholders' best interests by making decisions that increase the value of the stock. The appropriate goal for the financial manager can thus be stated quite easily:

The goal of financial management is to maximize the current value per share of the existing stock.

The goal of maximizing the value of the stock avoids the problems associated with the different goals we listed earlier. There is no ambiguity in the criterion, and there is no short-run versus long-run issue. We explicitly mean that our goal is to maximize the *current* stock value.

If this goal seems a little strong or one-dimensional to you, keep in mind that the stockholders in a firm are residual owners. By this we mean that they are only entitled to what is left after employees, suppliers, and creditors (and everyone else with legitimate claims) are paid their due. If any of these groups go unpaid, the stockholders get nothing. So, if the stockholders are winning in the sense that the leftover, residual portion is growing, it must be true that everyone else is winning also.

Because the goal of financial management is to maximize the value of the stock, we need to learn how to identify those investments and financing arrangements that favorably impact the value of the stock. This is precisely what we will be studying. In fact, we could have defined corporate finance as the study of the relationship between business decisions and the value of the stock in the business.

A More General Goal

Given our goal as stated in the preceding section (to maximize the value of the stock), an obvious question comes up: What is the appropriate goal when the firm has no traded stock? Corporations are certainly not the only type of business; and the stock in many corporations rarely changes hands, so it's difficult to say what the value per share is at any given time.

As long as we are dealing with for-profit businesses, only a slight modification is needed. The total value of the stock in a corporation is simply equal to the value of the owners' equity. Therefore, a more general way of stating our goal is as follows: Maximize the market value of the existing owners' equity.

Business ethics are considered at www.business-ethics.com.

With this in mind, it doesn't matter whether the business is a proprietorship, a partnership, or a corporation. For each of these, good financial decisions increase the market value of the owners' equity and poor financial decisions decrease it. In fact, although we choose to focus on corporations in the chapters ahead, the principles we develop apply to all forms of business. Many of them even apply to the not-for-profit sector.

Finally, our goal does not imply that the financial manager should take illegal or unethical actions in the hope of increasing the value of the equity in the firm. What we mean is that the financial manager best serves the owners of the business by identifying goods and services that add value to the firm because they are desired and valued in the free marketplace.

1.4 THE AGENCY PROBLEM AND CONTROL OF THE CORPORATION

We've seen that the financial manager acts in the best interests of the stockholders by taking actions that increase the value of the stock. However, in large corporations ownership can be spread over a huge number of stockholders. This dispersion of ownership arguably means that management effectively controls the firm. In this case, will management necessarily act in the best interests of the stockholders? Put another way, might not management pursue its own goals at the stockholders' expense? In the following pages, we briefly consider some of the arguments relating to this question.

Agency Relationships

The relationship between stockholders and management is called an *agency relationship*. Such a relationship exists whenever someone (the principal) hires another (the agent) to represent his/her interests. For example, you might hire someone (an agent) to sell a car that you own while you are away at school. In all such relationships, there is a possibility of a conflict of interest between the principal and the agent. Such a conflict is called an **agency problem**.

Suppose you hire someone to sell your car and you agree to pay that person a flat fee when he/she sells the car. The agent's incentive in this case is to make the sale, not necessarily to get you the best price. If you offer a commission of, say, 10 percent of the sales price instead of a flat fee, then this problem might not exist. This example illustrates that the way in which an agent is compensated is one factor that affects agency problems.

Management Goals

To see how management and stockholder interests might differ, imagine that the firm is considering a new investment. The new investment is expected to favorably impact the share value, but it is also a relatively risky venture. The owners of the firm will wish to take the investment (because the stock value will rise), but management may not because there is the possibility that things will turn out badly and management jobs will be lost. If management does not take the investment, then the stockholders may lose a valuable opportunity. This is one example of an *agency cost*.

More generally, the term agency costs refers to the costs of the conflict of interest between stockholders and management. These costs can be indirect or direct. An indirect agency cost is a lost opportunity, such as the one we have just described.

Direct agency costs come in two forms. The first type is a corporate expenditure that benefits management but costs the stockholders. Perhaps the purchase of a luxurious and unneeded corporate jet would fall under this heading. The second type of direct agency cost is an expense that arises from the need to monitor management actions. Paying outside auditors to assess the accuracy of financial statement information could be one example.

It is sometimes argued that, left to themselves, managers would tend to maximize the amount of resources over which they have control or, more generally, corporate power or wealth. This goal could lead to an overemphasis on corporate size or growth. For example, cases in which management is accused of overpaying to buy up another company just to increase the size of the business or to demonstrate corporate power are not uncommon. Obviously, if overpayment does take place, such a purchase does not benefit the stockholders of the purchasing company.

Our discussion indicates that management may tend to overemphasize organizational survival to protect job security. Also, management may dislike outside interference, so independence and corporate self-sufficiency may be important goals.

Do Managers Act in the Stockholders' Interests?

Whether managers will, in fact, act in the best interests of stockholders depends on two factors. First, how closely are management goals aligned with stockholder goals? This question relates, at least in part, to the way managers are compensated. Second, can management be replaced if they do not pursue stockholder goals? This issue relates to control of the firm. As we will discuss, there are a number of reasons to think that, even in the largest firms, management has a significant incentive to act in the interests of stockholders.

MANAGERIAL COMPENSATION Management will frequently have a significant economic incentive to increase share value for two reasons. First, managerial compensation, particularly at the top, is usually tied to financial performance in general and oftentimes to share value in particular. For example, managers are frequently given the option to buy stock at a bargain price. The more the stock is worth, the more valuable is this option. In fact, options are often used to motivate employees of all types, not just top management.

The second incentive managers have relates to job prospects. Better performers within the firm will tend to get promoted. More generally, those managers who are successful in pursuing stockholder goals will be in greater demand in the labor market and thus command higher salaries.

In fact, managers who are successful in pursuing stockholder goals can reap enormous rewards. For example, one of America's best paid executives in 2004 was Rueben Mark, the CEO of Colgate-Palmolive for the past 20 years; according to *Forbes* magazine, he made $148 million in that year. By way of comparison, Mark made less than Mel Gibson and Oprah Winfrey ($210 million each) but more than Tiger Woods ($80 million). Over the period 2000–2004, Oracle CEO Larry Ellison was the highest paid executive, earning about $836 million. Dell CEO Michael Dell earned slightly less over the same period, only $526 million.

CONTROL OF THE FIRM Control of the firm ultimately rests with stockholders. They elect the board of directors, who, in turn, hire and fire management. The fact that stockholders control the corporation was made abundantly clear by Carly Fiorina's experience at HP, which we described to open the chapter. Even though she had reorganized the corporation, there came a time when shareholders, through their elected directors, decided that HP would be better off without her, so out she went.

An important mechanism by which unhappy stockholders can act to replace existing management is called a *proxy fight.* A proxy is the authority to vote someone else's stock. A proxy fight develops when a group solicits proxies in order to replace the existing board, and thereby replace existing management. For example, the proposed merger between HP and Compaq, which we mentioned in our chapter opener, triggered one of the most widely followed, bitterly contested, and expensive proxy fights in history, with an estimated price tag of well over $100 million.

Another way that management can be replaced is by takeover. Those firms that are poorly managed are more attractive as acquisitions than well-managed firms because a greater profit potential exists. Thus, avoiding a takeover by another firm gives management another incentive to act in the stockholders' interests. For example, in 2004, Comcast, the cable television giant, announced a surprise bid to buy Disney at a time when Disney's management was under close scrutiny for its performance. Not too surprisingly, Disney's management strongly opposed being acquired, and Comcast ultimately decided to withdraw, in part because of improvements in Disney's financial performance.

CONCLUSION The available theory and evidence are consistent with the view that stockholders control the firm and that stockholder wealth maximization is the relevant goal of the corporation. Even so, there will undoubtedly be times when management goals are pursued at the expense of the stockholders, at least temporarily.

Stakeholders

Our discussion thus far implies that management and stockholders are the only parties with an interest in the firm's decisions. This is an oversimplification, of course. Employees, customers, suppliers, and even the government all have a financial interest in the firm.

Taken together, these various groups are called **stakeholders** in the firm. In general, a stakeholder is someone other than a stockholder or creditor who potentially has a claim on the cash flows of the firm. Such groups will also attempt to exert control over the firm, perhaps to the detriment of the owners.

1.5 FINANCIAL MARKETS

As indicated in Section 1.1, firms offer two basic types of securities to investors. *Debt securities* are contractual obligations to repay corporate borrowing. *Equity securities* are shares of common stock and preferred stock that represent noncontractual claims to the residual cash flow of the firm. Issues of debt and stock that are publicly sold by the firm are then traded on the financial markets.

The financial markets are composed of the **money markets** and the **capital markets**. Money markets are the markets for debt securities that will pay off in the short term (usually less than one year). Capital markets are the markets for long-term debt (with a maturity at over one year) and for equity shares.

The term *money market* applies to a group of loosely connected markets. They are dealer markets. Dealers are firms that make continuous quotations of prices for which they stand ready to buy and sell money market instruments for their own inventory and at their own risk. Thus, the dealer is a principal in most transactions. This is different from a stockbroker acting as an agent for a customer in buying or selling common stock on most stock exchanges; an agent does not actually acquire the securities.

At the core of the money markets are the money market banks (these are large banks mostly in New York), government securities dealers (some of which are the large banks), and a large number of money brokers. Money brokers specialize in finding short-term money for borrowers and placing money for lenders. The financial markets can be classified further as the *primary market* and the *secondary markets.*

The Primary Market: New Issues

The primary market is used when governments and corporations initially sell securities. Corporations engage in two types of primary market sales of debt and equity: public offerings and private placements.

Most publicly offered corporate debt and equity come to the market underwritten by a syndicate of investment banking firms. The *underwriting* syndicate buys the new securities from the firm for the syndicate's own account and resells them at a higher price. Publicly issued debt and equity must be registered with the United States Securities and Exchange Commission (SEC). *Registration* requires the corporation to disclose all of the material information in a registration statement.

The legal, accounting, and other costs of preparing the registration statement are not negligible. In part to avoid these costs, privately placed debt and equity are sold on the basis of private negotiations to large financial institutions, such as insurance companies and mutual funds, and other investors. Private placements are not registered with the SEC.

Secondary Markets

A secondary market transaction involves one owner or creditor selling to another. It is therefore the secondary markets that provide the means for transferring ownership of corporate securities. Although a corporation is only directly involved in a primary market transaction (when it sells securities to raise cash), the secondary markets are still critical to large corporations. The reason is that investors are much more willing to purchase securities in a primary market transaction when they know that those securities can later be resold if desired.

DEALER VERSUS AUCTION MARKETS There are two kinds of secondary markets: *dealer* markets and *auction* markets. Generally speaking, dealers buy and sell for themselves, at their own risk. A car dealer, for example, buys and sells automobiles. In contrast, brokers and agents match buyers and sellers, but they do not actually own the commodity that is bought or sold. A real estate agent, for example, does not normally buy and sell houses.

Dealer markets in stocks and long-term debt are called *over-the-counter* (OTC) markets. Most trading in debt securities takes place over the counter. The expression *over the counter* refers to days of old when securities were literally bought and sold at counters in offices around the country. Today, a significant fraction of the market for stocks and almost all of the market for long-term debt have no central location; the many dealers are connected electronically.

Auction markets differ from dealer markets in two ways. First, an auction market or exchange has a physical location (like Wall Street). Second, in a dealer market, most of the buying and selling is done by the dealer. The primary purpose of an auction market, on the other hand, is to match those who wish to sell with those who wish to buy. Dealers play a limited role.

TRADING IN CORPORATE SECURITIES The equity shares of most of the large firms in the United States trade in organized auction markets. The largest such market is the New York Stock Exchange (NYSE), which accounts for more than 85 percent of all the shares traded in auction markets. Other auction exchanges include the American Stock Exchange (AMEX) and regional exchanges such as the Pacific Stock Exchange.

In addition to the stock exchanges, there is a large OTC market for stocks. In 1971, the National Association of Securities Dealers (NASD) made available to dealers and brokers an electronic quotation system called NASDAQ (which originally stood for NASD Automated Quotation system and is pronounced "naz-dak"). There are roughly two times as many companies on NASDAQ as there are on NYSE, but they tend to be much smaller in size and trade less actively. There are exceptions, of course. Both Microsoft and Intel trade OTC, for example. Nonetheless, the total value of NASDAQ stocks is much less than the total value of NYSE stocks.

To learn more about the exchanges, visit www.nyse.com and www.nasdaq.com.

There are many large and important financial markets outside the United States, of course, and U.S. corporations are increasingly looking to these markets to raise cash. The Tokyo Stock Exchange and the London Stock Exchange (TSE and LSE, respectively) are two well-known examples. The fact that OTC markets have no physical location means that national borders do not present a great barrier, and there is now a huge international OTC debt market. Because of globalization, financial markets have reached the point where trading in many investments never stops; it just travels around the world.

Exchange Trading of Listed Stocks

Auction markets are different from dealer markets in two ways. First, trading in a given auction exchange takes place at a single site on the floor of the exchange. Second, transaction prices of shares traded on auction exchanges are communicated almost immediately to the public by computer and other devices.

The NYSE is one of the preeminent securities exchanges in the world. All transactions in stocks listed on the NYSE occur at a particular place on the floor of the exchange called a *post.* At the heart of the market is the specialist. Specialists are members of the NYSE who *make a market* in designated stocks. Specialists have an obligation to offer to buy and sell shares of their assigned NYSE stocks. It is believed that this makes the market liquid because the specialist assumes the role of a buyer for investors if they wish to sell and a seller if they wish to buy.

TABLE 1.3

Market Value of NYSE-Listed Securities

Source: Data from the NYSE Web site, www.nyse.com.

END-OF-YEAR	NUMBER OF LISTED COMPANIES	MARKET VALUE (IN $ TRILLIONS)
NYSE-listed stocks*		
2005, as of July 30	2,779	$20.8
2004	2,768	19.8
2003	2,750	17.3
2002	2,783	13.4
2001	2,798	16.0
2000	2,862	17.1
END-OF-YEAR	**NUMBER OF ISSUES**	**MARKET VALUE (IN $ MILLIONS)**
NYSE-listed bonds**		
2004	1,059	$1,079,531
2003	1,273	1,354,753
2002	1,323	1,378,275
2001	1,447	1,653,549
2000	1,627	2,124,789

* Includes preferred stock and common stock.

** Includes bonds issued by U.S. companies, foreign companies, the U.S. government, international banks, foreign governments, and municipalities. The bond value shown is the face value.

THE REAL WORLD

SARBANES-OXLEY

In response to corporate scandals at companies such as Enron, WorldCom, Tyco, and Adelphia, Congress enacted the Sarbanes-Oxley Act in 2002. The act, better known as "Sarbox," is intended to protect investors from corporate abuses. For example, one section of Sarbox prohibits personal loans from a company to its officers, such as the ones that were received by WorldCom CEO Bernie Ebbers.

One of the key sections of Sarbox took effect on November 15, 2004. Section 404 requires, among other things, that each company's annual report must have an assessment of the company's internal control structure and financial reporting. The auditor must then evaluate and attest to management's assessment of these issues.

Sarbox contains other key requirements. For example, the officers of the corporation must review and sign the annual reports. They must explicitly declare that the annual report does not contain any false statements or material omissions; that the financial statements fairly represent the financial results; and that they are responsible for all internal controls. Finally, the annual report must list any deficiencies in internal controls. In essence, Sarbox makes company management responsible for the accuracy of the company's financial statements.

Of course, as with any law, there are compliance costs, and Sarbox has increased the cost of corporate audits, sometimes dramatically. Estimates of the increase in company audit costs to comply with Sarbox range from $500,000 to over $5 million, which has led to some unintended consequences. For example, in 2003, 198 firms delisted their shares from exchanges, or "went dark." This was up from 30 delistings in 1999. For 2004, estimates of the number of companies that would go dark ranged from 134 to 250. Most of the companies that delisted stated that their reason was to avoid the cost of compliance with Sarbox. Some conservative estimates put the national Sarbox compliance tab at $35 billion in the first year alone, which is roughly 20 times the amount originally estimated by the SEC. For a large multibillion-dollar revenue company, the cost might be .05 percent of revenues, but it could be 3 percent or so for smaller companies, an enormous cost.

A company that goes dark does not have to file quarterly or annual reports. Annual audits by independent auditors are not required, and executives do not have to certify the accuracy of the financial statements, so the savings can be huge. Of course, there are costs. Stock prices typically fall when a company announces it is going dark. Further, such companies will typically have limited access to capital markets and usually will have a higher interest cost on bank loans.

Foreign companies have also been affected. Lastminute, a British online travel group, and Lion Bioscience, a German software company, have already initiated the process to withdraw from U.S. exchanges. And it is not just smaller foreign companies that are considering delisting from U.S. exchanges. German conglomerate Siemens AG, with worldwide sales approaching $100 billion, is considering delisting, and the London Stock Exchange has reported that several companies have discussed going public on that exchange rather than list on a U.S. exchange, to avoid the compliance costs of Sarbox.

To find out more about Sarbanes-Oxley, go to: www.sarbanes-oxley.com.

Listing

Stocks that trade on an organized exchange are said to be *listed* on that exchange. In order to be listed, firms must meet certain minimum criteria concerning, for example, asset size and number of shareholders. These criteria differ from one exchange to another.

NYSE has the most stringent requirements of the exchanges in the United States. For example, to be listed on NYSE, a company is expected to have a market value for its publicly held shares of at least $100 million. There are additional minimums on earnings, assets, and number of shares outstanding. The listing requirements for non–U.S. companies are somewhat more stringent. As *The Real World* box on this page discusses, listed companies also face significant costs arising from disclosure requirements. Table 1.3 (on p. 17) gives the market value of NYSE-listed stocks and bonds.

SUMMARY AND CONCLUSIONS

This chapter introduced you to some of the basic ideas in corporate finance. In it, we saw that:

1. Corporate finance has three main areas of concern:
   a. Capital budgeting. What long-term investments should the firm take?
   b. Capital structure. Where will the firm get the long-term financing to pay for its investments? Also, what mixture of debt and equity should we use to fund our operations?
   c. Working capital management. How should the firm manage its everyday financial activities?
2. The goal of financial management in a for-profit business is to make decisions that increase the value of the stock, or, more generally, increase the market value of the equity.
3. The corporate form of organization is superior to other forms when it comes to raising money and transferring ownership interests, but it has the significant disadvantage of double taxation.
4. There is the possibility of conflicts between stockholders and management in a large corporation. We called these conflicts agency problems and discussed how they might be controlled and reduced.
5. The advantages of the corporate form are enhanced by the existence of financial markets. Financial markets function as both primary and secondary markets for corporate securities and can be organized as either dealer or auction markets.

Of the topics we've discussed thus far, the most important is the goal of financial management: maximizing the value of the stock. Throughout the text, we will be analyzing many different financial decisions, but we will always ask the same question: How does the decision under consideration affect the value of the stock?

CONCEPT QUESTIONS

1. **Forms of Business** What are the three basic legal forms of organizing a business? What are the advantages and disadvantages of each? What business form do most start-up companies take? Why?
2. **Goal of Financial Management** What goal should always motivate the actions of the firm's financial manager?
3. **Agency Problems** Who owns a corporation? Describe the process whereby the owners control the firm's management. What is the main reason that an agency relationship exists in the corporate form of organization? In this context, what kinds of problems can arise?
4. **Not-for-Profit Firm Goals** Suppose you were the financial manager of a not-for-profit business (a not-for-profit hospital, perhaps). What kinds of goals do you think would be appropriate?
5. **Goal of the Firm** Evaluate the following statement: Managers should not focus on the current stock value because doing so will lead to an overemphasis on short-term profits at the expense of long-term profits.
6. **Ethics and Firm Goals** Can our goal of maximizing the value of the stock conflict with other goals, such as avoiding unethical or illegal behavior? In particular, do you think subjects like customer and employee safety, the environment, and the general good of society fit in this framework, or are they essentially ignored? Try to think of some specific scenarios to illustrate your answer.
7. **International Firm Goal** Would our goal of maximizing the value of the stock be different if we were thinking about financial management in a foreign country? Why or why not?

8. **Agency Problems** Suppose you own stock in a company. The current price per share is $25. Another company has just announced that it wants to buy your company and will pay $35 per share to acquire all the outstanding stock. Your company's management immediately begins fighting off this hostile bid. Is management acting in the shareholders' best interests? Why or why not?
9. **Agency Problems and Corporate Ownership** Corporate ownership varies around the world. Historically, individuals have owned the majority of shares in public corporations in the United States. In Germany and Japan, however, banks, other large financial institutions, and other companies own most of the stock in public corporations. Do you think agency problems are likely to be more or less severe in Germany and Japan than in the United States? Why? In recent years, large financial institutions such as mutual funds and pension funds have been becoming the dominant owners of stock in the United States, and these institutions are becoming more active in corporate affairs. What are the implications of this trend for agency problems and corporate control?
10. **Executive Compensation** Critics have charged that compensation to top management in the United States is simply too high and should be cut back. For example, focusing on large corporations, Larry Ellison of Oracle has been one of the best compensated CEOs in the United States, earning about $41 million in 2004 alone and $836 million over the 2000–2004 period. Are such amounts excessive? In answering, it might be helpful to recognize that superstar athletes such as Tiger Woods, top entertainers such as Mel Gibson and Oprah Winfrey, and many others at the top of their respective fields earn at least as much, if not a great deal more.

STANDARD & POOR'S

S&P PROBLEMS

www.mhhe.com/edumarketinsight

1. **Industry Comparison** On the Market Insight home page, follow the "Industry" link at the top of the page. You will be on the industry page. You can use the drop-down menu to select different industries. Answer the following questions for these industries: Airlines, Automobile Manufacturers, Biotechnology, Computer Hardware, Homebuilding, Marine, Restaurants, Soft Drinks, and Wireless Telecommunications.
   a. How many companies are in each industry?
   b. What are the total sales for each industry?
   c. Do the industries with the largest total sales have the most companies in the industry? What does this tell you about competition in the various industries?

WHAT'S ON THE WEB?

1. **Listing Requirements** This chapter discussed some of the listing requirements for the NYSE and NASDAQ. Find the complete listing requirements for the New York Stock Exchange at www.nyse.com and NASDAQ at www.nasdaq.com. Which exchange has more stringent listing requirements? Why don't the exchanges have the same listing requirements?
2. **Business Formation** As you may (or may not) know, many companies incorporate in Delaware for a variety of reasons. Visit Bizfilings at www.bizfilings.com to find out why. Which state has the highest fee for incorporation? For an LLC? While at the site, look at the FAQ section regarding corporations and LLCs.

CLOSING CASE

THE McGEE CAKE COMPANY

In early 2000, Doc and Lyn McGee formed the McGee Cake Company. The company produced a full line of cakes, and its specialties included chess cake, lemon pound cake, and double-iced, double-chocolate cake. The couple formed the company as an outside interest, and both continued to work at their current jobs. Doc did all the baking, and Lyn handled the marketing and distribution. With good product quality and a sound marketing plan, the company grew rapidly. In early 2003, the company was featured in a widely-distributed entrepreneurial magazine. Later that year, the company was featured in *Gourmet Desserts,* a leading specialty food magazine. After the article appeared in *Gourmet Desserts,* sales exploded, and the company began receiving orders from all over the world.

Because of the increased sales, Doc left his other job, followed shortly by Lyn. The company hired additional workers to meet demand. Unfortunately, the fast growth experienced by the company led to cash flow and capacity problems. The company is currently producing as many cakes as possible with the assets it owns, but demand for its cakes is still growing. Further, the company has been approached by a national supermarket with a proposal to put four of its cakes in all of the chain's stores, and a national restaurant chain has contacted the company about selling McGee cakes in its restaurants. The restaurant would sell the cakes without a brand name.

Doc and Lyn have operated the company as a sole proprietorship. They have approached you to help manage and direct the company's growth. Specifically, they have asked you to answer the following questions.

1. What are the advantages and disadvantages of changing the company organization from a sole proprietorship to an LLC?
2. What are the advantages and disadvantages of changing the company organization from a sole proprietorship to a corporation?
3. Ultimately, what action would you recommend the company undertake? Why?

CHAPTER 2

Financial Statements and Cash Flow

OPENING CASE

In early 2005, entertainment giant Viacom announced that it would take a charge of $18 billion, meaning that it was reducing the stated value of its assets by that amount. About $11 billion was attributable to write-offs related to radio holdings, and the remainder was associated with its outdoor advertising unit. In fact, it was a bad time for media companies. A week earlier, Clear Channel Communications, the largest owner of radio stations in the United States, announced a charge of $5 billion. This was not the first time for Clear Channel; it had taken a charge of about $11 billion in 2002 for similar reasons.

The company with possibly the largest write-offs in history is yet another media company, Time Warner, which took a charge of $45.5 billion in the fourth quarter of 2002. This enormous write-off followed an earlier, even larger, charge of $54 billion.

So, did the stockholders in these companies lose billions of dollars when these assets were written off? Fortunately for them, the answer is probably not. Understanding why ultimately leads us to the main subject of this chapter, that all-important substance known as *cash flow*.

2.1 THE BALANCE SHEET

The **balance sheet** is an accountant's snapshot of the firm's accounting value on a particular date, as though the firm stood momentarily still. The balance sheet has two sides: On the left are the *assets* and on the right are the *liabilities* and *stockholders' equity*. The balance sheet states what the firm owns and how it is financed. The accounting definition that underlies the balance sheet and describes the balance is

Assets ≡ Liabilities + Stockholders' equity

We have put a three-line equality in the balance equation to indicate that it must always hold, by definition. In fact, the stockholders' equity is *defined* to be the difference between the assets and the liabilities of the firm. In principle, equity is what the stockholders would have remaining after the firm discharged its obligations.

Table 2.1 gives the 2006 and 2005 balance sheet for the fictitious U.S. Composite Corporation. The assets in the balance sheet are listed in order by the length of time it normally would take an ongoing firm to convert them to cash. The asset side depends on the nature of the business and how management chooses to conduct it. Management must make decisions about cash versus marketable securities, credit versus cash sales,

Two excellent sources for company financial information are finance.yahoo.com and money.cnn.com.

TABLE 2.1

The Balance Sheet of the U.S. Composite Corporation

U.S. COMPOSITE CORPORATION
Balance Sheet
2006 and 2005
(in $ millions)

ASSETS	2006	2005	LIABILITIES (DEBT) AND STOCKHOLDERS' EQUITY	2006	2005
Current assets:			Current liabilities:		
Cash and equivalents	$ 140	$ 107	Accounts payable	$ 213	$ 197
Accounts receivable	294	270	Notes payable	50	53
Inventories	269	280	Accrued expenses	223	205
Other	58	50	Total current liabilities	$ 486	$ 455
Total current assets	$ 761	$ 707	Long-term liabilities:		
Fixed assets:			Deferred taxes	$ 117	$ 104
Property, plant, and equipment	$1,423	$1,274	Long-term debt*	471	458
Less accumulated depreciation	550	460	Total long-term liabilities	$ 588	$ 562
Net property, plant, and equipment	873	814	Stockholders' equity:		
Intangible assets and others	245	221	Preferred stock	$ 39	$ 39
Total fixed assets	$1,118	$1,035	Common stock ($1 par value)	55	32
			Capital surplus	347	327
			Accumulated retained earnings	390	347
			Less treasury stock†	26	20
			Total equity	$ 805	$ 725
Total assets	$1,879	$1,742	Total liabilities and stockholders' equity‡	$1,879	$1,742

*Long-term debt rose by $471 million − 458 million = $13 million. This is the difference between $86 million new debt and $73 million in retirement of old debt.

†Treasury stock rose by $6 million. This reflects the repurchase of $6 million of U.S. Composite's company stock.

‡U.S. Composite reports $43 million in new equity. The company issued 23 million shares at a price of $1.87. The par value of common stock increased by $23 million, and capital surplus increased by $20 million.

whether to make or buy commodities, whether to lease or purchase items, the types of business in which to engage, and so on. The liabilities and the stockholders' equity are listed in the order in which they would typically be paid over time.

The liabilities and stockholders' equity side reflects the types and proportions of financing, which depend on management's choice of capital structure, as between debt and equity and between current debt and long-term debt.

When analyzing a balance sheet, the financial manager should be aware of three concerns: accounting liquidity, debt versus equity, and value versus cost.

Accounting Liquidity

Annual and quarterly financial statements for most public U.S. corporations can be found in the EDGAR database at www.sec.gov.

Accounting liquidity refers to the ease and quickness with which assets can be converted to cash. *Current assets* are the most liquid and include cash and those assets that will be turned into cash within a year from the date of the balance sheet. *Accounts receivable* are amounts not yet collected from customers for goods or services sold to them (after adjustment for potential bad debts). *Inventory* is composed of raw materials to be used in production, work in process, and finished goods. *Fixed assets* are the least liquid kind of assets. Tangible fixed assets include property, plant, and equipment. These assets do not convert to cash from normal business activity, and they are not usually used to pay expenses such as payroll.

Some fixed assets are not tangible. Intangible assets have no physical existence but can be very valuable. Examples of intangible assets are the value of a trademark or the value of a patent. The more liquid a firm's assets, the less likely the firm is to experience problems meeting short-term obligations. Thus, the probability that a firm will avoid financial distress can be linked to the firm's liquidity. Unfortunately, liquid assets frequently have lower rates of return than fixed assets; for example, cash generates no investment income. To the extent a firm invests in liquid assets, it sacrifices an opportunity to invest in more profitable investment vehicles.

Debt versus Equity

Liabilities are obligations of the firm that require a payout of cash within a stipulated time period. Many liabilities involve contractual obligations to repay a stated amount and interest over a period. Thus, liabilities are debts and are frequently associated with nominally fixed cash burdens, called *debt service,* that put the firm in default of a contract if they are not paid. *Stockholders' equity* is a claim against the firm's assets that is residual and not fixed. In general terms, when the firm borrows, it gives the bondholders first claim on the firm's cash flow.[1] Bondholders can sue the firm if the firm defaults on its bond contracts. This may lead the firm to declare itself bankrupt. Stockholders' equity is the residual difference between assets and liabilities:

Assets − Liabilities ≡ Stockholders' equity

This is the stockholders' share in the firm stated in accounting terms. The accounting value of stockholders' equity increases when retained earnings are added. This occurs when the firm retains part of its earnings instead of paying them out as dividends.

Value versus Cost

The home page for the Financial Accounting Standards Board (FASB) is www.fasb.org.

The accounting value of a firm's assets is frequently referred to as the *carrying value* or the *book value* of the assets.[2] Under **generally accepted accounting principles (GAAP)**,

[1]Bondholders are investors in the firm's debt. They are creditors of the firm. In this discussion, the term *bondholder* means the same thing as *creditor.*

[2]Confusion often arises because many financial accounting terms have the same meaning. This presents a problem with jargon for the reader of financial statements. For example, the following terms usually refer to the same thing: assets minus liabilities, net worth, stockholders' equity, owners' equity, book equity, and equity capitalization.

audited financial statements of firms in the United States carry the assets at cost.[3] Thus the terms *carrying value* and *book value* are unfortunate. They specifically say "value," when in fact the accounting numbers are based on cost. This misleads many readers of financial statements to think that the firm's assets are recorded at true market values. *Market value* is the price at which willing buyers and sellers would trade the assets. It would be only a coincidence if accounting value and market value were the same. In fact, management's job is to create value for the firm that exceeds its cost.

Many people use the balance sheet, but the information each may wish to extract is not the same. A banker may look at a balance sheet for evidence of accounting liquidity and working capital. A supplier may also note the size of accounts payable and therefore the general promptness of payments. Many users of financial statements, including managers and investors, want to know the value of the firm, not its cost. This information is not found on the balance sheet. In fact, many of the true resources of the firm do not appear on the balance sheet: good management, proprietary assets, favorable economic conditions, and so on. Henceforth, whenever we speak of the value of an asset or the value of the firm, we will normally mean its market value. So, for example, when we say the goal of the financial manager is to increase the value of the stock, we mean the market value of the stock.

EXAMPLE 2.1 Market Value versus Book Value

The Cooney Corporation has fixed assets with a book value of $700 and an appraised market value of about $1,000. Net working capital is $400 on the books, but approximately $600 would be realized if all the current accounts were liquidated. Cooney has $500 in long-term debt, both book value and market value. What is the book value of the equity? What is the market value?

We can construct two simplified balance sheets, one in accounting (book value) terms and one in economic (market value) terms:

COONEY CORPORATION
Balance Sheets
Market Value versus Book Value

Assets			Liabilities and Shareholders' Equity		
	BOOK	MARKET		BOOK	MARKET
Net working capital	$ 400	$ 600	Long-term debt	$ 500	$ 500
Net fixed assets	700	1,000	Shareholders' equity	600	1,100
	$1,100	$1,600		$1,100	$1,600

In this example, shareholders' equity is actually worth almost twice as much as what is shown on the books. The distinction between book and market values is important precisely because book values can be so different from true economic value.

2.2 THE INCOME STATEMENT

The **income statement** measures performance over a specific period of time, say, a year. The accounting definition of income is:

Revenue − Expenses ≡ Income

[3]Generally, GAAP requires assets to be carried at the lower of cost or market value. In most instances, cost is lower than market value. However, in some cases when a fair market value can be readily determined, the assets have their value adjusted to the fair market value.

TABLE 2.2
The Income Statement of the U.S. Composite Corporation

U.S. COMPOSITE CORPORATION Income Statement 2006 (in $ millions)	
Total operating revenues	$2,262
Cost of goods sold	1,655
Selling, general, and administrative expenses	327
Depreciation	90
Operating income	$ 190
Other income	29
Earnings before interest and taxes (EBIT)	$ 219
Interest expense	49
Pretax income	$ 170
Taxes	84
Current: $71	
Deferred: $13	
Net income	$ 86
Addition to retained earnings:	$ 43
Dividends:	43

Note: There are 29 million shares outstanding. Earnings per share and dividends per share can be calculated as follows:

$$\text{Earnings per share} = \frac{\text{Net income}}{\text{Total shares outstanding}} = \frac{\$86}{29} = \$2.97 \text{ per share}$$

$$\text{Dividends per share} = \frac{\text{Dividends}}{\text{Total shares outstanding}} = \frac{\$43}{29} = \$1.48 \text{ per share}$$

If the balance sheet is like a snapshot, the income statement is like a video recording of what the people did between two snapshots. Table 2.2 gives the income statement for the U.S. Composite Corporation for 2006.

The income statement usually includes several sections. The operations section reports the firm's revenues and expenses from principal operations. One number of particular importance is earnings before interest and taxes (EBIT), which summarizes earnings before taxes and financing costs. Among other things, the nonoperating section of the income statement includes all financing costs, such as interest expense. Usually a second section reports as a separate item the amount of taxes levied on income. The last item on the income statement is the bottom line, or net income. Net income is frequently expressed per share of common stock, that is, earnings per share.

When analyzing an income statement, the financial manager should keep in mind GAAP, noncash items, time, and costs.

Generally Accepted Accounting Principles

Revenue is recognized on an income statement when the earnings process is virtually completed and an exchange of goods or services has occurred. Therefore, the unrealized appreciation from owning property will not be recognized as income. This provides a device for smoothing income by selling appreciated property at convenient times. For example, if the firm owns a tree farm that has doubled in value, then, in a year when its earnings from other businesses are down, it can raise overall earnings by selling some trees.

The matching principle of GAAP dictates that revenues be matched with expenses. Thus, income is reported when it is earned, or accrued, even though no cash flow has necessarily occurred (for example, when goods are sold for credit, sales and profits are reported).

Noncash Items

The economic value of assets is intimately connected to their future incremental cash flows. However, cash flow does not appear on an income statement. There are several **noncash items** that are expenses against revenues, but that do not affect cash flow. The most important of these is *depreciation.* Depreciation reflects the accountant's estimate of the cost of equipment used up in the production process. For example, suppose an asset with a five-year life and no resale value is purchased for $1,000. According to accountants, the $1,000 cost must be expensed over the useful life of the asset. If straight-line depreciation is used, there will be five equal installments and $200 of depreciation expense will be incurred each year. From a finance perspective, the cost of the asset is the actual negative cash flow incurred when the asset is acquired (that is, $1,000, *not* the accountant's smoothed $200-per-year depreciation expense).

Another noncash expense is *deferred taxes.* Deferred taxes result from differences between accounting income and true taxable income.[4] Notice that the accounting tax shown on the income statement for the U.S. Composite Corporation is $84 million. It can be broken down as current taxes and deferred taxes. The current tax portion is actually sent to the tax authorities (for example, the Internal Revenue Service). The deferred tax portion is not. However, the theory is that if taxable income is less than accounting income in the current year, it will be more than accounting income later on. Consequently, the taxes that are not paid today will have to be paid in the future, and they represent a liability of the firm. This shows up on the balance sheet as deferred tax liability. From the cash flow perspective, though, deferred tax is not a cash outflow.

In practice, the difference between cash flows and accounting income can be quite dramatic, so it is important to understand the difference. For example, industrial products and services company SPX Corp. reported a net loss of about $111 million for the fourth quarter of 2004. That sounds bad, but SPX also reported a positive cash flow of $124 million for the same quarter!

Time and Costs

It is often useful to think of all of future time as having two distinct parts, the *short run* and the *long run.* The short run is that period of time in which certain equipment, resources, and commitments of the firm are fixed; but the time is long enough for the firm to vary its output by using more labor and raw materials. The short run is not a precise period of time that will be the same for all industries. However, all firms making decisions in the short run have some fixed costs, that is, costs that will not change because of fixed commitments. In real business activity, examples of fixed costs are bond interest, overhead, and property taxes. Costs that are not fixed are variable. Variable costs change as the output of the firm changes; some examples are raw materials and wages for laborers on the production line.

In the long run, all costs are variable. Financial accountants do not distinguish between variable costs and fixed costs. Instead, accounting costs usually fit into a classification that distinguishes product costs from period costs. Product costs are the total production costs incurred during a period–raw materials, direct labor, and manufacturing overhead–and are reported on the income statement as cost of goods sold. Both variable and fixed costs are included in product costs. Period costs are costs that are allocated to a time period; they are called *selling, general, and administrative expenses.* One period cost would be the company president's salary.

[4]One situation in which taxable income may be lower than accounting income is when the firm uses accelerated depreciation expense procedures for the IRS but uses straight-line procedures allowed by GAAP for reporting purposes.

2.3 TAXES

Taxes can be one of the largest cash outflows that a firm experiences. For example, for the fiscal year 2004, ExxonMobil's earnings before taxes were about $41.2 billion. Its tax bill, including all taxes paid worldwide, was a whopping $15.9 billion, or about 39 percent of its pretax earnings. The size of the tax bill is determined through the tax code, an often amended set of rules. In this section, we examine corporate tax rates and how taxes are calculated.

If the various rules of taxation seem a little bizarre or convoluted to you, keep in mind that the tax code is the result of political, not economic, forces. As a result, there is no reason why it has to make economic sense.

Corporate Tax Rates

Corporate tax rates in effect for 2005 are shown in Table 2.3. A peculiar feature of taxation instituted by the Tax Reform Act of 1986 and expanded in the 1993 Omnibus Budget Reconciliation Act is that corporate tax rates are not strictly increasing. As shown, corporate tax rates rise from 15 percent to 39 percent, but they drop back to 34 percent on income over $335,000. They then rise to 38 percent and subsequently fall to 35 percent.

According to the originators of the current tax rules, there are only four corporate rates: 15 percent, 25 percent, 34 percent, and 35 percent. The 38 and 39 percent brackets arise because of "surcharges" applied on top of the 34 and 35 percent rates. A tax is a tax is a tax, however, so there are really six corporate tax brackets, as we have shown.

Average versus Marginal Tax Rates

In making financial decisions, it is frequently important to distinguish between average and marginal tax rates. Your **average tax rate** is your tax bill divided by your taxable income, in other words, the percentage of your income that goes to pay taxes. Your **marginal tax rate** is the tax you would pay (in percent) if you earned one more dollar. The percentage tax rates shown in Table 2.3 are all marginal rates. Put another way, the tax rates apply to the part of income in the indicated range only, not all income.

The difference between average and marginal tax rates can best be illustrated with a simple example. Suppose our corporation has a taxable income of $200,000. What is the tax bill? Using Table 2.3, we can figure our tax bill as:

.15($ 50,000) = $ 7,500
.25($ 75,000 − 50,000) = 6,250
.34($100,000 − 75,000) = 8,500
.39($200,000 − 100,000) = 39,000
$61,250

The IRS has a great Web site! (www.irs.gov)

Our total tax is thus $61,250.

In our example, what is the average tax rate? We had a taxable income of $200,000 and a tax bill of $61,250, so the average tax rate is $61,250/200,000 = 30.625%. What

TABLE 2.3
Corporate Tax Rates

TAXABLE INCOME	TAX RATE
$ 0– 50,000	15%
50,001– 75,000	25
75,001– 100,000	34
100,001– 335,000	39
335,001–10,000,000	34
10,000,001–15,000,000	35
15,000,001–18,333,333	38
18,333,334+	35

is the marginal tax rate? If we made one more dollar, the tax on that dollar would be 39 cents, so our marginal rate is 39 percent.

EXAMPLE 2.2 Deep in the Heart of Taxes

Algernon, Inc., has a taxable income of $85,000. What is its tax bill? What is its average tax rate? Its marginal tax rate?

From Table 2.3, we see that the tax rate applied to the first $50,000 is 15 percent; the rate applied to the next $25,000 is 25 percent, and the rate applied after that up to $100,000 is 34 percent. So Algernon must pay .15 × $50,000 + .25 × 25,000 + .34 × (85,000 − 75,000) = $17,150. The average tax rate is thus $17,150/85,000 = 20.18%. The marginal rate is 34 percent because Algernon's taxes would rise by 34 cents if it had another dollar in taxable income.

Table 2.4 summarizes some different taxable incomes, marginal tax rates, and average tax rates for corporations. Notice how the average and marginal tax rates come together at 35 percent.

With a *flat-rate* tax, there is only one tax rate, so the rate is the same for all income levels. With such a tax, the marginal tax rate is always the same as the average tax rate. As it stands now, corporate taxation in the United States is based on a modified flat-rate tax, which becomes a true flat rate for the highest incomes.

In looking at Table 2.4, notice that the more a corporation makes, the greater is the percentage of taxable income paid in taxes. Put another way, under current tax law, the average tax rate never goes down, even though the marginal tax rate does. As illustrated, for corporations, average tax rates begin at 15 percent and rise to a maximum of 35 percent.

It will normally be the marginal tax rate that is relevant for financial decision making. The reason is that any new cash flows will be taxed at that marginal rate. Because financial decisions usually involve new cash flows or changes in existing ones, this rate will tell us the marginal effect of a decision on our tax bill.

There is one last thing to notice about the tax code as it affects corporations. It's easy to verify that the corporate tax bill is just a flat 35 percent of taxable income if our taxable income is more than $18.33 million. Also, for the many midsize corporations with taxable incomes in the range of $335,000 to $10,000,000, the tax rate is a flat 34 percent. Because we will normally be talking about large corporations, you can assume that the average and marginal tax rates are 35 percent unless we explicitly say otherwise.

Before moving on, we should note that the tax rates we have discussed in this section relate to federal taxes only. Overall tax rates can be higher once state, local, and any other taxes are considered.

TABLE 2.4
Corporate Taxes and Tax Rates

(1) TAXABLE INCOME	(2) MARGINAL TAX RATE	(3) TOTAL TAX	(3)/(1) AVERAGE TAX RATE
$ 45,000	15%	$ 6,750	15.00%
70,000	25	12,500	17.86
95,000	34	20,550	21.63
250,000	39	80,750	32.30
1,000,000	34	340,000	34.00
17,500,000	38	6,100,000	34.86
50,000,000	35	17,500,000	35.00
100,000,000	35	35,000,000	35.00

2.4 NET WORKING CAPITAL

Net working capital is current assets minus current liabilities. Net working capital is positive when current assets are greater than current liabilities. This means the cash that will become available over the next 12 months will be greater than the cash that must be paid out. The net working capital of the U.S. Composite Corporation is $275 million in 2006 and $252 million in 2005:

	Current assets ($ millions)	−	Current liabilities ($ millions)	=	Net working capital ($ millions)
2006	$761	−	$486	=	$275
2005	707	−	455	=	252

In addition to investing in fixed assets (i.e., capital spending), a firm can invest in net working capital. This is called the **change in net working capital**. The change in net working capital in 2006 is the difference between the net working capital in 2006 and 2005; that is, $275 million − $252 million = $23 million. The change in net working capital is usually positive in a growing firm.

2.5 FINANCIAL CASH FLOW

Perhaps the most important item that can be extracted from financial statements is the actual **cash flow** of the firm. There is an official accounting statement called the *statement of cash flows*. This statement helps to explain the change in accounting cash and equivalents, which for U.S. Composite is $33 million in 2006. (See Section 2.6.) Notice in Table 2.1 that cash and equivalents increase from $107 million in 2005 to $140 million in 2006. However, we will look at cash flow from a different perspective, the perspective of finance. In finance, the value of the firm is its ability to generate financial cash flow. (We will talk more about financial cash flow in Chapter 8.)

The first point we should mention is that cash flow is not the same as net working capital. For example, increasing inventory requires using cash. Because both inventories and cash are current assets, this does not affect net working capital. In this case, an increase in a particular net working capital account, such as inventory, is associated with decreasing cash flow.

Just as we established that the value of a firm's assets is always equal to the value of the liabilities and the value of the equity, the cash flows received from the firm's assets (that is, its operating activities), CF(A), must equal the cash flows to the firm's creditors, CF(B), and equity investors, CF(S):

$$\mathbf{CF}(A) \equiv \mathbf{CF}(B) + \mathbf{CF}(S)$$

The first step in determining cash flows of the firm is to figure out the *cash flow from operations*. As can be seen in Table 2.5, operating cash flow is the cash flow generated by business activities, including sales of goods and services. Operating cash flow reflects tax payments, but not financing, capital spending, or changes in net working capital.

	IN $ MILLIONS
Earnings before interest and taxes	$219
Depreciation	90
Current taxes	− 71
Operating cash flow	$238

Another important component of cash flow involves *changes in fixed assets*. For example, when U.S. Composite sold its power systems subsidiary in 2006, it generated $25 in cash

U.S. COMPOSITE CORPORATION Financial Cash Flow 2006 (in $ millions)	
Cash Flow of the Firm	
Operating cash flow (Earnings before interest and taxes plus depreciation minus taxes)	$238
Capital spending (Acquisitions of fixed assets minus sales of fixed assets)	− 173
Additions to net working capital	− 23
Total	$ 42
Cash Flow to Investors in the Firm	
Debt (Interest plus retirement of debt minus long-term debt financing)	$ 36
Equity (Dividends plus repurchase of equity minus new equity financing)	6
Total	$ 42

TABLE 2.5

Financial Cash Flow of the U.S. Composite Corporation

flow. The net change in fixed assets equals sales of fixed assets minus the acquisition of fixed assets. The result is the cash flow used for capital spending:

Acquisition of fixed assets	$198	
Sales of fixed assets	− 25	
Capital spending	$173	($149 + 24 = Increase in property, plant, and equipment + Increase in intangible assets)

We can also calculate capital spending simply as:

$$\begin{aligned}\textbf{Capital spending} &= \textbf{Ending net fixed assets} - \textbf{Beginning net fixed assets} \\ &\quad + \textbf{Depreciation} \\ &= \$1{,}118 - 1{,}035 + 90 \\ &= \$173\end{aligned}$$

Cash flows are also used for making investments in net working capital. In U.S. Composite Corporation in 2006, *additions to net working capital* are:

Additions to net working capital	$23

Note that this $23 is the change in net working capital we previously calculated.

Total cash flows generated by the firm's assets are the sum of:

Operating cash flow	$238
Capital spending	− 173
Additions to net working capital	− 23
Total cash flow of the firm	$ 42

The total outgoing cash flow of the firm can be separated into cash flow paid to creditors and cash flow paid to stockholders. The cash flow paid to creditors represents a regrouping of the data in Table 2.5 and an explicit recording of interest expense. Creditors are paid an amount generally referred to as *debt service.* Debt service is interest payments plus repayments of principal (that is, retirement of debt).

An important source of cash flow is the sale of new debt. U.S. Composite's long-term debt increased by $13 million (the difference between $86 million in new debt and $73 million in retirement of old debt).[5] Thus, an increase in long-term debt is the net effect of new borrowing and repayment of maturing obligations plus interest expense.

CASH FLOW PAID TO CREDITORS (in $ millions)	
Interest	$ 49
Retirement of debt	73
Debt service	122
Proceeds from long-term debt sales	− 86
Total	$ 36

Cash flow paid to creditors can also be calculated as:

$$
\begin{aligned}
\textbf{Cash flow paid to creditors} &= \textbf{Interest paid} - \textbf{Net new borrowing}\\
&= \textbf{Interest paid} - \textbf{(Ending long-term debt}\\
&\quad - \textbf{Beginning long-term debt)}\\
&= \$49 - (471 - 458)\\
&= \$36
\end{aligned}
$$

Cash flow of the firm also is paid to the stockholders. It is the net effect of paying dividends plus repurchasing outstanding shares of stock and issuing new shares of stock.

CASH FLOW TO STOCKHOLDERS (in $ millions)	
Dividends	$43
Repurchase of stock	6
Cash to stockholders	49
Proceeds from new stock issue	− 43
Total	$ 6

In general, cash flow to stockholders can be determined as:

$$
\begin{aligned}
\textbf{Cash flow to stockholders} &= \textbf{Dividends paid} - \textbf{Net new equity raised}\\
&= \textbf{Dividends paid} - \textbf{(Stock sold}\\
&\quad - \textbf{Stock repurchased)}
\end{aligned}
$$

To determine stock sold, notice that the common stock and capital surplus accounts went up by a combined $23 + 20 = $43, which implies that the company sold $43 million worth of stock. Second, Treasury stock went up by $6, indicating that the company bought back $6 million worth of stock. Net new equity is thus $43 − 6 = $37. Dividends paid were $43, so the cash flow to stockholders was:

$$\textbf{Cash flow to stockholders} = \$43 - (43 - 6) = \$6,$$

which is what we previously calculated.

Some important observations can be drawn from our discussion of cash flow:

1. Several types of cash flow are relevant to understanding the financial situation of the firm. **Operating cash flow**, defined as earnings before interest and depreciation minus taxes, measures the cash generated from operations not counting capital spending or working capital requirements. It is usually positive; a firm is in trouble if operating cash flow is negative for a long time because the firm is not generating enough cash to pay operating costs.

[5]New debt and the retirement of old debt are usually found in the "notes" to the balance sheet.

Total cash flow of the firm includes adjustments for capital spending and additions to net working capital. It will frequently be negative. When a firm is growing at a rapid rate, the spending on inventory and fixed assets can be higher than cash flow from sales.

2. Net income is not cash flow. The net income of the U.S. Composite Corporation in 2006 was $86 million, whereas cash flow was $42 million. The two numbers are not usually the same. In determining the economic and financial condition of a firm, cash flow is more revealing.

A firm's total cash flow sometimes goes by a different name, **free cash flow**. Of course, there is no such thing as "free" cash (we wish!). Instead, the name refers to cash that the firm is free to distribute to creditors and stockholders because it is not needed for working capital or fixed asset investments. We will stick with "total cash flow of the firm" as our label for this important concept because, in practice, there is some variation in exactly how free cash flow is computed; different users calculate it in different ways. Nonetheless, whenever you hear the phrase "free cash flow," you should understand that what is being discussed is cash flow from assets or something quite similar.

2.6 THE ACCOUNTING STATEMENT OF CASH FLOWS

As previously mentioned, there is an official accounting statement called the statement of cash flows. This statement helps explain the change in accounting cash, which for U.S. Composite is $33 million in 2006. It is very useful in understanding financial cash flow.

The first step in determining the change in cash is to figure out cash flow from operating activities. This is the cash flow that results from the firm's normal activities producing and selling goods and services. The second step is to make an adjustment for cash flow from investing activities. The final step is to make an adjustment for cash flow from financing activities. Financing activities are the net payments to creditors and owners (excluding interest expense) made during the year.

The three components of the statement of cash flows are determined below.

Cash Flow from Operating Activities

To calculate cash flow from operating activities we start with net income. Net income can be found on the income statement and is equal to $86 million. We now need to add back noncash expenses and adjust for changes in current assets and liabilities (other than cash and notes payable). The result is cash flow from operating activities.

U.S. COMPOSITE CORPORATION
Cash Flow from Operating Activities
2006
(in $ millions)

Net income	$ 86
Depreciation	90
Deferred taxes	13
Change in assets and liabilities	
Accounts receivable	− 24
Inventories	11
Accounts payable	16
Accrued expense	18
Other	− 8
Cash flow from operating activities	$202

THE REAL WORLD

PUTTING A SPIN ON CASH FLOWS

One of the reasons why cash flow analysis is popular is the difficulty in manipulating, or spinning, cash flows. GAAP accounting principles allow for significant subjective decisions to be made regarding many key areas. The use of cash flow as a metric to evaluate a company comes from the idea that there is less subjectivity involved, and, therefore, it is harder to spin the numbers. But several recent examples have shown that companies can still find ways to do it.

For example, in March 2005, General Electric was forced to revise its 2003 operating cash flow by more than $1 billion and its 2002 operating cash flow by $1.2 billion. The reason was GE's classification of accounts receivable. The SEC argued that the company was placing its receivables from loans provided to customers in the investing portion of the cash flow statement instead of the operation portion. This maneuver had the effect of decreasing the investing cash flows and increasing the operating cash flows by the same amount.

Tyco used several ploys to alter cash flows. For example, the company purchased more than $800 million of customer security alarm accounts from dealers. The cash flows from these transactions were reported in the financing activity section of the accounting statement of cash flows. When Tyco received payments from customers, the cash inflows were reported as operating cash flows. Another method used by Tyco was to have acquired companies prepay operating expenses. In other words, the company acquired by Tyco would pay vendors for items not yet received. In one case, the payments totaled more than $50 million. When the acquired company was consolidated with Tyco, the prepayments reduced Tyco's cash outflows, thus increasing the operating cash flows.

Dynegy, the energy giant, was accused of engaging in a number of complex "round trip trades." The round trip trades essentially involved the sale of natural resources to a counterparty, with the repurchase of the resources from the same party at the same price. In essence, Dynegy would sell an asset for $100, and immediately repurchase it from the buyer for $100. The problem arose with the treatment of the cash flows from the sale. Dynegy treated the cash from the sale of the asset as an operating cash flow, but classified the repurchase as an investing cash outflow. The total cash flows of the contracts traded by Dynegy in these round trip trades totaled $300 million.

Adelphia Communications was another company that apparently manipulated cash flows. In Adelphia's case, the company capitalized the labor required to install cable. In other words, the company classified this labor expense as a fixed asset. While this practice is fairly common in the telecommunications industry, Adelphia capitalized a higher percentage of labor than is common. The effect of this classification was that the labor was treated as an investment cash flow, which increased the operating cash flow.

In each of these examples, the companies were trying to boost operating cash flows by shifting cash flows to a different heading. The important thing to notice is that these movements don't affect the total cash flow of the firm, which is why we recommend focusing on this number, not just operating cash flow.

Cash Flow from Investing Activities

Cash flow from investing activities involves changes in capital assets: acquisition of fixed assets and sales of fixed assets (i.e., net capital expenditures). The result for U.S. Composite is below.

U.S. COMPOSITE CORPORATION Cash Flow from Investing Activities 2006 (in $ millions)	
Acquisition of fixed assets	−$198
Sales of fixed assets	25
Cash flow from investing activities	**−$173**

Cash Flow from Financing Activities

Cash flows to and from creditors and owners include changes in equity and debt.

U.S. COMPOSITE CORPORATION Cash Flow from Financing Activities 2006 (in $ millions)	
Retirement of long-term debt	−$73
Proceeds from long-term debt sales	86
Change in notes payable	3
Dividends	− 43
Repurchase of stock	− 6
Proceeds from new stock issue	43
Cash flow from financing activities	$ 4

The statement of cash flows is the addition of cash flows from operations, cash flows from investing activities, and cash flows from financing activities, and is produced in Table 2.6. When we add all the cash flows together, we get the change in cash on the balance sheet of $33 million.

There is a close relationship between the official accounting statement called the statement of cash flows and the total cash flow of the firm used in finance. Going back to the previous section, you should note a slight conceptual problem here. Interest paid should

TABLE 2.6

Statement of Consolidated Cash Flows of the U.S. Composite Corporation

U.S. COMPOSITE CORPORATION Statement of Cash Flows 2006 (in $ millions)	
Operations	
Net income	$ 86
Depreciation	90
Deferred taxes	13
Changes in assets and liabilities	
Accounts receivable	− 24
Inventories	11
Accounts payable	16
Accrued expenses	18
Other	− 8
Total cash flow from operations	$202
Investing activities	
Acquisition of fixed assets	−$198
Sales of fixed assets	25
Total cash flow from investing activities	−$173
Financing activities	
Retirement of long-term debt	−$ 73
Proceeds from long-term debt sales	86
Change in notes payable	3
Dividends	− 43
Repurchase of stock	− 6
Proceeds from new stock issue	43
Total cash flow from financing activities	$ 4
Change in cash (on the balance sheet)	$ 33

really go under financing activities, but unfortunately that is not how the accounting is handled. The reason is that interest is deducted as an expense when net income is computed. As a consequence, a primary difference between the accounting cash flow and the financial cash flow of the firm (see Table 2.5) is interest expense. *The Real World* box on page 34 discusses some ways in which companies have attempted to "spin the numbers" in the accounting statement of cash flows.

SUMMARY AND CONCLUSIONS

Besides introducing you to corporate accounting, the purpose of this chapter has been to teach you how to determine cash flow from the accounting statements of a typical company.

1. Cash flow is generated by the firm and paid to creditors and shareholders. It can be classified as:
   a. Cash flow from operations.
   b. Cash flow from changes in fixed assets.
   c. Cash flow from changes in working capital.
2. Calculations of cash flow are not difficult, but they require care and particular attention to detail in properly accounting for noncash expenses such as depreciation and deferred taxes. It is especially important that you do not confuse cash flow with changes in net working capital and net income.

CONCEPT QUESTIONS

1. **Liquidity** What does liquidity measure? Explain the trade-off a firm faces between high liquidity and low liquidity levels.
2. **Accounting and Cash Flows** Why is it that the revenue and cost figures shown on a standard income statement may not be representative of the actual cash inflows and outflows that occurred during a period?
3. **Accounting Statement of Cash Flows** Looking at the accounting statement of cash flows, what does the bottom line number mean? How useful is this number for analyzing a company?
4. **Cash Flows** How do financial cash flows and the accounting statement of cash flows differ? Which is more useful when analyzing a company?
5. **Book Values versus Market Values** Under standard accounting rules, it is possible for a company's liabilities to exceed its assets. When this occurs, the owners' equity is negative. Can this happen with market values? Why or why not?
6. **Cash Flow from Assets** Suppose a company's cash flow from assets was negative for a particular period. Is this necessarily a good sign or a bad sign?
7. **Operating Cash Flow** Suppose a company's operating cash flow was negative for several years running. Is this necessarily a good sign or a bad sign?
8. **Net Working Capital and Capital Spending** Could a company's change in net working capital be negative in a given year? (Hint: Yes.) Explain how this might come about. What about net capital spending?

9. **Cash Flow to Stockholders and Creditors** Could a company's cash flow to stockholders be negative in a given year? (Hint: Yes.) Explain how this might come about. What about cash flow to creditors?

10. **Firm Values** Referring back to the Viacom example used at the beginning of the chapter, note that we suggested that Viacom's stockholders probably didn't suffer as a result of the reported loss. What do you think was the basis for our conclusion?

QUESTIONS AND PROBLEMS

Basic
(Questions 1–10)

1. **Building a Balance Sheet** Culligan, Inc., has current assets of $5,000, net fixed assets of $23,000, current liabilities of $4,300, and long-term debt of $13,000. What is the value of the shareholders' equity account for this firm? How much is net working capital?

2. **Building an Income Statement** Ragsdale, Inc., has sales of $527,000, costs of $280,000, depreciation expense of $38,000, interest expense of $15,000, and a tax rate of 35 percent. What is the net income for the firm? Suppose the company paid out $48,000 in cash dividends. What is the addition to retained earnings?

3. **Market Values and Book Values** Klingon Cruisers, Inc., purchased new cloaking machinery three years ago for $7 million. The machinery can be sold to the Romulans today for $3.2 million. Klingon's current balance sheet shows net fixed assets of $4,000,000, current liabilities of $2,200,000, and net working capital of $900,000. If all the current assets were liquidated today, the company would receive $2.8 million cash. What is the book value of Klingon's assets today? What is the market value?

4. **Calculating Taxes** The Herrera Co. had $273,000 in taxable income. Using the rates from Table 2.3 in the chapter, calculate the company's income taxes. What is the average tax rate? What is the marginal tax rate?

5. **Calculating OCF** Ranney, Inc., has sales of $13,500, costs of $5,400, depreciation expense of $1,200, and interest expense of $680. If the tax rate is 35 percent, what is the operating cash flow, or OCF?

6. **Calculating Net Capital Spending** Gordon Driving School's 2005 balance sheet showed net fixed assets of $4.2 million, and the 2006 balance sheet showed net fixed assets of $4.7 million. The company's 2006 income statement showed a depreciation expense of $925,000. What was Gordon's net capital spending for 2006?

7. **Building a Balance Sheet** The following table presents the long-term liabilities and stockholders' equity of Information Control Corp. one year ago:

Long-term debt	$60,000,000
Preferred stock	18,000,000
Common stock ($1 par value)	25,000,000
Accumulated retained earnings	89,000,000
Capital surplus	49,000,000

During the past year, Information Control issued 10 million shares of new stock at a total price of $26 million, and issued $8 million in new long-term debt. The company generated $7 million in net income and paid $4 million in dividends. Construct the current balance sheet reflecting the changes that occurred at Information Control Corp. during the year.

8. **Cash Flow to Creditors** The 2005 balance sheet of Anna's Tennis Shop, Inc., showed long-term debt of $2.8 million, and the 2006 balance sheet showed long-term debt of $3.1 million. The 2006 income statement showed an interest expense of $340,000. What was the firm's cash flow to creditors during 2006?

9. **Cash Flow to Stockholders** The 2005 balance sheet of Anna's Tennis Shop, Inc., showed $820,000 in the common stock account and $6.8 million in the additional paid-in surplus account. The 2006 balance sheet showed $855,000 and $7.6 million in the same two accounts, respectively. If the company paid out $600,000 in cash dividends during 2006, what was the cash flow to stockholders for the year?

10. **Calculating Total Cash Flows** Given the information for Anna's Tennis Shop, Inc., in the previous two problems, suppose you also know that the firm's net capital spending for 2006 was $760,000, and that the firm reduced its net working capital investment by $165,000. What was the firm's 2006 operating cash flow, or OCF?

Intermediate
(Questions 11–24)

11. **Cash Flows** Ritter Corporation's accountants prepared the following financial statements for year-end 2006.

RITTER CORPORATION
Income Statement
2006

Revenue	$500
Expenses	300
Depreciation	75
Net income	$125
Dividends	$ 65

RITTER CORPORATION
Balance Sheets
December 31

	2006	2005
Assets		
Cash	$ 45	$ 10
Other current assets	145	120
Net fixed assets	250	150
Total assets	$440	$280
Liabilities and Equity		
Current liabilities	$ 70	$ 60
Long-term debt	90	0
Stockholders' equity	280	220
Total liabilities and equity	$440	$280

a. Explain the change in cash during the year 2006.

b. Determine the change in net working capital in 2006.

c. Determine the cash flow generated by the firm's assets during the year 2006.

12. **Financial Cash Flows** The Stancil Corporation provided the following current information:

Proceeds from short-term borrowing	$ 7,000
Proceeds from long-term borrowing	18,000
Proceeds from the sale of common stock	2,000
Purchases of fixed assets	3,000
Purchases of inventories	1,000
Payment of dividends	23,000

Determine the cash flows from the firm and the cash flows to investors of the firm.

13. **Building an Income Statement** During the year, the Senbet Discount Tire Company had gross sales of $1 million. The firm's cost of goods sold and selling expenses were $300,000 and $200,000, respectively. Senbet also had notes payable of $1 million. These notes carried an interest rate of 10 percent. Depreciation was $100,000. Senbet's tax rate was 35 percent. 

    a. What was Senbet's net income?

    b. What was Senbet's operating cash flow?

14. **Calculating Total Cash Flows** Schwert Corp. shows the following information on its 2006 income statement: sales = $145,000; costs = $86,000; other expenses = $4,900; depreciation expense = $7,000; interest expense = $15,000; taxes = $12,840; dividends = $8,700. In addition, you're told that the firm issued $6,450 in new equity during 2006, and redeemed $6,500 in outstanding long-term debt.

    a. What is the 2006 operating cash flow?

    b. What is the 2006 cash flow to creditors?

    c. What is the 2006 cash flow to stockholders?

    d. If net fixed assets increased by $5,000 during the year, what was the addition to NWC?

15. **Using Income Statements** Given the following information for O'Hara Marine Co., calculate the depreciation expense: sales = $29,000; costs = $13,000; addition to retained earnings = $4,500; dividends paid = $900; interest expense = $1,600; tax rate = 35 percent.

16. **Preparing a Balance Sheet** Prepare a 2006 balance sheet for Jarrow Corp. based on the following information: cash = $175,000; patents and copyrights = $720,000; accounts payable = $430,000; accounts receivable = $140,000; tangible net fixed assets = $2,900,000; inventory = $265,000; notes payable = $180,000; accumulated retained earnings = $1,240,000; long-term debt = $1,430,000. 

17. **Residual Claims** Huang, Inc., is obligated to pay its creditors $3,500 very soon.

    a. What is the market value of the shareholders' equity if assets have a market value of $4,300?

    b. What if assets equal $3,200?

18. **Marginal versus Average Tax Rates** (Refer to Table 2.3.) Corporation Growth has $85,000 in taxable income, and Corporation Income has $8,500,000 in taxable income.

    a. What is the tax bill for each firm?

    b. Suppose both firms have identified a new project that will increase taxable income by $10,000. How much in additional taxes will each firm pay? Why is this amount the same?

19. **Net Income and OCF** During 2006, Raines Umbrella Corp. had sales of $850,000. Cost of goods sold, administrative and selling expenses, and depreciation expenses were $630,000, $120,000, and $130,000, respectively. In addition, the company had an interest expense of $85,000 and a tax rate of 35 percent. (Ignore any tax loss carry-back or carry-forward provisions.)

    a. What is Raines's net income for 2006?

    b. What is its operating cash flow?

    c. Explain your results in (a) and (b).

20. **Accounting Values versus Cash Flows** In Problem 19, suppose Raines Umbrella Corp. paid out $30,000 in cash dividends. Is this possible? If spending on net fixed assets and net working capital was zero, and if no new stock was issued during the year, what was the change in the firm's long-term debt account?

21. **Calculating Cash Flows** Cusic Industries had the following operating results for 2006: sales = $12,800; cost of goods sold = $10,400; depreciation expense = $1,900; interest expense = $450; dividends paid = $500. At the beginning of the year, net fixed assets were $9,100, current assets were $3,200, and current liabilities were $1,800. At the end of the year, net fixed assets were

$9,700, current assets were $3,850, and current liabilities were $2,100. The tax rate for 2006 was 34 percent.

a. What is net income for 2006?

b. What is the operating cash flow for 2006?

c. What is the cash flow from assets for 2006? Is this possible? Explain.

d. If no new debt was issued during the year, what is the cash flow to creditors? What is the cash flow to stockholders? Explain and interpret the positive and negative signs of your answers in (a) through (d).

22. **Calculating Cash Flows** Consider the following abbreviated financial statements for Weston Enterprises:

WESTON ENTERPRISES
2005 and 2006 Partial Balance Sheets

Assets	2005	2006	Liabilities and Owners' Equity	2005	2006
Current assets	$ 650	$ 705	Current liabilities	$ 265	$ 290
Net fixed assets	2,900	3,400	Long-term debt	1,500	1,720

WESTON ENTERPRISES
2006 Income Statement

Sales	$8,600
Costs	4,150
Depreciation	800
Interest paid	216

a. What is owners' equity for 2005 and 2006?

b. What is the change in net working capital for 2006?

c. In 2006, Weston Enterprises purchased $1,500 in new fixed assets. How much in fixed assets did Weston Enterprises sell? What is the cash flow from assets for the year? (The tax rate is 35 percent.)

d. During 2006, Weston Enterprises raised $300 in new long-term debt. How much long-term debt must Weston Enterprises have paid off during the year? What is the cash flow to creditors?

Use the following information for Ingersoll, Inc., for Problems 23 and 24 (assume the tax rate is 34 percent):

	2005	2006
Sales	$ 4,018	$ 4,312
Depreciation	577	578
Cost of goods sold	1,382	1,569
Other expenses	328	274
Interest	269	309
Cash	2,107	2,155
Accounts receivable	2,789	3,142
Short-term notes payable	407	382
Long-term debt	7,056	8,232
Net fixed assets	17,669	18,091
Accounts payable	2,213	2,146
Inventory	4,959	5,096
Dividends	490	539

23. **Financial Statements** Draw up an income statement and balance sheet for this company for 2005 and 2006.

24. **Calculating Cash Flow** For 2006, calculate the cash flow from assets, cash flow to creditors, and cash flow to stockholders.

25. **Cash Flows** You are researching Time Manufacturing and have found the following accounting statement of cash flows for the most recent year. You also know that the company paid $110 million in current taxes and had an interest expense of $57 million. Use the accounting statement of cash flows to construct the financial statement of cash flows.

Challenge (Questions 25–27)

TIME MANUFACTURING Statement of Cash Flows (in $ millions)	
Operations	
Net income	$192
Depreciation	105
Deferred taxes	21
Changes in assets and liabilities	
Accounts receivable	− 31
Inventories	24
Accounts payable	19
Accrued expenses	− 10
Other	2
Total cash flow from operations	$322
Investing activities	
Acquisition of fixed assets	−$198
Sale of fixed assets	25
Total cash flow from investing activities	−$173
Financing activities	
Retirement of long-term debt	−$ 84
Proceeds from long-term debt sales	129
Change in notes payable	6
Dividends	− 94
Repurchase of stock	− 15
Proceeds from new stock issue	49
Total cash flow from financing activities	−$ 9
Change in cash (on balance sheet)	$140

26. **Net Fixed Assets and Depreciation** On the balance sheet, the net fixed assets (NFA) account is equal to the gross fixed assets (FA) account, which records the acquisition cost of fixed assets, minus the accumulated depreciation (AD) account, which records the total depreciation taken by the firm against its fixed assets. Using the fact that NFA = FA − AD, show that the expression given in the chapter for net capital spending, $NFA_{end} - NFA_{beg} + D$ (where D is the depreciation expense during the year), is equivalent to $FA_{end} - FA_{beg}$.

27. **Tax Rates** Refer to the corporate marginal tax rate information in Table 2.3.
    a. Why do you think the marginal tax rate jumps up from 34 percent to 39 percent at a taxable income of $100,001, and then falls back to a 34 percent marginal rate at a taxable income of $335,001?
    b. Compute the average tax rate for a corporation with exactly $335,001 in taxable income. Does this confirm your explanation in part (a)? What is the average tax rate for a corporation with exactly $18,333,334? Is the same thing happening here?
    c. The 39 percent and 38 percent tax rates both represent what is called a tax "bubble." Suppose the government wanted to lower the upper threshold of the 39 percent marginal tax bracket from $335,000 to $200,000. What would the new 39 percent bubble rate have to be?

S&P PROBLEMS

www.mhhe.com/edumarketinsight

1. **Marginal and Average Tax Rates** Download the annual income statements for Sharper Image (SHRP). Looking back at Table 2.3, what is the marginal income tax rate for Sharper Image? Using the total income tax and the pretax income numbers calculate the average tax rate for Sharper Image. Is this number greater than 35 percent? Why or why not?
2. **Net Working Capital** Find the annual balance sheets for American Electric Power (AEP) and HJ Heinz (HNZ). Calculate the net working capital for each company. Is American Electric Power's net working capital negative? If so, does this indicate potential financial difficulty for the company? What about Heinz?
3. **Per Share Earnings and Dividends** Find the annual income statements for Harley-Davidson (HDI), Hawaiian Electric Industries (HE), and Time Warner (TWX). What are the earnings per share (EPS Basic from operations) for each of these companies? What are the dividends per share for each company? Why do these companies pay out a different portion of income in the form of dividends?
4. **Cash Flow Identity** Download the annual balance sheets and income statements for Landry's Seafood Restaurants (LNY). Using the most recent year calculate the cash flow identity for Landry Seafood. Explain your answer.

WHAT'S ON THE WEB?

1. **Change in Net Working Capital** Find the most recent abbreviated balance sheets for General Dynamics at finance.yahoo.com. Enter the ticker symbol "GD," follow the "Research" link, and the "Financials" link. Using the two most recent balance sheets, calculate the change in net working capital. What does this number mean?
2. **Book Values versus Market Values** The home page for Coca-Cola Company can be found at www.coca-cola.com. Locate the most recent annual report, which contains a balance sheet for the company. What is the book value of equity for Coca-Cola? The market value of a company is the number of shares of stock outstanding times the price per share. This information can be found at finance.yahoo.com using the ticker symbol for Coca-Cola (KO). What is the market value of equity? Which number is more relevant for shareholders?
3. **Cash Flows to Stockholders and Creditors** Cooper Tire and Rubber Company provides financial information for investors on its Web site at www.coopertires.com. Follow the "Investor Information" link and find the most recent annual report. Using the consolidated statements of cash flows, calculate the cash flow to stockholders and the cash flow to creditors.

CLOSING CASE

CASH FLOWS AT WARF COMPUTERS, INC.

Warf Computers, Inc., was founded 15 years ago by Nick Warf, a computer programmer. The small initial investment made to start the company was made by Nick and his friends. Over the years, this same group has supplied the limited additional investment needed by the company in the form of both equity and short- and long-term debt. Recently the company has developed a virtual keyboard (VK). The VK uses sophisticated artificial intelligence algorithms that allow the user to speak naturally and have the computer input the text, correct spelling and grammatical errors, and format the document according to preset user guidelines. The VK even suggests alternative phrasing and sentence structure, and it provides detailed stylistic diagnostics. Based on a proprietary, and very advanced, software/hardware hybrid technology, the system is a full generation beyond what is currently on the market. To introduce the VK, the company will require significant outside investment.

Nick has made the decision to seek this outside financing in the form of new equity investors and bank loans. Naturally, these new investors and the banks will require a detailed financial analysis. Your employer, Angus Jones & Partners, LLC, has asked you to examine the financial statements provided by Nick. Below you will find the balance sheet for the two most recent years and the most recent income statement.

WARF COMPUTERS
Balance Sheet
(in $ thousands)

	2006	2005
Current assets:		
Cash and equivalents	$ 232	$ 201
Accounts receivable	367	342
Inventories	329	340
Other	47	40
Total current assets	$ 975	$ 923
Fixed assets:		
Property, plant, and equipment	$2,105	$1,630
Less accumulated depreciation	687	560
Net property, plant, and equipment	$1,418	$1,070
Intangible assets and others	406	363
Total fixed assets	$1,824	$1,433
Total assets	$2,799	$2,356

	2006	2005
Current liabilities:		
Accounts payable	$ 263	$ 197
Notes payable	68	53
Accrued expenses	126	205
Total current liabilities	$ 457	$ 455
Long-term liabilities:		
Deferred taxes	$ 143	$ 82
Long-term debt	629	589
Total long-term liabilities	$ 772	$ 671
Stockholders' equity:		
Preferred stock	$ 10	$ 10
Common stock	72	64
Capital surplus	438	399
Accumulated retained earnings	1,147	822
Less treasury stock	− 97	− 65
Total equity	$1,570	$1,230
Total liabilities and shareholders' equity	$2,799	$2,356

WARF COMPUTERS Income Statement (in $ thousands)	
Sales	$3,875
Cost of goods sold	2,286
Selling, general, and administrative expense	434
Depreciation	127
Operating income	$1,028
Other income	38
Earnings before interest and taxes (EBIT)	$1,066
Interest expense	76
Pretax income	$ 990
Taxes	347
Current: $286	
Deferred: $61	
Net income	$ 643
Addition to retained earnings	$ 325
Dividends	$ 318

Nick has also provided the following information. During the year, the company raised $94,000 in new long-term debt and retired $54,000 in long-term debt. The company also sold $47,000 in new stock and repurchased $32,000 in stock. The company purchased $629,000 in fixed assets, and sold $111,000 in fixed assets.

Angus has asked you to prepare the financial statement of cash flows and the accounting statement of cash flows. He has also asked you to answer the following questions:

1. How would you describe Warf Computers's cash flows?
2. Which cash flows statement more accurately describes the cash flows at the company?
3. In light of your previous answers, comment on Nick's expansion plans.

CHAPTER 3

Financial Statements Analysis and Long-Term Planning

OPENING CASE

In March 2005, shares of stock in shipping company FedEx were trading for about $95. At that price, FedEx had a price-earnings ratio, or PE, of 20, meaning that investors were willing to pay $20 for every dollar in income earned by FedEx. At the same time, investors were willing to pay a whopping $746 for each dollar earned by Computer Associates, but only $11 and $6 for each dollar earned by Allstate and United States Steel, respectively. Meanwhile, the average stock in the Standard and Poor's (S&P) 500 Index, which contains 500 of the largest publicly traded companies in the United States, had a PE of about 20, so FedEx was about average in this regard. What do PE ratios tell us and why are they important? To find out, this chapter explores a variety of ratios and their use in financial analysis and planning.

3.1 FINANCIAL STATEMENTS ANALYSIS

In Chapter 2, we discussed some of the essential concepts of financial statements and cash flows. This chapter continues where our earlier discussion left off. Our goal here is to expand your understanding of the uses (and abuses) of financial statement information.

A good working knowledge of financial statements is desirable simply because such statements, and numbers derived from those statements, are the primary means of communicating financial information both within the firm and outside the firm. In short, much of the language of business finance is rooted in the ideas we discuss in this chapter.

Clearly, one important goal of the accountant is to report financial information to the user in a form useful for decision making. Ironically, the information frequently does not come to the user in such a form. In other words, financial statements don't come with a user's guide. This chapter is a first step in filling this gap.

Standardizing Statements

One obvious thing we might want to do with a company's financial statements is to compare them to those of other, similar companies. We would immediately have a problem, however. It's almost impossible to directly compare the financial statements for two companies because of differences in size.

For example, Ford and GM are obviously serious rivals in the auto market, but GM is much larger (in terms of assets), so it is difficult to compare them directly. For that matter, it's difficult to even compare financial statements from different points in time for the same company if the company's size has changed. The size problem is compounded if we try to compare GM and, say, Toyota. If Toyota's financial statements are denominated in yen, then we have a size *and* a currency difference.

To start making comparisons, one obvious thing we might try to do is to somehow standardize the financial statements. One very common and useful way of doing this is to work with percentages instead of total dollars. The resulting financial statements are called **common-size statements**. We consider these next.

Common-Size Balance Sheets

For easy reference, Prufrock Corporation's 2005 and 2006 balance sheets are provided in Table 3.1. Using these, we construct common-size balance sheets by expressing each item as a percentage of total assets. Prufrock's 2005 and 2006 common-size balance sheets are shown in Table 3.2.

Notice that some of the totals don't check exactly because of rounding errors. Also notice that the total change has to be zero since the beginning and ending numbers must add up to 100 percent.

In this form, financial statements are relatively easy to read and compare. For example, just looking at the two balance sheets for Prufrock, we see that current assets were 19.7 percent of total assets in 2006, up from 19.1 percent in 2005. Current liabilities declined from 16.0 percent to 15.1 percent of total liabilities and equity over that same time. Similarly, total equity rose from 68.1 percent of total liabilities and equity to 72.2 percent.

Overall, Prufrock's liquidity, as measured by current assets compared to current liabilities, increased over the year. Simultaneously, Prufrock's indebtedness diminished as a percentage of total assets. We might be tempted to conclude that the balance sheet has grown "stronger."

TABLE 3.1

PRUFROCK CORPORATION
Balance Sheets as of December 31, 2005 and 2006
($ in millions)

	2005	2006
Assets		
Current assets		
Cash	$ 84	$ 98
Accounts receivable	165	188
Inventory	393	422
Total	$ 642	$ 708
Fixed assets		
Net plant and equipment	$2,731	$2,880
Total assets	$3,373	$3,588
Liabilities and Owners' Equity		
Current liabilities		
Accounts payable	$ 312	$ 344
Notes payable	231	196
Total	$ 543	$ 540
Long-term debt	$ 531	$ 457
Owners' equity		
Common stock and paid-in surplus	$ 500	$ 550
Retained earnings	1,799	2,041
Total	$2,299	$2,591
Total liabilities and owners' equity	$3,373	$3,588

TABLE 3.2

PRUFROCK CORPORATION
Common-Size Balance Sheets
December 31, 2005 and 2006

	2005	2006	Change
Assets			
Current assets			
Cash	2.5%	2.7%	+ .2%
Accounts receivable	4.9	5.2	+ .3
Inventory	11.7	11.8	+ .1
Total	19.1	19.7	+ .6
Fixed assets			
Net plant and equipment	80.9	80.3	− .6
Total assets	100.0%	100.0%	.0%
Liabilities and Owners' Equity			
Current liabilities			
Accounts payable	9.2%	9.6%	+ .4%
Notes payable	6.8	5.5	−1.3
Total	16.0	15.1	− .9
Long-term debt	15.7	12.7	−3.0
Owners' equity			
Common stock and paid-in surplus	14.8	15.3	+ .5
Retained earnings	53.3	56.9	+3.6
Total	68.1	72.2	+4.1
Total liabilities and owners' equity	100.0%	100.0%	.0%

TABLE 3.3

PRUFROCK CORPORATION 2006 Income Statement ($ in millions)		
Sales		$2,311
Cost of goods sold		1,344
Depreciation		276
Earnings before interest and taxes		$ 691
Interest paid		141
Taxable income		$ 550
Taxes (34%)		187
Net income		$ 363
Dividends	$121	
Addition to retained earnings	242	

TABLE 3.4

PRUFROCK CORPORATION Common-Size Income Statement 2006		
Sales		100.0%
Cost of goods sold		58.2
Depreciation		11.9
Earnings before interest and taxes		29.9
Interest paid		6.1
Taxable income		23.8
Taxes (34%)		8.1
Net income		15.7%
Dividends	5.2%	
Addition to retained earnings	10.5	

Common-Size Income Statements

A useful way of standardizing the income statement shown in Table 3.3 is to express each item as a percentage of total sales, as illustrated for Prufrock in Table 3.4.

This income statement tells us what happens to each dollar in sales. For Prufrock, interest expense eats up $.061 out of every sales dollar, and taxes take another $.081. When all is said and done, $.157 of each dollar flows through to the bottom line (net income), and that amount is split into $.105 retained in the business and $.052 paid out in dividends.

These percentages are very useful in comparisons. For example, a very relevant figure is the cost percentage. For Prufrock, $.582 of each $1.00 in sales goes to pay for goods sold. It would be interesting to compute the same percentage for Prufrock's main competitors to see how Prufrock stacks up in terms of cost control.

3.2 RATIO ANALYSIS

Another way of avoiding the problems involved in comparing companies of different sizes is to calculate and compare **financial ratios**. Such ratios are ways of comparing and investigating the relationships between different pieces of financial information. We cover some of the more common ratios next, but there are many others that we don't touch on.

One problem with ratios is that different people and different sources frequently don't compute them in exactly the same way, and this leads to much confusion. The specific definitions we use here may or may not be the same as ones you have seen or will see elsewhere. If you are ever using ratios as tools for analysis, you should be careful to document how you calculate each one, and, if you are comparing your numbers to those of another source, be sure you know how their numbers are computed.

We will defer much of our discussion of how ratios are used and some problems that come up with using them until a bit later in the chapter. For now, for each of the ratios we discuss, several questions come to mind:

1. How is it computed?
2. What is it intended to measure, and why might we be interested?
3. What is the unit of measurement?
4. What might a high or low value be telling us? How might such values be misleading?
5. How could this measure be improved?

Financial ratios are traditionally grouped into the following categories:

1. Short-term solvency, or liquidity, ratios.
2. Long-term solvency, or financial leverage, ratios.
3. Asset management, or turnover, ratios.
4. Profitability ratios.
5. Market value ratios.

We will consider each of these in turn. In calculating these numbers for Prufrock, we will use the ending balance sheet (2006) figures unless we explicitly say otherwise.

Go to www.marketguide.com and find the ratios link to examine comparative ratios for a huge number of companies.

Short-Term Solvency or Liquidity Measures

As the name suggests, short-term solvency ratios as a group are intended to provide information about a firm's liquidity, and these ratios are sometimes called *liquidity measures*. The primary concern is the firm's ability to pay its bills over the short run without undue stress. Consequently, these ratios focus on current assets and current liabilities.

For obvious reasons, liquidity ratios are particularly interesting to short-term creditors. Since financial managers are constantly working with banks and other short-term lenders, an understanding of these ratios is essential.

One advantage of looking at current assets and liabilities is that their book values and market values are likely to be similar. Often (though not always), these assets and liabilities just don't live long enough for the two to get seriously out of step. On the other hand, like any type of near-cash, current assets and liabilities can and do change fairly rapidly, so today's amounts may not be a reliable guide to the future.

CURRENT RATIO One of the best-known and most widely used ratios is the *current ratio*. As you might guess, the current ratio is defined as:

$$\textbf{Current ratio} = \frac{\textbf{Current assets}}{\textbf{Current liabilities}} \tag{3.1}$$

For Prufrock, the 2006 current ratio is:

$$\textbf{Current ratio} = \frac{\$708}{\$540} = \textbf{1.31 times}$$

Because current assets and liabilities are, in principle, converted to cash over the following 12 months, the current ratio is a measure of short-term liquidity. The unit of measurement is either dollars or times. So, we could say Prufrock has $1.31 in current assets for every $1 in current liabilities, or we could say Prufrock has its current liabilities covered 1.31 times over.

To a creditor, particularly a short-term creditor such as a supplier, the higher the current ratio, the better. To the firm, a high current ratio indicates liquidity, but it also may indicate an inefficient use of cash and other short-term assets. Absent some extraordinary circumstances, we would expect to see a current ratio of at least 1, because a current ratio of less than 1 would mean that net working capital (current assets less current liabilities) is negative. This would be unusual in a healthy firm, at least for most types of businesses.

The current ratio, like any ratio, is affected by various types of transactions. For example, suppose the firm borrows over the long term to raise money. The short-run effect would be an increase in cash from the issue proceeds and an increase in long-term debt. Current liabilities would not be affected, so the current ratio would rise.

Finally, note that an apparently low current ratio may not be a bad sign for a company with a large reserve of untapped borrowing power.

EXAMPLE 3.1 Current Events

Suppose a firm were to pay off some of its suppliers and short-term creditors. What would happen to the current ratio? Suppose a firm buys some inventory. What happens in this case? What happens if a firm sells some merchandise?

The first case is a trick question. What happens is that the current ratio moves away from 1. If it is greater than 1 (the usual case), it will get bigger, but if it is less than 1, it will get smaller. To see this, suppose the firm has $4 in current assets and $2 in current liabilities for a current ratio of 2. If we use $1 in cash to reduce current liabilities, then the new current ratio is ($4 − 1)/($2 − 1) = 3. If we reverse the original situation to $2 in current assets and $4 in current liabilities, then the change will cause the current ratio to fall to 1/3 from 1/2.

The second case is not quite as tricky. Nothing happens to the current ratio because cash goes down while inventory goes up—total current assets are unaffected.

In the third case, the current ratio would usually rise because inventory is normally shown at cost and the sale would normally be at something greater than cost (the difference is the markup). The increase in either cash or receivables is therefore greater than the decrease in inventory. This increases current assets, and the current ratio rises.

QUICK (OR ACID-TEST) RATIO Inventory is often the least liquid current asset. It's also the one for which the book values are least reliable as measures of market value since the quality of the inventory isn't considered. Some of the inventory may later turn out to be damaged, obsolete, or lost.

More to the point, relatively large inventories are often a sign of short-term trouble. The firm may have overestimated sales and overbought or overproduced as a result. In this case, the firm may have a substantial portion of its liquidity tied up in slow-moving inventory.

To further evaluate liquidity, the *quick, or acid-test, ratio* is computed just like the current ratio, except inventory is omitted:

$$\textbf{Quick ratio} = \frac{\textbf{Current assets} - \textbf{Inventory}}{\textbf{Current liabilities}} \tag{3.2}$$

Notice that using cash to buy inventory does not affect the current ratio, but it reduces the quick ratio. Again, the idea is that inventory is relatively illiquid compared to cash.

For Prufrock, this ratio in 2006 was:

$$\textbf{Quick ratio} = \frac{\$708 - 422}{\$540} = .53 \textbf{ times}$$

The quick ratio here tells a somewhat different story than the current ratio, because inventory accounts for more than half of Prufrock's current assets. To exaggerate the point, if this inventory consisted of, say, unsold nuclear power plants, then this would be a cause for concern.

To give an example of current versus quick ratios, based on recent financial statements Wal-Mart and Manpower, Inc., had current ratios of .89 and 1.54, respectively. However, Manpower carries no inventory to speak of, whereas Wal-Mart's current assets are virtually all inventory. As a result, Wal-Mart's quick ratio was only .17, and Manpower's was 1.45, almost the same as its current ratio.

CASH RATIO A very short-term creditor might be interested in the *cash ratio:*

$$\textbf{Cash ratio} = \frac{\textbf{Cash}}{\textbf{Current liabilities}} \tag{3.3}$$

You can verify that this works out to be .18 times for Prufrock.

Long-Term Solvency Measures

Long-term solvency ratios are intended to address the firm's long-run ability to meet its obligations, or, more generally, its financial leverage. These ratios are sometimes called *financial leverage ratios* or just *leverage ratios.* We consider three commonly used measures and some variations.

TOTAL DEBT RATIO The *total debt ratio* takes into account all debts of all maturities to all creditors. It can be defined in several ways, the easiest of which is:

$$\begin{aligned}\textbf{Total debt ratio} &= \frac{\textbf{Total assets} - \textbf{Total equity}}{\textbf{Total assets}} \\ &= \frac{\$3{,}588 - 2{,}591}{\$3{,}588} = .28 \textbf{ times}\end{aligned} \tag{3.4}$$

In this case, an analyst might say that Prufrock uses 28 percent debt.[1] Whether this is high or low or whether it even makes any difference depends on whether or not capital structure matters, a subject we discuss in a later chapter.

Prufrock has \$.28 in debt for every \$1 in assets. Therefore, there is \$.72 in equity (\$1 − .28) for every \$.28 in debt. With this in mind, we can define two useful variations on the total debt ratio, the *debt-equity ratio* and the *equity multiplier:*

$$\begin{aligned}\textbf{Debt-equity ratio} &= \textbf{Total debt/Total equity} \\ &= \$.28/\$.72 = .39 \textbf{ times}\end{aligned} \tag{3.5}$$

$$\begin{aligned}\textbf{Equity multiplier} &= \textbf{Total assets/Total equity} \\ &= \$1/\$.72 = 1.39 \textbf{ times}\end{aligned} \tag{3.6}$$

The online Women's Business Center has more information on financial statements, ratios, and small business topics **www.onlinewbc.gov**.

The fact that the equity multiplier is 1 plus the debt-equity ratio is not a coincidence:

$$\begin{aligned}\textbf{Equity multiplier} &= \textbf{Total assets/Total equity} = \$1/\$.72 = 1.39 \textbf{ times} \\ &= \textbf{(Total equity + Total debt)/Total equity} \\ &= \textbf{1 + Debt-equity ratio} = 1.39 \textbf{ times}\end{aligned}$$

The thing to notice here is that given any one of these three ratios, you can immediately calculate the other two, so they all say exactly the same thing.

TIMES INTEREST EARNED Another common measure of long-term solvency is the *times interest earned* (TIE) *ratio.* Once again, there are several possible (and common) definitions,

[1]Total equity here includes preferred stock, if there is any. An equivalent numerator in this ratio would be (Current liabilities + Long-term debt).

but we'll stick with the most traditional:

$$\textbf{Times interest earned ratio} = \frac{\textbf{EBIT}}{\textbf{Interest}} \tag{3.7}$$

$$= \frac{\$691}{\$141} = 4.9 \text{ times}$$

As the name suggests, this ratio measures how well a company has its interest obligations covered, and it is often called the interest coverage ratio. For Prufrock, the interest bill is covered 4.9 times over.

CASH COVERAGE A problem with the TIE ratio is that it is based on EBIT, which is not really a measure of cash available to pay interest. The reason is that depreciation, a noncash expense, has been deducted out. Since interest is most definitely a cash outflow (to creditors), one way to define the *cash coverage ratio* is

$$\textbf{Cash coverage ratio} = \frac{\textbf{EBIT + Depreciation}}{\textbf{Interest}} \tag{3.8}$$

$$= \frac{\$691 + 276}{\$141} = \frac{\$967}{\$141} = 6.9 \text{ times}$$

The numerator here, EBIT plus depreciation, is often abbreviated EBITD (earnings before interest, taxes, and depreciation). It is a basic measure of the firm's ability to generate cash from operations, and it is frequently used as a measure of cash flow available to meet financial obligations.

Asset Management or Turnover Measures

We next turn our attention to the efficiency with which Prufrock uses its assets. The measures in this section are sometimes called *asset utilization ratios.* The specific ratios we discuss can all be interpreted as measures of turnover. What they are intended to describe is how efficiently, or intensively, a firm uses its assets to generate sales. We first look at two important current assets: inventory and receivables.

INVENTORY TURNOVER AND DAYS' SALES IN INVENTORY During the year, Prufrock had a cost of goods sold of $1,344. Inventory at the end of the year was $422. With these numbers, *inventory turnover* can be calculated as:

$$\textbf{Inventory turnover} = \frac{\textbf{Cost of goods sold}}{\textbf{Inventory}} \tag{3.9}$$

$$= \frac{\$1,344}{\$422} = 3.2 \text{ times}$$

In a sense, we sold off, or turned over, the entire inventory 3.2 times. As long as we are not running out of stock and thereby forgoing sales, the higher this ratio is, the more efficiently we are managing inventory.

If we know that we turned our inventory over 3.2 times during the year, then we can immediately figure out how long it took us to turn it over on average. The result is the average *days' sales in inventory:*

$$\textbf{Days' sales in inventory} = \frac{\textbf{365 days}}{\textbf{Inventory turnover}} \tag{3.10}$$

$$= \frac{365}{3.2} = 114 \text{ days}$$

This tells us that, roughly speaking, inventory sits 114 days on average before it is sold. Alternatively, assuming we used the most recent inventory and cost figures, it will take about 114 days to work off our current inventory.

For example, in February 2005, General Motors had a 123-day supply of the slow-selling Pontiac G6 and a 122-day supply of the Buick LaCrosse. This means that, at the then-current rate of sales, it would have taken General Motors 123 days to deplete the available supply, whereas a 60-day supply is considered normal in the industry. Of course the days in inventory is much lower for better selling models. DaimlerChrysler had no such problem with its new (and tough-looking) Chrysler 300C. This popular model flew off dealer lots, and DaimlerChrysler had only 28 days of inventory on hand.

RECEIVABLES TURNOVER AND DAYS' SALES IN RECEIVABLES Our inventory measures give some indication of how fast we can sell products. We now look at how fast we collect on those sales. The *receivables turnover* is defined in the same way as inventory turnover:

$$\textbf{Receivables turnover} = \frac{\textbf{Sales}}{\textbf{Accounts receivable}} \tag{3.11}$$

$$= \frac{\$2{,}311}{\$188} = 12.3 \text{ times}$$

Loosely speaking, we collected our outstanding credit accounts and reloaned the money 12.3 times during the year.[2]

This ratio makes more sense if we convert it to days, so the *days' sales in receivables* is:

$$\textbf{Days' sales in receivables} = \frac{\textbf{365 days}}{\textbf{Receivables turnover}} \tag{3.12}$$

$$= \frac{365}{12.3} = 30 \text{ days}$$

Therefore, on average, we collect on our credit sales in 30 days. For obvious reasons, this ratio is very frequently called the *average collection period* (ACP). Also note that if we are using the most recent figures, we can also say that we have 30 days' worth of sales currently uncollected.

EXAMPLE 3.2 Payables Turnover

Here is a variation on the receivables collection period. How long, on average, does it take for Prufrock Corporation to *pay* its bills? To answer, we need to calculate the accounts payable turnover rate using cost of goods sold. We will assume that Prufrock purchases everything on credit.

The cost of goods sold is $1,344, and accounts payable are $344. The turnover is therefore $1,344/$344 = 3.9 times. So, payables turned over about every 365/3.9 = 94 days. On average, then, Prufrock takes 94 days to pay. As a potential creditor, we might take note of this fact.

TOTAL ASSET TURNOVER Moving away from specific accounts like inventory or receivables, we can consider an important "big picture" ratio, the *total asset turnover* ratio. As the name suggests, total asset turnover is:

$$\textbf{Total asset turnover} = \frac{\textbf{Sales}}{\textbf{Total assets}} \tag{3.13}$$

$$= \frac{\$2{,}311}{\$3{,}588} = .64 \text{ times}$$

In other words, for every dollar in assets, we generated $.64 in sales.

PricewaterhouseCoopers has a useful utility for extracting EDGAR data. Try it at www.edgarscan.pwcglobal.com.

[2]Here we have implicitly assumed that all sales are credit sales. If they were not, then we would simply use total credit sales in these calculations, not total sales.

EXAMPLE 3.3 More Turnover

Suppose you find that a particular company generates $.40 in sales for every dollar in total assets. How often does this company turn over its total assets?

The total asset turnover here is .40 times per year. It takes $1/.40 = 2.5$ years to turn assets over completely.

Profitability Measures

The three measures we discuss in this section are probably the best known and most widely used of all financial ratios. In one form or another, they are intended to measure how efficiently the firm uses its assets and how efficiently the firm manages its operations. The focus in this group is on the bottom line–net income.

PROFIT MARGIN Companies pay a great deal of attention to their *profit margin:*

$$\text{Profit margin} = \frac{\text{Net income}}{\text{Sales}} \tag{3.14}$$

$$= \frac{\$363}{\$2{,}311} = 15.7\%$$

This tells us that Prufrock, in an accounting sense, generates a little less than 16 cents in profit for every dollar in sales.

All other things being equal, a relatively high profit margin is obviously desirable. This situation corresponds to low expense ratios relative to sales. However, we hasten to add that other things are often not equal.

For example, lowering our sales price will usually increase unit volume, but will normally cause profit margins to shrink. Total profit (or, more importantly, operating cash flow) may go up or down, so the fact that margins are smaller isn't necessarily bad. After all, isn't it possible that, as the saying goes, "Our prices are so low that we lose money on everything we sell, but we make it up in volume!"?[3]

Profit margins are very different for different industries. For example, grocery stores have a notoriously low profit margin, generally around 2 percent. In contrast, the profit margin for the pharmaceutical industry is about 18 percent.

RETURN ON ASSETS *Return on assets* (ROA) is a measure of profit per dollar of assets. It can be defined several ways, but the most common is:

$$\text{Return on assets} = \frac{\text{Net income}}{\text{Total assets}} \tag{3.15}$$

$$= \frac{\$363}{\$3{,}588} = 10.12\%$$

RETURN ON EQUITY *Return on equity* (ROE) is a measure of how the stockholders fared during the year. Since benefiting shareholders is our goal, ROE is, in an accounting sense, the true bottom-line measure of performance. ROE is usually measured as:

$$\text{Return on equity} = \frac{\text{Net income}}{\text{Total equity}} \tag{3.16}$$

$$= \frac{\$363}{\$2{,}591} = 14\%$$

[3]No, it's not.

Therefore, for every dollar in equity, Prufrock generated 14 cents in profit, but, again, this is only correct in accounting terms.

Because ROA and ROE are such commonly cited numbers, we stress that it is important to remember they are accounting rates of return. For this reason, these measures should properly be called *return on book assets* and *return on book equity*. In addition, ROE is sometimes called *return on net worth*. Whatever it's called, it would be inappropriate to compare the result to, for example, an interest rate observed in the financial markets.

The fact that ROE exceeds ROA reflects Prufrock's use of financial leverage. We will examine the relationship between these two measures in more detail below.

Market Value Measures

Our final group of measures is based, in part, on information not necessarily contained in financial statements–the market price per share of the stock. Obviously, these measures can be calculated directly only for publicly traded companies.

We assume that Prufrock has 33 million shares outstanding and the stock sold for $88 per share at the end of the year. If we recall that Prufrock's net income was $363 million, then we can calculate that its earnings per share were:

$$\textbf{EPS} = \frac{\textbf{Net income}}{\textbf{Shares outstanding}} = \frac{\$363}{33} = \$11 \tag{3.17}$$

PRICE-EARNINGS RATIO The first of our market value measures, the *price-earnings* or PE *ratio* (or multiple), is defined as:

$$\textbf{PE ratio} = \frac{\textbf{Price per share}}{\textbf{Earnings per share}} \tag{3.18}$$

$$= \frac{\$88}{\$11} = 8 \text{ times}$$

In the vernacular, we would say that Prufrock shares sell for eight times earnings, or we might say that Prufrock shares have, or "carry," a PE multiple of 8.

Since the PE ratio measures how much investors are willing to pay per dollar of current earnings, higher PEs are often taken to mean that the firm has significant prospects for future growth. Of course, if a firm had no or almost no earnings, its PE would probably be quite large; so, as always, care is needed in interpreting this ratio.

MARKET-TO-BOOK RATIO A second commonly quoted measure is the *market-to-book ratio:*

$$\textbf{Market-to-book ratio} = \frac{\textbf{Market value per share}}{\textbf{Book value per share}} \tag{3.19}$$

$$= \frac{\$88}{2{,}591/33} = \frac{\$88}{\$78.5} = 1.12 \text{ times}$$

Notice that book value per share is total equity (not just common stock) divided by the number of shares outstanding.

Since book value per share is an accounting number, it reflects historical costs. In a loose sense, the market-to-book ratio therefore compares the market value of the firm's investments to their cost. A value less than 1 could mean that the firm has not been successful overall in creating value for its stockholders.

This completes our definition of some common ratios. We could tell you about more of them, but these are enough for now. We'll leave it here and go on to discuss some ways of using these ratios instead of just how to calculate them. Table 3.5 summarizes the ratios we've discussed.

TABLE 3.5

Common Financial Ratios

I. Short-term solvency, or liquidity, ratios

$$\text{Current ratio} = \frac{\text{Current assets}}{\text{Current liabilities}}$$

$$\text{Quick ratio} = \frac{\text{Current assets} - \text{Inventory}}{\text{Current liabilities}}$$

$$\text{Cash ratio} = \frac{\text{Cash}}{\text{Current liabilities}}$$

II. Long-term solvency, or financial leverage, ratios

$$\text{Total debt ratio} = \frac{\text{Total assets} - \text{Total equity}}{\text{Total assets}}$$

Debt-equity ratio = Total debt/Total equity

Equity multiplier = Total assets/Total equity

$$\text{Times interest earned ratio} = \frac{\text{EBIT}}{\text{Interest}}$$

$$\text{Cash coverage ratio} = \frac{\text{EBIT} + \text{Depreciation}}{\text{Interest}}$$

III. Asset utilization, or turnover, ratios

$$\text{Inventory turnover} = \frac{\text{Cost of goods sold}}{\text{Inventory}}$$

$$\text{Days' sales in inventory} = \frac{365 \text{ days}}{\text{Inventory turnover}}$$

$$\text{Receivables turnover} = \frac{\text{Sales}}{\text{Accounts receivable}}$$

$$\text{Days' sales in receivables} = \frac{365 \text{ days}}{\text{Receivables turnover}}$$

$$\text{Total asset turnover} = \frac{\text{Sales}}{\text{Total assets}}$$

$$\text{Capital intensity} = \frac{\text{Total assets}}{\text{Sales}}$$

IV. Profitability ratios

$$\text{Profit margin} = \frac{\text{Net income}}{\text{Sales}}$$

$$\text{Return on assets (ROA)} = \frac{\text{Net income}}{\text{Total assets}}$$

$$\text{Return on equity (ROE)} = \frac{\text{Net income}}{\text{Total equity}}$$

$$\text{ROE} = \frac{\text{Net income}}{\text{Sales}} \times \frac{\text{Sales}}{\text{Assets}} \times \frac{\text{Assets}}{\text{Equity}}$$

V. Market value ratios

$$\text{Price-earnings ratio} = \frac{\text{Price per share}}{\text{Earnings per share}}$$

$$\text{Market-to-book ratio} = \frac{\text{Market value per share}}{\text{Book value per share}}$$

3.3 THE DU PONT IDENTITY

As we mentioned in discussing ROA and ROE, the difference between these two profitability measures is a reflection of the use of debt financing, or financial leverage. We illustrate the relationship between these measures in this section by investigating a famous way of decomposing ROE into its component parts.

A Closer Look at ROE

To begin, let's recall the definition of ROE:

$$\textbf{Return on equity} = \frac{\textbf{Net income}}{\textbf{Total equity}}$$

If we were so inclined, we could multiply this ratio by Assets/Assets without changing anything:

$$\begin{aligned}\textbf{Return on equity} &= \frac{\textbf{Net income}}{\textbf{Total equity}} = \frac{\textbf{Net income}}{\textbf{Total equity}} \times \frac{\textbf{Assets}}{\textbf{Assets}} \\ &= \frac{\textbf{Net income}}{\textbf{Assets}} \times \frac{\textbf{Assets}}{\textbf{Total equity}}\end{aligned}$$

Notice that we have expressed the ROE as the product of two other ratios–ROA and the equity multiplier:

$$\textbf{ROE} = \textbf{ROA} \times \textbf{Equity multiplier} = \textbf{ROA} \times (1 + \textbf{Debt-equity ratio})$$

Looking back at Prufrock, for example, we see that the debt-equity ratio was .39 and ROA was 10.12 percent. Our work here implies that Prufrock's ROE, as we previously calculated, is:

$$\text{ROE} = 10.12\% \times 1.39 = 14\%$$

The difference between ROE and ROA can be substantial, particularly for certain businesses. For example, BankAmerica has an ROA of only 1.23 percent, which is actually fairly typical for a bank. However, banks tend to borrow a lot of money, and, as a result, have relatively large equity multipliers. For BankAmerica, ROE is about 16 percent, implying an equity multiplier of 13.

We can further decompose ROE by multiplying the top and bottom by total sales:

$$\text{ROE} = \frac{\text{Sales}}{\text{Sales}} \times \frac{\text{Net income}}{\text{Assets}} \times \frac{\text{Assets}}{\text{Total equity}}$$

If we rearrange things a bit, ROE is:

$$\text{ROE} = \underbrace{\frac{\text{Net income}}{\text{Sales}} \times \frac{\text{Sales}}{\text{Assets}}}_{\text{Return on assets}} \times \frac{\text{Assets}}{\text{Total equity}} \tag{3.20}$$

$$= \text{Profit margin} \times \text{Total asset turnover} \times \text{Equity multiplier}$$

What we have now done is to partition ROA into its two component parts, profit margin and total asset turnover. The last expression of the preceding equation is called the **Du Pont identity**, after the Du Pont Corporation, which popularized its use.

We can check this relationship for Prufrock by noting that the profit margin was 15.7 percent and the total asset turnover was .64. ROE should thus be:

$$\begin{aligned} \text{ROE} &= \text{Profit margin} \times \text{Total asset turnover} \times \text{Equity multiplier} \\ &= 15.7\% \times .64 \times 1.39 \\ &= 14\% \end{aligned}$$

This 14 percent ROE is exactly what we had before.

The Du Pont identity tells us that ROE is affected by three things:

1. Operating efficiency (as measured by profit margin)
2. Asset use efficiency (as measured by total asset turnover)
3. Financial leverage (as measured by the equity multiplier)

Weakness in either operating or asset use efficiency (or both) will show up in a diminished return on assets, which will translate into a lower ROE.

Considering the Du Pont identity, it appears that the ROE could be leveraged up by increasing the amount of debt in the firm. However, notice that increasing debt also increases interest expense, which reduces profit margins, which acts to reduce ROE. So, ROE could go up or down, depending. More important, the use of debt financing has a number of other effects, and, as we discuss at some length in later chapters, the amount of leverage a firm uses is governed by its capital structure policy.

The decomposition of ROE we've discussed in this section is a convenient way of systematically approaching financial statement analysis. If ROE is unsatisfactory by some measure, then the Du Pont identity tells you where to start looking for the reasons.

General Motors provides a good example of how Du Pont analysis can be very useful and also illustrates why care must be taken in interpreting ROE values. In 1989, GM had an ROE of 12.1 percent. By 1993, its ROE had improved to 44.1 percent, a dramatic improvement. On closer inspection, however, we find that, over the same period, GM's

THE REAL WORLD

WHAT'S IN A RATIO?

Abraham Briloff, a well-known financial commentator, famously remarked that "financial statements are like fine perfume; to be sniffed but not swallowed." As you have probably figured out by now, his point is that information gleaned from financial statements—and ratios and growth rates computed from that information—should be taken with a grain of salt.

For example, looking back at the beginning of the chapter, investors must really think that Computer Associates will have extraordinary growth. After all, they are willing to pay about $750 for every dollar the company earns, which means they must be expecting much greater earnings in the future. Of course, this PE ratio is too high to even be realistically considered. The reason it was so high was that Computer Associates's earnings for 2004 were very small. Had the PE been calculated using projected 2005 earnings, it would have been a more reasonable 28.

Delta Airlines illustrates another problem. If you calculated its ROE in 2004, you would get about 89.66 percent, which is quite good. What's strange is the company reported a loss of about $5.2 billion dollars during 2004! What's going on is that Delta had a book value of equity balance of *negative* $5.80 billion. In this situation, the more Delta loses, the higher the ROE becomes. Of course, Delta's market-to-book and PE ratios are also both negative. How do you interpret a negative PE? We're not really sure, either. Whenever a company has a negative book value of equity, it means that losses have been so large that book equity has been wiped out. In such cases, the ROE, PE ratio, and market-to-book ratio are often not reported because they are meaningless.

Even if a company's book equity is positive, you still have to be careful. For example, consider venerable Maytag, which had a market-to-book ratio of about 30 at the end of 2004. Since the market-to-book ratio measures the value created by the company for shareholders, this would seem to be a good sign. But a closer look shows that Maytag's book value of equity per share was $5.18 in 1999, but then dropped to $.28 in 2000. This drop had to do with accounting for stock repurchases made by the company, not gains or losses, but it nonetheless dramatically increased the market-to-book ratio in that year and subsequent years as well.

Financial ratios are important tools used in evaluating companies of all types, but you cannot simply take a number as given. Instead, before doing any analysis, the first step is to ask whether the number actually makes sense.

profit margin had declined from 3.4 to 1.8 percent, and ROA had declined from 2.4 to 1.3 percent. The decline in ROA was moderated only slightly by an increase in total asset turnover from .71 to .73 over the period.

Given this information, how is it possible for GM's ROE to have climbed so sharply? From our understanding of the Du Pont identity, it must be the case that GM's equity multiplier increased substantially. In fact, what happened was that GM's book equity value was almost wiped out overnight in 1992 by changes in the accounting treatment of pension liabilities. If a company's equity value declines sharply, its equity multiplier rises. In GM's case, the multiplier went from 4.95 in 1989 to 33.62 in 1993. In sum, the dramatic "improvement" in GM's ROE was almost entirely due to an accounting change that affected the equity multiplier and doesn't really represent an improvement in financial performance at all. A nearby *The Real World* box discusses some additional issues along these lines.

An Expanded Du Pont Analysis

So far, we've seen how the Du Pont equation lets us break down ROE into its basic three components: profit margin, total asset turnover, and financial leverage. We now extend this analysis to take a closer look at how key parts of a firm's operations feed into

TABLE 3.6

FINANCIAL STATEMENTS FOR H.J. HEINZ 12 months ending April 27, 2005 (All numbers are in $ millions)					
INCOME STATEMENT		**BALANCE SHEET**			
Sales	$8,912	Current assets		Current liabilities	
CoGS	5,706	Cash	$ 1,084	Accounts payable	$ 1,063
Gross profit	$3,206	Accounts receivable	1,305	Notes payable	573
SG&A expense	1,692	Inventory	1,257	Other	951
Depreciation	252	Total	$ 3,646	Total	$ 2,587
EBIT	$1,262				
Interest	204	Fixed assets	$ 6,932	Total long-term debt	$ 5,388
EBT	$1,058				
Taxes	306			Total equity	$ 2,603
Net income	$ 752	Total assets	$10,578	Total liabilities and equity	$10,578

ROE. To get going, we went to the *S&P Market Insight* Web page (www.mhhe.com/edumarketinsight) and pulled abbreviated financial statements for food products company H.J. Heinz. What we found is summarized in Table 3.6.

Using the information in Table 3.6, Figure 3.1 shows how we can construct an expanded Du Pont analysis for H.J. Heinz and present that analysis in chart form. The advantage of the extended Du Pont chart is that it lets us examine several ratios at once, thereby getting a better overall picture of a company's performance and also allowing us to determine possible items to improve.

Looking at the left-hand side of our Du Pont chart in Figure 3.1, we see items related to profitability. As always, profit margin is calculated as net income divided by sales. But, as our chart emphasizes, net income depends on sales and a variety of costs, such as cost of goods sold (CoGS) and selling, general, and administrative expenses (SG&A expense). H.J. Heinz can increase its ROE by increasing sales and also by reducing one or more of these costs. In other words, if we want to improve profitability, our chart clearly shows us the areas on which we should focus.

Turning to the right-hand side of Figure 3.1, we have an analysis of the key factors underlying total asset turnover. Thus, for example, we see that reducing inventory holdings through more efficient management reduces current assets, which reduces total assets, which then improves total asset turnover.

3.4 USING FINANCIAL STATEMENT INFORMATION

Our next task is to discuss in more detail some practical aspects of financial statement analysis. In particular, we will look at reasons for doing financial statement analysis, how to go about getting benchmark information, and some of the problems that come up in the process.

Choosing a Benchmark

Given that we want to evaluate a division or a firm based on its financial statements, a basic problem immediately comes up. How do we choose a benchmark, or a standard of comparison? We describe some ways of getting started in this section.

FIGURE 3.1

Extended Du Pont Chart for H.J. Heinz

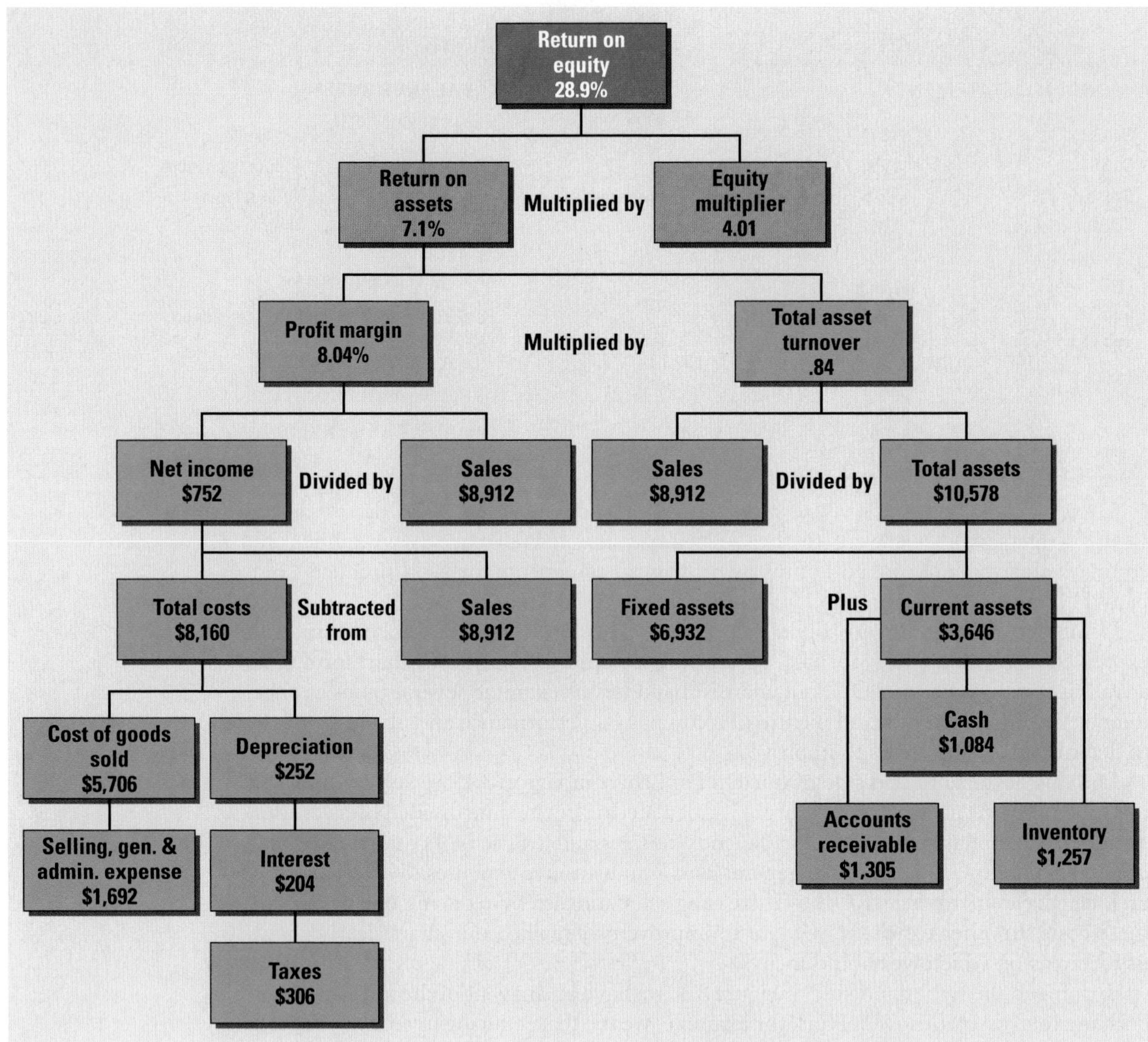

TIME-TREND ANALYSIS One standard we could use is history. Suppose we found that the current ratio for a particular firm is 2.4 based on the most recent financial statement information. Looking back over the last 10 years, we might find that this ratio had declined fairly steadily over that period.

Based on this, we might wonder if the liquidity position of the firm has deteriorated. It could be, of course, that the firm has made changes that allow it to more efficiently use its current assets, that the nature of the firm's business has changed, or that business practices have changed. If we investigate, we might find any of these possible explanations behind the decline. This is an example of what we mean by management by exception—a deteriorating time trend may not be bad, but it does merit investigation.

PEER GROUP ANALYSIS The second means of establishing a benchmark is to identify firms similar in the sense that they compete in the same markets, have similar assets, and operate in similar ways. In other words, we need to identify a *peer group*. There are obvious problems with doing this since no two companies are identical. Ultimately, the choice of which companies to use as a basis for comparison is subjective.

One common way of identifying potential peers is based on **Standard Industrial Classification (SIC) codes**. These are four-digit codes established by the U.S. government for statistical reporting purposes. Firms with the same SIC code are frequently assumed to be similar.

The first digit in an SIC code establishes the general type of business. For example, firms engaged in finance, insurance, and real estate have SIC codes beginning with 6. Each additional digit narrows down the industry. So, companies with SIC codes beginning with 60 are mostly banks and banklike businesses, those with codes beginning with 602 are mostly commercial banks, and SIC code 6025 is assigned to national banks that are members of the Federal Reserve system. Table 3.7 is a list of selected two-digit codes (the first two digits of the four-digit SIC codes) and the industries they represent.

SIC codes are far from perfect. For example, suppose you were examining financial statements for Wal-Mart, the largest retailer in the United States. The relevant SIC code is 5310, Department Stores. In a quick scan of the nearest financial database, you would find about 20 large, publicly owned corporations with this same SIC code, but you might not be too comfortable with some of them. Target would seem to be a reasonable peer,

TABLE 3.7
Selected Two-Digit SIC Codes

AGRICULTURE, FORESTRY, AND FISHING	WHOLESALE TRADE
01 Agriculture production—crops	50 Wholesale trade—durable goods
08 Forestry	51 Wholesale trade—nondurable goods
09 Fishing, hunting, and trapping	
MINING	**RETAIL TRADE**
10 Metal mining	54 Food stores
12 Bituminous coal and lignite mining	55 Automobile dealers and gas stations
13 Oil and gas extraction	58 Eating and drinking places
CONSTRUCTION	**FINANCE, INSURANCE, AND REAL ESTATE**
15 Building construction	60 Banking
16 Construction other than building	63 Insurance
17 Construction—special trade contractors	65 Real estate
MANUFACTURING	**SERVICES**
28 Chemicals and allied products	78 Motion pictures
29 Petroleum refining and related industries	80 Health services
35 Machinery, except electrical	82 Educational services
37 Transportation equipment	
TRANSPORTATION, COMMUNICATION, ELECTRIC, GAS, AND SANITARY SERVICE	
40 Railroad transportation	
45 Transportation by air	
49 Electric, gas, and sanitary services	

but Neiman-Marcus also carries the same industry code. Are Wal-Mart and Neiman-Marcus really comparable?

As this example illustrates, it is probably not appropriate to blindly use SIC code–based averages. Instead, analysts often identify a set of primary competitors and then compute a set of averages based on just this group. Also, we may be more concerned with a group of the top firms in an industry, not the average firm. Such a group is called an *aspirant group,* because we aspire to be like its members. In this case, a financial statement analysis reveals how far we have to go.

Learn more about NAICS at www.naics.com.

Beginning in 1997, a new industry classification system was initiated. Specifically, the North American Industry Classification System (NAICS, pronounced "nakes") is intended to replace the older SIC codes, and it will eventually. Currently, however, SIC codes are still widely used.

With these caveats about SIC codes in mind, we can now take a look at a specific industry. Suppose we are in the retail hardware business. Table 3.8 contains some condensed common-size financial statements for this industry from the Risk Management Association (RMA, formerly known as Robert Morris Associates), one of many sources of such information. Table 3.9 contains selected ratios from the same source.

There is a large amount of information here, most of which is self-explanatory. On the right in Table 3.8, we have current information reported for different groups based on sales. Within each sales group, common-size information is reported. For example, firms with sales in the $10 million to $25 million range have cash and equivalents equal to 5 percent of total assets. There are 31 companies in this group, out of 309 in all.

On the left, we have three years' worth of summary historical information for the entire group. For example, operating profit rose from 1.9 percent of sales to 2.5 percent over that time.

Table 3.9 contains some selected ratios, again reported by sales groups on the right and time period on the left. To see how we might use this information, suppose our firm has a current ratio of 2. Based on these ratios, is this value unusual?

Looking at the current ratio for the overall group for the most recent year (third column from the left in Table 3.9), we see that three numbers are reported. The one in the middle, 2.2, is the median, meaning that half of the 309 firms had current ratios that were lower and half had bigger current ratios. The other two numbers are the upper and lower quartiles. So, 25 percent of the firms had a current ratio larger than 3.7 and 25 percent had a current ratio smaller than 1.5. Our value of 2 falls comfortably within these bounds, so it doesn't appear too unusual. This comparison illustrates how knowledge of the range of ratios is important in addition to knowledge of the average. Notice how stable the current ratio has been for the last three years.

EXAMPLE 3.4 More Ratios

Take a look at the most recent numbers reported for Sales/Receivables and EBIT/Interest in Table 3.9. What are the overall median values? What are these ratios?

If you look back at our discussion, you will see that these are the receivables turnover and the times interest earned, or TIE, ratios. The median value for receivables turnover for the entire group is 26.5 times. So, the days in receivables would be 365/26.5 = 14, which is the bold-faced number reported. The median for the TIE is 2.8 times. The number in parentheses indicates that the calculation is meaningful for, and therefore based on, only 269 of the 309 companies. In this case, the reason is that only 269 companies paid any significant amount of interest.

There are many sources of ratio information in addition to the one we examine here. For example, www.investor.reuters.com shows a variety of ratios for publicly traded

TABLE 3.8

Selected Financial Statement Information

Retail—Hardware Stores SIC# 5072, 5251 (NAICS 444130)									
COMPARATIVE HISTORICAL DATA				CURRENT DATA SORTED BY SALES					
			Type of Statement						
9	11	17	Unqualified	1	1	2	1	4	8
38	42	54	Reviewed		8	10	16	14	6
88	85	110	Compiled	19	48	18	17	5	3
44	34	52	Tax Returns	10	30	5	1	5	1
67	57	76	Other	14	25	13	11	3	10
				58 (4/1-9/30/02)		251 (10/1/02-3/31/03)			
4/1/00-3/31/01 ALL	4/1/01-3/31/02 ALL	4/1/02-3/31/03 ALL		0-1 MM	1-3 MM	3-5 MM	5-10 MM	10-25 MM	25MM & OVER
246	229	309	NUMBER OF STATEMENTS	44	112	48	46	31	28
			Assets						
5.9%	6.1%	6.0%	Cash & Equivalents	5.3%	7.1%	7.4%	5.0%	5.0%	3.5%
12.2	13.3	13.8	Trade Receivables (net)	7.4	11.6	15.3	19.9	20.4	13.5
52.0	48.9	50.5	Inventory	62.4	50.1	47.8	47.3	44.5	50.4
1.3	1.3	1.8	All Other Current	1.8	1.7	1.7	2.1	.7	2.7
71.4	69.6	72.2	Total Current	76.8	70.4	72.2	74.2	70.5	70.1
17.3	17.8	17.0	Fixed Assets (net)	14.7	17.4	16.4	16.0	18.3	20.2
1.9	3.1	1.7	Intangibles (net)	1.1	1.6	1.5	2.0	.5	3.5
9.4	9.5	9.2	All Other Non-Current	7.3	10.5	9.9	7.8	10.7	6.2
100.0	100.0	100.0	Total	100.0	100.0	100.0	100.0	100.0	100.0
			Liabilities						
8.7	8.0	11.3	Notes Payable-Short Term	11.1	10.1	8.0	13.3	11.1	18.5
3.7	3.8	3.5	Cur. Mat.-L/T/D	2.9	3.6	3.5	5.2	2.6	2.0
15.7	15.6	15.5	Trade Payables	13.2	14.6	15.8	19.4	15.4	15.3
.2	.2	.2	Income Taxes Payable	.0	.5	.1	.2	.3	.1
7.1	8.1	7.0	All Other Current	7.8	7.3	5.8	6.0	7.1	8.2
35.3	35.6	37.4	Total Current	35.0	36.0	33.3	44.1	36.5	44.1
19.1	20.6	19.0	Long-Term Debt	29.0	20.6	17.9	13.6	13.7	13.9
.1	.1	.1	Deferred Taxes	.1	.0	.0	.1	.3	.2
4.8	6.3	5.0	All Other Non-Current	8.9	4.8	5.4	1.3	3.5	6.4
40.6	37.4	38.5	Net Worth	27.0	38.6	43.3	40.9	46.0	35.5
100.0	100.0	100.0	Total Liabilities & Net Worth	100.0	100.0	100.0	100.0	100.0	100.0
			Income Data						
100.0	100.0	100.0	Net Sales	100.0	100.0	100.0	100.0	100.0	100.0
35.0	35.3	35.7	Gross Profit	39.8	37.3	36.4	32.9	29.9	32.3
33.1	33.1	33.1	Operating Expenses	38.3	34.7	33.6	30.1	27.9	29.0
1.9	2.2	2.5	Operating Profit	1.5	2.7	2.8	2.8	2.0	3.4
.1	.4	.2	All Other Expenses (net)	.6	.2	.1	.2	−.3	.7
1.8	1.8	2.3	Profit Before Taxes	.9	2.5	2.7	2.6	2.3	2.7

MM = $ million.

Interpretation of Statement Studies Figures: RMA cautions that the studies be regarded only as a general guideline and not as an absolute industry norm. This is due to limited samples within categories, the categorization of companies by their primary Standard Industrial Classification (SIC) number only, and different methods of operations by companies within the same industry. For these reasons, RMA recommends that the figures be used only as general guidelines in addition to other methods of financial analysis.

TABLE 3.9

Selected Ratios

Retail—Hardware Stores SIC# 5072, 5251 (NAICS 444130)									
COMPARATIVE HISTORICAL DATA				CURRENT DATA SORTED BY SALES					
			Type of Statement						
9	11	17	Unqualified	1	1	2	1	4	8
38	42	54	Reviewed		8	10	16	14	6
88	85	110	Compiled	19	48	18	17	5	3
44	34	52	Tax Returns	10	30	5	1	5	1
67	57	76	Other	14	25	13	11	3	10
				58 (4/1-9/30/02)		251 (10/1/02-3/31/03)			
4/1/00-3/31/01 ALL	4/1/01-3/31/02 ALL	4/1/02-3/31/03 ALL	NUMBER OF	0-1 MM	1-3 MM	3-5 MM	5-10 MM	10-25 MM	25MM & OVER
246	229	309	STATEMENTS	44	112	48	46	31	28
			Ratios						
3.8%	3.7%	3.7%		6.6%	4.0%	3.4%	2.6%	2.8%	2.4%
2.1	2.2	2.2	Current	2.5	2.5	2.6	1.8	1.7	1.8
1.5	1.4	1.5		1.4	1.5	1.5	1.8	1.5	1.3
1.0	1.0	1.1		.9	1.1	1.2	1.0	1.1	.7
.5	.5	(308) .5	Quick	.4	.5	(47) .6	.5	.7	.5
.3	.2	.2		.2	.2	.3	.2	.4	.2
8 43.2	**7** 49.8	**7** 49.8		**4** 91.2	**8** 48.6	**6** 65.0	**11** 33.2	**11** 34.6	**5** 68.4
14 26.7	**15** 24.5	**14** 26.5	Sales/	**11** 32.1	**12** 29.3	**15** 25.0	**20** 18.4	**26** 14.0	**15** 24.5
25 14.6	**27** 13.4	**29** 12.4	Receivables	**20** 18.4	**25** 14.6	**34** 10.8	**43** 8.4	**39** 9.4	**38** 9.7
88 4.2	**81** 4.5	**85** 4.3		**137** 2.7	**93** 3.9	**78** 4.7	**70** 5.2	**57** 6.4	**81** 4.5
120 3.0	**121** 3.0	**120** 3.0	Cost of Sales/	**179** 2.0	**121** 3.0	**114** 3.2	**108** 3.4	**83** 4.4	**104** 3.5
178 2.0	**163** 2.2	**171** 2.1	Inventory	**262** 1.4	**172** 2.1	**167** 2.2	**161** 2.3	**120** 3.0	**149** 2.5
17 21.3	**18** 20.0	**17** 21.3		**0** UND	**17** 22.0	**17** 22.0	**22** 16.3	**15** 23.8	**18** 19.8
29 12.8	**29** 12.7	**30** 12.3	Cost of Sales/	**25** 14.3	**30** 12.3	**29** 12.7	**34** 10.6	**22** 16.4	**30** 12.1
48 7.7	**46** 7.9	**50** 7.4	Payables	**68** 5.4	**43** 8.5	**53** 6.9	**59** 6.2	**41** 8.8	**44** 8.3
4.2	4.4	4.2		2.6	4.1	4.4	5.4	5.7	5.7
6.4	6.7	7.0	Sales/	4.0	6.5	6.8	9.1	7.0	10.2
11.8	12.9	12.3	Working Capital	10.5	11.2	10.2	14.9	12.4	16.4
5.0	4.8	8.1		7.7	7.8	8.4	15.1	9.5	8.3
(225) 2.1	(213) 2.1	(269) 2.8	EBIT/Interest	(36) 2.4	(93) 2.5	(43) 4.0	(43) 3.2	(27) 4.1	(27) 3.2
.7	1.1	1.1		−.7	1.2	1.4	1.0	1.6	1.1
3.8	4.5	5.5	Net Profit + Depr.,		5.2	12.4	2.6	6.1	13.4
(58) 1.7	(53) 2.0	(73) 2.4	Dep., Amort./Cur.		(21) 1.9	(10) 2.0	(15) .6	(14) 2.8	(11) 5.3
.7	1.1	.5	Mat. L/T/D		.7	.1	.0	1.3	.5
.1	.2	.2		.0	.2	.1	.1	.1	.3
.4	.4	.4	Fixed/Worth	.4	.4	.4	.3	.3	.6
1.1	1.1	1.0		8.1	1.1	.9	.7	.8	1.2
.7	.6	.7		.8	.6	.7	.6	.6	1.2
1.6	1.7	1.5	Debt/Worth	2.8	1.6	1.4	1.7	1.0	2.2
3.8	4.8	3.7		NM	4.2	2.9	2.9	1.9	3.6
27.7	27.6	29.2	% Profit Before	46.5	25.3	28.4	31.0	17.6	40.4
(224) 9.9	(203) 10.4	(277) 11.9	Taxes/Tangible	(33) 12.3	(98) 11.5	(45) 15.0	(45) 10.9	(30) 9.6	(26) 23.7
.1	1.6	2.2	Net Worth	.4	.9	3.3	1.8	.3	2.5
9.4	9.1	11.5	% Profit	10.6	10.5	12.4	12.7	9.2	11.3
3.6	3.2	4.7	Before Taxes/	4.9	4.6	4.7	5.4	5.2	4.9
−1.2	.2	.2	Total Assets	−6.0	.2	1.5	.5	.2	.4
49.2	40.5	41.1		97.7	42.1	42.7	40.3	55.4	29.1
21.0	20.4	19.6	Sales/Net	21.2	23.1	18.6	20.1	17.6	14.3
9.4	8.7	9.2	Fixed Assets	7.1	9.4	9.6	12.2	7.6	9.1
3.1	3.0	3.1		2.8	3.0	3.2	3.2	3.0	3.3
2.3	2.4	2.4	Sales/	2.0	2.5	2.4	2.5	2.4	2.3
1.8	1.8	1.8	Total Assets	1.1	1.9	1.8	1.7	2.2	1.9
.7	.7	.7		.8	.7	.7	.7	.8	.8
(222) 1.1	(200) 1.2	(266) 1.2	% Depr., Dep.,	(31) 1.2	(102) 1.5	(41) 1.2	(40) 1.0	(29) 1.1	(23) 1.2
2.0	2.2	2.0	Amort./Sales	2.4	2.5	1.6	1.3	1.8	1.7
2.9	2.0	2.3	% Officers',	3.7	2.7	2.0	2.1	1.3	
(132) 4.6	(136) 4.0	(168) 4.0	Directors', Owners'	(21) 5.3	(75) 4.5	(32) 3.8	(22) 3.0	(14) 2.0	
7.0	6.1	7.0	Comp/Sales	11.6	7.1	6.7	6.2	3.3	
2771100M	**2517327M**	**3762671M**	Net Sales ($)	**27586M**	**204026M**	**188955M**	**328481M**	**469173M**	**2544450M**
990644M	**1153657M**	**1607310M**	Total Assets ($)	**18552M**	**93100M**	**86254M**	**158179M**	**191739M**	**1059486M**

M = $ thousand; MM = $ million.

companies. Below we show the profitability (called "Management Effectiveness" on this Web site) ratios for Johnson & Johnson.

Management Effectiveness				
Management Effectiveness (%)	**Company**	**Industry**	**Sector**	**S&P 500**
Return On Assets (TTM)	18.57	12.06	8.58	7.59
Return On Assets - 5 Yr. Avg.	15.58	13.31	8.52	6.63
Return On Investment (TTM)	24.97	16.03	11.58	11.41
Return On Investment - 5 Yr. Avg.	20.70	18.88	12.42	10.50
Return On Equity (TTM)	32.02	24.14	18.05	19.89
Return On Equity - 5 Yr. Avg.	27.25	28.74	20.04	18.69

In looking at numbers such as these, recall our caution about analyzing ratios that you don't calculate yourself: Different sources frequently do their calculations somewhat differently, even if the ratio names are the same.

Problems with Financial Statement Analysis

We continue our chapter on financial statements by discussing some additional problems that can arise in using financial statements. In one way or another, the basic problem with financial statement analysis is that there is no underlying theory to help us identify which quantities to look at and to guide us in establishing benchmarks.

As we discuss in other chapters, there are many cases in which financial theory and economic logic provide guidance in making judgments about value and risk. Very little such help exists with financial statements. This is why we can't say which ratios matter the most and what a high or low value might be.

One particularly severe problem is that many firms are conglomerates, owning more-or-less unrelated lines of business. GE is a well-known example. The consolidated financial statements for such firms don't really fit any neat industry category. More generally, the kind of peer group analysis we have been describing is going to work best when the firms are strictly in the same line of business, the industry is competitive, and there is only one way of operating.

Another problem that is becoming increasingly common is that major competitors and natural peer group members in an industry may be scattered around the globe. The automobile industry is an obvious example. The problem here is that financial statements from outside the United States do not necessarily conform at all to GAAP. The existence of different standards and procedures makes it very difficult to compare financial statements across national borders.

Even companies that are clearly in the same line of business may not be comparable. For example, electric utilities engaged primarily in power generation are all classified in the same group (SIC 4911). This group is often thought to be relatively homogeneous. However, most utilities operate as regulated monopolies, so they don't compete very much with each other, at least not historically. Many have stockholders, and many are organized as cooperatives with no stockholders. There are several different ways of generating power, ranging from hydroelectric to nuclear, so the operating activities of these utilities can differ quite a bit. Finally, profitability is strongly affected by the regulatory environment, so utilities in different locations can be very similar but show very different profits.

Several other general problems frequently crop up. First, different firms use different accounting procedures–for inventory, for example. This makes it difficult to compare statements. Second, different firms end their fiscal years at different times. For firms in seasonal businesses (such as a retailer with a large Christmas season), this can lead to difficulties in comparing balance sheets because of fluctuations in accounts during the year. Finally, for any particular firm, unusual or transient events, such as a one-time profit from an asset sale, may affect financial performance. In comparing firms, such events can give misleading signals.

3.5 LONG-TERM FINANCIAL PLANNING

Long-term planning is another important use of financial statements. Most financial planning models output pro forma financial statements, where pro forma means "as a matter of form." In our case, this means that financial statements are the form we use to summarize the projected future financial status of a company.

A Simple Financial Planning Model

We can begin our discussion of long-term planning models with a relatively simple example. The Computerfield Corporation's financial statements from the most recent year are as follows:

COMPUTERFIELD CORPORATION
Financial Statements

INCOME STATEMENT		BALANCE SHEET			
Sales	$1,000	Assets	$500	Debt	$250
Costs	800			Equity	250
Net income	$ 200	Total	$500	Total	$500

Unless otherwise stated, the financial planners at Computerfield assume that all variables are tied directly to sales and current relationships are optimal. This means that all items will grow at exactly the same rate as sales. This is obviously oversimplified; we use this assumption only to make a point.

Suppose sales increase by 20 percent, rising from $1,000 to $1,200. Planners would then also forecast a 20 percent increase in costs, from $800 to $800 × 1.2 = $960. The pro forma income statement would thus be:

Pro Forma Income Statement

Sales	$1,200
Costs	960
Net income	$ 240

The assumption that all variables will grow by 20 percent will enable us to easily construct the pro forma balance sheet as well:

Pro Forma Balance Sheet

Assets	$600 (+100)	Debt	$300 (+ 50)
		Equity	300 (+ 50)
Total	$600 (+100)	Total	$600 (+100)

Notice we have simply increased every item by 20 percent. The numbers in parentheses are the dollar changes for the different items.

Now we have to reconcile these two pro formas. How, for example, can net income be equal to \$240 and equity increase by only \$50? The answer is that Computerfield must have paid out the difference of \$240 − 50 = \$190, possibly as a cash dividend. In this case, dividends are the "plug" variable.

Suppose Computerfield does not pay out the \$190. In this case, the addition to retained earnings is the full \$240. Computerfield's equity will thus grow to \$250 (the starting amount) plus \$240 (net income), or \$490, and debt must be retired to keep total assets equal to \$600.

With \$600 in total assets and \$490 in equity, debt will have to be \$600 − 490 = \$110. Since we started with \$250 in debt, Computerfield will have to retire \$250 − 110 = \$140 in debt. The resulting pro forma balance sheet would look like this:

Planware provides insight into cash flow forecasting in its "White Papers" Section (www.planware.org).

Pro Forma Balance Sheet			
Assets	\$600 (+100)	Debt	\$110 (−140)
		Equity	490 (+240)
Total	\$600 (+100)	Total	\$600 (+100)

In this case, debt is the plug variable used to balance out projected total assets and liabilities.

This example shows the interaction between sales growth and financial policy. As sales increase, so do total assets. This occurs because the firm must invest in net working capital and fixed assets to support higher sales levels. Because assets are growing, total liabilities and equity, the right-hand side of the balance sheet, will grow as well.

The thing to notice from our simple example is that the way the liabilities and owners' equity change depends on the firm's financing policy and its dividend policy. The growth in assets requires that the firm decide on how to finance that growth. This is strictly a managerial decision. Note that, in our example, the firm needed no outside funds. This won't usually be the case, so we explore a more detailed situation in the next section.

The Percentage of Sales Approach

In the previous section, we described a simple planning model in which every item increased at the same rate as sales. This may be a reasonable assumption for some elements. For others, such as long-term borrowing, it probably is not, because the amount of long-term borrowing is something set by management, and it does not necessarily relate directly to the level of sales.

In this section, we describe an extended version of our simple model. The basic idea is to separate the income statement and balance sheet accounts into two groups, those that do vary directly with sales and those that do not. Given a sales forecast, we will then be able to calculate how much financing the firm will need to support the predicted sales level.

The financial planning model we describe next is based on the **percentage of sales approach**. Our goal here is to develop a quick and practical way of generating pro forma statements. We defer discussion of some "bells and whistles" to a later section.

THE INCOME STATEMENT We start out with the most recent income statement for the Rosengarten Corporation, as shown in Table 3.10. Notice we have still simplified things by including costs, depreciation, and interest in a single cost figure.

TABLE 3.10

ROSENGARTEN CORPORATION Income Statement		
Sales		$1,000
Costs		800
Taxable income		$ 200
Taxes (34%)		68
Net income		$ 132
Dividends	$44	
Addition to retained earnings	88	

TABLE 3.11

ROSENGARTEN CORPORATION Pro Forma Income Statement	
Sales (projected)	$1,250
Costs (80% of sales)	1,000
Taxable income	$ 250
Taxes (34%)	85
Net income	$ 165

Rosengarten has projected a 25 percent increase in sales for the coming year, so we are anticipating sales of $\$1{,}000 \times 1.25 = \$1{,}250$. To generate a pro forma income statement, we assume that total costs will continue to run at $\$800/1{,}000 = 80$ percent of sales. With this assumption, Rosengarten's pro forma income statement is as shown in Table 3.11. The effect here of assuming that costs are a constant percentage of sales is to assume that the profit margin is constant. To check this, notice that the profit margin was $\$132/1{,}000 =$ 13.2 percent. In our pro forma, the profit margin is $\$165/1{,}250 = 13.2$ percent; so it is unchanged.

Next, we need to project the dividend payment. This amount is up to Rosengarten's management. We will assume Rosengarten has a policy of paying out a constant fraction of net income in the form of a cash dividend. For the most recent year, the **dividend payout ratio** was:

$$\textbf{Dividend payout ratio} = \textbf{Cash dividends/Net income} \qquad (3.21)$$
$$= \$44/132 = 33\ 1/3\%$$

We can also calculate the ratio of the addition to retained earnings to net income as:

$$\textbf{Addition to retained earnings/Net income} = \$88/132 = 66\ 2/3\%$$

This ratio is called the **retention ratio** or **plowback ratio**, and it is equal to 1 minus the dividend payout ratio because everything not paid out is retained. Assuming that the payout ratio is constant, the projected dividends and addition to retained earnings will be:

Projected dividends paid to shareholders	**= $165 × 1/3 =**	**$ 55**
Projected addition to retained earnings	**= $165 × 2/3 =**	**110**
		$165

THE BALANCE SHEET To generate a pro forma balance sheet, we start with the most recent statement, as shown in Table 3.12.

On our balance sheet, we assume that some of the items vary directly with sales and others do not. For those items that do vary with sales, we express each as a percentage of

TABLE 3.12

ROSENGARTEN CORPORATION Balance Sheet					
Assets			**Liabilities and Owners' Equity**		
	$	**PERCENTAGE OF SALES**		**$**	**PERCENTAGE OF SALES**
Current assets			Current liabilities		
Cash	$ 160	16%	Accounts payable	$ 300	30%
Accounts receivable	440	44	Notes payable	100	n/a
Inventory	600	60	Total	$ 400	n/a
Total	$1,200	120	Long-term debt	$ 800	n/a
Fixed assets			Owners' equity		
Net plant and equipment	$1,800	180	Common stock and paid-in surplus	$ 800	n/a
			Retained earnings	1,000	n/a
			Total	$1,800	n/a
Total assets	$3,000	300%	Total liabilities and owners' equity	$3,000	n/a

sales for the year just completed. When an item does not vary directly with sales, we write "n/a" for "not applicable."

For example, on the asset side, inventory is equal to 60 percent of sales ($600/1,000) for the year just ended. We assume this percentage applies to the coming year, so for each $1 increase in sales, inventory will rise by $.60. More generally, the ratio of total assets to sales for the year just ended is $3,000/1,000 = 3, or 300 percent.

This ratio of total assets to sales is sometimes called the **capital intensity ratio**. It tells us the amount of assets needed to generate $1 in sales; so the higher the ratio is, the more capital intensive is the firm. Notice also that this ratio is just the reciprocal of the total asset turnover ratio we defined previously.

For Rosengarten, assuming that this ratio is constant, it takes $3 in total assets to generate $1 in sales (apparently Rosengarten is in a relatively capital intensive business). Therefore, if sales are to increase by $100, then Rosengarten will have to increase total assets by three times this amount, or $300.

On the liability side of the balance sheet, we show accounts payable varying with sales. The reason is that we expect to place more orders with our suppliers as sales volume increases, so payables will change "spontaneously" with sales. Notes payable, on the other hand, represents short-term debt such as bank borrowing. This will not vary unless we take specific actions to change the amount, so we mark this item as "n/a."

Similarly, we use "n/a" for long-term debt because it won't automatically change with sales. The same is true for common stock and paid-in surplus. The last item on the right-hand side, retained earnings, will vary with sales, but it won't be a simple percentage of sales. Instead, we will explicitly calculate the change in retained earnings based on our projected net income and dividends.

We can now construct a partial pro forma balance sheet for Rosengarten. We do this by using the percentages we have just calculated wherever possible to calculate the projected amounts. For example, net fixed assets are 180 percent of sales; so, with a new sales level of $1,250, the net fixed asset amount will be 1.80 × $1,250 = $2,250, representing an increase of $2,250 − 1,800 = $450 in plant and equipment. It is important to note that for those items that don't vary directly with sales, we initially assume no change and simply write in the original amounts. The result is shown in Table 3.13. Notice that the change in retained earnings is equal to the $110 addition to retained earnings we calculated earlier.

TABLE 3.13

ROSENGARTEN CORPORATION Partial Pro Forma Balance Sheet					
Assets			**Liabilities and Owners' Equity**		
	NEXT YEAR	**CHANGE FROM CURRENT YEAR**		**NEXT YEAR**	**CHANGE FROM CURRENT YEAR**
Current assets			Current liabilities		
Cash	$ 200	$ 40	Accounts payable	$ 375	$ 75
Accounts receivable	550	110	Notes payable	100	0
Inventory	750	150	Total	$ 475	$ 75
Total	$1,500	$300	Long-term debt	$ 800	$ 0
Fixed assets					
Net plant and equipment	$2,250	$450	Owners' equity		
			Common stock and paid-in surplus	$ 800	$ 0
			Retained earnings	1,110	110
			Total	$1,910	$110
Total assets	$3,750	$750	Total liabilities and owners' equity	$3,185	$185
			External financing needed	$ 565	$565

Inspecting our pro forma balance sheet, we notice that assets are projected to increase by \$750. However, without additional financing, liabilities and equity will only increase by \$185, leaving a shortfall of \$750 − 185 = \$565. We label this amount *external financing needed* (EFN).

Rather than create pro forma statements, if we were so inclined we could calculate EFN directly as follows:

$$EFN = \frac{\textbf{Assets}}{\textbf{Sales}} \times \Delta\textbf{Sales} - \frac{\textbf{Spontaneous liabilities}}{\textbf{Sales}} \times \Delta\textbf{Sales} - PM \times \textbf{Projected sales} \times (1 - d) \qquad (3.22)$$

In this expression, "ΔSales" is the projected change is sales (in dollars). In our example, projected sales for next year are \$1,250, an increase of \$250 over the previous year, so ΔSales = \$250. By "Spontaneous liabilities," we mean liabilities that naturally move up and down with sales. For Rosengarten, the spontaneous liabilities are the \$300 in accounts payable. Finally, *PM* and *d* are the profit margin and dividend payout ratios, which we previously calculated as 13.2 percent and 33 1/3 percent, respectively. Total assets and sales are \$3,000 and \$1,000, respectively, so we have:

$$EFN = \frac{\$3{,}000}{1{,}000} \times \$250 - \frac{\$300}{1{,}000} \times \$250 - .132 \times \$1{,}250 \times \left(1 - \frac{1}{3}\right) = \$565$$

In this calculation, notice that there are three parts. The first part is the projected increase in assets, which is calculated using the capital intensity ratio. The second is the spontaneous increase in liabilities. The third part is the product of profit margin and projected sales, which is projected net income, multiplied by the retention ratio. Thus, the third part is the projected addition to retained earnings.

A PARTICULAR SCENARIO Our financial planning model now reminds us of one of those good news–bad news jokes. The good news is we're projecting a 25 percent increase in sales. The bad news is this isn't going to happen unless Rosengarten can somehow raise \$565 in new financing.

TABLE 3.14

ROSENGARTEN CORPORATION Pro Forma Balance Sheet					
Assets			**Liabilities and Owners' Equity**		
	NEXT YEAR	**CHANGE FROM CURRENT YEAR**		**NEXT YEAR**	**CHANGE FROM CURRENT YEAR**
Current assets			Current liabilities		
Cash	$ 200	$ 40	Accounts payable	$ 375	$ 75
Accounts receivable	550	110	Notes payable	325	225
Inventory	750	150	Total	$ 700	$300
Total	$1,500	$300	Long-term debt	$1,140	$340
Fixed assets					
Net plant and equipment	$2,250	$450	Owners' equity		
			Common stock and paid-in surplus	$ 800	$ 0
			Retained earnings	1,110	110
			Total	$1,910	$110
Total assets	$3,750	$750	Total liabilities and owners' equity	$3,750	$750

This is a good example of how the planning process can point out problems and potential conflicts. If, for example, Rosengarten has a goal of not borrowing any additional funds and not selling any new equity, then a 25 percent increase in sales is probably not feasible.

If we take the need for $565 in new financing as given, we know that Rosengarten has three possible sources: short-term borrowing, long-term borrowing, and new equity. The choice of some combination among these three is up to management; we will illustrate only one of the many possibilities.

Suppose Rosengarten decides to borrow the needed funds. In this case, the firm might choose to borrow some over the short term and some over the long term. For example, current assets increased by $300 whereas current liabilities rose by only $75. Rosengarten could borrow $300 − 75 = $225 in short-term notes payable and leave total net working capital unchanged. With $565 needed, the remaining $565 − 225 = $340 would have to come from long-term debt. Table 3.14 shows the completed pro forma balance sheet for Rosengarten.

We have used a combination of short- and long-term debt as the plug here, but we emphasize that this is just one possible strategy; it is not necessarily the best one by any means. There are many other scenarios we could (and should) investigate. The various ratios we discussed earlier come in very handy here. For example, with the scenario we have just examined, we would surely want to examine the current ratio and the total debt ratio to see if we were comfortable with the new projected debt levels.

3.6 EXTERNAL FINANCING AND GROWTH

External financing needed and growth are obviously related. All other things staying the same, the higher the rate of growth in sales or assets, the greater will be the need for external financing. In the previous section, we took a growth rate as given, and then we determined the amount of external financing needed to support that growth. In this section, we turn things around a bit. We will take the firm's financial policy as given and then examine the relationship between that financial policy and the firm's ability to finance new investments and thereby grow.

We emphasize that we are focusing on growth not because growth is an appropriate goal; instead, for our purposes, growth is simply a convenient means of examining the interactions between investment and financing decisions. In effect, we assume that the use of growth as a basis for planning is just a reflection of the very high level of aggregation used in the planning process.

EFN and Growth

The first thing we need to do is establish the relationship between EFN and growth. To do this, we introduce the simplified income statement and balance sheet for the Hoffman Company in Table 3.15. Notice we have simplified the balance sheet by combining short-term and long-term debt into a single total debt figure. Effectively, we are assuming that none of the current liabilities vary spontaneously with sales. This assumption isn't as restrictive as it sounds. If any current liabilities (such as accounts payable) vary with sales, we can assume that any such accounts have been netted out in current assets. Also, we continue to combine depreciation, interest, and costs on the income statement.

Suppose the Hoffman Company is forecasting next year's sales level at $600, a $100 increase. Notice that the percentage increase in sales is $100/500 = 20 percent. Using the percentage of sales approach and the figures in Table 3.15, we can prepare a pro forma income statement and balance sheet as in Table 3.16. As Table 3.16 illustrates, at a 20 percent growth rate, Hoffman needs $100 in new assets (assuming full capacity). The projected addition to retained earnings is $52.8, so the external financing needed, EFN, is $100 − 52.8 = $47.2.

Notice that the debt-equity ratio for Hoffman was originally (from Table 3.15) equal to $250/250 = 1.0. We will assume that the Hoffman Company does not wish to sell new equity. In this case, the $47.2 in EFN will have to be borrowed. What will the new debt-equity ratio be? From Table 3.16, we know that total owners' equity is projected at $302.8. The new total debt will be the original $250 plus $47.2 in new borrowing, or $297.2 total. The debt-equity ratio thus falls slightly from 1.0 to $297.2/302.8 = .98.

TABLE 3.15

HOFFMAN COMPANY
Income Statement and Balance Sheet

Income Statement

Sales		$500
Costs		400
Taxable income		$100
Taxes (34%)		34
Net income		$ 66
Dividends	$22	
Addition to retained earnings	44	

Balance Sheet

Assets	$	PERCENTAGE OF SALES	Liabilities and Owners' Equity	$	PERCENTAGE OF SALES
Current assets	$200	40%	Total debt	$250	n/a
Net fixed assets	300	60	Owners' equity	250	n/a
Total assets	$500	100%	Total liabilities and owners' equity	$500	n/a

TABLE 3.16

HOFFMAN COMPANY Pro Forma Income Statement and Balance Sheet		
Income Statement		
Sales (projected)		$600.0
Costs (80% of sales)		480.0
Taxable income		$120.0
Taxes (34%)		40.8
Net income		$ 79.2
Dividends	$26.4	
Addition to retained earnings	52.8	

Balance Sheet

Assets	$	PERCENTAGE OF SALES	Liabilities and Owners' Equity	$	PERCENTAGE OF SALES
Current assets	$240.0	40%	Total debt	$250.0	n/a
Net fixed assets	360.0	60	Owners' equity	302.8	n/a
Total assets	$600.0	100%	Total liabilities and owners' equity	$552.8	n/a
			External financing needed	$ 47.2	n/a

PROJECTED SALES GROWTH	INCREASE IN ASSETS REQUIRED	ADDITION TO RETAINED EARNINGS	EXTERNAL FINANCING NEEDED, EFN	PROJECTED DEBT-EQUITY RATIO
0%	$ 0	$44.0	−$44.0	.70
5	25	46.2	− 21.2	.77
10	50	48.4	1.6	.84
15	75	50.6	24.4	.91
20	100	52.8	47.2	.98
25	125	55.0	70.0	1.05

TABLE 3.17

Growth and Projected EFN for the Hoffman Company

Table 3.17 shows EFN for several different growth rates. The projected addition to retained earnings and the projected debt-equity ratio for each scenario are also given (you should probably calculate a few of these for practice). In determining the debt-equity ratios, we assumed that any needed funds were borrowed, and we also assumed any surplus funds were used to pay off debt. Thus, for the zero growth case, the debt falls by $44, from $250 to $206. In Table 3.17, notice that the increase in assets required is simply equal to the original assets of $500 multiplied by the growth rate. Similarly, the addition to retained earnings is equal to the original $44 plus $44 times the growth rate.

Table 3.17 shows that for relatively low growth rates, Hoffman will run a surplus, and its debt-equity ratio will decline. Once the growth rate increases to about 10 percent, however, the surplus becomes a deficit. Furthermore, as the growth rate exceeds approximately 20 percent, the debt-equity ratio passes its original value of 1.0.

Figure 3.2 illustrates the connection between growth in sales and external financing needed in more detail by plotting asset needs and additions to retained earnings from Table 3.17 against the growth rates. As shown, the need for new assets grows at a much faster rate than the addition to retained earnings, so the internal financing provided by the addition to retained earnings rapidly disappears.

As this discussion shows, whether a firm runs a cash surplus or deficit depends on growth. Microsoft is a good example. Its revenue growth in the 1990s was amazing,

FIGURE 3.2

Growth and Related Financing Needed for the Hoffman Company

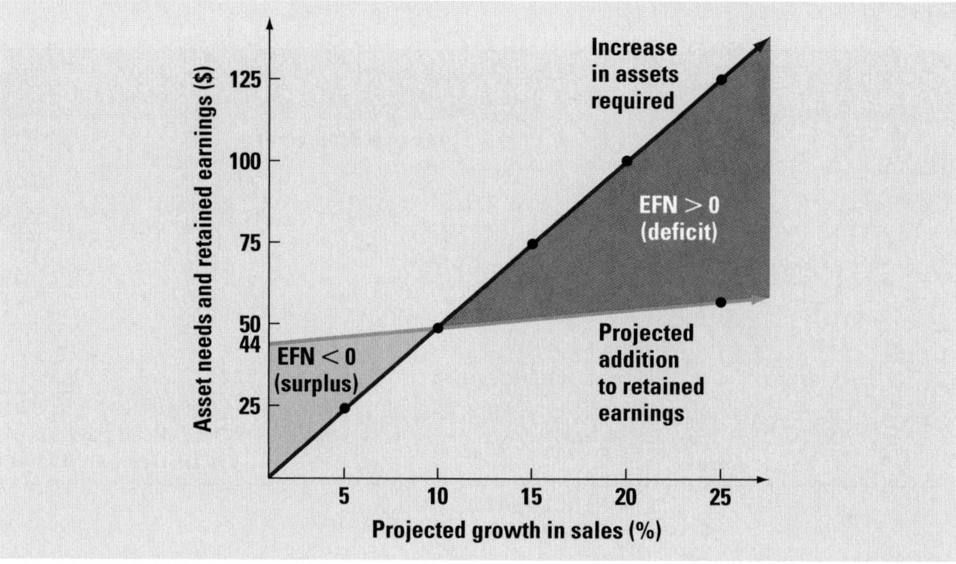

averaging well over 30 percent per year for the decade. Growth slowed down noticeably over the 2000–2004 period, but nonetheless, Microsoft's combination of growth and substantial profit margins led to enormous cash surpluses. In part because Microsoft paid few or no dividends, the cash really piled up; in 2004, Microsoft's cash horde exceeded $50 billion.

Financial Policy and Growth

Based on our discussion just preceding, we see that there is a direct link between growth and external financing. In this section, we discuss two growth rates that are particularly useful in long-range planning.

THE INTERNAL GROWTH RATE The first growth rate of interest is the maximum growth rate that can be achieved with no external financing of any kind. We will call this the **internal growth rate** because this is the rate the firm can maintain with internal financing only. In Figure 3.2, this internal growth rate is represented by the point where the two lines cross. At this point, the required increase in assets is exactly equal to the addition to retained earnings, and EFN is therefore zero. We have seen that this happens when the growth rate is slightly less than 10 percent. With a little algebra (see Problem 28 at the end of the chapter), we can define this growth rate more precisely as:

$$\text{Internal growth rate} = \frac{\text{ROA} \times b}{1 - \text{ROA} \times b} \tag{3.23}$$

where ROA is the return on assets we discussed earlier, and b is the plowback, or retention, ratio also defined earlier in this chapter.

For the Hoffman Company, net income was $66 and total assets were $500. ROA is thus $66/500 = 13.2 percent. Of the $66 net income, $44 was retained, so the plowback ratio, b, is $44/66 = 2/3. With these numbers, we can calculate the internal growth rate as:

$$\begin{aligned} \text{Internal growth rate} &= \frac{\text{ROA} \times b}{1 - \text{ROA} \times b} \\ &= \frac{.132 \times (2/3)}{1 - .132 \times (2/3)} \\ &= 9.65\% \end{aligned}$$

Thus, the Hoffman Company can expand at a maximum rate of 9.65 percent per year without external financing.

THE SUSTAINABLE GROWTH RATE We have seen that if the Hoffman Company wishes to grow more rapidly than at a rate of 9.65 percent per year, then external financing must be arranged. The second growth rate of interest is the maximum growth rate a firm can achieve with no external *equity* financing while it maintains a constant debt-equity ratio. This rate is commonly called the **sustainable growth rate** because it is the maximum rate of growth a firm can maintain without increasing its financial leverage.

There are various reasons why a firm might wish to avoid equity sales. For example, new equity sales can be very expensive because of the substantial fees that may be involved. Alternatively, the current owners may not wish to bring in new owners or contribute additional equity. Why a firm might view a particular debt-equity ratio as optimal is discussed in Chapters 14 and 15; for now, we will take it as given.

Based on Table 3.17, the sustainable growth rate for Hoffman is approximately 20 percent because the debt-equity ratio is near 1.0 at that growth rate. The precise value can be calculated as (see Problem 28 at the end of the chapter):

$$\textbf{Sustainable growth rate} = \frac{\text{ROE} \times b}{1 - \text{ROE} \times b} \qquad (3.24)$$

This is identical to the internal growth rate except that ROE, return on equity, is used instead of ROA.

For the Hoffman Company, net income was \$66 and total equity was \$250; ROE is thus \$66/250 = 26.4 percent. The plowback ratio, b, is still 2/3, so we can calculate the sustainable growth rate as:

$$\begin{aligned}\textbf{Sustainable growth rate} &= \frac{\text{ROE} \times b}{1 - \text{ROE} \times b} \\ &= \frac{.264 \times (2/3)}{1 - .264 \times (2/3)} \\ &= 21.36\%\end{aligned}$$

Thus, the Hoffman Company can expand at a maximum rate of 21.36 percent per year without external equity financing.

EXAMPLE 3.5 Sustainable Growth

Suppose Hoffman grows at exactly the sustainable growth rate of 21.36 percent. What will the pro forma statements look like?

At a 21.36 percent growth rate, sales will rise from \$500 to \$606.8. The pro forma income statement will look like this:

HOFFMAN COMPANY Pro Forma Income Statement		
Sales (projected)		\$606.8
Costs (80% of sales)		485.4
Taxable income		\$121.4
Taxes (34%)		41.3
Net income		\$ 80.1
Dividends	\$26.7	
Addition to retained earnings	53.4	

(continued)

We construct the balance sheet just as we did before. Notice, in this case, that owners' equity will rise from $250 to $303.4 because the addition to retained earnings is $53.4.

HOFFMAN COMPANY
Pro Forma Balance Sheet

Assets	$	PERCENTAGE OF SALES	Liabilities and Owners' Equity	$	PERCENTAGE OF SALES
Current assets	$242.7	40%	Total debt	$250.0	n/a
Net fixed assets	364.1	60	Owners' equity	303.4	n/a
Total assets	$606.8	100%	Total liabilities and owners' equity	$553.4	n/a
			External financing needed	$ 53.4	n/a

As illustrated, EFN is $53.4. If Hoffman borrows this amount, then total debt will rise to $303.4, and the debt-equity ratio will be exactly 1.0, which verifies our earlier calculation. At any other growth rate, something would have to change.

DETERMINANTS OF GROWTH Earlier in this chapter, we saw that the return on equity, ROE, could be decomposed into its various components using the Du Pont identity. Because ROE appears so prominently in the determination of the sustainable growth rate, it is obvious that the factors important in determining ROE are also important determinants of growth.

From our previous discussions, we know that ROE can be written as the product of three factors:

$$\textbf{ROE} = \textbf{Profit margin} \times \textbf{Total asset turnover} \times \textbf{Equity multiplier}$$

If we examine our expression for the sustainable growth rate, we see that anything that increases ROE will increase the sustainable growth rate by making the top bigger and the bottom smaller. Increasing the plowback ratio will have the same effect.

Putting it all together, what we have is that a firm's ability to sustain growth depends explicitly on the following four factors:

1. **Profit margin.** An increase in profit margin will increase the firm's ability to generate funds internally and thereby increase its sustainable growth.
2. **Dividend policy.** A decrease in the percentage of net income paid out as dividends will increase the retention ratio. This increases internally generated equity and thus increases sustainable growth.
3. **Financial policy.** An increase in the debt-equity ratio increases the firm's financial leverage. Because this makes additional debt financing available, it increases the sustainable growth rate.
4. **Total asset turnover.** An increase in the firm's total asset turnover increases the sales generated for each dollar in assets. This decreases the firm's need for new assets as sales grow and thereby increases the sustainable growth rate. Notice that increasing total asset turnover is the same thing as decreasing capital intensity.

The sustainable growth rate is a very useful planning number. What it illustrates is the explicit relationship between the firm's four major areas of concern: its operating efficiency as measured by profit margin, its asset use efficiency as measured by total asset turnover, its dividend policy as measured by the retention ratio, and its financial policy as measured by the debt-equity ratio.

EXAMPLE 3.6 Profit Margins and Sustainable Growth

The Sandar Co. has a debt-equity ratio of .5, a profit margin of 3 percent, a dividend payout ratio of 40 percent, and a capital intensity ratio of 1. What is its sustainable growth rate? If Sandar desired a 10 percent sustainable growth rate and planned to achieve this goal by improving profit margins, what would you think?

ROE is $.03 \times 1 \times 1.5 = 4.5$ percent. The retention ratio is $1 - .40 = .60$. Sustainable growth is thus $.045(.60)/[1 - .045(.60)] = 2.77$ percent.

For the company to achieve a 10 percent growth rate, the profit margin will have to rise. To see this, assume that sustainable growth is equal to 10 percent and then solve for profit margin, PM:

$$.10 = \text{PM}(1.5)(.6)/[1 - \text{PM}(1.5)(.6)]$$
$$\text{PM} = .1/.99 = 10.1\%$$

For the plan to succeed, the necessary increase in profit margin is substantial, from 3 percent to about 10 percent. This may not be feasible.

Given values for all four of these, there is only one growth rate that can be achieved. This is an important point, so it bears restating:

If a firm does not wish to sell new equity and its profit margin, dividend policy, financial policy, and total asset turnover (or capital intensity) are all fixed, then there is only one possible growth rate.

One of the primary benefits of financial planning is that it ensures internal consistency among the firm's various goals. The concept of the sustainable growth rate captures this element nicely. Also, we now see how a financial planning model can be used to test the feasibility of a planned growth rate. If sales are to grow at a rate higher than the sustainable growth rate, the firm must increase profit margins, increase total asset turnover, increase financial leverage, increase earnings retention, or sell new shares.

The two growth rates, internal and sustainable, are summarized in Table 3.18.

TABLE 3.18 Summary of Internal and Sustainable Growth Rates

I. Internal Growth Rate

$$\textit{Internal growth rate} = \frac{\text{ROA} \times b}{1 - \text{ROA} \times b}$$

where

ROA = Return on assets = Net income/Total assets

b = Plowback (retention) ratio

= Addition to retained earnings/Net income

The internal growth rate is the maximum growth rate than can be achieved with no external financing of any kind.

II. Sustainable Growth Rate

$$\textit{Sustainable growth rate} = \frac{\text{ROE} \times b}{1 - \text{ROE} \times b}$$

where

ROE = Return on equity = Net income/Total equity

b = Plowback (retention) ratio

= Addition to retained earnings/Net income

The sustainable growth rate is the maximum growth rate than can be achieved with no external equity financing while maintaining a constant debt-equity ratio.

A Note on Sustainable Growth Rate Calculations

Very commonly, the sustainable growth rate is calculated using just the numerator in our expression, ROE $\times$ b. This causes some confusion, which we can clear up here. The issue has to do with how ROE is computed. Recall that ROE is calculated as net income divided by total equity. If total equity is taken from an ending balance sheet (as we have done consistently, and is commonly done in practice), then our formula is the right one. However, if total equity is from the beginning of the period, then the simpler formula is the correct one.

In principle, you'll get exactly the same sustainable growth rate regardless of which way you calculate it (as long as you match up the ROE calculation with the right formula). In reality, you may see some differences because of accounting-related complications. By the way, if you use the average of beginning and ending equity (as some advocate), yet another formula is needed. Also, all of our comments here apply to the internal growth rate as well.

3.7 SOME CAVEATS REGARDING FINANCIAL PLANNING MODELS

Financial planning models do not always ask the right questions. A primary reason is that they tend to rely on accounting relationships and not financial relationships. In particular, the three basic elements of firm value tend to get left out, namely, cash flow size, risk, and timing.

Because of this, financial planning models sometimes do not produce output that gives the user many meaningful clues about what strategies will lead to increases in value. Instead, they divert the user's attention to questions concerning the association of, say, the debt-equity ratio and firm growth.

The financial model we used for the Hoffman Company was simple–in fact, too simple. Our model, like many in use today, is really an accounting statement generator at heart. Such models are useful for pointing out inconsistencies and reminding us of financial needs, but they offer very little guidance concerning what to do about these problems.

In closing our discussion, we should add that financial planning is an iterative process. Plans are created, examined, and modified over and over. The final plan will be a result negotiated between all the different parties to the process. In fact, long-term financial planning in most corporations relies on what might be called the Procrustes approach.[4] Upper-level management has a goal in mind, and it is up to the planning staff to rework and to ultimately deliver a feasible plan that meets that goal.

The final plan will therefore implicitly contain different goals in different areas and also satisfy many constraints. For this reason, such a plan need not be a dispassionate assessment of what we think the future will bring; it may instead be a means of reconciling the planned activities of different groups and a way of setting common goals for the future.

However it is done, the important thing to remember is that financial planning should not become a purely mechanical exercise. If it does, it will probably focus on the wrong things. Nevertheless, the alternative to planning is stumbling into the future. Perhaps the immortal Yogi Berra (the baseball catcher, not the cartoon character), said it best: "Ya gotta watch out if you don't know where you're goin.' You just might not get there."[5]

[4]In Greek mythology, Procrustes is a giant who seizes travelers and ties them to an iron bed. He stretches them or cuts off their legs as needed to make them fit the bed.

[5]We're not *exactly* sure what this means, either, but we like the sound of it.

SUMMARY AND CONCLUSIONS

This chapter focuses on working with information contained in financial statements. Specifically, we studied standardized financial statements, ratio analysis, and long-term financial planning.

1. We explained that differences in firm size make it difficult to compare financial statements, and we discussed how to form common-size statements to make comparisons easier and more meaningful.
2. Evaluating ratios of accounting numbers is another way of comparing financial statement information. We defined a number of the most commonly used ratios, and we discussed the famous Du Pont identity.
3. We showed how pro forma financial statements can be generated and used to plan for future financing needs.

After you have studied the chapter, we hope that you have some perspective on the uses and abuses of financial statement information. You should also find that your vocabulary of business and financial terms has grown substantially.

CONCEPT QUESTIONS

1. **Financial Ratio Analysis** A financial ratio by itself tells us little about a company since financial ratios vary a great deal across industries. There are two basic methods for analyzing financial ratios for a company: time trend analysis and peer group analysis. Why might each of these analysis methods be useful? What does each tell you about the company's financial health?
2. **Industry-Specific Ratios** So-called "same-store sales" are a very important measure for companies as diverse as McDonald's and Sears. As the name suggests, examining same-store sales means comparing revenues from the same stores or restaurants at two different points in time. Why might companies focus on same-store sales rather than total sales?
3. **Sales Forecast** Why do you think most long-term financial planning begins with sales forecasts? Put differently, why are future sales the key input?
4. **Sustainable Growth** In the chapter, we used Rosengarten Corporation to demonstrate how to calculate EFN. The ROE for Rosengarten is about 7.3 percent, and the plowback ratio is about 67 percent. If you calculate the sustainable growth rate for Rosengarten, you will find it is only 5.14 percent. In our calculation for EFN, we used a growth rate of 25 percent. Is this possible? (Hint: Yes. How?)
5. **EFN and Growth Rate** Broslofski Co. maintains a positive retention ratio and keeps its debt-equity ratio constant every year. When sales grow by 20 percent, the firm has a negative projected EFN. What does this tell you about the firm's sustainable growth rate? Do you know, with certainty, if the internal growth rate is greater than or less than 20 percent? Why? What happens to the projected EFN if the retention ratio is increased? What if the retention ratio is decreased? What if the retention ratio is zero?
6. **Common-Size Financials** One tool of financial analysis is common-size financial statements. Why do you think common-size income statements and balance sheets are used? Note that the accounting statement of cash flows is not converted into a common-size statement. Why do you think this is?
7. **Asset Utilization and EFN** One of the implicit assumptions we made in calculating the external funds needed was that the company was operating at full capacity. If the company is operating at less than full capacity, how will this affect the external funds needed?

Use the following information to answer the next five questions: A small business called The Grandmother Calendar Company began selling personalized photo calendar kits. The kits were a hit, and sales soon sharply exceeded forecasts. The rush of orders created a huge backlog, so the company leased more space and expanded capacity, but it still could not keep up with demand. Equipment failed from overuse and quality suffered. Working capital was drained to expand production, and, at the same time, payments from customers were often delayed until the product was shipped. Unable to deliver on orders, the company became so strapped for cash that employee paychecks began to bounce. Finally, out of cash, the company ceased operations entirely three years later.

8. **Product Sales** Do you think the company would have suffered the same fate if its product had been less popular? Why or why not?
9. **Cash Flow** The Grandmother Calendar Company clearly had a cash flow problem. In the context of the cash flow analysis we developed in Chapter 2, what was the impact of customers' not paying until orders were shipped?
10. **Corporate Borrowing** If the firm was so successful at selling, why wouldn't a bank or some other lender step in and provide it with the cash it needed to continue?
11. **Cash Flow** Which is the biggest culprit here: too many orders, too little cash, or too little production capacity?
12. **Cash Flow** What are some of the actions that a small company like The Grandmother Calendar Company can take (besides expansion of capacity) if it finds itself in a situation in which growth in sales outstrips production?
13. **Comparing ROE and ROA** Both ROA and ROE measure profitability. Which one is more useful for comparing two companies? Why?
14. **Ratio Analysis** Consider the ratio EBITD/Assets. What does this ratio tell us? Why might it be more useful than ROA in comparing two companies?

QUESTIONS AND PROBLEMS

Basic
(Questions 1–10)

1. **Du Pont Identity** If Roten, Inc., has an equity multiplier of 1.75, total asset turnover of 1.30, and a profit margin of 8.5 percent, what is its ROE?
2. **Equity Multiplier and Return on Equity** Thomsen Company has a debt-equity ratio of 1.40. Return on assets is 8.7 percent, and total equity is $520,000. What is the equity multiplier? Return on equity? Net income?
3. **Using the Du Pont Identity** Y3K, Inc., has sales of $2,700, total assets of $1,185, and a debt-equity ratio of 1.00. If its return on equity is 16 percent, what is its net income?

4. **EFN** The most recent financial statements for Martin, Inc., are shown here:

INCOME STATEMENT		BALANCE SHEET			
Sales	$19,200	Assets	$93,000	Debt	$20,400
Costs	15,550			Equity	72,600
Taxable income	$ 3,650	Total	$93,000	Total	$93,000
Taxes (34%)	1,241				
Net income	$ 2,409				

Assets and costs are proportional to sales. Debt and equity are not. A dividend of $963.60 was paid, and Martin wishes to maintain a constant payout ratio. Next year's sales are projected to be $23,040. What is the external financing needed?

5. **Sales and Growth** The most recent financial statements for Fontenot Co. are shown here:

INCOME STATEMENT		BALANCE SHEET			
Sales	$54,000	Current assets	$ 26,000	Long-term debt	$ 58,000
Costs	34,800	Fixed assets	105,000	Equity	73,000
Taxable income	$19,200	Total	$131,000	Total	$131,000
Taxes (34%)	6,528				
Net income	$12,672				

Assets and costs are proportional to sales. The company maintains a constant 30 percent dividend payout ratio and a constant debt-equity ratio. What is the maximum increase in sales that can be sustained assuming no new equity is issued?

6. **Sustainable Growth** If the Layla Corp. has a 19 percent ROE and a 25 percent payout ratio, what is its sustainable growth rate?

7. **Sustainable Growth** Assuming the following ratios are constant, what is the sustainable growth rate? 

   Total asset turnover = 1.40
   Profit margin = 7.6%
   Equity multiplier = 1.50
   Payout ratio = 40%

8. **Calculating EFN** The most recent financial statements for Bradley, Inc., are shown here (assuming no income taxes):

INCOME STATEMENT		BALANCE SHEET			
Sales	$4,400	Assets	$13,400	Debt	$ 9,100
Costs	2,685			Equity	4,300
Net income	$1,715	Total	$13,400	Total	$13,400

Assets and costs are proportional to sales. Debt and equity are not. No dividends are paid. Next year's sales are projected to be $5,192. What is the external financing needed?

9. **External Funds Needed** Cheryl Colby, CFO of Charming Florist Ltd., has created the firm's pro forma balance sheet for the next fiscal year. Sales are projected to grow by 10 percent to $440 million. Current assets, fixed assets, and short-term debt are 20 percent, 140 percent, and 15 percent of sales, respectively. Charming Florist pays out 40 percent of its net income in dividends. The company currently has $145 million of long-term debt, and $50 million in common stock par value. The profit margin is 12 percent.

   a. Construct the current balance sheet for the firm using the projected sales figure.

   b. Based on Ms. Colby's sales growth forecast, how much does Charming Florist need in external funds for the upcoming fiscal year?

   c. Construct the firm's pro forma balance sheet for the next fiscal year and confirm the external funds needed you calculated in part (b).

10. **Sustainable Growth Rate** The Steiben Company has a ROE of 8.50 percent and a payout ratio of 35 percent.

   a. What is the company's sustainable growth rate?

   b. Can the company's actual growth rate be different from its sustainable growth rate? Why or why not?

   c. How can the company change its sustainable growth rate?

Intermediate (Questions 11–23)

11. **Return on Equity** Firm A and Firm B have debt/total asset ratios of 60 percent and 40 percent and returns on total assets of 20 percent and 30 percent, respectively. Which firm has a greater return on equity?

12. **Ratios and Foreign Companies** Prince Albert Canning PLC had a net loss of £13,156 on sales of £147,318 (both in thousands of pounds). What was the company's profit margin? Does the fact that these figures are quoted in a foreign currency make any difference? Why? In dollars, sales were $267,661. What was the net loss in dollars?

13. **External Funds Needed** The Optical Scam Company has forecast a 20 percent sales growth rate for next year. The current financial statements are shown below.

INCOME STATEMENT		
Sales		$38,000,000
Costs		33,400,000
Taxable income		$ 4,600,000
Taxes		1,610,000
Net income		$ 2,990,000
Dividends	$1,196,000	
Additions to retained earnings	$1,794,000	

BALANCE SHEET			
Assets		**Liabilities and Equity**	
Current assets	$ 9,000,000	Short-term debt	$ 8,000,000
		Long-term debt	6,000,000
Fixed assets	22,000,000		
		Common stock	$ 4,000,000
		Accumulated retained earnings	13,000,000
		Total equity	$17,000,000
Total assets	$31,000,000	Total liabilities and equity	$31,000,000

a. Using the equation from the chapter, calculate the external funds needed for next year.

b. Construct the firm's pro forma balance sheet for next year and confirm the external funds needed you calculated in part (a).

c. Calculate the sustainable growth rate for the company.

d. Can Optical Scam eliminate the need for external funds by changing its dividend policy? What other options are available to the company to meet its growth objectives?

14. **Days' Sales in Receivables** A company has net income of $173,000, a profit margin of 8.6 percent, and an accounts receivable balance of $143,200. Assuming 75 percent of sales are on credit, what is the company's days' sales in receivables?

15. **Ratios and Fixed Assets** The Le Bleu Company has a ratio of long-term debt to total assets of 0.70 and a current ratio of 1.20. Current liabilities are $850, sales are $4,310, profit margin is 9.5 percent, and ROE is 21.5 percent. What is the amount of the firm's net fixed assets?

16. **Calculating the Cash Coverage Ratio** Titan Inc.'s net income for the most recent year was $7,850. The tax rate was 34 percent. The firm paid $2,108 in total interest expense and deducted $1,687 in depreciation expense. What was Titan's cash coverage ratio for the year?

17. **Cost of Goods Sold** Guthrie Corp. has current liabilities of $340,000, a quick ratio of 1.8, inventory turnover of 4.2, and a current ratio of 3.3. What is the cost of goods sold for the company?

18. **Common-Size and Common-Base Year Financial Statements** In addition to common-size financial statements, common-base year financial statements are often used. Common-base year financial statements are constructed by dividing the current year account value by the base year account value. Thus, the result shows the growth rate in the account. Using the financial statements below, construct the common-size balance sheet and common-base year balance sheet for the company. Use 2005 as the base year. 

JARROW CORPORATION
2005 and 2006 Balance Sheets

Assets	2005	2006	Liabilities and Owners' Equity	2005	2006
Current assets			Current liabilities		
Cash	$ 10,168	$ 10,683	Accounts payable	$ 73,185	$ 59,309
Accounts receivable	27,145	28,613	Notes payable	39,125	48,168
Inventory	59,324	64,853	Total	$112,310	$107,477
Total	$ 96,637	$104,149	Long-term debt	$ 50,000	$ 62,000
Fixed assets			Owners' equity		
Net plant and equipment	$304,165	$347,168	Common stock and paid-in surplus	$ 80,000	$ 80,000
			Retained earnings	158,492	201,840
			Total	$238,492	$281,840
Total assets	$400,802	$451,317	Total liabilities and owners' equity	$400,802	$451,317

Use the following information for Problems 19, 20, and 22.

The discussion of EFN in the chapter implicitly assumed that the company was operating at full capacity. Often, this is not the case. For example, assume that Rosengarten was operating at 90 percent capacity. Full capacity sales would be $1,000/.90 = $1,111. The balance sheet shows $1,800 in fixed assets. The capital intensity ratio for the company is:

Capital intensity ratio = Fixed assets/Full-capacity sales = $1,800/$1,111 = 1.62

This means that Rosengarten needs $1.62 in fixed assets for every dollar in sales when it reaches full capacity. At the projected sales level of $1,250, it needs $1,250 × 1.62 = $2,025 in fixed assets, which is $225 lower than our projection of $2,250 in fixed assets. So, EFN is only $565 − 225 = $340.

19. **Full-Capacity Sales** Thorpe Mfg., Inc., is currently operating at only 85 percent of fixed asset capacity. Current sales are $510,000. How fast can sales grow before any new fixed assets are needed?

20. **Fixed Assets and Capacity Usage** For the company in the previous problem, suppose fixed assets are $415,000 and sales are projected to grow to $680,000. How much in new fixed assets are required to support this growth in sales?

21. **Calculating EFN** The most recent financial statements for Moose Tours, Inc., follow. Sales for 2006 are projected to grow by 20 percent. Interest expense will remain constant; the tax rate and the dividend payout rate will also remain constant. Costs, other expenses, current assets, and accounts payable increase spontaneously with sales. If the firm is operating at full capacity and no new debt or equity is issued, what is the external financing needed to support the 20 percent growth rate in sales?

MOOSE TOURS, INC.
2005 Income Statement

Sales		$905,000
Costs		710,000
Other expenses		12,000
Earnings before interest and taxes		$183,000
Interest paid		19,700
Taxable income		$163,300
Taxes (35%)		57,155
Net income		$106,145
Dividends	$42,458	
Addition to retained earnings	63,687	

MOOSE TOURS, INC.
Balance Sheet as of December 31, 2005

Assets		Liabilities and Owners' Equity	
Current assets		Current liabilities	
Cash	$ 25,000	Accounts payable	$ 65,000
Accounts receivable	43,000	Notes payable	9,000
Inventory	76,000	Total	$ 74,000
Total	$144,000	Long-term debt	$156,000
Fixed assets		Owners' equity	
Net plant and equipment	$364,000	Common stock and paid-in surplus	$ 21,000
		Retained earnings	257,000
		Total	$278,000
Total assets	$508,000	Total liabilities and owners' equity	$508,000

22. **Capacity Usage and Growth** In the previous problem, suppose the firm was operating at only 80 percent capacity in 2005. What is EFN now?

23. **Calculating EFN** In Problem 21, suppose the firm wishes to keep its debt-equity ratio constant. What is EFN now?

Challenge
(Questions 24–30)

24. **EFN and Internal Growth** Redo Problem 21 using sales growth rates of 15 and 25 percent in addition to 20 percent. Illustrate graphically the relationship between EFN and the growth rate, and use this graph to determine the relationship between them.

25. **EFN and Sustainable Growth** Redo Problem 23 using sales growth rates of 30 and 35 percent in addition to 20 percent. Illustrate graphically the relationship between EFN and the growth rate, and use this graph to determine the relationship between them.

26. **Constraints on Growth** Bulla Recording, Inc., wishes to maintain a growth rate of 14 percent per year and a debt-equity ratio of .30. Profit margin is 6.2 percent, and the ratio of total assets to sales is constant at 1.55. Is this growth rate possible? To answer, determine what the dividend payout ratio must be. How do you interpret the result?

27. **EFN** Define the following:

    S = Previous year's sales

    A = Total assets

    D = Total debt

    E = Total equity

    g = Projected growth in sales

PM = Profit margin

b = Retention (plowback) ratio

Show that EFN can be written as:

$$\text{EFN} = -\text{PM(S)}b + [\text{A} - \text{PM(S)}b] \times g$$

Hint: Asset needs will equal $\text{A} \times g$. The addition to retained earnings will equal $\text{PM(S)}b \times (1 + g)$.

28. **Sustainable Growth Rate** Based on the results in Problem 27, show that the internal and sustainable growth rates can be calculated as shown in equations 3.23 and 3.24. Hint: For the internal growth rate, set EFN equal to zero and solve for *g*.

29. **Sustainable Growth Rate** In the chapter, we discussed one calculation of the sustainable growth rate as:

$$\text{Sustainable growth rate} = \frac{\text{ROE} \times b}{1 - \text{ROE} \times b}$$

In practice, probably the most commonly used calculation of the sustainable growth rate is $\text{ROE} \times b$. This equation is identical to the two sustainable growth rate equations presented in the chapter if the ROE is calculated using the beginning of period equity. Derive this equation from the equation presented in the chapter.

30. **Sustainable Growth Rate** Use the sustainable growth rate equations from the previous problem to answer the following questions. No Return, Inc., had total assets of $210,000 and equity of $165,000 at the beginning of the year. At the end of the year, the company had total assets of $250,000. During the year the company sold no new equity. Net income for the year was $80,000 and dividends were $49,000. What is the approximate sustainable growth rate for the company? What is the exact sustainable growth rate? What is the approximate sustainable growth rate if you calculate ROE based on the beginning of period equity? Is this number too high or too low? Why?

S&P PROBLEMS

www.mhhe.com/edumarketinsight

STANDARD & POOR'S

1. **Calculating the Du Pont Identity** Find the annual income statements and balance sheets for Dow Chemical (DOW) and Gateway (GTW). Calculate the Du Pont identity for each company for the most recent three years. Comment on the changes in each component of the Du Pont identity for each company over this period and compare the components between the two companies. Are the results what you expected? Why or why not?

2. **Ratio Analysis** Find and download the "Profitability" spreadsheet for Southwest Airlines (LUV) and Continental Airlines (CAL). Find the ROA (Net ROA), ROE (Net ROE), PE ratio (P/E-high and P/E-low), and the market-to-book ratio (Price/Book-high and Price/Book-low) for each company. Since stock prices change daily, PE and market-to-book ratios are often reported as the highest and lowest values over the year, as is done in this instance. Look at these ratios for both companies over the past five years. Do you notice any trends in these ratios? Which company appears to be operating at a more efficient level based on these four ratios? If you were going to invest in an airline, which one (if either) of these companies would you choose based on this information? Why?

3. **Sustainable Growth Rate** Use the annual income statements and balance sheets under the "Excel Analytics" link to calculate the sustainable growth rate for Coca-Cola (KO) each year for the past four years. Is the sustainable growth rate the same for every year? What are possible reasons the sustainable growth rate may vary from year to year?

4. **External Funds Needed** Look up Black & Decker (BDK). Under the "Financial Highlights" link you can find a five-year growth rate for sales. Using this growth rate and the most recent income statement and balance sheet, compute the external funds needed for BDK next year.

WHAT'S ON THE WEB?

1. **Du Pont Identity** You can find financial statements for Walt Disney Company at Disney's home page, disney.go.com. For the three most recent years, calculate the Du Pont identity for Disney. How has ROE changed over this period? How have changes in each component of the Du Pont identity affected ROE over this period?
2. **Ratio Analysis** You want to examine the financial ratios for Dell Computer Corporation. Go to www.investor.reuters.com and type in the ticker symbol for the company (DELL). Now find financial ratios for Dell and the industry, sector, and S&P 500 averages for each ratio.
   a. What do TTM and MRQ mean?
   b. How do Dell's recent profitability ratios compare to their values over the past five years? To the industry averages? To the sector averages? To the S&P 500 averages? Which is the better comparison group for Dell: the industry, sector, or S&P 500 averages? Why?
   c. In what areas does Dell seem to outperform its competitors based on the financial ratios? Where does Dell seem to lag behind its competitors?
   d. Dell's inventory turnover ratio is much larger than that for all comparison groups. Why do you think this is?
3. **Applying Percentage of Sales** Locate the most recent annual financial statements for Du Pont at www.dupont.com under the "Investor Center" link. Locate the annual report. Using the growth in sales for the most recent year as the projected sales growth for next year, construct a pro forma income statement and balance sheet. Based on these projections, what are the external funds needed?
4. **Growth Rates** You can find the home page for Caterpillar, Inc., at www.cat.com. Go to the Web page and find the most recent annual report. Using the information from the financial statements, what is the sustainable growth rate?

CLOSING CASE

RATIOS AND FINANCIAL PLANNING AT EAST COAST YACHTS

Dan Ervin was recently hired by East Coast Yachts to assist the company with its short-term financial planning and also to evaluate the company's financial performance. Dan graduated from college five years ago with a finance degree, and he has been employed in the treasury department of a Fortune 500 company since then.

East Coast Yachts was founded 10 years ago by Larisa Warren. The company's operations are located near Hilton Head Island, South Carolina, and the company is structured as an LLC. The company has manufactured custom midsize, high-performance yachts for clients over this period, and its products have received high reviews for safety and reliability. The company's yachts have also recently received the highest award for customer satisfaction. The yachts are primarily purchased by wealthy individuals for pleasure use. Occasionally, a yacht is manufactured for purchase by a company for business purposes.

The custom yacht industry is fragmented, with a number of manufacturers. As with any industry, there are market leaders, but the diverse nature of the industry ensures that no manufacturer dominates the market. The competition in the market, as well as the product cost, ensures that attention to detail is a necessity. For instance, East Coast Yachts will spend 80 to 100 hours on hand-buffing the stainless steel stem-iron, which is the metal cap on the yacht's bow that conceivably could collide with a dock or another boat.

To get Dan started with his analyses, Larisa has provided the following financial statements. Dan has gathered the industry ratios for the yacht manufacturing industry.

EAST COAST YACHTS
2005 Income Statement

Sales		$128,700,000
Cost of goods sold		90,700,000
Other expenses		15,380,000
Depreciation		4,200,000
Earnings before interest and taxes (EBIT)		$ 18,420,000
Interest		2,315,000
Taxable income		$ 16,105,000
Taxes (40%)		6,442,000
Net income		$ 9,663,000
Dividends	$5,797,800	
Addition to retained earnings	$3,865,200	

EAST COAST YACHTS
Balance Sheet as of December 31, 2005

Assets		Liabilities & Equity	
Current assets		Current liabilities	
Cash	$ 2,340,000	Accounts payable	$ 4,970,000
Accounts receivable	4,210,000	Notes payable	10,060,000
Inventory	4,720,000		
Total	$11,270,000	Total	$15,030,000
Fixed assets		Long-term debt	$25,950,000
Net plant and equipment	$72,280,000		
		Shareholders' equity	
		Common stock	$ 4,000,000
		Retained earnings	38,570,000
		Total equity	$42,570,000
Total assets	$83,550,000	Total liabilities and equity	$83,550,000

Yacht Industry Ratios

	Lower Quartile	Median	Upper Quartile
Current ratio	0.50	1.43	1.89
Quick ratio	0.21	0.38	0.62
Total asset turnover	0.68	0.85	1.38
Inventory turnover	4.89	6.15	10.89
Receivables turnover	6.27	9.82	14.11
Debt ratio	0.44	0.52	0.61
Debt-equity ratio	0.79	1.08	1.56
Equity multiplier	1.79	2.08	2.56
Interest coverage	5.18	8.06	9.83
Profit margin	4.05%	6.98%	9.87%
Return on assets	6.05%	10.53%	13.21%
Return on equity	9.93%	16.54%	26.15%

1. Calculate all of the ratios listed in the industry table for East Coast Yachts.
2. Compare the performance of East Coast Yachts to the industry as a whole. For each ratio, comment on why it might be viewed as positive or negative relative to the industry. Suppose you create an inventory ratio calculated as inventory divided by current liabilities. How do you interpret this ratio? How does East Coast Yachts compare to the industry average?
3. Calculate the sustainable growth rate of East Coast Yachts. Calculate external funds needed (EFN) and prepare pro forma income statements and balance sheets assuming growth at precisely this rate. Recalculate the ratios in the previous question. What do you observe?
4. As a practical matter, East Coast Yachts is unlikely to be willing to raise external equity capital, in part because the owners don't want to dilute their existing ownership and control positions. However, East Coast Yachts is planning for a growth rate of 20 percent next year. What are your conclusions and recommendations about the feasibility of East Coast's expansion plans?
5. Most assets can be increased as a percentage of sales. For instance, cash can be increased by any amount. However, fixed assets often must be increased in specific amounts since it is impossible, as a practical matter, to buy part of a new plant or machine. In this case, a company has a "staircase" or "lumpy" fixed cost structure. Assume that East Coast Yachts is currently producing at 100 percent of capacity. As a result, to expand production, the company must set up an entirely new line at a cost of $25,000,000. Calculate the new EFN with this assumption. What does this imply about capacity utilization for East Coast Yachts next year?

CHAPTER 4

Discounted Cash Flow Valuation

OPENING CASE

What do Jason Varitek, Michael Vick, and Carlos Beltran have in common? All three are star athletes who signed big-money contracts at the end of 2004 or the beginning of 2005. Their contract values were reported as $40 million, $119 million, and $130 million, respectively. But reported numbers can be misleading. For example, in December 2004, catcher Jason Varitek re-signed with the world champion Boston Red Sox. His deal called for a signing bonus of $4 million and a salary of $9 million per year over each of the next four years. Not bad, especially for someone who makes a living using the "tools of ignorance" (jock jargon for catcher's equipment).

A closer look at the numbers shows that Jason, Michael, and Carlos did pretty well, but nothing like the quoted figures. Using Carlos's contract as an example, the value was reported to be $119 million, but it was actually payable over several years. The terms called for a $7 million signing bonus. The remaining $112 million was to be distributed as $12 million in 2005, $14 million in 2006, $12 million in 2007, and $18.5 million per year for 2008 through 2011. Since the payments were spread out over time, we must consider the time value of money, which means his contract was worth less than reported. How much did he really get? This chapter gives you the "tools of knowledge" to answer this question.

4.1 VALUATION: THE ONE-PERIOD CASE

Keith Vaughn is trying to sell a piece of raw land in Alaska. Yesterday, he was offered \$10,000 for the property. He was about ready to accept the offer when another individual offered him \$11,424. However, the second offer was to be paid a year from now. Keith has satisfied himself that both buyers are honest and financially solvent, so he has no fear that the offer he selects will fall through. These two offers are pictured as cash flows in Figure 4.1. Which offer should Mr. Vaughn choose?

Mike Tuttle, Keith's financial advisor, points out that if Keith takes the first offer, he could invest the \$10,000 in the bank at an insured rate of 12 percent. At the end of one year, he would have

$$\underset{\text{Return of principal}}{\$10{,}000} + \underset{\text{Interest}}{(0.12 \times \$10{,}000)} = \$10{,}000 \times 1.12 = \$11{,}200$$

Because this is less than the \$11,424 Keith could receive from the second offer, Mr. Tuttle recommends that he take the latter. This analysis uses the concept of **future value** or **compound value**, which is the value of a sum after investing over one or more periods. The compound or future value of \$10,000 at 12 percent is \$11,200.

An alternative method employs the concept of **present value**. One can determine present value by asking the following question: How much money must Keith put in the bank today so that he will have \$11,424 next year? We can write this algebraically as

$$PV \times 1.12 = \$11{,}424$$

We want to solve for present value (PV), the amount of money that yields \$11,424 if invested at 12 percent today. Solving for PV, we have

$$PV = \frac{\$11{,}424}{1.12} = \$10{,}200$$

The formula for PV can be written as

Present Value of Investment:

$$PV = \frac{C_1}{1 + r} \tag{4.1}$$

where C_1 is cash flow at date 1 and r is the rate of return that Keith Vaughn requires on his land sale. It is sometimes referred to as the *discount rate*.

Present value analysis tells us that a payment of \$11,424 to be received next year has a present value of \$10,200 today. In other words, at a 12-percent interest rate, Mr. Vaughn is indifferent between \$10,200 today or \$11,424 next year. If you gave him \$10,200 today, he could put it in the bank and receive \$11,424 next year.

Because the second offer has a present value of \$10,200, whereas the first offer is for only \$10,000, present value analysis also indicates that Mr. Vaughn should take the second offer. In other words, both future value analysis and present value analysis lead to the same decision. As it turns out, present value analysis and future value analysis must always lead to the same decision.

FIGURE 4.1 Cash Flow for Mr. Vaughn's Sale

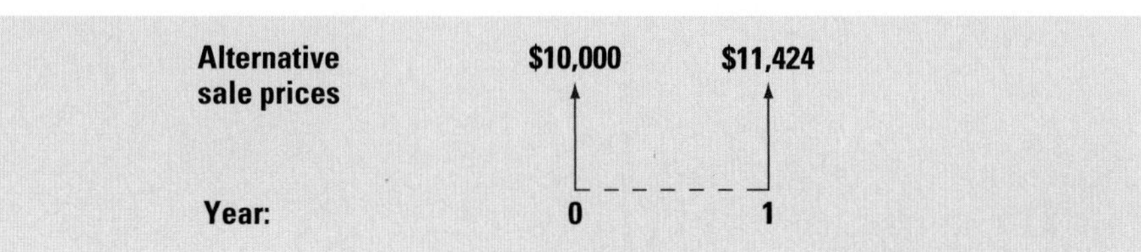

As simple as this example is, it contains the basic principles that we will be working with over the next few chapters. We now use another example to develop the concept of net present value.

EXAMPLE 4.1 Present Value

Lida Jennings, a financial analyst at Kaufman & Broad, a leading real estate firm, is thinking about recommending that Kaufman & Broad invest in a piece of land that costs $85,000. She is certain that next year the land will be worth $91,000, a sure $6,000 gain. Given that the guaranteed interest rate in the bank is 10 percent, should Kaufman & Broad undertake the investment in land? Ms. Jennings's choice is described in Figure 4.2 with the cash flow time chart.

A moment's thought should be all it takes to convince her that this is not an attractive business deal. By investing $85,000 in the land, she will have $91,000 available next year. Suppose, instead, that Kaufman & Broad puts the same $85,000 into the bank. At the interest rate of 10 percent, this $85,000 would grow to

$$(1 + .10) \times \$85{,}000 = \$93{,}500$$

next year.

FIGURE 4.2
Cash Flows for Land Investment

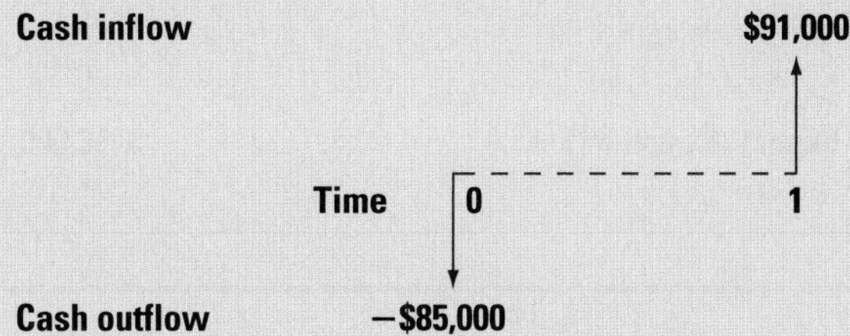

It would be foolish to buy the land when investing the same $85,000 in the financial market would produce an extra $2,500 (that is, $93,500 from the bank minus $91,000 from the land investment). This is a future value calculation.

Alternatively, she could calculate the present value of the sale price next year as

$$\text{Present value} = \frac{\$91{,}000}{1.10} = \$82{,}727.27$$

Because the present value of next year's sales price is less than this year's purchase price of $85,000, present value analysis also indicates that she should not recommend purchasing the property.

Frequently, businesspeople want to determine the exact *cost* or *benefit* of a decision. The decision to buy this year and sell next year can be evaluated as

Net Present Value of Investment:

$$-\$2{,}273 = \underset{\text{Cost of land today}}{-\$85{,}000} + \underset{\text{Present value of next year's sales price}}{\frac{\$91{,}000}{1.10}}$$

The formula for NPV can be written as

$$\text{NPV} = -\text{Cost} + \text{PV} \tag{4.2}$$

Equation (4.2) says that the value of the investment is −\$2,273, after stating all the benefits and all the costs as of date 0. We say that −\$2,273 is the **net present value** (NPV) of the investment. That is, NPV is the present value of future cash flows minus the present value of the cost of the investment. Because the net present value is negative, Lida Jennings should not recommend purchasing the land.

Both the Vaughn and the Jennings examples deal with perfect certainty. That is, Keith Vaughn knows with perfect certainty that he could sell his land for \$11,424 next year. Similarly, Lida Jennings knows with perfect certainty that Kaufman & Broad could receive \$91,000 for selling its land. Unfortunately, businesspeople frequently do not know future cash flows. This uncertainty is treated in the next example.

EXAMPLE 4.2 Uncertainty and Valuation

Professional Artworks, Inc., is a firm that speculates in modern paintings. The manager is thinking of buying an original Picasso for \$400,000 with the intention of selling it at the end of one year. The manager expects that the painting will be worth \$480,000 in one year. The relevant cash flows are depicted in Figure 4.3.

Of course, this is only an expectation—the painting could be worth more or less than \$480,000. Suppose the guaranteed interest rate granted by banks is 10 percent. Should the firm purchase the piece of art?

FIGURE 4.3
Cash Flows for Investment in Painting

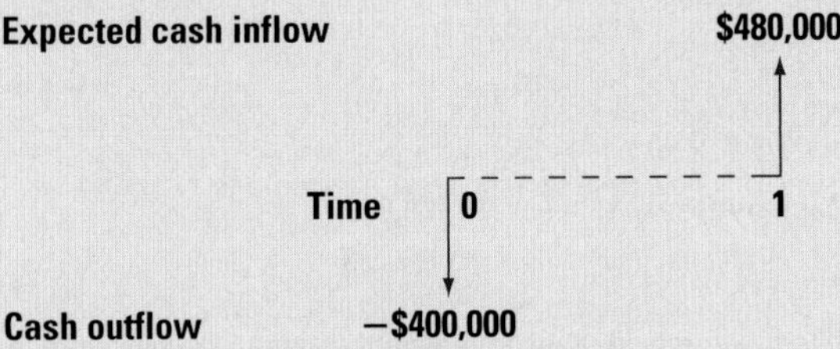

Our first thought might be to discount at the interest rate, yielding

$$\frac{\$480{,}000}{1.10} = \$436{,}364$$

Because \$436,364 is greater than \$400,000, it looks at first glance as if the painting should be purchased. However, 10 percent is the return one can earn on a riskless investment. Because the painting is quite risky, a higher *discount rate* is called for. The manager chooses a rate of 25 percent to reflect this risk. In other words, he argues that a 25 percent expected return is fair compensation for an investment as risky as this painting.

The present value of the painting becomes

$$\frac{\$480{,}000}{1.25} = \$384{,}000$$

Thus, the manager believes that the painting is currently overpriced at \$400,000 and does not make the purchase.

The preceding analysis is typical of decision making in today's corporations, though real world examples are, of course, much more complex. Unfortunately, any example with risk poses a problem not faced by a riskless example. In an example with riskless cash flows, the appropriate interest rate can be determined by simply checking with a few banks. The selection of the discount rate for a risky investment is quite a difficult task. We simply don't know at this point whether the discount rate on the painting should be 11 percent, 25 percent, 52 percent, or some other percentage.

Because the choice of a discount rate is so difficult, we merely wanted to broach the subject here. We must wait until the specific material on risk and return is covered in later chapters before a risk-adjusted analysis can be presented.

4.2 THE MULTIPERIOD CASE

The previous section presented the calculation of future value and present value for one period only. We will now perform the calculations for the multiperiod case.

Future Value and Compounding

Suppose an individual were to make a loan of \$1. At the end of the first year, the borrower would owe the lender the principal amount of \$1 plus the interest on the loan at the interest rate of r. For the specific case where the interest rate is, say, 9 percent, the borrower owes the lender

$$\$1 \times (1 + r) = \$1 \times 1.09 = \$1.09$$

At the end of the year, though, the lender has two choices. She can either take the \$1.09–or, more generally, $(1 + r)$–out of the financial market, or she can leave it in and lend it again for a second year. The process of leaving the money in the financial market and lending it for another year is called **compounding**.

Suppose that the lender decides to compound her loan for another year. She does this by taking the proceeds from her first one-year loan, \$1.09, and lending this amount for the next year. At the end of next year, then, the borrower will owe her

$$\$1 \times (1 + r) \times (1 + r) = \$1 \times (1 + r)^2 = 1 + 2r + r^2$$
$$\$1 \times (1.09) \times (1.09) = \$1 \times (1.09)^2 = \$1 + \$0.18 + \$0.0081 = \$1.1881$$

This is the total she will receive two years from now by compounding the loan.

In other words, the capital market enables the investor, by providing a ready opportunity for lending, to transform \$1 today into \$1.1881 at the end of two years. At the end of three years, the cash will be $\$1 \times (1.09)^3 = \$1.2950$.

The most important point to notice is that the total amount that the lender receives is not just the \$1 that she lent out plus two years' worth of interest on \$1:

$$2 \times r = 2 \times \$0.09 = \$0.18$$

The lender also gets back an amount r^2, which is the interest in the second year on the interest that was earned in the first year. The term, $2 \times r$, represents **simple interest** over the two years, and the term, r^2, is referred to as the *interest on interest.* In our example this latter amount is exactly

$$r^2 = (\$0.09)^2 = \$0.0081$$

When cash is invested at **compound interest**, each interest payment is reinvested. With simple interest, the interest is not reinvested. Benjamin Franklin's statement, "Money makes money and the money that money makes makes more money," is a colorful way of explaining compound interest. The difference between compound interest and simple interest is illustrated in Figure 4.4. In this example, the difference does not amount to much because the loan is for \$1. If the loan were for \$1 million, the lender would receive \$1,188,100 in two years' time. Of this amount, \$8,100 is interest on interest.

FIGURE 4.4
Simple and Compound Interest

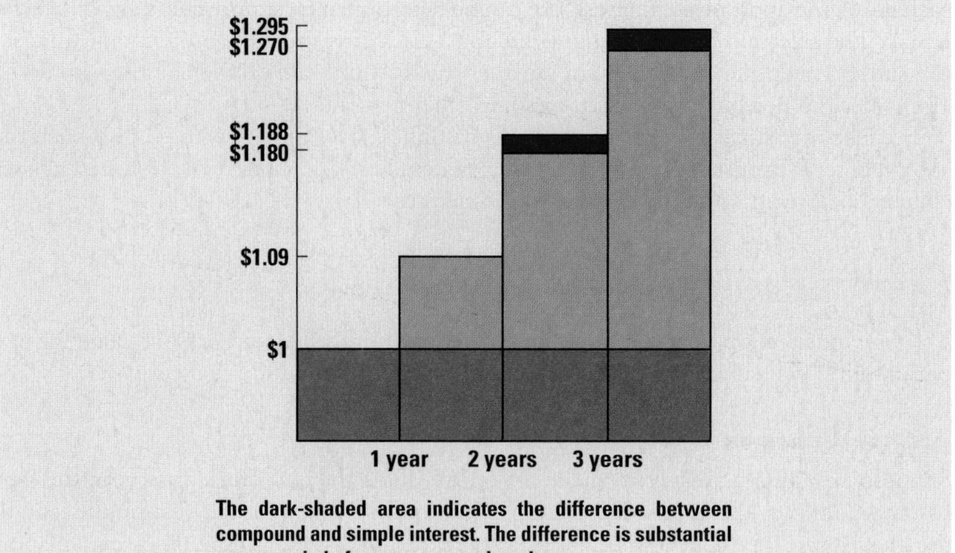

The dark-shaded area indicates the difference between compound and simple interest. The difference is substantial over a period of many years or decades.

The lesson is that those small numbers beyond the decimal point can add up to big dollar amounts when the transactions are for big amounts. In addition, the longer-lasting the loan, the more important interest on interest becomes.

The general formula for an investment over many periods can be written as

Future Value of an Investment:

$$FV = C_0 \times (1 + r)^T \tag{4.3}$$

where C_0 is the cash to be invested at date 0 (i.e., today), r is the interest rate per period, and T is the number of periods over which the cash is invested.

EXAMPLE 4.3 Interest on Interest

Suh-Pyng Ku has put $500 in a savings account at the First National Bank of Kent. The account earns 7 percent, compounded annually. How much will Ms. Ku have at the end of three years?

$$\$500 \times 1.07 \times 1.07 \times 1.07 = \$500 \times (1.07)^3 = \$612.52$$

Figure 4.5 illustrates the growth of Ms. Ku's account.

FIGURE 4.5
Suh-Pyng Ku's Savings Account

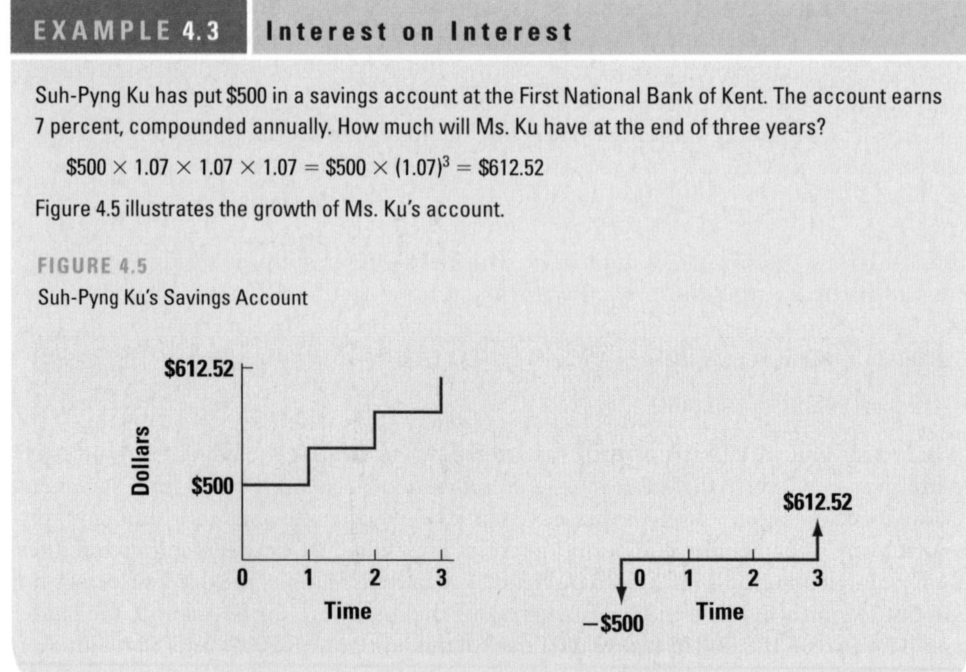

EXAMPLE 4.4 Compound Growth

Jay Ritter invested \$1,000 in the stock of the SDH Company. The company pays a current dividend of \$2, which is expected to grow by 20 percent per year for the next two years. What will the dividend of the SDH Company be after two years?

$\$2 \times (1.20)^2 = \$2.88$

Figure 4.6 illustrates the increasing value of SDH's dividends.

FIGURE 4.6

The Growth of the SDH Dividends

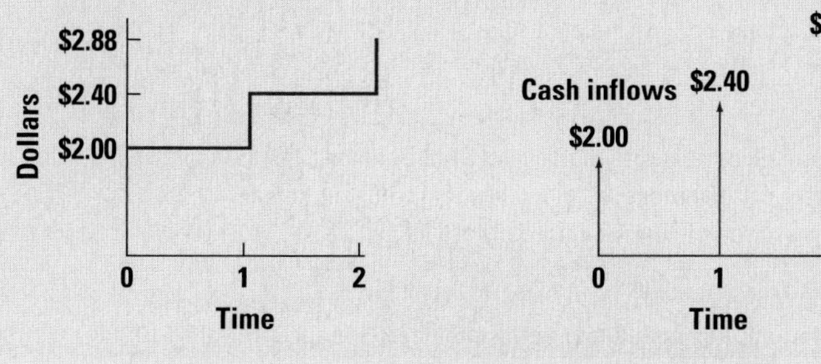

The two previous examples can be calculated in any one of three ways. The computations could be done by hand, by calculator, or with the help of a table. The appropriate table is Table A.3, which appears in the back of the text. This table presents *future value of \$1 at the end of T periods.* The table is used by locating the appropriate interest rate on the horizontal and the appropriate number of periods on the vertical.

For example, Suh-Pyng Ku would look at the following portion of Table A.3:

	Interest Rate		
PERIOD	6%	7%	8%
1	1.0600	1.0700	1.0800
2	1.1236	1.1449	1.1664
3	1.1910	1.2250	1.2597
4	1.2625	1.3108	1.3605

She could calculate the future value of her \$500 as

\$500	×	1.2250	=	\$612.50
Initial investment		Future value of \$1		

In the example concerning Suh-Pyng Ku, we gave you both the initial investment and the interest rate and then asked you to calculate the future value. Alternatively, the interest rate could have been unknown, as shown in the following example.

EXAMPLE 4.5 Finding the Rate

Carl Voigt, who recently won \$10,000 in the lottery, wants to buy a car in five years. Carl estimates that the car will cost \$16,105 at that time. His cash flows are displayed in Figure 4.7.

What interest rate must he earn to be able to afford the car?

(continued)

FIGURE 4.7
Cash Flows for Purchase of Carl Voigt's Car

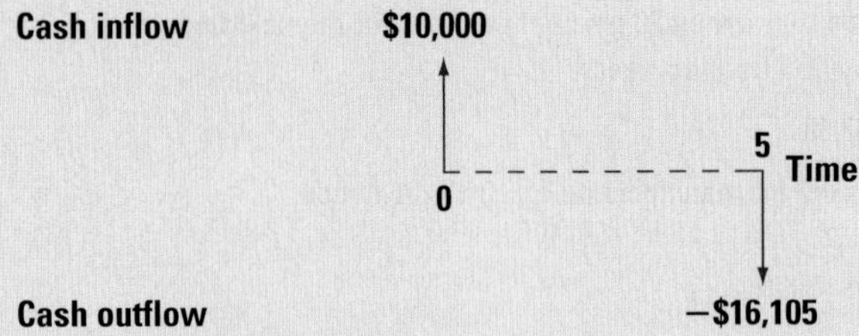

The ratio of purchase price to initial cash is

$$\frac{\$16{,}105}{\$10{,}000} = 1.6105$$

Thus, he must earn an interest rate that allows $1 to become $1.6105 in five years. Table A.3 tells us that an interest rate of 10 percent will allow him to purchase the car.

One can express the problem algebraically as

$$\$10{,}000 \times (1 + r)^5 = \$16{,}105$$

where r is the interest rate needed to purchase the car. Because $16,105/$10,000 = 1.6105, we have

$$(1 + r)^5 = 1.6105$$

Either the table or a hand calculator solves for r.

The Power of Compounding: A Digression

Most people who have had any experience with compounding are impressed with its power over long periods of time. Take the stock market, for example. Ibbotson and Sinquefield have calculated what the stock market returned as a whole from 1926 through 2004.[1] They find that one dollar placed in these stocks at the beginning of 1926 would have been worth $2,533.20 at the end of 2004. This is 10.43 percent compounded annually for 79 years, i.e., $(1.1043)^{79} = \$2{,}533.20$, ignoring a small rounding error.

The example illustrates the great difference between compound and simple interest. At 10.43 percent, simple interest on $1 is 10.43 cents a year. Simple interest over 79 years is $8.24 (79 × $.1043). That is, an individual withdrawing 10.43 cents every year would have withdrawn $8.24 (79 × $0.1043) over 79 years. This is quite a bit below the $2,533.20 that was obtained by reinvestment of all principal and interest.

The results are more impressive over even longer periods of time. A person with no experience in compounding might think that the value of $1 at the end of 158 years would be twice the value of $1 at the end of 79 years, if the yearly rate of return stayed the same. Actually the value of $1 at the end of 158 years would be the *square* of the value of $1 at the end of 79 years. That is, if the annual rate of return remained the same, a $1 investment in common stocks should be worth $6,417,102.24 [$1 × (2,533.20 × 2,533.20)].

A few years ago, an archaeologist unearthed a relic stating that Julius Caesar lent the Roman equivalent of one penny to someone. Since there was no record of the penny ever being repaid, the archaeologist wondered what the interest and principal would be if a descendant of Caesar tried to collect from a descendant of the borrower in the 20th century. The archaeologist felt that a rate of 6 percent might be appropriate. To his surprise, the principal and interest due after more than 2,000 years was vastly greater than the entire wealth on earth.

[1] *Stocks, Bonds, Bills and Inflation* [SBBI]. 2005 Yearbook. Ibbotson Associates, Chicago, 2005.

The power of compounding can explain why the parents of well-to-do families frequently bequeath wealth to their grandchildren rather than to their children. That is, they skip a generation. The parents would rather make the grandchildren very rich than make the children moderately rich. We have found that in these families the grandchildren have a more positive view of the power of compounding than do the children.

EXAMPLE 4.6 How Much for That Island?

Some people have said that it was the best real estate deal in history. Peter Minuit, director-general of New Netherlands, the Dutch West India Company's Colony in North America, in 1626 allegedly bought Manhattan Island for 60 guilders' worth of trinkets from native Americans. By 1667, the Dutch were forced to exchange it for Suriname with the British (perhaps the worst real estate deal ever). This sounds cheap but did the Dutch really get the better end of the deal? It is reported that 60 guilders was worth about $24 at the prevailing exchange rate. If the native Americans had sold the trinkets at a fair market value and invested the $24 at 5 percent (tax free), it would now, about 380 years later, be worth more than $2.5 billion. Today, Manhattan is undoubtedly worth more than $2.5 billion, and so, at a 5 percent rate of return, the native Americans got the worst of the deal. However, if invested at 10 percent, the amount of money they received would be worth about

$$\$24(1 + r)^T = 24 \times 1.1^{380} \cong \$129 \text{ quadrillion}$$

This is a lot of money. In fact, $129 quadrillion is more than all the real estate in the world is worth today. Note that no one in the history of the world has ever been able to find an investment yielding 10 percent every year for 380 years.

Present Value and Discounting

We now know that an annual interest rate of 9 percent enables the investor to transform $1 today into $1.1881 two years from now. In addition, we would like to know:

> How much would an investor need to lend today so that she could receive $1 two years from today?

Algebraically, we can write this as

$$\text{PV} \times (1.09)^2 = \$1$$

In the preceding equation, PV stands for present value, the amount of money we must lend today in order to receive $1 in two years' time.

Solving for PV in this equation, we have

$$\text{PV} = \frac{\$1}{1.1881} = \$.84$$

This process of calculating the present value of a future cash flow is called **discounting**. It is the opposite of compounding. The difference between compounding and discounting is illustrated in Figure 4.8.

To be certain that $.84 is in fact the present value of $1 to be received in two years, we must check whether or not, if we loaned out $.84 and rolled over the loan for two years, we would get exactly $1 back. If this were the case, the capital markets would be saying that $1 received in two years' time is equivalent to having $.84 today. Checking the exact numbers, we get

$$\$.84168 \times 1.09 \times 1.09 = \$1$$

In other words, when we have capital markets with a sure interest rate of 9 percent, we are indifferent between receiving $.84 today or $1 in two years. We have no reason to treat these two choices differently from each other, because if we had $.84 today and loaned it out for two years, it would return $1 to us at the end of that time. The value

FIGURE 4.8
Compounding and Discounting

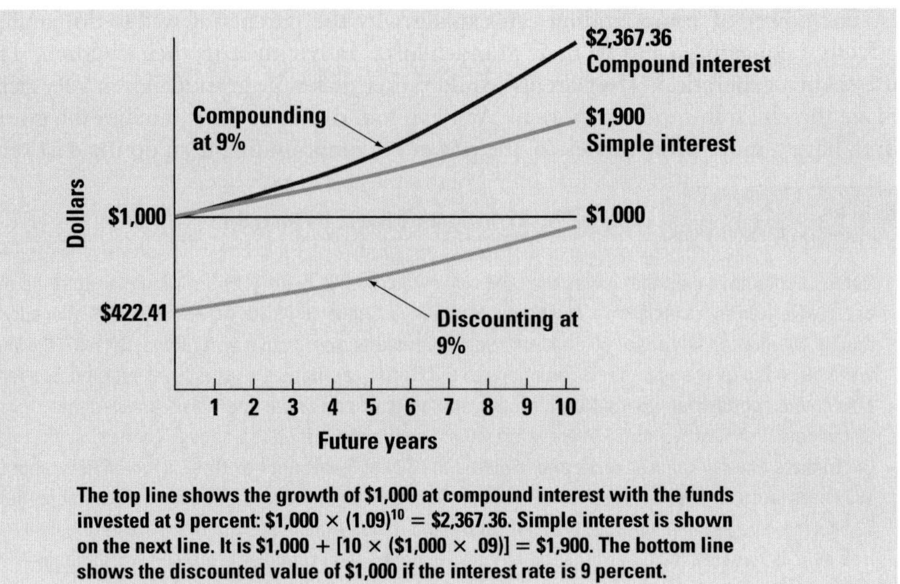

The top line shows the growth of $1,000 at compound interest with the funds invested at 9 percent: $\$1,000 \times (1.09)^{10} = \$2,367.36$. Simple interest is shown on the next line. It is $\$1,000 + [10 \times (\$1,000 \times .09)] = \$1,900$. The bottom line shows the discounted value of $1,000 if the interest rate is 9 percent.

.84 $[1/(1.09)^2]$ is called the **present value factor**. It is the factor used to calculate the present value of a future cash flow.

In the multiperiod case, the formula for PV can be written as

Present Value of Investment:

$$\text{PV} = \frac{C_T}{(1 + r)^T} \tag{4.4}$$

where C_T is cash flow at date T and r is the appropriate discount rate.

EXAMPLE 4.7 Multiperiod Discounting

Bernard Dumas will receive $10,000 three years from now. Bernard can earn 8 percent on his investments, and so the appropriate discount rate is 8 percent. What is the present value of his future cash flow?

$$\begin{aligned} \text{PV} &= \$10,000 \times \left(\frac{1}{1.08}\right)^3 \\ &= \$10,000 \times .7938 \\ &= \$7,938 \end{aligned}$$

Figure 4.9 illustrates the application of the present value factor to Bernard's investment.

FIGURE 4.9
Discounting Bernard Dumas's Opportunity

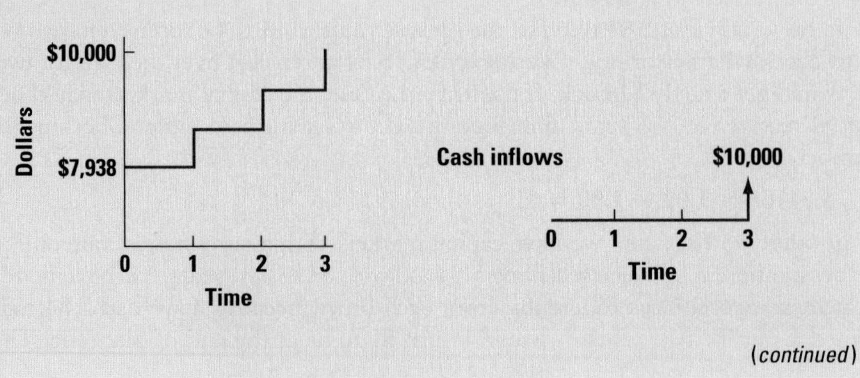

(*continued*)

When his investments grow at an 8 percent rate of interest, Bernard Dumas is equally inclined toward receiving $7,938 now and receiving $10,000 in three years' time. After all, he could convert the $7,938 he receives today into $10,000 in three years by lending it at an interest rate of 8 percent.

Bernard Dumas could have reached his present value calculation in one of three ways. The computation could have been done by hand, by calculator, or with the help of Table A.1, which appears in the back of the text. This table presents *present value of $1 to be received after T periods.* The table is used by locating the appropriate interest rate on the horizontal and the appropriate number of periods on the vertical. For example, Bernard Dumas would look at the following portion of Table A.1:

	Interest Rate		
PERIOD	**7%**	**8%**	**9%**
1	.9346	.9259	.9174
2	.8734	.8573	.8417
3	.8163	.7938	.7722
4	.7629	.7350	.7084

The appropriate present value factor is .7938.

In the preceding example, we gave both the interest rate and the future cash flow. Alternatively, the interest rate could have been unknown.

EXAMPLE 4.8 Finding the Rate

A customer of the Chaffkin Corp. wants to buy a tugboat today. Rather than paying immediately, he will pay $50,000 in three years. It will cost the Chaffkin Corp. $38,610 to build the tugboat immediately. The relevant cash flows to Chaffkin Corp. are displayed in Figure 4.10. By charging what interest rate would the Chaffkin Corp. neither gain nor lose on the sale?

FIGURE 4.10
Cash Flows for Tugboat

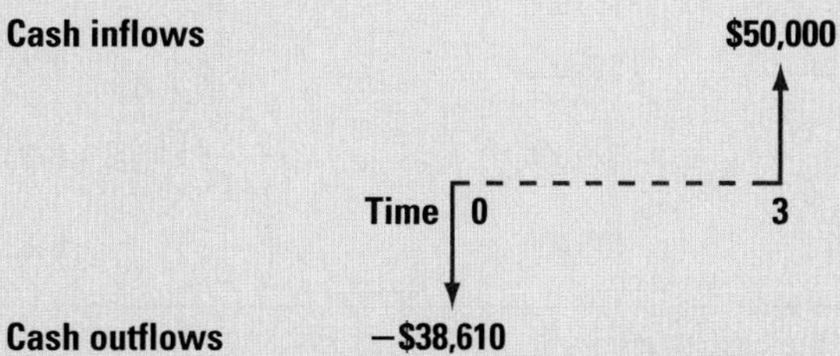

The ratio of construction cost to sale price is

$$\frac{\$38,610}{\$50,000} = 0.7722$$

We must determine the interest rate that allows $1 to be received in three years to have a present value of $.7722. Table A.1 tells us that 9 percent is that interest rate.

Frequently, an investor or a business will receive more than one cash flow. The present value of the set of cash flows is simply the sum of the present values of the individual cash flows. This is illustrated in the following example.

EXAMPLE 4.9 Cash Flow Valuation

Dennis Draper has won the Kentucky state lottery and will receive the following set of cash flows over the next two years:

YEAR	CASH FLOW
1	\$2,000
2	\$5,000

Mr. Draper can currently earn 6 percent in his money market account, and so, the appropriate discount rate is 6 percent. The present value of the cash flows is

YEAR	CASH FLOW × PRESENT VALUE FACTOR = PRESENT VALUE		
1	$\$2{,}000 \times \frac{1}{1.06} = \$2{,}000 \times .943$	=	\$1,887
2	$\$5{,}000 \times \left(\frac{1}{1.06}\right)^2 = \$5{,}000 \times .890$	=	\$4,450
	Total		\$6,337

In other words, Mr. Draper is equally inclined toward receiving \$6,337 today and receiving \$2,000 and \$5,000 over the next two years.

EXAMPLE 4.10 NPV

Finance.com has an opportunity to invest in a new high-speed computer that costs \$50,000. The computer will generate cash flows (from cost savings) of \$25,000 one year from now, \$20,000 two years from now, and \$15,000 three years from now. The computer will be worthless after three years, and no additional cash flows will occur. Finance.com has determined that the appropriate discount rate is 7 percent for this investment. Should Finance.com make this investment in a new high-speed computer? What is the present value of the investment?

The cash flows and present value factors of the proposed computer are as follows.

	CASH FLOWS	PRESENT VALUE FACTOR
Year 0	−\$50,000	$1 = 1$
1	\$25,000	$\frac{1}{1.07} = .9346$
2	\$20,000	$\left(\frac{1}{1.07}\right)^2 = .8734$
3	\$15,000	$\left(\frac{1}{1.07}\right)^3 = .8163$

The present values of the cash flows are:

Cash flows × Present value factor = Present value

Year 0	−\$50,000 × 1	=	−\$50,000
1	\$25,000 × .9346	=	\$23,365
2	\$20,000 × .8734	=	\$17,468
3	\$15,000 × .8163	=	\$12,244.5
		Total:	\$ 3,077.5

Finance.com should invest in a new high-speed computer because the present value of its future cash flows is greater than its cost. The NPV is \$3,077.5.

The Algebraic Formula

To derive an algebraic formula for net present value of a cash flow, recall that the PV of receiving a cash flow one year from now is

$$\text{PV} = C_1/(1 + r)$$

and the PV of receiving a cash flow two years from now is

$$\text{PV} = C_2/(1 + r)^2$$

We can write the NPV of a T-period project as

$$\text{NPV} = -C_0 + \frac{C_1}{1+r} + \frac{C_2}{(1+r)^2} + \cdots + \frac{C_T}{(1+r)^T} = -C_0 + \sum_{i=1}^{T} \frac{C_i}{(1+r)^i} \quad (4.5)$$

The initial flow, $-C_0$, is assumed to be negative because it represents an investment. The Σ is shorthand for the sum of the series.

We will close out this section by answering the question we posed at the beginning of the chapter concerning baseball player Carlos Beltran's contract. Recall that the contract called for a signing bonus of $7 million to be paid immediately, plus a salary and bonus of $112 million to be distributed as $12 million in 2005, $14 million in 2006, $12 million in 2007, and $18.5 million per year for 2008 through 2011. If 12 percent is the appropriate interest rate, what kind of deal did the Mets' new centerfielder catch?

To answer, we can calculate the present value by discounting each year's salary back to the present as follows (notice we assumed the future salaries will be paid at the end of the year):

Year 0:	$ 7,000,000	=	$ 7,000,000
Year 1:	$12,000,000 $\times$ 1/1.12^1	=	$10,714,285.71
Year 2:	$14,000,000 $\times$ 1/1.12^2	=	$11,160,714.29
Year 3:	$12,000,000 $\times$ 1/1.12^3	=	$ 8,541,362.97
.	.		.
.	.		.
.	.		.
Year 7:	$18,500,000 $\times$ 1/1.12^7	=	$ 8,368,460.48

If you fill in the missing rows and then add (do it for practice), you will see that Beltran's contract had a present value of about $77.41 million, less than two-thirds of the $119 million value reported, but still pretty good. And of course, playing for the Mets, Beltran will probably have his Octobers free as well.

As you have probably noticed, doing extensive present value calculations can get to be pretty tedious, so a nearby *Spreadsheet Techniques* box shows how we recommend doing them. As an application, we take a look at lottery payouts in a *The Real World* box on p. 104.

4.3 COMPOUNDING PERIODS

So far we have assumed that compounding and discounting occur yearly. Sometimes compounding may occur more frequently than just once a year. For example, imagine that a bank pays a 10-percent interest rate "compounded semiannually." This means that a $1,000 deposit in the bank would be worth $1,000 $\times$ 1.05 = $1,050 after six months, and $1,050 $\times$ 1.05 = $1,102.50 at the end of the year.

The end-of-the-year wealth can be written as

$$\$1{,}000\left(1 + \frac{.10}{2}\right)^2 = \$1{,}000 \times (1.05)^2 = \$1{,}102.50$$

SPREADSHEET TECHNIQUES How to Calculate Present Values with Multiple Future Cash Flows Using a Spreadsheet

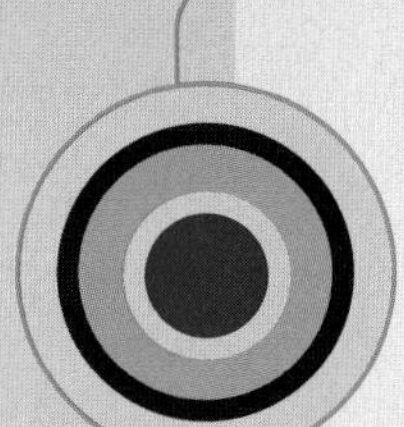

We can set up a basic spreadsheet to calculate the present values of the individual cash flows as follows. Notice that we have simply calculated the present values one at a time and added them up:

	A	B	C	D	E
1					
2	**Using a spreadsheet to value multiple future cash flows**				
3					
4	What is the present value of $200 in one year, $400 the next year, $600 the next year, and				
5	$800 the last year if the discount rate is 12 percent?				
6					
7	Rate:	0.12			
8					
9	Year	Cash flows	Present values	Formula used	
10	1	$200	$178.57	=PV(B7,A10,0,−B10)	
11	2	$400	$318.88	=PV(B7,A11,0,−B11)	
12	3	$600	$427.07	=PV(B7,A12,0,−B12)	
13	4	$800	$508.41	=PV(B7,A13,0,−B13)	
14					
15		Total PV:	**$1,432.93**	=SUM(C10:C13)	
16					
17	Notice the negative signs inserted in the PV formulas. These just make the present values have				
18	positive signs. Also, the discount rate in cell B7 is entered as B7 (an "absolute" reference)				
19	because it is used over and over. We could have just entered ".12" instead, but our approach is more				
20	flexible.				
21					
22					

Of course, a $1,000 deposit would be worth $1,100 ($1,000 × 1.10) with yearly compounding. Note that the future value at the end of one year is greater with semiannual compounding than with yearly compounding. With yearly compounding, the original $1,000 remains the investment base for the full year. The original $1,000 is the investment base only for the first six months with semiannual compounding. The base over the second six months is $1,050. Hence, one gets *interest on interest* with semiannual compounding.

Because $1,000 × 1.1025 = $1,102.50, 10 percent compounded semiannually is the same as 10.25 percent compounded annually. In other words, a rational investor could not care less whether she is quoted a rate of 10 percent compounded semiannually, or a rate of 10.25 percent compounded annually.

Quarterly compounding at 10 percent yields wealth at the end of one year of

$$\$1{,}000\left(1+\frac{.10}{4}\right)^4 = \$1{,}103.81$$

More generally, compounding an investment m times a year provides end-of-year wealth of

$$C_0\left(1+\frac{r}{m}\right)^m \tag{4.6}$$

where C_0 is one's initial investment and r is the **stated annual interest rate.** The stated annual interest rate is the annual interest rate without consideration of compounding. Banks and other financial institutions may use other names for the stated annual interest rate. **Annual percentage rate (APR)** is perhaps the most common synonym.

EXAMPLE 4.11 EARs

What is the end-of-year wealth if Jane Christine receives a stated annual interest rate of 24 percent compounded monthly on a $1 investment?

Using (4.6), her wealth is

$$\$1\left(1+\frac{.24}{12}\right)^{12} = \$1 \times (1.02)^{12}$$
$$= \$1.2682$$

The annual rate of return is 26.82 percent. This annual rate of return is either called the **effective annual rate (EAR)** or the **effective annual yield (EAY)**. Due to compounding, the effective annual interest rate is greater than the stated annual interest rate of 24 percent. Algebraically, we can rewrite the effective annual interest rate as

Effective Annual Rate:

$$\left(1+\frac{r}{m}\right)^{m} - 1 \tag{4.7}$$

Students are often bothered by the subtraction of 1 in (4.7). Note that end-of-year wealth is composed of both the interest earned over the year and the original principal. We remove the original principal by subtracting 1 in (4.7).

EXAMPLE 4.12 Compounding Frequencies

If the stated annual rate of interest, 8 percent, is compounded quarterly, what is the effective annual rate?

Using (4.7), we have

$$\left(1+\frac{r}{m}\right)^{m} - 1 = \left(1+\frac{.08}{4}\right)^{4} - 1 = .0824 = 8.24\%$$

Referring back to our original example where $C_0 = \$1{,}000$ and $r = 10\%$, we can generate the following table:

C_0	COMPOUNDING FREQUENCY (m)	C_1	EFFECTIVE ANNUAL RATE = $\left(1+\frac{r}{m}\right)^{m} - 1$
$1,000	Yearly ($m = 1$)	$1,100.00	.10
1,000	Semiannually ($m = 2$)	1,102.50	.1025
1,000	Quarterly ($m = 4$)	1,103.81	.10381
1,000	Daily ($m = 365$)	1,105.16	.10516

Distinction between Stated Annual Interest Rate and Effective Annual Rate

The distinction between the stated annual interest rate (SAIR), or APR, and the effective annual rate (EAR) is frequently quite troubling to students. One can reduce the confusion by noting that the SAIR becomes meaningful only if the compounding interval is given. For example, for an SAIR of 10 percent, the future value at the end of one year with semiannual compounding is $[1 + (.10/2)]^2 = 1.1025$. The future value with quarterly compounding is $[1 + (.10/4)]^4 = 1.1038$. If the SAIR is 10 percent but no

THE REAL WORLD

JACKPOT!

If you or someone you know is a regular lottery player, you probably already understand that you are 20 times more likely to get struck by lightning than you are to win a big lottery jackpot. What are your odds of winning? Below you will find a table with your chances of winning the Mega Millions Lottery compared to other events.

Odds of winning a Mega Millions jackpot	1:135,145,920*
Odds of being killed by a venomous spider	1:57,018,763
Odds of being killed by a dog bite	1:11,403,753
Odds of being killed by lightning	1:6,479,405
Odds of being killed by drowning	1:690,300
Odds of being killed falling from a bed or other furniture	1:388,411
Odds of being killed in a car crash	1:6,029

*Source: Virginia Lottery Web site. All other odds from the National Safety Council.

Sweepstakes may have different odds than lotteries, but these odds may not be much better. Probably the largest advertised potential grand prize ever was Pepsi's "Play for a Billion," which, you guessed it, had a $1 billion (*billion!*) prize. Not bad for a day's work, but you still have to read the fine print. It turns out that the winner would be paid $5 million per year for the next 20 years, $10 million per year for years 21 through 39, and a lump sum $710 million in 40 years. From what you have learned, you know the value of the sweepstakes wasn't even close to $1 billion. In fact, at an interest rate of 10 percent, the present value is about $70.7 million.

Lottery jackpots are often paid out over 20 or more years, but the winner can often choose to take a lump sum instead. For some, the cash option is a lot better. In December 2004, an ex-waitress in Massachusetts lost a lawsuit against the lottery in her state because they wouldn't pay out the winnings as a lump sum. She had won $5.6 million, which was to be paid out as $280,000 immediately and $280,000 per year for the next 19 years. However, since she was 94, she argued that she wouldn't be around to enjoy the money. When a lottery does allow the cash option, the rule of thumb used is that the cash option will be about one-half of the reported prize. Using this rule of thumb on the waitress's winnings, she would have received about $2.8 million in cash. So, what discount rate does this imply? Remembering that this is an annuity due, we find the interest rate using this rule of thumb is about 8.92 percent.

Some lotteries make your decision a little tougher. The Ontario Lottery wil pay you either $2,000 a week for the rest of your life or $1.3 million now. (That's in Canadian dollars or "loonies," by the way.) Of course, there is the chance you might die in the near future, so the lottery guarantees that your heirs will collect the $2,000 weekly payments until the twentieth anniversary of the first payment, or until you would have turned 91, whichever comes first. This payout scheme complicates your decision quite a bit. If you live for only the 20-year minimum, the break-even interest rate between the two options is about 5.13 percent per year, compounded weekly. If you expect to live longer than the 20-year minimum, you might be better off accepting $2,000 per week for life. Of course, if you manage to invest the $1.3 million lump sum at a rate of return of about 8 percent per year (compounded weekly), you can have your cake and eat it too because the investment will return $2,000 at the end of each week forever! Taxes complicate the decision in this case because the lottery payments are all on an aftertax basis. Thus, the rates of return in this example would have to be aftertax as well.

compounding interval is given, one cannot calculate future value. In other words, one does not know whether to compound semiannually, quarterly, or over some other interval.

By contrast, the EAR is meaningful *without* a compounding interval. For example, an EAR of 10.25 percent means that a $1 investment will be worth $1.1025 in one year. One can think of this as an SAIR of 10 percent with semiannual compounding or an SAIR of 10.25 percent with annual compounding, or some other possibility.

There can be a big difference between an SAIR and an EAR when interest rates are large. For example, consider "payday loans." Payday loans are short-term term loans made to consumers, often for less than two weeks, and are offered by companies such as AmeriCash Advance and National Payday. The loans work like this: You write a check today that is postdated. When the check date arrives, you go to the store and pay the cash for the check, or the company cashes the check. For example, AmeriCash Advance allows you to write a postdated check for $125 for 15 days later. In this case, they would give you $100 today. So what is the APR and EAR of this arrangement? First we need to find the interest rate, which we can find by the FV equation as:

$$\begin{aligned} \text{FV} &= \text{PV}\ (1 + r)^t \\ \$125 &= \$100 \times (1 + r)^1 \\ 1.25 &= (1 + r) \\ r &= .25 \text{ or } 25\% \end{aligned}$$

That doesn't seem too bad until you remember this is the interest rate for *15 days!* The APR of the loan is:

$$\begin{aligned} \text{APR} &= .25 \times 365/15 \\ \text{APR} &= 6.0833 \text{ or } 608.33\% \end{aligned}$$

And the EAR for this loan is:

$$\begin{aligned} \text{EAR} &= (1 + \text{Quoted rate}/m)^m - 1 \\ \text{EAR} &= (1 + .25)^{365/15} - 1 \\ \text{EAR} &= 227.1096 \text{ or } 22{,}710.96\% \end{aligned}$$

Now that's an interest rate! Just to see what a difference a day (or three) makes, let's look at National Payday's terms. This company will allow you to write a postdated check for the same amount, but will allow you 18 days to repay. Check for yourself that the APR of this arrangement is 506.94 percent and the EAR is 9,128.26 percent. This is lower, but still not a loan we recommend you take out!

Compounding over Many Years

Formula (4.6) applies for an investment over one year. For an investment over one or more (T) years, the formula becomes

Future Value with Compounding:

$$\text{FV} = C_0\left(1 + \frac{r}{m}\right)^{mT} \tag{4.8}$$

EXAMPLE 4.13 Multiyear Compounding

Harry DeAngelo is investing $5,000 at a stated annual interest rate of 12 percent per year, compounded quarterly, for five years. What is his wealth at the end of five years?

Using formula (4.8), his wealth is

$$\$5{,}000 \times \left(1 + \frac{.12}{4}\right)^{4\times5} = \$5{,}000 \times (1.03)^{20} = \$5{,}000 \times 1.8061 = \$9{,}030.50$$

Continuous Compounding

The previous discussion shows that one can compound much more frequently than once a year. One could compound semiannually, quarterly, monthly, daily, hourly, each minute, or even more often. The limiting case would be to compound every infinitesimal instant, which is commonly called **continuous compounding**. Surprisingly, banks and other financial institutions sometimes quote continuously compounded rates, which is why we study them.

Though the idea of compounding this rapidly may boggle the mind, a simple formula is involved. With continuous compounding, the value at the end of T years is expressed as

$$C_0 \times e^{rT} \qquad (4.9)$$

where C_0 is the initial investment, r is the stated annual interest rate, and T is the number of years over which the investment runs. The number e is a constant and is approximately equal to 2.718. It is not an unknown like C_0, r, and T.

EXAMPLE 4.14 Continuous Compounding

Linda DeFond invested $1,000 at a continuously compounded rate of 10 percent for one year. What is the value of her wealth at the end of one year?

From formula (4.9) we have

$\$1,000 \times e^{0.10} = \$1,000 \times 1.1052 = \$1,105.20$

This number can easily be read from our Table A.5. One merely sets r, the value on the horizontal dimension, to 10 percent and T, the value on the vertical dimension, to 1. For this problem, the relevant portion of the table is

PERIOD (T)	Continuously Compounded Rate (r)		
	9%	10%	11%
1	1.0942	1.1052	1.1163
2	1.1972	1.2214	1.2461
3	1.3100	1.3499	1.3910

Note that a continuously compounded rate of 10 percent is equivalent to an annually compounded rate of 10.52 percent. In other words, Linda DeFond would not care whether her bank quoted a continuously compounded rate of 10 percent or a 10.52-percent rate, compounded annually.

EXAMPLE 4.15 Continuous Compounding, Continued

Linda DeFond's brother, Mark, invested $1,000 at a continuously compounded rate of 10 percent for two years.

The appropriate formula here is

$\$1,000 \times e^{.10 \times 2} = \$1,000 \times e^{.20} = \$1,221.40$

Using the portion of the table of continuously compounded rates reproduced above, we find the value to be 1.2214.

Figure 4.11 illustrates the relationship among annual, semiannual, and continuous compounding. Semiannual compounding gives rise to both a smoother curve and a higher ending value than does annual compounding. Continuous compounding has both the smoothest curve and the highest ending value of all.

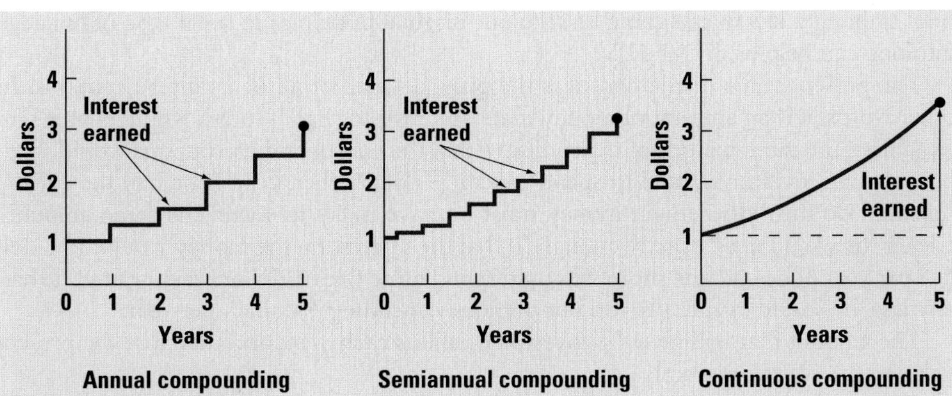

FIGURE 4.11
Annual, Semiannual, and Continuous Compounding

EXAMPLE 4.16 Present Value with Continuous Compounding

The Michigan state lottery is going to pay you $1,000 at the end of four years. If the annual continuously compounded rate of interest is 8 percent, what is the present value of this payment?

$$\$1{,}000 \times \frac{1}{e^{.08\times 4}} = \$1{,}000 \times \frac{1}{1.3771} = \$726.16$$

4.4 SIMPLIFICATIONS

The first part of this chapter has examined the concepts of future value and present value. Although these concepts allow one to answer a host of problems concerning the time value of money, the human effort involved can frequently be excessive. For example, consider a bank calculating the present value on a 20-year monthly mortgage. Because this mortgage has 240 (20 × 12) payments, a lot of time is needed to perform a conceptually simple task.

Because many basic finance problems are potentially so time-consuming, we search out simplifications in this section. We provide simplifying formulas for four classes of cash flow streams:

- Perpetuity
- Growing perpetuity
- Annuity
- Growing annuity

Perpetuity

A **perpetuity** is a constant stream of cash flows without end. If you are thinking that perpetuities have no relevance to reality, it will surprise you that there is a well-known case of an unending cash flow stream: the British bonds called *consols*. An investor purchasing a consol is entitled to receive yearly interest from the British government forever.

How can the price of a consol be determined? Consider a consol that pays a coupon of C dollars each year and will do so forever. Simply applying the PV formula gives us

$$\text{PV} = \frac{C}{1+r} + \frac{C}{(1+r)^2} + \frac{C}{(1+r)^3} + \cdots$$

where the dots at the end of the formula stand for the infinite string of terms that continues the formula. Series like the preceding one are called *geometric series*. It is well known that even though they have an infinite number of terms, the whole series has a finite sum because each term is only a fraction of the preceding term. Before turning to our calculus books, though, it is worth going back to our original principles to see if a bit of financial intuition can help us find the PV.

The present value of the consol is the present value of all of its future coupons. In other words, it is an amount of money that, if an investor had it today, would enable him to achieve the same pattern of expenditures that the consol and its coupons would. Suppose that an investor wanted to spend exactly *C* dollars each year. If he had the consol, he could do this. How much money must he have today to spend the same amount? Clearly he would need exactly enough so that the interest on the money would be *C* dollars per year. If he had any more, he could spend more than *C* dollars each year. If he had any less, he would eventually run out of money spending *C* dollars per year.

The amount that will give the investor *C* dollars each year, and therefore the present value of the consol, is simply

$$\mathbf{PV} = \frac{C}{r} \tag{4.10}$$

To confirm that this is the right answer, notice that if we lend the amount C/r, the interest it earns each year will be

$$\mathbf{Interest} = \frac{C}{r} \times r = C$$

which is exactly the consol payment. To sum up, we have shown that for a consol

Formula for Present Value of Perpetuity:

$$\begin{aligned}\mathbf{PV} &= \frac{C}{1+r} + \frac{C}{(1+r)^2} + \frac{C}{(1+r)^3} + \cdots \\ &= \frac{C}{r}\end{aligned} \tag{4.11}$$

It is comforting to know how easily we can use a bit of financial intuition to solve this mathematical problem.

EXAMPLE 4.17 Perpetuities

Consider a perpetuity paying $100 a year. If the relevant interest rate is 8 percent, what is the value of the consol?

Using formula (4.10), we have

$$\text{PV} = \frac{\$100}{.08} = \$1{,}250$$

Now suppose that interest rates fall to 6 percent. Using (4.10), the value of the perpetuity is

$$\text{PV} = \frac{\$100}{.06} = \$1{,}666.67$$

Note that the value of the perpetuity rises with a drop in the interest rate. Conversely, the value of the perpetuity falls with a rise in the interest rate.

Growing Perpetuity

Imagine an apartment building where cash flows to the landlord after expenses will be $100,000 next year. These cash flows are expected to rise at 5 percent per year. If one assumes that this rise will continue indefinitely, the cash flow stream is termed a **growing perpetuity**. The relevant interest rate is 11 percent. Therefore, the appropriate discount rate is 11 percent and the present value of the cash flows can be represented as

$$\begin{aligned}\mathbf{PV} &= \frac{\$100{,}000}{1.11} + \frac{\$100{,}000(1.05)}{(1.11)^2} + \frac{\$100{,}000(1.05)^2}{(1.11)^3} + \cdots \\ &\quad + \frac{\$100{,}000(1.05)^{N-1}}{(1.11)^N} + \cdots\end{aligned}$$

Algebraically, we can write the formula as

$$PV = \frac{C}{1+r} + \frac{C \times (1+g)}{(1+r)^2} + \frac{C \times (1+g)^2}{(1+r)^3} + \cdots + \frac{C \times (1+g)^{N-1}}{(1+r)^N} + \cdots$$

where C is the cash flow to be received one period hence, g is the rate of growth per period, expressed as a percentage, and r is the appropriate discount rate.

Fortunately, this formula reduces to the following simplification:

Formula for Present Value of Growing Perpetuity:

$$PV = \frac{C}{r-g} \tag{4.12}$$

From formula (4.12), the present value of the cash flows from the apartment building is

$$\frac{\$100{,}000}{.11 - .05} = \$1{,}666{,}667$$

There are three important points concerning the growing perpetuity formula:

1. *The Numerator.* The numerator in (4.12) is the cash flow one period hence, not at date 0. Consider the following example:

EXAMPLE 4.18 Paying Dividends

Rothstein Corporation is *just about* to pay a dividend of \$3.00 per share. Investors anticipate that the annual dividend will rise by 6 percent a year forever. The applicable discount rate is 11 percent. What is the price of the stock today?

The numerator in formula (4.12) is the cash flow to be received next period. Since the growth rate is 6 percent, the dividend next year is \$3.18 (\$3.00 × 1.06). The price of the stock today is

$$\$66.60 = \$3.00 + \frac{\$3.18}{.11 - .06}$$

\$66.60	=	\$3.00	+	\$3.18 / (.11 − .06)
		Imminent dividend		Present value of all dividends beginning a year from now

The price of \$66.60 includes both the dividend to be received immediately and the present value of all dividends beginning a year from now. Formula (4.12) only makes it possible to calculate the present value of all dividends beginning a year from now. Be sure you understand this example; test questions on this subject always seem to trip up a few of our students.

2. *The Discount Rate and the Growth Rate.* The discount rate r must be greater than the growth rate g for the growing perpetuity formula to work. Consider the case in which the growth rate approaches the interest rate in magnitude. Then the denominator in the growing perpetuity formula gets infinitesimally small and the present value grows infinitely large. The present value is in fact undefined when r is less than g.
3. *The Timing Assumption.* Cash generally flows into and out of real world firms both randomly and nearly continuously. However, formula (4.12) assumes that cash flows are received and disbursed at regular and discrete points in time. In the example of the apartment, we assumed that the net cash flows of \$100,000 only occurred once a year. In reality, rent checks are commonly received every month. Payments for maintenance and other expenses may occur anytime within the year.

   The growing perpetuity formula of (4.12) can be applied only by assuming a regular and discrete pattern of cash flow. Although this assumption is sensible because the formula saves so much time, the user should never forget that it is an *assumption.* This point will be mentioned again in the chapters ahead.

A few words should be said about terminology. Authors of financial textbooks generally use one of two conventions to refer to time. A minority of financial writers treat cash flows as being received on exact *dates,* for example date 0, date 1, and so forth. Under this convention, date 0 represents the present time. However, because a year is an interval, not a specific moment in time, the great majority of authors refer to cash flows that occur at the end of a year (or alternatively, the end of a *period*). Under this *end-of-the-year* convention, the end of year 0 is the present, the end of year 1 occurs one period hence, and so on. (The beginning of year 0 has already passed and is not generally referred to.)[2]

The interchangeability of the two conventions can be seen from the following chart:

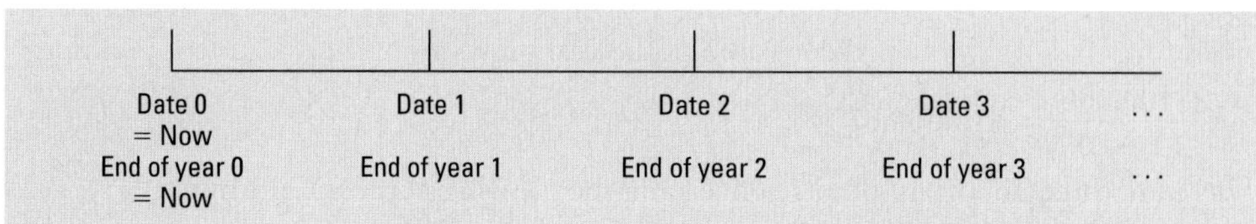

We strongly believe that the *dates convention* reduces ambiguity. However, we use both conventions because you are likely to see the *end-of-year convention* in later courses. In fact, both conventions may appear in the same example for the sake of practice.

Annuity

An **annuity** is a level stream of regular payments that lasts for a fixed number of periods. Not surprisingly, annuities are among the most common kinds of financial instruments. The pensions that people receive when they retire are often in the form of an annuity. Leases and mortgages are also often annuities.

To figure out the present value of an annuity we need to evaluate the following equation:

$$\frac{C}{1+r} + \frac{C}{(1+r)^2} + \frac{C}{(1+r)^3} + \cdots + \frac{C}{(1+r)^T}$$

The present value of only receiving the coupons for T periods must be less than the present value of a consol, but how much less? To answer this we have to look at consols a bit more closely.

Consider the following time chart:

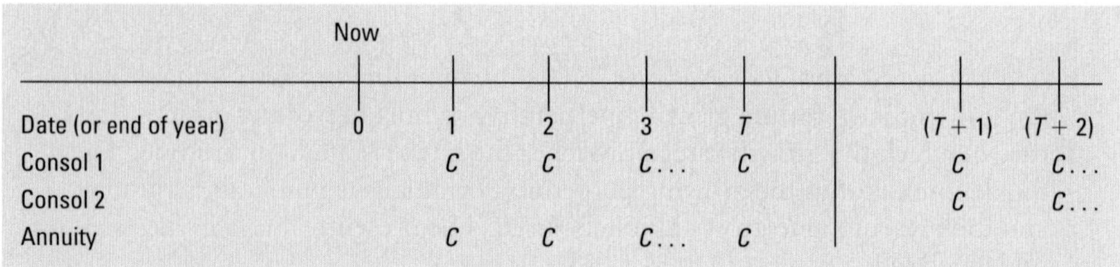

Consol 1 is a normal consol with its first payment at date 1. The first payment of consol 2 occurs at date $T + 1$.

The present value of having a cash flow of C at each of T dates is equal to the present value of consol 1 minus the present value of consol 2. The present value of consol 1 is given by

$$\text{PV} = \frac{C}{r} \qquad \textbf{(4.13)}$$

[2]Sometimes financial writers merely speak of a cash flow in year *x*. Although this terminology is ambiguous, such writers generally mean the *end of year x*.

Consol 2 is just a consol with its first payment at date $T + 1$. From the perpetuity formula, this consol will be worth C/r at date T.[3] However, we do not want the value at date T. We want the value now; in other words, the present value at date 0. We must discount C/r back by T periods. Therefore, the present value of consol 2 is

$$\text{PV} = \frac{C}{r}\left[\frac{1}{(1+r)^T}\right] \tag{4.14}$$

The present value of having cash flows for T years is the present value of a consol with its first payment at date 1 minus the present value of a consol with its first payment at date $T + 1$. Thus, the present value of an annuity is formula (4.13) minus formula (4.14). This can be written as

$$\frac{C}{r} - \frac{C}{r}\left[\frac{1}{(1+r)^T}\right]$$

This simplifies to

Formula for Present Value of Annuity:

$$\text{PV} = C\left[\frac{1}{r} - \frac{1}{r(1+r)^T}\right] \tag{4.15}$$

This can also be written as

$$\text{PV} = C\left[\frac{1 - \dfrac{1}{(1+r)^T}}{r}\right]$$

EXAMPLE 4.19 Lottery Valuation

Mark Young has just won the state lottery, paying $50,000 a year for 20 years. He is to receive his first payment a year from now. The state advertises this as the Million Dollar Lottery because $1,000,000 = $50,000 × 20. If the interest rate is 8 percent, what is the true value of the lottery?

Formula (4.15) yields

$$\text{Present value of Million Dollar Lottery} = \$50{,}000 \times \left[\frac{1 - \dfrac{1}{(1.08)^{20}}}{.08}\right]$$

$$\begin{aligned} &\text{Periodic payment} \qquad \text{Annuity factor} \\ &= \$50{,}000 \qquad\qquad \times\ 9.8181 \\ &= \$490{,}905 \end{aligned}$$

Rather than being overjoyed at winning, Mr. Young sues the state for misrepresentation and fraud. His legal brief states that he was promised $1 million but received only $490,905.

The term we use to compute the present value of the stream of level payments, C, for T years is called an **annuity factor**. The annuity factor in the current example is 9.8181. Because the annuity factor is used so often in PV calculations, we have included it in Table A.2 in the back of this book. The table gives the values of these factors for a range of interest rates, r, and maturity dates, T.

The annuity factor as expressed in the brackets of (4.15) is a complex formula. For simplification, we may from time to time refer to the annuity factor as

$$A_r^T$$

That is, the above expression stands for the present value of $1 a year for T years at an interest rate of r.

[3]Students frequently think that C/r is the present value at date $T + 1$ because the consol's first payment is at date $T + 1$. However, the formula values the annuity as of one period prior to the first payment.

We can also provide a formula for the future value of an annuity:

$$\mathrm{FV} = C\left[\frac{(1+r)^T}{r} - \frac{1}{r}\right] = C\left[\frac{(1+r)^T - 1}{r}\right] \tag{4.16}$$

As with present value factors for annuities, we have compiled future value factors in Table A.3 in the back of this book. Of course, you can also use a spreadsheet as we illustrate in a nearby box.

SPREADSHEET TECHNIQUES Annuity Present Values

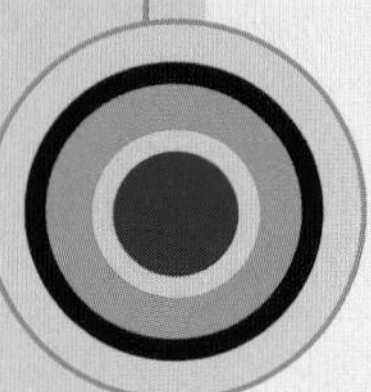

Using a spreadsheet to find annuity present values goes like this:

	A	B	C	D	E	F	G
1							
2	**Using a spreadsheet to find annuity present values**						
3							
4	What is the present value of $500 per year for 3 years if the discount rate is 10 percent?						
5	We need to solve for the unknown present value, so we use the formula PV(rate, nper, pmt, fv).						
6							
7	Payment amount per period:	$500					
8	Number of payments:	3					
9	Discount rate:	0.1					
10							
11	Annuity present value:	**$1,243.43**					
12							
13	The formula entered in cell B11 is =PV(B9,B8,-B7,0); notice that fv is zero and that						
14	pmt has a negative sign on it. Also notice that rate is entered as a decimal, not a percentage.						
15							
16							
17							

EXAMPLE 4.20 Retirement Investing

Suppose you put $3,000 per year into a Roth IRA. The account pays 6 percent per year. How much will you have when you retire in 30 years?

This question asks for the future value of an annuity of $3,000 per year for 30 years at 6 percent, which we can calculate as follows:

$$\mathrm{FV} = C\left[\frac{(1+r)^T - 1}{r}\right] = \$3{,}000 \times \left[\frac{1.06^{30} - 1}{.06}\right]$$

$$= \$3{,}000 \times 79.0582$$

$$= \$237{,}174.56$$

So, you'll have close to a quarter million dollars in the account.

Our experience is that annuity formulas are not hard, but tricky, for the beginning student. We present four tricks below.

TRICK 1: A DELAYED ANNUITY One of the tricks in working with annuities or perpetuities is getting the timing exactly right. This is particularly true when an annuity or perpetuity begins at a date many periods in the future. We have found that even the brightest beginning student can make errors here. Consider the following example.

EXAMPLE 4.21 Delayed Annuities

Danielle Caravello will receive a four-year annuity of $500 per year, beginning at date 6. If the interest rate is 10 percent, what is the present value of her annuity? This situation can be graphed as:

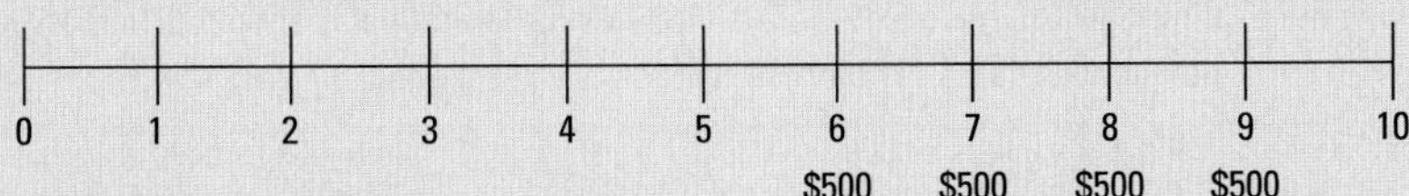

The analysis involves two steps:

1. Calculate the present value of the annuity using (4.15). This is

   Present Value of Annuity at Date 5:

$$\$500\left[\frac{1-\frac{1}{(1.10)^4}}{.10}\right] = \$500 \times A^4_{.10}$$
$$= \$500 \times 3.1699$$
$$= \$1{,}584.95$$

Note that $1,584.95 represents the present value at *date 5.*

Students frequently think that $1,584.95 is the present value at date 6, because the annuity begins at date 6. However, our formula values the annuity as of one period prior to the first payment. This can be seen in the most typical case where the first payment occurs at date 1. The formula values the annuity as of date 0 in that case.

2. Discount the present value of the annuity back to date 0. That is

   Present Value at Date 0:

$$\frac{\$1{,}584.95}{(1.10)^5} = \$984.13$$

Again, it is worthwhile mentioning that, because the annuity formula brings Danielle's annuity back to date 5, the second calculation must discount over the remaining 5 periods. The two-step procedure is graphed in Figure 4.12.

FIGURE 4.12
Discounting Danielle Caravello's Annuity

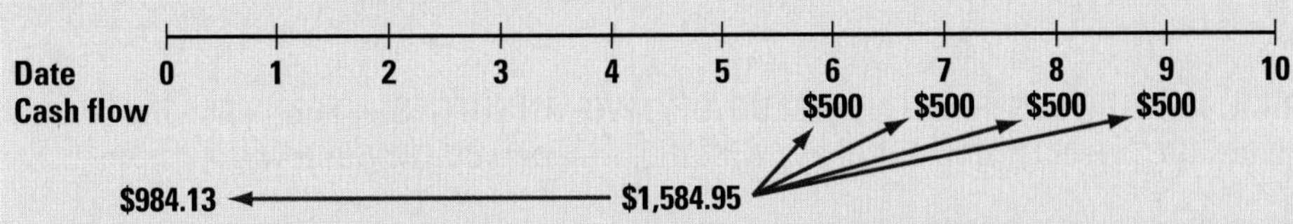

Step one: Discount the four payments back to date 5 by using the annuity formula.
Step two: Discount the present value at date 5 ($1,584.95) back to present value at date 0.

TRICK 2: ANNUITY DUE The annuity formula of (4.15) assumes that the first annuity payment begins a full period hence. This type of annuity is sometimes called an *annuity in arrears* or an *ordinary annuity*. What happens if the annuity begins today, in other words, at date 0?

EXAMPLE 4.22 Annuity Due

In a previous example, Mark Young received \$50,000 a year for 20 years from the state lottery. In that example, he was to receive the first payment a year from the winning date. Let us now assume that the first payment occurs immediately. The total number of payments remains 20.

Under this new assumption, we have a 19-date annuity with the first payment occurring at date 1—plus an extra payment at date 0. The present value is

$$\underset{\text{Payment at date 0}}{\$50{,}000} + \underset{\text{19-year annuity}}{\$50{,}000 \times A^{19}_{.08}}$$

$$= \$50{,}000 + (\$50{,}000 \times 9.6036)$$

$$= \$530{,}180$$

\$530,180, the present value in this example, is greater than \$490,905, the present value in the earlier lottery example. This is to be expected because the annuity of the current example begins earlier. An annuity with an immediate initial payment is called an *annuity in advance* or, more commonly, an *annuity due*. Always remember that formula (4.15), as well as Table A.2, in this book refers to an *ordinary annuity*.

TRICK 3: THE INFREQUENT ANNUITY The following example treats an annuity with payments occurring less frequently than once a year.

EXAMPLE 4.23 Infrequent Annuities

Ms. Ann Chen receives an annuity of \$450, payable once every two years. The annuity stretches out over 20 years. The first payment occurs at date 2, that is, two years from today. The annual interest rate is 6 percent.

The trick is to determine the interest rate over a two-year period. The interest rate over two years is

$$(1.06 \times 1.06) - 1 = 12.36\%$$

That is, \$100 invested over two years will yield \$112.36.

What we want is the present value of a \$450 annuity over 10 periods, with an interest rate of 12.36 percent per period. This is

$$\$450\left[\frac{1 - \frac{1}{(1 + .1236)^{10}}}{.1236}\right] = \$450 \times A^{10}_{.1236} = \$2{,}505.57$$

TRICK 4: EQUATING PRESENT VALUE OF TWO ANNUITIES The following example equates the present value of inflows with the present value of outflows.

EXAMPLE 4.24 Working with Annuities

Harold and Helen Nash are saving for the college education of their newborn daughter, Susan. The Nashes estimate that college expenses will run \$30,000 per year when their daughter reaches college in 18 years. The annual interest rate over the next few decades will be 14 percent. How much money must they deposit in the bank each year so that their daughter will be completely supported through four years of college?

To simplify the calculations, we assume that Susan is born today. Her parents will make the first of her four annual tuition payments on her 18th birthday. They will make equal bank deposits on each

(*continued*)

of her first 17 birthdays, but no deposit at date 0. This is illustrated as

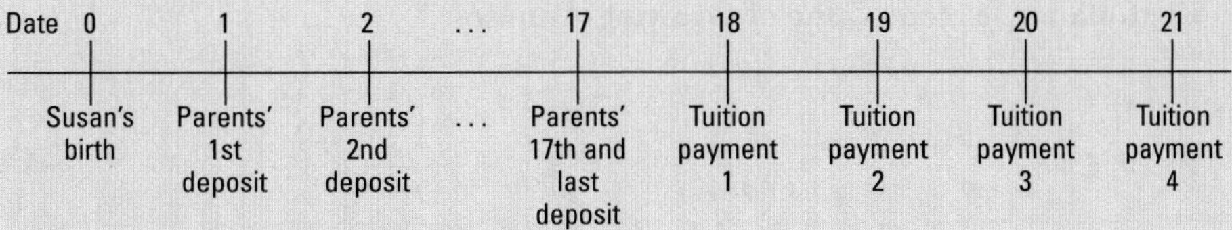

Mr. and Ms. Nash will be making deposits to the bank over the next 17 years. They will be withdrawing \$30,000 per year over the following four years. We can be sure they will be able to withdraw fully \$30,000 per year if the present value of the deposits is equal to the present value of the four \$30,000 withdrawals.

This calculation requires three steps. The first two determine the present value of the withdrawals. The final step determines yearly deposits that will have a present value equal to that of the withdrawals.

1. We calculate the present value of the four years at college using the annuity formula.

$$\$30{,}000 \times \left[\frac{1-\frac{1}{(1.14)^4}}{.14}\right] = \$30{,}000 \times A^4_{.14}$$
$$= \$30{,}000 \times 2.9137 = \$87{,}411$$

   We assume that Susan enters college on her 18th birthday. Given our discussion in Trick 1, \$87,411 represents the present value at date 17.

2. We calculate the present value of the college education at date 0 as

$$\frac{\$87{,}411}{(1.14)^{17}} = \$9{,}422.91$$

3. Assuming that Helen and Harold Nash make deposits to the bank at the end of each of the 17 years, we calculate the annual deposit that will yield a present value of all deposits of \$9,422.91. This is calculated as

$$C \times A^{17}_{.14} = \$9{,}422.91$$

   Because $A^{17}_{.14} = 6.3729$,

$$C = \frac{\$9{,}422.91}{6.3729} = \$1{,}478.59$$

Thus, deposits of \$1,478.59 made at the end of each of the first 17 years and invested at 14 percent will provide enough money to make tuition payments of \$30,000 over the following four years.

An alternative method would be to (1) calculate the present value of the tuition payments at Susan's 18th birthday and (2) calculate annual deposits such that the future value of the deposits at her 18th birthday equals the present value of the tuition payments at that date. Although this technique can also provide the right answer, we have found that it is more likely to lead to errors. Therefore, we only equate present values in our presentation.

Growing Annuity

Cash flows in business are very likely to grow over time, due either to real growth or to inflation. The growing perpetuity, which assumes an infinite number of cash flows, provides one formula to handle this growth. We now consider a **growing annuity**, which is a *finite* number of growing cash flows. Because perpetuities of any kind are rare, a formula for a growing annuity would be useful indeed. The formula is

Formula for Present Value of Growing Annuity:

$$\text{PV} = C\left[\frac{1}{r-g} - \frac{1}{r-g} \times \left(\frac{1+g}{1+r}\right)^T\right] = C\left[\frac{1-\left(\frac{1+g}{1+r}\right)^T}{r-g}\right] \quad \textbf{(4.17)}$$

where, as before, C is the payment to occur at the end of the first period, r is the interest rate, g is the rate of growth per period, expressed as a percentage, and T is the number of periods for the annuity.

EXAMPLE 4.25 Growing Annuities

Stuart Gabriel, a second-year MBA student, has just been offered a job at $80,000 a year. He anticipates his salary increasing by 9 percent a year until his retirement in 40 years. Given an interest rate of 20 percent, what is the present value of his lifetime salary?

We simplify by assuming he will be paid his $80,000 salary exactly one year from now, and that his salary will continue to be paid in annual installments. The appropriate discount rate is 20 percent. From (4.17), the calculation is

$$\begin{array}{c}\text{Present value} \\ \text{of Stuart's} \\ \text{lifetime salary}\end{array} = \$80{,}000 \times \left[\frac{1-\left(\frac{1.09}{1.20}\right)^{40}}{.20-.09}\right] = \$711{,}731$$

Though the growing annuity is quite useful, it is more tedious than the other simplifying formulas. Whereas most sophisticated calculators have special programs for perpetuity, growing perpetuity, and annuity, there is no special program for growing annuity. Hence, one must calculate all the terms in formula (4.17) directly.

EXAMPLE 4.26 More Growing Annuities

In a previous example, Harold and Helen Nash planned to make 17 identical payments in order to fund the college education of their daughter, Susan. Alternatively, imagine that they planned to increase their payments at 4 percent per year. What would their first payment be?

The first two steps of the previous Nash family example showed that the present value of the college costs was $9,422.91. These two steps would be the same here. However, the third step must be altered. Now we must ask, How much should their first payment be so that, if payments increase by 4 percent per year, the present value of all payments will be $9,422.91?

We set the growing-annuity formula equal to $9,422.91 and solve for C.

$$C\left[\frac{1-\left(\frac{1+g}{1+r}\right)^T}{r-g}\right] = C\left[\frac{1-\left(\frac{1.04}{1.14}\right)^{17}}{.14-.04}\right]$$

$$= \$9{,}422.91$$

Here, C = $1,192.78. Thus, the deposit on their daughter's first birthday is $1,192.78, the deposit on the second birthday is $1,240.49 (1.04 × $1,192.78), and so on.

4.5 WHAT IS A FIRM WORTH?

Suppose you are in the business of trying to determine the value of small companies. (You are a business appraiser.) How can you determine what a firm is worth? One way to think about the question of how much a firm is worth is to calculate the present value of its future cash flows.

Let us consider the example of a firm that is expected to generate net cash flows (cash inflows minus cash outflows) of $5,000 in the first year and $2,000 for each of the next five years. The firm can be sold for $10,000 seven years from now. The owners of the firm would like to be able to make 10 percent on their investment in the firm.

The value of the firm is found by multiplying the net cash flows by the appropriate present-value factor. The value of the firm is simply the sum of the present values of the individual net cash flows.

The present value of the net cash flows is given next.

The Present Value of the Firm

END OF YEAR	NET CASH FLOW OF THE FIRM	PRESENT VALUE FACTOR (10%)	PRESENT VALUE OF NET CASH FLOWS
1	$ 5,000	.90909	$ 4,545.45
2	2,000	.82645	1,652.90
3	2,000	.75131	1,502.62
4	2,000	.68301	1,366.02
5	2,000	.62092	1,241.84
6	2,000	.56447	1,128.94
7	10,000	.51316	5,131.58
		Present value of firm	$16,569.35

We can also use the simplifying formula for an annuity to give us

$$\frac{\$5{,}000}{1.1} + \frac{(2{,}000 \times A^{5}_{.10})}{1.1} + \frac{10{,}000}{(1.1)^7} = \$16{,}569.35$$

Suppose you have the opportunity to acquire the firm for $12,000. Should you acquire the firm? The answer is yes because the NPV is positive.

$$\begin{aligned} \text{NPV} &= \text{PV} - \text{Cost} \\ \$4{,}569.35 &= \$16{,}569.35 - \$12{,}000 \end{aligned}$$

The incremental value (NPV) of acquiring the firm is $4,569.35.

EXAMPLE 4.27 Firm Valuation

The Trojan Pizza Company is contemplating investing $1 million in four new outlets in Los Angeles. Andrew Lo, the firm's chief financial officer (CFO), has estimated that the investments will pay out cash flows of $200,000 per year for nine years and nothing thereafter. (The cash flows will occur at the end of each year and there will be no cash flow after year 9.) Mr. Lo has determined that the relevant discount rate for this investment is 15 percent. This is the rate of return that the firm can earn at comparable projects. Should the Trojan Pizza Company make the investments in the new outlets?

(continued)

The decision can be evaluated as:

$$\begin{aligned}\text{NPV} &= -\$1{,}000{,}000 + \frac{\$200{,}000}{1.15} + \frac{\$200{,}000}{(1.15)^2} + \cdots + \frac{\$200{,}000}{(1.15)^9} \\ &= -\$1{,}000{,}000 + \$200{,}000 \times A^{9}_{.15} \\ &= -\$1{,}000{,}000 + \$954{,}316.78 \\ &= -\$45{,}683.22\end{aligned}$$

The present value of the four new outlets is only $954,316.78. The outlets are worth less than they cost. The Trojan Pizza Company should not make the investment because the NPV is −$45,683.22. If the Trojan Pizza Company requires a 15 percent rate of return, the new outlets are not a good investment.

SUMMARY AND CONCLUSIONS

1. Two basic concepts, *future value* and *present value*, were introduced in the beginning of this chapter. With a 10 percent interest rate, an investor with $1 today can generate a future value of $1.10 in a year, $1.21 [$\$1 \times (1.10)^2$] in two years, and so on. Conversely, present value analysis places a current value on a later cash flow. With the same 10 percent interest rate, a dollar to be received in one year has a present value of $0.909 ($1/1.10) in year 0. A dollar to be received in two years has a present value of $0.826 [$\$1/(1.10)^2$].
2. One commonly expresses the interest rate as, say, 12 percent per year. However, one can speak of the interest rate as 3 percent per quarter. Although the stated annual interest rate remains 12 percent (3 percent × 4), the effective annual interest rate is 12.55 percent [$(1.03)^4 - 1$]. In other words, the compounding process increases the future value of an investment. The limiting case is continuous compounding, where funds are assumed to be reinvested every infinitesimal instant.
3. A basic quantitative technique for financial decision making is net present value analysis. The net present value formula for an investment that generates cash flows (C_i) in future periods is

$$\text{NPV} = -C_0 + \frac{C_1}{(1+r)} + \frac{C_2}{(1+r)^2} + \cdots + \frac{C_N}{(1+r)^N} = -C_0 + \sum_{i=1}^{T} \frac{C_i}{(1+r)^i}$$

   The formula assumes that the cash flow at date 0 is the initial investment (a cash outflow).
4. Frequently, the actual calculation of present value is long and tedious. The computation of the present value of a long-term mortgage with monthly payments is a good example of this. We presented four simplifying formulas:

$$\textbf{Perpetuity: } \text{PV} = \frac{C}{r}$$

$$\textbf{Growing perpetuity: } \text{PV} = \frac{C}{r-g}$$

$$\textbf{Annuity: } \text{PV} = C\left[\frac{1 - \frac{1}{(1+r)^T}}{r}\right]$$

Growing annuity: $\text{PV} = C\left[\frac{1-\left(\frac{1+g}{1+r}\right)^T}{r-g}\right]$

5. We stressed a few practical considerations in the application of these formulas:
   a. The numerator in each of the formulas, C, is the cash flow to be received *one full period hence.*
   b. Cash flows are generally irregular in practice. To avoid unwieldy problems, assumptions to create more regular cash flows are made both in this textbook and in the real world.
   c. A number of present value problems involve annuities (or perpetuities) beginning a few periods hence. Students should practice combining the annuity (or perpetuity) formula with the discounting formula to solve these problems.
   d. Annuities and perpetuities may have periods of every two or every n years, rather than once a year. The annuity and perpetuity formulas can easily handle such circumstances.
   e. One frequently encounters problems where the present value of one annuity must be equated with the present value of another annuity.

CONCEPT QUESTIONS

1. **Compounding and Period** As you increase the length of time involved, what happens to future values? What happens to present values?
2. **Interest Rates** What happens to the future value of an annuity if you increase the rate r? What happens to the present value?
3. **Present Value** Suppose two athletes sign 10-year contracts for $80 million. In one case, we're told that the $80 million will be paid in 10 equal installments. In the other case, we're told that the $80 million will be paid in 10 installments, but the installments will increase by 5 percent per year. Who got the better deal?
4. **APR and EAR** Should lending laws be changed to require lenders to report EARs instead of APRs? Why or why not?
5. **Time Value** On subsidized Stafford loans, a common source of financial aid for college students, interest does not begin to accrue until repayment begins. Who receives a bigger subsidy, a freshman or a senior? Explain.

Use the following information for the next five questions:

On December 2, 1982, General Motors Acceptance Corporation (GMAC), a subsidiary of General Motors, offered some securities for sale to the public. Under the terms of the deal, GMAC promised to repay the owner of one of these securities $10,000 on December 1, 2012, but the investors would receive nothing until then. Investors paid GMAC $500 for each of these securities on December 2, 1982, for the promise of a $10,000 payment 30 years later.

6. **Time Value of Money** Why would GMAC be willing to accept such a small amount today ($500) in exchange for a promise to repay 20 times that amount ($10,000) in the future?
7. **Call Provisions** GMAC has the right to buy back the securities anytime it wishes by paying $10,000 (this is a term of this particular deal). What impact does this feature have on the desirability of this security as an investment?
8. **Time Value of Money** Would you be willing to pay $500 today in exchange for $10,000 in 30 years? What would be the key considerations in answering yes or no? Would your answer depend on who is making the promise to repay?

9. **Investment Comparison** Suppose that when GMAC offered the security for $500, the U.S. Treasury had offered an essentially identical security. Do you think it would have had a higher or lower price? Why?
10. **Length of Investment** The GMAC security is bought and sold on the New York Stock Exchange. If you looked at the price today, do you think the price would exceed the $500 original price? Why? If you looked in the year 2008, do you think the price would be higher or lower than today's price? Why?

QUESTIONS AND PROBLEMS

Basic
(Questions 1–20)

1. **Simple Interest versus Compound Interest** First City Bank pays 7 percent simple interest on its savings account balances, whereas Second City Bank pays 7 percent interest compounded annually. If you made a $5,000 deposit in each bank, how much more money would you earn from your Second City Bank account at the end of 10 years?
2. **Calculating Future Values** Compute the future value of $1,000 compounded annually for
   a. 10 years at 5 percent
   b. 10 years at 7 percent
   c. 20 years at 5 percent
   d. Why is the interest earned in part (c) not twice the amount earned in part (a)?
3. **Calculating Present Values** For each of the following, compute the present value:

PRESENT VALUE	YEARS	INTEREST RATE	FUTURE VALUE
	6	5%	$ 15,451
	9	11	51,557
	23	16	886,073
	18	19	550,164

4. **Calculating Interest Rates** Solve for the unknown interest rate in each of the following:

PRESENT VALUE	YEARS	INTEREST RATE	FUTURE VALUE
$ 265	2		$ 307
360	9		896
39,000	15		162,181
46,523	30		483,500

5. **Calculating the Number of Periods** Solve for the unknown number of years in each of the following:

PRESENT VALUE	YEARS	INTEREST RATE	FUTURE VALUE
$ 625		8%	$ 1,284
810		7	4,341
18,400		21	402,662
21,500		29	173,439

6. **Calculating the Number of Periods** At 7 percent interest, how long does it take to double your money? To quadruple it?

7. **Calculating Present Values** Imprudential, Inc., has an unfunded pension liability of $800 million that must be paid in 20 years. To assess the value of the firm's stock, financial analysts want to discount this liability back to the present. If the relevant discount rate is 9.5 percent, what is the present value of this liability?

8. **Calculating Rates of Return** Although appealing to more refined tastes, art as a collectible has not always performed so profitably. During 2003, Sothebys sold the Edgar Degas bronze sculpture *Petite Danseuse de Quartorze Ans* at auction for a price of $10,311,500. Unfortunately for the previous owner, he had purchased it in 1999 at a price of $12,377,500. What was his annual rate of return on this sculpture?

9. **Perpetuities** An investor purchasing a British consol is entitled to receive annual payments from the British government forever. What is the price of a consol that pays $120 annually if the next payment occurs one year from today? The market interest rate is 15 percent.

10. **Continuous Compounding** Compute the future value of $1,000 continuously compounded for 
    a. Five years at a stated annual interest rate of 12 percent.
    b. Three years at a stated annual interest rate of 10 percent.
    c. 10 years at a stated annual interest rate of 5 percent.
    d. Eight years at a stated annual interest rate of 7 percent.

11. **Present Value and Multiple Cash Flows** Conoly Co. has identified an investment project with the following cash flows. If the discount rate is 10 percent, what is the present value of these cash flows? What is the present value at 18 percent? At 24 percent?

YEAR	CASH FLOW
1	$1,200
2	600
3	855
4	1,480

12. **Present Value and Multiple Cash Flows** Investment X offers to pay you $4,000 per year for nine years, whereas Investment Y offers to pay you $6,000 per year for five years. Which of these cash flow streams has the higher present value if the discount rate is 5 percent? If the discount rate is 22 percent?

13. **Calculating Annuity Present Value** An investment offers $3,600 per year for 15 years, with the first payment occurring one year from now. If the required return is 10 percent, what is the value of the investment? What would the value be if the payments occurred for 40 years? For 75 years? Forever?

14. **Calculating Perpetuity Values** The Perpetual Life Insurance Co. is trying to sell you an investment policy that will pay you and your heirs $15,000 per year forever. If the required return on this investment is 8 percent, how much will you pay for the policy? Suppose the Perpetual Life Insurance Co. told you the policy costs $195,000. At what interest rate would this be a fair deal?

15. **Calculating EAR** Find the EAR in each of the following cases:

STATED RATE (APR)	NUMBER OF TIMES COMPOUNDED	EFFECTIVE RATE (EAR)
11%	Quarterly	
7	Monthly	
9	Daily	
17	Infinite	

16. **Calculating APR** Find the APR, or stated rate, in each of the following cases:

STATED RATE (APR)	NUMBER OF TIMES COMPOUNDED	EFFECTIVE RATE (EAR)
	Semiannually	8.1%
	Monthly	7.6
	Weekly	16.8
	Infinite	26.2

17. **Calculating EAR** First National Bank charges 12.2 percent compounded monthly on its business loans. First United Bank charges 12.4 percent compounded semiannually. As a potential borrower, which bank would you go to for a new loan?

18. **Interest Rates** Well-known financial writer Andrew Tobias argues that he can earn 177 percent per year buying wine by the case. Specifically, he assumes that he will consume one $10 bottle of fine Bordeaux per week for the next twelve weeks. He can either pay $10 per week or buy a case of 12 bottles today. If he buys the case, he receives a 10 percent discount, and, by doing so, earns the 177 percent. Assume he buys the wine and consumes the first bottle today. Do you agree with his analysis? Do you see a problem with his numbers?

19. **Calculating Number of Periods** One of your customers is delinquent on his accounts payable balance. You've mutually agreed to a repayment schedule of $500 per month. You will charge .9 percent per month interest on the overdue balance. If the current balance is $16,500, how long will it take for the account to be paid off?

20. **Calculating EAR** Friendly's Quick Loans, Inc., offers you "three for four or I knock on your door." This means you get $3 today and repay $4 when you get your paycheck in one week (or else). What's the effective annual return Friendly's earns on this lending business? If you were brave enough to ask, what APR would Friendly's say you were paying?

Intermediate (Questions 21–50)

21 **Future Value** What is the future value in three years of $1,000 invested in an account with a stated annual interest rate of 8 percent,

a. Compounded annually?

b. Compounded semiannually?

c. Compounded monthly?

d. Compounded continuously?

e. Why does the future value increase as the compounding period shortens?

22. **Simple Interest versus Compound Interest** First Simple Bank pays 8 percent simple interest on its investment accounts. If First Complex Bank pays interest on its accounts compounded annually, what rate should the bank set if it wants to match First Simple Bank over an investment horizon of 10 years?

23. **Calculating Annuities** You are planning to save for retirement over the next 30 years. To do this, you will invest $700 a month in a stock account and $300 a month in a bond account. The return of the stock account is expected to be 11 percent, and the bond account will pay 7 percent. When you retire, you will combine your money into an account with a 9 percent return. How much can you withdraw each month from your account assuming a 25-year withdrawal period?

24. **Calculating Rates of Return** Suppose an investment offers to triple your money in 12 months (don't believe it). What rate of return per quarter are you being offered?

25. **Calculating Rates of Return** You're trying to choose between two different investments, both of which have up-front costs of $50,000. Investment G returns $85,000 in five years. Investment H returns $175,000 in 11 years. Which of these investments has the higher return?

26. **Growing Perpetuities** Mark Weinstein has been working on an advanced technology in laser eye surgery. His technology will be available in the near term. He anticipates his first annual cash flow from the technology to be $200,000, received two years from today. Subsequent annual cash flows will grow at 5 percent, in perpetuity. What is the present value of the technology if the discount rate is 10 percent? 

27. **Perpetuities** A prestigious investment bank designed a new security that pays a quarterly dividend of $10 in perpetuity. The first dividend occurs one quarter from today. What is the price of the security if the stated annual interest rate is 12 percent, compounded quarterly?

28. **Annuity Present Values** What is the present value of an annuity of $2,000 per year, with the first cash flow received three years from today and the last one received 22 years from today? Use a discount rate of 8 percent.

29. **Annuity Present Values** What is the value today of a 15-year annuity that pays $500 a year? The annuity's first payment occurs at the end of year 6. The annual interest rate is 12 percent for years 1 through 5, and 15 percent thereafter.

30. **Balloon Payments** Mike Bayles has just arranged to purchase a $400,000 vacation home in the Bahamas with a 20 percent down payment. The mortgage has an 8 percent stated annual interest rate, compounded monthly, and calls for equal monthly payments over the next 30 years. His first payment will be due one month from now. However, the mortgage has an eight-year balloon payment, meaning that the balance of the loan must be paid off at the end of year 8. There were no other transaction costs or finance charges. How much will Mike's balloon payment be in eight years?

31. **Calculating Interest Expense** You receive a credit card application from Shady Banks Savings and Loan offering an introductory rate of 1.90 percent per year, compounded monthly for the first six months, increasing thereafter to 16 percent compounded monthly. Assuming you transfer the $4,000 balance from your existing credit card and make no subsequent payments, how much interest will you owe at the end of the first year?

32. **Perpetuities** Barrett Pharmaceuticals is considering a drug project that costs $240,000 today and is expected to generate end-of-year annual cash flows of $21,000, forever. At what discount rate would Barrett be indifferent between accepting or rejecting the project?

33. **Growing Annuity** Southern California Publishing Company is trying to decide whether or not to revise its popular textbook, *Financial Psychoanalysis Made Simple*. They have estimated that the revision will cost $50,000. Cash flows from increased sales will be $12,000 the first year. These cash flows will increase by 6 percent per year. The book will go out of print five years from now. Assume that the initial cost is paid now and revenues are received at the end of each year. If the company requires an 11 percent return for such an investment, should it undertake the revision?

34. **Growing Annuity** Your job pays you only once a year, for all the work you did over the previous 12 months. Today, December 31, you just received your salary of $50,000 and you plan to spend all of it. However, you want to start saving for retirement beginning next year. You have decided that one year from today you will begin depositing 2 percent of your annual salary in an account that will earn 8 percent per year. Your salary will increase at 4 percent per year throughout your career. How much money will you have on the date of your retirement 40 years from today?

35. **Present Value and Interest Rates** What is the relationship between the value of an annuity and the level of interest rates? Suppose you just bought a 10-year annuity of $5,000 per year at the current interest rate of 10 percent per year. What happens to the value of your investment if interest rates suddenly drop to 5 percent? What if interest rates suddenly rise to 15 percent?

36. **Calculating the Number of Payments** You're prepared to make monthly payments of $125, beginning at the end of this month, into an account that pays 10 percent interest compounded monthly. How many payments will you have made when your account balance reaches $20,000?

37. **Calculating Annuity Present Values** You want to borrow $45,000 from your local bank to buy a new sailboat. You can afford to make monthly payments of $950, but no more. Assuming monthly compounding, what is the highest rate you can afford on a 60-month APR loan?

38. **Calculating Loan Payments** You need a 30-year, fixed-rate mortgage to buy a new home for $200,000. Your mortgage bank will lend you the money at a 6.8 percent APR for this 360-month loan. However, you can only afford monthly payments of $1,000, so you offer to pay off any remaining loan balance at the end of the loan in the form of a single balloon payment. How large will this balloon payment have to be for you to keep your monthly payments at $1,000?

39. **Present and Future Values** The present value of the following cash flow stream is $5,979 when discounted at 10 percent annually. What is the value of the missing cash flow?

YEAR	CASH FLOW
1	$1,000
2	?
3	2,000
4	2,000

40. **Calculating Present Values** You just won the TVM Lottery. You will receive $1 million today plus another 10 annual payments that increase by $400,000 per year. Thus, in one year you receive $1.4 million. In two years, you get $1.8 million, and so on. If the appropriate interest rate is 10 percent, what is the present value of your winnings?

41. **EAR versus APR** You have just purchased a new warehouse. To finance the purchase, you've arranged for a 30-year mortgage loan for 80 percent of the $1,600,000 purchase price. The monthly payment on this loan will be $10,000. What is the APR on this loan? The EAR?

42. **Present Value and Break-Even Interest** Consider a firm with a contract to sell an asset for $115,000 three years from now. The asset costs $72,000 to produce today. Given a relevant discount rate on this asset of 13 percent per year, will the firm make a profit on this asset? At what rate does the firm just break even?

43. **Present Value and Multiple Cash Flows** What is the present value of $2,000 per year, at a discount rate of 12 percent, if the first payment is received 9 years from now and the last payment is received 25 years from now?

44. **Variable Interest Rates** A 15-year annuity pays $1,500 per month, and payments are made at the end of each month. If the interest rate is 15 percent compounded monthly for the first seven years, and 12 percent compounded monthly thereafter, what is the present value of the annuity?

45. **Comparing Cash Flow Streams** You have your choice of two investment accounts. Investment A is a 15-year annuity that features end-of-month $1,000 payments and has an interest rate of 10.5 percent compounded monthly. Investment B is a 9 percent continuously compounded lump-sum investment, also good for 15 years. How much money would you need to invest in B today for it to be worth as much as Investment A 15 years from now?

46. **Calculating Present Value of a Perpetuity** Given an interest rate of 6.5 percent per year, what is the value at date $t = 7$ of a perpetual stream of $3,000 payments that begin at date $t = 15$?

47. **Calculating EAR** A local finance company quotes a 14 percent interest rate on one-year loans. So, if you borrow $20,000, the interest for the year will be $2,800. Because you must repay a total of $22,800 in one year, the finance company requires you to pay $22,800/12, or $1,900, per month over the next 12 months. Is this a 14 percent loan? What rate would legally have to be quoted? What is the effective annual rate?

48. **Calculating Present Values** A 5-year annuity of ten $6,000 semiannual payments will begin 9 years from now, with the first payment coming 9.5 years from now. If the discount rate is

12 percent compounded monthly, what is the value of this annuity five years from now? What is the value three years from now? What is the current value of the annuity?

49. **Calculating Annuities Due** As discussed in the text, an ordinary annuity assumes equal payments at the end of each period over the life of the annuity. An *annuity due* is the same thing except the payments occur at the beginning of each period instead. Thus, a three-year annual annuity due would have periodic payment cash flows occurring at Years 0, 1, and 2, whereas a three-year annual ordinary annuity would have periodic payment cash flows occurring at Years 1, 2, and 3.
    a. At a 9.5 percent annual discount rate, find the present value of a six-year ordinary annuity contract of $525 payments.
    b. Find the present value of the same contract if it is an annuity due.

50. **Calculating Annuities Due** You want to buy a new sports car from Muscle Motors for $56,000. The contract is in the form of a 48-month annuity due at an 8.15 percent APR. What will your monthly payment be?

Challenge (Questions 51–75)

51. **Calculating Annuities Due** You want to lease a set of golf clubs from Pings Ltd. The lease contract is in the form of 24 equal monthly payments at a 12 percent stated annual interest rate, compounded monthly. Since the clubs cost $4,000 retail, Pings wants the PV of the lease payments to equal $4,000. Suppose that your first payment is due immediately. What will your monthly lease payments be?

52. **Annuities** You are saving for the college education of your two children. They are two years apart in age; one will begin college 15 years from today and the other will begin 17 years from today. You estimate your children's college expenses to be $23,000 per year per child, payable at the beginning of each school year. The annual interest rate is 6.5 percent. How much money must you deposit in an account each year to fund your children's education? Your deposits begin one year from today. You will make your last deposit when your oldest child enters college. Assume four years of college.

53. **Growing Annuities** Tom Adams has received a job offer from a large investment bank as a clerk to an associate banker. His base salary will be $35,000. He will receive his first annual salary payment one year from the day he begins to work. In addition, he will get an immediate $10,000 bonus for joining the company. His salary will grow at 4 percent each year. Each year he will receive a bonus equal to 10 percent of his salary. Mr. Adams is expected to work for 25 years. What is the present value of the offer if the discount rate is 12 percent?

54. **Calculating Annuities** You have recently won the super jackpot in the Washington state lottery. On reading the fine print, you discover that you have the following two options:
    a. You will receive 31 annual payments of $160,000, with the first payment being delivered today. The income will be taxed at a rate of 28 percent. Taxes will be withheld when the checks are issued.
    b. You will receive $446,000 now, and you will not have to pay taxes on this amount. In addition, beginning one year from today, you will receive $101,055 each year for 30 years. The cash flows from this annuity will be taxed at 28 percent.

    Using a discount rate of 10 percent, which option should you select?

55. **Calculating Growing Annuities** You have 30 years left until retirement and want to retire with $1 million. Your salary is paid annually and you will receive $55,000 at the end of the current year. Your salary will increase at 3 percent per year, and you can earn a 10 percent return on the money you invest. If you save a constant percentage of your salary, what percentage of your salary must you save each year?

56. **Balloon Payments** On September 1, 2004, Susan Chao bought a motorcycle for $15,000. She paid $1,000 down and financed the balance with a five-year loan at a stated annual interest rate

of 9.6 percent, compounded monthly. She started the monthly payments exactly one month after the purchase (i.e., October 1, 2004). Two years later, at the end of October 2006, Susan got a new job and decided to pay off the loan. If the bank charges her a 1 percent prepayment penalty based on the loan balance, how much must she pay the bank on November 1, 2006?

57. **Calculating Annuity Values** Bilbo Baggins wants to save money to meet three objectives. First, he would like to be able to retire 30 years from now with a retirement income of $25,000 per month for 20 years, with the first payment received 30 years and 1 month from now. Second, he would like to purchase a cabin in Rivendell in 10 years at an estimated cost of $350,000. Third, after he passes on at the end of the 20 years of withdrawals, he would like to leave an inheritance of $750,000 to his nephew Frodo. He can afford to save $2,100 per month for the next 10 years. If he can earn an 11 percent EAR before he retires and an 8 percent EAR after he retires, how much will he have to save each month in years 11 through 30?

58. **Calculating Annuity Values** After deciding to buy a new car, you can either lease the car or purchase it with a 3-year loan. The car you wish to buy costs $35,000. The dealer has a special leasing arrangement where you pay $1 today and $450 per month for the next three years. If you purchase the car, you will pay it off in monthly payments over the next three years at an 8 percent APR. You believe that you will be able to sell the car for $23,000 in three years. Should you buy or lease the car? What break-even resale price in three years would make you indifferent between buying and leasing?

59. **Calculating Annuity Values** An All-Pro defensive lineman is in contract negotiations. The team has offered the following salary structure:

TIME	SALARY
0	$8,000,000
1	$4,000,000
2	$4,800,000
3	$5,700,000
4	$6,400,000
5	$7,000,000
6	$7,500,000

All salaries are to be paid in a lump sum. The player has asked you as his agent to renegotiate the terms. He wants a $9 million signing bonus payable today and a contract value increase of $750,000. He also wants an equal salary paid every three months, with the first paycheck three months from now. If the interest rate is 4.5 percent compounded daily, what is the amount of his quarterly check? Assume 365 days in a year.

60. **Discount Interest Loans** This question illustrates what is known as *discount interest.* Imagine you are discussing a loan with a somewhat unscrupulous lender. You want to borrow $20,000 for one year. The interest rate is 12 percent. You and the lender agree that the interest on the loan will be .12 $\times$ $20,000 = $2,400. So the lender deducts this interest amount from the loan up front and gives you $17,600. In this case, we say that the discount is $2,400. What's wrong here?

61. **Calculating Annuity Values** You are serving on a jury. A plaintiff is suing the city for injuries sustained after a freak street sweeper accident. In the trial, doctors testified that it will be five years before the plaintiff is able to return to work. The jury has already decided in favor of the plaintiff. You are the foreperson of the jury and propose that the jury give the plaintiff an award to cover the following: 1) The present value of two years' back pay. The plaintiff's annual salary for the last two years would have been $40,000 and $43,000, respectively. 2) The present value of five years' future salary. You assume the salary will be $45,000 per year. 3) $100,000 for pain and suffering. 4) $20,000 for court costs. Assume that the salary payments are equal amounts

paid at the end of each month. If the interest rate you choose is a 9 percent EAR, what is the size of the settlement? If you were the plaintiff, would you like to see a higher or lower interest rate?

62. **Calculating EAR with Points** You are looking at a one-year loan of $10,000. The interest rate is quoted as 10 percent plus three points. A *point* on a loan is simply 1 percent (one percentage point) of the loan amount. Quotes similar to this one are very common with home mortgages. The interest rate quotation in this example requires the borrower to pay three points to the lender up front and repay the loan later with 10 percent interest. What rate would you actually be paying here?

63. **Calculating EAR with Points** The interest rate on a one-year loan is quoted as 13 percent plus two points (see the previous problem). What is the EAR? Is your answer affected by the loan amount?

64. **EAR versus APR** There are two banks in the area that offer 30-year, $200,000 mortgages at 7.5 percent and charge a $1,500 loan application fee. However, the application fee charged by Insecurity Bank and Trust is refundable if the loan application is denied, whereas that charged by I. M. Greedy and Sons Mortgage Bank is not. The current disclosure law requires that any fees that will be refunded if the applicant is rejected be included in calculating the APR, but this is not required with nonrefundable fees (presumably because refundable fees are part of the loan rather than a fee). What are the EARs on these two loans? What are the APRs?

65. **Calculating EAR with Add-On Interest** This problem illustrates a deceptive way of quoting interest rates called *add-on interest.* Imagine that you see an advertisement for Crazy Judy's Stereo City that reads something like this: "$1,000 Instant Credit! 15% Simple Interest! Three Years to Pay! Low, Low Monthly Payments!" You're not exactly sure what all this means and somebody has spilled ink over the APR on the loan contract, so you ask the manager for clarification.

    Judy explains that if you borrow $1,000 for three years at 15 percent interest, in three years you will owe:

    $\$1{,}000 \times 1.15^3 = \$1{,}000 \times 1.52088 = \$1{,}520.88$

    Now, Judy recognizes that coming up with $1,520.88 all at once might be a strain, so she lets you make "low, low monthly payments" of $1,520.88/36 = $42.25 per month, even though this is extra bookkeeping work for her.

    Is this a 15 percent loan? Why or why not? What is the APR on this loan? What is the EAR? Why do you think this is called add-on interest?

66. **Calculating Annuity Payments** This is a classic retirement problem. A time line will help in solving it. Your friend is celebrating her 35th birthday today and wants to start saving for her anticipated retirement at age 65. She wants to be able to withdraw $90,000 from her savings account on each birthday for 15 years following her retirement; the first withdrawal will be on her 66th birthday. Your friend intends to invest her money in the local credit union, which offers 8 percent interest per year. She wants to make equal annual payments on each birthday into the account established at the credit union for her retirement fund.

    a. If she starts making these deposits on her 36th birthday and continues to make deposits until she is 65 (the last deposit will be on her 65th birthday), what amount must she deposit annually to be able to make the desired withdrawals at retirement?

    b. Suppose your friend has just inherited a large sum of money. Rather than making equal annual payments, she has decided to make one lump-sum payment on her 35th birthday to cover her retirement needs. What amount does she have to deposit?

    c. Suppose your friend's employer will contribute $1,500 to the account every year as part of the company's profit-sharing plan. In addition, your friend expects a $25,000 distribution from a family trust fund on her 55th birthday, which she will also put into the retirement account. What amount must she deposit annually now to be able to make the desired withdrawals at retirement?

67. **Calculating the Number of Periods** Your Christmas ski vacation was great, but it unfortunately ran a bit over budget. All is not lost, because you just received an offer in the mail to transfer your $10,000 balance from your current credit card, which charges an annual rate of 19.2 percent, to a new credit card charging a rate of 9.2 percent. How much faster could you pay the loan off by making your planned monthly payments of $200 with the new card? What if there was a 2 percent fee charged on any balances transferred?

68. **Future Value and Multiple Cash Flows** An insurance company is offering a new policy to its customers. Typically, the policy is bought by a parent or grandparent for a child at the child's birth. The details of the policy are as follows: The purchaser (say, the parent) makes the following six payments to the insurance company:

First birthday:	$750
Second birthday:	$750
Third birthday:	$850
Fourth birthday:	$850
Fifth birthday:	$950
Sixth birthday:	$950

After the child's sixth birthday, no more payments are made. When the child reaches age 65, he or she receives $250,000. If the relevant interest rate is 11 percent for the first six years and 7 percent for all subsequent years, is the policy worth buying?

69. **Annuity Present Values and Effective Rates** You have just won the lottery. You will receive $1,000,000 today, and then receive 40 payments of $500,000. These payments will start one year from now and will be paid every six months. A representative from Greenleaf Investments has offered to purchase all the payments from you for $10 million. If the appropriate interest rate is a 9 percent APR compounded daily, should you take the offer? Assume there are 12 months in a year, each with 30 days.

70. **Calculating Interest Rates** A financial planning service offers a college savings program. The plan calls for you to make six annual payments of $8,000 each, with the first payment occurring today, your child's 12th birthday. Beginning on your child's 18th birthday, the plan will provide $20,000 per year for four years. What return is this investment offering?

71. **Break-Even Investment Returns** Your financial planner offers you two different investment plans. Plan X is a $10,000 annual perpetuity. Plan Y is a 10-year, $22,000 annual annuity. Both plans will make their first payment one year from today. At what discount rate would you be indifferent between these two plans?

72. **Perpetual Cash Flows** What is the value of an investment that pays $6,700 every *other* year forever, if the first payment occurs one year from today and the discount rate is 13 percent compounded daily? What is the value today if the first payment occurs four years from today?

73. **Ordinary Annuities and Annuities Due** As discussed in the text, an annuity due is identical to an ordinary annuity except that the periodic payments occur at the beginning of each period and not at the end of the period. Show that the relationship between the value of an ordinary annuity and the value of an otherwise equivalent annuity due is:

$$\text{Annuity due value} = \text{Ordinary annuity value} \times (1 + r)$$

Show this for both present and future values.

74. **Calculating Annuities Due** A 10-year annual annuity due with the first payment occurring at date $t = 7$ has a current value of $75,000. If the discount rate is 10 percent per year, what is the annuity payment amount?

75. **Calculating EAR** A check-cashing store is in the business of making personal loans to walk-up customers. The store makes only one-week loans at 10 percent interest per week.

a. What APR must the store report to its customers? What is the EAR that the customers are actually paying?

b. Now suppose the store makes one-week loans at 10 percent discount interest per week (see Question 60). What's the APR now? The EAR?

c. The check-cashing store also makes one-month add-on interest loans at 9 percent discount interest per week. Thus, if you borrow \$100 for one month (four weeks), the interest will be ($\$100 \times 1.09^4$) $-$ 100 $=$ \$41.16. Because this is discount interest, your net loan proceeds today will be \$58.84. You must then repay the store \$100 at the end of the month. To help you out, though, the store lets you pay off this \$100 in installments of \$25 per week. What is the APR of this loan? What is the EAR?

S&P PROBLEMS

www.mhhe.com/edumarketinsight

STANDARD
&POOR'S

1. **Calculating Future Values** Under the "Excel Analytics" link find the "Mthly. Adj. Price" for Elizabeth Arden (RDEN) stock. What was your annual return over the last four years assuming you purchased the stock at the close price four years ago? (Assume no dividends were paid.) Using this same return, what price will Elizabeth Arden stock sell for five years from now? Ten years from now? What if the stock price increases at 11 percent per year?
2. **Calculating the Number of Periods** Find the monthly adjusted stock prices for Southwest Airlines (LUV). You find an analyst who projects the stock price will increase 12 percent per year for the foreseeable future. Based on the most recent monthly stock price, if the projection holds true, when will the stock price reach \$150? When will it reach \$200?

WHAT'S ON THE WEB?

1. **Calculating Future Values** Go to www.dinkytown.net and follow the "Savings Calculator" link. If you currently have \$10,000 and invest this money at 9 percent, how much will you have in 30 years? Assume you will not make any additional contributions. How much will you have if you can earn 11 percent?
2. **Calculating the Number of Periods** Go to www.dinkytown.net and follow the "Cool Million" link. You want to be a millionaire. You can earn 11.5 percent per year. Using your current age, at what age will you become a millionaire if you have \$25,000 to invest, assuming you make no other deposits (assume inflation is zero)?
3. **Future Values and Taxes** Taxes can greatly affect the future value of your investment. The Financial Calculators Web site at www.fincalc.com has a financial calculator that adjusts your return for taxes. Suppose you have \$50,000 to invest today. If you can earn a 12 percent return and no additional annual savings, how much will you have in 20 years? (Enter 0 percent as the tax rate.) Now, assume that your marginal tax rate is 27.5 percent. How much will you have at this tax rate?

CLOSING CASE

THE MBA DECISION

Ben Bates graduated from college six years ago with a finance undergraduate degree. Although he is satisfied with his current job, his goal is to become an investment banker. He feels that a MBA degree would allow him to achieve this goal. After examining schools, he has narrowed his choice to either Wilton University or Mount Perry College. Although internships are encouraged by both schools, to get class credit for the internship, no salary can be paid. Other than internships, neither school will allow its students to work while enrolled in its MBA program.

Ben currently works at the money management firm of Dewey and Louis. His annual salary at the firm is $50,000 per year, and his salary is expected to increase at 3 percent per year until retirement. He is currently 28 years old and expects to work for 35 more years. His current job includes a fully paid health insurance plan, and his current average tax rate is 26 percent. Ben has a savings account with enough money to cover the entire cost of his MBA program.

The Ritter College of Business at Wilton University is one of the top MBA programs in the country. The MBA degree requires two years of full-time enrollment at the university. The annual tuition is $60,000, payable at the beginning of each school year. Books and other supplies are estimated to cost $2,500 per year. Ben expects that after graduation from Wilton, he will receive a job offer for about $95,000 per year, with a $15,000 signing bonus. The salary at this job will increase at 4 percent per year. Because of the higher salary, his average income tax rate will increase to 31 percent.

The Bradley School of Business at Mount Perry College began its MBA program 16 years ago. The Bradley School is smaller and less well known than the Ritter College. Bradley offers an accelerated, one-year program, with a tuition cost of $75,000 to be paid upon matriculation. Books and other supplies for the program are expected to cost $3,500. Ben thinks that he will receive an offer of $78,000 per year upon graduation, with a $10,000 signing bonus. His average tax rate at this level of income will be 29 percent.

Both schools offer a health insurance plan that will cost $3,000 per year, payable at the beginning of the year. Ben also estimates that room and board expenses will cost $20,000 per year at both schools. The appropriate discount rate is 6.5 percent.

1. How does Ben's age affect his decision to get an MBA?
2. What other, perhaps nonquantifiable factors, affect Ben's decision to get an MBA?
3. Assuming all salaries are paid at the end of each year, what is the best option for Ben—from a strictly financial standpoint?
4. Ben believes that the appropriate analysis is to calculate the future value of each option. How would you evaluate this statement?
5. What initial salary would Ben need to receive to make him indifferent between attending Wilton University and staying in his current position?
6. Suppose, instead of being able to pay cash for his MBA, Ben must borrow the money. The current borrowing rate is 5.4 percent. How would this affect his decision?

CHAPTER 5

Interest Rates and Bond Valuation

OPENING CASE

In its most basic form, a bond is a pretty simple financial instrument. You loan a company some money, say $10,000. The company pays you interest on a regular basis, and it repays the original loan amount of $10,000 at some point in the future. But bonds also can have unusual characteristics. For example, in 2002, Berkshire Hathaway, the company run by legendary investor Warren Buffett, issued some bonds with a surprising feature. Basically, bond buyers were required to *make* interest payments to Berkshire Hathaway for the privilege of owning the bonds, and the interest payments had to be made upfront! Furthermore, if you paid $10,663.63 for one of these bonds, Berkshire Hathaway promised to pay you $10,000 in five years. Does this sound like a good deal? Investors must have thought it did; they bought $400 million worth!

This chapter takes what we have learned about the time value of money and shows how it can be used to value one of the most common of all financial assets, a bond. It then discusses bond features, bond types, and the operation of the bond market. What we will see is that bond prices depend critically on interest rates, so we will go on to discuss some very fundamental issues regarding interest rates. Clearly, interest rates are important to everybody because they underlie what businesses of all types—small and large—must pay to borrow money.

Our goal in this chapter is to introduce you to bonds. We begin by showing how the techniques we developed in Chapter 4 can be applied to bond valuation. From there, we go on to discuss bond features and how bonds are bought and sold. One important thing we learn is that bond values depend, in large part, on interest rates. We therefore close out the chapter with an examination of interest rates and their behavior.

5.1 BONDS AND BOND VALUATION

When a corporation (or government) wishes to borrow money from the public on a long-term basis, it usually does so by issuing or selling debt securities that are generically called bonds. In this section, we describe the various features of corporate bonds and some of the terminology associated with bonds. We then discuss the cash flows associated with a bond and how bonds can be valued using our discounted cash flow procedure.

Bond Features and Prices

As we mentioned in our previous chapter, a bond is normally an interest-only loan, meaning that the borrower will pay the interest every period, but none of the principal will be repaid until the end of the loan. For example, suppose the Beck Corporation wants to borrow $1,000 for 30 years. The interest rate on similar debt issued by similar corporations is 12 percent. Beck will thus pay $.12 \times \$1{,}000 = \$120$ in interest every year for 30 years. At the end of 30 years, Beck will repay the $1,000. As this example suggests, a bond is a fairly simple financing arrangement. There is, however, a rich jargon associated with bonds, so we will use this example to define some of the more important terms.

In our example, the $120 regular interest payments that Beck promises to make are called the bond's **coupons**. Because the coupon is constant and paid every year, the type of bond we are describing is sometimes called a *level coupon bond.* The amount that will be repaid at the end of the loan is called the bond's **face value**, or **par value**. As in our example, this par value is usually $1,000 for corporate bonds, and a bond that sells for its par value is called a *par value bond.* Government bonds frequently have much larger face, or par, values. Finally, the annual coupon divided by the face value is called the **coupon rate** on the bond; in this case, because $\$120/1{,}000 = 12$ percent, the bond has a 12 percent coupon rate.

The number of years until the face value is paid is called the bond's time to **maturity**. A corporate bond will frequently have a maturity of 30 years when it is originally issued, but this varies. Once the bond has been issued, the number of years to maturity declines as time goes by.

Bond Values and Yields

As time passes, interest rates change in the marketplace. The cash flows from a bond, however, stay the same. As a result, the value of the bond will fluctuate. When interest rates rise, the present value of the bond's remaining cash flows declines, and the bond is worth less. When interest rates fall, the bond is worth more.

To determine the value of a bond at a particular point in time, we need to know the number of periods remaining until maturity, the face value, the coupon, and the market interest rate for bonds with similar features. This interest rate required in the market on a bond is called the bond's **yield to maturity (YTM)**. This rate is sometimes called the bond's *yield* for short. Given all this information, we can calculate the present value of the cash flows as an estimate of the bond's current market value.

For example, suppose the Xanth (pronounced "zanth") Co. were to issue a bond with 10 years to maturity. The Xanth bond has an annual coupon of $80. Similar bonds have a yield to maturity of 8 percent. Based on our preceding discussion, the Xanth bond will

FIGURE 5.1

Cash Flows for Xanth Co. Bond

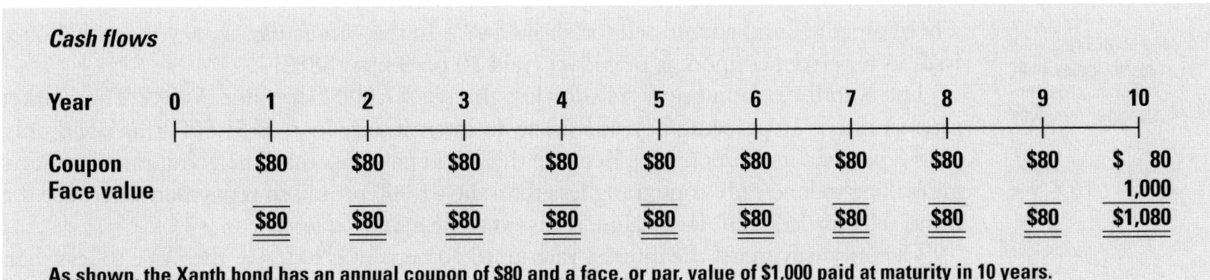

pay $80 per year for the next 10 years in coupon interest. In 10 years, Xanth will pay $1,000 to the owner of the bond. The cash flows from the bond are shown in Figure 5.1. What would this bond sell for?

As illustrated in Figure 5.1, the Xanth bond's cash flows have an annuity component (the coupons) and a lump sum (the face value paid at maturity). We thus estimate the market value of the bond by calculating the present value of these two components separately and adding the results together. First, at the going rate of 8 percent, the present value of the $1,000 paid in 10 years is:

$$\textbf{Present value} = \$1{,}000/1.08^{10} = \$1{,}000/2.1589 = \$463.19$$

Second, the bond offers $80 per year for 10 years; the present value of this annuity stream is:

$$\begin{aligned}\textbf{Annuity present value} &= \$80 \times (1 - 1/1.08^{10})/.08 \\ &= \$80 \times (1 - 1/2.1589)/.08 \\ &= \$80 \times 6.7101 \\ &= \$536.81\end{aligned}$$

We can now add the values for the two parts together to get the bond's value:

$$\textbf{Total bond value} = \$463.19 + 536.81 = \$1{,}000$$

This bond sells for exactly its face value. This is not a coincidence. The going interest rate in the market is 8 percent. Considered as an interest-only loan, what interest rate does this bond have? With an $80 coupon, this bond pays exactly 8 percent interest only when it sells for $1,000.

To illustrate what happens as interest rates change, suppose that a year has gone by. The Xanth bond now has nine years to maturity. If the interest rate in the market has risen to 10 percent, what will the bond be worth? To find out, we repeat the present value calculations with 9 years instead of 10, and a 10 percent yield instead of an 8 percent yield. First, the present value of the $1,000 paid in nine years at 10 percent is:

$$\textbf{Present value} = \$1{,}000/1.10^{9} = \$1{,}000/2.3579 = \$424.10$$

Second, the bond now offers $80 per year for nine years; the present value of this annuity stream at 10 percent is:

$$\begin{aligned}\textbf{Annuity present value} &= \$80 \times (1 - 1/1.10^{9})/.10 \\ &= \$80 \times (1 - 1/2.3579)/.10 \\ &= \$80 \times 5.7590 \\ &= \$460.72\end{aligned}$$

We can now add the values for the two parts together to get the bond's value:

$$\textbf{Total bond value} = \$424.10 + 460.72 = \$884.82$$

A good bond site to visit is bonds.yahoo.com, which has loads of useful information.

Therefore, the bond should sell for about \$885. In the vernacular, we say that this bond, with its 8 percent coupon, is priced to yield 10 percent at \$885.

The Xanth Co. bond now sells for less than its \$1,000 face value. Why? The market interest rate is 10 percent. Considered as an interest-only loan of \$1,000, this bond only pays 8 percent, its coupon rate. Because this bond pays less than the going rate, investors are willing to lend only something less than the \$1,000 promised repayment. Because the bond sells for less than face value, it is said to be a *discount bond.*

The only way to get the interest rate up to 10 percent is to lower the price to less than \$1,000 so that the purchaser, in effect, has a built-in gain. For the Xanth bond, the price of \$885 is \$115 less than the face value, so an investor who purchased and kept the bond would get \$80 per year and would have a \$115 gain at maturity as well. This gain compensates the lender for the below-market coupon rate.

Another way to see why the bond is discounted by \$115 is to note that the \$80 coupon is \$20 below the coupon on a newly issued par value bond, based on current market conditions. The bond would be worth \$1,000 only if it had a coupon of \$100 per year. In a sense, an investor who buys and keeps the bond gives up \$20 per year for nine years. At 10 percent, this annuity stream is worth:

$$\begin{aligned}\textbf{Annuity present value} &= \$20 \times (1 - 1/1.10^9)/.10\\ &= \$20 \times 5.7590\\ &= \$115.18\end{aligned}$$

This is just the amount of the discount.

Online bond calculators are available at personal.fidelity.com; interest rate information is available at money.cnn.com/markets/bondcenter and www.bankrate.com.

What would the Xanth bond sell for if interest rates had dropped by 2 percent instead of rising by 2 percent? As you might guess, the bond would sell for more than \$1,000. Such a bond is said to sell at a *premium* and is called a *premium bond.*

This case is just the opposite of that of a discount bond. The Xanth bond now has a coupon rate of 8 percent when the market rate is only 6 percent. Investors are willing to pay a premium to get this extra coupon amount. In this case, the relevant discount rate is 6 percent, and there are nine years remaining. The present value of the \$1,000 face amount is:

$$\textbf{Present value} = \$1{,}000/1.06^9 = \$1{,}000/1.6895 = \$591.89$$

The present value of the coupon stream is:

$$\begin{aligned}\textbf{Annuity present value} &= \$80 \times (1 - 1/1.06^9)/.06\\ &= \$80 \times (1 - 1/1.6895)/.06\\ &= \$80 \times 6.8017\\ &= \$544.14\end{aligned}$$

We can now add the values for the two parts together to get the bond's value:

$$\textbf{Total bond value} = \$591.89 + 544.14 = \$1{,}136.03$$

Total bond value is therefore about \$136 in excess of par value. Once again, we can verify this amount by noting that the coupon is now \$20 too high, based on current market conditions. The present value of \$20 per year for nine years at 6 percent is:

$$\begin{aligned}\textbf{Annuity present value} &= \$20 \times (1 - 1/1.06^9)/.06\\ &= \$20 \times 6.8017\\ &= \$136.03\end{aligned}$$

This is just as we calculated.

Based on our examples, we can now write the general expression for the value of a bond. If a bond has (1) a face value of F paid at maturity, (2) a coupon of C paid per period, (3) T periods to maturity, and (4) a yield of r per period, its value is:

$$\textbf{Bond value} = C \times [1 - 1/(1 + r)^T]/r \quad + \quad F/(1 + r)^T \tag{5.1}$$

$$\textbf{Bond value} = \begin{array}{c}\textbf{Present value}\\ \textbf{of the coupons}\end{array} + \begin{array}{c}\textbf{Present value of}\\ \textbf{the face amount}\end{array}$$

EXAMPLE 5.1 Semiannual Coupons

In practice, bonds issued in the United States usually make coupon payments twice a year. So, if an ordinary bond has a coupon rate of 14 percent, then the owner will get a total of $140 per year, but this $140 will come in two payments of $70 each. Suppose we are examining such a bond. The yield to maturity is quoted at 16 percent.

Bond yields are quoted like APRs; the quoted rate is equal to the actual rate per period multiplied by the number of periods. In this case, with a 16 percent quoted yield and semiannual payments, the true yield is 8 percent per six months. The bond matures in seven years. What is the bond's price? What is the effective annual yield on this bond?

Based on our discussion, we know the bond will sell at a discount because it has a coupon rate of 7 percent every six months when the market requires 8 percent every six months. So, if our answer exceeds $1,000, we know that we have made a mistake.

To get the exact price, we first calculate the present value of the bond's face value of $1,000 paid in seven years. This seven-year period has 14 periods of six months each. At 8 percent per period, the value is:

$$\text{Present value} = \$1{,}000/1.08^{14} = \$1{,}000/2.9372 = \$340.46$$

The coupons can be viewed as a 14-period annuity of $70 per period. At an 8 percent discount rate, the present value of such an annuity is:

$$\begin{aligned}\text{Annuity present value} &= \$70 \times (1 - 1/1.08^{14})/.08\\ &= \$70 \times (1 - .3405)/.08\\ &= \$70 \times 8.2442\\ &= \$577.10\end{aligned}$$

The total present value gives us what the bond should sell for:

$$\text{Total present value} = \$340.46 + 577.10 = \$917.56$$

To calculate the effective yield on this bond, note that 8 percent every six months is equivalent to:

$$\text{Effective annual rate} = (1 + .08)^2 - 1 = 16.64\%$$

The effective yield, therefore, is 16.64 percent.

As we have illustrated in this section, bond prices and interest rates always move in opposite directions. When interest rates rise, a bond's value, like any other present value, will decline. Similarly, when interest rates fall, bond values rise. Even if we are considering a bond that is riskless in the sense that the borrower is certain to make all the payments, there is still risk in owning a bond. We discuss this next.

Learn more about bonds at investorguide.com.

Interest Rate Risk

The risk that arises for bond owners from fluctuating interest rates is called *interest rate risk*. How much interest rate risk a bond has depends on how sensitive its price is to interest rate changes. This sensitivity directly depends on two things: the time to maturity and the coupon rate. As we will see momentarily, you should keep the following in mind when looking at a bond:

1. All other things being equal, the longer the time to maturity, the greater the interest rate risk.
2. All other things being equal, the lower the coupon rate, the greater the interest rate risk.

We illustrate the first of these two points in Figure 5.2. As shown, we compute and plot prices under different interest rate scenarios for 10 percent coupon bonds with maturities of 1 year and 30 years. Notice how the slope of the line connecting the prices is much steeper for the 30-year maturity than it is for the 1-year maturity. This steepness tells us that a relatively small change in interest rates will lead to a substantial change in the bond's value. In comparison, the one-year bond's price is relatively insensitive to interest rate changes.

Intuitively, we can see that the reason that longer-term bonds have greater interest rate sensitivity is that a large portion of a bond's value comes from the $1,000 face amount. The present value of this amount isn't greatly affected by a small change in interest rates if the amount is to be received in one year. Even a small change in the interest rate, however, once it is compounded for 30 years, can have a significant effect on the present value. As a result, the present value of the face amount will be much more volatile with a longer-term bond.

FIGURE 5.2
Interest Rate Risk and Time to Maturity

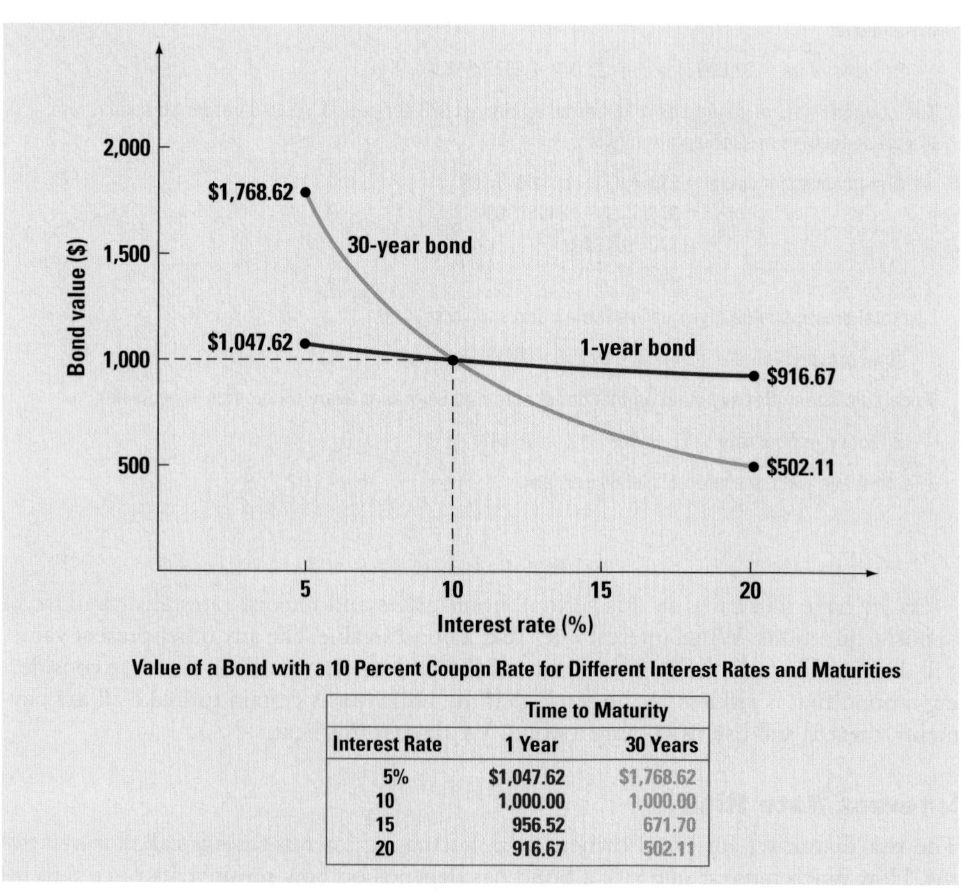

Value of a Bond with a 10 Percent Coupon Rate for Different Interest Rates and Maturities

	Time to Maturity	
Interest Rate	1 Year	30 Years
5%	$1,047.62	$1,768.62
10	1,000.00	1,000.00
15	956.52	671.70
20	916.67	502.11

The other thing to know about interest rate risk is that, like most things in finance and economics, it increases at a decreasing rate. In other words, if we compared a 10-year bond to a 1-year bond, we would see that the 10-year bond has much greater interest rate risk. However, if you were to compare a 20-year bond to a 30-year bond, you would find that the 30-year bond has somewhat greater interest rate risk because it has a longer maturity, but the difference in the risk would be fairly small.

The reason that bonds with lower coupons have greater interest rate risk is essentially the same. As we discussed earlier, the value of a bond depends on the present value of its coupons and the present value of the face amount. If two bonds with different coupon rates have the same maturity, then the value of the one with the lower coupon is proportionately more dependent on the face amount to be received at maturity. As a result, all other things being equal, its value will fluctuate more as interest rates change. Put another way, the bond with the higher coupon has a larger cash flow early in its life, so its value is less sensitive to changes in the discount rate.

Bonds are rarely issued with maturities longer than 30 years. However, low interest rates in recent years have led to the issuance of much longer-term issues. In the 1990s, Walt Disney issued "Sleeping Beauty" bonds with a 100-year maturity. Similarly, BellSouth, Coca-Cola, and Dutch banking giant ABN AMRO all issued bonds with 100-year maturities. These companies evidently wanted to lock in the historical low interest rates for a *long* time. The current record holder for corporations looks to be Republic National Bank, which sold bonds with 1,000 years to maturity. Before these fairly recent issues, it appears the last time 100-year bonds were issued was in May 1954, by the Chicago and Eastern Railroad. Just in case you are wondering when the next 100-year bonds will be issued, you might have a long wait. The IRS has warned companies about such long-term issues and threatened to disallow the interest payment deduction on these bonds.

We can illustrate the effect of interest rate risk using the 100-year BellSouth issue and one other BellSouth issue. The following table provides some basic information on the two issues, along with their prices on December 31, 1995, July 31, 1996, and March 23, 2005.

MATURITY	COUPON RATE	PRICE ON 12/31/95	PRICE ON 7/31/96	PERCENTAGE CHANGE IN PRICE 1995–96	PRICE ON 3/23/05	PERCENTAGE CHANGE IN PRICE 1996–05
2095	7.00%	$1,000.00	$800.00	−20.0%	$1,172.50	+46.6%
2033	6.75	976.25	886.25	− 9.2	$1,033.30	+16.6

Several things emerge from this table. First, interest rates apparently rose between December 31, 1995, and July 31, 1996 (why?). After that, however, they fell (why?). Second, the longer-term bond's price first lost 20 percent and then gained 46.6 percent. These swings are much greater than those on the shorter-lived issue, which illustrates that longer-term bonds have greater interest rate risk.

Finding the Yield to Maturity: More Trial and Error

Frequently, we will know a bond's price, coupon rate, and maturity date, but not its yield to maturity. For example, suppose we are interested in a six-year, 8 percent coupon bond. A broker quotes a price of $955.14. What is the yield on this bond?

We've seen that the price of a bond can be written as the sum of its annuity and lump-sum components. Knowing that there is an \$80 coupon for six years and a \$1,000 face value, we can say that the price is:

$$\$955.14 = \$80 \times [1 - 1/(1 + r)^6]/r + 1{,}000/(1 + r)^6$$

where r is the unknown discount rate, or yield to maturity. We have one equation here and one unknown, but we cannot solve it for r explicitly. The only way to find the answer is to use trial and error.

This problem is essentially identical to the one we examined in the last chapter when we tried to find the unknown interest rate on an annuity. However, finding the rate (or yield) on a bond is even more complicated because of the \$1,000 face amount.

We can speed up the trial-and-error process by using what we know about bond prices and yields. In this case, the bond has an \$80 coupon and is selling at a discount. We thus know that the yield is greater than 8 percent. If we compute the price at 10 percent:

$$\begin{aligned}\textbf{Bond value} &= \$80 \times (1 - 1/1.10^6)/.10 + 1{,}000/1.10^6 \\ &= \$80 \times 4.3553 + 1{,}000/1.7716 \\ &= \$912.89\end{aligned}$$

Current market rates are available at www.bankrate.com.

At 10 percent, the value we calculate is lower than the actual price, so 10 percent is too high. The true yield must be somewhere between 8 and 10 percent. At this point, it's "plug and chug" to find the answer. You would probably want to try 9 percent next. If you did, you would see that this is in fact the bond's yield to maturity.

A bond's yield to maturity should not be confused with its **current yield**, which is simply a bond's annual coupon divided by its price. In the example we just worked, the bond's annual coupon was \$80, and its price was \$955.14. Given these numbers, we see that the current yield is \$80/955.14 = 8.38 percent, which is less than the yield to maturity of 9 percent. The reason the current yield is too low is that it only considers the coupon portion of your return; it doesn't consider the built-in gain from the price discount. For a premium bond, the reverse is true, meaning that current yield would be higher because it ignores the built-in loss.

Our discussion of bond valuation is summarized in Table 5.1. A nearby *Spreadsheet Techniques* box shows how to find prices and yields the easy way.

EXAMPLE 5.2 Current Events

A bond has a quoted price of \$1,080.42. It has a face value of \$1,000, a semiannual coupon of \$30, and a maturity of five years. What is its current yield? What is its yield to maturity? Which is bigger? Why?

Notice that this bond makes semiannual payments of \$30, so the annual payment is \$60. The current yield is thus \$60/1,080.42 = 5.55 percent. To calculate the yield to maturity, refer back to Example 5.1. Now, in this case, the bond pays \$30 every six months and it has 10 six-month periods until maturity. So, we need to find r as follows:

$$\$1{,}080.42 = \$30 \times [1 - 1/(1 + r)^{10}]/r + 1{,}000/(1 + r)^{10}$$

After some trial and error, we find that r is equal to 2.1 percent. But, the tricky part is that this 2.1 percent is the yield *per six months.* We have to double it to get the yield to maturity, so the yield to maturity is 4.2 percent, which is less than the current yield. The reason is that the current yield ignores the built-in loss of the premium between now and maturity.

TABLE 5.1 Summary of Bond Valuation

I. Finding the Value of a Bond

Bond value $= C \times [1 - 1/(1 + r)^T]/r + F/(1 + r)^T$

where

$C =$ Coupon paid each period
$r =$ Rate per period
$T =$ Number of periods
$F =$ Bond's face value

II. Finding the Yield on a Bond

Given a bond value, coupon, time to maturity, and face value, it is possible to find the implicit discount rate, or yield to maturity, by trial and error only. To do this, try different discount rates until the calculated bond value equals the given value (or let a spreadsheet do it for you). Remember that increasing the rate *decreases* the bond value.

EXAMPLE 5.3 Bond Yields

You're looking at two bonds identical in every way except for their coupons and, of course, their prices. Both have 12 years to maturity. The first bond has a 10 percent coupon rate and sells for \$935.08. The second has a 12 percent coupon rate. What do you think it would sell for?

Because the two bonds are very similar, they will be priced to yield about the same rate. We first need to calculate the yield on the 10 percent coupon bond. Proceeding as before, we know that the yield must be greater than 10 percent because the bond is selling at a discount. The bond has a fairly long maturity of 12 years. We've seen that long-term bond prices are relatively sensitive to interest rate changes, so the yield is probably close to 10 percent. A little trial and error reveals that the yield is actually 11 percent:

$$\begin{aligned}\text{Bond value} &= \$100 \times (1 - 1/1.11^{12})/.11 + 1{,}000/1.11^{12} \\ &= \$100 \times 6.4924 + 1{,}000/3.4985 \\ &= \$649.24 + 285.84 \\ &= \$935.08\end{aligned}$$

With an 11 percent yield, the second bond will sell at a premium because of its \$120 coupon. Its value is:

$$\begin{aligned}\text{Bond value} &= \$120 \times (1 - 1/1.11^{12})/.11 + 1{,}000/1.11^{12} \\ &= \$120 \times 6.4924 + 1{,}000/3.4985 \\ &= \$779.08 + 285.84 \\ &= \$1{,}064.92\end{aligned}$$

5.2 MORE ON BOND FEATURES

In this section, we continue our discussion of corporate debt by describing in some detail the basic terms and features that make up a typical long-term corporate bond. We discuss additional issues associated with long-term debt in subsequent sections.

Securities issued by corporations may be classified roughly as *equity securities* and *debt securities.* At the crudest level, a debt represents something that must be repaid; it is the result of borrowing money. When corporations borrow, they generally promise to make regularly scheduled interest payments and to repay the original amount borrowed (that is, the principal). The person or firm making the loan is called the *creditor,* or *lender.* The corporation borrowing the money is called the *debtor,* or *borrower.*

SPREADSHEET TECHNIQUES How to Calculate Bond Prices and Yields Using a Spreadsheet

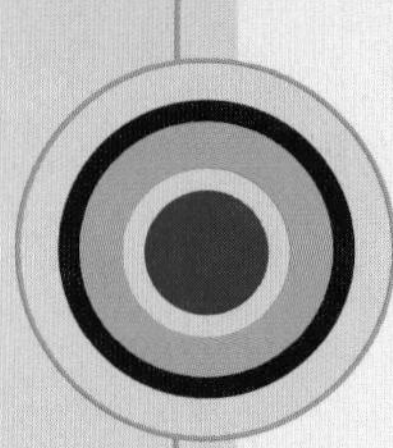

Most spreadsheets have fairly elaborate routines available for calculating bond values and yields; many of these routines involve details that we have not discussed. However, setting up a simple spreadsheet to calculate prices or yields is straightforward, as our next two spreadsheets show:

	A	B	C	D	E	F	G	H
1								
2	**Using a spreadsheet to calculate bond values**							
3								
4	Suppose we have a bond with 22 years to maturity, a coupon rate of 8 percent, and a yield to							
5	maturity of 9 percent. If the bond makes semiannual payments, what is its price today?							
6								
7	Settlement date:	1/1/00						
8	Maturity date:	1/1/22						
9	Annual coupon rate:	.08						
10	Yield to maturity:	.09						
11	Face value (% of par):	100						
12	Coupons per year:	2						
13	Bond price (% of par):	**90.49**						
14								
15	The formula entered in cell B13 is =PRICE(B7,B8,B9,B10,B11,B12); notice that face value and bond							
16	price are given as a percentage of face value.							

	A	B	C	D	E	F	G	H
1								
2	**Using a spreadsheet to calculate bond yields**							
3								
4	Suppose we have a bond with 22 years to maturity, a coupon rate of 8 percent, and a price of							
5	$960.17. If the bond makes semiannual payments, what is its yield to maturity?							
6								
7	Settlement date:	1/1/00						
8	Maturity date:	1/1/22						
9	Annual coupon rate:	.08						
10	Bond price (% of par):	96.017						
11	Face value (% of par):	100						
12	Coupons per year:	2						
13	Yield to maturity:	**.084**						
14								
15	The formula entered in cell B13 is =YIELD(B7,B8,B9,B10,B11,B12); notice that face value and bond							
16	price are entered as a percentage of face value.							
17								

In our spreadsheets, notice that we had to enter two dates, a settlement date and a maturity date. The settlement date is just the date you actually pay for the bond, and the maturity date is the day the bond actually matures. In most of our problems, we don't explicitly have these dates, so we have to make them up. For example, since our bond has 22 years to maturity, we just picked 1/1/2000 (January 1, 2000) as the settlement date and 1/1/2022 (January 1, 2022) as the maturity date. Any two dates would do as long as they are exactly 22 years apart, but these are particularly easy to work with. Finally, notice that we had to enter the coupon rate and yield to maturity in annual terms and then explicitly provide the number of coupon payments per year.

From a financial point of view, the main differences between debt and equity are the following:

1. Debt is not an ownership interest in the firm. Creditors generally do not have voting power.
2. The corporation's payment of interest on debt is considered a cost of doing business and is fully tax deductible. Dividends paid to stockholders are *not* tax deductible.
3. Unpaid debt is a liability of the firm. If it is not paid, the creditors can legally claim the assets of the firm. This action can result in liquidation or reorganization, two of the possible consequences of bankruptcy. Thus, one of the costs of issuing debt is the possibility of financial failure. This possibility does not arise when equity is issued.

Information for bond investors can be found at www.investinginbonds.com.

Is It Debt or Equity?

Sometimes it is not clear if a particular security is debt or equity. For example, suppose a corporation issues a perpetual bond with interest payable solely from corporate income if and only if earned. Whether or not this is really a debt is hard to say and is primarily a legal and semantic issue. Courts and taxing authorities would have the final say.

Corporations are very adept at creating exotic, hybrid securities that have many features of equity but are treated as debt. Obviously, the distinction between debt and equity is very important for tax purposes. So, one reason that corporations try to create a debt security that is really equity is to obtain the tax benefits of debt and the bankruptcy benefits of equity.

As a general rule, equity represents an ownership interest, and it is a residual claim. This means that equity holders are paid after debt holders. As a result of this, the risks and benefits associated with owning debt and equity are different. To give just one example, note that the maximum reward for owning a debt security is ultimately fixed by the amount of the loan, whereas there is no upper limit to the potential reward from owning an equity interest.

Long-Term Debt: The Basics

Ultimately, all long-term debt securities are promises made by the issuing firm to pay principal when due and to make timely interest payments on the unpaid balance. Beyond this, there are a number of features that distinguish these securities from one another. We discuss some of these features next.

The maturity of a long-term debt instrument is the length of time the debt remains outstanding with some unpaid balance. Debt securities can be short term (with maturities of one year or less) or long term (with maturities of more than one year).[1] Short-term debt is sometimes referred to as *unfunded debt*.[2]

Debt securities are typically called *notes, debentures,* or *bonds*. Strictly speaking, a bond is a secured debt. However, in common usage, the word *bond* refers to all kinds of secured and unsecured debt. We will therefore continue to use the term generically to refer to long-term debt. Also, usually, the only difference between a note and a bond is the original maturity. Issues with an original maturity of 10 years or less are often called notes. Longer-term issues are called bonds.

[1]There is no universally agreed-upon distinction between short-term and long-term debt. In addition, people often refer to intermediate-term debt, which has a maturity of more than 1 year and less than 3 to 5, or even 10, years.

[2]The word *funding* is part of the jargon of finance. It generally refers to the long term. Thus, a firm planning to "fund" its debt requirements may be replacing short-term debt with long-term debt.

The two major forms of long-term debt are public issue and privately placed. We concentrate on public-issue bonds. Most of what we say about them holds true for private-issue, long-term debt as well. The main difference between public-issue and privately placed debt is that the latter is directly placed with a lender and not offered to the public. Because this is a private transaction, the specific terms are up to the parties involved.

Information on individual bonds can be found at www.nasdbondinfo.com and www.bondresources.com.

There are many other dimensions to long-term debt, including such things as security, call features, sinking funds, ratings, and protective covenants. The following table illustrates these features for a bond issued by Southern California Edison. If some of these terms are unfamiliar, have no fear. We will discuss them all presently.

Features of a Southern California Edison Bond

TERM		EXPLANATION
Amount of issue	$250 million	The company issued $250 million worth of bonds.
Date of issue	1/19/2005	The bonds were sold on 1/19/2005.
Maturity	1/15/2036	The bonds mature on 1/15/2036.
Face value	$1,000	The denomination of the bonds is $1,000.
Annual coupon	5.55	Each bondholder will receive $55.50 per bond per year (5.55% of face value).
Offer price	99.707	The offer price will be 99.707% of the $1,000 face value, or $997.07, per bond.
Coupon payment dates	1/15, 7/15	Coupons of $55.50/2 = $27.75 will be paid on these dates.
Security	Mortgage	The bonds are secured with the first claim on all property owned by the company.
Sinking fund	No	The bonds do not have a sinking fund.
Call provision	At any time	The bonds do not have a deferred call.
Call price	Treasury rate plus 0.15%	The bonds have a "make-whole" call price.
Rating	Moody's A3 S&P BBB	The bonds are at the lower end of the investment grade rating.

Many of these features will be detailed in the bond indenture, so we discuss this first.

The Indenture

The **indenture** is the written agreement between the corporation (the borrower) and its creditors. It is sometimes referred to as the *deed of trust*.[3] Usually, a trustee (a bank perhaps) is appointed by the corporation to represent the bondholders. The trust company must (1) make sure the terms of the indenture are obeyed, (2) manage the sinking fund (described in the following pages), and (3) represent the bondholders in default, that is, if the company defaults on its payments to them.

The bond indenture is a legal document. It can run several hundred pages and generally makes for very tedious reading. It is an important document, however, because it generally includes the following provisions:

1. The basic terms of the bonds
2. The total amount of bonds issued
3. A description of property used as security
4. The repayment arrangements

[3]The words *loan agreement* or *loan contract* are usually used for privately placed debt and term loans.

5. The call provisions
6. Details of the protective covenants

We discuss these features next.

TERMS OF A BOND Corporate bonds usually have a face value (that is, a denomination) of $1,000. This is called the *principal value* and it is stated on the bond certificate. So, if a corporation wanted to borrow $1 million, 1,000 bonds would have to be sold. The par value (that is, initial accounting value) of a bond is almost always the same as the face value, and the terms are used interchangeably in practice.

Corporate bonds are usually in **registered form**. For example, the indenture might read as follows:

> **Interest is payable semiannually on July 1 and January 1 of each year to the person in whose name the bond is registered at the close of business on June 15 or December 15, respectively.**

This means that the company has a registrar who will record the ownership of each bond and record any changes in ownership. The company will pay the interest and principal by check mailed directly to the address of the owner of record. A corporate bond may be registered and have attached "coupons." To obtain an interest payment, the owner must separate a coupon from the bond certificate and send it to the company registrar (the paying agent).

Alternatively, the bond could be in **bearer form**. This means that the certificate is the basic evidence of ownership, and the corporation will "pay the bearer." Ownership is not otherwise recorded, and, as with a registered bond with attached coupons, the holder of the bond certificate detaches the coupons and sends them to the company to receive payment.

There are two drawbacks to bearer bonds. First, they are difficult to recover if they are lost or stolen. Second, because the company does not know who owns its bonds, it cannot notify bondholders of important events. Bearer bonds were once the dominant type, but they are now much less common (in the United States) than registered bonds.

SECURITY Debt securities are classified according to the collateral and mortgages used to protect the bondholder.

Collateral is a general term that frequently means securities (for example, bonds and stocks) that are pledged as security for payment of debt. For example, collateral trust bonds often involve a pledge of common stock held by the corporation. However, the term *collateral* is commonly used to refer to any asset pledged on a debt.

Mortgage securities are secured by a mortgage on the real property of the borrower. The property involved is usually real estate, for example, land or buildings. The Southern California Edison bond examined in the table is an example. The legal document that describes the mortgage is called a *mortgage trust indenture* or *trust deed.*

Sometimes mortgages are on specific property, for example, a railroad car. More often, blanket mortgages are used. A blanket mortgage pledges all the real property owned by the company.[4]

Bonds frequently represent unsecured obligations of the company. A **debenture** is an unsecured bond, for which no specific pledge of property is made. The term **note** is generally used for such instruments if the maturity of the unsecured bond is less than 10 or so years when the bond is originally issued. Debenture holders have a claim only on

[4]Real property includes land and things "affixed thereto." It does not include cash or inventories.

property not otherwise pledged, in other words, the property that remains after mortgages and collateral trusts are taken into account.

The terminology that we use here and elsewhere in this chapter is standard in the United States. Outside the United States, these same terms can have different meanings. For example, bonds issued by the British government ("gilts") are called treasury "stock." Also, in the United Kingdom, a debenture is a *secured* obligation.

At the current time, public bonds issued in the United States by industrial and financial companies are typically debentures. However, most utility and railroad bonds are secured by a pledge of assets.

The Bond Market Association Web site is www.bondmarkets.com.

SENIORITY In general terms, *seniority* indicates preference in position over other lenders, and debts are sometimes labeled as *senior* or *junior* to indicate seniority. Some debt is *subordinated,* as in, for example, a subordinated debenture.

In the event of default, holders of subordinated debt must give preference to other specified creditors. Usually, this means that the subordinated lenders will be paid off only after the specified creditors have been compensated. However, debt cannot be subordinated to equity.

REPAYMENT Bonds can be repaid at maturity, at which time the bondholder will receive the stated, or face, value of the bond, or they may be repaid in part or in entirety before maturity. Early repayment in some form is more typical and is often handled through a sinking fund.

A **sinking fund** is an account managed by the bond trustee for the purpose of repaying the bonds. The company makes annual payments to the trustee, who then uses the funds to retire a portion of the debt. The trustee does this by either buying up some of the bonds in the market or calling in a fraction of the outstanding bonds. This second option is discussed in the next section.

There are many different kinds of sinking fund arrangements, and the details would be spelled out in the indenture. For example:

1. Some sinking funds start about 10 years after the initial issuance.
2. Some sinking funds establish equal payments over the life of the bond.
3. Some high-quality bond issues establish payments to the sinking fund that are not sufficient to redeem the entire issue. As a consequence, there is the possibility of a large "balloon payment" at maturity.

THE CALL PROVISION A **call provision** allows the company to repurchase or "call" part or all of the bond issue at stated prices over a specific period. Corporate bonds are usually callable.

Generally, the call price is above the bond's stated value (that is, the par value). The difference between the call price and the stated value is the **call premium**. The amount of the call premium may become smaller over time. One arrangement is to initially set the call premium equal to the annual coupon payment and then make it decline to zero as the call date moves closer to the time of maturity.

Call provisions are often not operative during the first part of a bond's life. This makes the call provision less of a worry for bondholders in the bond's early years. For example, a company might be prohibited from calling its bonds for the first 10 years. This is a **deferred call provision**. During this period of prohibition, the bond is said to be **call protected**.

In just the last few years, a new type of call provision, a "make-whole" call, has become very widespread in the corporate bond market. With such a feature, bondholders receive approximately what the bonds are worth if they are called. Because when bondholders don't suffer a loss in the event of a call, they are "made whole."

To determine the make-whole call price, we calculate the present value of the remaining interest and principal payments at a rate specified in the indenture. For example, looking at our Southern California Edison issue, we see that the discount rate is "Treasury rate plus .15%." What this means is that we determine the discount rate by first finding a U.S. Treasury issue with the same maturity. We calculate the yield to maturity on the Treasury issue and then add on an additional .15 percent to get the discount rate we use.

Notice that, with a make-whole call provision, the call price is higher when interest rates are lower and vice versa (why?). Also notice that, as is common with a make-whole call, the Southern California Edison issue does not have a deferred call feature. Why might investors not be too concerned about the absence of this feature?

PROTECTIVE COVENANTS A **protective covenant** is that part of the indenture or loan agreement that limits certain actions a company might otherwise wish to take during the term of the loan. Protective covenants can be classified into two types: negative covenants and positive (or affirmative) covenants.

A *negative covenant* is a "thou shalt not" type of covenant. It limits or prohibits actions that the company might take. Here are some typical examples:

1. The firm must limit the amount of dividends it pays according to some formula.
2. The firm cannot pledge any assets to other lenders.
3. The firm cannot merge with another firm.
4. The firm cannot sell or lease any major assets without approval by the lender.
5. The firm cannot issue additional long-term debt.

A *positive covenant* is a "thou shalt" type of covenant. It specifies an action that the company agrees to take or a condition the company must abide by. Here are some examples:

Want detailed information on the amount and terms of the debt issued by a particular firm? Check out their latest financial statements by searching SEC filings at www.sec.gov.

1. The company must maintain its working capital at or above some specified minimum level.
2. The company must periodically furnish audited financial statements to the lender.
3. The firm must maintain any collateral or security in good condition.

This is only a partial list of covenants; a particular indenture may feature many different ones.

5.3 BOND RATINGS

Firms frequently pay to have their debt rated. The two leading bond-rating firms are Moody's and Standard & Poor's (S&P). The debt ratings are an assessment of the creditworthiness of the corporate issuer. The definitions of creditworthiness used by Moody's and S&P are based on how likely the firm is to default and the protection creditors have in the event of a default.

It is important to recognize that bond ratings are concerned *only* with the possibility of default. Earlier, we discussed interest rate risk, which we defined as the risk of a change in the value of a bond resulting from a change in interest rates. Bond ratings do not address this issue. As a result, the price of a highly rated bond can still be quite volatile.

Bond ratings are constructed from information supplied by the corporation and other sources. The rating classes and some information concerning them are shown in the following table.

	Investment-Quality Bond Ratings				Low-Quality, Speculative, and/or "Junk" Bond Ratings					
	High Grade		Medium Grade		Low Grade		Very Low Grade			
STANDARD & POOR's	AAA	AA	A	BBB	BB	B	CCC	CC	C	D
MOODY's	Aaa	Aa	A	Baa	Ba	B	Caa	Ca	C	D

MOODY's	S&P	
Aaa	AAA	Debt rated Aaa and AAA has the highest rating. Capacity to pay interest and principal is extremely strong.
Aa	AA	Debt rated Aa and AA has a very strong capacity to pay interest and repay principal. Together with the highest rating, this group comprises the high-grade bond class.
A	A	Debt rated A has a strong capacity to pay interest and repay principal, although it is somewhat more susceptible to the adverse effects of changes in circumstances and economic conditions than debt in high-rated categories.
Baa	BBB	Debt rated Baa and BBB is regarded as having an adequate capacity to pay interest and repay principal. Whereas it normally exhibits adequate protection parameters, adverse economic conditions or changing circumstances are more likely to lead to a weakened capacity to pay interest and repay principal for debt in this category than in higher-rated categories. These bonds are medium-grade obligations.
Ba; B Caa Ca	BB; B CCC CC	Debt rated in these categories is regarded, on balance, as predominantly speculative with respect to capacity to pay interest and repay principal in accordance with the terms of the obligation. BB and Ba indicate the lowest degree of speculation, and CC and Ca the highest degree of speculation. Although such debt is likely to have some quality and protective characteristics, these are outweighed by large uncertainties or major risk exposures to adverse conditions. Some issues may be in default.
C	C	This rating is reserved for income bonds on which no interest is being paid.
D	D	Debt rated D is in default, and payment of interest and/or repayment of principal is in arrears.

Note: At times, both Moody's and S&P use adjustments (called notches) to these ratings. S&P uses plus and minus signs: A+ is the strongest A rating and A− the weakest. Moody's uses a 1, 2, or 3 designation, with 1 being the highest.

Want to know what criteria are commonly used to rate corporate and municipal bonds? Go to www.standardandpoors.com, www.moodys.com, or www.fitchinv.com.

The highest rating a firm's debt can have is AAA or Aaa, and such debt is judged to be the best quality and to have the lowest degree of risk. For example, the 100-year BellSouth issue we discussed earlier was rated AAA. This rating is not awarded very often; AA or Aa ratings indicate very good quality debt and are much more common. The lowest rating is D, for debt that is in default.

A large part of corporate borrowing takes the form of low-grade, or "junk," bonds. If these low-grade corporate bonds are rated at all, they are rated below investment grade by the major rating agencies. Investment-grade bonds are bonds rated at least BBB by S&P or Baa by Moody's.

Rating agencies don't always agree. For example, some bonds are known as "crossover" or "5B" bonds. The reason is that they are rated triple-B (or Baa) by one rating agency and double-B (or Ba) by another, a "split rating." For example, in January 2005, Coventry Health sold $250 million of 10-year notes rated BBB− by S&P and Ba1 by Moody's. Notice that the Southern California Edison issue we discussed earlier was also split-rated.

A bond's credit rating can change as the issuer's financial strength improves or deteriorates. For example, in February 2005, Fitch (another well-known rating agency) downgraded camera giant Eastman Kodak from BBB− to BB+, pushing it from investment grade status into junk bond territory. Bonds that drop into junk status like this are called "fallen angels." Why were the Eastman Kodak bonds downgraded? A lot of reasons, but

Fitch was particularly concerned that the company's profit and cash flow outlook were not strong enough to support its previous credit rating.

Credit ratings are important because defaults really do occur, and, when they do, investors can lose heavily. For example, in 2000, AmeriServe Food Distribution, Inc., which supplied restaurants such as Burger King with everything from burgers to give-away toys, defaulted on $200 million in junk bonds. After the default, the bonds traded at just 18 cents on the dollar, leaving investors with a loss of more than $160 million.

Even worse in AmeriServe's case, the bonds had been issued only four months earlier, thereby making AmeriServe an NCAA champion. While that might be a good thing for a college basketball team such as the University of Kentucky Wildcats, in the bond market it means "No Coupon At All," and it's not a good thing for investors.

5.4 SOME DIFFERENT TYPES OF BONDS

Thus far, we have considered only "plain vanilla" corporate bonds. In this section, we briefly look at bonds issued by governments and also at bonds with unusual features.

Government Bonds

The biggest borrower in the world–by a wide margin–is everybody's favorite family member, Uncle Sam. In 2005, the total debt of the U.S. government was about $8 *trillion,* or approximately $26,000 per citizen (and growing!). When the government wishes to borrow money for more than one year, it sells what are known as Treasury notes and bonds to the public (in fact, it does so every month). Currently, outstanding Treasury notes and bonds have original maturities ranging from 2 to 30 years.

If you're nervous about the level of debt piled up by the U.S. government, *don't* go to www.publicdebt.treas.gov, or to www.brillig.com/debt_clock! Learn all about government bonds at www.ny.frb.org.

Most U.S. Treasury issues are just ordinary coupon bonds. Some older issues are callable, and a very few have some unusual features. There are two important things to keep in mind, however. First, U.S. Treasury issues, unlike essentially all other bonds, have no default risk because (we hope) the Treasury can always come up with the money to make the payments. Second, Treasury issues are exempt from state income taxes (though not federal income taxes). In other words, the coupons you receive on a Treasury note or bond are only taxed at the federal level.

State and local governments also borrow money by selling notes and bonds. Such issues are called *municipal* notes and bonds, or just "munis." Unlike Treasury issues, munis have varying degrees of default risk, and, in fact, they are rated much like corporate issues. Also, they are almost always callable. The most intriguing thing about munis is that their coupons are exempt from federal income taxes (though not necessarily state income taxes), which makes them very attractive to high-income, high–tax bracket investors.

Because of the enormous tax break they receive, the yields on municipal bonds are much lower than the yields on taxable bonds. For example, in Fall 2005, long-term AAA-rated corporate bonds were yielding about 5.38 percent. At the same time, long-term AAA munis were yielding about 4.35 percent. Suppose an investor was in a 30 percent tax bracket. All else being the same, would this investor prefer a AAA corporate bond or a AAA municipal bond?

To answer, we need to compare the *aftertax* yields on the two bonds. Ignoring state and local taxes, the muni pays 4.35 percent on both a pretax and an aftertax basis. The corporate issue pays 5.38 percent before taxes, but it only pays $.0538 \times (1 - .30) = .038$, or 3.8 percent, once we account for the 30 percent tax bite. Given this, the muni has a better yield.

Another good bond market site is money.cnn.com.

EXAMPLE 5.4 Taxable versus Municipal Bonds

Suppose taxable bonds are currently yielding 8 percent, while at the same time, munis of comparable risk and maturity are yielding 6 percent. Which is more attractive to an investor in a 40 percent bracket? What is the break-even tax rate? How do you interpret this rate?

For an investor in a 40 percent tax bracket, a taxable bond yields $8 \times (1 - .40) = 4.8$ percent after taxes, so the muni is much more attractive. The break-even tax rate is the tax rate at which an investor would be indifferent between a taxable and a nontaxable issue. If we let t^* stand for the break-even tax rate, then we can solve for it as follows:

$$.08 \times (1 - t^*) = .06$$
$$1 - t^* = .06/.08 = .75$$
$$t^* = .25$$

Thus, an investor in a 25 percent tax bracket would make 6 percent after taxes from either bond.

Zero Coupon Bonds

A bond that pays no coupons at all must be offered at a price that is much lower than its stated value. Such bonds are called **zero coupon bonds**, or just *zeroes*.[5]

Suppose the Eight-Inch Nails (EIN) Company issues a $1,000 face value, five-year zero coupon bond. The initial price is set at $497. It is straightforward to verify that at this price, the bond yields 15 percent to maturity. The total interest paid over the life of the bond is $1,000 − 497 = $503.

For tax purposes, the issuer of a zero coupon bond deducts interest every year even though no interest is actually paid. Similarly, the owner must pay taxes on interest accrued every year, even though no interest is actually received. Such interest is called "phantom" interest.

The way in which the yearly interest on a zero coupon bond is calculated is governed by tax law. Before 1982, corporations could calculate the interest deduction on a straight-line basis. For EIN, the annual interest deduction would have been $503/5 = $100.60 per year.

Some bonds are zero coupon bonds for only part of their lives. For example, General Motors has a debenture outstanding that matures on March 15, 2036. For the first 20 years of its life, no coupon payments will be made, but, after 20 years, it begins paying coupons at a rate of 7.75 percent per year, payable semiannually.

Floating-Rate Bonds

The conventional bonds we have talked about in this chapter have fixed-dollar obligations because the coupon rate is set as a fixed percentage of the par value. Similarly, the principal is set equal to the par value. Under these circumstances, the coupon payment and principal are completely fixed.

With *floating-rate bonds (floaters)*, the coupon payments are adjustable. The adjustments are tied to an interest rate index such as the Treasury bill interest rate or the 30-year Treasury bond rate.

The value of a floating-rate bond depends on exactly how the coupon payment adjustments are defined. In most cases, the coupon adjusts with a lag to some base rate. For example, suppose a coupon rate adjustment is made on June 1. The adjustment

[5]A bond issued with a very low coupon rate (as opposed to a zero coupon rate) is an original-issue discount (OID) bond.

might be based on the simple average of Treasury bond yields during the previous three months. In addition, the majority of floaters have the following features:

1. The holder has the right to redeem his/her note at par on the coupon payment date after some specified amount of time. This is called a *put* provision, and it is discussed in the following section.
2. The coupon rate has a floor and a ceiling, meaning that the coupon is subject to a minimum and a maximum. In this case, the coupon rate is said to be "capped," and the upper and lower rates are sometimes called the *collar*.

A particularly interesting type of floating-rate bond is an *inflation-linked* bond. Such bonds have coupons that are adjusted according to the rate of inflation (the principal amount may be adjusted as well). The U.S. Treasury began issuing such bonds in January of 1997. The issues are sometimes called "TIPS," or Treasury Inflation Protection Securities. Other countries, including Canada, Israel, and Britain, have issued similar securities.

Official information on U.S. inflation-indexed bonds is at www.publicdebt.treas.gov/gsr/gsrlist.htm.

Other Types of Bonds

Many bonds have unusual or exotic features. One such feature explains why the Berkshire Hathaway bond we described at the beginning of the chapter actually had what amounts to a negative coupon rate. The buyers of these bonds also received the right to purchase shares of stock in Berkshire at a fixed price per share over the subsequent five years. Such a right, which is called a warrant, would be very valuable if the stock price climbed substantially (a later chapter discusses this subject in greater depth).

Bond features are really only limited by the imaginations of the parties involved. Unfortunately, there are far too many variations for us to cover in detail here. We therefore close out this section by mentioning only a few of the more common types. A nearby *The Real World* box has some additional discussion on bond features.

Income bonds are similar to conventional bonds, except that coupon payments are dependent on company income. Specifically, coupons are paid to bondholders only if the firm's income is sufficient. This would appear to be an attractive feature, but income bonds are not very common.

A *convertible bond* can be swapped for a fixed number of shares of stock anytime before maturity at the holder's option. Convertibles are relatively common, but the number has been decreasing in recent years.

A *put bond* allows the *holder* to force the issuer to buy the bond back at a stated price. For example, International Paper Co. has bonds outstanding that allow the holder to force International Paper to buy the bonds back at 100 percent of face value given that certain "risk" events happen. One such event is a change in credit rating from investment grade to lower than investment grade by Moody's or S&P. The put feature is therefore just the reverse of the call provision.

A given bond may have many unusual features. Two of the most recent exotic bonds are CoCo bonds, which have a coupon payment, and NoNo bonds, which are zero coupon bonds. CoCo and NoNo bonds are contingent convertible, putable, callable, subordinated bonds. The contingent convertible clause is similar to the normal conversion feature, except the contingent feature must be met. For example, a contingent feature may require that the company stock trade at 110 percent of the conversion price for 20 out of the most recent 30 days. Valuing a bond of this sort can be quite complex, and the yield to maturity calculation is often meaningless. For example, in 2005, a NoNo issued by Merrill Lynch was selling at a price of $1,018.75, with a yield to maturity of negative 6.88 percent. At the same time, a NoNo issued by Countrywide Financial was selling for $1,520, which implied a yield to maturity of negative 64.48 percent!

THE REAL WORLD

BEAUTY IS IN THE EYE OF THE BONDHOLDER

Many bonds have unusual or exotic features. One of the most common types is an asset-backed, or securitized, bond. In fact, sales of new asset-backed securities in the United States were about the same as new corporate debt issues in 2004. Bondholders of a securitized bond receive interest and principal payments from a specific asset (or pool of assets) rather than a specific company. For example, at one point rock legend David Bowie sold $55 million in bonds backed by future royalties from his albums and songs (that's some serious ch-ch-ch-change!). Owners of these "Bowie" bonds receive the royalty payments, so if Bowie's record sales fall, there is a possibility the bonds would default. Other artists have sold bonds backed by future royalties, including James Brown, Iron Maiden, and the estate of the legendary Marvin Gaye.

Mortgage-backs are the best known type of asset-backed security. With a mortgage-backed bond, a trustee purchases mortgages from banks and merges them into a pool. Bonds are then issued, and the bondholders receive payments derived from payments on the underlying mortgages. One unusual twist with mortgage bonds is that if interest rates decline, the bonds can actually decrease in value. This can occur because homeowners are likely to refinance at the lower rates, paying off their mortgages in the process.

Securitized bonds are usually backed by assets with long-term payments, such as mortgages. However, there are bonds securitized by car loans and credit card payments, among other assets, and a growing market exists for bonds backed by automobile leases.

5.5 BOND MARKETS

Bonds are bought and sold in enormous quantities every day. You may be surprised to learn that the trading volume in bonds on a typical day is many, many times larger than the trading volume in stocks (by trading volume, we simply mean the amount of money that changes hands). Here is a finance trivia question: What is the largest securities market in the world? Most people would guess the New York Stock Exchange. In fact, the largest securities market in the world in terms of trading volume is the U.S. Treasury market.

How Bonds Are Bought and Sold

As we mentioned all the way back in Chapter 1, most trading in bonds takes place over the counter, or OTC. Recall that this means that there is no particular place where buying and selling occur. Instead, dealers around the country (and around the world) stand ready to buy and sell. The various dealers are connected electronically.

One reason the bond markets are so big is that the number of bond issues far exceeds the number of stock issues. There are two reasons for this. First, a corporation would typically have only one common stock issue outstanding (there are exceptions to this that we discuss in our next chapter). However, a single large corporation could easily have a dozen or more note and bond issues outstanding. Beyond this, federal, state, and local borrowing is simply enormous. For example, even a small city would usually have a wide variety of notes and bonds outstanding, representing money borrowed to pay for things like roads, sewers, and schools. When you think about how many small cities there are in the United States, you begin to get the picture!

Because the bond market is almost entirely OTC, it has historically had little or no *transparency*. A financial market is transparent if it is possible to easily observe its prices and trading volume. On the New York Stock Exchange, for example, it is possible to see the price and quantity for every single transaction. In contrast, in the bond market, it is often not possible to observe either. Transactions are privately negotiated between parties, and there is little or no centralized reporting of transactions.

Although the total volume of trading in bonds far exceeds that in stocks, only a very small fraction of the total bond issues that exist actually trade on a given day. This fact, combined with the lack of transparency in the bond market, means that getting up-to-date prices on individual bonds can be difficult or impossible, particularly for smaller corporate or municipal issues. Instead, a variety of sources of estimated prices exist and are very commonly used.

Bond Price Reporting

In 2002, transparency in the corporate bond market began to improve dramatically. Under new regulations, corporate bond dealers are now required to report trade information through what is known as the Transactions Report and Compliance Engine (TRACE). As this is written, transaction prices are now reported on more than 4,000 bonds, amounting to approximately 75 percent of the investment grade market. More bonds will be added over time.

TRACE bond quotes are available at www.nasdbondinfo.com. We went to the site and entered "Deere" for the well-known manufacturer of green tractors. We found a total of ten bond issues outstanding. Below you can see the information we found for three of these.

To learn more about TRACE, visit www.nasd.com.

Issue: DE.GG DEERE & CO. 7.125 03/03/2031 — Time and Sales — Descriptive Data

In Portfolio	Rating Moody's/S&P/Fitch	Last Sale Date	Last Sale Price	Last Sale Yield	Most Recent Date	Most Recent Price	Most Recent Yield
☐	A3 / A- / A	03/24/2005	120.862	5.591001	03/24/2005	120.86	5.591001

Issue: DE.GA DEERE & COMPANY 8.95 06/15/2019 — Time and Sales — Descriptive Data

In Portfolio	Rating Moody's/S&P/Fitch	Last Sale Date	Last Sale Price	Last Sale Yield	Most Recent Date	Most Recent Price	Most Recent Yield
☐	A3 / A- / A	03/24/2005	116.00	4.710887	03/24/2005	116.00	4.710887

Issue: DE.GB DEERE & COMPANY 8.50 01/09/2022 — Time and Sales — Descriptive Data

In Portfolio	Rating Moody's/S&P/Fitch	Last Sale Date	Last Sale Price	Last Sale Yield	Most Recent Date	Most Recent Price	Most Recent Yield
☐	A3 / A- / A	03/16/2005	134.518	5.357066	03/16/2005	134.52	5.357066

Most of the information is self-explanatory. The price and yield columns show the price and yield to maturity of the most recent sales. Notice the last sale dates for the issue maturing in 2022. This bond had not had a reported trade for the last week. A great feature of this Web site is the "Descriptive Data" link, which gives you more information about the bond issue such as call dates and coupon dates.

As shown in Figure 5.3, *The Wall Street Journal* provides a daily snapshot of the data from TRACE by reporting the 40 most active issues. The information reported is largely self-explanatory. The EST Spread is the estimated yield spread over a particular Treasury issue (a yield spread is just the difference in yields). The spread is reported in basis points, where 1 basis point is equal to .01 percent. The selected Treasury issue's maturity is given under UST, which is a standard abbreviation in the bond markets for U.S. Treasury. A "hot run" Treasury is the most recently issued of a particular maturity, better known as an on-the-run issue. Finally, the reported volume is the face value of bonds traded.

The Federal Reserve Bank of St. Louis maintains dozens of online files containing macroeconomic data as well as rates on U.S. Treasury issues. Go to www.stls.frb.org/fred/files.

As we mentioned before, the U.S. Treasury market is the largest securities market in the world. As with bond markets in general, it is an OTC market, so there is limited transparency. However, unlike the situation with bond markets in general, trading in Treasury issues, particularly recently issued ones, is very heavy. Each day, representative prices for outstanding Treasury issues are reported.

FIGURE 5.3
Sample *Wall Street Journal* Bond Quotation

Source: Reprinted by permission of *The Wall Street Journal,* via Copyright Clearance Center © 2005 Dow Jones and Company, Inc., March 22, 2005. All Rights Reserved Worldwide.

Corporate Bonds

Monday, March 21, 2005

Forty most active fixed-coupon corporate bonds

COMPANY (TICKER)	COUPON	MATURITY	LAST PRICE	LAST YIELD	*EST SPREAD	UST†	EST $ VOL (000's)
General Motors Acceptance (GM)	6.750	Dec 01, 2014	87.873	8.619	410	10	418,894
General Motors (GM)	8.375	Jul 15, 2033	86.615	9.775	495	30	221,290
Ford Motor Credit (F)	6.500	Jan 25, 2007	100.938	5.947	224	2	136,319
General Motors Acceptance (GM)	6.125	Aug 28, 2007	97.000	7.469	376	2	130,585
General Motors Acceptance (GM)	7.750	Jan 19, 2010	95.271	8.975	480	5	121,983
Ford Motor Credit (F)	6.875	Feb 01, 2006	101.250	5.345	164	2	106,174
General Motors Acceptance (GM)	6.875	Sep 15, 2011	90.600	8.810	464	5	99,036
General Motors Acceptance (GM)	6.750	Jan 15, 2006	100.125	6.572	287	2	94,066
Clear Channel Communications Inc (CCU)	5.500	Sep 15, 2014	96.138	6.041	151	10	91,420
Ford Motor Credit (F)	7.375	Oct 28, 2009	99.633	7.468	330	5	86,536
General Motors Acceptance (GM)	5.625	May 15, 2009	90.550	8.368	420	5	85,278
AT&T Wireless Services Inc (CNG)	8.750	Mar 01, 2031	132.521	6.210	139	30	75,360
General Motors (GM)	7.200	Jan 15, 2011	90.838	9.271	510	5	73,367
Ford Motor Co (F)	7.450	Jul 16, 2031	89.719	8.426	360	30	67,515
Ford Motor Credit (F)	4.950	Jan 15, 2008	96.235	6.433	253	3	67,293
Ford Motor Credit (F)	7.000	Oct 01, 2013	96.715	7.529	301	10	65,379
JP Morgan Chase and Co (JPM)	5.125	Sep 15, 2014	98.737	5.296	79	10	62,556
Morgan Stanley (MWD)	4.750	Apr 01, 2014	95.632	5.367	85	10	60,475
Sprint Capital (FON)	8.750	Mar 15, 2032	130.539	6.366	154	30	50,861
General Motors Acceptance (GM)	6.125	Feb 01, 2007	97.965	7.313	361	2	47,956
General Motors Acceptance (GM)	7.250	Mar 02, 2011	93.057	8.773	460	5	47,096
Sprint Capital (FON)	6.900	May 01, 2019	109.769	5.871	135	10	44,721
General Motors Acceptance (GM)	6.125	Sep 15, 2006	100.125	6.034	232	2	41,530
General Motors Acceptance (GM)	8.000	Nov 01, 2031	89.759	9.020	420	30	41,293
DaimlerChrysler North America Holding (DCX)	6.500	Nov 15, 2013	105.119	5.739	122	10	41,076
Berkshire Hathaway Finance (BRK)	4.625	Oct 15, 2013	97.405	5.001	48	10	40,035
Boeing Capital (BA)	6.500	Feb 15, 2012	108.897	4.959	44	10	39,543
General Motors Acceptance (GM)	6.875	Aug 28, 2012	90.548	8.623	410	10	38,778
Grupo Televisa, S.A. de C.V. (TELVIS)	8.000	Sep 13, 2011	117.754	4.777	61	5	37,877
BellSouth Corp (BLS)	6.000	Nov 15, 2034	99.950	6.003	118	30	37,145
Goldman Sachs Group (GS)	5.250	Oct 15, 2013	100.017	5.247	73	10	36,420
JP Morgan Chase and Co (JPM)	4.750	Mar 01, 2015	96.162	5.250	74	10	36,235
Comcast Holdings (CMCSA)	6.500	Jan 15, 2015	107.752	5.467	95	10	36,160
Boeing Capital (BA)	6.125	Feb 15, 2033	107.152	5.614	80	30	36,015
General Motors (GM)	7.125	Jul 15, 2013	87.547	9.307	479	10	35,624
Goldman Sachs Group (GS)	5.125	Jan 15, 2015	98.179	5.365	85	10	33,469
General Motors (GM)	8.250	Jul 15, 2023	86.376	9.870	505	30	32,462
Albertson's Inc (ABS)	7.450	Aug 01, 2029	111.988	6.465	164	30	32,000
BellSouth Corp (BLS)	5.200	Sep 15, 2014	99.474	5.271	75	10	30,961
Valero Energy Corp (VLO)	7.500	Apr 15, 2032	121.303	5.912	109	30	30,400
Ford Motor Credit (F)	7.375	Feb 01, 2011	98.731	7.645	347	5	30,216

Volume represents total volume for each issue; price/yield data are for trades of $1 million and greater. * Estimated spreads, in basis points (100 basis points is one percentage point), over the 2, 3, 5, 10 or 30-year hot run Treasury note/bond. 2-year: 3.375 02/07; 3-year: 3.375 02/08; 5-year: 4.000 03/10; 10-year: 4.000 02/15; 30-year: 5.375 02/31. †Comparable U.S. Treasury issue.

Figure 5.4 shows a portion of the daily Treasury note and bond listings from *The Wall Street Journal.* The entry that begins "8.000 Nov 21" is highlighted. Reading from left to right, the 8.000 is the bond's coupon rate, and the "Nov 21" tells us that the bond's maturity is November of 2021. Treasury bonds all make semiannual payments and have a face value of $1,000, so this bond will pay $40 per six months until it matures.

The next two pieces of information are the **bid** and **asked prices.** In general, in any OTC or dealer market, the bid price represents what a dealer is willing to pay for a security, and the asked price (or just "ask" price) is what a dealer is willing to take for it. The difference between the two prices is called the **bid-ask spread** (or just "spread"), and it represents the dealer's profit.

For historical reasons, Treasury prices are quoted in 32nds. Thus, the bid price on the 8.000 Nov 21 bond, 135:01, actually translates into 135 1/32, or 135.03125 percent of face value. With a $1,000 face value, this represents $1,350.3125. Because prices are quoted in 32nds, the smallest possible price change is 1/32. This is called the "tick" size.

The next number quoted is the change in the asked price from the previous day, measured in ticks (i.e., in 32nds), so this issue's asked price fell by 8/32 of 1 percent, or .25 percent, of face value from the previous day. Finally, the last number reported is the yield to maturity, based on the asked price. Notice that this is a premium bond because

Treasury Bonds, Notes and Bills — March 21, 2005

Explanatory Notes

Representative Over-the-Counter quotation based on transactions of $1 million or more. Treasury bond, note and bill quotes are as of mid-afternoon. Colons in bid-and-asked quotes represent 32nds; 101:01 means 101 1/32. Net changes in 32nds. n-Treasury note. i-Inflation-Indexed issue. Treasury bill quotes in hundredths, quoted on terms of a rate of discount. Days to maturity calculated from settlement date. All yields are to maturity and based on the asked quote. Latest 13-week and 26-week bills are boldfaced. For bonds callable prior to maturity, yields are computed to the earliest call date for issues quoted above par and to the maturity date for issues below par. *When issued.
Source: eSpeed/Cantor Fitzgerald

U.S. Treasury strips as of 3 p.m. Eastern time, also based on transactions of $1 million or more. Colons in bid and asked quotes represent 32nds; 99:01 means 99 1/32. Net changes in 32nds. Yields calculated on the asked quotation. ci-stripped coupon interest. bp-Treasury bond, stripped principal. np-Treasury note, stripped principal. For bonds callable prior to maturity, yields are computed to the earliest call date for issues quoted above par and to the maturity date for issues below par.
Source: Bear, Stearns & Co. via Street Software Technology Inc.

RATE	MATURITY MO/YR	BID	ASKED	CHG	ASK YLD
Government Bonds & Notes					
1.625	Mar 05n	100:00	100:00	1	1.61
1.625	Apr 05n	99:27	99:28	...	2.63
6.500	May 05n	100:17	100:18	...	2.55
6.750	May 05n	100:18	100:19	...	2.59
12.000	May 05	101:13	101:14	...	2.24
1.250	May 05n	99:22	99:23	...	2.63
1.125	Jun 05n	99:16	99:17	...	2.77
1.500	Jul 05n	99:15	99:16	...	2.85
6.500	Aug 05n	101:12	101:13	−1	2.91
10.750	Aug 05	103:04	103:05	...	2.81
2.000	Aug 05n	99:17	99:18	...	2.97
1.625	Sep 05n	99:07	99:08	...	3.05
1.625	Oct 05n	99:03	99:04	1	3.09
5.750	Nov 05n	101:20	101:21	...	3.15
5.875	Nov 05n	101:22	101:23	−1	3.15
1.875	Nov 05n	99:03	99:04	...	3.16
1.875	Dec 05n	98:30	98:31	...	3.23
1.875	Jan 06n	98:25	98:26	...	3.26
5.625	Feb 06n	102:02	102:03	...	3.25
9.375	Feb 06	105:12	105:13	...	3.23
1.625	Feb 06n	98:12	98:13	...	3.34
1.500	Mar 06n	98:03	98:04	...	3.36
2.250	Apr 06n	98:22	98:23	...	3.42
2.000	May 06n	98:12	98:13	...	3.42
4.625	May 06n	101:10	101:11	...	3.42
6.875	May 06n	103:26	103:27	−1	3.42
2.500	May 06n	98:28	98:29	...	3.44
2.750	Jun 06n	99:02	99:03	...	3.48
7.000	Jul 06n	104:13	104:14	...	3.52
2.750	Jul 06n	99:00	99:00	...	3.51
2.375	Aug 06n	98:12	98:13	−1	3.54
2.375	Aug 06n	98:10	98:11	...	3.55
2.500	Sep 06n	98:12	98:13	...	3.58
6.500	Oct 06n	104:11	104:12	−1	3.59
2.500	Oct 06n	98:08	98:09	...	3.61
2.625	Nov 06n	98:12	98:13	...	3.62
3.500	Nov 06n	99:25	99:26	...	3.61
2.875	Nov 06n	98:23	98:24	...	3.64
3.000	Dec 06n	98:26	98:27	−1	3.67
3.375	Jan 07i	105:04	105:05	−1	0.52
3.125	Jan 07n	99:00	99:00	...	3.68
2.250	Feb 07n	97:11	97:12	...	3.68
6.250	Feb 07n	104:22	104:23	...	3.66
3.375	Feb 07n	99:11	99:12	−1	3.70
6.625	May 07n	105:28	105:29	−1	3.74
4.375	May 07n	101:08	101:09	−1	3.75
3.125	May 07n	98:22	98:23	...	3.75
2.750	Aug 07n	97:18	97:19	−1	3.81
3.250	Aug 07n	98:23	98:24	−1	3.79
6.125	Aug 07n	105:09	105:10	−1	3.79
3.000	Nov 07n	97:27	97:28	−1	3.84
3.625	Jan 08i	107:22	107:23	−3	0.84

RATE	MATURITY MO/YR	BID	ASKED	CHG	ASK YLD
3.000	Feb 08n	97.16	97:17	−1	3.90
5.500	Feb 08n	104:12	104:13	−1	3.88
3.375	Feb 08n	98:17	98:18	...	3.90
2.625	May 08n	96:03	96:04	−1	3.94
5.625	May 08n	104:29	104:30	−1	3.94
3.250	Aug 08n	97:21	97:22	−1	3.98
3.125	Sep 08n	97:05	97:06	−1	4.00
3.125	Oct 08n	97:02	97:03	−1	4.01
3.375	Nov 08n	97:25	97:26	−1	4.02
4.750	Nov 08n	102:15	102:16	−1	4.00
3.375	Dec 08n	97:23	97:24	...	4.03
3.250	Jan 09n	97:07	97:08	...	4.03
3.875	Jan 09i	110:14	110:15	−2	1.06
3.000	Feb 09n	96:06	96:07	...	4.06
2.625	Mar 09n	94:24	94:25	−1	4.05
3.125	Apr 09n	96:15	96:16	...	4.07
3.875	May 09n	99:07	99:08	−1	4.07
5.500	May 09n	105:15	105:16	...	4.05
4.000	Jun 09n	99:20	99:21	−1	4.08
3.625	Jul 09n	98:04	98:05	−1	4.09
3.500	Aug 09n	97:19	97:20	...	4.09
6.000	Aug 09n	107:17	107:18	−1	4.10
3.375	Sep 09n	96:29	96:30	−1	4.13
3.375	Oct 09n	96.26	96.27	−1	4.14
3.500	Nov 09n	97:10	97:11	−1	4.13
3.500	Dec 09n	97:06	97:07	−1	4.15
3.625	Jan 10n	97:19	97:20	−1	4.17
4.250	Jan 10i	114:02	114:03	−2	1.22
3.500	Feb 10n	97:01	97:02	−1	4.17
6.500	Feb 10n	110:05	110:06	−2	4.18
4.000	Mar 10n	99:06	99:07	−1	4.18
0.875	Apr 10i	98:01	98:02	−1	1.27
10.000	May 10	101:00	101:01	−1	2.85
5.750	Aug 10n	107:10	107:11	−1	4.22
12.750	Nov 10	106:00	106:01	−2	3.24
3.500	Jan 11i	111:30	111:31	−4	1.35
5.000	Feb 11n	103:27	103:28	−2	4.25
13.875	May 11	111:17	111:18	−3	3.50
5.000	Aug 11n	103:26	103:27	−3	4.30
14.000	Nov 11	116:07	116:08	−2	3.73
3.375	Jan 12i	112:13	112:14	−5	1.45
4.875	Feb 12n	103:05	103:06	−2	4.34
3.000	Jul 12i	110:06	110:07	−4	1.52
4.375	Aug 12n	100:00	100:01	−3	4.37
4.000	Nov 12n	97:14	97:15	−3	4.39
10.375	Nov 12	116:06	116:07	−2	3.86
3.875	Feb 13n	96:11	96:12	−2	4.42
3.625	May 13n	94:23	94:24	−3	4.40
1.875	Jul 13i	101:26	101:27	−6	1.63
4.250	Aug 13n	98:12	98:13	−3	4.48
12.000	Aug 13	125:06	125:07	−2	3.99
4.250	Nov 13n	98:08	98:09	−3	4.49
2.000	Jan 14i	102:15	102:16	−5	1.69

RATE	MATURITY MO/YR	BID	ASKED	CHG	ASK YLD
4.000	Feb 14n	96:09	96:10	−3	4.51
4.750	May 14n	101:20	101:21	−3	4.53
13.250	May 14	134:22	134:23	−2	4.06
2.000	Jul 14i	102:07	102:08	−7	1.74
4.250	Aug 14n	97:26	97:27	−2	4.53
12.500	Aug 14	133:15	133:16	−2	4.10
11.750	Nov 14	131:27	131:28	−3	4.14
4.250	Nov 14n	97:22	97:23	−3	4.54
1.625	Jan 15i	98:19	98:20	−8	1.78
4.000	Feb 15n	95:26	95:27	−4	4.52
11.250	Feb 15	152:30	152:31	−6	4.54
10.625	Aug 15	149:20	149:21	−6	4.57
9.875	Nov 15	144:00	144:00	−6	4.60
9.250	Feb 16	139:10	139:11	−6	4.61
7.250	May 16	122:11	122:12	−4	4.65
7.500	Nov 16	125:01	125:02	−5	4.68
8.750	May 17	137:00	137:00	−6	4.71
8.875	Aug 17	138:18	138:19	−6	4.72
9.125	May 18	142:12	142:13	−7	4.75
9.000	Nov 18	141:29	141:30	−8	4.78
8.875	Feb 19	141:00	141:00	−8	4.80
8.125	Aug 19	133:30	133:31	−7	4.82
8.500	Feb 20	138:12	138:13	−8	4.85
8.750	May 20	141:15	141:16	−7	4.85
8.750	Aug 20	141:25	141:26	−7	4.86
7.875	Feb 21	132:24	132:25	−8	4.88
8.125	May 21	135:27	135:28	−8	4.89
8.125	Aug 21	136:05	136:06	−8	4.89
8.000	Nov 21	135:01	135:02	−8	4.89
7.250	Aug 22	127:02	127:03	−8	4.91
7.625	Nov 22	131:21	131:22	−8	4.92
7.125	Feb 23	125:29	125:30	−8	4.93
6.250	Aug 23	115:22	115:23	−8	4.94
7.500	Nov 24	132:02	132:03	−8	4.93
2.375	Jan 25i	107:01	107:02	−10	1.94
7.625	Feb 25	133:29	133:30	−10	4.93
6.875	Aug 25	124:23	124:24	−9	4.94
6.000	Feb 26	113:21	113:22	−9	4.94
6.750	Aug 26	123:25	123:26	−8	4.94
6.500	Nov 26	120:19	120:20	−10	4.94
6.625	Feb 27	122:14	122:15	−10	4.93
6.375	Aug 27	119:12	119:13	−10	4.93
6.125	Nov 27	116:05	116:06	−9	4.93
3.625	Apr 28i	130:29	130:30	−7	1.95
5.500	Aug 28	107:27	107:28	−10	4.93
5.250	Nov 28	104:13	104:14	−8	4.93
5.250	Feb 29	104:17	104:18	−8	4.92
3.875	Apr 29i	136:30	136:31	−8	1.94
6.125	Aug 29	116:30	116:31	−11	4.92
6.250	May 30	119:10	119:11	−8	4.90
5.375	Feb 31	108:01	108:02	−9	4.83
3.375	Apr 32i	131:27	131:28	−11	1.87

FIGURE 5.4

Sample *Wall Street Journal* U.S. Treasury Note and Bond Prices

Source: Reprinted by permission of *The Wall Street Journal,* via Copyright Clearance Center © 2005 Dow Jones and Company, Inc., March 22, 2005. All Rights Reserved Worldwide.

it sells for more than its face value. Not surprisingly, its yield to maturity (4.89 percent) is less than its coupon rate (8 percent).

Some of the maturity dates in Figure 5.4 have an "n" after them. This just means that these issues are notes rather than bonds. The bonds with an "i" after them are the inflation-linked bonds, or TIPS, which we discussed in a previous section.

The very last ordinary bond listed, the 5.375 Feb 31, is often called the "bellwether" bond. This bond's yield is the one that is usually reported in the evening news. So, for example, when you hear that long-term interest rates rose, what is really being said is that the yield on this bond went up (and its price went down). Beginning in 2001, the Treasury announced that it would no longer sell 30-year bonds, leaving the 10-year note as the longest maturity issue sold. However, in 2006, the 30-year bond was resurrected and once again assumed bellwether status.

Current and historical Treasury yield information is available at www.publicdebt.treas.gov/of/ofaucrt.htm.

If you examine the yields on the various issues in Figure 5.4, you will clearly see that they vary by maturity. Why this occurs and what it might mean is one of the things we discuss in our next section.

EXAMPLE 5.5 Treasury Quotes

Locate the Treasury note in Figure 5.4 maturing in October 2008. What is its coupon rate? What is its bid price? What was the *previous day's* asked price?

The note listed as 3.125 Oct 08 is the one we seek. Its coupon rate is 3.125, or 3.125 percent of face value. The bid price is 97:02, or 97.0625 percent of face value. The ask price is 97:03, which is down by one tick from the previous day. This means that the ask price on the previous day was equal to 97 $\frac{3}{32}$ + 1/32 = 97 $\frac{4}{32}$ = 97:04.

A Note on Bond Price Quotes

If you buy a bond between coupon payment dates, the price you pay is usually more than the price you are quoted. The reason is that standard convention in the bond market is to quote prices net of "accrued interest," meaning that accrued interest is deducted to arrive at the quoted price. This quoted price is called the **clean price**. The price you actually pay, however, includes the accrued interest. This price is the **dirty price**, also known as the "full" or "invoice" price.

An example is the easiest way to understand these issues. Suppose you buy a bond with a 12 percent annual coupon, payable semiannually. You actually pay $1,080 for this bond, so $1,080 is the dirty, or invoice, price. Further, on the day you buy it, the next coupon is due in four months, so you are between coupon dates. Notice that the next coupon will be $60.

The accrued interest on a bond is calculated by taking the fraction of the coupon period that has passed, in this case two months out of six, and multiplying this fraction by the next coupon, $60. So, the accrued interest in this example is 2/6 × $60 = $20. The bond's quoted price (i.e., its clean price) would be $1,080 − $20 = $1,060.[6]

5.6 INFLATION AND INTEREST RATES

So far, we haven't considered the role of inflation in our various discussions of interest rates, yields, and returns. Because this is an important consideration, we consider the impact of inflation next.

Real versus Nominal Rates

In examining interest rates, or any other financial market rates such as discount rates, bond yields, rates of return, and required returns, it is often necessary to distinguish between **real rates** and **nominal rates**. Nominal rates are called "nominal" because they have not been adjusted for inflation. Real rates are rates that have been adjusted for inflation.

To see the effect of inflation, suppose prices are currently rising by 5 percent per year. In other words, the rate of inflation is 5 percent. An investment is available that will be worth $115.50 in one year. It costs $100 today. Notice that with a present value of $100

[6]The way accrued interest is calculated actually depends on the type of bond being quoted, for example, Treasury or corporate. The difference has to do with exactly how the fractional coupon period is calculated. In our example above, we implicitly treated the months as having exactly the same length (i.e., 30 days each, 360 days in a year), which is consistent with the way corporate bonds are quoted. In contrast, for Treasury bonds, actual day counts are used.

and a future value in one year of $115.50, this investment has a 15.5 percent rate of return. In calculating this 15.5 percent return, we did not consider the effect of inflation, however, so this is the nominal return.

What is the impact of inflation here? To answer, suppose pizzas cost $5 apiece at the beginning of the year. With $100, we can buy 20 pizzas. Because the inflation rate is 5 percent, pizzas will cost 5 percent more, or $5.25, at the end of the year. If we take the investment, how many pizzas can we buy at the end of the year? Measured in pizzas, what is the rate of return on this investment?

Our $115.50 from the investment will buy us $115.50/5.25 = 22 pizzas. This is up from 20 pizzas, so our pizza rate of return is 10 percent. What this illustrates is that even though the nominal return on our investment is 15.5 percent, our buying power goes up by only 10 percent because of inflation. Put another way, we are really only 10 percent richer. In this case, we say that the real return is 10 percent.

Alternatively, we can say that with 5 percent inflation, each of the $115.50 nominal dollars we get is worth 5 percent less in real terms, so the real dollar value of our investment in a year is:

$$\$115.50/1.05 = \$110$$

What we have done is to *deflate* the $115.50 by 5 percent. Because we give up $100 in current buying power to get the equivalent of $110, our real return is again 10 percent. Because we have removed the effect of future inflation here, this $110 is said to be measured in current dollars.

The difference between nominal and real rates is important and bears repeating:

The nominal rate on an investment is the percentage change in the number of dollars you have.

The real rate on an investment is the percentage change in how much you can buy with your dollars, in other words, the percentage change in your buying power.

The Fisher Effect

Our discussion of real and nominal returns illustrates a relationship often called the **Fisher effect** (after the great economist Irving Fisher). Because investors are ultimately concerned with what they can buy with their money, they require compensation for inflation. Let R stand for the nominal rate and r stand for the real rate. The Fisher effect tells us that the relationship between nominal rates, real rates, and inflation can be written as:

$$1 + R = (1 + r) \times (1 + h) \tag{5.2}$$

where h is the inflation rate.

In the preceding example, the nominal rate was 15.50 percent and the inflation rate was 5 percent. What was the real rate? We can determine it by plugging in these numbers:

$$\begin{aligned} 1 + .1550 &= (1 + r) \times (1 + .05) \\ 1 + r &= 1.1550/1.05 = 1.10 \\ r &= 10\% \end{aligned}$$

This real rate is the same as we had before. If we take another look at the Fisher effect, we can rearrange things a little as follows:

$$\begin{aligned} 1 + R &= (1 + r) \times (1 + h) \\ R &= r + h + r \times h \end{aligned} \tag{5.3}$$

What this tells us is that the nominal rate has three components. First, there is the real rate on the investment, r. Next, there is the compensation for the decrease in the value of the money originally invested because of inflation, h. The third component represents compensation for the fact that the dollars earned on the investment are also worth less because of the inflation.

This third component is usually small, so it is often dropped. The nominal rate is then approximately equal to the real rate plus the inflation rate:

$$R \approx r + h \tag{5.4}$$

EXAMPLE 5.6 The Fisher Effect

If investors require a 10 percent real rate of return, and the inflation rate is 8 percent, what must be the approximate nominal rate? The exact nominal rate?

First of all, the nominal rate is approximately equal to the sum of the real rate and the inflation rate: 10 percent + 8 percent = 18 percent. From the Fisher effect, we have:

$$\begin{aligned} 1 + R &= (1 + r) \times (1 + h) \\ &= 1.10 \times 1.08 \\ &= 1.1880 \end{aligned}$$

Therefore, the nominal rate will actually be closer to 19 percent.

It is important to note that financial rates, such as interest rates, discount rates, and rates of return, are almost always quoted in nominal terms. To remind you of this, we will henceforth use the symbol R instead of r in most of our discussions about such rates.

5.7 DETERMINANTS OF BOND YIELDS

We are now in a position to discuss the determinants of a bond's yield. As we will see, the yield on any particular bond is a reflection of a variety of factors, some common to all bonds and some specific to the issue under consideration.

The Term Structure of Interest Rates

At any point in time, short-term and long-term interest rates will generally be different. Sometimes short-term rates are higher, sometimes lower. Figure 5.5 gives us a long range perspective on this by showing almost two centuries of short- and long-term interest rates. As shown, through time, the difference between short- and long-term rates has ranged from essentially zero to up to several percentage points, both positive and negative.

The relationship between short- and long-term interest rates is known as the **term structure of interest rates**. To be a little more precise, the term structure of interest rates tells us what *nominal* interest rates are on *default-free, pure discount* bonds of all maturities. These rates are, in essence, "pure" interest rates because they involve no risk of default and a single, lump-sum future payment. In other words, the term structure tells us the pure time value of money for different lengths of time.

When long-term rates are higher than short-term rates, we say that the term structure is upward sloping, and, when short-term rates are higher, we say it is downward sloping. The term structure can also be "humped." When this occurs, it is usually because rates increase at first, but then begin to decline as we look at longer- and longer-term rates. The most common shape of the term structure, particularly in modern times, is upward sloping, but the degree of steepness has varied quite a bit.

FIGURE 5.5

U.S. Interest Rates: 1800–2005

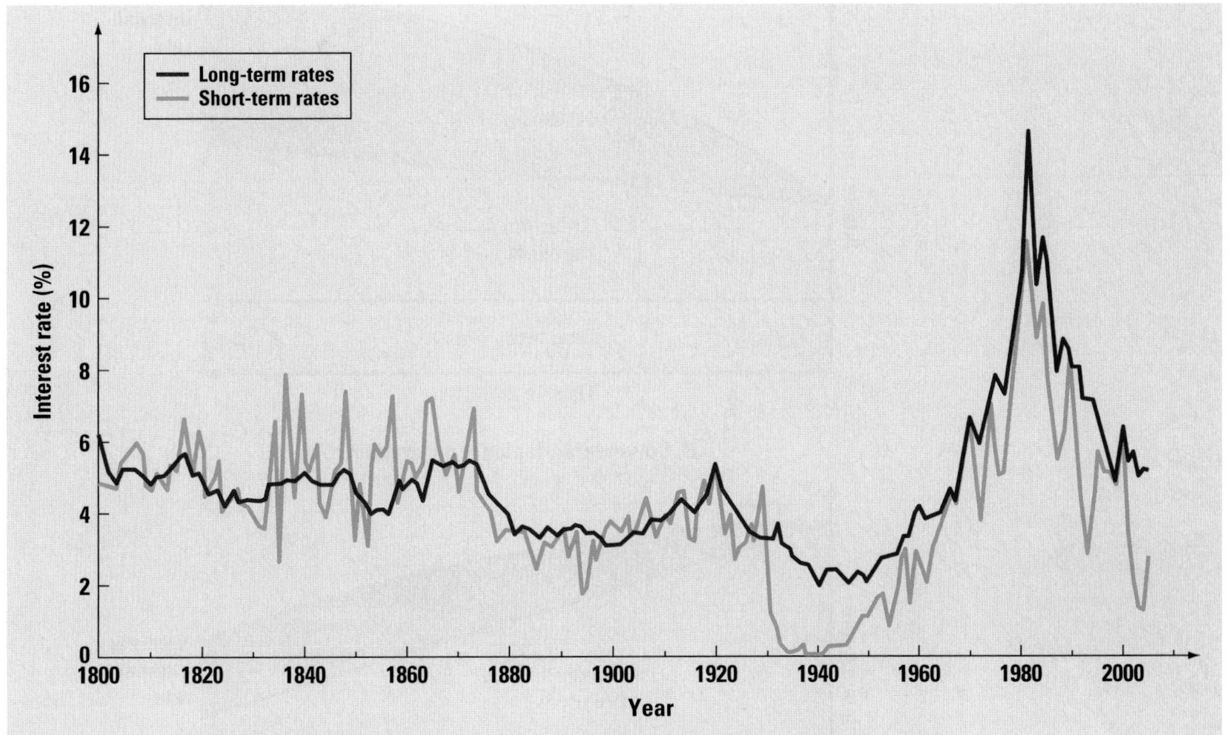

Source: Jeremy J. Siegel, *Stocks for the Long Run*, 3rd edition, © McGraw-Hill, 2004, updated by the authors.

What determines the shape of the term structure? There are three basic components. The first two are the ones we discussed in our previous section, the real rate of interest and the rate of inflation. The real rate of interest is the compensation investors demand for forgoing the use of their money. You can think of it as the pure time value of money after adjusting for the effects of inflation.

The real rate of interest is the basic component underlying every interest rate, regardless of the time to maturity. When the real rate is high, all interest rates will tend to be higher, and vice versa. Thus, the real rate doesn't really determine the shape of the term structure; instead, it mostly influences the overall level of interest rates.

In contrast, the prospect of future inflation very strongly influences the shape of the term structure. Investors thinking about loaning money for various lengths of time recognize that future inflation erodes the value of the dollars that will be returned. As a result, investors demand compensation for this loss in the form of higher nominal rates. This extra compensation is called the **inflation premium**.

If investors believe that the rate of inflation will be higher in the future, then long-term nominal interest rates will tend to be higher than short-term rates. Thus, an upward-sloping term structure may be a reflection of anticipated increases in inflation. Similarly, a downward-sloping term structure probably reflects the belief that inflation will be falling in the future.

You can actually see the inflation premium in U.S. Treasury yields. Look back at Figure 5.4 and recall that the entries with an "i" after them are Treasury Inflation Protection Securities (TIPS). If you compare the yields on a TIPS to a regular note or bond with a similar maturity, the difference in the yields is the inflation premium. For the issues

FIGURE 5.6

The Term Structure of Interest Rates

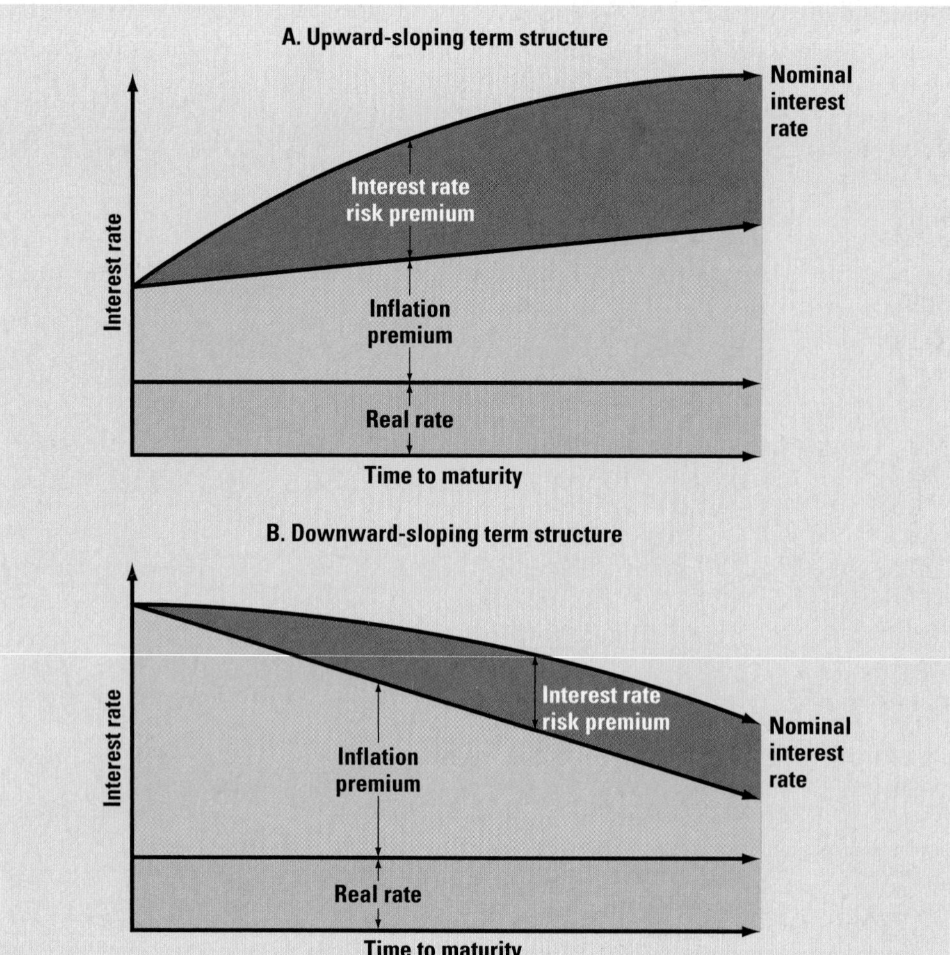

in Figure 5.4, check that the spread is about 2 to 3 percent, meaning that investors demand an extra 2 or 3 percent in yield as compensation for potential future inflation.

The third, and last, component of the term structure has to do with interest rate risk. As we discussed earlier in the chapter, longer-term bonds have much greater risk of loss resulting from changes in interest rates than do shorter-term bonds. Investors recognize this risk, and they demand extra compensation in the form of higher rates for bearing it. This extra compensation is called the **interest rate risk premium**. The longer the term to maturity, the greater is the interest rate risk, so the interest rate risk premium increases with maturity. However, as we discussed earlier, interest rate risk increases at a decreasing rate, so the interest rate risk premium does as well.[7]

Putting the pieces together, we see that the term structure reflects the combined effect of the real rate of interest, the inflation premium, and the interest rate risk premium. Figure 5.6 shows how these can interact to produce an upward-sloping term structure (in the top part of Figure 5.6) or a downward-sloping term structure (in the bottom part).

[7]In days of old, the interest rate risk premium was called a "liquidity" premium. Today, the term *liquidity premium* has an altogether different meaning, which we explore in our next section. Also, the interest rate risk premium is sometimes called a maturity risk premium. Our terminology is consistent with the modern view of the term structure.

In the top part of Figure 5.6, notice how the rate of inflation is expected to rise gradually. At the same time, the interest rate risk premium increases at a decreasing rate, so the combined effect is to produce a pronounced upward-sloping term structure. In the bottom part of Figure 5.6, the rate of inflation is expected to fall in the future, and the expected decline is enough to offset the interest rate risk premium and produce a downward-sloping term structure. Notice that if the rate of inflation was expected to decline by only a small amount, we could still get an upward-sloping term structure because of the interest rate risk premium.

We assumed in drawing Figure 5.6 that the real rate would remain the same. Actually, expected future real rates could be larger or smaller than the current real rate. Also, for simplicity, we used straight lines to show expected future inflation rates as rising or declining, but they do not necessarily have to look like this. They could, for example, rise and then fall, leading to a humped yield curve.

Bond Yields and the Yield Curve: Putting It All Together

Going back to Figure 5.4, recall that we saw that the yields on Treasury notes and bonds of different maturities are not the same. Each day, in addition to the Treasury prices and yields shown in Figure 5.4, *The Wall Street Journal* provides a plot of Treasury yields relative to maturity. This plot is called the **Treasury yield curve** (or just the yield curve). Figure 5.7 shows the yield curve drawn from the yields in Figure 5.4.

Online yield curve information is available at www.bloomberg.com/markets.

As you probably now suspect, the shape of the yield curve is a reflection of the term structure of interest rates. In fact, the Treasury yield curve and the term structure of interest rates are almost the same thing. The only difference is that the term structure is based on pure discount bonds, whereas the yield curve is based on coupon bond yields. As a result, Treasury yields depend on the three components that underlie the term structure—the real rate, expected future inflation, and the interest rate risk premium.

Treasury notes and bonds have three important features that we need to remind you of: they are default-free, they are taxable, and they are highly liquid. This is not true of bonds in general, so we need to examine what additional factors come into play when we look at bonds issued by corporations or municipalities.

The first thing to consider is credit risk, that is, the possibility of default. Investors recognize that issuers other than the Treasury may or may not make all the promised

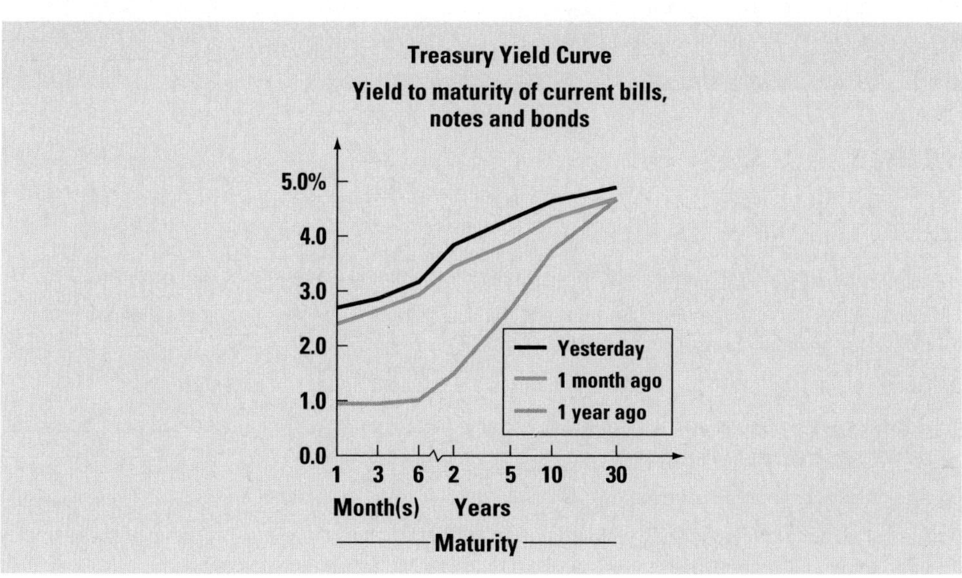

FIGURE 5.7

The Treasury Yield Curve: March, 2005

Source: Reprinted by permission of *The Wall Street Journal,* via Copyright Clearance Center © 2005 by Dow Jones & Company, Inc., 2005. All Rights Reserved Worldwide.

payments on a bond, so they demand a higher yield as compensation for this risk. This extra compensation is called the **default risk premium**. Earlier in the chapter, we saw how bonds were rated based on their credit risk. What you will find if you start looking at bonds of different ratings is that lower-rated bonds have higher yields.

An important thing to recognize about a bond's yield is that it is calculated assuming that all the promised payments will be made. As a result, it is really a promised yield, and it may or may not be what you will earn. In particular, if the issuer defaults, your actual yield will be lower, probably much lower. This fact is particularly important when it comes to junk bonds. Thanks to a clever bit of marketing, such bonds are now commonly called high-yield bonds, which has a much nicer ring to it; but now you recognize that these are really high *promised* yield bonds.

Next, recall that we discussed earlier how municipal bonds are free from most taxes and, as a result, have much lower yields than taxable bonds. Investors demand the extra yield on a taxable bond as compensation for the unfavorable tax treatment. This extra compensation is the **taxability premium**.

Finally, bonds have varying degrees of liquidity. As we discussed earlier, there are an enormous number of bond issues, most of which do not trade on a regular basis. As a result, if you wanted to sell quickly, you would probably not get as good a price as you could otherwise. Investors prefer liquid assets to illiquid ones, so they demand a **liquidity premium** on top of all the other premiums we have discussed. As a result, all else being the same, less liquid bonds will have higher yields than more liquid bonds.

Conclusion

If we combine all of the things we have discussed regarding bond yields, we find that bond yields represent the combined effect of no fewer than six things. The first is the real rate of interest. On top of the real rate are five premiums representing compensation for (1) expected future inflation, (2) interest rate risk, (3) default risk, (4) taxability, and (5) lack of liquidity. As a result, determining the appropriate yield on a bond requires careful analysis of each of these effects.

SUMMARY AND CONCLUSIONS

This chapter has explored bonds, bond yields, and interest rates. We saw that:

1. Determining bond prices and yields is an application of basic discounted cash flow principles.
2. Bond values move in the direction opposite that of interest rates, leading to potential gains or losses for bond investors.
3. Bonds have a variety of features spelled out in a document called the indenture.
4. Bonds are rated based on their default risk. Some bonds, such as Treasury bonds, have no risk of default, whereas so-called junk bonds have substantial default risk.
5. A wide variety of bonds exist, many of which contain exotic or unusual features.
6. Almost all bond trading is OTC, with little or no market transparency in many cases. As a result, bond price and volume information can be difficult to find for some types of bonds.

7. Bond yields and interest rates reflect the effect of six different things: the real interest rate and five premiums that investors demand as compensation for inflation, interest rate risk, default risk, taxability, and lack of liquidity.

In closing, we note that bonds are a vital source of financing to governments and corporations of all types. Bond prices and yields are a rich subject, and our one chapter, necessarily, touches on only the most important concepts and ideas. There is a great deal more we could say, but, instead, we will move on to stocks in our next chapter.

CONCEPT QUESTIONS

1. **Treasury Bonds** Is it true that a U.S. Treasury security is risk-free?
2. **Interest Rate Risk** Which has greater interest rate risk, a 30-year Treasury bond or a 30-year BB corporate bond?
3. **Treasury Pricing** With regard to bid and ask prices on a Treasury bond, is it possible for the bid price to be higher? Why or why not?
4. **Yield to Maturity** Treasury bid and ask quotes are sometimes given in terms of yields, so there would be a bid yield and an ask yield. Which do you think would be larger? Explain.
5. **Call Provisions** A company is contemplating a long-term bond issue. It is debating whether or not to include a call provision. What are the benefits to the company from including a call provision? What are the costs? How do these answers change for a put provision?
6. **Coupon Rate** How does a bond issuer decide on the appropriate coupon rate to set on its bonds? Explain the difference between the coupon rate and the required return on a bond.
7. **Real and Nominal Returns** Are there any circumstances under which an investor might be more concerned about the nominal return on an investment than the real return?
8. **Bond Ratings** Companies pay rating agencies such as Moody's and S&P to rate their bonds, and the costs can be substantial. However, companies are not required to have their bonds rated in the first place; doing so is strictly voluntary. Why do you think they do it?
9. **Bond Ratings** U.S. Treasury bonds are not rated. Why? Often, junk bonds are not rated. Why?
10. **Term Structure** What is the difference between the term structure of interest rates and the yield curve?
11. **Crossover Bonds** Looking back at the crossover bonds we discussed in the chapter, why do you think split ratings such as these occur?
12. **Municipal Bonds** Why is it that municipal bonds are not taxed at the federal level, but are taxable across state lines? Why is it that U.S. Treasury bonds are not taxable at the state level? (You may need to dust off the history books for this one.)
13. **Bond Market** What are the implications for bond investors of the lack of transparency in the bond market?
14. **Treasury Market** All Treasury bonds are relatively liquid, but some are more liquid than others. Take a look back at Figure 5.4. Which issues appear to be the most liquid? The least liquid?
15. **Rating Agencies** A controversy erupted regarding bond-rating agencies when some agencies began to provide unsolicited bond ratings. Why do you think this is controversial?
16. **Bonds as Equity** The 100-year bonds we discussed in the chapter have something in common with junk bonds. Critics charge that, in both cases, the issuers are really selling equity in disguise. What are the issues here? Why would a company want to sell "equity in disguise"?
17. **Bond Prices versus Yields**
    a. What is the relationship between the price of a bond and its YTM?

b. Explain why some bonds sell at a premium over par value while other bonds sell at a discount. What do you know about the relationship between the coupon rate and the YTM for premium bonds? What about for discount bonds? For bonds selling at par value?

c. What is the relationship between the current yield and YTM for premium bonds? For discount bonds? For bonds selling at par value?

18. **Interest Rate Risk** All else the same, which has more interest rate risk, a long-term bond or a short-term bond? What about a low coupon bond compared to a high coupon bond? What about a long-term, high coupon bond compared to a short-term, low coupon bond?

QUESTIONS AND PROBLEMS

Basic
(Questions 1–10)

1. **Valuing Bonds** What is the price of a 10-year, pure discount bond paying $1,000 at maturity if the YTM is:

   a. 5 percent

   b. 10 percent

   c. 15 percent

2. **Valuing Bonds** Microhard has issued a bond with the following characteristics:

   Par: $1,000

   Time to maturity: 20 years

   Coupon rate: 8 percent

   Semiannual payments

   Calculate the price of this bond if the YTM is:

   a. 8 percent

   b. 10 percent

   c. 6 percent

3. **Bond Yields** Raines Umbrella Corp. issued 12-year bonds 2 years ago at a coupon rate of 8.6 percent. The bonds make semiannual payments. If these bonds currently sell for 97 percent of par value, what is the YTM?

4. **Coupon Rates** Rhiannon Corporation has bonds on the market with 14.5 years to maturity, a YTM of 7.5 percent, and a current price of $1,145. The bonds make semiannual payments. What must the coupon rate be on these bonds?

5. **Calculating Real Rates of Return** If Treasury bills are currently paying 6 percent and the inflation rate is 4.5 percent, what is the approximate real rate of interest? The exact real rate?

6. **Inflation and Nominal Returns** Suppose the real rate is 4 percent and the inflation rate is 2.5 percent. What rate would you expect to see on a Treasury bill?

7. **Nominal and Real Returns** An investment offers a 15 percent total return over the coming year. Alan Wingspan thinks the total real return on this investment will be only 9 percent. What does Alan believe the inflation rate will be over the next year?

8. **Nominal versus Real Returns** Say you own an asset that had a total return last year of 13.4 percent. If the inflation rate last year was 4.5 percent, what was your real return?

9. **Using Treasury Quotes** Locate the Treasury issue in Figure 5.4 maturing in November 2027. Is this a note or a bond? What is its coupon rate? What is its bid price? What was the *previous day's* asked price?

10. **Using Treasury Quotes** Locate the Treasury bond in Figure 5.4 maturing in November 2024. Is this a premium or a discount bond? What is its current yield? What is its yield to maturity? What is the bid-ask spread?

Intermediate (Questions 11–20)

11. **Bond Price Movements** Miller Corporation has a premium bond making semiannual payments. The bond pays an 8 percent coupon, has a YTM of 6 percent, and has 13 years to maturity. The Modigliani Company has a discount bond making semiannual payments. This bond pays a 6 percent coupon, has a YTM of 8 percent, and also has 13 years to maturity. If interest rates remain unchanged, what do you expect the price of these bonds to be 1 year from now? In 3 years? In 8 years? In 12 years? In 13 years? What's going on here? Illustrate your answers by graphing bond prices versus time to maturity.

12. **Interest Rate Risk** Evans, Inc., and Troxel Corp. both have 10 percent coupon bonds outstanding, with semiannual interest payments, and both are priced at par value. The Evans, Inc., bond has 2 years to maturity, whereas the Troxel Corp. bond has 15 years to maturity. If interest rates suddenly rise by 2 percent, what is the percentage change in the price of these bonds? If interest rates were to suddenly fall by 2 percent instead, what would the percentage change in the price of these bonds be then? Illustrate your answers by graphing bond prices versus YTM. What does this problem tell you about the interest rate risk of longer-term bonds?

13. **Interest Rate Risk** The Faulk Corp. has a 5 percent coupon bond outstanding. The Gonas Company has an 11 percent bond outstanding. Both bonds have 8 years to maturity, make semiannual payments, and have a YTM of 7 percent. If interest rates suddenly rise by 2 percent, what is the percentage change in the price of these bonds? What if interest rates suddenly fall by 2 percent instead? What does this problem tell you about the interest rate risk of lower coupon bonds?

14. **Bond Yields** Stealers Wheel Software has 8.4 percent coupon bonds on the market with 9 years to maturity. The bonds make semiannual payments and currently sell for 104 percent of par. What is the current yield on the bonds? The YTM? The effective annual yield?

15. **Bond Yields** Petty Co. wants to issue new 20-year bonds for some much-needed expansion projects. The company currently has 8 percent coupon bonds on the market that sell for $1,095, make semiannual payments, and mature in 20 years. What coupon rate should the company set on its new bonds if it wants them to sell at par?

16. **Accrued Interest** You purchase a bond with an invoice price of $1,140. The bond has a coupon rate of 7.2 percent, and there are 5 months to the next semiannual coupon date. What is the clean price of the bond?

17. **Accrued Interest** You purchase a bond with a coupon rate of 6.5 percent and a clean price of $865. If the next semiannual coupon payment is due in three months, what is the invoice price?

18. **Finding the Bond Maturity** Jude Corp. has 11 percent coupon bonds making annual payments with a YTM of 8.5 percent. The current yield on these bonds is 9.06 percent. How many years do these bonds have left until they mature?

19. **Using Bond Quotes** Suppose the following bond quotes for IOU Corporation appear in the financial page of today's newspaper. Assume the bond has a face value of $1,000 and the current date is April 15, 2006. What is the yield to maturity of the bond? What is the current yield? What is the yield to maturity on a comparable U.S. Treasury issue?

COMPANY (TICKER)	COUPON	MATURITY	LAST PRICE	LAST YIELD	EST SPREAD	UST	EST VOL (000s)
IOU (IOU)	7.375	Apr 15, 2016	769.355	??	468	10	1,827

20. **Finding the Maturity** You've just found a 10 percent coupon bond on the market that sells for par value. What is the maturity on this bond?

Challenge (Questions 21–28)

21. **Components of Bond Returns** Bond P is a premium bond with a 10 percent coupon. Bond D is a 6 percent coupon bond currently selling at a discount. Both bonds make annual payments, have a YTM of 8 percent, and have five years to maturity. What is the current yield for Bond P? For Bond D? If interest rates remain unchanged, what is the expected capital gains yield over the next year for Bond P? For Bond D? Explain your answers and the interrelationship among the various types of yields.

22. **Holding Period Yield** The YTM on a bond is the interest rate you earn on your investment if interest rates don't change. If you actually sell the bond before it matures, your realized return is known as the holding period yield (HPY).

    a. Suppose that today you buy an 8 percent annual coupon bond for $1,150. The bond has 10 years to maturity. What rate of return do you expect to earn on your investment?

    b. Two years from now, the YTM on your bond has declined by 1 percent, and you decide to sell. What price will your bond sell for? What is the HPY on your investment? Compare this yield to the YTM when you first bought the bond. Why are they different?

23. **Valuing Bonds** The Mallory Corporation has two different bonds currently outstanding. Bond M has a face value of $20,000 and matures in 20 years. The bond makes no payments for the first six years, then pays $1,200 every six months over the subsequent eight years, and finally pays $1,500 every six months over the last six years. Bond N also has a face value of $20,000 and a maturity of 20 years; it makes no coupon payments over the life of the bond. If the required return on both these bonds is 10 percent compounded semiannually, what is the current price of Bond M? Of Bond N?

24. **Valuing the Call Feature** Consider the prices in the following three Treasury issues as of February 24, 2006:

6.500	May 12n	106:10	106:12	−13	5.28
8.250	May 12	103:14	103:16	− 3	5.24
12.000	May 12	134:25	134:31	−15	5.32

    The bond in the middle is callable in February 2007. What is the implied value of the call feature? (Hint: Is there a way to combine the two noncallable issues to create an issue that has the same coupon as the callable bond?)

25. **Treasury Bonds** The following Treasury bond quote appeared in *The Wall Street Journal* on May 11, 2004:

9.125	May 09	100:03	100:04	. . .	−2.15

    Why would anyone buy this Treasury bond with a negative yield to maturity? How is this possible?

26. **Real Cash Flows** When Marilyn Monroe died, ex-husband Joe DiMaggio vowed to place fresh flowers on her grave every Sunday as long as he lived. The week after she died in 1962, a bunch of fresh flowers that the former baseball player thought appropriate for the star cost about $5. Based on actuarial tables, "Joltin' Joe" could expect to live for 30 years after the actress died. Assume that the EAR is 10.4 percent. Also, assume that the price of the flowers will increase at 3.9 percent per year, when expressed as an EAR. Assuming that each year has exactly 52 weeks, what is the present value of this commitment? Joe began purchasing flowers the week after Marilyn died.

27. **Real Cash Flows** You are planning to save for retirement over the next 30 years. To save for retirement, you will invest $700 a month in a stock account in real dollars and $300 a month in a bond account in real dollars. The effective annual return of the stock account is expected to be 11 percent, and the bond account will earn 7 percent. When you retire, you will combine your money into an account with a 9 percent effective return. The inflation rate over this period is expected to be 4 percent. How much can you withdraw each month from your account in real terms assuming a 25-year withdrawal period? What is the nominal dollar amount of your last withdrawal?

28. **Real Cash Flows** Paul Adams owns a health club in downtown Los Angeles. He charges his customers an annual fee of $400 and has an existing customer base of 500. Paul plans to raise the annual fee by 10 percent every year and expects the club membership to grow at a constant rate of 3 percent for the next five years. The overall expenses of running the health club are $80,000 a year and are expected to grow at the inflation rate of 2 percent annually. After five years, Paul plans to buy a luxury boat for $500,000, close the health club, and travel the world in his boat for the rest of his life. What is the annual amount that Paul can spend while on his world tour if he will have no money left in the bank when he dies? Assume Paul has a remaining life of 15 years and earns 8 percent on his savings.

S&P PROBLEM

www.mhhe.com/edumarketinsight

1. **Bond Ratings** Look up Coca-Cola (KO), Gateway (GTW), AT&T (T), and Navistar International (NAV). For each company, follow the "Financial Highlights" link and find the bond rating. Which companies have an investment grade rating? Which companies are rated below investment grade? Are any unrated? When you find the credit rating for one of the companies, click on the "S&P Issuer Credit Rating" link. What are the three considerations listed that Standard & Poor's uses to issue a credit rating?

WHAT'S ON THE WEB?

1. **Bond Quotes** You can find current bond prices at www.nasdbondinfo.com. You want to find the bond prices and yields for bonds issued by Georgia Pacific. You can enter the ticker symbol "GP" to do a search. What is the shortest maturity bond issued by Georgia Pacific that is outstanding? What is the longest maturity bond? What is the credit rating for Georgia Pacific's bonds? Do all of the bonds have the same credit rating? Why do you think this is?

2. **Yield Curves** You can find information regarding the most current bond yields at money.cnn.com. Find the "Bonds & Rates" link and then find the yield curve for U.S. Treasury bonds. What is the general shape of the yield curve? What does this imply about the expected future inflation? Now graph the yield curve for AAA, AA and A rated corporate bonds. Is the corporate yield curve the same shape as the Treasury yield curve? Why or why not?

3. **Default Premiums** The St. Louis Federal Reserve Board has files listing historical interest rates on its Web site www.stls.frb.org. Find the link for "FRED" data, then "Interest Rates." You will find listings for Moody's Seasoned Aaa Corporate Bond Yield and Moody's Seasoned Baa Corporate Bond Yield. A default premium can be calculated as the difference between the Aaa bond yield and the Baa bond yield. Calculate the default premium using these two bond indices for the most recent 36 months. Is the default premium the same for every month? Why do you think this is?

FINANCING EAST COAST YACHTS'S EXPANSION PLANS WITH A BOND ISSUE

CLOSING CASE

Larisa Warren, the owner of East Coast Yachts, has decided to expand her operations. She asked her newly hired financial analyst, Dan Ervin, to enlist an underwriter to help sell $30 million in new 20-year bonds to finance new construction. Dan has entered into discussions with Robin Perry, an underwriter from the firm of Crowe & Mallard, about which bond features East Coast Yachts should consider and also what coupon rate the issue will likely have. Although Dan is aware of bond features, he is uncertain as to the costs and benefits of some features, so he isn't clear on how each feature would affect the coupon rate of the bond issue.

1. You are Robin's assistant, and she has asked you to prepare a memo to Dan describing the effect of each of the following bond features on the coupon rate of the bond. She would also like you to list any advantages or disadvantages of each feature.

a. The security of the bond, that is, whether or not the bond has collateral.

b. The seniority of the bond.

c. The presence of a sinking fund.

d. A call provision with specified call dates and call prices.

e. A deferred call accompanying the above call provision.

f. A make-whole call provision.

g. Any positive covenants. Also, discuss several possible positive covenants East Coast Yachts might consider.

h. Any negative covenants. Also, discuss several possible negative covenants East Coast Yachts might consider.

i. A conversion feature (note that East Coast Yachts is not a publicly traded company).

j. A floating rate coupon.

Dan is also considering whether to issue coupon bearing bonds or zero coupon bonds. The YTM on either bond issue will be 8 percent. The coupon bond would have an 8 percent coupon rate. The company's tax rate is 35 percent.

2. How many of the coupon bonds must East Coast Yachts issue to raise the $30 million? How many of the zeroes must it issue?
3. In 20 years, what will be the principal repayment due if East Coast Yachts issues the coupon bonds? What if it issues the zeroes?
4. What are the company's considerations in issuing a coupon bond compared to a zero coupon bond?
5. Suppose East Coast Yachts issues the coupon bonds with a make-whole call provision. The make-whole call rate is the Treasury rate plus .40 percent. If East Coast calls the bonds in 7 years when the Treasury rate is 5.6 percent, what is the call price of the bond? What if it is 9.1 percent?
6. Are investors really made whole with a make-whole call provision?
7. After considering all the relevant factors, would you recommend a zero coupon issue or a regular coupon issue? Why? Would you recommend an ordinary call feature or a make-whole call feature? Why?

CHAPTER 6

Stock Valuation

OPENING CASE

When the stock market closed on March 24, 2005, the common stock of McGraw-Hill, publisher of fine quality college textbooks, was selling for $87.79 per share. On that same day, AutoZone, the car parts retailer, closed at $85.13 per share, while cigarette manufacturer Reynolds American closed at $78.52. Since the stock prices of these three companies were so similar, you might expect that the three companies would be offering similar dividends to their stockholders, but you would be wrong. In fact, Reynolds American's annual dividend was $3.80 per share, McGraw-Hill's was $1.32 per share, and AutoZone was paying no dividends at all!

In our previous chapter, we introduced you to bonds and bond valuation. In this chapter, we turn to the other major source of financing for corporations, common and preferred stock. We first describe the cash flows associated with a share of stock and then go on to develop a very famous result, the dividend growth model. From there, we move on to examine various important features of common and preferred stock, focusing on shareholder rights. We close out the chapter with a discussion of how shares of stock are traded and how stock prices and other important information are reported in the financial press.

6.1 THE PRESENT VALUE OF COMMON STOCKS

Dividends versus Capital Gains

Our goal in this section is to value common stocks. We learned in the previous chapter that an asset's value is determined by the present value of its future cash flows. A stock provides two kinds of cash flows. First, most stocks pay dividends on a regular basis. Second, the stockholder receives the sale price when she sells the stock. Thus, in order to value common stocks, we need to answer an interesting question: Is the value of a stock equal to:

1. The discounted present value of the sum of next period's dividend plus next period's stock price, or
2. The discounted present value of all future dividends?

This is the kind of question that students would love to see on a multiple-choice exam, because both (1) and (2) are right.

To see that (1) and (2) are the same, let's start with an individual who will buy the stock and hold it for one year. In other words, she has a one-year *holding period.* In addition, she is willing to pay P_0 for the stock today. That is, she calculates:

$$P_0 = \frac{\text{Div}_1}{1 + R} + \frac{P_1}{1 + R} \tag{6.1}$$

Div_1 is the dividend paid at year's end and P_1 is the price at year's end. P_0 is the PV of the common stock investment. The term in the denominator, R, is the appropriate discount rate for the stock.

That seems easy enough, but where does P_1 come from? P_1 is not pulled out of thin air. Rather, there must be a buyer at the end of year 1 who is willing to purchase the stock for P_1. This buyer determines price by:

$$P_1 = \frac{\text{Div}_2}{1 + R} + \frac{P_2}{1 + R} \tag{6.2}$$

Substituting the value of P_1 from (6.2) into equation (6.1) yields:

$$\begin{aligned} P_0 &= \frac{1}{1 + R}\left[\text{Div}_1 + \left(\frac{\text{Div}_2 + P_2}{1 + R}\right)\right] \\ &= \frac{\text{Div}_1}{1 + R} + \frac{\text{Div}_2}{(1 + R)^2} + \frac{P_2}{(1 + R)^2} \end{aligned} \tag{6.3}$$

We can ask a similar question for formula (6.3): Where does P_2 come from? An investor at the end of year 2 is willing to pay P_2 because of the dividend and stock price

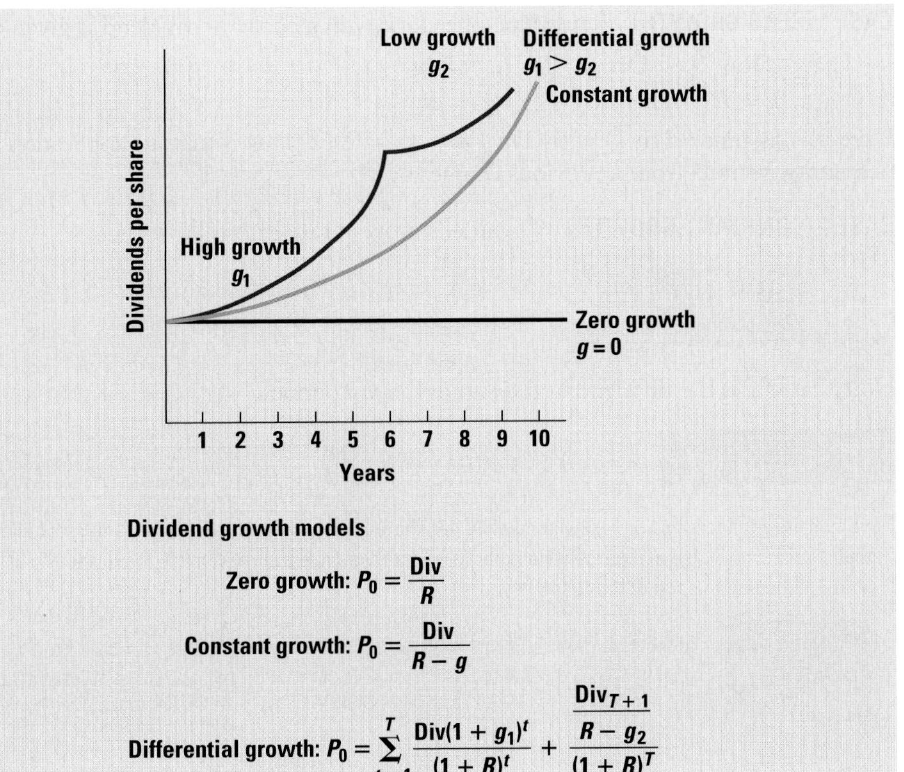

FIGURE 6.1
Zero Growth, Constant Growth, and Differential Growth Patterns

at year 3. This process can be repeated *ad nauseam*.[1] At the end, we are left with

$$P_0 = \frac{\text{Div}_1}{1+R} + \frac{\text{Div}_2}{(1+R)^2} + \frac{\text{Div}_3}{(1+R)^3} + \cdots = \sum_{t=1}^{\infty} \frac{\text{Div}_t}{(1+R)^t} \tag{6.4}$$

Thus the value of a firm's common stock to the investor is equal to the present value of all of the expected future dividends.

This is a very useful result. A common objection to applying present value analysis to stocks is that investors are too shortsighted to care about the long-run stream of dividends. These critics argue that an investor will generally not look past his or her time horizon. Thus, prices in a market dominated by short-term investors will reflect only near-term dividends. However, our discussion shows that a long-run dividend discount model holds even when investors have short-term time horizons. Although an investor may want to cash out early, she must find another investor who is willing to buy. The price this second investor pays is dependent on dividends *after* his date of purchase.

Valuation of Different Types of Stocks

The above discussion shows that the value of the firm is the present value of its future dividends. How do we apply this idea in practice? Equation (6.4) represents a very general model and is applicable regardless of whether the level of expected dividends is growing, fluctuating, or constant. The general model can be simplified if the firm's dividends are expected to follow some basic patterns: (1) zero growth, (2) constant growth, and (3) differential growth. These cases are illustrated in Figure 6.1.

[1]This procedure reminds us of the physicist lecturing on the origins of the universe. He was approached by an elderly gentleman in the audience who disagreed with the lecture. The attendee said that the universe rests on the back of a huge turtle. When the physicist asked what the turtle rested on, the gentleman said another turtle. Anticipating the physicist's objections, the attendee said, "Don't tire yourself out, young fellow. It's turtles all the way down."

CASE 1 (ZERO GROWTH) The value of a stock with a constant dividend is given by

$$P_0 = \frac{\text{Div}_1}{1+R} + \frac{\text{Div}_2}{(1+R)^2} + \cdots = \frac{\text{Div}}{R}$$

Here it is assumed that $\text{Div}_1 = \text{Div}_2 = \cdots = \text{Div}$. This is just an application of the perpetuity formula from a previous chapter.

CASE 2 (CONSTANT GROWTH) Dividends grow at rate g, as follows:

End of Year	1	2	3	4	. . .
Dividend	Div	$\text{Div}(1+g)$	$\text{Div}(1+g)^2$	$\text{Div}(1+g)^3$	

Note that Div is the dividend at the end of the *first* period.

EXAMPLE 6.1 Projected Dividends

Hampshire Products will pay a dividend of $4 per share a year from now. Financial analysts believe that dividends will rise at 6 percent per year for the foreseeable future. What is the dividend per share at the end of each of the first five years?

End of Year	1	2	3	4	5
Dividend	$4.00	$\$4 \times (1.06)$ = $4.24	$\$4 \times (1.06)^2$ = $4.4944	$\$4 \times (1.06)^3$ = $4.7641	$\$4 \times (1.06)^4$ = $5.0499

The value of a common stock with dividends growing at a constant rate is

$$P_0 = \frac{\text{Div}}{1+R} + \frac{\text{Div}(1+g)}{(1+R)^2} + \frac{\text{Div}(1+g)^2}{(1+R)^3} + \frac{\text{Div}(1+g)^3}{(1+R)^4} + \cdots = \frac{\text{Div}}{R-g}$$

where g is the growth rate. Div is the dividend on the stock at the end of the first period. This is the formula for the present value of a growing perpetuity, which we derived in a previous chapter.

EXAMPLE 6.2 Stock Valuation

Suppose an investor is considering the purchase of a share of the Utah Mining Company. The stock will pay a $3 dividend a year from today. This dividend is expected to grow at 10 percent per year ($g = 10\%$) for the foreseeable future. The investor thinks that the required return (R) on this stock is 15 percent, given her assessment of Utah Mining's risk. (We also refer to R as the discount rate of the stock.) What is the value of a share of Utah Mining Company's stock?

Using the constant growth formula of case 2, we assess the value to be $60:

$$\$60 = \frac{\$3}{.15 - .10}$$

P_0 is quite dependent on the value of g. If g had been estimated to be 12½ percent, the value of the share would have been:

$$\$120 = \frac{\$3}{.15 - .125}$$

The stock price doubles (from $60 to $120) when g only increases 25 percent (from 10 percent to 12.5 percent). Because of P_0's dependency on g, one must maintain a healthy sense of skepticism when using this constant growth of dividends model.

Furthermore, note that P_0 is equal to infinity when the growth rate, g, equals the discount rate, R. Because stock prices do not grow infinitely, an estimate of g greater than R implies an error in estimation. More will be said of this point later.

CASE 3 (DIFFERENTIAL GROWTH) In this case, an algebraic formula would be too unwieldy. Instead, we present examples.

EXAMPLE 6.3 Differential Growth

Consider the stock of Elixir Drug Company, which has a new back-rub ointment and is enjoying rapid growth. The dividend for a share of stock a year from today will be $1.15. During the next four years, the dividend will grow at 15 percent per year ($g_1 = 15\%$). After that, growth (g_2) will be equal to 10 percent per year. Can you calculate the present value of the stock if the required return (R) is 15 percent?

Figure 6.2 displays the growth in the dividends. We need to apply a two-step process to discount these dividends. We first calculate the present value of the dividends growing at 15 percent per annum. That is, we first calculate the present value of the dividends at the end of each of the first five years. Second, we calculate the present value of the dividends beginning at the end of year 6.

FIGURE 6.2
Growth in Dividends for Elixir Drug Company

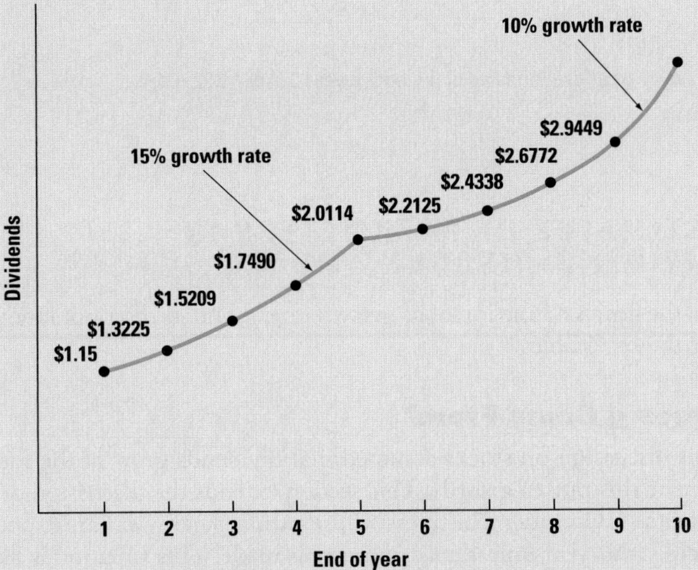

Calculate Present Value of First Five Dividends The present value of dividend payments in years 1 through 5 is as follows:

FUTURE YEAR	GROWTH RATE (g_1)	EXPECTED DIVIDEND	PRESENT VALUE
1	.15	$1.15	$1
2	.15	1.3225	1
3	.15	1.5209	1
4	.15	1.7490	1
5	.15	2.0114	1
Years 1–5		The present value of dividends =	$5

The growing annuity formula of the previous chapter could normally be used in this step. However, note that dividends grow at 15 percent, which is also the discount rate. Since $g = R$, the growing annuity formula cannot be used in this example.

(continued)

Calculate Present Value of Dividends Beginning at End of Year 6 This is the procedure for deferred perpetuities and deferred annuities that we mentioned in a previous chapter. The dividends beginning at the end of year 6 are

End of Year	6	7	8	9
Dividend	$\text{Div}_5 \times (1 + g_2)$ $2.0114 × 1.10 = $2.2125	$\text{Div}_5 \times (1 + g_2)^2$ $2.0114 \times (1.10)^2$ = $2.4338	$\text{Div}_5 \times (1 + g_2)^3$ $2.0114 \times (1.10)^3$ = $2.6772	$\text{Div}_5 \times (1 + g_2)^4$ $2.0114 \times (1.10)^4$ = $2.9449

As stated in the previous chapter, the growing perpetuity formula calculates present value as of one year prior to the first payment. Because the payment begins at the end of year 6, the present value formula calculates present value as of the end of year 5.

The price at the end of year 5 is given by

$$P_5 = \frac{\text{Div}_6}{R - g_2} = \frac{\$2.2125}{.15 - .10}$$
$$= \$44.25$$

The present value of P_5 at the end of year 0 is

$$\frac{P_5}{(1 + R)^5} = \frac{\$44.25}{(1.15)^5} = \$22$$

The present value of *all* dividends as of the end of year 0 is \$27 (\$22 + \$5).

6.2 ESTIMATES OF PARAMETERS IN THE DIVIDEND-DISCOUNT MODEL

The value of the firm is a function of its growth rate, *g*, and its discount rate, *R*. How does one estimate these variables?

Where Does *g* Come From?

The previous discussion on stocks assumed that dividends grow at the rate *g*. We now want to estimate this rate of growth. This section extends the discussion of growth contained in Chapter 3. Consider a business whose earnings next year are expected to be the same as earnings this year unless a *net investment* is made. This situation is likely to occur, because net investment is equal to gross, or total, investment less depreciation. A net investment of zero occurs when *total investment* equals depreciation. If total investment is equal to depreciation, the firm's physical plant is maintained, consistent with no growth in earnings.

Net investment will be positive only if some earnings are not paid out as dividends, that is, only if some earnings are retained.[2] This leads to the following equation:

$$\underset{\text{year}}{\overset{\text{Earnings}}{\text{next}}} = \underset{\text{year}}{\overset{\text{Earnings}}{\text{this}}} + \underbrace{\underset{\text{this year}}{\overset{\text{Retained}}{\text{earnings}}} \times \underset{\text{earnings}}{\overset{\text{Return on}}{\text{retained}}}}_{\text{Increase in earnings}} \qquad (6.5)$$

The increase in earnings is a function of both the *retained earnings* and the *return on the retained earnings.*

[2]We ignore the possibility of the issuance of stocks or bonds in order to raise capital. These possibilities are considered in later chapters.

We now divide both sides of (6.5) by earnings this year, yielding

$$\frac{\textbf{Earnings next year}}{\textbf{Earnings this year}} = \frac{\textbf{Earnings this year}}{\textbf{Earnings this year}} + \left(\frac{\textbf{Retained earnings this year}}{\textbf{Earnings this year}}\right) \times \textbf{Return on retained earnings} \qquad (6.6)$$

The left-hand side of (6.6) is simply one plus the growth rate in earnings, which we write as $1 + g$. The ratio of retained earnings to earnings is called the **retention ratio**. Thus, we can write

$$\mathbf{1 + g = 1 + \text{Retention ratio} \times \text{Return on retained earnings}} \qquad (6.7)$$

It is difficult for a financial analyst to determine the return to be expected on currently retained earnings, because the details on forthcoming projects are not generally public information. However, it is frequently assumed that the projects selected in the current year have an anticipated return equal to returns from projects in other years. Here, we can estimate the anticipated return on current retained earnings by the historical **return on equity** or ROE. After all, ROE is simply the return on the firm's entire equity, which is the return on the cumulation of all the firm's past projects.

From (6.7), we have a simple way to estimate growth:

Formula for Firm's Growth Rate:

$$\mathbf{g = \text{Retention ratio} \times \text{Return on retained earnings (ROE)}} \qquad (6.8)$$

Previously g referred to growth in dividends. However, the growth in earnings is equal to the growth rate in dividends in this context, because as we will presently see, the ratio of dividends to earnings is held constant. In fact, as you have probably figured out, g is the sustainable growth rate we introduced in Chapter 3.

EXAMPLE 6.4 Earnings Growth

Pagemaster Enterprises just reported earnings of $2 million. It plans to retain 40 percent of its earnings. The historical return on equity (ROE) has been .16, a figure that is expected to continue into the future. How much will earnings grow over the coming year?

We first perform the calculation without reference to equation (6.8). Then we use (6.8) as a check.

Calculation without Reference to Equation (6.8) The firm will retain $800,000 (40% × $2 million). Assuming that historical ROE is an appropriate estimate for future returns, the anticipated increase in earnings is

$$\$800{,}000 \times .16 = \$128{,}000$$

The percentage growth in earnings is

$$\frac{\text{Change in earnings}}{\text{Total earnings}} = \frac{\$128{,}000}{\$2\text{ million}} = .064$$

This implies that earnings in one year will be $2,128,000 (= $2,000,000 × 1.064).

Check Using Equation (6.8) We use g = Retention ratio × ROE. We have

$$g = .4 \times .16 = .064$$

Where Does R Come From?

Thus far, we have taken the required return, or discount rate R, as given. We will have quite a bit to say on this subject in later chapters. For now, we want to examine the implications of the dividend growth model for this required return. Earlier, we calculated P_0 as:

$$P_0 = \text{Div}/(R - g)$$

If we rearrange this to solve for R, we get:

$$\begin{aligned} R - g &= \text{Div}/P_0 \\ R &= \text{Div}/P_0 + g \end{aligned} \tag{6.9}$$

This tells us that the total return, R, has two components. The first of these, Div/P_0, is called the **dividend yield**. Because this is calculated as the expected cash dividend divided by the current price, it is conceptually similar to the current yield on a bond.

The second part of the total return is the growth rate, g. As we will verify shortly, the dividend growth rate is also the rate at which the stock price grows. Thus, this growth rate can be interpreted as the **capital gains yield**, that is, the rate at which the value of the investment grows.

To illustrate the components of the required return, suppose we observe a stock selling for \$20 per share. The next dividend will be \$1 per share. You think that the dividend will grow by 10 percent per year more or less indefinitely. What return does this stock offer you if this is correct?

The dividend growth model calculates total return as:

$$\begin{aligned} R &= \text{Dividend yield} + \text{Capital gains yield} \\ R &= \text{Div}/P_0 \quad + \quad g \end{aligned}$$

In this case, total return works out to be:

$$\begin{aligned} R &= \$1/20 + 10\% \\ &= 5\% + 10\% \\ &= 15\% \end{aligned}$$

This stock, therefore, has an expected return of 15 percent.

We can verify this answer by calculating the price in one year, P_1, using 15 percent as the required return. Based on the dividend growth model, this price is:

$$\begin{aligned} P_1 &= \text{Div} \times (1 + g)/(R - g) \\ &= \$1 \times 1.10/(.15 - .10) \\ &= \$1.10/.05 \\ &= \$22 \end{aligned}$$

Notice that this \$22 is \$20 × 1.1, so the stock price has grown by 10 percent as it should. If you pay \$20 for the stock today, you will get a \$1 dividend at the end of the year, and you will have a \$22 − 20 = \$2 gain. Your dividend yield is thus \$1/20 = 5 percent. Your capital gains yield is \$2/20 = 10 percent, so your total return would be 5 percent + 10 percent = 15 percent.

To get a feel for actual numbers in this context, consider that, according to the 2005 Value Line *Investment Survey*, Procter & Gamble's dividends were expected to grow by 9.5 percent over the next 5 or so years, compared to a historical growth rate of 10.5 percent over the preceding 5 years and 11.5 percent over the preceding 10 years. In 2005, the projected dividend for the coming year was given as \$1.00. The stock price at that time was about \$55 per share. What is the return investors require on P&G? Here, the dividend yield is 1.8 percent and the capital gains yield is 9.5 percent, giving a total required return of 11.3 percent on P&G stock.

EXAMPLE 6.5 Calculating the Required Return

Pagemaster Enterprises, the company examined in the previous example, has 1,000,000 shares of stock outstanding. The stock is selling at $10. What is the required return on the stock?

Because the retention ratio is 40 percent, the **payout ratio** is 60 percent (1 − Retention ratio). The payout ratio is the ratio of dividends/earnings. Because earnings a year from now will be $2,128,000 ($2,000,000 × 1.064), dividends will be $1,276,800 (.60 × $2,128,000). Dividends per share will be $1.28 ($1,276,800/1,000,000). Given our previous result that $g = .064$, we calculate R from (6.9) as follows:

$$.192 = \frac{\$1.28}{10.00} + .064$$

A Healthy Sense of Skepticism

It is important to emphasize that our approach merely *estimates* g; our approach does not *determine* g precisely. We mentioned earlier that our estimate of g is based on a number of assumptions. For example, we assume that the return on reinvestment of future retained earnings is equal to the firm's past ROE. We assume that the future retention ratio is equal to the past retention ratio. Our estimate for g will be off if these assumptions prove to be wrong.

Unfortunately, the determination of R is highly dependent on g. For example, if g is estimated to be 0, R equals 12.8 percent ($1.28/$10.00). If g is estimated to be 12 percent, R equals 24.8 percent ($1.28/$10.00 + 12%). Thus, one should view estimates of R with a healthy sense of skepticism.

Because of the preceding, some financial economists generally argue that the estimation error for R or a single security is too large to be practical. Therefore, they suggest calculating the average R for an entire industry. This R would then be used to discount the dividends of a particular stock in the same industry.

One should be particularly skeptical of two polar cases when estimating R for individual securities. First, consider a firm currently paying no dividend. The stock price will be above zero because investors believe that the firm may initiate a dividend at some point or the firm may be acquired at some point. However, when a firm goes from no dividends to a positive number of dividends, the implied growth rate is *infinite*. Thus, equation (6.9) must be used with extreme caution here, if at all–a point we emphasize later in this chapter.

Second, we mentioned earlier that the value of the firm is infinite when g is equal to R. Because prices for stocks do not grow infinitely, an analyst whose estimate of g for a particular firm is equal to or above R must have made a mistake. Most likely, the analyst's high estimate for g is correct for the next few years. However, firms simply cannot maintain an abnormally high growth rate *forever*. The analyst's error was to use a short-run estimate of g in a model requiring a perpetual growth rate. A nearby *The Real World* box discusses the consequences of long-term growth at unrealistic rates.

6.3 GROWTH OPPORTUNITIES

We previously spoke of the growth rate of dividends. We now want to address the related concept of growth opportunities. Imagine a company with a level stream of earnings per share in perpetuity. The company pays all of these earnings out to stockholders as dividends. Hence,

$$\text{EPS} = \text{Div}$$

THE REAL WORLD

HOW FAST IS TOO FAST?

Growth rates are an important tool for evaluating a company, and as we have seen, an important part of valuing a company's stock. When you're thinking about (and calculating) growth rates, a little common sense goes a long way. For example, in 2005 retailing giant Wal-Mart had about 1 billion square feet of stores, distribution centers, and so forth. The company expected to increase its square footage by about 8.5 percent over the next year. This doesn't sound too outrageous, but can Wal-Mart grow its square footage at 8.5 percent indefinitely?

Using the compound growth calculation we discussed in an earlier chapter, see if you agree that if Wal-Mart grows at 8.5 percent per year over the next 141 years, the company will have about 99 trillion square feet under roof, which is about the total land mass of the entire United States! In other words, if Wal-Mart keeps growing at 8.5 percent, the entire country will eventually be one big Wal-Mart. Scary.

XM Satellite Radio is another example. The company had total revenues of about $500,000 in 2001 and was projected to have revenues of about $470 million in 2005. This represents an annual increase of 454 percent! How likely do you think it is that the company can continue this growth rate? If this growth continued, the company would have revenues of about $14 trillion in just six years, which exceeds the gross domestic product (GDP) of the United States. Obviously, XM Radio's growth rate will slow substantially in the next several years.

What about growth in cash flow? As of the end of 2004, cash flow for Quest Diagnostics, a medical diagnostics company, had grown at an annual rate of about 85.5 percent for the previous five years. The company generated about $650 million in cash flow for 2004. If the company's cash flow grew at that same rate for the next 15 years, it would generate over $6.4 trillion per year, which is about the total amount of U.S. currency in the world.

As these examples show, growth rates shouldn't just be extrapolated into the future. It is fairly easy for a small company to grow very fast. If a company has $100 in sales, it only has to increase sales by another $100 to have a 100 percent increase in sales. If the company's sales are $10 billion, it has to increase sales by another $10 billion to achieve the same 100 percent increase. So, long-term growth rate estimates must be chosen very carefully. As a rule of thumb, for really long-term growth rate estimates, you should probably assume that a company will not grow much faster than the economy as a whole, which is probably noticeably less than five percent (inflation adjusted).

where EPS is *earnings per share* and Div is dividends per share. A company of this type is frequently called a *cash cow*.

From the perpetuity formula of the previous chapter, the value of a share of stock is:

Value of a Share of Stock When Firm Acts as a Cash Cow:

$$\frac{\textbf{EPS}}{R} = \frac{\textbf{Div}}{R}$$

where R is the discount rate on the firm's stock.

This policy of paying out all earnings as dividends may not be the optimal one. Many firms have *growth* opportunities, that is, opportunities to invest in profitable projects. Because these projects can represent a significant fraction of the firm's value, it would be foolish to forgo them in order to pay out all earnings as dividends.

Although firms frequently think in terms of a *set* of growth opportunities, let's focus on only one opportunity, that is, the opportunity to invest in a single project. Suppose the firm retains the entire dividend at date 1 in order to invest in a particular capital budgeting project. The net present value *per share* of the project as of date 0 is *NPVGO,* which stands for the *net present value (per share) of the growth opportunity.*

What is the price of a share of stock at date 0 if the firm decides to take on the project at date 1? Because the per share value of the project is added to the original stock price, the stock price must now be:

Stock Price after Firm Commits to New Project:

$$\frac{\text{EPS}}{R} + \text{NPVGO} \tag{6.10}$$

Thus, equation (6.10) indicates that the price of a share of stock can be viewed as the sum of two different items. The first term (EPS/R) is the value of the firm if it rested on its laurels, that is, if it simply distributed all earnings to the stockholders. The second term is the *additional* value if the firm retains earnings in order to fund new projects.

EXAMPLE 6.6 Growth Opportunities

Sarro Shipping, Inc., expects to earn $1 million per year in perpetuity if it undertakes no new investment opportunities. There are 100,000 shares of stock outstanding, so earnings per share equal $10 ($1,000,000/100,000). The firm will have an opportunity at date 1 to spend $1,000,000 on a new marketing campaign. The new campaign will increase earnings in every subsequent period by $210,000 (or $2.10 per share). This is a 21 percent return per year on the project. The firm's discount rate is 10 percent. What is the value per share before and after deciding to accept the marketing campaign?

The value of a share of Sarro Shipping before the campaign is:

Value of a Share of Sarro When Firm Acts as a Cash Cow:

$$\frac{\text{EPS}}{R} = \frac{\$10}{.1} = \$100$$

The value of the marketing campaign as of date 1 is:

Value of Marketing Campaign at Date 1:

$$-\$1{,}000{,}000 + \frac{\$210{,}000}{.1} = \$1{,}100{,}000 \tag{6.11}$$

Because the investment is made at date 1 and the first cash inflow occurs at date 2, equation (6.11) represents the value of the marketing campaign as of date 1. We determine the value at date 0 by discounting back one period as follows:

Value of Marketing Campaign at Date 0:

$$\frac{\$1{,}100{,}000}{1.1} = \$1{,}000{,}000$$

Thus, NPVGO per share is $10 ($1,000,000/100,000).

The price per share is:

$$\text{EPS}/R + \text{NPVGO} = \$100 + \$10 = \$110$$

The calculation can also be made on a straight net present value basis. Because all the earnings at date 1 are spent on the marketing effort, no dividends are paid to stockholders at that date. Dividends in all subsequent periods are $1,210,000 ($1,000,000 + 210,000). In this case, $1,000,000 is the annual dividend when Sarro is a cash cow. The additional contribution to the dividend from the marketing effort is $210,000. Dividends per share are $12.10 ($1,210,000/100,000). Because these dividends start at date 2, the price per share at date 1 is $121 ($12.10/.1). The price per share at date 0 is $110 ($121/1.1).

Note that value is created in this example because the project earned a 21 percent rate of return when the discount rate was only 10 percent. No value would have been created had the project earned a 10 percent rate of return. The NPVGO would have been zero, and value would have been negative had the project earned a percentage return below 10 percent. The NPVGO would be negative in that case.

Two conditions must be met in order to increase value.

1. Earnings must be retained so that projects can be funded.[3]
2. The projects must have positive net present value.

Surprisingly, a number of companies seem to invest in projects known to have *negative* net present values. For example, in the late 1970s, oil companies and tobacco companies were flush with cash. Due to declining markets in both industries, high dividends and low investment would have been the rational action. Unfortunately, a number of companies in both industries reinvested heavily in what were widely perceived to be negative NPVGO projects.

Given that NPV analysis (such as that presented in the previous chapter) is common knowledge in business, why would managers choose projects with negative NPVs? One conjecture is that some managers enjoy controlling a large company. Because paying dividends in lieu of reinvesting earnings reduces the size of the firm, some managers find it emotionally difficult to pay high dividends.

Growth in Earnings and Dividends versus Growth Opportunities

As mentioned earlier, a firm's value increases when it invests in growth opportunities with positive NPVGOs. A firm's value falls when it selects opportunities with negative NPVGOs. However, dividends grow whether projects with positive NPVs or negative NPVs are selected. This surprising result can be explained by the following example.

EXAMPLE 6.7 NPV versus Dividends

Lane Supermarkets, a new firm, will earn $100,000 a year in perpetuity if it pays out all its earnings as dividends. However, the firm plans to invest 20 percent of its earnings in projects that earn 10 percent per year. The discount rate is 18 percent. An earlier formula tells us that the growth rate of dividends is

$$g = \text{Retention ratio} \times \text{Return on retained earnings} = .2 \times .10 = 2\%$$

For example, in this first year of the new policy, dividends are $80,000 [$=(1-.2)\times$ $100,000]. Dividends next year are $81,600 ($=$ $80,000 $\times$ 1.02). Dividends the following year are $83,232 [$=$ $80,000 $\times (1.02)^2$] and so on. Because dividends represent a fixed percentage of earnings, earnings must grow at 2 percent a year as well.

However, note that the policy reduces value because the rate of return on the projects of 10 percent is less than the discount rate of 18 percent. That is, the firm would have had a higher value at date 0 if it had a policy of paying all its earnings out as dividends. Thus, a policy of investing in projects with negative NPVs rather than paying out earnings as dividends will lead to growth in dividends and earnings, but will reduce value.

Dividends or Earnings: Which to Discount?

As mentioned earlier, this chapter applied the growing perpetuity formula to the valuation of stocks. In our application, we discounted dividends, not earnings. This is sensible

[3]Later in the text, we speak of issuing stock or debt in order to fund projects.

since investors select a stock for what they can get out of it. They only get two things out of a stock: dividends and the ultimate sales price, which is determined by what future investors expect to receive in dividends.

The calculated stock price would be too high were earnings to be discounted instead of the dividends. As we saw in our estimation of a firm's growth rate, only a portion of earnings goes to the stockholders as dividends. The remainder is retained to generate future dividends. In our model, retained earnings are equal to the firm's investment. To discount earnings instead of dividends would be to ignore the investment that a firm must make today in order to generate future returns.

The No-Dividend Firm

Students frequently ask the following questions: If the dividend discount model is correct, why aren't no-dividend stocks selling at zero? This is a good question and gets at the goals of the firm. A firm with many growth opportunities is faced with a dilemma. The firm can pay out dividends now, or it can forgo dividends now so that it can make investments that will generate even greater dividends in the future.[4] This is often a painful choice, because a strategy of dividend deferment may be optimal yet unpopular among certain stockholders.

Many firms choose to pay no dividends–and these firms sell at positive prices. For example, most Internet firms, such as Amazon.com, Google, and eBay, pay no dividends. Rational shareholders believe that they will either receive dividends at some point or they will receive something just as good. That is, the firm will be acquired in a merger, with the stockholders receiving either cash or shares of stock at that time.

Of course, the actual application of the dividend discount model is difficult for firms of this type. Clearly, the model for constant growth of dividends does not apply. Though the differential growth model can work in theory, the difficulties of estimating the date of first dividend, the growth rate of dividends after that date, and the ultimate merger price make application of the model quite difficult in reality.

Empirical evidence suggests that firms with high growth rates are likely to pay lower dividends, a result consistent with the above analysis. For example, consider McDonald's Corporation. The company started in the 1950s and grew rapidly for many years. It paid its first dividend in 1975, though it was a billion-dollar company (in both sales and market value of stockholders' equity) prior to that date. Why did it wait so long to pay a dividend? It waited because it had so many positive growth opportunities, that is, additional locations for new hamburger outlets, to take advantage of.

6.4 THE DIVIDEND GROWTH MODEL AND THE NPVGO MODEL

This chapter has revealed that the price of a share of stock is the sum of its price as a cash cow plus the per-share value of its growth opportunities. The Sarro Shipping example illustrated this formula using only one growth opportunity. We also used the growing perpetuity formula to price a stock with a steady growth in dividends. When the formula is applied to stocks, it is typically called the *dividend growth model.* A steady growth in dividends results from a continual investment in growth opportunities, not just investment in a single opportunity. Therefore, it is worthwhile to compare the dividend growth model with the *NPVGO model* when growth occurs through continual investing.

We can use an example to illustrate the main points. Suppose Cumberland Book Publishers has EPS of $10 at the end of the first year, a dividend-payout ratio of 40 percent,

[4]A third alternative is to issue stock so that the firm has enough cash both to pay dividends and to invest. This possibility is explored in a later chapter.

a discount rate of 16 percent, and a return on its retained earnings of 20 percent. Because the firm retains some of its earnings each year, it is selecting growth opportunities each year. This is different from Sarro Shipping, which had a growth opportunity in only one year. We wish to calculate the price per share using both the dividend growth model and the NPVGO model.

The Dividend Growth Model

The dividends at date 1 are .40 × \$10 = \$4 per share. The retention ratio is .60 (1 − .40), implying a growth rate in dividends of .12 (.60 × .20).

From the dividend growth model, the price of a share of stock is:

$$\frac{\textbf{Div}}{R - g} = \frac{\$4}{.16 - .12} = \$100$$

The NPVGO Model

Using the NPVGO model, it is more difficult to value a firm with growth opportunities each year (like Cumberland) than a firm with growth opportunities in only one year (like Sarro). In order to value according to the NPVGO model, we need to calculate on a per-share basis (1) the net present value of a single growth opportunity, (2) the net present value of all growth opportunities, and (3) the stock price if the firm acts as a cash cow, that is, the value of the firm without these growth opportunities. The value of the firm is the sum of (2) + (3).

1. ***Value per Share of a Single Growth Opportunity*** Out of the earnings per share of \$10 at date 1, the firm retains \$6 (.6 × \$10) at that date. The firm earns \$1.20 (\$6 × .20) per year in perpetuity on that \$6 investment. The NPV from the investment is:

Per-Share NPV Generated from Investment at Date 1:

$$-\$6 + \frac{\$1.20}{.16} = \$1.50 \qquad (6.12)$$

That is, the firm invests \$6 in order to reap \$1.20 per year on the investment. The earnings are discounted at .16, implying a value per share from the project of \$1.50. Because the investment occurs at date 1 and the first cash flow occurs at date 2, \$1.50 is the value of the investment at *date 1*. In other words, the NPV from the date 1 investment has *not* yet been brought back to date 0.

2. ***Value per Share of All Opportunities*** As pointed out earlier, the growth rate of earnings and dividends is 12 percent. Because retained earnings are a fixed percentage of total earnings, retained earnings must also grow at 12 percent a year. That is, retained earnings at date 2 are \$6.72 (\$6 × 1.12), retained earnings at date 3 are \$7.5264 [\$6 × $(1.12)^2$], and so on.

Let's analyze the retained earnings at date 2 in more detail. Because projects will always earn 20 percent per year, the firm earns \$1.344 (\$6.72 × .20) in each future year on the \$6.72 investment at date 2.

The NPV from the investment is:

NPV per Share Generated from Investment at Date 2:

$$-\$6.72 + \frac{\$1.344}{.16} = \$1.68 \qquad (6.13)$$

\$1.68 is the NPV as of date 2 of the investment made at date 2. The NPV from the date 2 investment has *not* yet been brought back to date 0.

Now consider the retained earnings at date 3 in more detail. The firm earns \$1.5053 (\$7.5264 × .20) per year on the investment of \$7.5264 at date 3.

The NPV from the investment is:

NPV per Share Generated from Investment at Date 3:

$$-\$7.5264 + \frac{\$1.5053}{.16} = \$1.882 \tag{6.14}$$

From equations (6.12), (6.13), and (6.14), the NPV per share of all of the growth opportunities, discounted back to date 0, is:

$$\frac{\$1.50}{1.16} + \frac{\$1.68}{(1.16)^2} + \frac{\$1.882}{(1.16)^3} + \cdots \tag{6.15}$$

Because it has an infinite number of terms, this expression looks quite difficult to compute. However, there is an easy simplification. Note that retained earnings are growing at 12 percent per year. Because all projects earn the same rate of return per year, the NPVs in (6.12), (6.13), and (6.14) are also growing at 12 percent per year. Hence, we can write equation (6.15) as:

$$\frac{\$1.50}{1.16} + \frac{\$1.50 \times 1.12}{(1.16)^2} + \frac{\$1.50 \times (1.12)^2}{(1.16)^3} + \cdots$$

This is a growth perpetuity whose value is:

$$\text{NPVGO} = \$\frac{1.50}{.16 - .12} = \$37.50$$

Because the first NPV of \$1.50 occurs at date 1, the NPVGO is \$37.50 as of date 0. In other words, the firm's policy of investing in new projects from retained earnings has an NPV of \$37.50.

3. ***Value per Share If Firm Is a Cash Cow*** We now assume that the firm pays out all of its earnings as dividends. The dividends would be \$10 per year in this case. Since there would be no growth, the value per share would be evaluated by the perpetuity formula:

$$\frac{\text{Div}}{R} = \frac{\$10}{.16} = \$62.50$$

Summation

Formula (6.10) states that value per share is the value of a cash cow plus the value of the growth opportunities. This is:

$$\$100 = \$62.50 + 37.50$$

Hence, value is the same whether calculated by a discounted dividend approach or a growth opportunities approach. The share prices from the two approaches must be equal, because the approaches are different yet equivalent methods of applying concepts of present value.

6.5 PRICE-EARNINGS RATIO

We argued earlier that one should not discount earnings in order to determine price per share. Nevertheless, financial analysts frequently relate earnings and price per share, as made evident by their heavy reliance on the price-earnings (or PE) ratio.

Our previous discussion stated that

$$\textbf{Price per share} = \frac{\textbf{EPS}}{R} + \textbf{NPVGO}$$

Dividing by EPS yields

$$\frac{\textbf{Price per share}}{\textbf{EPS}} = \frac{1}{R} + \frac{\textbf{NPVGO}}{\textbf{EPS}}$$

The left-hand side is the formula for the price-earnings ratio. The equation shows that the PE ratio is related to the net present value of growth opportunities. As an example, consider two firms, each having just reported earnings per share of $1. However, one firm has many valuable growth opportunities, while the other firm has no growth opportunities at all. The firm with growth opportunities should sell at a higher price, because an investor is buying both current income of $1 and growth opportunities. Suppose that the firm with growth opportunities sells for $16 and the other firm sells for $8. The $1 earnings per share number appears in the denominator of the PE ratio for both firms. Thus, the PE ratio is 16 for the firm with growth opportunities, but only 8 for the firm without the opportunities.

This explanation seems to hold fairly well in the real world. Electronic and other high-tech stocks generally sell at very high PE ratios (or *multiples,* as they are often called) because they are perceived to have high growth rates. In fact, some technology stocks sell at high prices even though the companies have never earned a profit. The PE ratios of these companies are infinite. Conversely, railroads, utilities, and steel companies sell at lower multiples because of the prospects of lower growth. Table 6.1 contains PE ratios in 2005 for some well-known companies and the S&P 500 Index. Notice the variations across industries.

Of course, the market is merely pricing *perceptions* of the future, not the future itself. We will argue later in the text that the stock market generally has realistic perceptions of a firm's prospects. However, this is not always true. In the late 1960s, many electronics firms were selling at multiples of 200 times earnings. The high perceived growth rates did not materialize, causing great declines in stock prices during the early 1970s. In earlier decades, fortunes were made in stocks like IBM and Xerox because the high growth rates were not anticipated by investors. Most recently we have experienced the dot-com collapse when many Internet stocks were trading at multiples of thousands of times annual earnings. In fact, most Internet stocks had no earnings.

There are two additional factors explaining the PE ratio. The first is the discount rate, R. The above formula shows that the PE ratio is *negatively* related to the firm's discount rate. We have already suggested that the discount rate is positively related to the stock's risk or variability. Thus, the PE ratio is negatively related to the stock's risk. To see that this is a sensible result, consider two firms, A and B, behaving as cash cows. The stock market *expects* both firms to have annual earnings of $1 per share forever. However, the

TABLE 6.1
Selected PE Ratios

COMPANY	INDUSTRY	PE RATIO
General Motors	Automobiles	5.96
Bear Stearns	Investment banking	10.22
Caterpillar	Heavy equipment	15.96
S&P 500 average	n/a	20.00
Cisco Systems	Computer networking	22.91
Amgen	Biotechnology	32.86
Starbucks	Expensive coffee	51.22

earnings of firm *A* are known with certainty while the earnings of firm *B* are quite variable. A rational stockholder is likely to pay more for a share of firm *A* because of the absence of risk. If a share of firm *A* sells at a higher price and both firms have the same EPS, the PE ratio of firm *A* must be higher.

The second additional factor concerns the firm's choice of accounting methods. Under current accounting rules, companies are given a fair amount of leeway. For example, consider inventory accounting where either FIFO or LIFO may be used. In an inflationary environment, *FIFO* (*first in–first out*) accounting understates the true cost of inventory and hence inflates reported earnings. Inventory is valued according to more recent costs under *LIFO* (*last in–first out*), implying that reported earnings are lower here than they would be under FIFO. Thus, LIFO inventory accounting is a more *conservative* method than FIFO. Similar accounting leeway exists for construction costs (*completed contracts* versus *percentage-of-completion methods*) and depreciation (*accelerated depreciation* versus *straight-line depreciation*).

As an example, consider two identical firms, *C* and *D*. Firm *C* uses LIFO and reports earnings of $2 per share. Firm *D* uses the less conservative accounting assumptions of FIFO and reports earnings of $3 per share. The market knows that both firms are identical and prices both at $18 per share. This price-earnings ratio is 9 ($18/$2) for firm *C* and 6 ($18/$3) for firm *D*. Thus, the firm with the more conservative principles has the higher PE ratio.

This last example depends on the assumption that the market sees through differences in accounting treatments. A significant portion of the academic community believes that the market sees through virtually all accounting differences. These academics are adherents of the hypothesis of *efficient capital markets,* a theory that we explore in great detail later in the text. Though many financial people might be more moderate in their beliefs regarding this issue, the consensus view is certainly that many of the accounting differences are seen through. Thus, the proposition that firms with conservative accountants have high PE ratios is widely accepted.

6.6 SOME FEATURES OF COMMON AND PREFERRED STOCKS

In discussing common stock features, we focus on shareholder rights and dividend payments. For preferred stock, we explain what the "preferred" means, and we also debate whether preferred stock is really debt or equity.

Common Stock Features

The term **common stock** means different things to different people, but it is usually applied to stock that has no special preference either in receiving dividends or in bankruptcy.

SHAREHOLDER RIGHTS The conceptual structure of the corporation assumes that shareholders elect directors who, in turn, hire management to carry out their directives. Shareholders, therefore, control the corporation through the right to elect the directors. Generally, only shareholders have this right.

Directors are elected each year at an annual meeting. Although there are exceptions (discussed next), the general idea is "one share, one vote" (*not* one *shareholder,* one vote). Corporate democracy is thus very different from our political democracy. With corporate democracy, the "golden rule" prevails absolutely.[5]

Directors are elected at an annual shareholders' meeting by a vote of the holders of a majority of shares who are present and entitled to vote. However, the exact mechanism

[5]The golden rule: Whosoever has the gold makes the rules.

for electing directors differs across companies. The most important difference is whether shares must be voted cumulatively or voted straight.

To illustrate the two different voting procedures, imagine that a corporation has two shareholders: Smith with 20 shares and Jones with 80 shares. Both want to be a director. Jones does not want Smith, however. We assume there are a total of four directors to be elected.

The effect of **cumulative voting** is to permit minority participation.[6] If cumulative voting is permitted, the total number of votes that each shareholder may cast is determined first. This is usually calculated as the number of shares (owned or controlled) multiplied by the number of directors to be elected.

With cumulative voting, the directors are elected all at once. In our example, this means that the top four vote getters will be the new directors. A shareholder can distribute votes however he/she wishes.

Will Smith get a seat on the board? If we ignore the possibility of a five-way tie, then the answer is yes. Smith will cast $20 \times 4 = 80$ votes, and Jones will cast $80 \times 4 = 320$ votes. If Smith gives all his votes to himself, he is assured of a directorship. The reason is that Jones can't divide 320 votes among four candidates in such a way as to give all of them more than 80 votes, so Smith will finish fourth at worst.

In general, if there are N directors up for election, then $1/(N + 1)$ percent of the stock plus one share will guarantee you a seat. In our current example, this is $1/(4 + 1) = 20$ percent. So the more seats that are up for election at one time, the easier (and cheaper) it is to win one.

With **straight voting**, the directors are elected one at a time. Each time, Smith can cast 20 votes and Jones can cast 80. As a consequence, Jones will elect all of the candidates. The only way to guarantee a seat is to own 50 percent plus one share. This also guarantees that you will win every seat, so it's really all or nothing.

EXAMPLE 6.8 Buying the Election

Stock in JRJ Corporation sells for $20 per share and features cumulative voting. There are 10,000 shares outstanding. If three directors are up for election, how much does it cost to ensure yourself a seat on the board?

The question here is how many shares of stock it will take to get a seat. The answer is 2,501, so the cost is 2,501 × $20 = $50,020. Why 2,501? Because there is no way the remaining 7,499 votes can be divided among three people to give all of them more than 2,501 votes. For example, suppose two people receive 2,502 votes and the first two seats. A third person can receive at most 10,000 − 2,502 − 2,502 − 2,501 = 2,495, so the third seat is yours.

As we've illustrated, straight voting can "freeze out" minority shareholders; that is the reason many states have mandatory cumulative voting. In states where cumulative voting is mandatory, devices have been worked out to minimize its impact.

One such device is to stagger the voting for the board of directors. With staggered elections, only a fraction of the directorships are up for election at a particular time. Thus, if only two directors are up for election at any one time, it will take $1/(2 + 1) = 33.33$ percent of the stock plus one share to guarantee a seat.

Overall, staggering has two basic effects:

1. Staggering makes it more difficult for a minority to elect a director when there is cumulative voting because there are fewer directors to be elected at one time.
2. Staggering makes takeover attempts less likely to be successful because it makes it more difficult to vote in a majority of new directors.

[6]By minority participation, we mean participation by shareholders with relatively small amounts of stock.

We should note that staggering may serve a beneficial purpose. It provides "institutional memory," that is, continuity on the board of directors. This may be important for corporations with significant long-range plans and projects.

PROXY VOTING A **proxy** is the grant of authority by a shareholder to someone else to vote his/her shares. For convenience, much of the voting in large public corporations is actually done by proxy.

As we have seen, with straight voting, each share of stock has one vote. The owner of 10,000 shares has 10,000 votes. Large companies have hundreds of thousands or even millions of shareholders. Shareholders can come to the annual meeting and vote in person, or they can transfer their right to vote to another party.

Obviously, management always tries to get as many proxies as possible transferred to it. However, if shareholders are not satisfied with management, an "outside" group of shareholders can try to obtain votes via proxy. They can vote by proxy in an attempt to replace management by electing enough directors. The resulting battle is called a *proxy fight.*

CLASSES OF STOCK Some firms have more than one class of common stock. Often, the classes are created with unequal voting rights. The Ford Motor Company, for example, has Class B common stock, which is not publicly traded (it is held by Ford family interests and trusts). This class has 40 percent of the voting power, even though it represents less than 10 percent of the total number of shares outstanding.

There are many other cases of corporations with different classes of stock. For example, Adolph Coors Class B shares, which are owned by the public, have no votes at all except in the case of a merger. The CEO of cable TV giant Comcast, Brian Roberts, owns about .4 percent of the company's equity, but he has a third of all the votes, thanks to a special class of stock. Another good example is Google, the Web search company, which only recently became publicly owned. Google has two classes of common stock, A and B. The Class A shares are held by the public, and each share has one vote. The Class B shares are held by company insiders, and each Class B share has 10 votes. As a result, Google's founders and management control the company.

Historically, the New York Stock Exchange did not allow companies to create classes of publicly traded common stock with unequal voting rights. Exceptions (e.g., Ford) appear to have been made. In addition, many non-NYSE companies have dual classes of common stock.

A primary reason for creating dual or multiple classes of stock has to do with control of the firm. If such stock exists, management of a firm can raise equity capital by issuing nonvoting or limited-voting stock while maintaining control.

The subject of unequal voting rights is controversial in the United States, and the idea of one share, one vote has a strong following and a long history. Interestingly, however, shares with unequal voting rights are quite common in the United Kingdom and elsewhere around the world.

OTHER RIGHTS The value of a share of common stock in a corporation is directly related to the general rights of shareholders. In addition to the right to vote for directors, shareholders usually have the following rights:

1. The right to share proportionally in dividends paid.
2. The right to share proportionally in assets remaining after liabilities have been paid in a liquidation.
3. The right to vote on stockholder matters of great importance, such as a merger. Voting is usually done at the annual meeting or a special meeting.

In addition, stockholders sometimes have the right to share proportionally in any new stock sold. This is called the *preemptive right.*

Essentially, a preemptive right means that a company that wishes to sell stock must first offer it to the existing stockholders before offering it to the general public. The purpose is to give a stockholder the opportunity to protect his/her proportionate ownership in the corporation.

DIVIDENDS A distinctive feature of corporations is that they have shares of stock on which they are authorized by law to pay dividends to their shareholders. **Dividends** paid to shareholders represent a return on the capital directly or indirectly contributed to the corporation by the shareholders. The payment of dividends is at the discretion of the board of directors.

Some important characteristics of dividends include the following:

1. Unless a dividend is declared by the board of directors of a corporation, it is not a liability of the corporation. A corporation cannot default on an undeclared dividend. As a consequence, corporations cannot become bankrupt because of nonpayment of dividends. The amount of the dividend and even whether it is paid are decisions based on the business judgment of the board of directors.
2. The payment of dividends by the corporation is not a business expense. Dividends are not deductible for corporate tax purposes. In short, dividends are paid out of the corporation's aftertax profits.
3. Dividends received by individual shareholders are for the most part considered ordinary income by the IRS and are fully taxable. However, corporations that own stock in other corporations are permitted to exclude 70 percent of the dividend amounts they receive and are taxed only on the remaining 30 percent.[7]

Preferred Stock Features

Preferred stock differs from common stock because it has preference over common stock in the payment of dividends and in the distribution of corporation assets in the event of liquidation. *Preference* means only that the holders of the preferred shares must receive a dividend (in the case of an ongoing firm) before holders of common shares are entitled to anything.

Preferred stock is a form of equity from a legal and tax standpoint. It is important to note, however, that holders of preferred stock sometimes have no voting privileges.

STATED VALUE Preferred shares have a stated liquidating value, usually $100 per share. The cash dividend is described in terms of dollars per share. For example, General Motors "$5 preferred" easily translates into a dividend yield of 5 percent of stated value.

CUMULATIVE AND NONCUMULATIVE DIVIDENDS A preferred dividend is *not* like interest on a bond. The board of directors may decide not to pay the dividends on preferred shares, and their decision may have nothing to do with the current net income of the corporation.

Dividends payable on preferred stock are either *cumulative* or *noncumulative;* most are cumulative. If preferred dividends are cumulative and are not paid in a particular year, they will be carried forward as an *arrearage.* Usually, both the accumulated (past) preferred dividends and the current preferred dividends must be paid before the common shareholders can receive anything.

[7]For the record, the 70 percent exclusion applies when the recipient owns less than 20 percent of the outstanding stock in a corporation. If a corporation owns more than 20 percent but less than 80 percent, the exclusion is 80 percent. If more than 80 percent is owned, the corporation can file a single "consolidated" return and the exclusion is effectively 100 percent.

Unpaid preferred dividends are *not* debts of the firm. Directors elected by the common shareholders can defer preferred dividends indefinitely. However, in such cases, common shareholders must also forgo dividends. In addition, holders of preferred shares are sometimes granted voting and other rights if preferred dividends have not been paid for some time.

IS PREFERRED STOCK REALLY DEBT? A good case can be made that preferred stock is really debt in disguise, a kind of equity bond. Preferred shareholders receive a stated dividend only, and, if the corporation is liquidated, preferred shareholders get a stated value. Often, preferred stocks carry credit ratings much like those of bonds. Furthermore, preferred stock is sometimes convertible into common stock, and preferred stocks are often callable.

In addition, many issues of preferred stock have obligatory sinking funds. The existence of such a sinking fund effectively creates a final maturity because it means that the entire issue will ultimately be retired. For these reasons, preferred stock seems to be a lot like debt. However, for tax purposes, preferred dividends are treated like common stock dividends.

In the 1990s, firms began to sell securities that look a lot like preferred stocks but are treated as debt for tax purposes. The new securities were given interesting acronyms like TOPrS (trust-originated preferred securities, or toppers), MIPS (monthly income preferred securities), and QUIPS (quarterly income preferred securities), among others. Because of various specific features, these instruments can be counted as debt for tax purposes, making the interest payments tax deductible. Payments made to investors in these instruments are treated as interest for personal income taxes for individuals. Until 2003, interest payments and dividends were taxed at the same marginal tax rate. When the tax rate on dividend payments was reduced, these instruments were not included, so individuals must still pay their higher income tax rate on dividend payments received from these instruments.

6.7 THE STOCK MARKETS

Back in Chapter 1, we briefly mentioned that shares of stock are bought and sold on various stock exchanges, the two most important of which (in the U.S.) are the New York Stock Exchange and the NASDAQ. From our earlier discussion, recall that the stock market consists of a **primary market** and a **secondary market**. In the primary, or new-issue market, shares of stock are first brought to the market and sold to investors. In the secondary market, existing shares are traded among investors.

In the primary market, companies sell securities to raise money. We will discuss this process in detail in a later chapter. We therefore focus mainly on secondary-market activity in this section. We conclude with a discussion of how stock prices are quoted in the financial press.

Dealers and Brokers

Because most securities transactions involve dealers and brokers, it is important to understand exactly what is meant by the terms *dealer* and *broker*. A **dealer** maintains an inventory and stands ready to buy and sell at any time. In contrast, a **broker** brings buyers and sellers together, but does not maintain an inventory. Thus, when we speak of used car dealers and real estate brokers, we recognize that the used car dealer maintains an inventory, whereas the real estate broker does not.

In the securities markets, a dealer stands ready to buy securities from investors wishing to sell them and sell securities to investors wishing to buy them. Recall from our previous chapter that the price the dealer is willing to pay is called the bid price. The price at which the dealer will sell is called the ask price (sometimes called the asked, offered, or offering price). The difference between the bid and ask prices is called the spread, and it is the basic source of dealer profits.

How big is the bid-ask spread on your favorite stock? Check out the latest quotes at www.bloomberg.com.

Dealers exist in all areas of the economy, not just the stock markets. For example, your local college bookstore is probably both a primary and a secondary market textbook dealer. If you buy a new book, this is a primary market transaction. If you buy a used book, this is a secondary market transaction, and you pay the store's ask price. If you sell the book back, you receive the store's bid price, often half of the ask price. The bookstore's spread is the difference between the two prices.

In contrast, a securities broker arranges transactions between investors, matching investors wishing to buy securities with investors wishing to sell securities. The distinctive characteristic of security brokers is that they do not buy or sell securities for their own accounts. Facilitating trades by others is their business.

Organization of the NYSE

The New York Stock Exchange, or NYSE, popularly known as the Big Board, celebrated its bicentennial a few years ago. It has occupied its current location on Wall Street since the turn of the twentieth century. Measured in terms of dollar volume of activity and the total value of shares listed, it is the largest stock market in the world.

MEMBERS The NYSE has about 1,400 exchange **members**, who are said to own "seats" on the exchange. Collectively, the members of the exchange are its owners. However, in fall 2005, the NYSE was planning to go public, so this ownership structure will probably change. Exchange seat owners can buy and sell securities on the exchange floor without paying commissions. For this and other reasons, exchange seats are valuable assets and are regularly bought and sold. As of December 2005, the record price is $4 million. Interestingly, prior to 1986, the highest seat price paid was $625,000, just before the 1929 market crash. Since then, the lowest seat price paid has been $55,000, in 1977.

The largest number of NYSE members are registered as **commission brokers**. The business of a commission broker is to execute customer orders to buy and sell stocks. A commission broker's primary responsibility to customers is to get the best possible prices for their orders. The exact number varies, but, usually, about 500 NYSE members are commission brokers. NYSE commission brokers typically are employees of brokerage companies such as Merrill Lynch.

Second in number of NYSE members are **specialists**, so named because each of them acts as an assigned dealer for a small set of securities. With a few exceptions, each security listed for trading on the NYSE is assigned to a single specialist. Specialists are also called "market makers" because they are obligated to maintain a fair, orderly market for the securities assigned to them.

Specialists post bid prices and ask prices for securities assigned to them. Specialists make a market by standing ready to buy at bid prices and sell at asked prices when there is a temporary disparity between the flow of buy orders and that of sell orders for a security. In this capacity, they act as dealers for their own accounts.

Third in number of exchange members are **floor brokers**. Floor brokers are used by commission brokers who are too busy to handle certain orders themselves. Such commission brokers will delegate some orders to floor brokers for execution. Floor brokers are sometimes called $2 brokers, a name earned at a time when the standard fee for their service was only $2.

In recent years, floor brokers have become less important on the exchange floor because of the efficient **SuperDOT system** (the *DOT* stands for Designated Order Turnaround), which allows orders to be transmitted electronically directly to the specialist. SuperDOT trading now accounts for a substantial percentage of all trading on the NYSE, particularly on smaller orders.

Finally, a small number of NYSE members are **floor traders** who independently trade for their own accounts. Floor traders try to anticipate temporary price fluctuations and profit from them by buying low and selling high. In recent decades, the number of floor traders has declined substantially, suggesting that it has become increasingly difficult to profit from short-term trading on the exchange floor.

OPERATIONS Now that we have a basic idea of how the NYSE is organized and who the major players are, we turn to the question of how trading actually takes place. Fundamentally, the business of the NYSE is to attract and process **order flow**. The term *order flow* means the flow of customer orders to buy and sell stocks. The customers of the NYSE are the millions of individual investors and tens of thousands of institutional investors who place their orders to buy and sell shares in NYSE-listed companies. The NYSE has been quite successful in attracting order flow. Currently, it is not unusual for well over a billion shares to change hands in a single day.

FLOOR ACTIVITY It is quite likely that you have seen footage of the NYSE trading floor on television, or you may have visited the NYSE and viewed exchange floor activity from the visitors' gallery (it's worth the trip). Either way, you would have seen a big room, about the size of a basketball gym. This big room is called, technically, "the Big Room." There are a few other, smaller rooms that you normally don't see, one of which is called "the Garage" because that is what it was before it was taken over for trading.

Take a virtual field trip to the New York Stock Exchange at www.nyse.com.

On the floor of the exchange are a number of stations, each with a roughly figure-eight shape. These stations have multiple counters with numerous terminal screens above and on the sides. People operate behind and in front of the counters in relatively stationary positions.

Other people move around on the exchange floor, frequently returning to the many telephones positioned along the exchange walls. In all, you may be reminded of worker ants moving around an ant colony. It is natural to wonder: "What are all those people doing down there (and why are so many wearing funny-looking coats)?"

As an overview of exchange floor activity, here is a quick look at what goes on. Each of the counters at a figure-eight–shaped station is a **specialist's post**. Specialists normally operate in front of their posts to monitor and manage trading in the stocks assigned to them. Clerical employees working for the specialists operate behind the counter. Moving from the many telephones lining the walls of the exchange out to the exchange floor and back again are swarms of commission brokers, receiving telephoned customer orders, walking out to specialists' posts where the orders can be executed, and returning to confirm order executions and receive new customer orders.

To better understand activity on the NYSE trading floor, imagine yourself as a commission broker. Your phone clerk has just handed you an order to sell 20,000 shares of Wal-Mart for a customer of the brokerage company that employs you. The customer wants to sell the stock at the best possible price as soon as possible. You immediately walk (running violates exchange rules) to the specialist's post where Wal-Mart stock is traded.

As you approach the specialist's post where Wal-Mart is traded, you check the terminal screen for information on the current market price. The screen reveals that the last executed trade was at $60.25 and that the specialist is bidding $60 per share. You could immediately sell to the specialist at $60, but that would be too easy.

Instead, as the customer's representative, you are obligated to get the best possible price. It is your job to "work" the order, and your job depends on providing satisfactory order execution service. So, you look around for another broker who represents a customer who wants to buy Wal-Mart stock. Luckily, you quickly find another broker at the specialist's post with an order to buy 20,000 shares. Noticing that the dealer is asking $60.10 per share, you both agree to execute your orders with each other at a price of $60.05. This price is exactly halfway between the specialist's bid and ask prices, and it saves each of your customers .05 × 20,000 = $1,000 as compared to dealing at the posted prices.

For a very actively traded stock, there may be many buyers and sellers around the specialist's post, and most of the trading will be done directly between brokers. This is called trading in the "crowd." In such cases, the specialist's responsibility is to maintain order and to make sure that all buyers and sellers receive a fair price. In other words, the specialist essentially functions as a referee.

More often, however, there will be no crowd at the specialist's post. Going back to our Wal-Mart example, suppose you are unable to quickly find another broker with an order to buy 20,000 shares. Because you have an order to sell immediately, you may have no choice but to sell to the specialist at the bid price of $60. In this case, the need to execute an order quickly takes priority, and the specialist provides the liquidity necessary to allow immediate order execution.

Finally, note that colored coats are worn by many of the people on the floor of the exchange. The color of the coat indicates the person's job or position. Clerks, runners, visitors, exchange officials, and so on wear particular colors to identify themselves. Also, things can get a little hectic on a busy day, with the result that good clothing doesn't last long; the cheap coats offer some protection.

NASDAQ Operations

In terms of total dollar volume of trading, the second largest stock market in the United States is NASDAQ (say "Naz-dak"). The somewhat odd name originally was an acronym for the National Association of Securities Dealers Automated Quotations system, but NASDAQ is now a name in its own right.

Introduced in 1971, the NASDAQ market is a computer network of securities dealers and others that disseminates timely security price quotes to computer screens worldwide. NASDAQ dealers act as market makers for securities listed on NASDAQ. As market makers, NASDAQ dealers post bid and ask prices at which they accept sell and buy orders, respectively. With each price quote, they also post the number of stock shares that they obligate themselves to trade at their quoted prices.

Like NYSE specialists, NASDAQ market makers trade on an inventory basis, that is, using their inventory as a buffer to absorb buy and sell order imbalances. Unlike the NYSE specialist system, NASDAQ features multiple market makers for actively traded stocks. Thus, there are two key differences between the NYSE and NASDAQ:

1. NASDAQ is a computer network and has no physical location where trading takes place.
2. NASDAQ has a multiple market maker system rather than a specialist system.

Traditionally, a securities market largely characterized by dealers who buy and sell securities for their own inventories is called an **over-the-counter (OTC) market.** Consequently, NASDAQ is often referred to as an OTC market. However, in their efforts to promote a distinct image, NASDAQ officials prefer that the term OTC not be used when referring to the NASDAQ market. Nevertheless, old habits die hard, and many people still refer to NASDAQ as an OTC market.

By 2005, the NASDAQ had grown to the point that it was, by some measures, as big as the NYSE. For example, on May 3, 2005, 1.9 billion shares were traded on the NASDAQ versus 1.7 billion on the NYSE. In dollars, NASDAQ trading volume for the day was $42 billion compared to $54 billion for the NYSE.

NASDAQ (www.nasdaq.com) has a *great* Web site; check it out!

The NASDAQ is actually made up of two separate markets, the NASDAQ National Market (NNM) and the NASDAQ SmallCap Market. As the market for NASDAQ's larger and more actively traded securities, the NASDAQ National Market lists about 3,000 companies, including some of the best-known companies in the world. The NASDAQ SmallCap Market is for small companies and lists about 400 individual companies. As you might guess, an important difference in the two markets is that the National Market has more stringent listing requirements. Of course, as SmallCap companies become more established, they may move up to the National Market.

NASDAQ PARTICIPANTS As we mentioned previously, the NASDAQ has historically been a dealer market, characterized by competing market makers. Typically, there have been about a dozen or so per stock. The biggest market makers cover thousands of stocks.

In a very important development, in the late 1990s, the NASDAQ system was opened to so-called **electronic communications networks (ECNs)**. ECNs are basically Web sites that allow investors to trade directly with one another. You can actually watch trading taking place by visiting one of the biggest ECNs, INET, at www.island.com. (The previous name for INET was Island.) INET is somewhat unique in that the "order book," meaning the list of all buy and sell orders, is public in real time. In Figure 6.3, we have captured a sample of the order book for IBM. On the left side are buy orders (bids);

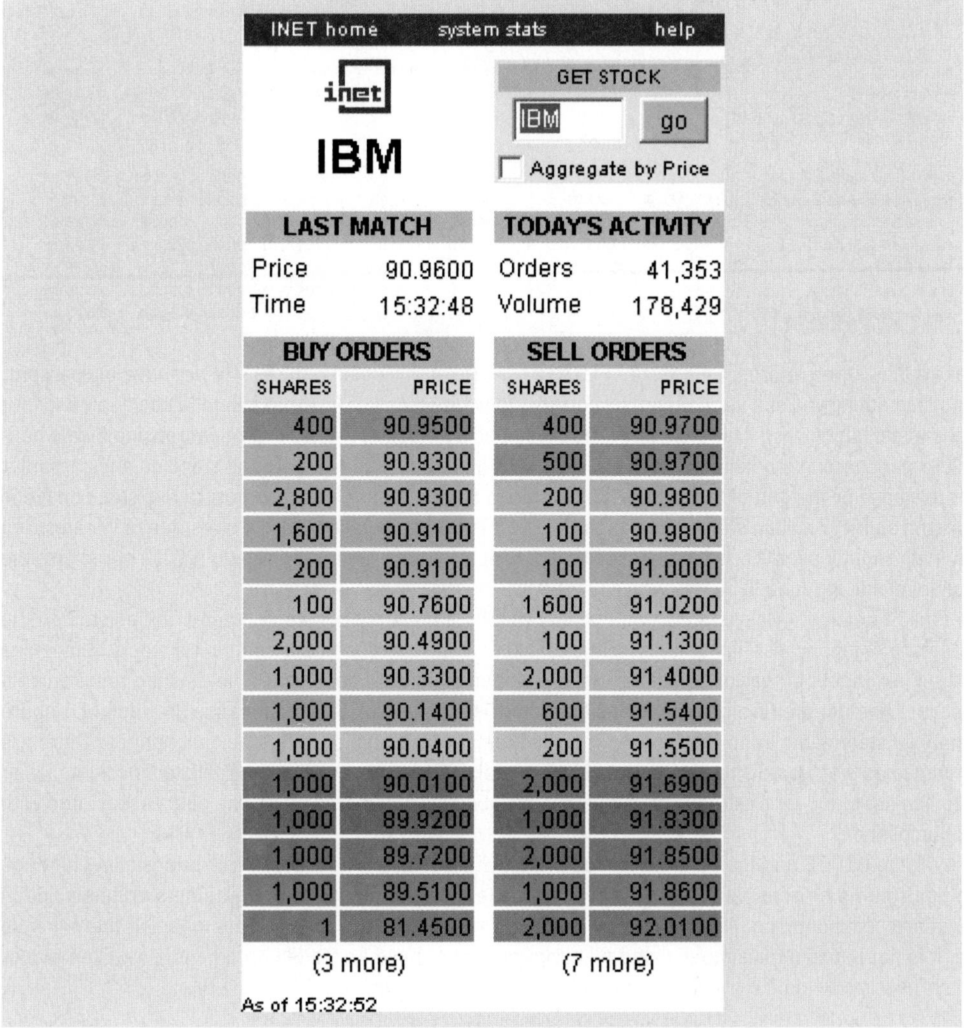

INET home | system stats | help

inet

IBM

GET STOCK: IBM go

Aggregate by Price

LAST MATCH		TODAY'S ACTIVITY	
Price	90.9600	Orders	41,353
Time	15:32:48	Volume	178,429

BUY ORDERS		SELL ORDERS	
SHARES	PRICE	SHARES	PRICE
400	90.9500	400	90.9700
200	90.9300	500	90.9700
2,800	90.9300	200	90.9800
1,600	90.9100	100	90.9800
200	90.9100	100	91.0000
100	90.7600	1,600	91.0200
2,000	90.4900	100	91.1300
1,000	90.3300	2,000	91.4000
1,000	90.1400	600	91.5400
1,000	90.0400	200	91.5500
1,000	90.0100	2,000	91.6900
1,000	89.9200	1,000	91.8300
1,000	89.7200	2,000	91.8500
1,000	89.5100	1,000	91.8600
1	81.4500	2,000	92.0100
(3 more)		(7 more)	

As of 15:32:52

FIGURE 6.3
An ECN Order Book

THE REAL WORLD

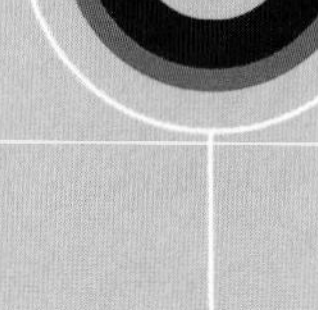

THE WILD, WILD WEST OF STOCK TRADING

Where do companies go when they can't (or don't want to) meet the listing requirements of the larger stock markets? Two options are the Over-the-Counter Bulletin Board (OTCBB) and the Pink Sheets. These two electronic markets are part of the Wild, Wild West of stock trading. The somewhat odd names have simple explanations. The OTCBB began as an electronic bulletin board that was created to facilitate OTC trading in nonlisted stocks. The name "Pink Sheets" just reflects the fact that, at one time, prices for such stocks were quoted on pink sheets of paper.

The well-known markets such as NASDAQ and the NYSE have relatively strict listing requirements. If a company fails to meet these requirements, it can be delisted. The OTCBB and the Pink Sheets, on the other hand, have no listing requirements. The OTCBB does require that companies file financial statements with the SEC (or other relevant agency), but the Pink Sheets does not.

Stocks traded on these markets often have very low prices and are frequently referred to as "penny stocks," "microcaps," or even "nanocaps." Relatively few brokers do any research on these companies, so information is often spread through word of mouth or the Internet, not the most reliable of sources. In fact, for many stocks, these markets often look like big electronic rumor mills and gossip factories. To get a feel for what trading looks like, we captured a typical screen from the OTCBB Web site (www.otcbb.com):

Market Statistics — Data delayed 15-20 minutes

OTCBB | Vol Actives | GO

Name	Symbol	Last	Tick	Chg	% Chg	Open	High	Low	Volume
Smartforce Plc	THTHF	0.000	▼	-0.0001	-100%	0.0002	0.0002	0.000	190.33 m
Reality Wireless Networks Inc	RWLN	0.0041	▲	0.001	32.26%	0.0035	0.0069	0.0034	93.79 m
Alpha Wireless Broadband Inc	AWBI	0.0002	▲	0.0001	100%	0.0002	0.0002	0.0002	79.77 m
Conectisys Cp	CNES	0.0025	▼	-0.0002	-7.41%	0.0027	0.0029	0.0025	68.81 m
Reward Companies Corp	RWRD	0.015	▼	-0.001	-6.25%	0.019	0.020	0.012	55.1 m
Ivoice Inc	IVOC	0.0006	–	0.000	0%	0.0006	0.0007	0.0005	54.69 m
Jackson Rivers Company	JRVC	0.0003	–	0.000	0%	0.0002	0.0004	0.0002	47.24 m
Gfy Foos Inc	GFYO	0.0002	–	0.000	0%	0.0002	0.0002	0.0001	45.75 m
Marmion Industries Corp	MMON	0.0003	–	0.000	0%	0.0004	0.0004	0.0002	41.09 m
Eworldmedia Holdings Inc	EWMD	0.0004	▼	-0.0002	-33.33%	0.0005	0.0005	0.0004	37.25 m

First, take a look at the returns. Smartforce PLC had a return at this point in the day of *negative* 100 percent! That's not something you see very often. The current stock price was so low that it couldn't be quoted to four decimal places. In contrast, Alpha Wireless stock jumped by a positive 100 percent, increasing by a whopping $.0001 per share. A stock listed on the OTCBB is often the most actively traded stock on any particular day. For example, by the end of this particular day, Sirius Satellite Radio was the most active stock on NASDAQ, trading about 97 million shares. Six stocks on the OTCBB traded even more shares. Alpha Wireless led the way with slightly over 390 million shares traded. But, at an average price of, say $.0002 per share, the total dollar volume in Alpha Wireless was all of $78,000.

The Pink Sheets (www.pinksheets.com) is operated by a privately owned company. To be listed on the Pink Sheets, a company just has to find a market maker willing to trade in the company's stock. Companies list on the Pink Sheets for various reasons. Small companies that do not wish to meet listing requirements are one type. Another are foreign companies that often list on the Pink Sheets because they do not prepare their financial statements according to GAAP, a requirement for listing on U.S. stock exchanges. There are many companies that were formerly listed on bigger stock markets that were either delisted involuntarily, or chose to "go dark" for various reasons, including, as we discussed in Chapter 1, the costs associated with Sarbox compliance.

All in all, the OTCBB and Pink Sheets can be pretty wild places to trade. Low stock prices allow for huge percentage returns on small stock price movements. Be advised, however, that attempts at manipulation and fraud are commonplace. Also, stocks on these markets are often thinly traded, meaning there is little volume. It is not unusual for a stock listed on either market to have no trades on a given day. Even two or three days in a row without a trade in a particular stock is not uncommon.

sell orders (asks) are on the right. All orders are "limit" orders, which means the customer has specified the most he or she will pay (for buy orders) or the least he or she will accept (for sell orders). The **inside quotes** (the highest bid, or buy, and the lowest ask, or sell) in the market are the ones at the top, so we sometimes hear the expression "top of the book" quotes.

If you visit the site, you can see trading take place as orders are entered and executed. Notice that on this particular day, by 3:32 P.M., 178,429 shares of IBM had traded on INET. At that time, the inside quotes for IBM were 400 shares bid at $90.95 and 400 shares offered at $90.97. Also notice that this is not the entire book for IBM. There are three more buy orders at $81.45 or less and seven more sell orders at $92.01 or higher.

Investor buy and sell orders placed on ECNs are transmitted to the NASDAQ and displayed along with market maker bid and ask prices. As a result, the ECNs open up the NASDAQ by essentially allowing individual investors to enter orders, not just market makers. Thus, the ECNs act to increase liquidity and competition.

If you check prices on the Web for both NASDAQ- and NYSE-listed stocks, you'll notice an interesting difference. For NASDAQ issues, you can actually see the bid and ask prices as well as recent transactions information. The bid and ask prices for the NASDAQ listings represent the inside quotes, which, as we noted previously, are the highest bid and the lowest ask prices. For a relatively small fee (or possibly free from your broker), you can even have access to "Level II" quotes, which show all of the posted bid and ask prices and, frequently, the identity of the market maker. Of course, NYSE specialists post bid and ask prices as well; they are just not disclosed to the general public (they are available by subscription at a cost substantially higher than that for Level II NASDAQ quotes).

The success of the NASDAQ National Market as a competitor to the NYSE and other organized exchanges can be judged by its ability to attract stock listings by companies that traditionally might have chosen to be listed on the NYSE. Such well-known companies as Microsoft, Apple Computer, Intel, Dell, Yahoo!, and Starbucks list their securities on NASDAQ. Stock Markets other than the NYSE and NASDAQ exist, of course. See our nearby *The Real World* box for a description of one of the more interesting such markets.

Stock Market Reporting

If you look through the pages of *The Wall Street Journal* (or other financial newspaper), you will find information on a large number of stocks in several different markets. Figure 6.4 reproduces a small section of the stock page for the New York Stock Exchange from May 3, 2005. Information on most NASDAQ issues is reported in the same way. In Figure 6.4, locate the line for motorcycle maker Harley-Davidson (HarleyDav). With the column headings, the line reads:

YTD	52 WEEK			YLD			VOL		NET
% CHG	HI	LO	STOCK (SYM)	DIV	%	PE	100s	CLOSE	CHG
−20.7	63.75	45.14	HarleyDav **HDI**	.64f	1.3	16	34048	48.17	1.15

You can get real-time stock quotes on the Web. See finance.yahoo.com for details.

The first number, −20.7, tells us that Harley's stock price has fallen by 20.7 percent on a year-to-date (YTD) basis. The next two numbers, 63.75 and 45.14, are the highest and lowest prices for the stock over the past 52 weeks. The .64 is the annual dividend in dollars. Because Harley, like most companies, pays dividends quarterly, this $.64 is actually the latest quarterly dividend multiplied by 4. So, the cash dividend paid was $.64/4 = $.16, or 16 cents per share. The small *f* following the .64 indicates a footnote, which in this case tells us the dividend was just increased.

FIGURE 6.4

Sample Stock Quotation from *The Wall Street Journal*

Source: Reprinted by permission of *The Wall Street Journal,* May 3, 2005. Reprinted by permission of Dow Jones & Company, Inc. via Copyright Clearance Center, Inc.

THE WALL STREET JOURNAL.

NEW YORK STOCK EXCHANGE COMPOSITE TRANSACTIONS

YTD % CHG	52-WEEK HI	LO	STOCK (SYM)	DIV	YLD %	PE	VOL 100s	CLOSE	NET CHG
1.3	71.42	45.50	FrnklnRes **BEN**	.40a	.6	21	9833	68.51	−0.17
−15.9	74.20	56.45	FredMac **FRE**	1.40f	2.3	...	16563	61.97	0.45
−7.9	43.36	27.24	FrptMcCG B **FCX**	1.00a	2.9	...	24509	34.78	0.12
2.6	19.67	12.06	FreescleSemi **FSL** n		...	...	12622	18.29	−0.43
0.8	19.93	16.20	FreescleSemi B **FSLB** n		...	...	15017	18.51	−0.35
−13.2	26.99	16.76	FremontGen **FMT**	.28	1.3	4	3750	21.85	0.16
−0.6	30.16	22.25	FresensMed **FMS**	.41e	1.6	23	116	26.64	−0.16
−2.4	33.94	22.62	FrshDlMnte **FDP**	.80	2.8	11	1423	28.89	−0.01
▼ **−42.1**	**20.94**	**12.08**	**FrdmnBillRm FBR**	**1.36a**	**12.1**	**5**	**70050**	**11.23**	**−0.86**
60.7	45.50	17.43	FrontrOil **FTO**	.32f	.7	17	4236	42.85	0.77
18.9	55.52	14.94	Frontln **FRO** s	14.40e	32.0	6	8953	45.04	1.13
▲ 7.7	30.71	25.23	FullrHB **FUL**	.49f	1.6	23	2519	30.71	0.39
−22.1	29.22	19.14	FurnBrndInt **FBN**	.60	3.1	13	6967	19.51	0.13
			G						
12.8	34.48	22.05	GATX **GMT**	.80	2.4	10	3652	33.33	0.61
−14.9	14.15	11.30	GMH CmntiesTr **GCT** n	.39e	3.3	...	652	12	0.25
−8.6	34	16.40	GolLinhas **GOL** n	.25e	.9	...	2824	29.14	0.77
2.6	8.60	5.33	GP Strategs **GPX**		...	6	46	7.64	−0.11
−17.5	49.89	35.99	Gabelli A **GBL**	.08a	.2	20	826	40.02	0.10
1.4	37.41	29.84	GblsRsdntl **GBP**	2.41	6.6	13	2646	36.30	−0.35
−14.2	34.12	25.42	Gallagr **AJG**	1.12f	4.0	36	3908	27.90	0.06
2.0	64.45	44.60	GallaherGp **GLH**	2.39e	3.9	...	304	61.93	−0.32
▲ 14.7	25.70	14.37	GameStop A **GME**		...	24	6237	25.64	1.03
8.9	25.20	18.65	GameStop B **GMEB** n		...	...	1287	24.40	1.06
−6.4	88.81	74.80	♣Gannett **GCI**	1.08	1.4	15	12009	76.48	−0.52
1.1	25.72	18.12	Gap Inc **GPS**	.18f	.8	18	39961	21.35	...
4.4	43.13	24.55	♣GardnrDenvr **GDI**		...	19	5405	37.89	1.35
−32.4	13.38	8.06	Gartner **IT**		...	70	2071	8.42	−0.02
−32.5	13.06	7.96	Gartner B **ITB**		...	69	605	8.30	−0.10
▼ −41.8	6.92	3.40	Gateway **GTW**		...	dd	32970	3.50	0.09
−1.3	44.19	26.55	GaylEnt **GET**		...	dd	2828	40.99	0.99
0.6	21.25	10.18	GenCorp **GY**		...	dd	5227	18.69	−0.32
29.1	75.50	41	♣Genentech **DNA** s		...	85	37754	70.28	−0.66
−13.4	14.10	6.79	GenlCbl **BGC**		...	52	3411	11.99	−0.16
0.9	109.98	90.61	GenDynam **GD**	1.60f	1.5	16	6958	105.51	0.46
−0.7	37.75	29.55	GenElec **GE**	.88	2.4	22	137260	36.25	0.05
▲ 6.2	39.15	24.31	GenGrthProp **GGP**	1.44	3.8	32	11204	38.39	−0.72
12.9	53.98	17.75	GenMaritime **GMR**	1.77p	...	6	5151	45.10	1.25
−0.9	53.89	43.01	GenMills **GIS**	1.24	2.5	18	9138	49.28	−0.12
−32.2	48.85	24.67	GenMotor **GM**	2.00	7.4	27	58286	27.16	0.48
−14.9	31.50	18.77	Genesco **GCO**		...	13	1260	26.50	0.77
−12.8	29.85	21.11	♣GeneseWY A **GWR**		...	18	1422	24.52	0.54
−2.9	44.77	35.05	GenuinePart **GPC**	1.25	2.9	19	3649	42.80	−0.10
1.6	29.80	18.75	GnwrthFnl A **GNW** n	.26	.9	11	9981	27.42	−0.53
−1.5	34.30	25	GnwrthFnl un n	1.50	4.7	...	82	31.93	−0.12
5.3	**32.70**	**17.02**	**♣GeoGrp GGI**		**...**	**16**	**394**	**27.99**	**1.73**
−26.1	58.75	29.47	GA Gulf **GGC**	.32	.9	10	5194	36.81	0.10
−8.0	38.45	31.25	♣GA Pac **GP**	.70f	2.0	13	12199	34.47	0.20
−7.0	8.09	5.50	♣GerbScnfc **GRB**		...	51	64	7.08	...
−27.4	7.39	4.42	Gerdau AmerSt **GNA** n	.02e	.4	...	1527	4.91	−0.03
−19.9	13.85	5.31	Gerdau **GGB** s	.68	7.1	...	3688	9.61	−0.14
5.0	79.77	50.28	GettyImages **GYI**		...	39	5214	72.30	0.75
−12.2	30.10	21.35	GettyRlty **GTY**	1.74f	6.9	16	424	25.22	−0.01
0.6	31.81	15.37	GiantInd **GI**		...	18	1037	26.66	0.55
			H						
39.3	56.67	34.70	HCA **HCA**	.60f	1.1	20	23050	55.65	−0.19
8.8	39.25	27.53	♣HCC InsHldg **HCC**	.34	.9	15	3996	36.04	0.47
−4.6	50	19.60	HDFC Bnk **HDB**	.54e	1.2	...	2921	43.28	−0.13
▲ 19.7	50.71	36.65	HNI **HNI**	.62f	1.2	25	3396	51.51	0.85
−9.0	13.20	8.25	HRPT Prop **HRP**	.84	7.2	18	5224	11.68	−0.07
−6.1	88.37	69.85	HSBC ADS **HBC**	3.30e	4.1	...	4315	79.97	−0.08
16.6	45.23	24.95	Haemonetic **HAE**		...	28	2407	42.21	−0.56
9.0	46.26	26.45	Hallibrtn **HAL**	.50	1.2	dd	39040	42.78	1.19
−42.1	15.20	5.67	HnckFabrcs **HKF**	.24m	4.0	75	639	6	0.08
−18.3	23.84	17.06	Handleman **HDL**	.32	1.8	11	782	17.54	0.19
−28.0	16.70	4.15	HangerOrtho **HGR**		...	dd	633	5.83	−0.01
−24.2	14.87	10.23	HanovrCmprsr **HC**		...	dd	6198	10.71	0.34
6.9	50.85	33.40	Hanson ADS **HAN**	1.71e	3.7	...	51	45.90	−0.12
2.1	38.40	26.91	Harland **JH**	.50	1.4	19	819	36.87	0.87
−20.7	63.75	45.14	HarleyDav **HDI**	.64f	1.3	16	34048	48.17	1.15
−38.3	131.74	70.33	HarmanInt **HAR**	.05	.1	26	6226	78.31	−0.27
−31.8	14.29	5.96	HrmnyGld ADS **HMY**	.05e	.8	...	7083	6.32	0.05
−1.2	72.60	43.94	HarrahEntn **HET**	1.32	2.0	19	10328	66.11	0.49
−8.4	35	21.19	Harris **HRS** s	.24	.8	22	7935	28.30	0.10
−3.1	61.35	40.10	Harsco **HSC**	1.20	2.2	18	3763	53.99	0.34
10.9	29.48	22.51	HarteHanks **HHS**	.20f	.7	24	2583	28.80	0.30
5.7	74.07	52.73	HrtfrdFnl **HIG**	1.16	1.6	10	26736	73.27	0.90
1.7	68.30	54.10	HrtfrdFnl 7.0un	3.50	5.2	...	3295	67.06	1.06
2.1	67.45	52.70	HrtfrdFnl un	3.00	4.5	...	750	66.11	0.70
12.1	10.29	5.64	♣Hartmarx **HMX**		...	18	925	8.71	0.08
−38.6	18.50	10.19	HarvstNatRes **HNR**		...	9	3748	10.60	−0.19
−2.6	21.50	16.90	Hasbro **HAS**	.36f	1.9	20	8188	18.88	−0.04
−21.1	21.09	14.20	HavrtyFurn **HVT**	.25	1.7	15	345	14.60	0.25
−12.3	29.79	22.97	HawEllnd **HE** s	1.24	4.9	20	4041	25.55	0.25
−11.7	4.40	2.40	Head **HED**		...	dd	14	3.25	...
12.3	34.96	19.50	Headwaters **HW**		...	19	4233	32	0.03
−7.4	28.85	20	HlthCrProp **HCP**	1.68	6.6	23	4057	25.64	...
−12.2	38.15	27.70	HlthCr Reit **HCN**	2.48f	7.4	24	1527	33.48	−0.02
9.2	27	18.80	HlthMgt A **HMA**	.16	.6	18	9234	24.80	0.07
18.4	35.41	21.60	HealthNet **HNT**		...	95	7483	34.18	0.15
−5.2	42.11	32.45	HlthcrRlty **HR** lf	2.62f	6.8	26	1586	38.59	−0.02
−5.1	26.75	22.57	♣HearstArgyl **HTV**	.28	1.1	19	1390	25.03	−0.07
▼ −22.0	7.50	4.55	HeclaMin **HL**		...	dd	7477	4.55	−0.11
−15.3	23.41	14.45	Heico **HEI**	.05b	.3	23	176	19.14	0.16
−11.7	17.80	11.55	Heico A **HEIA**	.05b	.3	18	622	15.26	0.06
−5.6	40.61	34.53	Heinz **HNZ**	1.14	3.1	18	6533	36.79	−0.06
7.0	10.01	5.74	Hellenic **OTE**	.21e	2.2	...	221	9.42	0.07
17.2	41.43	23.93	HelmPayne **HP**	.33	.8	38	4011	39.89	1.45
−8.6	16.85	14	Herbalife **HLF** n		...	...	181	14.85	−0.25
−9.6	15.55	9.93	Hercules **HPC**		...	cc	4930	13.43	0.20
−3.9	34	24.11	HeritageProp **HTG**	2.10	6.8	32	379	30.85	0.05
14.7	64.95	43.52	Hershey **HSY** s	.88	1.4	27	8941	63.71	−0.19
−17.0	32.42	24.40	Hewitt **HEW**		...	22	2667	26.58	−0.03
0.0	22.26	16.08	HewlettPk **HPQ**	.32	1.5	18	124329	20.97	0.50
14.5	17.92	7.70	Hexcel **HXL**		...	dd	3144	16.60	0.20
5.9	33.10	21.68	Hibernia **HIB**	.80	2.6	16	6110	31.25	0.02
−5.2	12	9.89	HighlndHspty **HIH**	.50e	4.7	cc	427	10.66	0.17
1.6	28.14	20.68	HighwdProp **HIW** lf	1.70	6.0	97	2163	28.13	...
−1.8	37.64	30.77	♣HilbRogl **HRH**	.42	1.2	15	2184	35.60	0.59

Jumping ahead just a bit, "CLOSE" is the closing price on the day (i.e., the last price at which a trade took place before the NYSE closed for the day). The "Net Chg" of 1.15 tells us that the closing price of \$48.17 is \$1.15 higher than it was the day before; so, we say that Harley was up 1.15 for the day.

The column marked "YLD %" gives the dividend yield based on the current dividend and the closing price. For Harley, this is \$.64/48.17 = .0133, or about 1.3 percent, the number shown. The next column, labeled "PE," is the price-earnings ratio we discussed earlier. It is calculated as the closing price divided by annual earnings per share (based on the most recent four quarters). In the jargon of Wall Street, we might say that Harley "sells for 16 times earnings."

Finally, the column marked "Vol 100s" tells us how many shares traded during the day (in hundreds). For example, the 34048 for Harley tells us that about 3.4 million shares changed hands on this day alone. If the average price during the day was \$48 or so, then the dollar volume of transactions was on the order of \$48 × 3.4 million = \$163 million worth for Harley alone. This was a fairly routine day of trading in Harley shares, so this amount is not unusual and serves to illustrate how active the market can be for well-known companies.

If you look over Figure 6.4, you will notice quite a few other footnote indicators (small letters) and special symbols. To learn more about these, pick up any *Wall Street Journal* and consult the stock pages.

SUMMARY AND CONCLUSIONS

This chapter has covered the basics of stocks and stock valuations. The key points include:

1. A stock can be valued by discounting its dividends. We mention three types of situations:
   a. The case of zero growth of dividends.
   b. The case of constant growth of dividends.
   c. The case of differential growth.
2. An estimate of the growth rate of a stock is needed for the dividend discount model. A useful estimate of the growth rate is

   g = Retention ratio × Return on retained earnings (ROE)
3. It is worthwhile to view a share of stock as the sum of its worth—if the company behaves like a cash cow (the company does no investing)—and the value per share of its growth opportunities. We write the value of a share as

   $$\frac{\text{EPS}}{R} + \text{NPVGO}$$

   We show that, in theory, share price must be the same whether the dividend growth model or the above formula is used.
4. From accounting, we know that earnings are divided into two parts: dividends and retained earnings. Most firms continually retain earnings in order to create future dividends. One should not discount earnings to obtain price per share since part of earnings must be reinvested. Only dividends reach the stockholders and only they should be discounted to obtain share price.
5. We suggest that a firm's price-earnings ratio is a function of three factors:
   a. The per-share amount of the firm's valuable growth opportunities.
   b. The risk of the stock.
   c. The type of accounting method used by the firm.
6. As the owner of shares of common stock in a corporation, you have various rights, including the right to vote to elect corporate directors. Voting in corporate elections can be either cumulative or straight. Most voting is actually done by proxy, and a proxy battle breaks out when competing sides try to gain enough votes to have their candidates for the board elected.
7. In addition to common stock, some corporations have issued preferred stock. The name stems from the fact that preferred stockholders must be paid first, before common stockholders can receive anything. Preferred stock has a fixed dividend.
8. The two biggest stock markets in the United States are the NYSE and the NASDAQ. We discussed the organization and operation of these two markets, and we saw how stock price information is reported in the financial press.

CONCEPT QUESTIONS

1. **Stock Valuation** Why does the value of a share of stock depend on dividends?
2. **Stock Valuation** A substantial percentage of the companies listed on the NYSE and the NASDAQ don't pay dividends, but investors are nonetheless willing to buy shares in them. How is this possible given your answer to the previous question?
3. **Dividend Policy** Referring to the previous questions, under what circumstances might a company choose not to pay dividends?
4. **Dividend Growth Model** Under what two assumptions can we use the dividend growth model presented in the chapter to determine the value of a share of stock? Comment on the reasonableness of these assumptions.
5. **Common versus Preferred Stock** Suppose a company has a preferred stock issue and a common stock issue. Both have just paid a $2 dividend. Which do you think will have a higher price, a share of the preferred or a share of the common?
6. **Dividend Growth Model** Based on the dividend growth model, what are the two components of the total return on a share of stock? Which do you think is typically larger?
7. **Growth Rate** In the context of the dividend growth model, is it true that the growth rate in dividends and the growth rate in the price of the stock are identical?
8. **Price-Earnings Ratio** What are the three factors that determine a company's price-earnings ratio?
9. **Voting Rights** When it comes to voting in elections, what are the differences between U.S. political democracy and U.S. corporate democracy?
10. **Corporate Ethics** Is it unfair or unethical for corporations to create classes of stock with unequal voting rights?
11. **Voting Rights** Some companies, such as Reader's Digest, have created classes of stock with no voting rights at all. Why would investors buy such stock?
12. **Stock Valuation** Evaluate the following statement: Managers should not focus on the current stock value because doing so will lead to an overemphasis on short-term profits at the expense of long-term profits.

QUESTIONS AND PROBLEMS

Basic
(Questions 1–9)

1. **Stock Values** The Brennan Co. just paid a dividend of $1.40 per share on its stock. The dividends are expected to grow at a constant rate of 6 percent per year, indefinitely. If investors require a 12 percent return on The Brennan Co. stock, what is the current price? What will the price be in three years? In 15 years?
2. **Stock Values** The next dividend payment by MUG, Inc., will be $3.10 per share. The dividends are anticipated to maintain a 5 percent growth rate, forever. If MUG stock currently sells for $48.00 per share, what is the required return?
3. **Stock Values** For the company in the previous problem, what is the dividend yield? What is the expected capital gains yield?
4. **Stock Values** Warren Corporation will pay a $3.60 per share dividend next year. The company pledges to increase its dividend by 4.5 percent per year, indefinitely. If you require a 13 percent return on your investment, how much will you pay for the company's stock today?
5. **Stock Valuation** Elton Co. is expected to maintain a constant 6 percent growth rate in its dividends, indefinitely. If the company has a dividend yield of 3.9 percent, what is the required return on the company's stock?

6. **Stock Valuation** Suppose you know that a company's stock currently sells for $70 per share and the required return on the stock is 12 percent. You also know that the total return on the stock is evenly divided between a capital gains yield and a dividend yield. If it's the company's policy to always maintain a constant growth rate in its dividends, what is the current dividend per share?
7. **Stock Valuation** Gruber Corp. pays a constant $12 dividend on its stock. The company will maintain this dividend for the next eight years and will then cease paying dividends forever. If the required return on this stock is 10 percent, what is the current share price?
8. **Valuing Preferred Stock** Ayden, Inc., has an issue of preferred stock outstanding that pays an $8.25 dividend every year, in perpetuity. If this issue currently sells for $113 per share, what is the required return?
9. **Growth Rate** The newspaper reported last week that Bradley Enterprises earned $20 million this year. The report also stated that the firm's return on equity is 14 percent. Bradley retains 60 percent of its earnings. What is the firm's earnings growth rate? What will next year's earnings be?

Intermediate
(Questions 10–31)

10. **Stock Valuation** Ferson, Inc., just paid a dividend of $3.00 on its stock. The growth rate in dividends is expected to be a constant 5 percent per year, indefinitely. Investors require a 16 percent return on the stock for the first three years, a 14 percent return for the next three years, and then an 11 percent return thereafter. What is the current share price for Ferson stock?
11. **Nonconstant Growth** Metallica Bearings, Inc., is a young start-up company. No dividends will be paid on the stock over the next nine years, because the firm needs to plow back its earnings to fuel growth. The company will pay an $8 per share dividend in 10 years and will increase the dividend by 6 percent per year thereafter. If the required return on this stock is 13 percent, what is the current share price?
12. **Nonconstant Dividends** Corn, Inc., has an odd dividend policy. The company has just paid a dividend of $9 per share and has announced that it will increase the dividend by $3 per share for each of the next four years, and then never pay another dividend. If you require an 11 percent return on the company's stock, how much will you pay for a share today?
13. **Nonconstant Dividends** South Side Corporation is expected to pay the following dividends over the next four years: $8, $6, $3, and $2. Afterwards, the company pledges to maintain a constant 5 percent growth rate in dividends forever. If the required return on the stock is 13 percent, what is the current share price?

14. **Supernormal Growth** Rizzi Co. is growing quickly. Dividends are expected to grow at a 25 percent rate for the next three years, with the growth rate falling off to a constant 7 percent thereafter. If the required return is 13 percent and the company just paid a $2.80 dividend, what is the current share price?
15. **Supernormal Growth** Janicek Corp. is experiencing rapid growth. Dividends are expected to grow at 30 percent per year during the next three years, 18 percent over the following year, and then 8 percent per year indefinitely. The required return on this stock is 14 percent, and the stock currently sells for $70.00 per share. What is the projected dividend for the coming year?
16. **Negative Growth** Antiques R Us is a mature manufacturing firm. The company just paid a $10 dividend, but management expects to reduce the payout by 8 percent per year, indefinitely. If you require an 11 percent return on this stock, what will you pay for a share today?

17. **Finding the Dividend** Hollin Corporation stock currently sells for $50 per share. The market requires a 14 percent return on the firm's stock. If the company maintains a constant 8 percent growth rate in dividends, what was the most recent dividend per share paid on the stock?
18. **Valuing Preferred Stock** Mark Bank just issued some new preferred stock. The issue will pay a $9 annual dividend in perpetuity, beginning six years from now. If the market requires a 7 percent return on this investment, how much does a share of preferred stock cost today?

19. **Using Stock Quotes** You have found the following stock quote for RJW Enterprises, Inc., in the financial pages of today's newspaper. What was the closing price for this stock that appeared in *yesterday's* paper? If the company currently has 25 million shares of stock outstanding, what was net income for the most recent four quarters?

YTD	52 WEEK				YLD			VOL		NET
% CHG	HI	LO	STOCK	SYM	DIV	%	PE	100s	CLOSE	CHG
22.4	70.80	39.93	RJW	RJW	.15	.2	14	35215	??	2.20

20. **Taxes and Stock Price** You own $100,000 worth of Smart Money stock. One year from now, you will receive a dividend of $2 per share. You will receive a $4 dividend two years from now. You will sell the stock for $50 per share three years from now. Dividends are taxed at the rate of 28 percent. Assume there is no capital gains tax. The required rate of return is 15 percent. How many shares of stock do you own?

21. **Negative Growth** Calamity Mining Company's iron ore reserves are being depleted, and its costs of recovering a declining quantity of ore are rising each year. As a result, the company's earnings are declining at a rate of 10 percent per year. If the dividend per share to be paid tomorrow is $5 and the required rate of return is 14 percent, what is the value of the firm's stock? Assume that the dividend payments are based on a fixed percentage of the firm's earnings.

22. **Nonconstant Growth and Quarterly Dividends** Pasqually Mineral Water, Inc., will pay a quarterly dividend per share of $1 at the end of each of the next 12 quarters. Thereafter, the dividend will grow at a quarterly rate of 0.5 percent, forever. The appropriate rate of return on the stock is 10 percent, compounded quarterly. What is the current stock price?

23. **Nonconstant Growth** In order to buy back its own shares, Pennzoil Co. has decided to suspend its dividends for the next two years. It will resume its annual cash dividend of $2.00 in year 3 and year 4. Thereafter, its dividend payments will grow at an annual growth rate of 6 percent, forever. The required rate of return on Pennzoil's stock is 16 percent. According to the discounted-dividend model, what should Pennzoil's current share price be?

24. **Finding the Dividend** Allen, Inc., is expected to pay equal dividends at the end of each of the next two years. Thereafter, the dividend will grow at a constant annual rate of 4 percent forever. The current stock price is $30. What is next year's dividend payment if the required rate of return is 12 percent?

25. **Finding the Required Return** Juggernaut Satellite Corporation earned $10 million for the fiscal year ending yesterday. The firm also paid out 25 percent of its earnings as dividends yesterday. The firm will continue to pay out 25 percent of its earnings as annual, end-of-year dividends. The remaining 75 percent of earnings is retained by the company for use in projects. The company has 1.25 million shares of common stock outstanding. The current stock price is $40. The historical return on equity (ROE) of 11 percent is expected to continue in the future. What is the required rate of return on the stock?

26. **Dividend Growth** Four years ago, Bling Diamond, Inc., paid a dividend of $.90 per share. Bling paid a dividend of $1.66 per share yesterday. Dividends will grow over the next five years at the same rate they grew over the last four years. Thereafter, dividends will grow at 8 percent per year. The required return on the stock is 18 percent. What will Bling Diamond's cash dividend be in seven years?

27. **Price-Earnings Ratio** Consider Pacific Energy Company and U.S. Bluechips, Inc., both of which reported earnings of $800,000. Without new projects, both firms will continue to generate earnings of $800,000 in perpetuity. Assume that all earnings are paid as dividends and that both firms require a 15 percent rate of return.

a. What is the current PE ratio for each company?

b. Pacific Energy Company has a new project that will generate additional earnings of $100,000 each year in perpetuity. Calculate the new PE ratio of the company.

c. U.S. Bluechips has a new project that will increase earnings by $200,000 in perpetuity. Calculate the new PE ratio of the firm.

28. **Growth Opportunities** The Stambaugh Corporation currently has earnings per share of $7.00. The company has no growth and pays out all earnings as dividends. It has a new project which will require an investment of $1.75 per share in one year. The project is only a two-year project, and will increase earnings in the two years following the investment by $1.90 and $2.10, respectively. Investors require a 12 percent return on Stambaugh stock.

    a. What is the value per share of the company's stock assuming the firm does not undertake the investment opportunity?

    b. If the company does undertake the investment, what is the value per share now?

    c. Again, assume the company undertakes the investment. What will the price per share be four years from today?

29. **Growth Opportunities** Rite Bite Enterprises sells toothpicks. Gross revenues last year were $3 million, and total costs were $1.5 million. Rite Bite has 1 million shares of common stock outstanding. Gross revenues and costs are expected to grow at 5 percent per year. Rite Bite pays no income taxes. All earnings are paid out as dividends.

    a. If the appropriate discount rate is 15 percent and all cash flows are received at year's end, what is the price per share of Rite Bite stock?

    b. Rite Bite has decided to produce toothbrushes. The project requires an immediate outlay of $15 million. In one year, another outlay of $5 million will be needed. The year after that, earnings will increase by $6 million. That profit level will be maintained in perpetuity. What effect will undertaking this project have on the price per share of the stock?

30. **Growth Opportunities** California Real Estate, Inc., expects to earn $110 million per year in perpetuity if it does not undertake any new projects. The firm has an opportunity to invest $12 million today and $7 million in one year in real estate. The new investment will generate annual earnings of $10 million in perpetuity, beginning two years from today. The firm has 20 million shares of common stock outstanding, and the required rate of return on the stock is 15 percent. Land investments are not depreciable. Ignore taxes.

    a. What is the price of a share of stock if the firm does not undertake the new investment?

    b. What is the value of the investment?

    c. What is the per-share stock price if the firm undertakes the investment?

31. **Growth Opportunities** The annual earnings of Avalanche Skis, Inc., will be $5 per share in perpetuity if the firm makes no new investments. Under such a situation, the firm would pay out all of its earnings as dividends. Assume the first dividend will be received exactly one year from now.

    Alternatively, assume that three years from now, and in every subsequent year in perpetuity, the company can invest 25 percent of its earnings in new projects. Each project will earn 40 percent at year-end in perpetuity. The firm's discount rate is 14 percent.

    a. What is the price per share of Avalanche Skis, Inc., stock today without the company making the new investment?

    b. If Avalanche announces that the new investment will be made, what will the per-share stock price be today?

Challenge
(Questions 32–37)

32. **Capital Gains versus Income** Consider four different stocks, all of which have a required return of 15 percent and a most recent dividend of $4.50 per share. Stocks W, X, and Y are

expected to maintain constant growth rates in dividends for the foreseeable future of 10 percent, 0 percent, and −5 percent per year, respectively. Stock Z is a growth stock that will increase its dividend by 20 percent for the next two years and then maintain a constant 12 percent growth rate thereafter. What is the dividend yield for each of these four stocks? What is the expected capital gains yield? Discuss the relationship among the various returns that you find for each of these stocks.

33. **Stock Valuation** Most corporations pay quarterly dividends on their common stock rather than annual dividends. Barring any unusual circumstances during the year, the board raises, lowers, or maintains the current dividend once a year and then pays this dividend out in equal quarterly installments to its shareholders.

    a. Suppose a company currently pays a $3.00 annual dividend on its common stock in a single annual installment, and management plans on raising this dividend by 6 percent per year indefinitely. If the required return on this stock is 14 percent, what is the current share price?

    b. Now suppose that the company in (a) actually pays its annual dividend in equal quarterly installments; thus, this company has just paid a $.75 dividend per share, as it has for the previous three quarters. What is your value for the current share price now? (Hint: Find the equivalent annual end-of-year dividend for each year.) Comment on whether or not you think that this model of stock valuation is appropriate.

34. **Growth Opportunities** Lewin Skis, Inc., (today) expects to earn $6 per share for each of the future operating periods (beginning at time 1) if the firm makes no new investments and returns the earnings as dividends to the shareholders. However, Clint Williams, president and CEO, has discovered an opportunity to retain and invest 30 percent of the earnings beginning three years from today. This opportunity to invest will continue for each period indefinitely. He expects to earn 12 percent on this new equity investment, the return beginning one year after each investment is made. The firm's equity discount rate is 14 percent throughout.

    a. What is the price per share of Lewin Skis, Inc., stock without making the new investment?

    b. If the new investment is expected to be made, per the preceding information, what would the price of the stock be now?

    c. Suppose the company could increase the investment in the project by whatever amount it chose. What would the retention ratio need to be to make this project attractive?

35. **Nonconstant Growth** Storico Co. just paid a dividend of $3.50 per share. The company will increase its dividend by 20 percent next year and will then reduce its dividend growth rate by 5 percentage points per year until it reaches the industry average of 5 percent dividend growth, after which the company will keep a constant growth rate forever. If the required return on Storico stock is 13 percent, what will a share of stock sell for today?

36. **Nonconstant Growth** This one's a little harder. Suppose the current share price for the firm in the previous problem is $98.65 and all the dividend information remains the same. What required return must investors be demanding on Storico stock? (Hint: Set up the valuation formula with all the relevant cash flows, and use trial and error to find the unknown rate of return.)

37. **Growth Opportunities** Shane, Inc., has earnings of $10 million and is projected to grow at a constant rate of 5 percent forever because of the benefits gained from the learning curve. Currently, all earnings are paid out as dividends. The company plans to launch a new project two years from now which would be completely internally funded and require 20 percent of the earnings that year. The project would start generating revenues one year after the launch of the project and the earnings from the new project in any year are estimated to be constant at $5 million. The company has 10 million shares of stock outstanding. Estimate the value of Shane stock. The discount rate is 10 percent.

S&P PROBLEMS

www.mhhe.com/edumarketinsight

STANDARD &POOR'S

1. **Dividend Discount Model** Enter the ticker symbol "WMT" for Wal-Mart. Using the most recent balance sheet and income statement under the "Excel Analytics" link, calculate the sustainable growth rate for Wal-Mart. Now download the "Mthly. Adj. Price" and find the closing stock price for the same month as the balance sheet and income statement you used. What is the implied required return on Wal-Mart according to the dividend growth model? Does this number make sense? Why or why not?
2. **Growth Opportunities** Assume that investors require an 11 percent return on Harley-Davidson (HDI) stock. Under the "Excel Analytics" link find the "Mthly. Adj. Price" and find the closing price for the month of the most recent fiscal year-end for HDI. Using this stock price and the EPS for the most recent year, calculate the NPVGO for Harley-Davidson. What is the appropriate PE ratio for Harley-Davidson using these calculations?

WHAT'S ON THE WEB?

1. **Dividend Discount Model** According to the 2005 Value Line *Investment Survey*, the dividend growth for ConocoPhillips (COP) is 5 percent. Find the current price quote and dividend information at finance.yahoo.com. If the growth rate given in the Value Line *Investment Survey* is correct, what is the required return for ConocoPhillips? Does this number make sense to you?
2. **Dividend Discount Model** Go to www.dividenddiscountmodel.com and enter JNJ (for Johnson & Johnson) as the ticker symbol. You can enter a required return in the Discount Rate box and the site will calculate the stock price using the dividend discount model. If you want a return 5 percent greater than the projected growth rate, what price should you be willing to pay for the stock? At what required return does the current stock price make sense? You will need to enter different required returns until you arrive at the current stock price. Does this required return make sense? Using this market required return for Johnson & Johnson, how does the price change if the required return increases by 1 percent? What does this tell you about the sensitivity of the dividend discount model to the inputs of the equation?
3. **Market Operations** How does a stock trade take place? Go to www.nyse.com and click on "The Trading Floor" and find the discussion of how trades take place. Summarize the trading process.

CLOSING CASE

STOCK VALUATION AT RAGAN THERMAL SYSTEMS

Ragan Thermal Systems, Inc., was founded nine years ago by brother and sister Carrington and Genevieve Ragan. The company manufactures and installs commercial heating and cooling (HVAC) units. Ragan has experienced rapid growth because of a proprietary technology that increases the energy efficiency of its systems. The company is equally owned by Carrington and Genevieve. The original agreement between the siblings gave each 50,000 shares of stock. In the event either wished to sell the stock, the shares first had to be offered to the other at a discounted price.

Although neither sibling wants to sell any shares at this time, they have decided they should value their holdings in the company for financial planning purposes. To accomplish this, they have gathered the following information about their main competitors:

RAGAN THERMAL SYSTEMS, INC., COMPETITORS					
	EPS	DPS	STOCK PRICE	ROE	*R*
Artic Cooling, Inc.	$ .82	$ .16	$15.19	11%	10%
National Heating & Cooling	1.32	.52	12.49	14	13
Expert HVAC Corp.	– .47	.54	48.60	14	12
Industry average	$0.72	$0.41	$25.43	13%	11.67%

Expert HVAC Corp.'s negative earnings per share (EPS) were the result of an accounting write-off last year. Without the write-off, EPS for the company would have been $2.34.

Last year, Ragan had an EPS of $4.32 and paid a dividend to Carrington and Genevieve of $54,000 each. The company also had a return on equity of 25 percent. The siblings believe a required return for the company of 20 percent is appropriate.

1. Assuming the company continues its current growth rate, what is the value per share of the company's stock?
2. To verify their calculations, Carrington and Genevieve have hired Josh Schlessman as a consultant. Josh was previously an equity analyst, and he has covered the HVAC industry. Josh has examined the company's financial statements, as well as examining those of its competitors. Although Ragan currently has a technological advantage, Josh's research indicates that Ragan's competitors are investigating other methods to improve efficiency. Given this, Josh believes that Ragan's technological advantage will only last for the next five years. After that period, the company's growth will likely slow to the industry average. Additionally, Josh believes that the required return the company uses is too high. He believes the industry average required return is more appropriate. Under Josh's assumptions, what is the estimated stock price?
3. What is the industry average price-earnings ratio? What is Ragan's price-earnings ratio? Comment on any differences and explain why they may exist.
4. Assume the company's growth rate declines to the industry average after five years. What percentage of the stock's value is attributable to growth opportunities?
5. Assume the company's growth rate slows to the industry average in five years. What future return on equity does this imply?
6. After discussions with Josh, Carrington and Genevieve agree that they would like to try and increase the value of the company stock. Like many small business owners, they want to retain control of the company and do not want to sell stock to outside investors. They also feel that the company's debt is at a manageable level and do not want to borrow more money. What steps can they take to try and increase the price of the stock? Are there any conditions under which this strategy would not increase the stock price?

CHAPTER 7

Net Present Value and Other Investment Rules

OPENING CASE

In 2005, the automobile market in North America was faced with chronic overcapacity. By some estimates, General Motors may have had as many as 15 factories more than it needed. But not all automobile manufacturers faced this problem. For example, Toyota Motors was expected to announce plans for its seventh North American assembly plant by the end of 2005, and then begin a search for a site to accommodate its eighth North American plant. Each plant represents an investment of $1 billion or more. For example, Toyota's truck factory in southern Indiana was built at a cost of $2.5 billion.

Toyota's new plants are an example of a capital budgeting decision. Decisions such as these, with a price tag of over $1 billion each, are obviously major undertakings, and the risks and rewards must be carefully weighed. In this chapter, we discuss the basic tools used in making such decisions.

In Chapter 1, we saw that increasing the value of the stock in a company is the goal of financial management. Thus, what we need to know is how to tell whether a particular investment will achieve that or not. This chapter considers a variety of techniques that are used in practice for this purpose. More importantly, it shows how many of these techniques can be misleading, and it explains why the net present value approach is the right one.

7.1 WHY USE NET PRESENT VALUE?

This chapter, as well as the next two, focuses on *capital budgeting,* the decision-making process for accepting or rejecting projects. This chapter develops the basic capital budgeting methods, leaving much of the practical application to Chapters 8 and 9. But we don't have to develop these methods from scratch. In Chapter 4, we pointed out that a dollar received in the future is worth less than a dollar received today. The reason, of course, is that today's dollar can be reinvested, yielding a greater amount in the future. And we showed in Chapter 4 that the exact worth of a dollar to be received in the future is its present value. Furthermore, Section 4.1 suggested calculating the *net present value* of any project. That is, the section suggested calculating the difference between the sum of the present values of the project's future cash flows and the initial cost of the project.

Find out more about capital budgeting for small businesses at www.missouribusiness.net.

The net present value (NPV) method is the first one to be considered in this chapter. We begin by reviewing the approach with a simple example. Next, we ask why the method leads to good decisions.

EXAMPLE 7.1 Net Present Value

The Alpha Corporation is considering investing in a riskless project costing \$100. The project receives \$107 in one year and has no other cash flows. The discount rate is 6 percent.

The NPV of the project can easily be calculated as:

$$\$.94 = -\$100 + \frac{\$107}{1.06} \tag{7.1}$$

From Chapter 4, we know that the project should be accepted since its NPV is positive. Had the NPV of the project been negative, as would have been the case with an interest rate greater than 7 percent, the project should be rejected.

The basic investment rule can be generalized to:

Accept a project if the NPV is greater than zero.

Reject a project if NPV is less than zero.

We refer to this as the **NPV rule.**

Now why does the NPV rule lead to good decisions? Consider the following two strategies available to the managers of Alpha Corporation:

1. Use \$100 of corporate cash to invest in the project. The \$107 will be paid as a dividend in one year.
2. Forgo the project and pay the \$100 of corporate cash as a dividend today.

If strategy 2 is employed, the stockholder might deposit the dividend in his bank for one year. With an interest rate of 6 percent, strategy 2 would produce cash of \$106 (\$100 × 1.06) at the end of the year. The stockholder would prefer strategy 1, since strategy 2 produces less than \$107 at the end of the year.

Thus, our basic point is:

Accepting positive NPV projects benefits the stockholders.

You can get a freeware NPV calculator at www.wheatworks.com.

How do we interpret the exact NPV of \$0.94? This is the increase in the value of the firm from the project. For example, imagine that the firm today has productive assets worth \$V and has \$100 of cash. If the firm foregoes the project, the value of the firm today would simply be:

$$\$V + \$100$$

If the firm accepts the project, the firm will receive \$107 in one year but will have no cash today. Thus, the firm's value today would be:

$$\$V + \frac{\$107}{1.06}$$

The difference between the above equations is just \$0.94, the present value of equation (7.1). Thus:

The value of the firm rises by the NPV of the project.

Note that the value of the firm is merely the sum of the values of the different projects, divisions, or other entities within the firm. This property, called **value additivity**, is quite important. It implies that the contribution of any project to a firm's value is simply the NPV of the project. As we will see later, alternative methods discussed in this chapter do not generally have this nice property.

One detail remains. We assumed that the project was riskless, a rather implausible assumption. Future cash flows of real-world projects are invariably risky. In other words, cash flows can only be estimated, rather than known. Imagine that the managers of Alpha *expect* the cash flow of the project to be \$107 next year. That is, the cash flow could be higher, say \$117, or lower, say \$97. With this slight change, the project is risky. Suppose the project is about as risky as the stock market as a whole, where the expected return this year is, say 10 percent. Well, 10 percent becomes the discount rate, implying that the NPV of the project would be:

$$-\$2.73 = -\$100 + \frac{\$107}{1.10}$$

Since the NPV is negative, the project should be rejected. This makes sense since a stockholder of Alpha receiving a \$100 dividend today could invest it in the stock market, expecting a 10 percent return. Why accept a project with the same risk as the market but with an expected return of only 7 percent?

Conceptually, the discount rate on a risky project is the return that one can expect to earn on a financial asset of comparable risk. This discount rate is often referred to as an *opportunity cost,* since corporate investment in the project takes away the stockholder's opportunity to invest the dividend in a financial asset. If the actual calculation of the discount rate strikes you as extremely difficult in the real world, you are probably right. While you can call a bank to find out the interest rate, whom do you call to find the expected return on the market this year? And, if the risk of the project differs from that of the market, how do you make the adjustment? However, the calculation is by no means impossible. While we forgo the calculation in this chapter, we present it in later chapters of the text.

Having shown that NPV is a sensible approach, how can we tell whether alternative methods are as good as NPV? The key to NPV is its three attributes:

1. *NPV Uses Cash Flows.* Cash flows from a project can be used for other corporate purposes (e.g., dividend payments, other capital budgeting projects, or payments of corporate interest). By contrast, earnings are an artificial construct. While earnings are useful to accountants, they should not be used in capital budgeting because they do not represent cash.

2. *NPV Uses All the Cash Flows of the Project.* Other approaches ignore cash flows beyond a particular date; beware of these approaches.
3. *NPV Discounts the Cash Flows Properly.* Other approaches may ignore the time value of money when handling cash flows. Beware of these approaches as well.

Calculating NPVs by hand can be tedious. A nearby *Spreadsheet Techniques* box shows how to do it the easy way and also illustrates an important *caveat calculator.*

SPREADSHEET TECHNIQUES **Calculating NPVs with a Spreadsheet**

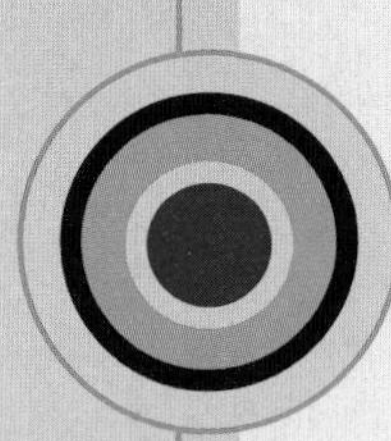

Spreadsheets are commonly used to calculate NPVs. Examining the use of spreadsheets in this context also allows us to issue an important warning. Consider the following:

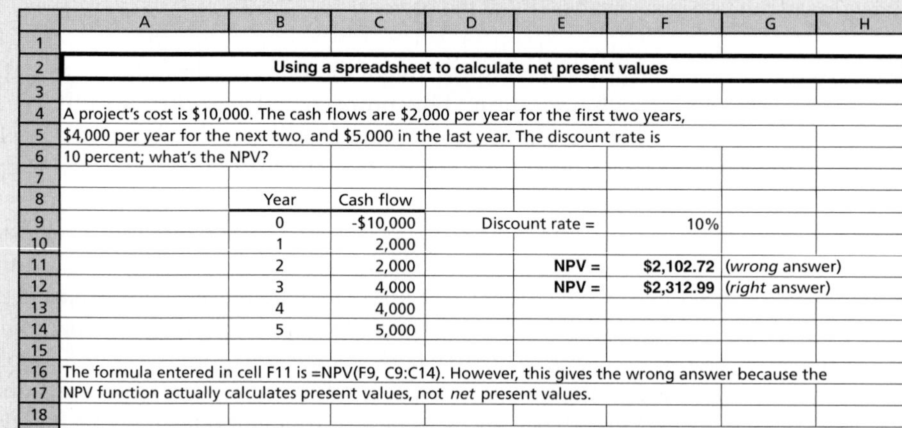

	A	B	C	D	E	F	G	H
1								
2	**Using a spreadsheet to calculate net present values**							
3								
4	A project's cost is $10,000. The cash flows are $2,000 per year for the first two years,							
5	$4,000 per year for the next two, and $5,000 in the last year. The discount rate is							
6	10 percent; what's the NPV?							
7								
8		Year	Cash flow					
9		0	-$10,000	Discount rate =		10%		
10		1	2,000					
11		2	2,000		**NPV =**	**$2,102.72**	(*wrong* answer)	
12		3	4,000		**NPV =**	**$2,312.99**	(*right* answer)	
13		4	4,000					
14		5	5,000					
15								
16	The formula entered in cell F11 is =NPV(F9, C9:C14). However, this gives the wrong answer because the							
17	NPV function actually calculates present values, not *net* present values.							
18								
19	The formula entered in cell F12 is =NPV(F9, C10:C14) + C9. This gives the right answer because the							
20	NPV function is used to calculate the present value of the cash flows and then the initial cost is							
21	subtracted to calculate the answer. Notice that we added cell C9 because it is already negative.							

In our spreadsheet example, notice that we have provided two answers. The first answer is wrong even though we used the spreadsheet's NPV formula. What happened is that the "NPV" function in our spreadsheet is actually a PV function; unfortunately, one of the original spreadsheet programs many years ago got the definition wrong, and subsequent spreadsheets have copied it! Our second answer shows how to use the formula properly.

The example here illustrates the danger of blindly using calculators or computers without understanding what is going on; we shudder to think of how many capital budgeting decisions in the real world are based on incorrect use of this particular function.

7.2 THE PAYBACK PERIOD METHOD

Defining the Rule

One of the most popular alternatives to NPV is **payback**. Here is how payback works: Consider a project with an initial investment of −$50,000. Cash flows are $30,000, $20,000, and $10,000 in the first three years, respectively. These flows are illustrated in Figure 7.1. A useful way of writing down investments like the preceding is with the notation:

(−$50,000, $30,000, $20,000, $10,000)

The minus sign in front of the $50,000 reminds us that this is a cash outflow for the investor, and the commas between the different numbers indicate that they are received–or if they are cash outflows, that they are paid out–at different times. In this example we

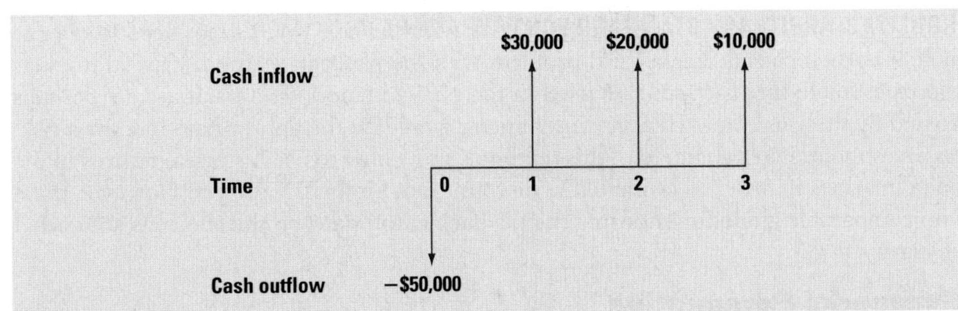

FIGURE 7.1
Cash Flows of an Investment Project

TABLE 7.1
Expected Cash Flows for Projects *A* through *C* ($)

YEAR	*A*	*B*	*C*
0	−100	−100	− 100
1	20	50	50
2	30	30	30
3	50	20	20
4	60	60	60,000
Payback period (years)	3	3	3

are assuming that the cash flows occur one year apart, with the first one occurring the moment we decide to take on the investment.

The firm receives cash flows of $30,000 and $20,000 in the first two years, which add up to the $50,000 original investment. This means that the firm has recovered its investment within two years. In this case two years is the *payback period* of the investment.

The **payback period rule** for making investment decisions is simple. A particular cutoff date, say two years, is selected. All investment projects that have payback periods of two years or less are accepted and all of those that pay off in more than two years–if at all–are rejected.

Problems with the Payback Method

There are at least three problems with payback. To illustrate the first two problems, we consider the three projects in Table 7.1. All three projects have the same three-year payback period, so they should all be equally attractive–right?

Actually, they are not equally attractive, as can be seen by a comparison of different *pairs* of projects.

PROBLEM 1: TIMING OF CASH FLOWS WITHIN THE PAYBACK PERIOD Let us compare project *A* with project *B*. In years 1 through 3, the cash flows of project *A* rise from $20 to $50, while the cash flows of project *B* fall from $50 to $20. Because the large cash flow of $50 comes earlier with project *B*, its net present value must be higher. Nevertheless, we saw above that the payback periods of the two projects are identical. Thus, a problem with the payback method is that it does not consider the timing of the cash flows within the payback period. This example shows that the payback method is inferior to NPV because, as we pointed out earlier, the NPV method *discounts the cash flows properly*.

PROBLEM 2: PAYMENTS AFTER THE PAYBACK PERIOD Now consider projects *B* and *C*, which have identical cash flows within the payback period. However, project *C* is clearly preferred because it has a cash flow of $60,000 in the fourth year. Thus, another problem with the payback method is that it ignores all cash flows occurring after the payback period. Because of the short-term orientation of the payback method, some valuable long-term projects are likely to be rejected. The NPV method does not have this flaw since, as we pointed out earlier, this method *uses all the cash flows of the project*.

PROBLEM 3: ARBITRARY STANDARD FOR PAYBACK PERIOD We do not need to refer to Table 7.1 when considering a third problem with the payback method. Capital markets help us estimate the discount rate used in the NPV method. The riskless rate, perhaps proxied by the yield on a Treasury instrument, would be the appropriate rate for a riskless investment. Later chapters of this textbook show how to use historical returns in the capital markets in order to estimate the discount rate for a risky project. However, there is no comparable guide for choosing the payback cutoff date, so the choice is somewhat arbitrary.

Managerial Perspective

The payback method is often used by large, sophisticated companies when making relatively small decisions. The decision to build a small warehouse, for example, or to pay for a tune-up for a truck is the sort of decision that is often made by lower-level management. Typically, a manager might reason that a tune-up would cost, say, \$200, and if it saved \$120 each year in reduced fuel costs, it would pay for itself in less than two years. On such a basis the decision would be made.

Although the treasurer of the company might not have made the decision in the same way, the company endorses such decision making. Why would upper management condone or even encourage such retrograde activity in its employees? One answer would be that it is easy to make decisions using payback. Multiply the tune-up decision into 50 such decisions a month, and the appeal of this simple method becomes clearer.

The payback method also has some desirable features for managerial control. Just as important as the investment decision itself is the company's ability to evaluate the manager's decision-making ability. Under the NPV method, a long time may pass before one decides whether or not a decision was correct. With the payback method we know in two years whether the manager's assessment of the cash flows was correct.

It has also been suggested that firms with good investment opportunities but no available cash may justifiably use payback. For example, the payback method could be used by small, privately held firms with good growth prospects but limited access to the capital markets. Quick cash recovery enhances the reinvestment possibilities for such firms.

Finally, practitioners often argue that standard academic criticisms of payback overstate any real world problems with the method. For example, textbooks typically make fun of payback by positing a project with low cash inflows in the early years but a huge cash inflow right after the payback cutoff date. This project is likely to be rejected under the payback method, though its acceptance would, in truth, benefit the firm. Project *C* in our Table 7.1 is an example of such a project. Practitioners point out that the pattern of cash flows in these textbook examples is much too stylized to mirror the real world. In fact, a number of executives have told us that, for the overwhelming majority of real world projects, both payback and NPV lead to the same decision. In addition, these executives indicate that, if an investment like project *C* were encountered in the real world, decision makers would almost certainly make *ad hoc* adjustments to the payback rule so that the project would be accepted.

Notwithstanding all of the preceding rationale, it is not surprising to discover that as the decisions grow in importance, which is to say when firms look at bigger projects, NPV becomes the order of the day. When questions of controlling and evaluating the manager become less important than making the right investment decision, payback is used less frequently. For big-ticket decisions, such as whether or not to buy a machine, build a factory, or acquire a company, the payback method is seldom used.

Summary of Payback

The payback method differs from NPV and is therefore conceptually wrong. With its arbitrary cutoff date and its blindness to cash flows after that date, it can lead to some flagrantly foolish decisions if it is used too literally. Nevertheless, because of its simplicity, as well as its other advantages mentioned above, companies often use it as a screen for making the myriad of minor investment decisions they continually face.

Although this means that you should be wary of trying to change approaches such as the payback method when you encounter them in companies, you should probably be careful not to accept the sloppy financial thinking they represent. After this course, you would do your company a disservice if you used payback instead of NPV when you had a choice.

7.3 THE DISCOUNTED PAYBACK PERIOD METHOD

Aware of the pitfalls of payback, some decision makers use a variant called the **discounted payback period method**. Under this approach, we first discount the cash flows. Then we ask how long it takes for the discounted cash flows to equal the initial investment.

For example, suppose that the discount rate is 10 percent and the cash flows on a project are given by:

$$(-\$100, \$50, \$50, \$20)$$

This investment has a payback period of two years, because the investment is paid back in that time.

To compute the project's discounted payback period, we first discount each of the cash flows at the 10 percent rate. These discounted cash flows are:

$$[-\$100, \$50/1.1, \$50/(1.1)^2, \$20/(1.1)^3] = (-\$100, \$45.45, \$41.32, \$15.03)$$

The discounted payback period of the original investment is simply the payback period for these discounted cash flows. The payback period for the discounted cash flows is slightly less than three years since the discounted cash flows over the three years are \$101.80 (\$45.45 + 41.32 + 15.03). As long as the cash flows are positive, the discounted payback period will never be smaller than the payback period, because discounting reduces the value of the cash flows.

At first glance, discounted payback may seem like an attractive alternative, but on closer inspection we see that it has some of the same major flaws as payback. Like payback, discounted payback first requires us to make a somewhat magical choice of an arbitrary cutoff period, and then it ignores all of the cash flows after that date.

If we have already gone to the trouble of discounting the cash flows, any small appeal to simplicity or to managerial control that payback may have has been lost. We might just as well add up all the discounted cash flows and use NPV to make the decision. Although discounted payback looks a bit like NPV, it is just a poor compromise between the payback method and NPV.

7.4 THE AVERAGE ACCOUNTING RETURN METHOD

Defining the Rule

Another attractive, but fatally flawed, approach to financial decision making is the **average accounting return**. The average accounting return is the average project earnings after taxes and depreciation, divided by the average book value of the investment during its life. In spite of its flaws, the average accounting return method is worth examining because it is used frequently in the real world.

EXAMPLE 7.2 Average Accounting Return

Consider a company that is evaluating whether to buy a store in a new mall. The purchase price is $500,000. We will assume that the store has an estimated life of five years and will need to be completely scrapped or rebuilt at the end of that time. The projected yearly sales and expense figures are shown in Table 7.2.

TABLE 7.2

Projected Yearly Revenue and Costs for Average Accounting Return

	YEAR 1	YEAR 2	YEAR 3	YEAR 4	YEAR 5
Revenue	$433,333	$450,000	$266,667	$200,000	$133,333
Expenses	200,000	150,000	100,000	100,000	100,000
Before-tax cash flow	233,333	300,000	166,667	100,000	33,333
Depreciation	100,000	100,000	100,000	100,000	100,000
Earnings before taxes	133,333	200,000	66,667	0	−66,667
Taxes ($t_c = .25$)*	33,333	50,000	16,667	0	−16,667
Net income	$100,000	$150,000	$ 50,000	$ 0	−$ 50,000

$$\text{Average net income} = \frac{(\$100{,}000 + 150{,}000 + 50{,}000 + 0 - 50{,}000)}{5} = \$50{,}000$$

$$\text{Average investment} = \frac{\$500{,}000 + 0}{2} = \$250{,}000$$

$$\text{AAR} = \frac{\$50{,}000}{\$250{,}000} = 20\%$$

*Corporate tax rate = t_c. The tax rebate in year 5 of −$16,667 occurs if the rest of the firm is profitable. Here, the loss in the project reduces taxes of entire firm.

It is worth examining this table carefully. In fact, the first step in any project assessment is a careful look at projected cash flows. First-year sales for the store are estimated to be $433,333. Before-tax cash flow will be $233,333. Sales are expected to rise and expenses are expected to fall in the second year, resulting in a before-tax cash flow of $300,000. Competition from other stores and the loss in novelty will reduce before-tax cash flow to $166,667, $100,000, and $33,333, respectively, in the next three years.

To compute the average accounting return (AAR) on the project, we divide the average net income by the average amount invested. This can be done in three steps.

STEP 1: DETERMINING AVERAGE NET INCOME Net income in any year is net cash flow minus depreciation and taxes. Depreciation is *not* a cash outflow.[1] Rather, it is a charge reflecting the fact that the investment in the store becomes less valuable every year.

We assume the project has a useful life of five years, at which time it will be worthless. Because the initial investment is $500,000 and because it will be worthless in five years, we assume that it loses value at the rate of $100,000 each year. This steady loss in value of $100,000 is called *straight-line depreciation.* We subtract both depreciation and taxes from before-tax cash flow to derive net income, as shown in Table 7.2. Net income is $100,000 in the first year, $150,000 in year 2, $50,000 in year 3, zero in year 4, and −$50,000 in the last year. The average net income over the life of the project is therefore:

[1]Depreciation will be treated in more detail in the next chapter.

Average Net Income:

$$[\$100{,}000 + 150{,}000 + 50{,}000 + 0 + (-50{,}000)]/5 = \$50{,}000$$

STEP 2: DETERMINING AVERAGE INVESTMENT We stated earlier that, due to depreciation, the investment in the store becomes less valuable every year. Because depreciation is $100,000 per year, the value at the end of year zero is $500,000, the value at the end of year 1 is $400,000 and so on. What is the average value of the investment over the life of the investment?

The mechanical calculation is:

Average Investment:

$$(\$500{,}000 + 400{,}000 + 300{,}000 + 200{,}000 + 100{,}000 + 0)/6 = \$250{,}000 \qquad (7.2)$$

We divide by 6 and not 5, because $500,000 is what the investment is worth at the beginning of the five years and $0 is what it is worth at the beginning of the sixth year. In other words, there are six terms in the parentheses of equation (7.2).

STEP 3: DETERMINING AAR The average return is simply:

$$\text{AAR} = \frac{\$50{,}000}{\$250{,}000} = 20\%$$

If the firm had a targeted accounting rate of return greater than 20 percent, the project would be rejected, and if its targeted return were less than 20 percent, it would be accepted.

Analyzing the Average Accounting Return Method

By now you should be able to see what is wrong with the AAR method.

The most important flaw with AAR is that it does not work with the right raw materials. It uses net income and book value of the investment, both of which come from the accounting books. Accounting numbers are somewhat arbitrary. For example, certain cash outflows, such as the cost of a building, are depreciated under current accounting rules. Other flows, such as maintenance, are expensed. In real world situations, the decision to depreciate or expense an item involves judgment. Thus, the basic inputs of the AAR method, income and average investment, are affected by the accountant's judgment. Conversely, the NPV method *uses cash flows.* Accounting judgments do not affect cash flow.

Second, AAR takes no account of timing. In the previous example, the AAR would have been the same if the $100,000 net income in the first year had occurred in the last year. However, delaying an inflow for five years would have lowered the NPV of the investment. As mentioned earlier in this chapter, the NPV approach *discounts properly.*

Third, just as payback requires an arbitrary choice of the cutoff date, the AAR method offers no guidance on what the right targeted rate of return should be. It could be the discount rate in the market. But then again, because the AAR method is not the same as the present value method, it is not obvious that this would be the right choice.

Given these problems, is the AAR method employed in practice? Like the payback method, the AAR (and variations of it) is frequently used as a "backup" to discounted cash flow methods. Perhaps this is so because it is easy to calculate and uses accounting numbers readily available from the firm's accounting system. In addition, both stockholders and the media pay a lot of attention to the overall profitability of a firm. Thus, some managers may feel pressured to select projects that are profitable in the near term, even if the projects come up short in terms of NPV. These managers may focus on the AAR of individual projects more than they should.

7.5 THE INTERNAL RATE OF RETURN

Now we come to the most important alternative to the NPV method, the internal rate of return, universally known as the IRR. The IRR is about as close as you can get to the NPV without actually being the NPV. The basic rationale behind the IRR method is that it provides a single number summarizing the merits of a project. That number does not depend on the interest rate prevailing in the capital market. That is why it is called the internal rate of return; the number is internal or intrinsic to the project and does not depend on anything except the cash flows of the project.

For example, consider the simple project (−$100, $110) in Figure 7.2. For a given rate, the net present value of this project can be described as:

$$\mathbf{NPV} = -\$100 + \frac{\$110}{1 + R}$$

where R is the discount rate. What must the discount rate be to make the NPV of the project equal to zero?

We begin by using an arbitrary discount rate of .08, which yields:

$$\$1.85 = -\$100 + \frac{\$110}{1.08}$$

Since the NPV in this equation is positive, we now try a higher discount rate, say, .12. This yields:

$$-\$1.79 = -\$100 + \frac{\$110}{1.12}$$

Since the NPV in the equation above is negative, we lower the discount rate to, say, .10. This yields:

$$0 = -\$100 + \frac{\$110}{1.10}$$

This trial-and-error procedure tells us that the NPV of the project is zero when R equals 10 percent.[2] Thus, we say that 10 percent is the project's **internal rate of return** (IRR). In general, the IRR is the rate that causes the NPV of the project to be zero. The implication of this exercise is very simple. The firm should be equally willing to accept or reject the project if the discount rate is 10 percent. The firm should accept the project if the discount rate is below 10 percent. The firm should reject the project if the discount rate is above 10 percent.

The general investment rule is clear:

Accept the project if IRR is greater than the discount rate. Reject the project if IRR is less than the discount rate.

We refer to this as the **basic IRR rule**. Now we can try the more complicated example (−$200, $100, $100, $100) in Figure 7.3.

As we did previously, let's use trial and error to calculate the internal rate of return. We try 20 percent and 30 percent, yielding:

DISCOUNT RATE	NPV
20%	$10.65
30	− 18.39

[2] Of course, we could have directly solved for R in this example after setting NPV equal to zero. However, with a long series of cash flows, one cannot generally directly solve for R. Instead, one is forced to use trial and error.

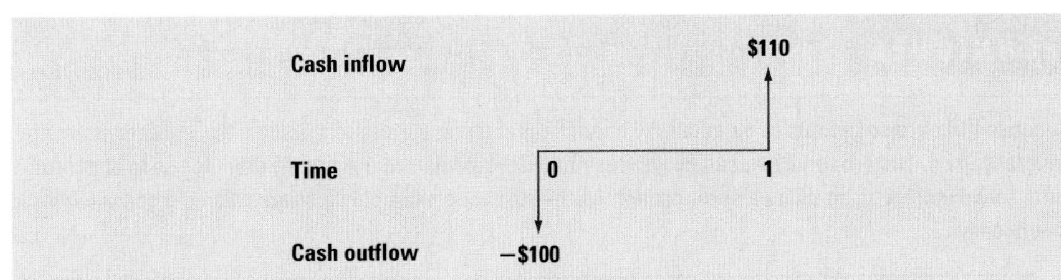

FIGURE 7.2
Cash Flows for a Simple Project

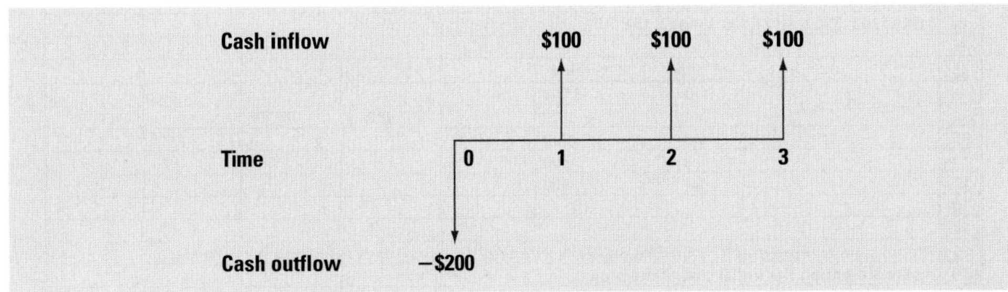

FIGURE 7.3
Cash Flows for a More Complex Project

After much more trial and error, we find that the NPV of the project is zero when the discount rate is 23.37 percent. Thus, the IRR is 23.37 percent. With a 20 percent discount rate the NPV is positive and we would accept it. However, if the discount rate were 30 percent, we would reject it.

Algebraically, IRR is the unknown in the following equation:[3]

$$0 = -\$200 + \frac{\$100}{1 + \text{IRR}} + \frac{\$100}{(1 + \text{IRR})^2} + \frac{\$100}{(1 + \text{IRR})^3}$$

Figure 7.4 illustrates what the IRR of a project means. The figure plots the NPV as a function of the discount rate. The curve crosses the horizontal axis at the IRR of 23.37 percent because this is where the NPV equals zero.

It should also be clear that the NPV is positive for discount rates below the IRR and negative for discount rates above the IRR. This means that if we accept projects like this one when the discount rate is less than the IRR, we will be accepting positive NPV projects. Thus, the IRR rule coincides exactly with the NPV rule.

If this were all there were to it, the IRR rule would always coincide with the NPV rule. This would be a wonderful discovery because it would mean that just by computing the IRR for a project we would be able to tell where it ranks among all of the projects we are considering. For example, if the IRR rule really works, a project with an IRR of 20 percent will always be at least as good as one with an IRR of 15 percent.

But the world of finance is not so kind. Unfortunately, the IRR rule and the NPV rule are the same only for examples like the ones above. Several problems with the IRR approach occur in more complicated situations. In the real world, spreadsheets are used to avoid boring trial-and-error calculations. A nearby *Spreadsheet Techniques* box shows how.

[3]One can derive the IRR directly for a problem with an initial outflow and up to four subsequent inflows. In the case of two subsequent inflows for example, the quadratic formula is needed. In general, however, only trial and error will work for an outflow and five or more subsequent inflows.

SPREADSHEET TECHNIQUES Calculating IRRs with a Spreadsheet

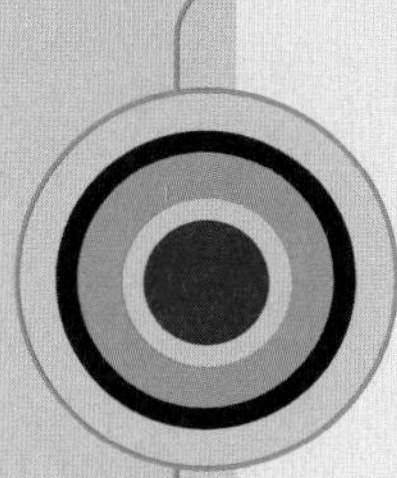

Because IRRs are so tedious to calculate by hand, financial calculators and, especially, spreadsheets are generally used. The procedures used by various financial calculators are too different for us to illustrate here, so we will focus on using a spreadsheet. As the following example illustrates, using a spreadsheet is very easy.

	A	B	C	D	E	F	G	H
1								
2	Using a spreadsheet to calculate internal rates of return							
3								
4	Suppose we have a four-year project that costs $500. The cash flows over the four-year life will be							
5	$100, $200, $300, and $400. What is the IRR?							
6								
7		Year	Cash flow					
8		0	-$500					
9		1	100		IRR =	27.3%		
10		2	200					
11		3	300					
12		4	400					
13								
14								
15	The formula entered in cell F9 is =IRR(C8:C12). Notice that the Year 0 cash flow has a negative							
16	sign representing the initial cost of the project.							
17								

FIGURE 7.4
Net Present Value (NPV) and Discount Rates for a More Complex Project

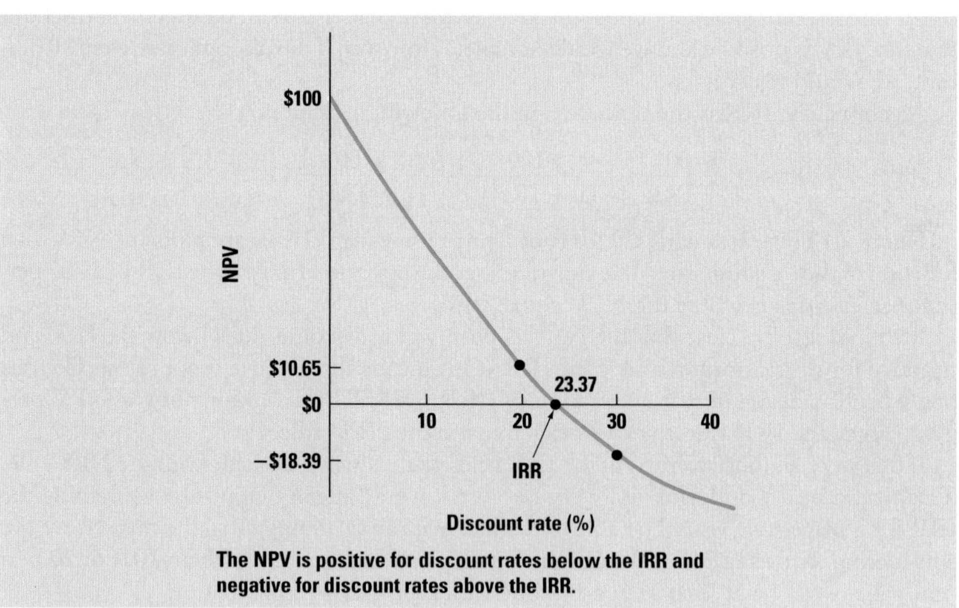

The NPV is positive for discount rates below the IRR and negative for discount rates above the IRR.

7.6 PROBLEMS WITH THE IRR APPROACH

Definition of Independent and Mutually Exclusive Projects

An **independent project** is one whose acceptance or rejection is independent of the acceptance or rejection of other projects. For example, imagine that McDonald's is considering putting a hamburger outlet on a remote island. Acceptance or rejection of this unit is likely to be unrelated to the acceptance or rejection of any other restaurant in its system. The remoteness of the outlet in question ensures that it will not pull sales away from other outlets.

Now consider the other extreme, **mutually exclusive investments**. What does it mean for two projects, *A* and *B*, to be mutually exclusive? You can accept *A* or you can accept *B* or you can reject both of them, but you cannot accept both of them. For example, *A* might be a decision to build an apartment house on a corner lot that you own, and *B* might be a decision to build a movie theater on the same lot.

We now present two general problems with the IRR approach that affect both independent and mutually exclusive projects. Next, we deal with two problems affecting mutually exclusive projects only.

Two General Problems Affecting Both Independent and Mutually Exclusive Projects

We begin our discussion with project *A*, which has the following cash flows:

(−$100, $130)

The IRR for project *A* is 30 percent. Table 7.3 provides other relevant information on the project. The relationship between NPV and the discount rate is shown for this project in Figure 7.5. As you can see, the NPV declines as the discount rate rises.

TABLE 7.3

The Internal Rate of Return and Net Present Value

	Project *A*			Project *B*			Project *C*		
DATES:	0	1	2	0	1	2	0	1	2
Cash flows	−$100	$130		$100	−$130		−$100	$230	−$132
IRR		30%			30%		10%	and	20%
NPV @10%		$18.2			−$18.2			0	
Accept if market rate		<30%			>30%		>10%	but	<20%
Financing or investing		Investing			Financing			Mixture	

FIGURE 7.5

Net Present Value and Discount Rates for Projects *A*, *B*, and *C*

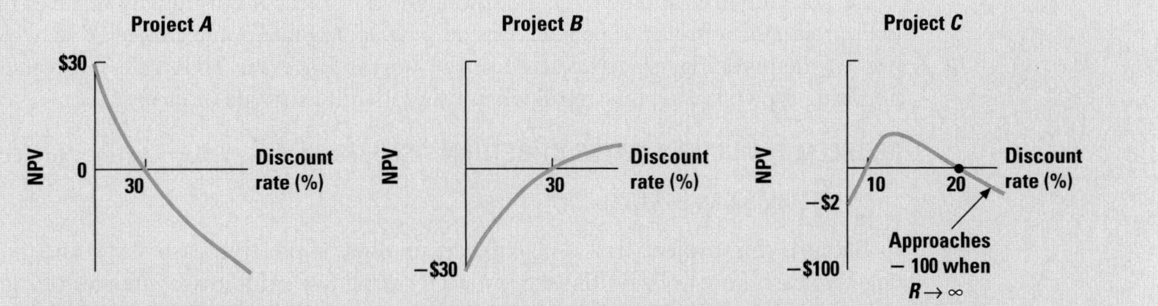

Project *A* has a cash outflow at date 0 followed by a cash inflow at date 1. Its NPV is negatively related to the discount rate. Project *B* has a cash inflow at date 0 followed by a cash outflow at date 1. Its NPV is positively related to the discount rate. Project *C* has two changes of sign in its cash flows. It has an outflow at date 0, an inflow at date 1, and an outflow at date 2. Projects with more than one change of sign can have multiple rates of return.

PROBLEM 1: INVESTING OR FINANCING? Now consider project *B*, with cash flows of:

($100, −$130)

These cash flows are exactly the reverse of the flows for project *A*. In project *B*, the firm receives funds first and then pays out funds later. While unusual, projects of this type do exist. For example, consider a corporation conducting a seminar where the participants pay in advance. Because large expenses are frequently incurred at the seminar date, cash inflows precede cash outflows.

Consider our trial-and-error method to calculate IRR:

$$-\$4 = +\$100 - \frac{\$130}{1.25}$$

$$\$0 = +\$100 - \frac{\$130}{1.30}$$

$$\$3.70 = +\$100 - \frac{\$130}{1.35}$$

As with project *A*, the internal rate of return is 30 percent. However, notice that the net present value is *negative* when the discount rate is *below* 30 percent. Conversely, the net present value is positive when the discount rate is above 30 percent. The decision rule is exactly the opposite of our previous result. For this type of a project, the rule is:

Accept the project when IRR is less than the discount rate. Reject the project when IRR is greater than the discount rate.

This unusual decision rule follows from the graph of project *B* in Figure 7.5. The curve is upward sloping, implying that NPV is *positively* related to the discount rate.

The graph makes intuitive sense. Suppose that the firm wants to obtain $100 immediately. It can either (1) accept project *B* or (2) borrow $100 from a bank. Thus, the project is actually a substitute for borrowing. In fact, because the IRR is 30 percent, taking on project *B* is tantamount to borrowing at 30 percent. If the firm can borrow from a bank at, say, only 25 percent, it should reject the project. However, if a firm can only borrow from a bank at, say, 35 percent, it should accept the project. Thus, project *B* will be accepted if and only if the discount rate is *above* the IRR.[4]

This should be contrasted with project *A*. If the firm has $100 of cash to invest, it can either (1) accept project *A* or (2) lend $100 to the bank. The project is actually a substitute for lending. In fact, because the IRR is 30 percent, taking on project *A* is tantamount to lending at 30 percent. The firm should accept project *A* if the lending rate is below 30 percent. Conversely, the firm should reject project *A* if the lending rate is above 30 percent.

Because the firm initially pays out money with project *A* but initially receives money with project *B*, we refer to project *A* as an *investing type project* and project *B* as a *financing type project*. Investing type projects are the norm. Since the IRR rule is reversed for financing type projects, be careful when using it with this type of project.

PROBLEM 2: MULTIPLE RATES OF RETURN Suppose the cash flows from a project are:

(−$100, $230, −$132)

Because this project has a negative cash flow, a positive cash flow, and another negative cash flow, we say that the project's cash flows exhibit two changes of signs, or

[4]This paragraph implicitly assumes that the cash flows of the project are risk-free. In this way, we can treat the borrowing rate as the discount rate for a firm needing $100. With risky cash flows, another discount rate would be chosen. However, the intuition behind the decision to accept when IRR is less than the discount rate would still apply.

"flip-flops." While this pattern of cash flows might look a bit strange at first, many projects require outflows of cash after receiving some inflows. An example would be a strip-mining project. The first stage in such a project is the initial investment in excavating the mine. Profits from operating the mine are received in the second stage. The third stage involves a further investment to reclaim the land and satisfy the requirements of environmental protection legislation. Cash flows are negative at this stage.

Projects financed by lease arrangements may produce a similar pattern of cash flows. Leases often provide substantial tax subsidies, generating cash inflows after an initial investment. However, these subsidies decline over time, frequently leading to negative cash flows in later years. (The details of leasing will be discussed in a later chapter.)

It is easy to verify that this project has not one but two IRRs, 10 percent and 20 percent.[5] In a case like this, the IRR does not make any sense. What IRR are we to use, 10 percent or 20 percent? Because there is no good reason to use one over the other, IRR simply cannot be used here.

Why does this project have multiple rates of return? Project *C* generates multiple internal rates of return because both an inflow and an outflow occur after the initial investment. In general, these flip-flops or changes in sign produce multiple IRRs. In theory, a cash flow stream with *K* changes in sign can have up to *K* sensible internal rates of return (IRRs above −100 percent). Therefore, since project *C* has two changes in sign, it can have as many as two IRRs. As we pointed out, projects whose cash flows change sign repeatedly can occur in the real world.

NPV RULE Of course, we should not be too worried about multiple rates of return. After all, we can always fall back on the NPV rule. Figure 7.5 plots the NPV of project *C* (−\$100, \$230, −\$132) as a function of the discount rate. As the figure shows, the NPV is zero at both 10 percent and 20 percent and negative outside the range. Thus, the NPV rule tells us to accept the project if the appropriate discount rate is between 10 percent and 20 percent. The project should be rejected if the discount rate lies outside of this range.

MODIFIED IRR As an alternative to NPV, we now introduce the **modified IRR (MIRR)** method, which handles the multiple IRR problem by combining cash flows until only one change in sign remains. To see how it works, consider project *C* again. With a discount rate of, say, 14 percent, the value of the last cash flow, −\$132, is:

$$-\$132/1.14 = -\$115.79$$

as of date 1. Since \$230 is already received at that time, the "adjusted" cash flow at date 1 is \$114.21 (= \$230 − 115.79). Thus, the MIRR approach produces the following two cash flows for the project:

$$(-\$100, \$114.21)$$

Note that, by discounting and then combining cash flows, we are left with only one change in sign. The IRR rule can now be applied. The IRR of these two cash flows is

[5]The calculations are:

$$-\$100 + \frac{\$230}{1.1} - \frac{\$132}{(1.1)^2}$$

$$0 = -\$100 + 209.09 - 109.09$$

and:

$$-\$100 + \frac{\$230}{1.2} - \frac{\$132}{(1.2)^2}$$

$$0 = -\$100 + 191.67 - 91.67$$

Thus, we have multiple rates of return.

14.21 percent, implying that the project should be accepted given our assumed discount rate of 14 percent.

Of course, project *C* is relatively simple to begin with, since it has only three cash flows and two changes in sign. However, the same procedure can easily be applied to more complex projects; that is, just keep discounting and combining the later cash flows until only one change of sign remains.

While this adjustment does correct for multiple IRRs, it appears, at least to us, to violate the "spirit" of the IRR approach. As stated earlier, the basic rationale behind the IRR method is that it provides a single number summarizing the merits of a project. That number does not depend on the discount rate. In fact, that is why it is called the internal rate of return; the number is *internal,* or intrinsic, to the project and does not depend on anything except the cash flows of the project. By contrast, MIRR is clearly a function of the discount rate. However, a firm using this adjustment will avoid the multiple IRR problem, just as a firm using the NPV rule will avoid it.

THE GUARANTEE AGAINST MULTIPLE IRRs If the first cash flow of a project is negative–because it is the initial investment–and if all of the remaining flows are positive, there can be only a single, unique IRR, no matter how many periods the project lasts. This is easy to understand by using the concept of the time value of money. For example, it is simple to verify that project *A* in Table 7.3 has an IRR of 30 percent, because using a 30-percent discount rate gives

$$\begin{aligned} \textbf{NPV} &= -\$100 + \$130/(1.3) \\ &= 0 \end{aligned}$$

How do we know that this is the only IRR? Suppose that we were to try a discount rate greater than 30 percent. In computing the NPV, changing the discount rate does not change the value of the initial cash flow of −\$100 because that cash flow is not discounted. But raising the discount rate can only lower the present value of the future cash flows. In other words, because the NPV is zero at 30 percent, any increase in the rate will push the NPV into the negative range. Similarly, if we try a discount rate of less than 30 percent, the overall NPV of the project will be positive. Though this example has only one positive flow, the above reasoning still implies a single, unique IRR if there are many inflows (but no outflows) after the initial investment.

If the initial cash flow is positive–and if all of the remaining flows are negative–there can only be a single, unique IRR. This result follows from reasoning similar to that above. Both these cases have only one change of sign or flip-flop in the cash flows. Thus, we are safe from multiple IRRs whenever there is only one sign change in the cash flows.

GENERAL RULES The following chart summarizes our rules:

FLOWS	NUMBER OF IRRs	IRR CRITERION	NPV CRITERION
First cash flow is negative and all remaining cash flows are positive.	1	Accept if IRR $>$ *R* Reject if IRR $<$ *R*	Accept if NPV $>$ 0 Reject if NPV $<$ 0
First cash flow is positive and all remaining cash flows are negative.	1	Accept if IRR $<$ *R* Reject if IRR $>$ *R*	Accept if NPV $>$ 0 Reject if NPV $<$ 0
Some cash flows after first are positive and some cash flows after first are negative.	May be more than 1	No valid IRR	Accept if NPV $>$ 0 Reject if NPV $<$ 0

Note that the NPV criterion is the same for each of the three cases. In other words, NPV analysis is always appropriate. Conversely, the IRR can be used only in certain cases. When it comes to NPV, the preacher's words, "You just can't lose with the stuff I use," clearly apply.

Problems Specific to Mutually Exclusive Projects

As mentioned earlier, two or more projects are mutually exclusive if the firm can, at most, accept only one of them. We now present two problems dealing with the application of the IRR approach to mutually exclusive projects. These two problems are quite similar, though logically distinct.

THE SCALE PROBLEM A professor we know motivates class discussions on this topic with the statement: "Students, I am prepared to let one of you choose between two mutually exclusive 'business' propositions. Opportunity 1–You give me $1 now and I'll give you $1.50 back at the end of the class period. Opportunity 2–You give me $10 and I'll give you $11 back at the end of the class period. You can only choose one of the two opportunities. And you cannot choose either opportunity more than once. I'll pick the first volunteer."

Which would you choose? The correct answer is opportunity 2.[6] To see this, look at the following chart:

	CASH FLOW AT BEGINNING OF CLASS	CASH FLOW AT END OF CLASS (90 MINUTES LATER)	NPV[7]	IRR
Opportunity 1	−$ 1	+$ 1.50	$ .50	50%
Opportunity 2	− 10	+ 11.00	1.00	10

As we have stressed earlier in the text, one should choose the opportunity with the highest NPV. This is opportunity 2 in the example. Or, as one of the professor's students explained it: "I'm bigger than the professor, so I know I'll get my money back. And I have $10 in my pocket right now so I can choose either opportunity. At the end of the class, I'll be able to play two rounds of my favorite electronic game with opportunity 2 and still have my original investment, safe and sound.[8] The profit on opportunity 1 buys only one round."

This business proposition illustrates a defect with the internal rate of return criterion. The basic IRR rule indicates the selection of opportunity 1, because the IRR is 50 percent. The IRR is only 10 percent for opportunity 2.

Where does IRR go wrong? The problem with IRR is that it ignores issues of *scale*. While opportunity 1 has a greater IRR, the investment is much smaller. In other words, the high percentage return on opportunity 1 is more than offset by the ability to earn at least a decent return[9] on a much bigger investment under opportunity 2.

Since IRR seems to be misguided here, can we adjust or correct it? We illustrate how in the next example.

[6]The professor uses real money here. Though many students have done poorly on the professor's exams over the years, no student ever chose opportunity 1. The professor claims that his students are "money players."

[7]We assume a zero rate of interest because his class lasted only 90 minutes. It just seemed like a lot longer.

[8]At press time for this text, electronic games cost $0.50 apiece.

[9]A 10 percent return is more than decent over a 90-minute interval!

EXAMPLE 7.3 NPV versus IRR

Stanley Jaffe and Sherry Lansing have just purchased the rights to *Corporate Finance: The Motion Picture.* They will produce this major motion picture on either a small budget or a big budget. The estimated cash flows are:

	CASH FLOW AT DATE 0	CASH FLOW AT DATE 1	NPV @25%	IRR
Small budget	−\$10 million	\$40 million	\$22 million	300%
Large budget	− 25 million	65 million	27 million	160

Because of high risk, a 25 percent discount rate is considered appropriate. Sherry wants to adopt the large budget because the NPV is higher. Stanley wants to adopt the small budget because the IRR is higher. Who is right?

For the reasons espoused in the classroom example above, NPV is correct. Hence, Sherry is right. However, Stanley is very stubborn where IRR is concerned. How can Sherry justify the large budget to Stanley using the IRR approach?

This is where *incremental IRR* comes in. Sherry calculates the incremental cash flows from choosing the large budget instead of the small budget as:

	CASH FLOW AT DATE 0 (IN \$ MILLIONS)	CASH FLOW AT DATE 1 (IN \$ MILLIONS)
Incremental cash flows from choosing large budget instead of small budget	−\$25 − (−10) = −\$15	\$65 − 40 = \$25

This chart shows that the incremental cash flows are −\$15 million at date 0 and \$25 million at date 1. Sherry calculates incremental IRR as:

Formula for Calculating the Incremental IRR:

$$0 = -\$15 \text{ million} + \frac{\$25 \text{ million}}{1 + \text{IRR}}$$

IRR equals 66.67 percent in this equation, implying that the **incremental IRR** is 66.67 percent. Incremental IRR is the IRR on the incremental investment from choosing the large project instead of the small project.

In addition, we can calculate the NPV of the incremental cash flows:

NPV of Incremental Cash Flows:

$$-\$15 \text{ million} + \frac{\$25 \text{ million}}{1.25} = \$5 \text{ million}$$

We know the small-budget picture would be acceptable as an independent project since its NPV is positive. We want to know whether it is beneficial to invest an additional \$15 million in order to make the large-budget picture instead of the small-budget picture. In other words, is it beneficial to invest an additional \$15 million in order to receive an additional \$25 million next year? First, the above calculations show the NPV on the incremental investment to be positive. Second, the incremental IRR of 66.67 percent is higher than the discount rate of 25 percent. For both reasons, the incremental investment can be justified. Hence, the large-budget movie should be made. The second reason is what Stanley needed to hear to be convinced.

In review, we can handle this example (or any mutually exclusive example) in one of three ways:

1. *Compare the NPVs of the two choices.* The NPV of the large-budget picture is greater than the NPV of the small-budget picture. That is, \$27 million is greater than \$22 million.
2. *Calculate the incremental NPV from making the large-budget picture instead of the small-budget picture.* Because the incremental NPV equals \$5 million, we choose the large-budget picture.
3. *Compare the incremental IRR to the discount rate.* Because the incremental IRR is 66.67 percent and the discount rate is 25 percent, we take the large-budget picture.

All three approaches always give the same decision. However, we must *not* compare the IRRs of the two pictures. If we did, we would make the wrong choice. That is, we would accept the small-budget picture.

While students frequently think that problems of scale are relatively unimportant, the truth is just the opposite. A well-known chef on TV often says, "I don't know about your flour, but the flour I buy don't come seasoned." The same thing applies to capital budgeting. No real world project comes in one clear-cut size. Rather, the firm has to *determine* the best size for the project. The movie budget of \$25 million is not fixed in stone. Perhaps an extra \$1 million to hire a bigger star or to film at a better location will increase the movie's gross. Similarly, an industrial firm must decide whether it wants a warehouse of, say, 500,000 square feet or 600,000 square feet. And, earlier in the chapter, we imagined McDonald's opening an outlet on a desert island. If it does this, it must decide how big the outlet should be. For almost any project, someone in the firm has to decide on its size, implying that problems of scale abound in the real world.

One final note here. Students often ask which project should be subtracted from the other in calculating incremental flows. Notice that we are subtracting the smaller project's cash flows from the bigger project's cash flows. This leaves an *outflow* at date 0. We then use the basic IRR rule on the incremental flows.[10]

THE TIMING PROBLEM Next we illustrate another, but quite similar, problem with the IRR approach when evaluating mutually exclusive projects.

EXAMPLE 7.4 Mutually Exclusive Investments

Suppose that the Kaufold Corporation has two alternative uses for a warehouse. It can store toxic waste containers (investment *A*) or electronic equipment (investment *B*). The cash flows are as follows:

	Cash Flow at Year				NPV			
YEAR:	**0**	**1**	**2**	**3**	**@0%**	**@10%**	**@15%**	**IRR**
Investment *A*	−\$10,000	\$10,000	\$1,000	\$ 1,000	\$2,000	\$669	\$109	16.04%
Investment *B*	− 10,000	1,000	1,000	12,000	4,000	751	− 484	12.94

(continued)

[10]Alternatively, we could have subtracted the larger project's cash flows from the smaller project's cash flows. This would have left an *inflow* at date 0, making it necessary to use the IRR rule for financing situations. This would work but we find it more confusing.

We find that the NPV of investment *B* is higher with low discount rates, and the NPV of investment *A* is higher with high discount rates. This is not surprising if you look closely at the cash flow patterns. The cash flows of *A* occur early, whereas the cash flows of *B* occur later. If we assume a high discount rate, we favor investment *A* because we are implicitly assuming that the early cash flow (for example, $10,000 in year 1) can be reinvested at that rate. Because most of investment *B*'s cash flows occur in year 3, *B*'s value is relatively high with low discount rates.

The patterns of cash flow for both projects appear in Figure 7.6. Project *A* has an NPV of $2,000 at a discount rate of zero. This is calculated by simply adding up the cash flows without discounting them. Project *B* has an NPV of $4,000 at the zero rate. However, the NPV of project *B* declines more rapidly as the discount rate increases than does the NPV of project *A*. As we mentioned above, this occurs because the cash flows of *B* occur later. Both projects have the same NPV at a discount rate of 10.55 percent. The IRR for a project is the rate at which the NPV equals zero. Because the NPV of *B* declines more rapidly, *B* actually has a lower IRR.

As with the movie example presented above, we can select the better project with one of three different methods:

1. *Compare NPVs of the Two Projects*. Figure 7.6 aids our decision. If the discount rate is below 10.55 percent, one should choose project *B* because *B* has a higher NPV. If the rate is above 10.55 percent, one should choose project *A* because *A* has a higher NPV.
2. *Compare Incremental IRR to Discount Rate*. The above method employed NPV. Another way of determining that *B* is a better project is to subtract the cash flows of *A* from the cash flows of *B* and then to calculate the IRR. This is the incremental IRR approach we spoke of earlier.

   The incremental cash flows are:

						NPV of Incremental Cash Flows		
YEAR:	0	1	2	3	INCREMENTAL IRR	@0%	@10%	@15%
B − *A*	0	−$9,000	0	$11,000	10.55%	$2,000	$83	−$593

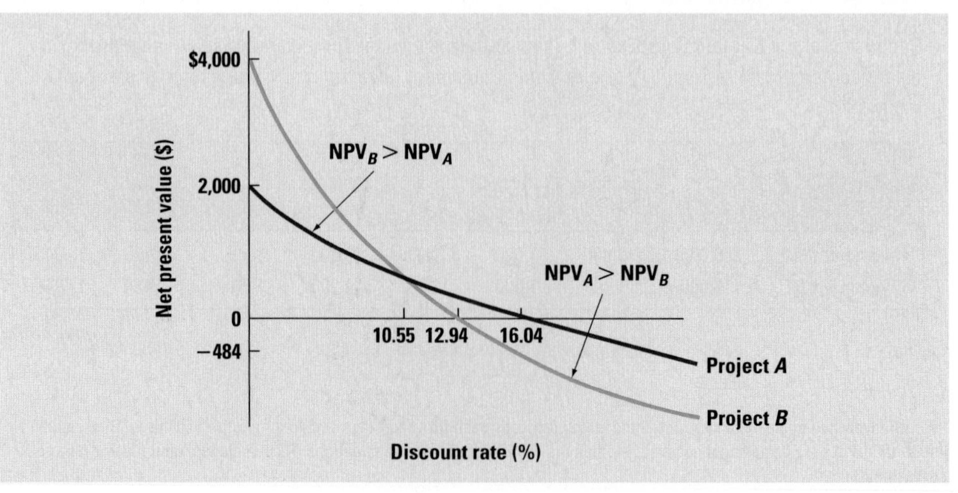

FIGURE 7.6
Net Present Value and the Internal Rate of Return for Mutually Exclusive Projects

This chart shows that the incremental IRR is 10.55 percent. In other words, the NPV on the incremental investment is zero when the discount rate is 10.55 percent. Thus, if the relevant discount rate is below 10.55 percent, project *B* is preferred to project *A*. If the relevant discount rate is above 10.55 percent, project *A* is preferred to project *B*.[11]

3. *Calculate NPV on Incremental Cash Flows.* Finally, one could calculate the NPV on the incremental cash flows. The chart that appears with the previous method displays these NPVs. We find that the incremental NPV is positive when the discount rate is either 0 percent or 10 percent. The incremental NPV is negative if the discount rate is 15 percent. If the NPV is positive on the incremental flows, one should choose *B*. If the NPV is negative, one should choose *A*.

In summary, the same decision is reached whether one (*a*) compares the NPVs of the two projects, (*b*) compares the incremental IRR to the relevant discount rate, or (*c*) examines the NPV of the incremental cash flows. However, as mentioned earlier, one should *not* compare the IRR of project *A* with the IRR of project *B*.

We suggested earlier that one should subtract the cash flows of the smaller project from the cash flows of the bigger project. What do we do here since the two projects have the same initial investment? Our suggestion in this case is to perform the subtraction so that the *first* nonzero cash flow is negative. In the Kaufold Corp. example, we achieved this by subtracting *A* from *B*. In this way, we can still use the basic IRR rule for evaluating cash flows.

The preceding examples illustrate problems with the IRR approach in evaluating mutually exclusive projects. Both the professor-student example and the motion picture example illustrate the problem that arises when mutually exclusive projects have different initial investments. The Kaufold Corp. example illustrates the problem that arises when mutually exclusive projects have different cash flow timing. When working with mutually exclusive projects, it is not necessary to determine whether it is the scale problem or the timing problem that exists. Very likely both occur in any real world situation. Instead, the practitioner should simply use either an incremental IRR or an NPV approach.

Redeeming Qualities of IRR

IRR probably survives because it fills a need that NPV does not. People seem to want a rule that summarizes the information about a project in a single rate of return. This single rate provides people with a simple way of discussing projects. For example, one manager in a firm might say to another, "Remodeling the north wing has a 20 percent IRR."

To their credit, however, companies that employ the IRR approach seem to understand its deficiencies. For example, companies frequently restrict managerial projections of cash flows to be negative at the beginning and strictly positive later. Perhaps, then, the ability of the IRR approach to capture a complex investment project in a single number and the ease of communicating that number explain the survival of the IRR.

A Test

To test your knowledge, consider the following two statements:

1. You must know the discount rate to compute the NPV of a project but you compute the IRR without referring to the discount rate.
2. Hence, the IRR rule is easier to apply than the NPV rule because you don't use the discount rate when applying IRR.

[11]In this example, we first showed that the NPVs of the two projects are equal when the discount rate is 10.55 percent. We next showed that the incremental IRR is also 10.55 percent. This is not a coincidence; this equality must *always* hold. The incremental IRR is the rate that causes the incremental cash flows to have zero NPV. The incremental cash flows have zero NPV when the two projects have the same NPV.

The first statement is true. The discount rate is needed to *compute* NPV. The IRR is *computed* by solving for the rate where the NPV is zero. No mention is made of the discount rate in the mere computation. However, the second statement is false. In order to *apply* IRR, you must compare the internal rate of return with the discount rate. Thus, the discount rate is needed for making a decision under either the NPV or IRR approach.

7.7 THE PROFITABILITY INDEX

Another method that is used to evaluate projects is called the **profitability index**. It is the ratio of the present value of the future expected cash flows *after* initial investment divided by the amount of the initial investment. The profitability index can be represented as:

$$\textbf{Profitability index (PI)} = \frac{\textbf{PV of cash flows } \textbf{\textit{subsequent}} \textbf{ to initial investment}}{\textbf{Initial investment}}$$

EXAMPLE 7.5 Profitability Index

Hiram Finnegan, Inc. (HFI), applies a 12 percent discount rate to two investment opportunities.

PROJECT	Cash Flows ($000,000) C_0	C_1	C_2	PV @12% OF CASH FLOWS SUBSEQUENT TO INITIAL INVESTMENT ($000,000)	PROFIT-ABILITY INDEX	NPV @12% ($000,000)
1	−$20	$70	$10	$70.5	3.53	$50.5
2	−10	15	40	45.3	4.53	35.3

Calculation of Profitability Index

The profitability index is calculated for project 1 as follows. The present value of the cash flows *after* the initial investment is:

$$\$70.5 = \frac{\$70}{1.12} + \frac{\$10}{(1.12)^2}$$

The profitability index is obtained by dividing the result of the above equation by the initial investment of $20. This yields:

$$3.53 = \frac{\$70.5}{\$20}$$

APPLICATION OF THE PROFITABILITY INDEX How do we use the profitability index? We consider three situations:

1. *Independent Projects.* Assume that HFI's two projects are independent. According to the NPV rule, both projects should be accepted since NPV is positive in each case. The profitability index (PI) is greater than one whenever the NPV is positive. Thus, the PI *decision rule* is:

- Accept an independent project if PI > 1.
- Reject if PI < 1.

2. *Mutually Exclusive Projects.* Let us now assume that HFI can only accept one of its two projects. NPV analysis says accept project 1 because this project has the bigger NPV. Since project 2 has the higher PI, the profitability index leads to the wrong selection.

The problem with the profitability index for mutually exclusive projects is the same as the scale problem with the IRR that we mentioned earlier. Project 2 is smaller than project 1. Because the PI is a ratio, this index misses the fact that project 1 has a larger investment than project 2 has. Thus, like IRR, PI ignores differences of scale for mutually exclusive projects.

However, like IRR, the flaw with the PI approach can be corrected using incremental analysis. We write the incremental cash flows after subtracting project 2 from project 1 as follows:

PROJECT	Cash Flows ($000,000) C_0	C_1	C_2	PV @12% OF CASH FLOWS SUBSEQUENT TO INITIAL INVESTMENT ($000,000)	PROFIT-ABILITY INDEX	NPV @12% ($000,000)
1 – 2	–$10	$55	–$30	$25.2	2.52	$15.2

Because the profitability index on the incremental cash flows is greater than 1.0, we should choose the bigger project, that is, project 1. This is the same decision we get with the NPV approach.

3. *Capital Rationing.* The two cases above implicitly assumed that HFI could always attract enough capital to make any profitable investments. Now consider the case when the firm does not have enough capital to fund all positive NPV projects. This is the case of **capital rationing**.

Imagine that the firm has a third project, as well as the first two. Project 3 has the following cash flows:

PROJECT	Cash Flows ($000,000) C_0	C_1	C_2	PV @12% OF CASH FLOWS SUBSEQUENT TO INITIAL INVESTMENT ($000,000)	PROFIT-ABILITY INDEX	NPV @12% ($000,000)
3	–$10	–$5	$60	$43.4	4.34	$33.4

Further, imagine that (*a*) the projects of Hiram Finnegan, Inc., are independent, but (*b*) the firm has only $20 million to invest. Because project 1 has an initial investment of $20 million, the firm cannot select both this project and another one. Conversely, because projects 2 and 3 have initial investments of $10 million each, both these projects can be chosen. In other words, the cash constraint forces the firm to choose either project 1 or projects 2 and 3.

What should the firm do? Individually, projects 2 and 3 have lower NPVs than project 1 has. However, when the NPVs of projects 2 and 3 are added together, the sum is higher than the NPV of project 1. Thus, common sense dictates that projects 2 and 3 should be accepted.

What does our conclusion have to say about the NPV rule or the PI rule? In the case of limited funds, we cannot rank projects according to their NPVs. Instead, we should rank them according to the ratio of present value to initial investment. This is the PI rule. Both project 2 and project 3 have higher PI ratios than does project 1. Thus, they should be ranked ahead of project 1 when capital is rationed.

The usefulness of the profitability index under capital rationing can be explained in military terms. The Pentagon speaks highly of a weapon with a lot of "bang for the buck." In capital budgeting, the profitability index measures the bang (the dollar return) for the buck invested. Hence, it is useful for capital rationing.

It should be noted that the profitability index does not work if funds are also limited beyond the initial time period. For example, if heavy cash outflows elsewhere in the firm were to occur at date 1, project 3, which also has a cash outflow at date 1, might need to be rejected. In other words, the profitability index cannot handle capital rationing over multiple time periods.

In addition, what economists term *indivisibilities* may reduce the effectiveness of the PI rule. Imagine that HFI has $30 million available for capital investment, not just $20 million. The firm now has enough cash for projects 1 and 2. Since the sum of the NPVs of these two projects is greater than the sum of the NPVs of projects 2 and 3, the firm would be better served by accepting projects 1 and 2. Since projects 2 and 3 still have the highest profitability indexes, the PI rule now leads to the wrong decision. Why does the PI rule lead us astray here? The key is that projects 1 and 2 use up all of the $30 million, while projects 2 and 3 have a combined initial investment of only $20 million (= $10 + 10). If projects 2 and 3 are accepted, the remaining $10 million must be left in the bank.

The above situation points out that care should be exercised when using the profitability index in the real world. Nevertheless, while not perfect, the profitability index goes a long way towards handling capital rationing.

7.8 THE PRACTICE OF CAPITAL BUDGETING

So far, this chapter has asked the question: Which capital budgeting methods should companies be using? An equally important question is: Which methods *are* companies using? Table 7.4 goes a long way towards answering this question. As can be seen from the table, approximately three-quarters of U.S. and Canadian companies use the IRR and NPV methods. This is not surprising, given the theoretical advantages of these approaches. Over one-half of these companies use the payback method, a rather surprising result given the conceptual problems with this approach. And while discounted payback represents a theoretical improvement over regular payback, the usage here is far less. Perhaps companies are attracted to the user-friendly nature of payback. In addition, the flaws of this approach, as mentioned in the current chapter, may be relatively easy to correct. For example, while the payback method ignores all cash flows after the payback period, an alert manager can make ad hoc adjustments for a project with back-loaded cash flows.

Capital expenditures by individual corporations can add up to enormous sums for the economy as a whole. For example, in early 2005 ExxonMobil announced that it expected to spend between $15 and $16 billion on capital expenditures in 2005. The company's capital spending had totaled $14.95 billion in 2004. About the same time, competitor ChevronTexaco announced it would increase its capital budgeting for 2005 to $10 billion, up from $8.3 billion in 2004. Other companies with large capital spending budgets in 2005 were Ford, which projected capital spending of just under $7 billion, and chipmaker Intel, which projected capital spending between $5.4 and $5.8 billion.

TABLE 7.4

Percent of CFOs Who Always or Almost Always Use a Given Technique

Source: Figure 2 from John R. Graham and Campbell R. Harvey, "The Theory and Practice of Corporate Finance: Evidence from the Field," *Journal of Financial Economics* 60 (2001). Based on a survey of 392 CFOs.

	% ALWAYS OR ALMOST ALWAYS
Internal rate of return (IRR)	75.6%
Net present value (NPV)	74.9
Payback method	56.7
Discounted payback	29.5
Accounting rate of return	30.3
Profitability index	11.9

	LARGE FIRMS	SMALL FIRMS
Internal rate of return (IRR)	3.41	2.87
Net present value (NPV)	3.42	2.83
Payback method	2.25	2.72
Discounted payback	1.55	1.58
Accounting rate of return	1.25	1.41
Profitability index	0.75	0.78

Firms indicate frequency of use on a scale from 0 (never) to 4 (always). Numbers in table are averages across respondents.

TABLE 7.5
Frequency of Use of Various Capital Budgeting Methods

Source: Table 2 from Graham and Harvey (2001), op. cit.

Large-scale capital spending is often an industrywide occurrence. For example, in 2005, capital spending in the 12 largest dynamic random access memory (DRAM) chipmakers was expected to reach $12.6 billion. This represented a 20 percent increase over the industry capital spending in 2004, which was $10.5 billion. The 20 percent increase in capital spending from 2004 to 2005 was actually a decrease; capital spending had grown an astonishing 65 percent from 2003 to 2004.

According to information released by the Census Bureau in 2005, capital investment for the economy as a whole was $1.01 trillion in 2002, $1.11 trillion in 2001, and $1.17 trillion in 2000. The totals for the three years therefore exceeded $3 trillion! Given the sums at stake, it is not too surprising that successful corporations seek to become adept at careful analysis of capital expenditures.

One might expect the capital budgeting methods of large firms to be more sophisticated than the methods of small firms. After all, large firms have the financial resources to hire more sophisticated employees. Table 7.5 provides some support for this idea. Here, firms indicate frequency of use of the various capital budgeting methods on a scale of 0 (never) to 4 (always). Both the IRR and NPV methods are used more frequently, and payback less frequently, in large firms than in small firms. Conversely, large and small firms employ the last three approaches about equally.

The use of quantitative techniques in capital budgeting varies with the industry. As one would imagine, firms that are better able to estimate cash flows are more likely to use NPV. For example, estimation of cash flow in certain aspects of the oil business is quite feasible. Because of this, energy-related firms were among the first to use NPV analysis. Conversely, the cash flows in the motion-picture business are very hard to project. The grosses of the great hits like *Titanic, Harry Potter,* and *Star Wars* were far, far greater than anyone imagined. The big failures like *Alamo* and *Waterworld* were unexpected as well. Because of this, NPV analysis is frowned upon in the movie business.

How does Hollywood perform capital budgeting? The information that a studio uses to accept or reject a movie idea comes from the *pitch.* An independent movie producer schedules an extremely brief meeting with a studio to pitch his or her idea for a movie. Consider the following four paragraphs of quotes concerning the pitch from the thoroughly delightful book *Reel Power.*[12]

> "They [studio executives] don't want to know too much," says Ron Simpson. "They want to know concept . . . . They want to know what the three-liner is, because they want it to suggest the ad campaign. They want a title . . . . They don't want to hear any esoterica. And if the meeting lasts more than five minutes, they're probably not going to do the project."
>
> "A guy comes in and says this is my idea: '*Jaws* on a spaceship,'" says writer Clay Frohman (*Under Fire*). "And they say, 'Brilliant, fantastic.' Becomes *Alien.* That is *Jaws* on a spaceship, ultimately . . . . And that's it. That's all they want to hear. Their attitude is 'Don't confuse us with the details of the story.'"

[12]Mark Litwak, *Reel Power: The Struggle for Influence and Success in the New Hollywood* (New York: William Morrow and Company, Inc., 1986), pp. 73, 74, and 77.

". . . Some high-concept stories are more appealing to the studios than others. The ideas liked best are sufficiently original that the audience will not feel it has already seen the movie, yet similar enough to past hits to reassure executives wary of anything too far-out. Thus, the frequently used shorthand: It's *Flashdance* in the country (*Footloose*) or *High Noon* in outer space (*Outland*)."

". . . One gambit not to use during a pitch," says executive Barbara Boyle, "is to talk about big box-office grosses your story is sure to make. Executives know as well as anyone that it's impossible to predict how much money a movie will make, and declarations to the contrary are considered pure malarkey."

SUMMARY AND CONCLUSIONS

1. In this chapter, we cover different investment decision rules. We evaluate the most popular alternatives to the NPV: the payback period, the discounted payback period, the accounting rate of return, the internal rate of return, and the profitability index. In doing so, we learn more about the NPV.
2. While we find that the alternatives have some redeeming qualities, when all is said and done, they are not the NPV rule; for those of us in finance, that makes them decidedly second-rate.
3. Of the competitors to NPV, IRR must be ranked above both payback and accounting rate of return. In fact, IRR always reaches the same decision as NPV in the normal case where the initial outflows of an independent investment project are only followed by a series of inflows.
4. We classified the flaws of IRR into two types. First, we considered the general case applying to both independent and mutually exclusive projects. There appeared to be two problems here:
   a. Some projects have cash inflows followed by one or more outflows. The IRR rule is inverted here: One should accept when the IRR is *below* the discount rate.
   b. Some projects have a number of changes of sign in their cash flows. Here, there are likely to be multiple internal rates of return. The practitioner must use either NPV or modified internal rate of return here.
5. Next, we considered the specific problems with the NPV for mutually exclusive projects. We showed that, either due to differences in size or in timing, the project with the highest IRR need not have the highest NPV. Hence, the IRR rule should not be applied. (Of course, NPV can still be applied.)

   However, we then calculated incremental cash flows. For ease of calculation, we suggested subtracting the cash flows of the smaller project from the cash flows of the larger project. In that way, the incremental initial cash flow is negative. One can always reach a correct decision by accepting the larger project if the incremental IRR is greater than the discount rate.
6. We describe capital rationing as the case where funds are limited to a fixed dollar amount. With capital rationing the profitability index is a useful method of adjusting the NPV.

CONCEPT QUESTIONS

1. **Payback Period and Net Present Value** If a project with conventional cash flows has a payback period less than the project's life, can you definitively state the algebraic sign of the NPV? Why or why not? If you know that the discounted payback period is less than the project's life, what can you say about the NPV? Explain.

2. **Net Present Value** Suppose a project has conventional cash flows and a positive NPV. What do you know about its payback? Its discounted payback? Its profitability index? Its IRR? Explain.
3. **Comparing Investment Criteria** Define each of the following investment rules and discuss any potential shortcomings of each. In your definition, state the criterion for accepting or rejecting independent projects under each rule.
   a. Payback period
   b. Average accounting return
   c. Internal rate of return
   d. Profitability index
   e. Net present value
4. **Payback and Internal Rate of Return** A project has perpetual cash flows of *C* per period, a cost of *I*, and a required return of *R*. What is the relationship between the project's payback and its IRR? What implications does your answer have for long-lived projects with relatively constant cash flows?
5. **International Investment Projects** In November 2004, automobile manufacturer Honda announced plans to build an automatic transmission plant in Georgia and expand its transmission plant in Ohio. Honda apparently felt that it would be better able to compete and create value with U.S.-based facilities. Other companies such as Fuji Film and Swiss chemical company Lonza have reached similar conclusions and taken similar actions. What are some of the reasons that foreign manufacturers of products as diverse as automobiles, film, and chemicals might arrive at this same conclusion?
6. **Capital Budgeting Problems** What are some of the difficulties that might come up in actual applications of the various criteria we discussed in this chapter? Which one would be the easiest to implement in actual applications? The most difficult?
7. **Capital Budgeting in Not-for-Profit Entities** Are the capital budgeting criteria we discussed applicable to not-for-profit corporations? How should such entities make capital budgeting decisions? What about the U.S. government? Should it evaluate spending proposals using these techniques?
8. **Net Present Value** The investment in project *A* is $1 million, and the investment in project *B* is $2 million. Both projects have a unique internal rate of return of 20 percent. Is the following statement true or false?

   For any discount rate from zero percent to 20 percent, project *B* has an NPV twice as great as that of project *A*.

   Explain your answer.
9. **Net Present Value versus Profitability Index** Consider the following two mutually exclusive projects available to Global Investments, Inc.

	C_0	C_1	C_2	PROFITABILITY INDEX	NPV
A	−$1,000	$1,000	$500	1.32	$322
B	− 500	500	400	1.57	285

   The appropriate discount rate for the projects is 10 percent. Global Investments chose to undertake project *A*. At a luncheon for shareholders, the manager of a pension fund that owns a substantial amount of the firm's stock asks you why the firm chose project *A* instead of project *B* when project *B* has a higher profitability index.

   How would you, the CFO, justify your firm's action? Are there any circumstances under which Global Investments should choose project *B*?

10. **Internal Rate of Return** Projects *A* and *B* have the following cash flows:

YEAR	PROJECT *A*	PROJECT *B*
0	−$1,000	−$2,000
1	C1A	C1B
2	C2A	C2B
3	C3A	C3B

a. If the cash flows from the projects are identical, which of the two projects would have a higher IRR? Why?

b. If C1B = 2C1A, C2B = 2C2A, and C3B = 2C3A, then is $IRR_A = IRR_B$?

11. **Net Present Value** You are evaluating two projects, Project *A* and Project *B*. Project *A* has a short period of future cash flows, while Project *B* has relatively long future cash flows. Which project will be more sensitive to changes in the required return? Why?

12. **Modified Internal Rate of Return** One of the less flattering interpretations of the acronym MIRR is "meaningless internal rate of return." Why do you think this term is applied to MIRR?

13. **Net Present Value** One potential criticism of the net present value technique is that there is an implicit assumption that this technique assumes the intermediate cash flows of the project are reinvested at the required return. In other words, if you calculate the future value of the intermediate cash flows to the end of the project at the required return, sum the future values, and find the net present value of the two cash flows, you will get the same net present value as the original calculation. If the reinvestment rate used to calculate the future value is lower than the required return, the net present value will decrease. How would you evaluate this criticism?

14. **Internal Rate of Return** One potential criticism of the internal rate of return technique is that there is an implicit assumption that this technique assumes the intermediate cash flows of the project are reinvested at the internal rate of return. In other words, if you calculate the future value of the intermediate cash flows to the end of the project at the required return, sum the future values, and calculate the internal rate of return of the two cash flows, you will get the same internal rate of return as the original calculation. If the reinvestment rate used to calculate the future value is different than the internal rate of return, the internal rate of return calculated for the two cash flows will be different. How would you evaluate this criticism?

QUESTIONS AND PROBLEMS

TM

Basic
(Questions 1–10)

1. **Calculating Payback Period and NPV** Fuji Software, Inc., has the following mutually exclusive projects.

YEAR	PROJECT *A*	PROJECT *B*
0	−$7,500	−$5,000
1	4,000	2,500
2	3,500	1,200
3	1,500	3,000

a. Suppose Fuji's payback period cutoff is two years. Which of these two projects should be chosen?

b. Suppose Fuji uses the NPV rule to rank these two projects. Which project should be chosen if the appropriate discount rate is 15 percent?

2. **Calculating Payback** An investment project provides cash inflows of $840 per year for eight years. What is the project payback period if the initial cost is $3,000? What if the initial cost is $5,000? What if it is $7,000?

3. **Calculating Discounted Payback** An investment project has annual cash inflows of $7,000, $7,500, $8,000, and $8,500, and a discount rate of 14 percent. What is the discounted payback period for these cash flows if the initial cost is $8,000? What if the initial cost is $13,000? What if it is $18,000? 

4. **Calculating Discounted Payback** An investment project costs $10,000 and has annual cash flows of $2,100 for six years. What is the discounted payback period if the discount rate is zero percent? What if the discount rate is 5 percent? If it is 15 percent?

5. **Average Accounting Return** Your firm is considering purchasing a machine with the following annual, end-of-year, book investment accounts.

	PURCHASE DATE	YEAR 1	YEAR 2	YEAR 3	YEAR 4
Gross investment	$16,000	$16,000	$16,000	$16,000	$16,000
Less: Accumulated depreciation	0	4,000	8,000	12,000	16,000
Net investment	$16,000	$12,000	$ 8,000	$ 4,000	$ 0

The machine generates, on average, $4,500 per year in additional net income.

a. What is the average accounting return for this machine?

b. What three flaws are inherent in this decision rule?

6. **Average Accounting Return** The Bluerock Group has invested $8,000 in a high-tech project lasting three years. Depreciation is $4,000, $2,500, and $1,500 in years 1, 2, and 3, respectively. The project generates pretax income of $2,000 each year. The pretax income already includes the depreciation expense. If the tax rate is 25 percent, what is the project's average accounting return (AAR)?

7. **Calculating IRR** Teddy Bear Planet, Inc., has a project with the following cash flows. 

YEAR	CASH FLOWS ($)
0	−8,000
1	4,000
2	3,000
3	2,000

The company evaluates all projects by applying the IRR rule. If the appropriate interest rate is 8 percent, should the company accept the project?

8. **Calculating IRR** Compute the internal rate of return for the cash flows of the following two projects.

	Cash Flows ($)	
YEAR	PROJECT *A*	PROJECT *B*
0	−2,000	−1,500
1	1,000	500
2	1,500	1,000
3	2,000	1,500

9. **Calculating Profitability Index** Bill plans to open a self-serve grooming center in a storefront. The grooming equipment will cost $160,000, to be paid immediately. Bill expects aftertax cash

inflows of $40,000 annually for seven years, after which he plans to scrap the equipment and retire to the beaches of Nevis. The first cash inflow occurs at the end of the first year. Assume the required return is 15 percent. What is the project's PI? Should it be accepted?

10. **Calculating Profitability Index** Suppose the following two independent investment opportunities are available to Greenplain, Inc. The appropriate discount rate is 10 percent.

YEAR	PROJECT ALPHA	PROJECT BETA
0	−$500	−$2,000
1	300	300
2	700	1,800
3	600	1,700

a. Compute the profitability indices for each of the two projects.

b. Which project(s) should Greenplain accept based on the profitability index rule?

Intermediate (Questions 11–23)

11. **Cash Flow Intuition** A project has an initial cost of I, has a required return of R, and pays C annually for N years.

a. Find C in terms of I and N such that the project has a payback period just equal to its life.

b. Find C in terms of I, N, and R such that this is a profitable project according to the NPV decision rule.

c. Find C in terms of I, N, and R such that the project has a benefit-cost ratio of 2.

12. **Problems with IRR** Suppose you are offered $5,000 today but must make the following payments.

YEAR	CASH FLOWS ($)
0	5,000
1	−2,500
2	−2,000
3	−1,000
4	−1,000

a. What is the IRR of this offer?

b. If the appropriate discount rate is 10 percent, should you accept this offer?

c. If the appropriate discount rate is 20 percent, should you accept this offer?

d. What is the NPV of the offer if the appropriate discount rate is 10 percent? 20 percent?

e. Are the decisions under the NPV rule in part (d) consistent with those of the IRR rule?

13. **NPV versus IRR** Consider the following cash flows on two mutually exclusive projects for the Bahamas Recreation Corporation (BRC). Both projects require an annual return of 15 percent.

YEAR	DEEPWATER FISHING	NEW SUBMARINE RIDE
0	−$600,000	−$1,800,000
1	270,000	1,000,000
2	350,000	700,000
3	300,000	900,000

As a financial analyst for BRC, you are asked the following questions.

a. If your decision rule is to accept the project with the greater IRR, which project should you choose?

b. Since you are fully aware of the IRR rule's scale problem, you calculate the incremental IRR for the cash flows. Based on your computation, which project should you choose?

c. To be prudent, you compute the NPV for both projects. Which project should you choose? Is it consistent with the incremental IRR rule?

14. **Problems with Profitability Index** The Robb Computer Corporation is trying to choose between the following two mutually exclusive design projects:

YEAR	CASH FLOW (I)	CASH FLOW (II)
0	−$30,000	−$5,000
1	15,000	2,800
2	15,000	2,800
3	15,000	2,800

a. If the required return is 10 percent and Robb Computer applies the profitability index decision rule, which project should the firm accept?

b. If the company applies the NPV decision rule, which project should it take?

c. Explain why your answers in (a) and (b) are different.

15. **Problems with IRR** Cutler Petroleum, Inc., is trying to evaluate a generation project with the following cash flows:

YEAR	CASH FLOW
0	−$28,000,000
1	53,000,000
2	− 8,000,000

a. If the company requires a 10 percent return on its investments, should it accept this project? Why?

b. Compute the IRR for this project. How many IRRs are there? If you apply the IRR decision rule, should you accept the project or not? What's going on here?

16. **Comparing Investment Criteria** Mario Brothers, a game manufacturer, has a new idea for an adventure game. It can either market the game as a traditional board game or as an interactive CD-ROM, but not both. Consider the following cash flows of the two mutually exclusive projects for Mario Brothers. Assume the discount rate for Mario Brothers is 10 percent.

YEAR	BOARD GAME	CD-ROM
0	−$300	−$1,500
1	400	1,100
2	100	800
3	100	400

a. Based on the payback period rule, which project should be chosen?

b. Based on the NPV, which project should be chosen?

c. Based on the IRR, which project should be chosen?

d. Based on the incremental IRR, which project should be chosen?

17. **Profitability Index versus NPV** Hanmi Group, a consumer electronics conglomerate, is reviewing its annual budget in wireless technology. It is considering investments in three different technologies to develop wireless communication devices. Consider the following cash flows of the three independent projects for Hanmi. Assume the discount rate for Hanmi is 10 percent. Further, Hanmi Group has only $30 million to invest in new projects this year.

	Cash Flows (in $ millions)		
YEAR	CDMA	G4	WI-FI
0	−$10	−$20	−$ 30
1	25	20	20
2	15	50	40
3	5	40	100

a. Based on the profitability index decision rule, rank these investments.

b. Based on the NPV, rank these investments.

c. Based on your findings in (a) and (b), what would you recommend to the CEO of Hanmi Group and why?

18. **Comparing Investment Criteria** Consider the following cash flows of two mutually exclusive projects for AZ-Motorcars. Assume the discount rate for AZ-Motorcars is 10 percent.

YEAR	AZM MINI-SUV	AZF FULL-SUV
0	−$200,000	−$500,000
1	200,000	200,000
2	150,000	300,000
3	150,000	300,000

a. Based on the payback period, which project should be taken?

b. Based on the NPV, which project should be taken?

c. Based on the IRR, which project should be taken?

d. Based on the above analysis, is incremental IRR analysis necessary? If yes, please conduct the analysis.

19. **Comparing Investment Criteria** The treasurer of Amaro Canned Fruits, Inc., has projected the cash flows of projects *A*, *B*, and *C* as follows.

YEAR	PROJECT *A*	PROJECT *B*	PROJECT *C*
0	−$100,000	−$200,000	−$100,000
1	70,000	130,000	75,000
2	70,000	130,000	60,000

Suppose the relevant discount rate is 12 percent a year.

a. Compute the profitability index for each of the three projects.

b. Compute the NPV for each of the three projects.

c. Suppose these three projects are independent. Which project(s) should Amaro accept based on the profitability index rule?

d. Suppose these three projects are mutually exclusive. Which project(s) should Amaro accept based on the profitability index rule?

e. Suppose Amaro's budget for these projects is $300,000. The projects are not divisible. Which project(s) should Amaro accept?

20. **Comparing Investment Criteria** Consider the following cash flows of two mutually exclusive projects for Tokyo Rubber Company. Assume the discount rate for Tokyo Rubber Company is 10 percent.

YEAR	DRY PREPREG	SOLVENT PREPREG
0	−$1,000,000	−$500,000
1	600,000	300,000
2	400,000	500,000
3	1,000,000	100,000

a. Based on the payback period, which project should be taken?

b. Based on the NPV, which project should be taken?

c. Based on the IRR, which project should be taken?

d. Based on the above analysis, is incremental IRR analysis necessary? If yes, please conduct the analysis.

21. **Comparing Investment Criteria** Consider two mutually exclusive new product launch projects that Nagano Golf is considering. Assume the discount rate for Nagano Golf is 15 percent.

Project *A*: Nagano NP-30
Professional clubs that will take an initial investment of $100,000 at time 0.
Next five years (years 1–5) of sales will generate a consistent cash flow of $40,000 per year.
Introduction of new product at year 6 will terminate further cash flows from this project.

Project *B*: Nagano NX-20
High-end amateur clubs that will take an initial investment of $30,000 at time 0.
Cash profit at year 1 is $20,000. In each subsequent year cash flow will grow at 15 percent per year.
Introduction of new product at year 6 will terminate further cash flows from this project.

YEAR	NP-30	NX-20
0	−$100,000	−$30,000
1	40,000	20,000
2	40,000	23,000
3	40,000	26,450
4	40,000	30,418
5	40,000	34,980

Please fill in the following table:

	NP-30	NX-20	IMPLICATIONS
NPV			
IRR			
Incremental IRR			
PI			

22. **Comparing Investment Criteria** Consider two mutually exclusive R&D projects that ADM is considering. Assume the discount rate for ADM is 15 percent.

Project *A*: Server CPU .13 micron processing project
By shrinking the die size to .13 micron, ADM will be able to offer server CPU chips with lower power consumption and heat generation, meaning faster CPUs.

Project *B*: New telecom chip project
Entry into this industry will require introduction of a new chip for cellphones. The know-how will require a large amount of upfront capital, but success of the project will lead to large cash flows later on.

YEAR	*A*	*B*
0	−$100,000	−$200,000
1	50,000	60,000
2	50,000	60,000
3	40,000	60,000
4	30,000	100,000
5	20,000	200,000

Please fill in the following table:

	A	*B*	IMPLICATIONS
NPV			
IRR			
Incremental IRR			
PI			

23. **Comparing Investment Criteria** You are a senior manager at Poeing Aircrafts and have been authorized to spend up to $200,000 for projects. The three projects that you are considering have the following characteristics:

Project *A*: Initial investment of $150,000. Cash flow of $50,000 at year 1 and $100,000 at year 2. This is a plant expansion project, where the required rate of return is 10 percent.

Project *B*: Initial investment of $200,000. Cash flow of $200,000 at year 1 and $111,000 at year 2.
This is a new product development project, where the required rate of return is 20 percent.

Project *C*: Initial investment of $100,000. Cash flow of $100,000 at year 1 and $100,000 at year 2.
This is a market expansion project, where the required rate of return is 20 percent.

Assume the corporate discount rate is 10 percent.
Please offer your recommendations, backed by your analysis.

	A	*B*	*C*	IMPLICATIONS
Payback				
IRR				
Incremental IRR				
PI				
NPV				

24. **Payback and NPV** An investment under consideration has a payback of seven years and a cost of $483,000. If the required return is 12 percent, what is the worst-case NPV? The best-case NPV? Explain. Assume the cash flows are conventional.

Challenge (Questions 24–30)

25. **Multiple IRRs** This problem is useful for testing the ability of financial calculators and computer software. Consider the following cash flows. How many different IRRs are there? (Hint: Search between 20 percent and 70 percent.) When should we take this project?

YEAR	CASH FLOW
0	−$ 504
1	2,862
2	− 6,070
3	5,700
4	− 2,000

26. **NPV Valuation** The Yurdone Corporation wants to set up a private cemetery business. According to the CFO, Barry M. Deep, business is "looking up." As a result, the cemetery project will provide a net cash inflow of $50,000 for the firm during the first year, and the cash flows are projected to grow at a rate of 6 percent per year forever. The project requires an initial investment of $780,000.

    a. If Yurdone requires a 13 percent return on such undertakings, should the cemetery business be started?

    b. The company is somewhat unsure about the assumption of a 6 percent growth rate in its cash flows. At what constant growth rate would the company just break even if it still required a 13 percent return on investment?

27. **Calculating IRR** The Utah Mining Corporation is set to open a gold mine near Provo, Utah. According to the treasurer, Monty Goldstein, "This is a golden opportunity." The mine will cost $600,000 to open and will have an economic life of 11 years. It will generate a cash inflow of $100,000 at the end of the first year and the cash inflows are projected to grow at 8 percent per year for the next 10 years. After 11 years, the mine will be abandoned. Abandonment costs will be $50,000 at the end of year 11.

    a. What is the IRR for the gold mine?

    b. The Utah Mining Corporation requires a 10 percent return on such undertakings. Should the mine be opened?

28. **Calculating IRR** Consider two streams of cash flows, *A* and *B*. Stream *A*'s first cash flow is $5,000 and is received three years from today. Future cash flows in stream *A* grow by 4 percent in perpetuity. Stream *B*'s first cash flow is −$6,000 and is received two years from today and will continue in perpetuity. Assume that the appropriate discount rate is 12 percent.

    a. What is the present value of each stream?

    b. Suppose that the two streams are combined into one project, called *C*. What is the IRR of project *C*?

    c. What is the correct IRR rule for project *C*?

29. **Calculating Incremental Cash Flows** Darin Clay, the CFO of MakeMoney.com, has to decide between the following two projects:

YEAR	PROJECT MILLION	PROJECT BILLION
0	−$1,500	−$$I_0$
1	I_0 + 200	I_0 + 500
2	1,200	1,500
3	1,500	2,000

The expected rate of return for either of the two projects is 12 percent. What is the range of initial investment (I_0) for which Project Billion is more financially attractive than Project Million?

30. **Problems with IRR** McKeekin Corp. has a project with the following cash flows:

YEAR	CASH FLOW
0	$20,000
1	− 26,000
2	13,000

What is the IRR of the project? What is happening here?

WHAT'S ON THE WEB?

1. **Net Present Value** You have a project that has an initial cash outflow of −$20,000 and cash inflows of $6,000, $5,000, $4,000, and $6,000, respectively, for the next four years. Go to www.datadynamica.com, and follow the "Online IRR NPV Calculator" link. Enter the cash flows. If the required return is 12 percent, what is the IRR of the project? The NPV?
2. **Internal Rate of Return** Using the online calculator from the previous problem, find the IRR for a project with cash flows of −$500, $1,200, and −$400. What is going on here?

CLOSING CASE

BULLOCK GOLD MINING

Seth Bullock, the owner of Bullock Gold Mining, is evaluating a new gold mine in South Dakota. Dan Dority, the company's geologist, has just finished his analysis of the mine site. He has estimated that the mine would be productive for eight years, after which the gold would be completely mined. Dan has taken an estimate of the gold deposits to Alma Garrett, the company's financial officer. Alma has been asked by Seth to perform an analysis of the new mine and present her recommendation on whether the company should open the new mine.

Alma has used the estimates provided by Dan to determine the revenues that could be expected from the mine. She has also projected the expense of opening the mine and the annual operating expenses. If the company opens the mine, it will cost $500 million today, and it will have a cash outflow of $80 million nine years from today in costs associated with closing the mine and reclaiming the area surrounding it. The expected cash flows each year from the mine are shown in the table on the next page. Bullock Mining has a 12 percent required return on all of its gold mines.

YEAR	CASH FLOW
0	−$500,000,000
1	60,000,000
2	90,000,000
3	170,000,000
4	230,000,000
5	205,000,000
6	140,000,000
7	110,000,000
8	70,000,000
9	− 80,000,000

1. Construct a spreadsheet to calculate the payback period, internal rate of return, modified internal rate of return, and net present value of the proposed mine.
2. Based on your analysis, should the company open the mine?
3. Bonus question: Most spreadsheets do not have a built-in formula to calculate the payback period. Write a VBA script that calculates the payback period for a project.

CHAPTER 8

Making Capital Investment Decisions

OPENING CASE

In February 2005, South Korean giant Samsung Electronics, the world's largest maker of flat panel displays, announced it was spending 2.08 trillion won ($2.04 billion) to build its second seventh-generation liquid crystal display (LCD) production line. The announcement followed an earlier expenditure of 286.7 billion won ($281 million) to construct the foundation for the second line. The plant was expected to manufacture 45,000 panels per month, and Samsung said it may further increase production capacity at the plant. The company was already selling 50,000 32-inch and 10,000 40-inch and larger flat panel screens per month. Of course, this new line was just the latest investment in plants designed to manufacture flat panel displays. Late in 2004, LG Philips LCD announced plans to build a seventh-generation LCD plant of its own at a cost of $5.3 trillion won ($5.2 billion).

This chapter follows up on our previous one by delving more deeply into capital budgeting and the evaluation of projects such as these flat panel manufacturing facilities. We identify the relevent cash flows of a project, including initial investment outlays, requirements for net working capital, and operating cash flows. Further, we look at the effects of depreciation and taxes. We also examine the impact of inflation, and show how to evaluate consistently the NPV analysis of a project.

8.1 INCREMENTAL CASH FLOWS

Cash Flows—Not Accounting Income

You may not have thought about it, but there is a big difference between corporate finance courses and financial accounting courses. Techniques in corporate finance generally use cash flows, whereas financial accounting generally stresses income or earnings numbers. Certainly, our text has followed this tradition since our net present value techniques discounted cash flows, not earnings. When considering a single project, we discounted the cash flows that the firm receives from the project. When valuing the firm as a whole, we discounted dividends–not earnings–because dividends are the cash flows that an investor receives.

EXAMPLE 8.1 **Relevant Cash Flows**

The Weber-Decker Co. just paid $1 million in cash for a building, as part of a new capital budgeting project. This entire $1 million is an immediate cash outflow. However, assuming straight-line depreciation over 20 years, only $50,000 ($1 million/20) is considered an accounting expense in the current year. Current earnings are thereby reduced by only $50,000. The remaining $950,000 is expensed over the following 19 years. For capital budgeting purposes, the relevant cash outflow at date 0 is the full $1 million, not the reduction in earnings of only $50,000.

Always discount cash flows, not earnings, when performing a capital budgeting calculation. Earnings do not represent real money. You can't spend out of earnings, you can't eat out of earnings, and you can't pay dividends out of earnings. You can only do these things out of cash flow.

In addition, it is not enough to use cash flows. In calculating the NPV of a project, only cash flows that are *incremental* to the project should be used. These cash flows are the changes in the firm's cash flows that occur as a direct consequence of accepting the project. That is, we are interested in the difference between the cash flows of the firm with the project and the cash flows of the firm without the project.

The use of incremental cash flows sounds easy enough, but pitfalls abound in the real world. We describe below how to avoid some of the pitfalls of determining incremental cash flows.

Sunk Costs

A **sunk cost** is a cost that has already occurred. Because sunk costs are in the past, they cannot be changed by the decision to accept or reject the project. Just as we "let bygones be bygones," we should ignore such costs. Sunk costs are not incremental cash outflows.

EXAMPLE 8.2 **Sunk Costs**

The General Milk Company is currently evaluating the NPV of establishing a line of chocolate milk. As part of the evaluation, the company had paid a consulting firm $100,000 to perform a test-marketing analysis. This expenditure was made last year. Is this cost relevant for the capital budgeting decision now confronting the management of General Milk Company?

The answer is no. The $100,000 is not recoverable, so the $100,000 expenditure is a sunk cost, or spilled milk. Of course, the decision to spend $100,000 for a marketing analysis was a capital budgeting decision itself and was perfectly relevant *before* it was sunk. Our point is that once the company incurred the expense, the cost became irrelevant for any future decision.

Opportunity Costs

Your firm may have an asset that it is considering selling, leasing, or employing elsewhere in the business. If the asset is used in a new project, potential revenues from alternative uses are lost. These lost revenues can meaningfully be viewed as costs. They are called **opportunity costs** because, by taking the project, the firm forgoes other opportunities for using the assets.

EXAMPLE 8.3 Opportunity Costs

Suppose the Weinstein Trading Company has an empty warehouse in Philadelphia that can be used to store a new line of electronic pinball machines. The company hopes to sell these machines to affluent northeastern consumers. Should the warehouse be considered a cost in the decision to sell the machines?

The answer is yes. The company could sell the warehouse, if the firm decides not to market the pinball machines. Thus, the sales price of the warehouse is an opportunity cost in the pinball machine decision.

Side Effects

Another difficulty in determining incremental cash flows comes from the side effects of the proposed project on other parts of the firm. A side effect is classified as either **erosion** or **synergy**. Erosion occurs when a new product reduces the sales and, hence, the cash flows, of existing products. Synergy occurs when a new project increases the cash flows of existing projects.

EXAMPLE 8.4 Synergies

Suppose the Innovative Motors Corporation (IMC) is determining the NPV of a new convertible sports car. Some of the customers who would purchase the car are owners of IMC's compact sedans. Are all sales and profits from the new convertible sports car incremental?

The answer is no because some of the cash flow represents transfers from other elements of IMC's product line. This is erosion, which must be included in the NPV calculation. Without taking erosion into account, IMC might erroneously calculate the NPV of the sports car to be, say $100 million. If half the customers are transfers from the sedan and lost sedan sales have an NPV of −$150 million, the true NPV is −$50 million ($100 million − $150 million).

IMC is also contemplating the formation of a racing team. The team is forecasted to lose money for the foreseeable future, with perhaps the best projection showing an NPV of −$35 million for the operation. However, IMC's managers are aware that the team will likely generate great publicity for all of IMC's products. A consultant estimates that the increase in cash flows elsewhere in the firm has a present value of $65 million. Assuming that the consultant's estimates of synergy are trustworthy, the net present value of the team is $30 million ($65 million − $35 million). The managers should form the team.

Allocated Costs

Frequently a particular expenditure benefits a number of projects. Accountants allocate this cost across the different projects when determining income. However, for capital budgeting purposes, this **allocated cost** should be viewed as a cash outflow of a project only if it is an incremental cost of the project.

EXAMPLE 8.5 Allocated Costs

The Voetmann Consulting Corp. devotes one wing of its suite of offices to a library requiring a cash outflow of $100,000 a year in upkeep. A proposed capital budgeting project is expected to generate revenue equal to 5 percent of the overall firm's sales. An executive at the firm, H. Sears, argues that $5,000 (5 percent × $100,000) should be viewed as the proposed project's share of the library's costs. Is this appropriate for capital budgeting?

The answer is no. One must ask the question: What is the difference between the cash flows of the entire firm with the project and the cash flows of the entire firm without the project? The firm will spend $100,000 on library upkeep whether or not the proposed project is accepted. Since acceptance of the proposed project does not affect this cash flow, the cash flow should be ignored when calculating the NPV of the project.

8.2 THE BALDWIN COMPANY: AN EXAMPLE

We next consider the example of a proposed investment in machinery and related items. Our example involves the Baldwin Company and colored bowling balls.

The Baldwin Company, originally established in 1965 to make footballs, is now a leading producer of tennis balls, baseballs, footballs, and golf balls. In 1973, the company introduced "High Flite," its first line of high-performance golf balls. The Baldwin management has sought opportunities in whatever businesses seem to have some potential for cash flow. In 2004, W. C. Meadows, vice president of the Baldwin Company, identified another segment of the sports ball market that looked promising and that he felt was not adequately served by larger manufacturers. That market was for brightly colored bowling balls, and he believed a large number of bowlers valued appearance and style above performance. He also believed that it would be difficult for competitors to take advantage of the opportunity because of both Baldwin's cost advantages and its highly developed marketing skills.

As a result, in late 2005, the Baldwin Company investigated the marketing potential of brightly colored bowling balls. Baldwin sent a questionnaire to consumers in three markets: Philadelphia, Los Angeles, and New Haven. The results of the three questionnaires were much better than expected and supported the conclusion that the brightly colored bowling ball could achieve a 10 to 15 percent share of the market. Of course, some people at Baldwin complained about the cost of the test marketing, which was $250,000. (As we shall see later, this is a sunk cost and should not be included in project evaluation.)

In any case, the Baldwin Company is now considering investing in a machine to produce bowling balls. The bowling balls would be manufactured in a building owned by the firm and located near Los Angeles. This building, which is vacant, and the land can be sold for $150,000 after taxes.

Working with his staff, Meadows is preparing an analysis of the proposed new product. He summarizes his assumptions as follows: The cost of the bowling ball machine is $100,000. The machine has an estimated market value at the end of five years of $30,000. Production by year during the five-year life of the machine is expected to be as follows: 5,000 units, 8,000 units, 12,000 units, 10,000 units, and 6,000 units. The price of bowling balls in the first year will be $20. The bowling ball market is highly competitive, so Meadows believes that the price of bowling balls will increase at only 2 percent per year, as compared to the anticipated general inflation rate of 5 percent. Conversely, the plastic used to produce bowling balls is rapidly becoming more expensive. Because of this, production cash outflows are expected to grow at 10 percent per year. First-year production costs will be $10 per unit. Meadows has determined, based upon Baldwin's taxable income, that the appropriate incremental corporate tax rate in the bowling ball project is 34 percent.

Net working capital is defined as the difference between current assets and current liabilities. Like any other manufacturing firm, Baldwin finds that it must maintain an investment in working capital. It will purchase raw materials before production and sale, giving rise to an investment in inventory. It will maintain cash as a buffer against unforeseen expenditures. And, its credit sales will generate accounts receivable. Management determines that an immediate (year 0) investment in the different items of working capital of $10,000 is required. Working capital is forecasted to rise in the early years of the project but to fall to $0 by the project's end. In other words, the investment in working capital is to be completely recovered by the end of the project's life.

Projections based on these assumptions and Meadows's analysis appear in Tables 8.1 through 8.4. In these tables all cash flows are assumed to occur at the *end* of the year. Because of the large amount of information in these tables, it is important to see how the tables are related. Table 8.1 shows the basic data for both investment and income. Supplementary schedules on operations and depreciation, as presented in Tables 8.2 and 8.3, help explain where the numbers in Table 8.1 come from. Our goal is to obtain projections of cash flow. The data in Table 8.1 are all that are needed to calculate the relevant cash flows, as shown in Table 8.4.

An Analysis of the Project

INVESTMENTS The investment outlays for the project are summarized in the top segment of Table 8.1. They consist of three parts:

TABLE 8.1

The Worksheet for Cash Flows of the Baldwin Company (in $ thousands) (All cash flows occur at the *end* of the year.)

	YEAR 0	YEAR 1	YEAR 2	YEAR 3	YEAR 4	YEAR 5
Investments:						
(1) Bowling ball machine	−$100.00					$ 21.76*
(2) Accumulated depreciation		$ 20.00	$ 52.00	$ 71.20	$ 82.72	94.24
(3) Adjusted basis of machine after depreciation (end of year)		80.00	48.00	28.80	17.28	5.76
(4) Opportunity cost (warehouse)	− 150.00					150.00
(5) Net working capital (end of year)	10.00	10.00	16.32	24.97	21.22	0
(6) Change in net working capital	− 10.00		− 6.32	− 8.65	3.75	21.22
(7) Total cash flow of investment [(1) + (4) + (6)]	− 260.00		− 6.32	− 8.65	3.75	192.98
Income:						
(8) Sales revenues		$100.00	$163.20	$249.72	$212.20	$129.90
(9) Operating costs		− 50.00	− 88.00	− 145.20	− 133.10	− 87.84
(10) Depreciation		− 20.00	− 32.00	− 19.20	− 11.52	− 11.52
(11) Income before taxes [(8) + (9) + (10)]		− 30.00	− 43.20	− 85.32	− 67.58	− 30.54
(12) Tax at 34 percent		− 10.20	− 14.69	− 29.01	− 22.98	− 10.38
(13) Net income		19.80	28.51	56.31	44.60	20.16

*We assume that the ending market value of the capital investment at year 5 is $30 (in thousands). The taxable amount is $24.24 ($30 − $5.76). The aftertax salvage value is $30 − [.34 × ($30 − $5.76)] = $21.76.

1. *The Bowling Ball Machine.* The purchase requires an immediate (year 0) cash outflow of $100,000. The firm realizes a cash inflow when the machine is sold in year 5. These cash flows are shown in line 1 of Table 8.1. As indicated in the footnote to the table, taxes are incurred when the asset is sold.

2. *The Opportunity Cost of Not Selling the Warehouse.* If Baldwin accepts the bowling-ball project, it will use a warehouse and land that could otherwise be sold. The estimated sales price of the warehouse and land is therefore included as an *opportunity cost* in year 0, as presented in line 4. Opportunity costs are treated as cash outflows for purposes of capital budgeting. However, note that if the project is accepted, management assumes that the warehouse will be sold for $150,000 (after taxes) in year 5.

The test marketing cost of $250,000 is not included. The tests occurred in the past and should be viewed as a *sunk cost.*

3. *The Investment in Working Capital.* Required working capital appears in line 5. Working capital rises over the early years of the project as expansion occurs. However, all working capital is assumed to be recovered at the end, a common assumption in capital budgeting. In other words, all inventory is sold by the end, the cash balance maintained as a buffer is liquidated, and all accounts receivable are collected. Increases in working capital in the early years must be funded by cash generated elsewhere in the firm. Hence, these increases are viewed as cash *outflows.* To reiterate, it is the *increase* in working capital over a year that leads to a cash outflow in that year. Even if working capital is at a high level, there will be no cash outflow over a year if working capital stays constant over that year. Conversely, decreases in working capital in the later years are viewed as cash inflows. All of these cash flows are presented in line 6. A more complete discussion of working capital is provided later in this section.

To recap, there are three investments in this example: the bowling ball machine (line 1 in Table 8.1), the opportunity cost of the warehouse (line 4), and the changes in working capital (line 6). The total cash flow from the above three investments is shown in line 7.

INCOME AND TAXES Next, the determination of income is presented in the bottom segment of Table 8.1. While we are ultimately interested in cash flow–not income–we need the income calculation in order to determine taxes. Lines 8 and 9 of Table 8.1 show sales revenues and operating costs, respectively. The projections in these lines are based on the sales revenues and operating costs computed in columns 4 and 6 of Table 8.2. The estimates of revenues and costs follow from assumptions made by the corporate planning staff at Baldwin. In other words, the estimates critically depend on the fact that product prices are projected to increase at 2 percent per year and costs per unit are projected to increase at 10 percent per year.

Depreciation of the $100,000 capital investment is shown in line 10 of Table 8.1. Where do these numbers come from? Depreciation for tax purposes for U.S. companies is based on the Modified Accelerated Cost Recovery System (MACRS). Each asset is assigned a useful life under MACRS, with an accompanying depreciation schedule as shown in Table 8.3. The IRS ruled that Baldwin is to depreciate its capital investment over five years, so the second column of the table applies in this case. Since depreciation in the table is expressed as a percentage of the asset's cost, multiply the percentages in this column by $100,000 to arrive at depreciation in dollars.

Income before taxes is calculated in line 11 of Table 8.1. Taxes are provided in line 12 of this table, and net income is calculated in line 13.

TABLE 8.2
Operating Revenues and Costs of the Baldwin Company

(1) YEAR	(2) PRODUCTION	(3) PRICE	(4) SALES REVENUES	(5) COST PER UNIT	(6) OPERATING COSTS
1	5,000	$20.00	$100,000	$10.00	$ 50,000
2	8,000	20.40	163,200	11.00	88,000
3	12,000	20.81	249,720	12.10	145,200
4	10,000	21.22	212,200	13.31	133,100
5	6,000	21.65	129,900	14.64	87,840

Prices rise at 2% a year.
Unit costs rise at 10% a year.

TABLE 8.3
Depreciation (in percent) under Modified Accelerated Cost Recovery System (MACRS)

	Recovery Period Class					
YEAR	3 YEARS	5 YEARS	7 YEARS	10 YEARS	15 YEARS	20 YEARS
1	.333	.200	.143	.100	.050	.038
2	.444	.320	.245	.180	.095	.072
3	.148	.192	.175	.144	.086	.067
4	.074	.115	.125	.115	.077	.062
5		.115	.089	.092	.069	.057
6		.058	.089	.074	.062	.053
7			.089	.066	.059	.049
8			.045	.066	.059	.045
9				.066	.059	.045
10				.066	.059	.045
11				.033	.059	.045
12–15					.059	.045
16					.030	.045
17–20						.045
21						.022

Depreciation is expressed as a percent of the asset's cost. These schedules are based on the IRS publication *Depreciation*. Details on depreciation are presented later in the chapter. Three-year depreciation actually carries over four years because the IRS assumes purchase is made in midyear.

TABLE 8.4
Incremental Cash Flows for the Baldwin Company (in $ thousands)

	YEAR 0	YEAR 1	YEAR 2	YEAR 3	YEAR 4	YEAR 5
(1) Sales revenue [line 8, Table 8.1]		$100.00	$163.20	$249.72	$212.20	$129.90
(2) Operating costs [line 9, Table 8.1]		− 50.00	− 88.00	− 145.20	− 133.10	− 87.84
(3) Taxes [line 12, Table 8.1]		− 10.20	− 14.69	− 29.01	− 22.98	− 10.38
(4) Cash flow from operations [(1) + (2) + (3)]		39.80	60.51	75.51	56.12	31.68
(5) Total cash flow of investment [line 7, Table 8.1]	−$260.00		− 6.32	− 8.65	3.75	192.98
(6) Total cash flow of project [(4) + (5)]	− 260.00	39.80	54.19	66.86	59.87	224.66
NPV @ 4% $123.641						
10% $51.588						
15% $5.472						
15.67% $0						
20% −$31.351						

SALVAGE VALUE In calculating depreciation under current tax law, the expected economic life and future value of an asset are not issues. As a result, the book value of an asset can differ substantially from its actual market value. For example, consider the bowling machine the Baldwin Company is considering for its new project. The book value after the first year is $100,000 less the first year's depreciation of $20,000, or $80,000. After six years, the book value of the machine is zero.

Suppose, at the end of the project, Baldwin sold the machine. At the end of the fifth year, the book value of the machine would be $5,760, but based on Baldwin's experience, it would probably be worth about $30,000. If the company actually sold it for this amount, then it would pay taxes at the ordinary income tax rate on the difference between the sale price of $30,000 and the book value of $5,760. With a 34 percent tax rate, the tax liability would be .34 × ($30,000 − 5,760) = $8,241.60. So, the aftertax salvage value of the equipment, a cash inflow to the company, would be $30,000 − 8,241.60 = $21,758.40.

Taxes must be paid in this case because the difference between the market value and the book value is "excess" depreciation, and it must be "recaptured" when the asset is sold. In this case, Baldwin would have overdepreciated the asset by $30,000 − 5,760 = $24,240. Because the depreciation was too high, the company paid too little in taxes.

Notice this is not a tax on a long-term capital gain. Further, what is and what is not a capital gain is ultimately up to taxing authorities, and the specific rules can be very complex. We will ignore capital gains taxes for the most part.

Finally, if the book value exceeds the market value, then the difference is treated as a loss for tax purposes. For example, if Baldwin sold the machine for $4,000, then the book value exceeds the market value by $1,760. In this case, a tax savings of .34 × $1,760 = $598.40 occurs.

CASH FLOW Cash flow is finally determined in Table 8.4. We begin by reproducing lines 8, 9, and 12 in Table 8.1 as lines 1, 2, and 3 in Table 8.4. Cash flow from operations, which is sales minus both operating costs and taxes, is provided in line 4 of Table 8.4. Total investment cash flow, taken from line 7 of Table 8.1, appears as line 5 of Table 8.4. Cash flow from operations plus total cash flow of the investment equals total cash flow of the project, which is displayed as line 6 of Table 8.4.

NET PRESENT VALUE The NPV of the Baldwin bowling ball project can be calculated from the cash flows in line 6. As can be seen at the bottom of Table 8.4, the NPV is $51,588 if 10 percent is the appropriate discount rate and −$31,351 if 20 percent is the appropriate discount rate. If the discount rate is 15.67 percent, the project will have a zero NPV. In other words, the project's internal rate of return is 15.67 percent. If the discount rate of the Baldwin bowling ball project is above 15.67 percent, it should not be accepted because its NPV would be negative.

Which Set of Books?

It should be noted that the firm's management generally keeps two sets of books, one for the IRS (called the *tax books*) and another for its annual report (called the *stockholders' books*). The tax books follow the rules of the IRS. The stockholders' books follow the rules of the *Financial Accounting Standards Board* (FASB), the governing body in accounting. The two sets of rules differ widely in certain areas. For example, income on municipal bonds is ignored for tax purposes while being treated as income by the FASB. The differences almost always benefit the firm, because the rules permit income on the stockholders' books to be higher than income on the tax books. That is, management can look profitable to the stockholders without needing to pay taxes on all of the reported profit. In fact, there are plenty of large companies that consistently report positive earnings to the stockholders while reporting losses to the IRS.

A Note on Net Working Capital

The investment in net working capital is an important part of any capital budgeting analysis. While we explicitly considered net working capital in lines 5 and 6 of Table 8.1, students may be wondering where the numbers in these lines came from. An investment in net working capital arises whenever (1) inventory is purchased, (2) cash is kept in the project as a buffer against unexpected expenditures, and (3) credit sales are made, generating accounts receivable rather than cash. (The investment in net working capital is reduced by credit purchases, which generate accounts payable.) This investment in net working capital represents a cash outflow, because cash generated elsewhere in the firm is tied up in the project.

To see how the investment in net working capital is built from its component parts, we focus on year 1. We see in Table 8.1 that Baldwin's managers predict sales in year 1 to be \$100,000 and operating costs to be \$50,000. If both the sales and costs were cash transactions, the firm would receive \$50,000 (\$100,000 − \$50,000). As stated earlier, this cash flow would occur at the *end* of year 1.

Now let's give you more information. The managers:

1. Forecast that \$9,000 of the sales will be on credit, implying that cash receipts at the end of year 1 will be only \$91,000 (\$100,000 − \$9,000). The accounts receivable of \$9,000 will be collected at the end of year 2.
2. Believe that they can defer payment on \$3,000 of the \$50,000 of costs, implying that cash disbursements at the end of year 1 will be only \$47,000 (\$50,000 − \$3,000). Baldwin will pay off the \$3,000 of accounts payable at the end of year 2.
3. Decide that inventory of \$2,500 should be left on hand at the end of year 1 to avoid *stockouts* (that is, running out of inventory).
4. Decide that cash of \$1,500 should be earmarked for the project at the end of year 1 to avoid running out of cash.

Thus, net working capital at the end of year 1 is:

\$9,000	−	\$3,000	+	\$2,500	+	\$1,500	=	\$10,000
Accounts receivable		**Accounts payable**		**Inventory**		**Cash**		**Net working capital**

Because \$10,000 of cash generated elsewhere in the firm must be used to offset this requirement for net working capital, Baldwin's managers correctly view the investment in net working capital as a cash outflow of the project. As the project grows over time, needs for net working capital increase. *Changes* in net working capital from year to year represent further cash flows, as indicated by the negative numbers for the first few years of line 6 of Table 8.1. However, in the declining years of the project, net working capital is reduced–ultimately to zero. That is, accounts receivable are finally collected, the project's cash buffer is returned to the rest of the corporation, and all remaining inventory is sold off. This frees up cash in the later years, as indicated by positive numbers in years 4 and 5 on line 6.

Typically, corporate worksheets (such as Table 8.1) treat net working capital as a whole. The individual components of working capital (receivables, inventory, etc.) do not generally appear in the worksheets. However, the reader should remember that the working capital numbers in the worksheets are not pulled out of thin air. Rather, they result from a meticulous forecast of the components, just as we illustrated for year 1.

A Note on Depreciation

The Baldwin case made some assumptions about depreciation. Where did these assumptions come from? Assets are currently depreciated for tax purposes according to the provisions of the 1986 Tax Reform Act. There are seven classes of depreciable property.

- The three-year class includes certain specialized short-lived property. Tractor units and racehorses over two years old are among the very few items fitting into this class.
- The five-year class includes (a) cars and trucks; (b) computers and peripheral equipment, as well as calculators, copiers, and typewriters; and (c) specific items used for research purposes.
- The seven-year class includes office furniture, equipment, books, and single-purpose agricultural structures. It is also a catchall category, because any asset not designated to be in another class is included here.
- The 10-year class includes vessels, barges, tugs, and similar equipment related to water transportation.
- The 15-year class encompasses a variety of specialized items. Included are equipment of telephone distribution plants and similar equipment used for voice and data communications, and sewage treatment plants.
- The 20-year class includes farm buildings, sewer pipe, and other very long-lived equipment.
- Real property that is depreciable is separated into two classes: residential and nonresidential. The cost of residential property is recovered over 27½ years and nonresidential property over 31½ years.

Items in the three-, five-, and seven-year classes are depreciated using the 200 percent declining-balance method, with a switch to straight-line depreciation at a point specified in the Tax Reform Act. Items in the 15- and 20-year classes are depreciated using the 150 percent declining-balance method, with a switch to straight-line depreciation at a specified point. All real estate is depreciated on a straight-line basis.

All calculations of depreciation include a half-year convention, which treats all property as if it were placed in service at midyear. To be consistent, the IRS allows half a year of depreciation for the year in which property is disposed of or retired. The effect of this is to spread the deductions for property over one year more than the name of its class, for example, six tax years for five-year property.

Interest Expense

It may have bothered you that interest expense was ignored in the Baldwin example. After all, many projects are at least partially financed with debt, particularly a bowling ball machine that is likely to increase the debt capacity of the firm. As it turns out, our approach of assuming no debt financing is rather standard in the real world. Firms typically calculate a project's cash flows under the assumption that the project is financed only with equity. Any adjustments for debt financing are reflected in the discount rate, not the cash flows. The treatment of debt in capital budgeting will be covered in depth later in the text. Suffice it to say at this time that the full ramifications of debt financing are well beyond our current discussion.

8.3 INFLATION AND CAPITAL BUDGETING

Inflation is an important fact of economic life, and it must be considered in capital budgeting. Capital budgeting requires data on cash flows as well as on interest rates. Like interest rates, cash flows can be expressed in either nominal or real terms. A **nominal**

cash flow refers to the actual dollars to be received (or paid out). A **real cash flow** refers to the cash flow's purchasing power. Like most definitions, these definitions are best explained by examples.

EXAMPLE 8.6 **Nominal versus Real Cash Flow**

Burrows Publishing has just purchased the rights to the next book of famed romantic novelist Barbara Musk. Still unwritten, the book should be available to the public in four years. Currently, romantic novels sell for $10.00 in softcover. The publishers believe that inflation will be 6 percent a year over the next four years. Since romantic novels are so popular, the publishers anticipate that their prices will rise about 2 percent per year more than the inflation rate over the next four years. Burrows Publishing plans to sell the novel at $13.60 [$=(1.08)^4 \times$ $10.00] four years from now, anticipating sales of 100,000 copies.

The expected cash flow in the fourth year of $1.36 million ($13.60 × 100,000) is a *nominal cash flow*. That is, the firm expects to receive $1.36 million at that time. In other words, a nominal cash flow refers to the actual dollars to be received in the future.

The purchasing power of $1.36 million in four years is determined by deflating the $1.36 million at 6 percent for four years:

$$\$1.08 \text{ million} = \frac{\$1.36 \text{ million}}{(1.06)^4}$$

The figure, $1.08 million, is a *real cash flow* since it is expressed in terms of purchasing power.

EXAMPLE 8.7 **Depreciation**

EOBII Publishers, a competitor of Burrows, recently bought a printing press for $2,000,000 to be depreciated by the straight-line method over five years. This implies yearly depreciation of $400,000 ($2,000,000/5). Is this $400,000 figure a real or a nominal quantity?

Depreciation is a *nominal* quantity because $400,000 is the actual tax deduction over each of the next four years. Depreciation becomes a real quantity if it is adjusted for purchasing power. Hence, $316,837 [$\$400{,}000/(1.06)^4$] is depreciation in the fourth year, expressed as a real quantity.

Discounting: Nominal or Real?

Our examples show that cash flows can be expressed in either nominal or real terms. Given these choices, how should one express discount rates and cash flows when performing capital budgeting?

Financial practitioners correctly stress the need to maintain *consistency* between cash flows and discount rates. That is,

> ***Nominal* cash flows must be discounted at the *nominal* rate.**
> ***Real* cash flows must be discounted at the *real* rate.**

As long as one is consistent, either approach is correct. In order to minimize computational error, it is generally advisable in practice to choose the approach that is easiest. This idea is illustrated in the following two examples.

EXAMPLE 8.8 Real and Nominal Discounting

Shields Electric forecasts the following nominal cash flows on a particular project:

DATE	0	1	2
CASH FLOW	−$1,000	$600	$650

The nominal discount rate is 14 percent, and the inflation rate is forecast to be 5 percent. What is the value of the project?

Using Nominal Quantities The NPV can be calculated as:

$$\$26.47 = -\$1{,}000 + \frac{\$600}{1.14} + \frac{\$650}{(1.14)^2}$$

The project should be accepted.

Using Real Quantities The real cash flows are:

DATE	0	1	2
CASH FLOW	−$1,000	$571.43	$589.57
		$\left(\frac{\$600}{1.05}\right)$	$\left(\frac{\$650}{(1.05)^2}\right)$

As we saw in an earlier chapter, from the Fisher equation, the real discount rate is 8.57143 percent (1.14/1.05 − 1).

The NPV can be calculated as:

$$\$26.47 = -\$1{,}000 + \frac{\$571.43}{1.0857143} + \frac{\$589.57}{(1.0857143)^2}$$

The NPV is the same whether cash flows are expressed in nominal or in real quantities. It must always be the case that the NPV is the same under the two different approaches.

Because both approaches always yield the same result, which one should be used? As mentioned above, use the approach that is simpler, since the simpler approach generally leads to fewer computational errors. Because the Shields Electric example begins with nominal cash flows, nominal quantities produce a simpler calculation here.

EXAMPLE 8.9 Real and Nominal NPV

Altshuler, Inc., generated the following forecast for a capital budgeting project:

	Year		
	0	1	2
Capital expenditure	$1,210		
Revenues (in real terms)		$1,900	$2,000
Cash expenses (in real terms)		950	1,000
Depreciation (straight line)		605	605

The president, David Altshuler, estimates inflation to be 10 percent per year over the next two years. In addition, he believes that the cash flows of the project should be discounted at the nominal rate of 15.5 percent. His firm's tax rate is 40 percent.

(*continued*)

Mr. Altshuler forecasts all cash flows in *nominal* terms, leading to the following spreadsheet:

	Year		
	0	1	2
Capital expenditure	−$1,210		
Revenues		$2,090 (= 1,900 × 1.10)	$2,420 [= 2,000 × (1.10)²]
−Expenses		− 1,045 (= 950 × 1.10)	− 1,210 [= 1,000 × (1.10)²]
−Depreciation		− 605 (= 1,210/2)	− 605
Taxable income		$ 440	$ 605
−Taxes (40%)		− 176	− 242
Income after taxes		$ 264	$ 363
+Depreciation		+ 605	+ 605
Cash flow		$ 869	$ 968

$$\text{NPV} = -\$1{,}210 + \frac{\$869}{1.155} + \frac{\$968}{(1.155)^2} = \$268$$

Mr. Altshuler's sidekick, Stuart Weiss, prefers working in real terms. He first calculates the real rate to be 5 percent (=1.155/1.10 − 1). Next, he generates the following spreadsheet in *real* quantities:

	Year		
	0	1	2
Capital expenditure	−$1,210		
Revenues		$1,900	$2,000
−Expenses		− 950	− 1,000
−Depreciation		− 550 (= 605/1.1)	− 500 [= 605/(1.1)²]
Taxable income		$ 400	$ 500
−Taxes (40%)		− 160	− 200
Income after taxes		$ 240	$ 300
+Depreciation		+ 550	+ 500
Cash flow		$ 790	$ 800

$$\text{NPV} = -\$1{,}210 + \frac{\$790}{1.05} + \frac{\$800}{(1.05)^2} = \$268$$

In explaining his calculations to Mr. Altshuler, Mr. Weiss points out:

1. Since the capital expenditure occurs at date 0 (today), its nominal value and its real value are equal.
2. Because yearly depreciation of $605 is a nominal quantity, one converts it to a real quantity by discounting at the inflation rate of 10 percent.

It is no coincidence that both Mr. Altshuler and Mr. Weiss arrive at the same NPV number. Both methods must always generate the same NPV.

8.4 ALTERNATIVE DEFINITIONS OF OPERATING CASH FLOW

The analysis we went through in the previous section is quite general and can be adapted to just about any capital investment problem. In the next section, we illustrate a particularly useful variation. Before we do so, we need to discuss the fact that there are different definitions of project operating cash flow that are commonly used, both in practice and in finance texts.

As we will see, the different approaches to operating cash flow that exist all measure the same thing. If they are used correctly, they all produce the same answer, and one is not necessarily any better or more useful than another. Unfortunately, the fact that alternative definitions are used does sometimes lead to confusion. For this reason, we examine several of these variations next to see how they are related.

In the discussion that follows, keep in mind that when we speak of cash flow, we literally mean dollars in less dollars out. This is all we are concerned with. Different definitions of operating cash flow simply amount to different ways of manipulating basic information about sales, costs, depreciation, and taxes to get at cash flow.

For a particular project and year under consideration, suppose we have the following estimates:

Sales = $1,500
Costs = $700
Depreciation = $600

With these estimates, notice that EBIT is:

EBIT = Sales − Costs − Depreciation
= $1,500 − 700 − 600
= $200

Once again, we assume that no interest is paid, so the tax bill is:

Taxes = EBIT × t_c
= $200 × .34 = $68

where t_c, the corporate tax rate, is 34 percent.

When we put all of this together, we see that project operating cash flow, OCF, is:

OCF = EBIT + Depreciation − Taxes
= $200 + 600 − 68 = $732

It turns out there are some other ways to determine OCF that could be (and are) used. We consider these next.

The Bottom-Up Approach

Because we are ignoring any financing expenses, such as interest, in our calculations of project OCF, we can write project net income as:

Project net income = EBIT − Taxes
= $200 − 68
= $132

If we simply add the depreciation to both sides, we arrive at a slightly different and very common expression for OCF:

OCF = Net income + Depreciation
= $132 + 600 **(8.1)**
= $732

This is the *bottom-up* approach. Here, we start with the accountant's bottom line (net income) and add back any noncash deductions such as depreciation. It is crucial to remember that this definition of operating cash flow as net income plus depreciation is correct only if there is no interest expense subtracted in the calculation of net income.

The Top-Down Approach

Perhaps the most obvious way to calculate OCF is:

OCF = Sales − Costs − Taxes **(8.2)**
= $1,500 − 700 − 68 = $732

This is the *top-down* approach, the second variation on the basic OCF definition. Here, we start at the top of the income statement with sales and work our way down to net cash flow by subtracting costs, taxes, and other expenses. Along the way, we simply leave out any strictly noncash items such as depreciation.

The Tax Shield Approach

The third variation on our basic definition of OCF is the *tax shield* approach. This approach will be very useful for some problems we consider in the next section. The tax shield definition of OCF is:

$$\textbf{OCF} = \textbf{(Sales} - \textbf{Costs)} \times (1 - t_c) + \textbf{Depreciation} \times t_c \qquad (8.3)$$

where t_c is again the corporate tax rate. Assuming that $t_c = 34$ percent, the OCF works out to be:

$$\begin{aligned} \text{OCF} &= (\$1{,}500 - 700) \times .66 + 600 \times .34 \\ &= \$528 + 204 \\ &= \$732 \end{aligned}$$

This is just as we had before.

This approach views OCF as having two components. The first part is what the project's cash flow would be if there were no depreciation expense. In this case, this would-have-been cash flow is \$528.

The second part of OCF in this approach is the depreciation deduction multiplied by the tax rate. This is called the **depreciation tax shield**. We know that depreciation is a noncash expense. The only cash flow effect of deducting depreciation is to reduce our taxes, a benefit to us. At the current 34 percent corporate tax rate, every dollar in depreciation expense saves us 34 cents in taxes. So, in our example, the \$600 depreciation deduction saves us \$600 × .34 = \$204 in taxes.

Conclusion

Now that we've seen that all of these approaches are the same, you're probably wondering why everybody doesn't just agree on one of them. One reason is that different approaches are useful in different circumstances. The best one to use is whichever happens to be the most convenient for the problem at hand.

8.5 INVESTMENTS OF UNEQUAL LIVES: THE EQUIVALENT ANNUAL COST METHOD

Suppose a firm must choose between two machines of unequal lives. Both machines can do the same job, but they have different operating costs and will last for different time periods. A simple application of the NPV rule suggests taking the machine whose costs have the lower present value. This choice might be a mistake, however, because the lower-cost machine may need to be replaced before the other one.

Let's consider an example. The Downtown Athletic Club must choose between two mechanical tennis ball throwers. Machine *A* costs less than machine *B* but will not last as long. The cash *outflows* from the two machines are:

	Date				
MACHINE	**0**	**1**	**2**	**3**	**4**
A	\$500	\$120	\$120	\$120	
B	\$600	\$100	\$100	\$100	\$100

Machine *A* costs \$500 and lasts three years. There will be maintenance expenses of \$120 to be paid at the end of each of the three years. Machine *B* costs \$600 and lasts four years. There will be maintenance expenses of \$100 to be paid at the end of each of the four years. We place all costs in real terms, an assumption greatly simplifying the analysis. Revenues per year are assumed to be the same, regardless of machine, so they are ignored in the analysis. Note that all numbers in the above chart are *outflows*.

To get a handle on the decision, let's take the present value of the costs of each of the two machines. Assuming a discount rate of 10 percent, we have:

$$\textbf{Machine } A\textbf{: } \$798.42 = \$500 + \frac{\$120}{1.1} + \frac{\$120}{(1.1)^2} + \frac{\$120}{(1.1)^3}$$

$$\textbf{Machine } B\textbf{: } \$916.99 = \$600 + \frac{\$100}{1.1} + \frac{\$100}{(1.1)^2} + \frac{\$100}{(1.1)^3} + \frac{\$100}{(1.1)^4}$$

Machine *B* has a higher present value of outflows. A naive approach would be to select machine *A* because of its lower present value. However, machine *B* has a longer life so perhaps its cost per year is actually lower.

How might one properly adjust for the difference in useful life when comparing the two machines? Perhaps the easiest approach involves calculating something called the *equivalent annual cost* of each machine. This approach puts costs on a per-year basis.

The above equation showed that payments of (\$500, \$120, \$120, \$120) are equivalent to a single payment of \$798.42 at date 0. We now wish to equate the single payment of \$798.42 at date 0 with a three-year annuity. Using techniques of previous chapters, we have:

$$\$798.42 = C \times A^3_{.10}$$

$A^3_{.10}$ is an annuity of \$1 a year for three years, discounted at 10 percent. C is the unknown–the annuity payment per year such that the present value of all payments equals \$798.42. Because $A^3_{.10}$ equals 2.4869, C equals \$321.05 (\$798.42/2.4869). Thus, a payment stream of (\$500, \$120, \$120, \$120) is equivalent to annuity payments of \$321.05 made at the *end* of each year for three years. We refer to \$321.05 as the *equivalent annual cost* of machine *A*.

This idea is summarized in the little chart below:

	Date			
	0	1	2	3
Cash outflows of Machine *A*	\$500	\$120	\$120	\$120
Equivalent annual cost of Machine *A*		\$321.05	\$321.05	\$321.05

The Downtown Athletic Club should be indifferent between cash outflows of (\$500, \$120, \$120, \$120) and cash outflows of (\$0, \$321.05, \$321.05, \$321.05). Alternatively, one can say that the purchase of the machine is financially equivalent to a rental agreement calling for annual lease payments of \$321.05.

Now let's turn to machine *B*. We calculate its equivalent annual cost from:

$$\$916.99 = C \times A^4_{.10}$$

Because $A^4_{.10}$ equals 3.1699, C equals \$916.99/3.1699, or \$289.28.

As we did above for machine *A*, the following chart can be created for machine *B*:

	Date				
	0	1	2	3	4
Cash outflows of Machine *B*	\$600	\$100	\$100	\$100	\$100
Equivalent annual cost of Machine *B*		\$289.28	\$289.28	\$289.28	\$289.28

The decision is easy once the charts of the two machines are compared. Would you rather make annual lease payments of $321.05 or $289.28? Put this way, the problem becomes a no-brainer. Clearly, a rational person would rather pay the lower amount. Thus, machine *B* is the preferred choice.

Two final remarks are in order. First, it is no accident that we specified the costs of the tennis ball machines in real terms. While *B* would still have been the preferred machine had the costs been stated in nominal terms, the actual solution would have been much more difficult. As a general rule, always convert cash flows to real terms when working through problems of this type.

Second, the above analysis applies only if one anticipates that both machines can be replaced. The analysis would differ if no replacement were possible. For example, imagine that the only company that manufactured tennis ball throwers just went out of business and no new producers are expected to enter the field. In this case, machine *B* would generate revenues in the fourth year whereas machine *A* would not. Here, simple net present value analysis for mutually exclusive projects including both revenues and costs would be appropriate.

The General Decision to Replace

The previous analysis concerned the choice between machine *A* and machine *B*, both of which were new acquisitions. More typically, firms must decide when to replace an existing machine with a new one. This decision is actually quite straightforward. One should replace if the annual cost of the new machine is less than the annual cost of the old machine. As with much else in finance, an example clarifies this approach better than further explanation.

EXAMPLE 8.10 Replacement Decisions

Consider the situation of BIKE, which must decide whether to replace an existing machine. BIKE currently pays no taxes. The replacement machine costs $9,000 now and requires maintenance of $1,000 at the end of every year for eight years. At the end of eight years, the machine would be sold for $2,000.

The existing machine requires increasing amounts of maintenance each year, and its salvage value falls each year, as shown:

YEAR	MAINTENANCE	SALVAGE
Present	$ 0	$4,000
1	1,000	2,500
2	2,000	1,500
3	3,000	1,000
4	4,000	0

This chart tells us that the existing machine can be sold for $4,000 now. If it is sold one year from now, the resale price will be $2,500, and $1,000 must be spent on maintenance during the year to keep it running. For ease of calculation, we assume that this maintenance fee is paid at the end of the year. The machine will last for four more years before it falls apart. In other words, salvage value will be zero at the end of year 4. If BIKE faces an opportunity cost of capital of 15 percent, when should it replace the machine?

As we said above, our approach is to compare the annual cost of the replacement machine with the annual cost of the old machine. The annual cost of the replacement machine is simply its *equivalent annual cost* (EAC). Let's calculate that first.

(*continued*)

Equivalent Annual Cost of New Machine The present value of the cost of the new replacement machine is as follows:

$$\begin{aligned} PV_{costs} &= \$9{,}000 + \$1{,}000 \times A^8_{.15} - \frac{\$2{,}000}{(1.15)^8} \\ &= \$9{,}000 + \$1{,}000 \times (4.4873) - \$2{,}000 \times (.3269) \\ &= \$12{,}833 \end{aligned}$$

Notice that the $2,000 salvage value is an inflow. It is treated as a *negative* number in the above equation because it *offsets* the cost of the machine.

The EAC of a new replacement machine equals:

$$PV/8\text{-year annuity factor at } 15\% = \frac{PV}{A^8_{.15}} = \frac{\$12{,}833}{4.4873} = \$2{,}860$$

This calculation implies that buying a replacement machine is financially equivalent to renting this machine for $2,860 per year.

Cost of Old Machine This calculation is a little trickier. If BIKE keeps the old machine for one year, the firm must pay maintenance costs of $1,000 a year from now. But this is not BIKE's only cost from keeping the machine for one year. BIKE will receive $2,500 at date 1 if the old machine is kept for one year but would receive $4,000 today if the old machine were sold immediately. This reduction in sales proceeds is clearly a cost as well.

Thus, the PV of the costs of keeping the machine one more year before selling it equals:

$$\$4{,}000 + \frac{\$1{,}000}{1.15} - \frac{\$2{,}500}{1.15} = \$2{,}696$$

That is, if BIKE holds the old machine for one year, BIKE does *not* receive the $4,000 today. This $4,000 can be thought of as an opportunity cost. In addition, the firm must pay $1,000 a year from now. Finally, BIKE does receive $2,500 a year from now. This last item is treated as a negative number because it offsets the other two costs.

While we normally express cash flows in terms of present value, the analysis to come is made easier if we express the cash flow in terms of its future value one year from now. This future value is:

$$\$2{,}696 \times 1.15 = \$3{,}100$$

In other words, the cost of keeping the machine for one year is equivalent to paying $3,100 at the end of the year.

Making the Comparison Now let's review the cash flows. If we replace the machine immediately, we can view our annual expense as $2,860, beginning at the end of the year. This annual expense occurs forever, if we replace the new machine every eight years. This cash flow stream can be written as:

	YEAR 1	YEAR 2	YEAR 3	YEAR 4	. . .
Expenses from replacing machine immediately	$2,860	$2,860	$2,860	$2,860	. . .

If we replace the old machine in one year, our expense from using the old machine for that final year can be viewed as $3,100, payable at the end of the year. After replacement, our annual expense is $2,860, beginning at the end of two years. This annual expense occurs forever, if we replace the new machine every eight years. This cash flow stream can be written as:

	YEAR 1	YEAR 2	YEAR 3	YEAR 4	. . .
Expenses from using old machine for one year and then replacing it	$3,100	$2,860	$2,860	$2,860	. . .

(*continued*)

Put this way, the choice is a no-brainer. Anyone would rather pay $2,860 at the end of the year than $3,100 at the end of the year. Thus, BIKE should replace[1] the old machine immediately in order to minimize the expense at year 1.

Two final points should be made on the decision to replace. First, we have examined a situation where both the old machine and the replacement machine generate the same revenues. Because revenues are unaffected by the choice of machine, revenues do not enter into our analysis. This situation is common in business. For example, the decision to replace either the heating system or the air conditioning system in one's home office will likely not affect firm revenues. However, sometimes revenues will be greater with a new machine. The above approach can easily be amended to handle differential revenues.

Second, we want to stress the importance of the above approach. Applications of the above approach are pervasive in business, since *every* machine must be replaced at some point.

[1]One caveat is in order. Perhaps the old machine's maintenance is high in the first year but drops after that. A decision to replace immediately might be premature in that case. Therefore, we need to check the cost of the old machine in future years.

The cost of keeping the existing machine a second year is:

$$\text{PV of costs at time 1} = \$2{,}500 + \frac{\$2{,}000}{1.15} - \frac{\$1{,}500}{1.15} = \$2{,}935$$

which has a future value of $3,375 ($2,935 × 1.15).

The costs of keeping the existing machine for years 3 and 4 are also greater than the EAC of buying a new machine. Thus, BIKE's decision to replace the old machine immediately is still valid.

www.mhhe.com/rwj

SUMMARY AND CONCLUSIONS

This chapter discusses a number of practical applications of capital budgeting.

1. Capital budgeting must be placed on an incremental basis. This means that sunk costs must be ignored, while both opportunity costs and side effects must be considered.
2. In the Baldwin case, we computed NPV using the following two steps:
   a. Calculate the net cash flow from all sources for each period.
   b. Calculate the NPV using the cash flows calculated above.
3. Inflation must be handled consistently. One approach is to express both cash flows and the discount rate in nominal terms. The other approach is to express both cash flows and the discount rate in real terms. Because either approach yields the same NPV calculation, the simpler method should be used. The simpler method will generally depend on the type of capital budgeting problem.
4. A firm should use the equivalent annual cost approach when choosing between two machines of unequal lives.

CONCEPT QUESTIONS

1. **Opportunity Cost** In the context of capital budgeting, what is an opportunity cost?
2. **Incremental Cash Flows** Which of the following should be treated as an incremental cash flow when computing the NPV of an investment?
   a. A reduction in the sales of a company's other products caused by the investment.
   b. An expenditure on plant and equipment that has not yet been made and will be made only if the project is accepted.
   c. Costs of research and development undertaken in connection with the product during the past three years.
   d. Annual depreciation expense from the investment.
   e. Dividend payments by the firm.
   f. The resale value of plant and equipment at the end of the project's life.
   g. Salary and medical costs for production personnel who will be employed only if the project is accepted.
3. **Incremental Cash Flows** Your company currently produces and sells steel shaft golf clubs. The board of directors wants you to consider the introduction of a new line of titanium bubble woods with graphite shafts. Which of the following costs are *not* relevant?
   a. Land you already own that will be used for the project, but otherwise will be sold for $700,000, its market value.
   b. A $300,000 drop in your sales of steel shaft clubs if the titanium woods with graphite shafts are introduced.
   c. $200,000 spent on research and development last year on graphite shafts.
4. **Depreciation** Given the choice, would a firm prefer to use MACRS depreciation or straight-line depreciation? Why?
5. **Net Working Capital** In our capital budgeting examples, we assumed that a firm would recover all of the working capital it invested in a project. Is this a reasonable assumption? When might it not be valid?
6. **Stand-Alone Principle** Suppose a financial manager is quoted as saying, "Our firm uses the stand-alone principle. Because we treat projects like minifirms in our evaluation process, we include financing costs because they are relevant at the firm level." Critically evaluate this statement.
7. **Equivalent Annual Cost** When is EAC analysis appropriate for comparing two or more projects? Why is this method used? Are there any implicit assumptions required by this method that you find troubling? Explain.
8. **Cash Flow and Depreciation** "When evaluating projects, we're only concerned with the relevant incremental aftertax cash flows. Therefore, because depreciation is a noncash expense, we should ignore its effects when evaluating projects." Critically evaluate this statement.
9. **Capital Budgeting Considerations** A major college textbook publisher has an existing finance textbook. The publisher is debating whether or not to produce an "essentialized" version, meaning a shorter (and lower-priced) book. What are some of the considerations that should come into play?

To answer the next three questions, refer to the following example. In 2003, Porsche unveiled its new sports-utility vehicle (SUV), the Cayenne. With a price tag of over $40,000, the Cayenne goes from zero to 62 mph in 9.7 seconds. Porsche's decision to enter the SUV market was in response to the runaway success of other high-priced SUVs such as the Mercedes-Benz M-class. Vehicles in this class had generated years of very high profits. The Cayenne certainly spiced up the market, and Porsche subsequently introduced the Cayenne Turbo, which goes from zero to 62 mph in 5.6 seconds and has a top speed of 165 mph. The price tag for the Cayenne Turbo? Almost $100,000!

Some analysts questioned Porsche's entry into the luxury SUV market. The analysts were concerned not only that Porsche was a late entry into the market, but also that the introduction of the Cayenne would damage Porsche's reputation as a maker of high-performance automobiles.

10. **Erosion** In evaluating the Cayenne, would you consider the possible damage to Porsche's reputation as erosion?

11. **Capital Budgeting** Porsche was one of the last manufacturers to enter the sports-utility vehicle market. Why would one company decide to proceed with a product when other companies, at least initially, decide not to enter the market?

12. **Capital Budgeting** In evaluating the Cayenne, what do you think Porsche needs to assume regarding the substantial profit margins that exist in this market? Is it likely that they will be maintained as the market becomes more competitive, or will Porsche be able to maintain the profit margin because of its image and the performance of the Cayenne?

QUESTIONS AND PROBLEMS

Basic
(Questions 1–10)

1. **Calculating Project NPV** Raphael Restaurant is considering the purchase of a $10,000 souffle maker. The souffle maker has an economic life of five years and will be fully depreciated by the straight-line method. The machine will produce 2,000 souffles per year, with each costing $2 to make and priced at $5. Assume that the discount rate is 17 percent and the tax rate is 34 percent. Should Raphael make the purchase?

2. **Calculating Project NPV** The Best Manufacturing Company is considering a new investment. Financial projections for the investment are tabulated below. The corporate tax rate is 34 percent. Assume all sales revenue is received in cash, all operating costs and income taxes are paid in cash, and all cash flows occur at the end of the year. All net working capital is recovered at the end of the project.

	YEAR 0	YEAR 1	YEAR 2	YEAR 3	YEAR 4
Investment	$10,000	—	—	—	—
Sales revenue	—	$7,000	$7,000	$7,000	$7,000
Operating costs	—	2,000	2,000	2,000	2,000
Depreciation	—	2,500	2,500	2,500	2,500
Net working capital spending	200	250	300	200	?

a. Compute the incremental net income of the investment for each year.

b. Compute the incremental cash flows of the investment for each year.

c. Suppose the appropriate discount rate is 12 percent. What is the NPV of the project?

3. **Calculating Project NPV** Down Under Boomerang, Inc., is considering a new three-year expansion project that requires an initial fixed asset investment of $2.7 million. The fixed asset will be depreciated straight-line to zero over its three-year tax life, after which time it will be worthless. The project is estimated to generate $2,400,000 in annual sales, with costs of $960,000. The tax rate is 35 percent and the required return is 15 percent. What is the project's NPV?

4. **Calculating Project Cash Flow from Assets** In the previous problem, suppose the project requires an initial investment in net working capital of $300,000 and the fixed asset will have

a market value of $210,000 at the end of the project. What is the project's Year 0 net cash flow? Year 1? Year 2? Year 3? What is the new NPV?

5. **NPV and Modified ACRS** In the previous problem, suppose the fixed asset actually falls into the three-year MACRS class. All the other facts are the same. What is the project's Year 1 net cash flow now? Year 2? Year 3? What is the new NPV?

6. **Project Evaluation** Your firm is contemplating the purchase of a new $925,000 computer-based order entry system. The system will be depreciated straight-line to zero over its five-year life. It will be worth $90,000 at the end of that time. You will save $360,000 before taxes per year in order processing costs and you will be able to reduce working capital by $125,000 (this is a one-time reduction). If the tax rate is 35 percent, what is the IRR for this project?

7. **Project Evaluation** Dog Up! Franks is looking at a new sausage system with an installed cost of $390,000. This cost will be depreciated straight-line to zero over the project's five-year life, at the end of which the sausage system can be scrapped for $60,000. The sausage system will save the firm $120,000 per year in pretax operating costs, and the system requires an initial investment in net working capital of $28,000. If the tax rate is 34 percent and the discount rate is 10 percent, what is the NPV of this project?

8. **Calculating Salvage Value** An asset used in a four-year project falls in the five-year MACRS class for tax purposes. The asset has an acquisition cost of $9,300,000 and will be sold for $2,100,000 at the end of the project. If the tax rate is 35 percent, what is the aftertax salvage value of the asset?

9. **Calculating NPV** Howell Petroleum is considering a new project that complements its existing business. The machine required for the project costs $2 million. The marketing department predicts that sales related to the project will be $1.2 million per year for the next four years, after which the market will cease to exist. The machine will be depreciated down to zero over its four-year economic life using the straight-line method. Cost of goods sold and operating expenses related to the project are predicted to be 25 percent of sales. Howell also needs to add net working capital of $100,000 immediately. The additional net working capital will be recovered in full at the end of the project's life. The corporate tax rate is 35 percent. The required rate of return for Howell is 14 percent. Should Howell proceed with the project?

10. **Calculating EAC** You are evaluating two different silicon wafer milling machines. The Techron I costs $210,000, has a three-year life, and has pretax operating costs of $34,000 per year. The Techron II costs $320,000, has a five-year life, and has pretax operating costs of $23,000 per year. For both milling machines, use straight-line depreciation to zero over the project's life and assume a salvage value of $20,000. If your tax rate is 35 percent and your discount rate is 14 percent, compute the EAC for both machines. Which do you prefer? Why?

Intermediate
(Questions 11–29)

11. **Cost-Cutting Proposals** Massey Machine Shop is considering a four-year project to improve its production efficiency. Buying a new machine press for $480,000 is estimated to result in $160,000 in annual pretax cost savings. The press falls in the MACRS five-year class, and it will have a salvage value at the end of the project of $70,000. The press also requires an initial investment in spare parts inventory of $20,000, along with an additional $3,000 in inventory for each succeeding year of the project. If the shop's tax rate is 35 percent and its discount rate is 14 percent, should Massey buy and install the machine press?

12. **Comparing Mutually Exclusive Projects** Hagar Industrial Systems Company (HISC) is trying to decide between two different conveyor belt systems. System A costs $430,000, has a four-year life, and requires $120,000 in pretax annual operating costs. System B costs $540,000, has a six-year life, and requires $80,000 in pretax annual operating costs. Both systems are to be depreciated straight-line to zero over their lives and will have zero salvage value. Whichever project is chosen, it will *not* be replaced when it wears out. If the tax rate is 34 percent and the discount rate is 20 percent, which project should the firm choose?

13. **Comparing Mutually Exclusive Projects** Suppose in the previous problem that HISC always needs a conveyor belt system; when one wears out, it must be replaced. Which project should the firm choose now?

14. **Comparing Mutually Exclusive Projects** Vandalay Industries is considering the purchase of a new machine for the production of latex. Machine A costs $2,100,000 and will last for six years. Variable costs are 35 percent of sales, and fixed costs are $150,000 per year. Machine B costs $4,500,000 and will last for nine years. Variable costs for this machine are 30 percent and fixed costs are $100,000 per year. The sales for each machine will be $9 million per year. The required return is 10 percent and the tax rate is 35 percent. Both machines will be depreciated on a straight-line basis. If the company plans to replace the machine when it wears out on a perpetual basis, which machine should you choose?

15. **Capital Budgeting with Inflation** Consider the following cash flows on two mutually exclusive projects.

YEAR	PROJECT *A*	PROJECT *B*
0	−$40,000	−$50,000
1	20,000	10,000
2	15,000	20,000
3	15,000	40,000

The cash flows of Project *A* are expressed in real terms while those of Project *B* are expressed in nominal terms. The appropriate nominal discount rate is 15 percent and the inflation rate is 4 percent. Which project should you choose?

16. **Inflation and Company Value** Sparkling Water, Inc., expects to sell 2 million bottles of drinking water each year in perpetuity. This year, each bottle will sell for $1.25 in real terms and will cost $0.70 in real terms. Sales income and costs occur at year-end. Revenues will rise at a real rate of 6 percent annually, while real costs will rise at a real rate of 5 percent annually. The real discount rate is 10 percent. The corporate tax rate is 34 percent. What is Sparkling worth today?

17. **Calculating Nominal Cash Flow** Etonic Inc. is considering an investment of $250,000 in an asset with an economic life of five years. The firm estimates that the nominal annual cash revenues and expenses at the end of the first year will be $200,000 and $50,000, respectively. Both revenues and expenses will grow thereafter at the annual inflation rate of 3 percent. Etonic will use the straight-line method to depreciate its asset to zero over five years. The salvage value of the asset is estimated to be $30,000 in nominal terms at that time. The one-time net working capital investment of $10,000 is required immediately and will be recovered at the end of the project. All corporate cash flows are subject to a 34 percent tax rate. What is the project's total nominal cash flow from assets for each year?

18. **Cash Flow Valuation** Phillips Industries runs a small manufacturing operation. For this fiscal year, it expects real net cash flows of $120,000. Phillips is an ongoing operation, but it expects competitive pressures to erode its real net cash flows at 6 percent per year in perpetuity. The appropriate real discount rate for Phillips is 11 percent. All net cash flows are received at year-end. What is the present value of the net cash flows from Phillips's operations?

19. **Equivalent Annual Cost** Bridgton Golf Academy is evaluating different golf practice equipment. The "Dimple-Max" equipment costs $45,000, has a three-year life, and costs $5,000 per year to operate. The relevant discount rate is 12 percent. Assume that the straight-line depreciation method is used and that the equipment is fully depreciated to zero. Furthermore, assume the equipment has a salvage value of $10,000 at the end of the project's life. The relevant tax rate is 34 percent. All cash flows occur at the end of the year. What is the equivalent annual cost (EAC) of this equipment?

20. **Equivalent Annual Cost** Harwell University must purchase word processors for its typing lab. The university can buy 10 EVF word processors that cost $8,000 each and have annual, year-end maintenance costs of $2,000 per machine. The EVF word processors will be replaced at the end of Year 4 and have no value at that time. Alternatively, Harwell can buy 11 AEH word processors to accomplish the same work. The AEH word processors will be replaced after three years. They each cost $5,000, and have annual, year-end maintenance costs of $2,500 per machine. Each AEH word processor will have a resale value of $500 at the end of three years. The university's opportunity cost of funds for this type of investment is 14 percent. Because the university is a nonprofit institution, it does not pay taxes. It is anticipated that whichever manufacturer is chosen now will be the supplier of future machines. Would you recommend purchasing 10 EVF word processors or 11 AEH machines?

21. **Calculating Project NPV** Scott Investors, Inc., is considering the purchase of a $500,000 computer with an economic life of five years. The computer will be fully depreciated over five years using the straight-line method. The market value of the computer will be $100,000 in five years. The computer will replace five office employees whose combined annual salaries are $120,000. The machine will also immediately lower the firm's required net working capital by $100,000. This amount of net working capital will need to be replaced once the machine is sold. The corporate tax rate is 34 percent. Is it worthwhile to buy the computer if the appropriate discount rate is 12 percent?

22. **Calculating NPV and IRR for a Replacement** A firm is considering an investment in a new machine with a price of $32 million to replace its existing machine. The current machine has a book value of $8 million, and a market value of $9 million. The new machine is expected to have a four-year life, and the old machine has four years left in which it can be used. If the firm replaces the old machine with the new machine, it expects to save $5 million in operating costs each year over the next four years. Both machines will have no salvage value in four years. If the firm purchases the new machine, it will also need an investment of $500,000 in net working capital. The required return on the investment is 10 percent, and the tax rate is 39 percent. 

    a. What is the NPV and IRR of the decision to replace the old machine?

    b. Ignoring the time value of money, the new machine saves only $20 million over the next four years, and has a cost of $32 million. How is it possible that the NPV of the decision to replace the old machine has a positive NPV?

23. **Project Analysis and Inflation** Sanders Enterprises, Inc., has been considering the purchase of a new manufacturing facility for $120,000. The facility is to be fully depreciated on a straight-line basis over seven years. It is expected to have no resale value after the seven years. Operating revenues from the facility are expected to be $50,000, in nominal terms, at the end of the first year. The revenues are expected to increase at the inflation rate of 5 percent. Production costs at the end of the first year will be $20,000, in nominal terms, and they are expected to increase at 7 percent per year. The real discount rate is 14 percent. The corporate tax rate is 34 percent. Sanders has other ongoing profitable operations. Should the company accept the project?

24. **Calculating Project NPV** With the growing popularity of casual surf print clothing, two recent MBA graduates decided to broaden this casual surf concept to encompass a "surf lifestyle for the home." With limited capital, they decided to focus on surf print table and floor lamps to accent people's homes. They projected unit sales of these lamps to be 5,000 in the first year, with growth of 15 percent each year for the next five years. Production of these lamps will require $28,000 in net working capital to start. Total fixed costs are $75,000 per year, variable production costs are $20 per unit, and the units are priced at $45 each. The equipment needed to begin production will cost $60,000. The equipment will be depreciated using the straight-line method over a five-year life and is not expected to have a salvage value. The effective tax rate is 34 percent and the required rate of return is 25 percent. What is the NPV of this project?

25. **Calculating Project NPV** You have been hired as a consultant for Pristine Urban-Tech Zither, Inc. (PUTZ), manufacturers of fine zithers. The market for zithers is growing quickly. The company bought some land three years ago for $1 million in anticipation of using it as a toxic waste dump site but has recently hired another company to handle all toxic materials. Based on a recent appraisal, the company believes it could sell the land for $800,000 on an aftertax basis. The company also hired a marketing firm to analyze the zither market, at a cost of $125,000. An excerpt of the marketing report is as follows:

    The zither industry will have a rapid expansion in the next four years. With the brand name recognition that PUTZ brings to bear, we feel that the company will be able to sell 2,900, 3,800, 2,700, 1,900 units each year for the next four years, respectively. Again, capitalizing on the name recognition of PUTZ, we feel that a premium price of $700 can be charged for each zither. Since zithers appear to be a fad, we feel at the end of the four-year period, sales should be discontinued.

    PUTZ feels that fixed costs for the project will be $350,000 per year, and variable costs are 15 percent of sales. The equipment necessary for production will cost $3.8 million and will be depreciated according to a three-year MACRS schedule. At the end of the project, the equipment can be scrapped for $400,000. Net working capital of $120,000 will be required by the end of the first year. PUTZ has a 38 percent tax rate and the required return on the project is 13 percent. What is the NPV of the project? Assume the company has other profitable projects.

26. **Calculating Project NPV** Pilot Plus Pens is deciding when to replace its old machine. The machine's current salvage value is $2 million. Its current book value is $1 million. If not sold, the old machine will require maintenance costs of $400,000 at the end of the year for the next five years. Depreciation on the old machine is $200,000 per year. At the end of five years, it will have a salvage value of $200,000 and a book value of $0. A replacement machine costs $3 million now and requires maintenance costs of $500,000 at the end of each year during its economic life of five years. At the end of the five years, the new machine will have a salvage value of $500,000. It will be fully depreciated by the straight-line method. In five years, a replacement machine will cost $3,500,000. Pilot will need to purchase this machine regardless of what choice it makes today. The corporate tax rate is 34 percent and the appropriate discount rate is 12 percent. The company is assumed to earn sufficient revenues to generate tax shields from depreciation. Should Pilot Plus Pens replace the old machine now or at the end of five years?

27. **Calculating EAC** Gold Star Industries is contemplating a purchase of computers. The firm has narrowed its choices to the SAL 5000 and the DET 1000. Gold Star would need 10 SALs, and each SAL costs $3,750 and requires $500 of maintenance each year. At the end of the computer's eight-year life, Gold Star expects to sell each one for $500. Alternatively, Gold Star could buy seven DETs. Each DET costs $5,250 and requires $700 of maintenance every year. Each DET lasts for six years and has a resale value of $600 at the end of its economic life. Gold Star will continue to purchase the model that it chooses today into perpetuity. Gold Star has a 34 percent tax rate. Assume that the maintenance costs occur at year-end. Depreciation is straight-line to zero. Which model should Gold Star buy if the appropriate discount rate is 11 percent?

28. **EAC and Inflation** Office Automation, Inc., must choose between two copiers, the XX40 or the RH45. The XX40 costs $700 and will last for three years. The copier will require an aftertax cost of $100 per year after all relevant expenses. The RH45 costs $900 and will last five years. The real aftertax cost for the RH45 will be $110 per year. All cash flows occur at the end of the year. The inflation rate is expected to be 5 percent per year, and the nominal discount rate is 14 percent. Which copier should the company choose?

29. **Project Analysis and Inflation** Dickinson Brothers, Inc., is considering investing in a machine to produce computer keyboards. The price of the machine will be $400,000 and its economic life is five years. The machine will be fully depreciated by the straight-line method. The machine will produce 10,000 keyboards each year. The price of each keyboard will be $40 in the first year and

will increase by 5 percent per year. The production cost per keyboard will be $20 in the first year and will increase by 10 percent per year. The project will have an annual fixed cost of $50,000 and require an immediate investment of $25,000 in net working capital. The corporate tax rate for the company is 34 percent. If the appropriate discount rate is 15 percent, what is the NPV of the investment?

Challenge (Questions 30–40)

30. **Project Evaluation** Aguilera Acoustics (AAI), Inc., projects unit sales for a new 7-octave voice emulation implant as follows:

YEAR	UNIT SALES
1	85,000
2	98,000
3	106,000
4	114,000
5	93,000

Production of the implants will require $1,500,000 in net working capital to start and additional net working capital investments each year equal to 15 percent of the projected sales increase for the following year. Total fixed costs are $900,000 per year, variable production costs are $240 per unit, and the units are priced at $325 each. The equipment needed to begin production has an installed cost of $21,000,000. Because the implants are intended for professional singers, this equipment is considered industrial machinery and thus qualifies as seven-year MACRS property. In five years, this equipment can be sold for about 20 percent of its acquisition cost. AAI is in the 35 percent marginal tax bracket and has a required return on all its projects of 18 percent. Based on these preliminary project estimates, what is the NPV of the project? What is the IRR?

31. **Calculating Required Savings** A proposed cost-saving device has an installed cost of $480,000. The device will be used in a five-year project, but is classified as three-year MACRS property for tax purposes. The required initial net working capital investment is $40,000, the marginal tax rate is 35 percent, and the project discount rate is 12 percent. The device has an estimated Year 5 salvage value of $45,000. What level of pretax cost savings do we require for this project to be profitable?

32. **Calculating a Bid Price** Another utilization of cash flow analysis is setting the bid price on a project. To calculate the bid price, we set the project NPV equal to zero and find the required price. Thus, the bid price represents a financial break-even level for the project. Guthrie Enterprises needs someone to supply it with 150,000 cartons of machine screws per year to support its manufacturing needs over the next five years, and you've decided to bid on the contract. It will cost you $780,000 to install the equipment necessary to start production; you'll depreciate this cost straight-line to zero over the project's life. You estimate that in five years, this equipment can be salvaged for $50,000. Your fixed production costs will be $240,000 per year, and your variable production costs should be $8.50 per carton. You also need an initial investment in net working capital of $75,000. If your tax rate is 35 percent and you require a 16 percent return on your investment, what bid price should you submit?

33. **Financial Break-Even Analysis** The technique for calculating a bid price can be extended to many other types of problems. Answer the following questions using the same technique as setting a bid price, that is, set the project NPV to zero and solve for the variable in question.

    a. In the previous problem, assume that the price per carton is $13 and find the project NPV. What does your answer tell you about your bid price? What do you know about the number of cartons you can sell and still break even? How about your level of costs?

    b. Solve the previous problem again with the price still at $13 but find the quantity of cartons per year that you can supply and still break even. (Hint: It's less than 150,000.)

c. Repeat (b) with a price of $13 and a quantity of 150,000 cartons per year, and find the highest level of fixed costs you could afford and still break even. (Hint: It's more than $240,000.)

34. **Calculating a Bid Price** Your company has been approached to bid on a contract to sell 10,000 voice recognition (VR) computer keyboards a year for four years. Due to technological improvements, beyond that time they will be outdated and no sales will be possible. The equipment necessary for the production will cost $2.4 million and will be depreciated on a straight-line basis to a zero salvage value. Production will require an investment in net working capital of $75,000 to be returned at the end of the project and the equipment can be sold for $200,000 at the end of production. Fixed costs are $500,000 per year, and variable costs are $165 per unit. In addition to the contract, you feel your company can sell 3,000, 6,000, 8,000, and 5,000 additional units to companies in other countries over the next four years, respectively, at a price of $275. This price is fixed. The tax rate is 40 percent, and the required return is 13 percent. Additionally, the president of the company will only undertake the project if it has an NPV of $100,000. What bid price should you set for the contract?

35. **Replacement Decisions** Suppose we are thinking about replacing an old computer with a new one. The old one cost us $390,000; the new one will cost $780,000. The new machine will be depreciated straight-line to zero over its five-year life. It will probably be worth about $140,000 after five years.

    The old computer is being depreciated at a rate of $130,000 per year. It will be completely written off in three years. If we don't replace it now, we will have to replace it in two years. We can sell it now for $230,000; in two years, it will probably be worth $90,000. The new machine will save us $125,000 per year in operating costs. The tax rate is 38 percent and the discount rate is 14 percent.

    a. Suppose we recognize that if we don't replace the computer now, we will be replacing it in two years. Should we replace now or should we wait? (Hint: What we effectively have here is a decision either to "invest" in the old computer—by not selling it—or to invest in the new one. Notice that the two investments have unequal lives.)

    b. Suppose we only consider whether or not we should replace the old computer now without worrying about what's going to happen in two years. What are the relevant cash flows? Should we replace it or not? (Hint: Consider the net change in the firm's aftertax cash flows if we do the replacement.)

36. **Project Analysis** Benson Enterprises is evaluating alternative uses for a three-story manufacturing and warehousing building that it has purchased for $225,000. The company can continue to rent the building to the present occupants for $12,000 per year. The present occupants have indicated an interest in staying in the building for at least another 15 years. Alternatively, the company could modify the existing structure to use for its own manufacturing and warehousing needs. Benson's production engineer feels the building could be adapted to handle one of two new product lines. The cost and revenue data for the two product alternatives are as follows:

	PRODUCT A	PRODUCT B
Initial cash outlay for building modifications	$ 36,000	$ 54,000
Initial cash outlay for equipment	144,000	162,000
Annual pretax cash revenues (generated for 15 years)	105,000	127,500
Annual pretax expenditures (generated for 15 years)	60,000	75,000

The building will be used for only 15 years for either Product A or Product B. After 15 years, the building will be too small for efficient production of either product line. At that time, Benson plans to rent the building to firms similar to the current occupants. To rent the building again, Benson will need to restore the building to its present layout. The estimated cash cost of restoring the building if Product A has been undertaken is $3,750. If Product B has been manufactured, the cash cost will be $28,125. These cash costs can be deducted for tax purposes in the year the expenditures occur.

Benson will depreciate the original building shell (purchased for $225,000) over a 30-year life to zero, regardless of which alternative it chooses. The building modifications and equipment purchases for either product are estimated to have a 15-year life. They will be depreciated by the straight-line method. The firm's tax rate is 34 percent, and its required rate of return on such investments is 12 percent.

For simplicity, assume all cash flows occur at the end of the year. The initial outlays for modifications and equipment will occur today (Year 0), and the restoration outlays will occur at the end of Year 15. Benson has other profitable ongoing operations that are sufficient to cover any losses. Which use of the building would you recommend to management?

37. **Project Analysis and Inflation** The Biological Insect Control Corporation (BICC) has hired you as a consultant to evaluate the NPV of its proposed toad ranch. BICC plans to breed toads and sell them as ecologically desirable insect control mechanisms. They anticipate that the business will continue into perpetuity. Following the negligible start-up costs, BICC expects the following nominal cash flows at the end of the year.

Revenues	$150,000
Labor costs	80,000
Other costs	40,000

The company will lease machinery for $20,000 per year. The lease payments start at the end of Year 1 and are expressed in nominal terms. Revenues will increase by 5 percent per year in real terms. Labor costs will increase by 3 percent per year in real terms. Other costs will decrease by 1 percent per year in real terms. The rate of inflation is expected to be 6 percent per year. BICC's required rate of return is 10 percent in real terms. The company has a 34 percent tax rate. All cash flows occur at year-end. What is the NPV of BICC's proposed toad ranch today?

38. **Project Analysis and Inflation** Sony International has an investment opportunity to produce a new stereo color TV. The required investment on January 1 of this year is $32 million. The firm will depreciate the investment to zero using the straight-line method over four years. The investment has no resale value after completion of the project. The firm is in the 34 percent tax bracket. The price of the product will be $400 per unit, in real terms, and will not change over the life of the project. Labor costs for Year 1 will be $15.30 per hour, in real terms, and will increase at 2 percent per year in real terms. Energy costs for Year 1 will be $5.15 per physical unit, in real terms, and will increase at 3 percent per year in real terms. The inflation rate is 5 percent per year. Revenues are received and costs are paid at year-end. Refer to the table below for the production schedule.

	YEAR 1	YEAR 2	YEAR 3	YEAR 4
Physical production, in units	100,000	200,000	200,000	150,000
Labor input, in hours	2,000,000	2,000,000	2,000,000	2,000,000
Energy input, physical units	200,000	200,000	200,000	200,000

The real discount rate for Sony is 8 percent. Calculate the NPV of this project.

39. **Project Analysis and Inflation** After extensive medical and marketing research, Pill, Inc., believes it can penetrate the pain reliever market. It is considering two alternative products. The first is to produce a medication for headache pain. The second is a pill for headache and arthritis pain. Both products would be introduced at a price of $4 per package in real terms. The headache-only medication is projected to sell 5 million packages a year, while the headache and arthritis remedy would sell 10 million packages a year. Cash costs of production in the first year are expected to be $1.50 per package in real terms for the headache-only brand.

Production costs are expected to be $1.70 in real terms for the headache and arthritis pill. All prices and costs are expected to rise at the general inflation rate of 5 percent.

Either product requires further investment. The headache-only pill could be produced using equipment costing $10.2 million. That equipment would last three years and have no resale value. The machinery required to produce the broader remedy would cost $12 million and last three years. The firm expects that equipment to have a $1 million resale value (in real terms) at the end of year 3.

Pill, Inc., uses straight-line depreciation. The firm faces a corporate tax rate of 34 percent and believes that the appropriate real discount rate is 13 percent. Which pain reliever should the firm produce?

40. **Calculating Project NPV** J. Smythe, Inc., manufactures fine furniture. The company is deciding whether to introduce a new mahogany dining room table set. The set will sell for $5,600, including a set of eight chairs. The company feels that sales will be 1,300; 1,325; 1,375; 1,450; and 1,320 sets per year for the next five years, respectively. Variable costs will amount to 45 percent of sales, and fixed costs are $1.7 million per year. The new tables will require inventory amounting to 10 percent of sales, produced and stockpiled in the year prior to sales. It is believed that the addition of the new table will cause a loss of 200 tables per year of the oak tables the company produces. These tables sell for $4,500 and have variable costs of 40 percent of sales. The inventory for this oak table is also 10 percent. J. Smythe currently has excess production capacity. If the company buys the necessary equipment today, it will cost $10.5 million. However, the excess production capacity means the company can produce the new table without buying the new equipment. The company controller has said that the current excess capacity will end in two years with current production. This means that if the company uses the current excess capacity for the new table, it will be forced to spend the $10.5 million in two years to accommodate the increased sales of its current products. In five years, the new equipment will have a market value of $2.8 million if purchased today, and $6.1 million if purchased in two years. The equipment is depreciated on a 7-year MACRS schedule. The company has a tax rate of 38 percent, and the required return for the project is 14 percent.

   a. Should J. Smythe undertake the new project?

   b. Can you perform an IRR analysis on this project? How many IRRs would you expect to find?

   c. How would you interpret the profitability index?

CLOSING CASES

BETHESDA MINING COMPANY

Bethesda Mining is a midsized coal mining company with 20 mines located in Ohio, Pennsylvania, West Virginia, and Kentucky. The company operates deep mines as well as strip mines. Most of the coal mined is sold under contract, with excess production sold on the spot market.

The coal mining industry, especially high-sulfur coal operations such as Bethesda, has been hard-hit by environmental regulations. Recently, however, a combination of increased demand for coal and new pollution reduction technologies has led to an improved market demand for high-sulfur coal. Bethesda has just been approached by Mid-Ohio Electric Company with a request to supply coal for its electric generators for the next four years. Bethesda Mining does not have enough excess capacity at its existing mines to guarantee the contract. The company is considering opening a strip mine in Ohio on 5,000 acres of land purchased 10 years ago for $6 million. Based on a recent appraisal, the company feels it could receive $5 million on an aftertax basis if it sold the land today.

Strip mining is a process where the layers of topsoil above a coal vein are removed and the exposed coal is removed. Some time ago, the company would simply remove the coal and leave the land in an unusable condition. Changes in mining regulations now force a company to reclaim the land; that is, when the mining is completed, the land must be restored to near its original condition. The land can then be used for other purposes. As they are currently operating at full capacity, Bethesda will need to purchase additional necessary equipment, which will cost $30 million. The equipment will be depreciated on a seven-year MACRS schedule. The contract only runs for four years. At that time the coal from the site will be entirely mined. The company feels that the equipment can be sold for 60 percent of its initial purchase price. However, Bethesda plans to open another strip mine at that time and will use the equipment at the new mine.

The contract calls for the delivery of 600,000 tons of coal per year at a price of $34 per ton. Bethesda Mining feels that coal production will be 650,000 tons, 725,000 tons, 810,000 tons, and 740,000 tons, respectively, over the next four years. The excess production will be sold in the spot market at an average of $40 per ton. Variable costs amount to $13 per ton and fixed costs are $2,500,000 per year. The mine will require a net working capital investment of 5 percent of sales. The NWC will be built up in the year prior to the sales.

Bethesda will be responsible for reclaiming the land at termination of the mining. This will occur in Year 5. The company uses an outside company for reclamation of all the company's strip mines. It is estimated the cost of reclamation will be $4 million. After the land is reclaimed, the company plans to donate the land to the state for use as a public park and recreation area. This will occur in Year 6 and result in a charitable expense deduction of $6 million. Bethesda faces a 38 percent tax rate and has a 12 percent required return on new strip mine projects. Assume a loss in any year will result in a tax credit.

You have been approached by the president of the company with a request to analyze the project. Calculate the payback period, profitability index, average accounting return, net present value, internal rate of return, and modified internal rate of return for the new strip mine. Should Bethesda Mining take the contract and open the mine?

GOODWEEK TIRES, INC.

After extensive research and development, Goodweek Tires, Inc., has recently developed a new tire, the SuperTread, and must decide whether to make the investment necessary to produce and market it. The tire would be ideal for drivers doing a large amount of wet weather and off-road driving in addition to normal freeway usage. The research and development costs so far have totaled about $10 million. The SuperTread would be put on the market beginning this year, and Goodweek expects it to stay on the market for a total of four years. Test marketing costing $5 million has shown that there is a significant market for a SuperTread–type tire.

As a financial analyst at Goodweek Tires, you have been asked by your CFO, Adam Smith, to evaluate the SuperTread project and provide a recommendation on whether to go ahead with the investment. Except for the initial investment that will occur immediately, assume all cash flows will occur at year-end.

Goodweek must initially invest $120 million in production equipment to make the SuperTread. This equipment can be sold for $51 million at the end of four years. Goodweek intends to sell the SuperTread to two distinct markets:

1. *The Original Equipment Manufacturer (OEM) Market* The OEM market consists primarily of the large automobile companies (e.g., General Motors) who buy tires for new cars. In the OEM market, the SuperTread is expected to sell for $36 per tire. The variable cost to produce each tire is $18.

2. *The Replacement Market* The replacement market consists of all tires purchased after the automobile has left the factory. This market allows higher margins and Goodweek expects to sell the SuperTread for $59 per tire there. Variable costs are the same as in the OEM market.

Goodweek Tires intends to raise prices at 1 percent above the inflation rate; variable costs will also increase 1 percent above the inflation rate. In addition, the SuperTread project will incur $25 million in marketing and general administration costs the first year. This cost is expected to increase at the inflation rate in the subsequent years.

Goodweek's corporate tax rate is 40 percent. Annual inflation is expected to remain constant at 3.25 percent. The company uses a 15.9 percent discount rate to evaluate new product decisions. Automotive industry analysts expect automobile manufacturers to produce 2 million new cars this year and production to grow at 2.5 percent per year thereafter. Each new car needs four tires (the spare tires are undersized and are in a different category). Goodweek Tires expects the SuperTread to capture 11 percent of the OEM market.

Industry analysts estimate that the replacement tire market size will be 14 million tires this year and that it will grow at 2 percent annually. Goodweek expects the SuperTread to capture an 8 percent market share.

The appropriate depreciation schedule for the equipment is the seven-year MACRS depreciation schedule. The immediate initial working capital requirement is $11 million. Thereafter, the net working capital requirements will be 15 percent of sales. What are the NPV, payback period, discounted payback period, AAR, IRR, and PI on this project?

CHAPTER

9

Risk Analysis, Real Options, and Capital Budgeting

OPENING CASE

In 1836, defenders of the Alamo in San Antonio, Texas, held out for 13 days against great odds, and "Remember the Alamo!" became a part of U.S. history. In contrast, Disney's 2004 movie *The Alamo,* starring Billy Bob Thornton as Davy Crockett, barely lasted a weekend at the box office, and the last thing Disney's management wants to do is remember that particular bomb. Disney spent close to $100 million making the movie, plus millions more for marketing and distribution, but the film pulled in only about $22.5 million. In fact, about four of ten movies lose money at the box office, though DVD sales often help the final tally. Of course, there are movies that do quite well. Also in 2004, the DreamWorks movie *Shrek 2* pulled in about $436 million at the box office at a production cost of $75 million.

Obviously, Disney didn't *plan* to lose $80 or so million on *The Alamo,* but it happened. As the short life and quick death of *The Alamo* shows, projects don't always go as companies think they will. This chapter explores how this can happen, and what companies can do to analyze and possibly avoid these situations.

9.1 DECISION TREES

There is usually a sequence of decisions in NPV project analysis. This section introduces the device of **decision trees** for identifying these sequential decisions.

Imagine you are the treasurer of the Solar Electronics Corporation (SEC), and the engineering group has recently developed the technology for solar-powered jet engines. The jet engine is to be used with 150-passenger commercial airplanes. The marketing staff has proposed that SEC develop some prototypes and conduct test marketing of the engine. A corporate planning group, including representatives from production, marketing, and engineering, estimates that this preliminary phase will take a year and will cost $100 million. Furthermore, the group believes there is a 75 percent chance that the marketing tests will prove successful.

If the initial marketing tests are *successful,* SEC can go ahead with full-scale production. This investment phase will cost $1,500 million. Production and sales will occur over the next five years. The preliminary cash flow projection appears in Table 9.1. Should SEC go ahead with investment and production on the jet engine, the NPV at a discount rate of 15 percent (in millions) is:

$$\begin{aligned} \textbf{NPV} &= -\$1{,}500 + \sum_{T=1}^{5} \frac{\$900}{(1.15)^T} \\ &= -\$1{,}500 + \$900 \times A_{.15}^{5} \\ &= \$1{,}517 \end{aligned}$$

Note that the NPV is calculated as of date 1, the date at which the investment of $1,500 million is made. Later, we bring this number back to date 0.

If the initial marketing tests are *unsuccessful,* SEC's $1,500 million investment has an NPV of −$3,611 million. This figure is also calculated as of date 1. (To save space, we will not provide the raw numbers leading to this calculation.)

Figure 9.1 displays the problem concerning the jet engine as a decision tree. If SEC decides to conduct test marketing, there is a 75 percent probability that the test marketing will be successful. If the tests are successful, the firm faces a second decision: whether to invest $1,500 million in a project that yields $1,517 million NPV or to stop. If the tests are unsuccessful, the firm faces a different decision: whether to invest $1,500 million in a project that yields −$3,611 million NPV or to stop.

To review, SEC has the following two decisions to make:

1. Whether to develop and test the solar-powered jet engine.
2. Whether to invest for full-scale production following the results of the test.

TABLE 9.1
Cash Flow Forecasts for Solar Electronics Corporation's Jet Engine Base Case (millions)*

INVESTMENT	YEAR 1	YEARS 2–6
Revenues		$6,000
Variable costs		− 3,000
Fixed costs		− 1,791
Depreciation		− 300
Pretax profit		$ 909
Tax (t_c = .34)		− 309
Net profit		$ 600
Cash flow		$ 900
Initial investment costs	−$1,500	

*Assumptions: (1) Investment is depreciated in years 2 through 6 using the straight-line method; (2) tax rate is 34 percent; (3) the company receives no tax benefits on initial development costs.

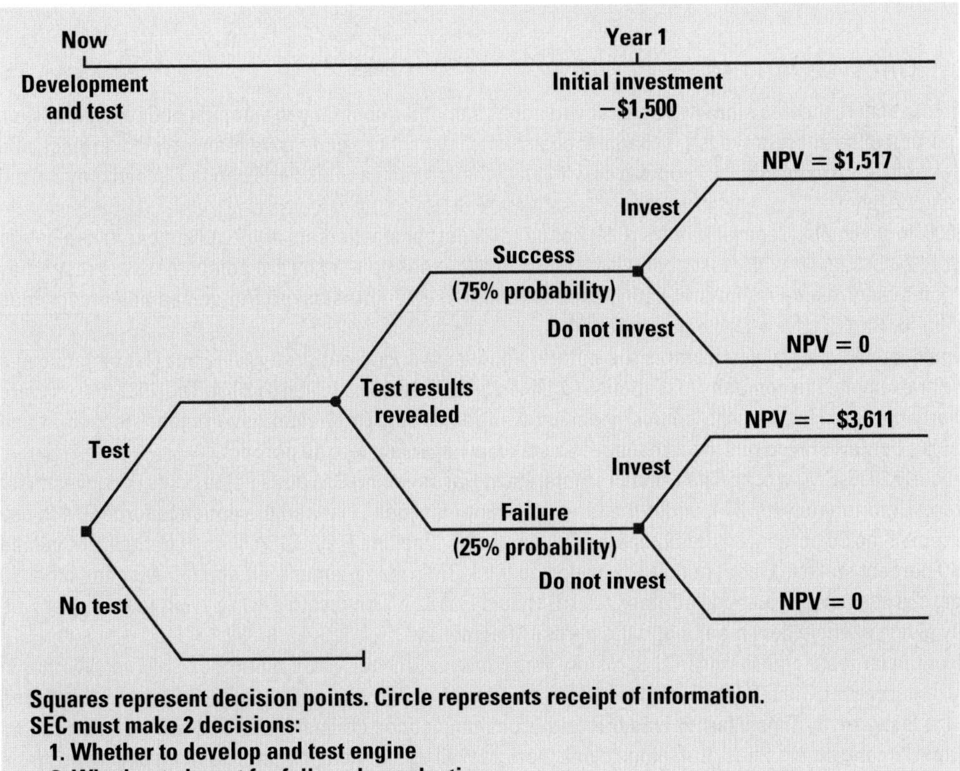

FIGURE 9.1

Decision Tree ($ millions) for SEC

One makes decisions in reverse order with decision trees. Thus we analyze the second-stage investment of $1,500 million first. If the tests are successful should SEC make the second-stage investment? The answer is obviously yes, since $1,517 million is greater than zero. If the tests are unsuccessful, should the second-stage investment be made? Just as obviously, the answer is no, since −$3,611 million is below zero.

Now we move back to the first stage, where the decision boils down to the question: Should SEC invest $100 million now to obtain a 75 percent chance of $1,517 million one year later? The expected payoff evaluated at date 1 (in millions) is:

$$\begin{aligned}\text{Expected payoff} &= \left(\begin{array}{c}\text{Probability}\\\text{of}\\\text{success}\end{array} \times \begin{array}{c}\text{Payoff}\\\text{if}\\\text{successful}\end{array}\right) + \left(\begin{array}{c}\text{Probability}\\\text{of}\\\text{failure}\end{array} \times \begin{array}{c}\text{Payoff}\\\text{if}\\\text{failure}\end{array}\right)\\ &= (.75 \times \$1{,}517) + (.25 \times \$0)\\ &= \$1{,}138\end{aligned}$$

The NPV of testing computed at date 0 (in millions) is:

$$\begin{aligned}\text{NPV} &= -\$100 + \frac{\$1{,}138}{1.15}\\ &= \$890\end{aligned}$$

Since the NPV is a positive number, the firm should test the market for solar-powered jet engines.

WARNING We have used a discount rate of 15 percent for both the testing and the investment decisions. Perhaps a higher discount rate should have been used for the initial test-marketing decision, which is likely to be riskier than the investment decision.

THE REAL WORLD

WHEN THINGS GO WRONG . . .

If you think about it, the decision by a company to acquire another company is a capital budgeting decision. One important difference, however, is that an acquisition may be more expensive than a typical project, and possibly much more expensive. Of course, as with any other project, acquisitions can fail. When they do, the losses can be huge.

In 2000, for example, General Motors (GM) acquired 20 percent ownership of the Italian carmaker Fiat for a price of $2.4 billion. As with most acquisitions, the initial outlook painted by the companies was rosy. They formed joint ventures in Europe and Latin America, and these ventures saved the companies a combined $2.6 billion for the first five years of the agreement.

It would seem with savings like this the partnership was working out pretty well, but Fiat began losing money. For example, the company lost about $1.7 billion in 2002 and $1.3 billion in 2004. The 2002 losses were particularly hard on Fiat, and the company almost went bankrupt. The Italian government stepped in and helped Fiat, but GM stayed out. As a result, GM's stake in Fiat was cut to 10 percent.

In early 2005, GM wrote off its remaining interest in Fiat, meaning GM put a value on its Fiat investment of zero. Unfortunately for GM, under the terms of the original deal, Fiat had the option to force GM to buy the remaining 90 percent of the company. The deal would include Fiat's $10 billion in debt. If GM valued its 10 percent stake in Fiat at nothing, how do you think GM's management felt about buying the other 90 percent? The answer came in February 2005. GM paid Fiat $2 billion just to *avoid* having to take over Fiat, thereby giving a whole new meaning to the phrase "fiat money."

One of the largest acquisitions in U.S. history was America Online's (AOL's) purchase of Time Warner in 2001. AOL purchased Time Warner under the assumption that AOL was part of the "new economy" and primed for fast growth. Time Warner was the "old" communications company, owning cable stations and a music label, among other things. But things didn't work as well as planned. Infighting among employees from the two companies hurt production and morale. In 2002, accounting irregularities were uncovered at AOL, and, as a result of the acquisition costs, the company was straddled with massive debt. To make matters worse, AOL began to lose customers and money. Although AOL was the acquirer, and once dominant partner, things got so bad at AOL that the company changed its name back to Time Warner. To cap things off, in 2002, Time Warner wrote off a stunning $54 billion in assets associated with the acquisition, which was, at the time, the largest such write-off in history.

9.2 SENSITIVITY ANALYSIS, SCENARIO ANALYSIS, AND BREAK-EVEN ANALYSIS

One thrust of this book is that NPV analysis is a superior capital budgeting technique. In fact, because the NPV approach uses cash flows rather than profits, uses all the cash flows, and discounts the cash flows properly, it is hard to find any theoretical fault with it. However, in our conversations with practical businesspeople, we hear the phrase "a false sense of security" frequently. These people point out that the documentation for capital budgeting proposals is often quite impressive. Cash flows are projected down to the last thousand dollars (or even the last dollar) for each year (or even each month). Opportunity costs and side effects are handled quite properly. Sunk costs are ignored—also quite properly. When a high net present value appears at the bottom, one's temptation is to say yes immediately. Nevertheless, the projected cash flow often goes unmet in practice, and the firm ends up with a money loser. A nearby *The Real World* box discusses some recent cases of plans gone awry.

Sensitivity Analysis and Scenario Analysis

How can the firm get the net present value technique to live up to its potential? One approach is **sensitivity analysis** (a.k.a. *what-if analysis* and *bop* analysis[1]), which examines how sensitive a particular NPV calculation is to changes in underlying assumptions. We illustrate the technique with Solar Electronics's solar-powered jet engine from the previous section. As pointed out earlier, the cash flow forecasts for this project appear in Table 9.1. We begin by considering the assumptions underlying revenues, costs, and aftertax cash flows shown in the table.

REVENUES Sales projections for the proposed jet engine have been estimated by the marketing department as:

$$\begin{array}{ccccc}
\textbf{Number of jet engines sold} & = & \textbf{Market share} & \times & \textbf{Size of jet engine market} \\
3{,}000 & = & .30 & \times & 10{,}000 \\
\textbf{Sales revenues} & = & \textbf{Number of jet engines sold} & \times & \textbf{Price per engine} \\
\$6{,}000 \text{ million} & = & 3{,}000 & \times & \$2 \text{ million}
\end{array}$$

Thus, it turns out that the revenue estimates depend on three assumptions.

1. Market share.
2. Size of jet engine market.
3. Price per engine.

COSTS Financial analysts frequently divide costs into two types: variable costs and fixed costs. **Variable costs** change as the output changes, and they are zero when production is zero. Costs of direct labor and raw materials are usually variable. It is common to assume that a variable cost is constant per unit of output, implying that total variable costs are proportional to the level of production. For example, if direct labor is variable and one unit of final output requires $10 of direct labor, then 100 units of final output should require $1,000 of direct labor.

Fixed costs are not dependent on the amount of goods or services produced during the period. Fixed costs are usually measured as costs per unit of time, such as rent per month or salaries per year. Naturally, fixed costs are not fixed forever. They are only fixed over a predetermined time period.

The engineering department has estimated variable costs to be $1 million per engine. Fixed costs are $1,791 million per year. The cost breakdowns are:

$$\begin{array}{ccccc}
\textbf{Variable cost} & = & \textbf{Variable cost per unit} & \times & \textbf{Number of jet engines sold} \\
\$3{,}000 \text{ million} & = & \$1 \text{ million} & \times & 3{,}000 \\
\textbf{Total cost before taxes} & = & \textbf{Variable cost} & + & \textbf{Fixed cost} \\
\$4{,}791 \text{ million} & = & \$3{,}000 \text{ million} & + & \$1{,}791 \text{ million}
\end{array}$$

The above estimates for market size, market share, price, variable cost, and fixed cost, as well as the estimate of initial investment, are presented in the middle column of Table 9.2. These figures represent the firm's expectations or best estimates of the different parameters. For purposes of comparison, the firm's analysts prepared both optimistic and pessimistic forecasts for the different variables. These are also provided in the table.

[1]Bop stands for best, optimistic, pessimistic.

TABLE 9.2
Different Estimates for Solar Electronics's Solar Jet Engine

VARIABLE	PESSIMISTIC	EXPECTED OR BEST	OPTIMISTIC
Market size (per year)	5,000	10,000	20,000
Market share	20%	30%	50%
Price	$1.9 million	$2 million	$2.2 million
Variable cost (per engine)	$1.2 million	$1 million	$0.8 million
Fixed cost (per year)	$1,891 million	$1,791 million	$1,741 million
Investment	$1,900 million	$1,500 million	$1,000 million

TABLE 9.3
NPV Calculations as of Date 1 (in $ millions) for the Solar Jet Engine Using Sensitivity Analysis

	PESSIMISTIC	EXPECTED OR BEST	OPTIMISTIC
Market size	−$1,802*	$1,517	$8,154
Market share	− 696*	1,517	5,942
Price	853	1,517	2,844
Variable cost	189	1,517	2,844
Fixed cost	1,295	1,517	1,628
Investment	1,208	1,517	1,903

Under sensitivity analysis, one input is varied while all other inputs are assumed to meet expectation. For example, an NPV of −$1,802 occurs when the pessimistic forecast of 5,000 is used for market size. However, the expected forecasts from Table 9.2 are used for all other variables when −$1,802 is generated.

*We assume that the other divisions of the firm are profitable, implying that a loss on this project can offset income elsewhere in the firm, thereby reducing the overall taxes of the firm.

Standard sensitivity analysis calls for an NPV calculation for all three possibilities of a single variable, along with the expected forecast for all other variables. This procedure is illustrated in Table 9.3. For example, consider the NPV calculation of $8,154 million provided in the upper right-hand corner of this table. This occurs when the optimistic forecast of 20,000 units per year is used for market size. However, the expected forecasts from Table 9.2 are employed for all other variables when the $8,154 million figure is generated. Note that the same number of $1,517 million appears in each row of the middle column of Table 9.3. This occurs because the expected forecast is used for the variable that was singled out, as well as for all other variables.

Table 9.3 can be used for a number of purposes. First, taken as a whole, the table can indicate whether NPV analysis should be trusted. In other words, it reduces the false sense of security we spoke of earlier. Suppose that NPV is positive when the expected forecast for each variable is used. However, further suppose that every number in the pessimistic column is highly negative and every number in the optimistic column is highly positive. Even a single error in this forecast greatly alters the estimate, making one leery of the net present value approach. A conservative manager might well scrap the entire NPV analysis in this situation. Fortunately, this does not seem to be the case in Table 9.3, because all but two of the numbers are positive. Managers viewing the table will likely consider NPV analysis to be useful for the solar-powered jet engine.

Second, sensitivity analysis shows where more information is needed. For example, an error in the estimate of investment appears to be relatively unimportant because, even under the pessimistic scenario, the NPV of $1,208 million is still highly positive. By contrast, the pessimistic forecast for market share leads to a negative NPV of −$696 million, and a pessimistic forecast for market size leads to a substantially negative NPV of −$1,802 million. Since the effect of incorrect estimates on revenues is so much greater than the effect of incorrect estimates on costs, more information on the factors determining revenues might be needed.

	YEAR 1	YEARS 2–6
Revenues		$2,800
Variable costs		− 1,400
Fixed costs		− 1,791
Depreciation		− 300
Pretax profit		−$ 691
Tax (t_c = .34)†		− 235
Net profit		−$ 456
Cash flow		− 156
Initial investment cost	−$1,500	

TABLE 9.4

Cash Flow Forecast (in $ millions) under the Scenario of a Plane Crash*

*Assumptions are

Market size 7,000 (70 percent of expectation)
Market share 20% (2/3 of expectation)

Forecasts for all other variables are the expected forecasts as given in Table 9.2.

†Tax loss offsets income elsewhere in firm.

Because of these advantages, sensitivity analysis is widely used in practice. Graham and Harvey[2] report that slightly over 50 percent of the 392 firms in their sample subject their capital budgeting calculations to sensitivity analysis. This number is particularly large when one considers that only about 75 percent of the firms in their sample use NPV analysis.

Unfortunately, sensitivity analysis also suffers from some drawbacks. For example, sensitivity analysis may unwittingly *increase* the false sense of security among managers. Suppose all pessimistic forecasts yield positive NPVs. A manager might feel that there is no way the project can lose money. Of course, the forecasters may simply have an optimistic view of a pessimistic forecast. To combat this, some companies do not treat optimistic and pessimistic forecasts subjectively. Rather, their pessimistic forecasts are always, say, 20 percent less than expected. Unfortunately, the cure in this case may be worse than the disease, because a deviation of a fixed percentage ignores the fact that some variables are easier to forecast than others.

In addition, sensitivity analysis treats each variable in isolation when, in reality, the different variables are likely to be related. For example, if ineffective management allows costs to get out of control, it is likely that variable costs, fixed costs, and investment will all rise above expectation at the same time. If the market is not receptive to a solar plane, both market share and price should decline together.

Managers frequently perform **scenario analysis**, a variant of sensitivity analysis, to minimize this problem. Simply put, this approach examines a number of different likely scenarios, where each scenario involves a confluence of factors. As a simple example, consider the effect of a few airline crashes. These crashes are likely to reduce flying in total, thereby limiting the demand for any new engines. Furthermore, even if the crashes did not involve solar-powered aircraft, the public could become more averse to any innovative and controversial technologies. Hence, SEC's market share might fall as well. Perhaps the cash flow calculations would look like those in Table 9.4 under the scenario of a plane crash. Given the calculations in the table, the NPV (in millions) would be:

$$-\$2{,}023 = -\$1{,}500 - \$156 \times A^{5}_{.15}$$

A series of scenarios like this might illuminate issues concerning the project better than the standard application of sensitivity analysis would.

[2]See Figure 2 of John Graham and Campbell Harvey, "The Theory and Practice of Corporate Finance: Evidence from the Field," *Journal of Financial Economics* (May/June 2001).

FIGURE 9.2

Break-Even Point Using Accounting Numbers

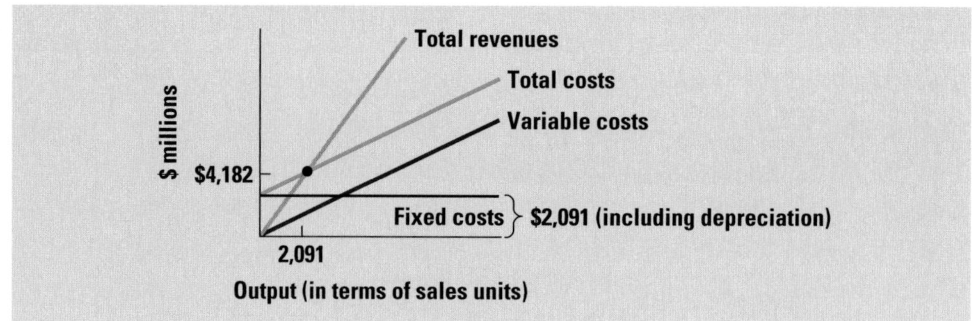

TABLE 9.5

Revenues and Costs of Project under Different Sales Assumptions (in $ millions, except unit sales)

Year 1	Years 2–6								NPV (EVALUATED DATE 1)
INITIAL INVEST-MENT	ANNUAL UNIT SALES	REVENUES	VARIABLE COSTS	FIXED COSTS	DEPRECI-ATION	TAXES* (t_c = .34)	NET PROFIT	OPERATING CASH FLOWS	
$1,500	0	$ 0	$ 0	−$1,791	−$300	$ 711	−$1,380	−$1,080	−$5,120
1,500	1,000	2,000	− 1,000	− 1,791	− 300	371	− 720	− 420	− 2,908
1,500	3,000	6,000	− 3,000	− 1,791	− 300	− 309	600	900	1,517
1,500	10,000	20,000	− 10,000	− 1,791	− 300	− 2,689	5,220	5,520	17,004

*Loss is incurred in the first two rows. For tax purposes, this loss offsets income elsewhere in the firm.

Break-Even Analysis

Our discussion of sensitivity analysis and scenario analysis suggests that there are many ways to examine variability in forecasts. We now present another approach, **break-even analysis**. As its name implies, this approach determines the sales needed to break even. The approach is a useful complement to sensitivity analysis, because it also sheds light on the severity of incorrect forecasts. We calculate the break-even point in terms of both accounting profit and present value.

ACCOUNTING PROFIT Net profit under four different sales forecasts is:

UNIT SALES	NET PROFIT ($ MILLIONS)
0	−$1,380
1,000	− 720
3,000	600
10,000	5,220

A more complete presentation of costs and revenues appears in Table 9.5.

We plot the revenues, costs, and profits under the different assumptions about sales in Figure 9.2. The revenue and cost curves cross at 2,091 jet engines. This is the break-even point, i.e., the point where the project generates no profits or losses. As long as sales are above 2,091 jet engines, the project will make a profit.

This break-even point can be calculated very easily. Because the sales price is $2 million per engine and the variable cost is $1 million per engine,[3] the aftertax difference per

[3]Though the previous section considered both optimistic and pessimistic forecasts for sales price and variable cost, break-even analysis uses just the expected or best estimates of these variables.

engine is:

$$(\text{Sales price} - \text{Variable cost}) \times (1 - t_c) = (\$2 \text{ million} - \$1 \text{ million}) \times (1 - .34) = \$.66 \text{ million}$$

where t_c is the corporate tax rate of 34 percent. This aftertax difference is called the **contribution margin** because each additional engine contributes this amount to aftertax profit.

Fixed costs are \$1,791 million and depreciation is \$300 million, implying that the aftertax sum of these costs is:

$$(\text{Fixed costs} + \text{Depreciation}) \times (1 - t_c) = (\$1{,}791 \text{ million} + \$300 \text{ million}) \times (1 - .34) = \$1{,}380 \text{ million}$$

That is, the firm incurs costs of \$1,380 million, regardless of the number of sales. Because each engine contributes \$.66 million, sales must reach the following level to offset the above costs:

Accounting Profit Break-Even Point:

$$\frac{(\text{Fixed costs} + \text{Depreciation}) \times (1 - t_c)}{(\text{Sales price} - \text{Variable costs}) \times (1 - t_c)} = \frac{\$1{,}380 \text{ million}}{\$.66 \text{ million}} = 2{,}091$$

Thus, 2,091 engines is the break-even point required for an accounting profit.

PRESENT VALUE As we stated many times in the text, we are more interested in present value than we are in net profits. Therefore, we must calculate the present value of the cash flows. Given a discount rate of 15 percent, we have:

UNIT SALES	NPV ($ MILLIONS)
0	−\$ 5,120
1,000	− 2,908
3,000	1,517
10,000	17,004

These NPV calculations are reproduced from the last column of Table 9.5. We can see that the NPV is negative if SEC produces 1,000 jet engines and positive if it produces 3,000 jet engines. Obviously, the zero NPV point occurs between 1,000 and 3,000 jet engines.

The present value break-even point can be calculated very easily. The firm originally invested \$1,500 million. This initial investment can be expressed as a five-year equivalent annual cost (EAC), determined by dividing the initial investment by the appropriate five-year annuity factor:

$$\text{EAC} = \frac{\text{Initial investment}}{\text{5-year annuity factor at 15\%}} = \frac{\text{Initial investment}}{A^5_{.15}}$$
$$= \frac{\$1{,}500 \text{ million}}{3.3522} = \$447.5 \text{ million}$$

Note that the EAC of \$447.5 million is greater than the yearly depreciation of \$300 million. This must occur since the calculation of EAC implicitly assumes that the \$1,500 million investment could have been invested at 15 percent.

Aftertax costs, regardless of output, can be viewed as:

$$\underset{\text{million}}{\$1{,}528} = \underset{\text{million}}{\$447.5} + \underset{\text{million}}{\$1{,}791} \times .66 - \underset{\text{million}}{\$300} \times .34$$
$$= \text{EAC} + \underset{\text{costs}}{\text{Fixed}} \times (1 - t_c) - \text{Depreciation} \times t_c$$

That is, in addition to the initial investment's equivalent annual cost of $447.5 million, the firm pays fixed costs each year and receives a depreciation tax shield each year. The depreciation tax shield is written as a negative number since it offsets the costs in the equation. Because each plane contributes $.66 million to aftertax profit, it will take the following sales to offset the above costs:

Present Value Break-Even Point:

$$\frac{\textbf{EAC + Fixed costs} \times (1 - t_c) - \textbf{Depreciation} \times t_c}{(\textbf{Sales price} - \textbf{Variable costs}) \times (1 - t_c)} = \frac{\$1{,}528 \textbf{ million}}{\$.66 \textbf{ million}} = 2{,}315$$

Thus, 2,315 planes is the break-even point from the perspective of present value.

Why is the accounting break-even point different from the financial break-even point? When we use accounting profit as the basis for the break-even calculation, we subtract depreciation. Depreciation for the solar jet engines project is $300 million. If 2,091 solar jet engines are sold, SEC will generate sufficient revenues to cover the $300 million depreciation expense plus other costs. Unfortunately, at this level of sales SEC will not cover the economic opportunity costs of the $1,500 million laid out for the investment. If we take into account that the $1,500 million could have been invested at 15 percent, the true annual cost of the investment is $447.5 million and not $300 million. Depreciation understates the true costs of recovering the initial investment. Thus, companies that break even on an accounting basis are really losing money. They are losing the opportunity cost of the initial investment.

9.3 MONTE CARLO SIMULATION

Both sensitivity analysis and scenario analysis attempt to answer the question, "What if?" However, while both analyses are frequently used in the real world, each has its own limitations. Sensitivity analysis allows only one variable to change at a time. By contrast, many variables are likely to move at the same time in the real world. Scenario analysis follows specific scenarios, such as changes in inflation, government regulation, or the number of competitors. While this methodology is often quite helpful, it cannot cover all sources of variability. In fact, projects are likely to exhibit a lot of variability under just one economic scenario.

> For a free demonstration of a spreadsheet application of Monte Carlo analysis, go to www.crystalball.com.

Monte Carlo simulation is a further attempt to model real world uncertainty. This approach takes its name from the famous European casino, because it analyzes projects the way one might analyze gambling strategies. Imagine a serious blackjack player who wonders if he should take a third card whenever his first two cards total 16. Most likely, a formal mathematical model would be too complex to be practical here. However, he could play thousands of hands in a casino, sometimes drawing a third card when his first two cards add to 16 and sometimes not drawing that third card. He could compare his winnings (or losings) under the two strategies in order to determine which was better. Of course, since he would probably lose a lot of money performing this test in a real casino, simulating the results from the two strategies on a computer might be cheaper. Monte Carlo simulation of capital budgeting projects is in this spirit.

Imagine that Backyard Barbeques, Inc. (BBI), a manufacturer of both charcoal and gas grills, has the blueprint for a new grill that cooks with compressed hydrogen. The CFO, Edward H. Comiskey, being dissatisfied with simpler capital budgeting techniques, wants a Monte Carlo simulation for this new grill. A consultant specializing in the Monte Carlo approach, Les Mauney, takes him through the five basic steps of the method.

STEP 1: SPECIFY THE BASIC MODEL Les Mauney breaks up cash flow into three components: annual revenue, annual costs, and initial investment. The revenue in any year is viewed as:

$$\text{Number of grills sold by entire industry} \times \text{Market share of BBI's hydrogen grill (in percent)} \times \text{Price per hydrogen grill}$$

The cost in any year is viewed as:

Fixed manufacturing costs + Variable manufacturing costs + Marketing costs + Selling costs

Initial investment is viewed as:

Cost of patent + Test-marketing costs + Cost of production facility

STEP 2: SPECIFY A DISTRIBUTION FOR EACH VARIABLE IN THE MODEL Here comes the hard part. Let's start with revenue, which has three components in the equation above. The consultant first models overall market size, that is, the number of grills sold by the entire industry. The trade publication, *Outdoor Food (OF),* reported that 10 million grills of all types were sold in the continental United States last year and it forecasts sales of 10.5 million next year. Mr. Mauney, using *OF*'s forecast and his own intuition, creates the following distribution for next year's sales of grills by the entire industry:

PROBABILITY	20%	60%	20%
NEXT YEAR'S INDUSTRYWIDE UNIT SALES	10 million	10.5 million	11 million

The tight distribution here reflects the slow but steady historical growth in the grill market.

Les Mauney realizes that estimating the market share of BBI's hydrogen grill is more difficult. Nevertheless, after a great deal of analysis, he determines the distribution of next year's market share to be:

PROBABILITY	10%	20%	30%	25%	10%	5%
MARKET SHARE OF BBI'S HYDROGEN GRILL NEXT YEAR	1%	2%	3%	4%	5%	8%

While the consultant assumed a symmetrical distribution for industrywide unit sales, he believes a skewed distribution makes more sense for the project's market share. In his mind, there is always the small possibility that sales of the hydrogen grill will really take off.

The above forecasts assume that unit sales for the overall industry are unrelated to the project's market share. In other words, the two variables are *independent* of each other. Mr. Mauney reasons that, while an economic boom might increase industrywide grill sales and a recession might decrease them, the project's market share is unlikely to be related to economic conditions.

Now Mr. Mauney must determine the distribution of price per grill. Mr. Comiskey, the CFO, informs him that the price will be in the area of $200 per grill, given what other competitors are charging. However, the consultant believes that the price per hydrogen grill will almost certainly depend on the size of the overall market for grills. As in any business, you can usually charge more if demand is high.

After rejecting a number of complex models for price, Mr. Mauney settles on the following specification:

$$\text{Next year's price per hydrogen grill} = \$190 + \$1 \times \text{Industrywide unit sales (in millions)} +/- \$3$$

The grill price in the above equation is dependent on the unit sales of the industry. In addition, random variation is modeled via the term "+/− $3," where a drawing of +$3 and a drawing of −$3 each occur 50 percent of the time. For example, if industrywide unit sales are 11 million, the price per share would be either:

$190 + $11 + $3 = $203 (50% probability)
$190 + $11 − $3 = $197 (50% probability)

The consultant now has distributions for each of the three components of next year's revenue. However, he needs distributions for future years as well. Using forecasts from *Outdoor Food* and other publications, Mr. Mauney forecasts the distribution of growth rates for the entire industry over the second year to be:

PROBABILITY	20%	60%	20%
GROWTH RATE OF INDUSTRYWIDE UNIT SALES IN SECOND YEAR	1%	3%	5%

Given both the distribution of next year's industrywide unit sales and the distribution of growth rates for this variable over the second year, we can generate the distribution of industrywide unit sales for the second year. A similar extension should give Mr. Mauney a distribution for later years as well, though we won't go into the details here. And, just as the consultant extended the first component of revenue (industrywide unit sales) to later years, he would want to do the same thing for market share and unit price.

The above discussion shows how the three components of revenue can be modeled. Step 2 would be complete once the components of cost and of investment are modeled in a similar way. Special attention must be paid to the interactions between variables here, since ineffective management will likely allow the different cost components to rise together. However, since you are probably getting the idea now, we will skip the rest of this step.

STEP 3: THE COMPUTER DRAWS ONE OUTCOME As we said above, next year's revenue in our model is the product of three components. Imagine that the computer randomly picks industrywide unit sales of 10 million, a market share for BBI's hydrogen grill of 2 percent and a +$3 random price variation. Given these drawings, next year's price per hydrogen grill will be:

$190 + $10 + $3 = $203

and next year's revenue for BBI's hydrogen grill will be:

10 million × .02 × $203 = $40.6 million

Of course, we are not done with the entire outcome yet. We would have to perform drawings for revenue in each future year. In addition, we would perform drawings for costs in each future year. Finally, a drawing for initial investment would have to be made as well. In this way, a single outcome would generate a cash flow from the project in each future year.

How likely is it that the specific outcome above would be drawn? We can answer this because we know the probability of each component. Since industry sales of $10 million has a 20 percent probability, a market share of 2 percent also has a 20 percent probability, and a random price variation of +$3 has a 50 percent probability, the probability of these three drawings together in the same outcome is:

.02 = .20 × .20 × .50

Of course, the probability would get even smaller once drawings for future revenues, future costs, and the initial investment are included in the outcome.

This step generates the cash flow for each year from a single outcome. What we are ultimately interested in is the *distribution* of cash flow each year across many outcomes.

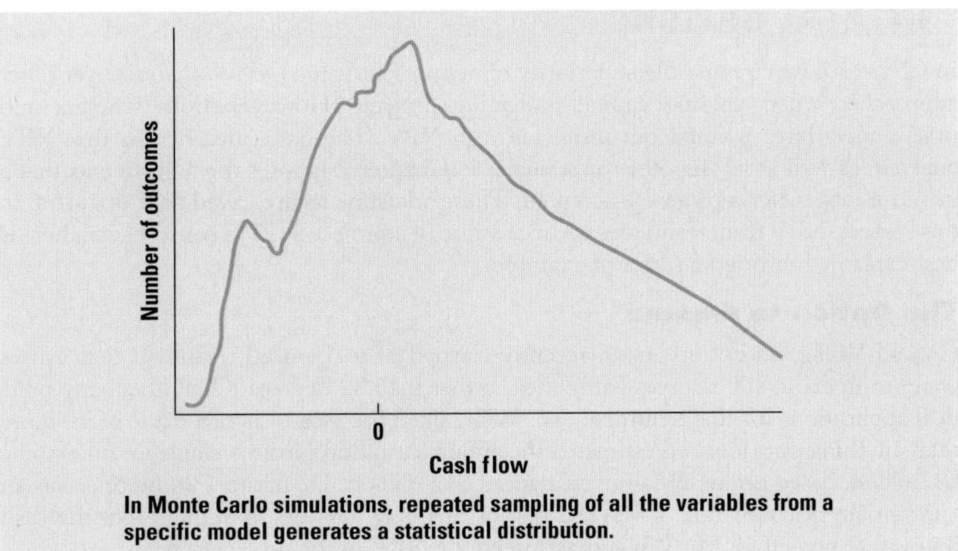

FIGURE 9.3

Simulated Distribution of the Third Year's Cash Flow for BBI's New Hydrogen Grill

We ask the computer to randomly draw over and over again to give us this distribution, which is just what is done in the next step.

STEP 4: REPEAT THE PROCEDURE While the above three steps generate one outcome, the essence of Monte Carlo simulation is repeated outcomes. Depending on the situation, the computer may be called on to generate thousands or even millions of outcomes. The result of all these drawings is a distribution of cash flow for each future year. This distribution is the basic output of Monte Carlo simulation.

Consider Figure 9.3. Here, repeated drawings have produced the simulated distribution of the third year's cash flow. There would be, of course, a distribution like the one in this figure for each future year. This leaves us with just one more step.

STEP 5: CALCULATE NPV Given the distribution of cash flow for the third year in Figure 9.3, one can determine the expected cash flow for this year. In a similar manner, one can also determine the expected cash flow for each future year and can then calculate the net present value of the project by discounting these expected cash flows at an appropriate rate.

Monte Carlo simulation is often viewed as a step beyond either sensitivity analysis or scenario analysis. Interactions between the variables are explicitly specified in Monte Carlo so, at least in theory, this methodology provides a more complete analysis. And, as a by-product, having to build a precise model deepens the forecaster's understanding of the project.

Since Monte Carlo simulations have been around for at least 35 years, you might think that most firms would be performing them by now. Surprisingly, this does not seem to be the case. In our experience, executives are frequently skeptical of all the complexity. It is difficult to model either the distributions of each variable or the interactions between variables. In addition, the computer output is often devoid of economic intuition. Thus, while Monte Carlo simulations are used in certain real world situations, the approach is not likely to be "the wave of the future." In fact, Graham and Harvey[4] report that only about 15 percent of the firms in their sample use capital budgeting simulations.

[4]See Figure 2 of Graham and Harvey, *op. cit.*

9.4 REAL OPTIONS

In Chapter 7, we stressed the superiority of net present value (NPV) analysis over other approaches when valuing capital budgeting projects. However, both scholars and practitioners have pointed out problems with NPV. The basic idea here is that NPV analysis, as well as all the other approaches in Chapter 7, ignores the adjustments that a firm can make after a project is accepted. These adjustments are called **real options**. In this respect, NPV underestimates the true value of a project. NPV's conservatism here is best explained through a series of examples.

The Option to Expand

Conrad Willig, an entrepreneur, recently learned of a chemical treatment that causes water to freeze at 100 degrees Fahrenheit, rather than 32 degrees. Of all the many practical applications for this treatment, Mr. Willig liked the idea of hotels made of ice more than anything else. Conrad estimated the annual cash flows from a single ice hotel to be \$2 million, based on an initial investment of \$12 million. He felt that 20 percent was an appropriate discount rate, given the risk of this new venture. Assuming that the cash flows were perpetual, Mr. Willig determined the NPV of the project to be:

$$-\$12{,}000{,}000 + \$2{,}000{,}000/.20 = -\$2 \text{ million}$$

Most entrepreneurs would have rejected this venture, given its negative NPV. But Conrad was not your typical entrepreneur. He reasoned that NPV analysis missed a hidden source of value. While he was pretty sure that the initial investment would cost \$12 million, there was some uncertainty concerning annual cash flows. His cash flow estimate of \$2 million per year actually reflected his belief that there was a 50 percent probability that annual cash flows would be \$3 million and a 50 percent probability that annual cash flows would be \$1 million.

The NPV calculations for the two forecasts are:

$$\textbf{Optimistic forecast: } -\$12 \text{ million} + \$3 \text{ million}/.20 = \$3 \text{ million}$$
$$\textbf{Pessimistic forecast: } -\$12 \text{ million} + \$1 \text{ million}/.20 = -\$7 \text{ million}$$

On the surface, this new calculation doesn't seem to help Mr. Willig very much since an average of the two forecasts yields an NPV for the project of:

$$.50 \times \$3 \text{ million} + .50 \times (-\$7 \text{ million}) = -\$2 \text{ million}$$

which is just the value he calculated in the first place.

However, if the optimistic forecast turns out to be correct, Mr. Willig would want to *expand*. If he believes that there are, say, 10 locations in the country that can support an ice hotel, the true NPV of the venture would be:

$$.50 \times 10 \times \$3 \text{ million} + .50 \times (-\$7 \text{ million}) = \$11.5 \text{ million}$$

The idea here, which is represented in Figure 9.4, is both basic and universal. The entrepreneur has the option to expand if the pilot location is successful. For example,

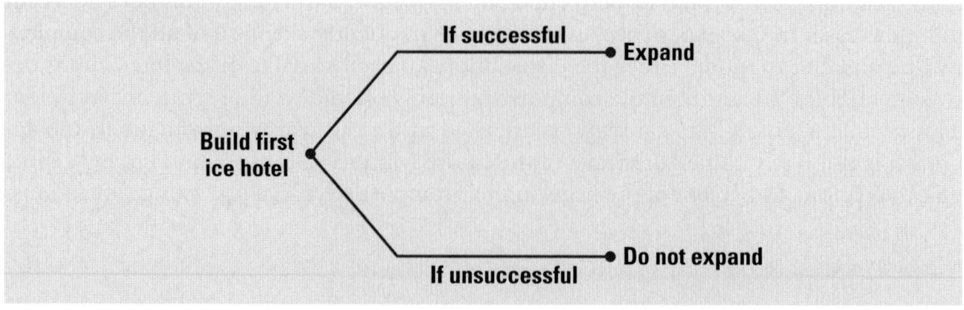

FIGURE 9.4 Decision Tree for Ice Hotel

think of all the people that start restaurants, most of them ultimately failing. These individuals are not necessarily overly optimistic. They may realize the likelihood of failure but go ahead anyway because of the small chance of starting the next McDonald's or Burger King.

The Option to Abandon

Managers also have the option to abandon existing projects. While abandonment may seem cowardly, it can often save companies a great deal of money. Because of this, the option to abandon increases the value of any potential project.

The above example on ice hotels, which illustrated the option to expand, can also illustrate the option to abandon. To see this, imagine that Mr. Willig now believes that there is a 50 percent probability that annual cash flows will be $6 million and a 50 percent probability that annual cash flows will be −$2 million. The NPV calculations under the two forecasts become:

Optimistic forecast: −$12 million + $6 million/.2 = $18 million
Pessimistic forecast: −$12 million − $2 million/.2 = −$22 million

yielding an NPV for the project of:

.50 × $18 million + .50 × (−$22 million) = −$2 million

Furthermore, now imagine that Mr. Willig wants to own, at most, just one ice hotel, implying that there is no option to expand. Since the NPV here is negative, it looks as if he will not build the hotel.

But things change when we consider the abandonment option. As of date 1, the entrepreneur will know which forecast has come true. If cash flows equal those under the optimistic forecast, Conrad will keep the project alive. If, however, cash flows equal those under the pessimistic forecast, he will abandon the hotel. Knowing these possibilities ahead of time, the NPV of the project becomes:

.50 × $18 million + .50 × (−$12 million − $2 million/1.20) = $2.17 million

Since Conrad abandons after experiencing the cash flow of −$2 million at date 1, he does not have to endure this outflow in any of the later years. Because the NPV is now positive, Conrad will accept the project.

The example here is clearly a stylized one. While many years may pass before a project is abandoned in the real world, our ice hotel was abandoned after just one year. And, while salvage values generally accompany abandonment, we assumed no salvage value for the ice hotel. Nevertheless, abandonment options are pervasive in the real world.

For example, consider the moviemaking industry, which we discussed to open the chapter. As shown in Figure 9.5, movies begin with either the purchase or development of a script. A completed script might cost a movie studio a few million dollars and potentially lead to actual production. However, the great majority of scripts (perhaps well in excess of 80 percent) are abandoned. Why would studios abandon scripts that they had commissioned in the first place? While the studios know ahead of time that only a few scripts will be promising, they don't know which ones. Thus, they cast a wide net, commissioning many scripts to get a few good ones. And the studios must be ruthless with the bad scripts, since the expenditure on a script pales in comparison to the huge losses from producing a bad movie.

The few lucky scripts will then move into production, where costs might be budgeted in the tens of millions of dollars, if not much more. At this stage, the dreaded phrase is that on-location production gets "bogged down," creating cost overruns. But the studios are equally ruthless here. Should these overruns become excessive, production is likely to be abandoned in midstream. Interestingly, abandonment almost always occurs due to

FIGURE 9.5

The Abandonment Option in the Movie Industry

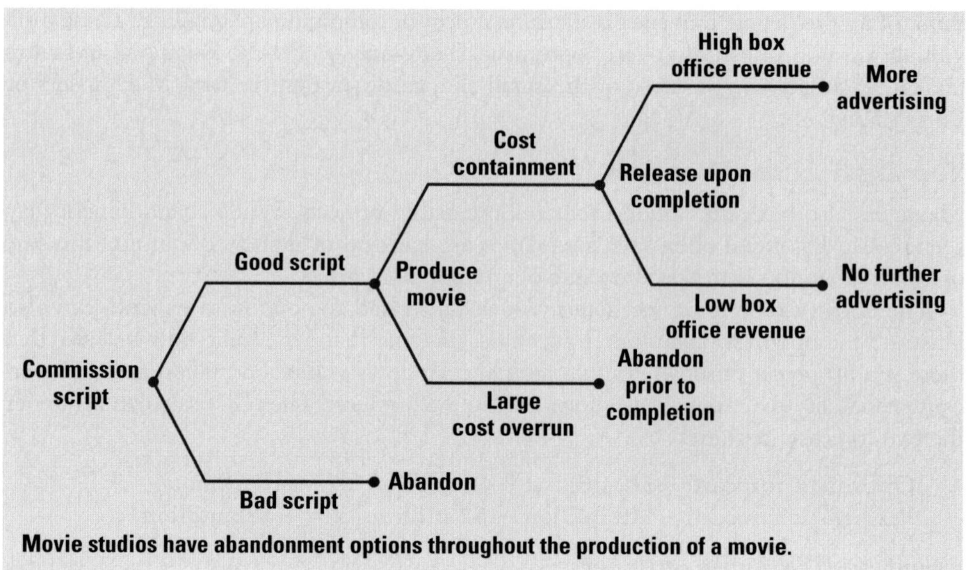

Movie studios have abandonment options throughout the production of a movie.

high costs, not due to the fear that the movie won't be able to find an audience. Little information on that score will be obtained until the movie is actually released.

Release of the movie is accompanied by significant advertising expenditures, perhaps in the range of $10 to $20 million. Box office success in the first few weeks is likely to lead to further advertising expenditures. Again, the studio has the option, but not the obligation, to increase advertising here.

Moviemaking is one of the riskiest businesses around, with studios receiving hundreds of millions of dollars in a matter of weeks from a blockbuster while receiving practically nothing during this period from a flop. The above abandonment options contain costs that might otherwise bankrupt the industry.

To illustrate some of these ideas, consider the case of Euro Disney. The deal to open Euro Disney occurred in 1987, and the park opened its doors outside of Paris in 1992. Disney's management thought Europeans would go goofy over the new park, but trouble soon began. The number of visitors never met expectations, in part because the company priced tickets too high. Disney also decided not to serve alcohol in a country that was accustomed to wine with meals. French labor inspectors fought Disney's strict dress codes, and so on.

After several years of operations, the park began serving wine in its restaurants, lowered ticket prices, and made other adjustments. In other words, management exercised its option to reformulate the product. The park began to make a small profit. Then, the company exercised the option to expand by adding a "second gate," which was another theme park next to Euro Disney named Walt Disney Studios. The second gate was intended to encourage visitors to extend their stays. But the new park flopped. The reasons ranged from high ticket prices, attractions geared toward Hollywood rather than European filmmaking, labor strikes in Paris, and a summer heat wave.

By the summer of 2003, Euro Disney was close to bankruptcy again. Executives discussed a range of options. These options ranged from letting the company go broke (the option to abandon) to pulling the Disney name from the park. In 2005, the company finally agreed to a restructuring with the help of the French government.

The whole idea of managerial options was summed up aptly by Jay Rasulo, the overseer of Disney's theme parks, when he said, "One thing we know for sure is that you never get it 100 percent right the first time. We open every one of our parks with the notion that we're going to add content."

A recent example of a company actually exercising the option to abandon occurred in early 2005 when Sony Corporation announced that it was withdrawing from the handheld computer, or PDA, market in Japan. What was somewhat surprising was that the company was the market leader in sales at the time, with about one-third of the market. However, PDA sales had been shrinking over the past three years, in large part due to increased competition from smart phones, which have PDA capabilities. So Sony concluded that the future market for stand-alone devices was limited and bailed out.

Timing Options

One often finds urban land that has been vacant for many years. Yet this land is bought and sold from time to time. Why would anyone pay a positive price for land that has no source of revenue? Certainly one could not arrive at this positive value through NPV analysis. However, the paradox can easily be explained in terms of real options.

Suppose that the land's highest and best use is as an office building. Total construction costs for the building are estimated to be $1 million. Currently, net rents (after all costs) are estimated to be $90,000 per year in perpetuity and the discount rate is 10 percent. The NPV of this proposed building would be:

$$-\$1 \text{ million} + \$90{,}000/.10 = -\$100{,}000$$

Since this NPV is negative, one would not currently want to build. In addition, it appears as if the land is worthless. However, suppose that the federal government is planning various urban revitalization programs for the city. Office rents will likely increase if the programs succeed. In this case, the property's owner might want to erect the office building after all. Conversely, office rents will remain the same, or even fall, if the programs fail. The owner will not build in this case.

We say that the property owner has a *timing option.* While he does not currently want to build, he will want to build in the future should rents in the area rise substantially. This timing option explains why vacant land often has value. While there are costs, such as taxes, from holding raw land, the value of an office building after a substantial rise in rents may more than offset these holding costs. Of course, the exact value of the vacant land depends on both the probability of success in the revitalization program and the extent of the rent increase. Figure 9.6 illustrates this timing option.

Mining operations almost always provide timing options as well. Suppose you own a copper mine where the cost of mining each ton of copper exceeds the sales revenue. It's a no-brainer to say that you would not want to mine the copper currently. And since there are costs of ownership such as property taxes, insurance, and security, you might

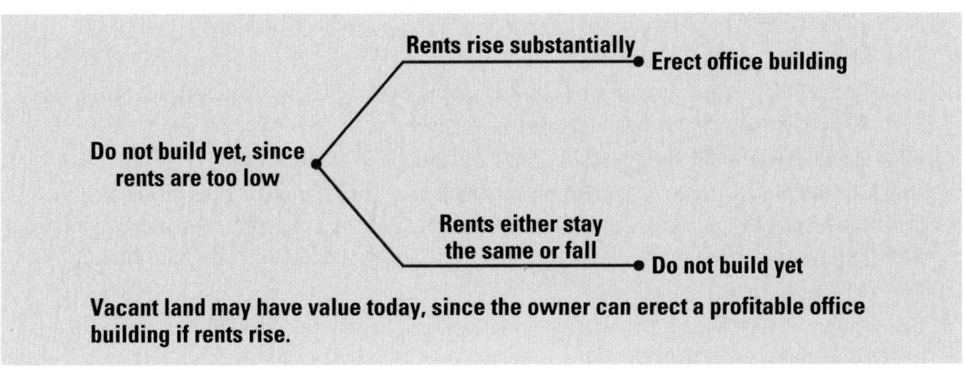

FIGURE 9.6
Decision Tree for Vacant Land

actually want to pay someone to take the mine off your hands. However, we would caution you not to do so hastily. Copper prices in the future might very well increase enough so that production is profitable. Given that possibility, you could likely find someone to pay a positive price for the property today.

SUMMARY AND CONCLUSIONS

This chapter discusses a number of practical applications of capital budgeting.

1. Though NPV is the best capital budgeting approach conceptually, it has been criticized in practice for providing managers with a false sense of security. Sensitivity analysis shows NPV under varying assumptions, giving managers a better feel for the project's risks. Unfortunately, sensitivity analysis modifies only one variable at a time, while many variables are likely to vary together in the real world. Scenario analysis examines a project's performance under different scenarios (e.g., war breaking out or oil prices skyrocketing). Finally, managers want to know how bad forecasts must be before a project loses money. Break-even analysis calculates the sales figure at which the project breaks even. Though break-even analysis is frequently performed on an accounting profit basis, we suggest that a net present value basis is more appropriate.
2. Monte Carlo simulation begins with a model of the firm's cash flows, based on both the interactions between different variables and the movement of each individual variable over time. Random sampling generates a distribution of these cash flows for each period, leading to a net present value calculation.
3. We analyze the hidden options in capital budgeting, such as the option to expand, the option to abandon, and timing options.

CONCEPT QUESTIONS

1. **Forecasting Risk** What is forecasting risk? In general, would the degree of forecasting risk be greater for a new product or a cost-cutting proposal? Why?
2. **Sensitivity Analysis and Scenario Analysis** What is the essential difference between sensitivity analysis and scenario analysis?
3. **Marginal Cash Flows** A co-worker claims that looking at all this marginal this and incremental that is just a bunch of nonsense, and states: "Listen, if our average revenue doesn't exceed our average cost, then we will have a negative cash flow, and we will go broke!" How do you respond?
4. **Break-Even Point** As a shareholder of a firm that is contemplating a new project, would you be more concerned with the accounting break-even point, the cash break-even point (i.e., the point at which operating cash flow is zero), or the financial break-even point? Why?
5. **Break-Even Point** Assume a firm is considering a new project that requires an initial investment and has equal sales and costs over its life. Will the project reach the accounting, cash, or financial break-even point first? Which will it reach next? Last? Will this ordering always apply?
6. **Real Options** Why does traditional NPV analysis tend to underestimate the true value of a capital budgeting project?

7. **Real Options** The Mango Republic has just liberalized its markets and is now permitting foreign investors. Tesla Manufacturing has analyzed starting a project in the country and has determined that the project has a negative NPV. Why might the company go ahead with the project? What type of option is most likely to add value to this project?

8. **Sensitivity Analysis and Breakeven** How does sensitivity analysis interact with break-even analysis?

9. **Option to Wait** An option can often have more than one source of value. Consider a logging company. The company can log the timber today, or wait another year (or more) to log the timber. What advantages would waiting one year potentially have?

10. **Project Analysis** You are discussing a project analysis with a co-worker. The project involves real options, such as expanding the project if successful, or abandoning the project if it fails. Your co-worker makes the following statement: "This analysis is ridiculous. We looked at expanding or abandoning the project in two years, but there are many other options we should consider. For example, we could expand in one year, and expand further in two years. Or we could expand in one year, and abandon the project in two years. There are too many options for us to examine. Because of this, anything this analysis would give us is worthless." How would you evaluate this statement? Considering that with any capital budgeting project there are an infinite number of real options, when do you stop the option analysis on an individual project?

QUESTIONS AND PROBLEMS

Basic
(Questions 1–10)

1. **Sensitivity Analysis and Break-Even Point** We are evaluating a project that costs $896,000, has an eight-year life, and has no salvage value. Assume that depreciation is straight-line to zero over the life of the project. Sales are projected at 100,000 units per year. Price per unit is $38, variable cost per unit is $25, and fixed costs are $900,000 per year. The tax rate is 35 percent, and we require a 15 percent return on this project.

   a. Calculate the accounting break-even point.

   b. Calculate the base-case cash flow and NPV. What is the sensitivity of NPV to changes in the sales figure? Explain what your answer tells you about a 500-unit decrease in projected sales.

   c. What is the sensitivity of OCF to changes in the variable cost figure? Explain what your answer tells you about a $1 decrease in estimated variable costs.

2. **Scenario Analysis** In the previous problem, suppose the projections given for price, quantity, variable costs, and fixed costs are all accurate to within ±10 percent. Calculate the best-case and worst-case NPV figures.

3. **Calculating Breakeven** In each of the following cases, find the unknown variable. Ignore taxes.

ACCOUNTING BREAKEVEN	UNIT PRICE	UNIT VARIABLE COST	FIXED COSTS	DEPRECIATION
130,200	$ 41	$30	$ 820,000	?
135,000	?	56	3,200,000	$1,150,000
5,478	105	?	160,000	105,000

4 **Financial Breakeven** L.J.'s Toys Inc. just purchased a $200,000 machine to produce toy cars. The machine will be fully depreciated by the straight-line method over its five-year economic life. Each toy sells for $25. The variable cost per toy is $5, and the firm incurs fixed costs of

$350,000 each year. The corporate tax rate for the company is 25 percent. The appropriate discount rate is 12 percent. What is the financial break-even point for the project?

5. **Option to Wait** Your company is deciding whether to invest in a new machine. The new machine will increase cash flow by $280,000 per year. You believe the technology used in the machine has a 10-year life; in other words, no matter when you purchase the machine, it will be obsolete 10 years from today. The machine is currently priced at $1,500,000. The cost of the machine will decline by $125,000 per year until it reaches $1,000,000, where it will remain. If your required return is 12 percent, should you purchase the machine? If so, when should you purchase it?

6. **Decision Trees** Ang Electronics, Inc., has developed a new VCR. If the VCR is successful, the present value of the payoff (at the time the product is brought to market) is $20 million. If the VCR fails, the present value of the payoff is $5 million. If the product goes directly to market, there is a 50 percent chance of success. Alternatively, Ang can delay the launch by one year and spend $2 million to test market the VCR. Test marketing would allow the firm to improve the product and increase the probability of success to 75 percent. The appropriate discount rate is 15 percent. Should the firm conduct test marketing?

7. **Decision Trees** The manager for a growing firm is considering the launch of a new product. If the product goes directly to market, there is a 50 percent chance of success. For $120,000, the manager can conduct a focus group that will increase the product's chance of success to 70 percent. Alternatively, the manager has the option to pay a consulting firm $400,000 to research the market and refine the product. The consulting firm successfully launches new products 90 percent of the time. If the firm successfully launches the product, the payoff will be $1.2 million. If the product is a failure, the NPV is $0. Which action will result in the highest expected payoff to the firm?

8. **Decision Trees** B&B has a new baby powder ready to market. If the firm goes directly to the market with the product, there is only a 55 percent chance of success. However, the firm can conduct customer segment research, which will take a year and cost $1 million. By going through research, B&B will be able to better target potential customers and will increase the probability of success to 70 percent. If successful, the baby powder will bring a present value profit (at time of initial selling) of $30 million. If unsuccessful, the present value payoff is only $3 million. Should the firm conduct customer segment research or go directly to market? The appropriate discount rate is 15 percent.

9. **Financial Break-Even Analysis** You are considering investing in a company that cultivates abalone for sale to local restaurants. Use the following information:

Sales price per abalone	= $2.00
Variable costs per abalone	= $.72
Fixed costs per year	= $340,000
Depreciation per year	= $20,000
Tax rate	= 35%

The discount rate for the company is 15 percent, the initial investment in equipment is $140,000, and the project's economic life is seven years. Assume the equipment is depreciated on a straight-line basis over the project's life.

a. What is the accounting break-even level for the project?

b. What is the financial break-even level for the project?

10. **Financial Breakeven** Niko has purchased a brand new machine to produce its High Flight line of shoes. The machine has an economic life of five years. The depreciation schedule for the machine is straight-line with no salvage value. The machine costs $300,000. The sales price per

pair of shoes is \$60, while the variable cost is \$8. \$100,000 of fixed costs per year are attributed to the machine. Assume that the corporate tax rate is 34 percent and the appropriate discount rate is 8 percent. What is the financial break-even point?

Intermediate (Questions 11–25)

11. **Break-Even Intuition** Consider a project with a required return of R percent that costs \$$I$ and will last for N years. The project uses straight-line depreciation to zero over the N-year life; there are neither salvage value nor net working capital requirements.
    a. At the accounting break-even level of output, what is the IRR of this project? The payback period? The NPV?
    b. At the cash break-even level of output, what is the IRR of this project? The payback period? The NPV?
    c. At the financial break-even level of output, what is the IRR of this project? The payback period? The NPV?
12. **Sensitivity Analysis** Consider a four-year project with the following information: initial fixed asset investment = \$420,000; straight-line depreciation to zero over the four-year life; zero salvage value; price = \$28; variable costs = \$19; fixed costs = \$190,000; quantity sold = 110,000 units; tax rate = 34 percent. How sensitive is OCF to changes in quantity sold?

13. **Project Analysis** You are considering a new product launch. The project will cost \$720,000, have a four-year life, and have no salvage value; depreciation is straight-line to zero. Sales are projected at 190 units per year; price per unit will be \$21,000, variable cost per unit will be \$15,000, and fixed costs will be \$225,000 per year. The required return on the project is 15 percent, and the relevant tax rate is 35 percent.
    a. Based on your experience, you think the unit sales, variable cost, and fixed cost projections given here are probably accurate to within ±10 percent. What are the upper and lower bounds for these projections? What is the base-case NPV? What are the best-case and worst-case scenarios?
    b. Evaluate the sensitivity of your base-case NPV to changes in fixed costs.
    c. What is the accounting break-even level of output for this project?
14. **Project Analysis** McGilla Golf has decided to sell a new line of golf clubs. The clubs will sell for \$700 per set and have a variable cost of \$320 per set. The company has spent \$150,000 for a marketing study that determined the company will sell 55,000 sets per year for seven years. The marketing study also determined that the company will lose sales of 13,000 sets of its high-priced clubs. The high-priced clubs sell at \$1,100 and have variable costs of \$600. The company will also increase sales of its cheap clubs by 10,000 sets. The cheap clubs sell for \$400 and have variable costs of \$180 per set. The fixed costs each year will be \$7,500,000. The company has also spent \$1,000,000 on research and development for the new clubs. The plant and equipment required will cost \$18,200,000 and will be depreciated on a straight-line basis. The new clubs will also require an increase in net working capital of \$950,000 that will be returned at the end of the project. The tax rate is 40 percent, and the cost of capital is 14 percent. Calculate the payback period, the NPV, and the IRR.
15. **Scenario Analysis** In the previous problem, you feel that the values are accurate to within only ±10 percent. What are the best-case and worst-case NPVs? (Hint: The price and variable costs for the two existing sets of clubs are known with certainty; only the sales gained or lost are uncertain.)
16. **Sensitivity Analysis** McGilla Golf would like to know the sensitivity of NPV to changes in the price of the new clubs and the quantity of new clubs sold. What is the sensitivity of the NPV to each of these variables?

17. **Abandonment Value** We are examining a new project. We expect to sell 7,000 units per year at \$60 net cash flow apiece for the next 10 years. In other words, the annual operating cash flow

is projected to be $60 × 7,000 = $420,000. The relevant discount rate is 16 percent, and the initial investment required is $1,800,000.

a. What is the base-case NPV?

b. After the first year, the project can be dismantled and sold for $1,400,000. If expected sales are revised based on the first year's performance, when would it make sense to abandon the investment? In other words, at what level of expected sales would it make sense to abandon the project?

c. Explain how the $1,400,000 abandonment value can be viewed as the opportunity cost of keeping the project in one year.

18. **Abandonment** In the previous problem, suppose you think it is likely that expected sales will be revised upwards to 9,000 units if the first year is a success and revised downwards to 4,000 units if the first year is not a success.

    a. If success and failure are equally likely, what is the NPV of the project? Consider the possibility of abandonment in answering.

    b. What is the value of the option to abandon?

19. **Abandonment and Expansion** In the previous problem, suppose the scale of the project can be doubled in one year in the sense that twice as many units can be produced and sold. Naturally, expansion would only be desirable if the project were a success. This implies that if the project is a success, projected sales after expansion will be 18,000. Again assuming that success and failure are equally likely, what is the NPV of the project? Note that abandonment is still an option if the project is a failure. What is the value of the option to expand?

20. **Break-Even Analysis** Your buddy comes to you with a sure fire way to make some quick money and help pay off your student loans. His idea is to sell T-shirts with the words "I get" on them. "You get it?" He says, "You see all those bumper stickers and T-shirts that say, 'got milk' or 'got surf.' So this says, 'I get.' It's funny! All we have to do is buy a used silk screen press for $2,000 and we are in business!" Assume there are no fixed costs, and you depreciate the $2,000 in the first period. Further, taxes are 30 percent.

    a. What is the accounting break-even point if each shirt costs $8 to make and you can sell them for $10 apiece?

    Now assume one year has passed and you have sold 5,000 shirts! You find out that the Dairy Farmers of America have copyrighted the "got milk" slogan and are requiring you to pay $10,000 to continue operations. You expect this craze will last for another three years and that your discount rate is 12 percent.

    b. What is the financial break-even point for your enterprise now?

21. **Decision Trees** Young screenwriter Carl Draper has just finished his first script. It has action, drama, humor, and he thinks it will be a blockbuster. He takes the script to every motion picture studio in town and tries to sell it but to no avail. Finally, ACME studios offers to buy the script, for either (a) $5,000 or (b) 1 percent of the movie's profits. There are two decisions the studio will have to make. First is to decide if the script is good or bad, and second if the movie is good or bad. First, there is a 90 percent chance that the script is bad. If it is bad, the studio does nothing more and throws the script out. If the script is good, they will shoot the movie. After the movie is shot, the studio will review it and there is a 70 percent chance that the movie is bad. If the movie is bad, the movie will not be promoted and will not turn a profit. If the movie is good, the studio will promote heavily and the average profit for this type of movie is $10 million. Carl rejects the $5,000 and says he wants the 1 percent of profits. Was this a good decision by Carl?

22. **Accounting Breakeven** Samuelson, Inc., has just purchased a $600,000 machine to produce calculators. The machine will be fully depreciated by the straight-line method over its economic

life of five years and will produce 20,000 calculators each year. The variable production cost per calculator is $15 and total fixed costs are $900,000 per year. The corporate tax rate for the company is 30 percent. For the firm to break even in terms of accounting profit, how much should the firm charge per calculator?

23. **Abandonment Decisions** Allied Products, Inc., is considering a new product launch. The firm expects to have annual operating cash flow of $25 million for the next ten years. Allied Products uses a discount rate of 20 percent for new product launches. The initial investment is $100 million. Assume that the project has no salvage value at the end of its economic life.

    a. What is the NPV of the new product?

    b. After the first year, the project can be dismantled and sold for $50 million. If the estimates of remaining cash flows are revised based on the first year's experience, at what level of expected cash flows does it make sense to abandon the project?

24. **Expansion Decisions** Applied Nanotech is thinking about introducing a new surface cleaning machine. The marketing department has come up with the estimate that Applied Nanotech can sell 10 units per year at $.3 million net cash flow per unit for the next five years. The engineering department has come up with the estimate that developing the machine will take a $10 million initial investment. The finance department has estimated that a 25 percent discount rate should be used.

    a. What is the base case NPV?

    b. If unsuccessful, after the first year the project can be dismantled and will have an aftertax salvage value of $5 million. Also, after the first year, expected cash flows will be revised up to 20 units per year or to 0 units, with equal probability. What is the revised NPV?

25. **Scenario Analysis** You are the financial analyst for a tennis racket manufacturer. The company is considering using a graphite-like material in its tennis rackets. The company has estimated the information in the table below about the market for a racket with the new material. The company expects to sell the racket for five years. The equipment required for the project has no salvage value. The required return for projects of this type is 13 percent, and the company has a 40 percent tax rate. Should you recommend the project?

	PESSIMISTIC	EXPECTED	OPTIMISTIC
Market size	110,000	120,000	130,000
Market share	22%	25%	27%
Selling price	$ 115	$ 120	$ 125
Variable costs per unit	$ 72	$ 70	$ 68
Fixed costs per year	$ 850,000	$ 800,000	$ 750,000
Initial investment	$1,500,000	$1,500,000	$1,500,000

Challenge
(Questions 26–30)

26. **Scenario Analysis** Consider a project to supply Detroit with 40,000 tons of machine screws annually for automobile production. You will need an initial $1,700,000 investment in threading equipment to get the project started; the project will last for five years. The accounting department estimates that annual fixed costs will be $450,000 and that variable costs should be $210 per ton; accounting will depreciate the initial fixed asset investment straight-line to zero over the five-year project life. It also estimates a salvage value of $500,000 after dismantling costs. The marketing department estimates that the automakers will let the contract at a selling price of $230 per ton. The engineering department estimates you will need an initial net working capital investment of $450,000. You require a 13 percent return and face a marginal tax rate of 38 percent on this project.

    a. What is the estimated OCF for this project? The NPV? Should you pursue this project?

b. Suppose you believe that the accounting department's initial cost and salvage value projections are accurate only to within ± 15 percent; the marketing department's price estimate is accurate only to within ± 10 percent; and the engineering department's net working capital estimate is accurate only to within ± 5 percent. What is your worst-case scenario for this project? Your best-case scenario? Do you still want to pursue the project?

27. **Sensitivity Analysis** In Problem 26, suppose you're confident about your own projections, but you're a little unsure about Detroit's actual machine screw requirement. What is the sensitivity of the project OCF to changes in the quantity supplied? What about the sensitivity of NPV to changes in quantity supplied? Given the sensitivity number you calculated, is there some minimum level of output below which you wouldn't want to operate? Why?

28. **Abandonment Decisions** Consider the following project for Hand Clapper, Inc. The company is considering a four-year project to manufacture clap-command garage door openers. This project requires an initial investment of $8 million that will be depreciated straight-line to zero over the project's life. An initial investment in net working capital of $2 million is required to support spare parts inventory; this cost is fully recoverable whenever the project ends. The company believes it can generate $7 million in pretax revenues with $3 million in total pretax operating costs. The tax rate is 38 percent and the discount rate is 16 percent. The market value of the equipment over the life of the project is as follows:

YEAR	MARKET VALUE ($ MILLIONS)
1	$6.50
2	6.00
3	3.00
4	0.00

a. Assuming Hand Clapper operates this project for four years, what is the NPV?

b. Now compute the project NPVs assuming the project is abandoned after only one year, after two years, and after three years. What economic life for this project maximizes its value to the firm? What does this problem tell you about not considering abandonment possibilities when evaluating projects?

29. **Abandonment Decisions** M.V.P. Games, Inc., has hired you to perform a feasibility study of a new video game that requires a $4 million initial investment. M.V.P. expects a total annual operating cash flow of $750,000 for the next 10 years. The relevant discount rate is 10 percent. Cash flows occur at year-end.

a. What is the NPV of the new video game?

b. After one year, the estimate of remaining annual cash flows will either be revised upward to $1.5 million or revised downward to $120,000. Each revision has an equal probability of occurring. At that time, the video game project can be sold for $800,000. What is the revised NPV given that the firm can abandon the project after one year?

30. **Financial Breakeven** The Cornchopper Company is considering the purchase of a new harvester. Cornchopper has hired you to determine the break-even purchase price in terms of present value of the harvester. This break-even purchase price is the price at which the project's NPV is zero. Base your analysis on the following facts:

- The new harvester is not expected to affect revenues, but pretax operating expenses will be reduced by $10,000 per year for 10 years.
- The old harvester is now 5 years old, with 10 years of its scheduled life remaining. It was originally purchased for $45,000 and has been depreciated by the straight-line method.
- The old harvester can be sold for $20,000 today.

- The new harvester will be depreciated by the straight-line method over its 10-year life.
- The corporate tax rate is 34 percent.
- The firm's required rate of return is 15 percent.
- The initial investment, the proceeds from selling the old harvester, and any resulting tax effects occur immediately.
- All other cash flows occur at year-end.
- The market value of each harvester at the end of its economic life is zero.

CLOSING CASE

BUNYAN LUMBER, LLC

Bunyan Lumber, LLC, harvests timber and delivers logs to timber mills for sale. The company was founded 70 years ago by Pete Bunyan. The current CEO is Paula Bunyan, the granddaughter of the founder. The company is currently evaluating a 5,000-acre forest it owns in Oregon. Paula has asked Steve Boles, the company's finance officer, to evaluate the project. Paula's concern is when the company should harvest the timber.

Lumber is sold by the company for its "pond value." Pond value is the amount a mill will pay for a log delivered to the mill location. The price paid for logs delivered to a mill is quoted in dollars per thousands of board feet (MBF), and the price depends on the grade of the logs. The forest Bunyan Lumber is evaluating was planted by the company 20 years ago and is made up entirely of Douglas fir trees. The table below shows the current price per MBF for the three grades of timber the company feels will come from the stand:

TIMBER GRADE	PRICE PER MBF
1P	$1,050
2P	925
3P	770

Steve believes that the pond value of lumber will increase at the inflation rate. The company is planning to thin the forest today, and it expects to realize a positive cash flow of $1,000 per acre from thinning. The thinning is done to increase the growth rate of the remaining trees, and it is always done 20 years following a planting.

The major decision the company faces is when to log the forest. When the company logs the forest, it will immediately replant saplings, which will allow for a future harvest. The longer the forest is allowed to grow, the larger the harvest becomes per acre. Additionally, an older forest has a higher grade of timber. Steve has compiled the following table with the expected harvest per acre in thousands of board feet, along with the breakdown of the timber grade.

YEARS FROM TODAY TO BEGIN HARVEST	HARVEST (MBF) PER ACRE	Timber Grade		
		1P	2P	3P
20	6	10%	40%	50%
25	7.6	12	42	46
30	9	15	42	43
35	10	16	43	41

The company expects to lose 5 percent of the timber it cuts due to defects and breakage.

The forest will be clear-cut when the company harvests the timber. This method of harvesting allows for faster growth of replanted trees. All of the harvesting, processing, replanting, and transportation are to be handled by subcontractors hired by Bunyan Lumber. The cost of the logging is expected to be $140 per MBF. A road system has to be constructed and is expected to cost $50 per MBF on average. Sales preparation and administrative costs, excluding office overhead costs, are expected to be $18 per MBF.

As soon as the harvesting is complete, the company will reforest the land. Reforesting costs include the following:

	PER ACRE COST
Excavator piling	$150
Broadcast burning	300
Site preparation	145
Planting costs	225

All costs are expected to increase at the inflation rate.

Assume all cash flows occur at the year of harvest. For example, if the company begins harvesting the timber 20 years from today, the cash flow from the harvest will be received 20 years from today. When the company logs the land, it will immediately replant the land with new saplings. The harvest period chosen will be repeated for the foreseeable future. The company's nominal required return is 10 percent, and the inflation rate is expected to be 3.7 percent per year. Bunyan Lumber has a 35 percent tax rate.

Clear-cutting is a controversial method of forest management. To obtain the necessary permits, Bunyan Lumber has agreed to contribute to a conservation fund every time it harvests the lumber. If the company harvested the forest today, the required contribution would be $100,000. The company has agreed that the required contribution will grow by 3.2 percent per year. When should the company harvest the forest?

CHAPTER 10

Risk and Return Lessons from Market History

OPENING CASE

With both the S&P 500 Index and NASDAQ stock market index up about 9 percent in 2004, stock market performance overall was a little below average. However, it was a great year for investors in Cheniere Energy, which gained a whopping 444 percent, and investors in Taser International, maker of stun guns, had to be shocked by the 361 percent gain in the price of that stock. Of course, not all stocks increased in value during the year. Stock in Ramp, a health care software firm, fell almost 90 percent during the year, and stock in aaiPharma, a pharmaceutical company, dropped 87 percent. These examples show that there were tremendous potential profits to be made during 2004, but there was also the risk of losing money, and lots of it. So what should you, as a stock market investor, expect when you invest your own money? In this chapter, we study almost eight decades of market history to find out.

10.1 RETURNS

Dollar Returns

Suppose the Video Concept Company has several thousand shares of stock outstanding and you are a shareholder. Further suppose that you purchased some of the shares of stock in the company at the beginning of the year; it is now year-end and you want to figure out how well you have done on your investment. The return you get on an investment in stocks, like that in bonds or any other investment, comes in two forms.

How did the market do today? Find out at finance.yahoo.com.

First, over the year most companies pay dividends to shareholders. As the owner of stock in the Video Concept Company, you are a part owner of the company. If the company is profitable, it generally will distribute some of its profits to the shareholders. Therefore, as the owner of shares of stock, you will receive some cash, called a *dividend,* during the year. This cash is the *income component* of your return. In addition to the dividends, the other part of your return is the *capital gain*—or, if it is negative, the *capital loss* (negative capital gain)—on the investment.

For example, suppose we are considering the cash flows of the investment in Figure 10.1 and you purchased 100 shares of stock at the beginning of the year at a price of $37 per share. Your total investment, then, would be:

$$C_0 = \$37 \times 100 = \$3{,}700$$

Suppose that over the year the stock paid a dividend of $1.85 per share. During the year, then, you would have received income of:

$$\text{Div} = \$1.85 \times 100 = \$185$$

Suppose, lastly, that at the end of the year the market price of the stock is $40.33 per share. Because the stock increased in price, you have a capital gain of:

$$\text{Gain} = (\$40.33 - \$37) \times 100 = \$333$$

The capital gain, like the dividend, is part of the return that shareholders require to maintain their investment in the Video Concept Company. Of course, if the price of Video Concept stock had dropped in value to, say, $34.78, you would have recorded a capital loss of:

$$\text{Loss} = (\$34.78 - \$37) \times 100 = -\$222$$

The *total dollar return* on your investment is the sum of the dividend income and the capital gain or loss on the investment:

$$\text{Total dollar return} = \text{Dividend income} + \text{Capital gain (or loss)}$$

FIGURE 10.1
Dollar Returns

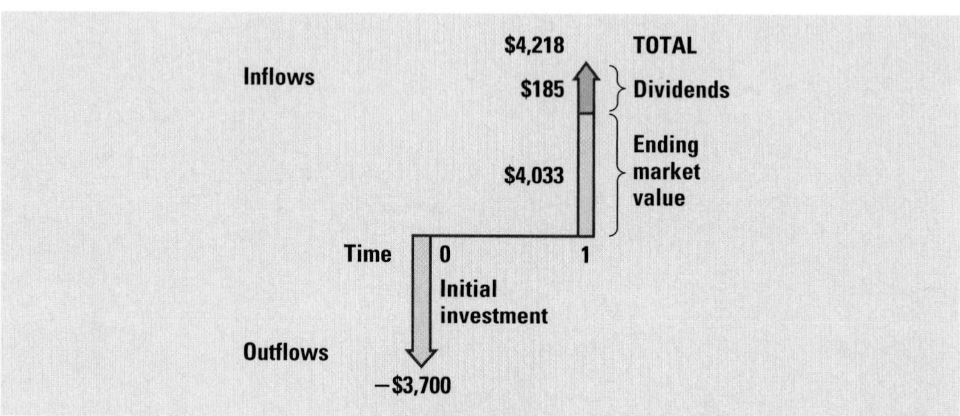

(From now on we will refer to *capital losses* as *negative capital gains* and not distinguish them.) In our first example, then, the total dollar return is given by:

Total dollar return = \$185 + \$333 = \$518

Notice that if you sold the stock at the end of the year, your total amount of cash would be the initial investment plus the total dollar return. In the preceding example, then, you would have:

Total cash if stock is sold = Initial investment + Total dollar return
= \$3,700 + \$518
= \$4,218

As a check, notice that this is the same as the proceeds from the sale of stock plus the dividends:

Proceeds from stock sale + Dividends
= \$40.33 × 100 + \$185
= \$4,033 + \$185
= \$4,218

Suppose, however, that you hold your Video Concept stock and don't sell it at year-end. Should you still consider the capital gain as part of your return? Does this violate our previous present value rule that only cash matters?

The answer to the first question is a strong yes, and the answer to the second question is an equally strong no. The capital gain is every bit as much a part of your return as is the dividend, and you should certainly count it as part of your total return. That you have decided to hold onto the stock and not sell or *realize* the gain or the loss in no way changes the fact that, if you want to, you could get the cash value of the stock. After all, you could always sell the stock at year-end and immediately buy it back. The total amount of cash you would have at year-end would be the \$518 gain plus your initial investment of \$3,700. You would not lose this return when you bought back 100 shares of stock. In fact, you would be in exactly the same position as if you had not sold the stock (assuming, of course, that there are no tax consequences and no brokerage commissions from selling the stock).

Percentage Returns

It is more convenient to summarize the information about returns in percentage terms than in dollars, because the percentages apply to any amount invested. The question we want to answer is: How much return do we get for each dollar invested? To find this out, let t stand for the year we are looking at, let P_t be the price of the stock at the beginning of the year, and let Div_{t+1} be the dividend paid on the stock during the year. Consider the cash flows in Figure 10.2.

In our example, the price at the beginning of the year was \$37 per share and the dividend paid during the year on each share was \$1.85. Hence the percentage income return, sometimes called the *dividend yield,* is:

Go to www.smartmoney.com/marketmap for a Java applet that shows today's returns by market sector.

$$\textbf{Dividend yield} = \mathbf{Div}_{t+1}/P_t$$
$$= \$1.85/\$37$$
$$= .05$$
$$= 5\%$$

The **capital gain** (or loss) is the change in the price of the stock divided by the initial price. Letting P_{t+1} be the price of the stock at year-end, the capital gain can be computed:

FIGURE 10.2
Percentage Returns

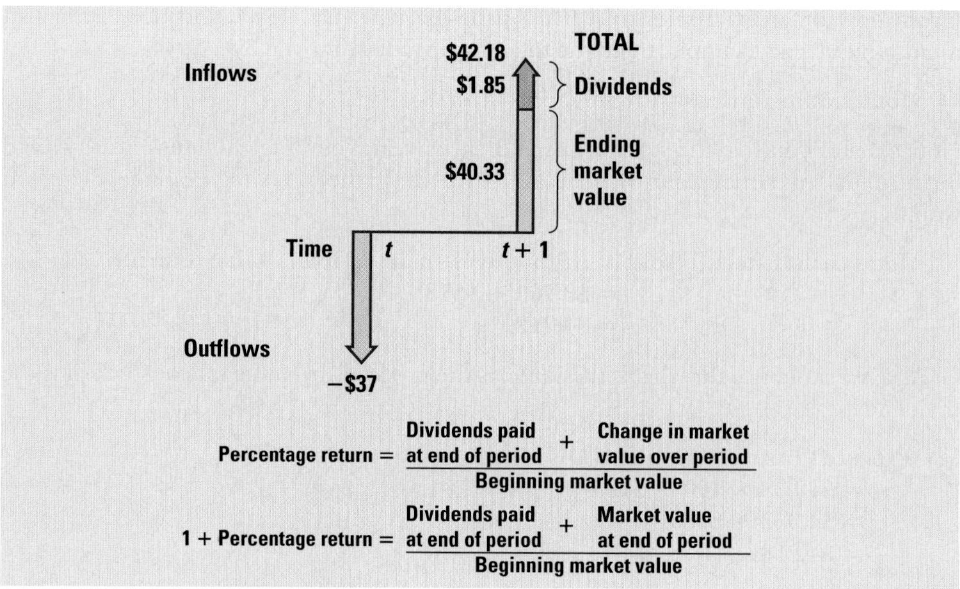

$$\begin{aligned}\textbf{Capital gain} &= (P_{t+1} - P_t)/P_t \\ &= (\$40.33 - \$37)/\$37 \\ &= \$3.33/\$37 \\ &= .09 \\ &= 9\%\end{aligned}$$

Combining these two results, we find that the *total return* on the investment in Video Concept stock over the year, which we will label R_{t+1}, was:

$$\begin{aligned}R_{t+1} &= \frac{\text{Div}_{t+1}}{P_t} + \frac{(P_{t+1} - P_t)}{P_t} \\ &= 5\% + 9\% \\ &= 14\%\end{aligned}$$

From now on we will refer to returns in percentage terms.

To give a more concrete example, stock in Stanley Works (SWK), the famous manufacturer of yellow tools, began 2004 at $36.93 a share. Stanley paid dividends of $1.08 during 2004, and the stock price at year-end was $48.99. What was the return on SWK for the year? For practice, see if you agree that the answer is 35.58 percent. Of course, negative returns occur as well. For example, in 2004 Maytag's stock price at the beginning of the year was $26.99 per share, and dividends of $.72 were paid. The stock ended the year at $21.10 per share. Verify that the loss was 19.16 percent for the year.

EXAMPLE 10.1 Calculating Returns

Suppose a stock begins the year with a price of $25 per share and ends with a price of $35 per share. During the year it paid a $2 dividend per share. What are its dividend yield, its capital gain, and its total return for the year? We can imagine the cash flows in Figure 10.3.

$$\begin{aligned}R_1 &= \frac{\text{Div}_1}{P_0} + \frac{P_1 - P_0}{P_0} \\ &= \frac{\$2}{\$25} + \frac{\$35 - 25}{\$25} = \frac{\$12}{\$25} \\ &= 8\% + 40\% = 48\%\end{aligned}$$

(*continued*)

Thus, the stock's dividend yield, its capital gain yield, and its total return are 8 percent, 40 percent, and 48 percent, respectively.

Suppose you had $5,000 invested. The total dollar return you would have received on an investment in the stock is $5,000 × .48 = $2,400. If you know the total dollar return on the stock, you do not need to know how many shares you would have had to purchase to figure out how much money you would have made on the $5,000 investment. You just use the total dollar return.

FIGURE 10.3
Cash Flow—An Investment Example

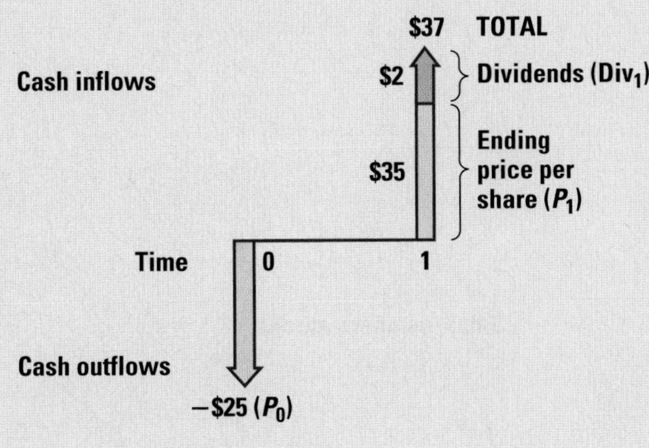

10.2 HOLDING PERIOD RETURNS

A famous set of studies dealing with rates of return on common stocks, bonds, and Treasury bills was conducted by Roger Ibbotson and Rex Sinquefield.[1] They present year-by-year historical rates of return for the following five important types of financial instruments in the United States:

1. *Large-Company Common Stocks.* The common stock portfolio is based on the Standard & Poor's (S&P) composite index. At present, the S&P composite includes 500 of the largest (in terms of market value) stocks in the United States.
2. *Small-Company Common Stocks.* This is a portfolio corresponding to the bottom fifth of stocks traded on the New York Stock Exchange in which stocks are ranked by market value (i.e., the price of the stock multiplied by the number of shares outstanding).
3. *Long-Term Corporate Bonds.* This is a portfolio of high-quality corporate bonds with a 20-year maturity.
4. *Long-Term U.S. Government Bonds.* This is based on U.S. government bonds with a maturity of 20 years.
5. *U.S. Treasury Bills.* This is based on Treasury bills with a three-month maturity.

For more on market history, visit www.globalfindata.com.

None of the returns are adjusted for taxes or transactions costs. In addition to the year-by-year returns on financial instruments, the year-to-year change in the consumer

[1]The most recent update of this work is *Stocks, Bonds, Bills and Inflation: 2005 Yearbook*™ (Chicago: Ibbotson Associates). All rights reserved.

price index is computed. This is a basic measure of inflation. Year-by-year real returns can be calculated by subtracting annual inflation.

Before looking closely at the different portfolio returns, we graphically present the returns and risks available from U.S. capital markets in the 79-year period from 1926 to 2004. Figure 10.4 shows the growth of $1 invested at the beginning of 1926. Notice that

FIGURE 10.4

Wealth Indices of Investments in the U.S. Capital Markets (Year-End 1925 = $1.00)

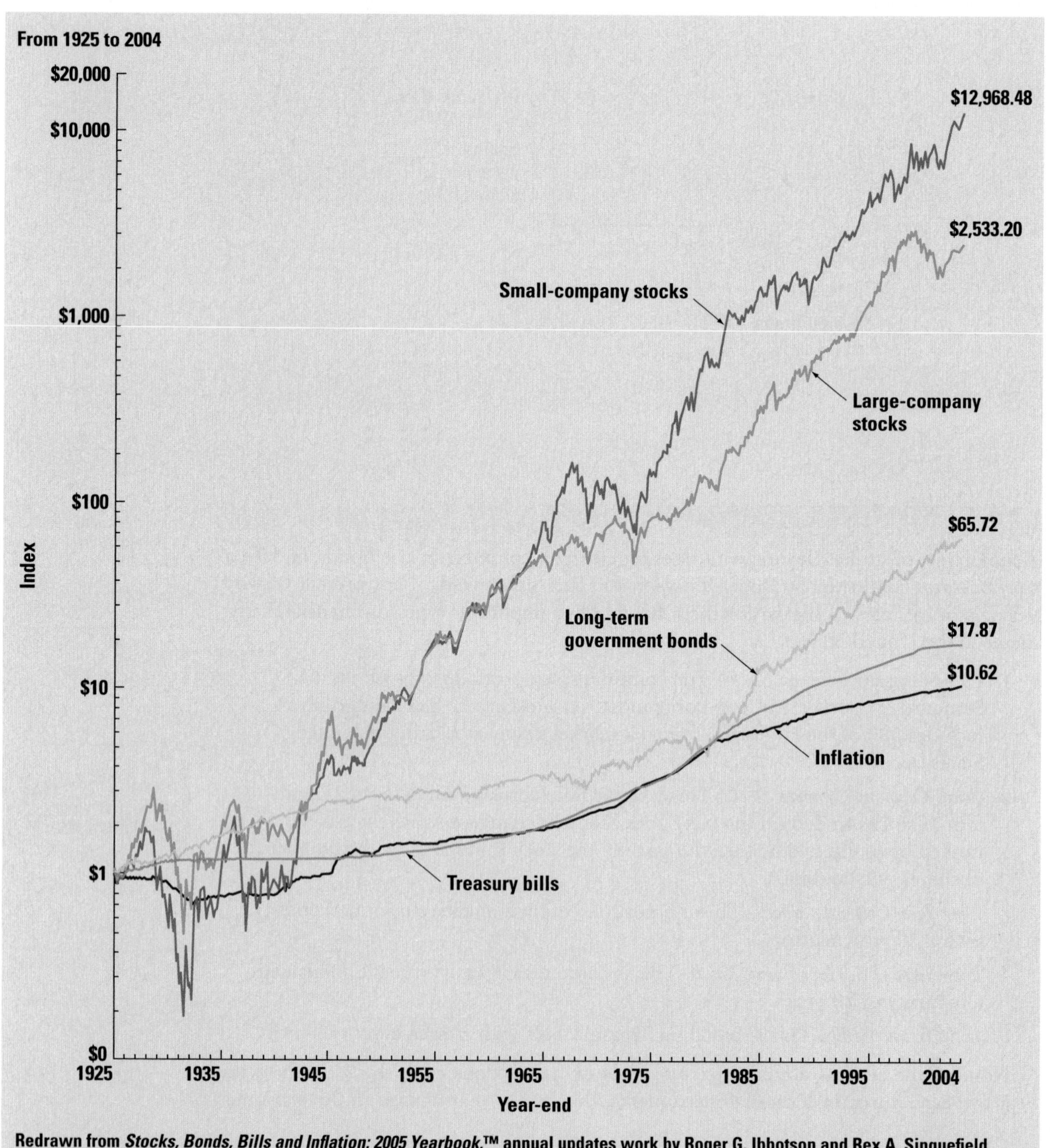

Redrawn from *Stocks, Bonds, Bills and Inflation: 2005 Yearbook,*™ annual updates work by Roger G. Ibbotson and Rex A. Sinquefield (Chicago: Ibbotson Associates). All rights reserved.

the vertical axis is logarithmic, so that equal distances measure the same percentage change. The figure shows that if $1 were invested in large-company common stocks and all dividends were reinvested, the dollar would have grown to $2,533.20 by the end of 2004. The biggest growth was in the small stock portfolio. If $1 were invested in small stocks in 1926, the investment would have grown to $12,968.48. However, when you look carefully at Figure 10.4, you can see great variability in the returns on small stocks, especially in the earlier part of the period. A dollar in long-term government bonds was very stable as compared with a dollar in common stocks. Figures 10.5 to 10.8 plot each

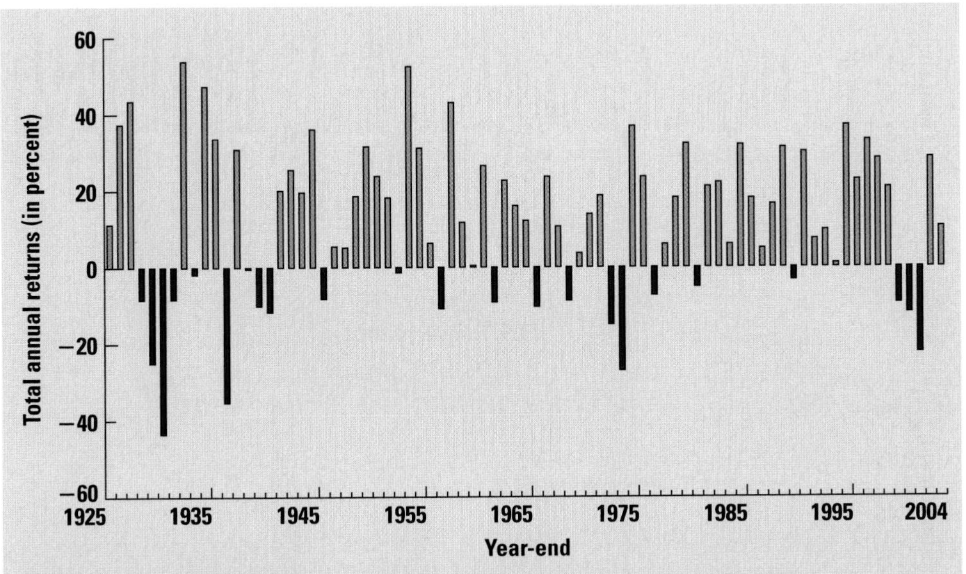

Redrawn from *Stocks, Bonds, Bills and Inflation: 2005 Yearbook,*™ annual updates work by Roger G. Ibbotson and Rex A. Sinquefield (Chicago: Ibbotson Associates).

FIGURE 10.5

Year-by-Year Total Returns on Large-Company Common Stocks

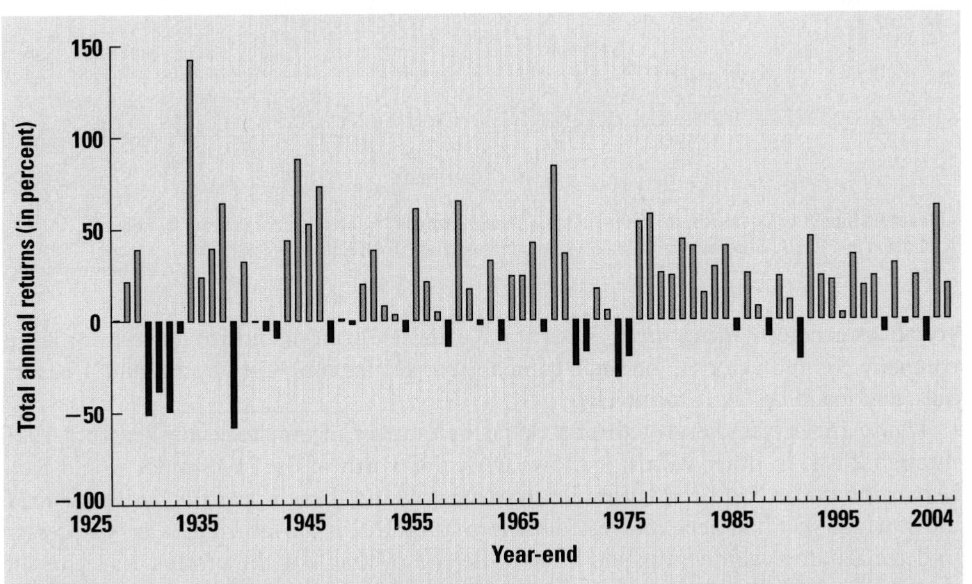

Redrawn from *Stocks, Bonds, Bills and Inflation: 2005 Yearbook,*™ annual updates work by Roger G. Ibbotson and Rex A. Sinquefield (Chicago: Ibbotson Associates).

FIGURE 10.6

Year-by-Year Total Returns on Small-Company Stocks

FIGURE 10.7
Year-by-Year Total Returns on Bonds and Bills

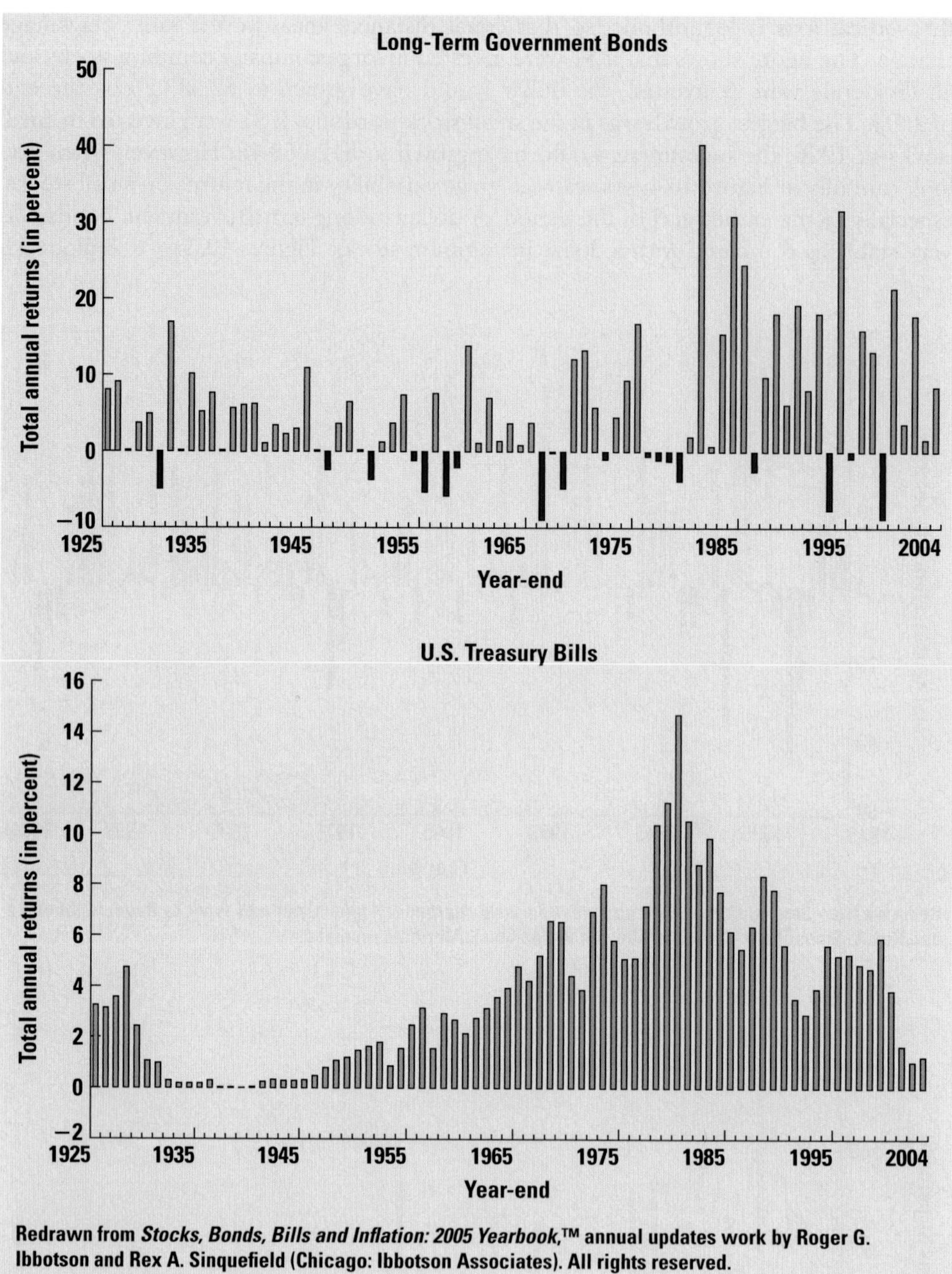

Redrawn from *Stocks, Bonds, Bills and Inflation: 2005 Yearbook,*™ annual updates work by Roger G. Ibbotson and Rex A. Sinquefield (Chicago: Ibbotson Associates).

year-to-year percentage return as a vertical bar drawn from the horizontal axis for large-company common stocks, for small-company stocks, for long-term bonds and Treasury bills, and for inflation, respectively.

Figure 10.4 gives the growth of a dollar investment in the stock market from 1926 through 2004. In other words, it shows what the worth of the investment would have been if the dollar had been left in the stock market and if each year the dividends from the previous year had been reinvested in more stock. If R_t is the return in year t (expressed in decimals), the value you would have at the end of year T is the product of 1 plus the return in each of the years:

$$(1 + R_1) \times (1 + R_2) \times \cdots \times (1 + R_t) \times \cdots \times (1 + R_T)$$

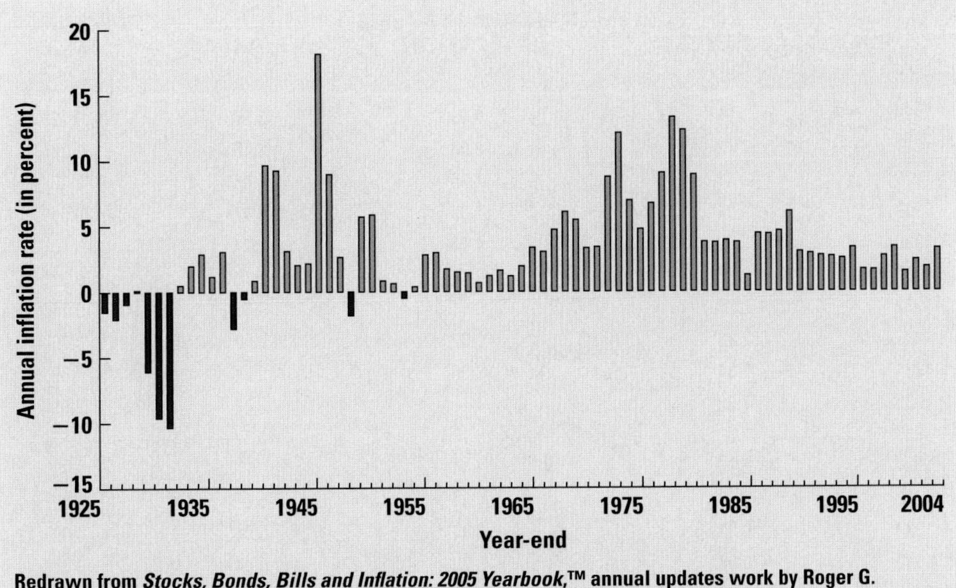

Redrawn from *Stocks, Bonds, Bills and Inflation: 2005 Yearbook,*™ annual updates work by Roger G. Ibbotson and Rex A. Sinquefield (Chicago: Ibbotson Associates). All rights reserved.

FIGURE 10.8
Year-by-Year Inflation

For example, if the returns were 11 percent, −5 percent, and 9 percent in a three-year period, an investment of $1 at the beginning of the period would be worth:

$$\begin{aligned}(1 + R_1) \times (1 + R_2) \times (1 + R_3) &= (\$1 + .11) \times (\$1 - .05) \times (\$1 + .09)\\ &= \$1.11 \times \$.95 \times \$1.09\\ &= \$1.15\end{aligned}$$

Go to bigcharts.marketwatch.com to see both intraday and long-term charts.

at the end of the three years. Notice that .15 or 15 percent is the total return and that it includes the return from reinvesting the first-year dividends in the stock market for two more years and reinvesting the second-year dividends for the final year. The 15 percent is called a three-year **holding period return**. Table 10.1 gives the annual returns each year for selected investments from 1926 to 2004. From this table, you can determine holding period returns for any combination of years.

10.3 RETURN STATISTICS

The history of capital market returns is too complicated to be handled in its undigested form. To use the history, we must first find some manageable ways of describing it, dramatically condensing the detailed data into a few simple statements.

This is where two important numbers summarizing the history come in. The first and most natural number is some single measure that best describes the past annual returns on the stock market. In other words, what is our best estimate of the return that an investor could have realized in a particular year over the 1926 to 2004 period? This is the *average return.*

Figure 10.9 plots the histogram of the yearly stock market returns given in Table 10.1. This plot is the **frequency distribution** of the numbers. The height of the graph gives the number of sample observations in the range on the horizontal axis.

Given a frequency distribution like that in Figure 10.9, we can calculate the **average** or **mean** of the distribution. To compute the average of the distribution, we add up all of the values and divide by the total (T) number (79 in our case because we have

TABLE 10.1
Year-by-Year Total Returns, 1926–2004

Source: Global Financial Data (www.globalfindata.com) copyright 2005.

YEAR	LARGE-COMPANY STOCKS	INTERMEDIATE-TERM GOVERNMENT BONDS	U.S. TREASURY BILLS	CONSUMER PRICE INDEX
1926	11.14%	5.69%	3.30%	− 1.12%
1927	37.13	6.58	3.15	− 2.26
1928	43.31	1.15	4.05	− 1.16
1929	− 8.91	4.39	4.47	0.58
1930	−25.26	4.47	2.27	− 6.40
1931	−43.86	− 2.15	1.15	− 9.32
1932	− 8.85	8.51	0.88	−10.27
1933	52.88	1.92	0.52	0.76
1934	− 2.34	7.59	0.27	1.52
1935	47.22	4.20	0.17	2.99
1936	32.80	5.13	0.17	1.45
1937	−35.26	1.44	0.27	2.86
1938	33.20	4.21	0.06	− 2.78
1939	− 0.91	3.84	0.04	0.00
1940	−10.08	5.70	0.04	0.71
1941	−11.77	0.47	0.14	9.93
1942	21.07	1.80	0.34	9.03
1943	25.76	2.01	0.38	2.96
1944	19.69	2.27	0.38	2.30
1945	36.46	5.29	0.38	2.25
1946	− 8.18	0.54	0.38	18.13
1947	5.24	− 1.02	0.62	8.84
1948	5.10	2.66	1.06	2.99
1949	18.06	4.58	1.12	− 2.07
1950	30.58	− 0.98	1.22	5.93
1951	24.55	− 0.20	1.56	6.00
1952	18.50	2.43	1.75	0.75
1953	− 1.10	2.28	1.87	0.75
1954	52.40	3.08	0.93	− 0.74
1955	31.43	− 0.73	1.80	0.37
1956	6.63	− 1.72	2.66	2.99
1957	−10.85	6.82	3.28	2.90
1958	43.34	− 1.72	1.71	1.76
1959	11.90	− 2.02	3.48	1.73
1960	0.48	11.21	2.81	1.36
1961	26.81	2.20	2.40	0.67
1962	− 8.78	5.72	2.82	1.33
1963	22.69	1.79	3.23	1.64
1964	16.36	3.71	3.62	0.97
1965	12.36	0.93	4.06	1.92
1966	−10.10	5.12	4.94	3.46
1967	23.94	− 2.86	4.39	3.04
1968	11.00	2.25	5.49	4.72
1969	− 8.47	− 5.63	6.90	6.20
1970	3.94	18.92	6.50	5.57
1971	14.30	11.24	4.36	3.27
1972	18.99	2.39	4.23	3.41
1973	−14.69	3.30	7.29	8.71

YEAR	LARGE-COMPANY STOCKS	INTERMEDIATE-TERM GOVERNMENT BONDS	U.S. TREASURY BILLS	CONSUMER PRICE INDEX
1974	−26.47%	4.00%	7.99%	12.34%
1975	37.23	5.52	5.87	6.94
1976	23.93	15.56	5.07	4.86
1977	− 7.16	0.38	5.45	6.70
1978	6.57	− 1.26	7.64	9.02
1979	18.61	1.26	10.56	13.29
1980	32.50	− 2.48	12.10	12.52
1981	− 4.92	4.04	14.60	8.92
1982	21.55	44.28	10.94	3.83
1983	22.56	1.29	8.99	3.79
1984	6.27	15.29	9.90	3.95
1985	31.73	32.27	7.71	3.80
1986	18.67	22.39	6.09	1.10
1987	5.25	− 3.03	5.88	4.43
1988	16.61	6.84	6.94	4.42
1989	31.69	18.54	8.44	4.65
1990	− 3.10	7.74	7.69	6.11
1991	30.46	19.36	5.43	3.06
1992	7.62	7.34	3.48	2.90
1993	10.08	13.06	3.03	2.75
1994	1.32	− 7.32	4.39	2.67
1995	37.58	25.94	5.61	2.54
1996	22.96	0.13	5.14	3.32
1997	33.36	12.02	5.19	1.70
1998	28.58	14.45	4.86	1.61
1999	21.04	− 7.51	4.80	2.68
2000	− 9.10	17.22	5.98	3.39
2001	−11.89	5.51	3.33	1.55
2002	−22.10	15.15	1.61	2.38
2003	28.68	0.54	1.03	1.88
2004	10.88	4.59	1.43	3.26

TABLE 10.1
Year-by-Year Total Returns, 1926–2004 (*concluded*)

79 years of data). The bar over the R is used to represent the mean, and the formula is the ordinary formula for the average:

$$\textbf{Mean} = \overline{R} = \frac{(R_1 + \cdots + R_T)}{T}$$

The mean of the 79 annual large-company stocks returns from 1926 to 2004 is 12.4 percent.

EXAMPLE 10.2 Calculating Average Returns

Suppose the returns on common stock from 1926 to 1929 are .1370, .3580, .4514, and −.0888, respectively. The average, or mean, return over these four years is:

$$\overline{R} = \frac{.1370 + .3580 + .4514 - .0888}{4} = .2144 \text{ or } 21.44\%.$$

FIGURE 10.9

Histogram of Returns on Common Stocks, 1926–2004

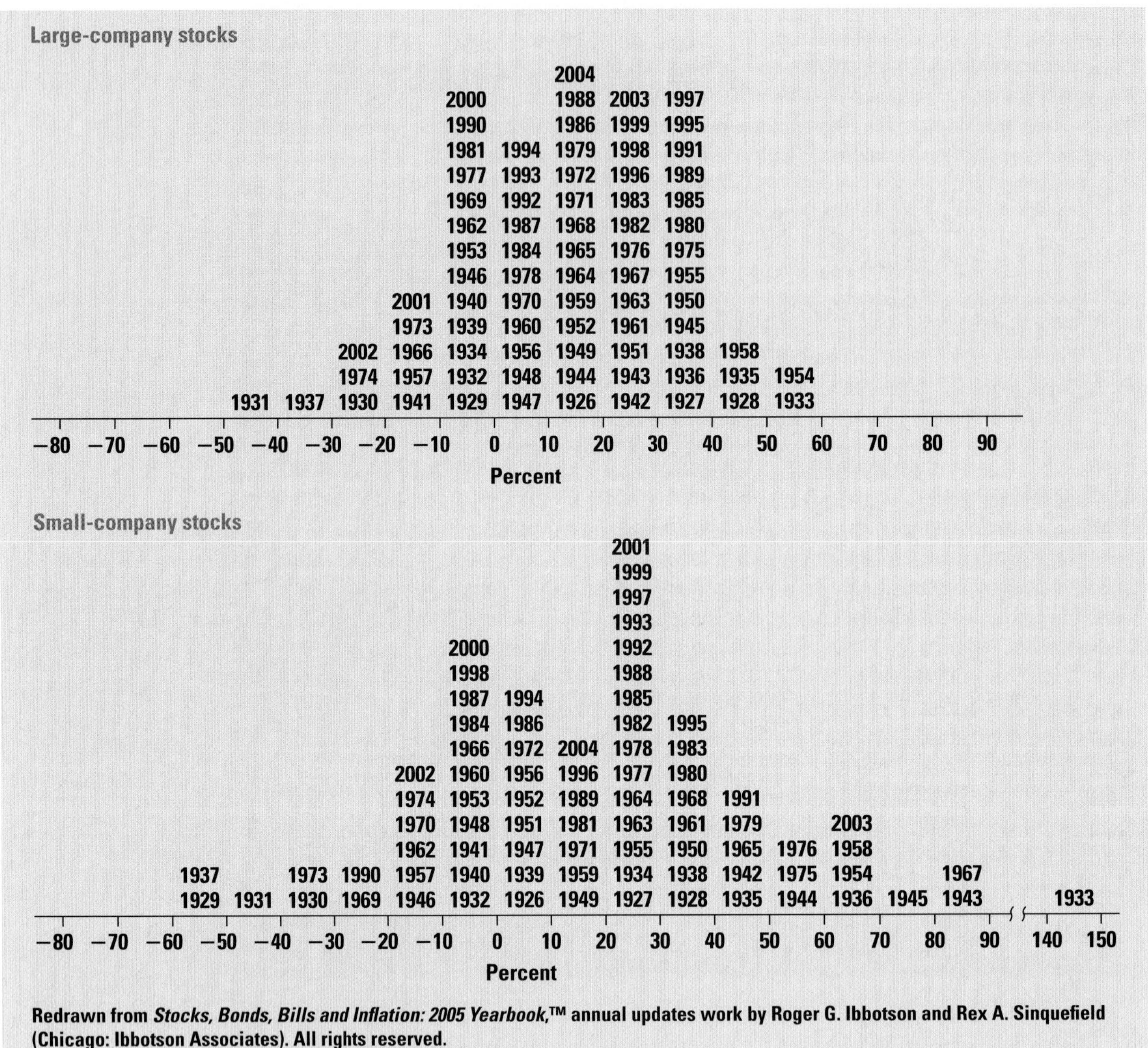

Redrawn from *Stocks, Bonds, Bills and Inflation: 2005 Yearbook,*™ annual updates work by Roger G. Ibbotson and Rex A. Sinquefield (Chicago: Ibbotson Associates).

10.4 AVERAGE STOCK RETURNS AND RISK-FREE RETURNS

Now that we have computed the average return on the stock market, it seems sensible to compare it with the returns on other securities. The most obvious comparison is with the low-variability returns in the government bond market. These are free of most of the volatility we see in the stock market.

The government borrows money by issuing bonds, which the investing public holds. As we discussed in an earlier chapter, these bonds come in many forms, and the ones we will look at here are called *Treasury bills,* or *T-bills.* Once a week the government sells some bills at an auction. A typical bill is a pure discount bond that will mature in a year or less. Because the government can raise taxes to pay for the debt it incurs—a trick that many of us would like to be able to perform—this debt is virtually free of the risk of default. Thus we will call this the *risk-free return* over a short time (one year or less).

An interesting comparison, then, is between the virtually risk-free return on T-bills and the very risky return on common stocks. This difference between risky returns and risk-free returns is often called the *excess return on the risky asset.* It is called *excess* because it is the additional return resulting from the riskiness of common stocks and is interpreted as an equity **risk premium**.

Table 10.2 shows the average stock return, bond return, T-bill return, and inflation rate for the period from 1926 through 2004. From this we can derive excess returns. The average excess return from large-company common stocks for the entire period was 8.6 percent (12.4 percent − 3.8 percent).

One of the most significant observations of stock market data is this long-run excess of the stock return over the risk-free return. An investor for this period was rewarded for

TABLE 10.2

Total Annual Returns, 1926–2004

Source: Modified from *Stocks, Bonds, Bills and Inflation: 2005 Yearbook,*™ annual updates work by Roger G. Ibbotson and Rex A. Sinquefield (Chicago: Ibbotson Associates). All rights reserved.

SERIES	AVERAGE RETURN	STANDARD DEVIATION	DISTRIBUTION
Large-company stocks	12.4%	20.3%	
Small-company stocks	17.5	33.1	*
Long-term corporate bonds	6.2	8.6	
Long-term government	5.8	9.3	
Intermediate-term government	5.5	5.7	
U.S. Treasury bills	3.8	3.1	
Inflation	3.1	4.3	−90% 0% 90%

*The 1933 small-company stock total return was 142.9 percent.

investment in the stock market with an extra or excess return over what would have been achieved by simply investing in T-bills.

Why was there such a reward? Does it mean that it never pays to invest in T-bills and that someone who invested in them instead of in the stock market needs a course in finance? A complete answer to these questions lies at the heart of modern finance, and Chapter 11 is devoted entirely to this. However, part of the answer can be found in the variability of the various types of investments. We see in Table 10.1 many years when an investment in T-bills achieved higher returns than an investment in large common stocks. Also, we note that the returns from an investment in common stocks are frequently negative whereas an investment in T-bills never produces a negative return. So, we now turn our attention to measuring the variability of returns and an introductory discussion of risk.

We first look more closely at Table 10.2. We see that the standard deviation of T-bills is substantially less than that of common stocks. This suggests that the risk of T-bills is less than that of common stocks. Because the answer turns on the riskiness of investments in common stock, we next turn our attention to measuring this risk.

10.5 RISK STATISTICS

For an easy-to-read review of basic stats, check out www.robertniles.com/stats.

The second number that we use to characterize the distribution of returns is a measure of the risk in returns. There is no universally agreed-upon definition of risk. One way to think about the risk of returns on common stock is in terms of how spread out the frequency distribution in Figure 10.9 is. The spread, or dispersion, of a distribution is a measure of how much a particular return can deviate from the mean return. If the distribution is very spread out, the returns that will occur are very uncertain. By contrast, a distribution whose returns are all within a few percentage points of each other is tight, and the returns are less uncertain. The measures of risk we will discuss are variance and standard deviation.

Variance

The **variance** and its square root, the **standard deviation**, are the most common measures of variability or dispersion. We will use Var and σ^2 to denote the variance and SD and σ to represent the standard deviation. σ is, of course, the Greek letter sigma.

EXAMPLE 10.3 Volatility

Suppose the returns on common stocks from 1926 to 1929 are (in decimals) .1370, .3580, .4514, and −.0888, respectively. The variance of this sample is computed as:

$$\text{Var} = \frac{1}{T-1}[(R_1 - \overline{R})^2 + (R_2 - \overline{R})^2 + (R_3 - \overline{R})^2 + (R_4 - \overline{R})^2]$$

$$.0582 = \tfrac{1}{3}[(.1370 - .2144)^2 + (.3580 - .2144)^2 + (.4514 - .2144)^2 + (-.0888 - .2144)^2]$$

$$\text{SD} = \sqrt{.0582} = .2413 \text{ or } 24.13\%.$$

This formula tells us just what to do: Take the T individual returns (R_1, R_2, . . .) and subtract the average return $\overline{R}$, square the result, and add them up. Finally, this total must be divided by the number of returns less one ($T - 1$). The standard deviation is always just the square root of the variance.

Using the stock returns for the 79-year period from 1926 through 2004 in the above formula, the resulting standard deviation of large-company stock returns is 20.3 percent. The standard deviation is the standard statistical measure of the spread of a sample, and it will be the measure we use most of the time. Its interpretation is facilitated by a discussion of the normal distribution.

Standard deviations are widely reported for mutual funds. For example, the Fidelity Magellan Fund is one of the largest mutual funds in the United States. How volatile is it? To find out, we went to www.morningstar.com, entered the ticker symbol FMAGX, and hit the "Risk/Measures" link. Here is what we found:

Fidelity Magellan FMAGX See Fund Family Data ▸▸

Volatility Measurements	Trailing 3-Yr through 03-31-05 | *Trailing 5-Yr through 03-31-05		
Standard Deviation	14.80	Sharpe Ratio	0.00
Mean	.43	Bear Market Decile Rank*	7

Modern Portfolio Theory Statistics		Trailing 3-Yr through 03-31-05
	Standard Index S&P 500	**Best Fit Index** S&P 500
R-Squared	99	99
Beta	.98	.98
Alpha	-2.27	-2.27

Over the last three years, the standard deviation of the return on the Fidelity Magellan Fund was 14.80 percent. When you consider the average stock has a standard deviation of about 50 percent, this seems like a low number, but the Magellan fund is a relatively well-diversified portfolio, so this is an illustration of the power of diversification, a subject we will discuss in detail later. The mean is the average return, so, over the last three years, investors in the Magellan Fund earned a .43 percent return per year. Also under the Volatility Measurements section, you will see the Sharpe ratio. The Sharpe ratio is calculated as the risk premium of the asset divided by the standard deviation. As such, it is a measure of return to the level of risk taken (as measured by standard deviation). This ratio is zero for the period covered because of the low return. The "beta" for the Fidelity Magellan Fund is .98. We will have more to say about this number–lots more–in the next chapter.

Normal Distribution and Its Implications for Standard Deviation

A large enough sample drawn from a **normal distribution** looks like the bell-shaped curve drawn in Figure 10.10. As you can see, this distribution is *symmetric* about its mean, not *skewed,* and has a much cleaner shape than the actual distribution of yearly returns drawn in Figure 10.9. Of course, if we had been able to observe stock market returns for 1,000 years, we might have filled in a lot of the jumps and jerks in Figure 10.9 and had a smoother curve.

In classical statistics, the normal distribution plays a central role, and the standard deviation is the usual way to represent the spread of a normal distribution. For the normal distribution, the probability of having a return that is above or below the mean by a certain amount depends only on the standard deviation. For example, the probability of having a return that is within one standard deviation of the mean of the distribution is approximately .68 or 2/3, and the probability of having a return that is within two standard deviations of the mean is approximately .95.

The 20.3 percent standard deviation we found for stock returns from 1926 through 2004 can now be interpreted in the following way: If stock returns are roughly normally distributed, the probability that a yearly return will fall within 20.3 percent of the mean of 12.4 percent will be approximately 2/3. That is, about 2/3 of the yearly returns will

FIGURE 10.10
The Normal Distribution

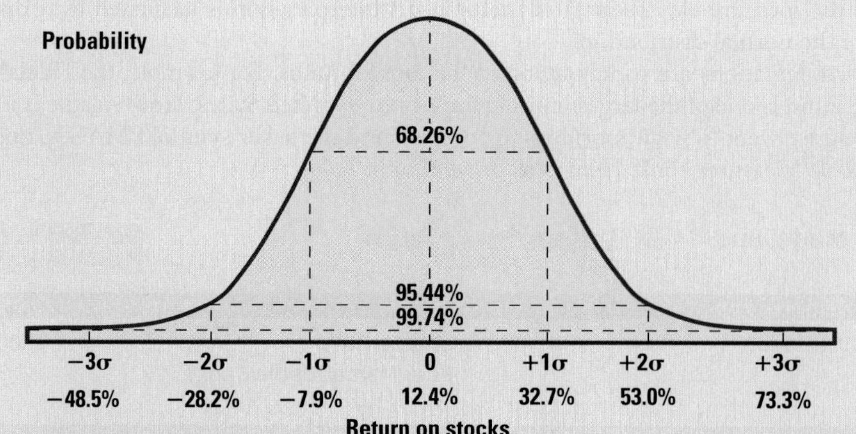

In the case of a normal distribution, there is a 68.26 percent probability that a return will be within one standard deviation of the mean. In this example, there is a 68.26 percent probability that a yearly return will be between −7.9 percent and 32.7 percent.

There is a 95.44 percent probability that a return will be within two standard deviations of the mean. In this example, there is a 95.44 percent probability that a yearly return will be between −28.2 percent and 53.0 percent.

Finally, there is a 99.74 percent probability that a return will be within three standard deviations of the mean. In this example, there is a 99.74 percent probability that a yearly return will be between −48.5 percent and 73.3 percent.

be between −7.9 percent and 32.7 percent. (Note that −7.9% = 12.4% − 20.3% and 32.7% = 12.4% + 20.3%.) The probability that the return in any year will fall within two standard deviations is about .95. That is, about 95 percent of yearly returns will be between −28.2 percent and 53.0 percent.

10.6 MORE ON AVERAGE RETURNS

Thus far in this chapter, we have looked closely at simple average returns. But there is another way of computing an average return. The fact that average returns are calculated two different ways leads to some confusion, so our goal in this section is to explain the two approaches and also the circumstances under which each is appropriate.

Arithmetic versus Geometric Averages

Let's start with a simple example. Suppose you buy a particular stock for $100. Unfortunately, the first year you own it, it falls to $50. The second year you own it, it rises back to $100, leaving you where you started (no dividends were paid).

What was your average return on this investment? Common sense seems to say that your average return must be exactly zero since you started with $100 and ended with $100. But if we calculate the returns year-by-year, we see that you lost 50 percent the first year (you lost half of your money). The second year, you made 100 percent (you doubled your money). Your average return over the two years was thus (−50 percent + 100 percent)/2 = 25 percent!

So which is correct, 0 percent or 25 percent? The answer is that both are correct; they just answer different questions. The 0 percent is called the **geometric average return**. The 25 percent is called the **arithmetic average return**. The geometric average return answers the question, *"What was your average compound return per year over a particular period?"* The arithmetic average return answers the question, *"What was your return in an average year over a particular period?"*

Notice that, in previous sections, the average returns we calculated were all arithmetic averages, so we already know how to calculate them. What we need to do now is (1) learn how to calculate geometric averages and (2) learn the circumstances under which one average is more meaningful than the other.

Calculating Geometric Average Returns

First, to illustrate how we calculate a geometric average return, suppose a particular investment had annual returns of 10 percent, 12 percent, 3 percent, and −9 percent over the last four years. The geometric average return over this four-year period is calculated as $(1.10 \times 1.12 \times 1.03 \times .91)^{1/4} - 1 = 3.66$ percent. In contrast, the average arithmetic return we have been calculating is $(.10 + .12 + .03 - .09)/4 = 4.0$ percent.

In general, if we have T years of returns, the geometric average return over these T years is calculated using this formula:

$$\textbf{Geometric average return} = [(1 + R_1) \times (1 + R_2) \times \cdots \times (1 + R_T)]^{1/T} - 1 \tag{10.1}$$

This formula tells us that four steps are required:

1. Take each of the T annual returns $R_1, R_2, \ldots, R_T$ and add a one to each (after converting them to decimals!).
2. Multiply all the numbers from step 1 together.
3. Take the result from step 2 and raise it to the power of $1/T$.
4. Finally, subtract one from the result of step 3. The result is the geometric average return.

EXAMPLE 10.4 Calculating the Geometric Average Return

Calculate the geometric average return for S&P 500 large-cap stocks for 1926–1930 using the numbers given here.

First, convert percentages to decimal returns, add one, and then calculate their product:

S&P 500 RETURNS	PRODUCT
13.75%	1.1375
35.70	× 1.3570
45.08	× 1.4508
− 8.80	× .9120
−25.13	× .7487
	1.5291

Notice that the number 1.5291 is what our investment is worth after five years if we started with a one dollar investment. The geometric average return is then calculated as:

Geometric average return $= 1.5291^{1/5} - 1 = .0887$, or 8.87%

Thus, the geometric average return is about 8.87 percent in this example. Here is a tip: If you are using a financial calculator, you can put $1 in as the present value, $1.5291 as the future value, and 5 as the number of periods. Then, solve for the unknown rate. You should get the same answer we did.

One thing you may have noticed in our examples thus far is that the geometric average returns seem to be smaller. It turns out that this will always be true (as long as the returns are not all identical, in which case the two "averages" would be the same).

TABLE 10.3 Geometric versus Arithmetic Average Returns: 1926–2004

SERIES	GEOMETRIC MEAN	ARITHMETIC MEAN	STANDARD DEVIATION
Large-company stocks	10.4%	12.4%	20.3%
Small-company stocks	12.7	17.5	33.1
Long-term corporate bonds	5.9	6.2	8.6
Long-term government bonds	5.4	5.8	9.3
Intermediate-term government bonds	5.4	5.5	5.7
U.S. Treasury bills	3.7	3.8	3.1
Inflation	3.0	3.1	4.3

To illustrate, Table 10.3 shows the arithmetic averages and standard deviations from Table 10.2, along with the geometric average returns.

As shown in Table 10.3, the geometric averages are all smaller, but the magnitude of the difference varies quite a bit. The reason is that the difference is greater for more volatile investments. In fact, there is useful approximation. Assuming all the numbers are expressed in decimals (as opposed to percentages), the geometric average return is approximately equal to the arithmetic average return minus half the variance. For example, looking at the large-company stocks, the arithmetic average is .124 and the standard deviation is .203, implying that the variance is .041209. The approximate geometric average is thus $.124 - .041209/2 = .1034$, which is quite close to the actual value.

EXAMPLE 10.5 More Geometric Averages

Take a look back at Figure 10.4. There, we showed the value of a $1 investment after 79 years. Use the value for the large-company stock investment to check the geometric average in Table 10.3.

In Figure 10.4, the large-company investment grew to $2,533.20 over 79 years. The geometric average return is thus:

$$\text{Geometric average return} = 2{,}533.20^{1/79} - 1 = .104, \text{ or } 10.4\%$$

This 10.4% is the value shown in Table 10.3. For practice, check some of the other numbers in Table 10.3 the same way.

Arithmetic Average Return or Geometric Average Return?

When we look at historical returns, the difference between the geometric and arithmetic average returns isn't too hard to understand. To put it slightly differently, the geometric average tells you what you actually earned per year on average, compounded annually. The arithmetic average tells you what you earned in a typical year. You should use whichever one answers the question you want answered.

A somewhat trickier question concerns forecasting the future, and there's a lot of confusion about this point among analysts and financial planners. The problem is this. If we have *estimates* of both the arithmetic and geometric average returns, then the arithmetic average is probably too high for longer periods and the geometric average is probably too low for shorter periods.

The good news is that there is a simple way of combining the two averages, which we will call *Blume's formula*.[2] Suppose we calculated geometric and arithmetic return averages from N years of data and we wish to use these averages to form a T-year average return

[2]This elegant result is due to Marshal Blume ("Unbiased Estimates of Long-Run Expected Rates of Return," *Journal of the American Statistical Association,* September 1974, pp. 634–638).

forecast, $R(T)$, where T is less than N. Here's how we do it:

$$R(T) = \frac{T-1}{N-1} \times \text{Geometric average} + \frac{N-T}{N-1} \times \text{Arithmetic average} \qquad (10.2)$$

For example, suppose that, from 25 years of annual returns data, we calculate an arithmetic average return of 12 percent and a geometric average return of 9 percent. From these averages, we wish to make 1-year, 5-year, and 10-year average return forecasts. These three average return forecasts are calculated as follows:

$$R(1) = \frac{1-1}{24} \times 9\% + \frac{25-1}{24} \times 12\% = 12\%$$

$$R(5) = \frac{5-1}{24} \times 9\% + \frac{25-5}{24} \times 12\% = 11.5\%$$

$$R(10) = \frac{10-1}{24} \times 9\% + \frac{25-10}{24} \times 12\% = 10.875\%$$

Thus, we see that 1-year, 5-year, and 10-year forecasts are 12 percent, 11.5 percent, and 10.875 percent, respectively.

This concludes our discussion of geometric versus arithmetic averages. One last note: In the future, when we say "average return," we mean arithmetic average unless we explicitly say otherwise.

SUMMARY AND CONCLUSIONS

1. This chapter presents returns for a number of different asset classes. The general conclusion is that stocks have outperformed bonds over most of the twentieth century, though stocks have also exhibited more risk.
2. The statistical measures in this chapter are necessary building blocks for the material of the next three chapters. In particular, standard deviation and variance measure the variability of the return on an individual security and on portfolios of securities. In the next chapter, we will argue that standard deviation and variance are appropriate measures of the risk of an individual security if an investor's portfolio is composed of that security only.

CONCEPT QUESTIONS

1. **Investment Selection** Given that Cheniere Energy was up by almost 444 percent for 2004, why didn't all investors hold Cheniere Energy?
2. **Investment Selection** Given that Ramp was down by 90 percent for 2004, why did some investors hold the stock? Why didn't they sell out before the price declined so sharply?
3. **Risk and Return** We have seen that over long periods of time stock investments have tended to substantially outperform bond investments. However, it is not at all uncommon to observe investors with long horizons holding their investments entirely in bonds. Are such investors irrational?
4. **Stocks versus Gambling** Critically evaluate the following statement: Playing the stock market is like gambling. Such speculative investing has no social value, other than the pleasure people get from this form of gambling.

5. **Effects of Inflation** Look at Table 10.1 and Figure 10.7 in the text. When were T-bill rates at their highest over the period from 1926 through 2004? Why do you think they were so high during this period? What relationship underlies your answer?
6. **Risk Premiums** Is it possible for the risk premium to be negative before an investment is undertaken? Can the risk premium be negative after the fact? Explain.
7. **Returns** Two years ago, General Materials's and Standard Fixtures's stock prices were the same. During the first year, General Materials's stock price increased by 10 percent while Standard Fixtures's stock price decreased by 10 percent. During the second year, General Materials's stock price decreased by 10 percent and Standard Fixtures's stock price increased by 10 percent. Do these two stocks have the same price today? Explain.
8. **Returns** Two years ago, the Lake Minerals and Small Town Furniture stock prices were the same. The annual return for both stocks over the past two years was 10 percent. Lake Minerals's stock price increased 10 percent each year. Small Town Furniture's stock price increased 25 percent in the first year, and lost 5 percent last year. Do these two stocks have the same price today?
9. **Arithmetic versus Geometric Returns** What is the difference between arithmetic and geometric returns? Suppose you have invested in a stock for the last ten years. Which number is more important to you, the arithmetic or geometric return?
10. **Historical Returns** The historical asset class returns presented in the chapter are not adjusted for inflation. What would happen to the estimated risk premium if we did account for inflation? The returns are also not adjusted for taxes. What would happen to the returns if we accounted for taxes? What would happen to the volatility?

QUESTIONS AND PROBLEMS

Basic
(Questions 1–20)

1. **Calculating Returns** Suppose a stock had an initial price of $83 per share, paid a dividend of $1.40 per share during the year, and had an ending share price of $91. Compute the percentage total return.
2. **Calculating Yields** In Problem 1, what was the dividend yield? The capital gains yield?
3. **Calculating Returns** Rework Problems 1 and 2 assuming the ending share price is $76.
4. **Calculating Returns** Suppose you bought a 9 percent coupon bond one year ago for $1,120. The bond sells for $1,074 today.
   a. Assuming a $1,000 face value, what was your total dollar return on this investment over the past year?
   b. What was your total nominal rate of return on this investment over the past year?
   c. If the inflation rate last year was 3 percent, what was your total real rate of return on this investment?
5. **Nominal versus Real Returns** What was the arithmetic average annual return on large-company stock from 1926 through 2004:
   a. In nominal terms?
   b. In real terms?
6. **Bond Returns** What is the historical real return on long-term government bonds? On long-term corporate bonds?

7. **Calculating Returns and Variability** Using the following returns, calculate the average returns, the variances, and the standard deviations for X and Y.

YEAR	Returns X	Returns Y
1	11%	36%
2	6	− 7
3	− 8	21
4	28	−12
5	13	43

8. **Risk Premiums** Refer to Table 10.1 in the text and look at the period from 1973 through 1978.
   a. Calculate the arithmetic average returns for large-company stocks and T-bills over this time period.
   b. Calculate the standard deviation of the returns for large-company stocks and T-bills over this time period.
   c. Calculate the observed risk premium in each year for the large-company stocks versus the T-bills. What was the arithmetic average risk premium over this period? What was the standard deviation of the risk premium over this period?
9. **Calculating Returns and Variability** You've observed the following returns on Mary Ann Data Corporation's stock over the past five years: −16 percent, 21 percent, 4 percent, 16 percent, and 19 percent.
   a. What was the arithmetic average return on Mary Ann's stock over this five-year period?
   b. What was the variance of Mary Ann's returns over this period? The standard deviation?
10. **Calculating Real Returns and Risk Premiums** In Problem 9, suppose the average inflation rate over this period was 4.2 percent and the average T-bill rate over the period was 5.1 percent.
    a. What was the average real return on Mary Ann's stock?
    b. What was the average nominal risk premium on Mary Ann's stock?
11. **Calculating Real Rates** Given the information in Problem 10, what was the average real risk-free rate over this time period? What was the average real risk premium?
12. **Holding Period Return** A stock has had returns of −4.91 percent, 21.67 percent, 22.57 percent, 6.19 percent, and 31.85 percent over the past five years, respectively. What was the holding period return for the stock?
13. **Calculating Returns** You purchased a zero coupon bond one year ago for $152.37. The market interest rate is now 10 percent. If the bond had 20 years to maturity when you originally purchased it, what was your total return for the past year?
14. **Calculating Returns** You bought a share of 5 percent preferred stock for $84.12 last year. The market price for your stock is now $80.27. What is your total return for last year?
15. **Calculating Returns** You bought a stock three months ago for $38.65 per share. The stock paid no dividends. The current share price is $42.02. What is the APR of your investment? The EAR?
16. **Calculating Real Returns** Refer to Table 10.1. What was the average real return for Treasury bills from 1926 through 1932?
17. **Return Distributions** Refer back to Figure 10.2. What range of returns would you expect to see 68 percent of the time for long-term corporate bonds? What about 95 percent of the time?

18. **Return Distributions** Refer back to Figure 10.2. What range of returns would you expect to see 68 percent of the time for large-company stocks? What about 95 percent of the time?

19. **Blume's Formula** Over a 30-year period an asset had an arithmetic return of 12.8 percent and a geometric return of 10.7 percent. Using Blume's formula, what is your best estimate of the future annual returns over 5 years? 10 years? 20 years?

20. **Blume's Formula** Assume that the historical return on large-company stocks is a predictor of the future returns. What return would you estimate for large-company stocks over the next year? The next 5 years? 20 years? 30 years?

Intermediate (Questions 21–28)

21. **Calculating Returns and Variability** You find a certain stock that had returns of 8 percent, −13 percent, −7 percent, and 29 percent for four of the last five years. If the average return of the stock over this period was 11 percent, what was the stock's return for the missing year? What is the standard deviation of the stock's returns?

22. **Arithmetic and Geometric Returns** A stock has had returns of 29 percent, 14 percent, 23 percent, −8 percent, 9 percent, and −14 percent over the last six years. What are the arithmetic and geometric returns for the stock?

23. **Arithmetic and Geometric Returns** A stock has had the following year-end prices and dividends:

YEAR	PRICE	DIVIDEND
1	$43.12	—
2	49.07	$0.55
3	51.19	0.60
4	47.24	0.63
5	56.09	0.72
6	67.21	0.81

What are the arithmetic and geometric returns for the stock?

24. **Calculating Returns** Refer to Table 10.1 in the text and look at the period from 1973 through 1980.
    a. Calculate the average return for Treasury bills and the average annual inflation rate (consumer price index) for this period.
    b. Calculate the standard deviation of Treasury bill returns and inflation over this time period.
    c. Calculate the real return for each year. What is the average real return for Treasury bills?
    d. Many people consider Treasury bills to be risk-free. What do these calculations tell you about the potential risks of Treasury bills?

25. **Calculating Investment Returns** You bought one of Bergen Manufacturing Co.'s 8 percent coupon bonds one year ago for $1,028.50. These bonds make annual payments and mature six years from now. Suppose you decide to sell your bonds today, when the required return on the bonds is 7 percent. If the inflation rate was 4.8 percent over the past year, what would be your total real return on the investment?

26. **Using Return Distributions** Suppose the returns on long-term government bonds are normally distributed. Based on the historical record, what is the approximate probability that your return on these bonds will be less than −3.5 percent in a given year? What range of returns would you expect to see 95 percent of the time? What range would you expect to see 99 percent of the time?

27. **Using Return Distributions** Assuming that the returns from holding small-company stocks are normally distributed, what is the approximate probability that your money will double in value in a single year? Triple in value?

28. **Distributions** In the previous problem, what is the probability that the return is less than −100 percent? (Think.) What are the implications for the distribution of returns?

Challenge (Questions 29–30)

29. **Using Probability Distributions** Suppose the returns on large-company stocks are normally distributed. Based on the historical record, use the cumulative normal probability table (rounded to the nearest table value) in Chapter 17 to determine the probability that in any given year you will lose money by investing in common stock.

30. **Using Probability Distributions** Suppose the returns on long-term corporate bonds and T-bills are normally distributed. Based on the historical record, use the cumulative normal probability table (rounded to the nearest table value) in Chapter 17 to answer the following questions:

    a. What is the probability that in any given year, the return on long-term corporate bonds will be greater than 10 percent? Less than 0 percent?

    b. What is the probability that in any given year, the return on T-bills will be greater than 10 percent? Less than 0 percent?

    c. In 1979, the return on long-term corporate bonds was −4.18 percent. How likely is it that this low of a return will recur at some point in the future? T-bills had a return of 10.32 percent in this same year. How likely is it that this high of a return on T-bills will recur at some point in the future?

S&P PROBLEMS

www.mhhe.com/edumarketinsight

1. **Calculating Yields** Download the historical stock prices for Duke Energy (DUK) under the "Mthly. Adj. Prices" link. Find the closing stock price for the beginning and end of the prior two years. Now use the annual financial statements to find the dividend for each of these years. What was the capital gains yield and dividend yield for Duke Energy stock for each of these years? Now calculate the capital gains yield and dividend yield for Tommy Hilfiger (TOM). How do the returns for these two companies compare?

2. **Calculating Average Returns** Download the Monthly Adjusted Prices for Microsoft (MSFT). What is the return on the stock over the past 12 months? Now use the 1 Month Total Return and calculate the average monthly return. Is this one-twelfth of the annual return you calculated? Why or why not? What is the monthly standard deviation of Microsoft's stock over the past year?

WHAT'S ON THE WEB?

1. **Market Risk Premium** You want to find the current market risk premium. Go to money.cnn.com and find current interest rates. What is the shortest maturity interest rate shown? What is the interest rate for this maturity? Using the large-company stock return in Table 10.3, what is the current market risk premium? What assumption are you making when calculating the risk premium?

2. **Historical Interest Rates** Go to the St. Louis Federal Reserve Web site at www.stls.frb.org and search "Treasury." You will find a list of links for different historical interest rates. Follow the "10-Year Treasury Constant Maturity Rate" link and you will find the monthly 10-year Treasury note interest rates. Calculate the average annual 10-year Treasury interest rate for 2004 and 2005 using the rates for each month. Compare this number to the long-term government bond returns and the U.S. Treasury bill returns found in Table 10.1. How does the 10-year Treasury interest rate compare to these numbers? Do you expect this relationship to always hold? Why or why not?

CLOSING CASE

A JOB AT EAST COAST YACHTS

You recently graduated from college, and your job search led you to East Coast Yachts. Since you felt the company's business was seaworthy, you accepted a job offer. The first day on the job, while you are finishing your employment paperwork, Dan Ervin, who works in Finance, stops by to inform you about the company's 401(k) plan.

A 401(k) plan is a retirement plan offered by many companies. Such plans are tax-deferred savings vehicles, meaning that any deposits you make into the plan are deducted from your current pretax income, so no current taxes are paid on the money. For example, assume your salary will be $50,000 per year. If you contribute $3,000 to the 401(k) plan, you will only pay taxes on $47,000 in income. There are also no taxes paid on any capital gains or income while you are invested in the plan, but you do pay taxes when you withdraw money at retirement. As is fairly common, the company also has a five percent match. This means that the company will match your contribution up to five percent of your salary, but you must contribute to get the match.

The 401(k) plan has several options for investments, most of which are mutual funds. A mutual fund is a portfolio of assets. When you purchase shares in a mutual fund, you are actually purchasing partial ownership of the fund's assets. The return of the fund is the weighted average of the return of the assets owned by the fund, minus any expenses. The largest expense is typically the management fee, paid to the fund manager. The management fee is compensation for the manager, who makes all of the investment decisions for the fund.

East Coast Yachts uses Bledsoe Financial Services as its 401(k) plan administrator. The investment options offered for employees are discussed below.

Company Stock One option in the 401(k) plan is stock in East Coast Yachts. The company is currently privately held. However, when you interviewed with the owner, Larissa Warren, she informed you the company stock was expected to go public in the next three to four years. Until then, a company stock price is simply set each year by the board of directors.

Bledsoe S&P 500 Index Fund This mutual fund tracks the S&P 500. Stocks in the fund are weighted exactly the same as the S&P 500. This means the fund return is approximately the return on the S&P 500, minus expenses. Since an index fund purchases assets based on the compensation of the index it is following, the fund manager is not required to research stocks and make investment decisions. The result is that the fund expenses are usually low. The Bledsoe S&P 500 Index Fund charges expenses of .15 percent of assets per year.

Bledsoe Small Cap Fund This fund primarily invests in small capitalization stocks. As such, the returns of the fund are more volatile. The fund can also invest 10 percent of its assets in companies based outside the United States. This fund charges 1.70 percent in expenses.

Bledsoe Large Company Stock Fund This fund invests primarily in large capitalization stocks of companies based in the United States. The fund is managed by Evan Bledsoe and has outperformed the market in six of the last eight years. The fund charges 1.50 percent in expenses.

Bledsoe Bond Fund This fund invests in long-term corporate bonds issued by U.S. domiciled companies. The fund is restricted to investments in bonds with an investment grade credit rating. This fund charges 1.40 percent in expenses.

Bledsoe Money Market Fund This fund invests in short-term, high credit quality debt instruments, which include Treasury bills. As such, the return on the money market fund is only slightly higher than the return on Treasury bills. Because of the credit quality and short-term nature of the investments, there is only a very slight risk of negative return. The fund charges .60 percent in expenses.

1. What advantages do the mutual funds offer compared to the company stock?
2. Assume that you invest five percent of your salary and receive the full five percent match from East Coast Yachts. What EAR do you earn from the match? What conclusions do you draw about matching plans?
3. Assume you decide you should invest at least part of your money in large capitalization stocks of companies based in the United States. What are the advantages and disadvantages of choosing the Bledsoe Large Company Stock Fund compared to the Bledsoe S&P 500 Index Fund?
4. The returns on the Bledsoe Small Cap Fund are the most volatile of all the mutual funds offered in the 401(k) plan. Why would you ever want to invest in this fund? When you examine the expenses of the mutual funds, you will notice that this fund also has the highest expenses. Does this affect your decision to invest in this fund?
5. A measure of risk-adjusted performance that is often used is the Sharpe ratio. The Sharpe ratio is calculated as the risk premium of an asset divided by its standard deviation. The standard deviation and return of the funds over the past 10 years are listed below. Calculate the Sharpe ratio for each of these funds. Assume that the expected return and standard deviation of the company stock will be 18 percent and 70 percent, respectively. Calculate the Sharpe ratio for the company stock. How appropriate is the Sharpe ratio for these assets? When would you use the Sharpe ratio?

	10-YEAR ANNUAL RETURN	STANDARD DEVIATION
Bledsoe S&P 500 Index Fund	11.48%	15.82%
Bledsoe Small Cap Fund	16.68	19.64
Bledsoe Large Company Stock Fund	11.85	15.41
Bledsoe Bond Fund	9.67	10.83

6. What portfolio allocation would you choose? Why? Explain your thinking carefully.

CHAPTER 11

Return and Risk: *The Capital Asset Pricing Model (CAPM)*

OPENING CASE

In February 2005, ExxonMobil, Amazon.com, and Cisco Systems joined a host of other companies in announcing operating results. As you might expect, news such as this tends to move stock prices.

ExxonMobil reported earnings of $1.30 per share, easily topping analyst estimates. In fact, the company reported a net income of $8.42 billion for the quarter, the highest quarterly profit ever by a company based in the United States. But investors didn't jump at the news: The stock price rose a mere .6 percent on the day. Amazon.com announced earnings that were nearly five times as large as the previous year, but did investors cheer? Not exactly: The stock price fell by 15 percent. Cisco Systems met a similar fate when it announced earnings that met expectations; the stock dropped 3.3 percent.

These three announcements all seem positive, but one stock rose only slightly in price and the other two fell. So when is good news really good news? The answer is fundamental to understanding risk and return, and—the good news is—this chapter explores it in some detail.

11.1 INDIVIDUAL SECURITIES

In the first part of Chapter 11, we will examine the characteristics of individual securities. In particular, we will discuss:

1. *Expected Return.* This is the return that an individual expects a stock to earn over the next period. Of course, because this is only an expectation, the actual return may be either higher or lower. An individual's expectation may simply be the average return per period a security has earned in the past. Alternatively, it may be based on a detailed analysis of a firm's prospects, on some computer-based model, or on special (or inside) information.
2. *Variance and Standard Deviation.* There are many ways to assess the volatility of a security's return. One of the most common is variance, which is a measure of the squared deviations of a security's return from its expected return. Standard deviation is the square root of the variance.
3. *Covariance and Correlation.* Returns on individual securities are related to one another. Covariance is a statistic measuring the interrelationship between two securities. Alternatively, this relationship can be restated in terms of the correlation between the two securities. Covariance and correlation are building blocks to an understanding of the beta coefficient.

11.2 EXPECTED RETURN, VARIANCE, AND COVARIANCE

Expected Return and Variance

Suppose financial analysts believe that there are four unequally likely states of the economy next year: depression, recession, normal, and boom times. The returns on the Supertech Company, R_A, are expected to follow the economy closely, while the returns on the Slowpoke Company, R_B, are not. The return predictions are as follows:

Want more information on investing? Take a look at TheStreet.com's investing basics at www.thestreet.com/basics.

STATE OF ECONOMY	PROBABILITY OF STATE OF ECONOMY	SUPERTECH RETURNS R_A	SLOWPOKE RETURNS R_B
Depression	.10	−30%	0%
Recession	.20	−10	5
Normal	.50	20	20
Boom	.20	50	− 5

Variance can be calculated in four steps. An additional step is needed to calculate standard deviation. (The calculations are presented in Table 11.1.) The steps are:

1. Calculate the expected returns, $E(R_A)$ and $E(R_B)$, by multiplying each possible return by the probability that it occurs and then add them up:

Supertech

$$.10(-.30) + .20(-.10) + .50(.20) + .20(.50) = .15 = 15\% = E(R_A)$$

Slowpoke

$$.10(.00) + .20(.05) + .50(.20) + .20(-.05) = .10 = 10\% = E(R_B)$$

2. As shown in the fourth column of Table 11.1, we next calculate the deviation of each possible return from the expected returns for the two companies.
3. Next, take the deviations from the fourth column and square them as we have done in the fifth column.

TABLE 11.1

Calculating Variance and Standard Deviation

(1) STATE OF ECONOMY	(2) PROBABILITY OF STATE OF ECONOMY	(3) RATE OF RETURN	(4) DEVIATION FROM EXPECTED RETURN	(5) SQUARED VALUE OF DEVIATION	(6) PRODUCT (2) × (5)
		Supertech (Expected return = .15)			
		R_A	$R_A - E(R_A)$	$(R_A - E(R_A))^2$	
Depression	.10	−.30	−.45	.2025	.02025
Recession	.20	−.10	−.25	.0625	.01250
Normal	.50	.20	.05	.0025	.00125
Boom	.20	.50	.35	.1225	.02450
				$\text{Var}(R_A) = \sigma_A^2 =$	.05850
		Slowpoke (Expected return = .10)			
		R_B	$R_B - E(R_B)$	$(R_B - E(R_B))^2$	
Depression	.10	.00	−.10	.0100	.00100
Recession	.20	.05	−.05	.0025	.00050
Normal	.50	.20	.10	.0100	.00500
Boom	.20	−.05	−.15	.0225	.00450
				$\text{Var}(R_B) = \sigma_B^2 =$	.01100

4. Finally, multiply each squared deviation by its associated probability and add the products up. As shown in Table 11.1, we get a variance of .0585 for Supertech and .0110 for Slowpoke.
5. As always, to get the standard deviations, we just take the square roots of the variances:

Supertech

$$\sqrt{.0585} = .242 = 24.2\% = \text{SD}(R_A) = \sigma_A$$

Slowpoke

$$\sqrt{.0110} = .105 = 10.5\% = \text{SD}(R_B) = \sigma_B$$

Covariance and Correlation

Variance and standard deviation measure the variability of individual stocks. We now wish to measure the relationship between the return on one stock and the return on another. Enter **covariance** and **correlation**.

Covariance and correlation measure how two random variables are related. We explain these terms by extending our Supertech and Slowpoke example presented earlier.

EXAMPLE 11.1 Calculating Covariance and Correlation

We have already determined the expected returns and standard deviations for both Supertech and Slowpoke. (The expected returns are .15 and .10 for Supertech and Slowpoke, respectively. The standard deviations are .242 and .105, respectively.) In addition, we calculated the deviation of each possible return from the expected return for each firm. Using these data, covariance can be calculated in two steps. An extra step is needed to calculate correlation.

1. For each state of the economy, multiply Supertech's deviation from its expected return and Slowpoke's deviation from its expected return together. For example, Supertech's rate of return in a depression is −.30, which is −.45 (= −.30 − .15) from its expected return. Slowpoke's rate

(continued)

TABLE 11.2

Calculating Covariance and Correlation

(1) STATE OF ECONOMY	(2) PROBABILITY OF STATE OF ECONOMY	(3) Deviations from Expected Returns SUPERTECH	(4) SLOWPOKE	(5) PRODUCT OF DEVIATIONS	(6) PRODUCT (2) × (5)
Depression	.10	−.45	−.10	.0450	.00450
Recession	.20	−.25	−.05	.0125	.00250
Normal	.50	.05	.10	.0050	.00250
Boom	.20	.35	−.15	−.0525	−.01050
				$\text{Cov}(R_A, R_B) = \sigma_{A,B} =$	−.001

of return in a depression is .00, which is −.10 (= .00 − .10) from its expected return. Multiplying the two deviations together yields .0450 [= (−.45) × (−.10)]. The actual calculations are given in the last column of Table 11.2.This procedure can be written algebraically as:

$$(R_A - \text{E}(R_A)) \times (R_B - \text{E}(R_B)) \quad (11.1)$$

where R_A and R_B are the returns on Supertech and Slowpoke. $\text{E}(R_A)$ and $\text{E}(R_B)$ are the expected returns on the two securities.

2. Once we have the products of the deviations, we multiply each one by its associated probability and sum to get the covariance.

Note that we represent the covariance between Supertech and Slowpoke as either $\text{Cov}(R_A, R_B)$ or $\sigma_{A,B}$. Equation (11.1) illustrates the intuition of covariance. Suppose Supertech's return is generally above its average when Slowpoke's return is above its average, and Supertech's return is generally below its average when Slowpoke's return is below its average. This is indicative of a positive dependency or a positive relationship between the two returns. Note that the term in equation (11.1) will be *positive* in any state where both returns are *above* their averages. In addition, (11.1) will still be *positive* in any state where both terms are *below* their averages. Thus, a positive relationship between the two returns will give rise to a positive value for covariance.

Conversely, suppose Supertech's return is generally above its average when Slowpoke's return is below its average, and Supertech's return is generally below its average when Slowpoke's return is above its average. This is indicative of a negative dependency or a negative relationship between the two returns. Note that the term in equation (11.1) will be *negative* in any state where one return is above its average and the other return is below its average. Thus, a negative relationship between the two returns will give rise to a negative value for covariance.

Finally, suppose there is no relation between the two returns. In this case, knowing whether the return on Supertech is above or below its expected return tells us nothing about the return on Slowpoke. In the covariance formula, then, there will be no tendency for the deviations to be positive or negative together. On average, they will tend to offset each other and cancel out, making the covariance zero.

Of course, even if the two returns are unrelated to each other, the covariance formula will not equal zero exactly in any actual history. This is due to sampling error; randomness alone will make the calculation positive or negative. But for a historical sample that is long enough, if the two returns are not related to each other, we should expect the covariance to come close to zero.

The covariance formula seems to capture what we are looking for. If the two returns are positively related to each other, they will have a positive covariance, and if they are negatively related to each other, the covariance will be negative. Last, and very important, if they are unrelated, the covariance should be zero.

The covariance we calculated is −.001. A negative number like this implies that the return on one stock is likely to be above its average when the return on the other stock is below its average, and vice versa. However, the size of the number is difficult to interpret. Like the variance figure, the

(continued)

covariance is in squared deviation units. Until we can put it in perspective, we don't know what to make of it.

We solve the problem by computing the correlation:

3. To calculate the correlation, divide the covariance by the product of the standard deviations of the two securities. For our example, we have:

$$\rho_{A,B} = \text{Corr}\,(R_A, R_B) = \frac{\text{Cov}(R_A, R_B)}{\sigma_A \times \sigma_B} = \frac{-.001}{.242 \times .105} = -.039 \tag{11.2}$$

where σ_A and σ_B are the standard deviations of Supertech and Slowpoke, respectively. Note that we represent the correlation between Supertech and Slowpoke either as $\text{Corr}(R_A, R_B)$ or $\rho_{A,B}$. Note also that the ordering of the two variables is unimportant. That is, the correlation of A with B is equal to the correlation of B with A. More formally, $\text{Corr}(R_A, R_B) = \text{Corr}(R_B, R_A)$ or $\rho_{A,B} = \rho_{B,A}$. The same is true for covariance.

Because the standard deviation is always positive, the sign of the correlation between two variables must be the same as that of the covariance between the two variables. If the correlation is positive, we say that the variables are *positively correlated*; if it is negative, we say that they are *negatively correlated*; and if it is zero, we say that they are *uncorrelated*. Furthermore, it can be

FIGURE 11.1

Examples of Different Correlation Coefficients—the Graphs in the Figure Plot the Separate Returns on the Two Securities through Time

Perfect Positive Correlation
Corr(R_A, R_B) = 1

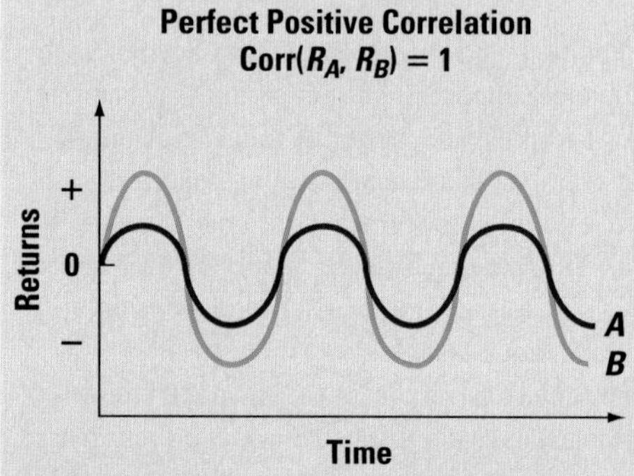

Both the return on security *A* and the return on security *B* are higher than average at the same time. Both the return on security *A* and the return on security *B* are lower than average at the same time.

Perfect Negative Correlation
Corr(R_A, R_B) = −1

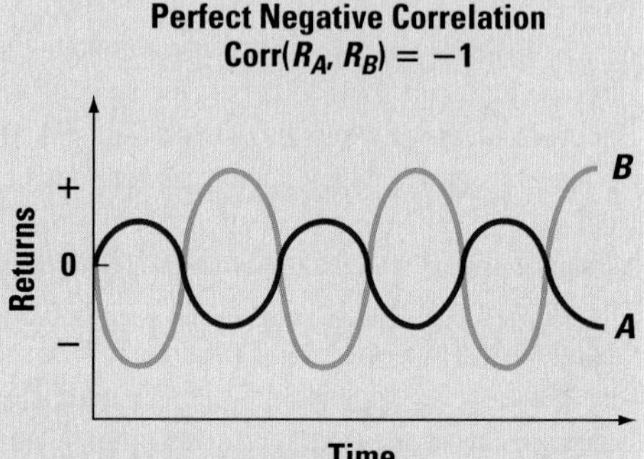

Security *A* has a higher-than-average return when security *B* has a lower-than-average return, and vice versa.

Zero Correlation
Corr(R_A, R_B) = 0

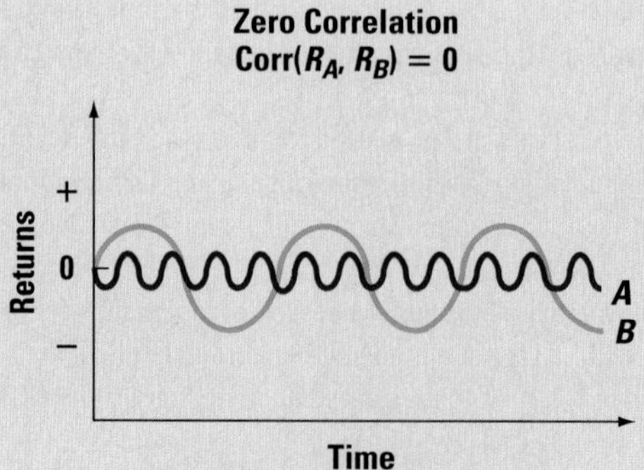

The return on security *A* is completely unrelated to the return on security *B*.

(*continued*)

proved that the correlation is always between +1 and −1. This is due to the standardizing procedure of dividing by the two standard deviations.

We can compare the correlation between different *pairs* of securities. For example, it turns out that the correlation between General Motors and Ford is much higher than the correlation between General Motors and IBM. Hence, we can state that the first pair of securities is more interrelated than the second pair.

Figure 11.1 shows the three benchmark cases for two assets, *A* and *B*. The figure shows two assets with return correlations of +1, −1, and 0. This implies perfect positive correlation, perfect negative correlation, and no correlation, respectively. The graphs in the figure plot the separate returns on the two securities through time.

11.3 THE RETURN AND RISK FOR PORTFOLIOS

Suppose that an investor has estimates of the expected returns and standard deviations on individual securities and the correlations between securities. How then does the investor choose the best combination or **portfolio** of securities to hold? Obviously, the investor would like a portfolio with a high expected return and a low standard deviation of return. It is therefore worthwhile to consider:

1. The relationship between the expected return on individual securities and the expected return on a portfolio made up of these securities.
2. The relationship between the standard deviations of individual securities, the correlations between these securities, and the standard deviation of a portfolio made up of these securities.

The Example of Supertech and Slowpoke

In order to analyze the above two relationships, we will use the same example of Supertech and Slowpoke that was presented previously. The relevant calculations are as follows.

The Expected Return on a Portfolio

The formula for expected return on a portfolio is very simple:

The expected return on a portfolio is simply a weighted average of the expected returns on the individual securities.

RELEVANT DATA FROM EXAMPLE OF SUPERTECH AND SLOWPOKE

ITEM	SYMBOL	VALUE
Expected return on Supertech	$E(R_{Super})$	.15 = 15%
Expected return on Slowpoke	$E(R_{Slow})$	.10 = 10%
Variance of Supertech	σ^2_{Super}	.0585
Variance of Slowpoke	σ^2_{Slow}	.0110
Standard deviation of Supertech	σ_{Super}	.242 = 24.2%
Standard deviation of Slowpoke	σ_{Slow}	.105 = 10.5%
Covariance between Supertech and Slowpoke	$\sigma_{Super, Slow}$	−.001
Correlation between Supertech and Slowpoke	$\rho_{Super, Slow}$	−.039

EXAMPLE 11.2 Portfolio Expected Returns

Consider Supertech and Slowpoke. From the preceding box, we find that the expected returns on these two securities are 15 percent and 10 percent, respectively.

The expected return on a portfolio of these two securities alone can be written as:

$$\text{Expected return on portfolio} = X_{\text{Super}}\,(15\%) + X_{\text{Slow}}\,(10\%) = R_P$$

where X_{Super} is the percentage of the portfolio in Supertech and X_{Slow} is the percentage of the portfolio in Slowpoke. If the investor with $100 invests $60 in Supertech and $40 in Slowpoke, the expected return on the portfolio can be written as:

$$\text{Expected return on portfolio} = .6 \times 15\% + .4 \times 10\% = 13\%$$

Algebraically, we can write:

$$\text{Expected return on portfolio} = X_A \text{E}(R_A) + X_B \text{E}(R_B) = \text{E}(R_P) \tag{11.3}$$

where X_A and X_B are the proportions of the total portfolio in the assets A and B, respectively. (Because our investor can only invest in two securities, $X_A + X_B$ must equal 1 or 100 percent.) $\text{E}(R_A)$ and $\text{E}(R_B)$ are the expected returns on the two securities.

Now consider two stocks, each with an expected return of 10 percent. The expected return on a portfolio composed of these two stocks must be 10 percent, regardless of the proportions of the two stocks held. This result may seem obvious at this point, but it will become important later. The result implies that you do not reduce or *dissipate* your expected return by investing in a number of securities. Rather, the expected return on your portfolio is simply a weighted average of the expected returns on the individual assets in the portfolio.

Variance and Standard Deviation of a Portfolio

THE VARIANCE The formula for the variance of a portfolio composed of two securities, A and B, is:

The Variance of the Portfolio

$$\textbf{Var (portfolio)} = X_A^2\sigma_A^2 + 2X_AX_B\sigma_{A,B} + X_B^2\sigma_B^2 \tag{11.4}$$

Note that there are three terms on the right-hand side of the equation (in addition to X_A and X_B, the investment proportions). The first term involves the variance of $A(\sigma_A^2)$ the second term involves the covariance between the two securities ($\sigma_{A,B}$), and the third term involves the variance of $B(\sigma_B^2)$. (As stated earlier in this chapter, $\sigma_{A,B} = \sigma_{B,A}$. That is, the ordering of the variables is not relevant when expressing the covariance between two securities.)

The formula indicates an important point. The variance of a portfolio depends on both the variances of the individual securities and the covariance between the two securities. The variance of a security measures the variability of an individual security's return. Covariance measures the relationship between the two securities. For given variances of the individual securities, a positive relationship or covariance between the two securities increases the variance of the entire portfolio. A negative relationship or covariance between the two securities decreases the variance of the entire portfolio. This important result seems to square with common sense. If one of your securities tends to go up when the other goes down, or vice versa, your two securities are offsetting each other. You are achieving what we call a *hedge* in finance, and the risk of your entire portfolio will be low. However, if both your securities rise and fall together, you are not hedging at all. Hence, the risk of your entire portfolio will be higher.

The variance formula for our two securities, Super and Slow, is:

$$\textbf{Var (portfolio)} = X_{\text{Super}}^2\sigma_{\text{Super}}^2 + 2X_{\text{Super}}X_{\text{Slow}}\sigma_{\text{Super, Slow}} + X_{\text{Slow}}^2\sigma_{\text{Slow}}^2$$

Given our earlier assumption that an individual with $100 invests $60 in Supertech and $40 in Slowpoke, $X_{\text{Super}} = .6$ and $X_{\text{Slow}} = .4$. Using this assumption and the relevant data from the previous box, the variance of the portfolio is:

$$.0223 = .36 \times .0585 + 2 \times [.6 \times .4 \times (-.001)] + .16 \times .0110$$

STANDARD DEVIATION OF A PORTFOLIO We can now determine the standard deviation of the portfolio's return. This is:

$$\sigma_P = \text{SD(portfolio)} = \sqrt{\text{Var (portfolio)}} = \sqrt{.0223} = .1495 = 14.95\% \tag{11.5}$$

The interpretation of the standard deviation of the portfolio is the same as the interpretation of the standard deviation of an individual security. The expected return on our portfolio is 13 percent. A return of −1.95 percent (13% − 14.95%) is one standard deviation below the mean and a return of 27.95 percent (13% + 14.95%) is one standard deviation above the mean. If the return on the portfolio is normally distributed, a return between −1.95 percent and +27.95 percent occurs about 68 percent of the time.[1]

THE DIVERSIFICATION EFFECT It is instructive to compare the standard deviation of the portfolio with the standard deviation of the individual securities. The weighted average of the standard deviations of the individual securities is:

$$\text{Weighted average of standard deviations} = X_{\text{Super}}\sigma_{\text{Super}} + X_{\text{Slow}}\sigma_{\text{Slow}} \tag{11.6}$$
$$.187 = .6 \times .242 + .4 \times .105$$

One of the most important results in this chapter concerns the difference between equations (11.5) and (11.6). In our example, the standard deviation of the portfolio is *less* than a weighted average of the standard deviations of the individual securities.

We pointed out earlier that the expected return on the portfolio is a weighted average of the expected returns on the individual securities. Thus, we get a different type of result for the standard deviation of a portfolio than we do for the expected return on a portfolio.

It is generally argued that our result for the standard deviation of a portfolio is due to diversification. For example, Supertech and Slowpoke are slightly negatively correlated ($\rho = -.039$). Supertech's return is likely to be a little below average if Slowpoke's return is above average. Similarly, Supertech's return is likely to be a little above average if Slowpoke's return is below average. Thus, the standard deviation of a portfolio composed of the two securities is less than a weighted average of the standard deviations of the two securities.

The above example has negative correlation. Clearly, there will be less benefit from diversification if the two securities exhibit positive correlation. How high must the positive correlation be before all diversification benefits vanish?

To answer this question, let us rewrite (11.4) in terms of correlation rather than covariance. First, note that the covariance can be rewritten as:

$$\sigma_{\text{Super, Slow}} = \rho_{\text{Super, Slow}}\sigma_{\text{Super}}\sigma_{\text{Slow}} \tag{11.7}$$

The formula states that the covariance between any two securities is simply the correlation between the two securities multiplied by the standard deviations of each. In other words, covariance incorporates both (1) the correlation between the two assets and (2) the variability of each of the two securities as measured by standard deviation.

From our calculations earlier in this chapter, we know that the correlation between the two securities is −.039. Thus, the variance of our portfolio can be expressed as:

[1]There are only four equally probable returns for Supertech and Slowpoke, so neither security possesses a normal distribution. Thus, probabilities would be somewhat different in our example.

Variance of the Portfolio's Return

$$= X^2_{\text{Super}}\sigma^2_{\text{Super}} + 2X_{\text{Super}}X_{\text{Slow}}\rho_{\text{Super, Slow}}\sigma_{\text{Super}}\sigma_{\text{Slow}} + X^2_{\text{Slow}}\sigma^2_{\text{Slow}} \quad (11.8)$$

$$.0223 = .36 \times .0585 + 2 \times .6 \times .4 \times (-.039) \times .242 \times .105 + .16 \times .0110$$

The middle term on the right-hand side is now written in terms of correlation, ρ, not covariance.

Suppose $\rho_{\text{Super, Slow}} = 1$, the highest possible value for correlation. Assume all the other parameters in the example are the same. The variance of the portfolio is:

$$\textbf{Variance of the portfolio's return} = .035 = .36 \times .0585 + 2 \times (.6 \times .4 \times 1 \times .242 \times .105) + .16 \times .0110$$

The standard deviation is:

$$\textbf{Standard deviation of portfolio's return} = \sqrt{.035} = .187 = 18.7\% \quad (11.9)$$

Note that equations (11.9) and (11.6) are equal. That is, the standard deviation of a portfolio's return is equal to the weighted average of the standard deviations of the individual returns when $\rho = 1$. Inspection of (11.8) indicates that the variance and hence the standard deviation of the portfolio must fall as the correlation drops below 1. This leads to:

As long as $\rho < 1$, the standard deviation of a portfolio of two securities is *less* than the weighted average of the standard deviations of the individual securities.

In other words, the diversification effect applies as long as there is less than perfect correlation (as long as $\rho < 1$). Thus, our Supertech-Slowpoke example is a case of overkill. We illustrated diversification by an example with negative correlation. We could have illustrated diversification by an example with positive correlation–as long as it was not *perfect* positive correlation.

AN EXTENSION TO MANY ASSETS The preceding insight can be extended to the case of many assets. That is, as long as correlations between pairs of securities are less than 1, the standard deviation of a portfolio of many assets is less than the weighted average of the standard deviations of the individual securities.

Now consider Table 11.3, which shows the standard deviation of the Standard & Poor's 500 Index and the standard deviations of some of the individual securities listed in the index over a recent 5-year period. Note that all of the individual securities in

TABLE 11.3
Standard Deviations for Standard & Poor's 500 Index and for Selected Stocks in the Index, 2000–2004

ASSET	STANDARD DEVIATION
S&P 500 Index	16.35%
Verizon	33.96
Ford Motor Co.	43.61
Walt Disney Co.	32.55
General Electric	25.18
IBM	35.96
McDonald's	28.61
Sears	44.06
Toys "R" Us Inc.	50.77
Amazon.com	69.19

As long as the correlations between pairs of securities are less than 1, the standard deviation of an index is less than the weighted average of the standard deviations of the individual securities within the index.

the table have higher standard deviations than that of the index. In general, the standard deviations of most of the individual securities in an index will be above the standard deviation of the index itself, though a few of the securities could have lower standard deviations than that of the index.

11.4 THE EFFICIENT SET

The Two-Asset Case

Our results on expected returns and standard deviations are graphed in Figure 11.2. In the figure, there is a dot labeled Slowpoke and a dot labeled Supertech. Each dot represents both the expected return and the standard deviation for an individual security. As can be seen, Supertech has both a higher expected return and a higher standard deviation.

You can find out more about the efficient frontier on the Web at www.efficientfrontier.com.

The box or "□" in the graph represents a portfolio with 60 percent invested in Supertech and 40 percent invested in Slowpoke. You will recall that we have previously calculated both the expected return and the standard deviation for this portfolio.

The choice of 60 percent in Supertech and 40 percent in Slowpoke is just one of an infinite number of portfolios that can be created. The set of portfolios is sketched by the curved line in Figure 11.3.

Consider portfolio *1*. This is a portfolio composed of 90 percent Slowpoke and 10 percent Supertech. Because it is weighted so heavily toward Slowpoke, it appears close to the Slowpoke point on the graph. Portfolio *2* is higher on the curve because it is composed of 50 percent Slowpoke and 50 percent Supertech. Portfolio *3* is close to the Supertech point on the graph because it is composed of 90 percent Supertech and 10 percent Slowpoke.

There are a few important points concerning this graph.

1. We argued that the diversification effect occurs whenever the correlation between the two securities is below 1. The correlation between Supertech and Slowpoke is −.039. The diversification effect can be illustrated by comparison with the straight line between the Supertech point and the Slowpoke point. The straight line represents points that would have been generated had the correlation coefficient between the two securities been 1. The diversification effect is illustrated in the figure since the curved line is always to the left of the straight line. Consider point *1′*. This represents a portfolio composed of 90 percent in Slowpoke and

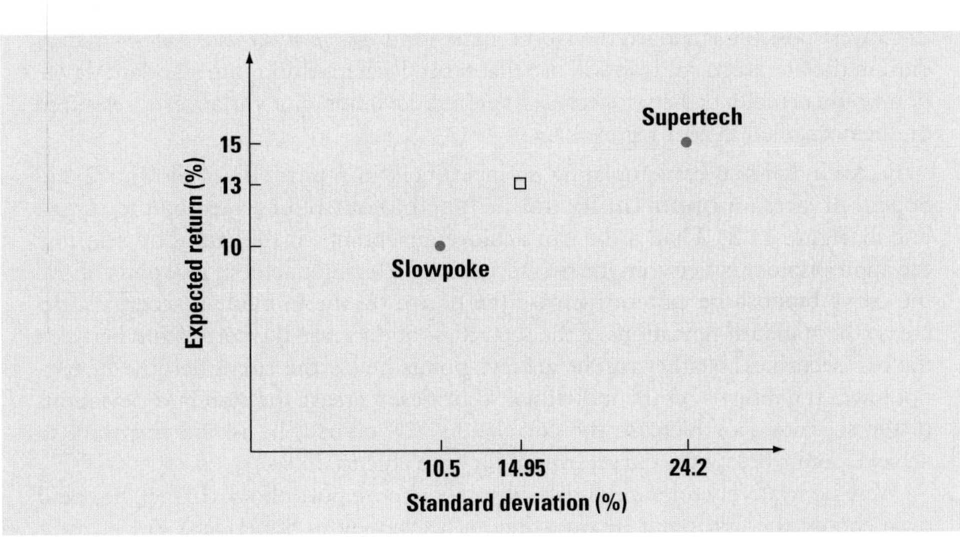

FIGURE 11.2 Expected Returns and Standard Deviations for Supertech, Slowpoke, and a Portfolio Composed of 60 Percent in Supertech and 40 Percent in Slowpoke

FIGURE 11.3 Set of Portfolios Composed of Holdings in Supertech and Slowpoke (correlation between the two securities is −.039)

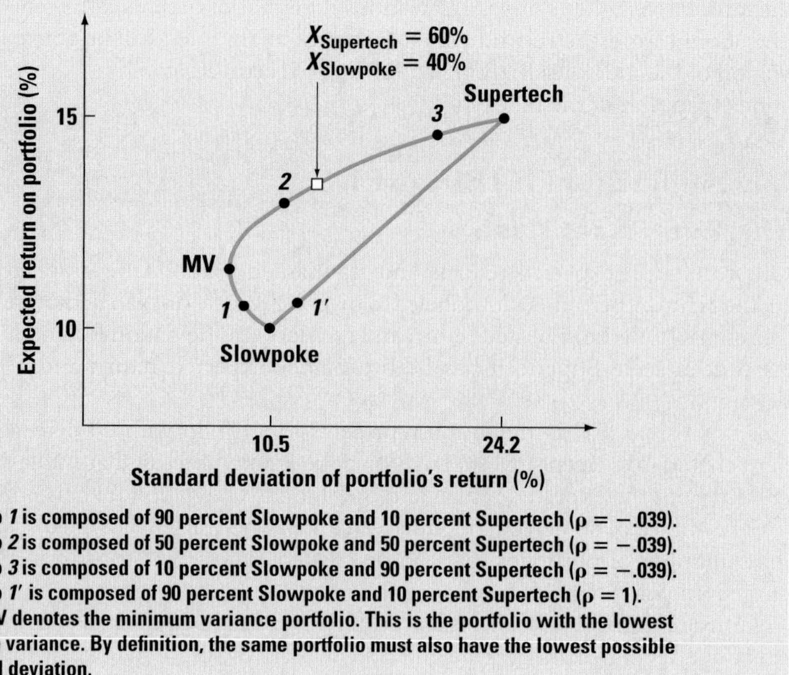

Portfolio *1* is composed of 90 percent Slowpoke and 10 percent Supertech ($\rho = -.039$).
Portfolio *2* is composed of 50 percent Slowpoke and 50 percent Supertech ($\rho = -.039$).
Portfolio *3* is composed of 10 percent Slowpoke and 90 percent Supertech ($\rho = -.039$).
Portfolio *1′* is composed of 90 percent Slowpoke and 10 percent Supertech ($\rho = 1$).
Point MV denotes the minimum variance portfolio. This is the portfolio with the lowest possible variance. By definition, the same portfolio must also have the lowest possible standard deviation.

10 percent in Supertech *if* the correlation between the two were exactly 1. We argue that there is no diversification effect if $\rho = 1$. However, the diversification effect applies to the curved line, because point *1* has the same expected return as point *1′* but has a lower standard deviation. (Points *2′* and *3′* are omitted to reduce the clutter of Figure 11.3.)

Though the straight line and the curved line are both represented in Figure 11.3, they do not simultaneously exist in the same world. *Either* $\rho = -.039$ and the curve exists *or* $\rho = 1$ and the straight line exists. In other words, though an investor can choose between different points on the curve if $\rho = -.039$, she cannot choose between points on the curve and points on the straight line.

2. The point MV represents the minimum variance portfolio. This is the portfolio with the lowest possible variance. By definition, this portfolio must also have the lowest possible standard deviation. (The term *minimum variance portfolio* is standard in the literature, and we will use that term. Perhaps minimum standard deviation would actually be better, because standard deviation, not variance, is measured on the horizontal axis of Figure 11.3.)

3. An individual contemplating an investment in a portfolio of Slowpoke and Supertech faces an **opportunity set** or **feasible set** represented by the curved line in Figure 11.3. That is, he can achieve any point on the curve by selecting the appropriate mix between the two securities. He cannot achieve any point above the curve because he cannot increase the return on the individual securities, decrease the standard deviations of the securities, or decrease the correlation between the two securities. Neither can he achieve points below the curve because he cannot lower the returns on the individual securities, increase the standard deviations of the securities, or increase the correlation. (Of course, he would not want to achieve points below the curve, even if he were able to do so.)

Were he relatively tolerant of risk, he might choose portfolio *3*. (In fact, he could even choose the end point by investing all his money in Supertech.) An investor with less tolerance for risk might choose portfolio *2*. An investor wanting as little risk as possible would choose MV, the portfolio with minimum variance or minimum standard deviation.

4. Note that the curve is backward bending between the Slowpoke point and MV. This indicates that, for a portion of the feasible set, standard deviation actually decreases as one increases expected return. Students frequently ask, "How can an increase in the proportion of the risky security, Supertech, lead to a reduction in the risk of the portfolio?"

This surprising finding is due to the diversification effect. The returns on the two securities are negatively correlated with each other. One security tends to go up when the other goes down and vice versa. Thus, an addition of a small amount of Supertech acts as a hedge to a portfolio composed only of Slowpoke. The risk of the portfolio is reduced, implying backward bending. Actually, backward bending always occurs if $\rho \leq 0$. It may or may not occur when $\rho > 0$. Of course, the curve bends backward only for a portion of its length. As one continues to increase the percentage of Supertech in the portfolio, the high standard deviation of this security eventually causes the standard deviation of the entire portfolio to rise.

5. No investor would want to hold a portfolio with an expected return below that of the minimum variance portfolio. For example, no investor would choose portfolio *1*. This portfolio has less expected return but more standard deviation than the minimum variance portfolio has. We say that portfolios such as portfolio *1* are *dominated* by the minimum variance portfolio. Though the entire curve from Slowpoke to Supertech is called the *feasible set,* investors only consider the curve from MV to Supertech. Hence, the curve from MV to Supertech is called the **efficient set** or the **efficient frontier**.

Figure 11.3 represents the opportunity set where $\rho = -.039$. It is worthwhile to examine Figure 11.4, which shows different curves for different correlations. As can be seen, the lower the correlation, the more bend there is in the curve. This indicates that the diversification effect rises as ρ declines. The greatest bend occurs in the limiting case where $\rho = -1$. This is perfect negative correlation. While this extreme case where $\rho = -1$ seems to fascinate students, it has little practical importance. Most pairs of securities

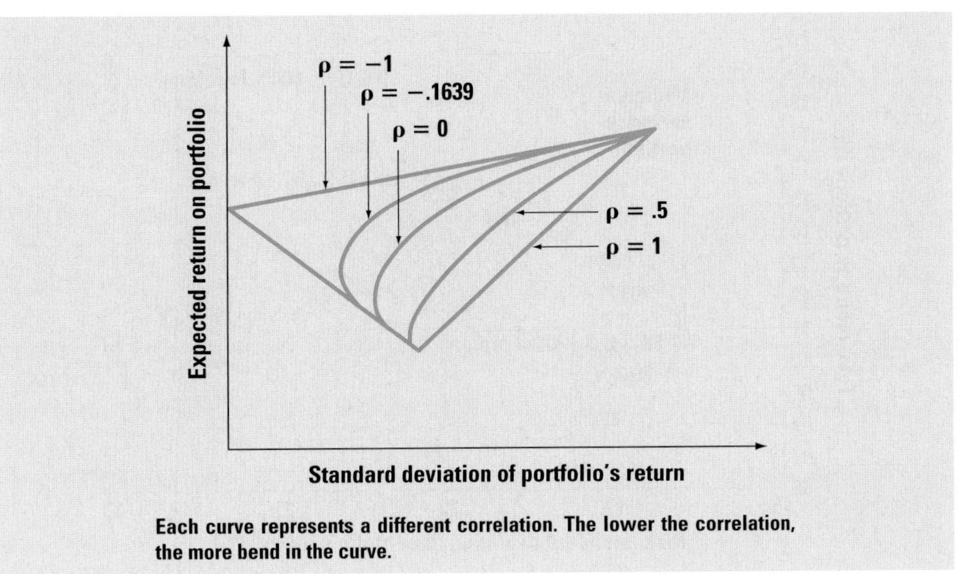

Each curve represents a different correlation. The lower the correlation, the more bend in the curve.

FIGURE 11.4 Opportunity Sets Composed of Holdings in Supertech and Slowpoke

exhibit positive correlation. Strong negative correlations, let alone perfect negative correlations, are uncommon occurrences for ordinary securities such as stocks and bonds.

Note that there is only one correlation between a pair of securities. We stated earlier that the correlation between Slowpoke and Supertech is −.039. Thus, the curve in Figure 11.3 representing this correlation is the correct one, and the other curves in Figure 11.4 should be viewed as merely hypothetical.

The graphs we examined are not mere intellectual curiosities. Rather, efficient sets can easily be calculated in the real world. As mentioned earlier, data on returns, standard deviations, and correlations are generally taken from past observations, though subjective notions can be used to determine the values of these parameters as well. Once the parameters have been determined, any one of a whole host of software packages can be purchased to generate an efficient set. However, the choice of the preferred portfolio within the efficient set is up to you. As with other important decisions like what job to choose, what house or car to buy, and how much time to allocate to this course, there is no computer program to choose the preferred portfolio.

An efficient set can be generated where the two individual assets are portfolios themselves. For example, the two assets in Figure 11.5 are a diversified portfolio of American stocks and a diversified portfolio of foreign stocks. Expected returns, standard deviations, and the correlation coefficient were calculated over the recent past. No subjectivity entered the analysis. The U.S. stock portfolio with a standard deviation of about .173 is less risky than the foreign stock portfolio, which has a standard deviation of about .222. However, combining a small percentage of the foreign stock portfolio with the U.S. portfolio actually reduces risk, as can be seen by the backward-bending nature of the curve. In other words, the diversification benefits from combining two different portfolios more than offset the introduction of a riskier set of stocks into one's holdings. The minimum variance portfolio occurs with about 80 percent of one's funds in American stocks and about 20 percent in foreign stocks. Addition of foreign securities beyond this point increases the risk of one's entire portfolio.

The backward-bending curve in Figure 11.5 is important information that has not bypassed American money managers. In recent years, pension fund and mutual fund managers in the United States have sought out investment opportunities overseas. Another point worth pondering concerns the potential pitfalls of using only past data to

FIGURE 11.5

Return/Risk Trade-off for World Stocks: Portfolio of U.S. and Foreign Stocks

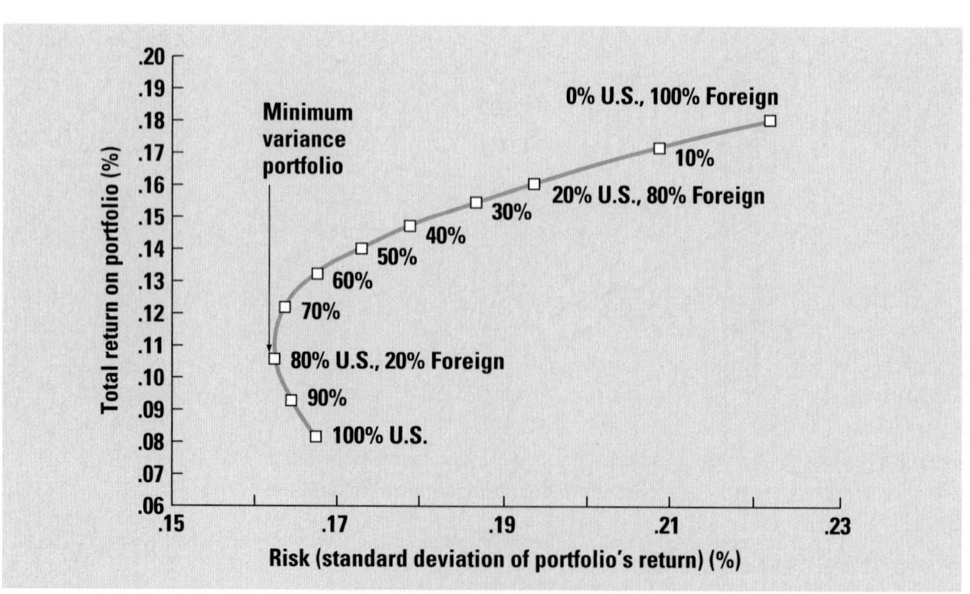

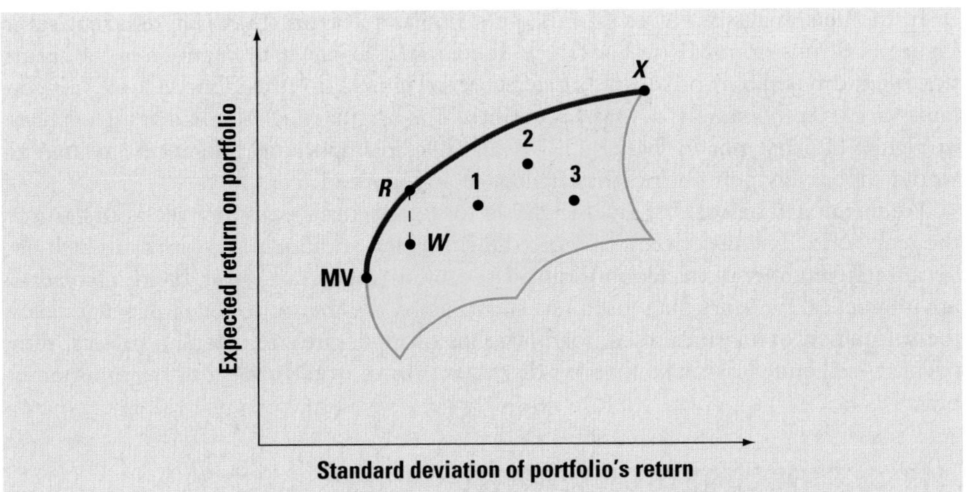

FIGURE 11.6

The Feasible Set of Portfolios Constructed from Many Securities

estimate future returns. The stock markets of many foreign countries have had phenomenal growth in the past 25 years. Thus, a graph like Figure 11.5 makes a large investment in these foreign markets seem attractive. However, because abnormally high returns cannot be sustained forever, some subjectivity must be used when forecasting future expected returns.

The Efficient Set for Many Securities

The previous discussion concerned two securities. We found that a simple curve sketched out all the possible portfolios. Because investors generally hold more than two securities, we should look at the same graph when more than two securities are held. The shaded area in Figure 11.6 represents the opportunity set or feasible set when many securities are considered. The shaded area represents all the possible combinations of expected return and standard deviation for a portfolio. For example, in a universe of 100 securities, point 1 might represent a portfolio of, say 40 securities. Point 2 might represent a portfolio of 80 securities. Point 3 might represent a different set of 80 securities, or the same 80 securities held in different proportions, or something else. Obviously, the combinations are virtually endless. However, note that all possible combinations fit into a confined region. No security or combination of securities can fall outside of the shaded region. That is, no one can choose a portfolio with an expected return above that given by the shaded region. Furthermore, no one can choose a portfolio with a standard deviation below that given in the shaded area. Perhaps more surprisingly, no one can choose an expected return below that given in the curve. In other words, the capital markets actually prevent a self-destructive person from taking on a guaranteed loss.[2]

So far, Figure 11.6 is different from the earlier graphs. When only two securities are involved, all the combinations lie on a single curve. Conversely, with many securities the combinations cover an entire area. However, notice that an individual will want to be somewhere on the upper edge between MV and *X*. The upper edge, which we indicate in Figure 11.6 by a thick curve, is called the *efficient set.* Any point below the efficient set would receive less expected return and the same standard deviation as a point on the efficient set. For example, consider *R* on the efficient set and *W* directly below it. If *W* contains the risk you desire, you should choose *R* instead in order to receive a higher expected return.

[2]Of course, someone dead set on parting with his money can do so. For example, he can trade frequently without purpose, so that commissions more than offset the positive expected returns on the portfolio.

In the final analysis, Figure 11.6 is quite similar to Figure 11.3. The efficient set in Figure 11.3 runs from MV to Supertech. It contains various combinations of the securities Supertech and Slowpoke. The efficient set in Figure 11.6 runs from MV to *X*. It contains various combinations of many securities. The fact that a whole shaded area appears in Figure 11.6 but not in Figure 11.3 is just not an important difference; no investor would choose any point below the efficient set in Figure 11.6 anyway.

We mentioned before that an efficient set for two securities can be traced out easily in the real world. The task becomes more difficult when additional securities are included because the number of calculations quickly becomes huge. As a result, hand calculations are impractical for more than just a few securities. A number of software packages allow the calculation of an efficient set for portfolios of moderate size. By all accounts, these packages sell quite briskly, so that our discussion above would appear to be important in practice.

11.5 RISKLESS BORROWING AND LENDING

Figure 11.6 assumes that all the securities on the efficient set are risky. Alternatively, an investor could combine a risky investment with an investment in a riskless or *risk-free* security, such as an investment in United States Treasury bills. This is illustrated in the following example.

EXAMPLE 11.3 Riskless Lending and Portfolio Risk

Ms. Bagwell is considering investing in the common stock of Merville Enterprises. In addition, Ms. Bagwell will either borrow or lend at the risk-free rate. The relevant parameters are:

	COMMON STOCK OF MERVILLE	RISK-FREE ASSET
Expected return	14%	10%
Standard deviation	.20	0

Suppose Ms. Bagwell chooses to invest a total of $1,000, $350 of which is to be invested in Merville Enterprises and $650 placed in the risk-free asset. The expected return on her total investment is simply a weighted average of the two returns:

$$\text{Expected return on portfolio composed of one riskless and one risky asset} = .114 = (.35 \times .14) + (.65 \times .10) \quad (11.10)$$

Because the expected return on the portfolio is a weighted average of the expected return on the risky asset (Merville Enterprises) and the risk-free return, the calculation is analogous to the way we treated two risky assets. In other words, equation (11.3) applies here.

Using equation (11.4), the formula for the variance of the portfolio can be written as:

$$X^2_{\text{Merville}}\sigma^2_{\text{Merville}} + 2X_{\text{Merville}}X_{\text{Risk-free}}\sigma_{\text{Merville, Risk-free}} + X^2_{\text{Risk-free}}\sigma^2_{\text{Risk-free}}$$

However, by definition, the risk-free asset has no variability. Thus, both $\sigma_{\text{Merville, Risk-free}}$ and $\sigma^2_{\text{Risk-free}}$ are equal to zero, reducing the above expression to:

$$\begin{aligned}\text{Variance of portfolio composed of one riskless and one risky asset} &= X^2_{\text{Merville}}\sigma^2_{\text{Merville}} \\ &= (.35)^2 \times (.20)^2 \\ &= .0049\end{aligned} \quad (11.11)$$

(continued)

FIGURE 11.7
Relationship between Expected Return and Risk for a Portfolio of One Risky Asset and One Riskless Asset

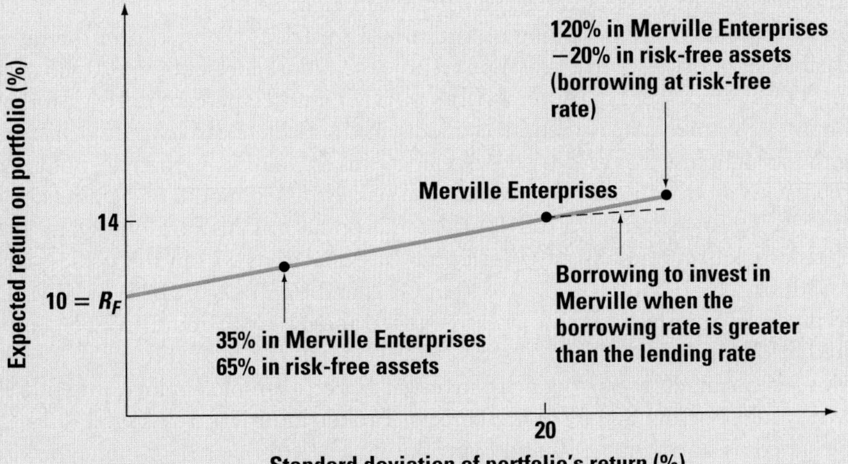

The standard deviation of the portfolio is:

$$\begin{aligned} \text{Standard deviation of portfolio composed of one riskless and one risky asset} &= X_{\text{Merville}}\sigma_{\text{Merville}} \quad (11.12) \\ &= .35 \times .20 \\ &= .07 \end{aligned}$$

The relationship between risk and expected return for one risky and one riskless asset can be seen in Figure 11.7. Ms. Bagwell's split of 35–65 percent between the two assets is represented on a *straight* line between the risk-free rate and a pure investment in Merville Enterprises. Note that, unlike the case of two risky assets, the opportunity set is straight, not curved.

Suppose that, alternatively, Ms. Bagwell borrows \$200 at the risk-free rate. Combining this with her original sum of \$1,000, she invests a total of \$1,200 in Merville. Her expected return would be

$$\text{Expected return on portfolio formed by borrowing to invest in risky asset} = 14.8\% = 1.20 \times .14 + (-.2 \times .10)$$

Here, she invests 120 percent of her original investment of \$1,000 by borrowing 20 percent of her original investment. Note that the return of 14.8 percent is greater than the 14 percent expected return on Merville Enterprises. This occurs because she is borrowing at 10 percent to invest in a security with an expected return greater than 10 percent.

The standard deviation is:

$$\text{Standard deviation of portfolio formed by borrowing to invest in risky asset} = .24 = 1.20 \times .2$$

The standard deviation of .24 is greater than .20, the standard deviation of the Merville investment, because borrowing increases the variability of the investment. This investment also appears in Figure 11.7.

So far, we have assumed that Ms. Bagwell is able to borrow at the same rate at which she can lend.[3] Now let us consider the case where the borrowing rate is above the lending rate. The dotted line in Figure 11.7 illustrates the opportunity set for borrowing opportunities in this case. The dotted line is below the solid line because a higher borrowing rate lowers the expected return on the investment.

[3]Surprisingly, this appears to be a decent approximation because a large number of investors are able to borrow from a stockbroker (called *going on margin*) when purchasing stocks. The borrowing rate here is very near the riskless rate of interest, particularly for large investors. More will be said about this in a later chapter.

The Optimal Portfolio

The previous section concerned a portfolio formed between one riskless asset and one risky asset. In reality, an investor is likely to combine an investment in the riskless asset with a *portfolio* of risky assets. This is illustrated in Figure 11.8.

Consider point *Q*, representing a portfolio of securities. Point *Q* is in the interior of the feasible set of risky securities. Let us assume the point represents a portfolio of 30 percent in AT&T, 45 percent in General Motors (GM), and 25 percent in IBM. Individuals combining investments in *Q* with investments in the riskless asset would achieve points along the straight line from R_F to *Q*. We refer to this as line *I*. For example, point *1* on the line represents a portfolio of 70 percent in the riskless asset and 30 percent in stocks represented by *Q*. An investor with \$100 choosing point *1* as his portfolio would put \$70 in the risk-free asset and \$30 in *Q*. This can be restated as \$70 in the riskless asset, \$9 (.3 × \$30) in AT&T, \$13.50 (.45 × \$30) in GM, and \$7.50 (.25 × \$30) in IBM. Point *2* also represents a portfolio of the risk-free asset and *Q*, with more (65 percent) being invested in *Q*.

Point *3* is obtained by borrowing to invest in *Q*. For example, an investor with \$100 of his own would borrow \$40 from the bank or broker in order to invest \$140 in *Q*. This can be stated as borrowing \$40 and contributing \$100 of one's own money in order to invest \$42 (.3 × \$140) in AT&T, \$63 (.45 × \$140) in GM, and \$35 (.25 × \$140) in IBM.

The above investments can be summarized as:

	POINT *Q*	POINT *1* (LENDING \$70)	POINT *3* (BORROWING \$40)
AT&T	\$ 30	\$ 9	\$ 42
GM	45	13.50	63
IBM	25	7.50	35
Risk-free	0	70	− 40
Total investment	\$100	\$100	\$100

Though any investor can obtain any point on line *I*, no point on the line is optimal. To see this, consider line *II*, a line running from R_F through *A*. Point *A* represents a portfolio of risky securities. Line *II* represents portfolios formed by combinations of the

FIGURE 11.8

Relationship between Expected Return and Standard Deviation for an Investment in a Combination of Risky Securities and the Riskless Asset

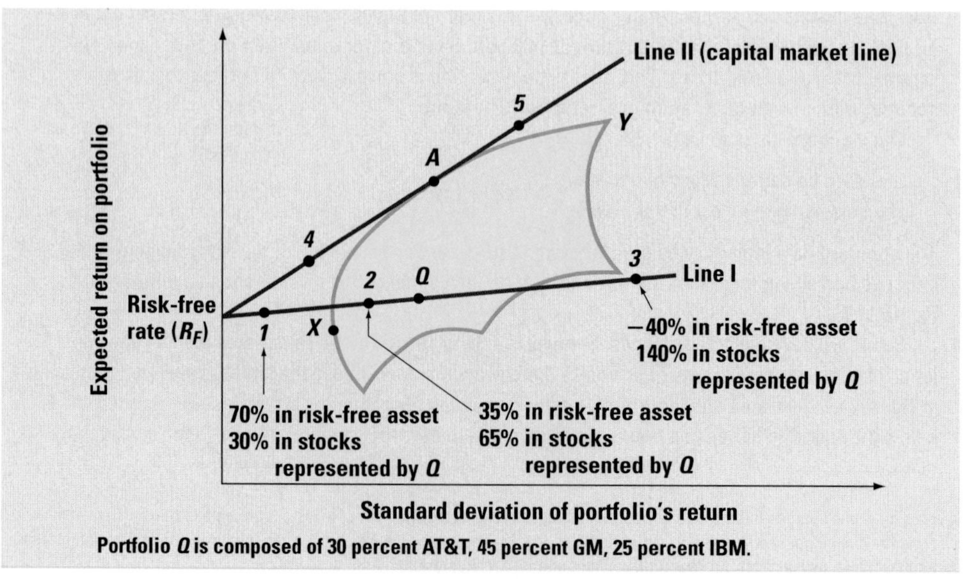

Portfolio *Q* is composed of 30 percent AT&T, 45 percent GM, 25 percent IBM.

risk-free asset and the securities in A. Points between R_F and A are portfolios in which some money is invested in the riskless asset and the rest is placed in A. Points past A are achieved by borrowing at the riskless rate to buy more of A than one could with one's original funds alone.

As drawn, line *II* is tangent to the efficient set of risky securities. Whatever point an individual can obtain on line *I*, he can obtain a point with the same standard deviation and a higher expected return on line *II*. In fact, because line *II* is tangent to the efficient set of risky assets, it provides the investor with the best possible opportunities. In other words, line *II* can be viewed as the efficient set of *all* assets, both risky and riskless. An investor with a fair degree of risk aversion might choose a point between R_F and A, perhaps point *4*. An individual with less risk aversion might choose a point closer to A or even beyond A. For example, point *5* corresponds to an individual borrowing money to increase his investment in A.

The graph illustrates an important point. With riskless borrowing and lending, the portfolio of *risky* assets held by any investor would always be point A. Regardless of the investor's tolerance for risk, he would never choose any other point on the efficient set of risky assets (represented by curve *XAY*) nor any point in the interior of the feasible region. Rather, he would combine the securities of A with the riskless assets if he had high aversion to risk. He would borrow the riskless asset to invest more funds in A if he had low aversion to risk.

This result establishes what financial economists call the **separation principle**. That is, the investor's investment decision consists of two separate steps:

1. After estimating (*a*) the expected returns and variances of individual securities, and (*b*) the covariances between pairs of securities, the investor calculates the efficient set of risky assets, represented by curve *XAY* in Figure 11.8. He then determines point A, the tangency between the risk-free rate and the efficient set of risky assets (curve *XAY*). Point A represents the portfolio of risky assets that the investor will hold. This point is determined solely from his estimates of returns, variances, and covariances. No personal characteristics, such as degree of risk aversion, are needed in this step.

2. The investor must now determine how he will combine point A, his portfolio of risky assets, with the riskless asset. He might invest some of his funds in the riskless asset and some in portfolio A. He would end up at a point on the line between R_F and A in this case. Alternatively, he might borrow at the risk-free rate and contribute some of his own funds as well, investing the sum in portfolio A. He would end up at a point on line *II* beyond A. His position in the riskless asset, that is, his choice of where on the line he wants to be, is determined by his internal characteristics, such as his ability to tolerate risk.

11.6 ANNOUNCEMENTS, SURPRISES, AND EXPECTED RETURNS

Now that we know how to construct portfolios and evaluate their returns, we begin to describe more carefully the risks and returns associated with individual securities. Thus far, we have measured volatility by looking at the difference between the actual return on an asset or portfolio, R, and the expected return, $E(R)$. We now look at why those deviations exist.

Expected and Unexpected Returns

To begin, for concreteness, we consider the return on the stock of a company called Flyers. What will determine this stock's return in, say, the coming year?

The return on any stock traded in a financial market is composed of two parts. First, the normal, or expected, return from the stock is the part of the return that shareholders in the market predict or expect. This return depends on the information shareholders have that bears on the stock, and it is based on the market's understanding today of the important factors that will influence the stock in the coming year.

The second part of the return on the stock is the uncertain, or risky, part. This is the portion that comes from unexpected information revealed within the year. A list of all possible sources of such information would be endless, but here are a few examples:

www.quicken.com is a great site for stock info.

News about Flyers research.

Government figures released on gross domestic product (GDP).

The results from the latest arms control talks.

The news that Flyers's sales figures are higher than expected.

A sudden, unexpected drop in interest rates.

Based on this discussion, one way to express the return on Flyers stock in the coming year would be:

$$\begin{aligned}\textbf{Total return} &= \textbf{Expected return} + \textbf{Unexpected return} \\ \boldsymbol{R} &= \mathbf{E}(\boldsymbol{R}) + \boldsymbol{U}\end{aligned} \tag{11.13}$$

where R stands for the actual total return in the year, $E(R)$ stands for the expected part of the return, and U stands for the unexpected part of the return. What this says is that the actual return, R, differs from the expected return, $E(R)$, because of surprises that occur during the year. In any given year, the unexpected return will be positive or negative, but, through time, the average value of U will be zero. This simply means that on average, the actual return equals the expected return.

Announcements and News

We need to be careful when we talk about the effect of news items on the return. For example, suppose Flyers's business is such that the company prospers when GDP grows at a relatively high rate and suffers when GDP is relatively stagnant. In this case, in deciding what return to expect this year from owning stock in Flyers, shareholders either implicitly or explicitly must think about what GDP is likely to be for the year.

When the government actually announces GDP figures for the year, what will happen to the value of Flyers's stock? Obviously, the answer depends on what figure is released. More to the point, however, the impact depends on how much of that figure is *new* information.

At the beginning of the year, market participants will have some idea or forecast of what the yearly GDP will be. To the extent that shareholders have predicted GDP, that prediction will already be factored into the expected part of the return on the stock, $E(R)$. On the other hand, if the announced GDP is a surprise, then the effect will be part of U, the unanticipated portion of the return. As an example, suppose shareholders in the market had forecast that the GDP increase this year would be .5 percent. If the actual announcement this year is exactly .5 percent, the same as the forecast, then the shareholders don't really learn anything, and the announcement isn't news. There will be no impact on the stock price as a result. This is like receiving confirmation of something that you suspected all along; it doesn't reveal anything new.

A common way of saying that an announcement isn't news is to say that the market has already "discounted" the announcement. The use of the word *discount* here is different from the use of the term in computing present values, but the spirit is the same. When we discount a dollar in the future, we say it is worth less to us because of the time value of money. When we discount an announcement or a news item, we say that it has less of an impact on the market because the market already knew much of it.

Going back to Flyers, suppose the government announces that the actual GDP increase during the year has been 1.5 percent. Now shareholders have learned something, namely, that the increase is one percentage point higher than they had forecast. This difference between the actual result and the forecast, one percentage point in this example, is sometimes called the *innovation* or the *surprise.*

This distinction explains why what seems to be good news can actually be bad news (and vice versa). For example, in May 2004, Deere & Company, makers of the famous green tractors, announced record net income of $477.3 million for the second quarter. The company had earnings per share of $1.88, which handily surpassed the market estimate of $1.76 per share. Good news, right? Wrong. The stock slid 1.3 percent on the announcement. Investors were concerned that the company's performance was so strong that there was little room for improvement. In fact, Deere announced that it had operated at 110 percent of normal market conditions, and operations for the company typically topped out at 120 percent of normal market conditions, so there was little room left for future growth.

A key idea to keep in mind about news and price changes is that news about the future is what matters. For example, to open the chapter, we compared ExxonMobil, Amazon.com, and Cisco Systems. In ExxonMobil's case, the company reported record profits, but on a percentage basis, the increase in net income was smaller than increases reported by competitors. The prior week, ChevronTexaco and ConocoPhillips reported net income that had nearly doubled. In Amazon.com's case, earnings were increased by tax credits. Excluding the tax credits, net income was actually below analyst estimates. Additionally, the company was feeling the pressure from increased competition, which increased marketing costs. In Cisco's case, the news was announced on a day when investors turned sour on the future of stocks in general. (Keep this case in mind as you read the next section.)

To summarize, an announcement can be broken into two parts, the anticipated, or expected, part and the surprise, or innovation:

$$\textbf{Announcement} = \textbf{Expected part} + \textbf{Surprise} \qquad \textbf{(11.14)}$$

The expected part of any announcement is the part of the information that the market uses to form the expectation, $E(R)$, of the return on the stock. The surprise is the news that influences the unanticipated return on the stock, U. Henceforth, when we speak of news, we will mean the surprise part of an announcement and not the portion that the market has expected and therefore already discounted.

11.7 RISK: SYSTEMATIC AND UNSYSTEMATIC

The unanticipated part of the return, that portion resulting from surprises, is the true risk of any investment. After all, if we always receive exactly what we expect, then the investment is perfectly predictable and, by definition, risk-free. In other words, the risk of owning an asset comes from surprises–unanticipated events.

There are important differences, though, among various sources of risk. Look back at our previous list of news stories. Some of these stories are directed specifically at Flyers, and some are more general. Which of the news items are of specific importance to Flyers?

Announcements about interest rates or GDP are clearly important for nearly all companies, whereas the news about Flyers's president, its research, or its sales is of specific interest to Flyers. We will distinguish between these two types of events, because, as we shall see, they have very different implications.

Systematic and Unsystematic Risk

The first type of surprise, the one that affects a large number of assets, we will label **systematic risk**. A systematic risk is one that influences a large number of assets, each to a greater or lesser extent. Because systematic risks have marketwide effects, they are sometimes called *market risks.*

The second type of surprise we will call **unsystematic risk**. An unsystematic risk is one that affects a single asset or a small group of assets. Because these risks are unique to individual companies or assets, they are sometimes called *unique* or *asset specific risks.* We will use these terms interchangeably.

As we have seen, uncertainties about general economic conditions, such as GDP, interest rates, or inflation, are examples of systematic risks. These conditions affect nearly all companies to some degree. An unanticipated increase, or surprise, in inflation, for example, affects wages and the costs of the supplies that companies buy; it affects the value of the assets that companies own; and it affects the prices at which companies sell their products. Forces such as these, to which all companies are susceptible, are the essence of systematic risk.

In contrast, the announcement of an oil strike by a company will primarily affect that company and, perhaps, a few others (such as primary competitors and suppliers). It is unlikely to have much of an effect on the world oil market, however, or on the affairs of companies not in the oil business, so this is an unsystematic event.

Systematic and Unsystematic Components of Return

The distinction between a systematic risk and an unsystematic risk is never really as exact as we make it out to be. Even the most narrow and peculiar bit of news about a company ripples through the economy. This is true because every enterprise, no matter how tiny, is a part of the economy. It's like the tale of a kingdom that was lost because one horse lost a shoe. This is mostly hairsplitting, however. Some risks are clearly much more general than others. We'll see some evidence on this point in just a moment.

The distinction between the types of risk allows us to break down the surprise portion, U, of the return on the Flyers stock into two parts. Earlier, we had the actual return broken down into its expected and surprise components:

$$\boldsymbol{R} = \mathrm{E}(\boldsymbol{R}) + \boldsymbol{U}$$

We now recognize that the total surprise component for Flyers, U, has a systematic and an unsystematic component, so:

$$\boldsymbol{R} = \mathrm{E}(\boldsymbol{R}) + \textbf{Systematic portion} + \textbf{Unsystematic portion} \qquad \textbf{(11.15)}$$

Systematic risks are often called market risks because they affect most assets in the market to some degree.

The important thing about the way we have broken down the total surprise, U, is that the unsystematic portion is more or less unique to Flyers. For this reason, it is unrelated to the unsystematic portion of return on most other assets. To see why this is important, we need to return to the subject of portfolio risk.

11.8 DIVERSIFICATION AND PORTFOLIO RISK

For more on risk and diversification, visit www.investopedia.com/university.

We've seen earlier that portfolio risks can, in principle, be quite different from the risks of the assets that make up the portfolio. We now look more closely at the riskiness of an individual asset versus the risk of a portfolio of many different assets. We will once again examine some market history to get an idea of what happens with actual investments in U.S. capital markets.

(1) NUMBER OF STOCKS IN PORTFOLIO	(2) AVERAGE STANDARD DEVIATION OF ANNUAL PORTFOLIO RETURNS	(3) RATIO OF PORTFOLIO STANDARD DEVIATION TO STANDARD DEVIATION OF A SINGLE STOCK
1	49.24%	1.00
2	37.36	.76
4	29.69	.60
6	26.64	.54
8	24.98	.51
10	23.93	.49
20	21.68	.44
30	20.87	.42
40	20.46	.42
50	20.20	.41
100	19.69	.40
200	19.42	.39
300	19.34	.39
400	19.29	.39
500	19.27	.39
1,000	19.21	.39

TABLE 11.4

Standard Deviations of Annual Portfolio Returns

Sources: These figures are from Table 1 in M. Statman, "How Many Stocks Make a Diversified Portfolio?" *Journal of Financial and Quantitative Analysis* 22 (September 1987), pp. 353–64. They were derived from E. J. Elton and M. J. Gruber, "Risk Reduction and Portfolio Size: An Analytic Solution," *Journal of Business* 50 (October 1977), pp. 415–37.

The Effect of Diversification: Another Lesson from Market History

In our previous chapter, we saw that the standard deviation of the annual return on a portfolio of 500 large common stocks has historically been about 20 percent per year. Does this mean that the standard deviation of the annual return on a typical stock in that group of 500 is about 20 percent? As you might suspect by now, the answer is *no*. This is an extremely important observation.

To allow examination of the relationship between portfolio size and portfolio risk, Table 11.4 illustrates typical average annual standard deviations for equally weighted portfolios that contain different numbers of randomly selected NYSE securities.

In Column 2 of Table 11.4, we see that the standard deviation for a "portfolio" of one security is about 49 percent. What this means is that if you randomly selected a single NYSE stock and put all your money into it, your standard deviation of return would typically be a substantial 49 percent per year. If you were to randomly select two stocks and invest half your money in each, your standard deviation would be about 37 percent on average, and so on.

The important thing to notice in Table 11.4 is that the standard deviation declines as the number of securities is increased. By the time we have 100 randomly chosen stocks, the portfolio's standard deviation has declined by about 60 percent, from 49 percent to about 20 percent. With 500 securities, the standard deviation is 19.27 percent, similar to the 20 percent we saw in our previous chapter for the large common stock portfolio. The small difference exists because the portfolio securities and time periods examined are not identical.

The Principle of Diversification

Figure 11.9 illustrates the point we've been discussing. What we have plotted is the standard deviation of return versus the number of stocks in the portfolio. Notice in Figure 11.9 that the benefit in terms of risk reduction from adding securities drops off as we add

FIGURE 11.9
Portfolio Diversification

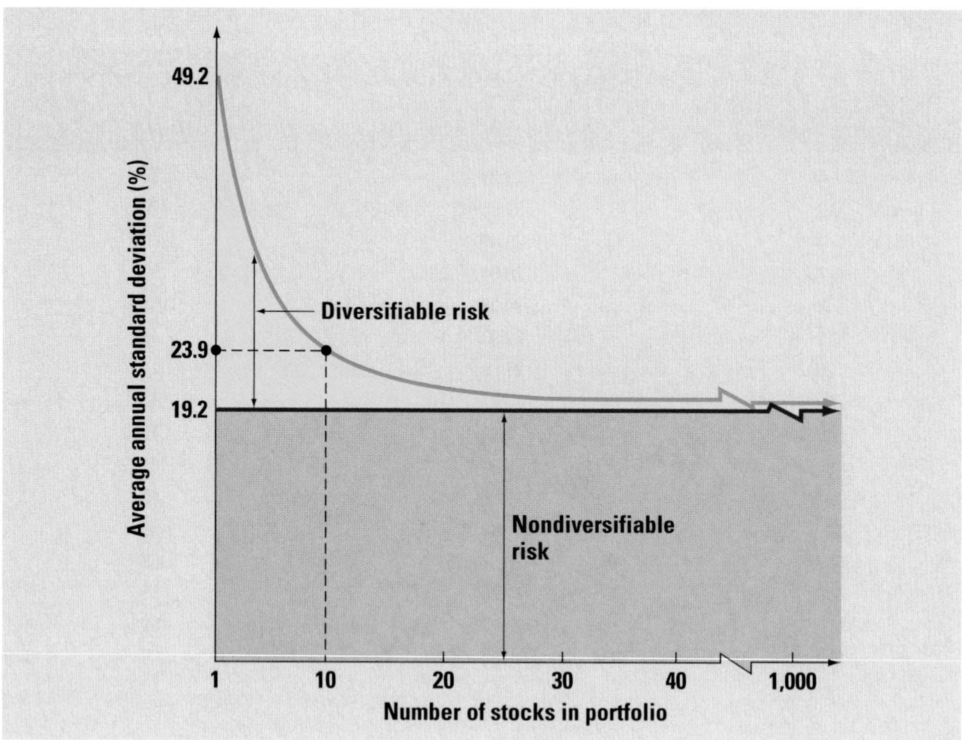

more and more. By the time we have 10 securities, most of the effect is already realized, and by the time we get to 30 or so, there is very little remaining benefit.

Figure 11.9 illustrates two key points. First, some of the riskiness associated with individual assets can be eliminated by forming portfolios. The process of spreading an investment across assets (and thereby forming a portfolio) is called *diversification.* The **principle of diversification** tells us that spreading an investment across many assets will eliminate some of the risk. The blue shaded area in Figure 11.9, labeled "diversifiable risk," is the part that can be eliminated by diversification.

The second point is equally important. There is a minimum level of risk that cannot be eliminated simply by diversifying. This minimum level is labeled "nondiversifiable risk" in Figure 11.9. Taken together, these two points are another important lesson from capital market history: Diversification reduces risk, but only up to a point. Put another way, some risk is diversifiable and some is not.

To give a recent example of the impact of diversification, the Dow Jones Industrial Average (DJIA), which is a widely followed stock market index of 30 large, well-known U.S. stocks, was up about 25 percent in 2003. As we saw in our previous chapter, this represents a pretty good year for a portfolio of large-cap stocks. The biggest individual gainers for the year were Intel (up 107 percent), Caterpillar (up 86 percent), and Alcoa (up 71 percent). But not all 30 stocks were up: The losers included Eastman Kodak (down 24 percent), AT&T (down 19 percent), and Merck (down 11 percent).

In contrast to 2003, consider 2002 when the DJIA was down about 17 percent, a fairly bad year. The big losers in this year were Home Depot (down 52 percent), and Intel (down 50 percent). Working to offset these losses was Eastman Kodak (up 20 percent). Again, the lesson is clear: Diversification reduces exposure to extreme outcomes, both good and bad.

Diversification and Unsystematic Risk

From our discussion of portfolio risk, we know that some of the risk associated with individual assets can be diversified away and some cannot. We are left with an obvious question: Why is this so? It turns out that the answer hinges on the distinction we made earlier between systematic and unsystematic risk.

By definition, an unsystematic risk is one that is particular to a single asset or, at most, a small group. For example, if the asset under consideration is stock in a single company, the discovery of positive NPV projects such as successful new products and innovative cost savings will tend to increase the value of the stock. Unanticipated lawsuits, industrial accidents, strikes, and similar events will tend to decrease future cash flows and thereby reduce share values.

Here is the important observation: If we only held a single stock, then the value of our investment would fluctuate because of company-specific events. If we hold a large portfolio, on the other hand, some of the stocks in the portfolio will go up in value because of positive company-specific events and some will go down in value because of negative events. The net effect on the overall value of the portfolio will be relatively small, however, because these effects will tend to cancel each other out.

Now we see why some of the variability associated with individual assets is eliminated by diversification. When we combine assets into portfolios, the unique, or unsystematic, events–both positive and negative–tend to "wash out" once we have more than just a few assets.

This is an important point that bears repeating:

Unsystematic risk is essentially eliminated by diversification, so a portfolio with many assets has almost no unsystematic risk.

In fact, the terms *diversifiable risk* and *unsystematic risk* are often used interchangeably.

Diversification and Systematic Risk

We've seen that unsystematic risk can be eliminated by diversifying. What about systematic risk? Can it also be eliminated by diversification? The answer is no because, by definition, a systematic risk affects almost all assets to some degree. As a result, no matter how many assets we put into a portfolio, the systematic risk doesn't go away. Thus, for obvious reasons, the terms *systematic risk* and *nondiversifiable risk* are used interchangeably.

Because we have introduced so many different terms, it is useful to summarize our discussion before moving on. What we have seen is that the total risk of an investment, as measured by the standard deviation of its return, can be written as:

$$\textbf{Total risk} = \textbf{Systematic risk} + \textbf{Unsystematic risk} \qquad \textbf{(11.16)}$$

Systematic risk is also called *nondiversifiable risk* or *market risk*. Unsystematic risk is also called *diversifiable risk, unique risk,* or *asset-specific risk*. For a well-diversified portfolio, the unsystematic risk is negligible. For such a portfolio, essentially all of the risk is systematic.

11.9 MARKET EQUILIBRIUM

Definition of the Market Equilibrium Portfolio

Much of our analysis thus far concerns one investor. His estimates of the expected returns and variances for individual securities and the covariances between pairs of securities are his and his alone. Other investors would obviously have different estimates of the above variables. However, the estimates might not vary much because all investors would be forming expectations from the same data on past price movements and other publicly available information.

Financial economists often imagine a world where all investors possess the *same* estimates on expected returns, variances, and covariances. Though this can never be literally true, it can be thought of as a useful simplifying assumption in a world where investors have access to similar sources of information. This assumption is called **homogeneous expectations.**[4]

If all investors had homogeneous expectations, Figure 11.8 would be the same for all individuals. That is, all investors would sketch out the same efficient set of risky assets because they would be working with the same inputs. This efficient set of risky assets is represented by the curve *XAY*. Because the same risk-free rate would apply to everyone, all investors would view point *A* as the portfolio of risky assets to be held.

This point *A* takes on great importance because all investors would purchase the risky securities that it represents. Those investors with a high degree of risk aversion might combine *A* with an investment in the riskless asset, achieving point *4*, for example. Others with low aversion to risk might borrow to achieve, say, point *5*. Because this is a very important conclusion, we restate it:

In a world with homogeneous expectations, all investors would hold the portfolio of risky assets represented by point *A*.

If all investors choose the same portfolio of risky assets, it is possible to determine what that portfolio is. Common sense tells us that it is a market value weighted portfolio of all existing securities. It is the **market portfolio**.

In practice, financial economists use a broad-based index such as the Standard & Poor's (S&P) 500 as a proxy for the market portfolio. Of course, all investors do not hold the same portfolio. However, we know that a large number of investors hold diversified portfolios, particularly when mutual funds or pension funds are included. A broad-based index is a good proxy for the highly diversified portfolios of many investors.

Definition of Risk When Investors Hold the Market Portfolio

The previous section states that many investors hold diversified portfolios similar to broad-based indices. This result allows us to be more precise about the risk of a security in the context of a diversified portfolio.

Researchers have shown that the best measure of the risk of a security in a large portfolio is the *beta* of the security. We illustrate beta by an example.

EXAMPLE 11.4 Beta

Consider the following possible returns on both the stock of Jelco, Inc., and on the market:

STATE	TYPE OF ECONOMY	RETURN ON MARKET (PERCENT)	RETURN ON JELCO, INC. (PERCENT)
I	Bull	15	25
II	Bull	15	15
III	Bear	− 5	− 5
IV	Bear	− 5	−15

Though the return on the market has only two possible outcomes (15% and −5%), the return on Jelco has four possible outcomes. It is helpful to consider the expected return on a security for a given return on the market. Assuming each state is equally likely, we have:

[4]The assumption of homogeneous expectations states that all investors have the same beliefs concerning returns, variances, and covariances. It does not say that all investors have the same aversion to risk.

TYPE OF ECONOMY	RETURN ON MARKET (PERCENT)	EXPECTED RETURN ON JELCO, INC. (PERCENT)
Bull	15%	20% = 25% × .50 + 15% × .50
Bear	− 5%	−10% = −5% × .50 + (−15%) × .50

Jelco, Inc., responds to market movements because its expected return is greater in bullish states than in bearish states. We now calculate exactly how responsive the security is to market movements. The market's return in a bullish economy is 20 percent [15% − (−5%)] greater than the market's return in a bearish economy. However, the expected return on Jelco in a bullish economy is 30 percent [20% − (−10%)] greater than its expected return in a bearish state. Thus, Jelco, Inc., has a responsiveness coefficient of 1.5 (30%/20%).

This relationship appears in Figure 11.10. The returns for both Jelco and the market in each state are plotted as four points. In addition, we plot the expected return on the security for each of the two possible returns on the market. These two points, each of which we designate by an X, are joined by a line called the **characteristic line** of the security. The slope of the line is 1.5, the number calculated in the previous paragraph. This responsiveness coefficient of 1.5 is the **beta** of Jelco.

The interpretation of beta from Figure 11.10 is intuitive. The graph tells us that the returns of Jelco are magnified 1.5 times over those of the market. When the market does well, Jelco's stock is expected to do even better. When the market does poorly, Jelco's stock is expected to do even worse. Now imagine an individual with a portfolio near that of the market who is considering the addition of Jelco to his portfolio. Because of Jelco's *magnification factor* of 1.5, he will view this stock as contributing much to the risk of the portfolio. (We will show shortly that the beta of the average security in the market is 1.) Jelco contributes more to the risk of a large, diversified portfolio than does an average security because Jelco is more responsive to movements in the market.

FIGURE 11.10

Performance of Jelco, Inc., and the Market Portfolio

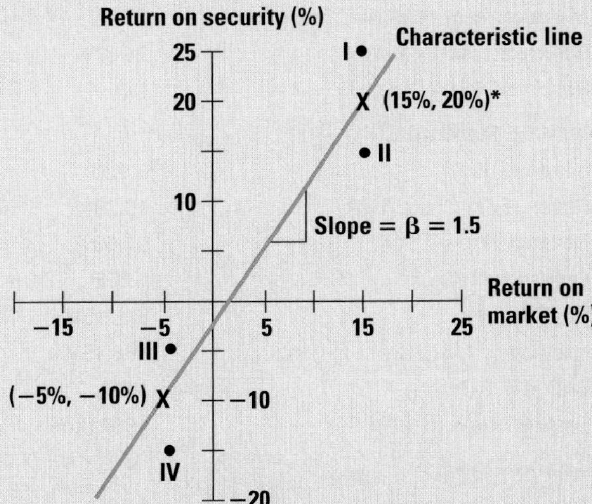

The two points marked X represent the expected return on Jelco for each possible outcome of the market portfolio. The expected return on Jelco is positively related to the return on the market. Because the slope is 1.5, we say that Jelco's beta is 1.5. Beta measures the responsiveness of the security's return to movements in the market.

***(15%, 20%) refers to the point where the return on the market is 15 percent and the return on the security is 20 percent.**

Further insight can be gleaned by examining securities with negative betas. One should view these securities as either hedges or insurance policies. The security is expected to do well when the market does poorly and vice versa. Because of this, adding a negative beta security to a large, diversified portfolio actually reduces the risk of the portfolio.[5]

Table 11.5 presents empirical estimates of betas for individual securities. As can be seen, some securities are more responsive to the market than others. For example, eBay has a beta of 2.07. This means that, for every 1 percent movement in the market, eBay is expected to move 2.07 percent in the same direction. Conversely, McDonald's has a beta of only .79. This means that, for every 1 percent movement in the market, McDonald's is expected to move .79 percent in the same direction.

We can summarize our discussion of beta by saying:

Beta measures the responsiveness of a security to movements in the market portfolio.

You can find beta estimates at many sites on the Web. One of the best is finance.yahoo.com. We went there and entered the ticker symbol AMZN for Amazon.com, and followed the "Key Statistics" link. Here is part of what we found:

Stock Price History	
Beta:	2.693
52-Week Change:	-28.62%
52-Week Change (relative to S&P500):	-29.34%
52-Week High (30-Jun-04):	54.70
52-Week Low (19-Apr-05):	32.01
50-Day Moving Average:	34.58
200-Day Moving Average:	38.76

Betas are easy to find on the Web. Try finance.yahoo.com and money.cnn.com.

Management Effectiveness	
Return on Assets (ttm):	24.37%
Return on Equity (ttm):	N/A
Income Statement	
Revenue (ttm):	6.92B
Revenue Per Share (ttm):	16.294
Revenue Growth (lfy)³:	31.50%
Gross Profit (ttm)²:	1.60B
EBITDA (ttm):	516.15M
Net Income Avl to Common (ttm):	588.45M
Diluted EPS (ttm):	1.39
Earnings Growth (lfy)³:	1567.90%
Balance Sheet	
Total Cash (mrq):	1.78B
Total Cash Per Share (mrq):	4.33
Total Debt (mrq)²:	1.86B
Total Debt/Equity (mrq):	N/A
Current Ratio (mrq):	1.567
Book Value Per Share (mrq):	-0.555

[5]Unfortunately, empirical evidence shows that virtually no stocks have negative betas.

STOCK	BETA
McGraw-Hill Co.	.55
MMM	.57
McDonald's	.79
Bed, Bath & Beyond	.80
Home Depot	1.28
Dell	1.51
eBay	2.07
Computer Associates	2.82

The beta is defined as $\text{Cov}(R_i, R_M)/\text{Var}(R_M)$, where $\text{Cov}(R_i, R_M)$ is the covariance of the return on an individual stock, R_i, and the return on the market, R_M. $\text{Var}(R_M)$ is the variance of the return on the market, R_M.

TABLE 11.5

Estimates of Beta for Selected Individual Stocks

The reported beta for Amazon.com is 2.69, which means that Amazon has about two and one-half times the systematic risk of a typical stock. You would expect that the company is very risky, and looking at the other numbers, we agree. Amazon's ROA is 24.37 percent, a relatively good number, but no ROE is reported. Why? If we try calculating the ROE using the earnings per share and the book value per share reported here, we will find that ROE is about *negative* 250 percent. That's not good! Digging deeper, the reason is that Amazon has a negative book value, which means that Amazon's assets are worth less than its liabilities. In all, Amazon appears to be a good candidate for a high beta. A nearby *The Real World* box contains some additional discussion on obtaining betas and some of the issues that arise in that context.

The Formula for Beta

Our discussion so far has stressed the intuition behind beta. The actual definition of beta is:

$$\beta_i = \frac{\text{Cov}(R_i, R_M)}{\sigma^2(R_M)} \qquad (11.17)$$

where $\text{Cov}(R_i, R_M)$ is the covariance between the return on asset i and the return on the market portfolio and $\sigma^2(R_M)$ is the variance of the market.

One useful property is that the average beta across all securities, when weighted by the proportion of each security's market value to that of the market portfolio, is 1. That is:

$$\sum_{i=1}^{N} X_i \beta_i = 1 \qquad (11.18)$$

where X_i is the proportion of security i's market value to that of the entire market and N is the number of securities in the market.

Equation (11.18) is intuitive, once you think about it. If you weight all securities by their market values, the resulting portfolio is the market. By definition, the beta of the market portfolio is 1. That is, for every 1 percent movement in the market, the market must move 1 percent—*by definition.*

For more on beta, visit moneycentral.msn.com.

A Test

We have put these questions on past corporate finance examinations:

1. What sort of investor rationally views the variance (or standard deviation) of an individual security's return as the security's proper measure of risk?
2. What sort of investor rationally views the beta of a security as the security's proper measure of risk?

THE REAL WORLD

BETA, BETA, WHO'S GOT THE BETA?

Based on what we've studied so far, you can see that beta is a pretty important topic. You might wonder then, are all published betas created equal? Read on for a partial answer to this question.

We did some checking on betas and found some interesting results. The Value Line *Investment Survey* is one of the best-known sources for information on publicly traded companies. However, with the explosion of online investing, there has been a corresponding increase in the amount of investment information available online. We decided to compare the betas presented by Value Line to those reported by Yahoo! Finance (finance.yahoo.com), Lycos (finance.lycos.com), and CNN Money (money.cnn.com). What we found leads to an important note of caution.

Consider Amazon.com, the big online retailer. The beta reported for it on the Internet was 2.69. This estimate was much larger than Value Line's beta for Amazon of 1.55. Amazon.com wasn't the only stock that showed a divergence in betas. In fact, for most of the technology companies we looked at, Value Line reported betas that were significantly lower than their online cousins. For example, the online beta for Yahoo! was 2.89, while Value Line reported 1.80. Similarly, the online beta for Sun Microsystems was 2.85 and the Value Line beta was 1.55. Interested in something less high-tech? The online beta for Coca-Cola was .24, compared to Value Line's .60. As you can see, Value Line's betas are not always lower.

We also found some unusual, and even hard to believe, estimates for beta. General Mills had a very low online beta of .00, while Value Line reported .55 for General Mills. The online beta estimate of J.M. Smucker, the jelly company, was .09, compared to Value Line's .65. Even more incredulous were the following online betas: Acme Metals was −100, and Kindred Healthcare had a reported beta of 1179. Perhaps the most outrageous reported betas were the online betas for Compare Generiks and Syndicated Food Service, with betas of 2220 and −464 (notice the minus sign!), respectively. Value Line did not report a beta for these companies. How do you suppose we should interpret a beta of −464?

There are a few lessons to be learned from all of this. First, not all betas are created equal. Some are computed using weekly returns and some using daily returns. Some are computed using 60 months of stock returns; some consider more or less returns. Some betas are computed by comparing the stock to the S&P 500 Index, while others use alternative indices. Finally, some reporting firms (including Value Line) make adjustments to raw betas to reflect information other than just the fluctuation in stock prices.

The second lesson is perhaps more subtle and comes from the betas of Compare Generiks and Syndicated Food Service. We are interested in knowing what the beta of the stock will be in the future, but betas have to be estimated using historical data. Anytime we use the past to predict the future, there is the danger of a poor estimate. In our case, it is very unlikely that Compare Generiks has a beta anything like 2220 or that Syndicated Food Service has a beta of −464. Instead, the estimates are almost certainly bad. The moral of the story is that, as with any financial tool, beta is not a black box that should be taken without question.

A good answer might be something like the following:

> A rational, risk-averse investor views the variance (or standard deviation) of her portfolio's return as the proper measure of the risk of her portfolio. If for some reason or another the investor can hold only one security, the variance of that security's return becomes the variance of the portfolio's return. Hence, the variance of the security's return is the security's proper measure of risk.
>
> If an individual holds a diversified portfolio, she still views the variance (or standard deviation) of her portfolio's return as the proper measure of the risk of her portfolio. However, she is no longer interested in the variance of each individual security's return. Rather, she is interested in the contribution of an individual security to the variance of the portfolio.

Under the assumption of homogeneous expectations, all individuals hold the market portfolio. Thus, we measure risk as the contribution of an individual security to the variance of the market portfolio. This contribution, when standardized properly, is the beta of the security. While very few investors hold the market portfolio exactly, many hold reasonably diversified portfolios. These portfolios are close enough to the market portfolio so that the beta of a security is likely to be a reasonable measure of its risk.

11.10 RELATIONSHIP BETWEEN RISK AND EXPECTED RETURN (CAPM)

It is commonplace to argue that the expected return on an asset should be positively related to its risk. That is, individuals will hold a risky asset only if its expected return compensates for its risk. In this section, we first estimate the expected return on the stock market as a whole. Next, we estimate expected returns on individual securities.

Expected Return on Market

Financial economists frequently argue that the expected return on the market can be represented as:

$$\mathrm{E}(R_M) = R_F + \textbf{Risk premium}$$

In words, the expected return on the market is the sum of the risk-free rate plus some compensation for the risk inherent in the market portfolio. Note that the equation refers to the *expected* return on the market, not the actual return in a particular month or year. Because stocks have risk, the actual return on the market over a particular period can, of course, be below R_F, or can even be negative.

Since investors want compensation for risk, the risk premium is presumably positive. But exactly how positive is it? It is generally argued that the place to start looking for the risk premium in the future is the average risk premium in the past. As reported in Chapter 10, Ibbotson and Sinquefield found that the average return on large-company common stocks was 12.4 percent over 1926–2004. The average risk-free rate over the same time interval was 3.8 percent. Thus, the average difference between the two was 8.6 percent (12.4 percent − 3.8 percent). Financial economists find this to be a useful estimate of the difference to occur in the future.

For example, if the risk-free rate, estimated by the current yield on a one-year Treasury bill, is 1 percent, the expected return on the market is:

$$9.6\% = 1\% + 8.6\%$$

Of course, the future equity risk premium could be higher or lower than the historical equity risk premium. This could be true if future risk is higher or lower than past risk or if individual risk aversions are higher or lower than those of the past.

Expected Return on Individual Security

Now that we have estimated the expected return on the market as a whole, what is the expected return on an individual security? We have argued that the beta of a security is the appropriate measure of risk in a large, diversified portfolio. Since most investors are diversified, the expected return on a security should be positively related to its beta. This is illustrated in Figure 11.11.

Actually, financial economists can be more precise about the relationship between expected return and beta. They posit that, under plausible conditions, the relationship between expected return and beta can be represented by the following equation:

Capital Asset Pricing Model

$$\mathrm{E}(R) = R_F + \beta \times [\mathrm{E}(R_M) - R_F] \tag{11.19}$$

Expected return on a security	=	Risk-free rate	+	Beta of the security	×	Difference between expected return on market and risk-free rate

For more on CAPM and the equity risk premium, visit www.investopedia.com/terms/c/capm.asp.

FIGURE 11.11

Relationship between Expected Return on an Individual Security and Beta of the Security

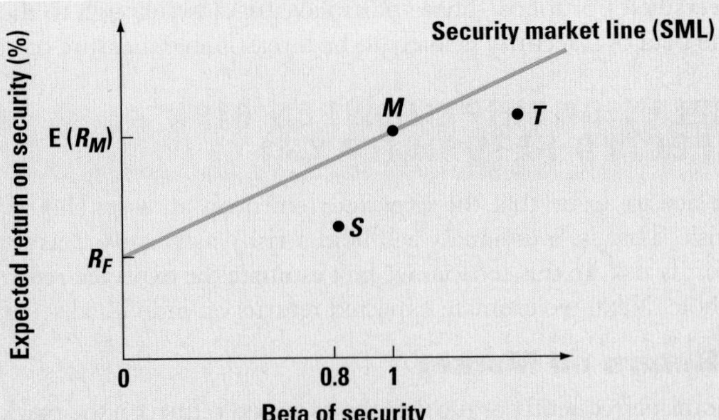

The security market line (SML) is the graphical depiction of the capital asset pricing model (CAPM).
The expected return on a stock with a beta of 0 is equal to the risk-free rate.
The expected return on a stock with a beta of 1 is equal to the expected return on the market.

This formula, which is called the **capital asset pricing model** (or CAPM for short), implies that the expected return on a security is linearly related to its beta. Since the average return on the market has been higher than the average risk-free rate over long periods of time, $E(R_M) - R_F$ is presumably positive. Thus, the formula implies that the expected return on a security is *positively* related to its beta. The formula can be illustrated by assuming a few special cases:

- *Assume that* $\beta = 0$. Here $E(R) = R_F$, that is, the expected return on the security is equal to the risk-free rate. Because a security with zero beta has no relevant risk, its expected return should equal the risk-free rate.
- *Assume that* $\beta = 1$. Equation (11.19) reduces to $E(R) = E(R_M)$. That is, the expected return on the security is equal to the expected return on the market. This makes sense since the beta of the market portfolio is also 1.

Formula (11.19) can be represented graphically by the upward-sloping line in Figure 11.11. Note that the line begins at R_F and rises to $E(R_M)$ when beta is 1. This line is frequently called the **security market line (SML)**.

As with any line, the SML has both a slope and an intercept. R_F, the risk-free rate, is the intercept. Because the beta of a security is the horizontal axis, $E(R_M) - R_F$ is the slope. The line will be upward sloping as long as the expected return on the market is greater than the risk-free rate. Because the market portfolio is a risky asset, theory suggests that its expected return is above the risk-free rate. As mentioned, the empirical evidence of the previous chapter showed that the average return per year on the market portfolio (e.g., large-company stocks) over the past 79 years was 8.6 percent above the risk-free rate.

EXAMPLE 11.5 CAPM

The stock of Aardvark Enterprises has a beta of 1.5 and that of Zebra Enterprises has a beta of .7. The risk-free rate is assumed to be 3 percent, and the difference between the expected return on the market and the risk-free rate is assumed to be 8.0 percent. The expected returns on the two securities are:

Expected Return for Aardvark

$15.0\% = 3\% + 1.5 \times 8.0\%$

Expected Return for Zebra

$8.6\% = 3\% + .7 \times 8.0\%$

Three additional points concerning the CAPM should be mentioned:

1. *Linearity.* The intuition behind an upwardly sloping curve is clear. Because beta is the appropriate measure of risk, high-beta securities should have an expected return above that of low-beta securities. However, both Figure 11.11 and equation (11.19) show something more than an upwardly sloping curve; the relationship between expected return and beta corresponds to a *straight* line.

It is easy to show that the line of Figure 11.11 is straight. To see this, consider security *S* with, say, a beta of .8. This security is represented by a point below the security market line in the figure. Any investor could duplicate the beta of security *S* by buying a portfolio with 20 percent in the risk-free asset and 80 percent in a security with a beta of 1. However, the homemade portfolio would itself lie on the SML. In other words, the portfolio dominates security *S* because the portfolio has a higher expected return and the same beta.

Now consider security *T* with, say, a beta greater than 1. This security is also below the SML in Figure 11.11. Any investor could duplicate the beta of security *T* by borrowing to invest in a security with a beta of 1. This portfolio must also lie on the SML, thereby dominating security *T*.

Because no one would hold either *S* or *T*, their stock prices would drop. This price adjustment would raise the expected returns on the two securities. The price adjustment would continue until the two securities lay on the security market line. The preceding example considered two overpriced stocks and a straight SML. Securities lying above the SML are *underpriced*. Their prices must rise until their expected returns lie on the line. If the SML is itself curved, many stocks would be mispriced. In equilibrium, all securities would be held only when prices changed so that the SML became straight. In other words, linearity would be achieved.

2. *Portfolios as well as securities.* Our discussion of the CAPM considered individual securities. Does the relationship in Figure 11.11 and equation (11.19) hold for portfolios as well?

Yes. To see this, consider a portfolio formed by investing equally in our two securities, Aardvark and Zebra. The expected return on the portfolio is:

Expected Return on Portfolio

$$11.8\% = .5 \times 15.0\% + .5 \times 8.6\% \qquad (11.20)$$

The beta of the portfolio is simply a weighted average of the betas of the two securities. Thus, we have:

Beta of Portfolio

$$1.1 = .5 \times 1.5 + .5 \times .7$$

Under the CAPM, the expected return on the portfolio is:

$$11.8\% = 3\% + 1.1 \times 8.0\%$$

Because the expected return in (11.20) is the same as the expected return in the above equation, the example shows that the CAPM holds for portfolios as well as for individual securities.

3. *A potential confusion.* Students often confuse the SML in Figure 11.11 with line *II* in Figure 11.8. Actually, the lines are quite different. Line *II* traces the efficient set of portfolios formed from both risky assets and the riskless asset. Each point on the line represents an entire portfolio. Point *A* is a portfolio composed entirely of risky assets. Every other point on the line represents a portfolio of the securities in *A* combined with the riskless asset. The axes on Figure 11.8 are the expected return on a *portfolio* and the standard deviation of a *portfolio*. Individual securities do not lie along line *II*.

The SML in Figure 11.11 relates expected return to beta. Figure 11.11 differs from Figure 11.8 in at least two ways. First, beta appears in the horizontal axis of Figure 11.11, but standard deviation appears in the horizontal axis of Figure 11.8. Second, the SML in Figure 11.11 holds both for all individual securities and for all possible portfolios, whereas line *II* in Figure 11.8 holds only for efficient portfolios.

We stated earlier that, under homogeneous expectations, point *A* in Figure 11.8 becomes the market portfolio. In this situation, line *II* is referred to as the **capital market line** (CML).

SUMMARY AND CONCLUSIONS

This chapter sets forth the fundamentals of modern portfolio theory. Our basic points are these:

1. This chapter shows us how to calculate the expected return and variance for individual securities, and the covariance and correlation for pairs of securities. Given these statistics, the expected return and variance for a portfolio of two securities *A* and *B* can be written as:

   Expected return on portfolio $= X_A \text{E}(R_A) + X_B \text{E}(R_B)$

   Var(portfolio) $X_A^2 \sigma_A^2 + 2X_A X_B \sigma_{A,B} + X_B^2 \sigma_B^2$

2. In our notation, *X* stands for the proportion of a security in one's portfolio. By varying *X*, one can trace out the efficient set of portfolios. We graphed the efficient set for the two asset case as a curve, pointing out that the degree of curvature or bend in the graph reflects the diversification effect: The lower the correlation between the two securities, the greater the bend. The same general shape of the efficient set holds in a world of many assets.
3. A diversified portfolio can only eliminate some, but not all, of the risk associated with individual securities. The reason is that part of the risk with an individual asset is unsystematic, meaning essentially unique to that asset. In a well-diversified portfolio, these unsystematic risks tend to cancel out. Systematic, or market, risks are not diversifiable.
4. The efficient set of risky assets can be combined with riskless borrowing and lending. In this case, a rational investor will always choose to hold the portfolio of risky securities represented by point *A* in Figure 11.8. Then he can either borrow or lend at the riskless rate to achieve any desired point on line *II* in the figure.
5. The contribution of a security to the risk of a large, well-diversified portfolio is proportional to the covariance of the security's return with the market's return. This contribution, when standardized, is called the beta. The beta of a security can also be interpreted as the responsiveness of a security's return to that of the market.
6. The CAPM states that

   $\text{E}(R) = R_F + \beta[\text{E}(R_M) - R_F]$

   In other words, the expected return on a security is positively (and linearly) related to the security's beta.

CONCEPT QUESTIONS

1. **Diversifiable and Nondiversifiable Risks** In broad terms, why is some risk diversifiable? Why are some risks nondiversifiable? Does it follow that an investor can control the level of unsystematic risk in a portfolio, but not the level of systematic risk?
2. **Information and Market Returns** Suppose the government announces that, based on a just-completed survey, the growth rate in the economy is likely to be 2 percent in the coming year, as compared to 5 percent for the year just completed. Will security prices increase, decrease, or stay the same following this announcement? Does it make any difference whether or not the 2 percent figure was anticipated by the market? Explain.
3. **Systematic versus Unsystematic Risk** Classify the following events as mostly systematic or mostly unsystematic. Is the distinction clear in every case?
   a. Short-term interest rates increase unexpectedly.
   b. The interest rate a company pays on its short-term debt borrowing is increased by its bank.
   c. Oil prices unexpectedly decline.
   d. An oil tanker ruptures, creating a large oil spill.
   e. A manufacturer loses a multimillion-dollar product liability suit.
   f. A Supreme Court decision substantially broadens producer liability for injuries suffered by product users.
4. **Systematic versus Unsystematic Risk** Indicate whether the following events might cause stocks in general to change price, and whether they might cause Big Widget Corp.'s stock to change price.
   a. The government announces that inflation unexpectedly jumped by 2 percent last month.
   b. Big Widget's quarterly earnings report, just issued, generally fell in line with analysts' expectations.
   c. The government reports that economic growth last year was at 3 percent, which generally agreed with most economists' forecasts.
   d. The directors of Big Widget die in a plane crash.
   e. Congress approves changes to the tax code that will increase the top marginal corporate tax rate. The legislation had been debated for the previous six months.
5. **Expected Portfolio Returns** If a portfolio has a positive investment in every asset, can the expected return on the portfolio be greater than that on every asset in the portfolio? Can it be less than that on every asset in the portfolio? If you answer yes to one or both of these questions, give an example to support your answer.
6. **Diversification** True or false: The most important characteristic in determining the expected return of a well-diversified portfolio is the variances of the individual assets in the portfolio. Explain.
7. **Portfolio Risk** If a portfolio has a positive investment in every asset, can the standard deviation on the portfolio be less than that on every asset in the portfolio? What about the portfolio beta?
8. **Beta and CAPM** Is it possible that a risky asset could have a beta of zero? Explain. Based on the CAPM, what is the expected return on such an asset? Is it possible that a risky asset could have a negative beta? What does the CAPM predict about the expected return on such an asset? Can you give an explanation for your answer?
9. **Corporate Downsizing** In recent years, it has been common for companies to experience significant stock price changes in reaction to announcements of massive layoffs. Critics charge that such events encourage companies to fire longtime employees and that Wall Street is cheering them on. Do you agree or disagree?

10. **Earnings and Stock Returns** As indicated by a number of examples in this chapter, earnings announcements by companies are closely followed by, and frequently result in, share price revisions. Two issues should come to mind. First, earnings announcements concern past periods. If the market values stocks based on expectations of the future, why are numbers summarizing past performance relevant? Second, these announcements concern accounting earnings. Going back to Chapter 2, such earnings may have little to do with cash flow, so, again, why are they relevant?
11. **Covariance** Briefly explain why the covariance of a security with the rest of a well-diversified portfolio is a more appropriate measure of the risk of the security than the security's variance.
12. **Beta** Consider the following quotation from a leading investment manager: "The shares of Southern Co. have traded close to $12 for most of the past three years. Since Southern's stock has demonstrated very little price movement, the stock has a low beta. Texas Instruments, on the other hand, has traded as high as $150 and as low as its current $75. Since TI's stock has demonstrated a large amount of price movement, the stock has a very high beta." Do you agree with this analysis? Explain.
13. **Risk** A broker has advised you not to invest in oil industry stocks because they have high standard deviations. Is the broker's advice sound for a risk-averse investor like yourself? Why or why not?
14. **Security Selection** Is the following statement true of false? A risky security cannot have an expected return that is less than the risk-free rate because no risk-averse investor would be willing to hold this asset in equilibrium. Explain.

QUESTIONS AND PROBLEMS

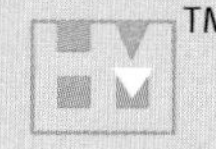

Basic
(Questions 1–20)

1. **Determining Portfolio Weights** What are the portfolio weights for a portfolio that has 70 shares of Stock A that sell for $40 per share and 110 shares of Stock B that sell for $22 per share?
2. **Portfolio Expected Return** You own a portfolio that has $1,200 invested in Stock A and $1,900 invested in Stock B. If the expected returns on these stocks are 11 percent and 16 percent, respectively, what is the expected return on the portfolio?
3. **Portfolio Expected Return** You own a portfolio that is 50 percent invested in Stock X, 30 percent in Stock Y, and 20 percent in Stock Z. The expected returns on these three stocks are 11 percent, 17 percent, and 14 percent, respectively. What is the expected return on the portfolio?

4. **Portfolio Expected Return** You have $10,000 to invest in a stock portfolio. Your choices are Stock X with an expected return of 14 percent and Stock Y with an expected return of 9 percent. If your goal is to create a portfolio with an expected return of 12.2 percent, how much money will you invest in Stock X? In Stock Y?
5. **Calculating Expected Return** Based on the following information, calculate the expected return.

STATE OF ECONOMY	PROBABILITY OF STATE OF ECONOMY	RATE OF RETURN IF STATE OCCURS
Recession	.20	−.05
Normal	.50	.12
Boom	.30	.25

6. **Calculating Returns and Standard Deviations** Based on the following information, calculate the expected return and standard deviation for the two stocks.

STATE OF ECONOMY	PROBABILITY OF STATE OF ECONOMY	Rate of Return If State Occurs	
		STOCK *A*	STOCK *B*
Recession	.10	.06	−.20
Normal	.60	.07	.13
Boom	.30	.11	.33

7. **Calculating Returns and Standard Deviations** Based on the following information, calculate the expected return and standard deviation of the following stock.

STATE OF ECONOMY	PROBABILITY OF STATE OF ECONOMY	RATE OF RETURN IF STATE OCCURS
Depression	.10	−.045
Recession	.20	.044
Normal	.50	.120
Boom	.20	.207

8. **Calculating Expected Returns** A portfolio is invested 20 percent in Stock G, 70 percent in Stock J, and 10 percent in Stock K. The expected returns on these stocks are 8 percent, 15 percent, and 24 percent, respectively. What is the portfolio's expected return? How do you interpret your answer?

9. **Returns and Standard Deviations** Consider the following information:

STATE OF ECONOMY	PROBABILITY OF STATE OF ECONOMY	Rate of Return If State Occurs		
		STOCK A	STOCK B	STOCK C
Boom	.70	.07	.15	.33
Bust	.30	.13	.03	−.06

a. What is the expected return on an equally weighted portfolio of these three stocks?

b. What is the variance of a portfolio invested 20 percent each in A and B, and 60 percent in C?

10. **Returns and Standard Deviations** Consider the following information:

STATE OF ECONOMY	PROBABILITY OF STATE OF ECONOMY	Rate of Return If State Occurs		
		STOCK A	STOCK B	STOCK C
Boom	.30	.30	.45	.33
Good	.40	.12	.10	.15
Poor	.25	.01	−.15	−.05
Bust	.05	−.06	−.30	−.09

a. Your portfolio is invested 30 percent each in A and C, and 40 percent in B. What is the expected return of the portfolio?

b. What is the variance of this portfolio? The standard deviation?

11. **Calculating Portfolio Betas** You own a stock portfolio invested 25 percent in Stock Q, 20 percent in Stock R, 15 percent in Stock S, and 40 percent in Stock T. The betas for these four stocks are .6, 1.70, 1.15, and 1.34, respectively. What is the portfolio beta?

12. **Calculating Portfolio Betas** You own a portfolio equally invested in a risk-free asset and two stocks. If one of the stocks has a beta of 1.9 and the total portfolio is equally as risky as the market, what must the beta be for the other stock in your portfolio?

13. **Using CAPM** A stock has a beta of 1.3, the expected return on the market is 14 percent, and the risk-free rate is 5 percent. What must the expected return on this stock be?

14. **Using CAPM** A stock has an expected return of 14 percent, the risk-free rate is 4 percent, and the market risk premium is 6 percent. What must the beta of this stock be?

15. **Using CAPM** A stock has an expected return of 11 percent, its beta is .85, and the risk-free rate is 5.5 percent. What must the expected return on the market be?

16. **Using CAPM** A stock has an expected return of 17 percent, a beta of 1.9, and the expected return on the market is 11 percent. What must the risk-free rate be?

17. **Using CAPM** A stock has a beta of 1.2 and an expected return of 16 percent. A risk-free asset currently earns 5 percent.
    a. What is the expected return on a portfolio that is equally invested in the two assets?
    b. If a portfolio of the two assets has a beta of .75, what are the portfolio weights?
    c. If a portfolio of the two assets has an expected return of 8 percent, what is its beta?
    d. If a portfolio of the two assets has a beta of 2.40, what are the portfolio weights? How do you interpret the weights for the two assets in this case? Explain.

18. **Using the SML** Asset W has an expected return of 16 percent and a beta of 1.3. If the risk-free rate is 5 percent, complete the following table for portfolios of Asset W and a risk-free asset. Illustrate the relationship between portfolio expected return and portfolio beta by plotting the expected returns against the betas. What is the slope of the line that results?

PERCENTAGE OF PORTFOLIO IN ASSET W	PORTFOLIO EXPECTED RETURN	PORTFOLIO BETA
0%		
25		
50		
75		
100		
125		
150		

19. **Reward-to-Risk Ratios** Stock Y has a beta of 1.50 and an expected return of 17 percent. Stock Z has a beta of .80 and an expected return of 10.5 percent. If the risk-free rate is 5.5 percent and the market risk premium is 7.5 percent, are these stocks correctly priced?

20. **Reward-to-Risk Ratios** In the previous problem, what would the risk-free rate have to be for the two stocks to be correctly priced?

Intermediate (Questions 21–33)

21. **Portfolio Returns** Using information from the previous chapter on capital market history, determine the return on a portfolio that is equally invested in large-company stocks and long-term government bonds. What is the return on a portfolio that is equally invested in small-company stocks and Treasury bills?

22. **CAPM** Using the CAPM, show that the ratio of the risk premiums on two assets is equal to the ratio of their betas.

23. **Portfolio Returns and Deviations** Consider the following information on three stocks:

STATE OF ECONOMY	PROBABILITY OF STATE OF ECONOMY	Rate of Return If State Occurs		
		STOCK A	STOCK B	STOCK C
Boom	.4	.20	.35	.60
Normal	.4	.15	.12	.05
Bust	.2	.01	−.25	−.50

a. If your portfolio is invested 40 percent each in A and B and 20 percent in C, what is the portfolio expected return? The variance? The standard deviation?

b. If the expected T-bill rate is 3.80 percent, what is the expected risk premium on the portfolio?

c. If the expected inflation rate is 3.50 percent, what are the approximate and exact expected real returns on the portfolio? What are the approximate and exact expected real risk premiums on the portfolio?

24. **Analyzing a Portfolio** You want to create a portfolio equally as risky as the market, and you have $1,000,000 to invest. Given this information, fill in the rest of the following table:

ASSET	INVESTMENT	BETA
Stock A	$200,000	.80
Stock B	$250,000	1.30
Stock C		1.50
Risk-free asset		

25. **Analyzing a Portfolio** You have $100,000 to invest in a portfolio containing Stock X, Stock Y, and a risk-free asset. You must invest all of your money. Your goal is to create a portfolio that has an expected return of 13.5 percent and that has only 70 percent of the risk of the overall market. If X has an expected return of 31 percent and a beta of 1.8, Y has an expected return of 20 percent and a beta of 1.3, and the risk-free rate is 7 percent, how much money will you invest in Stock X? How do you interpret your answer?

26. **Covariance and Correlation** Based on the following information, calculate the expected return and standard deviation of each of the following stocks. Assume each state of the economy is equally likely to happen. What is the covariance and correlation between the returns of the two stocks?

STATE OF ECONOMY	RETURN ON STOCK A	RETURN ON STOCK B
Bear	.063	−.037
Normal	.105	.064
Bull	.156	.253

27. **Covariance and Correlation** Based on the following information, calculate the expected return and standard deviation for each of the following stocks. What is the covariance and correlation between the returns of the two stocks?

STATE OF ECONOMY	PROBABILITY OF STATE OF ECONOMY	RETURN ON STOCK J	RETURN ON STOCK K
Bear	.25	−.020	.050
Normal	.60	.092	.062
Bull	.15	.154	.074

28. **Portfolio Standard Deviation** Security F has an expected return of 12 percent and a standard deviation of 34 percent per year. Security G has an expected return of 18 percent and a standard deviation of 50 percent per year.

a. What is the expected return on a portfolio composed of 30 percent of security F and 70 percent of security G?

b. If the correlation between the returns of security F and security G is .2, what is the standard deviation of the portfolio described in part (a)?

29. **Portfolio Standard Deviation** Suppose the expected returns and standard deviations of stocks A and B are $E(R_A) = .15$, $E(R_B) = .25$, $\sigma_A = .40$, and $\sigma_B = .65$, respectively.

   a. Calculate the expected return and standard deviation of a portfolio that is composed of 40 percent A and 60 percent B when the correlation between the returns on A and B is .5.

   b. Calculate the standard deviation of a portfolio that is composed of 40 percent A and 60 percent B when the correlation coefficient between the returns on A and B is −.5.

   c. How does the correlation between the returns on A and B affect the standard deviation of the portfolio?

30. **Correlation and Beta** You have been provided the following data on the securities of three firms, the market portfolio, and the risk-free asset:

SECURITY	EXPECTED RETURN	STANDARD DEVIATION	CORRELATION*	BETA
Firm A	.13	.38	(i)	.9
Firm B	.16	(ii)	.4	1.1
Firm C	.25	.65	.35	(iii)
The market portfolio	.15	.20	(iv)	(v)
The risk-free asset	.05	(vi)	(vii)	(viii)

*With the market portfolio.

   a. Fill in the missing values in the table.

   b. Is the stock of Firm A correctly priced according to the capital asset pricing model (CAPM)? What about the stock of Firm B? Firm C? If these securities are not correctly priced, what is your investment recommendation for someone with a well-diversified portfolio?

31. **CML** The market portfolio has an expected return of 12 percent and a standard deviation of 10 percent. The risk-free rate is 5 percent.

   a. What is the expected return on a well-diversified portfolio with a standard deviation of 7 percent?

   b. What is the standard deviation of a well-diversified portfolio with an expected return of 20 percent?

32. **Beta and CAPM** A portfolio that combines the risk-free asset and the market portfolio has an expected return of 12 percent and a standard deviation of 18 percent. The risk-free rate is 5 percent, and the expected return on the market portfolio is 14 percent. Assume the capital asset pricing model holds. What expected rate of return would a security earn if it had a .45 correlation with the market portfolio and a standard deviation of 40 percent?

33. **Beta and CAPM** Suppose the risk-free rate is 6.3 percent and the market portfolio has an expected return of 14.8 percent. The market portfolio has a variance of .0498. Portfolio Z has a correlation coefficient with the market of .45 and a variance of .1783. According to the capital asset pricing model, what is the expected return on portfolio Z?

Challenge (Questions 34–39)

34. **Systematic versus Unsystematic Risk** Consider the following information on Stocks I and II:

STATE OF ECONOMY	PROBABILITY OF STATE OF ECONOMY	Rate of Return If State Occurs	
		STOCK I	STOCK II
Recession	.15	.09	−.30
Normal	.70	.42	.12
Irrational exuberance	.15	.26	.44

The market risk premium is 10 percent, and the risk-free rate is 4 percent. Which stock has the most systematic risk? Which one has the most unsystematic risk? Which stock is "riskier"? Explain.

35. **SML** Suppose you observe the following situation:

SECURITY	BETA	EXPECTED RETURN
Pete Corp.	1.3	.23
Repete Co.	.6	.13

Assume these securities are correctly priced. Based on the CAPM, what is the expected return on the market? What is the risk-free rate?

36. **Covariance and Portfolio Standard Deviation** There are three securities in the market. The following chart shows their possible payoffs.

STATE	PROBABILITY OF OUTCOME	RETURN ON SECURITY 1	RETURN ON SECURITY 2	RETURN ON SECURITY 3
1	.10	.25	.25	.10
2	.40	.20	.15	.15
3	.40	.15	.20	.20
4	.10	.10	.10	.25

a. What is the expected return and standard deviation of each security?

b. What are the covariances and correlations between the pairs of securities?

c. What is the expected return and standard deviation of a portfolio with half of its funds invested in security 1 and half in security 2?

d. What is the expected return and standard deviation of a portfolio with half of its funds invested in security 1 and half in security 3?

e. What is the expected return and standard deviation of a portfolio with half of its funds invested in security 2 and half in security 3?

f. What do your answers in parts (a), (c), (d), and (e) imply about diversification?

37. **SML** Suppose you observe the following situation:

		Return If State Occurs	
STATE OF ECONOMY	PROBABILITY OF STATE	STOCK A	STOCK B
Bust	.25	−.10	−.30
Normal	.50	.10	.05
Boom	.25	.20	.40

a. Calculate the expected return on each stock.

b. Assuming the capital asset pricing model holds and stock A's beta is greater than stock B's beta by .25, what is the expected market risk premium?

38. **Standard Deviation and Beta** There are two stocks in the market, stock A and stock B. The price of stock A today is $50. The price of stock A next year will be $40 if the economy is in a recession, $55 if the economy is normal, and $60 if the economy is expanding. The probabilities of recession, normal times, and expansion are .1, .8, and .1, respectively. Stock A pays no dividends and has a correlation of .8 with the market portfolio. Stock B has an expected return of 9 percent, a standard deviation of 12 percent, a correlation with the market portfolio of .2, and

a correlation with stock A of .6. The market portfolio has a standard deviation of 10 percent. Assume the CAPM holds.

a. If you are a typical, risk-averse investor with a well-diversified portfolio, which stock would you prefer? Why?

b. What are the expected return and standard deviation of a portfolio consisting of 70 percent of stock A and 30 percent of stock B?

c. What is the beta of the portfolio in part (b)?

39. **Minimum Variance Portfolio** Assume stocks A and B have the following characteristics:

STOCK	EXPECTED RETURN (%)	STANDARD DEVIATION (%)
A	5	10
B	10	20

The covariance between the returns on the two stocks is .001.

a. Suppose an investor holds a portfolio consisting of only stock A and stock B. Find the portfolio weights, X_A and X_B, such that the variance of his portfolio is minimized. (Hint: Remember that the sum of the two weights must equal 1.)

b. What is the expected return on the minimum variance portfolio?

c. If the covariance between the returns on the two stocks is −.02, what are the minimum variance weights?

d. What is the variance of the portfolio in part (c)?

STANDARD &POOR'S

S&P PROBLEMS

www.mhhe.com/edumarketinsight

1. **Using CAPM** You can find estimates of beta for companies under the "Mthly. Val. Data" link. Locate the beta for Amazon.com (AMZN) and Dow Chemical (DOW). How has the beta for each of these companies changed over the period reported? Using the historical risk-free rate and market risk premium found in the chapter, calculate the expected return for each company based on the most recent beta. Is the expected return for each company what you would expect? Why or why not?

WHAT'S ON THE WEB?

1. **Expected Return** You want to find the expected return for Honeywell using the CAPM. First you need the market risk premium. Go to www.cnnfn.com and find current interest rates. Find the current interest rate for three-month Treasury bills. Use the average large-company stock return in Table 10.3 to calculate the market risk premium. Next, go to finance.yahoo.com, enter the ticker symbol HON for Honeywell, and follow the "Profile" link. In the Statistics at a Glance section you will find the beta for Honeywell. What is the expected return for Honeywell using CAPM? What assumptions have you made to arrive at this number?

2. **Portfolio Beta** You have decided to invest in an equally weighted portfolio consisting of American Express, Procter & Gamble, Home Depot, and Du Pont and need to find the beta of your portfolio. Go to finance.yahoo.com and follow the "Global Symbol Lookup" link to find the ticker symbols for each of these companies. Next, go back to finance.yahoo.com, enter one of

the ticker symbols and get a stock quote. Follow the "Profile" link to find the beta for this company. You will then need to find the beta for each of the companies. What is the beta for your portfolio?

3. **Beta** Which companies currently have the highest and lowest betas? Go to finance.yahoo.com and follow the "Screener" link. Enter 0 as the maximum beta and enter search. How many stocks currently have a beta less than 0? What is the lowest beta? Go back to the stock screener and enter 3 as the minimum. How many stocks have a beta above 3? What stock has the highest beta?
4. **Security Market Line** Go to finance.yahoo.com and enter the ticker symbol IP for International Paper. Follow the "Profile" link to get the beta for the company. Next, follow the "Research" link to find the estimated price in 12 months according to market analysts. Using the current share price and the mean target price, compute the expected return for this stock. Don't forget to include the expected dividend payments over the next year. Now go to money.cnn.com and find the current interest rate for three-month Treasury bills. Using this information, calculate the expected return on the market using the reward-to-risk ratio. Does this number make sense? Why or why not?

CLOSING CASE

A JOB AT EAST COAST YACHTS, PART 2

You are discussing your 401(k) with Dan Ervin, when he mentions that Sarah Brown, a representative from Bledsoe Financial Services, is visiting East Coast Yachts today. You decide that you should meet with Sarah, so Dan sets up an appointment for you later in the day.

When you sit down with Sarah, she discusses the various investment options available in the company's 401(k) account. You mention to Sarah that you researched East Coast Yachts before you accepted your new job. You are confident in management's ability to lead the company. Analysis of the company has led to your belief that the company is growing and will achieve a greater market share in the future. You also feel you should support your employer. Given these considerations, along with the fact that you are a conservative investor, you are leaning toward investing 100 percent of your 401(k) account in East Coast Yachts.

Assume the risk-free rate is the historical average risk-free rate (in Chapter 10). The correlation between the bond fund and the large cap stock fund is .27. Note the spreadsheet graphing and "solver" functions may assist you in answering the following questions.

1. Considering the effects of diversification, how should Sarah respond to the suggestion that you invest 100 percent of your 401(k) account in East Coast Yachts stock?
2. After hearing Sarah's response to investing your 401(k) account entirely in East Coast Yachts stock, she has convinced you that this may not be the best alternative. Since you are a conservative investor, you tell Sarah that a 100 percent investment in the bond fund may be the best alternative. Is it?
3. Using the returns for the Bledsoe Large-Cap Stock Fund and the Bledsoe Bond Fund, graph the opportunity set of feasible portfolios.
4. After examining the opportunity set, you notice that you can invest in a portfolio consisting of the bond fund and the large-cap stock fund that will have exactly the same standard deviation as the bond fund. This portfolio will also have a greater expected return. What are the portfolio weights and expected return of this portfolio?

5. Examining the opportunity set, notice there is a portfolio that has the lowest standard deviation. This is the minimum variance portfolio. What are the portfolio weights, expected return, and standard deviation of this portfolio? Why is the minimum variance portfolio important?
6. A measure of risk-adjusted performance that is often used is the Sharpe ratio. The Sharpe ratio is calculated as the risk premium of an asset divided by its standard deviation. The portfolio with the highest possible Sharpe ratio on the opportunity set is called the Sharpe optimal portfolio. What are the portfolio weights, expected return, and standard deviation of the Sharpe optimal portfolio? How does the Sharpe ratio of this portfolio compare to the Sharpe ratio of the bond fund and the large-cap stock fund? Do you see a connection between the Sharpe optimal portfolio and the CAPM? What is the connection?

CHAPTER 12

Risk, Cost of Capital, and Capital Budgeting

OPENING CASE

After it was introduced in 2004, the tough-looking Chrysler 300C was a huge hit and received more awards in its first year of sales than any other car in history. Designing, producing, and marketing a new car like the 300C represent a major undertaking in terms of time and money for an auto manufacturer. So, how do companies like DaimlerChrysler decide which projects to invest in and which to reject? The answer is that many companies rely heavily on their weighted average cost of capital (WACC).

The WACC is the return a company needs to earn to satisfy all of its investors, including stockholders, bondholders, and preferred stockholders. In 2005, for example, DaimlerChrysler announced that its WACC was 8 percent. Similarly, Whole Foods Market, an organic food retailer, said it uses a WACC of 9 percent, and PacificCorp, which operates the Idaho Power and Light Company, argued before the Idaho Public Utilities Commission that it should use a WACC of 8.633 percent. In this chapter, we learn how to compute a firm's cost of capital and find out what it means to the firm and its investors. We will also learn when to use the firm's cost of capital, and, perhaps more importantly, when not to use it.

12.1 THE COST OF EQUITY CAPITAL

Whenever a firm has extra cash, it can take one of two actions. On the one hand, it can pay out the cash immediately as a dividend. On the other hand, the firm can invest extra cash in a project, paying out the future cash flows of the project as dividends. Which procedure would the stockholders prefer? If a stockholder can reinvest the dividend in a financial asset (a stock or bond) with the same risk as that of the project, the stockholders would desire the alternative with the highest expected return. In other words, the project should be undertaken only if its expected return is greater than that of a financial asset of comparable risk. This is illustrated in Figure 12.1. This discussion implies a very simple capital budgeting rule:

The discount rate of a project should be the expected return on a financial asset of comparable risk.

From the firm's perspective, the expected return is the cost of equity capital. Under the CAPM, the expected return on the stock can be written as:

$$R_S = R_F + \beta \times (R_M - R_F) \tag{12.1}$$

where R_F is the risk-free rate and $R_M - R_F$ is the difference between the expected return on the market portfolio and the riskless rate. This difference is often called the expected *excess* market return or market risk premium. Note we have dropped the "E" denoting expectations from our expression to simplify the notation, but remember that we are always thinking about expected returns with the CAPM.

We now have the tools to estimate a firm's cost of equity capital. To do this, we need to know three things:

- The risk-free rate, R_F
- The market risk premium, $R_M - R_F$
- The company beta, β

FIGURE 12.1

Choices of a Firm with Extra Cash

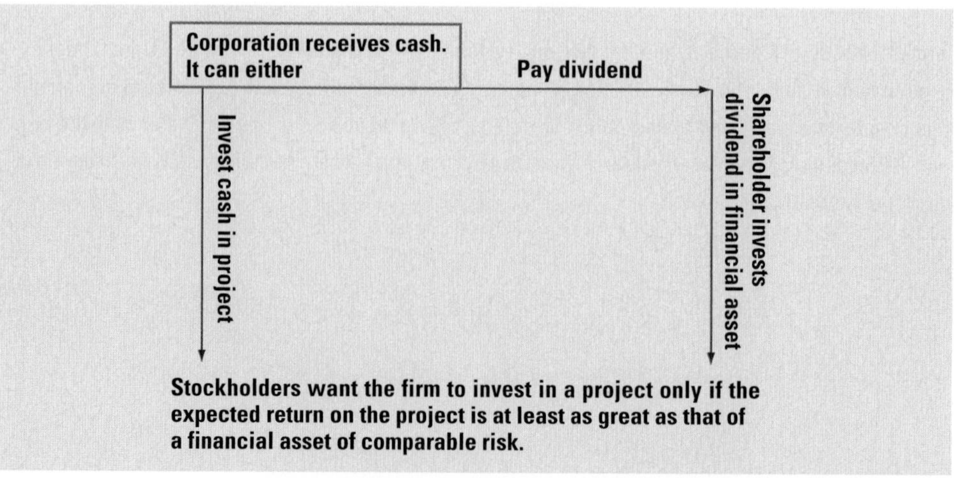

EXAMPLE 12.1 Cost of Equity

Suppose the stock of the Quatram Company, a publisher of college textbooks, has a beta (β) of 1.3. The firm is 100 percent equity financed; that is, it has no debt. Quatram is considering a number of capital budgeting projects that will double its size. Because these new projects are similar to the firm's existing ones, the average beta on the new projects is assumed to be equal to Quatram's existing beta. The risk-free rate is 5 percent. What is the appropriate discount rate for these new projects, assuming a market risk premium of 8.4 percent?

We estimate the cost of equity R_S for Quatram as:

$$\begin{aligned} R_S &= 5\% + (8.4\% \times 1.3) \\ &= 5\% + 10.92\% \\ &= 15.92\% \end{aligned}$$

Two key assumptions were made in this example: (1) The beta risk of the new projects is the same as the risk of the firm, and (2) The firm is all-equity financed. Given these assumptions, it follows that the cash flows of the new projects should be discounted at the 15.92 percent rate.

EXAMPLE 12.2 Project Evaluation and Beta

Suppose Alpha Air Freight is an all-equity firm with a beta of 1.21. Further suppose the market risk premium is 9.5 percent, and the risk-free rate is 5 percent. We can determine the expected return on the common stock of Alpha Air Freight by using the SML of equation (12.1). We find that the expected return is:

$$5\% + (1.21 \times 9.5\%) = 16.495\%$$

Because this is the return that shareholders can expect in the financial markets on a stock with a β of 1.21, it is the return they expect on Alpha Air Freight's stock.

Further suppose Alpha is evaluating the following non-mutually exclusive projects:

PROJECT	PROJECT'S BETA (β)	PROJECT'S EXPECTED CASH FLOWS NEXT YEAR	PROJECT'S INTERNAL RATE OF RETURN	PROJECT'S NPV WHEN CASH FLOWS ARE DISCOUNTED AT 16.495%	ACCEPT OR REJECT
A	1.21	$140	40%	$20.2	Accept
B	1.21	120	20	3.0	Accept
C	1.21	110	10	− 5.6	Reject

Each project initially costs $100. All projects are assumed to have the same risk as the firm as a whole. Because the cost of equity capital is 16.495 percent, projects in an all-equity firm are discounted at this rate. Projects *A* and *B* have positive NPVs, and *C* has a negative NPV. Thus, only *A* and *B* will be accepted. This is illustrated in Figure 12.2.

(*continued*)

FIGURE 12.2

Using the Security Market Line to Estimate the Risk-Adjusted Discount Rate for Risky Projects

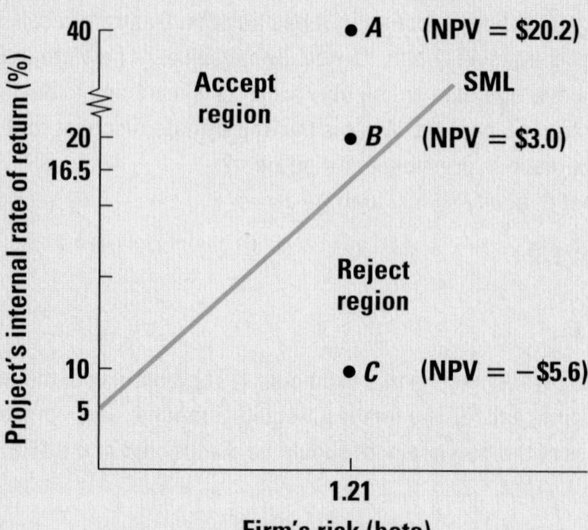

The diagonal line represents the relationship between the cost of equity capital and the firm's beta. An all-equity firm should accept a project whose internal rate of return is greater than the cost of equity capital, and should reject a project whose internal rate of return is less than the cost of equity capital. (The above graph assumes that all projects are as risky as the firm.)

12.2 ESTIMATION OF BETA

In the previous section we assumed that the beta of the company was known. Of course, beta must be estimated in the real world. We pointed out earlier that the beta of a security is the standardized covariance of a security's return with the return on the market portfolio. As we have seen, the formula for security *i* is:

$$\textbf{Beta of security } i = \frac{\text{Cov}(R_i, R_M)}{\text{Var}(R_M)} = \frac{\sigma_{i,M}}{\sigma_M^2}$$

In words, the beta is the covariance of a security with the market, divided by the variance of the market. Because we calculated both covariance and variance in earlier chapters, calculating beta involves no new material.

MEASURING COMPANY BETAS

The basic method of measuring company betas is to estimate:

$$\frac{\text{Cov}(R_i, R_M)}{\text{Var}(R_M)}$$

using $t = 1, 2, \ldots, T$ observations

Problems

1. Betas may vary over time.
2. The sample size may be inadequate.
3. Betas are influenced by changing financial leverage and business risk.

Solutions

1. Problems 1 and 2 (above) can be moderated by more sophisticated statistical techniques.
2. Problem 3 can be lessened by adjusting for changes in business and financial risk.
3. Look at average beta estimates of several comparable firms in the industry.

Real World Betas

It is instructive to see how betas are determined for actual real world companies. Figure 12.3 plots monthly returns for four large firms against monthly returns on the Standard & Poor's (S&P) 500 Index. Using a standard regression technique, we fit a straight line through data points. The result is called the "characteristic" line for the security. The slope of the characteristic line is beta. Though we have not shown it in the table, one can also determine the intercept (commonly called alpha) of the characteristic line by regression.

We use five years of monthly data for each plot. While this choice is arbitrary, it is in line with calculations performed in the real world. Practitioners know that the accuracy of the beta coefficient is suspect when too few observations are used. Conversely, since firms may change their industry over time, observations from the distant past are out-of-date.

We stated in Chapter 11 that the average beta across all stocks in an index is 1. Of course, this need not be true for a subset of the index. For example, of the four securities in our figure, two have betas above 1 and two have betas below 1. Since beta is a measure of the risk of a single security for someone holding a large, diversified portfolio, our results indicate that Philip Morris has relatively low risk and Amazon.com has relatively high risk. A more detailed discussion of the determinants of beta is presented in Section 12.3.

FIGURE 12.3

Plots of Five Years of Monthly Returns (2000–2004) on Four Individual Securities against Five Years of Monthly Returns on the Standard & Poor's (S&P) 500 Index

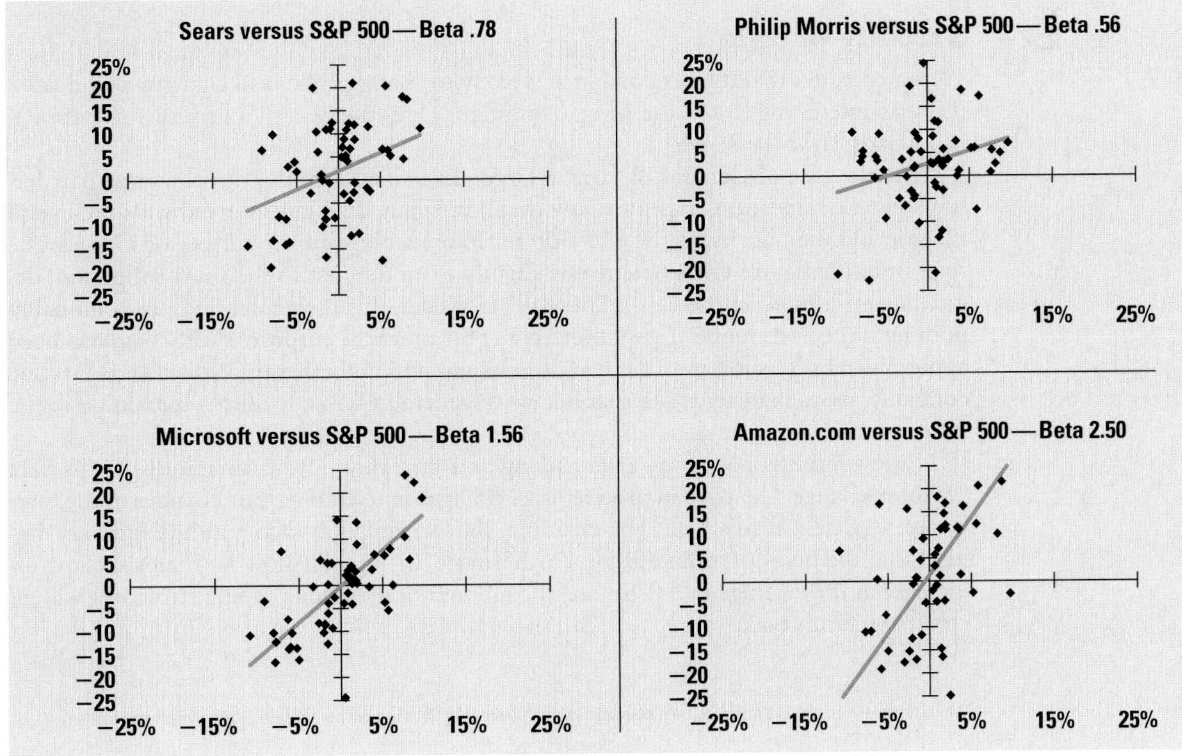

FIGURE 12.4

Plots of Monthly Returns on General Electric and on the Standard & Poor's 500 Index for Four Five-Year Periods

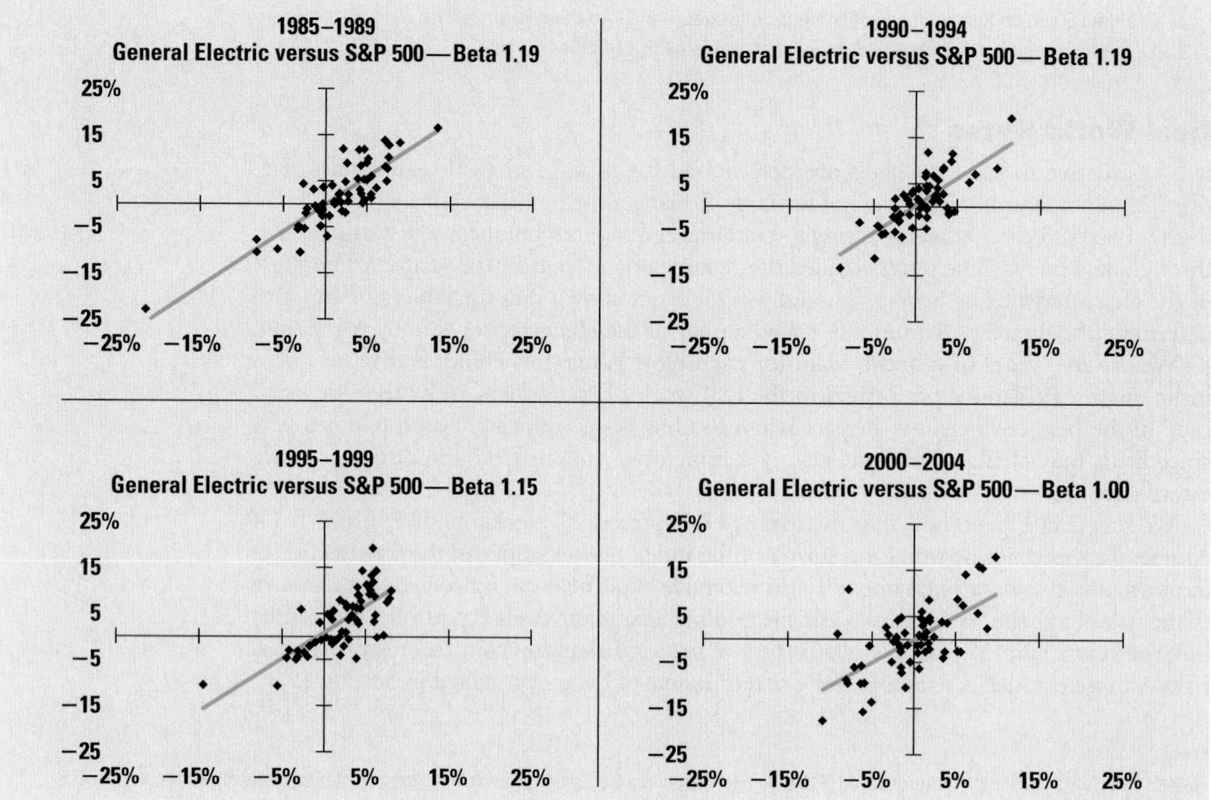

Stability of Beta

We stated above that the beta of a firm is likely to change if the firm changes its industry. It is also interesting to ask the reverse question: Does the beta of a firm stay the same if its industry stays the same?

Take the case of General Electric, a large, diversified firm that for the most part has stayed in the same industries for many decades. Figure 12.4 plots the returns on General Electric and the returns on the S&P 500 for four successive five-year periods. As can be seen from the figure, GE's beta drops slightly from the first to the third subperiod, decreasing a bit more in the last subperiod.[1] However, this movement in beta is probably nothing more than random variation. Thus, for practical purposes, GE's beta has been approximately constant over the two decades covered in the figure. While GE is just one company, most analysts argue that betas are generally stable for firms remaining in the same industry.

However, this is not to say that, as long as a firm stays in the same industry, its beta will *never* change. Changes in product line, changes in technology, or changes in the market may affect a firm's beta. For example, the deregulation of the airline industry has increased the betas of airline firms. Furthermore, as we will show in a later section, an increase in the leverage of a firm (i.e., the amount of debt in its capital structure) will increase the firm's beta.

[1]More precisely, one can say that the beta coefficients over the four periods are not statistically different from each other.

COMPANY	BETA
Microsoft	1.43
First Data Corp.	.89
Automatic Data Processing	.97
Electronic Data Systems	1.42
Oracle Corp.	1.59
Computer Sciences	1.64
Computer Associates	2.82
Fiserv Inc.	.81
Accenture Ltd.	1.68
SunGard Data	.93
Symantec Corp.	1.56
Paychex, Inc.	.72
Equally weighted portfolio	1.37

TABLE 12.1

Betas for Firms in the Computer Software Industry

Using an Industry Beta

Our approach to estimating the beta of a company from its own past data may seem commonsensical to you. However, it is frequently argued that one can better estimate a firm's beta by involving the whole industry. Consider Table 12.1, which shows the betas of some of the more prominent firms in the software industry. The average beta across all of the firms in the table is 1.37. Imagine a financial executive at Microsoft trying to estimate the firm's beta. Because beta estimation is subject to large random variation in this volatile industry, the executive may be uncomfortable with the estimate of 1.43. However, the error in beta estimation on a single stock is much higher than the error for a portfolio of securities. Thus, the executive of Microsoft may use the industry beta of 1.37 as the estimate of its own firm's beta. (As it turns out, the choice is unimportant here, since the industry beta is so close to that of the firm.)

In contrast, consider Computer Associates. Assuming a risk-free rate of 3.7 percent and a risk premium of 8.7 percent, Computer Associates might estimate its cost of equity capital as:

$$3.7\% + 2.82 \times 8.7\% = 28.23\%$$

However, if Computer Associates believed the industry beta contained less estimation error, it could estimate its cost of equity capital as:

$$3.7\% + 1.37 \times 8.7\% = 15.62\%$$

The difference is substantial here, presenting a difficult choice for a financial executive at Computer Associates.

While there is no formula for selecting the right beta, there is a very simple guideline. If one believes that the operations of the firm are similar to the operations of the rest of the industry, one should use the industry beta simply to reduce estimation error.[2] However, if an executive believes that the operations of the firm are fundamentally different from those in the rest of the industry, the firm's beta should be used.

When we discussed financial statements analysis in Chapter 3, we noted that a problem frequently comes up in practice; namely, what is the industry? For example, Value

[2]As we will see later, an adjustment must be made when the debt level in the industry is different from that of the firm. However, we ignore this adjustment here, since firms in the software industry generally have little debt.

Line's *Investment Survey* categorizes Accenture, Ltd. as a computer software company, while online financial providers such as investor.reuters.com categorize the same company in the business services industry.

12.3 DETERMINANTS OF BETA

The regression analysis approach in the previous section doesn't tell us where beta comes from. The beta of a stock does not come out of thin air. Rather, it is determined by the characteristics of the firm. We consider three factors: the cyclical nature of revenues, operating leverage, and financial leverage.

Cyclicality of Revenues

The revenues of some firms are quite cyclical. That is, these firms do well in the expansion phase of the business cycle and do poorly in the contraction phase. Empirical evidence suggests high-tech firms, retailers, and automotive firms fluctuate with the business cycle. Firms in industries such as utilities, railroads, food, and airlines are less dependent upon the cycle. Because beta is the standardized covariability of a stock's return with the market's return, it is not surprising that highly cyclical stocks have high betas.

It is worthwhile to point out that cyclicality is not the same as variability. For example, a moviemaking firm has highly variable revenues because hits and flops are not easily predicted. However, because the revenues of a studio are more dependent on the quality of its releases than upon the phase of the business cycle, motion-picture companies are not particularly cyclical. In other words, stocks with high standard deviations need not have high betas, a point we have stressed before.

Operating Leverage

We distinguished fixed costs from variable costs earlier in the text. At that time, we mentioned that fixed costs do not change as quantity changes. Conversely, variable costs increase as the quantity of output rises. This difference between variable and fixed costs allows us to define operating leverage.

EXAMPLE 12.3 Operating Leverage Illustrated

Consider a firm that can choose either technology *A* or technology *B* when making a particular product. The relevant differences between the two technologies are displayed below:

TECHNOLOGY *A*	TECHNOLOGY *B*
Fixed cost: $1,000/year	Fixed cost: $2,000/year
Variable cost: $8/unit	Variable cost: $6/unit
Price: $10/unit	Price: $10/unit
Contribution margin: $2 (= $10 − $8)	Contribution margin: $4 (= $10 − $6)

Technology *A* has lower fixed costs and higher variable costs than does technology *B*. Perhaps technology *A* involves less mechanization than does *B*. Or, the equipment in *A* may be leased, whereas the equipment in *B* must be purchased. Alternatively, perhaps technology *A* involves few employees but many subcontractors, whereas *B* involves only highly skilled employees who must be

(*continued*)

FIGURE 12.5
Illustration of Two Different Technologies

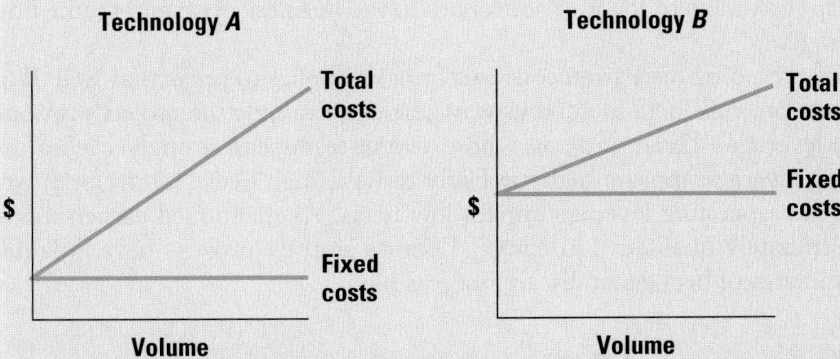

Technology A has higher variable costs and lower fixed costs than does technology *B*. Technology *B* has higher operating leverage.

FIGURE 12.6
Illustration of the Effect of a Change in Volume on the Change in Earnings before Interest and Taxes (EBIT)

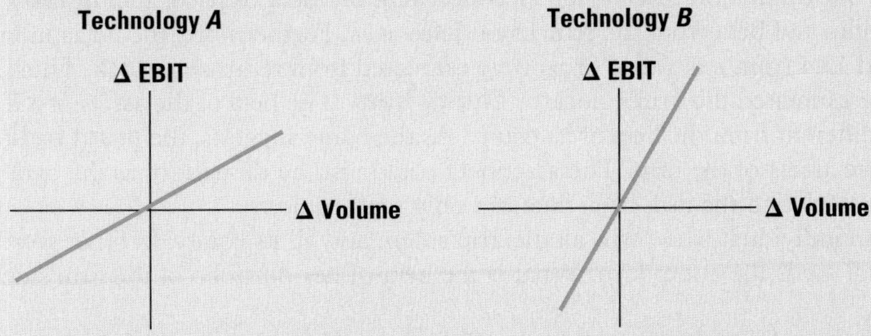

Technology *B* has lower variable costs than *A*, implying a higher contribution margin. The profits of the firm are more responsive to changes in volume under technology *B* than under *A*.

retained in bad times. Because technology *B* has both lower variable costs and higher fixed costs, we say that it has higher **operating leverage.**[3]

Figure 12.5 graphs the costs under both technologies. The slope of each total cost line represents variable costs under a single technology. The slope of *A*'s line is steeper, indicating greater variable costs.

Because the two technologies are used to produce the same products, a unit price of $10 applies for both cases. We mentioned in an earlier chapter that contribution margin is the difference between price and variable cost. It measures the incremental profit from one additional unit. Because the contribution margin in *B* is greater, its technology is riskier. An unexpected sale increases profit by $2 under *A* but increases profit by $4 under *B*. Similarly, an unexpected sale cancellation reduces profit by $2 under *A* but reduces profit by $4 under *B*. This is illustrated in Figure 12.6. This figure shows the change in earnings before interest and taxes for a given change in volume. The slope of the right-hand graph is greater, indicating that technology *B* is riskier.

[3]The actual definition of operating leverage is:

$$\frac{\text{Change in EBIT}}{\text{EBIT}} \times \frac{\text{Sales}}{\text{Change in sales}}$$

where EBIT is the earnings before interest and taxes. That is, operating leverage measures the percentage change in EBIT for a given percentage change in sales or revenues. It can be shown that operating leverage increases as fixed costs rise and as variable costs fall.

The cyclicality of a firm's revenues is a determinant of the firm's beta. Operating leverage magnifies the effect of cyclicality on beta. As mentioned earlier, business risk is generally defined as the risk of the firm without financial leverage. Business risk depends both on the responsiveness of the firm's revenues to the business cycle and on the firm's operating leverage.

Although the preceding discussion concerns firms, it applies to projects as well. If one cannot estimate a project's beta in another way, one can examine the project's revenues and operating leverage. Those projects whose revenues appear strongly cyclical and whose operating leverage appears high are likely to have high betas. Conversely, weak cyclicality and low operating leverage implies low betas. As mentioned earlier, this approach is unfortunately qualitative in nature. Because start-up projects have little data, quantitative estimates of beta generally are not feasible.

Financial Leverage and Beta

As suggested by their names, operating leverage and financial leverage are analogous concepts. Operating leverage refers to the firm's fixed costs of *production.* Financial leverage is the extent to which a firm relies on debt and a levered firm is a firm with some debt in its capital structure. Because a *levered* firm must make interest payments regardless of the firm's sales, financial leverage refers to the firm's fixed costs of *finance.*

Consider our discussion in Chapter 11 concerning the beta of Jelco, Inc. In that example, we estimated beta from the returns on Jelco *stock.* Furthermore, the betas in Figures 12.3 and 12.4 from real world firms were estimated from returns on stock. Thus, in each case, we estimated the firm's stock or **equity beta**. The beta of the assets of a levered firm is different from the beta of its equity. As the name suggests, the **asset beta** is the beta of the assets of the firm. The asset beta could also be thought of as the beta of the common stock had the firm been financed only with equity.

Imagine an individual who owns all the firm's debt and all its equity. In other words, this individual owns the entire firm. What is the beta of her portfolio of the firm's debt and equity?

As with any portfolio, the beta of this portfolio is a weighted average of the betas of the individual items in the portfolio. Let B stand for the market value of the firm's debt and S stand for the market value of the firm's equity, then we have:

$$\beta_{\text{Asset}} = \frac{S}{B+S} \times \beta_{\text{Equity}} + \frac{B}{B+S} \times \beta_{\text{Debt}} \tag{12.2}$$

where β_{Equity} is the beta of the stock of the *levered* firm. Notice that the beta of debt is multiplied by $B/(B + S)$, the percentage of debt in the capital structure. Similarly, the beta of equity is multiplied by the percentage of equity in the capital structure. Because the portfolio contains both the debt of the firm and the equity of the firm, the beta of the portfolio is the *asset beta.* As we said above, the asset beta can also be viewed as the beta of the common stock had the firm been all equity.

The beta of debt is very low in practice. If we make the commonplace assumption that the beta of debt is zero, we have:

$$\beta_{\text{Asset}} = \frac{S}{B+S} \times \beta_{\text{Equity}} \tag{12.3}$$

Because $S/(B + S)$ must be below 1 for a levered firm, it follows that $\beta_{\text{Asset}} < \beta_{\text{Equity}}$. Rearranging this equation, we have:

$$\beta_{\text{Equity}} = \beta_{\text{Asset}}\left(1 + \frac{B}{S}\right)$$

The equity beta will always be greater than the asset beta with financial leverage (assuming the asset beta is positive).[4]

EXAMPLE 12.4 Asset versus Equity Betas

Consider a tree growing company, Rapid Cedars, Inc., which is currently all equity and has a beta of .8. The firm has decided to move to a capital structure of one part debt to two parts equity. Because the firm is staying in the same industry, its asset beta should remain at .8. However, assuming a zero beta for its debt, its equity beta would become:

$$\beta_{\text{Equity}} = \beta_{\text{Asset}}\left(1 + \frac{B}{S}\right)$$

$$1.2 = .8\left(1 + \frac{1}{2}\right)$$

If the firm had one part debt to one part equity in its capital structure, its equity beta would be:

$$1.6 = .8(1 + 1)$$

However, as long as it stayed in the same industry, its asset beta would remain at .8. The effect of leverage, then, is to increase the equity beta.

12.4 EXTENSIONS OF THE BASIC MODEL

The Firm versus the Project: Vive la Différence

We now assume that the risk of a project differs from that of the firm, while going back to the all-equity assumption. We began the chapter by pointing out that each project should be paired with a financial asset of comparable risk. If a project's beta differs from that of the firm, the project should be discounted at the rate commensurate with its own beta. This is a very important point because firms frequently speak of a *corporate discount rate*. (*Hurdle rate, cutoff rate, benchmark,* and *cost of capital* are frequently used synonymously.) Unless all projects in the corporation are of the same risk, choosing the same discount rate for all projects is incorrect.

EXAMPLE 12.5 Project Risk

D. D. Ronnelley Co., a publishing firm, may accept a project in computer software. Noting that computer software companies have high betas, the publishing firm views the software venture as more risky than the rest of its business. It should discount the project at a rate commensurate with the risk of software companies. For example, it might use the average beta of a portfolio of publicly traded software firms. Instead, if all projects in D. D. Ronnelley Co. were discounted at the same rate, a bias would result. The firm would accept too many high-risk projects (software ventures) and reject too many low-risk projects (books and magazines). This point is illustrated in Figure 12.7.

(*continued*)

[4]It can be shown that the relationship between a firm's asset beta and its equity beta with corporate taxes is:

$$\beta_{\text{Equity}} = \beta_{\text{Asset}}\left[1 + (1 - t_C)\frac{B}{S}\right]$$

In this expression, t_C is the corporate tax rate. Tax effects are considered in more detail in a later chapter.

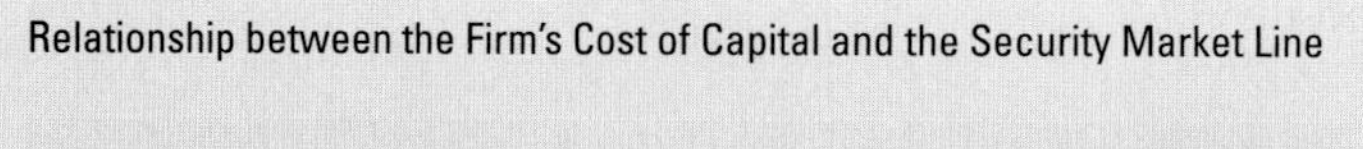

FIGURE 12.7
Relationship between the Firm's Cost of Capital and the Security Market Line

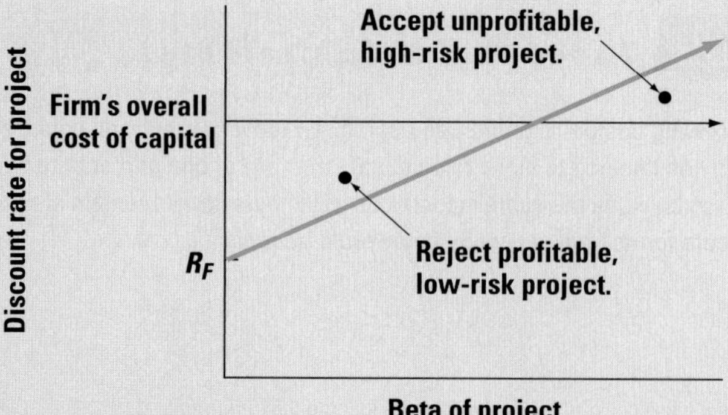

Use of a firm's cost of capital in calculations may lead to incorrect capital budgeting decisions. Projects with high risk, such as the software venture for D. D. Ronnelley Co., should be discounted at a high rate. By using the firm's cost of capital, the firm is likely to accept too many high-risk projects.

Projects with low risk should be discounted at a low rate. By using the firm's cost of capital, the firm is likely to reject too many low-risk projects.

The D. D. Ronnelley example assumes that the proposed project has identical risk to that of the software industry, allowing the industry beta to be used. However, the beta of a new project may be greater than the beta of existing firms in the same industry because the very newness of the project likely increases its responsiveness to economywide movements. For example, a start-up computer venture may fail in a recession, while IBM or Hewlett-Packard will still be around. Conversely, in an economywide expansion, the venture may grow much faster than the old-line computer firms.

Fortunately, a slight adjustment is all that is needed here. The new venture should be assigned a somewhat higher beta than that of the industry to reflect added risk. The adjustment is necessarily ad hoc, so no formula can be given. Our experience indicates that this approach is widespread in practice today.

However, a problem does arise for the rare project constituting its own industry. For example, consider the firms providing consumer shopping by television. Today, one can obtain a reasonable estimate for the beta of this industry, since a few of the firms have publicly traded stock. However, when the ventures began in the 1980s, any beta estimate was suspect. At that time, no one knew whether shopping by TV belonged in the television industry, the retail industry, or in an entirely new industry.

What beta should be used in the rare case when an industrywide beta is not appropriate? One approach, which considers the determinants of the project's beta, was treated earlier in this chapter. Unfortunately, that approach is only qualitative in nature.

The Cost of Capital with Debt

Section 12.1 showed how to choose the discount rate when a project is all-equity financed. In this section, we discuss an adjustment when the project is financed with both debt and equity.

Suppose a firm uses both debt and equity to finance its investments. If the firm pays R_B for its debt financing and R_S for its equity, what is the overall or average cost of its capital? The cost of equity is R_S, as discussed in earlier sections. The cost of debt is the firm's borrowing rate, R_B, which we can often observe by looking at the yield to maturity on the firm's debt. If a firm uses both debt and equity, the cost of capital is a weighted average of each. This works out to be:

$$\frac{S}{S+B} \times R_S + \frac{B}{S+B} \times R_B$$

The weights in the formula are, respectively, the proportion of total value represented by the equity:

$$\left(\frac{S}{S+B}\right)$$

and the proportion of total value represented by debt:

$$\left(\frac{B}{S+B}\right)$$

This is only natural. If the firm had issued no debt and was therefore an all-equity firm, its average cost of capital would equal its cost of equity, R_S. At the other extreme, if the firm had issued so much debt that its equity was valueless, it would be an all-debt firm, and its average cost of capital would be its cost of debt, R_B.

Of course, interest is tax deductible at the corporate level, a point to be treated in more detail in a later chapter. The aftertax cost of debt is:

$$\textbf{Cost of debt (after corporate tax)} = R_B \times (1 - t_C)$$

where t_C is the corporation's tax rate.

Assembling these results, we get the average cost of capital (after tax) for the firm:

$$\textbf{Average cost of capital} = \left(\frac{S}{S+B}\right) \times R_S + \left(\frac{B}{S+B}\right) \times R_B \times (1 - t_C) \qquad (12.4)$$

Because the average cost of capital is a weighting of its cost of equity and its cost of debt, it is usually referred to as the **weighted average cost of capital, R_{WACC}**, and from now on we will use this term.

EXAMPLE 12.6 WACC

Consider a firm whose debt has a market value of $40 million and whose stock has a market value of $60 million (3 million outstanding shares of stock, each selling for $20 per share). The firm pays a 15 percent rate of interest on its new debt and has a beta of 1.41. The corporate tax rate is 34 percent. (Assume that the SML holds, that the risk premium on the market is 9.5 percent [slightly higher than the historical equity risk premium], and that the current Treasury bill rate is 11 percent [much higher than the current Treasury bill rate].) What is this firm's R_{WACC}?

To compute the R_{WACC} using equation (12.4), we must know (1) the aftertax cost of debt, $R_B \times (1 - t_C)$, (2) the cost of equity, R_S, and (3) the proportions of debt and equity used by the firm. These three values are computed below.

1. The pretax cost of debt is 15 percent, implying an aftertax cost of 9.9 percent [15% × (1 − .34)].
2. The cost of equity capital is computed by using the SML:

$$\begin{aligned} R_S &= R_F + \beta \times [R_M - R_F] \\ &= 11\% + 1.41 \times 9.5\% \\ &= 24.40\% \end{aligned}$$

(continued)

3. The proportions of debt and equity are computed from the market values of debt and equity. Because the market value of the firm is $100 million ($40 million + $60 million), the proportions of debt and equity are 40 and 60 percent, respectively.

The cost of equity, R_S, is 24.40 percent, and the aftertax cost of debt, $R_B \times (1 - t_C)$, is 9.9 percent. *B* is $40 million and *S* is $60 million. Therefore:

$$R_{\text{WACC}} = \frac{S}{B+S} \times R_S + \frac{B}{B+S} \times R_B \times (1 - t_C)$$

$$= \left(\frac{40}{100} \times 9.9\%\right) + \left(\frac{60}{100} \times 24.40\%\right) = 18.60\%$$

This procedure is presented in chart form next:

(1) FINANCING COMPONENTS	(2) MARKET VALUES	(3) WEIGHT	(4) COST OF CAPITAL (AFTER CORPORATE TAX)	(5) WEIGHTED COST OF CAPITAL
Debt	$ 40,000,000	.40	15% × (1 − .34) = 9.9%	3.96%
Equity	60,000,000	.60	11% + 1.41 × 9.5% = 24.40%	14.64
	$100,000,000	1.00		18.60%

The weights we used in the previous example were market value weights. Market value weights are more appropriate than book value weights because the market values of the securities are closer to the actual dollars that would be received from their sale. Actually, it is usually useful to think in terms of "target" market weights. These are the market weights expected to prevail over the life of the firm or project.

EXAMPLE 12.7

Suppose that a firm has both a current and a target debt-equity ratio of .6, a cost of debt of 15.15 percent, and a cost of equity of 20 percent. The corporate tax rate is 34 percent.

Our first step calls for transforming the debt-to-equity (*B/S*) ratio to a debt-to-value ratio. A *B/S* ratio of .6 implies 6 parts debt for 10 parts equity. Since value is equal to the sum of the debt plus the equity, the debt-to-value ratio is 6/(6 + 10) = .375. Similarly, the equity-to-value ratio is 10/(6 + 10) = .625. The R_{WACC} will then be:

$$R_{\text{WACC}} = \left(\frac{S}{S+B}\right) \times R_S + \left(\frac{B}{S+B}\right) \times R_B \times (1 - t_C)$$

$$= .625 \times 20\% + .375 \times 15.15\% \times .66 = 16.25\%$$

Suppose the firm is considering taking on a warehouse renovation costing $50 million that is expected to yield cost savings of $12 million a year for six years. Using the NPV equation and discounting the six years of expected cash flows from the renovation at the R_{WACC}, we have:

$$\text{NPV} = -\$50 + \frac{\$12}{(1 + R_{\text{WACC}})} + \cdots + \frac{\$12}{(1 + R_{\text{WACC}})^6}$$

$$= -\$50 + \$12 \times A^6_{.1625}$$

$$= -\$50 + (12 \times 3.66)$$

$$= -\$6.07$$

Should the firm take on the warehouse renovation? The project has a negative NPV using the firm's R_{WACC}. This means that the financial markets offer superior projects in the same risk class (namely, the firm's risk class). The answer is clear: The firm should reject the project.

12.5 ESTIMATING EASTMAN CHEMICAL'S COST OF CAPITAL

In our previous sections, we calculated the cost of capital in examples. We will now calculate the cost of capital for a real company, Eastman Chemical Co., a leading international chemical company and maker of plastics such as that used in soft drink containers. It was created in 1993, when its former parent company, Eastman Kodak, split off the division as a separate company.

EASTMAN'S COST OF EQUITY Our first stop for Eastman is finance.yahoo.com (ticker: "EMN"). As of April 2005, the relevant pieces of what we found are shown in the next two boxes.

EASTMAN CHEM CO (NYSE:EMN) Delayed quote data			
Last Trade:	**48.09**	Day's Range:	47.93 - 49.45
Trade Time:	4:02PM ET	52wk Range:	41.97 - 61.80
Change:	↓1.36 (2.75%)	Volume:	1,445,300
Prev Close:	49.45	Avg Vol (3m):	707,681
Open:	49.45	Market Cap:	3.81B
Bid:	N/A	P/E (ttm):	22.21
Ask:	N/A	EPS (ttm):	2.165
1y Target Est:	56.50	Div & Yield:	1.76 (3.56%)

TRADING INFORMATION	
Stock Price History	
Beta:	0.71
52-Week Change:	14.26%
52-Week Change (relative to S&P500):	12.90%
52-Week High (9-Mar-05):	61.80
52-Week Low (29-Apr-04):	41.97
50-Day Moving Average:	57.36
200-Day Moving Average:	51.24
Share Statistics	
Average Volume (3 month):	707,681
Average Volume (10 day):	1,081,000
Shares Outstanding:	79.21M
Float:	78.50M
% Held by Insiders:	0.90%
% Held by Institutions:	83.81%
Shares Short (as of 8-Apr-05):	1.41M
Daily Volume (as of 8-Apr-05):	N/A
Short Ratio (as of 8-Apr-05):	2.164
Short % of Float (as of 8-Apr-05):	1.80%
Shares Short (prior month):	1.25M

Balance Sheet	
Total Cash (mrq):	325.00M
Total Cash Per Share (mrq):	4.1
Total Debt (mrq)[2]:	2.06B
Total Debt/Equity (mrq):	1.742
Current Ratio (mrq):	1.609
Book Value Per Share (mrq):	14.948

According to this screen, Eastman has 79.21 million shares of stock outstanding. The book value per share is $14.948, but the stock sells for $48.09. Total equity is therefore about $1.184 billion on a book value basis, but it is closer to $3.809 billion on a market value basis.

To estimate Eastman's cost of equity, we will assume a market risk premium of 8.7 percent, similar to what we calculated in Chapter 10. Eastman's beta on Yahoo! is .71. Table 12.2 shows the betas for other U.S.-based diversified chemical companies. As you can see, the industry average beta is .81, which is slightly higher than Eastman's beta. According to the bond section of finance.yahoo.com, T-bills were paying about 2.72 percent. Using Eastman's own beta in the CAPM to estimate the cost of equity, we find:

$$R_S = .0272 + .71(.087) = .0890 \text{ or } 8.90\%$$

If we use the industry beta, we would find the estimate for the cost of equity capital is:

$$R_S = .0272 + .81(.087) = .0977 \text{ or } 9.77\%$$

Notice that the estimates for the cost of equity are close because Eastman's beta is relatively close to the industry beta. The decision of which cost of equity estimate to use is up to the financial executive, based on the knowledge and experience of both the company and the industry. In this case, we will choose to use the cost of equity using Eastman's estimated beta.

EASTMAN'S COST OF DEBT Eastman has six long-term bond issues that account for essentially all of its long-term debt. To calculate the cost of debt, we will have to combine these six issues and compute a weighted average. We will go to www.nasdbondinfo.com to find quotes on the bonds. We should note here that finding the yield to maturity for all of a company's outstanding bond issues on a single day is unusual. In our previous discussion on bonds, we found that the bond market is not as liquid as the stock market

TABLE 12.2 Betas for Companies in the Diversified Chemical Industry

COMPANY	BETA
3M Company	.57
Air Products & Chemical	.66
Monsanto Co.	.99
PPG Industries	.83
Eastman Chemical	.71
Albermarle Corp.	.93
Cabot Corp.	.86
Pall Corp.	.86
Cytec Industries	.66
Millipore Corp.	1.13
Cambrex Corp.	.75
Equally weighted portfolio	.81

and on many days, individual bond issues may not trade. To find the book value of the bonds, we go to www.sec.gov and find the 10K report (i.e., the most recent annual financial report) dated December 31, 2004, and filed with the SEC on March 15, 2005. The basic information is as follows:

COUPON RATE	MATURITY	BOOK VALUE (FACE VALUE, $ MILLIONS)	PRICE (% OF PAR)	YIELD TO MATURITY
3.25 %	2008	$250	96.58%	4.43%
7.00	2012	399	111.84	4.97
6.30	2018	253	108.14	5.42
7.25	2024	497	117.78	5.69
7.625	2024	200	123.57	5.61
7.60	2027	297	121.94	5.84

To calculate the weighted average cost of debt, we take the percentage of the total debt represented by each issue and multiply by the yield on the issue. We then add to get the overall weighted average debt cost. We use both book values and market values here for comparison. The results of the calculations are as follows:

COUPON RATE	BOOK VALUE (FACE VALUE, $ MILLIONS)	PERCENTAGE OF TOTAL	MARKET VALUE ($ MILLIONS)	PERCENTAGE OF TOTAL	YIELD TO MATURITY	BOOK VALUES	MARKET VALUES
3.25%	$ 250	.13	$ 241.45	.11	4.43%	.58%	.50%
7.00	399	.21	446.24	.21	4.97	1.05	1.03
6.30	253	.13	273.59	.13	5.42	.72	.69
7.60	497	.26	585.37	.27	5.69	1.49	1.54
7.625	200	.11	247.14	.11	5.61	.59	.64
7.60	297	.16	362.16	.17	5.84	.91	.98
Total	$1,896	1.00	$2,155.95	1.00		5.35%	5.38%

As these calculations show, Eastman's cost of debt is 5.35 percent on a book value basis and 5.38 percent on a market value basis. Thus, for Eastman, whether market values or book values are used makes no difference. The reason is simply that the market values and book values are similar. This will often be the case and explains why companies frequently use book values for debt in WACC calculations.

EASTMAN'S WACC We now have the various pieces necessary to calculate Eastman's WACC. First, we need to calculate the capital structure weights. On a book value basis, Eastman's equity and debt are worth $1.184 billion and $1.896 billion, respectively. The total value is $3.08 billion, so the equity and debt percentages are $1.184 billion/ $3.08 billion = .38 and $1.896 billion/$3.08 billion = .62. Assuming a tax rate of 35 percent, Eastman's WACC is:

$$\begin{aligned} R_{\text{WACC}} &= .38 \times 8.90\% + .62 \times 5.35\% \times (1 - .35) \\ &= 5.54\% \end{aligned}$$

Thus, using book value capital structure weights, we get about 5.54 percent for Eastman's R_{WACC}.

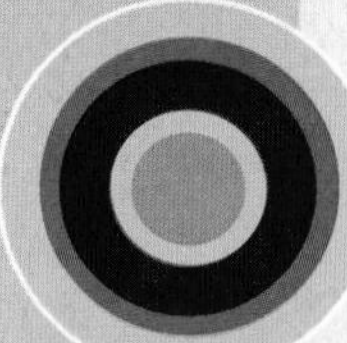

THE COST OF OIL

We have discussed the weighted average cost of capital and its uses in the corporate world. WACC is also used by governments as well. One of the most important tasks undertaken by a state government is property valuation. This valuation determines the amount of property tax revenue to be received by the state (and paid by property owners). Property valuation is a difficult process. The value of a home depends on what it could be sold for, but how do you value an oil or gas field? The Texas Comptroller of Public Accounts does it by calculating the present value of the future cash flows of the property. As you know by now, the cost of capital depends on the use of funds, not the source of funds. So, Texas calculates the WACC for companies in the oil industry and adjusts the industry average WACC for company-specific factors. The table below shows the Texas calculations for integrated oil companies.

Integrated Petroleum Companies

Company Name	Total Capital	Total Equity	Total Convertible Preferred Stock	Total Debt	Equity % of Capital	Convertible Preferred Stock % of Capital	Debt % of Capital	Beta Factor	After Income Tax Cost of Equity, %	Before Income Tax Cost of Equity, %	Cost of Convertible Preferred Stock %	Cost of Debt %	Before Income Tax WACC %
Amerada Hess	$8,756,531,560	$4,778,281,560	$47,250,000	$3,931,000,000	54.57	0.01	44.89	0.90	12.14	18.68	0.07	5.61	12.75
Anadarko	$18,066,550,000	$13,007,550,000	$0	$5,059,000,000	72.00	0.00	28.00	0.85	11.81	18.17	0.00	4.66	14.39
Apache	$15,160,427,641	$12,833,461,641	$0	$2,326,966,000	84.65	0.00	15.35	0.80	11.48	17.66	0.00	5.07	15.73
Burlington Resources	$14,818,790,710	$10,945,790,710	$0	$3,873,000,000	73.86	0.00	26.14	0.75	11.15	17.15	0.00	5.24	14.04
Chevron Texaco	$103,257,671,531	$92,363,671,531	$0	$10,894,000,000	89.45	0.00	10.55	0.80	11.48	17.66	0.00	3.62	16.18
Conoco Phillips	$62,769,139,810	$46,429,139,810	$0	$16,340,000,000	73.97	0.00	26.03	0.85	11.81	18.17	0.00	4.47	14.60
Exxon Mobil	$274,044,000,000	$269,288,000,000	$0	$4,756,000,000	98.26	0.00	1.74	0.80	11.48	17.66	0.00	4.43	17.43
Kerr-McGee	$7,770,001,391	$4,689,001,391	$0	$3,081,000,000	60.35	0.00	39.65	0.95	12.47	19.18	0.00	4.79	13.48
Marathon	$14,356,851,009	$10,271,851,009	$0	$4,085,000,000	71.55	0.00	28.45	0.85	11.81	18.17	0.00	4.88	14.39
Murphy	$7,090,375,755	$6,000,068,755	$0	$1,090,307,000	84.62	0.00	15.38	0.85	11.81	18.17	0.00	5.44	16.21
Occidental	$20,367,905,324	$16,348,905,324	$0	$4,019,000,000	80.27	0.00	19.73	0.85	6.20	18.17	0.00	4.27	15.43
Unocal	$12,232,677,020	$9,597,677,020	$0	$2,635,000,000	78.46	0.00	21.54	0.85	11.81	18.17	0.00	4.38	15.20
TOTAL	$558,690,921,750	$496,553,398,750	$47,250,000	$62,090,273,000	922.01	0.01	277.45	10.10	135.45	217.02	0.07	56.85	179.82
ENTRIES					12	1	12	12	12	12	1	12	**12**
AVERAGE					76.83	0.005	23.12	0.84	11.29	18.08	0.07	4.74	**14.98**
STANDARD DEVIATION					12.02	0.002	11.93	0.05	1.64	0.52	0.02	0.56	1.31

As you can see, the WACC numbers for the companies are similar. Amerada Hess has the lowest WACC at 12.75 percent and ExxonMobil has the highest at 17.43 percent, but most other companies' WACCs are in the 13 to 15 percent range. The average WACC for a company in this industry is 14.98 percent, with a standard deviation of 1.31 percent. When Texas uses this calculation, a 2 percent adjustment factor is added, plus any property-specific risk adjustment. The range used by the state for 2004 was from 16.97 percent to 22.55 percent, before any property-specific factor.

Notice one major difference between the calculations of WACC that we have discussed and the calculations from the Texas Comptroller of Public Accounts: The Texas state government calculated these numbers on a pretax basis. In other words, Texas did not account for the tax deductibility of interest payments in this calculation. The reason is that the government adjusts the cost of capital for taxes on a company-by-company basis.

If we use market value weights, however, the R_{WACC} will be higher. To see why, notice that on a market value basis, Eastman's equity and debt are worth \$3.809 billion and \$2.156 billion, respectively. The capital structure weights are therefore \$3.809 billion/\$5.965 billion = .64 and \$2.156 billion/\$5.965 billion = .36, so the equity percentage is much higher. With these weights, Eastman's R_{WACC} is:

$$\begin{aligned} R_{WACC} &= .64 \times 8.90\% + .36 \times 5.38\% \times (1 - .35) \\ &= 6.95\% \end{aligned}$$

Thus, using market value weights, we get 6.95 percent for Eastman's R_{WACC}, which is more than a full percent higher than the 5.54 percent R_{WACC} we got using book value weights.

So how does our estimate of the R_{WACC} for Eastman compare to others? One place to find estimates for a company's R_{WACC} is www.valuepro.net. We went there and found the following information for Eastman:

Online Valuation for EMN - 4 / 27 / 2005

Intrinsic Stock Value	168.67	Recalculate	Value Another Stock

Excess Return Period (yrs)	10	Depreciation Rate (% of Rev)	6.33
Revenues ($mil)	6580.0	Investment Rate (% of Rev)	3.97
Growth Rate (%)	31.5	Working Capital (% of Rev)	5.84
Net Oper. Profit Margin (%)	1.64	Short-Term Assets ($mil)	1553.0
Tax Rate (%)	21.053	Short-Term Liab. ($mil)	812
Stock Price ($)	51.7100	Equity Risk Premium (%)	3
Shares Outstanding (mil)	77.8	Company Beta	1.1025
10-Yr Treasury Yield (%)	5	Value Debt Out. ($mil)	2066
Bond Spread Treasury (%)	1.5	Value Pref. Stock Out. ($mil)	0
Preferred Stock Yield (%)	7.5	Company WACC (%)	7.23

As you can see, ValuePro estimates the R_{WACC} for Eastman as 7.23 percent, which is very close to our estimate of 6.95 percent. The methods used by this site are not identical to ours, but they are similar in the most important regards. You can visit the site to learn more if you are so inclined. A nearby *The Real World* box illustrates the use of R_{WACC} in the context of tax assessments by state governments.

SUMMARY AND CONCLUSIONS

Earlier chapters on capital budgeting assumed that projects generate riskless cash flows. The appropriate discount rate in that case is the riskless interest rate. Of course, most cash flows from real world capital budgeting projects are risky. This chapter discusses the discount rate when cash flows are risky.

1. A firm with excess cash can either pay a dividend or make a capital expenditure. Because stockholders can reinvest the dividend in risky financial assets, the expected return on a capital budgeting project should be at least as great as the expected return on a financial asset of comparable risk.
2. The expected return on any asset is dependent upon its beta. Thus, we showed how to estimate the beta of a stock. The appropriate procedure employs regression analysis on historical returns.
3. We considered the case of a project whose beta risk was equal to that of the firm. If the firm is unlevered, the discount rate on the project is equal to:

   $$R_F + \beta \times (R_M - R_F)$$

   where R_M is the expected return on the market portfolio and R_F is the risk-free rate. In words, the discount rate on the project is equal to the CAPM's estimate of the expected return on the security.
4. If the project's beta differs from that of the firm, the discount rate should be based on the project's beta. The project's beta can generally be estimated by determining the average beta of the project's industry.
5. The beta of a company is a function of a number of factors. Perhaps the three most important are:
   - Cyclicality of revenues
   - Operating leverage
   - Financial leverage
6. Sometimes one cannot use the average beta of the project's industry as an estimate of the beta of the project. For example, a new project may not fall neatly into any existing industry. In this case, one can estimate the project's beta by considering the project's cyclicality of revenues and its operating leverage. This approach is qualitative in nature.
7. If a firm uses debt, the discount rate to use is the R_{WACC}. In order to calculate R_{WACC}, the cost of equity and the cost of debt applicable to a project must be estimated. If the project is similar to the firm, the cost of equity can be estimated using the SML for the firm's equity. Conceptually, a dividend growth model could be used as well, though it is likely to be far less accurate in practice.

CONCEPT QUESTIONS

1. **WACC** On the most basic level, if a firm's WACC is 12 percent, what does this mean?
2. **Book Values versus Market Values** In calculating the WACC, if you had to use book values for either debt or equity, which would you choose? Why?
3. **Project Risk** If you can borrow all the money you need for a project at 6 percent, doesn't it follow that 6 percent is your cost of capital for the project?
4. **WACC and Taxes** Why do we use an aftertax figure for cost of debt but not for cost of equity?
5. **SML Cost of Equity Estimation** If you use the stock beta and the security market line to compute the discount rate for a project, what assumptions are you implicitly making?

6. **SML Cost of Equity Estimation** What are the advantages of using the SML approach to finding the cost of equity capital? What are the disadvantages? What are the specific pieces of information needed to use this method? Are all of these variables observable, or do they need to be estimated? What are some of the ways in which you could get these estimates?
7. **Cost of Debt Estimation** How do you determine the appropriate cost of debt for a company? Does it make a difference if the company's debt is privately placed as opposed to being publicly traded? How would you estimate the cost of debt for a firm whose only debt issues are privately held by institutional investors?
8. **Cost of Capital** Suppose Tom O'Bedlam, president of Bedlam Products, Inc., has hired you to determine the firm's cost of debt and cost of equity capital.
   a. The stock currently sells for $50 per share, and the dividend per share will probably be about $5. Tom argues, "It will cost us $5 per share to use the stockholders' money this year, so the cost of equity is equal to 10 percent ($5/50)." What's wrong with this conclusion?
   b. Based on the most recent financial statements, Bedlam Products' total liabilities are $8 million. Total interest expense for the coming year will be about $1 million. Tom therefore reasons, "We owe $8 million, and we will pay $1 million interest. Therefore, our cost of debt is obviously $1 million/8 million = 12.5 percent." What's wrong with this conclusion?
   c. Based on his own analysis, Tom is recommending that the company increase its use of equity financing, because "debt costs 12.5 percent, but equity only costs 10 percent; thus equity is cheaper." Ignoring all the other issues, what do you think about the conclusion that the cost of equity is less than the cost of debt?
9. **Company Risk versus Project Risk** Both Dow Chemical Company, a large natural gas user, and Superior Oil, a major natural gas producer, are thinking of investing in natural gas wells near Houston. Both are all-equity financed companies. Dow and Superior are looking at identical projects. They've analyzed their respective investments, which would involve a negative cash flow now and positive expected cash flows in the future. These cash flows would be the same for both firms. No debt would be used to finance the projects. Both companies estimate that their project would have a net present value of $1 million at an 18 percent discount rate and a −$1.1 million NPV at a 22 percent discount rate. Dow has a beta of 1.25, whereas Superior has a beta of .75. The expected risk premium on the market is 8 percent, and risk-free bonds are yielding 12 percent. Should either company proceed? Should both? Explain.
10. **Divisional Cost of Capital** Under what circumstances would it be appropriate for a firm to use different costs of capital for its different operating divisions? If the overall firm WACC were used as the hurdle rate for all divisions, would the riskier divisions or the more conservative divisions tend to get most of the investment projects? Why? If you were to try to estimate the appropriate cost of capital for different divisions, what problems might you encounter? What are two techniques you could use to develop a rough estimate for each division's cost of capital?
11. **Leverage** Consider a levered firm's projects that have similar risks to the firm as a whole. Is the discount rate for the projects higher or lower than the rate computed using the security market line? Why?
12. **Beta** What factors determine the beta of a stock? Define and describe each.

QUESTIONS AND PROBLEMS

1. **Calculating Cost of Equity** The Dybvig Corporation's common stock has a beta of 1.3. If the risk-free rate is 4.5 percent and the expected return on the market is 12 percent, what is Dybvig's cost of equity capital?

Basic
(Questions 1–13)

2. **Calculating Cost of Debt** Advance, Inc., is trying to determine its cost of debt. The firm has a debt issue outstanding with 12 years to maturity that is quoted at 105 percent of face value. The issue makes semiannual payments and has a coupon rate of 8 percent annually. What is Advance's pretax cost of debt? If the tax rate is 35 percent, what is the aftertax cost of debt?

3. **Calculating Cost of Debt** Shanken Corp. issued a 30-year, 10 percent semiannual bond 7 years ago. The bond currently sells for 108 percent of its face value. The company's tax rate is 35 percent.

   a. What is the pretax cost of debt?

   b. What is the aftertax cost of debt?

   c. Which is more relevant, the pretax or the aftertax cost of debt? Why?

4. **Calculating Cost of Debt** For the firm in the previous problem, suppose the book value of the debt issue is $20 million. In addition, the company has a second debt issue on the market, a zero coupon bond with seven years left to maturity; the book value of this issue is $80 million and the bonds sell for 58 percent of par. What is the company's total book value of debt? The total market value? What is your best estimate of the aftertax cost of debt now?

5. **Calculating WACC** Mullineaux Corporation has a target capital structure of 55 percent common stock and 45 percent debt. Its cost of equity is 16 percent, and the cost of debt is 9 percent. The relevant tax rate is 35 percent. What is Mullineaux's WACC?

6. **Taxes and WACC** Miller Manufacturing has a target debt-equity ratio of .60. Its cost of equity is 18 percent and its cost of debt is 10 percent. If the tax rate is 35 percent, what is Miller's WACC?

7. **Finding the Capital Structure** Fama's Llamas has a weighted average cost of capital of 11.5 percent. The company's cost of equity is 16 percent and its cost of debt is 8.5 percent. The tax rate is 35 percent. What is Fama's debt-equity ratio?

8. **Book Value versus Market Value** Filer Manufacturing has 9.5 million shares of common stock outstanding. The current share price is $53, and the book value per share is $5. Filer Manufacturing also has two bond issues outstanding. The first bond issue has a face value of $75 million, an 8 percent coupon, and sells for 93 percent of par. The second issue has a face value of $60 million, a 7.5 percent coupon, and sells for 96.5 percent of par. The first issue matures in 10 years, the second in 6 years.

   a. What are Filer's capital structure weights on a book value basis?

   b. What are Filer's capital structure weights on a market value basis?

   c. Which are more relevant, the book or market value weights? Why?

9. **Calculating the WACC** In the previous problem, suppose the company's stock has a beta of 1.2. The risk-free rate is 5.2 percent, and the market risk premium is 9 percent. Assume that the overall cost of debt is the weighted average implied by the two outstanding debt issues. Both bonds make semiannual payments. The tax rate is 35 percent. What is the company's WACC?

10. **WACC** Kose, Inc., has a target debt-equity ratio of .80. Its WACC is 10.5 percent, and the tax rate is 35 percent.

    a. If Kose's cost of equity is 15 percent, what is its pretax cost of debt?

    b. If instead you know that the aftertax cost of debt is 6.4 percent, what is the cost of equity?

11. **Finding the WACC** Given the following information for Huntington Power Co., find the WACC. Assume the company's tax rate is 35 percent.

    Debt: 4,000 7 percent coupon bonds outstanding, $1,000 par value, 20 years to maturity, selling for 103 percent of par; the bonds make semiannual payments.

Common stock: 90,000 shares outstanding, selling for $57 per share; the beta is 1.10.

Market: 8 percent market risk premium and 6 percent risk-free rate.

12. **Finding the WACC** Titan Mining Corporation has 9 million shares of common stock outstanding and 120,000 8.5 percent semiannual bonds outstanding, par value $1,000 each. The common stock currently sells for $34 per share and has a beta of 1.20, and the bonds have 15 years to maturity and sell for 93 percent of par. The market risk premium is 10 percent, T-bills are yielding 5 percent, and Titan Mining's tax rate is 35 percent.
    a. What is the firm's market value capital structure?
    b. If Titan Mining is evaluating a new investment project that has the same risk as the firm's typical project, what rate should the firm use to discount the project's cash flows?
13. **SML and WACC** An all-equity firm is considering the following projects:

PROJECT	BETA	EXPECTED RETURN
W	.60	11%
X	.90	13
Y	1.20	14
Z	1.70	16

The T-bill rate is 5 percent, and the expected return on the market is 12 percent.
    a. Which projects have a higher expected return than the firm's 12 percent cost of capital?
    b. Which projects should be accepted?
    c. Which projects would be incorrectly accepted or rejected if the firm's overall cost of capital were used as a hurdle rate?

Intermediate
(Questions 14–15)

14. **WACC and NPV** Och, Inc., is considering a project that will result in initial aftertax cash savings of $3.5 million at the end of the first year, and these savings will grow at a rate of 5 percent per year indefinitely. The firm has a target debt-equity ratio of .65, a cost of equity of 15 percent, and an aftertax cost of debt of 5.5 percent. The cost-saving proposal is somewhat riskier than the usual project the firm undertakes; management uses the subjective approach and applies an adjustment factor of +2 percent to the cost of capital for such risky projects. Under what circumstances should Och take on the project?
15. **Preferred Stock and WACC** The Saunders Investment Bank has the following financing outstanding. What is the WACC for the company?

Debt: 50,000 bonds with an 8 percent coupon rate and a current price of $119.80. The bonds have 25 years to maturity. 150,000 zero coupon bonds with a price of $13.85 and 30 years until maturity.

Preferred Stock: 120,000 shares of 6.5 percent preferred with a current price of $112, and a par value = $100.

Common Stock: 2,000,000 shares of common stock. The current price is $65, and the beta of the stock is 1.1.

Market: The corporate tax rate is 40 percent, the market risk premium is 9 percent, and the risk-free rate is 4 percent.

Challenge
(Questions 16–17)

16. **WACC and NPV** Photochronograph Corporation (PC) manufactures time series photographic equipment. It is currently at its target debt-equity ratio of 1.3. It's considering building a new $45 million manufacturing facility. This new plant is expected to generate aftertax cash flows of

$5.7 million in perpetuity. There are three financing options:

1. A new issue of common stock. The required return on the company's equity is 17 percent.
2. A new issue of 20-year bonds. If the company issues these new bonds at an annual coupon rate of 9 percent, they will sell at par.
3. Increased use of accounts payable financing. Because this financing is part of the company's ongoing daily business, the company assigns it a cost that is the same as the overall firm WACC. Management has a target ratio of accounts payable to long-term debt of .20. (Assume there is no difference between the pretax and aftertax accounts payable cost.)

What is the NPV of the new plant? Assume that PC has a 35 percent tax rate.

17. **Project Evaluation** This is a comprehensive project evaluation problem bringing together much of what you have learned in this and previous chapters. Suppose you have been hired as a financial consultant to Defense Electronics, Inc. (DEI), a large, publicly traded firm that is the market share leader in radar detection systems (RDSs). The company is looking at setting up a manufacturing plant overseas to produce a new line of RDSs. This will be a five-year project. The company bought some land three years ago for $7 million in anticipation of using it as a toxic dump site for waste chemicals, but it built a piping system to safely discard the chemicals instead. If the company sold the land today, it would receive $6.5 million after taxes. In five years, the land can be sold for $4.5 million after taxes and reclamation costs. The company wants to build its new manufacturing plant on this land; the plant will cost $15 million to build. The following market data on DEI's securities are current:

    Debt: 15,000 7 percent coupon bonds outstanding, 15 years to maturity, selling for 92 percent of par; the bonds have a $1,000 par value each and make semiannual payments.

    Common stock: 300,000 shares outstanding, selling for $75 per share; the beta is 1.3.

    Preferred stock: 20,000 shares of 5 percent preferred stock outstanding, selling for $72 per share.

    Market: 8 percent expected market risk premium; 5 percent risk-free rate.

    DEI's tax rate is 35 percent. The project requires $900,000 in initial net working capital investment to get operational.

    a. Calculate the project's initial Time 0 cash flow, taking into account all side effects.
    b. The new RDS project is somewhat riskier than a typical project for DEI, primarily because the plant is being located overseas. Management has told you to use an adjustment factor of +2 percent to account for this increased riskiness. Calculate the appropriate discount rate to use when evaluating DEI's project.
    c. The manufacturing plant has an eight-year tax life, and DEI uses straight-line depreciation. At the end of the project (i.e., the end of Year 5), the plant can be scrapped for $5 million. What is the aftertax salvage value of this manufacturing plant?
    d. The company will incur $400,000 in annual fixed costs. The plan is to manufacture 12,000 RDSs per year and sell them at $10,000 per machine; the variable production costs are $9,000 per RDS. What is the annual operating cash flow, OCF, from this project?
    e. DEI's comptroller is primarily interested in the impact of DEI's investments on the bottom line of reported accounting statements. What will you tell her is the accounting break-even quantity of RDSs sold for this project?
    f. Finally, DEI's president wants you to throw all your calculations, assumptions, and everything else into the report for the chief financial officer; all he wants to know is what the RDS project's internal rate of return, IRR, and net present value, NPV, are. What will you report?

CLOSING CASE

THE COST OF CAPITAL FOR GOFF COMPUTER, INC.

You have recently been hired by Goff Computer, Inc. (GCI), in the finance area. GCI was founded eight years ago by Chris Goff and currently operates 74 stores in the Southeast. GCI is privately owned by Chris and his family and had sales of $97 million last year.

GCI primarily sells to in-store customers. Customers come to the store and talk with a sales representative. The sales representative assists the customer in determining the type of computer and peripherals that are necessary for the individual customer's computing needs. After the order is taken, the customer pays for the order immediately, and the computer is assembled to fill the order. Delivery of the computer averages 15 days, but is guaranteed in 30 days.

GCI's growth to date has been financed from its profits. Whenever the company had sufficient capital, it would open a new store. Relatively little formal analysis has been used in the capital budgeting process. Chris has just read about capital budgeting techniques and has come to you for help. The company has never attempted to determine its cost of capital, and Chris would like you to perform the analysis. Since the company is privately owned, it is difficult to determine the cost of equity for the company. You have determined that to estimate the cost of capital for GCI, you will use Dell as a representative company. The following steps will allow you to calculate this estimate.

1. Most publicly traded corporations are required to submit 10Q (quarterly) and 10K (annual) reports to the SEC detailing their financial operations over the previous quarter or year, respectively. These corporate filings are available on the SEC Web site at www.sec.gov. Go to the SEC Web site, follow the "Search for Company Filings" link, the "Companies & Other Filers" link, enter "Dell Computer," and search for SEC filings made by Dell. Find the most recent 10Q and 10K and download the forms. Look on the balance sheet to find the book value of debt and the book value of equity. If you look further down the report, you should find a section titled either "Long-term Debt" or "Long-term Debt and Interest Rate Risk Management" that will list a breakdown of Dell's long-term debt.
2. To estimate the cost of equity for Dell, go to finance.yahoo.com and enter the ticker symbol "DELL." Follow the various links to find answers to the following questions: What is the most recent stock price listed for Dell? What is the market value of equity, or market capitalization? How many shares of stock does Dell have outstanding? What is the beta for Dell? Now go back to finance.yahoo.com and follow the "Bonds" link. What is the yield on 3-month Treasury bills? Using the historical market risk premium, what is the cost of equity for Dell using the CAPM?
3. Go to investor.reuters.com and find the list of competitors in the industry. Find the beta for each of these competitors, and then calculate the industry average beta. Using the industry average beta, what is the cost of equity? Does it matter if you use the beta for Dell or the beta for the industry in this case?
4. You now need to calculate the cost of debt for Dell. Go to www.nasdbondinfo.com, enter Dell as the company and find the yield to maturity for each of Dell's bonds. What is the weighted average cost of debt for Dell using the book value weights and the market value weights? Does it make a difference in this case if you use book value weights or market value weights?
5. You now have all the necessary information to calculate the weighted average cost of capital for Dell. Calculate the weighted average cost of capital for Dell using book value weights and market value weights assuming Dell has a 35 percent marginal tax rate. Which cost of capital number is more relevant?
6. You used Dell as a representative company to estimate the cost of capital for GCI. What are some of the potential problems with this approach in this situation? What improvements might you suggest?

13

CHAPTER

Corporate Financing Decisions and Efficient Capital Markets

OPENING CASE

The NASDAQ stock market was raging in the late 1990s, gaining about 23 percent, 14 percent, 35 percent, and 62 percent in 1996 to 1999, respectively. Of course, that spectacular run came to a jarring halt, and the NASDAQ lost about 40 percent in 2000, followed by another 30 percent in 2001. The ISDEX, an index of Internet-related stocks, rose from 100 in January 1996 to 1100 in February 2000, a gain of about 1,000 percent! It then fell like a rock to 600 by May 2000.

The performance of the NASDAQ over this period, and particularly the rise and fall of Internet stocks, has been described by many as one of the greatest market "bubbles" in history. The argument is that prices were inflated to economically ridiculous levels before investors came to their senses, which then caused the bubble to pop and prices to plunge. Debate over whether the stock market of the late 1990s really was a bubble has generated much controversy. In this chapter, we will discuss the competing ideas, present some evidence on both sides, and then examine the implications for financial managers.

13.1 CAN FINANCING DECISIONS CREATE VALUE?

Earlier parts of the book show how to evaluate projects according to the net present value criterion. The real world is a competitive one where projects with positive net present value are not always easy to come by. However, through hard work or through good fortune, a firm can identify winning projects. For example, to create value from capital budgeting decisions, the firm is likely to:

1. Locate an unsatisfied demand for a particular product or service.
2. Create a barrier to make it more difficult for other firms to compete.
3. Produce products or services at lower cost than the competition.
4. Be the first to develop a new product.

The next five chapters concern *financing* decisions. Typical financing decisions include how much debt and equity to sell, what types of debt and equity to sell, and when to sell them. Just as the net present value criterion was used to evaluate capital budgeting projects, we now want to use the same criterion to evaluate financing decisions.

Though the procedure for evaluating financing decisions is identical to the procedure for evaluating projects, the results are different. It turns out that the typical firm has many more capital expenditure opportunities with positive net present values than financing opportunities with positive net present values. In fact, we later show that some plausible financial models imply that no valuable financial opportunities exist at all.

Though this dearth of profitable financing opportunities will be examined in detail later, a few remarks are in order now. We maintain that there are basically three ways to create valuable financing opportunities:

1. *Fool Investors.* Assume that a firm can raise capital either by issuing stock or by issuing a more complex security, say, a combination of stock and warrants. Suppose that, in truth, 100 shares of stock are worth the same as 50 units of our complex security. If investors have a misguided, overly optimistic view of the complex security, perhaps the 50 units can be sold for more than the 100 shares of stock can be. Clearly this complex security provides a valuable financing opportunity because the firm is getting more than fair value for it.

   Financial managers try to package securities to receive the greatest value. A cynic might view this as attempting to fool investors.

   However, the theory of efficient capital markets implies that investors cannot easily be fooled. It says that securities are appropriately priced at all times, implying that the market as a whole is very shrewd indeed. In our example, 50 units of the complex security would sell for the same price as 100 shares of stock. Thus, corporate managers cannot attempt to create value by fooling investors. Instead, managers must create value in other ways.

2. *Reduce Costs or Increase Subsidies.* We show later in the book that certain forms of financing have greater tax advantages than other forms. Clearly, a firm packaging securities to minimize taxes can increase firm value. In addition, any financing technique involves other costs. For example, investment bankers, lawyers, and accountants must be paid. A firm packaging securities to minimize these costs can also increase its value.

EXAMPLE 13.1 Valuing Financial Subsidies

Suppose Vermont Electronics Company is thinking about relocating its plant to Mexico where labor costs are lower. In the hope that it can stay in Vermont, the company has submitted an application to the state of Vermont to issue $2 million in five-year, tax-exempt industrial bonds. The coupon rate on industrial revenue bonds in Vermont is currently 5 percent. This is an attractive rate because the normal cost of debt capital for Vermont Electronics Company is 10 percent. What is the NPV of this potential financing transaction?

If the application is accepted and the industrial revenue bonds are issued by the Vermont Electronics Company, the NPV (ignoring corporate taxes) is:

$$\begin{aligned} NPV &= \$2{,}000{,}000 - \left[\frac{\$100{,}000}{1.1} + \frac{\$100{,}000}{(1.1)^2} + \frac{\$100{,}000}{(1.1)^3} + \frac{\$100{,}000}{(1.1)^4} + \frac{\$2{,}100{,}000}{(1.1)^5}\right] \\ &= \$2{,}000{,}000 - \$1{,}620{,}921 \\ &= \$379{,}079 \end{aligned}$$

This transaction has a positive NPV. The Vermont Electronics Company obtains subsidized financing where the value of the subsidy is $379,079.

3. *Create a New Security.* There has been a surge in financial innovation in recent years. For example, in a speech on financial innovation, Nobel laureate Merton Miller asked the rhetorical question, "Can any twenty-year period in recorded history have witnessed even a tenth as much new development? Where corporations once issued only straight debt and straight common stock, they now issue zero coupon bonds, adjustable rate notes, floating-rate notes, putable bonds, credit enhanced debt securities, receivable-backed securities, adjusted-rate preferred stock, convertible adjustable preferred stock, auction rate preferred stock, single-point adjustable rate stock, convertible exchangeable preferred stock, adjustable-rate convertible debt, zero coupon convertible debt, debt with mandatory common stock purchase contracts–to name just a few!"[1] And, financial innovation has occurred even more rapidly in the years following Miller's speech.

Though the advantage of each instrument is different, one general theme is that these new securities cannot easily be duplicated by combinations of existing securities. Thus, a previously unsatisfied clientele may pay extra for a specialized security catering to its needs. For example, putable bonds let the purchaser sell the bond at a fixed price back to the firm. This innovation creates a price floor, allowing the investor to reduce his or her downside risk. Perhaps risk-averse investors or investors with little knowledge of the bond market would find this feature particularly attractive.

Corporations gain by issuing these unique securities at high prices. However, the value captured by the innovator may well be small in the long run because the innovator usually cannot patent or copyright his idea. Soon many firms are issuing securities of the same kind, forcing prices down as a result.

This brief introduction sets the stage for the next several chapters of the book. The rest of this chapter examines the efficient capital markets hypothesis. We show that if capital markets are efficient, corporate managers cannot create value by fooling investors. This is quite important, because managers must create value in other, perhaps more difficult, ways. The following chapters concern the costs and subsidies of various forms of financing.

[1]M. Miller, "Financial Innovation: The Last Twenty Years and the Next," *Journal of Financial and Quantitative Analysis* (December 1986). However, Peter Tufano, "Securities Innovations: A Historical and Functional Perspective," *Journal of Applied Corporate Finance* (Winter 1995), shows that many securities commonly believed to have been invented in the 1970s and 1980s can be traced as far back as the 1830s.

13.2 A DESCRIPTION OF EFFICIENT CAPITAL MARKETS

An efficient capital market is one in which stock prices fully reflect available information. To illustrate how an efficient market works, suppose the F-stop Camera Corporation (FCC) is attempting to develop a camera that will double the speed of the auto-focusing system now available. FCC believes this research has positive NPV.

Now consider a share of stock in FCC. What determines the willingness of investors to hold shares of FCC at a particular price? One important factor is the probability that FCC will be the first company to develop the new auto-focusing system. In an efficient market, we would expect the price of the shares of FCC to increase if this probability increases.

Suppose FCC hires a well-known engineer to develop the new auto-focusing system. In an efficient market, what will happen to FCC's share price when this is announced? If the well-known scientist is paid a salary that fully reflects his or her contribution to the firm, the price of the stock will not necessarily change. Suppose, instead, that hiring the scientist is a positive NPV transaction. In this case, the price of shares in FCC will increase because the firm can pay the scientist a salary below his or her true value to the company.

When will the increase in the price of FCC's shares take place? Assume that the hiring announcement is made in a press release on Wednesday morning. In an efficient market, the price of shares in FCC will *immediately* adjust to this new information. Investors should not be able to buy the stock on Wednesday afternoon and make a profit on Thursday. This would imply that it took the stock market a day to realize the implication of the FCC press release. The efficient market hypothesis predicts that the price of shares of FCC stock on Wednesday afternoon will already reflect the information contained in the Wednesday morning press release.

The **efficient market hypothesis** (EMH) has implications for investors and for firms.

- Because information is reflected in prices immediately, investors should only expect to obtain a normal rate of return. Awareness of information when it is released does an investor no good. The price adjusts before the investor has time to trade on it.
- Firms should expect to receive fair value for securities that they sell. *Fair* means that the price they receive for the securities they issue is the present value. Thus, valuable financing opportunities that arise from fooling investors are unavailable in efficient capital markets.

Figure 13.1 presents several possible adjustments in stock prices. The solid line represents the path taken by the stock in an efficient market. In this case the price adjusts immediately to the new information with no further price changes. The dotted line depicts a delayed reaction. Here it takes the market 30 days to fully absorb the information. Finally, the broken line illustrates an overreaction and subsequent correction back to the true price. The broken line and the dotted line show the paths that the stock price might take in an inefficient market. If the price of the stock takes several days to adjust, trading profits would be available to investors who suitably timed their purchases and sales.[2]

[2]Now you should understand the following short story. A student was walking down the hall with his finance professor when they both saw a $20 bill on the ground. As the student bent down to pick it up, the professor shook his head slowly and, with a look of disappointment on his face, said patiently to the student, "Don't bother. If it was really there, someone else would have already picked it up."

The moral of the story reflects the logic of the efficient market hypothesis: If you think you have found a pattern in stock prices or a simple device for picking winners, you probably have not. If there were such a simple way to make money, someone else would have found it before. Furthermore, if people tried to exploit the information, their efforts would become self-defeating and the pattern would disappear.

FIGURE 13.1

Reaction of Stock Price to New Information in Efficient and Inefficient Markets

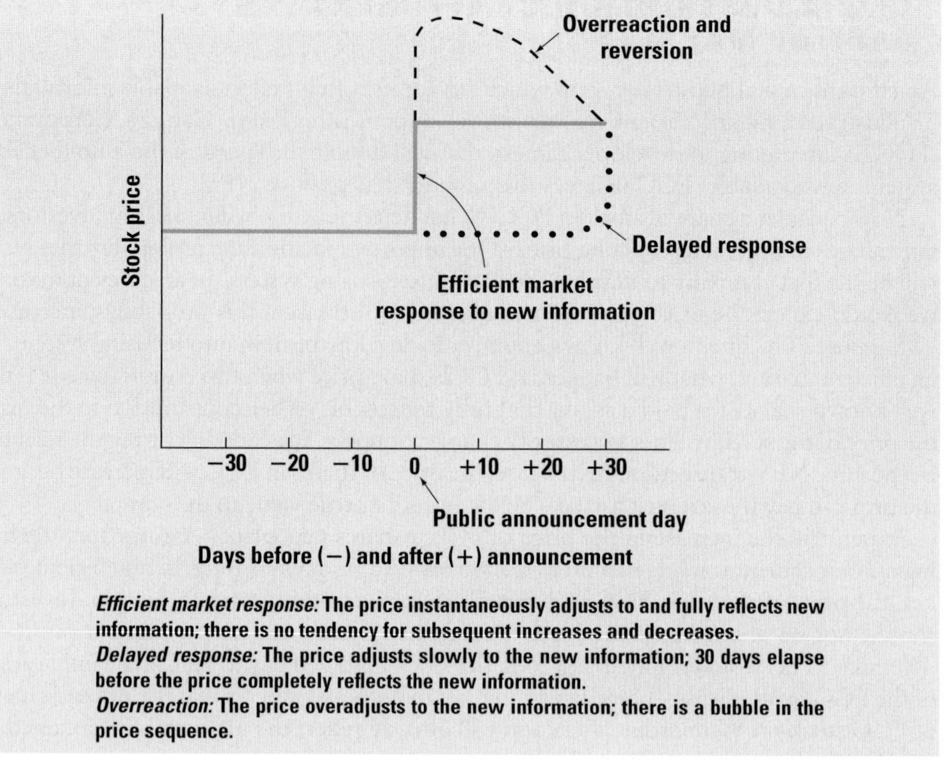

Efficient market response: **The price instantaneously adjusts to and fully reflects new information; there is no tendency for subsequent increases and decreases.**
Delayed response: **The price adjusts slowly to the new information; 30 days elapse before the price completely reflects the new information.**
Overreaction: **The price overadjusts to the new information; there is a bubble in the price sequence.**

Foundations of Market Efficiency

Figure 13.1 shows the consequences of market efficiency. But what are the conditions that *cause* market efficiency? Andrei Shleifer argues that there are three conditions, any one of which will lead to efficiency:[3] (1) rationality, (2) independent deviations from rationality, and (3) arbitrage. A discussion of these conditions follows.

RATIONALITY Imagine that all investors are rational. When new information is released in the marketplace, all investors will adjust their estimates of stock prices in a rational way. In our example, investors will use the information in FCC's press release, in conjunction with existing information on the firm, to determine the NPV of FCC's new venture. If the information in the press release implies that the NPV of the venture is $10 million and there are 2 million shares, investors will calculate that the NPV is $5 per share. While FCC's old price might be, say, $40, no one would now transact at that price. Anyone interested in selling would only sell at a price of at least $45 (= $40 + 5). And anyone interested in buying would now be willing to pay up to $45. In other words, the price would rise by $5. And the price would rise immediately, since rational investors would see no reason to wait before trading at the new price.

Of course, we all know times when family members, friends, and yes, even ourselves seem to behave less than perfectly rationally. Thus, perhaps it is too much to ask that *all* investors behave rationally. But the market will still be efficient if the following scenario holds.

INDEPENDENT DEVIATIONS FROM RATIONALITY Suppose that FCC's press release is not all that clear. How many new cameras are likely to be sold? At what price? What is

[3]Shleifer, Andrei, *Inefficient Markets: An Introduction to Behavioral Finance,* Oxford University Press, Oxford, United Kingdom (2000).

the likely cost per camera? Will other camera companies be able to develop competing products? How long will this likely take? If these, and other, questions cannot be answered easily, it will be difficult to estimate NPV.

Now imagine that, with so many questions going unanswered, many investors do not think clearly. Some investors might get caught up in the romance of a new product, hoping, and ultimately believing, in sales projections well above what is rational. They would overpay for new shares. And if they needed to sell shares (perhaps to finance current consumption), they would do so only at a high price. If these individuals dominate the market, the stock price would likely rise beyond what market efficiency would predict.

However, due to emotional resistance, investors could just as easily react to new information in a pessimistic manner. After all, business historians tell us that investors were initially quite skeptical about the benefits of the telephone, the copier, the automobile, and the motion picture. Certainly, they could be overly skeptical about this new camera. If investors were primarily of this type, the stock price would likely rise less than market efficiency would predict.

But suppose that about as many individuals were irrationally optimistic as were irrationally pessimistic. Prices would likely rise in a manner consistent with market efficiency, even though most investors would be classified as less than fully rational. Thus, market efficiency does not require rational individuals, only countervailing irrationalities.

However, this assumption of offsetting irrationalities at *all* times may be unrealistic. Perhaps, at certain times, most investors are swept away by excessive optimism and, at other times, are caught in the throes of extreme pessimism. But even here, there is an assumption that will produce efficiency.

ARBITRAGE Imagine a world with two types of individuals: the irrational amateurs and the rational professionals. The amateurs get caught up in their emotions, at times believing irrationally that a stock is undervalued and at other times believing the opposite. If the passions of the different amateurs do not cancel each other out, these amateurs, by themselves, would tend to carry stocks either above or below their efficient prices.

Now let's bring in the professionals. Suppose professionals go about their business methodically and rationally. They study companies thoroughly, they evaluate the evidence objectively, they estimate stock prices coldly and clearly, and they act accordingly. If a stock is underpriced, they would buy it. If overpriced, they would sell it. And their confidence would likely be greater than that of the amateurs. While an amateur might risk only a small sum, these professionals might risk large ones, *knowing* as they do that the stock is mispriced. Furthermore, they would be willing to rearrange their entire portfolio in search of a profit. If they find that General Motors is underpriced, they might sell the Ford stock they own in order to buy GM. *Arbitrage* is the word that comes to mind here, since arbitrage generates profit from the simultaneous purchase and sale of different, but substitute, securities. If the arbitrage of professionals dominates the speculation of amateurs, markets would still be efficient.

13.3 THE DIFFERENT TYPES OF EFFICIENCY

In our previous discussion, we assumed that the market responds immediately to all available information. In actuality, certain information may affect stock prices more quickly than other information. To handle differential response rates, researchers separate information into different types. The most common classification system identifies three types: information on past prices, publicly available information, and all information. The effect of these three information sets on prices is examined next.

FIGURE 13.2
Investor Behavior Tends to Eliminate Cyclical Patterns

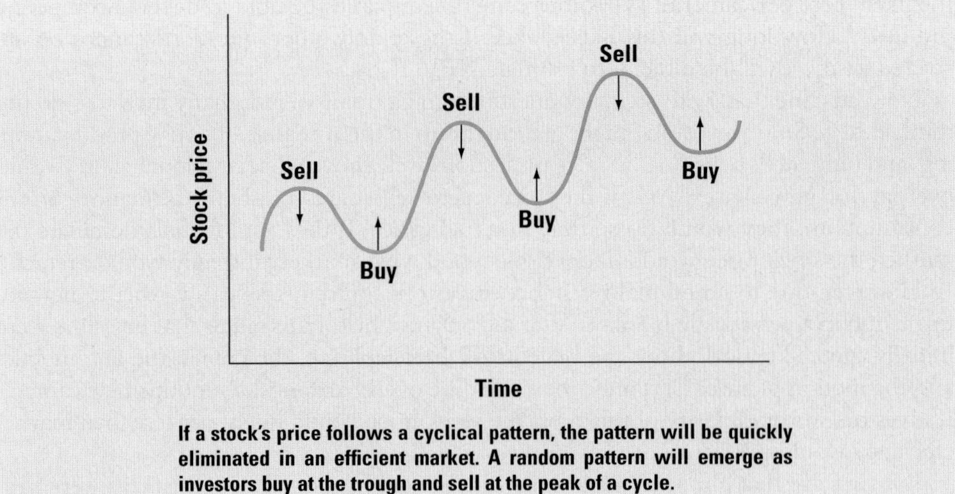

If a stock's price follows a cyclical pattern, the pattern will be quickly eliminated in an efficient market. A random pattern will emerge as investors buy at the trough and sell at the peak of a cycle.

The Weak Form

Imagine a trading strategy that recommends buying a stock after it has gone up three days in a row and recommends selling a stock after it has gone down three days in a row. This strategy uses information based only on past prices. It does not use any other information, such as earnings, forecasts, merger announcements, or money supply figures. A capital market is said to be *weakly efficient* or to satisfy **weak form efficiency** if it fully incorporates the information in past stock prices. Thus, the above strategy would not be able to generate profits if weak form efficiency holds.

Weak form efficiency is about the weakest type of efficiency that we would expect a financial market to display because historical price information is the easiest kind of information about a stock to acquire. If it were possible to make extraordinary profits simply by finding patterns in stock price movements, everyone would do it, and any profits would disappear in the scramble.

This effect of competition can be seen in Figure 13.2. Suppose the price of a stock displays a cyclical pattern, as indicated by the wavy curve. Shrewd investors would buy at the low points, forcing those prices up. Conversely, they would sell at the high points, forcing prices down. Via competition, cyclical regularities would be eliminated, leaving only random fluctuations.

The Semistrong and Strong Forms

If weak form efficiency is controversial, even more contentious are the two stronger types of efficiency, **semistrong form efficiency** and **strong form efficiency**. A market is semistrong form efficient if prices reflect (incorporate) all publicly available information, including information such as published accounting statements for the firm as well as historical price information. A market is strong form efficient if prices reflect all information, public or private.

The information set of past prices is a subset of the information set of publicly available information, which in turn is a subset of all information. This is shown in Figure 13.3. Thus, strong form efficiency implies semistrong form efficiency, and semistrong form efficiency implies weak form efficiency. The distinction between semistrong form efficiency and weak form efficiency is that semistrong form efficiency requires not only that the market be efficient with respect to historical price information, but that *all* of the information available to the public be reflected in prices.

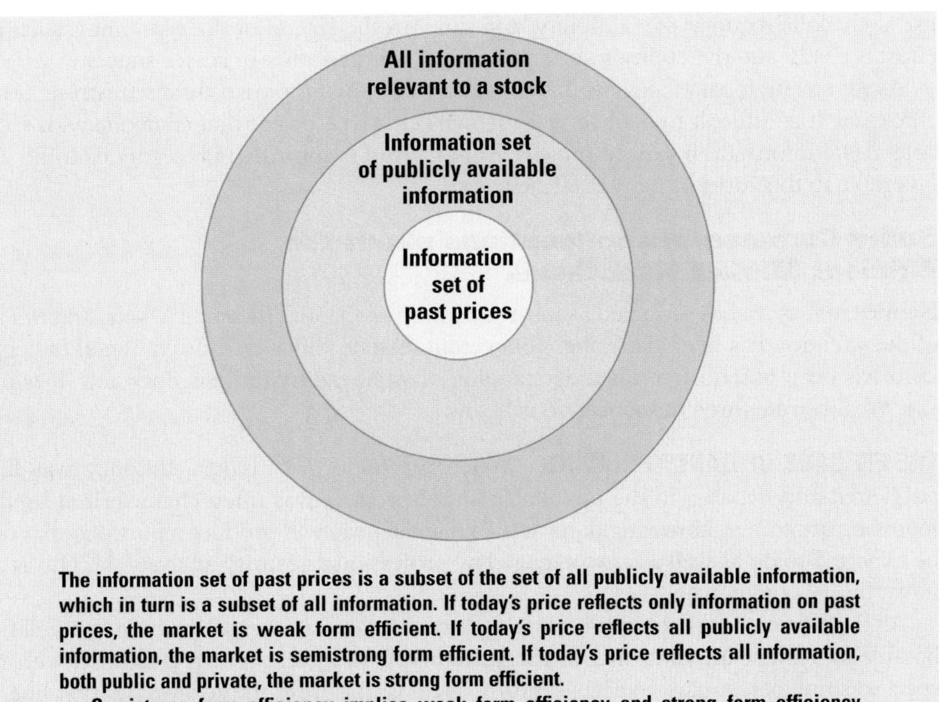

The information set of past prices is a subset of the set of all publicly available information, which in turn is a subset of all information. If today's price reflects only information on past prices, the market is weak form efficient. If today's price reflects all publicly available information, the market is semistrong form efficient. If today's price reflects all information, both public and private, the market is strong form efficient.

Semistrong form efficiency implies weak form efficiency and strong form efficiency implies semistrong form efficiency.

FIGURE 13.3

Relationship among Three Different Information Sets

To illustrate the different forms of efficiency, imagine an investor who always sold a particular stock after its price had risen. A market that was only weak form efficient and not semistrong form efficient would still prevent such a strategy from generating positive profits. According to weak form efficiency, a recent price rise does not imply that the stock is overvalued.

Now consider a firm reporting increased earnings. An individual might consider investing in the stock after hearing of the news release giving this information. However, if the market is semistrong form efficient, the price should rise immediately upon the news release. Thus, the investor would end up paying the higher price, eliminating all chance for profit.

At the furthest end of the spectrum is strong form efficiency. This form says that anything that is pertinent to the value of the stock and that is known to at least one investor is, in fact, fully incorporated into the stock price. A strict believer in strong form efficiency would deny that an insider who knew whether a company mining operation had struck gold could profit from that information. Such a devotee of the strong form efficient market hypothesis might argue that as soon as the insider tried to trade on his or her information, the market would recognize what was happening, and the price would shoot up before he or she could buy any of the stock. Alternatively, believers in strong form efficiency argue that there are no secrets, and as soon as the gold is discovered, the secret gets out.

One reason to expect that markets are weak form efficient is that it is so cheap and easy to find patterns in stock prices. Anyone who can program a computer and knows a little bit of statistics can search for such patterns. It stands to reason that if there were such patterns, people would find and exploit them, in the process causing them to disappear.

Semistrong form efficiency, though, implies more sophisticated investors than does weak form efficiency. An investor must be skilled at economics and statistics, and steeped in the idiosyncrasies of individual industries and companies. Furthermore, to acquire and use such skills requires talent, ability, and time. In the jargon of the economist, such an effort is costly and the ability to be successful at it is probably in scarce supply.

As for strong form efficiency, this is just farther down the road than semistrong form efficiency. It is difficult to believe that the market is so efficient that someone with valuable inside information cannot prosper from it. And empirical evidence tends to be unfavorable to this form of market efficiency.

Some Common Misconceptions about the Efficient Market Hypothesis

No idea in finance has attracted as much attention as that of efficient markets, and not all of the attention has been flattering. To a certain extent, this is because much of the criticism has been based on a misunderstanding of what the hypothesis does and does not say. We illustrate three misconceptions below.

THE EFFICACY OF DART THROWING When the notion of market efficiency was first publicized and debated in the popular financial press, it was often characterized by the following quote: ". . . throwing darts at the financial page will produce a portfolio that can be expected to do as well as any managed by professional security analysts."[4,5] This is almost, but not quite, true.

All the efficient market hypothesis really says is that, on average, the manager will not be able to achieve an abnormal or excess return. The excess return is defined with respect to some benchmark expected return, such as that from the security market line of Chapter 11 (SML). The investor must still decide how risky a portfolio he or she wants. In addition, a random dart thrower might wind up with all of the darts sticking into one or two high-risk stocks that deal in genetic engineering. Would you really want all of your stock investments in two such stocks?

The failure to understand this has often led to a confusion about market efficiency. For example, sometimes it is wrongly argued that market efficiency means that it does not matter what you do because the efficiency of the market will protect the unwary. However, someone once remarked, "The efficient market protects the sheep from the wolves, but nothing can protect the sheep from themselves."

What efficiency does say is that the price that a firm obtains when it sells a share of its stock is a fair price in the sense that it reflects the value of that stock given the information that is available about it. Shareholders need not worry that they are paying too much for a stock with a low dividend or some other characteristic, because the market has already incorporated it into the price. However, investors still have to worry about such things as their level of risk exposure and their degree of diversification.

PRICE FLUCTUATIONS Much of the public is skeptical of efficiency because stock prices fluctuate from day to day. However, daily price movement is in no way inconsistent with efficiency; a stock in an efficient market adjusts to new information by changing price. A great deal of new information comes into the stock market each day. In fact, the *absence* of daily price movements in a changing world might suggest an inefficiency.

STOCKHOLDER DISINTEREST Many laypersons are skeptical that the market price can be efficient if only a fraction of the outstanding shares changes hands on any given day. However, the number of traders in a stock on a given day is generally far less than the number of people following the stock. This is true because an individual will trade only when his appraisal of the value of the stock differs enough from the market price to

[4]B. G. Malkiel, *A Random Walk Down Wall Street,* 7th ed. (New York: Norton, 1999).

[5]Older articles often referred to the benchmark of "dart-throwing monkeys." As government involvement in the securities industry grew, the benchmark was oftentimes restated as "dart-throwing congressmen."

justify incurring brokerage commissions and other transaction costs. Furthermore, even if the number of traders following a stock is small relative to the number of outstanding shareholders, the stock can be expected to be efficiently priced as long as a number of interested traders use the publicly available information. That is, the stock price can reflect the available information even if many stockholders never follow the stock and are not considering trading in the near future.

13.4 THE EVIDENCE

The evidence on the efficient market hypothesis is extensive, with studies covering the broad categories of weak form, semistrong form, and strong form efficiency. In the first category we investigate whether stock price changes are random. We review both *event studies* and studies of the performance of mutual funds in the second category. In the third category, we look at the performance of corporate insiders.

The Weak Form

Weak form efficiency implies that a stock's price movement in the past is unrelated to its price movement in the future. The work of Chapter 11 allows us to test this implication. In that chapter, we discussed the concept of correlation between the returns on two different stocks. For example, the correlation between the return on General Motors and the return on Ford is likely to be relatively high because both stocks are in the same industry. Conversely, the correlation between the return on General Motors and the return on the stock of, say, a European fast-food chain is likely to be low.

Financial economists frequently speak of **serial correlation**, which involves only one security. This is the correlation between the current return on a security and the return on the same security over a later period. A positive coefficient of serial correlation for a particular stock indicates a tendency toward *continuation.* That is, a higher-than-average return today is likely to be followed by higher-than-average returns in the future. Similarly, a lower-than-average return today is likely to be followed by lower-than-average returns in the future.

A negative coefficient of serial correlation for a particular stock indicates a tendency toward *reversal.* A higher-than-average return today is likely to be followed by lower-than-average returns in the future. Similarly, a lower-than-average return today is likely to be followed by higher-than-average returns in the future. Both significantly positive and significantly negative serial correlation coefficients are indications of market inefficiencies; in either case, returns today can be used to predict future returns.

Serial correlation coefficients for stock returns near zero would be consistent with weak form efficiency. Thus, a current stock return that is higher than average is as likely to be followed by lower-than-average returns as by higher-than-average returns. Similarly, a current stock return that is lower than average is as likely to be followed by higher-than-average returns as by lower-than-average returns.

Table 13.1 shows the serial correlation for daily stock price changes for eight large U.S. companies. These coefficients indicate whether or not there are relationships between yesterday's return and today's return. As can be seen, the correlation coefficients are predominantly negative, implying that a higher-than-average return today makes a lower-than-average return tomorrow slightly more likely. Conversely, Coca-Cola's coefficient is slightly positive, implying that a higher-than-average return today makes a higher-than-average return tomorrow slightly more likely.

However, because correlation coefficients can, in principle, vary between −1 and 1, the reported coefficients are quite small. In fact, the coefficients are so small relative to both estimation errors and to transactions costs that the results are generally considered to be consistent with weak form efficiency.

TABLE 13.1
Serial Correlation Coefficients for Selected Companies, 2000–2004

COMPANY	SERIAL CORRELATION COEFFICIENT
Boeing	−.0066
Citigroup	−.0102
Coca-Cola	.0353
IBM	−.0599
McDonald's	.0168
Microsoft	−.0230
Pfizer	−.0007
Procter & Gamble	−.0220

McDonald's coefficient of .0168 is slightly positive, implying that a positive return today makes a positive return tomorrow slightly more likely. Citigroup's coefficient is negative, implying that a negative return today makes a positive return tomorrow slightly more likely. However, the coefficients are so small relative to estimation error and transaction costs that the results are generally considered to be consistent with efficient capital markets.

FIGURE 13.4
Simulated and Actual Stock Price Movements

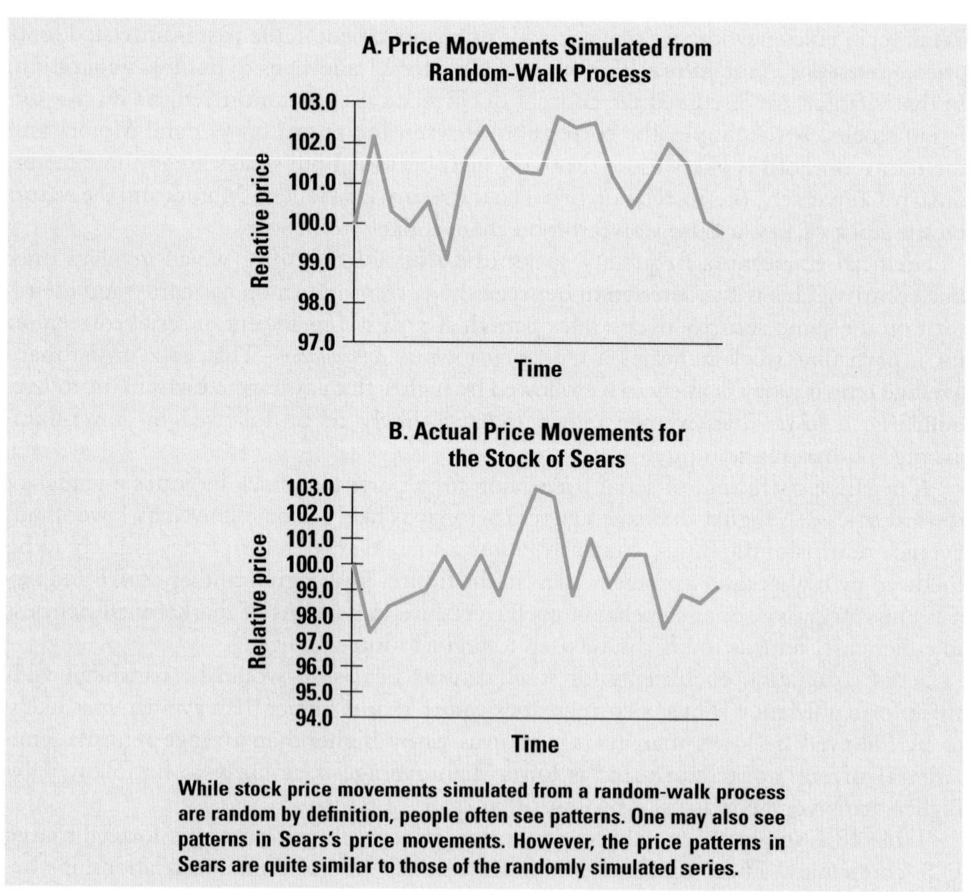

While stock price movements simulated from a random-walk process are random by definition, people often see patterns. One may also see patterns in Sears's price movements. However, the price patterns in Sears are quite similar to those of the randomly simulated series.

The weak form of the efficient market hypothesis has been tested in many other ways as well. Our view of the literature is that the evidence, taken as a whole, is consistent with weak form efficiency.

This finding raises an interesting thought: If price changes are truly random, why do so many believe that prices follow patterns? The work of both psychologists and statisticians suggests that most people simply do not know what randomness looks like. For example, consider Figure 13.4. The top graph was generated by a computer using random numbers. Yet, we have found that people examining the chart generally see patterns. Different people see different patterns and forecast different future price movements. However, in our experience, viewers are all quite confident of the patterns they see.

Next, consider the bottom graph, which tracks actual movements in Sears's stock price. This graph may look quite nonrandom to some, suggesting weak form inefficiency. However, it also bears a close visual resemblance to the simulated series above, and statistical tests indicate that it indeed behaves like a purely random series. Thus, in our opinion, people claiming to see patterns in stock price data are probably seeing optical illusions.

The Semistrong Form

The semistrong form of the efficient market hypothesis implies that prices should reflect all publicly available information. We present two types of tests of this form.

EVENT STUDIES The *abnormal return* (AR) on a given stock for a particular day can be calculated by subtracting the market's return on the same day (R_m)–as measured by a broad-based index such as the S&P composite index–from the actual return (R) on the stock for that day. We write this algebraically as:

$$\text{AR} = R - R_m$$

The following system will help us understand tests of the semistrong form:

Information released at time $t - 1 \rightarrow \text{AR}_{t-1}$
Information released at time $t \rightarrow \text{AR}_t$
Information released at time $t + 1 \rightarrow \text{AR}_{t+1}$

The arrows indicate that the abnormal return in any time period is related only to the information released during that period.

According to the efficient market hypothesis, a stock's abnormal return at time t, AR_t, should reflect the release of information at the same time, t. Any information released before then should have no effect on abnormal returns in this period, because all of its influence should have been felt before. In other words, an efficient market would already have incorporated previous information into prices. Because a stock's return today cannot depend on what the market does not yet know, information that will be known only in the future cannot influence the stock's return either. Hence the arrows point in the direction that is shown, with information in any one time period affecting only that period's abnormal return. *Event studies* are statistical studies that examine whether the arrows are as shown or whether the release of information influences returns on other days.

These studies also speak of *cumulative abnormal returns* (CARs), as well as abnormal returns (ARs). As an example, consider a firm with ARs of 1 percent, −3 percent, and 6 percent for dates −1, 0, and 1 relative to a corporate announcement. The CARs for dates −1, 0, and 1 would be 1 percent, −2 percent [1 percent + (−3 percent)], and 4 percent [1 percent + (−3 percent) + 6 percent], respectively.

As an example, consider the study by Szewczyk, Tsetsekos, and Zantout[6] on dividend omissions. Figure 13.5 shows the plot of CARs for a sample of companies announcing dividend omissions. Since dividend omissions are generally considered to be bad events, we would expect abnormal returns to be negative around the time of the announcements. They are, as evidenced by a drop in the CAR on both the day before the

[6]Samuel H. Szewczyk, George P. Tsetsekos, and Zaher Z. Zantout, "Do Dividend Omissions Signal Future Earnings or Past Earnings?" *Journal of Investing* (Spring 1997).

FIGURE 13.5

Cumulative Abnormal Returns for Companies Announcing Dividend Omissions

Source: From Exhibit 2 in S. H. Szewczyk, George P. Tsetsekos, and Zaher Z. Zantout, "Do Dividend Omissions Signal Future Earnings or Past Earnings?" *Journal of Investing* (Spring 1997).

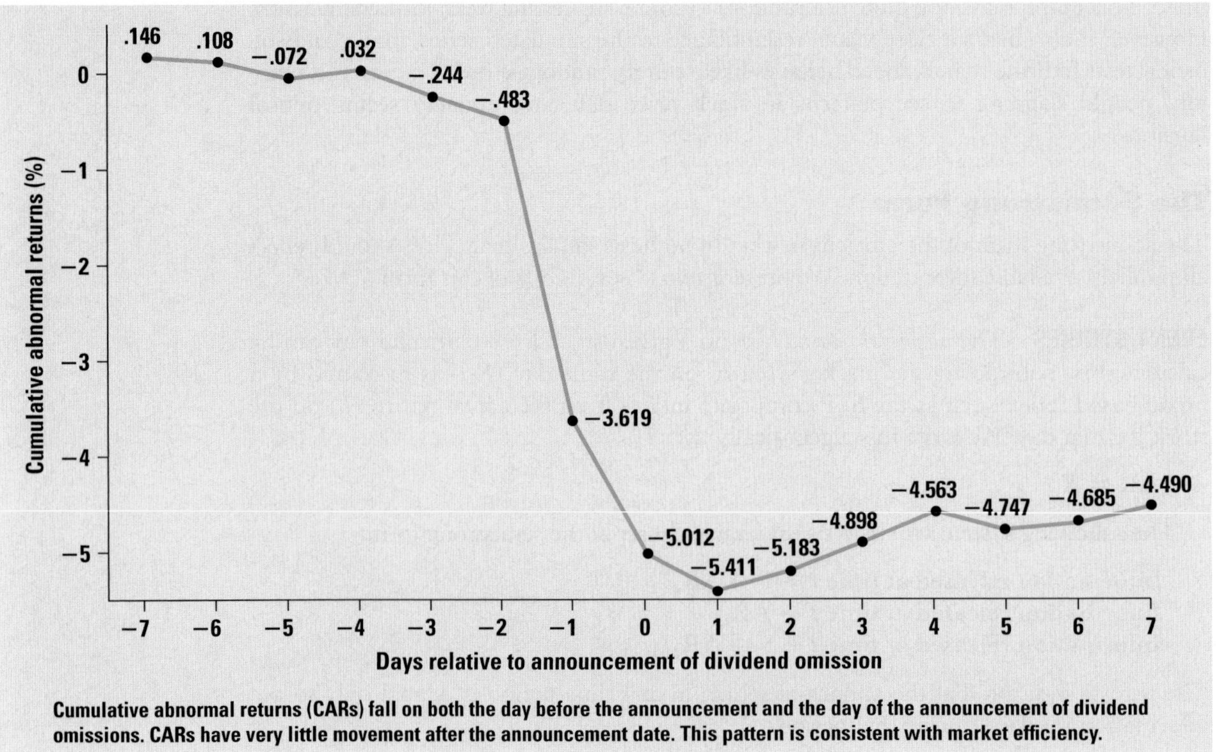

Cumulative abnormal returns (CARs) fall on both the day before the announcement and the day of the announcement of dividend omissions. CARs have very little movement after the announcement date. This pattern is consistent with market efficiency.

announcement (day −1) and the day of the announcement (day 0).[7] However, note that there is virtually no movement in the CARs in the days following the announcement. This implies that the bad news is fully incorporated into the stock price by the announcement day, a result consistent with market efficiency.

Over the years this type of methodology has been applied to a large number of events. Announcements of dividends, earnings, mergers, capital expenditures, and new issues of stock are a few examples of the vast literature in the area. The early event study tests generally supported the view that the market is semistrong form (and therefore also weak form) efficient. However, a number of more recent studies present evidence that the market does not impound all relevant information immediately. Some conclude from this that the market is not efficient. Others argue that this conclusion is unwarranted, given statistical and methodological problems in the studies. This issue will be addressed in more detail later in the chapter.

[7]An astute reader may wonder why the abnormal return is negative on day −1, as well as on day 0. To see why, first note that the announcement date is generally taken in academic studies to be the publication date of the story in *The Wall Street Journal (WSJ).* Then consider a company announcing a dividend omission via a press release at noon on Tuesday. The stock should fall on Tuesday. The announcement will be reported in the *WSJ* on Wednesday, because the Tuesday edition of the *WSJ* has already been printed. For this firm, the stock price falls on the day *before* the announcement in the *WSJ.*

Alternatively, imagine another firm announcing a dividend omission via a press release on Tuesday at 8 p.m. Since the stock market is closed at that late hour, the stock price will fall on Wednesday. Because the *WSJ* will report the announcement on Wednesday, the stock price falls on the day of the announcement in the *WSJ.*

Since firms may either make announcements during trading hours or after trading hours, stocks should fall on both day −1 and day 0 relative to publication in the *WSJ.*

FIGURE 13.6

Annual Return Performance* of Different Types of U.S. Mutual Funds Relative to a Broad-Based Market Index (1963–1998)

Source: Taken from Table 2 of Lubos Pastor and Robert F. Stambaugh, "Mutual Fund Performance and Seemingly Unrelated Assets," *Journal of Financial Economics,* 63 (2002).

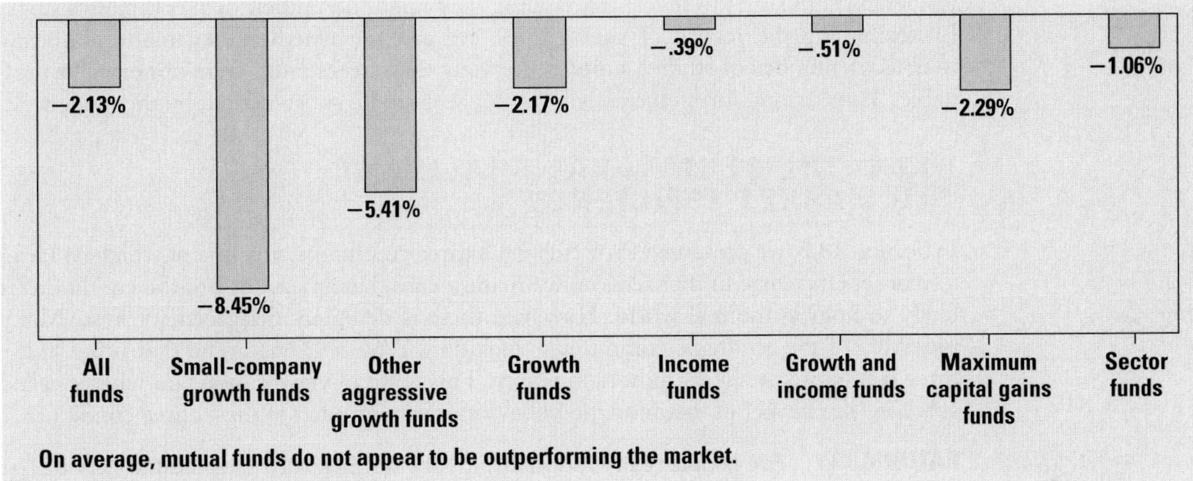

*Performance is relative to the market model.

THE RECORD OF MUTUAL FUNDS If the market is efficient in the semistrong form, then no matter what publicly available information mutual fund managers rely on to pick stocks, their average returns should be the same as those of the average investor in the market as a whole. We can test efficiency, then, by comparing the performance of these professionals with that of a market index.

Consider Figure 13.6, which presents the performance of various types of mutual funds relative to the stock market as a whole. The far left of the figure shows that the universe of all funds covered in the study underperforms the market by 2.13 percent per year, after an appropriate adjustment for risk. Thus, rather than outperforming the market, the evidence shows underperformance. This underperformance holds for a number of types of funds as well. Returns in this study are net of fees, expenses, and commissions, so fund returns would be higher if these costs were added back. However, the study shows no evidence that funds, as a whole, are *beating* the market.

Perhaps nothing rankles successful stock market investors more than to have some professor tell them that they are not necessarily smart, just lucky. However, while Figure 13.6 represents only one study, there have been many papers on mutual funds. The overwhelming evidence here is that mutual funds, on average, do not beat broad-based indices.

By and large, mutual fund managers rely on publicly available information. Thus, the finding that they do not outperform market indices is consistent with semistrong form and weak form efficiency.

However, this evidence does not imply that mutual funds are bad investments for individuals. Though these funds fail to achieve better returns than some indices of the market, they do permit the investor to buy a portfolio that has a large number of stocks in it (the phrase "a well-diversified portfolio" is often used). They might also be very good at providing a variety of services such as keeping custody and records of all the stocks.

The Strong Form

Even the strongest adherents to the efficient market hypothesis would not be surprised to find that markets are inefficient in the strong form. After all, if an individual has information that no one else has, it is likely that she can profit from it.

One group of studies of strong form efficiency investigates insider trading. Insiders in firms have access to information that is not generally available. But if the strong form of the efficient market hypothesis holds, they should not be able to profit by trading on their information. A government agency, the Securities and Exchange Commission, requires insiders in companies to reveal any trading they might do in their own company's stock. By examining the record of such trades, we can see whether they made abnormal returns. A number of studies support the view that these trades were abnormally profitable. Thus, strong form efficiency does not seem to be substantiated by the evidence.

13.5 THE BEHAVIORAL CHALLENGE TO MARKET EFFICIENCY

In Section 13.2, we presented Prof. Shleifer's three conditions, any one of which will lead to market efficiency. In that section, we made a case that at least one of the conditions is likely to hold in the real world. However, there is definitely disagreement here. Many members of the academic community (including Prof. Shleifer) argue that none of the three conditions are likely to hold in reality. This point of view is based on what is called *behavioral finance*. Let us examine the behavioral view on each of these three conditions.

RATIONALITY Are people really rational? Not always. Just travel to Atlantic City or Las Vegas to see people gambling, sometimes with large sums of money. The casino's take implies a negative expected return for the gambler. Since gambling is risky and has a negative expected return, it can never be on the efficient frontier of our Chapter 11. In addition, gamblers will often bet on black at a roulette table after black has occurred a number of consecutive times, thinking that the run will continue. This strategy is faulty, since roulette tables have no memory.

But, of course, gambling is only a sideshow as far as finance is concerned. Do we see irrationality in financial markets as well? The answer may very well be yes. Many investors do not achieve the degree of diversification that they should. Others trade frequently, generating both commissions and taxes. In fact, taxes can be handled optimally by selling losers and holding on to winners. While some individuals invest with tax minimization in mind, plenty of them do just the opposite. Many are more likely to sell their winners than their losers, a strategy leading to high tax payments. The behavioral view is not that *all* investors are irrational. Rather, it is that some, perhaps many, investors are.

INDEPENDENT DEVIATIONS FROM RATIONALITY Are deviations from rationality generally random, thereby likely to cancel out in a whole population of investors? To the contrary, psychologists have long argued that people deviate from rationality in accordance with a number of basic principles. While not all of these principles have an application to finance and market efficiency, at least two seem to do so.

The first principle, called *representativeness,* can be explained with the gambling example used above. The gambler believing a run of black will continue is in error since, in reality, the probability of a black spin is still only about 50 percent. Gamblers behaving in this way exhibit the psychological trait of representativeness. That is, they draw conclusions from too little data. In other words, the gambler believes the small sample he observed is more representative of the population than it really is.

How is this related to finance? Perhaps a market dominated by representativeness leads to bubbles. People see a sector of the market, for example, Internet stocks, having a short history of high revenue growth and extrapolate that it will continue forever. When the growth inevitably stalls, prices have nowhere to go but down.

The second principle is *conservatism,* which means that people are too slow in adjusting their beliefs to new information. Suppose that your goal since childhood was to become a dentist. Perhaps you came from a family of dentists, perhaps you liked the security and relatively high income that comes with that profession, or perhaps teeth always fascinated you. As things stand now, you could probably look forward to a long and productive career in that occupation. However, suppose that a new drug was developed that would prevent tooth decay. That drug would clearly reduce, or even eliminate, the demand for dentists. How quickly would you realize the implications as stated here? If you were emotionally attached to dentistry, you might adjust your beliefs very slowly. Family and friends could tell you to switch out of predental courses in college, but you just might not be psychologically ready to do that. Instead, you might cling to your rosy view of dentistry's future.

Perhaps there is a relationship to finance here. For example, many studies report that prices seem to adjust slowly to the information contained in earnings announcements. Could it be that, because of conservatism, investors are slow in adjusting their beliefs to new information? More will be said on this in the next section.

ARBITRAGE In Section 13.2, we suggested that professional investors, knowing that securities are mispriced, could buy the underpriced ones while selling correctly priced (or even overpriced) substitutes. This might well undo any mispricing caused by emotional amateurs.

However, trading of this sort is likely to be more risky than it appears at first glance. Suppose professionals generally believed that McDonald's stock was underpriced. They would buy it, while selling their holdings in, say, Burger King and Wendy's. However, if amateurs were taking opposite positions, prices would adjust to correct levels only if the positions of amateurs were small relative to those of the professionals. In a world of many amateurs, a few professionals would have to take big positions to bring prices into line, perhaps even engaging heavily in short selling. Buying large amounts of one stock and short selling large amounts of other stocks is quite risky, even if the two stocks are in the same industry. Here, unanticipated bad news about McDonald's and unanticipated good news about the other two stocks would cause the professionals to register large losses.

In addition, if amateurs mispriced McDonald's today, what is to prevent McDonald's from being even *more* mispriced tomorrow? This risk of further mispricing, even in the presence of no new information, may also cause professionals to cut back their arbitrage positions. As an example, imagine a shrewd professional who believed Internet stocks were overpriced in 1998. Had he bet on a decline at that time, he would have lost in the near term, since prices rose through March of 2000. Yet, he would have eventually made money, since prices later fell. However, near-term risk may reduce the size of arbitrage strategies.

In conclusion, the arguments presented here suggest that the theoretical underpinnings of the efficient capital markets hypothesis, presented in Section 13.2, might not hold in reality. That is, investors may be irrational, irrationality may be related across investors rather than canceling out across investors, and arbitrage strategies may involve too much risk to eliminate market efficiencies.

13.6 EMPIRICAL CHALLENGES TO MARKET EFFICIENCY

Section 13.4 presented empirical evidence supportive of market efficiency. We now present evidence challenging this hypothesis. (Adherents of market efficiency generally refer to results of this type as *anomalies.*)

1. *Limits to arbitrage.* Royal Dutch Petroleum and Shell Transport merged their interests in 1907, with all subsequent cash flows being split on a 60 percent–40 percent basis between the two companies. However, both companies continued to be publicly traded. One might imagine that the market value of Royal Dutch would

THE REAL WORLD

CAN STOCK MARKET INVESTORS ADD AND SUBTRACT?

On March 2, 2000, 3Com, a profitable provider of computer networking products and services, sold 5 percent of one of its subsidiaries to the public via an initial public offering (IPO). At the time, the subsidiary was known as Palm (now it is known as palmOne).

3Com planned to distribute the remaining Palm shares to 3Com shareholders at a later date. Under the plan, if you owned one share of 3Com, you would receive 1.5 shares of Palm. So, after 3Com sold part of Palm via the IPO, investors could buy Palm shares directly, or indirectly by purchasing shares of 3Com and waiting.

What makes this case interesting is what happened in the days that followed the Palm IPO. If you owned one 3Com share, you would be entitled, eventually, to 1.5 shares of Palm. Therefore, each 3Com share should be worth *at least* 1.5 times the value of each Palm share. We say at least, because the other parts of 3Com were profitable. As a result, each 3Com share should have been worth much more than 1.5 times the value of one Palm share. But, as you might guess, things did not work out this way.

The day before the Palm IPO, shares in 3Com sold for $104.13. After the first day of trading, Palm closed at $95.06 per share. Multiplying $95.06 by 1.5 results in $142.59, which is the minimum value one would expect to pay for 3Com. But, the day Palm closed at $95.06, 3Com shares closed at $81.81, more than $60 lower than the price implied by Palm. It gets stranger.

A 3Com price of $81.81 when Palm was selling for $95.06 implies that the market value the rest of 3Com's businesses (per share) at: $81.81 − 142.59 = −$60.78. Given the number of 3Com shares outstanding at the time, this means the market placed a *negative* value of about $22 billion for the rest of 3Com's businesses. Of course, a stock price cannot be negative. This means, then, that the price of Palm relative to 3Com was much too high.

To profit from this mispricing, investors would purchase shares of 3Com and sell shares of Palm. This trade is a no-brainer. In a well-functioning market, arbitrage traders would force the prices into alignment quite quickly. What happened?

As you can see in the accompanying figure, the market valued 3Com and Palm shares in such a way that the non-Palm part of 3Com had a negative value for about two months, from March 2, 2000, until May 8, 2000. Thus, the pricing error was corrected by market forces, but not instantly, which is consistent with the existence of limits to arbitrage.

The Percentage Difference between One Share of 3Com and One and One-Half Shares of Palm, March 2, 2000 to July 27, 2000

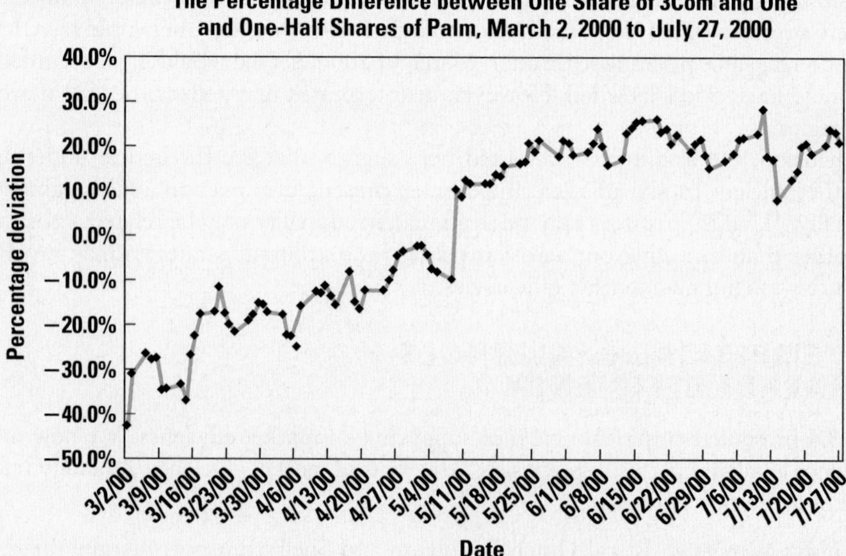

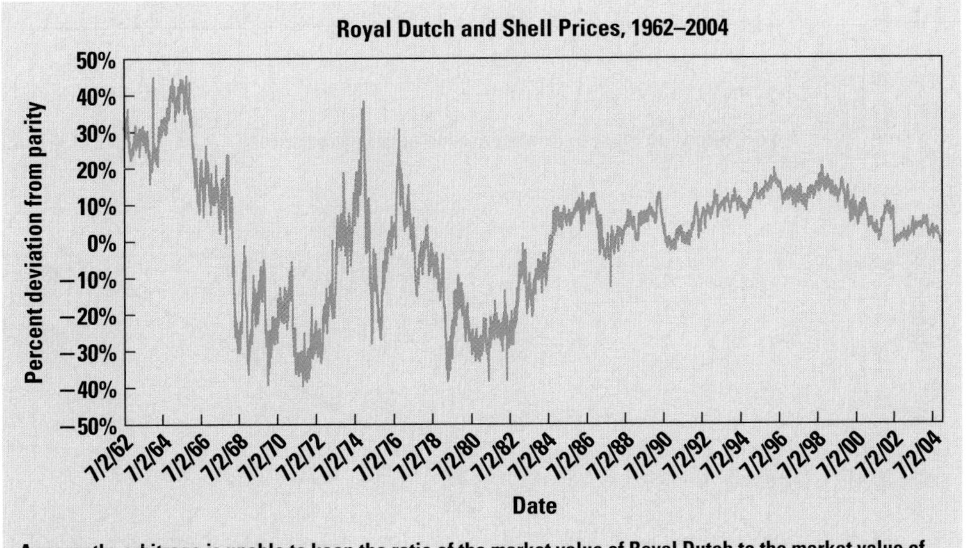

Apparently, arbitrage is unable to keep the ratio of the market value of Royal Dutch to the market value of Shell at parity.

FIGURE 13.7

Deviations of the Ratio of the Market Value of Royal Dutch to the Market Value of Shell from Parity

Source: Author calculations.

always be 1.5 (60/40) times that of Shell. That is, if Royal Dutch ever became overpriced, rational investors would buy Shell instead of Royal Dutch. If Royal Dutch were underpriced, investors would buy Royal Dutch. In addition, arbitrageurs would go further by buying the underpriced security and selling the overpriced security short.

However, Figure 13.7 shows that Royal Dutch and Shell have rarely traded at parity over the 1962 to 2004 period. Why would these deviations occur? As stated in the previous section, behavioral finance suggests that there are limits to arbitrage. That is, an investor buying the overpriced asset and selling the underpriced asset does not have a sure thing. Deviations from parity could actually *increase* in the short run, implying losses for the arbitrageur. The well-known statement, "Markets can stay irrational longer than you can stay solvent," attributed to John Maynard Keynes, applies here. Thus, risk considerations may force arbitrageurs to take positions that are too small to move prices back to parity. A nearby *The Real World* box nearby discusses another recent example of relative mispricing between two stocks.

2. *Earnings surprises.* Common sense suggests that prices should rise when earnings are reported to be higher than expected and prices should fall when the reverse occurs. However, market efficiency implies that prices will adjust immediately to the announcement, while behavioral finance would predict another pattern. Chan, Jegadeesh, and Lakonishok rank companies by the extent of their *earnings surprise,* that is, the difference between current quarterly earnings and quarterly earnings four quarters ago, divided by the standard deviation of quarterly earnings.[8] They form a portfolio of companies with the most extreme positive surprises and another portfolio of companies with the most extreme negative surprises. Figure 13.8 shows returns from buying the two portfolios. As can be seen, prices adjust slowly to the earnings announcements, with the portfolio with the positive surprises outperforming the portfolio with the negative surprises over both the next six months and the next year. Many other researchers obtain similar results.

[8]Chan, Louis K.C., Narasimhan Jegadeesh, and Josef Lakonishok, "Momentum Strategies," *Journal of Finance* (December 1996).

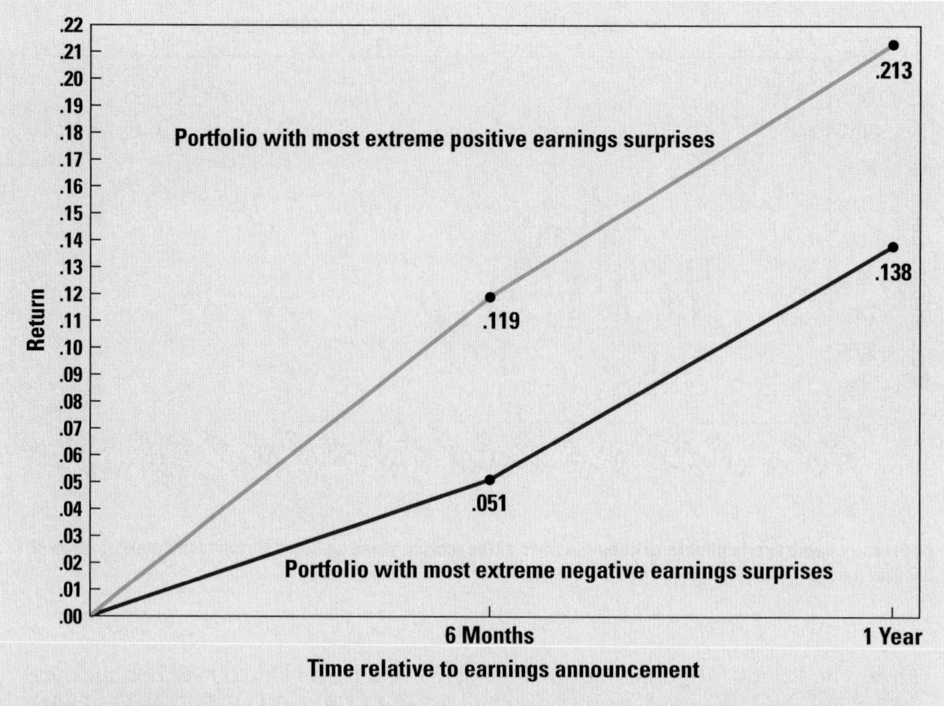

FIGURE 13.8

Returns to Two Investment Strategies Based on Earnings Surprise

Source: Adapted from Table III of L. C. Chan, N. Jegadeesh, and J. Lakonishok, "Momentum Strategies," *Journal of Finance* (December 1996).

This figure shows returns to a strategy of buying stocks with extremely high positive earnings surprise (the difference between current quarterly earnings and quarterly earnings four quarters ago, divided by the standard deviation of quarterly earnings) and to a strategy of buying stocks with extremely high negative earnings surprise. The graph shows a slow adjustment to the information in the earnings announcement.

Why do prices adjust slowly? Behavioral finance suggests that investors exhibit conservatism here, as they are slow to adjust to the information contained in the announcements.

3. *Size.* In 1981, two important papers presented evidence that, in the United States, the returns on stocks with small market capitalizations were greater than the returns on stocks with large market capitalizations over most of the 20th century.[9] The studies have since been replicated over different time periods and in different countries. For example, Figure 13.9 shows average returns over the period from 1963 to 1995 for five portfolios of U.S. stocks ranked on size. As can be seen, the average return on small stocks is quite a bit higher than the average return on large stocks. Although much of the differential performance is merely compensation for the extra risk of small stocks, researchers have generally argued that not all of it can be explained by risk differences. In addition, Donald Keim presented evidence that most of the difference in performance occurs in the month of January.[10]

4. *Value versus Growth.* A number of papers have argued that stocks with high book-value-to-stock-price ratios and/or high earnings-to-price ratios (generally called *value stocks*) outperform stocks with low ratios (growth stocks). For example, Fama and French find that, for 12 of 13 major international stock markets, the average

[9]See R. W. Banz, "The Relationship between Return and Market Value of Common Stocks," *Journal of Financial Economics* (March 1981), and M. R. Reinganum, "Misspecification of Capital Asset Pricing: Empirical Anomalies Based on Earnings Yields and Market Values," *Journal of Financial Economics* (March 1981).

[10]D. B. Keim, "Size-Related Anomalies and Stock Return Seasonality: Further Empirical Evidence," *Journal of Financial Economics* (June 1983).

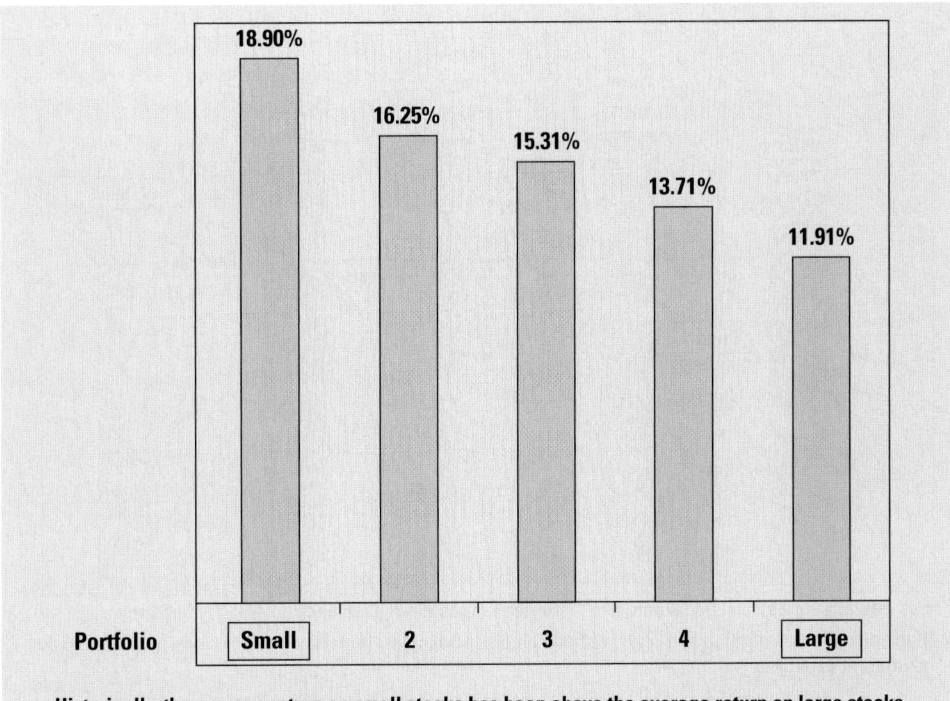

FIGURE 13.9

Annual Stock Returns on Portfolios Sorted by Size (Market Capitalization)

Source: Tim Loughran, "Book-to-Market across Firm Size, Exchange and Seasonality," *Journal of Financial and Quantitative Analysis* 32 (1997).

return on stocks with high book-value-to-stock-price ratios is above the average return on stocks with low book-value-to-stock-price ratios.[11] Figure 13.10 shows these returns for the world's five largest stock markets. Value stocks have outperformed growth stocks in each of these five markets.

Because the return difference is so large and because the above ratios can be obtained so easily for individual stocks, the results may constitute strong evidence against market efficiency. However, a number of papers suggest that the unusual returns are due to biases in the commercial databases or to differences in risk, not to a true inefficiency.[12] Since the debate revolves around arcane statistical issues, we will not pursue the issue further. However, it is safe to say that no conclusion is warranted at this time. As with so many other topics in finance and economics, further research is needed.

5. *Crashes and Bubbles.* The stock market crash of October 19, 1987, is extremely puzzling. The market dropped between 20 percent and 25 percent on a Monday following a weekend during which little surprising news was released. A drop of this magnitude for no apparent reason is not consistent with market efficiency. Because the crash of 1929 is still an enigma, it is doubtful that the more recent 1987 debacle will be explained anytime soon. The recent comments of an eminent historian are apt here: When asked what, in his opinion, the effect of the French Revolution of 1789 was, he replied that it was too early to tell.

Perhaps the two stock market crashes are evidence consistent with the **bubble theory** of speculative markets. That is, security prices sometimes move wildly

[11]Taken from Table III of Eugene F. Fama and Kenneth R. French, "Value versus Growth: The International Evidence," *Journal of Finance* 53 (December 1998).

[12]For example, see S. P. Kothari, J. Shanken, and R. G. Sloan, "Another Look at the Cross Section of Expected Stock Returns," *Journal of Finance* (March 1995), and E. F. Fama and K. R. French, "Multifactor Explanations of Asset Pricing Anomalies," *Journal of Finance* 51 (March 1996).

FIGURE 13.10
Annual U.S. Dollar Returns* (in percent) on Low Book-to-Price Firms and High Book-to-Price Firms in Selected Countries

Source: Eugene F. Fama and Kenneth R. French, "Value versus Growth: The International Evidence," *Journal of Finance* (December 1998).

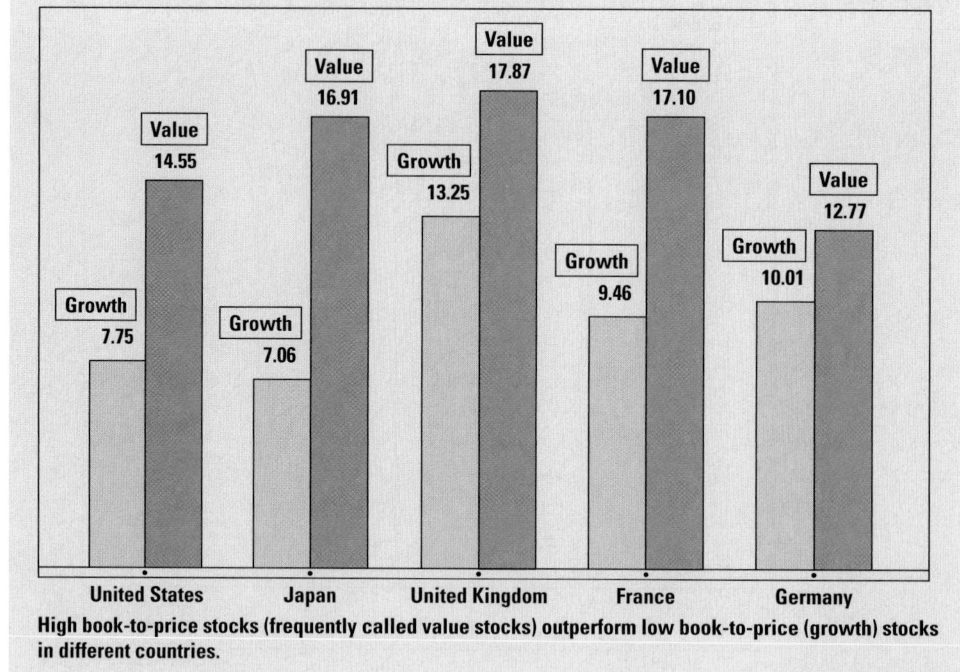

High book-to-price stocks (frequently called value stocks) outperform low book-to-price (growth) stocks in different countries.

*Returns are expressed as the excess over the return on U.S. Treasury bills.

FIGURE 13.11
Value of Index of Internet Stocks

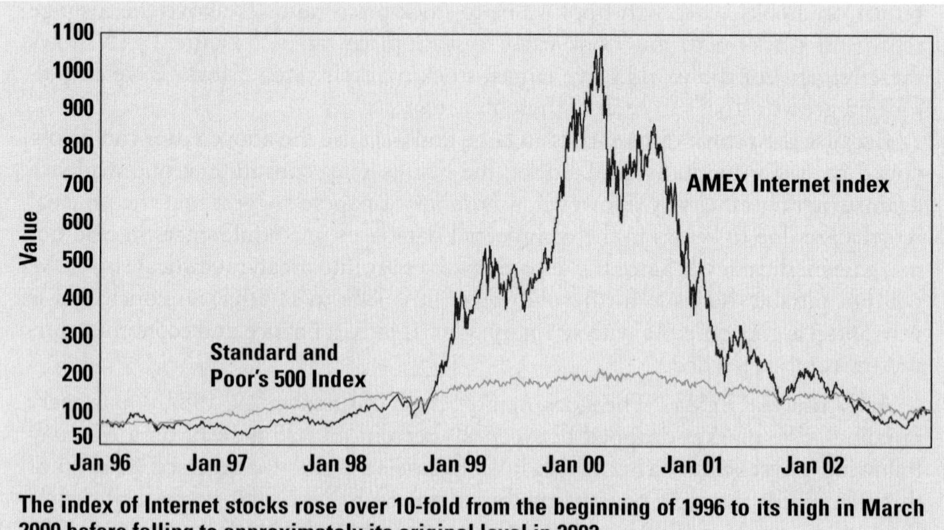

The index of Internet stocks rose over 10-fold from the beginning of 1996 to its high in March 2000 before falling to approximately its original level in 2002.

above their true values. Eventually, prices fall back to their original level, causing great losses for investors. Consider, for example, the behavior of Internet stocks of the late 1990s. Figure 13.11 shows values of an index of Internet stocks from 1996 through 2002. The index rose over 10-fold from January 1996 to its high in March 2000, before retreating to approximately its original level in 2002. For comparison, the figure also shows price movement for the Standard & Poor 500 Index. While this index rose and fell over the same period, the price movement was quite muted, relative to that of Internet stocks.

Many commentators describe the rise and fall of Internet stocks as a *bubble*. Is it correct to do so? Unfortunately, there is no precise definition of the term. Some academics argue that the price movement in the figure is consistent with rationality. Prices rose initially, they say, because it appeared that the Internet would soon capture a large chunk of international commerce. Prices fell when later evidence suggested this would not occur quite so quickly. However, others argue that the initial rosy scenario was never supported by the facts. Rather, prices rose due to nothing more than "irrational exuberance."

13.7 REVIEWING THE DIFFERENCES

It is fair to say that the controversy over efficient capital markets has not yet been resolved. Rather, academic financial economists have sorted themselves into three camps, with some adhering to market efficiency, some believing in behavioral finance, and others (perhaps the majority) not yet convinced that either side has won the argument. This state of affairs is certainly different from, say, 20 years ago, when market efficiency went unchallenged. In addition, the controversy here is perhaps the most contentious of any area of financial economics. Only in this area do grown-up finance professors come close to fisticuffs over an idea.

Because of the controversy, it does not appear that our textbook, or any textbook, can easily resolve the differing points of view. However, we can illustrate the differences between the two camps by relating the two psychological principles mentioned earlier, representativeness and conservatism, to stock returns.

Representativeness

This principle implies overweighting the results of small samples, as with the gambler who thinks a few consecutive spins of black on the roulette wheel make black a more likely outcome than red on the next spin. Financial economists have argued that representativeness leads to *overreaction* in stock returns. We mentioned earlier that financial bubbles are likely overreactions to news. Internet companies showed great revenue growth for a short time in the late 1990s, causing many to believe that this growth would continue indefinitely. Stock prices rose (too much) at this point. When, at last, investors realized that this growth could not be sustained, prices plummeted.

Conservatism

This principle states that individuals adjust their beliefs too slowly to new information. A market composed of this type of investor would likely lead to stock prices that *underreact* in the presence of new information. The example concerning earnings surprises may well illustrate this underreaction. Prices rose slowly following announcements of positive earnings surprises. Announcements of negative surprises had a similar, but opposite, reaction.

The two academic camps have different views of these results. The efficient market believers stress that representativeness and conservatism have opposite implications for stock prices. Which principle, they ask, should dominate in any particular situation? In other words, why should investors overreact to news about Internet stocks but underreact to earnings news? Fama reviewed the academic studies on anomalies, finding that about half of them show overreaction and about half show underreaction.[13] He concludes that this evidence is consistent with the market efficiency hypothesis that anomalies are chance events. In addition, he argues that behavioral finance must do better at specifying which types of information should lead to overreaction and which to underreaction before one rejects market efficiency in favor of behavioral finance.

[13]Fama, Eugene F., "Market Efficiency, Long-Term Returns and Behavioral Finance," *Journal of Financial Economics* 49 (September 1998).

Adherents of behavioral finance see things a little differently. First, they point out that, as discussed in Section 13.5, the three theoretical foundations of market efficiency appear to be violated in the real world. Second, there are simply too many anomalies, with a number of them being replicated in out-of-sample tests. This argues against anomalies being mere chance events. Finally, though the field has not yet determined why either overreaction or underreaction should dominate in a particular situation, much progress has already been made in a short period of time.

13.8 IMPLICATIONS FOR CORPORATE FINANCE

So far, the chapter has examined both theoretical arguments and empirical evidence concerning efficient markets. We now ask the question: Does market efficiency have any relevance for corporate financial managers? The answer is that it does. Below we consider four implications of efficiency for managers.

1. Accounting Choices, Financial Choices, and Market Efficiency

The accounting profession provides firms with a significant amount of leeway in their reporting practices. For example, companies may choose between the last-in, first-out (LIFO) or the first-in, first-out (FIFO) method in valuing inventories. They may choose either the percentage-of-completion or the completed-contract method for construction projects. They may depreciate physical assets by either accelerated or straight-line depreciation.

Managers clearly prefer high stock prices to low stock prices. Should managers use the leeway in accounting choices to report the highest possible income? Not necessarily, if markets are efficient. That is, accounting choice should not affect stock price if two conditions hold. First, enough information must be provided in the annual report so that financial analysts can construct earnings under the alternative accounting methods. This appears to be the case for many, though not necessarily all, accounting choices. Second, the market must be efficient in the semistrong form. In other words, the market must appropriately use all of this accounting information in determining the market price.

Of course, the issue of whether accounting choice affects stock price is ultimately an empirical matter. A number of academic papers have addressed this issue, and the evidence does not suggest that managers can boost stock price through accounting practices. In other words, the market appears efficient enough to see through different accounting choices.

One caveat is called for here. Our discussion specifically assumed that "financial analysts can construct earnings under the alternative accounting methods." However, companies like Enron, WorldCom, Global Crossing, and Xerox simply reported fraudulent numbers in recent years. There was no way for financial analysts to construct alternative earnings numbers, since these analysts were unaware how the reported numbers were determined. So it was not surprising that the prices of these stocks initially rose well above fair value. Yes, managers can boost prices in this way–as long as they are willing to serve time once they are caught!

Is there anything else that investors can be expected to see through in an efficient market? Consider stock splits and stock dividends. Today Amarillo Corporation has 1 million shares outstanding and reports $10 million of earnings. In the hopes of boosting stock price, the firm's chief financial officer (CFO), Ms. Green, recommends to the board of directors that Amarillo have a 2-for-1 stock split. That is, a shareholder with 100 shares prior to the split would have 200 shares after the split. The CFO contends that each investor would feel richer after the split because he would own more shares.

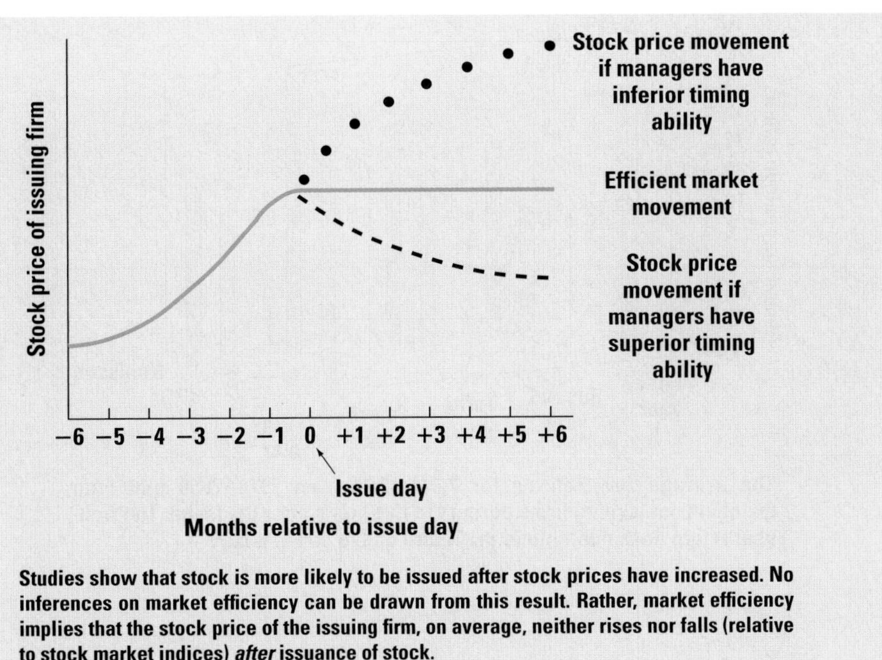

Studies show that stock is more likely to be issued after stock prices have increased. No inferences on market efficiency can be drawn from this result. Rather, market efficiency implies that the stock price of the issuing firm, on average, neither rises nor falls (relative to stock market indices) *after* issuance of stock.

FIGURE 13.12

Three Stock Price Adjustments after Issuing Equity

However, this thinking runs counter to market efficiency. A rational investor knows that he would own the same proportion of the firm after the split as before the split. For example, our investor with 100 shares owns 1/10,000 (100/1 million) of Amarillo's shares prior to the split. His share of the earnings would be $1,000 ($10 million/10,000). While he would own 200 shares after the split, there would now be 2 million shares outstanding. Thus, he still would own 1/10,000 of the firm. His share of the earnings would still be $1,000, since the stock split would not affect the earnings of the entire firm.

2. The Timing Decision

Imagine a firm whose managers are contemplating the date to issue equity. This decision is frequently called the *timing* decision. If managers believe that their stock is overpriced, they are likely to issue equity immediately. Here, they are creating value for their current stockholders because they are selling stock for more than it is worth. Conversely, if the managers believe that their stock is underpriced, they are more likely to wait, hoping that the stock price will eventually rise to its true value.

However, if markets are efficient, securities are always correctly priced. Since efficiency implies that stock is sold for its true worth, the timing decision becomes unimportant. Figure 13.12 shows three possible stock price adjustments to the issuance of new stock.

Of course, market efficiency is ultimately an empirical issue. Surprisingly, recent research has called market efficiency into question. Ritter presents evidence that the annual returns over the five years following an initial public offering (IPO) are about 2 percent less for the issuing company than the returns on a nonissuing company of similar book-to-market ratio.[14] Annual returns over this period following a seasoned equity offering (SEO) are between 3 percent and 4 percent less for the issuing company than for a comparable nonissuing company. A company's first public offering is called an IPO and all subsequent offerings are termed SEOs. The upper half of Figure 13.13 shows average annual returns of both IPOs and their control group, and the lower half of the figure shows average annual returns of both SEOs and their control group.

[14] Jay Ritter, "Investment Banking and Security Issuance," Chapter 9 of *Handbook of the Economics of Finance,* ed. George Constantinides, Milton Harris, and Rene Stulz, North Holland: Amsterdam, 2003.

FIGURE 13.13

Returns on Initial Public Offerings (IPOs) and Seasoned Equity Offerings (SEOs) in Years Following Issue

Source: Jay Ritter, "Investment Banking and Security Issuance," Chapter 9 of *Handbook of the Economics of Finance,* ed. George Constantinides, Milton Harris, and Rene Stulz, North Holland: Amsterdam, 2003.

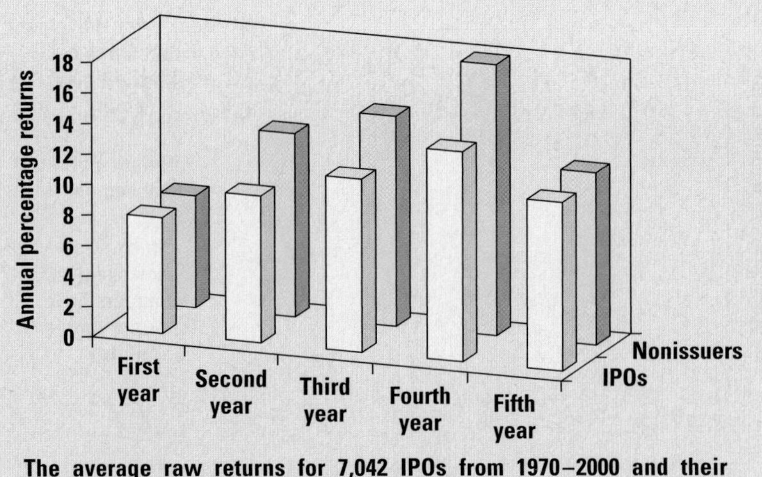

The average raw returns for 7,042 IPOs from 1970–2000 and their matching nonissuing firms during the five years after the issue. The first-year return does not include the return on the day of issue.

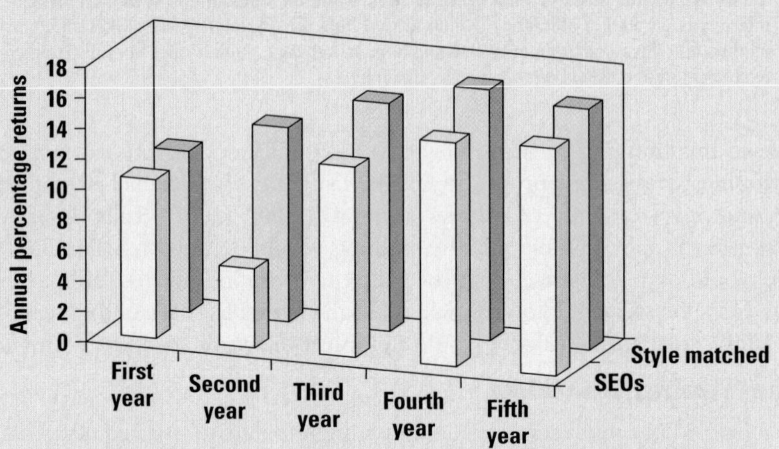

The average raw returns for 7,502 SEOs from 1970–2000 and their matching nonissuing firms during the five years after the issue. The first-year return does not include the return on the day of issue. On average, IPOs underperform their control groups by about 2% per year in the five years following issuance. SEOs underperform by about 3%–4% per year.

The evidence in Ritter's paper suggests that corporate managers issue SEOs when the company's stock is overpriced. In other words, managers appear to time the market successfully. The evidence that managers time their IPOs is less compelling, since returns following IPOs are closer to those of their control group.

Does the ability of a corporate official to issue an SEO when the security is overpriced indicate that the market is inefficient in the semistrong form or the strong form? The answer is actually somewhat more complex than it may first appear. On one hand, officials are likely to have special information that the rest of us do not have, suggesting that the market need only be inefficient in the strong form. On the other hand, if the market were truly semistrong efficient, the price would drop immediately and completely upon the announcement of an upcoming SEO. That is, rational investors would realize that stock is being issued because corporate officials have special information that the stock is overpriced. Indeed, many empirical studies report a price drop on the announcement date. However, Figure 13.13 indicates that there is a further price drop in the subsequent years, suggesting that the market is inefficient in the semistrong form.

If firms can time the issuance of common stock, perhaps they can also time the repurchase of stock. Here, a firm would like to repurchase when its stock is undervalued. Ikenberry, Lakonishok, and Vermaelen find that stock returns of repurchasing firms are abnormally high in the two years following repurchase, suggesting that timing is effective here.[15]

As is always the case, empirical research is never ultimately settled. However, in our opinion, the evidence strongly suggests that managers successfully engage in timing. If this conclusion stands the test of time, it would constitute evidence against market efficiency.

3. Speculation and Efficient Markets

We normally think of individuals and financial institutions as the primary speculators in financial markets. However, industrial corporations speculate as well. For example, many companies make interest rate bets. If the managers of a firm believe that interest rates are likely to rise, they have an incentive to borrow, because the present value of the liability will fall with the rate increase. In addition, these managers will have an incentive to borrow long term rather than short term in order to lock in the low rates for a longer period of time. The thinking can get more sophisticated. Suppose that the long-term rate is already higher than the short-term rate. The manager might argue that this differential reflects the market's view that rates will rise. However, perhaps he anticipates a rate increase even greater than what the market anticipates, as implied by the upward-sloping term structure. Again, the manager will want to borrow long term rather than short term.

Firms also speculate in foreign currencies. Suppose that the CFO of a multinational corporation based in the United States believes that the euro will decline relative to the dollar. He would probably issue euro-denominated debt rather than dollar-denominated debt, since he expects the value of the foreign liability to fall. Conversely, he would issue debt domestically if he believes foreign currencies will appreciate relative to the dollar.

We are perhaps getting a little ahead of our story, since the subtleties of the term structure and exchange rates are treated in other chapters, not this one. However, the big picture question is this: What does market efficiency have to say about the above activity? The answer is quite clear. If financial markets are efficient, managers should not waste their time trying to forecast the movements of interest rates and foreign currencies. Their forecasts will likely be no better than chance. And they will be using up valuable executive time. This is not to say, however, that firms should flippantly pick the maturity or the denomination of their debt in a random fashion. A firm must *choose* these parameters carefully. However, the choice should be based on other rationales, not on an attempt to beat the market. For example, a firm with a project lasting five years might decide to issue five-year debt. A firm might issue yen-denominated debt, because it anticipates expanding into Japan in a big way.

The same thinking applies to acquisitions. Many corporations buy up other firms because they think these targets are underpriced. Unfortunately, the empirical evidence suggests that the market is too efficient for this type of speculation to be profitable. And the acquirer never pays just the current market price. The bidding firm must pay a premium above market to induce a majority of shareholders of the target firm to sell their shares. However, this is not to say that firms should never be acquired. Rather, one should consider an acquisition if there are benefits, that is, synergies, from the union. Improved marketing, economies in production, replacement of bad management, and even

[15]D. Ikenberry, J. Lakonishok, and T. Vermaelen, "Market Underreaction to Open Market Share Repurchases," *Journal of Financial Economics* (October–November 1995).

tax reduction are typical synergies. These synergies are distinct from the perception that the acquired firm is underpriced.

One caveat should be mentioned. We talked earlier about empirical evidence suggesting that SEOs are timed to take advantage of overpriced stock. This makes sense, since managers are likely to know more about their own firm than the market does. However, while managers may very well have special information about their own firm, it is unlikely that they have special information about interest rates, foreign currencies, and other firms. There are simply too many participants in these markets, many of whom are devoting all of their time to forecasting. Managers typically spend most of their time running their own firms, with only a small amount devoted to studying financial markets.

4. Information in Market Prices

The previous section argued that it is quite difficult to forecast future market prices. However, the current and past prices of any asset are known–and of great use. Consider, for example, Becher's study of bank mergers.[16] The author finds that stock prices of acquired banks rise about 23 percent on average upon the first announcement of a merger. This is not surprising, since companies are generally bought out at a premium above current stock price. However, the same study shows that prices of acquiring banks fall almost 5 percent on average upon the same announcement. This is pretty strong evidence that bank mergers do not benefit, and may even hurt, acquiring companies. The reason for this result is unclear, though perhaps acquirers simply overpay for acquisitions. Regardless of the reason, the *implication* is clear. A bank should think deeply before making an acquisition of another bank.

Furthermore, suppose you are the CFO of a company whose stock price drops much more than 5 percent upon announcement of an acquisition. The market is telling you that the merger is quite bad for your firm. Serious consideration should be given to canceling the merger, even if, prior to the announcement, you thought the merger was a good idea.

Of course, mergers are only one type of corporate event. Managers should pay attention to the stock price reaction to any of their announcements, whether it concerns a new venture, a divestiture, a restructuring, or something else.

This is not the only way in which corporations can use the information in market prices. Suppose you are on the board of directors of a company whose stock price has declined precipitously since the current chief executive officer (CEO) was hired. In addition, the prices of competitors have risen over the same time. Though there may be extenuating circumstances, this can be viewed as evidence that the CEO is doing a poor job. Perhaps he should be fired. If this seems harsh, consider that Warner, Watts, and Wruck find a strong negative correlation between managerial turnover and prior stock performance.[17] Figure 13.14 shows that stocks fall on average about 40 percent in price (relative to market movements) in the three years prior to the forced departure of a top manager.

If managers are fired for bad stock price performance, perhaps they are rewarded for stock price appreciation. Hall and Liebman state:

> Our main empirical finding is that CEO wealth often changes by millions of dollars for typical changes in firm value. For example, the median total compensation for CEOs is about \$1 million if their firm's stock has a 30th percentile annual return (−7.0 percent) and is \$5 million if the firm's stock has a 70th percentile annual return (20.5 percent). Thus, there is a difference of about \$4 million in compensation for achieving a moderately above average performance relative to a moderately below average performance.[18]

[16]David A. Becher, "The Valuation Effects of Bank Mergers," *Journal of Corporate Finance* 6 (2000).

[17]Jerold B. Warner, Ross L. Watts, and Karen H. Wruck, "Stock Prices and Top Management Changes," *Journal of Financial Economics* 20 (1988).

[18]Brian J. Hall and Jeffrey B. Liebman, "Are CEOs Really Paid Like Bureaucrats?" *Quarterly Journal of Economics* (August 1998), p. 654.

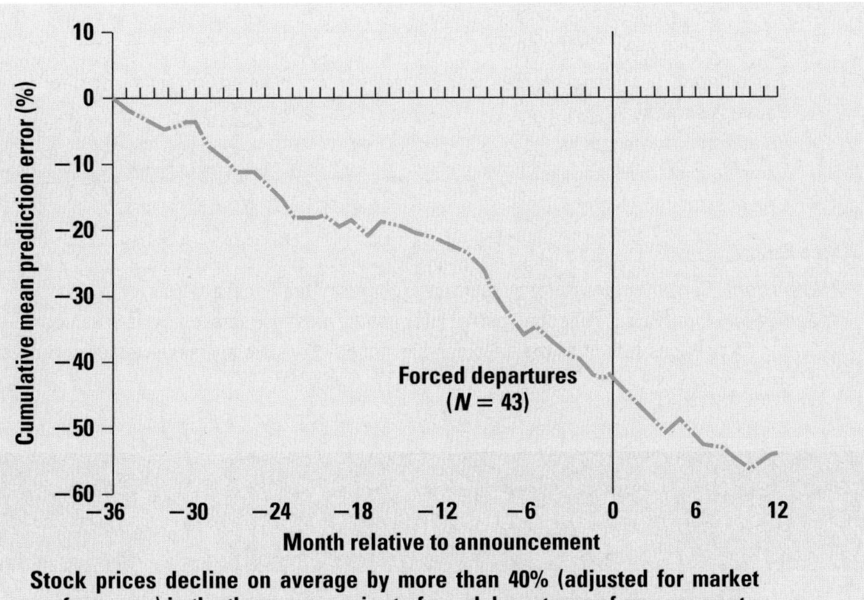

FIGURE 13.14

Stock Performance Prior to Forced Departures of Management

Source: Adapted from Figure 1 of Warner, Watts, and Wruck, "Stock Prices and Management Changes," *Journal of Financial Economics* 20 (1988).

Market efficiency implies that stock prices reflect all available information. We recommend using this information as much as possible in corporate decisions. And at least with respect to executive firings and executive compensation, it looks as if real world corporations do pay attention to market prices. The following box summarizes some key issues in the efficient markets debate.

EFFICIENT MARKET HYPOTHESIS: A SUMMARY

Does Not Say

- Prices are uncaused.
- Investors are foolish and too stupid to be in the market.
- All shares of stock have the same expected returns.
- Investors should throw darts to select stocks.
- There is no upward trend in stock prices.

Does Say

- Prices reflect underlying value.
- Financial managers cannot time stock and bond sales.
- Managers cannot profitably speculate in foreign currencies.
- Managers cannot boost stock prices through creative accounting.

Why Doesn't Everybody Believe It?

- There are optical illusions, mirages, and apparent patterns in charts of stock market returns.
- The truth is less interesting.

(*continued*)

- There is evidence against efficiency:
  - Two different, but financially identical, classes of stock of same firm selling at different prices.
  - Earnings surprises.
  - Small versus large stocks.
  - Value versus growth stocks.
  - Crashes and bubbles.

Three Forms

Weak form: Current prices reflect past prices; chartism (technical analysis) is useless.
Semistrong form: Prices reflect all public information; most financial analysis is useless.
Strong form: Prices reflect all that is knowable; nobody consistently makes superior profits.

SUMMARY AND CONCLUSIONS

1. An efficient financial market processes the information available to investors and incorporates it into the prices of securities. Market efficiency has two general implications. First, in any given time period, a stock's abnormal return depends on information or news received by the market in that period. Second, an investor who uses the same information as the market cannot expect to earn abnormal returns. In other words, systems for playing the market are doomed to fail.
2. What information does the market use to determine prices? The weak form of the efficient market hypothesis says that the market uses the past history of prices and is therefore efficient with respect to these past prices. This implies that stock selection based on patterns of past stock price movements is not better than random stock selection.
3. The semistrong form states that the market uses all publicly available information in setting prices.
4. Strong form efficiency states that the market uses all of the information that anybody knows about stocks, even inside information.
5. Much evidence from different financial markets supports weak form and semistrong form efficiency but not strong form efficiency.
6. Behavioral finance states that the market is not efficient. Adherents argue that:
   a. Investors are not rational.
   b. Deviations from rationality are similar across investors.
   c. Arbitrage, being costly, will not eliminate inefficiencies.
7. Behaviorists point to many studies, including those showing that small stocks outperform large stocks, value stocks outperform growth stocks, and stock prices adjust slowly to earnings surprises, as empirical confirmation of their beliefs.
8. Four implications of market efficiency for corporate finance are:
   a. Managers cannot fool the market through creative accounting.
   b. Firms cannot successfully time issues of debt and equity.
   c. Managers cannot profitably speculate in foreign currencies and other instruments.
   d. Managers can reap many benefits by paying attention to market prices.

CONCEPT QUESTIONS

1. **Firm Value** What rule should a firm follow when making financing decisions? How can firms create valuable financing opportunities?
2. **Efficient Market Hypothesis** Define the three forms of market efficiency.
3. **Efficient Market Hypothesis** Which of the following statements are true about the efficient market hypothesis?
   a. It implies perfect forecasting ability.
   b. It implies that prices reflect all available information.
   c. It implies an irrational market.
   d. It implies that prices do not fluctuate.
   e. It results from keen competition among investors.
4. **Market Efficiency Implications** Explain why a characteristic of an efficient market is that investments in that market have zero NPVs.
5. **Efficient Market Hypothesis** A stock market analyst is able to identify mispriced stocks by comparing the average price for the last 10 days to the average price for the last 60 days. If this is true, what do you know about the market?
6. **Semistrong Efficiency** If a market is semistrong form efficient, is it also weak form efficient? Explain.
7. **Efficient Market Hypothesis** What are the implications of the efficient market hypothesis for investors who buy and sell stocks in an attempt to "beat the market"?
8. **Stocks versus Gambling** Critically evaluate the following statement: Playing the stock market is like gambling. Such speculative investing has no social value, other than the pleasure people get from this form of gambling.
9. **Efficient Market Hypothesis** There are several celebrated investors and stock pickers frequently mentioned in the financial press who have recorded huge returns on their investments over the past two decades. Is the success of these particular investors an invalidation of the EMH? Explain.
10. **Efficient Market Hypothesis** For each of the following scenarios, discuss whether profit opportunities exist from trading in the stock of the firm under the conditions that (1) the market is not weak form efficient, (2) the market is weak form but not semistrong form efficient, (3) the market is semistrong form but not strong form efficient, and (4) the market is strong form efficient.
    a. The stock price has risen steadily each day for the past 30 days.
    b. The financial statements for a company were released three days ago, and you believe you've uncovered some anomalies in the company's inventory and cost control reporting techniques that are causing the firm's true liquidity strength to be understated.
    c. You observe that the senior management of a company has been buying a lot of the company's stock on the open market over the past week.

Use the following information for the next two questions:

Technical analysis is a controversial investment practice. Technical analysis covers a wide array of techniques, which are all used in an attempt to predict the direction of a particular stock, or the market. Technical analysts look at two major types of information: historical stock prices and investor sentiment. A technical analyst would argue these two information sets provide information on the future direction of a particular stock, or the market as a whole.

11. **Technical Analysis** What would a technical analyst say about market efficiency?

12. **Investor Sentiment** A technical analysis tool that is sometimes used to predict market movements is an investor sentiment index. AAII, the American Association of Individual Investors, publishes an investor sentiment index based on a survey of its members. In the table below you will find the percentage of investors who were bullish, bearish, or neutral during a four-week period.

WEEK	BULLISH	BEARISH	NEUTRAL
1	37%	25%	38%
2	52	14	34
3	29	35	36
4	43	26	31

What is the investor sentiment index intended to capture? How might it be useful in technical analysis?

13. **Performance of the Pros** In the mid- to late-1990s, the performance of the pros was unusually poor—on the order of 90 percent of all equity mutual funds underperformed a passively managed index fund. How does this bear on the issue of market efficiency?

14. **Efficient Market** A hundred years ago or so, companies did not compile annual reports. Even if you owned stock in a particular company, you were unlikely to be allowed to see the balance sheet and income statement for the company. Assuming the market is semistrong form efficient, what does this say about market efficiency then compared to now?

15. **Efficient Market Hypothesis** Aerotech, an aerospace technology research firm, announced this morning that it has hired the world's most knowledgeable and prolific space researchers. Before today, Aerotech's stock had been selling for $100. Assume that no other information is received over the next week and the stock market as a whole does not move.

    a. What do you expect will happen to Aerotech's stock?

    b. Consider the following scenarios:

        i. The stock price jumps to $118 on the day of the announcement. In subsequent days it floats up to $123, then falls back to $116.

        ii. The stock price jumps to $116 and remains at that level.

        iii. The stock price gradually climbs to $116 over the next week.

    Which scenario(s) indicate market efficiency? Which do not? Why?

16. **Efficient Market Hypothesis** When the 56-year-old founder of Gulf & Western, Inc., died of a heart attack, the stock price immediately jumped from $18.00 a share to $20.25, a 12.5 percent increase. This is evidence of market inefficiency, because an efficient stock market would have anticipated his death and adjusted the price beforehand. Assume that no other information is received and the stock market as a whole does not move. Is this statement about market efficiency true or false? Explain.

17. **Efficient Market Hypothesis** Today, the following announcement was made: "Early today the Justice Department reached a decision in the Universal Product Care (UPC) case. UPC has been found guilty of discriminatory practices in hiring. For the next five years, UPC must pay $2 million each year to a fund representing victims of UPC's policies." Assuming the market is efficient, should investors not buy UPC stock after the announcement because the litigation will cause an abnormally low rate of return? Explain.

18. **Efficient Market Hypothesis** Newtech Corp. is going to adopt a new chip-testing device that can greatly improve its production efficiency. Do you think the lead engineer can profit from

purchasing the firm's stock before the news release on the device? After reading the announcement in *The Wall Street Journal,* should you be able to earn an abnormal return from purchasing the stock if the market is efficient?

19. **Efficient Market Hypothesis** TransTrust Corp. has changed how it accounts for inventory. Taxes are unaffected, although the resulting earnings report released this quarter is 20 percent higher than what it would have been under the old accounting system. There is no other surprise in the earnings report and the change in the accounting treatment was publicly announced. If the market is efficient will the stock price be higher when the market learns that the reported earnings are higher?

20. **Efficient Market Hypothesis** The Durkin Investing Agency has been the best stock picker in the country for the past two years. Before this rise to fame occurred, the Durkin newsletter had 200 subscribers. Those subscribers beat the market consistently, earning substantially higher returns after adjustment for risk and transaction costs. Subscriptions have skyrocketed to 10,000. Now, when the Durkin Investing Agency recommends a stock, the price instantly rises several points. The subscribers currently earn only a normal return when they buy recommended stock because the price rises before anybody can act on the information. Briefly explain this phenomenon. Is Durkin's ability to pick stocks consistent with market efficiency?

21. **Efficient Market Hypothesis** Your broker commented that well-managed firms are better investments than poorly managed firms. As evidence, your broker cited a recent study examining 100 small manufacturing firms that eight years earlier had been listed in an industry magazine as the best-managed small manufacturers in the country. In the ensuing eight years, the 100 firms listed have not earned more than the normal market return. Your broker continued to say that if the firms were well managed, they should have produced better-than-average returns. If the market is efficient, do you agree with your broker?

22. **Efficient Market Hypothesis** A famous economist just announced in *The Wall Street Journal* his findings that the recession is over and the economy is again entering an expansion. Assume market efficiency. Can you profit from investing in the stock market after you read this announcement?

23. **Efficient Market Hypothesis** Suppose the market is semistrong form efficient. Can you expect to earn excess returns if you make trades based on:

    a. Your broker's information about record earnings for a stock?

    b. Rumors about a merger of a firm?

    c. Yesterday's announcement of a successful new product test?

24. **Efficient Market Hypothesis** Imagine that a particular macroeconomic variable that influences your firm's net earnings is positively serially correlated. Assume market efficiency. Would you expect price changes in your stock to be serially correlated? Why or why not?

25. **Efficient Market Hypothesis** The efficient market hypothesis implies that all mutual funds should obtain the same expected risk-adjusted returns. Therefore, we can simply pick mutual funds at random. Is this statement true or false? Explain.

26. **Efficient Market Hypothesis** Assume that markets are efficient. During a trading day, American Golf Inc. announces that it has lost a contract for a large golfing project, which, prior to the news, it was widely believed to have secured. If the market is efficient, how should the stock price react to this information if no additional information is released?

27. **Efficient Market Hypothesis** Prospectors, Inc., is a publicly traded gold prospecting company in Alaska. Although the firm's searches for gold usually fail, the prospectors occasionally find a rich vein of ore. What pattern would you expect to observe for Prospectors's cumulative abnormal returns if the market is efficient?

28. **Evidence on Market Efficiency** Some people argue that the efficient market hypothesis cannot explain the 1987 market crash or the high price-to-earnings ratio of Internet stocks during the late 1990s. What alternative hypothesis is currently used for these two phenomena?

QUESTIONS AND PROBLEMS

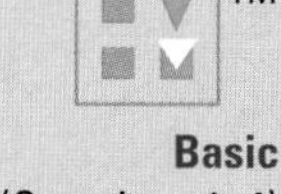

Basic
(Questions 1–4)

1. **Cumulative Abnormal Returns** Delta, United, and American Airlines announced purchases of planes on July 18 (7/18), February 12 (2/12), and October 7 (10/7), respectively. Given the information below, calculate the cumulative abnormal return (CAR) for these stocks as a group. Graph the result and provide an explanation. All of the stocks have a beta of one and no other announcements are made.

Delta			United			American		
DATE	MARKET RETURN	COMPANY RETURN	DATE	MARKET RETURN	COMPANY RETURN	DATE	MARKET RETURN	COMPANY RETURN
7/12	−.3	−.5	2/8	−.9	−1.1	10/1	.5	.3
7/13	.0	.2	2/9	−1.0	−1.1	10/2	.4	.6
7/16	.5	.7	2/10	.4	.2	10/3	1.1	1.1
7/17	−.5	−.3	2/11	.6	.8	10/6	.1	−.3
7/18	−2.2	1.1	2/12	−.3	−.1	10/7	−2.2	−.3
7/19	−.9	−.7	2/15	1.1	1.2	10/8	.5	.5
7/20	−1.0	−1.1	2/16	.5	.5	10/9	−.3	−.2
7/23	.7	.5	2/17	−.3	−.2	10/10	.3	.1
7/24	.2	.1	2/18	.3	.2	10/13	.0	−.1

2. **Cumulative Abnormal Returns** The following diagram shows the cumulative abnormal returns (CAR) for 386 oil exploration companies announcing oil discoveries over the period from 1950 to 1980. Month 0 in the diagram is the announcement month. Assume that no other information is received and the stock market as a whole does not move. Is the diagram consistent with market efficiency? Why or why not?

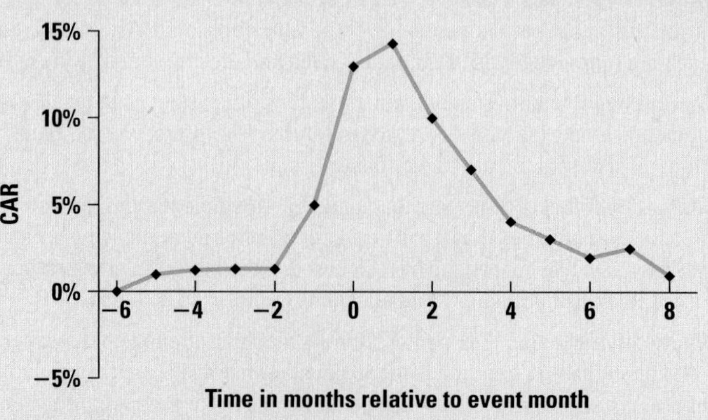

3. **Cumulative Abnormal Returns** The following figures present the results of four cumulative abnormal returns (CAR) studies. Indicate whether the results of each study support, reject, or are inconclusive about the semistrong form of the efficient market hypothesis. In each figure, time 0 is the date of an event.

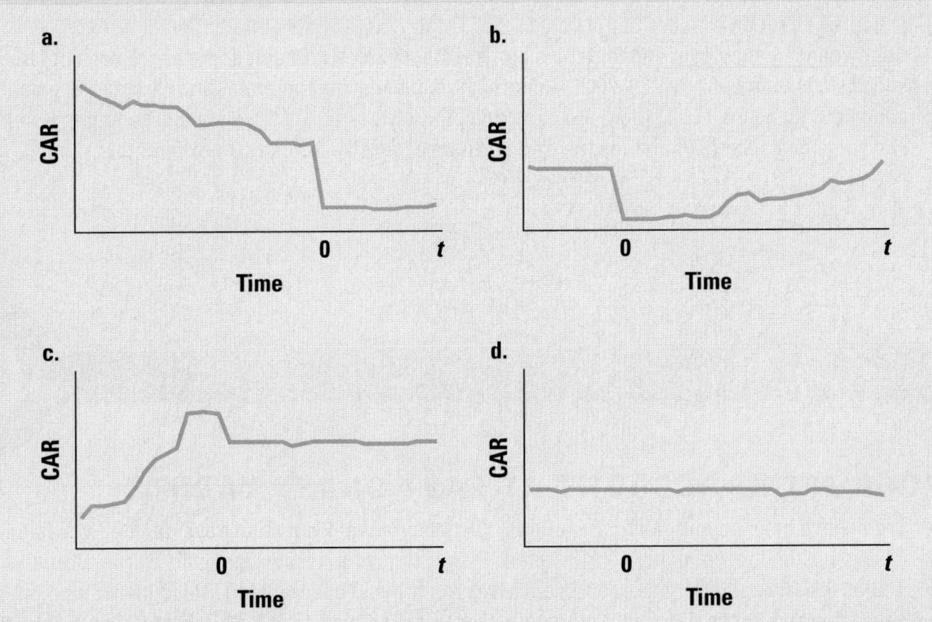

4. **Cumulative Abnormal Returns** A study analyzed the behavior of the stock prices of firms that had lost antitrust cases. Included in the diagram are all firms that lost the initial court decision, even if the decision was later overturned on appeal. The event at time 0 is the initial, preappeal court decision. Assume no other information was released, aside from that disclosed in the initial trial. The stock prices all have a beta of one. Is the diagram consistent with market efficiency? Why or why not?

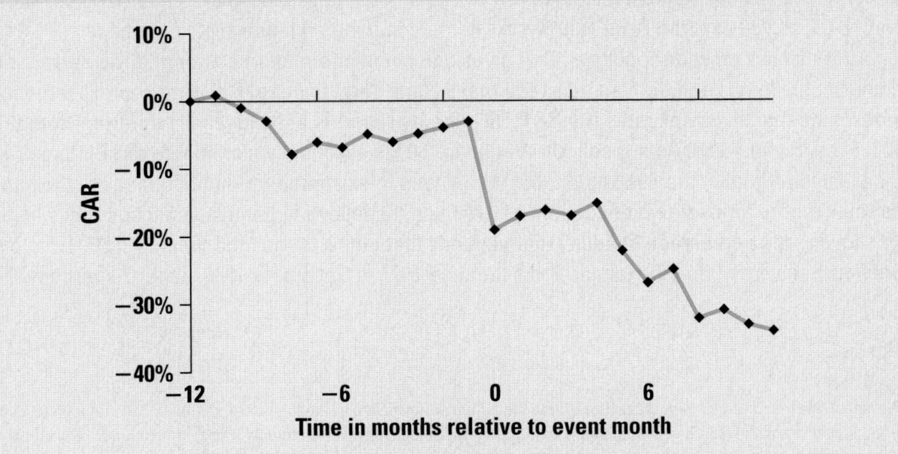

WHAT'S ON THE WEB?

1. **Cumulative Abnormal Returns** On February 28, 2005, Elan (ELN) and Biogen Idec (BIIB) suspended sales and clinical trials of their multiple sclerosis drug Tysabri because of a patient fatality. The decision to pull the drug was based on the fatality, and one other suspected case of a rare and often fatal disease of the central nervous system. According to the companies, both patients had received more than two years of Tysabri therapy plus the Biogen drug Avonex. Go to finance.yahoo.com and find the historical stock prices for each company 15 days before and 15 days after February 28, 2005. Construct the cumulative abnormal return for each company compared to the S&P 500 Index. Did each company's stock fall by the same percentage? How can you explain this? What does the trading volume look like for each stock over this same period?

CLOSING CASE

YOUR 401(K) ACCOUNT AT EAST COAST YACHTS

You have been at your job for East Coast Yachts for a week now and have decided you need to sign up for the company's 401(k) plan. Even after your discussion with Sarah Brown, the Bledsoe Financial Services representative, you are still unsure as to which investment option you should choose. Recall that the options available to you are stock in East Coast Yachts, the Bledsoe S&P 500 Index Fund, the Bledsoe Small-Cap Fund, the Bledsoe Large-Company Stock Fund, the Bledsoe Bond Fund, and the Bledsoe Money Market Fund. You have decided that you should invest in a diversified portfolio, with 70 percent of your investment in equity, 25 percent in bonds, and 5 percent in the money market fund. You have also decided to focus your equity investment on large-cap stocks, but you are debating whether to select the S&P 500 Index Fund or the Large-Company Stock Fund.

In thinking it over, you understand the basic difference in the two funds. One is a purely passive fund that replicates a widely followed large-cap index, the S&P 500, and has low fees. The other is actively managed with the intention that the skill of the portfolio manager will result in improved performance relative to an index. Fees are higher in the latter fund. You're just not certain on which way to go, so you ask Dan Ervin, who works in the company's finance area, for advice.

After discussing your concerns, Dan gives you some information comparing the performance of equity mutual funds and the Vanguard 500 Index Fund. The Vanguard 500 is the world's largest equity index mutual fund. It replicates the S&P 500, and its return is only negligibly different from the S&P 500. Fees are very low. As a result, the Vanguard 500 is essentially identical to the Bledsoe S&P 500 Index Fund offered in the 401(k) plan, but it has been in existence for much longer, so you can study its track record for over two decades. The graph on the following page summarizes Dan's comments by showing the percentage of equity mutual funds that outperformed the Vanguard 500 Fund over the previous ten years.[1] So for example, from January 1977 to December 1986, about 70 percent of equity

[1]Note that this graph is not hypothetical; it reflects the actual performance of the Vanguard 500 Index Fund relative to a very large population of diversified equity mutual funds. Specialty funds, such as international funds, are excluded. All returns are net of management fees, but do not include sales charges (which are known as "loads"), if any. As a result, the performance of actively managed funds is overstated.

mutual funds outperformed the Vanguard 500. Dan suggests that you study the graph and answer the following questions:

1. What implications do you draw from the graph for mutual fund investors?
2. Is the graph consistent or inconsistent with market efficiency? Explain carefully.
3. What investment decision would you make for the equity portion of your 401(k) account? Why?

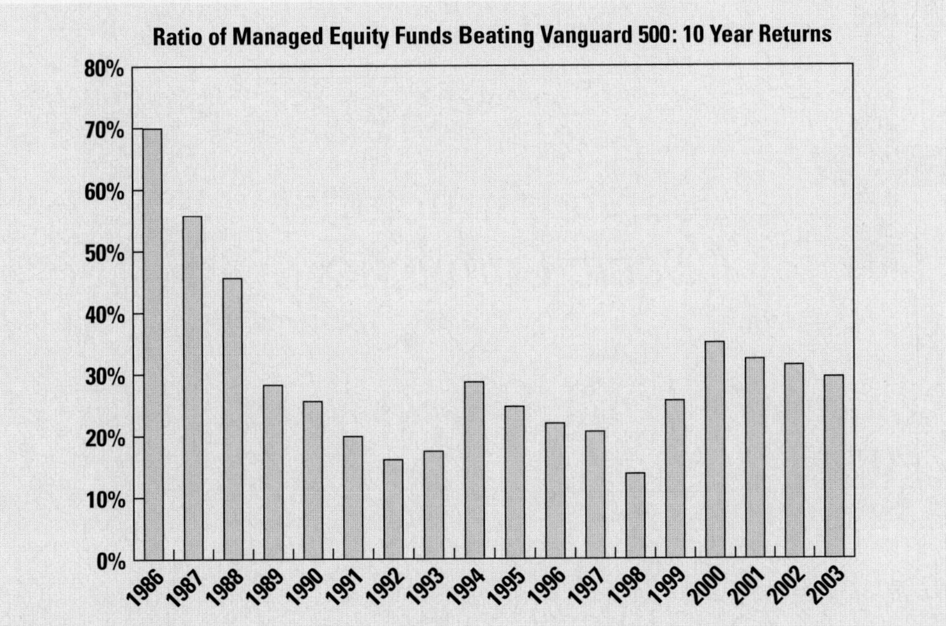

Source: Author calculations using data from the Center for Research in Security Prices (CRSP) Survivor Bias-Free U.S. Mutual Fund Database.

14 CHAPTER

Capital Structure: *Basic Concepts*

OPENING CASE

What do HCA, Inc., Limited Brands, and Pacific Gas and Electric have in common? In 2004, all three companies issued debt and used at least a part of the proceeds to buy back some of their own stock. HCA, the Nashville-based hospital operator, repurchased $2.5 billion of its stock, which amounted to about 13 percent of the company's outstanding stock. To pay for the repurchase, the company issued new bonds. This transaction essentially meant that the company was swapping debt for equity. Rating agencies looked unkindly on the action. Standard & Poor's and Fitch Ratings both downgraded the company's debt to junk status. In the same year, Limited Brands, the apparel company, borrowed 50 percent of the $2 billion in stock it planned to repurchase. Pacific Gas and Electric issued $1.9 billion in debt, with $975 million of the proceeds earmarked for a stock repurchase. Why did these companies decide to swap debt for equity? We will explore this question and other issues in this chapter.

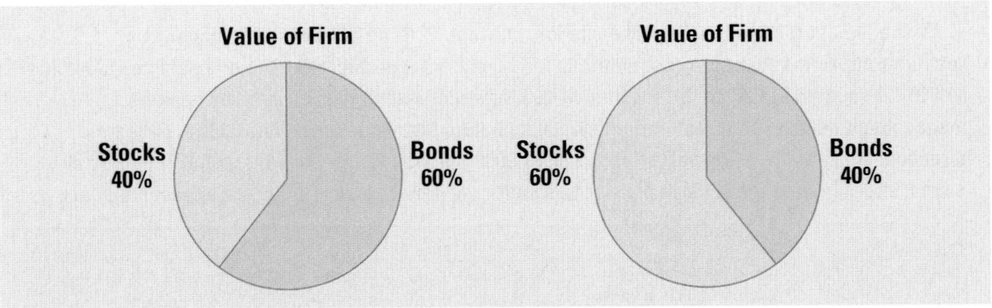

FIGURE 14.1
Two Pie Models of Capital Structure

14.1 THE CAPITAL STRUCTURE QUESTION AND THE PIE THEORY

How should a firm choose its debt-equity ratio? We call our approach to the capital structure question the **pie model**. If you are wondering why we chose this name, just take a look at Figure 14.1. The pie in question is the sum of the financial claims of the firm, debt and equity in this case. We *define* the value of the firm to be this sum. Hence, the value of the firm, V, is

$$V \equiv B + S \qquad (14.1)$$

where B is the market value of the debt and S is the market value of the equity. Figure 14.1 presents two possible ways of slicing this pie between stock and debt: 40 percent–60 percent and 60 percent–40 percent. If the goal of the management of the firm is to make the firm as valuable as possible, then the firm should pick the debt-equity ratio that makes the pie–the total value–as big as possible.

This discussion begs two important questions:

1. Why should the stockholders in the firm care about maximizing the value of the entire firm? After all, the value of the firm is, by definition, the sum of both the debt and the equity. Instead, why should the stockholders not prefer the strategy that maximizes their interests only?
2. What is the ratio of debt to equity that maximizes the shareholders' interests?

Let us examine each of the two questions in turn.

14.2 MAXIMIZING FIRM VALUE VERSUS MAXIMIZING STOCKHOLDER INTERESTS

The following example illustrates that the capital structure that maximizes the value of the firm is the one that financial managers should choose for the shareholders.

EXAMPLE 14.1 Debt and Firm Value

Suppose the market value of the J. J. Sprint Company is $1,000. The company currently has no debt, and each of J. J. Sprint's 100 shares of stock sells for $10. A company such as J. J. Sprint with no debt is called an *unlevered* company. Further suppose that J. J. Sprint plans to borrow $500 and pay the $500 proceeds to shareholders as an extra cash dividend of $5 per share. After the issuance of debt, the firm becomes *levered*. The investments of the firm will not change as a result of this transaction. What will the value of the firm be after the proposed restructuring?

(*continued*)

Management recognizes that, by definition, only one of three outcomes can occur from restructuring. Firm value after restructuring can be either (1) greater than the original firm value of $1,000, (2) equal to $1,000, or (3) less than $1,000. After consulting with investment bankers, management believes that restructuring will not change firm value more than $250 in either direction. Thus, it views firm values of $1,250, $1,000, and $750 as the relevant range. The original capital structure and these three possibilities under the new capital structure are presented next.

	NO DEBT (ORIGINAL CAPITAL STRUCTURE)	Value of Debt plus Equity after Payment of Dividend (three possibilities)		
		I	II	III
Debt	$ 0	$ 500	$ 500	$500
Equity	1,000	750	500	250
Firm value	$1,000	$1,250	$1,000	$750

Note that the value of equity is below $1,000 under any of the three possibilities. This can be explained in one of two ways. First, the table shows the value of the equity *after* the extra cash dividend is paid. Since cash is paid out, a dividend represents a partial liquidation of the firm. Consequently, there is less value in the firm for the equityholders after the dividend payment. Second, in the event of a future liquidation, stockholders will be paid only after bondholders have been paid in full. Thus, the debt is an encumbrance of the firm, reducing the value of the equity.

Of course, management recognizes that there are infinite possible outcomes. The above three are to be viewed as *representative* outcomes only. We can now determine the payoff to stockholders under the three possibilities.

	Payoff to Shareholders after Restructuring		
	I	II	III
Capital gains	−$250	−$500	−$750
Dividends	500	500	500
Net gain or loss to stockholders	$250	$ 0	−$250

No one can be sure ahead of time which of the three outcomes will occur. However, imagine that managers believe that outcome *I* is most likely. They should definitely restructure the firm because the stockholders would gain $250. That is, although the price of the stock declines by $250 to $750, they receive $500 in dividends. Their net gain is $250 = −$250 + $500. Also, notice that the value of the firm would rise by $250 = $1,250 − $1,000.

Alternatively, imagine that managers believe that outcome *III* is most likely. In this case, they should not restructure the firm because the stockholders would expect a $250 loss. That is, the stock falls by $750 to $250 and they receive $500 in dividends. Their net loss is −$250 = −$750 + $500. Also, notice that the value of the firm would change by −$250 = $750 − $1,000.

Finally, imagine that the managers believe that outcome *II* is most likely. Restructuring would not affect the stockholders' interest because the net gain to stockholders in this case is zero. Also, notice that the value of the firm is unchanged if outcome *II* occurs.

This example explains why managers should attempt to maximize the value of the firm. In other words, it answers question (1) in Section 14.1. We find in this example that:

Changes in capital structure benefit the stockholders *if and only if* the value of the firm increases.

	CURRENT	PROPOSED
Assets	$8,000	$8,000
Debt	$ 0	$4,000
Equity (market and book)	$8,000	$4,000
Interest rate	10%	10%
Market value/share	$ 20	$ 20
Shares outstanding	400	200

The proposed capital structure has leverage, whereas the current structure is all equity.

TABLE 14.1
Financial Structure of Trans Am Corporation

	RECESSION	EXPECTED	EXPANSION
Return on assets (ROA)	5%	15%	25%
Earnings	$ 400	$1,200	$2,000
Return on equity (ROE) = Earnings/Equity	5%	15%	25%
Earnings per share (EPS)	$1.00	$ 3.00	$ 5.00

TABLE 14.2
Trans Am's Current Capital Structure: No Debt

Conversely, these changes hurt the stockholders if and only if the value of the firm decreases. This result holds true for capital structure changes of many different types.[1] As a corollary, we can say:

Managers should choose the capital structure that they believe will have the highest firm value, because this capital structure will be most beneficial to the firm's stockholders.

Note however that this example does not tell us which of the three outcomes is most likely to occur. Thus, it does not tell us whether debt should be added to J. J. Sprint's capital structure. In other words, it does not answer question (2) in Section 14.1. This second question is treated in the next section.

14.3 FINANCIAL LEVERAGE AND FIRM VALUE: AN EXAMPLE

Leverage and Returns to Shareholders

The previous section shows that the capital structure producing the highest firm value is the one that maximizes shareholder wealth. In this section, we wish to determine that optimal capital structure. We begin by illustrating the effect of capital structure on returns to stockholders. We will use a detailed example which we encourage students to study carefully. Once we have this example under our belts, we will be ready to determine the optimal capital structure.

Trans Am Corporation currently has no debt in its capital structure. The firm is considering issuing debt to buy back some of its equity. Both its current and proposed capital structures are presented in Table 14.1. The firm's assets are $8,000. There are 400 shares of the all-equity firm, implying a market value per share of $20. The proposed debt issue is for $4,000, leaving $4,000 in equity. The interest rate is 10 percent.

The effect of economic conditions on earnings per share is shown in Table 14.2 for the current capital structure (all-equity). Consider first the middle column where earnings are *expected* to be $1,200. Since assets are $8,000, the return on assets (ROA) is 15 percent (= $1,200/$8,000). Because assets equal equity for this all-equity firm, return on equity

[1]This result may not hold exactly in a more complex case where debt has a significant possibility of default. Issues of default are treated in the next chapter.

TABLE 14.3
Trans Am's Proposed Capital Structure: Debt = $4,000

	RECESSION	EXPECTED	EXPANSION
Return on assets (ROA)	5%	15%	25%
Earnings before interest (EBI)	$400	$1,200	$2,000
Interest	− 400	− 400	− 400
Earnings after interest	$ 0	$ 800	$1,600
Return on equity (ROE) = Earnings after interest/Equity	0	20%	40%
Earnings per share (EPS)	0	$4.00	$8.00

FIGURE 14.2
Financial Leverage: EPS and EBI for the Trans Am Corporation

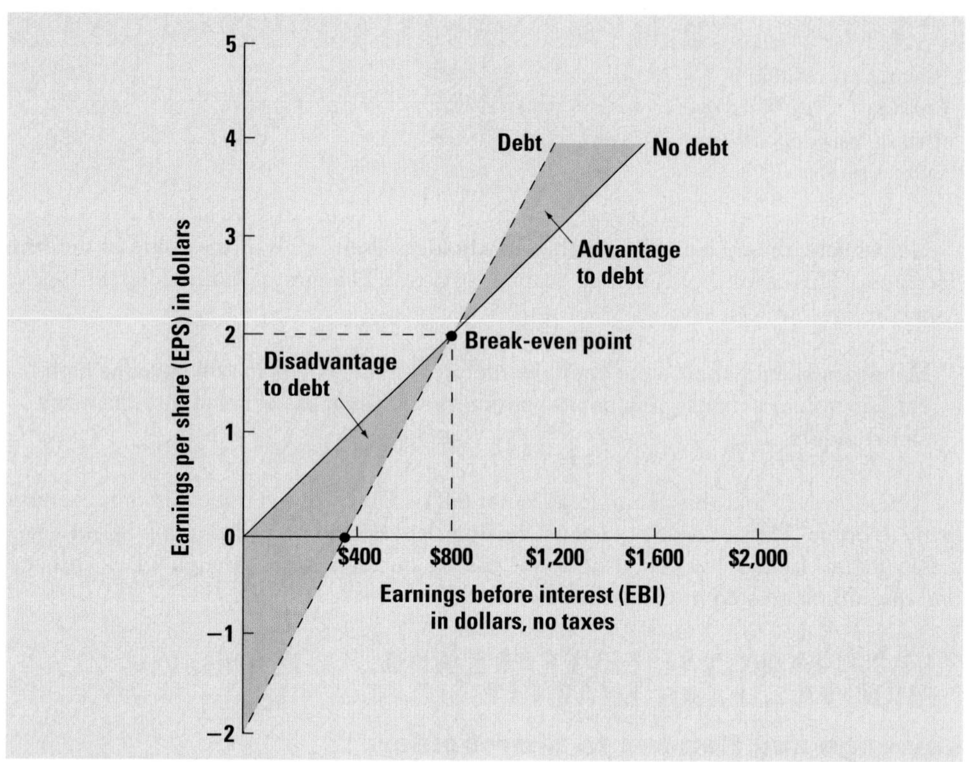

(ROE) is also 15 percent. Earnings per share (EPS) is $3.00 (= $1,200/400). Similar calculations yield EPS of $1.00 and $5.00 in the cases of recession and expansion, respectively.

The case of leverage is presented in Table 14.3. ROA in the three economic states is identical in Tables 14.2 and 14.3, because this ratio is calculated before interest is considered. Since debt is $4,000 here, interest is $400 (= .10 × $4,000). Thus, earnings after interest is $800 (= $1,200 − $400) in the middle (expected) case. Since equity is $4,000, ROE is 20 percent ($800/$4,000). Earnings per share is $4.00 (= $800/200). Similar calculations yield earnings of $0 and $8.00 for recession and expansion, respectively.

Tables 14.2 and 14.3 show that the effect of financial leverage depends on the company's earnings before interest. If earnings before interest is equal to $1,200, the return on equity (ROE) is higher under the proposed structure. If earnings before interest is equal to $400, the ROE is higher under the current structure.

This idea is represented in Figure 14.2. The solid line represents the case of no leverage. The line begins at the origin, indicating that earnings per share (EPS) would be zero if earnings before interest (EBI) were zero. The EPS rises in tandem with a rise in EBI.

The dotted line represents the case of $4,000 of debt. Here, EPS is negative if EBI is zero. This follows because $400 of interest must be paid regardless of the firm's profits.

Now consider the slopes of the two lines. The slope of the dotted line (the line with debt) is higher than the slope of the solid line. This occurs because the levered firm has *fewer* shares of stock outstanding than the unlevered firm. Therefore, any increase in EBI leads to a greater rise in EPS for the levered firm because the earnings increase is distributed over fewer shares of stock.

Because the dotted line has a lower intercept but a higher slope, the two lines must intersect. The *break-even* point occurs at $800 of EBI. Were earnings before interest to be $800, both firms would produce $2 of earnings per share (EPS). Because $800 is breakeven, earnings above $800 lead to greater EPS for the levered firm. Earnings below $800 lead to greater EPS for the unlevered firm.

The Choice between Debt and Equity

Tables 14.2 and 14.3 and Figure 14.2 are important because they show the effect of leverage on earnings per share. Students should study the tables and figure until they feel comfortable with the calculation of each number in them. However, we have not yet presented the punch line. That is, we have not yet stated which capital structure is better for Trans Am.

At this point, many students believe that leverage is beneficial, because EPS is expected to be $4.00 with leverage and only $3.00 without leverage. However, leverage also creates *risk*. Note that in a recession, EPS is higher ($1.00 versus $0) for the unlevered firm. Thus, a risk-averse investor might prefer the all-equity firm, while a risk-neutral (or less risk-averse) investor might prefer leverage. Given this ambiguity, which capital structure *is* better?

Modigliani and Miller (MM or M & M) have a convincing argument that a firm cannot change the total value of its outstanding securities by changing the proportions of its capital structure. In other words, the value of the firm is always the same under different capital structures. In *still* other words, no capital structure is any better or worse than any other capital structure for the firm's stockholders. This rather pessimistic result is the famous **MM Proposition I**.[2]

Their argument compares a simple strategy, which we call Strategy *A*, with a two-part strategy, which we call Strategy *B*. Both of these strategies for shareholders of Trans Am are illuminated in Table 14.4. Let us now examine the first strategy.

Strategy A–Buy 100 shares of the levered equity.

The first line in the top panel of Table 14.4 shows EPS for the proposed levered equity in the three economic states. The second line shows the earnings in the three states for an individual buying 100 shares. The next line shows that the cost of these 100 shares is $2,000.

Let us now consider the second strategy, which has two parts to it.

Strategy B:

1. Borrow $2,000 from either a bank or, more likely, a brokerage house. (If the brokerage house is the lender, we say that this activity is *going on margin.*)
2. Use the borrowed proceeds plus your own investment of $2,000 (a total of $4,000) to buy 200 shares of the current unlevered equity at $20 per share.

The bottom panel of Table 14.4 shows payoffs under Strategy *B*, which we call the *homemade leverage* strategy. First, observe the middle column, which indicates that 200 shares of the unlevered equity are *expected* to generate $600 of earnings. Assuming that the $2,000 is borrowed at a 10 percent interest rate, the interest expense is $200 (= .10 × $2,000). Thus, the net earnings are expected to be $400. A similar calculation generates net earnings of either $0 or $800 in recession or expansion, respectively.

[2]The original paper is F. Modigliani and M. Miller, "The Cost of Capital, Corporation Finance and the Theory of Investment," *American Economic Review* (June 1958).

TABLE 14.4

Payoff and Cost to Shareholders of Trans Am Corporation under the Proposed Structure and under the Current Structure with Homemade Leverage

	RECESSION	EXPECTED	EXPANSION
Strategy A: Buy 100 Shares of Levered Equity			
EPS of *levered* equity (taken from last line of Table 14.3)	$0	$ 4	$ 8
Earnings per 100 shares	0	400	800
Initial cost = 100 shares @ $20/share = $2,000			
Strategy B: Homemade Leverage			
Earnings per 200 shares in current *unlevered* Trans Am	$1 × 200 = 200	$3 × 200 = 600	$5 × 200 = 1,000
Interest at 10% on $2,000	−200	−200	−200
Net earnings	$ 0	$ 400	$ 800
Initial cost = 200 shares @ $20/share (Cost of stock) − $2,000 (Amount borrowed) = $2,000			

Investor receives the same payoff whether she (1) buys shares in a levered corporation or (2) buys shares in an unlevered firm and borrows on personal account. Her initial investment is the same in either case. Thus, the firm neither helps nor hurts her by adding debt to capital structure.

Now, let us compare these two strategies, both in terms of net earnings and in terms of initial cost. The top panel of the table shows that Strategy *A* generates earnings of $0, $400, and $800 in the three states. The bottom panel of the table shows that Strategy *B* generates the *same* net earnings in the three states.

The top panel of the table shows that Strategy *A* involves an initial cost of $2,000. Similarly, the bottom panel shows an *identical* net cost of $2,000 for Strategy *B*.

This shows a very important result. Both the cost and the payoff from the two strategies are the same. Thus, one must conclude that Trans Am is neither helping nor hurting its stockholders by restructuring. In other words, an investor is not receiving anything from corporate leverage that she could not receive on her own.

Note that, as shown in Table 14.1, the equity of the unlevered firm is valued at $8,000. Since the equity of the levered firm is $4,000 and its debt is $4,000, the value of the levered firm is also $8,000. Now suppose that, for whatever reason, the value of the levered firm were actually greater than the value of the unlevered firm. Here, Strategy *A* would cost more than Strategy *B*. In this case, an investor would prefer to borrow on his own account and invest in the stock of the unlevered firm. He would get the same net earnings each year as if he had invested in the stock of the levered firm. However, his cost would be less. The strategy would not be unique to our investor. Given the higher value of the levered firm, no rational investor would invest in the stock of the levered firm. Anyone desiring shares in the levered firm would get the same dollar return more cheaply by borrowing to finance a purchase of the unlevered firm's shares. The equilibrium result would be, of course, that the value of the levered firm would fall, and the value of the unlevered firm would rise until they became equal. At this point, individuals would be indifferent between Strategy *A* and Strategy *B*.

This example illustrates the basic result of Modigliani-Miller (MM) and is, as we have noted, commonly called their Proposition I. We restate this proposition as:

MM Proposition I (no taxes): The value of the levered firm is the same as the value of the unlevered firm.

This is perhaps the most important result in all of corporate finance. In fact, it is generally considered the beginning point of modern managerial finance. Before MM, the effect of leverage on the value of the firm was considered complex and convoluted. Modigliani and Miller showed a blindingly simple result: If levered firms are priced too high, rational investors will simply borrow on their personal accounts to buy shares in unlevered firms. This substitution is oftentimes called *homemade leverage.* As long as individuals borrow (and lend) on the same terms as the firms, they can duplicate the effects of corporate leverage on their own.

The example of Trans Am Corporation shows that leverage does not affect the value of the firm. Since we showed earlier that stockholders' welfare is directly related to the firm's value, the example indicates that changes in capital structure cannot affect the stockholders' welfare.

A Key Assumption

The MM result hinges on the assumption that individuals can borrow as cheaply as corporations. If, alternatively, individuals can only borrow at a higher rate, one can easily show that corporations can increase firm value by borrowing.

Is this assumption of equal borrowing costs a good one? Individuals who want to buy stock and borrow can do so by establishing a margin account with the broker. Under this arrangement, the broker loans the individual a portion of the purchase price. For example, the individual might buy $10,000 of stock by investing $6,000 of her own funds and borrowing $4,000 from the broker. Should the stock be worth $9,000 on the next day, the individual's net worth or equity in the account would be $5,000 = $9,000 − $4,000.[3]

The broker fears that a sudden price drop will cause the equity in the individual's account to be negative, implying that the broker may not get her loan repaid in full. To guard against this possibility, stock exchange rules require that the individual make additional cash contributions (replenish her margin account) as the stock price falls. Because (1) the procedures for replenishing the account have developed over many years, and (2) the broker holds the stock as collateral, there is little default risk to the broker.[4] In particular, if margin contributions are not made on time, the broker can sell the stock in order to satisfy her loan. Therefore, brokers generally charge low interest, with many rates being only slightly above the risk-free rate.

By contrast, corporations frequently borrow using illiquid assets (e.g., plant and equipment) as collateral. The costs to the lender of initial negotiation and ongoing supervision, as well as of working out arrangements in the event of financial distress, can be quite substantial. Thus, it is difficult to argue that individuals must borrow at higher rates than corporations.

14.4 MODIGLIANI AND MILLER: PROPOSITION II (NO TAXES)

Risk to Equityholders Rises with Leverage

At a Trans Am corporate meeting, a corporate officer said, "Well, maybe it does not matter whether the corporation or the individual levers–as long as some leverage takes place. Leverage benefits investors. After all, an investor's expected return rises with the amount of the leverage present." He then pointed out that, as shown in Tables 14.2 and 14.3, the expected return on unlevered equity is 15 percent while the expected return on levered equity is 20 percent.

However, another officer replied, "Not necessarily. Though the expected return rises with leverage, the *risk* rises as well." This point can be seen from an examination of

[3]We are ignoring the one-day interest charge on the loan.

[4]Had this text been published before October 19, 1987, when stock prices declined by more than 20 percent in a single day, we might have used the phrase "virtually no" risk instead of "little" risk.

Tables 14.2 and 14.3. With earnings before interest (EBI) varying between \$400 and \$2,000, earnings per share (EPS) for the stockholders of the unlevered firm vary between \$1.00 and \$5.00. EPS for the stockholders of the levered firm vary between \$0 and \$8.00. This greater range for the EPS of the levered firm implies greater risk for the levered firm's stockholders. In other words, levered stockholders have better returns in good times than do unlevered stockholders but have worse returns in bad times. The two tables also show greater range for the ROE of the levered firm's stockholders. The above interpretation concerning risk applies here as well.

The same insight can be taken from Figure 14.2. The slope of the line for the levered firm is greater than the slope of the line for the unlevered firm. This means that the levered stockholders have better returns in good times than do unlevered stockholders but have worse returns in bad times, implying greater risk with leverage. In other words, the slope of the line measures the risk to stockholders, since the slope indicates the responsiveness of ROE to changes in firm performance (earnings before interest).

Proposition II: Required Return to Equityholders Rises with Leverage

Since levered equity has greater risk, it should have a greater expected return as compensation. In our example, the market *requires* only a 15 percent expected return for the unlevered equity, but it requires a 20 percent expected return for the levered equity.

This type of reasoning allows us to develop **MM Proposition II**. Here, MM argue that the expected return on equity is positively related to leverage, because the risk to equityholders increases with leverage.

To develop this position recall that the firm's weighted average cost of capital, R_{WACC}, can be written as:[5]

$$R_{WACC} = \frac{S}{B+S} \times R_S + \frac{B}{B+S} \times R_B \qquad (14.2)$$

where

R_B	**is the cost of debt**
R_S	**is the expected return on equity or stock, also called the *cost of equity* or the *required return on equity***
R_{WACC}	**is the firm's weighted average cost of capital**
B	**is the value of the firm's debt or bonds**
S	**is the value of the firm's stock or equity**

Formula (14.2) is quite intuitive. It simply says that a firm's weighted average cost of capital is a weighted average of its cost of debt and its cost of equity. The weight applied to debt is the proportion of debt in the capital structure, and the weight applied to equity is the proportion of equity in the capital structure. Calculations of R_{WACC} from formula (14.2) for both the unlevered and the levered firm are presented in Table 14.5.

An implication of MM Proposition I is that R_{WACC} is a constant for a given firm, regardless of the capital structure.[6] For example, Table 14.5 shows that R_{WACC} for Trans Am is 15 percent, with or without leverage.

Let us now define R_0 to be the *cost of capital for an all-equity firm*. For the Trans Am Corp., R_0 is calculated as:

$$R_0 = \frac{\textbf{Expected earnings to unlevered firm}}{\textbf{Unlevered equity}} = \frac{\$1{,}200}{\$8{,}000} = 15\%$$

[5]Since we do not have taxes here, the cost of debt is R_B, not $R_B(1 - t_C)$ as it was in Chapter 12.

[6]This statement holds in a world of no taxes. It does not hold in a world with taxes, a point to be brought out later in this chapter (see Figure 14.6).

	$R_{WACC} =$	$\frac{B}{B+S} \times R_B + \frac{S}{B+S} \times R_S$
Unlevered firm:	$15\% =$	$\frac{0}{\$8{,}000} \times 10\%^* + \frac{\$8{,}000}{\$8{,}000} \times 15\%^{\dagger}$
Levered firm:	$15\% =$	$\frac{\$4{,}000}{\$8{,}000} \times 10\%^* + \frac{\$4{,}000}{\$8{,}000} \times 20\%^{\ddagger}$

TABLE 14.5

Cost of Capital Calculations for Trans Am

*10% is the cost of debt.

†From the "Expected" column in Table 14.2, we learn that expected earnings after interest for the unlevered firm are $1,200. From Table 14.1, we learn that equity for the unlevered firm is $8,000. Thus, R_S for the unlevered firm is:

$$\frac{\text{Expected earnings after interest}}{\text{Equity}} = \frac{\$1{,}200}{\$8{,}000} = 15\%$$

‡From the "Expected" column in Table 14.3, we learn that expected earnings after interest for the levered firm are $800. From Table 14.1, we learn that equity for the levered firm is $4,000. Thus R_S for the levered firm is:

$$\frac{\text{Expected earnings after interest}}{\text{Equity}} = \frac{\$800}{\$4{,}000} = 20\%$$

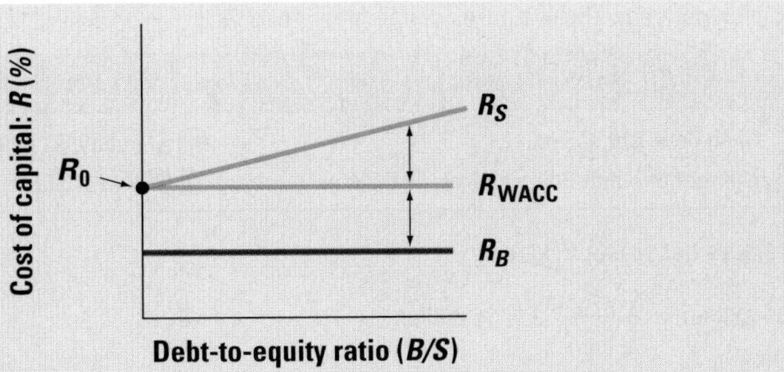

FIGURE 14.3

The Cost of Equity, the Cost of Debt, and the Weighted Average Cost of Capital: MM Proposition II with No Corporate Taxes

$R_S = R_0 + (R_0 - R_B)B/S$

R_S is the cost of equity

R_B is the cost of debt

R_0 is the cost of capital for an all-equity firm

R_{WACC} is a firm's weighted average cost of capital. In a world with no taxes, R_{WACC} for a levered firm is equal to R_0.

R_0 is a single point while R_S, R_B, and R_{WACC} are all entire lines.

The cost of equity capital, R_S, is positively related to the firm's debt-equity ratio. The firm's weighted average cost of capital, R_{WACC}, is invariant to the firm's debt-equity ratio.

As can be seen from Table 14.5, R_{WACC} is equal to R_0 for Trans Am. In fact, R_{WACC} must *always* equal R_0 in a world without corporate taxes.

Proposition II states the expected return of equity, R_S, in terms of leverage. The exact relationship, derived by setting $R_{WACC} = R_0$ and then rearranging formula (14.2), is:

MM Proposition II (no taxes):

$$R_S = R_0 + \frac{B}{S}(R_0 - R_B) \tag{14.3}$$

Equation (14.3) implies that the required return on equity is a linear function of the firm's debt-to-equity ratio. Examining equation (14.3), we see that if R_0 exceeds the debt rate, R_B, then the cost of equity rises with increases in the debt-equity ratio, B/S. Normally, R_0 should exceed R_B. That is, because even unlevered equity is risky, it should have an expected return greater than that of riskless debt. Note that equation (14.3) holds for Trans Am in its levered state:

$$.20 = .15 + \frac{\$4{,}000}{\$4{,}000}(.15 - .10)$$

Figure 14.3 graphs equation (14.3). As you can see, we have plotted the relation between the cost of equity, R_S, and the debt-equity ratio, B/S, as a straight line. What we witness in equation (14.3) and illustrate in Figure 14.3 is the effect of leverage on the cost of equity. As the firm raises the debt-equity ratio, each dollar of equity is levered with additional debt. This raises the risk of equity and therefore the required return, R_S, on the equity.

Figure 14.3 also shows that R_{WACC} is unaffected by leverage, a point we made above. (It is important for students to realize that R_0, the cost of capital for an all-equity firm, is represented by a single dot on the graph. By contrast, R_{WACC} is an entire line.)

EXAMPLE 14.2 MM Propositions I and II

Luteran Motors, an all-equity firm, has expected earnings of \$10 million per year in perpetuity. The firm pays all of its earnings out as dividends, so that the \$10 million may also be viewed as the stockholders' expected cash flow. There are 10 million shares outstanding, implying expected annual cash flow of \$1 per share. The cost of capital for this unlevered firm is 10 percent. In addition, the firm will soon build a new plant for \$4 million. The plant is expected to generate additional cash flow of \$1 million per year. These figures can be described as:

CURRENT COMPANY	NEW PLANT
Cash flow: \$10 million	Initial outlay: \$4 million
Number of outstanding shares: 10 million	Additional annual cash flow: \$1 million

The project's net present value is:

$$-\$4 \text{ million} + \frac{\$1 \text{ million}}{.1} = \$6 \text{ million}$$

assuming that the project is discounted at the same rate as the firm as a whole. Before the market knows of the project, the *market value* balance sheet of the firm is:

LUTERAN MOTORS Balance Sheet (all equity)			
Old assets:	$\frac{\$10 \text{ million}}{.1} = \$100 \text{ million}$	Equity:	\$100 million (10 million shares of stock)

The value of the firm is \$100 million, because the cash flow of \$10 million per year is capitalized (discounted) at 10 percent. A share of stock sells for \$10 (\$100 million/10 million) because there are 10 million shares outstanding.

The market value balance sheet is a useful tool of financial analysis. Because students are often thrown off guard by it initially, we recommend extra study here. The key is that the market value balance sheet has the same form as the balance sheet that accountants use. That is, assets are placed on the left-hand side whereas liabilities and owners' equity are placed on the right-hand side. In addition, the left-hand side and the right-hand side must be equal. The difference between a market value balance sheet and the accountant's balance sheet is in the numbers. Accountants value items in terms of historical cost (original purchase price less depreciation), whereas financial analysts value items in terms of market value.

The firm will either issue \$4 million of equity or debt. Let us consider the effect of equity and debt financing in turn.

Stock Financing Imagine that the firm announces that in the near future, it will raise \$4 million in equity in order to build a new plant. The stock price, and therefore the value of the firm, will rise to reflect the positive net present value of the plant. According to efficient markets, the increase occurs immediately. That is, the rise occurs on the day of the announcement, not on the date of either the onset of construction of the power plant or the forthcoming stock offering. The market value balance sheet becomes:

(*continued*)

LUTERAN MOTORS Balance Sheet (upon announcement of equity issue to construct plant)			
Old assets	\$100 million	Equity	\$106 million (10 million shares of stock)
NPV of plant:			
$-4 \text{ million} + \dfrac{\$1 \text{ million}}{.1} =$	6 million		
Total assets	\$106 million		

Note that the NPV of the plant is included in the market value balance sheet. Because the new shares have not yet been issued, the number of outstanding shares remains 10 million. The price per share has now risen to \$10.60 (\$106 million/10 million) to reflect news concerning the plant.

Shortly thereafter, \$4 million of stock is issued or *floated.* Because the stock is selling at \$10.60 per share, 377,358 (\$4 million/\$10.60) shares of stock are issued. Imagine that funds are put in the bank *temporarily* before being used to build the plant. The market value balance sheet becomes:

LUTERAN MOTORS Balance Sheet (upon issuance of stock but before construction begins on plant)			
Old assets	\$100 million	Equity	\$110 million (10,377,358 shares of stock)
NPV of plant	6 million		
Proceeds from new issue of stock (currently placed in bank)	4 million		
Total assets	\$110 million		

The number of shares outstanding is now 10,377,358 because 377,358 new shares were issued. The price per share is \$10.60 (\$110,000,000/10,377,358). Note that the price has not changed. This is consistent with efficient capital markets, because the stock price should only move due to new information.

Of course, the funds are placed in the bank only temporarily. Shortly after the new issue, the \$4 million is given to a contractor who builds the plant. To avoid problems in discounting, we assume that the plant is built immediately. The balance sheet then becomes:

LUTERAN MOTORS Balance Sheet (upon completion of the plant)			
Old assets	\$100 million	Equity	\$110 million (10,377,358 shares of stock)
PV of plant: $\dfrac{\$1 \text{ million}}{.1} =$	10 million		
Total assets	\$110 million		

Though total assets do not change, the composition of the assets does change. The bank account has been emptied to pay the contractor. The present value of cash flows of \$1 million a year from the plant is reflected as an asset worth \$10 million. Because the building expenditures of \$4 million have already been paid, they no longer represent a future cost. Hence, they no longer reduce the value of the plant. According to efficient capital markets, the price per share of stock remains \$10.60.

Expected yearly cash flow from the firm is \$11 million, \$10 million of which comes from the old assets and \$1 million from the new. The expected return to equityholders is:

$$R_S = \frac{\$11 \text{ million}}{\$110 \text{ million}} = .10$$

Because the firm is all equity, $R_S = R_0 = .10$.

(continued)

Debt Financing Alternatively, imagine the firm announces that, in the near future, it will borrow \$4 million at 6 percent to build a new plant. This implies yearly interest payments of \$240,000 (\$4,000,000 × 6%). Again, the stock price rises immediately to reflect the positive net present value of the plant. Thus, we have:

LUTERAN MOTORS Balance Sheet (upon announcement of debt issue to construct plant)			
Old assets	\$100 million	Equity	\$106 million (10 million shares of stock)
NPV of plant: $-\$4 \text{ million} + \dfrac{\$1 \text{ million}}{.1} =$	6 million		
Total assets	\$106 million		

The value of the firm is the same as in the equity financing case because (1) the same plant is to be built and (2) MM proved that debt financing is neither better nor worse than equity financing.

At some point, \$4 million of debt is issued. As before, the funds are placed in the bank temporarily. The market value balance sheet becomes:

LUTERAN MOTORS Balance Sheet (upon debt issuance but before construction begins on plant)			
Old assets	\$100 million	Debt	\$ 4 million
NPV of plant	6 million	Equity	106 million (10 million shares of stock)
Proceeds from debt issue (currently invested in bank)	4 million		
Total assets	\$110 million	Debt plus equity	\$110 million

Note that debt appears on the right-hand side of the balance sheet. The stock price is still \$10.60, in accordance with our discussion of efficient capital markets.

Finally, the contractor receives \$4 million and builds the plant. The market value balance sheet becomes:

LUTERAN MOTORS Balance Sheet (upon completion of the plant)			
Old assets	\$100 million	Debt	\$ 4 million
PV of plant	10 million	Equity	106 million (10 million shares of stock)
Total assets	\$110 million	Debt plus equity	\$110 million

The only change here is that the bank account has been depleted to pay the contractor. The equityholders expect yearly cash flow after interest of:

\$10,000,000	+	\$1,000,000	−	\$240,000	=	\$10,760,000
Cash flow on old assets		Cash flow on new assets		Interest: \$4 million × 6%		

The equityholders expect to earn a return of:

$$\frac{\$10{,}760{,}000}{\$106{,}000{,}000} = 10.15\%$$

(continued)

This return of 10.15 percent for levered equityholders is higher than the 10 percent return for the unlevered equityholders. This result is sensible because, as we argued earlier, levered equity is riskier. In fact, the return of 10.15 percent should be exactly what MM Proposition II predicts. This prediction can be verified by plugging values into:

$$R_S = R_0 + \frac{B}{S} \times (R_0 - R_B) \tag{14.3}$$

We obtain:

$$10.15\% = 10\% + \frac{\$4{,}000{,}000}{\$106{,}000{,}000} \times (10\% - 6\%)$$

This example was useful for two reasons. First, we wanted to introduce the concept of market value balance sheets, a tool that will prove useful elsewhere in the text. Among other things, this technique allows one to calculate the price per share of a new issue of stock. Second, the example illustrates three aspects of Modigliani and Miller:

1. The example is consistent with MM Proposition I because the value of the firm is $110 million after either equity or debt financing.
2. Students are often more interested in stock price than in firm value. We show that the stock price is always $10.60, regardless of whether debt or equity financing is used.
3. The example is consistent with MM Proposition II. The expected return to equityholders rises from 10 to 10.15 percent, just as formula (14.3) states. This rise occurs because the equityholders of a levered firm face more risk than do the equityholders of an unlevered firm.

MM: An Interpretation

The Modigliani-Miller results indicate that managers cannot change the value of a firm by repackaging the firm's securities. Though this idea was considered revolutionary when it was originally proposed in the late 1950s, the MM approach and proof have since met with wide acclaim.[7]

MM argue that the firm's overall cost of capital cannot be reduced as debt is substituted for equity, even though debt appears to be cheaper than equity. The reason for this is that as the firm adds debt, the remaining equity becomes more risky. As this risk rises, the cost of equity capital rises as a result. The increase in the cost of the remaining equity capital offsets the higher proportion of the firm financed by low-cost debt. In fact, MM prove that the two effects exactly offset each other, so that both the value of the firm and the firm's overall cost of capital are invariant to leverage.

MM use an interesting analogy to food. They consider a dairy farmer with two choices. On the one hand, he can sell whole milk. On the other hand, by skimming, he can sell a combination of cream and low-fat milk. Though the farmer can get a high price for the cream, he gets a low price for the low-fat milk, implying no net gain. In fact, imagine that the proceeds from the whole-milk strategy were less than those from the cream–low-fat milk strategy. Arbitrageurs would buy the whole milk, perform the skimming operation themselves, and resell the cream and low-fat milk separately. Competition between arbitrageurs would tend to boost the price of whole milk until proceeds from the two strategies became equal. Thus, the value of the farmer's milk is invariant to the way in which the milk is packaged.

Food found its way into this chapter earlier, when we viewed the firm as a pie. MM argue that the size of the pie does not change, no matter how stockholders and bondholders divide it. MM say that a firm's capital structure is irrelevant; it is what it is by some historical accident. The theory implies that firms' debt-equity ratios could be

[7]Both Merton Miller and Franco Modigliani were awarded separate Nobel Prizes, in part for their work on capital structure.

SUMMARY OF MODIGLIANI-MILLER PROPOSITIONS WITHOUT TAXES

Assumptions

- No taxes
- No transaction costs
- Individuals and corporations borrow at same rate

Results

Proposition I: $V_L = V_U$ (Value of levered firm equals value of unlevered firm)

Proposition II: $R_S = R_0 + \frac{B}{S}(R_0 - R_B)$

Intuition

Proposition I: Through homemade leverage, individuals can either duplicate or undo the effects of corporate leverage.

Proposition II: The cost of equity rises with leverage, because the risk to equity rises with leverage.

anything. They are what they are because of whimsical and random managerial decisions about how much to borrow and how much stock to issue.

Although scholars are always fascinated with far-reaching theories, students are perhaps more concerned with real world applications. Do real world managers follow MM by treating capital structure decisions with indifference? Unfortunately for the theory, virtually all companies in certain industries, such as banking, choose high debt-to-equity ratios. Conversely, companies in other industries, such as pharmaceuticals, choose low debt-to-equity ratios. In fact, almost any industry has a debt-to-equity ratio to which companies in that industry tend to adhere. Thus, companies do not appear to be selecting their degree of leverage in a frivolous or random manner. Because of this, financial economists (including MM themselves) have argued that real world factors may have been left out of the theory.

Though many of our students have argued that individuals can only borrow at rates above the corporate borrowing rate, we disagreed with this argument earlier in the chapter. But when we look elsewhere for unrealistic assumptions in the theory, we find two:[8]

1. Taxes were ignored.
2. Bankruptcy costs and other agency costs were not considered.

We turn to taxes in the next section. Bankruptcy costs and other agency costs will be treated in the next chapter. A summary of the main Modigliani-Miller results without taxes is presented in the nearby boxed section.

14.5 TAXES

The Basic Insight

The previous part of this chapter showed that firm value is unrelated to debt in a world without taxes. We now show that, in the presence of corporate taxes, the firm's value is positively related to its debt. The basic intuition can be seen from a pie chart, such as the one in Figure 14.4. Consider the all-equity firm on the left. Here, both equityholders and the IRS have claims on the firm. The value of the all-equity firm is, of course, that part of the pie owned by the equityholders. The proportion going to taxes is simply a cost.

[8]MM were aware of both of these issues, as can be seen in their original paper.

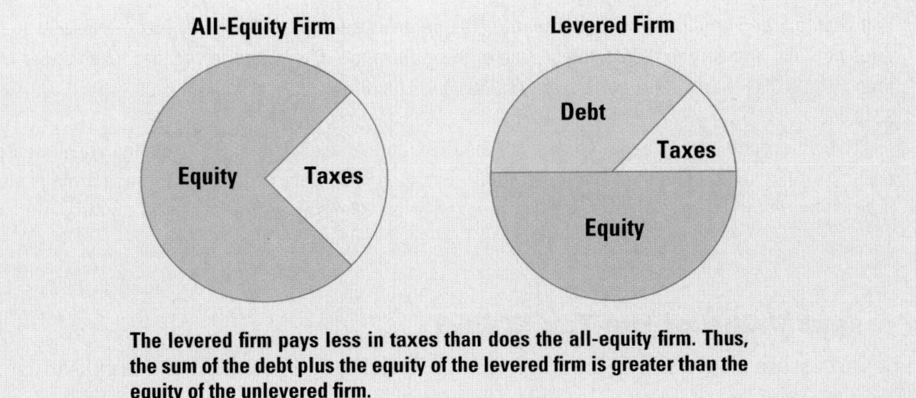

FIGURE 14.4
Two Pie Models of Capital Structure under Corporate Taxes

The pie on the right for the levered firm shows three claims: equityholders, debtholders, and taxes. The value of the levered firm is the sum of the value of the debt and the value of the equity. In selecting between the two capital structures in the picture, a financial manager should select the one with the higher value. Assuming that the total area is the same for both pies,[9] value is maximized for the capital structure paying the least in taxes. In other words, the manager should choose the capital structure that the IRS hates the most.

We will show that due to a quirk in U.S. tax law, the proportion of the pie allocated to taxes is less for the levered firm than it is for the unlevered firm. Thus, managers should select high leverage.

EXAMPLE 14.3 Taxes and Cash Flow

The Water Products Company has a corporate tax rate, t_C, of 35 percent and expected earnings before interest and taxes (EBIT) of $1 million each year. Its entire earnings after taxes are paid out as dividends.

The firm is considering two alternative capital structures. Under plan *I*, Water Products would have no debt in its capital structure. Under plan *II*, the company would have $4,000,000 of debt, *B*. The cost of debt, R_B, is 10 percent.

The chief financial officer for Water Products makes the following calculations:

	PLAN *I*	PLAN *II*
Earnings before interest and corporate taxes (EBIT)	$1,000,000	$1,000,000
Interest (R_BB)	0	400,000
Earnings before taxes (EBT) = (EBIT − R_BB)	1,000,000	600,000
Taxes (t_C = .35)	350,000	210,000
Earnings after corporate taxes (EAT) = [(EBIT − R_BB) × (1 − t_C)]	650,000	390,000
Total cash flow to both stockholders and bondholders [EBIT × (1 − t_C) + t_CR_BB]	$ 650,000	$ 790,000

The most relevant numbers for our purposes are the two on the bottom line. Dividends, which are equal to earnings after taxes in this example, are the cash flow to stockholders, and interest is the cash flow to bondholders. Here, we see that more cash flow reaches the owners of the firm (both

(*continued*)

[9]Under the MM propositions developed earlier, the two pies should be of the same size.

stockholders and bondholders) under plan *II*. The difference is $140,000 = $790,000 − $650,000. It does not take one long to realize the source of this difference. The IRS receives less taxes under plan *II* ($210,000) than it does under plan *I* ($350,000). The difference here is $140,000 = $350,000 − $210,000.

This difference occurs because the way the IRS treats interest is different from the way it treats earnings going to stockholders.[10] Interest totally escapes corporate taxation, whereas earnings after interest but before corporate taxes (EBT) are taxed at the 35 percent rate.

Present Value of the Tax Shield

The discussion above shows a tax advantage to debt or, equivalently, a tax disadvantage to equity. We now want to value this advantage. The dollar interest is:

$$\text{Interest} = \underbrace{R_B}_{\text{Interest rate}} \times \underbrace{B}_{\text{Amount borrowed}}$$

This interest is $400,000 (10 percent × $4,000,000) for Water Products. All this interest is tax deductible. That is, whatever the taxable income of Water Products would have been without the debt, the taxable income is now $400,000 *less* with the debt.

Because the corporate tax rate is .35 in our example, the reduction in corporate taxes is $140,000 (.35 × $400,000). This number is identical to the reduction in corporate taxes calculated previously.

Algebraically, the reduction in corporate taxes is:

$$\underbrace{t_C}_{\text{Corporate tax rate}} \times \underbrace{R_B \times B}_{\text{Dollar amount of interest}} \tag{14.4}$$

That is, whatever the taxes that a firm would pay each year without debt, the firm will pay $t_C R_B B$ less with the debt of B. Expression (14.4) is often called the *tax shield from debt*. Note that it is an *annual* amount.

As long as the firm expects to be in a positive tax bracket, we can assume that the cash flow in expression (14.4) has the same risk as the interest on the debt. Thus, its value can be determined by discounting at the cost of debt, R_B. Assuming that the cash flows are perpetual, the present value of the tax shield is:

$$\frac{t_C R_B B}{R_B} = t_C B$$

Value of the Levered Firm

We have just calculated the present value of the tax shield from debt. Our next step is to calculate the value of the levered firm. The annual aftertax cash flow of an unlevered firm is:

$$\text{EBIT} \times (1 - t_C)$$

where EBIT is earnings before interest and taxes. The value of an unlevered firm (that is, a firm with no debt) is the present value of EBIT × $(1 - t_C)$:

$$V_U = \frac{\text{EBIT} \times (1 - t_C)}{R_0}$$

[10]Note that stockholders actually receive more under plan *I* ($650,000) than under plan *II* ($390,000). Students are often bothered by this since it seems to imply that stockholders are better off without leverage. However, remember that there are more shares outstanding in plan *I* than in plan *II*. A full-blown model would show that earnings *per share* are higher with leverage.

where:

$$V_U = \text{Present value of an unlevered firm}$$
$$\text{EBIT} \times (1 - t_C) = \text{Firm cash flows after corporate taxes}$$
$$t_C = \text{Corporate tax rate}$$

R_0 = **The cost of capital to an all-equity firm. As can be seen from the formula, R_0 now discounts *aftertax* cash flows.**

As shown previously, leverage increases the value of the firm by the tax shield, which is $t_C B$ for perpetual debt. Thus, we merely add this tax shield to the value of the unlevered firm to get the value of the levered firm.

We can write this algebraically as:

MM Proposition I (corporate taxes):

$$V_L = \frac{\text{EBIT} \times (1 - t_C)}{R_0} + \frac{t_C R_B B}{R_B} = V_U + t_C B \qquad (14.5)$$

Equation (14.5) is MM Proposition I under corporate taxes. The first term in equation (14.5) is the value of the cash flows of the firm with no debt tax shield. In other words, this term is equal to V_U, the value of the all-equity firm. The value of the levered firm is the value of an all-equity firm plus $t_C B$, the tax rate times the value of the debt. $t_C B$ is the present value of the tax shield in the case of perpetual cash flows. Because the tax shield increases with the amount of debt, the firm can raise its total cash flow and its value by substituting debt for equity.

EXAMPLE 14.4 MM with Corporate Taxes

Divided Airlines is currently an unlevered firm. The company expects to generate $153.85 in earnings before interest and taxes (EBIT), in perpetuity. The corporate tax rate is 35 percent, implying aftertax earnings of $100. All earnings after tax are paid out as dividends.

The firm is considering a capital restructuring to allow $200 of debt. Its cost of debt capital is 10 percent. Unlevered firms in the same industry have a cost of equity capital of 20 percent. What will the new value of Divided Airlines be?

FIGURE 14.5

The Effect of Financial Leverage on Firm Value: MM with Corporate Taxes in the Case of Divided Airlines

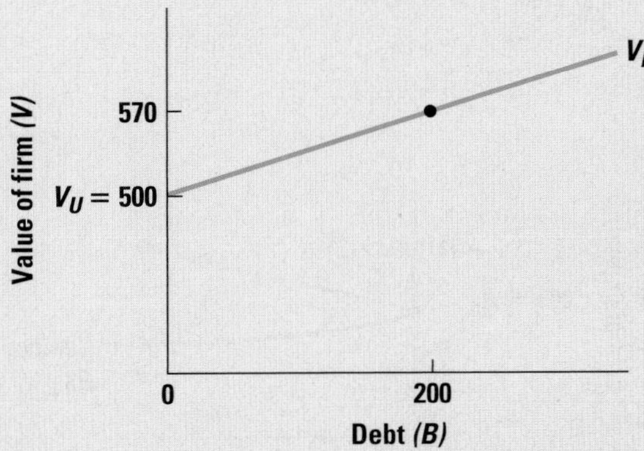

$V_L = V_U + t_C B$
$= \$500 + (.35 \times \$200)$
$= \$570$

Debt reduces Divided's tax burden. As a result, the value of the firm is positively related to debt.

(continued)

The value of Divided Airlines will be equal to:

$$V_L = \frac{\text{EBIT} \times (1 - t_C)}{R_0} + t_C B$$

$$= \frac{\$100}{.20} + (.35 \times \$200)$$

$$= \$500 + \$70$$

$$= \$570$$

The value of the levered firm is \$570, which is greater than the unlevered value of \$500. Because $V_L = B + S$, the value of levered equity, S, is equal to \$570 − \$200 = \$370. The value of Divided Airlines as a function of leverage is illustrated in Figure 14.5.

Expected Return and Leverage under Corporate Taxes

MM Proposition II under no taxes posits a positive relationship between the expected return on equity and leverage. This result occurs because the risk of equity increases with leverage. The same intuition also holds in a world of corporate taxes. The exact formula in a world of corporate taxes is:

MM Proposition II (corporate taxes):

$$R_S = R_0 + \frac{B}{S} \times (1 - t_C) \times (R_0 - R_B) \tag{14.6}$$

Applying the formula to Divided Airlines, we get:

$$R_S = .2351 = .20 + \frac{200}{370} \times (1 - .35) \times (.20 - .10)$$

This calculation is illustrated in Figure 14.6.

Whenever $R_0 > R_B$, R_S increases with leverage, a result that we also found in the no-tax case. As stated earlier in this chapter, R_0 should exceed R_B. That is, since equity (even unlevered equity) is risky, it should have an expected return greater than that on the less risky debt.

Let's check our calculations by determining the value of the levered equity in another way. The algebraic formula for the value of levered equity is:

$$S = \frac{(\text{EBIT} - R_B B) \times (1 - t_C)}{R_S}$$

FIGURE 14.6

The Effect of Financial Leverage on the Cost of Debt and Equity Capital

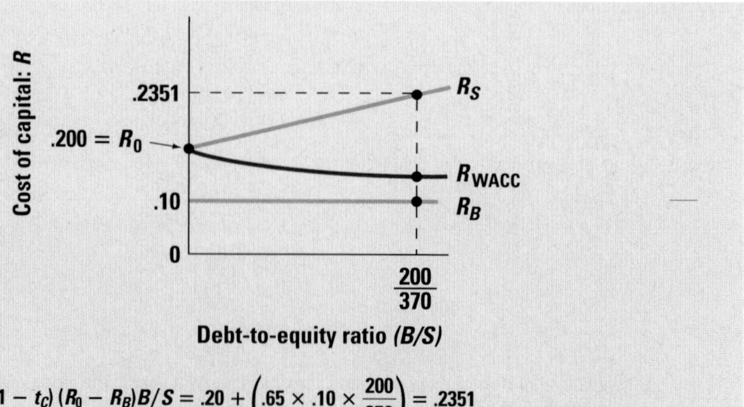

$$R_S = R_0 + (1 - t_C)(R_0 - R_B)B/S = .20 + \left(.65 \times .10 \times \frac{200}{370}\right) = .2351$$

Financial leverage adds risk to the firm's equity. As compensation, the cost of equity rises with the firm's risk. Note that R_0 is a single point, while R_S, R_B, and R_{WACC} are all entire lines.

The numerator is the expected cash flow to levered equity after interest and taxes. The denominator is the rate at which the cash flow to equity is discounted.

For Divided Airlines we get:

$$\frac{(\$153.85 - .10 \times \$200)(1 - .35)}{.2351} = \$370$$

the same result we obtained earlier (ignoring a small rounding error).

The Weighted Average Cost of Capital R_{WACC} and Corporate Taxes

In Chapter 12, we defined the weighted average cost of capital (with corporate taxes) as (note that $V_L = S + B$):

$$R_{WACC} = \frac{S}{V_L} R_S + \frac{B}{V_L} R_B(1 - t_C)$$

Note that the cost of debt capital, R_B, is multiplied by $(1 - t_C)$ because interest is tax-deductible at the corporate level. However, the cost of equity, R_S, is not multiplied by this factor because dividends are not deductible. In the no-tax case, R_{WACC} is not affected by leverage. This result is reflected in Figure 14.3, which we discussed earlier. However, since debt is tax-advantaged relative to equity, it can be shown that R_{WACC} declines with leverage in a world with corporate taxes. This result can be seen in Figure 14.6.

For Divided Airlines, R_{WACC} is equal to:

$$R_{WACC} = \left(\frac{370}{570} \times .2351\right) + \left(\frac{200}{570} \times .10 \times .65\right) = .1754$$

Divided Airlines has reduced its R_{WACC} from .20 (with no debt) to .1754 with reliance on debt. This result is intuitively pleasing because it suggests that, when a firm lowers its R_{WACC}, the firm's value will increase. Using the R_{WACC} approach, we can confirm that the value of Divided Airlines is \$570:

$$V_L = \frac{\text{EBIT} \times (1 - t_C)}{R_{WACC}} = \frac{\$100}{.1754} = \$570$$

Stock Price and Leverage under Corporate Taxes

At this point, students often believe the numbers–or at least are too intimidated to dispute them. However, they sometimes think we have asked the wrong question. "Why are we choosing to maximize the value of the firm?" they will say. "If managers are looking out for the stockholders' interest, why aren't they trying to maximize stock price?" If this question occurred to you, you have come to the right section.

Our response is twofold: First, we showed in the first section of this chapter that the capital structure that maximizes firm value is also the one that most benefits the interests of the stockholders.

However, that general explanation is not always convincing to students. As a second procedure, we calculate the stock price of Divided Airlines both before and after the exchange of debt for stock. We do this by presenting a set of market value balance sheets. The market value balance sheet for the company in its all-equity form can be represented as:

DIVIDED AIRLINES Balance Sheet (all-equity firm)		
Physical assets: $\frac{\$153.85}{.20} \times (1 - .35) = \$500$	Equity	\$500 (100 shares)

Assuming that there are 100 shares outstanding, each share is worth $5 = $500/100.

Next, imagine the company announces that, in the near future, it will issue $200 of debt to buy back $200 of stock. We know from our previous discussion that the value of the firm will rise to reflect the tax shield of debt. If we assume that capital markets efficiently price securities, the increase occurs immediately. That is, the rise occurs on the day of the announcement, not on the date of the debt-for-equity exchange. The market value balance sheet now becomes:

DIVIDED AIRLINES Balance Sheet (upon announcement of debt issue)			
Physical assets:	$500	Equity	$570 (100 shares)
Present value of tax shield: $t_C B$ = 35% × $200 =	70		
Total assets	$570		

Note that the debt has not yet been issued. Therefore, only equity appears on the right-hand side of the balance sheet. Each share is now worth $570/100 = $5.70, implying that the stockholders have benefited by $70. The equityholders gain because they are the owners of a firm that has improved its financial policy.

The introduction of the tax shield to the balance sheet is perplexing to many students. Although physical assets are tangible, the ethereal nature of the tax shield bothers these students. However, remember that an asset is any item with value. The tax shield has value because it reduces the stream of future taxes. The fact that one cannot touch the shield in the way that one can touch a physical asset is a philosophical, not financial, consideration.

At some point, the exchange of debt for equity occurs. Debt of $200 is issued, and the proceeds are used to buy back shares. How many shares of stock are repurchased? Because shares are now selling at $5.70 each, the number of shares that the firm acquires is $200/$5.70 = 35.09. This leaves 64.91 (100 − 35.09) shares of stock outstanding. The market value balance sheet is now:

DIVIDED AIRLINES Balance Sheet (after exchange has taken place)			
Physical assets:	$500	Equity	$370 (100 − 35.09 = 64.91 shares)
Present value of tax shield	70	Debt	200
Total assets	$570	Debt plus equity	$570

Each share of stock is worth $370/64.91 = $5.70 after the exchange. Notice that the stock price does not change on the exchange date. As we mentioned above, the stock price moves on the date of the announcement only. Because the shareholders participating in the exchange receive a price equal to the market price per share after the exchange, they do not care whether they exchange their stock or not.

This example was provided for two reasons. First, it shows that an increase in the value of the firm from debt financing leads to an increase in the price of the stock. In fact, the stockholders capture the entire $70 tax shield. Second, we wanted to provide more work with market value balance sheets.

A summary of the main results of Modigliani-Miller with corporate taxes is presented in the following boxed section.

SUMMARY OF MODIGLIANI-MILLER PROPOSITIONS WITH CORPORATE TAXES

Assumptions

- Corporations are taxed at the rate t_C, on earnings after interest.
- No transaction costs.
- Individuals and corporations borrow at same rate.

Results

Proposition I: $V_L = V_U + t_C B$ (for a firm with perpetual debt)

Proposition II: $R_S = R_0 + \frac{B}{S}(1 - t_C)(R_0 - R_B)$

Intuition

Proposition I: Since corporations can deduct interest payments but not dividend payments, corporate leverage lowers tax payments.

Proposition II: The cost of equity rises with leverage, because the risk to equity rises with leverage.

SUMMARY AND CONCLUSIONS

1. We began our discussion of the capital structure decision by arguing that the particular capital structure that maximizes the value of the firm is also the one that provides the most benefit to the stockholders.
2. In a world of no taxes, the famous Proposition I of Modigliani and Miller proves that the value of the firm is unaffected by the debt-to-equity ratio. In other words, a firm's capital structure is a matter of indifference in that world. The authors obtain their results by showing that either a high or a low corporate ratio of debt to equity can be offset by homemade leverage. The result hinges on the assumption that individuals can borrow at the same rate as corporations, an assumption we believe to be quite plausible.
3. MM's Proposition II in a world without taxes states that:

   $$R_S = R_0 + \frac{B}{S}(R_0 - R_B)$$

   This implies that the expected rate of return on equity (also called the *cost of equity* or the *required return on equity*) is positively related to the firm's leverage. This makes intuitive sense, because the risk of equity rises with leverage, a point illustrated by Figure 14.2.
4. While the above work of MM is quite elegant, it does not explain the empirical findings on capital structure very well. MM imply that the capital structure decision is a matter of indifference, while the decision appears to be a weighty one in the real world. To achieve real world applicability, we next considered corporate taxes.
5. In a world with corporate taxes but no bankruptcy costs, firm value is an increasing function of leverage. The formula for the value of the firm is:

   $$V_L = V_U + t_C B$$

Expected return on levered equity can be expressed as:

$$R_S = R_0 + (1 - t_C) \times (R_0 - R_B) \times \frac{B}{S}$$

Here, value is positively related to leverage. This result implies that firms should have a capital structure almost entirely composed of debt. Because real world firms select more moderate levels of debt, the next chapter considers modifications to the results of this chapter.

CONCEPT QUESTIONS

1. **MM Assumptions** List the three assumptions that lie behind the Modigliani-Miller theory in a world without taxes. Are these assumptions reasonable in the real world? Explain.
2. **MM Propositions** In a world with no taxes, no transaction costs, and no costs of financial distress, is the following statement true, false, or uncertain? If a firm issues equity to repurchase some of its debt, the price per share of the firm's stock will rise because the shares are less risky. Explain.
3. **MM Propositions** In a world with no taxes, no transaction costs, and no costs of financial distress, is the following statement true, false, or uncertain? Moderate borrowing will not increase the required return on a firm's equity. Explain.
4. **MM Propositions** What is the quirk in the tax code that makes a levered firm more valuable than an otherwise identical unlevered firm?
5. **Business Risk versus Financial Risk** Explain what is meant by business and financial risk. Suppose Firm A has greater business risk than Firm B. Is it true that Firm A also has a higher cost of equity capital? Explain.
6. **MM Propositions** How would you answer in the following debate?

   Q: Isn't it true that the riskiness of a firm's equity will rise if the firm increases its use of debt financing?

   A: Yes, that's the essence of MM Proposition II.

   Q: And isn't it true that, as a firm increases its use of borrowing, the likelihood of default increases, thereby increasing the risk of the firm's debt?

   A: Yes.

   Q: In other words, increased borrowing increases the risk of the equity *and* the debt?

   A: That's right.

   Q: Well, given that the firm uses only debt and equity financing, and given that the risks of both are increased by increased borrowing, does it not follow that increasing debt increases the overall risk of the firm and therefore decreases the value of the firm?

   A: ??
7. **Optimal Capital Structure** Is there an easily identifiable debt-equity ratio that will maximize the value of a firm? Why or why not?
8. **Financial Leverage** Why is the use of debt financing referred to as financial "leverage"?
9. **Homemade Leverage** What is homemade leverage?
10. **Capital Structure Goal** What is the basic goal of financial management with regard to capital structure?

Basic
(Questions 1–16)

1. **EBIT and Leverage** Money, Inc., has no debt outstanding and a total market value of $150,000. Earnings before interest and taxes, EBIT, are projected to be $14,000 if economic conditions are normal. If there is strong expansion in the economy, then EBIT will be 30 percent higher. If there is a recession, then EBIT will be 60 percent lower. Money is considering a $60,000 debt issue with a 5 percent interest rate. The proceeds will be used to repurchase shares of stock. There are currently 2,500 shares outstanding. Ignore taxes for this problem.
   a. Calculate earnings per share, EPS, under each of the three economic scenarios before any debt is issued. Also, calculate the percentage changes in EPS when the economy expands or enters a recession. 
   b. Repeat part (a) assuming that Money goes through with recapitalization. What do you observe?
2. **EBIT, Taxes, and Leverage** Repeat parts (a) and (b) in Problem 1 assuming Money has a tax rate of 35 percent.
3. **ROE and Leverage** Suppose the company in Problem 1 has a market-to-book ratio of 1.0.
   a. Calculate return on equity, ROE, under each of the three economic scenarios before any debt is issued. Also, calculate the percentage changes in ROE for economic expansion and recession, assuming no taxes.
   b. Repeat part (a) assuming the firm goes through with the proposed recapitalization.
   c. Repeat parts (a) and (b) of this problem assuming the firm has a tax rate of 35 percent.
4. **Break-Even EBIT** Rolston Corporation is comparing two different capital structures, an all-equity plan (Plan I) and a levered plan (Plan II). Under Plan I, Rolston would have 150,000 shares of stock outstanding. Under Plan II, there would be 60,000 shares of stock outstanding and $1.5 million in debt outstanding. The interest rate on the debt is 10 percent and there are no taxes. 
   a. If EBIT is $200,000, which plan will result in the higher EPS?
   b. If EBIT is $700,000, which plan will result in the higher EPS?
   c. What is the break-even EBIT?
5. **MM and Stock Value** In Problem 4, use MM Proposition I to find the price per share of equity under each of the two proposed plans. What is the value of the firm?
6. **Break-Even EBIT and Leverage** Kolby Corp. is comparing two different capital structures. Plan I would result in 1,100 shares of stock and $16,500 in debt. Plan II would result in 900 shares of stock and $27,500 in debt. The interest rate on the debt is 10 percent.
   a. Ignoring taxes, compare both of these plans to an all-equity plan assuming that EBIT will be $10,000. The all-equity plan would result in 1,400 shares of stock outstanding. Which of the three plans has the highest EPS? The lowest?
   b. In part (a), what are the break-even levels of EBIT for each plan as compared to that for an all-equity plan? Is one higher than the other? Why?
   c. Ignoring taxes, when will EPS be identical for Plans I and II?
   d. Repeat parts (a), (b), and (c) assuming that the corporate tax rate is 40 percent. Are the break-even levels of EBIT different from before? Why or why not?
7. **Leverage and Stock Value** Ignoring taxes in Problem 6, what is the price per share of equity under Plan I? Plan II? What principle is illustrated by your answers?
8. **Homemade Leverage** Star, Inc., a prominent consumer products firm, is debating whether or not to convert its all-equity capital structure to one that is 40 percent debt. Currently, there are 2,000 shares outstanding and the price per share is $70. EBIT is expected to remain at $16,000 per year forever. The interest rate on new debt is 8 percent, and there are no taxes. 

a. Ms. Brown, a shareholder of the firm, owns 100 shares of stock. What is her cash flow under the current capital structure, assuming the firm has a dividend payout rate of 100 percent?

b. What will Ms. Brown's cash flow be under the proposed capital structure of the firm? Assume that she keeps all 100 of her shares.

c. Suppose Star does convert, but Ms. Brown prefers the current all-equity capital structure. Show how she could unlever her shares of stock to recreate the original capital structure.

d. Using your answer to part (c), explain why Star's choice of capital structure is irrelevant.

9. **Homemade Leverage and WACC** ABC Co. and XYZ Co. are identical firms in all respects except for their capital structure. ABC is all-equity financed with $600,000 in stock. XYZ uses both stock and perpetual debt; its stock is worth $300,000 and the interest rate on its debt is 10 percent. Both firms expect EBIT to be $73,000. Ignore taxes.

a. Richard owns $30,000 worth of XYZ's stock. What rate of return is he expecting?

b. Show how Richard could generate exactly the same cash flows and rate of return by investing in ABC and using homemade leverage.

c. What is the cost of equity for ABC? What is it for XYZ?

d. What is the WACC for ABC? For XYZ? What principle have you illustrated?

10. **MM** Nina Corp. uses no debt. The weighted average cost of capital is 13 percent. If the current market value of the equity is $35 million and there are no taxes, what is EBIT?

11. **MM and Taxes** In the previous question, suppose the corporate tax rate is 35 percent. What is EBIT in this case? What is the WACC? Explain.

12. **Calculating WACC** Weston Industries has a debt-equity ratio of 1.5. Its WACC is 12 percent, and its cost of debt is 12 percent. The corporate tax rate is 35 percent.

a. What is Weston's cost of equity capital?

b. What is Weston's unlevered cost of equity capital?

c. What would the cost of equity be if the debt-equity ratio were 2? What if it were 1.0? What if it were zero?

13. **Calculating WACC** Shadow Corp. has no debt but can borrow at 8 percent. The firm's WACC is currently 12 percent, and the tax rate is 35 percent.

a. What is Shadow's cost of equity?

b. If the firm converts to 25 percent debt, what will its cost of equity be?

c. If the firm converts to 50 percent debt, what will its cost of equity be?

d. What is Shadow's WACC in part (b)? In part (c)?

14. **MM and Taxes** Bruce & Co. expects its EBIT to be $95,000 every year forever. The firm can borrow at 11 percent. Bruce currently has no debt, and its cost of equity is 22 percent. If the tax rate is 35 percent, what is the value of the firm? What will the value be if Bruce borrows $60,000 and uses the proceeds to repurchase shares?

15. **MM and Taxes** In Problem 14, what is the cost of equity after recapitalization? What is the WACC? What are the implications for the firm's capital structure decision?

16. **MM Proposition I** Levered, Inc., and Unlevered, Inc., are identical in every way except their capital structures. Each company expects to earn $96 million before interest per year in perpetuity, with each company distributing all its earnings as dividends. Levered's perpetual debt has a market value of $275 million and costs 8 percent per year. Levered has 4.5 million shares outstanding, currently worth $100 per share. Unlevered has no debt and 10 million shares outstanding, currently worth $80 per share. Neither firm pays taxes. Is Levered's stock a better buy than Unlevered's stock?

Intermediate (Questions 17–25)

17. **MM** Tool Manufacturing has an expected EBIT of $35,000 in perpetuity and a tax rate of 35 percent. The firm has $70,000 in outstanding debt at an interest rate of 9 percent, and its unlevered cost of capital is 14 percent. What is the value of the firm according to MM Proposition I with taxes? Should Tool change its debt-equity ratio if the goal is to maximize the value of the firm? Explain.

18. **Firm Value** Old School Corporation expects an EBIT of $9,000 every year forever. Old School currently has no debt, and its cost of equity is 17 percent. The firm can borrow at 10 percent. If the corporate tax rate is 35 percent, what is the value of the firm? What will the value be if Old School converts to 50 percent debt? To 100 percent debt?

19. **MM Proposition I with Taxes** The Maxwell Company is financed entirely with equity. The company is considering a loan of $1 million. The loan will be repaid in equal installments over the next two years, and it has an 8 percent interest rate. The company's tax rate is 35 percent. According to MM Proposition I with taxes, what would be the increase in the value of the company after the loan?

20. **MM Proposition I without Taxes** Alpha Corporation and Beta Corporation are identical in every way except their capital structures. Alpha Corporation, an all-equity firm, has 5,000 shares of stock outstanding, currently worth $20 per share. Beta Corporation uses leverage in its capital structure. The market value of Beta's debt is $25,000, and its cost of debt is 12 percent. Each firm is expected to have earnings before interest of $35,000 in perpetuity. Neither firm pays taxes. Assume that every investor can borrow at 12 percent per year.

    a. What is the value of Alpha Corporation?

    b. What is the value of Beta Corporation?

    c. What is the market value of Beta Corporation's equity?

    d. How much will it cost to purchase 20 percent of each firm's equity?

    e. Assuming each firm meets its earnings estimates, what will be the dollar return to each position in part (d) over the next year?

    f. Construct an investment strategy in which an investor purchases 20 percent of Alpha's equity and replicates both the cost and dollar return of purchasing 20 percent of Beta's equity.

    g. Is Alpha's equity more or less risky than Beta's equity? Explain.

21. **Cost of Capital** Acetate, Inc., has equity with a market value of $20 million and debt with a market value of $10 million. The cost of the debt is 14 percent per year. Treasury bills that mature in one year yield 8 percent per year, and the expected return on the market portfolio over the next year is 18 percent. The beta of Acetate's equity is .90. The firm pays no taxes.

    a. What is Acetate's debt-equity ratio?

    b. What is the firm's weighted average cost of capital?

    c. What is the cost of capital for an otherwise identical all-equity firm?

22. **Homemade Leverage** The Veblen Company and the Knight Company are identical in every respect except that Veblen is not levered. The market value of Knight Company's 6 percent bonds is $1 million. Financial information for the two firms appears below. All earnings streams are perpetuities. Neither firm pays taxes. Both firms distribute all earnings available to common stockholders immediately.

	VEBLEN	KNIGHT
Projected operating income	$ 300,000	$ 300,000
Year-end interest on debt	—	$ 60,000
Market value of stock	$2,400,000	$1,714,000
Market value of debt	—	$1,000,000

a. An investor who is able to borrow at 6 percent per year wishes to purchase 5 percent of Knight's equity. Can he increase his dollar return by purchasing 5 percent of Veblen's equity if he borrows so that the initial net costs of the two strategies are the same?

b. Given the two investment strategies in (a), which will investors choose? When will this process cease?

23. **MM Propositions** Locomotive Corporation is planning to repurchase part of its common stock by issuing corporate debt. As a result, the firm's debt-to-equity ratio is expected to rise from 40 percent to 50 percent. The firm currently has $7.5 million worth of debt outstanding. The cost of this debt is 10 percent per year. Locomotive expects to have an EBIT of $3.75 million per year in perpetuity. Locomotive pays no taxes.

   a. What is the market value of Locomotive Corporation before and after the repurchase announcement?

   b. What is the expected return on the firm's equity before the announcement of the stock repurchase plan?

   c. What is the expected return on the equity of an otherwise identical all-equity firm?

   d. What is the expected return on the firm's equity after the announcement of the stock repurchase plan?

24. **Stock Value and Leverage** Green Manufacturing, Inc., plans to announce that it will issue $2 million of perpetual debt and use the proceeds to repurchase common stock. The bonds will sell at par with a 6 percent annual coupon rate. Green is currently an all-equity firm worth $10 million with 500,000 shares of common stock outstanding. After the sale of the bonds, Green will maintain the new capital structure indefinitely. Green currently generates annual pretax earnings of $1.5 million. This level of earnings is expected to remain constant in perpetuity. Green is subject to a corporate tax rate of 40 percent.

   a. What is the expected return on Green's equity before the announcement of the debt issue?

   b. Construct Green's market value balance sheet before the announcement of the debt issue. What is the price per share of the firm's equity?

   c. Construct Green's market value balance sheet immediately after the announcement of the debt issue.

   d. What is Green's stock price per share immediately after the repurchase announcement?

   e. How many shares will Green repurchase as a result of the debt issue? How many shares of common stock will remain after the repurchase?

   f. Construct the market value balance sheet after the restructuring.

   g. What is the required return on Green's equity after the restructuring?

25. **MM with Taxes** Williamson, Inc., has a debt-to-equity ratio of 2.5. The firm's weighted average cost of capital is 15 percent, and its pretax cost of debt is 10 percent. Williamson is subject to a corporate tax rate of 35 percent.

   a. What is Williamson's cost of equity capital?

   b. What is Williamson's unlevered cost of equity capital?

   c. What would Williamson's weighted average cost of capital be if the firm's debt-to-equity ratio were .75? What if it were 1.5?

Challenge (Questions 26–30)

26. **Weighted Average Cost of Capital** In a world of corporate taxes only, show that the R_{WACC} can be written as $R_{WACC} = R_0 \times [1 - t_C(B/V)]$.

27. **Cost of Equity and Leverage** Assuming a world of corporate taxes only, show that the cost of equity, R_S, is as given in the chapter by MM Proposition II with corporate taxes.

28. **Business and Financial Risk** Assume a firm's debt is risk-free, so that the cost of debt equals the risk-free rate, R_f. Define β_A as the firm's *asset* beta, that is, the systematic risk of the firm's assets. Define β_S to be the beta of the firm's equity. Use the capital asset pricing model, CAPM, along with MM Proposition II to show that $\beta_S = \beta_A \times (1 + B/S)$, where B/S is the debt-equity ratio. Assume the tax rate is zero.

29. **Stockholder Risk** Suppose a firm's business operations are such that they mirror movements in the economy as a whole very closely, that is, the firm's asset beta is 1.0. Use the result of previous problem to find the equity beta for this firm for debt-equity ratios of 0, 1, 5, and 20. What does this tell you about the relationship between capital structure and shareholder risk? How is the shareholders' required return on equity affected? Explain.

30. **Unlevered Cost of Equity** Beginning with the cost of capital equation, that is:

$$R_{\text{WACC}} = \frac{S}{B+S} R_S + \frac{B}{B+S} R_B$$

show that the cost of equity capital for a levered firm can be written as:

$$R_S = R_0 + \frac{B}{S}(R_0 - R_B)$$

S&P PROBLEMS

www.mhhe.com/edumarketinsight

STANDARD &POOR'S

1. Locate the annual balance sheets for General Motors (GM), Merck (MRK), and Kellogg (K). For each company calculate the long-term debt-to-equity ratio for the prior two years. Why would these companies use such different capital structures?

2. Look up Georgia Pacific (GP) and download the annual income statements. For the most recent year, calculate the marginal tax and EBIT, and find the total interest expense. From the annual balance sheets calculate the total long-term debt (including the portion due within one year). Using the interest expense and total long-term debt, calculate the average cost of debt. Next, find the estimated beta for Georgia Pacific on the S&P Stock Report. Use this reported beta, a current T-bill rate, and the historical average market risk premium found in a previous chapter to calculate the levered cost of equity. Now calculate the unlevered cost of equity, then the unlevered EBIT. What is the unlevered value of Georgia Pacific? What is the value of the interest tax shield and the value of the levered Georgia Pacific?

WHAT'S ON THE WEB?

1. **Capital Structure** Go to investor.reuters.com and enter the ticker symbol AMGN for Amgen, a biotechnology company. Follow the "Ratio Comparison" link and find long-term debt-to-equity and total debt-to-equity ratios. How does Amgen compare to the industry, sector, and S&P 500 in these areas? Now answer the same question for Edison International (EIX), the parent company of Southern California Edison, a utility company. How do the capital structures of Amgen and Edison International compare? Can you think of possible explanations for the difference between these two companies?

2. **Capital Structure** Go to finance.yahoo.com and follow the "Screener" link. Using the Total Debt/Equity screen on the Java Screener, how many companies have debt-to-equity ratios greater than 2? Greater than 5? Greater than 10? What company has the highest debt-to-equity ratio? What is the ratio? Now find how many companies have a negative debt-to-equity ratio. What is the lowest debt-to-equity ratio? What does it mean if a company has a negative debt-to-equity ratio? Repeat these screens for the Long-Term Debt/Equity screen.

STEPHENSON REAL ESTATE RECAPITALIZATION

CLOSING CASE

Stephenson Real Estate Company was founded 25 years ago by the current CEO, Robert Stephenson. The company purchases real estate, including land and buildings, and rents the property to tenants. The company has shown a profit every year for the past 18 years, and the shareholders are satisfied with the company's management. Prior to founding Stephenson Real Estate, Robert was the founder and CEO of a failed alpaca farming operation. The resulting bankruptcy made him extremely averse to debt financing. As a result, the company is entirely equity financed, with 15 million shares of common stock outstanding. The stock currently trades at $32.50 per share.

Stephenson is evaluating a plan to purchase a huge tract of land in the southeastern United States for $100 million. The land will subsequently be leased to tenant farmers. This purchase is expected to increase Stephenson's annual pretax earnings by $25 million in perpetuity. Kim Weyand, the company's new CFO, has been put in charge of the project. Kim has determined that the company's current cost of capital is 12.5 percent. She feels that the company would be more valuable if it included debt in its capital structure, so she is evaluating whether the company should issue debt to entirely finance the project. Based on some conversations with investment banks, she thinks that the company can issue bonds at par value with an 8 percent coupon rate. Based on her analysis, she also believes that a capital structure in the range of 70 percent equity/30 percent debt would be optimal. If the company goes beyond 30 percent debt, its bonds would carry a lower rating and a much higher coupon because the possibility of financial distress and the associated costs would rise sharply. Stephenson has a 40 percent corporate tax rate (state and federal).

1. If Stephenson wishes to maximize its total market value, would you recommend that it issue debt or equity to finance the land purchase? Explain.
2. Construct Stephenson's market value balance sheet before it announces the purchase.
3. Suppose Stephenson decides to issue equity to finance the purchase.
   a. What is the net present value of the project?
   b. Construct Stephenson's market value balance sheet after it announces that the firm will finance the purchase using equity. What would be the new price per share of the firm's stock? How many shares will Stephenson need to issue in order to finance the purchase?
   c. Construct Stephenson's market value balance sheet after the equity issue, but before the purchase has been made. How many shares of common stock does Stephenson have outstanding? What is the price per share of the firm's stock?
   d. Construct Stephenson's market value balance sheet after the purchase has been made.
4. Suppose Stephenson decides to issue debt in order to finance the purchase.
   a. What will the market value of the Stephenson company be if the purchase is financed with debt?
   b. Construct Stephenson's market value balance sheet after both the debt issue and the land purchase. What is the price per share of the firm's stock?
5. Which method of financing maximizes the per-share stock price of Stephenson's equity?

CHAPTER 15

Capital Structure: *Limits to the Use of Debt*

OPENING CASE

Airlines traditionally rely heavily on debt financing. Unfortunately, this practice can have adverse consequences when things do not work out as planned. By August 2005, a variety of problems in the airline industry had led to widespread financial distress, particularly among the "legacy" carriers (the ones that have been in business for decades). For example, in an effort to avoid filing for bankruptcy, Delta Air Lines announced it was selling Atlantic Southeast Airlines, one of its regional feeder airlines, for $425 million in much-needed cash (it didn't prevent Delta from subsequently filing, however). Northwest Airlines was also considering bankruptcy. The company had piled up losses of about $3 billion in the previous four years, and its pension plan was underfunded by about $3.8 billion. Of course, other airlines were already in bankruptcy. United Airlines had been bankrupt since late 2002, and US Airways entered bankruptcy in September 2004, for the second time. Financial problems in the airline industry were not limited to U.S. carriers. In June 2005, the European Commission approved a plan to restructure Italy's state-owned Alitalia airline, and other big European carriers were experiencing difficulties staying aloft.

As these situations point out, there is a limit to the financial leverage a company can undertake, and the risk of too much leverage is bankruptcy. In this chapter, we discuss the costs associated with bankruptcies, and how companies attempt to avoid them.

15.1 COSTS OF FINANCIAL DISTRESS

One limiting factor affecting the amount of debt a firm might use comes in the form of *bankruptcy costs*. As the debt-equity ratio rises, so too does the probability that the firm will be unable to pay its bondholders what was promised to them. When this happens, ownership of the firm's assets is ultimately transferred from the stockholders to the bondholders.

In principle, a firm becomes bankrupt when the value of its assets equals the value of its debt. When this occurs, the value of equity is zero, and the stockholders turn over control of the firm to the bondholders. When this takes place, the bondholders hold assets whose value is exactly equal to what is owed on the debt. In a perfect world, there are no costs associated with this transfer of ownership, and the bondholders don't lose anything.

This idealized view of bankruptcy is not, of course, what happens in the real world. Ironically, it is expensive to go bankrupt. As we discuss, the costs associated with bankruptcy may eventually offset the tax-related gains from leverage.

Direct Bankruptcy Costs

When the value of a firm's assets equals the value of its debt, then the firm is economically bankrupt in the sense that the equity has no value. However, the formal turning over of the assets to the bondholders is a *legal* process, not an economic one. There are legal and administrative costs to bankruptcy, and it has been remarked that bankruptcies are to lawyers what blood is to sharks.

To give you some idea of the costs associated with a bankruptcy, consider the case of the energy giant Enron, which filed for bankruptcy in December 2001. The company wanted to reorganize through the bankruptcy process, but complications soon arose. In fact, the company filed at least six reorganization plans. By the end of 2004, lawyers, consultants, accountants, and other professionals had earned nearly *$1 billion* in fees, and the company was still in bankruptcy. The next largest fees appear to have been paid to those involved in the WorldCom bankruptcy. The fees in that case reached a mere $600 million.

Because of the expenses associated with bankruptcy, bondholders won't get all that they are owed. Some fraction of the firm's assets will "disappear" in the legal process of going bankrupt. These are the legal and administrative expenses associated with the bankruptcy proceeding. We call these costs **direct bankruptcy costs**.

These direct bankruptcy costs are a disincentive to debt financing. If a firm goes bankrupt, then, suddenly, a piece of the firm disappears. This amounts to a bankruptcy "tax." So, a firm faces a trade-off: borrowing saves a firm money on its corporate taxes, but the more a firm borrows, the more likely it is that the firm will become bankrupt and have to pay the bankruptcy tax.

Indirect Bankruptcy Costs

Because it is expensive to go bankrupt, a firm will spend resources to avoid doing so. When a firm is having significant problems in meeting its debt obligations, we say that it is experiencing financial distress. Some financially distressed firms ultimately file for bankruptcy, but most do not because they are able to recover or otherwise survive.

For example, in early 2005, most of the older, larger airlines in the United States were in financial distress. United Airlines and US Airways were in bankruptcy protection. Problems also existed at Delta Air Lines. Analysts estimated the company would be able to operate for only another six months unless wage concessions were reached with employees, particularly pilots. The company and its creditors had already met to attempt to find a way in which the company could avoid bankruptcy. By September of 2005, Delta was running out of cash, and the company's management decided that filing for bankruptcy was the only way to keep flying.

The costs of avoiding a bankruptcy filing incurred by a financially distressed firm are called **indirect bankruptcy costs**. We use the term **financial distress costs** to refer generically to the direct and indirect costs associated with going bankrupt and/or avoiding a bankruptcy filing.

Cutler and Summers examine the costs of the well-publicized Texaco bankruptcy.[1] In January 1984, Pennzoil reached what it believed to be a binding agreement to acquire three-sevenths of Getty Oil. However, less than a week later, Texaco acquired all of Getty at a higher per-share price. Pennzoil then sued Getty for breach of contract. Because Texaco had previously indemnified Getty against litigation, Texaco became liable for damages.

In November 1985, the Texas State Court awarded damages of $12 billion to Pennzoil, although this amount was later reduced. As a result, Texaco filed for bankruptcy. Cutler and Summers identify nine important events over the course of the litigation. They find that Texaco's market value (stock price times number of shares outstanding) fell a cumulative $4.1 billion over these events, whereas Pennzoil's value rose only $682 million. Thus, Pennzoil gained about one-sixth of what Texaco lost, resulting in a net loss to the two firms of almost $3.5 billion.

What could explain this net loss? Cutler and Summers suggest that it is likely due to costs that Texaco and Pennzoil incurred from the litigation and subsequent bankruptcy. The authors argue that direct bankruptcy fees represent only a small part of these costs, estimating Texaco's aftertax legal expenses to be about $165 million. Legal costs to Pennzoil were more difficult to assess, because Pennzoil's lead lawyer, Joe Jamail, stated publicly that he had no set fee. However, using a clever statistical analysis, the authors estimate his fee to be about $200 million. Thus, one must search elsewhere for the bulk of the costs.

Indirect costs of financial distress may be the culprit here. An affidavit by Texaco stated that, following the lawsuit, some of its suppliers were demanding cash payments. Other suppliers halted or canceled shipments of crude oil. Certain banks restricted Texaco's use of futures contracts on foreign exchange. The affidavit stressed that these constraints were reducing Texaco's ability to run its business, leading to deterioration of its financial condition. Could these sorts of indirect costs explain the $3.5 billion disparity between Texaco's drop and Pennzoil's rise in market value? Unfortunately, although it is quite likely that indirect costs play a role here, there is simply no way to obtain a decent, quantitative estimate for them.

Agency Costs

When a firm has debt, conflicts of interest arise between stockholders and bondholders. Because of this, stockholders are tempted to pursue selfish strategies. These conflicts of interest, which are magnified when financial distress is incurred, impose **agency costs** on the firm. We describe three kinds of selfish strategies that stockholders use to hurt the bondholders and help themselves. These strategies are costly because they will lower the market value of the whole firm.

Selfish Investment Strategy 1: *Incentive to Take Large Risks* Firms near bankruptcy often take great chances, because they believe that they are playing with someone else's money. To see this, imagine a levered firm considering two *mutually exclusive* projects, a low-risk one and a high-risk one. There are two equally likely outcomes, recession and boom. The firm is in such dire straits that should a recession hit, it will come near to

[1]David M. Cutler and Lawrence H. Summers, "The Costs of Conflict Resolution and Financial Distress: Evidence from the Texaco-Pennzoil Litigation," *Rand Journal of Economics* (Summer 1988).

bankruptcy with one project and actually fall into bankruptcy with the other. The cash flows for the entire firm if the low-risk project is taken can be described as:

Value of Entire Firm If Low-Risk Project Is Chosen						
	PROBABILITY	VALUE OF FIRM	=	STOCK	+	BONDS
Recession	.5	$100	=	$ 0	+	$100
Boom	.5	200	=	100	+	100

If recession occurs, the value of the firm will be $100, and if boom happens, the value of the firm will be $200. The expected value of the firm is $150 (.5 × $100 + .5 × $200).

The firm has promised to pay bondholders $100. Shareholders will obtain the difference between the total payoff and the amount paid to the bondholders. In other words, the bondholders have the prior claim on the payoffs, and the shareholders have the residual claim.

Now suppose that another, riskier project can be substituted for the low-risk project. The payoffs and probabilities are as follows:

Value of Entire Firm If High-Risk Project Is Chosen						
	PROBABILITY	VALUE OF FIRM	=	STOCK	+	BONDS
Recession	.5	$ 50	=	$ 0	+	$ 50
Boom	.5	240	=	140	+	100

The expected value of the *firm* is $145 (.5 × $50 + .5 × $240), which is lower than the expected value of the firm with the low-risk project. Thus, the low-risk project would be accepted if the firm were all equity. However, note that the expected value of the *stock* is $70 (.5 × 0 + .5 × $140) with the high-risk project, but only $50 (.5 × 0 + .5 × $100) with the low-risk project. Given the firm's present levered state, stockholders will select the high-risk project, even though the high-risk project has a *lower* NPV.

The key is that, relative to the low-risk project, the high-risk project increases firm value in a boom and decreases firm value in a recession. The increase in value in a boom is captured by the stockholders, because the bondholders are paid in full (they receive $100) regardless of which project is accepted. Conversely, the drop in value in a recession is lost by the bondholders, because they are paid in full with the low-risk project but receive only $50 with the high-risk one. The stockholders will receive nothing in a recession anyway, whether the high-risk or low-risk project is selected. Thus, financial economists argue that stockholders expropriate value from the bondholders by selecting high-risk projects.

A story, perhaps apocryphal, illustrates this idea. It seems that Federal Express was near financial collapse within a few years of its inception. The founder, Frederick Smith, took $20,000 of corporate funds to Las Vegas in despair. He won at the gaming tables, providing enough capital to allow the firm to survive. Had he lost, the banks would simply have received $20,000 less when the firm reached bankruptcy.

Selfish Investment Strategy 2: *Incentive toward Underinvestment* Stockholders of a firm with a significant probability of bankruptcy often find that new investment helps the bondholders at the stockholders' expense. The simplest case might be a real estate owner facing imminent bankruptcy. If he took $100,000 out of his own pocket to refurbish the

TABLE 15.1 Example Illustrating Incentive to Underinvest

	Firm without Project		Firm with Project	
	BOOM	RECESSION	BOOM	RECESSION
Firm cash flows	$5,000	$2,400	$6,700	$4,100
Bondholders' claim	4,000	2,400	4,000	4,000
Stockholders' claim	$1,000	$ 0	$2,700	$ 100

The project has positive NPV. However, much of its value is captured by bondholders. Rational managers, acting in the stockholders' interest, will reject the project.

building, he could increase the building's value by, say, $150,000. Though this investment has a positive net present value, he will turn it down if the increase in value cannot prevent bankruptcy. "Why," he asks, "should I use my own funds to improve the value of a building that the bank will soon repossess?"

This idea is formalized by the following simple example. Consider a firm with $4,000 of principal and interest payments due at the end of the year. It will be pulled into bankruptcy by a recession because its cash flows will be only $2,400 in that state. The firm's cash flows are presented in the left-hand side of Table 15.1. The firm could avoid bankruptcy in a recession by raising new equity to invest in a new project. The project costs $1,000 and brings in $1,700 in either state, implying a positive net present value. Clearly it would be accepted in an all-equity firm.

However, the project hurts the stockholders of the levered firm. To see this, imagine the old stockholders contribute the $1,000 *themselves*.[2] The expected value of the stockholders' interest without the project is $500 (.5 × $1,000 + .5 × 0). The expected value with the project is $1,400 (.5 × $2,700 + .5 × $100). The stockholders' interest rises by only $900 ($1,400 − $500) while costing $1,000.

The key is that the stockholders contribute the full $1,000 investment, but the stockholders and bondholders *share* the benefits. The stockholders take the entire gain if boom times occur. Conversely, the bondholders reap most of the cash flow from the project in a recession.

The discussion of selfish strategy 1 is quite similar to the discussion of selfish strategy 2. In both cases, an investment strategy for the levered firm is different from the one for the unlevered firm. Thus, leverage results in distorted investment policy. Whereas the unlevered corporation always chooses projects with positive net present value, the levered firm may deviate from this policy.

Selfish Investment Strategy 3: *Milking the Property* Another strategy is to pay out extra dividends or other distributions in times of financial distress, leaving less in the firm for the bondholders. This is known as *milking the property,* a phrase taken from real estate. Strategies 2 and 3 are very similar. In strategy 2, the firm chooses not to raise new equity. Strategy 3 goes one step further, because equity is actually withdrawn through the dividend.

SUMMARY OF SELFISH STRATEGIES The above distortions occur only when there is a probability of bankruptcy or financial distress. Thus, these distortions *should not* affect, say, General Electric because bankruptcy is not a realistic possibility for a diversified blue-chip firm such as this. In other words, General Electric's debt will be virtually risk-free, regardless of the projects it accepts. The same argument could be made for regulated companies that are protected by state utility commissions. However, smaller firms

[2]The same qualitative results will obtain if the $1,000 is raised from new stockholders. However, the arithmetic becomes much more difficult since we must determine how many new shares are issued.

in risky industries, such as computers, might be very much affected by these distortions. Firms in the computer industry generally have significant potential future investment opportunities as compared to assets in place and face intense competition and uncertain future revenues. Because the distortions are related to financial distress, we have included them in our discussion of the indirect costs of financial distress.

Who pays for the cost of selfish investment strategies? We argue that it is ultimately the stockholders. Rational bondholders know that, when financial distress is imminent, they cannot expect help from stockholders. Rather, stockholders are likely to choose investment strategies that reduce the value of the bonds. Bondholders protect themselves accordingly by raising the interest rate that they require on the bonds. Because the stockholders must pay these high rates, they ultimately bear the costs of selfish strategies. The relationship between stockholders and bondholders is very similar to the relationship between Erroll Flynn and David Niven, good friends and movie stars in the 1930s. Niven reportedly said that the good thing about Flynn was that you knew exactly where you stood with him. When you needed his help, you could always count on him to let you down.

For firms that face these distortions, debt will be difficult and costly to obtain. These firms will have low leverage ratios.

15.2 CAN COSTS OF DEBT BE REDUCED?

As U.S. senators are prone to say, "A billion here, a billion there. Pretty soon it all adds up."[3] Each of the costs of financial distress we mentioned above is substantial in its own right. The sum of them may well affect debt financing severely. Thus, managers have an incentive to reduce these costs. We now turn to some of their methods. However, it should be mentioned at the outset that the methods below can, at most, reduce the costs of debt. They cannot *eliminate* them entirely.

Protective Covenants

As we discussed in a previous chapter, loan agreements and bond indentures frequently include protective covenants. These covenants should reduce the costs of bankruptcy, ultimately increasing the value of the firm. Thus, stockholders are likely to favor all reasonable covenants. To see this, consider three choices by stockholders to reduce bankruptcy costs.

1. *Issue No Debt.* Because of the tax advantages to debt, this is a very costly way of avoiding conflicts.
2. *Issue Debt with No Restrictive and Protective Covenants.* In this case, bondholders will demand high interest rates to compensate for the unprotected status of their debt.
3. *Write Protective and Restrictive Covenants into the Loan Contracts.* If the covenants are clearly written, the creditors may receive protection without large costs being imposed on the shareholders. The creditors will gladly accept a lower interest rate.

Thus, bond covenants, even if they reduce flexibility, can increase the value of the firm. They can be the lowest cost solution to the stockholder-bondholder conflict. A list of typical bond covenants and their uses appears in Table 15.2.

[3]The original quote is generally attributed to Senator Everett Dirksen, though whether he actually said it is not known.

TABLE 15.2
Loan Covenants

COVENANT TYPE	SHAREHOLDER ACTION OR FIRM CIRCUMSTANCES	REASON FOR COVENANT
Financial statement signals 1. Working capital requirement 2. Interest coverage 3. Minimum net worth	As firm approaches financial distress, shareholders may want firm to make high-risk investments.	Shareholders lose value before bankruptcy; bondholders are hurt much more in bankruptcy than shareholders (limited liability); bondholders are hurt by *distortion of investment that leads to increases in risk.*
Restrictions on asset disposition 1. Limit dividends 2. Limit sale of assets 3. Collateral and mortgages	Shareholders attempt to transfer corporate assets to themselves.	This limits the ability of shareholders to transfer assets to themselves and to *underinvest.*
Restrictions on switching assets	Shareholders attempt to increase risk of firm.	Increased firm risk helps shareholders; bondholders are hurt by *distortion of investment that leads to increases in risk.*
Dilution 1. Limit on leasing 2. Limit on further borrowing	Shareholders may attempt to issue new debt of equal or greater priority.	This restricts *dilution of the claim of existing bondholders.*

Consolidation of Debt

One reason bankruptcy costs are so high is that different creditors (and their lawyers) contend with each other. This problem can be alleviated by proper arrangement of bondholders and stockholders. For example, perhaps one, or at most a few, lenders can shoulder the entire debt. Should financial distress occur, negotiating costs are minimized under this arrangement. In addition, bondholders can purchase stock as well. In this way, stockholders and debtholders are not pitted against each other, because they are not separate entities. This appears to be the approach in Japan, where large banks generally take significant stock positions in the firms to which they lend money. Debt-equity ratios in Japan are far higher than those in the United States.

15.3 INTEGRATION OF TAX EFFECTS AND FINANCIAL DISTRESS COSTS

Modigliani and Miller argue that the firm's value rises with leverage in the presence of corporate taxes. Because this implies that all firms should choose maximum debt, the theory does not predict the behavior of firms in the real world. Other authors have suggested that bankruptcy and related costs reduce the value of the levered firm.

The integration of tax effects and distress costs appears in Figure 15.1. At the top of the figure, the diagonal straight line in the figure represents the value of the firm in a world without bankruptcy costs. The ∩-shaped curve represents the value of the firm with these costs. This curve rises as the firm moves from all-equity to a small amount of debt. Here, the present value of the distress costs is minimal because the probability of distress is so small. However, as more and more debt is added, the present value of these costs rises at an *increasing* rate. At some point, the increase in the present value of these costs from an additional dollar of debt equals the increase in the present value of the tax shield. This is the debt level maximizing the value of the firm and is represented by B^* in Figure 15.1. In other words, B^* is the optimal amount of debt. Bankruptcy costs increase faster than the tax shield beyond this point, implying a reduction in firm value from further leverage. At the bottom of Figure 15.1, the weighted average cost of capital (R_{WACC}) goes down as debt is added to the capital structure. After reaching B^*, the weighted

FIGURE 15.1

The Optimal Amount of Debt and the Value of the Firm

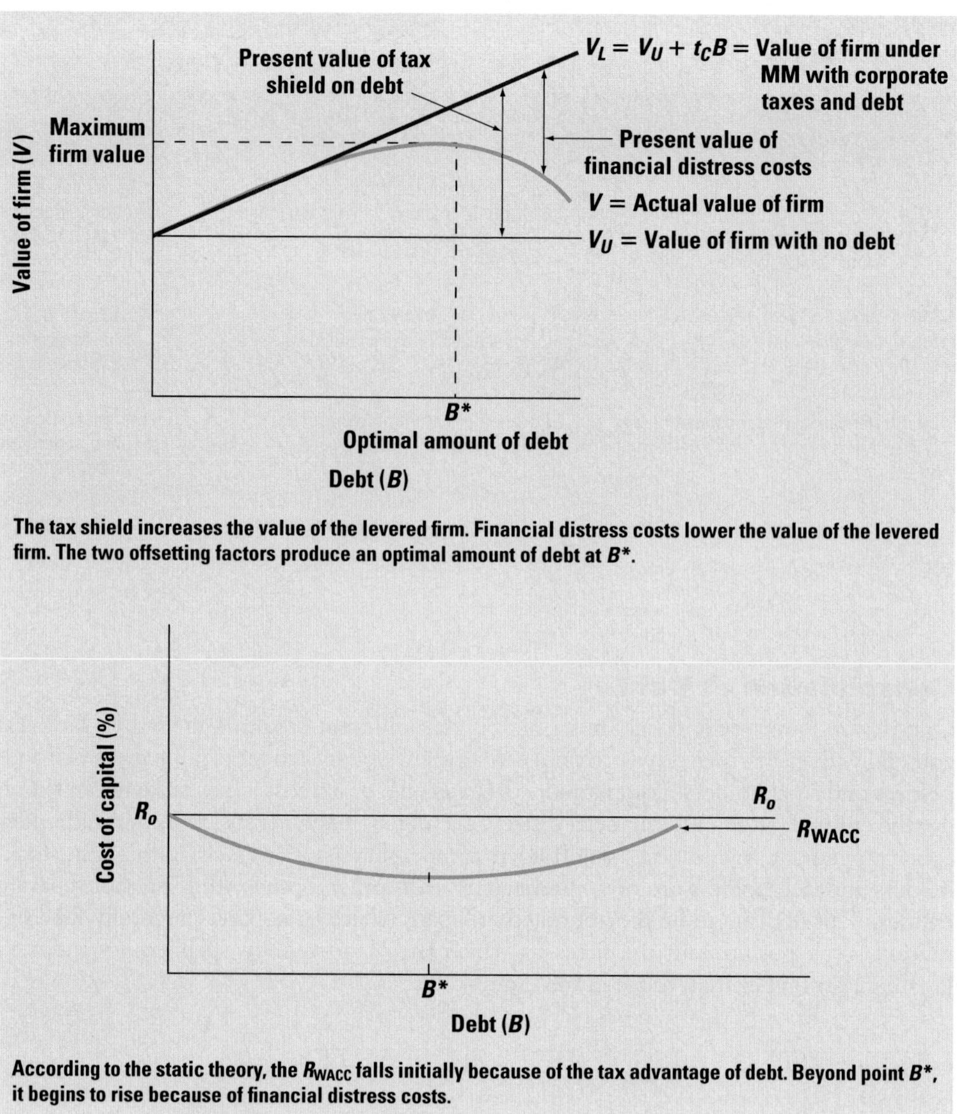

The tax shield increases the value of the levered firm. Financial distress costs lower the value of the levered firm. The two offsetting factors produce an optimal amount of debt at B^*.

According to the static theory, the R_{WACC} falls initially because of the tax advantage of debt. Beyond point B^*, it begins to rise because of financial distress costs.

average cost of capital goes up. The optimal amount of debt also produces the lowest weighted average cost of capital.

Our discussion implies that a firm's capital structure decisions involve a trade-off between the tax benefits of debt and the costs of financial distress. In fact, this approach is frequently called the *trade-off* or the *static trade-off* theory of capital structure. The implication is that there is an optimum amount of debt for any individual firm. This amount of debt becomes the firm's target debt level. (In the real world of finance, this optimum is frequently referred to as the firm's *debt capacity*.) Because financial distress costs cannot be expressed in a precise way, no formula has yet been developed to determine a firm's optimal debt level exactly. However, the last section of this chapter offers some rules of thumb for selecting a debt-equity ratio in the real world. Our situation reminds us of a quote of John Maynard Keynes. He reputedly said that, although most historians would agree that Queen Elizabeth I was both a better monarch and an unhappier woman than Queen Victoria, no one has yet been able to express the statement in a precise and rigorous formula.

Pie Again

Critics of the MM theory often say that MM fails when we add such real world issues as taxes and bankruptcy costs. Taking that view, however, blinds critics to the real value of the MM theory. The pie approach offers a more constructive way of thinking about these matters and the role of capital structure.

Taxes are just another claim on the cash flows of the firm. Let G (for government and taxes) stand for the value of the firm's taxes. Bankruptcy costs are also another claim on the cash flows. Let us label their value with an L (for lawyers?). The pie theory says that these claims are paid from only one source, the cash flows (CF) of the firm. Algebraically, we must have:

CF = Payments to stockholders (S)
+
Payments to bondholders (B)
+
Payments to the government (G)
+
Payments to lawyers (L)
+
Payments to any and all other claimants to the cash flows of the firm

Figure 15.2 shows the new pie. No matter how many slices we take and no matter who gets them, they must still add up to the total cash flow. The total value of the firm, V_T, is unaltered by the capital structure. Now, however, we must be broader in our definition of the firm's value:

$$V_T = S + B + G + L$$

We previously wrote the firm's value as:

$$S + B$$

when we ignored taxes and bankruptcy costs.

We have not even begun to exhaust the list of financial claims to the firm's cash flows. To give an unusual example, everyone reading this book has an economic claim to the cash flows of General Motors. After all, if you are injured in an accident, you might sue GM. Win or lose, GM will expend resources dealing with the matter. If you think this is

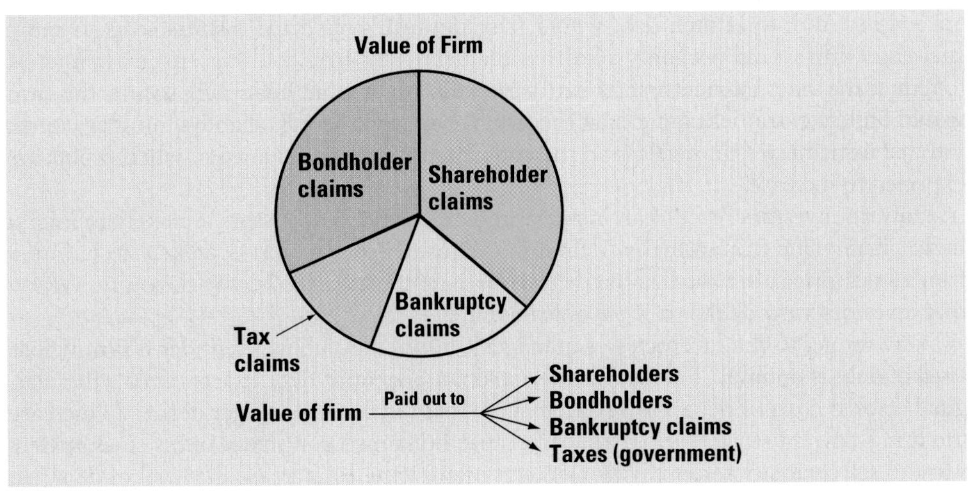

FIGURE 15.2 The Pie Model with Real World Factors

farfetched and unimportant, ask yourself what GM might be willing to pay every man, woman, and child in the country to have them promise that they would never sue GM, no matter what happened. The law does not permit such payments, but that does not mean that a value to all of those potential claims does not exist. We guess that it would run into the billions of dollars, and, for GM or any other company, there should be a slice of the pie labeled *LS* for "potential lawsuits."

This is the essence of the MM intuition and theory: V is V(CF) and depends on the total cash flow of the firm. The capital structure cuts it into slices.

There is, however, an important difference between claims such as those of stockholders and bondholders on the one hand and those of government and potential litigants in lawsuits on the other. The first set of claims are **marketed claims**, and the second set are **nonmarketed claims**. One difference is that the marketed claims can be bought and sold in financial markets, and the nonmarketed claims cannot.

When we speak of the *value of the firm,* we are referring just to the value of the marketed claims, V_M, and not the value of nonmarketed claims, V_N. What we have shown is that the total value:

$$\begin{aligned} V_T &= S + B + G + L \\ &= V_M + V_N \end{aligned}$$

is unaltered. But, as we saw, the value of the marketed claims, V_M, can change with changes in the capital structure.

By the pie theory, any increase in V_M must imply an identical decrease in V_N. Rational financial managers will choose a capital structure to maximize the value of the marketed claims, V_M. Equivalently, rational managers will work to minimize the value of the nonmarketed claims, V_N. These are taxes and bankruptcy costs in the previous example, but they also include all the other nonmarketed claims such as the *LS* claim.

15.4 SIGNALING

The previous section pointed out that the corporate leverage decision involves a trade-off between a tax subsidy and financial distress costs. This idea was graphed in Figure 15.1, where the marginal tax subsidy of debt exceeds the distress costs of debt for low levels of debt. The reverse holds for high levels of debt. The firm's capital structure is optimized where the marginal tax subsidy to debt equals the marginal cost.

Let's explore this idea a little more. What is the relationship between a company's profitability and its debt level? A firm with low anticipated profits will likely take on a low level of debt. A small interest deduction is all that is needed to offset all of this firm's pretax profits. And, too much debt would raise the firm's expected distress costs. A more successful firm would probably take on more debt. This firm could use the extra interest to reduce the taxes from its greater earnings. And, being more financially secure, this firm would find its extra debt increasing the risk of bankruptcy only slightly. In other words, rational firms raise debt levels (and the concomitant interest payments) when profits are expected to increase.

How do investors react to an increase in debt? Rational investors are likely to infer a higher firm value from a higher debt level. Thus, these investors are likely to bid up a firm's stock price after the firm has, say, issued debt in order to buy back equity. We say that investors view debt as a *signal* of firm value.

Now we get to the incentives of managers to fool the public. Consider a firm whose level of debt is optimal. That is, the marginal tax benefit of debt exactly equals the marginal distress costs of debt. However, imagine that the firm's manager desires to increase the firm's current stock price, perhaps because he knows that many of his stockholders want to sell their stock soon. This manager might want to increase the level of debt just to make investors *think* that the firm is more valuable than it really is. If the strategy works, investors will push up the price of the stock.

The above implies that firms can fool investors by taking on *some* additional leverage. Now let's ask the big question. Are there benefits to extra debt but no costs, implying that all firms will take on as much debt as possible? The answer, fortunately, is that there are costs as well. Imagine that a firm has issued extra debt just to fool the public. At some point, the market will learn that the company is not that valuable after all. At this time, the stock price should actually fall *below* what it would have been had the debt never been increased. Why? Because the firm's debt level is now above the optimal level. That is, the marginal tax benefit of debt is below the marginal cost of debt. Thus, if the current stockholders plan to sell, say, half of their shares now and retain the other half, an increase in debt will help them on immediate sales but likely hurt them on later ones.

Now here is the important point: We said earlier that, in a world where managers do not attempt to fool investors, valuable firms issue more debt than less valuable ones. It turns out that, even when managers attempt to fool investors, the more valuable firms will still want to issue more debt than the less valuable firms. That is, while all firms will increase debt levels somewhat to fool investors, the cost of extra debt prevents the less valuable firms from issuing more debt than the more valuable firms issue. Thus, investors can still treat debt level as a signal of firm value. In other words, investors can still view an announcement of debt as a positive sign for the firm.

The above is a simplified example of debt signaling and one can argue that it is too simplified. For example, perhaps the stockholders of some firms want to sell most of their stock immediately while the stockholders of other firms want to sell only a little of theirs now. It is impossible to tell here whether the firms with the most debt are the most valuable or merely the ones with the most impatient stockholders. Since other objections can be brought up as well, signaling theory is best validated by empirical evidence. And, fortunately, the empirical evidence tends to support the theory.

For example, consider the evidence concerning **exchange offers**. Firms often change their debt levels through exchange offers, of which there are two types. The first type of offer allows stockholders to exchange some of their stock for debt, thereby increasing leverage. The second type allows bondholders to exchange some of their debt for stock, decreasing leverage. Figure 15.3 shows the stock price behavior of firms that

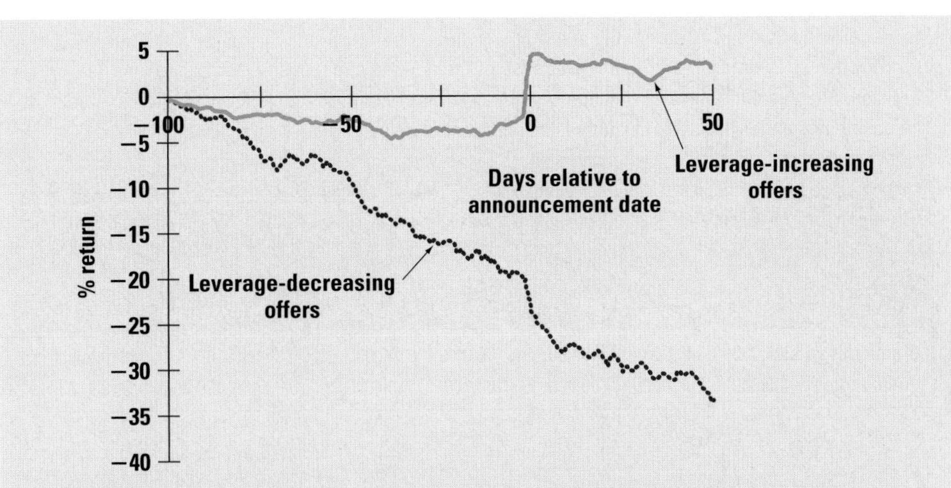

Exchange offers change the debt-to-equity ratios of firms. The graph shows that stock prices increase for firms whose exchange offers increase leverage. Conversely, stock prices decrease for firms whose offers decrease leverage.

FIGURE 15.3

Stock Returns at the Time of Announcements of Exchange Offers

Source: K. Shah, "The Nature of Information Conveyed by Pure Capital Structure Changes," *Journal of Financial Economics* 36 (August 1994).

change their proportions of debt and equity via exchange offers. The solid line in the figure indicates that stock prices rise substantially on the date when an exchange offering increasing leverage is announced. (This date is referred to as date 0 in the figure.) Conversely, the dotted line in the figure indicates that stock price falls substantially when an offer decreasing leverage is announced.

The market infers from an increase in debt that the firm is better off, leading to a stock price rise. Conversely, the market infers the reverse from a decrease in debt, implying a stock price fall. Thus, we say that managers signal information when they change leverage.

15.5 SHIRKING, PERQUISITES, AND BAD INVESTMENTS: A NOTE ON AGENCY COST OF EQUITY

The previous section introduced the static trade-off model, where a rise in debt increases both the tax shield and the costs of distress. We now extend the trade-off model by considering an important agency cost of equity. A discussion of this cost of equity is contained in a well-known quote from Adam Smith.[4]

> The directors of such [joint-stock] companies, however, being the managers of other people's money than of their own, it cannot well be expected that they should watch over it with the same anxious vigilance with which the partners in a private copartnery frequently watch over their own. Like the stewards of a rich man, they are apt to consider attention to small matters as not for their master's honor, and very easily give themselves a dispensation from having it. Negligence and profusion, therefore, must always prevail, more or less, in the management of the affairs of such a company.

This elegant prose can be restated in modern day vocabulary. An individual will work harder for a firm if she is one of its owners than if she is just an employee. In addition, the individual will work harder if she owns a large percentage of the company than if she owns a small percentage. This idea has an important implication for capital structure, which we illustrate with the following example.

EXAMPLE 15.1 Shirking and Perks

Ms. Pagell is an owner-entrepreneur running a computer services firm worth $1 million. She currently owns 100 percent of the firm. Because of the need to expand, she must raise another $2 million. She can either issue $2 million of debt at 12 percent interest or issue $2 million in stock. The cash flows under the two alternatives are presented below:

	Debt Issue				Stock Issue			
	CASH FLOW	INTEREST	CASH FLOW TO EQUITY	CASH FLOW TO MS. PAGELL (100% OF EQUITY)	CASH FLOW	INTEREST	CASH FLOW TO EQUITY	CASH FLOW TO MS. PAGELL ($33\frac{1}{3}$% OF EQUITY)
6-hour days	$300,000	$240,000	$ 60,000	$ 60,000	$300,000	0	$300,000	$100,000
10-hour days	400,000	240,000	160,000	160,000	400,000	0	400,000	133,333

(*continued*)

[4]Adam Smith, *The Wealth of Nations* [1776], Cannon edition (New York: Modern Library, 1937), p. 700, as quoted in M. C. Jensen and W. Meckling, "Theory of the Firm: Managerial Behavior, Agency Costs, and Ownership Structure," *Journal of Financial Economics* 3 (1978).

Like any entrepreneur, Ms. Pagell can choose the degree of intensity with which she works. In our example, she can either work a 6- or a 10-hour day. With the debt issue, the extra work brings her $100,000 ($160,000 − 60,000) more income. However, let's assume that with a stock issue she retains only a one-third interest in the equity. Here, the extra work brings her merely $33,333 ($133,333 − 100,000). Being only human, she is likely to work harder if she issues debt. In other words, she has more incentive to *shirk* if she issues equity.

In addition, she is likely to obtain more *perquisites* (a big office, a company car, more expense account meals) if she issues stock. If she is a one-third stockholder, two-thirds of these costs are paid for by the other stockholders. If she is the sole owner, any additional perquisites reduce her equity stake alone.

Finally, she is more likely to take on capital budgeting projects with negative net present values. It might seem surprising that a manager with any equity interest at all would take on negative NPV projects, since stock price would clearly fall here. However, managerial salaries generally rise with firm size, indicating that managers have an incentive to accept some unprofitable projects after all the profitable ones have been taken on. That is, when an unprofitable project is accepted, the loss in stock value to a manager with only a small equity interest may be less than the increase in salary. In fact, it is our opinion that losses from accepting bad projects are far greater than losses from either shirking or excessive perquisites. Hugely unprofitable projects have bankrupted whole firms, something that even the largest of expense accounts is unlikely to do.

Thus, as the firm issues more equity, our entrepreneur will likely increase leisure time, work-related perquisites, and unprofitable investments. These three items are called agency costs, because managers of the firm are agents of the stockholders.[5]

This example is quite applicable to a small company considering a large stock offering. Because a manager-owner will greatly dilute his or her share in the total equity in this case, a significant drop in work intensity or a significant increase in fringe benefits is possible. However, the example may be less applicable for a large corporation with many stockholders. For example, consider a large company such as General Motors going public for the umpteenth time. The typical manager there already has such a small percentage stake in the firm that any temptation for negligence has probably been experienced before. An additional offering cannot be expected to increase this temptation.

Who bears the burden of these agency costs? If the new stockholders invest with their eyes open, they do not. Knowing that Ms. Pagell may work shorter hours, they will pay only a low price for the stock. Thus, it is the owner who is hurt by agency costs. However, Ms. Pagell can protect herself to some extent. Just as stockholders reduce bankruptcy costs through protective covenants, an owner may allow monitoring by new stockholders. However, though proper reporting and surveillance may reduce the agency costs of equity, these techniques are unlikely to eliminate them.

It is commonly suggested that leveraged buyouts (LBOs) significantly reduce the cost of equity. In an LBO, a purchaser (usually a team of existing management) buys out the stockholders at a price above the current market. In other words, the company goes private since the stock is placed in the hands of only a few people. Because the managers now own a substantial chunk of the business, they are likely to work harder than when they were simply hired hands.[6]

[5]As previously discussed, agency costs are generally defined as the costs from the conflicts of interest among stockholders, bondholders, and managers.

[6]One professor we know introduces his classes to LBOs by asking the students three questions:

1. How many of you have ever owned your own car?
2. How many of you have ever rented a car?
3. How many of you took better care of the car you owned than the car you rented?

Just as it is human nature to take better care of your own car, it is human nature to work harder when you own more of the company.

Effect of Agency Costs of Equity on Debt-Equity Financing

The preceding discussion on the agency costs of equity should be viewed as an extension of the static trade-off model. That is, we stated in Section 15.3 that the change in the value of the firm when debt is substituted for equity is the difference between (1) the tax shield on debt and (2) the increase in the costs of financial distress (including the agency costs of debt). Now, the change in the value of the firm is (1) the tax shield on debt plus (2) the reduction in the agency costs of equity, minus (3) the increase in the costs of financial distress (including the agency costs of debt). The optimal debt-equity ratio would be higher in a world with agency costs of equity than in a world without these costs. However, because costs of financial distress are so significant, the costs of equity do not imply 100 percent debt financing.

Free Cash Flow

Any reader of murder mysteries knows that a criminal must have both motive and opportunity. The above discussion was about motive. Managers with only a small ownership interest have an incentive for wasteful behavior. For example, they bear only a small portion of the costs of, say, excessive expense accounts, and reap all of the benefits.

Now let's talk about opportunity. A manager can only pad his expense account if the firm has the cash flow to cover it. Thus, we might expect to see more wasteful activity in a firm with a capacity to generate large cash flows than in one with a capacity to generate only small flows. This very simple idea is formally called the *free cash flow hypothesis.*

A fair amount of academic work supports the hypothesis. For example, a frequently cited paper found that firms with high free cash flow are more likely to make bad acquisitions than firms with low free cash flow.[7]

The hypothesis has important implications for capital structure. Since dividends leave the firm, they reduce free cash flow. Thus, according to the free cash flow hypothesis, an increase in dividends should benefit the stockholders by reducing the ability of managers to pursue wasteful activities. Furthermore, since interest and principal also leave the firm, debt reduces free cash flow as well. In fact, interest and principal should have a greater effect than dividends on the free-spending ways of managers, because bankruptcy will occur if the firm is unable to make future debt payments. By contrast, a future dividend reduction will cause fewer problems to the managers, since the firm has no legal obligation to pay dividends. Because of this, the free cash flow hypothesis argues that a shift from equity to debt will boost firm value.

In summary, the free cash flow hypothesis provides still another reason for firms to issue debt. We previously discussed the cost of equity; new equity dilutes the holdings of managers with equity interests, increasing their *motive* to waste corporate resources. We now state that debt reduces free cash flow, because the firm must make interest and principal payments. The free cash flow hypothesis implies that debt reduces the *opportunity* for managers to waste resources.

15.6 THE PECKING-ORDER THEORY

Although the trade-off theory has dominated corporate finance circles for a long time, attention is also being paid to the *pecking-order theory.* To understand this view of the world, let's put ourselves in the position of a corporate financial manager whose firm needs new capital. The manager faces a choice between issuing debt and issuing equity. Previously, we evaluated the choice in terms of tax benefits, distress costs, and agency costs. However, there is one consideration that we have so far neglected: timing.

[7]L. Lang, R. Stulz, and R. Walkling, "Managerial Performance, Tobin's *Q* and the Gains in Tender Offers," *Journal of Financial Economics* (1989).

Imagine the manager saying:

> I want to issue stock in one situation only—when it is overvalued. If the stock of my firm is selling at $50 per share, but I think that it is actually worth $60, I will not issue stock. I would actually be giving new stockholders a gift, because they would receive stock worth $60, but would only have to pay $50 for it. More importantly, my current stockholders would be upset, because the firm would be receiving $50 in cash, but giving away something worth $60. So if I believe that my stock is undervalued, I would issue bonds. Bonds, particularly those with little or no risk of default, are likely to be priced correctly. Their value is primarily determined by the marketwide interest rate, a variable that is publicly known.
>
> But, suppose that our stock is selling at $70. Now I'd like to issue stock. If I can get some fool to buy our stock for $70 while the stock is really only worth $60, I will be making $10 for our current shareholders.

Now, although this may strike you as a cynical view, it seems to square well with reality. Before the United States adopted insider trading and disclosure laws, many managers were alleged to have unfairly trumpeted their firm's prospects prior to equity issuance. And, even today, managers seem more willing to issue equity after the price of their stock has risen than after their stock has fallen in price. Thus, timing might be an important motive in equity issuance, perhaps even more important than those motives in the trade-off model. After all, the firm in the preceding example *immediately* makes $10 by properly timing the issuance of equity. Ten dollars worth of agency costs and bankruptcy cost reduction might take many years to realize.

The key that makes the example work is asymmetric information; the manager must know more about his firm's prospects than does the typical investor. If the manager's estimate of the true worth of the company is no better than the estimate of a typical investor, any attempts by the manager to time will fail. This assumption of asymmetry is quite plausible. Managers should know more about their company than do outsiders, because managers work at the company every day. (One caveat is that some managers are perpetually optimistic about their firm, blurring good judgment.)

But we are not done with this example yet; we must consider the investor. Imagine an investor saying:

> I make investments carefully, because it involves my hard-earned money. However, even with all the time I put into studying stocks, I can't possibly know what the managers themselves know. After all, I've got a day job to be concerned with. So, I watch what the managers do. If a firm issues stock, the firm was likely overvalued beforehand. If a firm issues debt, it was likely undervalued.

When we look at both issuers and investors, we see a kind of poker game, with each side trying to outwit the other. There are two prescriptions to the issuer in this poker game. The first one, which is fairly straightforward, is to issue debt instead of equity when the stock is undervalued. The second, which is more subtle, is to issue debt also when the firm is *overvalued.* After all, if a firm issues equity, investors will infer that the stock is overvalued. They will not buy it until the stock has fallen enough to eliminate any advantage from equity issuance. In fact, only the most overvalued firms have any incentive to issue equity. Should even a moderately overpriced firm issue equity, investors will infer that this firm is among the *most* overpriced, causing the stock to fall more than is deserved. Thus, the end result is that virtually no one will issue equity.

This result that essentially all firms should issue debt is clearly an extreme one. It is as extreme as (1) the Modigliani-Miller (MM) result that, in a world without taxes, firms are indifferent to capital structure and (2) the MM result that, in a world of corporate taxes but no financial distress costs, all firms should be 100 percent debt financed. Perhaps we in finance have a penchant for extreme models!

But, just as one can temper MM's conclusions by combining financial distress costs with corporate taxes, we can temper those of the pure pecking-order theory. This pure version assumes that timing is the financial manager's only consideration. In reality, a manager must consider taxes, financial distress costs, and agency costs as well. Thus, a firm may issue debt only up to a point. If financial distress becomes a real possibility beyond that point, the firm may issue equity instead.

Rules of the Pecking Order

The above discussion presented the basic ideas behind the pecking-order theory. What are the practical implications of the theory for financial managers? The theory provides the following two rules for the real world.

RULE #1 USE INTERNAL FINANCING For expository purposes, we have oversimplified by comparing equity to *riskless* debt. Managers cannot use special knowledge of their firm to determine if this type of debt is mispriced, because the price of riskless debt is determined solely by the marketwide interest rate. However, in reality, corporate debt has the possibility of default. Thus, just as managers have a tendency to issue equity when they think it is overvalued, managers also have a tendency to issue debt when they think it is overvalued.

When would managers view their debt as overvalued? Probably in the same situations when they think their equity is overvalued. For example, if the public thinks that the firm's prospects are rosy but the managers see trouble ahead, these managers would view their debt—as well as their equity—as being overvalued. That is, the public might see the debt as nearly risk-free, whereas the managers see a strong possibility of default.

Thus, investors are likely to price a debt issue with the same skepticism that they have when pricing an equity issue. The way managers get out of this box is to finance projects out of retained earnings. You don't have to worry about investor skepticism if you can avoid going to investors in the first place. Thus, the first rule of the pecking order is:

Use Internal Financing.

RULE #2 ISSUE SAFE SECURITIES FIRST Although investors fear mispricing of both debt and equity, the fear is much greater for equity. Corporate debt still has relatively little risk compared to equity because, if financial distress is avoided, investors receive a fixed return. Thus, the pecking-order theory implies that, if outside financing is required, debt should be issued before equity. Only when the firm's debt capacity is reached should the firm consider equity.

Of course, there are many types of debt. For example, because convertible debt is more risky than straight debt, the pecking-order theory implies that one should issue straight debt before issuing convertibles. Thus, the second rule of pecking-order theory is:

Issue the Safest Securities First.

Implications

There are a number of implications associated with the pecking-order theory that are at odds with the trade-off theory.

1. *There is no target amount of leverage.* According to the trade-off model, each firm balances the benefits of debt, such as the tax shield, with the costs of debt, such as distress costs. The optimal amount of leverage occurs where the marginal benefit of debt equals the marginal cost of debt.

By contrast, the pecking-order theory does not imply a target amount of leverage. Rather, each firm chooses its leverage ratio based on financing needs. Firms first fund projects out of retained earnings. This should lower the percentage of debt in the capital structure, because profitable, internally funded projects raise both the book value and the market value of equity. Additional cash needs are met with debt, clearly raising the debt level. However, at some point the debt capacity of the firm may be exhausted, giving way to equity issuance. Thus, the amount of leverage is determined by the happenstance of available projects. Firms do not pursue a target ratio of debt to equity.

2. *Profitable firms use less debt.* Profitable firms generate cash internally, implying less need for outside financing. Because firms desiring outside capital turn to debt first, profitable firms end up relying on less debt. The trade-off model does not have this implication. The greater cash flow of more profitable firms creates greater debt capacity. These firms will use that debt capacity to capture the tax shield and the other benefits of leverage.

3. *Companies like financial slack.* The pecking-order theory is based on the difficulties of obtaining financing at a reasonable cost. A skeptical investing public thinks a stock is overvalued if the managers try to issue more of it, thereby leading to a stock-price decline. Because this happens with bonds only to a lesser extent, managers rely first on bond financing. However, firms can only issue so much debt before encountering the potential costs of financial distress.

Wouldn't it be easier to have the cash ahead of time? This is the idea behind *financial slack.* Because firms know that they will have to fund profitable projects at various times in the future, they accumulate cash today. They are then not forced to go to the capital markets when a project comes up. However, there is a limit to the amount of cash a firm will want to accumulate. As mentioned earlier in this chapter, too much free cash may tempt managers to pursue wasteful activities.

15.7 GROWTH AND THE DEBT-EQUITY RATIO

While the trade-off between the tax shield and bankruptcy costs (as illustrated in Figure 15.1) is often viewed as the "standard model" of capital structure, it has its critics. For example, some point out that bankruptcy costs in the real world appear to be much smaller than the tax subsidy. Thus, the model implies that the optimal debt/value ratio should be near 100 percent, an implication at odds with reality.

Perhaps the pecking-order theory is more consistent with the real world here. That is, firms are likely to have more equity in their capital structure than implied by the static trade-off theory, because internal financing is preferred to external financing.

In addition, Berens and Cuny argue that growth implies significant equity financing, even in a world with low bankruptcy costs.[8] To explain the idea, we first consider an example of a no-growth firm. Next, we examine the effect of growth on firm leverage.

No Growth

Imagine a world of perfect certainty[9] where a firm has annual earnings before interest and taxes (EBIT) of $100. In addition, the firm has issued $1,000 of debt at an interest rate of 10 percent, implying interest payments of $100 per year. The cash flows to the firm are:

[8]J. L. Berens and C. L. Cuny, "Inflation, Growth and Capital Structure," *Review of Financial Studies* 8 (Winter 1995).

[9]The same qualitative results occur under uncertainty, though the mathematics is more troublesome.

	Date			
	1	2	3	4 . . .
Earnings before interest and taxes (EBIT)	$100	$100	$100	$100 . . .
Interest	− 100	− 100	− 100	− 100 . . .
Taxable income	$ 0	$ 0	$ 0	$ 0

The firm has issued just enough debt so that all EBIT is paid out as interest. Since interest is tax deductible, the firm pays no taxes. In this example, the equity is worthless because stockholders receive no cash flows (we assume there are no noncash deductions such as depreciation). Since debt is worth $1,000, the firm is also valued at $1,000. Therefore, the debt-to-value ratio is 100 percent ($1,000/$1,000).

Had the firm issued less than $1,000 of debt, the corporation would have positive taxable income and, consequently, would have ended up paying some taxes. Had the firm issued more than $1,000 of debt, interest would have exceeded EBIT, causing default. Consequently, the optimal debt-to-value ratio is 100 percent.

Growth

Now imagine another firm where EBIT is also $100 at date 1 but is growing at 5 percent per year.[10] To eliminate taxes, this firm also wants to issue enough debt so that interest equals EBIT. Since EBIT is growing at 5 percent per year, interest must also grow at this rate. This is achieved by increasing debt by 5 percent per year.[11] The debt, EBIT, interest, and taxable income levels are:

	Date				
	0	1	2	3	4 . . .
Debt	$1,000	$1,050	$1,102.50	$1,157.63 . . .	
New debt issued		50	52.50	55.13 . . .	
EBIT		$ 100	$ 105	$ 110.25	$115.76 . . .
Interest		− 100	− 105	− 110.25	− 115.76 . . .
Taxable income		$ 0	$ 0	$ 0	$ 0

Note that interest on a particular date is always 10 percent of the debt on the previous date. Debt is set so that interest is exactly equal to EBIT. As in the no-growth case, the levered firm has the maximum amount of debt at each date. Default would occur if interest payments were increased.

Because growth is 5 percent per year, the value of the firm is:[12]

$$V_{\text{Firm}} = \frac{\$100}{.10 - .05} = \$2,000$$

[10]For simplicity, assume that growth is achieved without earnings retention. The same conclusions would be reached with retained earnings, though the arithmetic would become more involved. Of course, growth without earnings retention is less realistic than growth with retention.

[11]Since the firm makes no real investment, the new debt is used to buy back shares of stock.

[12]The firm can also be valued by a variant of (14.5):

$$V_L = V_U + PV \text{ of tax shield}$$
$$= \frac{\$100(1 - t_C)}{.10 - .05} + \frac{t_C \times \$100}{.10 - .05} = \$2,000$$

Because of firm growth, both V_U and PV of tax shield are growing perpetuities.

The equity at date 0 is the difference between the value of the firm at that time, \$2,000, and the debt of \$1,000. Hence, equity must be equal to \$1,000,[13] implying a debt-to-value ratio of 50 percent (= \$1,000/\$2,000). Note the important difference between the no-growth and the growth example. The no-growth example has no equity; the value of the firm is simply the value of the debt. With growth, there is equity as well as debt.

We can also value the equity in another way. It may appear at first glance that the stockholders receive nothing, since the EBIT is paid out as interest each year. However, the new debt issued each year can be paid as a dividend to the stockholders. Because the new debt is \$50 at date 1 and grows at 5 percent per year, the value of the stockholders' interest is:

$$\frac{\$50}{.10 - .05} = \$1{,}000$$

the same number that we obtained in the previous paragraph.

As we mentioned earlier, any further increase in debt above \$1,000 at date 0 would lower the value of the firm in a world with bankruptcy costs. Thus, with growth, the optimal amount of debt is less than 100 percent. Note, however, that bankruptcy costs need not be as large as the tax subsidy. In fact, even with infinitesimally small bankruptcy costs, firm value would decline if promised interest rose above \$100 in the first year. The key to this example is that *today's* interest is set equal to *today's* income. While the introduction of future growth opportunities increases firm value, it does not increase the current level of debt needed to shield today's income from today's taxes. Since equity is the difference between firm value and debt, growth increases the value of equity.

The preceding example captures an essential feature of the real world: growth. The same conclusion is reached in a world of inflation but with no growth opportunities. The result of this section, that 100 percent debt financing is suboptimal, holds whether growth opportunities and/or inflation is present. Since most firms have growth opportunities and since inflation has been with us for most of this century, this section's example is based on realistic assumptions. The basic point is this: High-growth firms will have lower debt ratios than low-growth firms.

15.8 HOW FIRMS ESTABLISH CAPITAL STRUCTURE

The theories of capital structure are among the most elegant and sophisticated in the field of finance. Financial economists should (and do!) pat themselves on the back for contributions in this area. However, the practical applications of the theories are less than fully satisfying. Consider that our work on net present value produced an *exact* formula for evaluating projects. Prescriptions for capital structure under either the trade-off model or the pecking-order theory are vague by comparison. No exact formula is available for evaluating the optimal debt-equity ratio. Because of this, we turn to evidence from the real world.

The following empirical regularities are worthwhile to consider when formulating capital-structure policy.

1. *Most corporations have low debt-asset ratios.* How much debt is used in the real world? Figures 15.4 and 15.5 present the debt-to-equity ratios for U.S. industrial firms in both book and market values for the years 1995 to 2004. The debt ratios are usually less than 100 percent. Figure 15.6 shows the debt-to-total-value ratios of firms in different countries in recent years. Differences in accounting procedures

[13]Students are often surprised that equity has value when taxable income is zero. Actually, the equityholders are receiving cash flow each period, since the proceeds from the new debt can be used either to pay dividends or to buy back stock.

FIGURE 15.4

Book Debt Ratio: Total Debt as a Percentage of Equity for U.S. Nonfarm, Nonfinancial Firms from 1995 to 2004

Source: Board of Governors of the Federal Reserve System, *Flow of Accounts.*

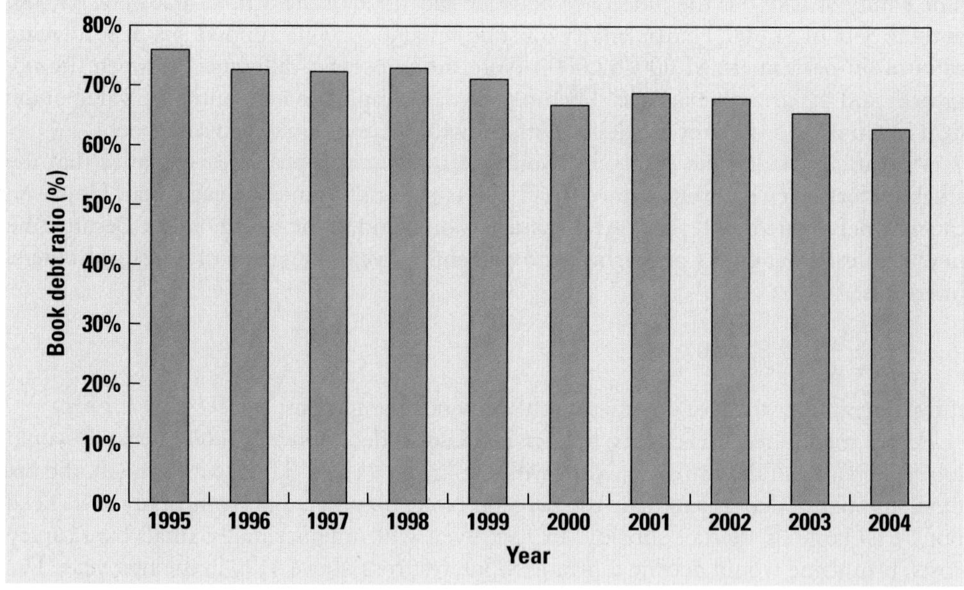

FIGURE 15.5

Market Debt Ratio: Total Debt as a Percentage of the Market Value of Equity for U.S. Nonfarm, Nonfinancial Firms from 1995 to 2004

Source: Board of Governors of the Federal Reserve System, *Flow of Funds.*

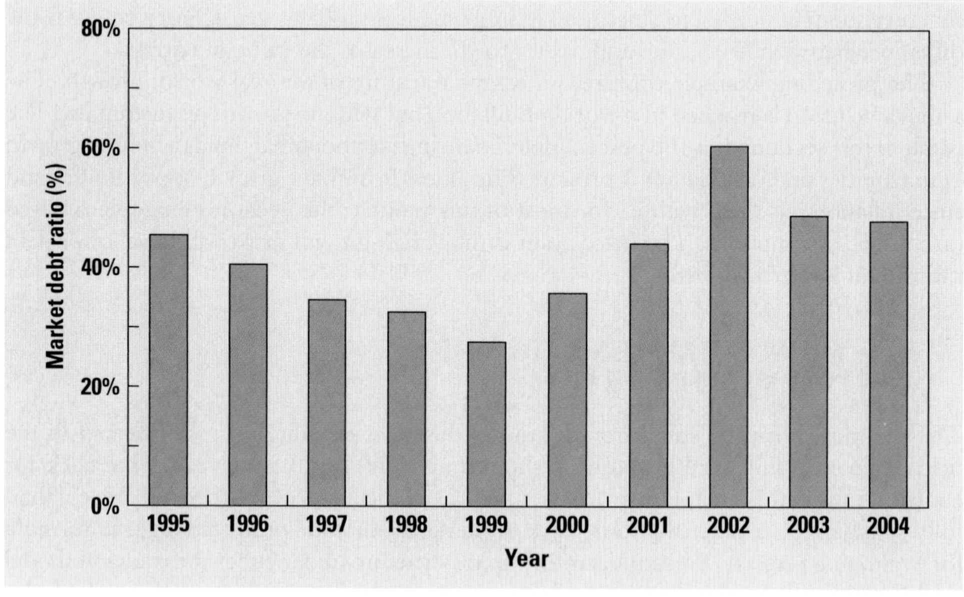

make the figures somewhat difficult to interpret. However, the debt ratios of U.S. and Canadian firms are the lowest.

Should we view these ratios as being high or low? As we discussed earlier, academics generally see corporate tax reduction as the chief motivation for debt. Thus, we might wonder if real world companies issue enough debt to greatly reduce, if not downright eliminate, corporate taxes. The empirical evidence suggests that this is not the case. For example, corporate taxes in the U.S. for 2004 were more than $200 billion. Thus, it is clear that corporations do not issue debt up to the point where tax shelters are completely used up. There are clearly limits to the amount of debt corporations can issue, perhaps because of the financial distress costs discussed earlier in this chapter.

FIGURE 15.6

Estimated Ratios of Debt to Total Value (accounting value) of Nonfinancial Firms, Various Countries

Source: OECD financial statistics.

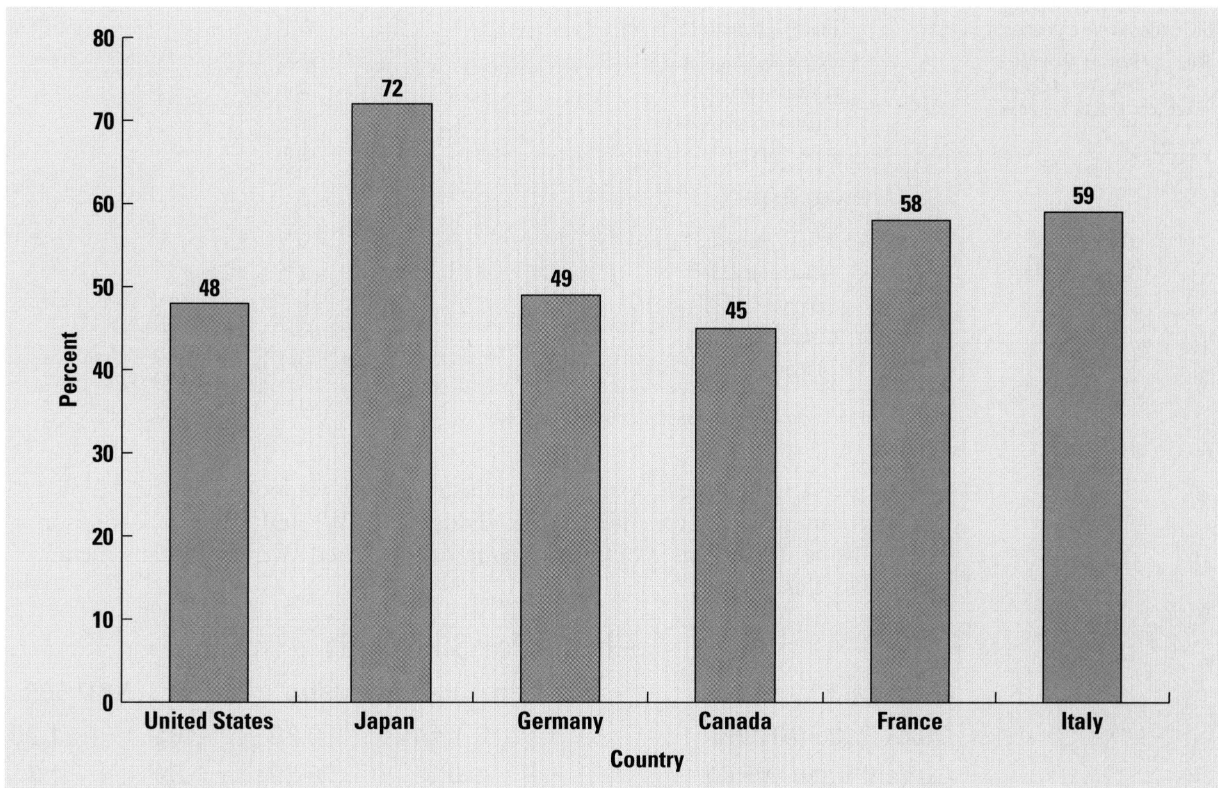

Definition: Debt is short-term debt plus long-term debt. Total value is debt plus equity (in book value terms).

2. *A number of firms use no debt.* In a fascinating study, Agrawal and Nagarajan examined approximately 100 firms on the New York Stock Exchange without long-term debt.[14] They found that these firms are averse to leverage of any kind, with little short-term debt as well. In addition, they have levels of cash and marketable securities well above their levered counterparts. Typically, the managers of these firms have high equity ownership. Furthermore, there is significantly greater family involvement in all-equity firms than in levered firms.

Thus, a story emerges. Managers of all-equity firms are less diversified than the managers of similar, but levered, firms. Because of this, significant leverage represents an added risk that the managers of all-equity firms are loathe to accept.

3. *There are differences in the capital structures of different industries.* There are very significant interindustry differences in debt ratios that persist over time. As can be seen in Table 15.3, debt ratios tend to be very low in high-growth industries with ample future investment opportunities such as the drugs and electronics industries. This is true even when the need for external financing is great. Industries such as air transport and paper, with relatively few investment opportunities and slow growth, tend to use the most debt.

[14]Anup Agrawal and Nandu Nagarajan, "Corporate Capital Structure, Agency Costs, and Ownership Control: The Case of All-Equity Firms," *Journal of Finance* 45 (September 1990).

TABLE 15.3

Capital Structure Ratios for Selected U.S. Nonfinancial Firms 5-Year Average (SIC codes in parentheses)

Source: Ibbotson Associates 2004, *Cost of Capital Quarterly*, 2004 Yearbook.

	DEBT AS A PERCENTAGE OF THE MARKET VALUE OF EQUITY AND DEBT
High Leverage	
Building construction (15)	47.1
Hotels and lodging (701)	55.4
Air transport (451)	47.6
Communications (48)	39.7
Paper (26)	49.6
Low Leverage	
Drugs (283)	5.7
Electronics (367)	6.3
Biological products (2836)	5.7
Computers (3571)	7.9
Educational services (82)	4.0

Definition: Debt is the total of short-term debt and long-term debt.

To give a more specific example of industry effects, we looked up some capital structure information on Allied Waste Industries (AW) and Johnson & Johnson (JNJ) using the ratio area of investor.reuters.com. Allied Waste's capital structure looks like this:

Financial Strength

Financial Strength	Company	Industry	Sector	S&P 500
Quick Ratio (MRQ)	0.51	0.79	0.85	1.20
Current Ratio (MRQ)	0.61	0.99	1.39	1.71
LT Debt to Equity (MRQ)	2.95	1.26	0.76	0.54
Total Debt to Equity (MRQ)	3.05	1.34	0.89	0.79
Interest Coverage (TTM)	1.11	5.12	8.66	12.51

For every dollar of equity, Allied Waste has long-term debt of $2.95 and total debt of $3.05. Compare this result to Johnson & Johnson:

Financial Strength

Financial Strength	Company	Industry	Sector	S&P 500
Quick Ratio (MRQ)	1.63	1.27	1.98	1.20
Current Ratio (MRQ)	2.18	1.77	2.61	1.71
LT Debt to Equity (MRQ)	0.09	0.27	0.36	0.54
Total Debt to Equity (MRQ)	0.11	0.38	0.43	0.79
Interest Coverage (TTM)	74.61	22.32	13.71	12.51

For every dollar of equity, Johnson & Johnson has only $.09 of long-term debt and total debt of $.11. When we examine the industry and sector averages, the differences are again apparent. The waste management industry on average has $1.26 of long-term debt and $1.34 of total debt for every dollar of equity. By comparison, the pharmaceutical industry on average has only $.27 of long-term debt and $.38 of total debt for every dollar of equity. Thus, we see that choice of capital structure is a management decision, but it is clearly also influenced by industry characteristics.

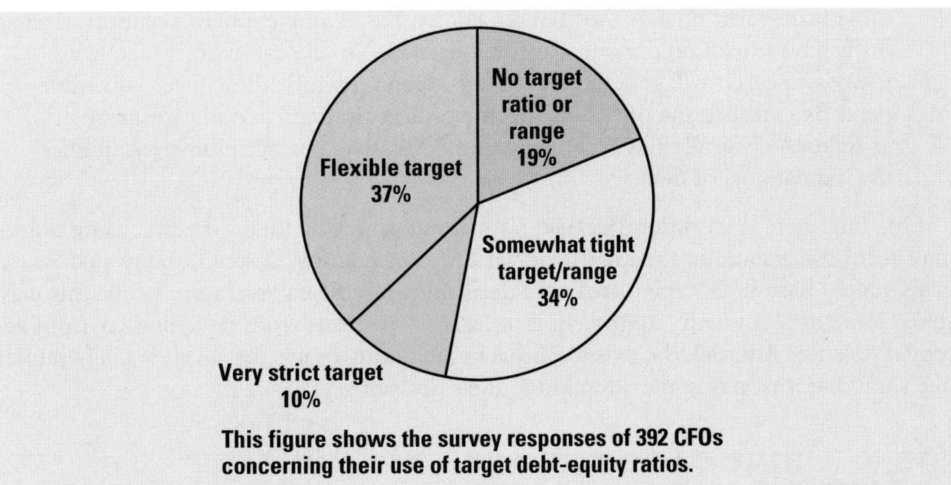

FIGURE 15.7

Survey Results on the Use of Target Debt-Equity Ratios

Source: Figure 6 of John Graham and Campbell Harvey, "The Theory and Practice of Corporate Finance," *Journal of Financial Economics* (May/June 2001).

4. *Most corporations employ target debt-equity ratios.* Graham and Harvey asked 392 chief financial officers (CFOs) whether their firms use target debt-equity ratios, with the results being presented in Figure 15.7.[15] As can be seen, the great majority of the firms use targets, though the strictness of the targets varies across companies. Only 19 percent of the firms avoid target ratios. Results elsewhere in the paper indicate that large firms are more likely than small firms to employ these targets. The CFOs did not specify what they meant by either *flexible* or *strict* targets. However, elsewhere in the study, the respondents indicated that, by and large, they did not rebalance in response to changes in their firm's stock price, suggesting some flexibility in target ratios.

How should companies establish target debt-equity ratios? While there is no mathematical formula for establishing a target ratio, we present three important factors affecting the ratio:

- *Taxes.* As pointed out earlier, firms can only deduct interest for tax purposes to the extent of their profits before interest. Thus, highly profitable firms are more likely to have larger target ratios than less profitable firms. By contrast, the pecking-order theory argues that profitable firms will employ less debt because they can invest out of retained earnings. However, the pecking-order theory argues against the use of *target* ratios in the first place.
- *Types of Assets.* Financial distress is costly, with or without formal bankruptcy proceedings. The costs of financial distress depend on the types of assets that the firm has. For example, if a firm has a large investment in land, buildings, and other tangible assets, it will have smaller costs of financial distress than a firm with a large investment in research and development. Research and development typically has less resale value than land; thus, most of its value disappears in financial distress. Therefore, firms with large investments in tangible assets are likely to have higher target debt-equity ratios than firms with large investments in research and development.
- *Uncertainty of Operating Income.* Firms with uncertain operating income have a high probability of experiencing financial distress, even without debt. Thus,

[15]Graham, John and Campbell Harvey, "The Theory and Practice of Corporate Finance," *Journal of Financial Economics* (May/June 2001).

these firms must finance mostly with equity. For example, pharmaceutical firms have uncertain operating income because no one can predict whether today's research will generate new drugs. Consequently, these firms issue little debt. By contrast, the operating income of firms in regulated industries, such as utilities, generally has little uncertainty. Relative to other industries, utilities use a great deal of debt.

One final note is in order. Because no formula supports them, the preceding points may seem too nebulous to assist financial decision making. Instead, many real world firms simply base their capital structure decisions on industry averages. While this may strike some as a cowardly approach, it at least keeps firms from deviating far from accepted practice. After all, the existing firms in any industry are the survivors. Therefore, one should at least pay some attention to their decisions.

15.9 A QUICK LOOK AT THE BANKRUPTCY PROCESS

As we have discussed, one of the consequences of using debt is the possibility of financial distress, which can be defined in several ways:

1. *Business failure.* This term is usually used to refer to a situation in which a business has terminated with a loss to creditors, but even an all-equity firm can fail.
2. *Legal bankruptcy.* Firms or creditors bring petitions to a federal court for bankruptcy. **Bankruptcy** is a legal proceeding for liquidating or reorganizing a business.
3. *Technical insolvency.* Technical insolvency occurs when a firm is unable to meet its financial obligations.
4. *Accounting insolvency.* Firms with negative net worth are insolvent on the books. This happens when the total book liabilities exceed the book value of the total assets.

The SEC has a good overview of the bankruptcy process in its "online publications" section: www.sec.gov.

We now very briefly discuss some of the terms and more relevant issues associated with bankruptcy and financial distress.

Liquidation and Reorganization

Firms that cannot or choose not to make contractually required payments to creditors have two basic options: liquidation or reorganization. **Liquidation** means termination of the firm as a going concern, and it involves selling off the assets of the firm. The proceeds, net of selling costs, are distributed to creditors in order of established priority. **Reorganization** is the option of keeping the firm a going concern; it often involves issuing new securities to replace old securities. Liquidation or reorganization is the result of a bankruptcy proceeding. Which occurs depends on whether the firm is worth more "dead or alive."

BANKRUPTCY LIQUIDATION Chapter 7 of the Federal Bankruptcy Reform Act of 1978 deals with "straight" liquidation. The following sequence of events is typical:

1. A petition is filed in a federal court. Corporations may file a voluntary petition, or involuntary petitions may be filed against the corporation by several of its creditors.
2. A trustee-in-bankruptcy is elected by the creditors to take over the assets of the debtor corporation. The trustee will attempt to liquidate the assets.

3. When the assets are liquidated, after payment of the bankruptcy administration costs, the proceeds are distributed among the creditors.
4. If any proceeds remain, after expenses and payments to creditors, they are distributed to the shareholders.

The distribution of the proceeds of the liquidation occurs according to the following priority list:

1. Administrative expenses associated with the bankruptcy.
2. Other expenses arising after the filing of an involuntary bankruptcy petition but before the appointment of a trustee.
3. Wages, salaries, and commissions.
4. Contributions to employee benefit plans.
5. Consumer claims.
6. Government tax claims.
7. Payment to unsecured creditors.
8. Payment to preferred stockholders.
9. Payment to common stockholders.

This priority list for liquidation is a reflection of the **absolute priority rule (APR)**. The higher a claim is on this list, the more likely it is to be paid. In many of these categories, there are various limitations and qualifications that we omit for the sake of brevity.

Two qualifications to this list are in order. The first concerns secured creditors. Such creditors are entitled to the proceeds from the sale of the security and are outside this ordering. However, if the secured property is liquidated and provides insufficient cash to cover the amount owed, the secured creditors join with unsecured creditors in dividing the remaining liquidated value. In contrast, if the secured property is liquidated for proceeds greater than the secured claim, the net proceeds are used to pay unsecured creditors and others. The second qualification to the APR is that, in reality, what happens and who gets what in the event of bankruptcy is subject to much negotiation, and, as a result, the APR is frequently not followed.

BANKRUPTCY REORGANIZATION Corporate reorganization takes place under Chapter 11 of the Federal Bankruptcy Reform Act of 1978. The general objective of a proceeding under Chapter 11 is to plan to restructure the corporation with some provision for repayment of creditors. A typical sequence of events follows:

Get the latest on bankruptcy at www.bankruptcydata.com.

1. A voluntary petition can be filed by the corporation, or an involuntary petition can be filed by creditors.
2. A federal judge either approves or denies the petition. If the petition is approved, a time for filing proofs of claims is set.
3. In most cases, the corporation (the "debtor in possession") continues to run the business.
4. The corporation (and, in certain cases, the creditors) submits a reorganization plan.
5. Creditors and shareholders are divided into classes. A class of creditors accepts the plan if a majority of the class agrees to the plan.
6. After its acceptance by creditors, the plan is confirmed by the court.

7. Payments in cash, property, and securities are made to creditors and shareholders. The plan may provide for the issuance of new securities.
8. For some fixed length of time, the firm operates according to the provisions of the reorganization plan.

The corporation may wish to allow the old stockholders to retain some participation in the firm. Needless to say, this may involve some protest by the holders of unsecured debt. In some cases, the bankruptcy procedure is needed to invoke the "cram-down" power of the bankruptcy court. Under certain circumstances, a class of creditors can be forced to accept a bankruptcy plan even if they vote not to approve it, hence the remarkably apt description "cram down."

So-called prepackaged bankruptcies are a relatively common phenomenon. What happens is that the corporation secures the necessary approval of a bankruptcy plan from a majority of its creditors first, and then it files for bankruptcy. As a result, the company enters bankruptcy and reemerges almost immediately.

For example, MTS Inc., better known as Tower Records, filed for Chapter 11 bankruptcy in February 2004. The company claimed it would not be able to meet debt payments without affecting daily operations. The problems experienced by Tower were increased competition from retailers such as Wal-Mart, Virgin Megastores, and Best Buy, as well as both legal and illegal digital downloading (particularly by college students). Tower and its bondholders therefore began negotiating a prepackaged bankruptcy, or prepack, which amounts to agreeing to terms prior to the bankruptcy filing. Tower's bondholders agreed to eliminate $80 million of the company's debt in exchange for equity interest in the company. As a result of the prepack, MTS was able to exit the Chapter 11 bankruptcy process in about two months.

To give another example, in November 2004, Trump Hotels and Casinos filed for Chapter 11 bankruptcy. This was the second bankruptcy proceeding for the company. Fortunately for "The Donald," creditors didn't say "You're fired!" Instead, under the terms of the prepack, Trump's stake in the company was cut, but he stayed on as chairman of the board and CEO. He also received, among other things, a 25 percent stake in the Miss America Pageant and four acres of land in Atlantic City. The current bondholders agreed to exchange their bonds for a combination of new bonds with a lower coupon rate, along with cash and stock.

Financial Management and the Bankruptcy Process

It may seem a little odd, but the right to go bankrupt is very valuable. There are several reasons why this is true. First of all, from an operational standpoint, when a firm files for bankruptcy, there is an immediate "stay" on creditors, usually meaning that payments to creditors will cease, and creditors will have to await the outcome of the bankruptcy process to find out if and how much they will be paid. This stay gives the firm time to evaluate its options, and it prevents what is usually termed a "race to the courthouse steps" by creditors and others.

Beyond this, some bankruptcy filings are actually strategic actions intended to improve a firm's competitive position, and firms have filed for bankruptcy even though they were not insolvent at the time. Probably the most famous example is Continental Airlines. In 1983, following deregulation of the airline industry, Continental found itself competing with newly established airlines that had much lower labor costs. Continental filed for reorganization under Chapter 11 even though it was not insolvent.

Continental argued that, based on pro forma data, it would become insolvent in the future, and a reorganization was therefore necessary. By filing for bankruptcy, Continental was able to terminate its existing labor agreements, lay off large numbers of workers, and slash wages for the remaining employees. In other words, at least in the eyes of critics, Continental essentially used the bankruptcy process as a vehicle for reducing labor costs. Congress subsequently modified bankruptcy laws to make it more difficult, though not impossible, for companies to abrogate a labor contract through the bankruptcy process.

Other famous examples of strategic bankruptcies exist. For example, Manville (then known as Johns-Manville) and Dow Corning filed for bankruptcy because of expected future losses resulting from litigation associated with asbestos and silicone breast implants, respectively. In fact, by 2004, at least 70 companies had filed for Chapter 11 bankruptcy because of asbestos litigation. In 2000, for example, Owens Corning, known for its pink fiberglass insulation, threw in the towel after settling about 240,000 cases with no end in sight. As of June 2004, the company was still in bankruptcy. In that month, the company reached a tentative agreement to repay senior trade creditors, bondholders, and holders of bank debt an estimated 35.8 percent of the debt owed. Other well-known companies that filed for bankruptcy due to the asbestos nightmare include Congoleum, Federal Mogul, and two subsidiaries of Halliburton.

Agreements to Avoid Bankruptcy

When a firm defaults on an obligation, it can avoid a bankruptcy filing. Because the legal process of bankruptcy can be lengthy and expensive, it is often in everyone's best interest to devise a "workout" that avoids a bankruptcy filing. Much of the time, creditors can work with the management of a company that has defaulted on a loan contract. Voluntary arrangements to restructure or "reschedule" the company's debt can be and often are made. This may involve *extension,* which postpones the date of payment, or *composition,* which involves a reduced payment.

www.mhhe.com/rwj

SUMMARY AND CONCLUSIONS

1. We mentioned in the last chapter that according to theory, firms should create all-debt capital structures under corporate taxation. Because firms generally assume moderate amounts of debt in the real world, the theory must have been missing something at that point. We state in this chapter that costs of financial distress cause firms to restrain their issuance of debt. These costs are of two types: direct and indirect. Lawyers' and accountants' fees during the bankruptcy process are examples of direct costs. We mention four examples of indirect costs:
   - Impaired ability to conduct business.
   - Incentive to take on risky projects.
   - Incentive toward underinvestment.
   - Distribution of funds to stockholders prior to bankruptcy.
2. Because the above costs are substantial and the stockholders ultimately bear them, firms have an incentive for cost reduction. We suggest three cost-reduction techniques:
   - Protective covenants.
   - Repurchase of debt prior to bankruptcy.
   - Consolidation of debt.

3. Because costs of financial distress can be reduced but not eliminated, firms will not finance entirely with debt. Figure 15.1 illustrates the relationship between firm value and debt. In the figure, firms select the debt-to-equity ratio at which firm value is maximized.
4. Signaling theory argues that profitable firms are likely to increase their leverage, since the extra interest payments will offset some of the pretax profits. Rational stockholders will infer higher firm value from a higher debt level. Thus, investors view debt as a signal of firm value.
5. Managers owning a small proportion of a firm's equity can be expected to work less, maintain more lavish expense accounts, and accept more pet projects with negative NPVs than managers owning a large proportion of equity. Since new issues of equity dilute a manager's percentage interest in the firm, the above agency costs are likely to increase when a firm's growth is financed through new equity, rather than through new debt.
6. The pecking-order theory implies that managers prefer internal to external financing. If external financing is required, managers tend to choose the safest securities, such as debt. Firms may accumulate slack to avoid external equity.
7. Berens and Cuny argue that significant equity financing can be explained by real growth and inflation, even in a world of low bankruptcy costs.
8. Debt-to-equity ratios vary across industries. We present three factors determining the target debt-to-equity ratio:
   a. *Taxes.* Firms with high taxable income should rely more on debt than firms with low taxable income.
   b. *Types of Assets.* Firms with a high percentage of intangible assets such as research and development should have low debt. Firms with primarily tangible assets should have higher debt.
   c. *Uncertainty of Operating Income.* Firms with high uncertainty of operating income should rely mostly on equity.
9. We closed the chapter with a brief look at the bankruptcy process and some financial aspects of bankruptcy.

CONCEPT QUESTIONS

1. **Bankruptcy Costs** What are the direct and indirect costs of bankruptcy? Briefly explain each.
2. **Stockholder Incentives** Do you agree or disagree with the following statement: A firm's stockholders will never want the firm to invest in projects with negative net present values. Why?
3. **Capital Structure Decisions** Due to large losses incurred in the past several years, a firm has $2 billion in tax loss carry-forwards. This means that the next $2 billion of the firm's income will be free from corporate income taxes. Security analysts estimate that it will take many years for the firm to generate $2 billion in earnings. The firm has a moderate amount of debt in its capital structure. The firm's CEO is deciding whether to issue debt or equity in order to raise the funds needed to finance an upcoming project. Which method of financing would you recommend? Why?
4. **Cost of Debt** What steps can stockholders take to reduce the costs of debt?
5. **M&M and Bankruptcy Costs** How do the existence of financial distress costs and agency costs affect Modigliani and Miller's theory in a world where corporations pay taxes?
6. **Agency Costs of Equity** What are the sources of the agency costs of equity?

7. **Observed Capital Structures** Refer to the observed capital structures given in Table 15.3 of the text. What do you notice about the types of industries with respect to their average debt-equity ratios? Are certain types of industries more likely to be highly leveraged than others? What are some possible reasons for this observed segmentation? Do the operating results and tax history of the firms play a role? How about their future earnings prospects? Explain.
8. **Bankruptcy and Corporate Ethics** As mentioned in the text, some firms have filed for bankruptcy because of actual or likely litigation-related losses. Is this a proper use of the bankruptcy process?
9. **Bankruptcy and Corporate Ethics** Firms sometimes use the threat of a bankruptcy filing to force creditors to renegotiate terms. Critics argue that in such cases, the firm is using bankruptcy laws "as a sword rather than a shield." Is this an ethical tactic?
10. **Bankruptcy and Corporate Ethics** As mentioned in the text, Continental Airlines filed for bankruptcy, at least in part, as a means of reducing labor costs. Whether this move was ethical or proper was hotly debated. Give both sides of the argument.

QUESTIONS & PROBLEMS

Basic
(Questions 1–5)

1. **Firm Value** Janetta Corp. has an EBIT of $750,000 per year that is expected to continue in perpetuity. The unlevered cost of equity for the company is 15 percent, and the corporate tax rate is 35 percent. The company also has a perpetual bond issue outstanding with a market value of $1.5 million.
   a. What is the value of the company?
   b. The CFO of the company informs the company president that the value of the company is $3.2 million. Is the CFO correct?
2. **Agency Costs** Tom Scott is the owner, president, and primary salesperson for Scott Manufacturing. Because of this, the company's profits are driven by the amount of work Tom does. If he works 40 hours each week, the company's EBIT will be $500,000 per year, and if he works a 50-hour week, the company's EBIT will be $600,000 per year. The company is currently worth $3 million. The company needs a cash infusion of $2 million, and it can issue equity or issue debt with an interest rate of 9 percent. Assume there are no corporate taxes.
   a. What are the cash flows to Tom under each scenario?
   b. Under which form of financing is Tom likely to work harder?
   c. What specific new costs will occur with each form of financing?
3. **Capital Structure and Growth** Edwards Construction currently has debt outstanding with a market value of $80,000 and a cost of 12 percent. The company has an EBIT of $9,600 that is expected to continue in perpetuity. Assume there are no taxes.

   a. What is the value of the company's equity? What is the debt to value ratio?
   b. What is the equity value and debt to value ratio if the company's growth rate is 5 percent?
   c. What is the equity value and debt to value ratio if the company's growth rate is 10 percent?
4. **Nonmarketed Claims** Dream, Inc., has debt outstanding with a face value of $4 million. The value of the firm if it were entirely financed by equity would be $12 million. The company also has 250,000 shares of stock outstanding that sell at a price of $35 per share. The corporate tax rate is 35 percent. What is the decrease in the value of the company due to expected bankruptcy costs?

5. **Capital Structure and Nonmarketed Claims** Suppose the president of the company in the previous problem stated that the company should increase the amount of debt in its capital structure because of the tax-advantaged status of its interest payments. His argument is that this action would increase the value of the company. How would you respond?

Intermediate
(Questions 6–8)

6. **Costs of Financial Distress** Steinberg Corporation and Dietrich Corporation are identical firms except that Dietrich is more levered. Both companies will remain in business for one more year. The companies' economists agree that the probability of the continuation of the current expansion is 80 percent for the next year, and the probability of a recession is 20 percent. If the expansion continues, each firm will generate earnings before interest and taxes (EBIT) of \$2 million. If a recession occurs, each firm will generate earnings before interest and taxes (EBIT) of \$800,000. Steinberg's debt obligation requires the firm to pay \$750,000 at the end of the year. Dietrich's debt obligation requires the firm to pay \$1 million at the end of the year. Neither firm pays taxes.

   a. What are the potential payoffs in one year to Steinberg's stockholders and bondholders? What about those for Dietrich's?

   b. Steinberg's CEO recently stated that Steinberg's value should be higher than Dietrich's since the firm has less debt, and, therefore, less bankruptcy risk. Do you agree or disagree with this statement?

7. **Agency Costs** Fountain Corporation economists estimate that a good business environment and a bad business environment are equally likely for the coming year. The managers of Fountain must choose between two mutually exclusive projects. Assume that the project Fountain chooses will be the firm's only activity and that the firm will close one year from today. Fountain is obligated to make a \$500 payment to bondholders at the end of the year. The projects have the same systematic risk, but different volatilities. Consider the following information pertaining to the two projects:

ECONOMY	PROBABILITY	LOW-VOLATILITY PROJECT PAYOFF	HIGH-VOLATILITY PROJECT PAYOFF
Bad	.50	\$500	\$100
Good	.50	700	800

   a. What is the expected value of the firm if the low-volatility project is undertaken? What if the high-volatility project is undertaken? Which of the two strategies maximizes the expected value of the firm?

   b. What is the expected value of the firm's equity if the low-volatility project is undertaken? What is it if the high-volatility project is undertaken?

   c. Which project would Fountain's stockholders prefer? Explain.

   d. Suppose bondholders are fully aware that stockholders might choose to maximize equity value rather than total firm value and opt for the high-volatility project. To minimize this agency cost, the firm's bondholders decide to use a bond covenant to stipulate that the bondholders can demand a higher payment if Fountain chooses to take on the high-volatility project. What payment to bondholders would make stockholders indifferent between the two projects?

8. **Financial Distress** Good Time Company is a regional chain department store. It will remain in business for one more year. The probability of a boom year is 60 percent and the probability of a recession is 40 percent. It is projected that the company will generate a total cash flow of \$250 million in a boom year and \$100 million in a recession. The company's required debt

payment at the end of the year is $150 million. The market value of the company's outstanding debt is $108.93 million. The company pays no taxes.

a. What payoff do bondholders expect to receive in the event of a recession?

b. What is the promised return on the company's debt?

c. What is the expected return on the company's debt?

Challenge (Questions 9–10)

9. **Personal Taxes, Bankruptcy Costs, and Firm Value** When personal taxes on interest income and bankruptcy costs are considered, the general expression for the value of a levered firm in a world in which the tax rate on equity distributions equals zero is:

$$V_L = V_U + \{1 - [(1 - t_C)/(1 - t_B)]\} \times B - C(B)$$

where:

V_L = the value of a levered firm
V_U = the value of an unlevered firm
B = the value of the firm's debt
t_C = the tax rate on corporate income
t_B = the personal tax rate on interest income
$C(B)$ = the present value of the costs of financial distress

a. In their no-tax model, what do Modigliani and Miller assume about t_C, t_B, and $C(B)$? What do these assumptions imply about a firm's optimal debt-equity ratio?

b. In their model with corporate taxes, what do Modigliani and Miller assume about t_C, t_B, and $C(B)$? What do these assumptions imply about a firm's optimal debt-equity ratio?

c. Consider an all-equity firm that is certain to be able to use interest deductions to reduce its corporate tax bill. If the corporate tax rate is 34 percent, the personal tax rate on interest income is 20 percent, and there are no costs of financial distress, by how much will the value of the firm change if it issues $1 million in debt and uses the proceeds to repurchase equity?

d. Consider another all-equity firm that does not pay taxes due to large tax loss carry-forwards from previous years. The personal tax rate on interest income is 20 percent, and there are no costs of financial distress. What would be the change in the value of this firm from adding $1 of perpetual debt rather than $1 of equity?

10. **Personal Taxes, Bankruptcy Costs, and Firm Value** Overnight Publishing Company (OPC) has $2 million in excess cash. The firm plans to use this cash either to retire all of its outstanding debt or to repurchase equity. The firm's debt is held by one institution that is willing to sell it back to OPC for $2 million. The institution will not charge OPC any transaction costs. Once OPC becomes an all-equity firm, it will remain unlevered forever. If OPC does not retire the debt, the company will use the $2 million in cash to buy back some of its stock on the open market. Repurchasing stock also has no transaction costs. The company will generate $1,100,000 of annual earnings before interest and taxes in perpetuity regardless of its capital structure. The firm immediately pays out all earnings as dividends at the end of each year. OPC is subject to a corporate tax rate of 35 percent, and the required rate of return on the firm's unlevered equity is 20 percent. The personal tax rate on interest income is 25 percent, and there are no taxes on equity distribution. Assume there are no bankruptcy costs.

a. What is the value of OPC if it chooses to retire all of its debt and become an unlevered firm?

b. What is the value of OPC if it decides to repurchase stock instead of retiring its debt? (Hint: Use the equation for the value of a levered firm with personal tax on interest income from the previous problem.)

c. Assume that expected bankruptcy costs have a present value of $300,000. How does this influence OPC's decision?

CLOSING CASE

McKENZIE CORPORATION'S CAPITAL BUDGETING

Sam McKenzie is the founder and CEO of McKenzie Restaurants, Inc., a regional company. Sam is considering opening several new restaurants. Sally Thornton, the company's CFO, has been put in charge of the capital budgeting analysis. She has examined the potential for the company's expansion and determined that the success of the new restaurants will depend critically on the state of the economy next year and over the next few years.

McKenzie currently has a bond issue outstanding with a face value of $25 million that is due in one year. Covenants associated with this bond issue prohibit the issuance of any additional debt. This restriction means that the expansion will be entirely financed with equity, at a cost of $9 million. Sally has summarized her analysis in the following table, which shows the value of the company in each state of the economy next year, both with and without expansion.

ECONOMIC GROWTH	PROBABILITY	WITHOUT EXPANSION	WITH EXPANSION
Low	.30	$20,000,000	$24,000,000
Normal	.50	$34,000,000	$45,000,000
High	.20	$41,000,000	$53,000,000

1. What is the expected value of the company in one year, with and without expansion? Would the company's stockholders be better off with or without expansion? Why?
2. What is the expected value of the company's debt in one year, with and without the expansion?
3. One year from now, how much value creation is expected from the expansion? How much value is expected for stockholders? Bondholders?
4. If the company announces that it is not expanding, what do you think will happen to the price of its bonds? What will happen to the price of the bonds if the company does expand?
5. If the company opts not to expand, what are the implications for the company's future borrowing needs? What are the implications if the company does expand?
6. Because of the bond covenant, the expansion would have to be financed with equity. How would it affect your answer if the expansion were financed with cash on hand instead of new equity?

CHAPTER 16

Dividends and Other Payouts

OPENING CASE

In July 2004, Microsoft was sitting on a cash hoard of nearly $60 billion. Under growing pressure from shareholders, the company announced it was going to use some of that cash to (1) increase the annual dividend to $.32 per share, (2) repurchase about $30 billion of the company's stock over the next four years, and (3) make a special dividend payment of $3 per share to shareholders. Microsoft has over 10 billion shares outstanding, so the special dividend payment totaled a remarkable $32.6 billion, making it the largest corporate cash disbursement in history.

To put the size of Microsoft's special dividend in perspective, the total dividends paid by all the companies in the S&P 500 for the year totaled $213.6 billion. This means Microsoft's special dividend amounted to about 15 percent of all dividends paid by 500 of the largest companies for the year. Still not impressed? Well, consider that when the dividend was sent to investors in December, personal income in the United States rose 3.7 percent. Without the dividend, personal income only rose .3 percent. This means the dividend payment accounted for over 3 percent of all personal income in the United States for the month!

16.1 DIFFERENT TYPES OF DIVIDENDS

The term *dividend* usually refers to a cash distribution of earnings. If a distribution is made from sources other than current or accumulated retained earnings, the term *distribution* rather than dividend is used. However, it is acceptable to refer to a distribution from earnings as a *dividend* and a distribution from capital as a *liquidating dividend.* More generally, any direct payment by the corporation to the shareholders may be considered part of dividend policy.

The most common type of dividend is in the form of cash. Public companies usually pay **regular cash dividends** four times a year. Sometimes firms will pay a regular cash dividend and an *extra cash dividend.* Paying a cash dividend reduces the corporate cash and retained earnings shown in the balance sheet–except in the case of a liquidating dividend (where paid-in capital may be reduced).

Another type of dividend is paid out in shares of stock. This dividend is referred to as a **stock dividend.** It is not a true dividend, because no cash leaves the firm. Rather, a stock dividend increases the number of shares outstanding, thereby reducing the value of each share. A stock dividend is commonly expressed as a ratio; for example, with a 2 percent stock dividend a shareholder receives one new share for every 50 currently owned.

When a firm declares a **stock split**, it increases the number of shares outstanding. Because each share is now entitled to a smaller percentage of the firm's cash flow, the stock price should fall. For example, if the managers of a firm whose stock is selling at $90 declare a 3:1 stock split, the price of a share of stock should fall to about $30. A stock split strongly resembles a stock dividend except that it is usually much larger.

16.2 STANDARD METHOD OF CASH DIVIDEND PAYMENT

The decision to pay a dividend rests in the hands of the board of directors of the corporation. A dividend is distributable to shareholders of record on a specific date. When a dividend has been declared, it becomes a liability of the firm and cannot be easily rescinded by the corporation. The amount of the dividend is expressed as dollars per share (*dividend per share*), as a percentage of the market price (*dividend yield*), or as a percentage of earnings per share (*dividend payout*).

The mechanics of a dividend payment can be illustrated by the example in Figure 16.1 and the following chronology.

FIGURE 16.1
Example of Procedure for Dividend Payment

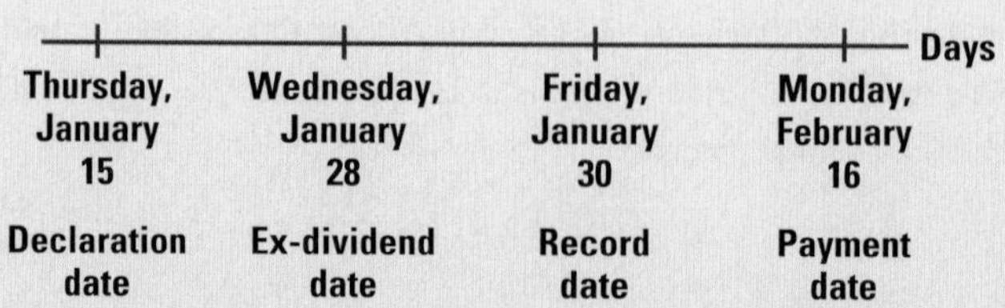

1. ***Declaration Date:*** **The board of directors declares a payment of dividends.**
2. ***Record Date:*** **The declared dividends are distributable to shareholders of record on a specific date.**
3. ***Ex-dividend Date:*** **A share of stock becomes ex dividend on the date the seller is entitled to keep the dividend; under NYSE rules, shares are traded ex dividend on and after the second business day before the record date.**
4. ***Payment Date:*** **The dividend checks are mailed to shareholders of record.**

1. **Declaration date**. On January 15 (the declaration date), the board of directors passes a resolution to pay a dividend of $1 per share on February 16 to all holders of record on January 30.
2. **Date of record**. The corporation prepares a list on January 30 of all individuals believed to be stockholders as of this date. The word *believed* is important here, because the dividend will not be paid to those individuals whose notification of purchase is received by the company after January 30.
3. **Ex-dividend date**. The procedure on the date of record would be unfair if efficient brokerage houses could notify the corporation by January 30 of a trade occurring on January 29, whereas the same trade might not reach the corporation until February 2 if executed by a less efficient house. To eliminate this problem, all brokerage firms entitle stockholders to receive the dividend if they purchased the stock three business days before the date of record. The second day before the date of record, which is Wednesday, January 28, in our example, is called the *ex-dividend date*. Before this date the stock is said to trade *cum dividend*.
4. **Date of payment**. The dividend checks are mailed to the stockholders on February 16.

For a list of today's dividends, go to www.company boardroom.com.

Obviously, the ex-dividend date is important, because an individual purchasing the security before the ex-dividend date will receive the current dividend, whereas another individual purchasing the security on or after this date will not receive the dividend. The stock price will therefore fall on the ex-dividend date (assuming no other events occur). It is worthwhile to note that this drop is an indication of efficiency, not inefficiency, because the market rationally attaches value to a cash dividend. In a world with neither taxes nor transaction costs, the stock price would be expected to fall by the amount of the dividend:

Before ex-dividend date	**Price = $\$(P + 1)$**
On or after ex-dividend date	**Price = $\$P$**

This is illustrated in Figure 16.2.

The amount of the price drop may depend on tax rates. For example, consider the case with no capital gains taxes. On the day before a stock goes ex dividend, shareholders must decide either (1) to buy the stock immediately and pay tax on the forthcoming dividend, or (2) to buy the stock tomorrow, thereby missing the dividend. If all investors are in the 15 percent bracket and the quarterly dividend is $1, the stock price should fall by $.85 on the ex-dividend date. That is, if the stock price falls by this amount on the ex-dividend date, purchasers will receive the same return from either strategy.

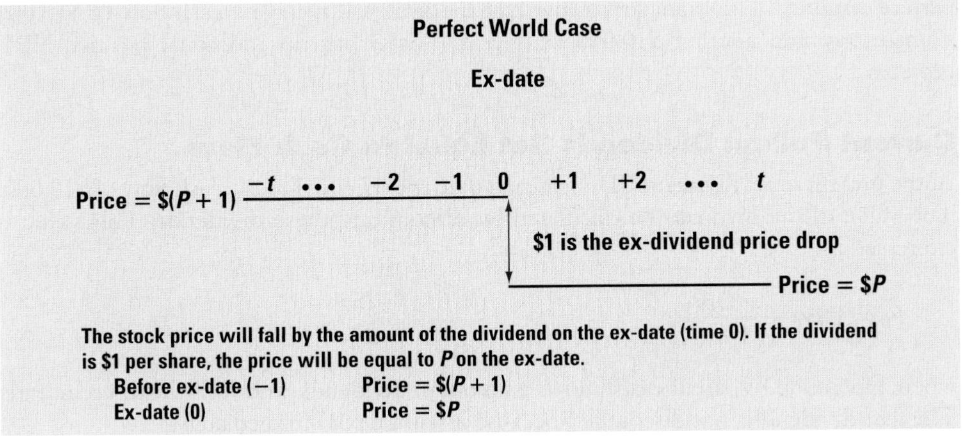

Perfect World Case

Ex-date

Price = $\$(P + 1)$ $-t$ ••• -2 -1 0 $+1$ $+2$ ••• t

$1 is the ex-dividend price drop

Price = $\$P$

The stock price will fall by the amount of the dividend on the ex-date (time 0). If the dividend is $1 per share, the price will be equal to *P* on the ex-date.

Before ex-date (−1)	**Price = $\$(P + 1)$**
Ex-date (0)	**Price = $\$P$**

FIGURE 16.2

Price Behavior around the Ex-Dividend Date for a $1 Cash Dividend

As an example of the price drop on the ex-dividend date, consider the Microsoft dividend we discussed at the beginning of the chapter. The stock went ex dividend on November 15, 2004, with a total dividend of \$3.08 per share, consisting of a \$3 special dividend and a \$.08 regular dividend. The stock price chart below shows the change in Microsoft stock the four days prior to the ex-dividend date and on the ex-dividend date.

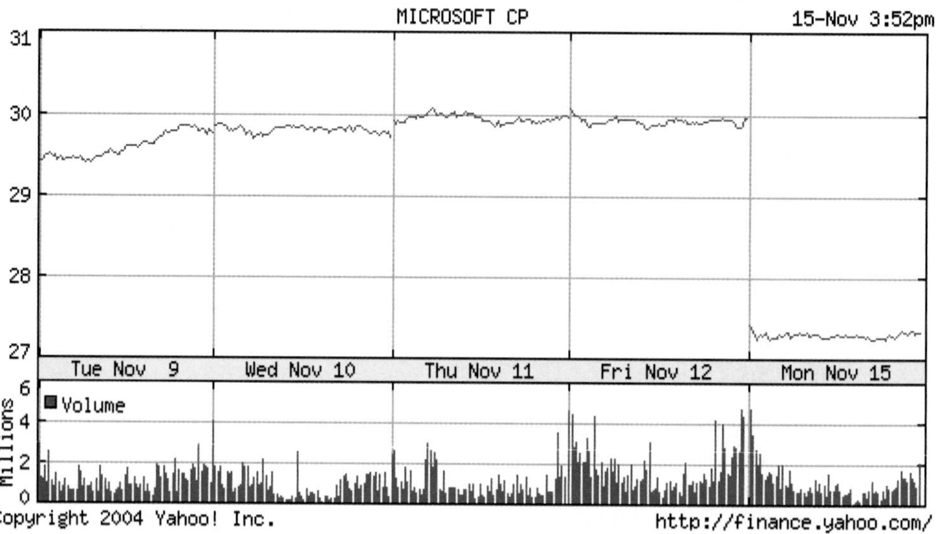

The stock closed at \$29.97 on November 12 (a Friday) and opened at \$27.34 on November 15, a drop of \$2.63. With a 15 percent tax rate on dividends, we would have expected a drop of \$2.62, and the actual price drop was almost exactly that amount.

16.3 THE BENCHMARK CASE: AN ILLUSTRATION OF THE IRRELEVANCE OF DIVIDEND POLICY

A powerful argument can be made that dividend policy does not matter. This will be illustrated with the Bristol Corporation. Bristol is an all-equity firm started 10 years ago. The current financial managers know at the present time (date 0) that the firm will dissolve in one year (date 1). At date 0, the managers are able to forecast cash flows with perfect certainty. The managers know that the firm will receive a cash flow of \$10,000 immediately and another \$10,000 next year. Bristol has no additional positive NPV projects.

Current Policy: Dividends Set Equal to Cash Flow

At the present time, dividends (Div) at each date are set equal to the cash flow of \$10,000. The value of the firm can be calculated by discounting these dividends. This value is expressed as:

$$V_0 = \text{Div}_0 + \frac{\text{Div}_1}{1 + R_S}$$

where Div_0 and Div_1 are the cash flows paid out in dividends, and R_S is the discount rate. The first dividend is not discounted because it will be paid immediately.

Assuming $R_S = 10$ percent, the value of the firm is:

$$\$19{,}090.91 = \$10{,}000 + \frac{\$10{,}000}{1.1}$$

If 1,000 shares are outstanding, the value of each share is:

$$\$19.09 = \$10 + \frac{\$10}{1.1} \tag{16.1}$$

To simplify the example, we assume that the ex-dividend date is the same as the date of payment. After the imminent dividend is paid, the stock price will immediately fall to \$9.09 (\$19.09 – \$10). Several members of the board of Bristol have expressed dissatisfaction with the current dividend policy and have asked you to analyze an alternative policy.

Alternative Policy: Initial Dividend Is Greater than Cash Flow

Another policy is for the firm to pay a dividend of \$11 per share immediately, which is, of course, a total dividend payout of \$11,000. Because the cash runoff is only \$10,000, the extra \$1,000 must be raised in one of a few ways. Perhaps the simplest would be to issue \$1,000 of bonds or stock now (at date 0). Assume that stock is issued and the new stockholders will desire enough cash flow at date 1 to let them earn the required 10 percent return on their date 0 investment. The new stockholders will demand \$1,100 of the date 1 cash flow, leaving only \$8,900 to the old stockholders. The dividends to the old stockholders will be:

	DATE 0	DATE 1
Aggregate dividends to old stockholders	\$11,000	\$8,900
Dividends per share	\$ 11.00	\$ 8.90

The present value of the dividends per share is therefore:

$$\$19.09 = \$11 + \frac{\$8.90}{1.1} \tag{16.2}$$

Students often find it instructive to determine the price at which the new stock is issued. Because the new stockholders are not entitled to the immediate dividend, they would pay \$8.09 (\$8.90/1.1) per share. Thus, 123.61 (\$1,000/\$8.09) new shares are issued.

The Indifference Proposition

Note that the values in equations (16.1) and (16.2) are equal. This leads to the initially surprising conclusion that the change in dividend policy did not affect the value of a share of stock. However, upon reflection, the result seems quite sensible. The new stockholders are parting with their money at date 0 and receiving it back with the appropriate return at date 1. In other words, they are taking on a zero NPV investment. As illustrated in Figure 16.3, old stockholders are receiving additional funds at date 0 but must pay the new stockholders their money with the appropriate return at date 1. Because the old stockholders must pay back principal plus the appropriate return, the act of issuing new stock at date 0 will not increase or decrease the value of the old stockholders' holdings. That is, they are giving up a zero NPV investment to the new stockholders. An increase in dividends at date 0 leads to the necessary reduction of dividends at date 1, so the value of the old stockholders' holdings remains unchanged.

This illustration is based on the pioneering work of Miller and Modigliani (MM). Although our presentation is in the form of a numerical example, the MM paper proves that investors are indifferent to dividend policy in a more general setting.

FIGURE 16.3

Current and Alternative Dividend Policies

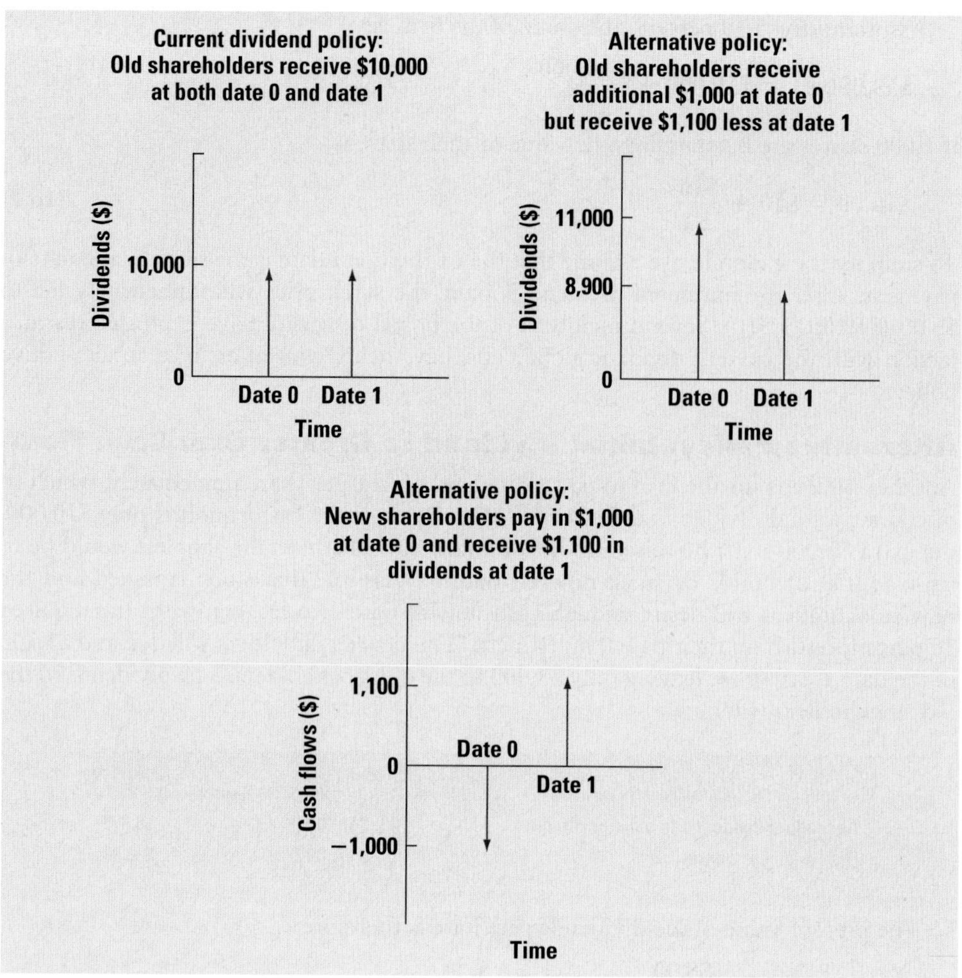

Homemade Dividends

To illustrate the indifference investors have toward dividend policy in our example, we used present value equations. An alternative and perhaps more intuitively appealing explanation avoids the mathematics of discounted cash flows.

Suppose individual investor *X* prefers dividends per share of $10 at both dates 0 and 1. Would she be disappointed when informed that the firm's management is adopting the alternative dividend policy (dividends of $11 and $8.90 on the two dates, respectively)? Not necessarily, because she could easily reinvest the $1 of unneeded funds received on date 0, yielding an incremental return of $1.10 at date 1. Thus, she would receive her desired net cash flow of $11 − $1 = $10 at date 0 and $8.90 + $1.10 = $10 at date 1.

Conversely, imagine investor *Z* preferring $11 of cash flow at date 0 and $8.90 of cash flow at date 1, who finds that management will pay dividends of $10 at both dates 0 and 1. Here he can sell off shares of stock at date 0 to receive the desired amount of cash flow. That is, if he sells off shares (or fractions of shares) at date 0 totaling $1, his cash flow at date 0 becomes $10 + $1 = $11. Because a $1 sale of stock at date 0 will reduce his dividends by $1.10 at date 1, his net cash flow at date 1 would be $10 − $1.10 = $8.90.

The example illustrates how investors can make **homemade dividends**. In this instance, corporate dividend policy is being undone by a potentially dissatisfied stockholder. This homemade dividend is illustrated by Figure 16.4. Here the firm's cash flows

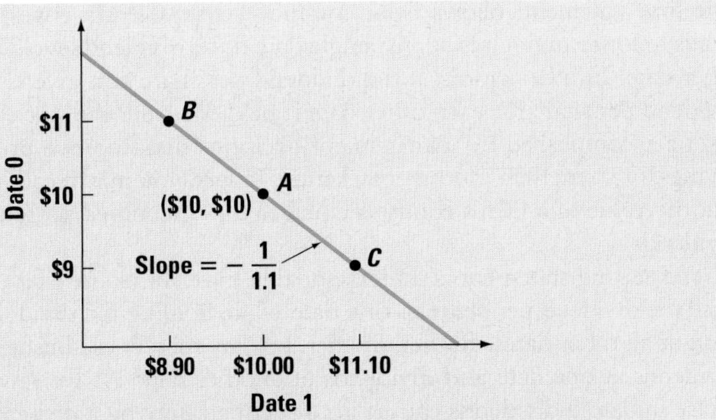

FIGURE 16.4

Homemade Dividends: A Trade-Off between Dividends per Share at Date 0 and Dividends per Share at Date 1

The graph illustrates both (1) how managers can vary dividend policy and (2) how individuals can undo the firm's dividend policy.

Managers varying dividend policy. **A firm paying out all cash flows immediately is at point *A* on the graph. The firm could achieve point *B* by issuing stock to pay extra dividends or achieve point *C* by buying back old stock with some of its cash.**

Individuals undoing the firm's dividend policy. **Suppose the firm adopts the dividend policy represented by point *B*: dividends per share of $11 at date 0 and $8.90 at date 1. An investor can reinvest $1 of the dividends at 10 percent, which will place her at point *A*. Suppose, alternatively, the firm adopts the dividend policy represented by point *A*. An individual can sell off $1 of stock at date 0, placing him at point *B*. No matter what dividend policy the firm establishes, a shareholder can undo it.**

of $10 per share at both dates 0 and 1 are represented by point *A*. This point also represents the initial dividend payout. However, as we just saw, the firm could alternatively pay out $11 per share at date 0 and $8.90 per share at date 1, a strategy represented by point *B*. Similarly, by either issuing new stock or buying back old stock, the firm could achieve a dividend payout represented by any point on the diagonal line.

The previous paragraph describes the choices available to the managers of the firm. The same diagonal line also represents the choices available to the shareholder. For example, if the shareholder receives a per-share dividend distribution of ($11, $8.90), he or she can either reinvest some of the dividends to move down and to the right on the graph or sell off shares of stock and move up and to the left.

The implications of the graph can be summarized in two sentences:

1. By varying dividend policy, the managers can achieve any payout along the diagonal line in Figure 16.4.
2. Either by reinvesting excess dividends at date 0 or by selling off shares of stock at this date, any individual investor can achieve any net cash payout along the diagonal line.

Thus, because both the corporation and the individual investor can move only along the diagonal line, dividend policy in this model is irrelevant. The changes the managers make in dividend policy can be undone by an individual who, by either reinvesting dividends or selling off stock, can move to a desired point on the diagonal line.

A Test

You can test your knowledge of this material by examining these true statements:

1. Dividends are relevant.
2. Dividend policy is irrelevant.

The first statement follows from common sense. Clearly, investors prefer higher dividends to lower dividends at any single date if the dividend level is held constant at every other date. In other words, if the dividend per share at a given date is raised while the dividend per share for each other date is held constant, the stock price will rise. This act can be accomplished by management decisions that improve productivity, increase tax savings, or strengthen product marketing. In fact, you may recall in Chapter 6 we argued that the value of a firm's equity is equal to the discounted present value of all its future dividends.

The second statement is understandable once we realize that dividend policy cannot raise the dividend per share at one date while holding the dividend level per share constant at all other dates. Rather, dividend policy merely establishes the trade-off between dividends at one date and dividends at another date. As we saw in Figure 16.4, an increase in date 0 dividends can be accomplished only by a decrease in date 1 dividends. The extent of the decrease is such that the present value of all dividends is not affected.

Thus, in this simple world, dividend policy does not matter. That is, managers choosing either to raise or to lower the current dividend do not affect the current value of their firm. The above theory is a powerful one, and the work of MM is generally considered a classic in modern finance. With relatively few assumptions, a rather surprising result is shown to be perfectly true. Because we want to examine many real world factors ignored by MM, their work is only a starting point in this chapter's discussion of dividends. The next part of the chapter investigates these real world considerations.

Dividends and Investment Policy

The preceding argument shows that an increase in dividends through issuance of new shares neither helps nor hurts the stockholders. Similarly, a reduction in dividends through share repurchase neither helps nor hurts stockholders.

What about reducing capital expenditures to increase dividends? Earlier chapters show that a firm should accept all positive net present value projects. To do otherwise would reduce the value of the firm. Thus, we have an important point:

Firms should never give up a positive NPV project to increase a dividend (or to pay a dividend for the first time).

This idea was implicitly considered by Miller and Modigliani. One of the assumptions underlying their dividend irrelevance proposition was, "The investment policy of the firm is set ahead of time and is not altered by changes in dividend policy."

16.4 REPURCHASE OF STOCK

Instead of paying dividends, a firm may use cash to repurchase shares of its own stock. Share repurchases have taken on increased importance in recent years. Consider Figure 16.5, which shows the dollar amount of both share repurchases and dividends for U.S. firms for each year between 1972 and 2000. As can be seen, the dollar amount of share repurchases was a small fraction of that of dividends in the early years. However, this fraction has risen over time, with the dollar amount of share repurchases actually exceeding that of dividends in the last two years of the sample period, 1999 and 2000.

Share repurchases are typically accomplished in one of three ways. First, companies may simply purchase their own stock, just as anyone would buy shares of a particular stock. In these *open market purchases,* the firm does not reveal itself as the buyer. Thus, the seller does not know whether the shares were sold back to the firm or to just another investor.

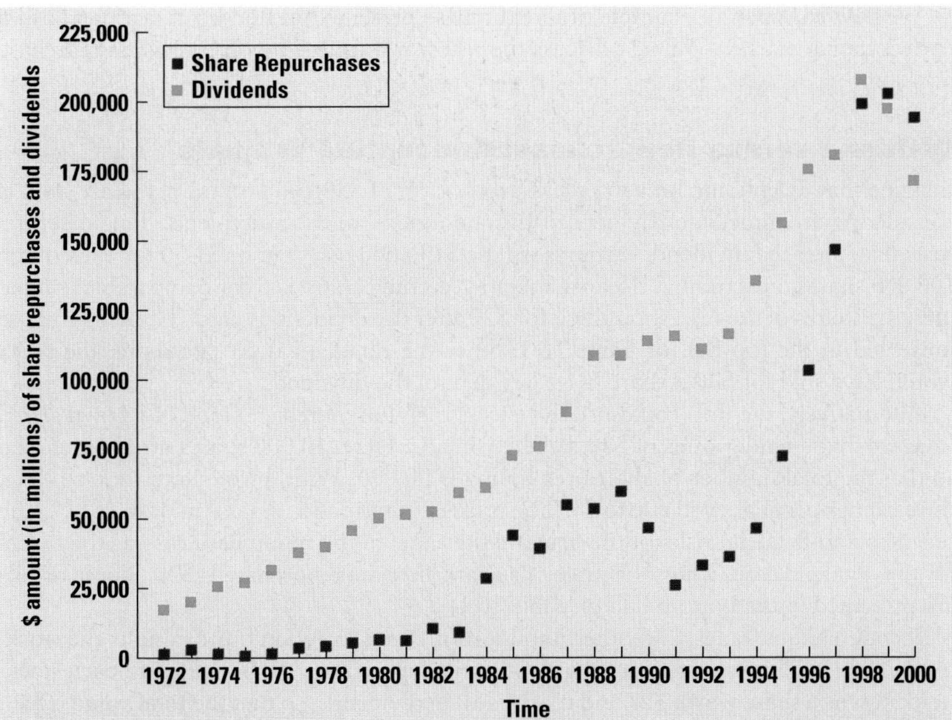

This figure shows the dollar amount of both share repurchases and dividends for U.S. firms for each year from 1972 to 2000. The dollar amount of share repurchases was actually greater than that of dividends for each of the last two years of the sample period.

FIGURE 16.5

Share Repurchases vs. Dividends

Source: Adapted from Table 1 of Grullon, Gustavo, and Michaely, "Dividends, Share Repurchases, and the Substitution Hypothesis," *Journal of Finance* (August 2002).

Second, the firm could institute a *tender offer*. Here, the firm announces to all of its stockholders that it is willing to buy a fixed number of shares at a specific price. For example, suppose Arts and Crafts (A&C), Inc., has 1 million shares of stock outstanding, with a stock price of $50 per share. The firm makes a tender offer to buy back 300,000 shares at $60 per share. A&C chooses a price above $50 to induce shareholders to sell, that is, tender, their shares. In fact, if the tender price is set high enough, shareholders may very well want to sell more than the 300,000 shares. In the extreme case where all outstanding shares are tendered, A&C will buy back 3 out of every 10 shares that a shareholder has.

Finally, firms may repurchase shares from specific individual stockholders. This procedure has been called a *targeted repurchase*. For example, suppose the International Biotechnology Corporation purchased approximately 10 percent of the outstanding stock of the Prime Robotics Company (P-R Co.) in April at around $38 per share. At that time, International Biotechnology announced to the Securities and Exchange Commission that it might eventually try to take control of P-R Co. In May, P-R Co. repurchased the International Biotechnology holdings at $48 per share, well above the market price at that time. This offer was not extended to other shareholders.

Companies engage in this type of repurchase for a variety of reasons. In some rare cases, a single large stockholder can be bought out at a price lower than that in a tender offer. The legal fees in a targeted repurchase may also be lower than those in a more typical buyback. More frequently, certain stockholders become nuisances to the repurchasing firm. Though targeted repurchases executed for these reasons are in the interest of the remaining shareholders, the shares of large stockholders are often repurchased to avoid a takeover unfavorable to management.

We now consider an example of a repurchase presented in the theoretical world of a perfect capital market. We next discuss the real world factors involved in the repurchase decision.

Dividend versus Repurchase: Conceptual Example

Imagine that Telephonic Industries has excess cash of $300,000 (or $3 per share) and is considering an immediate payment of this amount as an extra dividend. The firm forecasts that, after the dividend, earnings will be $450,000 per year, or $4.50 for each of the 100,000 shares outstanding. Because the price-earnings ratio is 6 for comparable companies, the shares of the firm should sell for $27 after the dividend is paid. These figures are presented in the top half of Table 16.1. Since the dividend is $3 per share, the stock would have sold for $30 a share *before* payment of the dividend.

Alternatively, the firm could use the excess cash to repurchase some of its own stock. Imagine that a tender offer of $30 a share is made. Here, 10,000 shares are repurchased so that the total number of shares remaining is 90,000. With fewer shares outstanding, the earnings per share will rise to $5. The price-earnings ratio remains at 6, since both the business and financial risks of the firm are the same in the repurchase case as they were for the dividend case. Thus, the price of a share after the repurchase is $30. These results are presented in the bottom half of Table 16.1.

If commissions, taxes, and other imperfections are ignored in our example, the stockholders are indifferent between a dividend and a repurchase. With dividends, each stockholder owns a share worth $27 and receives $3 in dividends, so that the total value is $30. This figure is the same as both the amount received by the selling stockholders and the value of the stock for the remaining stockholders in the repurchase case.

This example illustrates the important point that, in a perfect market, the firm is indifferent between a dividend payment and a share repurchase. This result is quite similar to the indifference propositions established by MM for debt versus equity financing and for dividends versus capital gains.

You may often read in the popular financial press that a repurchase agreement is beneficial because earnings per share increase. Earnings per share do rise for Telephonic Industries if a repurchase is substituted for a cash dividend: The EPS is $4.50 after a dividend and $5 after the repurchase. This result holds because the drop in shares after a repurchase implies a reduction in the denominator of the EPS ratio.

However, the financial press frequently places undue emphasis on EPS figures in a repurchase agreement. Given the irrelevance propositions we have discussed, an increase in EPS need not be beneficial. When a repurchase is financed by excess cash, we showed

TABLE 16.1

Dividend versus Repurchase Example for Telephonic Industries

	FOR ENTIRE FIRM	PER SHARE
Extra Dividend		**(100,000 shares outstanding)**
Proposed dividend	$ 300,000	$ 3.00
Forecasted annual earnings after dividend	450,000	4.50
Market value of stock after dividend	2,700,000	27.00
Repurchase		**(90,000 shares outstanding)**
Forecasted annual earnings after repurchase	$ 450,000	$ 5.00
Market value of stock after repurchase	2,700,000	30.00

that, in a perfect capital market, the total value to the stockholder is the same under the dividend payment strategy as under the repurchase strategy.

Dividends versus Repurchases: Real World Considerations

We previously referred to Figure 16.5, which showed the recent growth in share repurchases. Why do some firms choose repurchases over dividends? Here are perhaps five of the most common reasons.

1. FLEXIBILITY It is well known that firms view dividends as a commitment to their stockholders and are quite hesitant to reduce an existing dividend. Repurchases do not represent a similar commitment. Thus, a firm with a permanent increase in cash flow is likely to increase its dividend. Conversely, a firm whose cash flow increase is only temporary is likely to repurchase shares of stock.

2. EXECUTIVE COMPENSATION Executives are frequently given stock options as part of their overall compensation. Let's revisit the Telephonic Industries example of Table 16.1, where the firm's stock was selling at $30 when the firm was considering either a dividend or a repurchase. Further imagine that Telephonic had granted 1,000 stock options to its CEO, Ralph Taylor, two years before the decision was made. At that time, the stock price was, say, only $20. This means that Mr. Taylor can buy 1,000 shares for $20 a share at any time between the grant of the options and their expiration, a procedure called *exercising* the options. His gain from exercising is directly proportional to the rise in the stock price above $20. As we saw in the example, the price of the stock would fall to $27 following a dividend but would remain at $30 following a repurchase. The CEO would clearly prefer a repurchase to a dividend because the difference between the stock price and the exercise price of $20 would be $10 ($30 − $20) following the repurchase but only $7 ($27 − $20) following the dividend. Existing stock options will always have greater value when the firm repurchases shares instead of paying a dividend, since the stock price will be greater after a repurchase than after a dividend.

3. OFFSET TO DILUTION In addition, the exercise of stock options increases the number of shares outstanding. In other words, exercise causes dilution of the stock. Firms frequently buy back shares of stock to offset this dilution. However, it is hard to argue that this is a valid reason for repurchase. As we showed in Table 16.1, repurchase is neither better nor worse for the stockholders than a dividend. Our argument holds whether or not stock options have been exercised previously.

4. REPURCHASE AS INVESTMENT Many companies buy back stock because they believe that a repurchase is their best investment. This occurs more frequently when managers believe that the stock price is temporarily depressed. Here, it is likely thought that (1) investment opportunities in nonfinancial assets are few, and (2) the firm's own stock price should rise with the passage of time.

The fact that some companies repurchase their stock when they believe it is undervalued does not imply that the management of the company must be correct; only empirical studies can make this determination. The immediate stock market reaction to the announcement of a stock repurchase is usually quite favorable. In addition, some empirical work has shown that the long-term stock price performance of securities after a buyback is better than the stock price performance of comparable companies that do not repurchase.

5. TAXES Since taxes for both dividends and share repurchases are treated in depth in the next section, suffice it to say at this point that repurchases provide a tax advantage over dividends.

16.5 PERSONAL TAXES, ISSUANCE COSTS, AND DIVIDENDS

The model we used in Section 16.3 to determine the level of dividends assumed that there were no taxes, no transactions costs, and no uncertainty. It concluded that dividend policy is irrelevant. Although this model helps us to grasp some fundamentals of dividend policy, it ignores many real world factors. It is now time to investigate these practical considerations. We first examine the effect of taxes on the level of a firm's dividends.

In the United States, both cash dividends and capital gains are taxed at a maximum rate of 15 percent. However, since dividends are taxed when distributed, while the taxes on capital gains are deferred until the stock is sold, the tax rate on dividends is greater than the *effective* rate on capital gains. A discussion of dividend policy in the presence of personal taxes is facilitated by classifying firms into two types, those without sufficient cash to pay a dividend and those with sufficient cash to do so.

Firms without Sufficient Cash to Pay a Dividend

It is simplest to begin with a firm without cash and owned by a single entrepreneur. If this firm should decide to pay a dividend of $100, it must raise capital. The firm might choose among a number of different stock and bond issues in order to pay the dividend. However, for simplicity, we assume that the entrepreneur contributes cash to the firm by issuing stock to himself. This transaction, diagrammed in the left-hand side of Figure 16.6, would clearly be a *wash* in a world of no taxes. $100 cash goes into the firm when stock is issued and is immediately paid out as a dividend. Thus, the entrepreneur neither benefits nor loses when the dividend is paid, a result consistent with Miller-Modigliani.

Now assume that dividends are taxed at the owner's personal tax rate of 15 percent. The firm still receives $100 upon issuance of stock. However, the entrepreneur does not get to keep the full $100 dividend. Instead, the dividend payment is taxed, implying that the owner receives only $85 net after tax. Thus, the entrepreneur loses $15.

Though the example is clearly contrived and unrealistic, similar results can be reached for more plausible situations. Thus, financial economists generally agree that, in a world of personal taxes, one should not issue stock to pay a dividend.

The direct costs of issuance will add to this effect. Investment bankers must be paid when new capital is raised. Thus, the net receipts due to the firm from a new issue

FIGURE 16.6 Firm Issues Stock in Order to Pay a Dividend

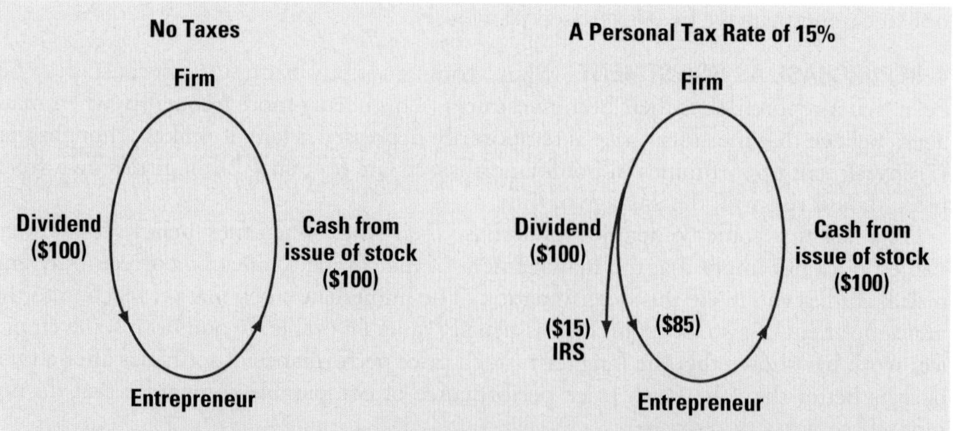

In the no-tax case, the entrepreneur receives the $100 in dividends that he gave to the firm when purchasing stock. The entire operation is called a *wash;* in other words, it has no economic effect. With taxes, the entrepreneur still receives $100 in dividends. However, he must pay $15 in taxes to the IRS. The entrepreneur loses and the IRS wins when a firm issues stock to pay a dividend.

are less than 100 percent of total capital raised. Because the size of new issues can be lowered by a reduction in dividends, we have another argument in favor of a low-dividend policy.

Of course, our advice not to finance dividends through new stock issues might need to be modified somewhat in the real world. A company with a large and steady cash flow for many years in the past might be paying a regular dividend. If the cash flow unexpectedly dried up for a single year, should new stock be issued so that dividends could be continued? While our above discussion would imply that new stock should not be issued, many managers might issue the stock anyway for practical reasons. In particular, stockholders appear to prefer dividend stability. Thus, managers might be forced to issue stock to achieve this stability, knowing full well the adverse tax consequences.

Firms with Sufficient Cash to Pay a Dividend

The previous discussion argues that, in a world with personal taxes, one should not issue stock to pay a dividend. Does the tax disadvantage of dividends imply the stronger policy, "Never pay dividends in a world with personal taxes"?

We argue below that this prescription does not necessarily apply to firms with excess cash. To see this, imagine a firm with $1 million in extra cash after selecting all positive NPV projects and determining the level of prudent cash balances. The firm might consider the following alternatives to a dividend:

1. *Select Additional Capital Budgeting Projects.* Because the firm has taken all the available positive NPV projects already, it must invest its excess cash in negative NPV projects. This is clearly a policy at variance with the principles of corporate finance.

   In spite of our distaste for this policy, researchers have suggested that many managers purposely take on negative NPV projects in lieu of paying dividends. The idea here is that managers would rather keep the funds in the firm, since their prestige, pay, and perquisites are often tied to the firm's size. While managers may help themselves here, they are hurting stockholders. We broached this subject in a previous chapter, and we will have more to say about it later in this chapter.

2. *Acquire Other Companies.* To avoid the payment of dividends, a firm might use excess cash to acquire another company. This strategy has the advantage of acquiring profitable assets. However, a firm often incurs heavy costs when it embarks on an acquisition program. In addition, acquisitions are invariably made above the market price. Premiums of 20 to 80 percent are not uncommon. Because of this, a number of researchers have argued that mergers are not generally profitable to the acquiring company, even when firms are merged for a valid business purpose. Therefore, a company making an acquisition merely to avoid a dividend is unlikely to succeed.

3. *Purchase Financial Assets.* Deciding whether to invest in financial assets or to pay a dividend is a complex question, depending on the tax rate of the firm, the marginal tax rates of its investors, and the application of the dividend exclusion. While there are likely many real world situations where the numbers favor investment in financial assets, few companies actually seem to hoard cash in this manner without limit. The reason is that Section 532 of the Internal Revenue Code penalizes firms exhibiting "improper accumulation of surplus." Thus, in the final analysis, the purchase of financial assets, like selecting negative NPV projects and acquiring other companies, does not obviate the need for companies with excess cash to pay dividends.

4. *Repurchase Shares.* The example we described in the previous section showed that investors are indifferent between share repurchase and dividends in a world without taxes and transaction costs. However, under current tax law, stockholders generally prefer a repurchase to a dividend.

THE REAL WORLD

STOCK BUYBACKS: NO END IN SIGHT

As we have seen, a strong case can be made for share repurchases as a means of distributing cash to stockholders, and corporate America seems to agree. For example, consider Microsoft's mammoth $30 billion stock "buyback" (another word for repurchase), which we discussed at the beginning of the chapter. At the then-current market value of the stock, this repurchase amounted to over 10 percent of all shares outstanding. And Microsoft was not alone. During 2004, U.S. companies announced $233 billion in stock buybacks. In fact, over the past several years, the number of share repurchases has been so large that U.S. corporations bought back more shares than they sold. In other words, the net equity raised by U.S. corporations has been negative.

Some companies appear to have become serial repurchasers. Take General Electric (GE), for example. In December 2004, the company announced a plan to buy back $15 billion worth of stock over the next three years. But the $15 billion buyback was nothing new to GE shareholders. The company had repurchased $12.8 billion worth of stock from 1998 to 2002. In 2003 and 2004, due to cash restraints caused by acquisitions, the company only repurchased about $500 million in stock each year.

Stock buybacks have evolved to the point where they are used for other purposes. For example, in January 2005, consumer products giant Procter & Gamble (P&G) announced that it was purchasing razor manufacturer Gillette for $54 billion. The purchase was paid for entirely by stock in P&G. This is important because if a company acquires another company for cash, the shareholders of the acquired company are forced to pay taxes. If shareholders receive stock, no taxes are due. What made the deal unique was that P&G announced at the same time that it would repurchase from $18 to $22 billion in stock. Thus, P&G essentially paid about 60 percent in stock and 40 percent in cash, but the way the deal was structured made it look like a 100 percent stock acquisition to Gillette's stockholders.

Stock buybacks are not limited to the United States. In August 2004, Matsushita Electric, manufacturer of Panasonic electronics products, announced a stock buyback of up to 80 million shares, or about 3.5 percent of the company's outstanding stock. The dollar amount of the buyback could be up to 100 billion yen, or about a billion dollars. In January 2005, the Brazilian phone company Tele Norte Leste Participacoes SA, or Telemar, announced a stock buyback of 3.46 million shares of common and 20.4 million shares of preferred stock. And in December 2004, South Korean tobacco company KT&G announced that it had bought back 10 million shares of its stock.

We haven't discussed what happens to the stock when a company does a buyback. There are actually several things the company can do. Many companies keep the stock and use the shares for employee stock option plans. When employee stock options are exercised by the employee, new shares are created, which increases the number of shares of stock outstanding. By using the repurchased shares, the company does not need to issue any new shares. A company can also keep the repurchased stock for itself as Treasury stock. Finally, the company can cancel the stock completely. In essence, it destroys the shares repurchased, which reduces the number of shares outstanding.

As an example, consider an individual receiving a dividend of $1 on each of 100 shares of a stock. With a 15 percent tax rate, that individual would pay taxes of $15 on the dividend. Selling shareholders would pay lower taxes if the firm repurchased $100 of existing shares. This occurs because taxes are paid only on the *profit* from a sale. The individual's gain on a sale would be only $40 if the shares sold for $100 were originally purchased for, say, $60. The capital gains tax would be $6 (.15 × $40), a number below the tax on dividends of $15. Note that the tax from a repurchase is less than the tax on a dividend even though the same 15 percent tax rate applies to both the repurchase and the dividend.

In fact, of all the alternatives to dividends mentioned in this section, the strongest case can be made for repurchases. A nearby *The Real World* box contains more on recent repurchase activity.

Summary on Personal Taxes

This section suggests that, because of personal taxes, firms have an incentive to reduce dividends. For example, they might increase capital expenditures, acquire other companies, or purchase financial assets. However, due to financial considerations and legal constraints, rational firms with large cash flows will likely exhaust these activities with plenty of cash left over for dividends.

It is harder to explain why firms pay dividends instead of repurchasing shares. The tax savings from buybacks are significant and fear of either the SEC or the IRS seems overblown. Academics are of two minds here. Some argue that corporations were simply slow to grasp the benefits from repurchases. However, since the idea has firmly caught on, the trend toward replacement of dividends with buybacks will continue. One might even conjecture that dividends will be as unimportant in the future as repurchases were in the past. Conversely, others argue that companies have paid dividends all along for good reason. Perhaps the legal hassles, particularly from the IRS, are significant after all. Or, there may be other, more subtle benefits from dividends. We consider potential benefits of dividends in the next section.

16.6 REAL WORLD FACTORS FAVORING A HIGH-DIVIDEND POLICY

In the previous section, we pointed out that taxes must be paid by the recipient of a dividend. Since the tax rate on dividends is above the *effective* tax rate on capital gains, financial managers will seek out ways to reduce dividends. While we discussed the problems with taking on more capital budgeting projects, acquiring other firms, and hoarding cash, we stated that share repurchase has many of the benefits of a dividend with less of a tax disadvantage. In this section, we consider reasons why a firm might pay its shareholders high dividends, even in the presence of personal taxes on these dividends.

Desire for Current Income

It has been argued that many individuals desire current income. The classic example is the group of retired people and others living on fixed incomes, proverbially known as "widows and orphans." The argument further states that these individuals would bid up the stock price should dividends rise and bid down the stock price should dividends fall.

Miller and Modigliani point out that this argument does not hold in their theoretical model. An individual preferring high current cash flow but holding low-dividend securities could easily sell off shares to provide the necessary funds. Thus, in a world of no transactions costs, a high current dividend policy would be of no value to the stockholder.

However, the current income argument does have relevance in the real world. The sale of stock involves brokerage fees and other transactions costs–direct cash expenses that could be avoided by an investment in high-dividend securities. In addition, the expenditure of one's time when selling securities might further lead many investors to buy high-dividend securities.

However, to put this argument in perspective, it should be remembered that financial intermediaries such as mutual funds can perform repackaging transactions at low cost. Such intermediaries could buy low-dividend stocks and, by a controlled policy of realizing gains, pay their investors at a higher rate.

Behavioral Finance

Suppose it turned out that the transaction costs in selling no-dividend securities could not account for the preference of investors for dividends. Would there still be a reason for high dividends? We introduced the topic of behavioral finance in an earlier chapter, pointing out that the ideas of behaviorists represent a strong challenge to the theory of efficient capital markets. It turns out that behavioral finance also has an argument for high dividends.

The basic idea here concerns *self-control,* a concept that, though quite important in psychology, has received virtually no emphasis in finance. While we cannot review all that psychology has to say about self-control, let's focus on one example–losing weight. Suppose Alfred Martin, a college student, just got back from the Christmas break more than a few pounds heavier than he would like. Everyone would probably agree that diet and exercise are the two ways to lose weight. But how should Alfred put this approach into practice? (We'll focus on exercise though the same principle would apply to diet as well.) One way, let's call it the economists' way, would involve trying to make rational decisions. Each day, Al would balance the costs and the benefits of exercising. Perhaps he would choose to exercise on most days, since losing the weight is important to him. However, when he is too busy with exams, he might rationally choose not to exercise because he cannot afford the time. And, he wants to be socially active as well. So he may rationally choose to avoid exercise on days when parties and other social commitments become too time-consuming.

This seems sensible–at first glance. The problem is that he must make a choice every day and there may simply be too many days when his lack of self-control gets the better of him. He may tell himself that he doesn't have the time to exercise on a particular day, simply because he is starting to find exercise boring, not because he really doesn't have the time. Before long, he is avoiding exercise on most days–and overeating in reaction to the guilt from not exercising!

What does this have to do with dividends? Investors must also deal with self-control. Suppose a retiree wants to consume $20,000 a year from savings, in addition to Social Security and her pension. On one hand, she could buy stocks with a dividend yield high enough to generate $20,000 in dividends. On the other hand, she could place her savings in no-dividend stocks, selling off $20,000 each year for consumption. Though these two approaches seem equivalent financially, the second one may allow for too much leeway. If lack of self-control gets the better of her, she might sell off too much, leaving little for her later years. Better, perhaps, to short-circuit this possibility by investing in dividend-paying stocks, with a firm personal rule of *never* "dipping into principal." While behaviorists do not claim that this approach is for everyone, they argue that enough people think this way to explain why firms pay dividends, even though, as we said earlier, dividends are tax disadvantaged.

Does behavioral finance argue for increased stock repurchases as well as increased dividends? The answer is no, since investors will sell the stock that firms repurchase. As we said above, selling stock involves too much leeway. Investors might sell too many shares of stock, leaving little for the later years. Thus, the behaviorist argument may explain why companies pay dividends in a world with personal taxes.

Agency Costs

Although stockholders, bondholders, and management form firms for mutually beneficial reasons, one party may later gain at the other's expense. For example, take the potential conflict between bondholders and stockholders. Bondholders would like stockholders to leave as much cash as possible in the firm so that this cash would be available to pay the bondholders during times of financial distress. Conversely, stockholders would like to keep this extra cash for themselves. That's where dividends come in. Managers, acting on behalf of the stockholders, may pay dividends simply to keep the cash away from the bondholders. In other words, a dividend can be viewed as a wealth transfer from bondholders to stockholders. Of course, bondholders know of the propensity of stockholders to transfer money out of the firm. To protect themselves, bondholders frequently create loan agreements stating that dividends can be paid only if the firm has earnings, cash flow, and working capital above prespecified levels.

Although the managers may be looking out for the stockholders in any conflict with bondholders, the managers may pursue selfish goals at the expense of stockholders in other situations. For example, as discussed in an earlier chapter, managers might pad expense accounts, take on pet projects with negative NPVs, or more simply, not work very hard. Managers find it easier to pursue these selfish goals when the firm has plenty of free cash flow. After all, one cannot squander funds if the funds are not available in the first place. And, that is where dividends come in. It has been suggested that dividends can serve as a way for the board of directors to reduce agency costs. By paying dividends equal to the amount of "surplus" cash flow, a firm can reduce management's ability to squander the firm's resources.

While the above discussion suggests a reason for increased dividends, the same argument applies to share repurchases as well. Managers, acting on behalf of stockholders, can just as easily keep cash from bondholders through repurchases as through dividends. And the board of directors, also acting on behalf of stockholders, can reduce the cash available to spendthrift managers just as easily through repurchases as through dividends. Thus, the presence of agency costs is not an argument for dividends over repurchases. Rather, agency costs imply firms may well increase either dividends or share repurchases rather than hoard large amounts of cash.

Information Content of Dividends and Dividend Signaling

INFORMATION CONTENT While there are many things researchers do not know about dividends, there is one thing that we know for sure: The stock price of a firm will generally rise when the firm announces an increase in the dividend and will generally fall when a dividend reduction is announced. The question is: How should one *interpret* this fact? Consider the following three positions on dividends:

1. From the homemade dividend argument of MM, dividend policy is irrelevant, given that future earnings (and cash flows) are held constant.
2. Because of tax effects, a firm's stock price is negatively related to the current dividend when future earnings (or cash flows) are held constant.
3. Because of stockholders' desire for current income, a firm's stock price is positively related to its current dividend, even when future earnings (or cash flows) are held constant.

At first glance, the empirical evidence that stock prices rise when dividend increases are announced may seem consistent with position 3 and inconsistent with positions 1 and 2. In fact, many writers have argued this. However, other authors have countered that the observation itself is consistent with all three positions. They point out that companies do not like to cut a dividend. Thus, firms will raise the dividend only when future earnings, cash flow, and so on are expected to rise enough so that the dividend is not likely to be reduced later to its original level. A dividend increase is management's *signal* to the market that the firm is expected to do well.

It is the expectation of good times, and not only the stockholder's affinity for current income, that raises stock price. The rise in the stock price following the dividend signal is called the **information content effect** of the dividend. To recapitulate, imagine that the stock price is unaffected or even negatively affected by the level of dividends, given that future earnings (or cash flows) are held constant. Nevertheless, the information content effect implies that stock price may rise when dividends are raised–if dividends simultaneously cause stockholders to *increase* their expectations of future earnings and cash flows.

16.7 THE CLIENTELE EFFECT: A RESOLUTION OF REAL WORLD FACTORS?

In the previous two sections, we pointed out that the existence of personal taxes favors a low-dividend policy, whereas other factors favor high dividends. The financial profession had hoped that it would be easy to determine which of these sets of factors dominates. Unfortunately, after years of research, no one has been able to conclude which of the two is more important. This is surprising, since one might be skeptical that the two sets of factors would cancel each other out so perfectly.

However, one particular idea, known as the *clientele effect,* implies that the two sets of factors are likely to cancel each other out after all. To understand this idea, let's separate those investors in high tax brackets from those in low tax brackets. Individuals in high tax brackets likely prefer either no or low dividends. Low tax bracket investors generally fall into three categories. First, there are individual investors in low brackets. They are likely to prefer some dividends if they desire current income. Second, pension funds pay no taxes on either dividends or capital gains. Because they face no tax consequences, pension funds will also prefer dividends if they have a preference for current income. Finally, corporations can exclude at least 70 percent of their dividend income but cannot exclude any of their capital gains. Thus, corporations would prefer to invest in high-dividend stocks, even without a preference for current income.

Suppose that 40 percent of all investors prefer high dividends and 60 percent prefer low dividends, yet only 20 percent of firms pay high dividends, while 80 percent pay low dividends. Here, the high-dividend firms will be in short supply; thus their stock should be bid up while the stock of low-dividend firms should be bid down.

However, the dividend policies of all firms need not be fixed in the long run. In this example, we would expect enough low-dividend firms to increase their payout so that 40 percent of the firms pay high dividends and 60 percent of the firms pay low dividends. After this has occurred, no type of firm will be better off from changing its dividend policy. Once payouts of corporations conform to the desires of stockholders, no single firm can affect its market value by switching from one dividend strategy to another.

Clienteles are likely to form in the following way:

GROUP	STOCKS
Individuals in high tax brackets	Zero-to-low payout stocks
Individuals in low tax brackets	Low-to-medium payout stocks
Tax-free institutions	Medium payout stocks
Corporations	High payout stocks

To see if you understand the clientele effect, consider the following question: "In spite of the theoretical argument that dividend policy is irrelevant or that firms should not pay dividends, many investors like high dividends. Because of this fact, a firm can boost its share price by having a higher dividend payout ratio." True or false?

The statement is likely to be false. As long as there are already enough high-dividend firms to satisfy dividend-loving investors, a firm will not be able to boost its share price by paying high dividends. A firm can boost its stock price only if an unsatisfied clientele exists. There is no evidence that this is the case.

FIGURE 16.7

Ratio of Aggregate Dividends to Aggregate Earnings in the United States

Source: Table 11 of E. F. Fama and K. R. French, "Disappearing Dividends: Changing Firm Characteristics or Lower Propensity to Pay?" *Journal of Financial Economics* (April 2001).

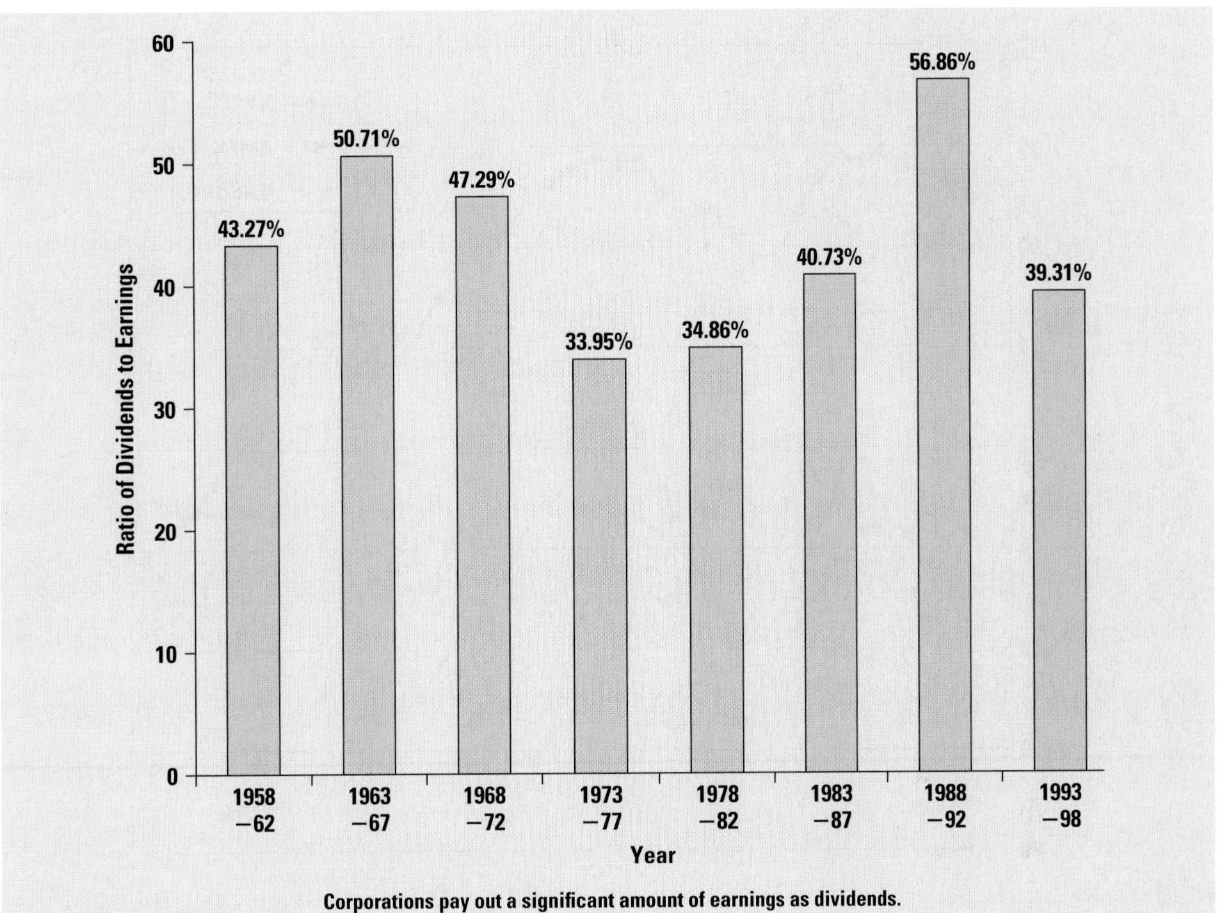

Corporations pay out a significant amount of earnings as dividends.

16.8 WHAT WE KNOW AND DO NOT KNOW ABOUT DIVIDEND POLICY

Corporate Dividends Are Substantial

We pointed out earlier in the chapter that dividends are tax disadvantaged relative to capital gains, because dividends are taxed upon payment while taxes on capital gains are deferred until sale. Nevertheless, dividends in the U.S. economy are substantial. For example, consider Figure 16.7, which shows the ratio of aggregate dividends to aggregate earnings for firms on the New York Stock Exchange (NYSE), the American Stock Exchange (AMEX), and NASDAQ over various time periods. The ratio is approximately 43 percent for the period from 1958 to 1998. This ratio varies from a low of 33.95 percent in the 1973–77 period to a high of 56.86 percent from 1988 to 1992.

While dividends are substantial, Fama and French (FF) point out that the percentage of companies paying dividends has fallen in recent years.[1] This insight is illustrated in Figure 16.8 for NYSE, AMEX, and NASDAQ firms. FF argue that the decline has been

[1] E. F. Fama and K. R. French, "Disappearing Dividends: Changing Firm Characteristics or Lower Propensity to Pay?" *Journal of Financial Economics* (April 2001).

FIGURE 16.8

Percent of Firms Paying Dividends

Source: Figure 5 of E. F. Fama and K. R. French, "Disappearing Dividends: Changing Firm Characteristics or Lower Propensity to Pay," *Journal of Financial Economics* (April 2001).

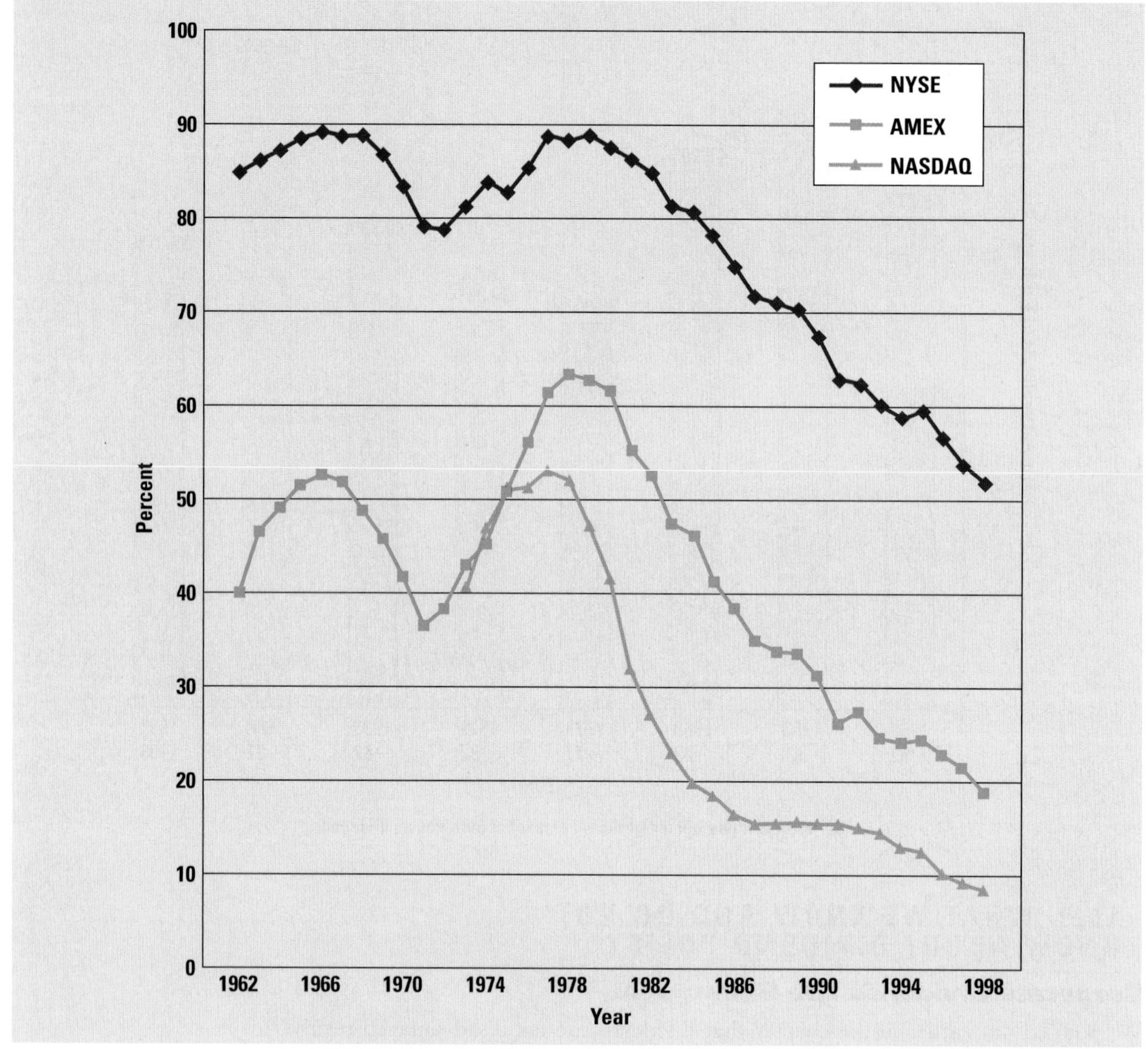

caused primarily by an explosion of small, currently unprofitable companies that have recently listed on the different exchanges. For the most part, firms of this type do not pay dividends. In addition, the authors argue that the percentage of firms of all types paying dividends has declined in recent years.

Corporations Smooth Dividends

In 1956, John Lintner made two important observations concerning dividend policy.[2] First, real world companies typically set long-run target ratios of dividends to earnings.

[2]J. Lintner, "Distribution and Incomes of Corporations among Dividends, Retained Earnings and Taxes," *American Economic Review* (May 1956).

A firm is likely to set a low target ratio if it has many positive NPV projects relative to available cash flow and a high ratio if it has few positive NPV projects. Second, managers know that only part of any change in earnings is likely to be permanent. Because managers need time to assess the permanence of any earnings rise, dividend changes appear to lag earnings changes by a number of periods.

Taken together, Lintner's observations suggest that two parameters describe dividend policy: the target payout ratio (t) and the speed of adjustment of current dividends to the target (s). Dividend changes will tend to conform to the following model:

$$\textbf{Dividend changes} = \text{Div}_1 - \text{Div}_0 = s \cdot (t\text{EPS}_1 - \text{Div}_1) \tag{16.3}$$

where Div_1 and Div_0 are dividends in the next year and dividends in the current year, respectively. EPS_1 is earnings per share in the next year.

EXAMPLE 16.1 Dividend Adjustments

Calculator Graphics, Inc. (CGI), has a target payout ratio of .30. Last year's earnings per share were \$10, and in accordance with the target, CGI paid dividends of \$3 per share last year. However, earnings have jumped to \$20 this year. Since the managers do not believe that this increase is permanent, they do *not* plan to raise dividends all the way to \$6 (.30 × \$20). Rather, their speed of adjustment coefficient, s, is .5, implying that the *increase* in dividends from last year to this year will be:

$$.5 \times (\$6 - \$3) = \$1.50$$

That is, the increase in dividends is the product of the speed of adjustment coefficient, .50, times the difference between what dividends would be with full adjustment [\$6 (.30 × \$20)] and last year's dividends. Since dividends will increase by \$1.50, dividends this year will be \$4.50 (\$3 + \$1.50).

Now, suppose that earnings stay at \$20 next year. The increase in dividends next year will be:

$$.5 \times (\$6 - \$4.50) = \$.75$$

In words, the increase in dividends from this year to next year will be the speed of adjustment coefficient (.50) times the difference between what dividends would have been next year with full adjustment (\$6) and this year's dividends (\$4.50). Since dividends will increase by \$.75, dividends next year will be \$5.25 (\$4.50 + \$.75). In this way, dividends will slowly rise every year, if earnings in all future years remain at \$20. However, dividends will reach \$6 only at infinity.

The limiting cases in (16.3) occur when $s = 1$ and $s = 0$. If $s = 1$, the actual change in dividends will be equal to the target change in dividends. Here, full adjustment occurs immediately. If $s = 0$, $\text{Div}_1 = \text{Div}_0$. In other words, there is no change in dividends at all. Real world companies can be expected to set s between 0 and 1.

An implication of Lintner's model is that the dividends-to-earnings ratio rises when a company begins a period of bad times, and the ratio falls when a company reaches a period of good times. Thus, dividends display less variability than do earnings. In other words, firms "smooth" dividends.

To show how important dividend stability and steady growth are to financial managers, consider that in 2004, 1,745 of the approximately 7,000 public companies in the United States increased their dividend payments. Dividend cuts or omissions totaled 64 for the same year. Two companies with long histories of dividend increases are Procter & Gamble and Colgate-Palmolive. At the end of 2004, Procter & Gamble had increased its dividend for 49 consecutive years, and Colgate-Palmolive had increased its dividend for 41 consecutive years. Overall, 85 companies in the S&P 500 had increased dividends for at least 25 consecutive years.

Payouts Provide Information to the Market

We previously observed that the price of a firm's stock frequently rises when either its current dividend is increased or a stock repurchase is announced. Conversely, the price of a firm's stock can fall significantly when its dividend is cut. In other words, there is information content in payouts. For example, consider what happened to Pacific Enterprises a number of years ago. Faced with poor operating results, Pacific Enterprises omitted its regular quarterly dividend. The next day the price of its common stock dropped from \$25 to \$19. One reason may be that investors are looking at current dividends for clues concerning the level of future earnings and dividends.

A Sensible Payout Policy

The knowledge of the finance profession varies across topic areas. For example, capital budgeting techniques are both powerful and precise. A single net present value equation can accurately determine whether a multimillion dollar project should be accepted or rejected. The capital asset pricing model and the arbitrage pricing model provide empirically validated relationships between expected return and risk.

Conversely, the field has less knowledge of capital structure policy. Though a number of elegant theories relate firm value to the level of debt, no formula can be used to calculate the firm's optimum debt-equity ratio. Our profession is forced too frequently to employ rules of thumb, such as treating the industry's average ratio as the optimal one for the firm. The field's knowledge of dividend policy is, perhaps, similar to its knowledge of capital structure policy. We do know that:

1. The intrinsic value of a firm is reduced when positive NPV projects are rejected in order to pay a dividend.
2. Firms should avoid issuing stock to pay a dividend in a world with personal taxes.
3. Stock repurchases represent a sensible alternative to dividends.

The preceding recommendations suggest that firms with many positive NPV projects relative to available cash flow should have low payout ratios. Firms with fewer positive

THE PROS AND CONS OF PAYING DIVIDENDS

PROS	CONS
1. Cash dividends can underscore good results and provide support to the stock price.	1. Dividends are taxed as ordinary income.
2. Dividends may attract institutional investors who prefer some return in the form of dividends. A mix of institutional and individual investors may allow a firm to raise capital at lower cost because of the ability of the firm to reach a wider market.	2. Dividends can reduce internal sources of financing. Dividends may force the firm to forgo positive NPV projects or to rely on costly external equity financing.
3. Stock price usually increases with the announcement of a new or increased dividend.	3. Once established, dividend cuts are hard to make without adversely affecting a firm's stock price.
4. Dividends absorb excess cash flow and may reduce agency costs that arise from conflicts between management and shareholders.	

NPV projects relative to available cash flow might want to consider higher payouts. In addition, there is some benefit to dividend stability, and unnecessary changes in dividend payout are avoided by most firms.

However, there is no formula for calculating the optimal dividend-to-earnings ratio. In addition, there is no formula for determining the optimal mix between repurchases and dividends. It can be argued that, for tax reasons, firms should always substitute stock repurchases for dividends. However, while the volume of repurchases has greatly increased over time, dividends do not appear to be on the way out. At the present time, the dollar volume of dividends is only slightly less than that of repurchases.

Some Survey Evidence on Dividends

A recent study surveyed a large number of financial executives regarding dividend policy. One of the questions asked was, "Do these statements describe factors that affect your company's dividend decisions?" Table 16.2 shows some of the results.

As shown in Table 16.2, financial managers are very disinclined to cut dividends. Moreover, they are very conscious of their previous dividends and desire to maintain a relatively steady dividend. In contrast, the cost of external capital and the desire to attract "prudent man" investors (those with fiduciary duties) are less important.

Table 16.3 is drawn from the same survey, but here the responses are to the question, "How important are the following factors to your company's dividend decision?" Not surprisingly given the responses in Table 16.2 and our earlier discussion, the highest priority is maintaining a consistent dividend policy. The next several items are also

TABLE 16.2

Survey Responses on Dividend Decisions*

Source: Adapted from Table 4 of A. Brav, J.R. Graham, C.R. Harvey, and R. Michaely, "Payout Policy in the 21st Century," *Journal of Financial Economics,* 2005.

POLICY STATEMENTS	PERCENT WHO AGREE OR STRONGLY AGREE
1. We try to avoid reducing dividends per share.	93.8%
2. We try to maintain a smooth dividend from year to year.	89.6
3. We consider the level of dividends per share that we have paid in recent quarters.	88.2
4. We are reluctant to make dividend changes that might have to be reversed in the future.	77.9
5. We consider the change or growth in dividends per share.	66.7
6. We consider the cost of raising external capital to be smaller than the cost of cutting dividends.	42.8
7. We pay dividends to attract investors subject to "prudent man" investment restrictions.	41.7

*Survey respondents were asked the question, "Do these statements describe factors that affect your company's dividend decisions?"

TABLE 16.3

Survey Responses on Dividend Decisions*

Source: Adapted from Table 5 of A. Brav, J.R. Graham, C.R. Harvey, and R. Michaely, "Payout Policy in the 21st Century," *Journal of Financial Economics,* 2005.

POLICY STATEMENTS	PERCENT WHO THINK THIS IS IMPORTANT OR VERY IMPORTANT
1. Maintaining consistency with our historic dividend policy.	84.1%
2. Stability of future earnings.	71.9
3. A sustainable change in earnings.	67.1
4. Attracting institutional investors to purchase our stock.	52.5
5. The availability of good investment opportunities for our firm to pursue.	47.6
6. Attracting retail investors to purchase our stock.	44.5
7. Personal taxes our stockholders pay when receiving dividends.	21.1
8. Flotation costs to issuing new equity.	9.3

*Survey respondents were asked the question, "How important are the following factors to your company's dividend decision?"

consistent with our previous analysis. Financial managers are very concerned about earnings stability and future earnings levels in making dividend decisions, and they consider the availability of good investment opportunities. Survey respondents also believed that attracting both institutional and individual (retail) investors was relatively important.

In contrast to our discussion in the earlier part of this chapter on taxes and flotation costs, the financial managers in this survey did not think that personal taxes paid on dividends by shareholders are very important. And even fewer think that equity flotation costs are relevant.

16.9 STOCK DIVIDENDS AND STOCK SPLITS

Another type of dividend is paid out in shares of stock. This type of dividend is called a **stock dividend**. A stock dividend is not a true dividend because it is not paid in cash. The effect of a stock dividend is to increase the number of shares that each owner holds. Because there are more shares outstanding, each is simply worth less.

A stock dividend is commonly expressed as a percentage; for example, a 20 percent stock dividend means that a shareholder receives one new share for every five currently owned (a 20 percent increase). Because every shareholder receives 20 percent more stock, the total number of shares outstanding rises by 20 percent. As we will see in a moment, the result is that each share of stock is worth about 20 percent less.

A **stock split** is essentially the same thing as a stock dividend, except that a split is expressed as a ratio instead of a percentage. When a split is declared, each share is split up to create additional shares. For example, in a three-for-one stock split, each old share is split into three new shares.

Some Details on Stock Splits and Stock Dividends

Stock splits and stock dividends have essentially the same impacts on the corporation and the shareholder: They increase the number of shares outstanding and reduce the value per share. The accounting treatment is not the same, however, and it depends on two things: (1) whether the distribution is a stock split or a stock dividend and (2) the size of the stock dividend if it is called a dividend.

By convention, stock dividends of less than 20 to 25 percent are called *small stock dividends*. The accounting procedure for such a dividend is discussed next. A stock dividend greater than this value of 20 to 25 percent is called a *large stock dividend*. Large stock dividends are not uncommon. For example, in April 2005, WellPoint (health insurer) and Gentex (manufacturer of automatic dimming rearview mirrors) both announced a 100 percent stock dividend, to name a few. Except for some relatively minor accounting differences, this has the same effect as a two-for-one stock split.

EXAMPLE OF A SMALL STOCK DIVIDEND The Peterson Co., a consulting firm specializing in difficult accounting problems, has 10,000 shares of stock outstanding, each selling at \$66. The total market value of the equity is \$66 × 10,000 = \$660,000. With a 10 percent stock dividend, each stockholder receives one additional share for each 10 owned, and the total number of shares outstanding after the dividend is 11,000.

Before the stock dividend, the equity portion of Peterson's balance sheet might look like this:

Common stock (\$1 par, 10,000 shares outstanding)	\$ 10,000
Capital in excess of par value	200,000
Retained earnings	290,000
Total owners' equity	\$500,000

A seemingly arbitrary accounting procedure is used to adjust the balance sheet after a small stock dividend. Because 1,000 new shares are issued, the common stock account is increased by $1,000 (1,000 shares at $1 par value each), for a total of $11,000. The market price of $66 is $65 greater than the par value, so the "excess" of $65 × 1,000 shares = $65,000 is added to the capital surplus account (capital in excess of par value), producing a total of $265,000.

Total owners' equity is unaffected by the stock dividend because no cash has come in or out, so retained earnings is reduced by the entire $66,000, leaving $224,000. The net effect of these machinations is that Peterson's equity accounts now look like this:

Common stock ($1 par, 11,000 shares outstanding)	$ 11,000
Capital in excess of par value	265,000
Retained earnings	224,000
Total owners' equity	$500,000

EXAMPLE OF A STOCK SPLIT A stock split is conceptually similar to a stock dividend, but it is commonly expressed as a ratio. For example, in a three-for-two split, each shareholder receives one additional share of stock for each two held originally, so a three-for-two split amounts to a 50 percent stock dividend. Again, no cash is paid out, and the percentage of the entire firm that each shareholder owns is unaffected.

The accounting treatment of a stock split is a little different from (and simpler than) that of a stock dividend. Suppose Peterson decides to declare a two-for-one stock split. The number of shares outstanding will double to 20,000, and the par value will be halved to $.50 per share. The owners' equity after the split is represented as:

Common stock ($.50 par, 20,000 shares outstanding)	$ 10,000
Capital in excess of par value	200,000
Retained earnings	290,000
Total owners' equity	$500,000

For a list of recent stock splits, try www.stocksplits.net.

Note that, for all three of the categories, the figures on the right are completely unaffected by the split. The only changes are in the par value per share and the number of shares outstanding. Because the number of shares has doubled, the par value of each is cut in half.

EXAMPLE OF A LARGE STOCK DIVIDEND In our example, if a 100 percent stock dividend were declared, 10,000 new shares would be distributed, so 20,000 shares would be outstanding. At a $1 par value per share, the common stock account would rise by $10,000, for a total of $20,000. The retained earnings account would be reduced by $10,000, leaving $280,000. The result would be the following:

Common stock ($1 par, 20,000 shares outstanding)	$ 20,000
Capital in excess of par value	200,000
Retained earnings	280,000
Total owners' equity	$500,000

Value of Stock Splits and Stock Dividends

The laws of logic tell us that stock splits and stock dividends can (1) leave the value of the firm unaffected, (2) increase its value, or (3) decrease its value. Unfortunately, the issues are complex enough that one cannot easily determine which of the three relationships holds.

THE BENCHMARK CASE A strong case can be made that stock dividends and splits do not change either the wealth of any shareholder or the wealth of the firm as a whole. In our preceding example, the equity had a total market value of $660,000. With the small stock dividend, the number of shares increased to 11,000, so it seems that each would be worth $660,000/11,000 = $60.

For example, a shareholder who had 100 shares worth $66 each before the dividend would have 110 shares worth $60 each afterwards. The total value of the stock is $6,600 either way; so the stock dividend doesn't really have any economic effect.

After the stock split, there are 20,000 shares outstanding, so each should be worth $660,000/20,000 = $33. In other words, the number of shares doubles and the price halves. From these calculations, it appears that stock dividends and splits are just paper transactions.

Although these results are relatively obvious, there are reasons that are often given to suggest that there may be some benefits to these actions. The typical financial manager is aware of many real world complexities, and, for that reason, the stock split or stock dividend decision is not treated lightly in practice.

POPULAR TRADING RANGE Proponents of stock dividends and stock splits frequently argue that a security has a proper **trading range**. When the security is priced above this level, many investors do not have the funds to buy the common trading unit of 100 shares, called a *round lot.* Although securities can be purchased in *odd-lot* form (fewer than 100 shares), the commissions are greater. Thus, firms will split the stock to keep the price in this trading range.

For example, in early 2003, Microsoft announced a two-for-one stock split. This was the ninth split for Microsoft since the company went public in 1986. The stock had split three-for-two on two occasions and two-for-one a total of seven times. So, for every share of Microsoft you owned in 1986 when the company first went public, you would own 288 shares as of the most recent stock split in 2003. Similarly, since Wal-Mart went public in 1970, it has split its stock two-for-one eleven times, and Dell Computer has split three-for-two once and two-for-one six times since going public in 1988.

Although this argument of a trading range is a popular one, its validity is questionable for a number of reasons. Mutual funds, pension funds, and other institutions have steadily increased their trading activity since World War II and now handle a sizable percentage of total trading volume (on the order of 80 percent of NYSE trading volume, for example). Because these institutions buy and sell in huge amounts, the individual share price is of little concern.

Furthermore, we sometimes observe share prices that are quite large that do not appear to cause problems. To take an extreme case, consider the Swiss chocolatier Lindt. In May 2005, Lindt shares were selling for around 18,850 Swiss francs each, or about $15,400. A round lot would have cost a cool $1.54 million. This is fairly expensive, but also consider Berkshire-Hathaway, the company run by legendary investor Warren Buffet. In May 2005, each share in the company sold for about $85,000, down from a high of $95,700 in February 2004.

Finally, there is evidence that stock splits may actually decrease the liquidity of the company's shares. Following a two-for-one split, the number of shares traded should more than double if liquidity is increased by the split. This doesn't appear to happen, and the reverse is sometimes observed.

Reverse Splits

A less frequently encountered financial maneuver is the **reverse split**. For example, in February 2005, Boston Life Sciences underwent a one-for-five reverse stock split, and ADC Telecommunications undertook a one-for-five reverse stock split in May 2005. In a one-for-five reverse split, each investor exchanges five old shares for one new share. The par value is quintupled in the process. As with stock splits and stock dividends, a case can be made that a reverse split has no real effect.

Given real world imperfections, three related reasons are cited for reverse splits. First, transaction costs to shareholders may be less after the reverse split. Second, the liquidity and marketability of a company's stock might be improved when its price is raised to the popular trading range. Third, stocks selling at prices below a certain level are not considered respectable, meaning that investors underestimate these firms' earnings, cash flow, growth, and stability. Some financial analysts argue that a reverse split can achieve instant respectability. As was the case with stock splits, none of these reasons is particularly compelling, especially not the third one.

There are two other reasons for reverse splits. First, stock exchanges have minimum price per share requirements. A reverse split may bring the stock price up to such a minimum. In 2001–2002, in the wake of a bear market, this motive became an increasingly important one. In 2001, 106 companies asked their shareholders to approve reverse splits. There were 111 reverse splits in 2002 and 75 in 2003, but only 14 by mid-year 2004. The most common reason for these reverse splits is that NASDAQ delists companies whose stock price drops below $1 per share for 30 days. A large number of companies, particularly Internet-related technology companies, found themselves in danger of being delisted and used reverse splits to boost their stock prices. Second, companies sometimes perform reverse splits and, at the same time, buy out any stockholders who end up with less than a certain number of shares.

For example, in May 2004, Detwiler, Mitchell & Co., a Boston-based investment bank, completed a 1-for-600 reverse stock split, followed by a cash purchase of all holdings less than one share in order to buy out all shareholders who held less than 600 shares to save mailing and other costs. The company ultimately repurchased about 64,000 shares from some 500 stockholders. What made the proposal especially imaginative was that immediately after the reverse stock split, the company underwent a 600-for-1 split to restore the stock to its original cost!

SUMMARY AND CONCLUSIONS

1. The dividend policy of the firm is irrelevant in a perfect capital market because the shareholder can effectively undo the firm's dividend strategy. If a shareholder receives a greater dividend than desired, he or she can reinvest the excess. Conversely, if the shareholder receives a smaller dividend than desired, he or she can sell off extra shares of stock. This argument is due to MM and is similar to their homemade leverage concept, discussed in a previous chapter.
2. Stockholders will be indifferent between dividends and share repurchases in a perfect capital market.
3. Since dividends in the United States are taxed, companies should not issue stock in order to pay out a dividend.
4. Also because of taxes, firms have an incentive to reduce dividends. For example, they might consider increasing capital expenditures, acquiring other companies, or purchasing financial assets. However, due to financial considerations and legal constraints, rational firms with large cash flows will likely exhaust these activities with plenty of cash left over for dividends.

5. In a world with personal taxes, a strong case can be made for repurchasing shares instead of paying dividends.
6. Nevertheless, there are a number of justifications for dividends even in a world with personal taxes:
   a. Investors in no-dividend stocks incur transaction costs when selling off shares for current consumption.
   b. Behavioral finance argues that investors with limited self-control can meet current consumption needs via high-dividend stocks while adhering to a policy of "never dipping into principal."
   c. Managers, acting on behalf of stockholders, can pay dividends to keep cash from bondholders. The board of directors, also acting on behalf of stockholders, can use dividends to reduce the cash available to spendthrift managers.
7. The stock market reacts positively to increases in dividends (or an initial payment) and negatively to decreases in dividends. This suggests that there is information content in dividend payments.
8. High (low) dividend firms should arise to meet the demands of dividend-preferring (capital gains–preferring) investors. Because of these clienteles, it is not clear that a firm can create value by changing its dividend policy.

CONCEPT QUESTIONS

1. **Dividend Policy Irrelevance** How is it possible that dividends are so important, but, at the same time, dividend policy is irrelevant?
2. **Stock Repurchases** What is the impact of a stock repurchase on a company's debt ratio? Does this suggest another use for excess cash?
3. **Dividend Policy** It is sometimes suggested that firms should follow a "residual" dividend policy. With such a policy, the main idea is that a firm should focus on meeting its investment needs and maintaining its desired debt-equity ratio. Having done so, any leftover, or residual, income is paid out as dividends. What do you think would be the chief drawback to a residual dividend policy?
4. **Dividend Chronology** On Tuesday, December 8, Hometown Power Co.'s board of directors declares a dividend of 75 cents per share payable on Wednesday, January 17, to shareholders of record as of Wednesday, January 3. When is the ex-dividend date? If a shareholder buys stock before that date, who gets the dividends on those shares, the buyer or the seller?
5. **Alternative Dividends** Some corporations, like one British company that offers its large shareholders free crematorium use, pay dividends in kind (that is, offer their services to shareholders at below-market cost). Should mutual funds invest in stocks that pay these dividends in kind? (The fundholders do not receive these services.)
6. **Dividends and Stock Price** If increases in dividends tend to be followed by (immediate) increases in share prices, how can it be said that dividend policy is irrelevant?
7. **Dividends and Stock Price** Last month, Central Virginia Power Company, which had been having trouble with cost overruns on a nuclear power plant that it had been building, announced that it was "temporarily suspending payments due to the cash flow crunch associated with its investment program." The company's stock price dropped from $28.50 to $25 when this announcement was made. How would you interpret this change in the stock price (that is, what would you say caused it)?
8. **Dividend Reinvestment Plans** The DRK Corporation has recently developed a dividend reinvestment plan, or DRIP. The plan allows investors to reinvest cash dividends automatically in DRK in exchange for new shares of stock. Over time, investors in DRK will be able to build their holdings by reinvesting dividends to purchase additional shares of the company.

Over 1,000 companies offer dividend reinvestment plans. Most companies with DRIPs charge no brokerage or service fees. In fact, the shares of DRK will be purchased at a 10 percent discount from the market price.

A consultant for DRK estimates that about 75 percent of DRK's shareholders will take part in this plan. This is somewhat higher than the average.

Evaluate DRK's dividend reinvestment plan. Will it increase shareholder wealth? Discuss the advantages and disadvantages involved here.

9. **Dividend Policy** For initial public offerings of common stock, 2000 was a very big year, with over $80.6 billion raised by the process. Relatively few of the 452 firms involved paid cash dividends. Why do you think that most chose not to pay cash dividends?

10. **Investment and Dividends** The Phew Charitable Trust pays no taxes on its capital gains or on its dividend income or interest income. Would it be irrational for it to have low-dividend, high-growth stocks in its portfolio? Would it be irrational for it to have municipal bonds in its portfolio? Explain.

Use the following information to answer the next two questions:

Historically, the U.S. tax code treated dividend payments made to shareholders as ordinary income. Thus, dividends were taxed at the investor's marginal tax rate, which was as high as 38.6 percent in 2002. Capital gains were taxed at a capital gains tax rate, which was the same for most investors, and fluctuated through the years. In 2002, the capital gains tax rate stood at 20 percent. In an effort to stimulate the economy, President George W. Bush presided over a tax plan overhaul that included changes in dividend and capital gains tax rates. The new tax plan, which was implemented in 2003, called for a 15 percent tax rate on both dividends and capital gains for investors in higher tax brackets. For lower tax bracket investors, the tax rate on dividends and capital gains was set at 5 percent through 2007, dropping to zero in 2008.

11. **Ex-Dividend Stock Prices** How do you think this tax law change affects ex-dividend stock prices?

12. **Stock Repurchases** How do you think this tax law change affected the relative attractiveness of stock repurchases compared to dividend payments?

13. **Dividends and Stock Value** The growing perpetuity model expresses the value of a share of stock as the present value of the expected dividends from that stock. How can you conclude that dividend policy is irrelevant when this model is valid?

14. **Bird-in-the-Hand Argument** The bird-in-the-hand argument, which states that a dividend today is safer than the uncertain prospect of a capital gain tomorrow, is often used to justify high dividend payout ratios. Explain the fallacy behind this argument.

15. **Dividends and Income Preference** The desire for current income is not a valid explanation for preference for high current dividend policy, as investors can always create homemade dividends by selling a portion of their stocks. Is this statement true or false? Why?

16. **Dividends and Clientele** Cap Henderson owns Neotech stock because its price has been steadily rising over the past few years and he expects this performance to continue. Cap is trying to convince Widow Jones to purchase some Neotech stock, but she is reluctant because Neotech has never paid a dividend. She depends on steady dividends to provide her with income.

    a. What preferences are these two investors demonstrating?

    b. What argument should Cap use to convince Widow Jones that Neotech stock is the stock for her?

    c. Why might Cap's argument not convince Widow Jones?

17. **Dividends and Taxes** Your aunt is in a high tax bracket and would like to minimize the tax burden of her investment portfolio. She is willing to buy and sell in order to maximize her after-tax returns and she has asked for your advice. What would you suggest she do?

18. **Dividends versus Capital Gains** If the market places the same value on $1 of dividends as on $1 of capital gains, then firms with different payout ratios will appeal to different clienteles of investors. One clientele is as good as another; therefore, a firm cannot increase its value by changing its dividend policy. Yet empirical investigations reveal a strong correlation between dividend payout ratios and other firm characteristics. For example, small, rapidly growing firms that have recently gone public almost always have payout ratios that are zero; all earnings are reinvested in the business. Explain this phenomenon if dividend policy is irrelevant.

19. **Dividend Irrelevancy** In spite of the theoretical argument that dividend policy should be irrelevant, the fact remains that many investors like high dividends. If this preference exists, a firm can boost its share price by increasing its dividend payout ratio. Explain the fallacy in this argument.

20. **Dividends and Stock Price** Empirical research found that there have been significant increases in stock price on the day an initial dividend (i.e., the first time a firm pays a cash dividend) is announced. What does this finding imply about the information content of initial dividends?

QUESTIONS AND PROBLEMS

Basic
(Questions 1–14)

1. **Dividends and Taxes** Lee Ann, Inc., has declared a $6 per-share dividend. Suppose capital gains are not taxed, but dividends are taxed at 15 percent. New IRS regulations require that taxes be withheld at the time the dividend is paid. Lee Ann sells for $80 per share, and the stock is about to go ex dividend. What do you think the ex-dividend price will be?

2. **Stock Dividends** The owners' equity accounts for Hexagon International are shown here:

Common stock ($1 par value)	$ 10,000
Capital surplus	180,000
Retained earnings	586,500
Total owners' equity	$776,500

   a. If Hexagon stock currently sells for $25 per share and a 10 percent stock dividend is declared, how many new shares will be distributed? Show how the equity accounts would change.

   b. If Hexagon declared a 25 percent stock dividend, how would the accounts change?

3. **Stock Splits** For the company in Problem 2, show how the equity accounts will change if:

   a. Hexagon declares a four-for-one stock split. How many shares are outstanding now? What is the new par value per share?

   b. Hexagon declares a one-for-five reverse stock split. How many shares are outstanding now? What is the new par value per share?

4. **Stock Splits and Stock Dividends** Roll Corporation (RC) currently has 150,000 shares of stock outstanding that sell for $65 per share. Assuming no market imperfections or tax effects exist, what will the share price be after:

   a. RC has a five-for-three stock split?

   b. RC has a 15 percent stock dividend?

   c. RC has a 42.5 percent stock dividend?

   d. RC has a four-for-seven reverse stock split?

   e. Determine the new number of shares outstanding in parts (a) through (d).

5. **Regular Dividends** The balance sheet for Levy Corp. is shown here in market value terms. There are 5,000 shares of stock outstanding.

MARKET VALUE BALANCE SHEET			
Cash	$ 20,000	Equity	$175,000
Fixed assets	155,000		
Total	$175,000	Total	$175,000

The company has declared a dividend of $1.50 per share. The stock goes ex dividend tomorrow. Ignoring any tax effects, what is the stock selling for today? What will it sell for tomorrow? What will the balance sheet look like after the dividends are paid?

6. **Share Repurchase** In the previous problem, suppose Levy has announced it is going to repurchase $4,025 worth of stock. What effect will this transaction have on the equity of the firm? How many shares will be outstanding? What will the price per share be after the repurchase? Ignoring tax effects, show how the share repurchase is effectively the same as a cash dividend.

7. **Stock Dividends** The market value balance sheet for Outbox Manufacturing is shown here. Outbox has declared a 25 percent stock dividend. The stock goes ex dividend tomorrow (the chronology for a stock dividend is similar to that for a cash dividend). There are 15,000 shares of stock outstanding. What will the ex-dividend price be?

MARKET VALUE BALANCE SHEET			
Cash	$190,000	Debt	$160,000
Fixed assets	330,000	Equity	360,000
Total	$520,000	Total	$520,000

8. **Stock Dividends** The company with the common equity accounts shown here has declared a 12 percent stock dividend at a time when the market value of its stock is $20 per share. What effects on the equity accounts will the distribution of the stock dividend have?

Common stock ($1 par value)	$ 350,000
Capital surplus	1,650,000
Retained earnings	3,000,000
Total owners' equity	$5,000,000

9. **Stock Splits** In the previous problem, suppose the company instead decides on a five-for-one stock split. The firm's 70-cent per share cash dividend on the new (post-split) shares represents an increase of 10 percent over last year's dividend on the pre-split stock. What effect does this have on the equity accounts? What was last year's dividend per share?

10. **Residual Dividend Policy** Soprano, Inc., a litter recycling company, uses a residual dividend policy (see Concept Question 3). A debt-equity ratio of .80 is considered optimal. Earnings for the period just ended were $1,200, and a dividend of $480 was declared. How much in new debt was borrowed? What were total capital outlays?

11. **Residual Dividend Policy** Worthington Corporation has declared an annual dividend of $0.80 per share. For the year just ended, earnings were $7 per share.
    a. What is Worthington's payout ratio?
    b. Suppose Worthington has seven million shares outstanding. Borrowing for the coming year is planned at $18 million. What are planned investment outlays assuming a residual dividend policy (see Concept Question 3)? What target capital structure is implicit in these calculations?

12. **Residual Dividend Policy** Red Zeppelin Corporation follows a strict residual dividend policy (see Concept Question 3). Its debt-equity ratio is 3.

    a. If earnings for the year are $180,000, what is the maximum amount of capital spending possible with no new equity?

    b. If planned investment outlays for the coming year are $760,000, will Red Zeppelin pay a dividend? If so, how much?

    c. Does Red Zeppelin maintain a constant dividend payout? Why or why not?

13. **Residual Dividend Policy** Preti Rock (PR), Inc., predicts that earnings in the coming year will be $56 million. There are 12 million shares, and PR maintains a debt-equity ratio of 2.

    a. Calculate the maximum investment funds available without issuing new equity and the increase in borrowing that goes along with it.

    b. Suppose the firm uses a residual dividend policy (see Concept Question 3). Planned capital expenditures total $72 million. Based on this information, what will the dividend per share be?

    c. In part (b), how much borrowing will take place? What is the addition to retained earnings?

    d. Suppose PR plans no capital outlays for the coming year. What will the dividend be under a residual policy? What will new borrowing be?

14. **Dividends and Stock Price** The Mann Company belongs to a risk class for which the appropriate discount rate is 10 percent. Mann currently has 100,000 outstanding shares selling at $100 each. The firm is contemplating the declaration of a $5 dividend at the end of the fiscal year that just began. Assume there are no taxes on dividends. Answer the following questions based on the Miller and Modigliani model, which is discussed in the text.

    a. What will be the price of the stock on the ex-dividend date if the dividend is declared?

    b. What will be the price of the stock at the end of the year if the dividend is not declared?

    c. If Mann makes $2 million of new investments at the beginning of the period, earns net income of $1 million, and pays the dividend at the end of the year, how many shares of new stock must the firm issue to meet its funding needs?

    d. Is it realistic to use the MM model in the real world to value stock? Why or why not?

Intermediate (Questions 15–20)

15. **Homemade Dividends** You own 1,000 shares of stock in Avondale Corporation. You will receive a 70-cent per share dividend in one year. In two years, Avondale will pay a liquidating dividend of $40 per share. The required return on Avondale stock is 15 percent. What is the current share price of your stock (ignoring taxes)? If you would rather have equal dividends in each of the next two years, show how you can accomplish this by creating homemade dividends. (Hint: Dividends will be in the form of an annuity.)

16. **Homemade Dividends** In the previous problem, suppose you want only $200 total in dividends the first year. What will your homemade dividend be in two years?

17. **Stock Repurchase** Flychucker Corporation is evaluating an extra dividend versus a share repurchase. In either case, $5,000 would be spent. Current earnings are $0.95 per share, and the stock currently sells for $40 per share. There are 200 shares outstanding. Ignore taxes and other imperfections in answering the first two questions.

    a. Evaluate the two alternatives in terms of the effect on the price per share of the stock and shareholder wealth.

    b. What will be the effect on Flychucker's EPS and PE ratio under the two different scenarios?

    c. In the real world, which of these actions would you recommend? Why?

18. **Dividends and Firm Value** The net income of Novis Corporation is $32,000. The company has 10,000 outstanding shares, and a 100 percent payout policy. The expected value of the firm one

year from now is $1,545,600. The appropriate discount rate for Novis is 12 percent, and the dividend tax rate is zero.

a. What is the current value of the firm assuming the current dividend has not yet been paid?

b. What is the ex-dividend price of Novis's stock if the board follows its current policy?

c. At the dividend declaration meeting, several board members claimed that the dividend is too meager and is probably depressing Novis's price. They proposed that Novis sell enough new shares to finance a $4.25 dividend.

   i. Comment on the claim that the low dividend is depressing the stock price. Support your argument with calculations.

   ii. If the proposal is adopted, at what price will the new shares sell and how many will be sold?

19. **Dividend Policy** Gibson Co. has a current period cash flow of $1.2 million and pays no dividends. The present value of the company's future cash flows is $15 million. The company is entirely financed with equity, and has 1 million shares outstanding. Assume the dividend tax rate is zero.

a. What is the share price of the Gibson stock?

b. Suppose the board of directors of Gibson Co. announces its plan to pay out 50 percent of its current cash flow as cash dividends to its shareholders. How can Jeff Miller, who owns 1,000 shares of Gibson stock, achieve a zero payout policy on his own?

20. **Dividend Smoothing** The Sharpe Co. just paid a dividend of $1.25 per share of stock. Its target payout ratio is 40 percent. The company expects to have an earnings per share of $4.50 one year from now.

a. If the adjustment rate is .3 as defined in the Lintner model, what is the dividend one year from now?

b. If the adjustment rate is .6 instead, what is the dividend one year from now?

c. Which adjustment rate is more conservative? Why?

Challenge (Questions 21–24)

21. **Expected Return, Dividends, and Taxes** The Gecko Company and the Gordon Company are two firms whose business risk is the same but that have different dividend policies. Gecko pays no dividend, whereas Gordon has an expected dividend yield of 6 percent. Suppose the capital gains tax rate is zero, whereas the dividend tax rate is 35 percent. Gecko has an expected earnings growth rate of 15 percent annually, and its stock price is expected to grow at this same rate. If the aftertax expected returns on the two stocks are equal (because they are in the same risk class), what is the pretax required return on Gordon's stock?

22. **Dividends and Taxes** As discussed in the text, in the absence of market imperfections and tax effects, we would expect the share price to decline by the amount of the dividend payment when the stock goes ex dividend. Once we consider the role of taxes, however, this is not necessarily true. One model has been proposed that incorporates tax effects into determining the ex-dividend price:[3]

$$(P_0 - P_X)/D = (1 - t_P)/(1 - t_G)$$

where P_0 is the price just before the stock goes ex, P_X is the ex-dividend share price, D is the amount of the dividend per share, t_P is the relevant marginal personal tax rate on dividends, and t_G is the effective marginal tax rate on capital gains.

a. If $t_P = t_G = 0$, how much will the share price fall when the stock goes ex?

b. If $t_P =$ 15 percent and $t_G = 0$, how much will the share price fall?

c. If $t_P =$ 15 percent and $t_G =$ 20 percent, how much will the share price fall?

[3] N. Elton and M. Gruber, "Marginal Stockholder Tax Rates and the Clientele Effect," *Review of Economics and Statistics* 52 (February 1970).

d. Suppose the only owners of stock are corporations. Recall that corporations get at least a 70 percent exemption from taxation on the dividend income they receive, but they do not get such an exemption on capital gains. If the corporation's income and capital gains tax rates are both 35 percent, what does this model predict the ex-dividend share price will be?

e. What does this problem tell you about real world tax considerations and the dividend policy of the firm?

23. **Dividends versus Reinvestment** National Business Machine Co. (NBM) has $2 million of extra cash after taxes have been paid. NBM has two choices to make use of this cash. One alternative is to invest the cash in financial assets. The resulting investment income will be paid out as a special dividend at the end of three years. In this case, the firm can invest in Treasury bills yielding 7 percent, or an 11 percent preferred stock. IRS regulations allow the company to exclude from taxable income 70 percent of the dividends received from investing in another company's stock. Another alternative is to pay out the cash now as dividends. This would allow the shareholders to invest on their own in Treasury bills with the same yield, or in preferred stock. The corporate tax rate is 35 percent. Assume the investor has a 31 percent personal income tax rate, which is applied to interest income and preferred stock dividends. The personal dividend tax rate is 15 percent on common stock dividends. Should the cash be paid today or in three years? Which of the two options generates the highest aftertax income for the shareholders?

24. **Dividends versus Reinvestment** After completing its capital spending for the year, Carlson Manufacturing has $1,000 extra cash. Carlson's managers must choose between investing the cash in Treasury bonds that yield 8 percent or paying the cash out to investors who would invest in the bonds themselves.

a. If the corporate tax rate is 35 percent, what personal tax rate would make the investors equally willing to receive the dividend or to let Carlson invest the money?

b. Is the answer to (a) reasonable? Why or why not?

c. Suppose the only investment choice is a preferred stock that yields 12 percent. The corporate dividend exclusion of 70 percent applies. What personal tax rate will make the stockholders indifferent to the outcome of Carlson's dividend decision?

d. Is this a compelling argument for a low dividend payout ratio? Why or why not?

STANDARD & POOR'S

S&P PROBLEM

www.mhhe.com/edumarketinsight

1. **Dividend Payouts** Use the annual financial statements for General Mills (GIS), Boston Beer (SAM), and US Steel (X) to find the dividend payout ratio for each company for the last three years. Why would these companies pay out a different percentage of income as dividends? Is there anything unusual about the dividends paid by US Steel? How is this possible?

WHAT'S ON THE WEB?

1. **Dividend Reinvestment Plans** Dividend reinvestment plans (DRIPs) permit shareholders to automatically reinvest cash dividends in the company. To find out more about DRIPs go to www.fool.com, follow the "Fool's School" link and then the "DRIP Investing" link. What are the advantages Motley Fool lists for DRIPs? What are the different types of DRIPs? What is a Direct Purchase Plan? How does a Direct Purchase Plan differ from a DRIP?

2. **Dividends** Go to www.companyboardroom.com and scroll down until you see the section titled Today's Highlighted Dividends and follow the "Full List" link. How many companies went "ex" on this day? What is the largest declared dividend? For the stocks going "ex" today, what is the longest time until the payable date?

3. **Stock Splits** Go to www.companyboardroom.com and scroll down until you see the section titled Today's Highlighted Splits and follow the "Full List" link. How many stock splits are listed? How many are reverse splits? What is the largest split and the largest reverse split in terms of shares? Pick a company and follow the link. What type of information do you find?
4. **Dividend Yields** Which stock has the highest dividend yield? To answer this (and more), go to finance.yahoo.com and follow the "Screener" link. Use the minimum value box for the dividend yield on the Java version of the screener to find out how many stocks have a dividend yield above 3 percent. Above 5 percent? Now use the dividend amount to find out how many stocks have an annual dividend above $2. Above $4?
5. **Stock Splits** How many times has Procter & Gamble's stock split? Go to the Web page at www.pg.com, and you will find a pull-down menu listed under "Investor." Follow the "Stock Information" link, then the "Splits & Dividends." When did Procter & Gamble's stock first split? What was the split? When was the most recent stock split?

CLOSING CASE

ELECTRONIC TIMING, INC.

Electronic Timing, Inc., (ETI) is a small company founded 15 years ago by electronics engineers Tom Miller and Jessica Kerr. ETI manufactures integrated circuits to capitalize on the complex mixed-signal design technology and has recently entered the market for frequency timing generators, or silicon timing devices, which provide the timing signals or "clocks" necessary to synchronize electronic systems. Its clock products originally were used in PC video graphics applications, but the market subsequently expanded to include motherboards, PC peripheral devices, and other digital consumer electronics, such as digital television boxes and game consoles. ETI also designs and markets custom application-specific integrated circuits (ASICs) for industrial customers. The ASIC's design combines analog and digital, or mixed-signal, technology. In addition to Tom and Jessica, Nolan Pittman, who provided capital for the company, is the third primary owner. Each owns 25 percent of the one million shares outstanding. The company has several other individuals, including current employees, who own the remaining shares.

Recently, the company designed a new computer motherboard. The company's design is both more efficient and less expensive to manufacture, and the ETI design is expected to become standard in many personal computers. After investigating the possibility of manufacturing the new motherboard, ETI determined that the costs involved in building a new plant would be prohibitive. The owners also decided that they were unwilling to bring in another large outside owner. Instead, ETI sold the design to an outside firm. The sale of the motherboard design was completed for an aftertax payment of $30 million.

1. Tom believes the company should use the extra cash to pay a special one-time dividend. How will this proposal affect the stock price? How will it affect the value of the company?
2. Jessica believes that the company should use the extra cash to pay off debt and upgrade and expand its existing manufacturing capability. How would Jessica's proposals affect the company?
3. Nolan is in favor of a share repurchase. He argues that a repurchase will increase the company's P/E ratio, return on assets, and return on equity. Are his arguments correct? How will a share repurchase affect the value of the company?

4. Another option discussed by Tom, Jessica, and Nolan would be to begin a regular dividend payment to shareholders. How would you evaluate this proposal?
5. One way to value a share of stock is the dividend growth, or growing perpetuity, model. Consider the following: The dividend payout ratio is one minus *b*, where *b* is the "retention" or "plowback" ratio. So, the dividend next year will be the earnings next year, E_1, times one minus the retention ratio. The most commonly used equation to calculate the sustainable growth rate is the return on equity times the retention ratio. Substituting these relationships into the dividend growth model, we get the following equation to calculate the price of a share of stock today:

$$P_0 = \frac{E_1(1 - b)}{R_S - \text{ROE} \times b}$$

   What are the implications of this result in terms of whether the company should pay a dividend or upgrade and expand its manufacturing capability? Explain.
6. Does the question of whether the company should pay a dividend depend on whether the company is organized as a corporation or an LLC?

CHAPTER 17

Options and Corporate Finance

OPENING CASE

On May 12, 2005, the closing stock prices for Procter & Gamble, Allstate, and Adobe Systems were $55.44, $56.79, and $57.78, respectively. Each company had a call option trading on the Chicago Board Options Exchange with a $55 strike price and an expiration date of July 15—64 days away. Given how close the stock prices are, you might expect that the prices on these call options would be similar, but they were not. The Procter & Gamble option sold for $1.80, Allstate options traded at $2.95, and Adobe Systems options traded at $5.40. Why would options on these three similarly priced stocks be priced so differently when the strike prices and the time to expiration were exactly the same? A big reason is that the volatility of the underlying stock is an important determinant of an option's underlying value, and, in fact, these three stocks had very different volatilities. In this chapter, we will explore this issue—and many others—in much greater depth using the Nobel prize–winning Black-Scholes option pricing model.

17.1 OPTIONS

An **option** is a contract giving its owner the right to buy or sell an asset at a fixed price on or before a given date. For example, an option on a building might give the buyer the right to buy the building for $1 million on or anytime before the Saturday prior to the third Wednesday in January 2010. Options are a unique type of financial contract because they give the buyer the right, but not the *obligation,* to do something. The buyer uses the option only if it is advantageous to do so; otherwise the option can be thrown away.

The Options Industry Council has a Web page with lots of educational material at www.888options.com.

There is a special vocabulary associated with options. Here are some important definitions:

1. **Exercising the option**. The act of buying or selling the underlying asset via the option contract is referred to as *exercising the option.*
2. **Strike or exercise price**. The fixed price in the option contract at which the holder can buy or sell the underlying asset is called the *strike price* or *exercise price.*
3. **Expiration date**. The maturity date of the option is referred to as the *expiration date.* After this date, the option is dead.
4. **American and European options**. An American option may be exercised anytime up to the expiration date. A European option differs from an American option in that it can be exercised only on the expiration date.

17.2 CALL OPTIONS

The most common type of option is a **call option**. A call option gives the owner the right to buy an asset at a fixed price during a particular time period. There is no restriction on the kind of asset, but the most common ones traded on exchanges are options on stocks and bonds.

For example, call options on IBM stock can be purchased on the Chicago Board Options Exchange. IBM does not issue (that is, sell) call options on its common stock. Instead, individual investors are the original buyers and sellers of call options on IBM common stock. A representative call option on IBM stock enables an investor to buy 100 shares of IBM on or before July 15, at an exercise price of $100. This is a valuable option if there is some probability that the price of IBM common stock will exceed $100 on or before July 15.

The Value of a Call Option at Expiration

What is the value of a call option contract on common stock at expiration? The answer depends on the value of the underlying stock at expiration.

Let's continue with the IBM example. Suppose the stock price is $130 at expiration. The buyer[1] of the call option has the right to buy the underlying stock at the exercise price of $100. In other words, he has the right to exercise the call. Having the right to buy something for $100 when it is worth $130 is obviously a good thing. The value of this right is $30 ($130 − $100) on the expiration day.[2]

The call would be worth even more if the stock price were higher on expiration day. For example, if IBM were selling for $150 on the date of expiration, the call would be worth $50 ($150 − $100) at that time. In fact, the call's value increases $1 for every $1 rise in the stock price.

If the stock price is greater than the exercise price, we say that the call is *in the money.* Of course, it is also possible that the value of the common stock will turn out to be less

[1]We use *buyer, owner,* and *holder* interchangeably.

[2]This example assumes that the call lets the holder purchase one share of stock at $100. In reality, one call option contract would let the holder purchase 100 shares. The profit would then equal $3,000 [($130 − $100) × 100].

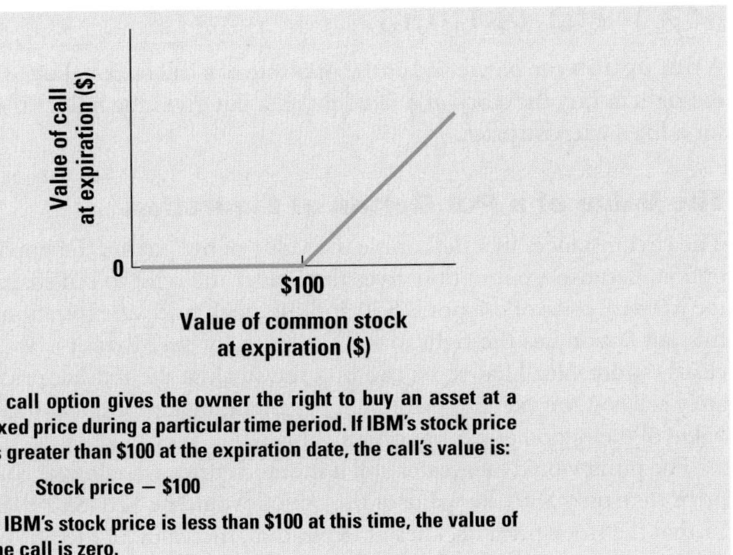

A call option gives the owner the right to buy an asset at a fixed price during a particular time period. If IBM's stock price is greater than $100 at the expiration date, the call's value is:

Stock price − $100

If IBM's stock price is less than $100 at this time, the value of the call is zero.

FIGURE 17.1
The Value of a Call Option on the Expiration Date

than the exercise price. In this case, we say that the call is *out of the money*. The holder will not exercise in this case. For example, if the stock price at the expiration date is $90, no rational investor would exercise. Why pay $100 for stock worth only $90? Because the option holder has no obligation to exercise the call, she can *walk away* from the option. As a consequence, if IBM's stock price is less than $100 on the expiration date, the value of the call option will be $0. In this case, the value of the call option is not the difference between IBM's stock price and $100, as it would be if the holder of the call option had the *obligation* to exercise the call.

The payoff of a call option at expiration is:

	Payoff on the Expiration Date	
	IF STOCK PRICE IS LESS THAN $100	IF STOCK PRICE IS GREATER THAN $100
Call option value:	$0	Stock price − $100

Figure 17.1 plots the value of the call at expiration against the value of IBM's stock. It is referred to as the *hockey stick diagram* of call option values. If the stock price is less than $100, the call is out of the money and worthless. If the stock price is greater than $100, the call is in the money and its value rises one-for-one with increases in the stock price. Notice that the call can never have a negative value. It is a *limited liability instrument,* which means that all the holder can lose is the initial amount she paid for it.

EXAMPLE 17.1 Call Option Payoffs

Suppose Mr. Optimist holds a one-year call option on TIX common stock. It is a European call option and can be exercised at $150. Assume that the expiration date has arrived. What is the value of the TIX call option on the expiration date? If TIX is selling for $200 per share, Mr. Optimist can exercise the option—purchase TIX at $150—and then immediately sell the share at $200. Mr. Optimist will have made $50 ($200 − $150).

Instead, assume that TIX is selling for $100 per share on the expiration date. If Mr. Optimist still holds the call option, he will throw it out. The value of the TIX call on the expiration date will be zero in this case.

17.3 PUT OPTIONS

A **put option** can be viewed as the opposite of a call option. Just as a call gives the holder the right to buy the stock at a fixed price, a put gives the holder the right to *sell* the stock for a fixed exercise price.

The Value of a Put Option at Expiration

The circumstances that determine the value of the put are the opposite of those for a call option, because a put option gives the holder the right to sell shares. Let us assume that the exercise price of the put is $50 and the stock price at expiration is $40. The owner of this put option has the right to sell the stock for *more* than it is worth, something that is clearly profitable. That is, he can buy the stock at the market price of $40 and immediately sell it at the exercise price of $50, generating a profit of $10 ($50 − $40). Thus, the value of the option at expiration must be $10.

The profit would be greater still if the stock price were lower. For example, if the stock price were only $30, the value of the option would be $20 ($50 − $30). In fact, for every $1 that the stock price declines at expiration, the value of the put rises by $1.

However, suppose that the stock at expiration is trading at $60—or any price above the exercise price of $50. The owner of the put would not want to exercise here. It is a losing proposition to sell stock for $50 when it trades in the open market at $60. Instead, the owner of the put will walk away from the option. That is, he will let the put option expire.

The payoff of this put option is:

	Payoff on the Expiration Date	
	IF STOCK PRICE IS LESS THAN $50	IF STOCK PRICE IS GREATER THAN $50
Put option value	$50 − Stock price	$0

Figure 17.2 plots the values of a put option for all possible values of the underlying stock. It is instructive to compare Figure 17.2 with Figure 17.1 for the call option. The call option is valuable whenever the stock is above the exercise price, and the put is valuable when the stock price is below the exercise price.

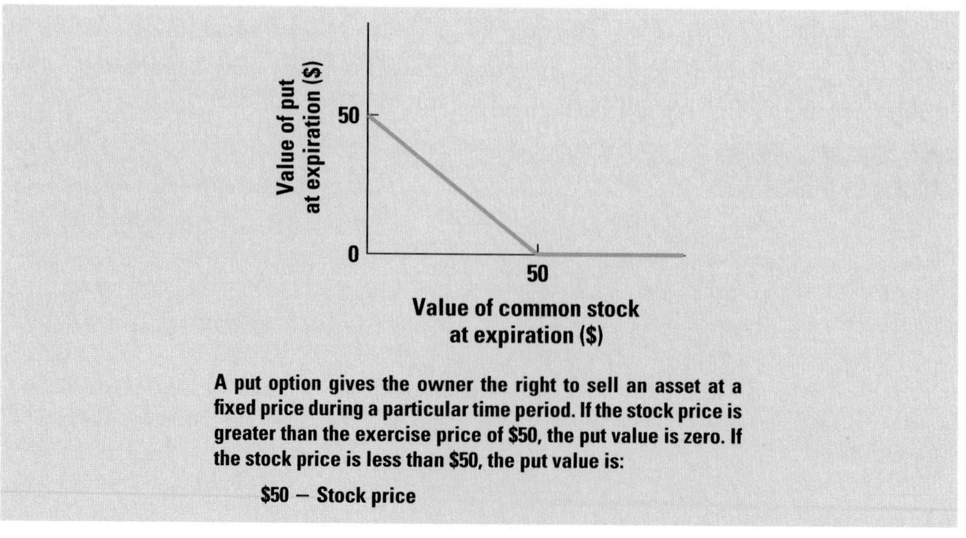

FIGURE 17.2
The Value of a Put Option on the Expiration Date

A put option gives the owner the right to sell an asset at a fixed price during a particular time period. If the stock price is greater than the exercise price of $50, the put value is zero. If the stock price is less than $50, the put value is:

$50 − Stock price

EXAMPLE 17.2 Put Option Payoffs

Ms. Pessimist feels quite certain that BMI will fall from its current $160 per-share price. She buys a put. Her put option contract gives her the right to sell a share of BMI stock at $150 one year from now. If the price of BMI is $200 on the expiration date, she will tear up the put option contract because it is worthless. That is, she will not want to sell stock worth $200 for the exercise price of $150.

On the other hand, if BMI is selling for $100 on the expiration date, she will exercise the option. In this case, she can buy a share of BMI in the market for $100 per share and turn around and sell the share at the exercise price of $150. Her profit will be $50 ($150 − $100). The value of the put option on the expiration date therefore will be $50.

17.4 SELLING OPTIONS

An investor who sells (or *writes*) a call on common stock promises to deliver shares of the common stock if required to do so by the call option holder. Notice that the seller is *obligated* to do so.

If, at expiration date, the price of the common stock is greater than the exercise price, the holder will exercise the call and the seller must give the holder shares of stock in exchange for the exercise price. The seller loses the difference between the stock price and the exercise price. For example, assume that the stock price is $60 and the exercise price is $50. Knowing that exercise is imminent, the option seller buys stock in the open market at $60. Because she is obligated to sell at $50, she loses $10 ($50 − $60). Conversely, if at the expiration date, the price of the common stock is below the exercise price, the call option will not be exercised and the seller's liability is zero.

Check out these option exchanges:
www.cboe.com
www.pacificex.com
www.phlx.com
www.kcbt.com
www.euronext.com

Why would the seller of a call place himself in such a precarious position? After all, the seller loses money if the stock price ends up above the exercise price and he merely avoids losing money if the stock price ends up below the exercise price. The answer is that the seller is paid to take this risk. On the day that the option transaction takes place, the seller receives the price that the buyer pays.

Now, let's look at the seller of puts. An investor who sells a put on common stock agrees to purchase shares of common stock if the put holder should so request. The seller loses on this deal if the stock price falls below the exercise price and the holder puts the stock to the seller. For example, assume that the stock price is $40 and the exercise price is $50. The holder of the put will exercise in this case. In other words, he will sell the underlying stock at the exercise price of $50. This means that the seller of the put must buy the underlying stock at the exercise price of $50. Because the stock is only worth $40, the loss here is $10 ($40 − $50).

The values of the "sell-a-call" and "sell-a-put" positions are depicted in Figure 17.3. The graph on the left-hand side of the figure shows that the seller of a call loses nothing when the stock price at expiration date is below $50. However, the seller loses a dollar for every dollar that the stock rises above $50. The graph in the center of the figure shows that the seller of a put loses nothing when the stock price at expiration date is above $50. However, the seller loses a dollar for every dollar that the stock falls below $50.

It is worthwhile to spend a few minutes comparing the graphs in Figure 17.3 to those in Figures 17.1 and 17.2. The graph of selling a call (the graph in the left-hand side of Figure 17.3) is the mirror image of the graph of buying a call (Figure 17.1).[3] This occurs because options are a zero-sum game. The seller of a call loses what the buyer makes. Similarly, the graph of selling a put (the middle graph in Figure 17.3) is the mirror image of the graph of buying a put (Figure 17.2). Again, the seller of a put loses what the buyer makes.

[3]Actually, because of differing exercise prices, the two graphs are not quite mirror images of each other. The exercise price in Figure 17.1 is $100 and the exercise price in Figure 17.3 is $50.

FIGURE 17.3

The Payoffs to Sellers of Calls and Puts, and to Buyers of Common Stock

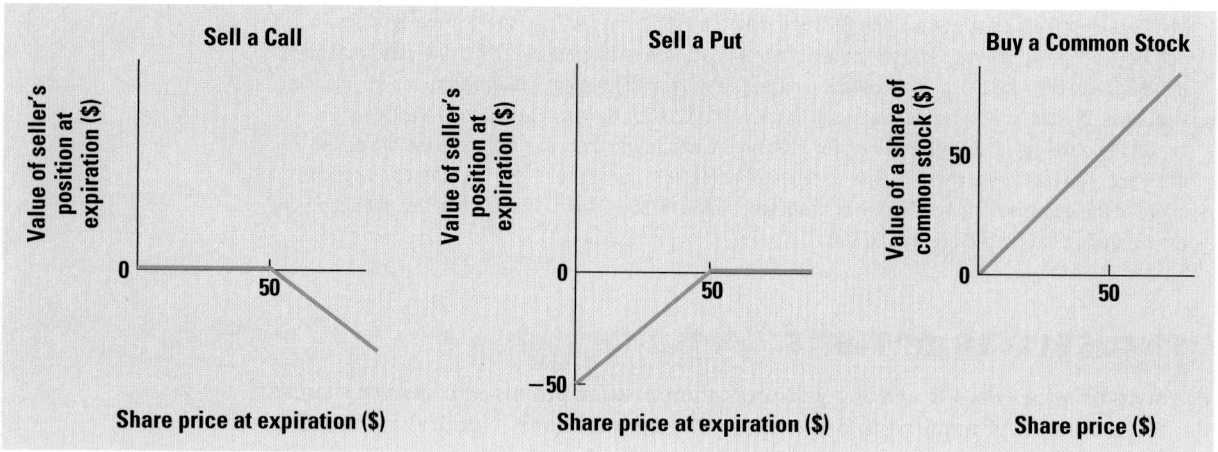

TABLE 17.1

Information on the Options of Intel Corporation

Options

View By Expiration: Nov 05 | **Dec 05** | Jan 06 | Apr 06 | Jan 07 | Jan 08

CALL OPTIONS				Expire at close Fri, Dec 16, 2005			
Strike	Symbol	Last	Chg	Bid	Ask	Vol	Open Int
20.00	NQLD.X	3.20	↑0.20	3.10	3.20	81	363
22.50	NQLX.X	1.20	↑0.15	1.15	1.20	5,480	1,099
25.00	INQLE.X	0.20	↓0.05	0.20	0.25	2,129	4,275

PUT OPTIONS				Expire at close Fri, Dec 16, 2005			
Strike	Symbol	Last	Chg	Bid	Ask	Vol	Open Int
17.50	NQXW.X	0.05	0.00	N/A	0.05	2,000	2,000
20.00	NQXD.X	0.10	0.00	0.05	0.15	2,000	1,394
22.50	NQXX.X	0.55	↓0.05	0.50	0.60	5,376	1,514
25.00	INQXE.X	2.00	↓0.35	2.10	2.20	392	447
27.50	INQXY.X	4.50	↑0.09	4.40	4.60	1,002	20

Figure 17.3 also shows the value at expiration of simply buying common stock. Notice that buying the stock is the same as buying a call option on the stock with an exercise price of zero. This is not surprising. If the exercise price is 0, the call holder can buy the stock for nothing, which is really the same as owning it.

17.5 OPTION QUOTES

For more on option ticker symbols, go to "Symbol Directory" link under "Trading Tools" at www.cboe.com.

Now that we understand the definitions for calls and puts, let's see how these options are quoted. Table 17.1 presents information on Intel Corporation options expiring in December 2005, obtained from finance.yahoo.com. At the time of these quotes, Intel was selling for $23.07.

In the center of the table are the available strike prices. To the left are call option quotes; put option quotes are to the right. Focusing on the call options, the first column contains ticker symbols, which uniquely indicate the underlying stock, the type of option, the expiration month, and the strike price. Next, we have the most recent prices on the options ("Last") and the change from the previous day ("Change"). Bid and ask prices follow. Note that option prices are quoted on a per-option basis, but trading actually occurs in standardized contracts, where each contract calls for the purchase (for calls) or sale (for puts) of 100 shares. Thus, the call option with a strike price of $25 last traded at $.20 per option, or $20 per contract. The final two columns contain volume, quoted in contracts, and the open interest ("Open Int"), which is the number of contracts currently outstanding.

17.6 COMBINATIONS OF OPTIONS

Puts and calls can serve as building blocks for more complex option contracts. For example, Figure 17.4 illustrates the payoff from buying a put option on a stock and simultaneously buying the stock.

For information on options and the underlying companies, see www.optionsnewsletter.com.

If the share price is greater than the exercise price, the put option is worthless, and the value of the combined position is equal to the value of the common stock. If instead the exercise price is greater than the share price, the decline in the value of the shares will be exactly offset by the rise in value of the put.

The strategy of buying a put and buying the underlying stock is called a *protective* put. It is as if one is buying insurance for the stock. The stock can always be sold at the exercise price, regardless of how far the market price of the stock falls.

Note that the combination of buying a put and buying the underlying stock has the same *shape* in Figure 17.4 as the call purchase in Figure 17.1. To pursue this point, let's consider the graph for buying a call, which is shown at the far left of Figure 17.5. This graph is the same as Figure 17.1, except that the exercise price is $50 here. Now, let's try the strategy of:

(Leg A) Buying a call.

(Leg B) Buying a risk-free, zero-coupon bond (i.e., a T-bill), with a face value of $50 that matures on the same day that the option expires.

We have drawn the graph of Leg A of this strategy at the far left of Figure 17.5, but what does the graph of Leg B look like? It looks like the middle graph of the figure. That

FIGURE 17.4

Payoff to the Combination of Buying a Put and Buying the Underlying Stock

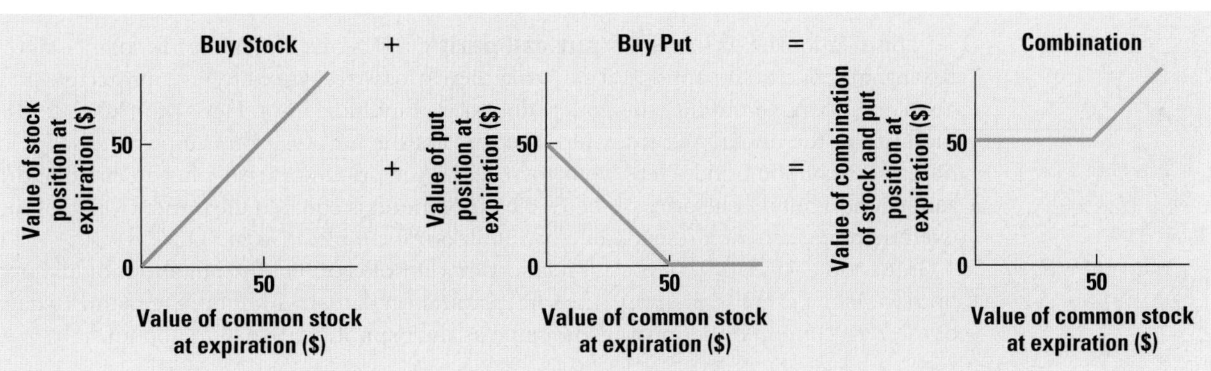

FIGURE 17.5

Payoff to the Combination of Buying a Call and Buying a Zero Coupon Bond

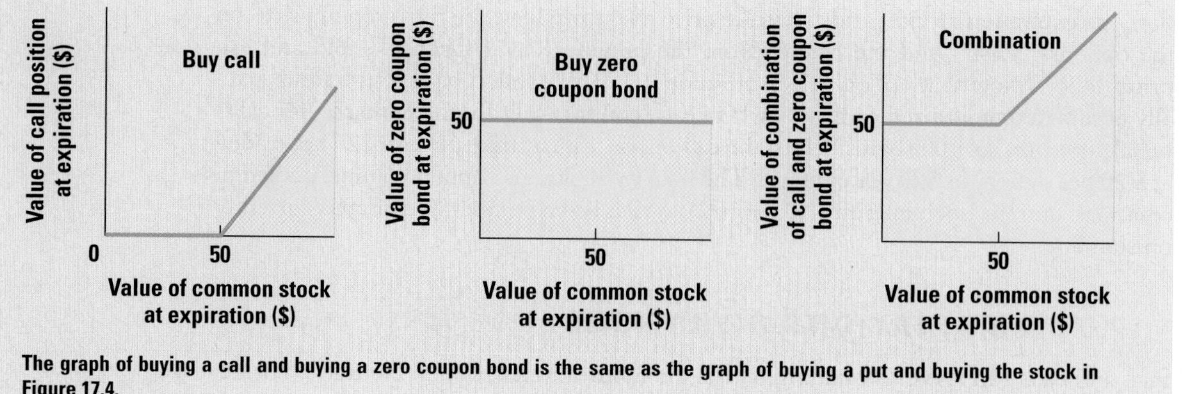

The graph of buying a call and buying a zero coupon bond is the same as the graph of buying a put and buying the stock in Figure 17.4.

is, anyone buying this zero coupon bond will be guaranteed to get \$50, regardless of the price of the stock at expiration.

What does the graph of *simultaneously* buying both Leg A and Leg B of this strategy look like? It looks like the far-right graph of Figure 17.5. That is, the investor receives a guaranteed \$50 from the bond, regardless of what happens to the stock. In addition, the investor receives a payoff from the call of \$1 for every \$1 that the price of the stock rises above the exercise price of \$50.

The far-right graph of Figure 17.5 looks *exactly* like the far-right graph of Figure 17.4. Thus, an investor gets the same payoff from the strategy of Figure 17.4 and the strategy of Figure 17.5, regardless of what happens to the price of the underlying stock. In other words, the investor gets the same payoff from:

1. Buying a put and buying the underlying stock.
2. Buying a call and buying a risk-free, zero coupon bond.

If investors have the same payoffs from the two strategies, the two strategies must have the *same* cost. Otherwise, all investors will choose the strategy with the lower cost and avoid the strategy with the higher cost. This leads to the interesting result that:

$$\underbrace{\textbf{Price of underlying stock} + \textbf{Price of put}}_{\textbf{Cost of first strategy}} = \underbrace{\textbf{Price of call} + \textbf{Present value of exercise price}}_{\textbf{Cost of second strategy}} \quad (17.1)$$

This relationship is known as **put-call parity** and is one of the most fundamental relationships concerning options. It says that there are two ways of buying a protective put. You can buy a put and buy the underlying stock simultaneously. Here, your total cost is the price of the underlying stock plus the price of the put. Or, you can buy the call and buy a zero coupon bond. Here, your total cost is the price of the call plus the price of the zero coupon bond. The price of the zero coupon bond is equal to the present value of the exercise price, i.e., the present value of \$50 in our example.

Equation (17.1) is a very precise relationship. It holds only if the put and the call have both the same exercise price and the same expiration date. In addition, the maturity date of the zero coupon bond must be the same as the expiration date of the options.

FIGURE 17.6
Payoff to the Combination of Buying a Stock and Selling a Call

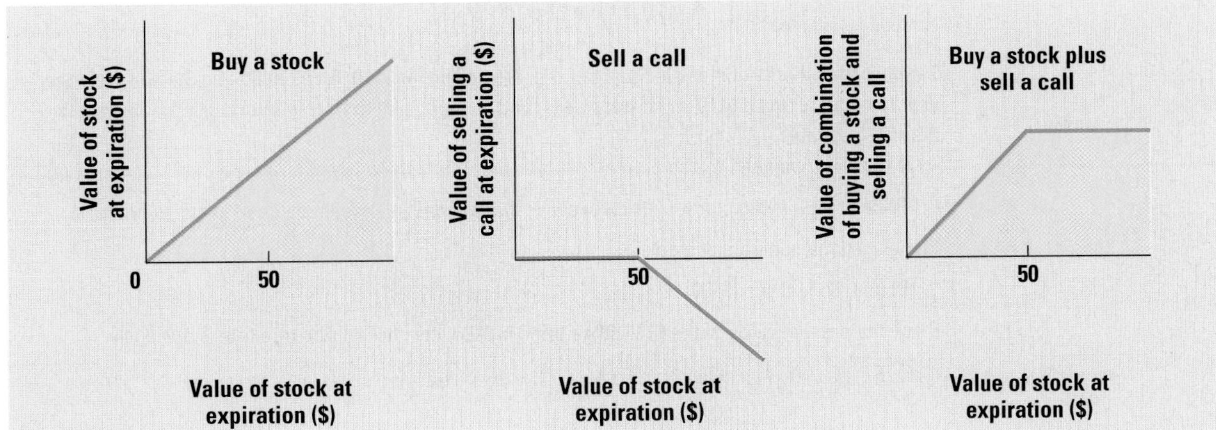

To see how fundamental put-call parity is, let's rearrange the formula, yielding:

$$\text{Price of underlying stock} = \text{Price of call} - \text{Price of put} + \text{Present value of exercise price}$$

This relationship now states that you can replicate the purchase of a share of stock by buying a call, selling a put, and buying a zero coupon bond. (Note that, because a minus sign comes before "Price of put," the put is sold, not bought.) Investors in this three-legged strategy are said to have purchased a *synthetic* stock.

Let's do one more transformation:

Covered-Call Strategy:

$$\text{Price of underlying stock} - \text{Price of call} = -\text{Price of put} + \text{Present value of exercise price}$$

Many investors like to buy a stock and write the call on the stock simultaneously. This is a conservative strategy known as *selling a covered call.* The preceding put-call parity relationship tells us that this strategy is equivalent to selling a put and buying a zero coupon bond. Figure 17.6 develops the graph for the covered call. You can verify that the covered call can be replicated by selling a put and simultaneously buying a zero coupon bond.

Of course, there are other ways of rearranging the basic put-call relationship. For each rearrangement, the strategy on the left-hand side is equivalent to the strategy on the right-hand side. The beauty of put-call parity is that it shows how any strategy in options can be achieved in two different ways.

To test your understanding of put-call parity, suppose shares of stock in Joseph-Belmont, Inc., are selling for \$80. A three-month call option with an \$85 strike price goes for \$6. The risk-free rate is .5 percent per month. What's the value of a three-month put option with an \$85 strike price?

We can rearrange the put-call parity relationship to solve for the price of the put as follows:

$$\begin{aligned}\text{Price of put} &= -\text{Price of underlying stock} + \text{Price of call} + \text{Present value of strike price} \\ &= -\$80 + \$6 + \$85/1.005^3 \\ &= \$9.74\end{aligned}$$

As illustrated, the value of the put is $9.74.

EXAMPLE 17.3 A Synthetic T-bill

Suppose that shares of stock in Smolira Corp. are selling for $110. A call option on Smolira with one year to maturity and a $110 strike price sells for $15. A put with the same terms sells for $5. What's the risk-free rate?

To answer, we need to use put-call parity to determine the price of a risk-free, zero-coupon bond:

Price of underlying stock + Price of put − Price of call = Present value of exercise price

Plugging in the numbers, we get:

$110 + $5 − $15 = $100

Since the present value of the $110 strike price is $100, the implied risk-free rate is obviously 10 percent.

17.7 VALUING OPTIONS

In the last section, we determined what options are worth on the expiration date. Now, we wish to determine the value of options when you buy them well before expiration.[4] We begin by considering the lower and upper bounds on the value of a call.

Bounding the Value of a Call

LOWER BOUND Consider an American call that is in the money prior to expiration. For example, assume that the stock price is $60 and the exercise price is $50. In this case, the option cannot sell below $10. To see this, note the simple strategy if the option sells at, say, $9.

DATE		TRANSACTION	
Today	(1)	Buy call.	−$ 9
Today	(2)	Exercise call, that is, buy underlying stock at exercise price.	−$50
Today	(3)	Sell stock at current market price.	+$60
Arbitrage profit			+$ 1

The type of profit that is described in this transaction is an *arbitrage* profit. Arbitrage profits come from transactions that have no risk or cost and cannot occur regularly in normal, well-functioning financial markets. The excess demand for these options would quickly force the option price up to at least $10 ($60 − $50).

Of course, the price of the option is likely to be above $10. Investors will rationally pay more than $10 because of the possibility that the stock will rise above $60 before expiration. For example, suppose the call actually sells for $12. In this case, we say that the *intrinsic value* of the option is $10, meaning it must always be worth at least this much. The remaining $12 − $10 = $2 is sometimes called the *time premium,* and it represents the extra that investors are willing to pay because of the possibility that the stock price will rise before the option expires.

[4]Our discussion in this section is of American options, because they are more commonly traded in the real world. As necessary, we will indicate differences for European options.

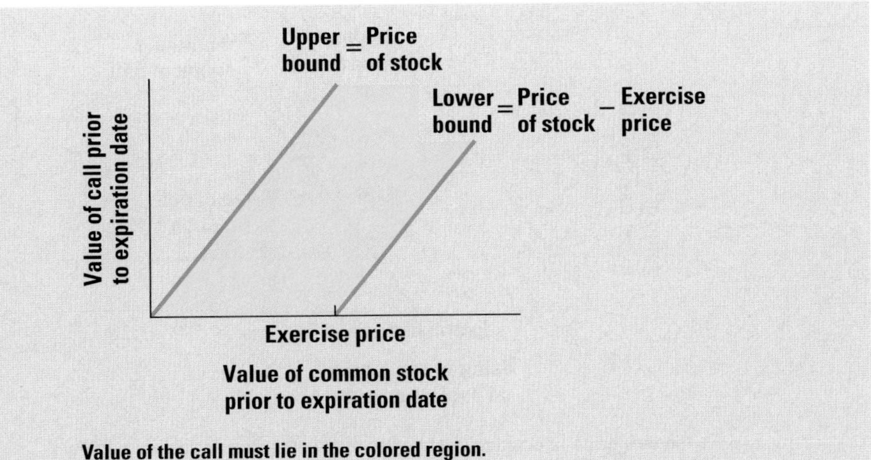

FIGURE 17.7

The Upper and Lower Boundaries of Call Option Values

TABLE 17.2

Factors Affecting American Option Values

INCREASE IN	CALL OPTION*	PUT OPTION*
Value of underlying asset (stock price)	+	−
Exercise price	−	+
Stock volatility	+	+
Interest rate	+	−
Time to exercise date	+	+

In addition to the preceding, we have presented the following four relationships for American calls:

1. The call price can never be greater than the stock price (*upper bound*).
2. The call price can never be less than either zero or the difference between the stock price and the exercise price (*lower bound*).
3. The call is worth zero if the stock is worth zero.
4. When the stock price is much greater than the exercise price, the call price tends toward the difference between the stock price and the present value of the exercise price.

*The signs (+, −) indicate the effect of the variables on the value of the option. For example, the two +s for stock volatility indicate that an increase in volatility will increase both the value of a call and the value of a put.

UPPER BOUND Is there an upper boundary for the option price as well? It turns out that the upper boundary is the price of the underlying stock. That is, an option to buy common stock cannot have a greater value than the common stock itself. A call option can be used to buy common stock with a payment of an exercise price. It would be foolish to buy stock this way if the stock could be purchased directly at a lower price.

The upper and lower bounds are represented in Figure 17.7. In addition, these bounds are summarized in the bottom half of Table 17.2.

The Factors Determining Call Option Values

The previous discussion indicated that the price of a call option must fall somewhere in the shaded region of Figure 17.7. We now will determine more precisely where in the shaded region it should be. The factors that determine a call's value can be broken into two sets. The first set contains the features of the option contract. The two basic contractual features are the expiration price and the exercise date. The second set of factors affecting the call price concerns characteristics of the stock and the market.

EXERCISE PRICE An increase in the exercise price reduces the value of the call. For example, imagine that there are two calls on a stock selling at $60. The first call has an

FIGURE 17.8
Value of an American Call as a Function of Stock Price

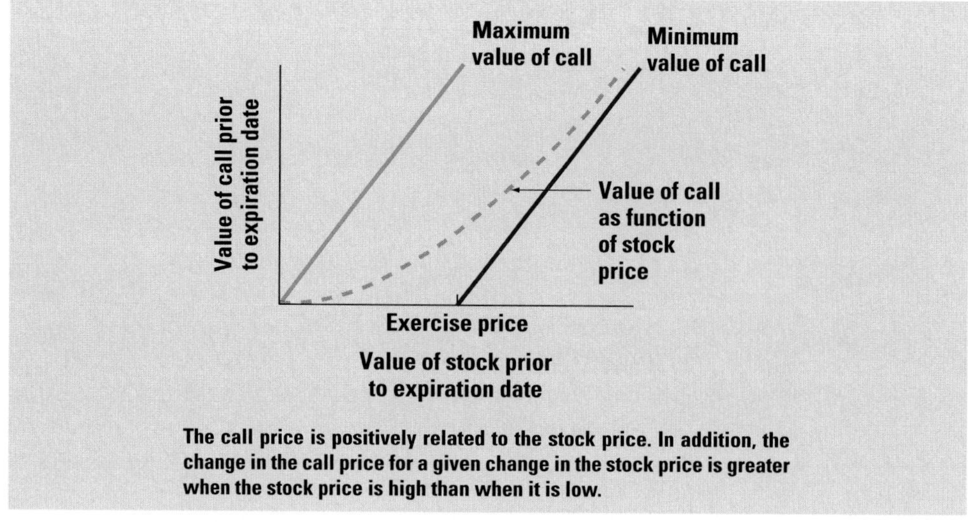

The call price is positively related to the stock price. In addition, the change in the call price for a given change in the stock price is greater when the stock price is high than when it is low.

exercise price of $50 and the second one has an exercise price of $40. Which call would you rather have? Clearly, you would rather have the call with an exercise price of $40, because that one is $20 ($60 − $40) in the money. In other words, the call with an exercise price of $40 should sell for more than an otherwise identical call with an exercise price of $50.

EXPIRATION DATE The value of an American call option must be at least as great as the value of an otherwise identical option with a shorter term to expiration. Consider two American calls: One has a maturity of nine months and the other expires in six months. Obviously, the nine-month call has the same rights as the six-month call, and also has an additional three months within which these rights can be exercised. It cannot be worth less and will generally be more valuable.[5]

The Philadelphia Stock Exchange has a good discussion of options at www.phlx.com/products.

STOCK PRICE Other things being equal, the higher the stock price, the more valuable the call option will be. For example, if a stock is worth $80, a call with an exercise price of $100 isn't worth very much. If the stock soars to $120, the call becomes much more valuable.

Now consider Figure 17.8, which shows the relationship between the call price and the stock price prior to expiration. The curve indicates that the call price increases as the stock price increases. Furthermore, it can be shown that the relationship is represented, not by a straight line, but by a *convex* curve. That is, the increase in the call price for a given change in the stock price is greater when the stock price is high than when the stock price is low.

There are two special points on the curve in Figure 17.8:

1. *The Stock Is Worthless.* The call must be worthless if the underlying stock is worthless. That is, if the stock has no chance of attaining any value, it is not worthwhile to pay the exercise price in order to obtain the stock.

[5]This relationship need not hold for a European call option. Consider a firm with two otherwise identical European call options, one expiring at the end of May and the other expiring a few months later. Further assume that a *huge* dividend is paid in early June. If the first call is exercised at the end of May, its holder will receive the underlying stock. If he does not sell the stock, he will receive the large dividend shortly thereafter. However, the holder of the second call will receive the stock through exercise after the dividend is paid. Because the market knows that the holder of this option will miss the dividend, the value of the second call option could be less than the value of the first.

2. *The Stock Price Is Very High Relative to the Exercise Price.* In this situation, the owner of the call knows that he will end up exercising the call. He can view himself as the owner of the stock now, with one difference. He must pay the exercise price at expiration.

Thus, the value of his position, i.e., the value of the call, is:

Stock price − Present value of exercise price

These two points on the curve are summarized in the bottom half of Table 17.2.

THE KEY FACTOR: THE VARIABILITY OF THE UNDERLYING ASSET The greater the variability of the underlying asset, the more valuable the call option will be. Consider the following example. Suppose that just before the call expires, the stock price will be either \$100 with probability .5 or \$80 with probability .5. What will be the value of a call with an exercise price of \$110? Clearly, it will be worthless because no matter what happens to the stock, its price will always be below the exercise price.

Now let us see what happens if the stock is more variable. Suppose that we add \$20 to the best case and take \$20 away from the worst case. Now the stock has a one-half chance of being worth \$60 and a one-half chance of being worth \$120. We have spread the stock returns, but, of course, the expected value of the stock has stayed the same:

$$(1/2 \times \$80) + (1/2 \times \$100) = \$90 = (1/2 \times \$60) + (1/2 \times \$120)$$

For an option-oriented site focusing on volatilities, visit www.ivolatility.com.

Notice that the call option has value now because there is a one-half chance that the stock price will be \$120, or \$10 above the exercise price of \$110. This illustrates a very important point. There is a fundamental distinction between holding an option on an underlying asset and holding the underlying asset. If investors in the marketplace are risk-averse, a rise in the variability of the stock will decrease its market value. However, the holder of a call receives payoffs from the positive tail of the probability distribution. As a consequence, a rise in the variability in the underlying stock increases the market value of the call.

This result can also be seen from Figure 17.9. Consider two stocks, *A* and *B,* each of which is normally distributed. For each security, the figure illustrates the probability of

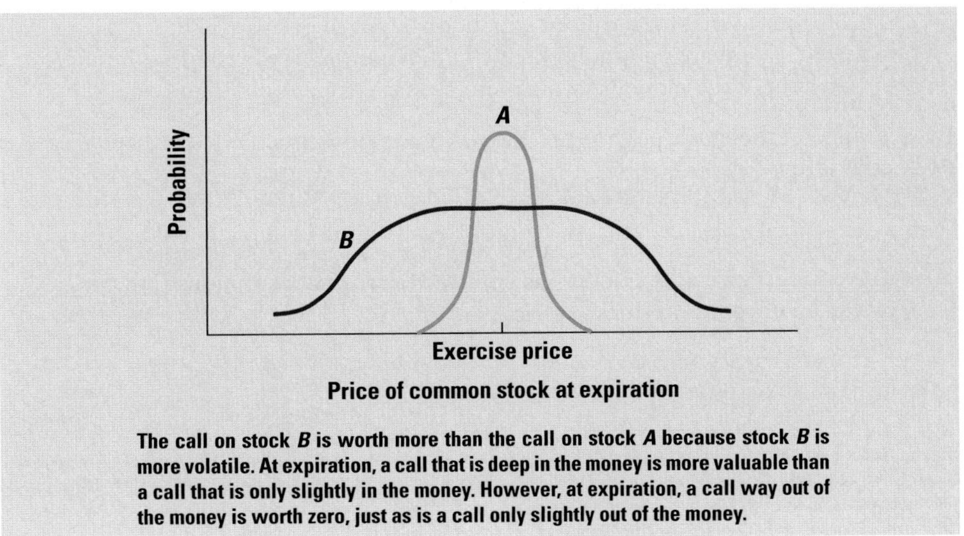

The call on stock *B* is worth more than the call on stock *A* because stock *B* is more volatile. At expiration, a call that is deep in the money is more valuable than a call that is only slightly in the money. However, at expiration, a call way out of the money is worth zero, just as is a call only slightly out of the money.

FIGURE 17.9

Distribution of Common Stock Price at Expiration for Both Security *A* and Security *B*. Options on the Two Securities Have the Same Exercise Price

different stock prices on the expiration date.[6] As can be seen from the figures, stock B has more volatility than does stock A. This means that stock B has higher probability of both abnormally high returns and abnormally low returns. Let us assume that options on each of the two securities have the same exercise price. To option holders, a return much below average on stock B is no worse than a return only moderately below average on stock A. In either situation, the option expires out of the money. However, to option holders, a return much above average on stock B is better than a return only moderately above average on stock A. Because a call's price at the expiration date is the difference between the stock price and the exercise price, the value of the call on B at expiration will be higher in this case.

THE INTEREST RATE Call prices are also a function of the level of interest rates. Buyers of calls do not pay the exercise price until they exercise the option, if they do so at all. The ability to delay payment is more valuable when interest rates are high and less valuable when interest rates are low. Thus, the value of a call is positively related to interest rates.

A Quick Discussion of Factors Determining Put Option Values

Given our extended discussion of the factors influencing a call's value, we can examine the effect of these factors on puts very easily. Table 17.2 summarizes the five factors influencing the prices of both American calls and American puts. The effect of three factors on puts are the opposite of the effect of these three factors on calls:

1. The put's market value *decreases* as the stock price increases because puts are in the money when the stock sells below the exercise price.
2. The value of a put with a high exercise price is *greater* than the value of an otherwise identical put with a low exercise price for the reason given in (1).
3. A high interest rate *adversely* affects the value of a put. The ability to sell a stock at a fixed exercise price sometime in the future is worth less if the present value of the exercise price is diminished by a high interest rate.

The effect of the other two factors on puts is the same as the effect of these factors on calls:

4. The value of an American put with a distant expiration date is greater than an otherwise identical put with an earlier expiration.[7] The longer time to maturity gives the put holder more flexibility, just as it did in the case of a call.
5. Volatility of the underlying stock increases the value of the put. The reasoning is analogous to that for a call. At expiration, a put that is way in the money is more valuable than a put only slightly in the money. However, at expiration, a put way out of the money is worth zero, just as is a put only slightly out of the money.

17.8 AN OPTION PRICING FORMULA

We have explained *qualitatively* that the value of a call option is a function of five variables:

1. The current price of the underlying asset, which for stock options is the price of a share of common stock.
2. The exercise price.
3. The time to expiration date.

[6]This graph assumes that, for each security, the exercise price is equal to the expected stock price. This assumption is employed merely to facilitate the discussion. It is not needed to show the relationship between a call's value and the volatility of the underlying stock.

[7]Though this result must hold in the case of an American put, it need not hold for a European put.

4. The variance of the underlying asset.
5. The risk-free interest rate.

It is time to replace the qualitative model with a precise option valuation model. The model we choose is the famous Black-Scholes option pricing model. You can put numbers into the Black-Scholes model and get values back.

The Black-Scholes model is represented by a rather imposing formula. A derivation of the formula is simply not possible in this textbook, as many students will be happy to learn. However, some appreciation for the achievement as well as some intuitive understanding is in order.

In the early chapters of this book, we showed how to discount capital budgeting projects, using the net present value formula. We also used this approach to value stocks and bonds. Why, students sometimes ask, can't the same NPV formula be used to value puts and calls? It is a good question because the earliest attempts at valuing options used NPV. Unfortunately, the attempts were simply not successful because no one could determine the appropriate discount rate. An option is generally riskier than the underlying stock, but no one knew exactly how much riskier.

Black and Scholes attacked the problem by pointing out that a strategy of borrowing to finance a stock purchase duplicates the risk of a call. Then, knowing the price of a stock already, one can determine the price of a call such that its return is identical to that of the stock-with-borrowing alternative.

We illustrate the intuition behind the Black-Scholes approach by considering a simple example where a combination of a call and a stock eliminates all risk. This example works because we let the future stock price be one of only *two* values. Hence, the example is called a *two-state option model.* By eliminating the possibility that the stock price can take on other values, we are able to duplicate the call exactly.

A Two-State Option Model

Consider the following example. Suppose the current market price of a stock is $50 and the stock will either be $60 or $40 at the end of the year. Further, imagine a call option on this stock with a one-year expiration date and a $50 exercise price. Investors can borrow at 10 percent. Our goal is to determine the value of the call.

In order to value the call correctly, we need to examine two strategies. The first is to simply buy the call. The second is to:

a. Buy one-half a share of stock.

b. Borrow $18.18, implying a payment of principal and interest at the end of the year of $20 ($18.18 × 1.10).

As you will see shortly, the cash flows from the second strategy exactly match the cash flows from buying a call. (A little later, we will show how we came up with the exact fraction of a share of stock to buy and the exact borrowing amount.) Because the cash flows match, we say that we are *duplicating* the call with the second strategy.

At the end of the year, the future payoffs are set out as follows:

	Future Payoffs			
INITIAL TRANSACTIONS	IF STOCK PRICE IS $60		IF STOCK PRICE IS $40	
1. Buy a call	$60 − $50 =	$10		$ 0
2. Buy $\frac{1}{2}$ share of stock	$\frac{1}{2}$ × $60 =	$30	$\frac{1}{2}$ × $40 =	$20
Borrow $18.18 at 10%	−($18.18 × 1.10) =	−$20		−$20
Total from stock and borrowing strategy		$20		0

Note that the future payoff structure of the "buy-a-call" strategy is duplicated by the strategy of "buy stock" and "borrow." That is, under either strategy, an investor would end up with $10 if the stock price rose and $0 if the stock price fell. Thus, these two strategies are equivalent as far as traders are concerned.

Now, if two strategies always have the same cash flows at the end of the year, how must their initial costs be related? The two strategies must have the *same* initial cost. Otherwise, there will be an arbitrage possibility. We can easily calculate this cost for our strategy of buying stock and borrowing. This cost is:

Buy $\frac{1}{2}$ share of stock	$\frac{1}{2} \times \$50 =$	$25.00
Borrow $18.18		−$18.18
		$ 6.82

Because the call option provides the same payoffs at expiration as does the strategy of buying stock and borrowing, the call must be priced at $6.82. This is the value of the call option in a market without arbitrage profits.

We left two issues unexplained in the preceding example.

DETERMINING THE DELTA How did we know to buy one-half share of stock in the duplicating strategy? Actually, the answer is easier than it might at first appear. The call price at the end of the year will be either $10 or $0, whereas the stock price will be either $60 or $40. Thus, the call price has a potential swing of $10 ($10 − $0) next period, whereas the stock price has a potential swing of $20 ($60 − $40). We can write this in terms of the following ratio:

$$\textbf{Delta} = \frac{\textbf{Swing of call}}{\textbf{Swing of stock}} = \frac{\$10 - \$0}{\$60 - \$40} = \frac{1}{2}$$

As indicated, this ratio is called the *delta* of the call. In words, a $1 swing in the price of the stock gives rise to a $1/2 swing in the price of the call. Because we are trying to duplicate the call with the stock, it seems sensible to buy one-half share of stock instead of buying one call. In other words, the risk of buying one-half share of stock should be the same as the risk of buying one call.

DETERMINING THE AMOUNT OF BORROWING How did we know how much to borrow? Buying one-half share of stock brings us either $30 or $20 at expiration, which is exactly $20 more than the payoffs of $10 and $0, respectively, from the call. To duplicate the call through a purchase of stock, we should also borrow enough money so that we have to pay back exactly $20 of interest and principal. This amount of borrowing is merely the present value of $20, which is $18.18 ($20/1.10).

Now that we know how to determine both the delta and the borrowing, we can write the value of the call as:

$$\begin{array}{ccccccc} \textbf{Value of call} & = & \textbf{Stock price} & \times & \textbf{Delta} & - & \textbf{Amount borrowed} \\ \$6.82 & = & \$50 & \times & \frac{1}{2} & - & \$18.18 \end{array} \quad (17.2)$$

We will find this intuition very useful in explaining the Black-Scholes model.

RISK-NEUTRAL VALUATION Before leaving this simple example, we should comment on a remarkable feature. We found the exact value of the option without even knowing the probability that the stock would go up or down! If an optimist thought the probability of an up move was very high and a pessimist thought it was very low, they would still agree on the option value. How could that be? The answer is that the current $50 stock price already balances the views of the optimists and the pessimists. The option reflects that balance because its value depends on the stock price.

This insight provides us with another approach to valuing the call. If we don't need the probabilities of the two states to value the call, perhaps we can select *any* probabilities we want and still come up with the right answer. Suppose we selected probabilities such that the return on the stock is equal to the risk-free rate of 10 percent. We know that the stock return given a rise is 20 percent ($60/$50 − 1) and the stock return given a fall is −20 percent ($40/$50 − 1). Thus, we can solve for the probability of a rise necessary to achieve an expected return of 10 percent as:

$$10\% = \textbf{Probability of a rise} \times 20\% + (1 - \textbf{Probability of rise}) \times -20\%$$

Solving this formula, we find that the probability of a rise is 3/4 and the probability of a fall is 1/4. If we apply these probabilities to the call, we can value it as:

$$\textbf{Value of call} = \frac{\frac{3}{4} \times \$10 + \frac{1}{4} \times \$0}{1.10} = \$6.82$$

the same value that we got from the duplicating approach.

Why did we select probabilities such that the expected return on the stock is 10 percent? We wanted to work with the special case where investors are *risk-neutral.* This case occurs when the expected return on *any* asset (including both the stock and the call) is equal to the risk-free rate. In other words, this case occurs when investors demand no additional compensation beyond the risk-free rate, regardless of the risk of the asset in question.

What would have happened if we had assumed that the expected return on a stock was greater than the risk-free rate? The value of the call would still be $6.82. However, the calculations would be difficult. For example, if we assumed that the expected return on the stock was, say 11 percent, we would have had to derive the expected return on the call. Although the expected return on the call would be higher than 11 percent, it would take a lot of work to determine it precisely. Why do any more work than you have to? Because we can't think of any good reason, we (and most other financial economists) choose to assume risk-neutrality.

Thus, the preceding material allows us to value a call in the following two ways:

1. Determine the cost of a strategy to duplicate the call. This strategy involves an investment in a fractional share of stock financed by partial borrowing.
2. Calculate the probabilities of a rise and a fall under the assumption of risk-neutrality.

Use those probabilities, in conjunction with the risk-free rate, to discount the payoffs of the call at expiration.

The Black-Scholes Model

The preceding example illustrates the duplicating strategy. Unfortunately, a strategy such as this will not work in the real world over, say, a one-year time frame, because there are many more than two possibilities for next year's stock price. However, the number of possibilities is reduced as the time period is shortened. In fact, the assumption that there are only two possibilities for the stock price over the next infinitesimal instant is quite plausible.[8]

There's a Black-Scholes calculator (and a lot more) at www.numa.com.

In our opinion, the fundamental insight of Black and Scholes is to shorten the time period. They show that a specific combination of stock and borrowing can indeed duplicate a call over an infinitesimal time horizon. Because the price of the stock will change over the first instant, another combination of stock and borrowing is needed to duplicate the call over the second instant and so on. By adjusting the combination from moment to moment, they can continually duplicate the call. It may boggle the mind that a formula can (1) determine the duplicating combination at any moment and (2) value the option based

[8]A full treatment of this assumption can be found in John C. Hull, *Options, Futures and Other Derivatives,* 5th ed. Upper Saddle River, N.J.: Prentice Hall (2003).

on this duplicating strategy. Suffice it to say that their dynamic strategy allows them to value a call in the real world, just as we showed how to value the call in the two-state model.

This is the basic intuition behind the Black-Scholes (BS) model. Because the actual derivation of their formula is, alas, far beyond the scope of this text, we simply present the formula itself. The formula is:

Black-Scholes Model:

$$C = S\text{N}(d_1) - Ee^{-Rt}\text{N}(d_2)$$

where:

$$d_1 = [\ln(S/E) + (R + \sigma^2/2)t]/\sqrt{\sigma^2 t}$$
$$d_2 = d_1 - \sqrt{\sigma^2 t}$$

This formula for the value of a call, C, is one of the most complex in finance. However, it involves only five parameters:

1. S = **Current stock price**
2. E = **Exercise price of call**
3. R = **Annual risk-free rate of return, continuously compounded**
4. σ^2 = **Variance (per year) of the continuous return on the stock**
5. t = **Time (in years) to expiration date**

In addition, there is the statistical concept:

$\text{N}(d)$ = **Probability that a standardized, normally distributed, random variable will be less than or equal to d**

Rather than discuss the formula in its algebraic state, we illustrate the formula with an example.

EXAMPLE 17.4 Black-Scholes

Consider Private Equipment Company (PEC). On October 4, of year 0, the PEC April 49 call option had a closing value of $4. The stock itself is selling at $50. On October 4, the option had 199 days to expiration (maturity date = April 21, Year 1). The annual risk-free interest rate, continuously compounded, is 7 percent.

This information determines three variables directly:

1. The stock price, S, is $50.
2. The exercise price, E, is $49.
3. The risk-free rate, R, is .07.

In addition, the time to maturity, t, can be calculated quickly: The formula calls for t to be expressed in *years.*

4. We express the 199-day interval in years as $t = 199/365$.

In the real world, an option trader would know S and E exactly. Traders generally view U.S. Treasury bills as riskless, so a current quote from *The Wall Street Journal* or a similar source would be obtained for the interest rate. The trader would also know (or could count) the number of days to expiration exactly. Thus, the fraction of a year to expiration, t, could be calculated quickly.

The problem comes in determining the variance of the stock's return. The formula calls for the variance in operation between the purchase date of October 4 and the expiration date. Unfortunately, this represents the future, so the correct value for variance is simply not available. Instead, traders frequently estimate variance from past data, just as we calculated variance in an earlier chapter. In addition, some traders may use intuition to adjust their estimate. For example, if anticipation of an upcoming event is currently increasing the volatility of the stock, the trader might adjust her estimate of variance upward to reflect this. (This problem was most severe right after the October 19, 1987, crash. The stock market was quite risky in the aftermath, so estimates using precrash data were too low.)

The above discussion was intended merely to mention the difficulties in variance estimation, not to present a solution. For our purposes, we assume that a trader has come up with an estimate of variance:

5. The variance of Private Equipment Co. has been estimated to be .09 per year.

Using the above five parameters, we calculate the Black-Scholes value of the PEC option in three steps:

Step 1: *Calculate d_1 and d_2.* These values can be determined by a straightforward, albeit tedious, insertion of our parameters into the basic formula. We have

$$\begin{aligned} d_1 &= \left[\ln\left(\frac{S}{E}\right) + (R + \sigma^2/2)t\right] \Big/ \sqrt{\sigma^2 t} \\ &= \left[\ln\left(\frac{50}{49}\right) + (.07 + .09/2) \times \frac{199}{365}\right] \Big/ \sqrt{.09 \times \frac{199}{365}} \\ &= [.0202 + .0627]/.2215 = .3742 \\ d_2 &= d_1 - \sqrt{\sigma^2 t} \\ &= .1527 \end{aligned}$$

Step 2: *Calculate* $N(d_1)$ *and* $N(d_2)$. The values $N(d_1)$ and $N(d_2)$ can best be understood by examining Figure 17.10. The figure shows the normal distribution with an expected value of 0 and a standard deviation of 1. This is frequently called the **standardized normal distribution**. We mentioned in an earlier chapter that the probability that a drawing from this distribution will be between -1 and $+1$ (within one standard deviation of its mean, in other words) is 68.26 percent.

Now, let us ask a different question. What is the probability that a drawing from the standardized normal distribution will be *below* a particular value? For example, the probability that a drawing will be below 0 is clearly 50 percent because the normal distribution is symmetric. Using statistical terminology, we say that the **cumulative probability** of 0 is 50 percent. Statisticians also say that $N(0) = 50\%$. It turns out that

$$\begin{aligned} N(d_1) &= N(.3742) = .6459 \\ N(d_2) &= N(.1527) = .5607 \end{aligned}$$

The first value means that there is a 64.59 percent probability that a drawing from the standardized normal distribution will be below .3742. The second value means that there is a 56.07 percent probability that a drawing from the standardized normal distribution will be below .1527. More

FIGURE 17.10

Graph of Cumulative Probability

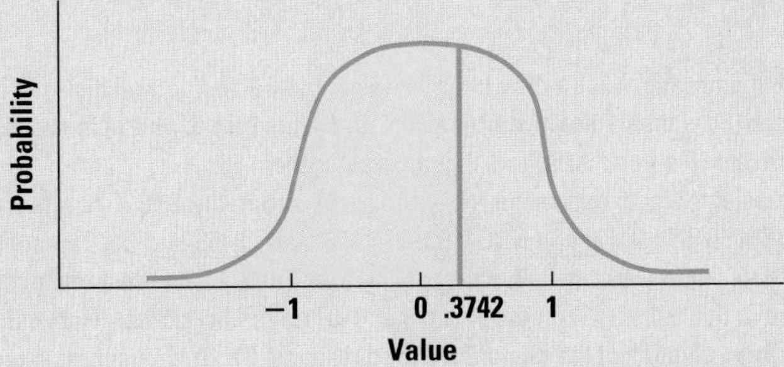

Shaded area represents cumulative probability. Because the probability is .6459 that a drawing from the standard normal distribution will be below .3742, we say that N(.3742) = .6459. That is, the cumulative probability of .3742 is .6459.

(continued)

TABLE 17.3

Cumulative Probabilities of the Standard Normal Distribution Function

d	.00	.01	.02	.03	.04	.05	.06	.07	.08	.09
.0	.0000	.0040	.0080	.0120	.0160	.0199	.0239	.0279	.0319	.0359
.1	.0398	.0438	.0478	.0517	.0557	.0596	.0636	.0675	.0714	.0753
.2	.0793	.0832	.0871	.0910	.0948	.0987	.1026	.1064	.1103	.1141
.3	.1179	.1217	.1255	.1293	.1331	.1368	.1406	.1443	.1480	.1517
.4	.1554	.1591	.1628	.1664	.1700	.1736	.1772	.1808	.1844	.1879
.5	.1915	.1950	.1985	.2019	.2054	.2088	.2123	.2157	.2190	.2224
.6	.2257	.2291	.2324	.2357	.2389	.2422	.2454	.2486	.2517	.2549
.7	.2580	.2611	.2642	.2673	.2704	.2734	.2764	.2794	.2823	.2852
.8	.2881	.2910	.2939	.2967	.2995	.3023	.3051	.3078	.3106	.3133
.9	.3159	.3186	.3212	.3238	.3264	.3289	.3315	.3340	.3365	.3389
1.0	.3413	.3438	.3461	.3485	.3508	.3531	.3554	.3577	.3599	.3621
1.1	.3643	.3665	.3686	.3708	.3729	.3749	.3770	.3790	.3810	.3830
1.2	.3849	.3869	.3888	.3907	.3925	.3944	.3962	.3980	.3997	.4015
1.3	.4032	.4049	.4066	.4082	.4099	.4115	.4131	.4147	.4162	.4177
1.4	.4192	.4207	.4222	.4236	.4251	.4265	.4279	.4292	.4306	.4319
1.5	.4332	.4345	.4357	.4370	.4382	.4394	.4406	.4418	.4429	.4441
1.6	.4452	.4463	.4474	.4484	.4495	.4505	.4515	.4525	.4535	.4545
1.7	.4554	.4564	.4573	.4582	.4591	.4599	.4608	.4616	.4625	.4633
1.8	.4641	.4649	.4656	.4664	.4671	.4678	.4686	.4693	.4699	.4706
1.9	.4713	.4719	.4726	.4732	.4738	.4744	.4750	.4756	.4761	.4767
2.0	.4773	.4778	.4783	.4788	.4793	.4798	.4803	.4808	.4812	.4817
2.1	.4821	.4826	.4830	.4834	.4838	.4842	.4846	.4850	.4854	.4857
2.2	.4861	.4866	.4830	.4871	.4875	.4878	.4881	.4884	.4887	.4890
2.3	.4893	.4896	.4898	.4901	.4904	.4906	.4909	.4911	.4913	.4916
2.4	.4918	.4920	.4922	.4925	.4927	.4929	.4931	.4932	.4934	.4936
2.5	.4938	.4940	.4941	.4943	.4945	.4946	.4948	.4949	.4951	.4952
2.6	.4953	.4955	.4956	.4957	.4959	.4960	.4961	.4962	.4963	.4964
2.7	.4965	.4966	.4967	.4968	.4969	.4970	.4971	.4972	.4973	.4974
2.8	.4974	.4975	.4976	.4977	.4977	.4978	.4979	.4979	.4980	.4981
2.9	.4981	.4982	.4982	.4982	.4984	.4984	.4985	.4985	.4986	.4986
3.0	.4987	.4987	.4987	.4988	.4988	.4989	.4989	.4989	.4990	.4990

N(d) represents areas under the standard normal distribution function. Suppose that $d_1 = .24$. This table implies a cumulative probability of .5000 + .0948 = .5948. If d_1 is equal to .2452, we must estimate the probability by interpolating between N(.25) and N(.24).

generally, N(d) is the notation that a drawing from the standardized normal distribution will be below d. In other words, N(d) is the cumulative probability of d. Note that d_1 and d_2 in our example are slightly above zero, so N(d_1) and N(d_2) are slightly greater than .50.

Perhaps the easiest way to determine N(d_1) and N(d_2) is from the EXCEL function NORMSDIST. In our example, NORMSDIST (.3742) and NORMSDIST (.1527) are .6459 and .5607, respectively.

We can also determine the cumulative probability from Table 17.3. For example, consider $d = .37$. This can be found in the table as .3 on the vertical and .07 on the horizontal. The value in the table for $d = .37$ is .1443. This value is *not* the cumulative probability of .37. One must first make an adjustment to determine cumulative probability. That is,

$$N(.37) = .50 + .1443 = .6443$$
$$N(-.37) = .50 - .1443 = .3557$$

(*continued*)

Unfortunately, our table handles only two significant digits, whereas our value of .3742 has four significant digits. Hence, we must interpolate to find N(.3742). Because N(.37) = .6443 and N(.38) = .6480, the difference between the two values is .0037 (.6480 − .6443). Because .3742 is 42 percent of the way between .37 and .38, we interpolate as:[9]

N(.3742) = .6443 + .42 × .0037 = .6459

Step 3: *Calculate C.* We have

$$\begin{aligned} C &= S \times [\mathrm{N}(d_1)] - Ee^{-Rt} \times [\mathrm{N}(d_2)] \\ &= \$50 \times [\mathrm{N}(d_1)] - \$49 \times [e^{-.07 \times (199/365)}] \times \mathrm{N}(d_2) \\ &= (\$50 \times .6459) - (\$49 \times .9626 \times .5607) \\ &= \$32.295 - \$26.447 \\ &= \$5.85 \end{aligned}$$

The estimated price of $5.85 is greater than the $4 actual price, implying that the call option is underpriced. A trader believing in the Black-Scholes model would buy a call. Of course, the Black-Scholes model is fallible. Perhaps the disparity between the model's estimate and the market price reflects error in the trader's estimate of variance.

The previous example stressed the calculations involved in using the Black-Scholes formula. Is there any intuition behind the formula? Yes, and that intuition follows from the stock purchase and borrowing strategy in our binomial example. The first line of the Black-Scholes equation is:

$$\boldsymbol{C = S \times \mathrm{N}(d_1) - Ee^{-Rt}\mathrm{N}(d_2)}$$

which is exactly analogous to equation (17.2):

Value of call = Stock price × Delta − Amount borrowed (17.2)

that we presented in the binomial example. It turns out that $\mathrm{N}(d_1)$ is the delta in the Black-Scholes model. $\mathrm{N}(d_1)$ is .6459 in the previous example. In addition, $Ee^{-Rt}\mathrm{N}(d_1)$ is the amount that an investor must borrow to duplicate a call. In the previous example, this value is $26.45 ($49 × .9626 × .5607). Thus, the model tells us that we can duplicate the call of the preceding example by both:

Another good options calculator can be found at www/margrabe.com/optionpricing.html.

1. Buying .6459 share of stock.
2. Borrowing $26.45.

It is no exaggeration to say that the Black-Scholes formula is among the most important contributions in finance. It allows anyone to calculate the value of an option given a few parameters. The attraction of the formula is that four of the parameters are observable: the current price of stock, *S*, the exercise price, *E*, the interest rate, *R*, and the time to expiration date, *t*. Only one of the parameters must be estimated: the variance of return, σ^2.

To see how truly attractive this formula is, note what parameters are not needed. First, the investor's risk aversion does not affect value. The formula can be used by anyone, regardless of willingness to bear risk. Second, it does not depend on the expected return on the stock! Investors with different assessments of the stock's expected return will nevertheless agree on the call price. As in the two-state example, this is because the call depends on the stock price and that price already balances investors' divergent views.

[9]This method is called *linear interpolation.* It is only one of a number of possible methods of interpolation.

17.9 STOCKS AND BONDS AS OPTIONS

The previous material in this chapter described, explained, and valued publicly traded options. This is important material to any finance student because much trading occurs in these listed options. The study of options has another purpose for the student of corporate finance.

You may have heard the one-liner about the elderly gentleman who was surprised to learn that he had been speaking prose all of his life. The same can be said about the corporate finance student and options. Although options were formally defined for the first time in this chapter, many corporate policies discussed earlier in the text were actually options in disguise. Though it is beyond the scope of this chapter to recast all of corporate finance in terms of options, the rest of the chapter considers the implicit options in three topics:

1. Stocks and bonds as options.
2. Capital structure decisions as options.
3. Capital budgeting decisions as options.

We begin by illustrating the implicit options in stocks and bonds through a simple example.

EXAMPLE 17.5 Stocks and Bonds as Options

The Popov Company has been awarded the concessions at next year's Olympic Games in Antarctica. Because the firm's principals live in Antarctica and because there is no other concession business in that continent, their enterprise will disband after the games. The firm has issued debt to help finance this venture. Interest and principal due on the debt next year will be $800, at which time the debt will be paid off in full. The firm's cash flows next year are forecasted as:

	Popov's Cash Flow Schedule			
	VERY SUCCESSFUL GAMES	MODERATELY SUCCESSFUL GAMES	MODERATELY UNSUCCESSFUL GAMES	OUTRIGHT FAILURE
Cash flow before interest and principal	$1,000	$850	$700	$550
−Interest and principal	− 800	− 800	− 700	− 550
Cash flow to stockholders	$ 200	$ 50	$ 0	$ 0

As can be seen, the principals forecasted four equally likely scenarios. If either of the first two scenarios occurs, the bondholders will be paid in full. The extra cash flow goes to the stockholders. However, if either of the last two scenarios occurs, the bondholders will not be paid in full. Instead, they will receive the firm's entire cash flow, leaving the stockholders with nothing.

This example is similar to the bankruptcy examples presented in our chapters on capital structure. Our new insight is that the relationship between the common stock and the firm can be expressed in terms of options. We consider call options first because the intuition is easier. The put option scenario is treated next.

The Firm Expressed in Terms of Call Options

THE STOCKHOLDERS We now show that stock can be viewed as a call option on the firm. To illustrate this, Figure 17.11 graphs the cash flow to the stockholders as a function

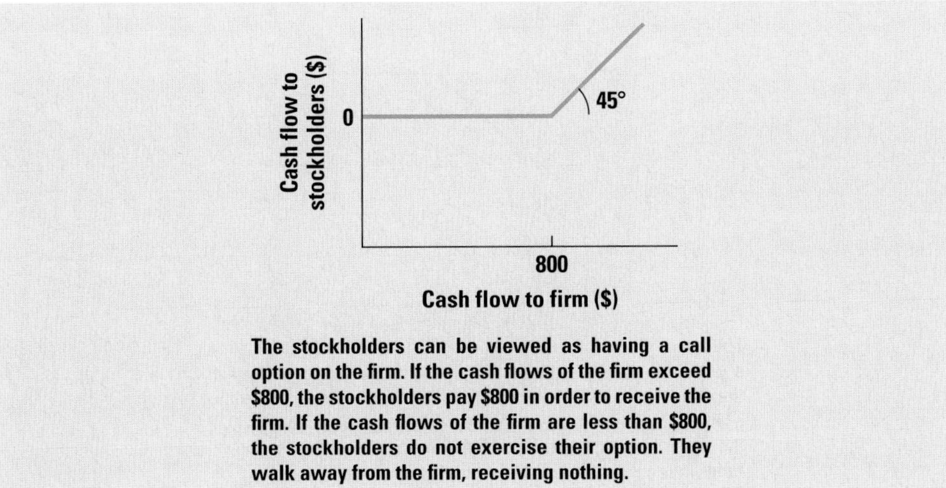

The stockholders can be viewed as having a call option on the firm. If the cash flows of the firm exceed $800, the stockholders pay $800 in order to receive the firm. If the cash flows of the firm are less than $800, the stockholders do not exercise their option. They walk away from the firm, receiving nothing.

FIGURE 17.11
Cash Flow to Stockholders of Popov Company as a Function of Cash Flow of Firm

of the cash flow to the firm. The stockholders receive nothing if the firm's cash flows are less than $800; here, all of the cash flows go to the bondholders. However, the stockholders earn a dollar for every dollar that the firm receives above $800. The graph looks exactly like the call option graphs that we considered earlier in this chapter.

But what is the underlying asset upon which the stock is a call option? The underlying asset is the firm itself. That is, we can view the *bondholders* as owning the firm. However, the stockholders have a call option on the firm with an exercise price of $800.

If the firm's cash flow is above $800, the stockholders would choose to exercise this option. In other words, they would buy the firm from the bondholders for $800. Their net cash flow is the difference between the firm's cash flow and their $800 payment. This would be $200 ($1,000 − $800) if the games are very successful and $50 ($850 − $800) if the games are moderately successful.

Should the value of the firm's cash flows be less than $800, the stockholders would not choose to exercise their option. Instead, they walk away from the firm, as any call option holder would do. The bondholders then receive the firm's entire cash flow.

This view of the firm is a novel one, and students are frequently bothered by it on first exposure. However, we encourage students to keep looking at the firm in this way until the view becomes second nature to them.

THE BONDHOLDERS What about the bondholders? Our earlier cash flow schedule showed that they would get the entire cash flow of the firm if the firm generates less cash than $800. Should the firm earn more than $800, the bondholders would receive only $800. That is, they are entitled only to interest and principal. This schedule is graphed in Figure 17.12.

In keeping with our view that the stockholders have a call option on the firm, what does the bondholders' position consist of? The bondholders' position can be described by two claims:

1. They own the firm.
2. They have written a call against the firm with an exercise price of $800.

As we mentioned before, the stockholders walk away from the firm if cash flows are less than $800. Thus, the bondholders retain ownership in this case. However, if the cash flows are greater than $800, the stockholders exercise their option. They call the stock away from the bondholders for $800.

FIGURE 17.12
Cash Flow to Bondholders as a Function of Cash Flow of Firm

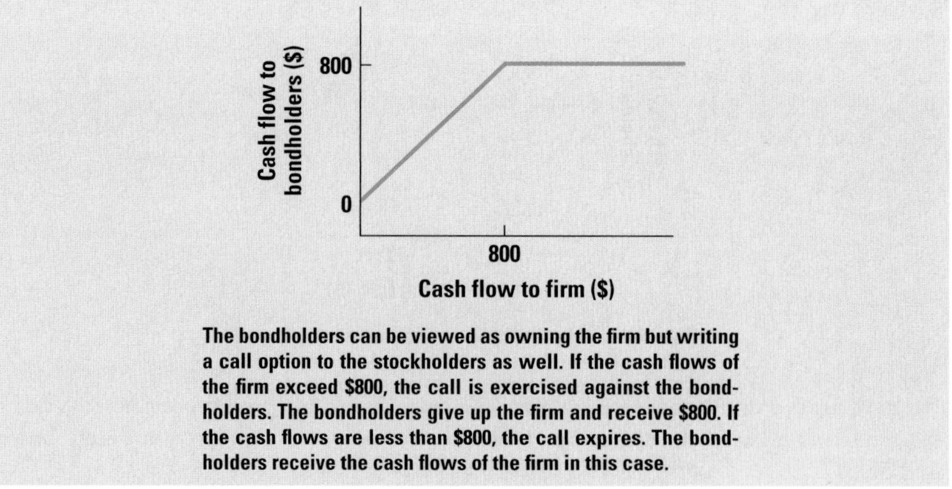

The bondholders can be viewed as owning the firm but writing a call option to the stockholders as well. If the cash flows of the firm exceed $800, the call is exercised against the bondholders. The bondholders give up the firm and receive $800. If the cash flows are less than $800, the call expires. The bondholders receive the cash flows of the firm in this case.

The Firm Expressed in Terms of Put Options

The preceding analysis expresses the positions of the stockholders and the bondholders in terms of call options. We can now express the situation in terms of put options.

THE STOCKHOLDERS The stockholders' position can be expressed by three claims:

1. They own the firm.
2. They owe $800 in interest and principal to the bondholders.

If the debt were risk-free, these two claims would fully describe the stockholders' situation. However, because of the possibility of default, we have a third claim as well.

3. The stockholders own a put option on the firm with an exercise price of $800. The group of bondholders is the seller of the put.

Now consider two possibilities.

Cash Flow Is Less Than $800 Because the put has an exercise price of $800, the put is in the money. The stockholders "put," that is, sell, the firm to the bondholders. Normally, the holder of a put receives the exercise price when the asset is sold. However, the stockholders already owe $800 to the bondholders. Thus, the debt of $800 is simply canceled–and no money changes hands–when the stock is delivered to the bondholders. Because the stockholders give up the stock in exchange for extinguishing the debt, the stockholders end up with nothing if the cash flow is below $800.

Cash Flow Is Greater Than $800 Because the put is out of the money here, the stockholders do not exercise. Thus, the stockholders retain ownership of the firm but pay $800 to the bondholders as interest and principal.

THE BONDHOLDERS The bondholders' position can be described by two claims:

1. The bondholders are owed $800.
2. They have sold a put option on the firm to the stockholders with an exercise price of $800.

Cash Flow Is Less Than $800 As mentioned before, the stockholders will exercise the put in this case. This means that the bondholders are obligated to pay $800 for the firm. Because they are owed $800, the two obligations offset each other. Thus, the bondholders simply end up with the firm in this case.

Cash Flow Is Greater Than $800 Here, the stockholders do not exercise the put. Thus, the bondholders merely receive the $800 that is due them.

Expressing the bondholders' position in this way is illuminating. With a riskless default-free bond, the bondholders are owed $800. Thus, we can express the risky bond in terms of a riskless bond and a put:

$$\textbf{Value of risky bond} = \textbf{Value of default-free bond} - \textbf{Value of put option}$$

That is, the value of the risky bond is the value of the default-free bond less the value of the stockholders' option to sell the company for $800.

A Resolution of the Two Views

We have argued above that the positions of the stockholders and the bondholders can be viewed either in terms of calls or in terms of puts. These two viewpoints are summarized in Table 17.4.

We have found from past experience that it is generally harder for students to think of the firm in terms of puts than in terms of calls. Thus, it would be helpful if there were a way to show that the two viewpoints are equivalent. Fortunately, there is *put-call parity*. In an earlier section, we presented the put-call parity relationship as equation (17.1), which we now repeat:

$$\textbf{Price of underlying stock} + \textbf{Price of put} = \textbf{Price of call} + \textbf{Present value of exercise price} \quad (17.1)$$

Using the results of this section, equation (17.1) can be rewritten as:

$$\textbf{Value of call on firm} = \textbf{Value of firm} + \textbf{Value of put on firm} - \textbf{Value of default-free bond} \quad (17.3)$$

Stockholders' position in terms of call options (left side); **Stockholders' position in terms of put options** (right side)

Going from equation (17.1) to equation (17.3) involves a few steps. First, we treat the firm, not the stock, as the underlying asset in this section. (In keeping with common convention, we refer to the *value* of the firm and the *price* of the stock.) Second, the exercise price is now $800, the principal and interest on the firm's debt. Taking the present value of this amount at the riskless rate yields the value of a default-free bond. Third, the order of the terms in equation (17.1) is rearranged in equation (17.3).

TABLE 17.4 Positions of Stockholders and Bondholders in Popov Company in Terms of Calls and Puts

STOCKHOLDERS	BONDHOLDERS
Positions viewed in terms of call options	
1. Stockholders own a call on the firm with exercise price of $800.	1. Bondholders own the firm. 2. Bondholders have sold a call on the firm to the stockholders.
Positions viewed in terms of put options	
1. Stockholders own the firm. 2. Stockholders owe $800 in interest and principal to bondholders. 3. Stockholders own a put option on the firm with exercise price of $800.	1. Bondholders are owed $800 in interest and principal. 2. Bondholders have sold a put on the firm to the stockholders.

Note that the left-hand side of equation (17.3) is the stockholders' position in terms of call options, as shown in Table 17.4. The right-hand side of equation (17.3) is the stockholders' position in terms of put options, as shown in the table. Thus, put-call parity shows that viewing the stockholders' position in terms of call options is equivalent to viewing the stockholders' position in terms of put options.

Now, let's rearrange terms in equation (17.3) to yield:

$$\underbrace{\textbf{Value of firm} - \textbf{Value of call on firm}}_{\textbf{Bondholders' position in terms of call options}} = \underbrace{\textbf{Value of default-free bond} - \textbf{Value of put on firm}}_{\textbf{Bondholders' position in terms of put options}} \qquad (17.4)$$

The left-hand side of equation (17.4) is the bondholders' position in terms of call options, as shown in Table 17.4. The right-hand side of the equation is the bondholders' position in terms of put options, as shown in Table 17.4. Thus, put-call parity shows that viewing the bondholders' position in terms of call options is equivalent to viewing the bondholders' position in terms of put options.

A Note on Loan Guarantees

In the Popov example given earlier, the bondholders bore the risk of default. Of course, bondholders generally ask for an interest rate that is enough to compensate them for bearing risk. When firms experience financial distress, they can no longer attract new debt at moderate interest rates. Thus, firms experiencing distress have frequently sought loan guarantees from the government. Our framework can be used to understand these guarantees.

If the firm defaults on a guaranteed loan, the government must make up the difference. In other words, a government guarantee converts a risky bond into a riskless bond. What is the value of this guarantee?

Recall that, with option pricing:

$$\textbf{Value of default-free bond} = \textbf{Value of risky bond} + \textbf{Value of put option}$$

This equation shows that the government is assuming an obligation that has a cost equal to the value of a put option.

This analysis differs from that of either politicians or company spokespeople. They generally say that the guarantee will cost the taxpayer nothing because the guarantee enables the firm to attract debt, thereby staying solvent. However, it should be pointed out that, although solvency may be a strong possibility, it is never a certainty. Thus, at the time when the guarantee is made, the government's obligation has a cost in terms of present value. To say that a government guarantee costs the government nothing is like saying a put on the stock of Microsoft has no value because the stock is *likely* to rise in price.

Actually, the government has had good fortune with loan guarantees. Its two biggest guarantees were to the Lockheed Corporation in 1971 and the Chrysler Corporation in 1980. Both firms nearly ran out of cash and defaulted on loans. In both cases, the U.S. government came to the rescue by agreeing to guarantee new loans. Under the guarantees, if Lockheed and Chrysler had defaulted on new loans, the lenders could have obtained the full value of their claims from the U.S. government. From the lender's point of view, the loans became as risk-free as Treasury bonds. These guarantees enabled Lockheed and Chrysler to borrow large amounts of cash and to get through a difficult time. As it turned out, neither firm defaulted.

Who benefits from a typical loan guarantee?

1. If existing risky bonds are guaranteed, all gains accrue to the existing bondholders. The stockholders gain nothing because the limited liability of corporations absolves the stockholders of any obligation in bankruptcy.

2. If new debt is being issued and guaranteed, the new debtholders do not gain. Rather, in a competitive market, they must accept a low interest rate because of the debt's low risk. The stockholders gain here because they are able to issue debt at a low interest rate. In addition, some of the gains accrue to the old bondholders because the firm's value is greater than would otherwise be true. Therefore, if shareholders want all the gains from loan guarantees, they should renegotiate or retire existing bonds before the guarantee is in place. This happened in the Chrysler case.

17.10 OPTIONS AND CORPORATE DECISIONS: SOME APPLICATIONS

In this section, we explore the implications of options analysis in two key areas, capital budgeting and mergers. We start with mergers and show a very surprising result. We then go on to show that the net present value rule has some important wrinkles in a leveraged firm.

Mergers and Diversification

Elsewhere in our book, we discuss mergers and acquisitions. There we mention that diversification is frequently cited as a reason for two firms to merge. Is diversification a good reason to merge? It might seem so. After all, in an earlier chapter, we spent a lot of time explaining why diversification is very valuable for investors in their own portfolios because of the elimination of unsystematic risk.

To investigate this issue, let's consider two companies, Sunshine Swimwear (SS) and Polar Winterwear (PW). For obvious reasons, both companies have very seasonal cash flows, and, in their respective off-seasons, both companies worry about cash flow. If the two companies were to merge, the combined company would have a much more stable cash flow. In other words, a merger would diversify away some of the seasonal variation and, in fact, would make bankruptcy much less likely.

Notice that the operations of the two firms are very different, so the proposed merger is a purely "financial" merger, which means that there are no "synergies" or other value-creating possibilities except, possibly, gains from risk reduction. Here is some premerger information:

	SUNSHINE SWIMWEAR	POLAR WINTERWEAR
Market value of assets	$30 million	$10 million
Face value of pure discount debt	$12 million	$4 million
Debt maturity	3 years	3 years
Asset return standard deviation	50%	60%

The risk-free rate, continuously compounded, is 5 percent. Given this, we can view the equity in each firm as a call option and calculate the following using Black-Scholes to determine equity values (check these for practice):

	SUNSHINE SWIMWEAR	POLAR WINTERWEAR
Market value of equity	$20.394 million	$6.992 million
Market value of debt	$ 9.606 million	$3.008 million

If you do check these, you may get slightly different answers if you use Table 17.3 (we used a spreadsheet). Notice that we calculated the market value of debt using the balance sheet identity.

After the merger, the combined firm's assets will simply be the sum of the premerger values, $30 + $10 = $40, because no value was created or destroyed. Similarly, the total face value of the debt is now $16 million. However, we will assume that the combined firm's asset return standard deviation is 40 percent. This is lower than for either of the two individual firms because of the diversification effect.

So, what is the impact of this merger? To find out, we compute the postmerger value of the equity. Based on our discussion, here is the relevant information:

	COMBINED FIRM
Market value of assets	$40 million
Face value of pure discount debt	$16 million
Debt maturity	3 years
Asset return standard deviation	40%

Once again, we can calculate equity and debt values:

	COMBINED FIRM
Market value of equity	$26.602 million
Market value of debt	$13.398 million

What we notice is that this merger is a terrible idea, at least for the stockholders! Before the merger, the stock in the two separate firms was worth a total of $20.394 + 6.992 = $27.386 million compared to only $26.602 million postmerger, so the merger vaporized $27.386 − 26.602 = $.784 million, or almost $1 million, in equity.

Where did $1 million in equity go? It went to the bondholders. Their bonds were worth $9.606 + 3.008 = $12.614 million before the merger and $13.398 million after, a gain of exactly $.784 million. Thus, this merger neither created nor destroyed value, but it shifted it from the stockholders to the bondholders.

Our example shows that pure financial mergers are a bad idea, and it also shows why. The diversification works in the sense that it reduces the volatility of the firm's return on assets. This risk reduction benefits the bondholders by making default less likely. This is sometimes called the "coinsurance" effect. Essentially, by merging, the firms insure each other's bonds. The bonds are thus less risky, and they rise in value. If the bonds increase in value, and there is no net increase in asset values, then the equity must decrease in value. Thus, pure financial mergers are good for creditors, but not stockholders.

Another way to see this is that since the equity is a call option, a reduction in return variance on the underlying asset has to reduce its value. The reduction in value in the case of a purely financial merger has an interesting interpretation. The merger makes default (and, thus, bankruptcy) *less* likely to happen. That is obviously a good thing from a bondholder's perspective, but why is it a bad thing from a stockholder's perspective? The answer is simple: The right to go bankrupt is a valuable stockholder option. A purely financial merger reduces the value of that option.

Options and Capital Budgeting

We now consider two issues regarding capital budgeting. What we will show is that, for a leveraged firm, the shareholders might prefer a lower NPV project to a higher one. We then show that they might even prefer a *negative* NPV project to a positive NPV project.

As usual, we will illustrate these points first with an example. Here is the basic background information on the firm:

Market value of assets	$20 million
Face value of pure discount debt	$40 million
Debt maturity	5 years
Asset return standard deviation	50%

The risk-free rate is 4 percent. As we have now done several times, we can calculate equity and debt values:

Market value of equity	$ 5.724 million
Market value of debt	$14.276 million

This firm has a fairly high degree of leverage; the debt/equity ratio based on market values is $14.276/5.724 = 2.5, or 250 percent. This is high, but not unheard-of. Notice also that the option here is out of the money; as a result, the delta is .546.

The firm has two mutually exclusive investments under consideration. The projects affect both the market value of the firm's assets and the firm's asset return standard deviation as follows:

	PROJECT *A*	PROJECT *B*
NPV	$4	$2
Market value of firm's assets ($20 + NPV)	$24	$22
Firm's asset return standard deviation	40%	60%

Which project is better? It is obvious that Project *A* has the higher NPV, but by now you are wary of the change in the firm's asset return standard deviation. One project reduces it, the other increases it. To see which project the stockholders like better, we have to go through our by now very familiar calculations:

	PROJECT *A*	PROJECT *B*
Market value of equity	$ 5.938	$ 8.730
Market value of debt	$18.062	$13.27

There is a dramatic difference between the two projects. Project *A* benefits both the stockholders and the bondholders, but most of the gain goes to the bondholders. Project *B* has a huge impact on the value of the equity plus it reduces the value of the debt. Clearly, the stockholders prefer *B*.

What are the implications of our analysis? Basically, what we have discovered is two things. First, when the equity has a delta significantly smaller than 1.0, any value created will go partially to bondholders. Second, stockholders have a strong incentive to increase the variance of the return on the firm's assets. More specifically, stockholders will have a strong preference for variance-increasing projects as opposed to variance-decreasing ones, even if that means a lower NPV.

Let's do one final example. Here is a different set of numbers:

Market value of assets	$20 million
Face value of pure discount debt	$100 million
Debt maturity	5 years
Asset return standard deviation	50%

The risk-free rate is 4 percent, so the equity and debt values are:

Market value of equity	$ 2 million
Market value of debt	$18 million

Notice that the change from our previous example is that the face value of the debt is now $100 million, so the option is far out of the money. The delta is only .24, so most of any value created will go to the bondholders.

The firm has an investment under consideration, which must be taken now or never. The project affects both the market value of the firm's assets and the firm's asset return standard deviation as follows:

Project NPV	−$ 1 million
Market value of firm's assets ($20 million + NPV)	$19 million
Firm's asset return standard deviation	70%

Thus, the project has a negative NPV, but it increases the standard deviation of the firm's return on assets. If the firm takes the project, here is the result:

Market value of equity	$ 4.821 million
Market value of debt	$14.179 million

This project more than doubles the value of the equity! Once again, what we are seeing is that stockholders have a strong incentive to increase volatility, particularly when the option is far out of the money. What is happening is that the shareholders have relatively little to lose because bankruptcy is the likely outcome. As a result, there is a strong incentive to go for a long shot, even if that long shot has a negative NPV. It's a bit like using your very last dollar on a lottery ticket. It's a bad investment, but there aren't a lot of other options!

17.11 INVESTMENT IN REAL PROJECTS AND OPTIONS

Let us quickly review the material on capital budgeting presented earlier in the text. We first considered projects where forecasts for future cash flows were made at date 0. The expected cash flow in each future period was discounted at an appropriate risky rate, yielding an NPV calculation. For independent projects, a positive NPV meant acceptance and a negative NPV meant rejection.

This approach treated risk through the discount rate. We later considered decision tree analysis, an approach that handles risk in a more sophisticated way. We pointed out that the firm will make investment and operating decisions on a project over its entire life. We value a project today, assuming that future decisions will be optimal. However, we do not yet know what these decisions will be, because much information remains to be discovered. The firm's ability to delay its investment and operating decisions until the release of information is an option. We now illustrate this option through an example.

EXAMPLE 17.6 Options and Capital Budgeting

Exoff Oil Corporation is considering the purchase of an oil field in a remote part of Alaska. The seller has listed the property for $10,000 and is eager to sell immediately. Initial drilling costs are $500,000. The firm anticipates that 10,000 barrels of oil can be extracted each year for many decades. Because the termination date is so far in the future and so hard to estimate, the firm views the cash flow stream from the oil as a perpetuity. With oil prices at $20 per barrel and extraction costs at $16 a barrel, the firm anticipates a net margin of $4 per barrel. Because oil prices are expected to rise

(*continued*)

at the inflation rate, the firm assumes that its cash flow per barrel will always be $4 in real terms. The appropriate real discount rate is 10 percent. The firm has enough tax credits from bad years in the past that it will not need to pay taxes on any profits from the oil field. Should Exoff buy the property?

The NPV of the oil field to Exoff is:

$$-\$110{,}000 = -\$10{,}000 - \$500{,}000 + \frac{\$4 \times 10{,}000}{.10}$$

According to this analysis, Exoff should not purchase the land.

Though this approach uses the standard capital budgeting techniques of this and other textbooks, it is actually inappropriate for this situation. To see this, consider the analysis of Kirtley Thornton, a consultant to Exoff. He agrees that the price of oil is *expected* to rise at the rate of inflation. However, he points out that the next year is quite perilous for oil prices. On the one hand, OPEC is considering a long-term agreement that would raise oil prices to $35 per barrel in real terms for many years in the future. On the other hand, National Motors recently indicated that cars using a mixture of sand and water for fuel are currently being tested. Thornton argues that oil will be priced at $5 in real terms for many years, should this development prove successful. Full information on both these developments will be released in exactly one year.

Should oil prices rise to $35 a barrel, the NPV of the project would be:

$$\$1{,}390{,}000 = -\$10{,}000 - \$500{,}000 + \frac{(\$35 - \$16) \times 10{,}000}{.10}$$

However, should oil prices fall to $5 a barrel, the NPV of the oil field will be even more negative than it is today.

Mr. Thornton makes two recommendations to Exoff's board. He argues that:

1. The land should be purchased.
2. The drilling decision should be delayed until information on both OPEC's new agreement and National Motors' new automobile is released.

Kirtley explains his recommendations to the board by first assuming that the land has already been purchased. He argues that, under this assumption, the drilling decision should be delayed. Second, he investigates his assumption that the land should have been purchased in the first place. This approach of examining the second decision (whether to drill) after assuming that the first decision (to buy the land) had been made was also used in our earlier presentation on decision trees. Let us now work through Mr. Thornton's analysis.

Assume the land has already been purchased. If the land has already been purchased, should drilling begin immediately? If drilling begins immediately, the NPV is −$110,000. If the drilling decision is delayed until new information is released in a year, the optimal choice can be made at that time. If oil prices drop to $5 a barrel, Exoff should not drill. Instead, the firm should walk away from the project, losing nothing beyond its $10,000 purchase price for the land. If oil prices rise to $35, drilling should begin.

Mr. Thornton points out that, by delaying, the firm will only invest the $500,000 of drilling costs if oil prices rise. Thus, by delaying, the firm saves $500,000 in the case where oil prices drop. Kirtley concludes that, once the land is purchased, the drilling decision should be delayed.[10]

Should the land have been purchased in the first place? We now know that if the land had been purchased, it is optimal to defer the drilling decision until the release of information. Given that we know this optimal decision concerning drilling, should the land be purchased in the first place? Without knowing the exact probability that oil prices will rise, Mr. Thornton is nevertheless confident that the land should be purchased. The NPV of the project at $35 oil prices is $1,390,000 whereas the cost of the land is only $10,000. Kirtley believes that an oil price rise is possible, though by no means probable. Even so, he argues that the high potential return is clearly worth the risk.

[10]Actually, there are three separate effects here. First, the firm avoids drilling costs in the case of low oil prices by delaying the decision. This is the effect discussed by Mr. Thornton. Second, the present value of the $500,000 payment is less when the decision is delayed, even if drilling eventually takes place. Third, the firm loses one year of cash inflows through delay.

The first two arguments support delaying the decision. The third argument supports immediate drilling. In this example, the first argument greatly outweighs the other two arguments. Thus, Mr. Thornton avoided the second and third arguments in his presentation.

This example presents an approach that is similar to our decision tree analysis of the Solar Equipment Company in a previous chapter. Our purpose in this section is to discuss this type of decision in an option framework. When Exoff purchases the land, it is actually purchasing a call option. That is, once the land has been purchased, the firm has an option to buy an active oil field at an exercise price of $500,000. As it turns out, one should generally not exercise a call option immediately.[11] In this case, the firm should delay exercise until relevant information concerning future oil prices is released.

This section points out a serious deficiency in classical capital budgeting: Net present value calculations typically ignore the flexibility that real world firms have. In our example, the standard techniques generated a negative NPV for the land purchase. Yet, by allowing the firm the option to change its investment policy according to new information, the land purchase can easily be justified.

We encourage the reader to look for hidden options in projects. Because options are beneficial, managers are shortchanging their firm's projects if capital budgeting calculations ignore flexibility.

[11]Actually, it can be shown that a call option that pays no dividend should *never* be exercised before expiration. However, for a dividend-paying stock, it may be optimal to exercise prior to the ex-dividend date. The analogy applies to our example of an option in real assets.

The firm would receive cash flows from oil earlier if drilling begins immediately. This is equivalent to the benefit from exercising a call on a stock prematurely in order to capture the dividend. However, in our example, this dividend effect is far outweighed by the benefits from waiting.

SUMMARY AND CONCLUSIONS

This chapter serves as an introduction to options.

1. The most familiar options are puts and calls. These options give the holder the right to sell or buy shares of common stock at a given exercise price. American options can be exercised any time up to and including the expiration date. European options can be exercised only on the expiration date.
2. We showed that a strategy of buying a stock and buying a put is equivalent to a strategy of buying a call and buying a zero-coupon bond. From this, the put-call parity relationship was established:

$$\text{Value of stock} + \text{Value of put} - \text{Value of call} = \text{Present value of exercise price}$$

3. The value of an option depends on five factors:
   a. The price of the underlying asset.
   b. The exercise price.
   c. The expiration date.

d. The variability of the underlying asset.

e. The interest rate on risk-free bonds.

The Black-Scholes model can determine the intrinsic price of an option from these five factors.

4. Much of corporate financial theory can be presented in terms of options. In this chapter, we pointed out that

a. Common stock can be represented as a call option on the firm.

b. Stockholders enhance the value of their call by increasing the risk of their firm.

c. Real projects have hidden options that enhance value.

CONCEPT QUESTIONS

1. **Options** What is a call option? A put option? Under what circumstances might you want to buy each? Which one has greater *potential* profit? Why?

2. **Options** Complete the following sentence for each of these investors:

 a. A buyer of call options

 b. A buyer of put options

 c. A seller (writer) of call options

 d. A seller (writer) of put options

 "The (buyer/seller) of a (put/call) option (pays/receives) money for the (right/obligation) to (buy/sell) a specified asset at a fixed price for a fixed length of time."

3. **American and European Options** What is the difference between an American option and a European option?

4. **Intrinsic Value** What is the intrinsic value of a call option? Of a put option? How do we interpret this value?

5. **Option Pricing** You notice that shares of stock in the Patel Corporation are going for $50 per share. Call options with an exercise price of $35 per share are selling for $10. What's wrong here? Describe how you can take advantage of this mispricing if the option expires today.

6. **Options and Stock Risk** If the risk of a stock increases, what is likely to happen to the price of call options on the stock? To the price of put options? Why?

7. **Option Rise** True or false: The unsystematic risk of a share of stock is irrelevant in valuing the stock because it can be diversified away; therefore, it is also irrelevant for valuing a call option on the stock. Explain.

8. **Option Pricing** Suppose a certain stock currently sells for $30 per share. If a put option and a call option are available with $30 exercise prices, which do you think will sell for more, the put or the call? Explain.

9. **Option Price and Interest Rates** Suppose the interest rate on T-bills suddenly and unexpectedly rises. All other things being the same, what is the impact on call option values? On put option values?

10. **Contingent Liabilities** When you take out an ordinary student loan, it is usually the case that whoever holds that loan is given a guarantee by the U.S. government, meaning that the government will make up any payments you skip. This is just one example of the many loan guarantees made by the U.S. government. Such guarantees don't show up in calculations of government spending or in official deficit figures. Why not? Should they show up?

11. **Options and Expiration Dates** What is the impact of lengthening the time to expiration on an option's value? Explain.

12. **Options and Stock Price Volatility** What is the impact of an increase in the volatility of the underlying stock's return on an option's value? Explain.
13. **Insurance as an Option** An insurance policy is considered analogous to an option. From the policyholder's point of view, what type of option is an insurance policy? Why?
14. **Equity as a Call Option** It is said that the equityholders of a levered firm can be thought of as holding a call option on the firm's assets. Explain what is meant by this statement.
15. **Option Valuation and NPV** You are CEO of Titan Industries and have just been awarded a large number of employee stock options. The company has two mutually exclusive projects available. The first project has a large NPV and will reduce the total risk of the company. The second project has a small NPV and will increase the total risk of the company. You have decided to accept the first project when you remember your employee stock options. How might this affect your decision?
16. **Put-Call Parity** You find a put and a call with the same exercise price and maturity. What do you know about the relative prices of the put and call? Prove your answer and provide an intuitive explanation.
17. **Put-Call Parity** A put and a call have the same maturity and strike price. If they have the same price, which one is in the money? Prove your answer and provide an intuitive explanation.
18. **Put-Call Parity** One thing put-call parity tells us is that given any three of a stock, a call, a put, and a T-bill, the fourth can be synthesized or replicated using the other three. For example, how can we replicate a share of stock using a call, a put, and a T-bill?

QUESTIONS AND PROBLEMS

Basic
(Questions 1–17)

1. **Two-State Option Pricing Model** T-bills currently yield 5.5 percent. Stock in Nina Manufacturing is currently selling for $55 per share. There is no possibility that the stock will be worth less than $50 per share in one year.
   a. What is the value of a call option with a $45 exercise price? What is the intrinsic value?
   b. What is the value of a call option with a $35 exercise price? What is the intrinsic value?
   c. What is the value of a put option with a $45 exercise price? What is the intrinsic value?
2. **Understanding Option Quotes** Use the option quote information shown here to answer the questions that follow. The stock is currently selling for $83.

OPTION AND NY CLOSE	EXPIRATION	STRIKE PRICE	Calls VOL.	Calls LAST	Puts VOL.	Puts LAST
RWJ						
	Mar	80	230	2.80	160	0.80
	Apr	80	170	6	127	1.40
	Jul	80	139	8.05	43	3.90
	Oct	80	60	10.20	11	3.65

   a. Are the call options in the money? What is the intrinsic value of an RWJ Corp. call option?
   b. Are the put options in the money? What is the intrinsic value of an RWJ Corp. put option?
   c. Two of the options are clearly mispriced. Which ones? At a minimum, what should the mispriced options sell for? Explain how you could profit from the mispricing in each case.
3. **Calculating Payoffs** Use the option quote information shown on the next page to answer the questions that follow. The stock is currently selling for $114.

OPTION AND NY CLOSE	EXPIRATION	STRIKE PRICE	Calls		Puts	
			VOL.	LAST	VOL.	LAST
Macrosoft						
	Feb	110	85	7.60	40	.60
	Mar	110	61	8.80	22	1.55
	May	110	22	10.25	11	2.85
	Aug	110	3	13.05	3	4.70

a. Suppose you buy 10 contracts of the February 110 call option. How much will you pay, ignoring commissions?

b. In part (a), suppose that Macrosoft stock is selling for $140 per share on the expiration date. How much is your options investment worth? What if the terminal stock price is $125? Explain.

c. Suppose you buy 10 contracts of the August 110 put option. What is your maximum gain? On the expiration date, Macrosoft is selling for $104 per share. How much is your options investment worth? What is your net gain?

d. In part (c), suppose you *sell* 10 of the August 110 put contracts. What is your net gain or loss if Macrosoft is selling for $103 at expiration? For $132? What is the break-even price, that is, the terminal stock price that results in a zero profit?

4. **Two-State Option Pricing Model** The price of Ervin Corp. stock will be either $75 or $95 at the end of the year. Call options are available with one year to expiration. T-bills currently yield 6 percent. 

a. Suppose the current price of Ervin stock is $80. What is the value of the call option if the exercise price is $70 per share?

b. Suppose the exercise price is $90 in part (a). What is the value of the call option now?

5. **Two-State Option Pricing Model** The price of Tara, Inc., stock will be either $60 or $80 at the end of the year. Call options are available with one year to expiration. T-bills currently yield 5 percent.

a. Suppose the current price of Tara stock is $70. What is the value of the call option if the exercise price is $45 per share?

b. Suppose the exercise price is $70 in part (a). What is the value of the call option now?

6. **Put-Call Parity** A stock is currently selling for $61 per share. A call option with an exercise price of $65 sells for $4.12 and expires in three months. If the risk-free rate of interest is 2.6 percent per year, compounded continuously, what is the price of a put option with the same exercise price? 

7. **Put-Call Parity** A put option that expires in six months with an exercise price of $50 sells for $4.89. The stock is currently priced at $53, and the risk-free rate is 3.6 percent per year, compounded continuously. What is the price of a call option with the same exercise price?

8. **Put-Call Parity** A put option and a call option with an exercise price of $70 and three months to expiration sell for $2.87 and $4.68, respectively. If the risk-free rate is 4.8 percent per year, compounded continuously, what is the current stock price?

9. **Put-Call Parity** A put option and a call option with an exercise price of $65 expire in two months and sell for $2.86 and $4.08, respectively. If the stock is currently priced at $65.80, what is the annual continuously compounded rate of interest?

10. **Black-Scholes** What are the prices of a call option and a put option with the following characteristics? 

Stock price =	\$38
Exercise price =	\$35
Risk-free rate =	6% per year, compounded continuously
Maturity =	3 months
Standard deviation =	54% per year

11. **Black-Scholes** What are the prices of a call option and a put option with the following characteristics?

Stock price =	\$86
Exercise price =	\$90
Risk-free rate =	4% per year, compounded continuously
Maturity =	8 months
Standard deviation =	62% per year

12. **Delta** What are the deltas of a call option and a put option with the following characteristics? What does the delta of the option tell you?

Stock price =	\$87
Exercise price =	\$85
Risk-free rate =	5% per year, compounded continuously
Maturity =	9 months
Standard deviation =	56% per year

13. **Black-Scholes and Asset Value** You own a lot in Key West, Florida, that is currently unused. Similar lots have recently sold for \$1.6 million. Over the past five years, the price of land in the area has increased 12 percent per year, with an annual standard deviation of 20 percent. A buyer has recently approached you and wants an option to buy the land in the next 12 months for \$1.75 million. The risk-free rate of interest is 5 percent per year, compounded continuously. How much should you charge for the option?
14. **Black-Scholes and Asset Value** In the previous problem, suppose you wanted the option to sell the land to the buyer in one year. Assuming all the facts are the same, describe the transaction that would occur today. What is the price of the transaction today?
15. **Time Value of Options** You are given the following information concerning options on a particular stock:

Stock price =	\$86
Exercise price =	\$90
Risk-free rate =	6% per year, compounded continuously
Maturity =	6 months
Standard deviation =	53% per year

   a. What is the intrinsic value of the call option? Of the put option?
   b. What is the time value of the call option? Of the put option?
   c. Does the call or the put have the larger time value component? Would you expect this to be true in general?
16. **Risk-Neutral Valuation** A stock is currently priced at \$75. The stock will either increase or decrease by 15 percent over the next year. There is a call option on the stock with a strike price of \$70 and one year until expiration. If the risk-free rate is 12 percent, what is the risk-neutral value of the call option?

17. **Risk-Neutral Valuation** In the previous problem, assume the risk-free rate is only 8 percent. What is the risk-neutral value of the option now? What happens to the risk-neutral probabilities of a stock price increase and a stock price decrease?

Intermediate (Questions 18–29)

18. **Black-Scholes** A call option matures in six months. The underlying stock price is $85, and the stock's return has a standard deviation of 20 percent per year. The risk-free rate is 4 percent per year, compounded continuously. If the exercise price is $0, what is the price of the call option?

19. **Black-Scholes** A call option has an exercise price of $80 and matures in six months. The current stock price is $84, and the risk-free rate is 5 percent per year, compounded continuously. What is the price of the call if the standard deviation of the stock is 0 percent per year?

20. **Black-Scholes** A stock is currently priced at $35. A call option with an expiration of one year has an exercise price of $50. The risk-free rate is 12 percent per year, compounded continuously, and the standard deviation of the stock's return is infinitely large. What is the price of the call option?

21. **Equity as an Option** Sunburn Sunscreen has a zero coupon bond issue outstanding with a $10,000 face value that matures in one year. The current market value of the firm's assets is $10,500. The standard deviation of the return on the firm's assets is 38 percent per year, and the annual risk-free rate is 5 percent per year, compounded continuously. Based on the Black-Scholes model, what is the market value of the firm's equity and debt?

22. **Equity as an Option and NPV** Suppose the firm in the previous problem is considering two mutually exclusive investments. Project A has an NPV of $700, and Project B has an NPV of $1,000. As the result of taking Project A, the standard deviation of the return on the firm's assets will increase to 55 percent per year. If Project B is taken, the standard deviation will fall to 34 percent per year.
    a. What is the value of the firm's equity and debt if Project A is undertaken? If Project B is undertaken?
    b. Which project would the stockholders prefer? Can you reconcile your answer with the NPV rule?
    c. Suppose the stockholders and bondholders are in fact the same group of investors. Would this affect your answer to (b)?
    d. What does this problem suggest to you about stockholder incentives?

23. **Equity as an Option** Frostbite Thermalwear has a zero coupon bond issue outstanding with a face value of $20,000 that matures in one year. The current market value of the firm's assets is $22,000. The standard deviation of the return on the firm's assets is 53 percent per year, and the annual risk-free rate is 5 percent per year, compounded continuously. Based on the Black-Scholes model, what is the market value of the firm's equity and debt? What is the firm's continuously compounded cost of debt?

24. **Mergers and Equity as an Option** Suppose Sunburn Sunscreen and Frostbite Thermalwear in the previous problems have decided to merge. Since the two companies have seasonal sales, the combined firm's return on assets will have a standard deviation of 31 percent per year.
    a. What is the combined value of equity in the two existing companies? Value of debt?
    b. What is the value of the new firm's equity? Value of debt?
    c. What was the gain or loss for shareholders? For bondholders?
    d. What happened to shareholder value here?

25. **Equity as an Option and NPV** A company has a single zero coupon bond outstanding which matures in 10 years with a face value of $30 million. The current value of the company's assets

is $22 million, and the standard deviation of the return on the firm's assets is 39 percent per year. The risk-free rate is 6 percent per year, compounded continuously.

a. What is the current market value of the company's equity?

b. What is the current market value of the company's debt?

c. What is the company's continuously compounded cost of debt?

d. The company has a new project available. The project has an NPV of $750,000. If the company undertakes the project, what will be the new market value of equity? Assume volatility is unchanged.

e. Assuming the company undertakes the new project and does not borrow any additional funds, what is the new continuously compounded cost of debt? What is happening here?

26. **Two-State Option Pricing Model** Ken is interested in buying a European call option written on Southeastern Airlines, Inc., a nondividend-paying common stock, with a strike price of $110 and one year until expiration. Currently, Southeastern's stock sells for $100 per share. In one year, Ken knows that Southeastern's stock will be trading at either $125 per share or $80 per share. Ken is able to borrow and lend at the risk-free EAR of 2.5 percent.

    a. What should the call option sell for today?

    b. If no options currently trade on the stock, is there a way to create a synthetic call option with identical payoffs to the call option described above? If there is, how would you do it?

    c. How much does the synthetic call option cost? Is this greater than, less than, or equal to what the actual call option costs? Does this make sense?

27. **Two-State Option Pricing Model** Rob wishes to buy a European put option on BioLabs, Inc., a nondividend-paying common stock, with a strike price of $40 and six months until expiration. BioLab's common stock is currently selling for $30 per share, and Rob expects that the stock price will either rise to $60 or fall to $15 in six months. Rob can borrow and lend at the risk-free EAR of 21 percent.

    a. What should the put option sell for today?

    b. If no options currently trade on the stock, is there a way to create a synthetic put option with identical payoffs to the put option described above? If there is, how would you do it?

    c. How much does the synthetic put option cost? Is this greater than, less than, or equal to what the actual put option costs? Does this make sense?

28. **Two-State Option Pricing Model** Maverick Manufacturing, Inc., must purchase gold in three months for use in its operations. Maverick's management has estimated that if the price of gold were to rise above $375 per ounce, the firm would go bankrupt. The current price of gold is $350 per ounce. The firm's chief financial officer believes that the price of gold will either rise to $400 per ounce or fall to $325 per ounce over the next three months. Management wishes to eliminate any risk of the firm going bankrupt. Maverick can borrow and lend at the risk-free EAR of 16.99 percent.

    a. Should the company buy a call option or a put option on gold? In order to avoid bankruptcy, what strike price and time to expiration would the company like this option to have?

    b. How much should such an option sell for in the open market?

    c. If no options currently trade on gold, is there a way for the company to create a synthetic option with identical payoffs to the option described above? If there is, how would the firm do it?

    d. How much does the synthetic option cost? Is this greater than, less than, or equal to what the actual option costs? Does this make sense?

29. **Black-Scholes and Collar Cost** An investor is said to take a position in a "collar" if he buys the asset, buys an out-of-the-money put option on the asset, and sells an out-of-the-money call

option on the asset. The two options should have the same time to expiration. Suppose Marie wishes to purchase a collar on Hollywood, Inc., a nondividend-paying common stock, with six months until expiration. She would like the put to have a strike price of $50 and the call to have a strike price of $120. The current price of Hollywood's stock is $80 per share. Marie can borrow and lend at the continuously compounded risk-free rate of 10 percent per annum, and the annual standard deviation of the stock's return is 50 percent. Use the Black-Scholes model to calculate the total cost of the collar that Marie is interested in buying. What is the effect of the collar?

Challenge (Questions 30–38)

30. **Debt Valuation and Time to Maturity** McLemore Industries has a zero coupon bond issue that matures in two years with a face value of $30,000. The current value of the company's assets is $13,000, and the standard deviation of the return on assets is 60 percent per year.
    a. Assume the risk-free rate is 5 percent per year, compounded continuously. What is the value of a risk-free bond with the same face value and maturity as the company's bond?
    b. What price would the bondholders have to pay for a put option on the firm's assets with a strike price equal to the face value of the debt?
    c. Using the answers from (a) and (b), what is the value of the firm's debt? What is the continuously compounded yield on the company's debt?
    d. From an examination of the value of the assets of McLemore Industries, and the fact that the debt must be repaid in two years, it seems likely that the company will default on its debt. Management has approached bondholders and proposed a plan whereby the company would repay the same face value of debt, but the repayment would not occur for five years. What is the value of the debt under the proposed plan? What is the new continuously compounded yield on the debt? Explain why this occurs.
31. **Debt Valuation and Asset Variance** Brozik Corp. has a zero coupon bond that matures in five years with a face value of $60,000. The current value of the company's assets is $57,000, and the standard deviation of its return on assets is 50 percent per year. The risk-free rate is 6 percent per year, compounded continuously.
    a. What is the value of a risk-free bond with the same face value and maturity as the current bond?
    b. What is the value of a put option on the firm's assets with a strike price equal to the face value of the debt?
    c. Using the answers from (a) and (b), what is the value of the firm's debt? What is the continuously compounded yield on the company's debt?
    d. Assume the company can restructure its assets so that the standard deviation of its return on assets increases to 60 percent per year. What happens to the value of the debt? What is the new continuously compounded yield on the debt? Reconcile your answers in (c) and (d).
    e. What happens to bondholders if the company restructures its assets? What happens to shareholders? How does this create an agency problem?
32. **Two-State Option Pricing and Corporate Valuation** Strudler Real Estate, Inc., a construction firm financed by both debt and equity, is undertaking a new project. If the project is successful, the value of the firm in one year will be $500 million, but if the project is a failure, the firm will only be worth $320 million. The current value of Strudler is $400 million, a figure that includes the prospects for the new project. Strudler has outstanding zero coupon bonds due in one year with a face value of $380 million. Treasury bills that mature in one year yield 7 percent EAR. Strudler pays no dividends.
    a. Use the two-state option pricing model to find the current value of Strudler's debt and equity.
    b. Suppose Strudler has 500,000 shares of common stock outstanding. What is the price per share of the firm's equity?

c. Compare the market value of Strudler's debt to the present value of an equal amount of debt that is riskless with one year until maturity. Is the firm's debt worth more than, less than, or the same as the riskless debt? Does this make sense? What factors might cause these two values to be different?

d. Suppose that in place of the project described above, Strudler's management decides to undertake a project that is even more risky. The value of the firm will either increase to $800 million or decrease to $200 million by the end of the year. Surprisingly, management concludes that the value of the firm today will remain at exactly $400 million if this risky project is substituted for the less risky one. Use the two-state option pricing model to determine the value of the firm's debt and equity if the firm plans on undertaking this new project. Which project do bondholders prefer?

33. **Black-Scholes and Dividends** In addition to the five factors discussed in the chapter, dividends also affect the price of an option. The Black-Scholes option pricing model with dividends is:

$$C = S \times e^{-dt} \times \mathrm{N}(d_1) - E \times e^{-Rt} \times \mathrm{N}(d_2)$$
$$d_1 = [\ln(S/E) + (R - d + \sigma^2/2) \times t]/(\sigma \times \sqrt{t})$$
$$d_2 = d_1 - \sigma \times \sqrt{t}$$

All of the variables are the same as the Black-Scholes model without dividends except for the variable d, which is the continuously compounded dividend yield on the stock.

a. What effect do you think the dividend yield will have on the price of a call option? Explain.

b. A stock is currently priced at $84 per share, the standard deviation of its return is 50 percent per year, and the risk-free rate is 5 percent per year compounded continuously. What is the price of a call option with a strike price of $80 and a maturity of 6 months if the stock has a dividend yield of 2 percent per year?

34. **Put-Call Parity and Dividends** The put-call parity condition is altered when dividends are paid. The dividend adjusted put-call parity formula is:

$$S \times e^{-dt} + P = E \times e^{-Rt} + C$$

where d is again the continuously compounded dividend yield.

a. What effect do you think the dividend yield will have on the price of a put option? Explain.

b. From the previous question, what is the price of a put option with the same strike price and time to expiration as the call option?

35. **Put Delta** In the chapter, we noted that the delta for a put option is $\mathrm{N}(d_1) - 1$. Is this the same thing as $-\mathrm{N}(-d_1)$? (Hint: Yes, but why?)

36. **Black-Scholes Put Pricing Model** Use the Black-Scholes model for pricing a call, put-call parity, and the previous question to show that the Black-Scholes model for directly pricing a put can be written as:

$$P = E \times e^{-Rt} \times \mathrm{N}(-d_2) - S \times \mathrm{N}(-d_1)$$

37. **Black-Scholes** A stock is currently priced at $50. The stock will never pay a dividend. The risk-free rate is 12 percent per year, compounded continuously, and the standard deviation of the stock's return is 60 percent. A European call option on the stock has a strike price of $100 and no expiration date, meaning that it has an infinite life. Based on Black-Scholes, what is the value of the call option? Do you see a paradox here? Do you see a way out of the paradox?

38. **Delta** You purchase one call and sell one put with the same strike price and expiration date. What is the delta of your portfolio? Why?

WHAT'S ON THE WEB?

1. **Black-Scholes** Go to www.cfo.com. Find the stock options calculator. The call option and put option on a stock expire in 30 days. The strike price is $50 and the current stock price is $51.20. The standard deviation of the stock is 60 percent per year, and the risk-free rate is 4.8 percent per year, compounded continuously. What is the price of the call and the put? What are the deltas?
2. **Black-Scholes** Go to www.cboe.com, click on the "Trading Tools" tab, then the "Volatility Optimizer" link to find the options calculator. A stock is currently priced at $93 per share, and its return has a standard deviation of 48 percent per year. Options are available with an exercise price of $90, and the risk-free rate is 5.2 percent per year, compounded continuously. What is the price of the call and the put that expire next month? What are the deltas? How do your answers change for an exercise price of $95?
3. **Black-Scholes with Dividends** Recalculate the first two problems assuming a dividend yield of 2 percent per year. How does this change your answers? Can you explain why dividends have the effect they do?

CLOSING CASE

EXOTIC CUISINE EMPLOYEE STOCK OPTIONS

As a newly minted MBA, you've taken a management position with Exotic Cuisines, Inc., a restaurant chain that just went public last year. The company's restaurants specialize in exotic main dishes, using ingredients such as alligator, buffalo, and ostrich. A concern you had going in was that the restaurant business is very risky. However, after some due diligence, you discovered a common misperception about the restaurant industry. It is widely thought that 90 percent of new restaurants close within three years; however, recent evidence suggests the failure rate is closer to 60 percent over three years. So, it is a risky business, although not as risky as you originally thought.

During your interview process, one of the benefits mentioned was employee stock options. Upon signing your employment contract, you received options with a strike price of $50 for 10,000 shares of company stock. As is fairly common, your stock options have a three-year vesting period and a 10-year expiration, meaning that you cannot exercise the options for a period of three years, and you lose them if you leave before they vest. After the three-year vesting period, you can exercise the options at any time. Thus, the employee stock options are European (and subject to forfeit) for the first three years and American afterward. Of course, you cannot sell the options, nor can you enter into any sort of hedging agreement. If you leave the company after the options vest, you must exercise within 90 days or forfeit.

Exotic Cuisines stock is currently trading at $24.38 per share, a slight increase from the initial offering price last year. There are no market traded options on the company's stock. Because the company has only been traded for about a year, you are reluctant to use the historical returns to estimate the standard deviation of the stock's return. However, you have estimated that the average annual standard deviation for restaurant company stocks is about 55 percent. Since Exotic Cuisines is a newer restaurant chain, you decide to use a 60 percent standard deviation in your calculations. The company is relatively young, and you expect that all earnings will be reinvested back into the company for the near future. Therefore, you expect no dividends will be paid for at least the next 10 years. A three-year Treasury note currently has a yield of 3.8 percent, and a 10-year Treasury note has a yield of 4.4 percent.

1. You're trying to value your options. What minimum value would you assign? What is the maximum value you would assign?
2. Suppose that, in three years, the company's stock is trading at $60. At that time, should you keep the options or exercise them immediately? What are some of the important determinants in making such a decision?
3. Your options, like most employee stock options, are not transferable or tradeable. Does this have a significant effect on the value of the options? Why?
4. Why do you suppose employee stock options usually have a vesting provision? Why must they be exercised shortly after you depart the company even after they vest?
5. A controversial practice with employee stock options is repricing. What happens is that a company experiences a stock price decrease, which leaves employee stock options far out of the money or "underwater." In such cases, many companies have "repriced" or "restruck" the options, meaning that the company leaves the original terms of the option intact, but lowers the strike price. Proponents of repricing argue that since the option is very unlikely to end in the money because of the stock price decline, the motivational force is lost. Opponents argue that repricing is in essence a reward for failure. How do you evaluate this argument? How does the possibility of repricing affect the value of an employee stock option at the time it is granted?
6. As we have seen, much of the volatility in a company's stock price is due to systematic or marketwide risks. Such risks are beyond the control of a company and its employees. What are the implications for employee stock options? In light of your answer, can you recommend an improvement over traditional employee stock options?

CHAPTER 18

Short-Term Finance and Planning

OPENING CASE

Most often, when news breaks about a firm's cash position, it's because the company is running low. That wasn't the case for many companies in early 2005. At the beginning of the year, the cash on hand for all companies in the S&P 500 was *$600 billion!* Insurance giant Cigna certainly had one of the largest cash reserves relative to its size, with a cash balance of $2.92 billion, or $22 per share. The stock was trading at about $81 per share, so cash made up over one-quarter of the company's value. Of course no company came close to Microsoft. Before paying a huge special dividend, the company's cash horde reached $64 billion. In examining these numbers, it is clear that these companies certainly had ample cash reserves; in fact, the word *enormous* might be more appropriate. Why would these firms hold such large quantities of cash? To find out, this chapter explores short-term finance and examines optimal investments in current assets such as cash.

To this point, we have described many of the decisions of long-term finance, such as those of capital budgeting, dividend policy, and financial structure. In this chapter, we begin to discuss short-term finance. Short-term finance is primarily concerned with the analysis of decisions that affect current assets and current liabilities.

Interested in a career in short-term finance? Visit the Treasury Management Association Web site at www.treasurymanagement.com.

Frequently, the term *net working capital* is associated with short-term financial decision making. As we have described in previous chapters, net working capital is the difference between current assets and current liabilities. Often, short-term financial management is called *working capital management.* These terms mean the same thing.

There is no universally accepted definition of short-term finance. The most important difference between short-term and long-term finance is in the timing of cash flows. Short-term financial decisions typically involve cash inflows and outflows that occur within a year or less. For example, short-term financial decisions are involved when a firm orders raw materials, pays in cash, and anticipates selling finished goods in one year for cash. In contrast, long-term financial decisions are involved when a firm purchases a special machine that will reduce operating costs over, say, the next five years.

What types of questions fall under the general heading of short-term finance? To name just a very few:

1. What is a reasonable level of cash to keep on hand (in a bank) to pay bills?
2. How much should the firm borrow in the short term?
3. How much credit should be extended to customers?

This chapter introduces the basic elements of short-term financial decisions. First, we discuss the short-term operating activities of the firm. We then identify some alternative short-term financial policies. Finally, we outline the basic elements in a short-term financial plan and describe short-term financing instruments.

18.1 TRACING CASH AND NET WORKING CAPITAL

In this section, we examine the components of cash and net working capital as they change from one year to the next. We have already discussed various aspects of this subject in Chapters 2 and 3. We briefly review some of that discussion as it relates to short-term financing decisions. Our goal is to describe the short-term operating activities of the firm and their impact on cash and working capital.

To begin, recall that *current assets* are cash and other assets that are expected to convert to cash within the year. Current assets are presented on the balance sheet in order of their accounting liquidity–the ease with which they can be converted to cash and the time it takes to convert them. Four of the most important items found in the current asset section of a balance sheet are cash and cash equivalents, marketable securities, accounts receivable, and inventories.

Analogous to their investment in current assets, firms use several kinds of short-term debt, called *current liabilities.* Current liabilities are obligations that are expected to require cash payment within one year (or within the operating period if it is longer than one year). Three major items found as current liabilities are accounts payable, expenses payable (including accrued wages and taxes), and notes payable.

Because we want to focus on changes in cash, we start off by defining cash in terms of the other elements of the balance sheet. This lets us isolate the cash account and explore the impact on cash from the firm's operating and financing decisions. The basic balance sheet identity can be written as:

$$\textbf{Net working capital} + \textbf{Fixed assets} = \textbf{Long-term debt} + \textbf{Equity} \qquad \textbf{(18.1)}$$

Net working capital is cash plus other current assets, less current liabilities, that is:

$$\textbf{Net working capital} = (\textbf{Cash} + \textbf{Other current assets}) - \textbf{Current liabilities} \tag{18.2}$$

If we substitute this for net working capital in the basic balance sheet identity and rearrange things a bit, we see that cash is:

$$\begin{aligned}\textbf{Cash} = {} & \textbf{Long-term debt} + \textbf{Equity} + \textbf{Current liabilities} \\ & - \textbf{Current assets other than cash} - \textbf{Fixed assets}\end{aligned} \tag{18.3}$$

This tells us in general terms that some activities naturally increase cash and some activities decrease it. We can list these various activities, along with an example of each, as follows:

Activities that increase cash

Increasing long-term debt (borrowing over the long term)

Increasing equity (selling some stock)

Increasing current liabilities (getting a 90-day loan)

Decreasing current assets other than cash (selling some inventory for cash)

Decreasing fixed assets (selling some property)

Activities that decrease cash

Decreasing long-term debt (paying off a long-term debt)

Decreasing equity (repurchasing some stock)

Decreasing current liabilities (paying off a 90-day loan)

Increasing current assets other than cash (buying some inventory for cash)

Increasing fixed assets (buying some property)

Notice that our two lists are exact opposites. For example, floating a long-term bond issue increases cash (at least until the money is spent). Paying off a long-term bond issue decreases cash.

Activities that increase cash are called *sources of cash*. Those activities that decrease cash are called *uses of cash*. Looking back at our list, we see that sources of cash always involve increasing a liability (or equity) account or decreasing an asset account. This makes sense because increasing a liability means that we have raised money by borrowing it or by selling an ownership interest in the firm. A decrease in an asset means that we have sold or otherwise liquidated an asset. In either case, there is a cash inflow.

Uses of cash are just the reverse. A use of cash involves decreasing a liability by paying it off, perhaps, or increasing assets by purchasing something. Both of these activities require that the firm spend some cash.

EXAMPLE 18.1 Sources and Uses

Here is a quick check of your understanding of sources and uses: If accounts payable go up by $100, does this indicate a source or a use? What if accounts receivable go up by $100?

Accounts payable are what we owe our suppliers. This is a short-term debt. If it rises by $100, we have effectively borrowed the money, which is a *source* of cash. Receivables are what our customers owe to us, so an increase of $100 in accounts receivable means that we have loaned the money; this is a *use* of cash.

18.2 THE OPERATING CYCLE AND THE CASH CYCLE

The primary concern in short-term finance is the firm's short-run operating and financing activities. For a typical manufacturing firm, these short-run activities might consist of the following sequence of events and decisions:

EVENT	DECISION
1. Buying raw materials	1. How much inventory to order
2. Paying cash	2. Whether to borrow or draw down cash balances
3. Manufacturing the product	3. What choice of production technology to use
4. Selling the product	4. Whether credit should be extended to a particular customer
5. Collecting cash	5. How to collect

These activities create patterns of cash inflows and cash outflows. These cash flows are both unsynchronized and uncertain. They are unsynchronized because, for example, the payment of cash for raw materials does not happen at the same time as the receipt of cash from selling the product. They are uncertain because future sales and costs cannot be precisely predicted.

Defining the Operating and Cash Cycles

We can start with a simple case. One day, call it Day 0, we purchase \$1,000 worth of inventory on credit. We pay the bill 30 days later, and, after 30 more days, someone buys the \$1,000 in inventory for \$1,400. Our buyer does not actually pay for another 45 days. We can summarize these events chronologically as follows:

DAY	ACTIVITY	CASH EFFECT
0	Acquire inventory	None
30	Pay for inventory	−\$1,000
60	Sell inventory on credit	None
105	Collect on sale	+\$1,400

THE OPERATING CYCLE There are several things to notice in our example. First, the entire cycle, from the time we acquire some inventory to the time we collect the cash, takes 105 days. This is called the **operating cycle**.

As we illustrate, the operating cycle is the length of time it takes to acquire inventory, sell it, and collect for it. This cycle has two distinct components. The first part is the time it takes to acquire and sell the inventory. This period, a 60-day span in our example, is called the **inventory period**. The second part is the time it takes to collect on the sale, 45 days in our example. This is called the **accounts receivable period**.

Based on our definitions, the operating cycle is obviously just the sum of the inventory and accounts receivable periods:

$$\begin{aligned}\textbf{Operating cycle} &= \textbf{Inventory period} + \textbf{Accounts receivable period} \\ \textbf{105 days} &= \textbf{60 days} + \textbf{45 days}\end{aligned} \tag{18.4}$$

What the operating cycle describes is how a product moves through the current asset accounts. The product begins life as inventory, it is converted to a receivable when it is sold, and it is finally converted to cash when we collect from the sale. Notice that, at each step, the asset is moving closer to cash.

THE CASH CYCLE The second thing to notice is that the cash flows and other events that occur are not synchronized. For example, we don't actually pay for the inventory until

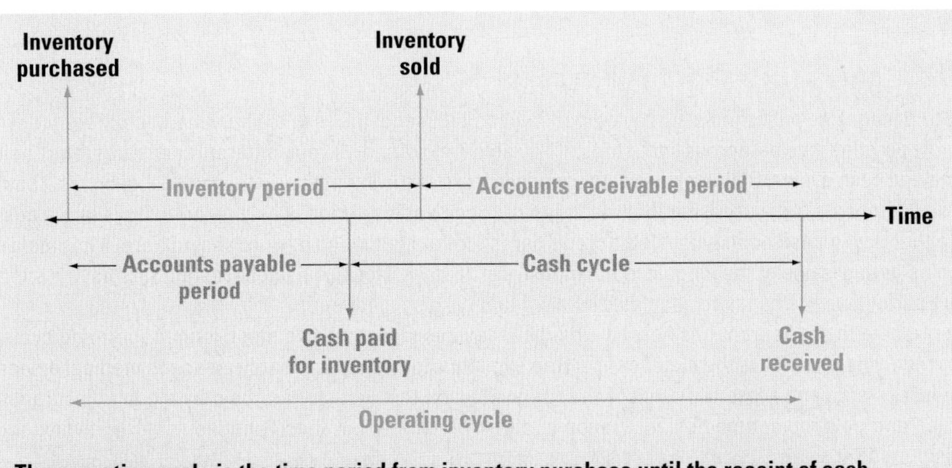

The operating cycle is the time period from inventory purchase until the receipt of cash. (The operating cycle may not include the time from placement of the order until arrival of the stock.) The cash cycle is the time period from when cash is paid out to when cash is received.

FIGURE 18.1

Cash Flow Time Line and the Short-Term Operating Activities of a Typical Manufacturing Firm

30 days after we acquire it. The intervening 30-day period is called the **accounts payable period**. Next, we spend cash on Day 30, but we don't collect until Day 105. Somehow, we have to arrange to finance the $1,000 for 105 − 30 = 75 days. This period is called the **cash cycle**.

The cash cycle, therefore, is the number of days that pass before we collect the cash from a sale, measured from when we actually pay for the inventory. Notice that, based on our definitions, the cash cycle is the difference between the operating cycle and the accounts payable period:

$$\begin{aligned}\textbf{Cash cycle} &= \textbf{Operating cycle} - \textbf{Accounts payable period} \\ \textbf{75 days} &= \textbf{105 days} - \textbf{30 days}\end{aligned} \tag{18.5}$$

Figure 18.1 depicts the short-term operating activities and cash flows for a typical manufacturing firm by way of a cash flow time line. As shown, the **cash flow time line** presents the operating cycle and the cash cycle in graphical form. In Figure 18.1, the need for short-term financial management is suggested by the gap between the cash inflows and the cash outflows. This is related to the lengths of the operating cycle and the accounts payable period.

The gap between short-term inflows and outflows can be filled either by borrowing or by holding a liquidity reserve in the form of cash or marketable securities. Alternatively, the gap can be shortened by changing the inventory, receivable, and payable periods. These are all managerial options that we discuss in the following sections.

Learn more about outsourcing accounts management at **www.businessdebts.com** and **www.opiglobal.com**.

Internet-based bookseller and retailer Amazon.com provides an interesting example of the importance of managing the cash cycle. In May 2005, the market value of Amazon.com was higher than (in fact more than five times as much as) that of Barnes & Noble, king of the brick-and-mortar bookstores, even though Barnes & Noble's sales were greater than Amazon's.

How could Amazon.com be worth so much more? There are multiple reasons, but short-term management is one factor. During 2003, Amazon turned over its inventory about 14 times per year, 5 times faster than Barnes & Noble, so its inventory period is dramatically shorter. Even more striking, Amazon charges a customer's credit card when it ships a book, and it usually gets paid by the credit card firm within a day. This means

THE REAL WORLD

A LOOK AT OPERATING AND CASH CYCLES

In 2004, *CFO* magazine published a survey of working capital usage; the results show marked differences in cash and operating cycles across industries. The table below shows four different industries and their operating and cash cycles. Of these, the restaurant industry has the lowest operating and cash cycles. Looking at its components, it is surprising that the industry's receivables period is as long as 10 days (most customers either pay in cash or else use debit/credit cards). In fact, although it is not shown here, McDonald's receivables period is one of the longest in the industry at 16 days. Not surprisingly, restaurants have a short inventory period (we are happy to see this, since we don't like spoiled food).

In contrast to the restaurant business, the medical devices industry has a much longer operating cycle. The long receivables period is the major cause. However, this does not necessarily mean the medical device industry is less efficient. Most, if not all, of the receivables in this industry are paid by medical insurance companies and government medical insurance such as Medicare, but these entities have relatively long payables periods.

	RECEIVABLES PERIOD (DAYS)	INVENTORY PERIOD (DAYS)	OPERATING CYCLE (DAYS)	PAYABLES PERIOD (DAYS)	CASH CYCLE (DAYS)
Apparel retailers	15	54	69	24	45
Clothing manufacturers	51	53	104	21	83
Medical devices firms	79	48	127	8	119
Restaurants	10	6	16	13	3

Operating and cash cycles can also be quite different for companies in the same industry. Below you will find the operating and cash cycles for selected apparel retailers. As you can see, there are major differences. American Eagle Outfitters and Gap have the best operating cycles and cash cycles in the industry. Notice how Kohl's receivables period stands out as being three to eight times larger than the others.

	RECEIVABLES PERIOD (DAYS)	INVENTORY PERIOD (DAYS)	OPERATING CYCLE (DAYS)	PAYABLES PERIOD (DAYS)	CASH CYCLE (DAYS)
American Eagle Outfitters	5	29	34	17	17
Gap	7	39	46	27	19
Kohl's	41	57	98	19	79
Saks	13	87	100	19	81

It is important to examine all parts of the cash cycle and conversion cycle to get the whole picture. For example, looking at the operating cycle for Kohl's and Saks, the companies appear to have similar cycles. However, Kohl's has a long receivables period and a long inventory period. On the other hand, Saks has a relatively short receivables period, but a very long inventory period.

When you look at the operating and cash cycles, consider that each is really a financial ratio. As with any financial ratio, firm and industry characteristics will have an effect, so take care in your interpretation. For example, in looking at Kohl's, we noted its seemingly long receivables period. Is that a bad thing? Maybe not. Many businesses encourage customers to open (and use) charge accounts. By extending credit in this way, companies can increase sales and also earn interest on consumers' outstanding balances. Of course, such operations result in increased receivables, but, properly managed, it can be a good thing.

TABLE 18.1

Managers Who Deal with Short-Term Financial Problems

TITLE OF MANAGER	DUTIES RELATED TO SHORT-TERM FINANCIAL MANAGEMENT	ASSETS/LIABILITIES INFLUENCED
Cash manager	Collection, concentration, disbursement; short-term investments; short-term borrowing; banking relations	Cash, marketable securities, short-term loans
Credit manager	Monitoring and control of accounts receivable; credit policy decisions	Accounts receivable
Marketing manager	Credit policy decisions	Accounts receivable
Purchasing manager	Decisions on purchases, suppliers; may negotiate payment terms	Inventory, accounts payable
Production manager	Setting of production schedules and materials requirements	Inventory, accounts payable
Payables manager	Decisions on payment policies and on whether to take discounts	Accounts payable
Controller	Accounting information on cash flows; reconciliation of accounts payable; application of payments to accounts receivable	Accounts receivable, accounts payable

Amazon has a *negative* cash cycle! In fact, during 2004, Amazon's cash cycle was a negative 41 days. Every sale therefore generates a cash inflow that can be put to work immediately.

To see how important the cash cycle is, consider the case of Sun Microsystems. At the end of 2004, the company had a cash cycle of 40 days, down from 52 days two years earlier. As a result, the company freed up $540 million in cash that it could redeploy along more profitable lines. Our nearby *The Real World* box discusses the cash cycle and operating cycle for several industries, as well as for some specific companies.

The Operating Cycle and the Firm's Organization Chart

Before we examine the operating and cash cycles in greater detail, it is useful for us to take a look at the people involved in managing a firm's current assets and liabilities. As Table 18.1 illustrates, short-term financial management in a large corporation involves a number of different financial and nonfinancial managers. Examining Table 18.1, we see that selling on credit involves at least three different entities: the credit manager, the marketing manager, and the controller. Of these three, only two are responsible to the vice president of finance (the marketing function is usually associated with the vice president of marketing). Thus, there is the potential for conflict, particularly if different managers concentrate on only part of the picture. For example, if marketing is trying to land a new account, it may seek more liberal credit terms as an inducement. However, this may increase the firm's investment in receivables or its exposure to bad-debt risk, and conflict can result.

Calculating the Operating and Cash Cycles

In our example, the lengths of time that made up the different periods were obvious. If all we have is financial statement information, we will have to do a little more work. We illustrate these calculations next.

To begin, we need to determine various things such as how long it takes, on average, to sell inventory and how long it takes, on average, to collect. We start by gathering some balance sheet information such as the following (in thousands):

ITEM	BEGINNING	ENDING	AVERAGE
Inventory	$2,000	$3,000	$2,500
Accounts receivable	1,600	2,000	1,800
Accounts payable	750	1,000	875

Also, from the most recent income statement, we might have the following figures (in thousands):

Net sales	$11,500
Cost of goods sold	8,200

We now need to calculate some financial ratios. We discussed these in some detail in Chapter 3; here, we just define them and use them as needed.

THE OPERATING CYCLE First of all, we need the inventory period. We spent $8.2 million on inventory (our cost of goods sold). Our average inventory was $2.5 million. We thus turned our inventory over $8.2/2.5 times during the year:[1]

$$\textbf{Inventory turnover} = \frac{\textbf{Cost of goods sold}}{\textbf{Average inventory}}$$
$$= \frac{\$8.2 \text{ million}}{2.5 \text{ million}} = 3.28 \text{ times}$$

Loosely speaking, this tells us that we bought and sold off our inventory 3.28 times during the year. This means that, on average, we held our inventory for:

$$\textbf{Inventory period} = \frac{\textbf{365 days}}{\textbf{Inventory turnover}}$$
$$= \frac{365}{3.28} = 111.3 \text{ days}$$

So, the inventory period is about 111 days. On average, in other words, inventory sat for about 111 days before it was sold.[2]

Similarly, receivables averaged $1.8 million, and sales were $11.5 million. Assuming that all sales were credit sales, the receivables turnover is:[3]

$$\textbf{Receivables turnover} = \frac{\textbf{Credit sales}}{\textbf{Average accounts receivable}}$$
$$= \frac{\$11.5 \text{ million}}{1.8 \text{ million}} = 6.4 \text{ times}$$

If we turn over our receivables 6.4 times, then the receivables period is:

$$\textbf{Receivables period} = \frac{\textbf{365 days}}{\textbf{Receivables turnover}}$$
$$= \frac{365}{6.4} = 57 \text{ days}$$

The receivables period is also called the *days' sales in receivables* or the *average collection period.* Whatever it is called, it tells us that our customers took an average of 57 days to pay.

The operating cycle is the sum of the inventory and receivables periods:

$$\textbf{Operating cycle} = \textbf{Inventory period} + \textbf{Accounts receivable period}$$
$$= 111 \text{ days} + 57 \text{ days} = 168 \text{ days}$$

This tells us that, on average, 168 days elapse between the time we acquire inventory and, having sold it, collect for the sale.

[1]Notice that in calculating inventory turnover here, we use the *average* inventory instead of using the ending inventory as we did in Chapter 3. Both approaches are used in the real world. To gain some practice using average figures, we will stick with this approach in calculating various ratios throughout this chapter.

[2]This measure is conceptually identical to the days' sales in inventory figure we discussed in Chapter 3.

[3]If less than 100 percent of our sales were credit sales, then we would just need a little more information, namely, credit sales for the year. See Chapter 3 for more discussion of this measure.

THE CASH CYCLE We now need the payables period. From the information given earlier, we know that average payables were $875,000 and cost of goods sold was $8.2 million. Our payables turnover is:

$$\begin{aligned}\textbf{Payables turnover} &= \frac{\textbf{Cost of goods sold}}{\textbf{Average payables}}\\ &= \frac{\$8.2 \textbf{ million}}{\$.875 \textbf{ million}} = 9.4 \textbf{ times}\end{aligned}$$

The payables period is:

$$\begin{aligned}\textbf{Payables period} &= \frac{\textbf{365 days}}{\textbf{Payables turnover}}\\ &= \frac{365}{9.4} = 39 \textbf{ days}\end{aligned}$$

Thus, we took an average of 39 days to pay our bills.

Finally, the cash cycle is the difference between the operating cycle and the payables period:

$$\begin{aligned}\textbf{Cash cycle} &= \textbf{Operating cycle} - \textbf{Accounts payable period}\\ &= \textbf{168 days} - \textbf{39 days} = \textbf{129 days}\end{aligned}$$

So, on average, there is a 129-day delay between the time we pay for merchandise and the time we collect on the sale.

EXAMPLE 18.2 The Operating and Cash Cycles

You have collected the following information for the Slowpay Company.

ITEM	BEGINNING	ENDING
Inventory	$5,000	$7,000
Accounts receivable	1,600	2,400
Accounts payable	2,700	4,800

Credit sales for the year just ended were $50,000, and cost of goods sold was $30,000. How long does it take Slowpay to collect on its receivables? How long does merchandise stay around before it is sold? How long does Slowpay take to pay its bills?

We can first calculate the three turnover ratios:

Inventory turnover = $30,000/6,000 = 5 times
Receivables turnover = $50,000/2,000 = 25 times
Payables turnover = $30,000/3,750 = 8 times

We use these to get the various periods:

Inventory period = 365/5 = 73 days
Receivables period = 365/25 = 14.6 days
Payables period = 365/8 = 45.6 days

All told, Slowpay collects on a sale in 14.6 days, inventory sits around for 73 days, and bills get paid after about 46 days. The operating cycle here is the sum of the inventory and receivables periods: 73 + 14.6 = 87.6 days. The cash cycle is the difference between the operating cycle and the payables period: 87.6 − 45.6 = 42 days.

Interpreting the Cash Cycle

Our examples show that the cash cycle depends on the inventory, receivables, and payables periods. The cash cycle increases as the inventory and receivables periods get longer. It decreases if the company is able to defer payment of payables and thereby lengthen the payables period.

Unlike Amazon.com, most firms have a positive cash cycle, and they thus require financing for inventories and receivables. The longer the cash cycle, the more financing is required. Also, changes in the firm's cash cycle are often monitored as an early-warning measure. A lengthening cycle can indicate that the firm is having trouble moving inventory or collecting on its receivables. Such problems can be masked, at least partially, by an increased payables cycle, so both cycles should be monitored.

The link between the firm's cash cycle and its profitability can be easily seen by recalling that one of the basic determinants of profitability and growth for a firm is its total asset turnover, which is defined as Sales/Total assets. In Chapter 3, we saw that the higher this ratio is, the greater is the firm's accounting return on assets, ROA, and return on equity, ROE. Thus, all other things being the same, the shorter the cash cycle is, the lower is the firm's investment in inventories and receivables. As a result, the firm's total assets are lower, and total turnover is higher.

18.3 SOME ASPECTS OF SHORT-TERM FINANCIAL POLICY

The short-term financial policy that a firm adopts will be reflected in at least two ways:

1. *The size of the firm's investment in current assets.* This is usually measured relative to the firm's level of total operating revenues. A *flexible,* or accommodative, short-term financial policy would maintain a relatively high ratio of current assets to sales. A *restrictive* short-term financial policy would entail a low ratio of current assets to sales.[4]
2. *The financing of current assets.* This is measured as the proportion of short-term debt (that is, current liabilities) and long-term debt used to finance current assets. A restrictive short-term financial policy means a high proportion of short-term debt relative to long-term financing, and a flexible policy means less short-term debt and more long-term debt.

If we take these two areas together, we see that a firm with a flexible policy would have a relatively large investment in current assets, and it would finance this investment with relatively less in short-term debt. The net effect of a flexible policy is thus a relatively high level of net working capital. Put another way, with a flexible policy, the firm maintains a higher overall level of liquidity.

The Size of the Firm's Investment in Current Assets

Short-term financial policies that are flexible with regard to current assets include such actions as:

1. Keeping large balances of cash and marketable securities.
2. Making large investments in inventory.
3. Granting liberal credit terms, which results in a high level of accounts receivable.

Restrictive short-term financial policies would be just the opposite:

1. Keeping low cash balances and making little investment in marketable securities.
2. Making small investments in inventory.
3. Allowing few or no credit sales, thereby minimizing accounts receivable.

[4]Some people use the term *conservative* in place of *flexible* and the term *aggressive* in place of *restrictive.*

Determining the optimal level of investment in short-term assets requires an identification of the different costs of alternative short-term financing policies. The objective is to trade off the cost of a restrictive policy against the cost of a flexible one to arrive at the best compromise.

Current asset holdings are highest with a flexible short-term financial policy and lowest with a restrictive policy. So, flexible short-term financial policies are costly in that they require a greater investment in cash and marketable securities, inventory, and accounts receivable. However, we expect that future cash inflows will be higher with a flexible policy. For example, sales are stimulated by the use of a credit policy that provides liberal financing to customers. A large amount of finished inventory on hand ("on the shelf") enables quick delivery service to customers and may increase sales. Similarly, a large inventory of raw materials may result in fewer production stoppages because of inventory shortages.

A more restrictive short-term financial policy probably reduces future sales to levels below those that would be achieved under flexible policies. It is also possible that higher prices can be charged to customers under flexible working capital policies. Customers may be willing to pay higher prices for the quick delivery service and more liberal credit terms implicit in flexible policies.

Managing current assets can be thought of as involving a trade-off between costs that rise and costs that fall with the level of investment. Costs that rise with increases in the level of investment in current assets are called **carrying costs**. The larger the investment a firm makes in its current assets, the higher its carrying costs will be. Costs that fall with increases in the level of investment in current assets are called **shortage costs**.

In a general sense, carrying costs are the opportunity costs associated with current assets. The rate of return on current assets is very low when compared to that on other assets. For example, the rate of return on U.S. Treasury bills is usually a good deal less than 10 percent. This is very low compared to the rate of return firms would like to achieve overall. (U.S. Treasury bills are an important component of cash and marketable securities.)

Shortage costs are incurred when the investment in current assets is low. If a firm runs out of cash, it will be forced to sell marketable securities. Of course, if a firm runs out of cash and cannot readily sell marketable securities, it may have to borrow or default on an obligation. This situation is called a *cash-out*. A firm may lose customers if it runs out of inventory (a *stock-out*) or if it cannot extend credit to customers.

More generally, there are two kinds of shortage costs:

1. *Trading, or order, costs.* Order costs are the costs of placing an order for more cash (brokerage costs, for example) or more inventory (production setup costs, for example).
2. *Costs related to lack of safety reserves.* These are costs of lost sales, lost customer goodwill, and disruption of production schedules.

The top part of Figure 18.2 illustrates the basic trade-off between carrying costs and shortage costs. On the vertical axis, we have costs measured in dollars, and, on the horizontal axis, we have the amount of current assets. Carrying costs start out at zero when current assets are zero and then climb steadily as current assets grow. Shortage costs start out very high and then decline as we add current assets. The total cost of holding current assets is the sum of the two. Notice how the combined costs reach a minimum at CA^*. This is the optimal level of current assets.

Optimal current asset holdings are highest under a flexible policy. This policy is one in which the carrying costs are perceived to be low relative to shortage costs. This is Case A in Figure 18.2. In comparison, under restrictive current asset policies, carrying costs are perceived to be high relative to shortage costs, resulting in lower current asset holdings. This is Case B in Figure 18.2.

FIGURE 18.2
Carrying Costs and Shortage Costs

Short-Term Financial Policy: the Optimal Investment in Current Assets

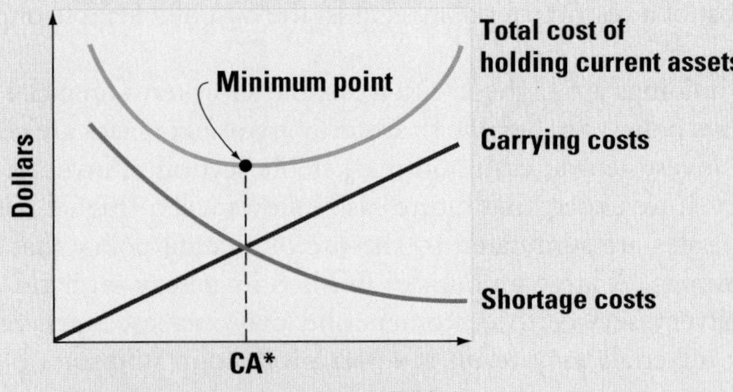

CA* represents the optimal amount of current assets. Holding this amount minimizes total costs.

Carrying costs increase with the level of investment in current assets. They include the costs of maintaining economic value and opportunity costs. Shortage costs decrease with increases in the level of investment in current assets. They include trading costs and the costs related to being short of the current asset (for example, being short of cash). The firm's policy can be characterized as flexible or restrictive.

A. Flexible Policy

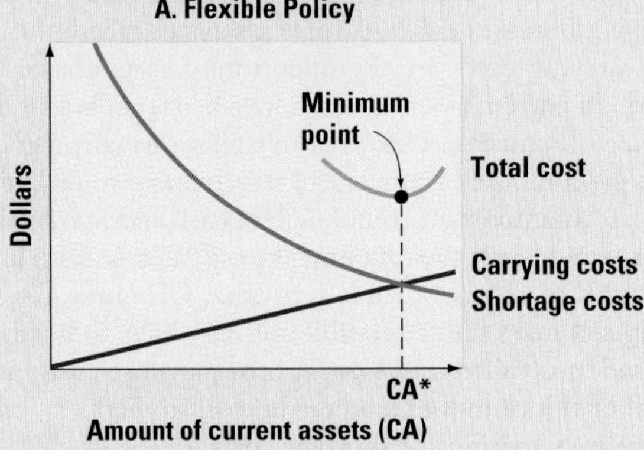

A flexible policy is most appropriate when carrying costs are low relative to shortage costs.

B. Restrictive Policy

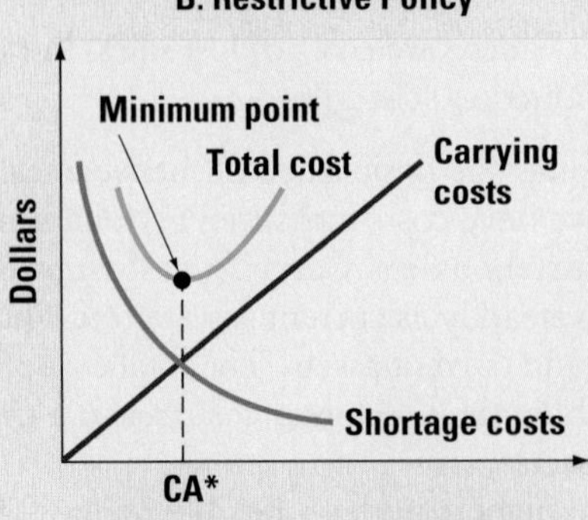

A restrictive policy is most appropriate when carrying costs are high relative to shortage costs.

Alternative Financing Policies for Current Assets

In previous sections, we looked at the basic determinants of the level of investment in current assets, and we thus focused on the asset side of the balance sheet. Now we turn to the financing side of the question. Here we are concerned with the relative amounts of short-term and long-term debt, assuming that the investment in current assets is constant.

AN IDEAL CASE We start off with the simplest possible case: an "ideal" economy. In such an economy, short-term assets can always be financed with short-term debt, and long-term assets can be financed with long-term debt and equity. In this economy, net working capital is always zero.

Consider a simplified case for a grain elevator operator. Grain elevator operators buy crops after harvest, store them, and sell them during the year. They have high inventories of grain after the harvest and end up with low inventories just before the next harvest.

Bank loans with maturities of less than one year are used to finance the purchase of grain and the storage costs. These loans are paid off from the proceeds of the sale of grain.

The situation is shown in Figure 18.3. Long-term assets are assumed to grow over time, whereas current assets increase at the end of the harvest and then decline during the year. Short-term assets end up at zero just before the next harvest. Current (short-term) assets are financed by short-term debt, and long-term assets are financed with long-term debt and equity. Net working capital–current assets minus current liabilities–is always zero. Figure 18.3 displays a "sawtooth" pattern that we will see again when we get to our discussion on cash management in the next chapter. For now, we need to discuss some alternative policies for financing current assets under less idealized conditions.

DIFFERENT POLICIES FOR FINANCING CURRENT ASSETS In the real world, it is not likely that current assets will ever drop to zero. For example, a long-term rising level of sales will result in some permanent investment in current assets. Moreover, the firm's investments in long-term assets may show a great deal of variation.

A growing firm can be thought of as having a total asset requirement consisting of the current assets and long-term assets needed to run the business efficiently. The total asset requirement may exhibit change over time for many reasons, including (1) a general growth trend, (2) seasonal variation around the trend, and (3) unpredictable day-to-day and month-to-month fluctuations. This fluctuation is depicted in Figure 18.4. (We have not tried to show the unpredictable day-to-day and month-to-month variations in the total asset requirement.)

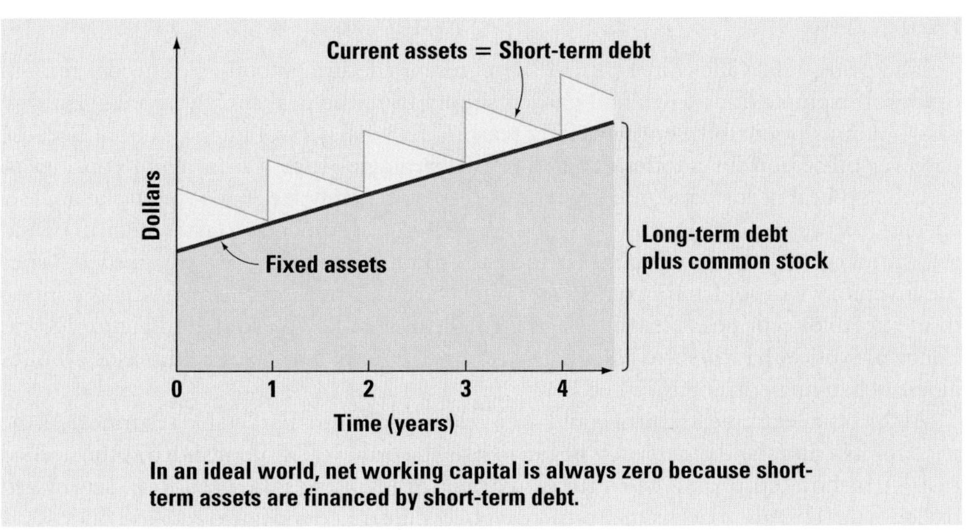

In an ideal world, net working capital is always zero because short-term assets are financed by short-term debt.

FIGURE 18.3
Financing Policy for an Ideal Economy

FIGURE 18.4
The Total Asset Requirement over Time

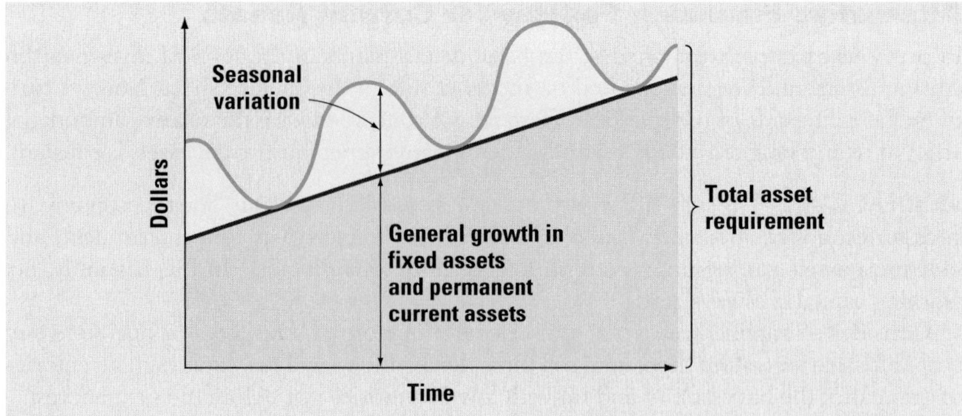

FIGURE 18.5
Alternative Asset Financing Policies

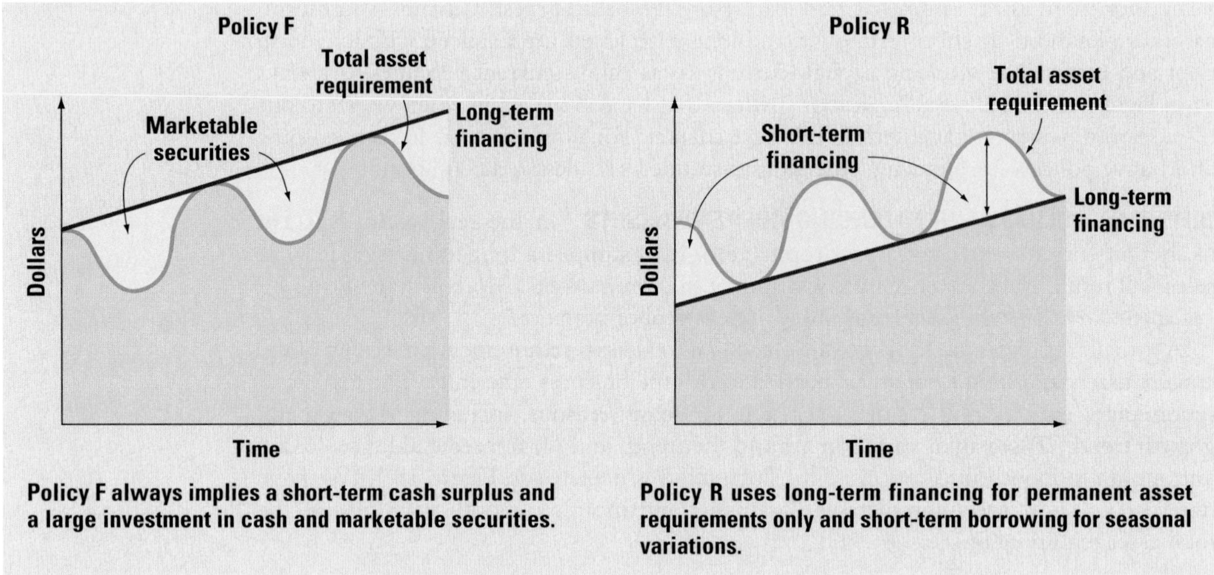

Policy F always implies a short-term cash surplus and a large investment in cash and marketable securities.

Policy R uses long-term financing for permanent asset requirements only and short-term borrowing for seasonal variations.

The peaks and valleys in Figure 18.4 represent the firm's total asset needs through time. For example, for a lawn and garden supply firm, the peaks might represent inventory buildups prior to the spring selling season. The valleys would come about because of lower off-season inventories. There are two strategies such a firm might consider to meet its cyclical needs. First, the firm could keep a relatively large pool of marketable securities. As the need for inventory and other current assets began to rise, the firm would sell off marketable securities and use the cash to purchase whatever was needed. Once the inventory was sold and inventory holdings began to decline, the firm would reinvest in marketable securities. This approach is the flexible policy illustrated in Figure 18.5 as Policy F. Notice that the firm essentially uses a pool of marketable securities as a buffer against changing current asset needs.

At the other extreme, the firm could keep relatively little in marketable securities. As the need for inventory and other assets began to rise, the firm would simply borrow the needed cash on a short-term basis. The firm would repay the loans as the need for assets cycled back down. This approach is the restrictive policy illustrated in Figure 18.5 as Policy R.

In comparing the two strategies illustrated in Figure 18.5, notice that the chief difference is the way in which the seasonal variation in asset needs is financed. In the flexible case, the firm finances internally, using its own cash and marketable securities. In the restrictive case, the firm finances the variation externally, borrowing the needed funds on a short-term basis. As we discussed previously, all else being the same, a firm with a flexible policy will have a greater investment in net working capital.

Which Financing Policy Is Best?

What is the most appropriate amount of short-term borrowing? There is no definitive answer. Several considerations must be included in a proper analysis:

1. *Cash reserves.* The flexible financing policy implies surplus cash and little short-term borrowing. This policy reduces the probability that a firm will experience financial distress. Firms may not have to worry as much about meeting recurring, short-run obligations. However, investments in cash and marketable securities are zero net present value investments at best.
2. *Maturity hedging.* Most firms attempt to match the maturities of assets and liabilities. They finance inventories with short-term bank loans and fixed assets with long-term financing. Firms tend to avoid financing long-lived assets with short-term borrowing. This type of maturity mismatching would necessitate frequent refinancing and is inherently risky because short-term interest rates are more volatile than longer-term rates.
3. *Relative interest rates.* Short-term interest rates are usually lower than long-term rates. This implies that it is, on the average, more costly to rely on long-term borrowing as compared to short-term borrowing.

The two policies, F and R, we depict in Figure 18.5 are, of course, extreme cases. With F, the firm never does any short-term borrowing, and with R, the firm never has a cash reserve (an investment in marketable securities). Figure 18.6 illustrates these two policies along with a compromise, Policy C.

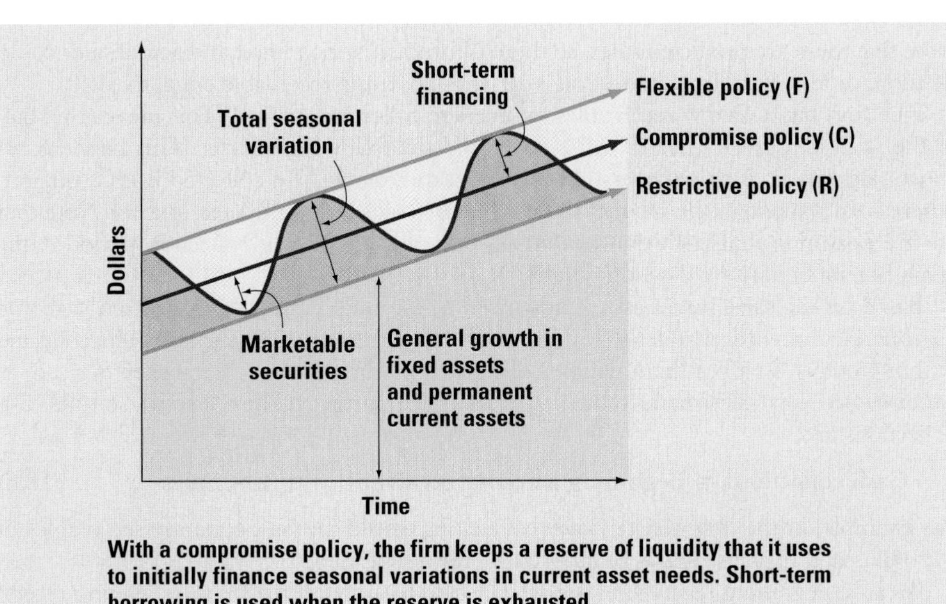

With a compromise policy, the firm keeps a reserve of liquidity that it uses to initially finance seasonal variations in current asset needs. Short-term borrowing is used when the reserve is exhausted.

FIGURE 18.6
A Compromise Financing Policy

With this compromise approach, the firm borrows in the short term to cover peak financing needs, but it maintains a cash reserve in the form of marketable securities during slow periods. As current assets build up, the firm draws down this reserve before doing any short-term borrowing. This allows for some run-up in current assets before the firm has to resort to short-term borrowing.

Current Assets and Liabilities in Practice

Short-term assets represent a significant portion of a typical firm's overall assets. For U.S. manufacturing, mining, and trade corporations, current assets were about 50 percent of total assets in the 1960s. Today, this figure is closer to 40 percent. Most of the decline is due to more efficient cash and inventory management. Over this same period, current liabilities rose from about 20 percent of total liabilities and equity to almost 30 percent. The result is that liquidity (as measured by the ratio of net working capital to total assets) has declined, signaling a move to more restrictive short-term policies.

18.4 THE CASH BUDGET

The **cash budget** is a primary tool in short-run financial planning. It allows the financial manager to identify short-term financial needs and opportunities. An important function of the cash budget is to help the manager explore the need for short-term borrowing. The idea of the cash budget is simple: It records estimates of cash receipts (cash in) and disbursements (cash out). The result is an estimate of the cash surplus or deficit.

Sales and Cash Collections

We start with an example involving the Fun Toys Corporation. We will prepare a quarterly cash budget. We could just as well use a monthly, weekly, or even daily basis. We choose quarters for convenience and also because a quarter is a common short-term business planning period. (Note that, throughout this example, all figures are in millions of dollars.)

All of Fun Toys's cash inflows come from the sale of toys. Cash budgeting for Fun Toys must therefore start with a sales forecast for the coming year, by quarter:

	Q1	Q2	Q3	Q4
Sales (in millions)	$200	$300	$250	$400

Note that these are predicted sales, so there is forecasting risk here, and actual sales could be more or less. Fun Toys started the year with accounts receivable equal to $120.

Fun Toys has a 45-day receivables, or average collection, period. This means that half of the sales in a given quarter will be collected the following quarter. This happens because sales made during the first 45 days of a quarter will be collected in that quarter, whereas sales made in the second 45 days will be collected in the next quarter. Note that we are assuming that each quarter has 90 days, so the 45-day collection period is the same as a half-quarter collection period.

Based on the sales forecasts, we now need to estimate Fun Toys's projected cash collections. First, any receivables that we have at the beginning of a quarter will be collected within 45 days, so all of them will be collected sometime during the quarter. Second, as we discussed, any sales made in the first half of the quarter will be collected, so total cash collections are:

$$\textbf{Cash collections} = \textbf{Beginning accounts receivable} + \mathbf{1/2} \times \textbf{Sales} \qquad \textbf{(18.6)}$$

For example, in the first quarter, cash collections would be the beginning receivables of $120 plus half of sales, $1/2 \times \$200 = \$100$, for a total of $220.

Because beginning receivables are all collected along with half of sales, ending receivables for a particular quarter will be the other half of sales. First-quarter sales are projected

	Q1	Q2	Q3	Q4
Beginning receivables	$120	$100	$150	$125
Sales	200	300	250	400
Cash collections	220	250	275	325
Ending receivables	100	150	125	200

Collections = Beginning receivables + 1/2 × Sales
Ending receivables = Beginning receivables + Sales − Collections
= 1/2 × Sales

TABLE 18.2
Cash Collection for Fun Toys (in millions)

	Q1	Q2	Q3	Q4
Payment of accounts (60% of sales)	$120	$180	$150	$240
Wages, taxes, other expenses	40	60	50	80
Capital expenditures	0	100	0	0
Long-term financing expenses (interest and dividends)	20	20	20	20
Total cash disbursements	$180	$360	$220	$340

TABLE 18.3
Cash Disbursements for Fun Toys (in millions)

at $200, so ending receivables will be $100. This will be the beginning receivables in the second quarter. Cash collections in the second quarter will thus be $100 plus half of the projected $300 in sales, or $250 total.

Continuing this process, we can summarize Fun Toys's projected cash collections as shown in Table 18.2.

In Table 18.2, collections are shown as the only source of cash. Of course, this need not be the case. Other sources of cash could include asset sales, investment income, and receipts from planned long-term financing.

See the Finance Tools section of www.toolkit.cch.com/tools/tools.asp for several useful templates, including a cash flow budget.

Cash Outflows

Next, we consider the cash disbursements, or payments. These come in four basic categories:

1. *Payments of accounts payable.* These are payments for goods or services rendered by suppliers, such as raw materials. Generally, these payments will be made sometime after purchases.
2. *Wages, taxes, and other expenses.* This category includes all other regular costs of doing business that require actual expenditures. Depreciation, for example, is often thought of as a regular cost of business, but it requires no cash outflow and is not included.
3. *Capital expenditures.* These are payments of cash for long-lived assets.
4. *Long-term financing expenses.* This category includes, for example, interest payments on long-term debt outstanding and dividend payments to shareholders.

Fun Toys's purchases from suppliers (in dollars) in a quarter are equal to 60 percent of the next quarter's predicted sales. Fun Toys's payments to suppliers are equal to the previous quarter's purchases, so the accounts payable period is 90 days. For example, in the quarter just ended, Fun Toys ordered .60 × $200 = $120 in supplies. This will actually be paid in the first quarter (Q1) of the coming year.

Wages, taxes, and other expenses are routinely 20 percent of sales; interest and dividends are currently $20 per quarter. In addition, Fun Toys plans a major plant expansion (a capital expenditure) costing $100 in the second quarter. If we put all this information together, the cash outflows are as shown in Table 18.3.

TABLE 18.4
Net Cash Inflow for Fun Toys (in millions)

	Q1	Q2	Q3	Q4
Total cash collections	$220	$250	$275	$325
Total cash disbursements	180	360	220	340
Net cash inflow	$ 40	−$110	$ 55	−$ 15

TABLE 18.5
Cash Balance for Fun Toys (in millions)

	Q1	Q2	Q3	Q4
Beginning cash balance	$20	$ 60	−$50	$ 5
Net cash inflow	40	− 110	55	− 15
Ending cash balance	$60	−$ 50	$ 5	−$10
Minimum cash balance	− 10	− 10	− 10	− 10
Cumulative surplus (deficit)	$50	−$ 60	−$ 5	−$20

The Cash Balance

The predicted *net cash inflow* is the difference between cash collections and cash disbursements. The net cash inflow for Fun Toys is shown in Table 18.4. What we see immediately is that there is a cash surplus in the first and third quarters and a cash deficit in the second and fourth.

We will assume that Fun Toys starts the year with a $20 cash balance. Furthermore, Fun Toys maintains a $10 minimum cash balance to guard against unforeseen contingencies and forecasting errors. So, the company starts the first quarter with $20 in cash. This amount rises by $40 during the quarter, and the ending balance is $60. Of this, $10 is reserved as a minimum, so we subtract it out and find that the first quarter surplus is $60 − 10 = $50.

Fun Toys starts the second quarter with $60 in cash (the ending balance from the previous quarter). There is a net cash inflow of −$110, so the ending balance is $60 − 110 = −$50. We need another $10 as a buffer, so the total deficit is −$60. These calculations and those for the last two quarters are summarized in Table 18.5.

At the beginning of the second quarter, Fun Toys has a cash shortfall of $60. This occurs because of the seasonal pattern of sales (higher towards the end of the second quarter), the delay in collections, and the planned capital expenditure.

The cash situation at Fun Toys is projected to improve to a $5 deficit in the third quarter, but, by year's end, Fun Toys still has a $20 deficit. Without some sort of financing, this deficit will carry over into the next year. We explore this subject in the next section.

For now, we can make the following general comments on Fun Toys's cash needs:

1. Fun Toys's large outflow in the second quarter is not necessarily a sign of trouble. It results from delayed collections on sales and a planned capital expenditure (presumably a worthwhile one).
2. The figures in our example are based on a forecast. Sales could be much worse (or better) than the forecasted figures.

18.5 SHORT-TERM BORROWING

Fun Toys has a short-term financing problem. It cannot meet the forecasted cash outflows in the second quarter using internal sources. How it will finance that shortfall depends on its financial policy. With a very flexible policy, Fun Toys might seek up to $60 million in long-term debt financing.

In addition, note that much of the cash deficit comes from the large capital expenditure. Arguably, this is a candidate for long-term financing. Nonetheless, because we have discussed long-term financing elsewhere, we will concentrate here on two short-term borrowing options: (1) unsecured borrowing and (2) secured borrowing.

Unsecured Loans

The most common way to finance a temporary cash deficit is to arrange a short-term unsecured bank loan. Firms that use short-term bank loans often arrange for a line of credit. A **line of credit** is an agreement under which a firm is authorized to borrow up to a specified amount. To ensure that the line is used for short-term purposes, the lender will sometimes require the borrower to pay the line down to zero and keep it there for some period during the year, typically 60 days (called a *cleanup period*).

Short-term lines of credit are classified as either *committed* or *noncommitted.* The latter type is an informal arrangement that allows firms to borrow up to a previously specified limit without going through the normal paperwork (much as they would with a credit card). A *revolving credit arrangement* (or just *revolver*) is similar to a line of credit, but it is usually open for two or more years, whereas a line of credit would usually be evaluated on an annual basis.

Committed lines of credit are more formal legal arrangements and usually involve a commitment fee paid by the firm to the bank (usually the fee is on the order of .25 percent of the total committed funds per year). The interest rate on the line of credit is usually set equal to the bank's prime lending rate plus an additional percentage, and the rate will usually float. A firm that pays a commitment fee for a committed line of credit is essentially buying insurance to guarantee that the bank can't back out of the agreement (absent some material change in the borrower's status).

COMPENSATING BALANCES As a part of a credit line or other lending arrangement, banks will sometimes require that the firm keep some amount of money on deposit. This is called a compensating balance. A **compensating balance** is some of the firm's money kept by the bank in low-interest or noninterest-bearing accounts. By leaving these funds with the bank and receiving little or no interest, the firm further increases the effective interest rate earned by the bank on the line of credit, thereby "compensating" the bank. A compensating balance might be on the order of 2 to 5 percent of the amount borrowed.

Firms also use compensating balances to pay for noncredit bank services such as cash management services. A traditionally contentious issue is whether the firm should pay for bank credit and noncredit services with fees or with compensating balances. Most major firms have now negotiated for banks to use the corporation's collected funds for compensation and use fees to cover any shortfall. Arrangements such as this one and some similar approaches discussed in the next chapter make the subject of minimum balances less of an issue than it once was.

COST OF A COMPENSATING BALANCE A compensating balance requirement has an obvious opportunity cost because the money often must be deposited in an account with a zero or low interest rate. For example, suppose that we have a $100,000 line of credit with a 10 percent compensating balance requirement. This means that 10 percent of the amount actually used must be left on deposit in a noninterest-bearing account.

The quoted interest rate on the credit line is 16 percent. Suppose we need $54,000 to purchase some inventory. How much do we have to borrow? What interest rate are we effectively paying?

If we need \$54,000, we have to borrow enough so that \$54,000 is left over after we take out the 10 percent compensating balance:

$$\$54{,}000 = (1 - .10) \times \text{Amount borrowed}$$
$$\$60{,}000 = \$54{,}000/.90 = \text{Amount borrowed}$$

The interest on the \$60,000 for one year at 16 percent is $\$60{,}000 \times .16 = \$9{,}600$. We're actually only getting \$54,000 to use, so the effective interest rate is:

$$\begin{aligned}\text{Effective interest rate} &= \text{Interest paid/Amount available}\\ &= \$9{,}600/54{,}000\\ &= 17.78\%\end{aligned}$$

Notice that what effectively happens here is that we pay 16 cents in interest on every 90 cents we borrow because we don't get to use the 10 cents tied up in the compensating balance. The interest rate is thus $.16/.90 = 17.78$ percent, as we calculated.

Several points bear mentioning. First, compensating balances are usually computed as a monthly *average* of the daily balances. This means that the effective interest rate may be lower than our example illustrates. Second, it has become common for compensating balances to be based on the *unused* amount of the credit line. The requirement of such a balance amounts to an implicit commitment fee. Third, and most important, the details of short-term business lending arrangements are highly negotiable. Banks will generally work with firms to design a package of fees and interest.

LETTERS OF CREDIT A *letter of credit* is a common arrangement in international finance. With a letter of credit, the bank issuing the letter promises to make a loan if certain conditions are met. Typically, the letter guarantees payment on a shipment of goods provided that the goods arrive as promised. A letter of credit can be revocable (subject to cancellation) or irrevocable (not subject to cancellation if the specified conditions are met).

Secured Loans

Banks and other finance companies often require security for a short-term loan just as they do for a long-term loan. Security for short-term loans usually consists of accounts receivable, inventories, or both.

ACCOUNTS RECEIVABLE FINANCING **Accounts receivable financing** involves either *assigning* receivables or *factoring* receivables. Under assignment, the lender has the receivables as security, but the borrower is still responsible if a receivable can't be collected. With *conventional factoring,* the receivable is discounted and sold to the lender (the factor). Once it is sold, collection is the factor's problem, and the factor assumes the full risk of default on bad accounts. With *maturity factoring,* the factor forwards the money on an agreed-upon future date.

For more on factoring, see www.factors.com.

Factors play a particularly important role in the retail industry. Retailers in the clothing business, for example, must buy large amounts of new clothes at the beginning of the season. Because this is typically a long time before they have sold anything, they wait to pay their suppliers, sometimes 30 to 60 days. If an apparel maker can't wait that long, it turns to factors, who buy the receivables and take over collection. In fact, the garment industry accounts for about 80 percent of all factoring in the United States.

Factoring can also be important elsewhere. For instance, in May 2004 Moody's upgraded the credit rating of graphite and carbon products specialist Graftech International. One of the reasons given for the upgrade was the increased liquidity Graftech had because of its accounts receivable factoring.

EXAMPLE 18.3 Cost of Factoring

For the year just ended, LuLu's Pies had an average of $50,000 in accounts receivable. Credit sales were $500,000. LuLu's factors its receivables by discounting them 3 percent, in other words, by selling them for 97 cents on the dollar. What is the effective interest rate on this source of short-term financing?

To determine the interest rate, we first have to know the accounts receivable, or average collection, period. During the year, LuLu's turned over its receivables $500,000/50,000 = 10 times. The average collection period is therefore 365/10 = 36.5 days.

The interest paid here is a form of discount interest (discussed in Chapter 4). In this case, LuLu's is paying 3 cents in interest on every 97 cents of financing. The interest rate per 36.5 days is thus .03/.97 = 3.09 percent. The APR is 10 × 3.09 percent = 30.9 percent, but the effective annual rate is:

$$\text{EAR} = 1.0309^{10} - 1 = 35.6\%$$

Factoring is a relatively expensive source of money in this case.

We should note that, if the factor takes on the risk of default by a buyer, then the factor is providing insurance as well as immediate cash. More generally, the factor essentially takes over the firm's credit operations. This can result in a significant savings. The interest rate we calculated is therefore overstated, particularly if default is a significant possibility.

INVENTORY LOANS **Inventory loans**, short-term loans to purchase inventory, come in three basic forms: blanket inventory liens, trust receipts, and field warehouse financing:

1. *Blanket inventory lien.* A blanket lien gives the lender a lien against all the borrower's inventories (the blanket "covers" everything).
2. *Trust receipt.* A trust receipt is a device by which the borrower holds specific inventory in "trust" for the lender. Automobile dealer financing, for example, is done by use of trust receipts. This type of secured financing is also called *floor planning,* in reference to inventory on the showroom floor. However, it is somewhat cumbersome to use trust receipts for, say, wheat grain.
3. *Field warehouse financing.* In field warehouse financing, a public warehouse company (an independent company that specializes in inventory management) acts as a control agent to supervise the inventory for the lender.

Other Sources

There are a variety of other sources of short-term funds employed by corporations. Two of the most important are *commercial paper* and *trade credit.*

Commercial paper consists of short-term notes issued by large and highly rated firms. Typically, these notes are of short maturity, ranging up to 270 days (beyond that limit, the firm must file a registration statement with the SEC). Because the firm issues these directly and because it usually backs the issue with a special bank line of credit, the interest rate the firm obtains is often significantly below the rate a bank would charge for a direct loan.

Another option available to a firm is to increase the accounts payable period; in other words, the firm may take longer to pay its bills. This amounts to borrowing from suppliers in the form of trade credit. This is an extremely important form of financing for smaller businesses in particular. However, a firm using trade credit may end up paying a much higher price for what it purchases, so this can be a very expensive source of financing.

18.6 A SHORT-TERM FINANCIAL PLAN

To illustrate a completed short-term financial plan, we will assume that Fun Toys arranges to borrow any needed funds on a short-term basis. The interest rate is a 20 percent APR, and it is calculated on a quarterly basis. From Chapter 4, we know that the rate is 20 percent/4 = 5 percent per quarter. We will assume that Fun Toys starts the year with no short-term debt.

From Table 18.5, we know that Fun Toys has a second-quarter deficit of $60 million. The firm will have to borrow this amount. Net cash inflow in the following quarter is $55 million. The firm will now have to pay $60 million × .05 = $3 million in interest out of that, leaving $52 million to reduce the borrowing.

Fun Toys still owes $60 million − 52 million = $8 million at the end of the third quarter. Interest in the last quarter will thus be $8 million × .05 = $.4 million. In addition, net inflows in the last quarter are −$15 million, so the company will have to borrow a total of $15.4 million, bringing total borrowing up to $15.4 million + 8 million = $23.4 million. Table 18.6 extends Table 18.5 to include these calculations.

Notice that the ending short-term debt is just equal to the cumulative deficit for the entire year, $20 million, plus the interest paid during the year, $3 million + .4 million = $3.4 million, for a total of $23.4 million.

Our plan is very simple. For example, we ignored the fact that the interest paid on the short-term debt is tax deductible. We also ignored the fact that the cash surplus in the first quarter would earn some interest (which would be taxable). We could add on a number of refinements. Even so, our plan highlights the fact that in about 90 days, Fun Toys will need to borrow $60 million or so on a short-term basis. It's time to start lining up the source of the funds.

Our plan also illustrates that financing the firm's short-term needs will cost about $3.4 million in interest (before taxes) for the year. This is a starting point for Fun Toys to begin evaluating alternatives to reduce this expense. For example, can the $100 million planned expenditure be postponed or spread out? At 5 percent per quarter, short-term credit is expensive.

Also, if Fun Toys's sales are expected to keep growing, then the deficit of $20 million–plus will probably also keep growing, and the need for additional financing will be permanent. Fun Toys may wish to think about raising money on a long-term basis to cover this need.

TABLE 18.6
Short-Term Financial Plan for Fun Toys (in millions)

	Q1	Q2	Q3	Q4
Beginning cash balance	$20	$ 60	$10	$10.0
Net cash inflow	40	− 110	55	− 15.0
New short-term borrowing	—	60	—	15.4
Interest on short-term borrowing	—	—	− 3	− .4
Short-term borrowing repaid	—	—	− 52	—
Ending cash balance	$60	$ 10	$10	$10.0
Minimum cash balance	− 10	− 10	− 10	− 10.0
Cumulative surplus (deficit)	$50	$ 0	$ 0	$ 0.0
Beginning short-term borrowing	0	0	60	8.0
Change in short-term debt	0	60	− 52	15.4
Ending short-term debt	$ 0	$ 60	$ 8	$23.4

SUMMARY AND CONCLUSIONS

1. This chapter has introduced the management of short-term finance. Short-term finance involves short-lived assets and liabilities. We trace and examine the short-term sources and uses of cash as they appear on the firm's financial statements. We see how current assets and current liabilities arise in the short-term operating activities and the cash cycle of the firm.
2. Managing short-term cash flows involves the minimizing of costs. The two major costs are carrying costs, the return forgone by keeping too much invested in short-term assets such as cash, and shortage costs, the cost of running out of short-term assets. The objective of managing short-term finance and doing short-term financial planning is to find the optimal trade-off between these two costs.
3. In an ideal economy, the firm could perfectly predict its short-term uses and sources of cash, and net working capital could be kept at zero. In the real world we live in, cash and net working capital provide a buffer that lets the firm meet its ongoing obligations. The financial manager seeks the optimal level of each of the current assets.
4. The financial manager can use the cash budget to identify short-term financial needs. The cash budget tells the manager what borrowing is required or what lending will be possible in the short run. The firm has available to it a number of possible ways of acquiring funds to meet short-term shortfalls, including unsecured and secured loans.

CONCEPT QUESTIONS

1. **Operating Cycle** What are some of the characteristics of a firm with a long operating cycle?
2. **Cash Cycle** What are some of the characteristics of a firm with a long cash cycle?
3. **Sources and Uses** For the year just ended, you have gathered the following information on the Holly Corporation:
   a. A $200 dividend was paid.
   b. Accounts payable increased by $500.
   c. Fixed asset purchases were $900.
   d. Inventories increased by $625.
   e. Long-term debt decreased by $1,200.

   Label each as a source or use of cash and describe its effect on the firm's cash balance.
4. **Cost of Current Assets** Loftis Manufacturing, Inc., has recently installed a just-in-time (JIT) inventory system. Describe the effect this is likely to have on the company's carrying costs, shortage costs, and operating cycle.
5. **Operating and Cash Cycles** Is it possible for a firm's cash cycle to be longer than its operating cycle? Explain why or why not.
6. **Shortage Costs** What are the costs of shortages? Describe them.
7. **Reasons for Net Working Capital** In an ideal economy, net working capital is always zero. Why might net working capital be positive in a real economy?

Use the following information to answer Questions 8–12: Last month, BlueSky Airline announced that it would stretch out its bill payments to 45 days from 30 days. The reason given was that the company wanted to "control costs and optimize cash flow." The increased payables period will be in effect for all of the company's 4,000 suppliers.

8. **Operating and Cash Cycles** What impact did this change in payables policy have on BlueSky's operating cycle? Its cash cycle?

9. **Operating and Cash Cycles** What impact did the announcement have on BlueSky's suppliers?
10. **Corporate Ethics** Is it ethical for large firms to unilaterally lengthen their payables periods, particularly when dealing with smaller suppliers?
11. **Payables Period** Why don't all firms simply increase their payables periods to shorten their cash cycles?
12. **Payables Period** BlueSky lengthened its payables period to "control costs and optimize cash flow." Exactly what is the cash benefit to BlueSky from this change?

QUESTIONS AND PROBLEMS

TM

Basic
(Questions 1–12)

1. **Changes in the Cash Account** Indicate the impact of the following corporate actions on cash, using the letter *I* for an increase, *D* for a decrease, or *N* when no change occurs.
   a. A dividend is paid with funds received from a sale of debt.
   b. Real estate is purchased and paid for with short-term debt.
   c. Inventory is bought on credit.
   d. A short-term bank loan is repaid.
   e. Next year's taxes are prepaid.
   f. Preferred stock is redeemed.
   g. Sales are made on credit.
   h. Interest on long-term debt is paid.
   i. Payments for previous sales are collected.
   j. The accounts payable balance is reduced.
   k. A dividend is paid.
   l. Production supplies are purchased and paid for with a short-term note.
   m. Utility bills are paid.
   n. Cash is paid for raw materials purchased for inventory.
   o. Marketable securities are sold.
2. **Cash Equation** McConnell Corp. has a book net worth of $9,300. Long-term debt is $1,900. Net working capital, other than cash, is $2,450. Fixed assets are $2,300. How much cash does the company have? If current liabilities are $1,250, what are current assets?
3. **Changes in the Operating Cycle** Indicate the effect that the following will have on the operating cycle. Use the letter *I* to indicate an increase, the letter *D* for a decrease, and the letter *N* for no change.
   a. Receivables average goes up.
   b. Credit repayment times for customers are increased.
   c. Inventory turnover goes from 3 times to 6 times.
   d. Payables turnover goes from 6 times to 11 times.
   e. Receivables turnover goes from 7 times to 9 times.
   f. Payments to suppliers are accelerated.
4. **Changes in Cycles** Indicate the impact of the following on the cash and operating cycles, respectively. Use the letter *I* to indicate an increase, the letter *D* for a decrease, and the letter *N* for no change.

a. The terms of cash discounts offered to customers are made less favorable.

b. The cash discounts offered by suppliers are increased; thus, payments are made earlier.

c. An increased number of customers begin to pay in cash instead of with credit.

d. Fewer raw materials than usual are purchased.

e. A greater percentage of raw material purchases are paid for with credit.

f. More finished goods are produced for inventory instead of for order.

5. **Calculating Cash Collections** The Litzenberger Company has projected the following quarterly sales amounts for the coming year: 

	Q1	Q2	Q3	Q4
Sales	$800	$760	$940	$870

a. Accounts receivable at the beginning of the year are $300. Litzenberger has a 45-day collection period. Calculate cash collections in each of the four quarters by completing the following:

	Q1	Q2	Q3	Q4
Beginning receivables				
Sales				
Cash collections				
Ending receivables				

b. Rework (a) assuming a collection period of 60 days.

c. Rework (a) assuming a collection period of 30 days.

6. **Calculating Cycles** Consider the following financial statement information for the Bulldog Icers Corporation:

ITEM	BEGINNING		ENDING
Inventory	$8,413		$10,158
Accounts receivable	5,108		5,439
Accounts payable	6,927		7,625
Net sales		$67,312	
Cost of goods sold		52,827	

Calculate the operating and cash cycles. How do you interpret your answer?

7. **Factoring Receivables** Your firm has an average collection period of 34 days. Current practice is to factor all receivables immediately at a 2 percent discount. What is the effective cost of borrowing in this case? Assume that default is extremely unlikely.

8. **Calculating Payments** Lewellen Products has projected the following sales for the coming year: 

	Q1	Q2	Q3	Q4
Sales	$540	$630	$710	$785

Sales in the year following this one are projected to be 15 percent greater in each quarter.

a. Calculate payments to suppliers assuming that Lewellen places orders during each quarter equal to 30 percent of projected sales for the next quarter. Assume that the company pays immediately. What is the payables period in this case?

	Q1	Q2	Q3	Q4
Payment of accounts	$	$	$	$

b. Rework (a) assuming a 90-day payables period.

	Q1	Q2	Q3	Q4
Payment of accounts	$	$	$	$

c. Rework (a) assuming a 60-day payables period.

	Q1	Q2	Q3	Q4
Payment of accounts	$	$	$	$

9. **Calculating Payments** The Thakor Corporation's purchases from suppliers in a quarter are equal to 75 percent of the next quarter's forecasted sales. The payables period is 60 days. Wages, taxes, and other expenses are 20 percent of sales, and interest and dividends are $60 per quarter. No capital expenditures are planned.

   Projected quarterly sales are:

	Q1	Q2	Q3	Q4
Sales	$750	$920	$890	$790

Sales for the first quarter of the following year are projected at $970. Calculate the company's cash outlays by completing the following:

	Q1	Q2	Q3	Q4
Payment of accounts				
Wages, taxes, other expenses				
Long-term financing expenses (interest and dividends)				
Total				

10. **Calculating Cash Collections** The following is the sales budget for Shleifer, Inc., for the first quarter of 2006:

	JANUARY	FEBRUARY	MARCH
Sales budget	$150,000	$173,000	$194,000

Credit sales are collected as follows:

65 percent in the month of the sale

20 percent in the month after the sale

15 percent in the second month after the sale

The accounts receivable balance at the end of the previous quarter was $57,000 ($41,000 of which was uncollected December sales).

a. Compute the sales for November.

b. Compute the sales for December.

c. Compute the cash collections from sales for each month from January through March.

11. **Calculating the Cash Budget** Here are some important figures from the budget of Cornell, Inc., for the second quarter of 2006:

	APRIL	MAY	JUNE
Credit sales	$380,000	$396,000	$438,000
Credit purchases	147,000	175,500	200,500
Cash disbursements			
Wages, taxes, and expenses	39,750	48,210	50,300
Interest	11,400	11,400	11,400
Equipment purchases	83,000	91,000	0

The company predicts that 5 percent of its credit sales will never be collected, 35 percent of its sales will be collected in the month of the sale, and the remaining 60 percent will be collected in the following month. Credit purchases will be paid in the month following the purchase.

In March 2006, credit sales were $210,000, and credit purchases were $156,000. Using this information, complete the following cash budget:

		APRIL	MAY	JUNE
Beginning cash balance	$280,000			
Cash receipts				
Cash collections from credit sales				
Total cash available				
Cash disbursements				
Purchases				
Wages, taxes, and expenses				
Interest				
Equipment purchases				
Total cash disbursements				
Ending cash balance				

12. **Sources and Uses** Below are the most recent balance sheets for Country Kettles, Inc. Excluding accumulated depreciation, determine whether each item is a source or a use of cash, and the amount.

COUNTRY KETTLES, INC.
Balance Sheet
December 31, 2006

	2006	2005
Assets		
Cash	$ 42,000	$ 35,000
Accounts receivable	94,250	84,500
Inventory	78,750	75,000
Property, plant, equipment	181,475	168,750
Less: Accumulated depreciation	61,475	56,250
Total assets	$335,000	$307,000
Liabilities and Equity		
Accounts payable	$ 60,500	$ 55,000
Accrued expenses	5,150	8,450
Long-term debt	15,000	30,000
Common stock	28,000	25,000
Accumulated retained earnings	226,350	188,550
Total liabilities and equity	$335,000	$307,000

Intermediate (Questions 13–16)

13. **Costs of Borrowing** You've worked out a line of credit arrangement that allows you to borrow up to $60 million at any time. The interest rate is .61 percent per month. In addition, 4 percent of the amount that you borrow must be deposited in a noninterest-bearing account. Assume that your bank uses compound interest on its line of credit loans.
    a. What is the effective annual interest rate on this lending arrangement?
    b. Suppose you need $15 million today and you repay it in six months. How much interest will you pay?
14. **Costs of Borrowing** A bank offers your firm a revolving credit arrangement for up to $100 million at an interest rate of 2.20 percent per quarter. The bank also requires you to maintain a compensating balance of 5 percent against the *unused* portion of the credit line, to be deposited in a noninterest-bearing account. Assume you have a short-term investment account at the bank that pays 1.40 percent per quarter, and assume that the bank uses compound interest on its revolving credit loans.
    a. What is your effective annual interest rate (an opportunity cost) on the revolving credit arrangement if your firm does not use it during the year?
    b. What is your effective annual interest rate on the lending arrangement if you borrow $60 million immediately and repay it in one year?
    c. What is your effective annual interest rate if you borrow $100 million immediately and repay it in one year?
15. **Calculating the Cash Budget** Wildcat, Inc., has estimated sales (in millions) for the next four quarters as:

	Q1	Q2	Q3	Q4
Sales	$230	$195	$270	$290

Sales for the first quarter of the year after this one are projected at $250 million. Accounts receivable at the beginning of the year were $79 million. Wildcat has a 45-day collection period.

Wildcat's purchases from suppliers in a quarter are equal to 45 percent of the next quarter's forecasted sales, and suppliers are normally paid in 36 days. Wages, taxes, and other expenses run about 30 percent of sales. Interest and dividends are $15 million per quarter.

Wildcat plans a major capital outlay in the second quarter of $90 million. Finally, the company started the year with a $73 million cash balance and wishes to maintain a $30 million minimum balance.

a. Complete a cash budget for Wildcat by filling in the following:

WILDCAT, INC. Cash Budget (in millions)				
	Q1	Q2	Q3	Q4
Beginning cash balance	$73			
Net cash inflow				
Ending cash balance				
Minimum cash balance	30			
Cumulative surplus (deficit)				

b. Assume that Wildcat can borrow any needed funds on a short-term basis at a rate of 3 percent per quarter, and can invest any excess funds in short-term marketable securities at a rate of 2 percent per quarter. Prepare a short-term financial plan by filling in the following schedule. What is the net cash cost (total interest paid minus total investment income earned) for the year?

WILDCAT, INC. Short-Term Financial Plan (in millions)				
	Q1	Q2	Q3	Q4
Beginning cash balance	$73			
Net cash inflow				
New short-term investments				
Income from short-term investments				
Short-term investments sold				
New short-term borrowing				
Interest on short-term borrowing				
Short-term borrowing repaid				
Ending cash balance				
Minimum cash balance	30			
Cumulative surplus (deficit)				
Beginning short-term investments				
Ending short-term investments				
Beginning short-term debt				
Ending short-term debt				

16. **Cash Management Policy** Rework Problem 15 assuming:

    a. Wildcat maintains a minimum cash balance of $45 million.

    b. Wildcat maintains a minimum cash balance of $15 million.

    Based on your answers in (a) and (b), do you think the firm can boost its profit by changing its cash management policy? Are there other factors that must be considered as well? Explain.

Challenge (Questions 17–18)

17. **Costs of Borrowing** In exchange for a $500 million fixed commitment line of credit, your firm has agreed to do the following:

    1. Pay 1.3 percent per quarter on any funds actually borrowed.
    2. Maintain a 4 percent compensating balance on any funds actually borrowed.
    3. Pay an up-front commitment fee of .105 percent of the amount of the line.

    Based on this information, answer the following:

    a. Ignoring the commitment fee, what is the effective annual interest rate on this line of credit?

    b. Suppose your firm immediately uses $210 million of the line and pays it off in one year. What is the effective annual interest rate on this $210 million loan?

18. **Costs of Borrowing** DeAngelo Bank offers your firm an 8 percent *discount* interest loan for up to $8 million, and in addition requires you to maintain a 6 percent compensating balance against the amount borrowed. What is the effective annual interest rate on this lending arrangement?

STANDARD
&POOR'S

S&P PROBLEMS

www.mhhe.com/edumarketinsight

1. **Cash and Operating Cycles** Find the most recent financial statements for Dell Computer (DELL) and Boeing (BA). Calculate the cash and operating cycle for each company for the most recent year. Are the numbers similar for these companies? Why or why not?
2. **Cash and Operating Cycles** Download the most recent quarterly financial statements for Wal-Mart (WMT). Calculate the operating and cash cycle for Wal-Mart over each of the last four quarters. Comment on any changes in the operating or cash cycle over this period.

WHAT'S ON THE WEB?

1. **Cash Cycle** Go to www.investor.reuters.com. You will need to find the most recent annual income statement and two most recent balance sheets for BJ Services Company (BJS) and Avon Products (AVP). Both companies are on the S&P 500 Index. BJS is a provider of pressure pumping and other oilfield services, while AVP is a manufacturer and marketer of beauty and related products. Calculate the cash cycle for each company and comment on any similarities or differences.
2. **Operating Cycle** Using the information you gathered in the previous problem, calculate the operating cycle for each company. What are the similarities or differences? Is this what you would expect from companies in each of these industries?

CLOSING CASE

KEAFER MANUFACTURING WORKING CAPITAL MANAGEMENT

You have recently been hired by Keafer Manufacturing to work in its newly established treasury department. Keafer Manufacturing is a small company that produces highly customized cardboard boxes in a variety of sizes for different purchasers. Adam Keafer, the owner of the company, works primarily in the sales and production areas of the company. Currently, the company basically puts all receivables in one pile and all payables in another, and a part-time bookkeeper periodically comes in and attacks the piles. Because of this disorganized system, the finance area needs work, and that's what you've been brought in to do.

The company currently has a cash balance of $115,000, and it plans to purchase new machinery in the third quarter at a cost of $200,000. The purchase of the machinery will be made with cash because of the discount offered for a cash purchase. Adam wants to maintain a minimum cash balance of $90,000 to guard against unforeseen contingencies. All of Keafer's sales to customers and purchases from suppliers are made with credit, and no discounts are offered or taken.

The company had the following sales each quarter of the year just ended:

	Q1	Q2	Q3	Q4
Gross sales	$565,000	$585,000	$628,000	$545,000

After some research and discussions with customers, you're projecting that sales will be 8 percent higher in each quarter next year. Sales for the first quarter of the following year are also expected to grow at 8 percent. You calculate that Keafer currently has an accounts receivable period of 57 days and an accounts receivable balance of $426,000. However, 10 percent of the accounts receivable balance is from a company that has just entered bankruptcy, and it is likely that this portion will never be collected.

You've also calculated that Keafer typically orders supplies each quarter in the amount of 50 percent of the next quarter's projected gross sales, and suppliers are paid in 53 days on average. Wages, taxes, and other costs run about 25 percent of gross sales. The company has a quarterly interest payment of $120,000 on its long-term debt. Finally, the company uses a local bank for its short-term financial needs. It currently pays 1.2 percent per quarter on all short-term borrowing and maintains a money market account that pays .5 percent per quarter on all short-term deposits.

Adam has asked you to prepare a cash budget and short-term financial plan for the company under the current policies. He has also asked you to prepare additional plans based on changes in several inputs.

1. Use the numbers given to complete the cash budget and short-term financial plan.
2. Rework the cash budget and short-term financial plan assuming Keafer changes to a minimum cash balance of $70,000.
3. Rework the sales budget assuming an 11 percent growth rate in sales and a 5 percent growth rate in sales. Assume a $90,000 target cash balance.
4. Assuming the company maintains its target cash balance at $90,000, what sales growth rate would result in a zero need for short-term financing? To answer this question, you may need to set up a spreadsheet and use the "Solver" function.
5. You have looked at competitors' credit policies and have determined that the industry standard credit policy is 1/10, net 45. The interpretation of these credit terms is that a purchaser will receive a 1 percent discount on sales if it pays within 10 days. If the purchaser does not pay within 10 days, the full sales price is due in 45 days. You want to examine how a switch to this credit policy would affect your cash budget and short-term financial plan. If this credit policy is implemented, you estimate that 25 percent of all customers will take advantage of it, and the accounts receivable period will decline to 38 days. Rework the cash budget and short-term financial plan under the new credit policy and a minimum cash balance of $90,000. What interest rate is implied by the credit terms?
6. You have talked to the company's main supplier about the credit terms Keafer receives. The supplier has stated that it would be willing to offer new credit terms of 2/15, net 40. The interpretation of these credit terms is that Keafer will receive a 2 percent discount on sales if it pays within 15 days. If it does not pay within 15 days, the full sales price will be due in 40 days. What interest rate are the suppliers offering the company? Rework the cash budget and short-term financial plan assuming you take the credit terms on all orders and the minimum cash balance is $90,000.

19 CHAPTER

Mergers and Acquisitions

OPENING CASE

In December 2004, communications companies Sprint and Nextel finalized a much-anticipated merger. The deal was structured as a "merger of equals," meaning that shareholders of the existing companies would each end up owning about 50 percent of the new company, Sprint Nextel. The new company would be the third-largest wireless phone service, with roughly 38.5 million subscribers. According to the companies, Sprint Nextel would achieve operating cost and capital investment synergies with an expected net present value of $12 billion, an enormous benefit. How do companies like Nextel and Sprint determine whether a merger is a good idea? This chapter explores reasons that mergers should take place, and, just as important, reasons why they should not.

There is no more dramatic or controversial activity in corporate finance than the acquisition of one firm by another or the merger of two firms. It is the stuff of headlines in the financial press, and it is occasionally an embarrassing source of scandal.

The acquisition of one firm by another is, of course, an investment made under uncertainty, and the basic principles of valuation apply. One firm should acquire another only if doing so generates a positive net present value for the shareholders of the acquiring firm. However, because the NPV of an acquisition candidate can be difficult to determine, mergers and acquisitions, or M&A activities, are interesting topics in their own right.

Some of the special problems that come up in this area of finance include the following:

1. The benefits from acquisitions can depend on such things as strategic fits. Strategic fits are difficult to define precisely, and it is not easy to estimate the value of strategic fits using discounted cash flow techniques.
2. There can be complex accounting, tax, and legal effects that must be taken into account when one firm is acquired by another.
3. Acquisitions are an important control device for shareholders. Some acquisitions are a consequence of an underlying conflict between the interests of existing managers and those of shareholders. Agreeing to be acquired by another firm is one way that shareholders can remove existing managers.
4. Mergers and acquisitions sometimes involve "unfriendly" transactions. In such cases, when one firm attempts to acquire another, the activity does not always confine itself to quiet, genteel negotiations. The sought-after firm often resists takeover and may resort to defensive tactics with exotic names such as poison pills, greenmail, and white knights.

For up-to-date information on happenings in the world of M&A, go to **cbs.marketwatch.com**, then type "merger" into its search option.

We discuss these and other issues associated with mergers in the sections that follow. We begin by introducing the basic legal, accounting, and tax aspects of acquisitions.

19.1 THE LEGAL FORMS OF ACQUISITIONS

There are three basic legal procedures that one firm can use to acquire another firm:

1. Merger or consolidation
2. Acquisition of stock
3. Acquisition of assets

Although these forms are different from a legal standpoint, the financial press frequently does not distinguish between them. The term *merger* is often used regardless of the actual form of the acquisition.

In our discussion, we will frequently refer to the acquiring firm as the *bidder*. This is the company that will make an offer to distribute cash or securities to obtain the stock or assets of another company. The firm that is sought (and perhaps acquired) is often called the *target firm*. The cash or securities offered to the target firm are the *consideration* in the acquisition.

Merger or Consolidation

A **merger** is the complete absorption of one firm by another. The acquiring firm retains its name and its identity, and it acquires all of the assets and liabilities of the acquired firm. After a merger, the acquired firm ceases to exist as a separate business entity.

A **consolidation** is the same as a merger except that an entirely new firm is created. In a consolidation, both the acquiring firm and the acquired firm terminate their previous legal existence and become part of a new firm. For this reason, the distinction between the acquiring and the acquired firm is not as important in a consolidation as it is in a merger.

The rules for mergers and consolidations are basically the same. Acquisition by merger or consolidation results in a combination of the assets and liabilities of acquired and acquiring firms; the only difference lies in whether or not a new firm is created. We will henceforth use the term *merger* to refer generically to both mergers and consolidations.

There are some advantages and some disadvantages to using a merger to acquire a firm:

1. A primary advantage is that a merger is legally simple and does not cost as much as other forms of acquisition. The reason is that the firms simply agree to combine their entire operations. Thus, for example, there is no need to transfer title to individual assets of the acquired firm to the acquiring firm.
2. A primary disadvantage is that a merger must be approved by a vote of the stockholders of each firm. Typically, two-thirds (or even more) of the share votes are required for approval. Obtaining the necessary votes can be time-consuming and difficult. Furthermore, as we discuss in greater detail a bit later, the cooperation of the target firm's existing management is almost a necessity for a merger. This cooperation may not be easily or cheaply obtained.

Acquisition of Stock

A second way to acquire another firm is to simply purchase the firm's voting stock with an exchange of cash, shares of stock, or other securities. This process will often start as a private offer from the management of one firm to that of another.

Regardless of how it starts, at some point the offer is taken directly to the target firm's stockholders. This can be accomplished by a tender offer. A **tender offer** is a public offer to buy shares. It is made by one firm directly to the shareholders of another firm.

Those shareholders who choose to accept the offer tender their shares by exchanging them for cash or securities (or both), depending on the offer. A tender offer is frequently contingent on the bidder's obtaining some percentage of the total voting shares. If not enough shares are tendered, then the offer might be withdrawn or reformulated.

The tender offer is communicated to the target firm's shareholders by public announcements such as those made in newspaper advertisements. Sometimes, a general mailing is used in a tender offer. This is not common, however, because a general mailing requires the names and addresses of the stockholders of record. Obtaining such a list without the target firm's cooperation is not easy.

The following are some factors involved in choosing between an acquisition by stock and a merger:

What's new in mergers and acquisitions? Visit www.advisor-alliance.com to find out.

1. In an acquisition by stock, no shareholder meetings have to be held and no vote is required. If the shareholders of the target firm don't like the offer, they are not required to accept it and need not tender their shares.
2. In an acquisition by stock, the bidding firm can deal directly with the shareholders of the target firm by using a tender offer. The target firm's management and board of directors can be bypassed.
3. Acquisition is occasionally unfriendly. In such cases, a stock acquisition is used in an effort to circumvent the target firm's management, which is usually actively resisting acquisition. Resistance by the target firm's management often makes the cost of acquisition by stock higher than the cost of a merger.

4. Frequently, a significant minority of shareholders will hold out in a tender offer. The target firm cannot be completely absorbed when this happens, and this may delay realization of the merger benefits or may be costly in some other way. For example, if the bidder ends up with less than 80 percent of the target firm's shares, it must pay tax on 20 to 30 percent of any dividends paid by the target firm to the bidder.
5. Complete absorption of one firm by another requires a merger. Many acquisitions by stock are followed up with a formal merger later.

Acquisition of Assets

A firm can effectively acquire another firm by buying most or all of its assets. This accomplishes the same thing as buying the company. In this case, however, the target firm will not necessarily cease to exist; it will have just sold off its assets. The "shell" will still exist unless its stockholders choose to dissolve it.

This type of acquisition requires a formal vote of the shareholders of the selling firm. One advantage to this approach is that there is no problem with minority shareholders holding out. However, acquisition of assets may involve transferring titles to individual assets. The legal process of transferring assets can be costly.

Acquisition Classifications

Financial analysts typically classify acquisitions into three types:

1. *Horizontal acquisition.* This is acquisition of a firm in the same industry as the bidder. The firms compete with each other in their product markets. The Sprint/Nextel acquisition we discussed to open the chapter is a good example. Additional examples are easy to find, including the combination of regional telephone companies Bell Atlantic and GTE that produced telecommunications giant Verizon. Such mergers have been common in the banking industry. A recent example would be the 2004 combination of Wachovia and SouthTrust.
2. *Vertical acquisition.* A vertical acquisition involves firms at different steps of the production process. The acquisition by an airline company of a travel agency would be a vertical acquisition.
3. *Conglomerate acquisition.* When the bidder and the target firm are not related to each other, the merger is called a conglomerate acquisition. The acquisition of a food products firm by a computer firm would be considered a conglomerate acquisition.

Got the urge to merge? See www.firstlist.com and www.mergernetwork.com for ideas.

A Note on Takeovers

Takeover is a general and imprecise term referring to the transfer of control of a firm from one group of shareholders to another. A takeover thus occurs whenever one group takes control from another. This can occur through any one of three means: acquisitions, proxy contests, and going-private transactions. Thus, takeovers encompass a broader set of activities than just acquisitions. These activities can be depicted as follows:

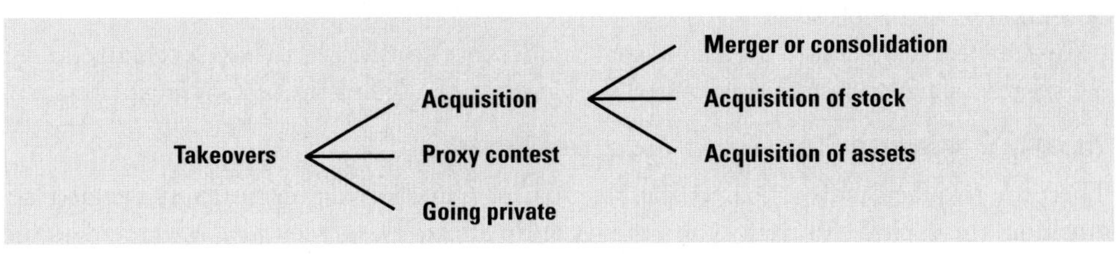

As we have mentioned before, a takeover achieved by acquisition will occur by merger, tender offer, or purchase of assets. In mergers and tender offers, the bidder buys the voting common stock of the target firm.

Takeovers can also occur with proxy contests. **Proxy contests** occur when a group attempts to gain controlling seats on the board of directors by voting in new directors. A proxy is the right to cast someone else's votes. In a proxy contest, proxies are solicited by an unhappy group of shareholders from the rest of the shareholders.

In **going-private transactions**, all of the equity shares of a public firm are purchased by a small group of investors. Usually, the group includes members of incumbent management and some outside investors. Such transactions have come to be known generically as **leveraged buyouts (LBOs)** because a large percentage of the money needed to buy up the stock is usually borrowed. Such transactions are also termed *management buyouts (MBOs)* when existing management is heavily involved. The shares of the firm are delisted from stock exchanges and can no longer be purchased in the open market.

LBOs are relatively common, and some have been quite large. For example, one of the largest cash acquisitions in history (and possibly the single largest private transaction ever of any kind) was the 1989 LBO of RJR Nabisco, the tobacco and food products giant. The acquisition price in that buyout was an astonishing $30.6 billion. In that LBO, as with most of the large ones, much of the financing came from junk bond sales (see Chapter 5 for a discussion of junk bonds).

Alternatives to Merger

Firms don't have to merge to combine their efforts. At a minimum, two (or more) firms can simply agree to work together. They can sell each other's products, perhaps under different brand names, or jointly develop a new product or technology. Firms will frequently establish a **strategic alliance**, which is usually a formal agreement to cooperate in pursuit of a joint goal. An even more formal arrangement is a **joint venture**, which commonly involves two firms putting up the money to establish a new firm. For example, Verizon Wireless is a joint venture between Verizon Communications and Vodaphone, and Cingular is a joint venture between SBC and BellSouth.

19.2 TAXES AND ACQUISITIONS

If one firm buys another firm, the transaction may be taxable or tax-free. In a *taxable acquisition,* the shareholders of the target firm are considered to have sold their shares, and they will have capital gains or losses that will be taxed. In a *tax-free acquisition,* the acquisition is considered an exchange instead of a sale, so no capital gain or loss occurs at the time of the transaction.

Determinants of Tax Status

The general requirements for tax-free status are that the acquisition be for a business purpose, and not to avoid taxes, and that there be a continuity of equity interest. In other words, the stockholders in the target firm must retain an equity interest in the bidder.

The specific requirements for a tax-free acquisition depend on the legal form of the acquisition, but, in general, if the buying firm offers the selling firm cash for its equity, it will be a taxable acquisition. If shares of stock are offered, the transaction will generally be a tax-free acquisition.

In a tax-free acquisition, the selling shareholders are considered to have exchanged their old shares for new ones of equal value, so that no capital gains or losses are experienced.

Taxable versus Tax-Free Acquisitions

There are two factors to consider when comparing a tax-free acquisition and a taxable acquisition: the capital gains effect and the write-up effect. The *capital gains effect* refers to the fact that the target firm's shareholders may have to pay capital gains taxes in a taxable acquisition. They may demand a higher price as compensation, thereby increasing the cost of the merger. This is a cost of a taxable acquisition.

The tax status of an acquisition also affects the appraised value of the assets of the selling firm. In a taxable acquisition, the assets of the selling firm are revalued or "written up" from their historic book value to their estimated current market value. This is the *write-up effect,* and it is important because it means that the depreciation expense on the acquired firm's assets can be increased in taxable acquisitions. Remember that an increase in depreciation is a noncash expense, but it has the desirable effect of reducing taxes.

The benefit from the write-up effect was sharply curtailed by the Tax Reform Act of 1986. The reason is that the increase in value from writing up the assets is now considered a taxable gain. Before this change, taxable mergers were much more attractive, because the write-up was not taxed.

19.3 ACCOUNTING FOR ACQUISITIONS

Prior to 2001, when one firm acquired another, the bidder had to decide whether the acquisition would be treated as a *purchase* or a *pooling of interests* for accounting purposes. Through the years, a great deal was written on the two approaches, discussing their pros and cons. This issue was made moot in 2001 because the Federal Accounting Standards Board (FASB) eliminated the pooling of interests option. We discuss both approaches next to illustrate some issues, but, because pooling is no longer allowed, our treatment of it is brief. In all of this, keep in mind that we are examining purely accounting-related issues. How a merger is treated for financial reporting purposes has no cash flow consequences.

The Purchase Method

The *purchase accounting method* of reporting acquisitions requires that the assets of the target firm be reported at their fair market value on the books of the bidder. With this method, an asset called *goodwill* is created for accounting purposes. Goodwill is the difference between the purchase price and the estimated fair market value of the net assets (assets less liabilities) acquired.

To illustrate, suppose Firm A acquires Firm B, thereby creating a new firm, AB. The balance sheets for the two firms on the date of the acquisition are shown in Table 19.1. Suppose Firm A pays $18 million in cash for Firm B. The money is raised by borrowing the full amount. The net fixed assets of Firm B, which are carried on the books at $8 million, are appraised at $14 million fair market value. Because the working capital is $2 million, the balance sheet assets are worth $16 million. Firm A thus pays $2 million in excess of the estimated market value of these net assets. This amount is the goodwill.[1]

The last balance sheet in Table 19.1 shows what the new firm looks like under purchase accounting. Notice that:

1. The total assets of Firm AB increase to $38 million. The fixed assets increase to $30 million. This is the sum of the fixed assets of Firm A and the revalued fixed assets of Firm B ($16 million + 14 million = $30 million).
2. The $2 million excess of the purchase price over the fair market value is reported as goodwill on the balance sheet.[2]

[1]Remember, there are assets such as employee talents, good customers, growth opportunities, and other intangibles that don't show up on the balance sheet. The $2 million excess pays for these.

[2]You might wonder what would happen if the purchase price were less than the estimated fair market value. Amusingly, to be consistent, it seems that the accountants would need to create a liability called *ill will!* Instead, the fair market value is revised downwards to equal the purchase price.

TABLE 19.1
Accounting for Acquisitions: Purchase (in millions)

FIRM A				FIRM B			
Working capital	$ 4	Equity	$20	Working capital	$ 2	Equity	$10
Fixed assets	16			Fixed assets	8		
Total	$20	Total	$20	Total	$10	Total	$10

FIRM AB			
Working capital	$ 6	Debt	$18
Fixed assets	30	Equity	20
Goodwill	2		
Total	$38	Total	$38

The market value of the fixed assets of Firm B is $14 million. Firm A pays $18 million for Firm B by issuing debt.

TABLE 19.2
Accounting for Acquisitions: Pooling of Interests (in millions)

FIRM A				FIRM B			
Working capital	$ 4	Equity	$20	Working capital	$ 2	Equity	$10
Fixed assets	16			Fixed assets	8		
Total	$20	Total	$20	Total	$10	Total	$10

FIRM AB			
Working capital	$ 6	Equity	$30
Fixed assets	24		
Total	$30	Total	$30

Pooling of Interests

Under a pooling of interests, the assets of the acquiring and acquired firms are pooled, meaning that the balance sheets are just added together. Using our previous example, assume that Firm A buys Firm B by giving B's shareholders $18 million worth of common stock. The result is shown in Table 19.2.

The new firm is owned jointly by all the stockholders of the previously separate firms. The accounting is much simpler here; we just add the two old balance sheets together. The total assets are unchanged by the acquisition, and no goodwill account is created.

More on Goodwill

As we just discussed, the purchase method generally leads to the creation of an intangible asset called goodwill. Pre-2001 guidelines required firms to amortize this goodwill, meaning that a portion of it was deducted as an expense every year over some period of time. In essence, the goodwill, like any asset, had to be depreciated until it was completely written off.

The amortization of goodwill was something that firms generally disliked because it reduced reported earnings. However, notice that the amortization deduction was strictly noncash. Unlike true depreciation, it was not even a tax-deductible expense, so financial analysts just routinely ignored it.

Despite the cash flow irrelevance of goodwill amortization, FASB's decision to require purchase accounting caused a great deal of protest, much of it due to the treatment of goodwill and its impact on reported earnings. As a compromise, in 2001 FASB eliminated the requirement that goodwill be amortized and put in place a new rule. In essence, the new rule says that each year firms must assess the value of the goodwill on their balance sheets. If the value has gone down (or become "impaired" in accounting-speak), the firm must deduct the decrease; otherwise, no amortization is required.

19.4 GAINS FROM ACQUISITION

To determine the gains from an acquisition, we need to first identify the relevant incremental cash flows, or, more generally, the source of value. In the broadest sense, acquiring another firm makes sense only if there is some concrete reason to believe that the target firm will somehow be worth more in our hands than it is worth now. As we will see, there are a number of reasons why this might be so.

Synergy

Try the "M&A" link at www.thedeal.com for current news.

Suppose Firm A is contemplating acquiring Firm B. The acquisition will be beneficial if the combined firm will have value that is greater than the sum of the values of the separate firms. If we let V_{AB} stand for the value of the merged firm, then the merger makes sense only if:

$$V_{AB} > V_A + V_B$$

where V_A and V_B are the separate values. A successful merger thus requires that the value of the whole exceed the sum of the parts.

The difference between the value of the combined firm and the sum of the values of the firms as separate entities is the incremental net gain from the acquisition, ΔV:

$$\Delta V = V_{AB} - (V_A + V_B)$$

When ΔV is positive, the acquisition is said to generate **synergy**. If Firm A buys Firm B, it gets a company worth V_B plus the incremental gain, ΔV. The value of Firm B to Firm A (V_B^*) is thus:

$$\textbf{Value of Firm B to Firm A} = V_B^* = \Delta V + V_B$$

We place an * on V_B^* to emphasize that we are referring to the value of Firm B to Firm A, not the value of Firm B as a separate entity.

V_B^* can be determined in two steps: (1) estimating V_B and (2) estimating ΔV. If B is a public company, then its market value as an independent firm under existing management (V_B) can be observed directly. If Firm B is not publicly owned, then its value will have to be estimated based on similar companies that are. Either way, the problem of determining a value for V_B^* requires determining a value for ΔV.

To determine the incremental value of an acquisition, we need to know the incremental cash flows. These are the cash flows for the combined firm less what A and B could generate separately. In other words, the incremental cash flow for evaluating a merger is the difference between the cash flow of the combined company and the sum of the cash flows for the two companies considered separately. We will label this incremental cash flow as ΔCF.

EXAMPLE 19.1 Synergy

Firms A and B are competitors with very similar assets and business risks. Both are all-equity firms with aftertax cash flows of \$10 per year forever, and both have an overall cost of capital of 10 percent. Firm A is thinking of buying Firm B. The aftertax cash flow from the merged firm would be \$21 per year. Does the merger generate synergy? What is V_B^*? What is ΔV?

(continued)

The merger does generate synergy because the cash flow from the merged firm is $\Delta CF = \$1$ greater than the sum of the individual cash flows ($21 versus $20). Assuming that the risks stay the same, the value of the merged firm is $21/.10 = $210. Firms A and B are each worth $10/.10 = $100, for a total of $200. The incremental gain from the merger, ΔV, is thus $210 − 200 = $10. The total value of Firm B to Firm A, V_B^*, is $100 (the value of B as a separate company) plus $10 (the incremental gain), or $110.

From our discussions in earlier chapters, we know that the incremental cash flow ΔCF can be broken down into four parts:

$$\begin{aligned}\Delta\textbf{CF} &= \Delta\textbf{EBIT} + \Delta\textbf{Depreciation} - \Delta\textbf{Tax} - \Delta\textbf{Capital requirements}\\ &= \Delta\textbf{Revenue} - \Delta\textbf{Cost} - \Delta\textbf{Tax} - \Delta\textbf{Capital requirements}\end{aligned}$$

where ΔRevenue is the difference in revenues, ΔCost is the difference in costs, ΔTax is the difference in taxes, and ΔCapital requirements is the change in new fixed assets and net working capital.

Based on this breakdown, the merger will make sense only if one or more of these cash flow components are beneficially affected by the merger. The possible cash flow benefits of mergers and acquisitions thus fall into four basic categories: revenue enhancement, cost reductions, lower taxes, and reductions in capital needs.

Revenue Enhancement

One important reason for an acquisition is that the combined firm may generate greater revenues than two separate firms. Increases in revenue may come from marketing gains, strategic benefits, and increases in market power.

MARKETING GAINS It is frequently claimed that mergers and acquisitions can produce greater operating revenues from improved marketing. For example, improvements might be made in the following areas:

1. Previously ineffective media programming and advertising efforts.
2. A weak existing distribution network.
3. An unbalanced product mix.

In the Sprint–Nextel merger we discussed to open the chapter, analysts noted enormous savings in marketing expenses. Cell phone providers advertise heavily, and much of the existing spending would no longer be necessary after the merger.

STRATEGIC BENEFITS Some acquisitions promise a strategic advantage. This is an opportunity to take advantage of the competitive environment if certain things occur or, more generally, to enhance management flexibility with regard to the company's future operations. In this latter regard, a strategic benefit is more like an option than a standard investment opportunity.

For example, suppose a sewing machine manufacturer can use its technology to enter other businesses. The small-motor technology from the original business can provide opportunities to begin manufacturing small appliances and electric typewriters. Similarly, electronics expertise gained in producing typewriters can be used to manufacture electronic printers.

The word *beachhead* has been used in describing the process of entering a new industry to exploit perceived opportunities. The beachhead is used to spawn new opportunities based on "intangible" relationships. One example is Procter & Gamble's initial acquisition of the Charmin Paper Company as a beachhead that allowed Procter & Gamble to develop a highly interrelated cluster of paper products–disposable diapers, paper towels, feminine hygiene products, and bathroom tissue.[3]

MARKET POWER One firm may acquire another to increase its market share and market power. In such mergers, profits can be enhanced through higher prices and reduced competition for customers. Of course, mergers that substantially reduce competition in the market may be challenged by the U.S. Department of Justice or the Federal Trade Commission on antitrust grounds.

Cost Reductions

One of the most basic reasons to merge is that a combined firm may operate more efficiently than two separate firms. A firm can achieve greater operating efficiency in several different ways through a merger or an acquisition.

ECONOMIES OF SCALE Economies of scale relate to the average cost per unit of producing goods and services. If the per-unit cost of production falls as the level of production increases, then an economy of scale exists:

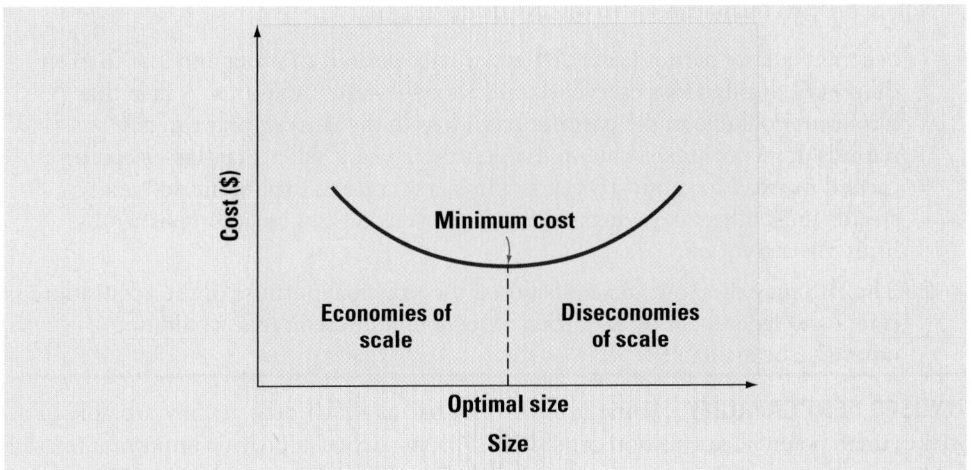

Frequently, the phrase *spreading overhead* is used in connection with economies of scale. This expression refers to the sharing of central facilities such as corporate headquarters, top management, and computer services.

ECONOMIES OF VERTICAL INTEGRATION Operating economies can be gained from vertical combinations as well as from horizontal combinations. The main purpose of vertical acquisitions is to make it easier to coordinate closely related operating activities. Benefits from vertical integration are probably the reason that most forest product firms that cut timber also own sawmills and hauling equipment. Economies of vertical integration may explain why some airline companies have purchased hotels and car rental companies.

Technology transfers are another reason for vertical integration. Very frequently, a company will decide that the cheapest–and fastest–way to acquire another firm's technological skills is to simply buy the firm. For obvious reasons, this rationale is particularly common in high-tech industries.

COMPLEMENTARY RESOURCES Some firms acquire others to make better use of existing resources or to provide the missing ingredient for success. Think of a ski equipment store that could merge with a tennis equipment store to produce more even sales over both the winter and summer seasons, and thereby better use store capacity.

[3]This example comes from Michael Porter, *Competitive Advantage* (New York: Free Press, 1985).

Lower Taxes

Tax gains are a powerful incentive for some acquisitions. The possible tax gains from an acquisition include the following:

1. The use of tax losses.
2. The use of unused debt capacity.
3. The use of surplus funds.
4. The ability to write up the value of depreciable assets.

NET OPERATING LOSSES Firms that lose money on a pretax basis will not pay taxes. Such firms can end up with tax losses they cannot use. These tax losses are referred to as *net operating losses (NOL).*

A firm with net operating losses may be an attractive merger partner for a firm with significant tax liabilities. Absent any other effects, the combined firm will have a lower tax bill than the two firms considered separately. This is a good example of how a firm can be more valuable merged than standing alone.

There are two qualifications to our NOL discussion:

1. Federal tax laws permit firms that experience periods of profit and loss to even things out through loss carryback and carryforward provisions. A firm that has been profitable in the past but has a loss in the current year can get refunds of income taxes paid in the past three years. After that, losses can be carried forward for up to 15 years. Thus, a merger to exploit unused tax shields must offer tax savings over and above what can be accomplished by firms via carryovers.[4]
2. The IRS may disallow an acquisition if the principal purpose of the acquisition is to avoid federal tax by acquiring a deduction or credit that would not otherwise be available.

UNUSED DEBT CAPACITY Some firms do not use as much debt as they are able. This makes them potential acquisition candidates. Adding debt can provide important tax savings, and many acquisitions are financed with debt. The acquiring company can deduct interest payments on the newly created debt and reduce taxes.

SURPLUS FUNDS Another quirk in the tax laws involves surplus funds. Consider a firm that has free cash flow—cash flow available after all taxes have been paid and after all positive net present value projects have been financed. In such a situation, aside from purchasing fixed-income securities, the firm has several ways to spend the free cash flow, including:

1. Paying dividends.
2. Buying back its own shares.
3. Acquiring shares in another firm.

We discussed the first two options in Chapter 16. We saw that an extra dividend will increase the income tax paid by some investors. A share repurchase will reduce the taxes paid by shareholders as compared to paying dividends, but this is not a legal option if the sole purpose is to avoid taxes that otherwise would have been paid by shareholders.

To avoid these problems, the firm can buy another firm. By doing this, the firm avoids the tax problem associated with paying a dividend. Also, the dividends received from the purchased firm are not taxed in a merger.

[4]The specific tax rules contain a number of complications, particularly when mergers or mergerlike transactions are involved.

ASSET WRITE-UPS We have previously observed that, in a taxable acquisition, the assets of the acquired firm can be revalued. If the value of the assets is increased, tax deductions for depreciation will be a benefit, but this benefit will usually be more than offset by taxes due on the write-up.

Reductions in Capital Needs

All firms must make investments in working capital and fixed assets to sustain an efficient level of operating activity. A merger may reduce the combined investments needed by the two firms. For example, it may be that Firm A needs to expand its manufacturing facilities whereas Firm B has significant excess capacity. It may be much cheaper for Firm A to buy Firm B than to build from scratch.

In addition, acquiring firms may see ways of more effectively managing existing assets. This can occur with a reduction in working capital resulting from more efficient handling of cash, accounts receivable, and inventory. Finally, the acquiring firm may also sell off certain assets that are not needed in the combined firm.

Firms will often cite a large number of reasons for merging. Typically, when firms agree to merge, they sign an *agreement of merger,* which contains, among other things, a list of the economic benefits that shareholders can expect from the merger. For example, in the Sprint–Nextel merger we discussed to open the chapter, the companies stated in the merger announcement that the $12 billion net present value was primarily attributable to the following synergies:

- Saving network operating expenses by reducing the number of cell sites and switches.
- Reducing overall capital expenditures by extending Sprint's current deployment of next-generation technology to the combined customer base.
- Migrating Nextel's telecommunications traffic to Sprint's long-haul infrastructure.
- Optimizing consumer care, billing, and IT costs by consolidating operations.
- Reducing combined sales and marketing costs.
- Lowering overall general and administrative costs.
- Reducing network capital expense after the merger by building a true IP-based multimedia network.

Notice that most of these synergies come in the form of operating and capital costs savings, so economies of scale and reductions in capital needs were the main value drivers.

Avoiding Mistakes

Evaluating the benefit of a potential acquisition is more difficult than a standard capital budgeting analysis because so much of the value can come from intangible, or otherwise difficult to quantify, benefits. Consequently, there is a great deal of room for error. Here are some general rules that should be remembered:

1. *Do not ignore market values.* There is no point to, and little gain from, estimating the value of a publicly traded firm when that value can be directly observed. The current market value represents a consensus opinion of investors concerning the firm's value (under existing management). Use this value as a starting point. If the firm is not publicly held, then the place to start is with similar firms that are publicly held.

2. *Estimate only incremental cash flows.* It is important to estimate the incremental cash flows that will result from the acquisition. Only incremental cash flows from an acquisition will add value to the acquiring firm. Acquisition analysis should thus

focus only on the newly created, incremental cash flows from the proposed acquisition.

3. *Use the correct discount rate.* The discount rate should be the required rate of return for the incremental cash flows associated with the acquisition. It should reflect the risk associated with the use of funds, not the source. In particular, if Firm A is acquiring Firm B, then Firm A's cost of capital is not particularly relevant. Firm B's cost of capital is a much more appropriate discount rate because it reflects the risk of Firm B's cash flows.

4. *Be aware of transactions costs.* An acquisition may involve substantial (and sometimes astounding) transactions costs. These will include fees to investment bankers, legal fees, and disclosure requirements.

A Note on Inefficient Management

There are firms whose value could be increased with a change in management. These are firms that are poorly run or otherwise do not efficiently use their assets to create shareholder value. Mergers are a means of replacing management in such cases.

The fact that a firm might benefit from a change in management does not necessarily mean that existing management is dishonest, incompetent, or negligent. Instead, just as some athletes are better than others, so might some management teams be better at running a business. This can be particularly true during times of technological change or other periods when innovations in business practice are occurring. In any case, to the extent that corporate "raiders" can identify poorly run firms or firms that, for other reasons, will benefit from a change in management, these raiders provide a valuable service to target-firm shareholders and society in general.

19.5 SOME FINANCIAL SIDE EFFECTS OF ACQUISITIONS

In addition to the various possibilities we have discussed thus far, mergers can have some purely financial side effects, that is, things that occur regardless of whether the merger makes economic sense or not. Two such effects are particularly worth mentioning: EPS growth and diversification.

EPS Growth

An acquisition can create the appearance of growth in earnings per share, or EPS. This may fool investors into thinking that the firm is doing better than it really is. What happens is easiest to see with an example.

Suppose Global Resources, Ltd., acquires Regional Enterprises. The financial positions of Global and Regional before the acquisition are shown in Table 19.3. We assume that the merger creates no additional value, so the combined firm (Global Resources after acquiring Regional) has a value that is equal to the sum of the values of the two firms before the merger.

Before the merger, both Global and Regional have 100 shares outstanding. However, Global sells for \$25 per share, versus a price of \$10 per share for Regional. Global therefore acquires Regional by exchanging 1 of its shares for every 2.5 Regional shares. Because there are 100 shares in Regional, this will take $100/2.5 = 40$ shares in all.

After the merger, Global will have 140 shares outstanding, and several things will happen (see the third column of Table 19.3):

1. The market value of the combined firm is \$3,500. This is equal to the sum of the values of the separate firms before the merger. If the market is "smart," it will realize that the combined firm is worth the sum of the values of the separate firms.

	GLOBAL RESOURCES BEFORE MERGER	REGIONAL ENTERPRISES BEFORE MERGER	Global Resources after Merger	
			THE MARKET IS SMART	THE MARKET IS FOOLED
Earnings per share	$ 1	$ 1	$ 1.43	$ 1.43
Price per share	$ 25	$ 10	$ 25	$ 35.71
Price-earnings ratio	25	10	17.5	25
Number of shares	100	100	140	140
Total earnings	$ 100	$ 100	$ 200	$ 200
Total value	$2,500	$1,000	$3,500	$5,000

Exchange ratio: 1 share in Global for 2.5 shares in Regional.

TABLE 19.3

Financial Positions of Global Resources and Regional Enterprises

2. The earnings per share of the merged firm are $1.43. The acquisition enables Global to increase its earnings per share from $1 to $1.43, an increase of 43 percent.
3. Because the stock price of Global after the merger is the same as that before the merger, the price-earnings ratio must fall. This is true as long as the market is smart and recognizes that the total market value has not been altered by the merger.

If the market is "fooled," it might mistake the 43 percent increase in earnings per share for true growth. In this case, the price-earnings ratio of Global may not fall after the merger. Suppose the price-earnings ratio of Global remains equal to 25. Because the combined firm has earnings of $200, the total value of the combined firm will increase to $5,000 (25 × $200). The per-share value for Global will increase to $35.71 ($5,000/140).

This is earnings growth magic. Like all good magic, it is just an illusion. For it to work, the shareholders of Global and Regional must receive something for nothing. This, of course, is unlikely with so simple a trick.

Diversification

Diversification is commonly mentioned as a benefit of a merger. The problem is that diversification per se probably does not create value.

Going back to Chapter 11, recall that diversification reduces unsystematic risk. We also saw that the value of an asset depends on its systematic risk, and systematic risk is not directly affected by diversification. Because the unsystematic risk is not especially important, there is no particular benefit from reducing it.

An easy way to see why diversification isn't an important benefit of a merger is to consider someone who owned stock in two companies that were proposing to merge. Such a stockholder was already diversified between these two investments. The merger didn't do anything the stockholders couldn't do for themselves.

More generally, stockholders can get all the diversification they want by buying stock in different companies. As a result, they won't pay a premium for a merged company just for the benefit of diversification. In fact, diversification may actually harm stockholders when one or both firms are leveraged. This point is discussed in Chapter 17, which should be consulted for greater detail on this important consideration.

19.6 THE COST OF AN ACQUISITION

We've discussed some of the benefits of acquisition. We now need to discuss the cost of a merger. We learned earlier that the net incremental gain from a merger is:

$$\Delta V = V_{AB} - (V_A + V_B)$$

Also, the total value of Firm B to Firm A, V_B^*, is:

$$V_B^* = V_B + \Delta V$$

The NPV of the merger is therefore:

$$\textbf{NPV} = V_B^* - \textbf{Cost to Firm A of the acquisition} \tag{19.1}$$

To illustrate, suppose we have the following premerger information for Firm A and Firm B:

	FIRM A	FIRM B
Price per share	\$ 20	\$ 10
Number of shares	25	10
Total market value	\$500	\$100

Both of these firms are 100 percent equity. You estimate that the incremental value of the acquisition, ΔV, is \$100.

The board of Firm B has indicated that it will agree to a sale if the price is \$150, payable in cash or stock. This price for Firm B has two parts. Firm B is worth \$100 as a stand-alone, so this is the minimum value that we could assign to Firm B. The second part, \$50, is called the merger premium, and it represents the amount paid above the stand-alone value.

Should Firm A acquire Firm B? Should it pay in cash or stock? To answer, we need to determine the NPV of the acquisition under both alternatives. We can start by noting that the value of Firm B to Firm A is:

$$\begin{aligned} V_B^* &= \Delta V + V_B \\ &= \$100 + 100 = \$200 \end{aligned}$$

The total value received by A as a result of buying Firm B is thus \$200. The question then is, How much does Firm A have to give up? The answer depends on whether cash or stock is used as the means of payment.

Case I: Cash Acquisition

The cost of an acquisition when cash is used is just the cash itself. So, if Firm A pays \$150 in cash to purchase all of the shares of Firm B, the cost of acquiring Firm B is \$150. The NPV of a cash acquisition is:

$$\begin{aligned} \text{NPV} &= V_B^* - \text{Cost} \\ &= \$200 - 150 = \$50 \end{aligned}$$

The acquisition is therefore profitable.

After the merger, Firm AB will still have 25 shares outstanding. The value of Firm A after the merger is:

$$\begin{aligned} V_{AB} &= V_A + (V_B^* - \text{Cost}) \\ &= \$500 + 200 - 150 \\ &= \$550 \end{aligned}$$

This is just the premerger value of \$500 plus the \$50 NPV. The price per share after the merger is \$550/25 = \$22, representing a gain of \$2 per share.

Case II: Stock Acquisition

Things are somewhat more complicated when stock is the means of payment. In a cash merger, the shareholders in B receive cash for their stock, and they no longer participate in the company. Thus, as we have seen, the cost of the acquisition in this case is the amount of cash needed to pay off B's stockholders.

In a stock merger, no cash actually changes hands. Instead, the shareholders of Firm B come in as new shareholders in the merged firm. The value of the merged firm in this case will be equal to the premerger values of Firms A and B plus the incremental gain from the merger, ΔV:

$$\begin{aligned} V_{AB} &= V_A + V_B + \Delta V \\ &= \$500 + 100 + 100 \\ &= \$700 \end{aligned}$$

To give $150 worth of stock for Firm B, Firm A will have to give up $150/20 = 7.5 shares. After the merger, there will be 25 + 7.5 = 32.5 shares outstanding, and the per-share value will be $700/32.5 = $21.54.

Notice that the per-share price after the merger is lower under the stock purchase option. The reason has to do with the fact that B's shareholders own stock in the new firm.

It appears that Firm A paid $150 for Firm B. However, it actually paid more than that. When all is said and done, B's stockholders own 7.5 shares of stock in the merged firm. After the merger, each of these shares is worth $21.54. The total value of the consideration received by B's stockholders is thus 7.5 × $21.54 = $161.55.

This $161.55 is the true cost of the acquisition because it is what the sellers actually end up receiving. The NPV of the merger to Firm A is:

$$\begin{aligned} \text{NPV} &= V_B^* - \text{Cost} \\ &= \$200 - 161.55 = \$38.45 \end{aligned}$$

We can check this by noting that A started with 25 shares worth $20 each. The gain to A of $38.45 works out to be $38.45/25 = $1.54 per share. The value of the stock has increased to $21.54, as we calculated.

When we compare the cash acquisition to the stock acquisition, we see that the cash acquisition is better in this case, because Firm A gets to keep all of the NPV if it pays in cash. If it pays in stock, Firm B's stockholders share in the NPV by becoming new stockholders in A.

Cash versus Common Stock

The distinction between cash and common stock financing in a merger is an important one. If cash is used, the cost of an acquisition is not dependent on the acquisition gains. All other things being the same, if common stock is used, the cost is higher because Firm A's shareholders must share the acquisition gains with the shareholders of Firm B. However, if the NPV of the acquisition is negative, then the loss will be shared between the two firms.

Whether a firm should finance an acquisition with cash or with shares of stock depends on several factors, including the following:

1. *Sharing gains.* If cash is used to finance an acquisition, the selling firm's shareholders will not participate in the potential gains from the merger. Of course, if the acquisition is not a success, the losses will not be shared, and shareholders of the acquiring firm will be worse off than if stock had been used.
2. *Taxes.* Acquisition by paying cash usually results in a taxable transaction. Acquisition by exchanging stock is generally tax-free.
3. *Control.* Acquisition by paying cash does not affect the control of the acquiring firm. Acquisition with voting shares may have implications for control of the merged firm.

In a typical year, in terms of the total number of deals, cash financing is much more common than stock financing. The same is usually true based on the total dollar values, though the difference is smaller. The reason is that stock financing becomes more common if we look at very large deals.

19.7 DEFENSIVE TACTICS

Target-firm managers frequently resist takeover attempts. Resistance usually starts with press releases and mailings to shareholders that present management's viewpoint. It can eventually lead to legal action and solicitation of competing bids. Managerial action to defeat a takeover attempt may make target-firm shareholders better off if it elicits a higher offer premium from the bidding firm or another firm.

Of course, management resistance may simply reflect pursuit of self-interest at the expense of shareholders. This is a controversial subject. At times, management resistance has greatly increased the amount ultimately received by their shareholders. At other times, management resistance appears to have defeated all takeover attempts to the detriment of their shareholders.

In this section, we describe various defensive tactics that have been used by target-firm management to resist unfriendly attempts. The law surrounding these defenses is not settled, and some of these maneuvers may ultimately be deemed illegal or otherwise unsuitable.

The Corporate Charter

The *corporate charter* consists of the articles of incorporation and corporate bylaws that establish the governance rules of the firm. The corporate charter establishes the conditions that allow for a takeover. Firms frequently amend corporate charters to make acquisitions more difficult. For example, usually, two-thirds (67 percent) of the shareholders of record must approve a merger. Firms can make it more difficult to be acquired by changing this required percentage to 80 percent or so. Such a change is called a *supermajority amendment.*

Another device is to stagger the election of the board members. This makes it more difficult to elect a new board of directors quickly. Such a board is sometimes called a classified board.

Repurchase and Standstill Agreements

Managers of target firms may attempt to negotiate *standstill agreements*. Standstill agreements are contracts wherein the bidding firm agrees to limit its holdings in the target firm. These agreements usually lead to the end of a takeover attempt.

Standstill agreements often occur at the same time that a *targeted repurchase* is arranged. In a targeted repurchase, a firm buys a certain amount of its own stock from an individual investor, usually at a substantial premium. These premiums can be thought of as payments to potential bidders to eliminate unfriendly takeover attempts. Critics of such payments view them as bribes and label them **greenmail**.

Poison Pills and Share Rights Plans

A **poison pill** is a tactic designed to repel would-be suitors. The term comes from the world of espionage. Agents are supposed to bite a pill of cyanide rather than permit capture. Presumably, this prevents enemy interrogators from learning important secrets.

In the equally colorful world of corporate finance, a poison pill is a financial device designed to make it impossible for a firm to be acquired without management's consent–unless the buyer is willing to commit financial suicide.

A majority of the largest firms in the United States have adopted poison pill provisions of one form or another, often calling them **share rights plans** (SRPs) or something similar. SRPs differ quite a bit in detail from company to company; we will describe a kind of generic approach here. In general, when a company adopts an SRP, it distributes share rights to its existing stockholders. These rights allow shareholders to buy shares of stock (or preferred stock) at some fixed price.

The rights issued with an SRP have a number of unusual features. First, the exercise or subscription price on the right is usually set high enough so that the rights are well out of the money, meaning that the purchase price is much higher than the current stock price. The rights will often be good for 10 years, and the purchase or exercise price is usually a reasonable estimate of what the stock will be worth at the end of that time.

In addition, unlike ordinary stock rights, these rights can't be exercised immediately, and they can't be bought and sold separately from the stock. Also, they can essentially be canceled by management at any time; often, they can be redeemed (bought back) for a penny apiece, or some similarly trivial amount.

Things get interesting when, under certain circumstances, the rights are "triggered." This means that the rights become exercisable, they can be bought and sold separately from the stock, and they are not easily canceled or redeemed. Typically, the rights will be triggered when someone acquires 20 percent of the common stock or announces a tender offer.

When the rights are triggered, they can be exercised. Because they are out of the money, this fact is not especially important. Certain other features come into play, however. The most important is the *flip-in provision.*

The flip-in provision is the "poison" in the pill. In the event of an unfriendly takeover attempt, the holder of a right can pay the exercise price and receive common stock in the target firm worth twice the exercise price. In other words, holders of the rights can buy stock in the target firm at half price. Simultaneously, the rights owned by the raider (the acquirer) are voided. The goal of the flip-in provision is to massively dilute the raider's ownership position.[5]

The rights issued in connection with an SRP are poison pills because anyone trying to force a merger will trigger the rights. When this happens, all the target firm's stockholders can effectively buy stock in the merged firm at half price. This greatly increases the cost of the merger to the bidder because the target firm's shareholders end up with a much larger percentage of the merged firm.

Notice that the flip-in provision doesn't prevent someone from acquiring control of a firm by purchasing a majority interest. It just acts to vastly increase the cost of doing so.

The intention of a poison pill is to force a bidder to negotiate with management. Frequently, merger offers are made with the contingency that the rights will be canceled by the target firm.

Some new varieties of poison pills have appeared on the scene in recent years. For example, a "chewable" pill, common in Canada but not in the United States, is a pill that is installed by shareholder vote and can be redeemed by shareholder vote. Then there's the "deadhand pill," which explicitly gives the directors who installed the pill, or their handpicked successors, the authority to remove the pill. This type of pill is controversial because it makes it virtually impossible for new directors elected by stockholders to remove an existing poison pill.

Going Private and Leveraged Buyouts

As we have previously discussed, going private is what happens when the publicly owned stock in a firm is replaced with complete equity ownership by a private group, which may include elements of existing management. As a consequence, the firm's stock is taken off the market (if it is an exchange-traded stock, it is delisted) and is no longer traded.

[5]Some plans also contain "flip-over" provisions. These allow the holders to buy stock in the merged company at half price.

One result of going private is that takeovers via tender offer can no longer occur since there are no publicly held shares. In this sense, an LBO (or, more specifically, an MBO) can be a takeover defense. However, it's only a defense for management. From the stockholders' point of view, an LBO is a takeover because they are bought out.

Other Devices and Jargon of Corporate Takeovers

As corporate takeovers have become more common, a new vocabulary has developed. The terms are colorful, and, in no particular order, some of them are listed here:

1. *Golden parachute.* Some target firms provide compensation to top-level management if a takeover occurs. For example, several months after the initial announcement of the proposed Procter & Gamble (P&G) acquisition of Gillette, P&G filings with the SEC indicated that Gillette CEO James Kilts and Gillette's four other highest-paid executives would receive a package worth about $284.5 million. Other Gillette officers would receive an additional $175.9 million. The opposite of a golden parachute is a "golden handcuff," which is an incentive package designed to get executives to stay on board once the acquisition is completed.

   Depending on your perspective and the amounts involved, golden parachutes can be viewed as a payment to management to make it less concerned for its own welfare and more interested in stockholders when considering a takeover bid.
2. *Poison put.* A poison put is a variation on the poison pill we described earlier. A poison put forces the firm to buy securities back at some set price.
3. *Crown jewel.* Firms often sell or threaten to sell major assets—crown jewels—when faced with a takeover threat. This is sometimes referred to as the "scorched earth" strategy. This tactic often involves a lockup, which we discuss shortly.
4. *White knight.* A firm facing an unfriendly merger offer might arrange to be acquired by a different, friendly firm. The firm is thereby rescued by a white knight. Alternatively, the firm may arrange for a friendly entity to acquire a large block of stock. So-called white squires or big brothers are individuals, firms, or even mutual funds involved in friendly transactions of these types. Sometimes white knights or others are granted exceptional terms or otherwise compensated. Inevitably it seems, this has been called *whitemail.*
5. *Lockup.* A lockup is an option granted to a friendly suitor (a white knight, perhaps) giving them the right to purchase stock or some of the assets (the crown jewels, possibly) of a target firm at a fixed price in the event of an unfriendly takeover.
6. *Shark repellent.* A shark repellent is any tactic (a poison pill, for example) designed to discourage unwanted merger offers.
7. *Bear hug.* A bear hug is an unfriendly takeover offer designed to be so attractive that the target firm's management has little choice but to accept it. For example, in May 2005, a "bear hug" offer made the news when online broker E*Trade Financial made an unsolicited bid for rival Internet broker Ameritrade.
8. *Fair price provision.* A fair price provision is a requirement that all selling shareholders receive the same price from a bidder. The provision prevents a "two-tier" offer. In such a deal, a bidder offers a premium price only for a large enough percentage of the shares to gain control. It offers a lower price for the remaining shares. Such an offer can set off a stampede among shareholders as they rush to get the better price.

9. *Dual class capitalization.* In an earlier chapter, we noted that some firms such as Google have more than one class of common stock and that voting power is typically concentrated in a class of stock not held by the public. Such a capital structure means that an unfriendly bidder will not succeed in gaining control.
10. *Countertender offer.* Better known as the "Pac-man" defense, the target responds to an unfriendly overture by offering to buy the bidder! This tactic is rarely used, in part because target firms are usually too small to realistically purchase the bidder.

19.8 SOME EVIDENCE ON ACQUISITIONS: DOES M&A PAY?

One of the most controversial issues surrounding our subject is whether mergers and acquisitions benefit shareholders. A very large number of studies have attempted to estimate the effect of mergers and takeovers on stock prices of the bidding and target firms. These studies have examined the gains and losses in stock value around the time of merger announcements.

One conclusion that clearly emerges is that M&A pays for target-firm shareholders. There is no mystery here. The premium typically paid by bidders represents an immediate, relatively large gain, often on the order of 20 percent or more.

Matters become much more murky when we look at bidders, and different studies reach different conclusions. One thing is clear, however. Shareholders in bidder firms seem to neither win nor lose very much, at least on average. This finding is a bit of a puzzle, and there are a variety of explanations:

1. Anticipated merger gains may not be completely achieved, and shareholders thus experience losses. This can happen if managers of bidding firms tend to overestimate the gains from acquisition.
2. The bidding firms are usually much larger than the target firms. Thus, even though the dollar gains to the bidder may be similar to the dollar gains earned by shareholders of the target firm, the percentage gains will be much lower.
3. Another possible explanation for the low returns to the shareholders of bidding firms in takeovers is simply that management may not be acting in the interest of shareholders when it attempts to acquire other firms. Perhaps it is attempting to increase the size of the firm, even if this reduces its value per share.
4. The market for takeovers may be sufficiently competitive that the NPV of acquiring is zero because the prices paid in acquisitions fully reflect the value of the acquired firms. In other words, the sellers capture all of the gain.
5. Finally, the announcement of a takeover may not convey much new information to the market about the bidding firm. This can occur because firms frequently announce intentions to engage in merger "programs" long before they announce specific acquisitions. In this case, the stock price for the bidding firm may already reflect anticipated gains from mergers.

19.9 DIVESTITURES AND RESTRUCTURINGS

In contrast to a merger or acquisition, a **divestiture** occurs when a firm sells assets, operations, divisions, and/or segments to a third party. Note that divestitures are an important part of M&A activity. After all, one company's acquisition is usually another's divestiture.

Also, following a merger, it is very common for certain assets or divisions to be sold. Such sales may be required by antitrust regulations; they may be needed to raise cash to help pay for a deal; or the divested units may simply be unwanted by the acquirer.

Divestitures also occur when a company decides to sell off a part of itself for reasons unrelated to mergers and acquisitions. This can happen when a particular unit is unprofitable or not a good strategic fit. Or, a firm may decide to cash out of a very profitable operation. Finally, a cash-strapped firm may have to sell assets just to raise capital (this commonly occurs in bankruptcy).

A divestiture usually occurs like any other sale. A company lets it be known that it has assets for sale and seeks offers. If a suitable offer is forthcoming, a sale occurs.

In some cases, particularly when the desired divestiture is a relatively large operating unit, companies will elect to do an **equity carve-out**. To do a carve-out, a parent company first creates a completely separate company of which the parent is the sole shareholder. Next, the parent company arranges an initial public offering (IPO) in which a fraction, perhaps 20 percent or so, of the parent's stock in the new firm is sold to the public, thus creating a publicly held company.

Instead of a carve-out, a company can elect to do a **spin-off**. In a spin-off, the company simply distributes shares in the subsidiary to its existing stockholders on a pro rata basis. Shareholders can keep the shares or sell them as they see fit. Very commonly, a company will first do an equity carve-out to create an active market for the shares and then subsequently do a spin-off of the remaining shares at a later date. Many well-known companies were created by this route. For example, insurance giant Allstate was spun off by Sears; Palm Computing was a 3Com spin-off; and Conoco was once a part of Du Pont.

In a less common, but more drastic move, a company can elect to do (or be forced to do) a **split-up**. A split-up is just what the name suggests: A company splits itself into two or more new companies. Shareholders have their shares in the old company swapped for shares in the new companies. Probably the most famous split-up occurred in the 1980s. As the result of an antitrust suit by the Justice Department, AT&T was forced to split up through the creation of seven regional phone companies (the so-called Baby Bells). Today, the Baby Bells survive as companies such as BellSouth, SBC Communications, and Verizon.

SUMMARY AND CONCLUSIONS

This chapter has introduced you to the extensive literature on mergers and acquisitions. We touched on a number of issues, including:

1. **Forms of merger** One firm can acquire another in several different ways. The three legal forms of acquisition are merger or consolidation, acquisition of stock, and acquisition of assets.
2. **Tax issues** Mergers and acquisitions can be taxable or tax-free transactions. The primary issue is whether the target firm's stockholders sell or exchange their shares. Generally, a cash purchase will be a taxable merger, whereas a stock exchange will not be taxable. In a taxable merger, there are capital gains effects and asset write-up effects to consider. In a stock exchange, the target firm's shareholders become shareholders in the merged firm.

3. **Accounting issues** Accounting for mergers and acquisitions traditionally involved either the purchase method or the pooling of interests method. In 2001, pooling was eliminated as an option. As a result, a merger or acquisition will generally result in the creation of goodwill, but, under the new guidelines, goodwill does not have to be amortized.
4. **Merger valuation** If Firm A is acquiring Firm B, the benefits (ΔV) from the acquisition are defined as the value of the combined firm (V_{AB}) less the value of the firms as separate entities (V_A and V_B), or:

   $$\Delta V = V_{AB} - (V_A + V_B)$$

   The gain to Firm A from acquiring Firm B is the increased value of the acquired firm, ΔV, plus the value of B as a separate firm, V_B. The total value of Firm B to Firm A, V_B^*, is thus:

   $$V_B^* = \Delta V + V_B$$

   An acquisition will benefit the shareholders of the acquiring firm if this value is greater than the cost of the acquisition.

   The cost of an acquisition can be defined in general terms as the price paid to the shareholders of the acquired firm. The cost frequently includes a merger premium paid to the shareholders of the acquired firm. Moreover, the cost depends on the form of payment, that is, the choice between paying with cash or paying with common stock.
5. **Benefits** The possible benefits of an acquisition come from several sources, including the following:
   a. Revenue enhancement
   b. Cost reductions
   c. Lower taxes
   d. Reductions in capital needs
6. **Defensive tactics** Some of the most colorful language of finance comes from defensive tactics used in acquisition battles. *Poison pills, golden parachutes, crown jewels,* and *greenmail* are terms that describe various antitakeover tactics.
7. **Effect on shareholders** Mergers and acquisitions have been extensively studied. The basic conclusions are that, on average, the shareholders of target firms do very well, whereas the shareholders of bidding firms do not appear to gain very much.
8. **Divestitures** For a variety of reasons, companies often wish to sell assets or operating units. For relatively large divestitures involving operating units, firms sometimes elect to do carve-outs, spin-offs, or split-ups.

CONCEPT QUESTIONS

1. **Merger Accounting** Explain the difference between purchase and pooling of interests accounting for mergers. What is the effect on cash flows of the choice of accounting method? On EPS?
2. **Merger Concepts** Indicate whether you think the following claims regarding takeovers are true or false. In each case, provide a brief explanation for your answer.
   a. By merging competitors, takeovers have created monopolies that will raise product prices, reduce production, and harm consumers.
   b. Managers act in their own interests at times and in reality may not be answerable to shareholders. Takeovers may reflect runaway management.

c. In an efficient market, takeovers would not occur because market price would reflect the true value of corporations. Thus, bidding firms would not be justified in paying premiums above market prices for target firms.

d. Traders and institutional investors, having extremely short time horizons, are influenced by their perceptions of what other market traders will be thinking of stock prospects and do not value takeovers based on fundamental factors. Thus, they will sell shares in target firms despite the true value of the firms.

e. Mergers are a way of avoiding taxes because they allow the acquiring firm to write up the value of the assets of the acquired firm.

f. Acquisitions analysis frequently focuses on the total value of the firms involved. An acquisition, however, will usually affect relative values of stocks and bonds, as well as their total value.

3. **Merger Rationale** Explain why diversification *per se* is probably not a good reason for merger.

4. **Corporate Split** In May 2005, high-end retailer Nieman Marcus announced plans to sell off its private label credit card business. Unlike other credit cards, private label credit cards can only be used in a particular merchant's store. Why might a company do this? Is there a possibility of reverse synergy?

5. **Poison Pills** Are poison pills good or bad for stockholders? How do you think acquiring firms are able to get around poison pills?

6. **Merger and Taxes** Describe the advantages and disadvantages of a taxable merger as opposed to a tax-free exchange. What is the basic determinant of tax status in a merger? Would an LBO be taxable or nontaxable? Explain.

7. **Economies of Scale** What does it mean to say that a proposed merger will take advantage of available economies of scale? Suppose Eastern Power Co. and Western Power Co. are located in different time zones. Both operate at 60 percent of capacity except for peak periods, when they operate at 100 percent of capacity. The peak periods begin at 9:00 a.m. and 5:00 p.m. local time and last about 45 minutes. Explain why a merger between Eastern and Western might make sense.

8. **Hostile Takeovers** What types of actions might the management of a firm take to fight a hostile acquisition bid from an unwanted suitor? How do the target-firm shareholders benefit from the defensive tactics of their management team? How are the target-firm shareholders harmed by such actions? Explain.

9. **Merger Offers** Suppose a company in which you own stock has attracted two takeover offers. Would it ever make sense for your company's management to favor the lower offer? Does the form of payment affect your answer at all?

10. **Merger Profit** Acquiring-firm stockholders seem to benefit very little from takeovers. Why is this finding a puzzle? What are some of the reasons offered for it?

QUESTIONS AND PROBLEMS

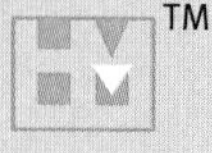

Basic
(Questions 1–10)

1. **Calculating Synergy** Evan Inc. has offered $740 million cash for all of the common stock in Tanner Corporation. Based on recent market information, Tanner is worth $650 million as an independent operation. If the merger makes economic sense for Evan, what is the minimum estimated value of the synergistic benefits from the merger?

2. **Balance Sheets for Mergers** Consider the following premerger information about Firm X and Firm Y:

	FIRM X	FIRM Y
Total earnings	$40,000	$15,000
Shares outstanding	20,000	20,000
Per-share values:		
Market	$ 49	$ 18
Book	$ 20	$ 7

Assume that Firm X acquires Firm Y by paying cash for all the shares outstanding at a merger premium of $5 per share. Assuming that neither firm has any debt before or after the merger, construct the postmerger balance sheet for Firm X assuming the use of (a) pooling of interests accounting methods and (b) purchase accounting methods.

3. **Balance Sheets for Mergers** Assume that the following balance sheets are stated at book value. Construct a postmerger balance sheet assuming that Jurion Co. purchases James, Inc., and the pooling of interests method of accounting is used. 

JURION CO.			
Current assets	$10,000	Current liabilities	$ 3,100
Net fixed assets	14,000	Long-term debt	1,900
		Equity	19,000
Total	$24,000	Total	$24,000

JAMES, INC.			
Current assets	$3,400	Current liabilities	$1,600
Net fixed assets	5,600	Long-term debt	900
		Equity	6,500
Total	$9,000	Total	$9,000

4. **Incorporating Goodwill** In the previous problem, suppose the fair market value of James's fixed assets is $12,000 versus the $5,600 book value shown. Jurion pays $17,000 for James and raises the needed funds through an issue of long-term debt. Construct the postmerger balance sheet now, assuming that the purchase method of accounting is used.

5. **Balance Sheets for Mergers** Silver Enterprises has acquired All Gold Mining in a merger transaction. Construct the balance sheet for the new corporation if the merger is treated as a pooling of interests for accounting purposes. The following balance sheets represent the premerger book values for both firms.

SILVER ENTERPRISES			
Current assets	$2,600	Current liabilities	$1,800
Other assets	800	Long-term debt	900
Net fixed assets	3,900	Equity	4,600
Total	$7,300	Total	$7,300

ALL GOLD MINING			
Current assets	$1,100	Current liabilities	$ 900
Other assets	350	Long-term debt	0
Net fixed assets	2,800	Equity	3,350
Total	$4,250	Total	$4,250

6. **Incorporating Goodwill** In the previous problem, construct the balance sheet for the new corporation assuming that the transaction is treated as a purchase for accounting purposes. The market value of All Gold Mining's fixed assets is $2,800; the market values for current and other assets are the same as the book values. Assume that Silver Enterprises issues $8,400 in new long-term debt to finance the acquisition.

7. **Cash versus Stock Payment** Penn Corp. is analyzing the possible acquisition of Teller Company. Both firms have no debt. Penn believes the acquisition will increase its total aftertax annual cash flows by $3.1 million indefinitely. The current market value of Teller is $78 million, and that of Penn is $135 million. The appropriate discount rate for the incremental cash flows is 12 percent. Penn is trying to decide whether it should offer 40 percent of its stock or $94 million in cash to Teller's shareholders.

   a. What is the cost of each alternative?

   b. What is the NPV of each alternative?

   c. Which alternative should Penn choose?

8. **EPS, PE, and Mergers** The shareholders of Flannery Company have voted in favor of a buyout offer from Stultz Corporation. Information about each firm is given here:

	FLANNERY	STULTZ
Price-earnings ratio	5.25	21
Shares outstanding	60,000	180,000
Earnings	$300,000	$675,000

   Flannery's shareholders will receive one share of Stultz stock for every three shares they hold in Flannery.

   a. What will the EPS of Stultz be after the merger? What will the PE ratio be if the NPV of the acquisition is zero?

   b. What must Stultz feel is the value of the synergy between these two firms? Explain how your answer can be reconciled with the decision to go ahead with the takeover.

9. **Merger Rationale** Cholern Electric Company (CEC) is a public utility that provides electricity to the central Colorado area. Recent events at its Mile-High Nuclear Station have been discouraging. Several shareholders have expressed concern over last year's financial statements.

INCOME STATEMENT LAST YEAR (IN $ MILLIONS)		BALANCE SHEET END OF YEAR (IN $ MILLIONS)	
Revenue	$110	Assets	$400
Fuel	50	Debt	300
Other expenses	30	Equity	100
Interest	30		
Net income	$ 0		

   Recently, a wealthy group of individuals has offered to purchase one-half of CEC's assets at fair market price. Management recommends that this offer be accepted because, "We believe our expertise in the energy industry can be better exploited by CEC if we sell our electricity generating and transmission assets and enter the telecommunications business. Although telecommunications is a riskier business than providing electricity as a public utility, it is also potentially very profitable."

   Should the management approve this transaction? Why or why not?

10. **Cash versus Stock as Payment** Consider the following premerger information about a bidding firm (Firm B) and a target firm (Firm T). Assume that both firms have no debt outstanding.

	FIRM B	FIRM T
Shares outstanding	1,500	900
Price per share	$34	$24

Firm B has estimated that the value of the synergistic benefits from acquiring Firm T is $3,000.

a. If Firm T is willing to be acquired for $27 per share in cash, what is the NPV of the merger?

b. What will the price per share of the merged firm be assuming the conditions in (a)?

c. In part (a), what is the merger premium?

d. Suppose Firm T is agreeable to a merger by an exchange of stock. If B offers three of its shares for every five of T's shares, what will the price per share of the merged firm be?

e. What is the NPV of the merger assuming the conditions in (d)?

Intermediate
(Questions 11–16)

11. **Cash versus Stock as Payment** In Problem 10, are the shareholders of Firm T better off with the cash offer or the stock offer? At what exchange ratio of B shares to T shares would the shareholders in T be indifferent between the two offers?

12. **Effects of a Stock Exchange** Consider the following premerger information about Firm A and Firm B:

	FIRM A	FIRM B
Total earnings	$900	$600
Shares outstanding	550	220
Price per share	$ 40	$ 15

Assume that Firm A acquires Firm B via an exchange of stock at a price of $20 for each share of B's stock. Both A and B have no debt outstanding.

a. What will the earnings per share, EPS, of Firm A be after the merger?

b. What will Firm A's price per share be after the merger if the market incorrectly analyzes this reported earnings growth (that is, the price-earnings ratio does not change)?

c. What will the price-earnings ratio of the postmerger firm be if the market correctly analyzes the transaction?

d. If there are no synergy gains, what will the share price of A be after the merger? What will the price-earnings ratio be? What does your answer for the share price tell you about the amount A bid for B? Was it too high? Too low? Explain.

13. **Merger NPV** Show that the NPV of a merger can be expressed as the value of the synergistic benefits, ΔV, less the merger premium.

14. **Merger NPV** Fly-By-Night Couriers is analyzing the possible acquisition of Flash-in-the-Pan Restaurants. Neither firm has debt. The forecasts of Fly-By-Night show that the purchase would increase its annual aftertax cash flow by $600,000 indefinitely. The current market value of Flash-in-the-Pan is $20 million. The current market value of Fly-By-Night is $35 million. The appropriate discount rate for the incremental cash flows is 8 percent. Fly-By-Night is trying to decide whether it should offer 25 percent of its stock or $25 million in cash to Flash-in-the-Pan.

a. What is the synergy from the merger?

b. What is the value of Flash-in-the-Pan to Fly-By-Night?

c. What is the cost to Fly-By-Night of each alternative?

d. What is the NPV to Fly-By-Night of each alternative?

e. Which alternative should Fly-By-Night use?

15. **Merger NPV** Harrods PLC has a market value of £600 million and 30 million shares outstanding. Selfridge Department Store has a market value of £200 million and 20 million shares outstanding. Harrods is contemplating acquiring Selfridge. Harrods's CFO concludes that the combined firm with synergy will be worth £1 billion and Selfridge can be acquired at a premium of £100 million.

    a. If Harrods offers 15 million shares of its stock in exchange for the 20 million shares of Selfridge, what will the stock price of Harrods be after the acquisition?

    b. What exchange ratio between the two stocks would make the value of a stock offer equivalent to a cash offer of £300 million?

16. **Mergers and Shareholder Value** Bentley Corp. and Rolls Manufacturing are considering a merger. The possible states of the economy and each company's value in that state are shown below:

STATE	PROBABILITY	BENTLEY	ROLLS
Boom	.70	$300,000	$260,000
Recession	.30	$110,000	$ 80,000

Bentley currently has a bond issue outstanding with a face value of $140,000. Rolls is an all-equity company.

    a. What is the value of each company before the merger?

    b. What is the value of each company's debt and equity before the merger?

    c. If the companies continue to operate separately, what is the total value of the companies, the total value of the equity, and the total value of the debt?

    d. What would be the value of the merged company? What would be the value of the merged company's debt and equity?

    e. Is there a transfer of wealth in this case? Why?

    f. Suppose that the face value of Bentley's debt was $100,000. Would this affect the transfer of wealth?

Challenge (Questions 17–18)

17. **Calculating NPV** Plant, Inc., is considering making an offer to purchase Palmer Corp. Plant's vice president of finance has collected the following information:

	PLANT	PALMER
Price-earnings ratio	12.5	9
Shares outstanding	1,000,000	550,000
Earnings	$2,000,000	$580,000
Dividends	600,000	290,000

Plant also knows that securities analysts expect the earnings and dividends of Palmer to grow at a constant rate of 5 percent each year. Plant management believes that the acquisition of Palmer will provide the firm with some economies of scale that will increase this growth rate to 7 percent per year.

    a. What is the value of Palmer to Plant?

    b. What would Plant's gain be from this acquisition?

c. If Plant were to offer $18 in cash for each share of Palmer, what would the NPV of the acquisition be?

d. What's the most Plant should be willing to pay in cash per share for the stock of Palmer?

e. If Plant were to offer 100,000 of its shares in exchange for the outstanding stock of Palmer, what would the NPV be?

f. Should the acquisition be attempted, and, if so, should it be as in (c) or as in (e)?

g. Plant's outside financial consultants think that the 7 percent growth rate is too optimistic and a 6 percent rate is more realistic. How does this change your previous answers?

18. **Mergers and Shareholder Value** The Chocolate Ice Cream Company and the Vanilla Ice Cream Company have agreed to merge and form Fudge Swirl Consolidated. Both companies are exactly alike except that they are located in different towns. The end-of-period value of each firm is determined by the weather, as shown below. There will be no synergy to the merger.

STATE	PROBABILITY	VALUE
Rainy	.1	$100,000
Warm	.4	200,000
Hot	.5	400,000

The weather conditions in each town are independent of those in the other. Furthermore, each company has an outstanding debt claim of $200,000. Assume that no premiums are paid in the merger.

a. What are the possible values of the combined company?

b. What are the possible values of end-of-period debt values and stock values after the merger?

c. Show that the bondholders are better off and the stockholders are worse off in the combined firm than they would have been if the firms had remained separate.

CLOSING CASE

THE BIRDIE GOLF–HYBRID GOLF MERGER

Birdie Golf, Inc., has been in merger talks with Hybrid Golf Company for the past six months. After several rounds of negotiations, the offer under discussion is a cash offer of $550 million for Hybrid Golf. Both companies have niche markets in the golf club industry, and the companies believe a merger will result in significant synergies due to economies of scale in manufacturing and marketing, as well as significant savings in general and administrative expenses.

Bryce Adams, the financial officer for Birdie, has been instrumental in the merger negotiations. Bryce has prepared the following pro forma financial statements for Hybrid Golf assuming the merger takes place. The financial statements include all synergistic benefits from the merger.

	2007	2008	2009	2010	2011
Sales	$800,000,000	$900,000,000	$1,000,000,000	$1,125,000,000	$1,250,000,000
Production costs	562,000,000	630,000,000	700,000,000	790,000,000	875,000,000
Depreciation	75,000,000	80,000,000	82,000,000	83,000,000	83,000,000
Other expenses	80,000,000	90,000,000	100,000,000	113,000,000	125,000,000
EBIT	$ 83,000,000	$100,000,000	$ 118,000,000	$ 139,000,000	$ 167,000,000
Interest	19,000,000	22,000,000	24,000,000	25,000,000	27,000,000
Taxable income	$ 64,000,000	$ 78,000,000	$ 94,000,000	$ 114,000,000	$ 140,000,000
Taxes (40%)	25,600,000	31,200,000	37,600,000	45,600,000	56,000,000
Net income	$ 38,400,000	$ 46,800,000	$ 56,400,000	$ 68,400,000	$ 84,000,000

Bryce is also aware that the Hybrid Golf division will require investments each year for continuing operations, along with sources of financing. The table below outlines the required investments and sources of financing.

	2007	2008	2009	2010	2011
Investments:					
Net working capital	$20,000,000	$25,000,000	$25,000,000	$30,000,000	$30,000,000
Fixed assets	15,000,000	25,000,000	18,000,000	12,000,000	7,000,000
Total	$35,000,000	$50,000,000	$43,000,000	$42,000,000	$37,000,000
Sources of Financing:					
New debt	$35,000,000	$16,000,000	$16,000,000	$15,000,000	$12,000,000
Profit retention	0	34,000,000	27,000,000	27,000,000	25,000,000
Total	$35,000,000	$50,000,000	$43,000,000	$42,000,000	$37,000,000

The management of Birdie Golf feels that the capital structure at Hybrid Golf is not optimal. If the merger takes place, Hybrid Golf will immediately increase its leverage with a $110 million debt issue, which would be followed by a $150 million dividend payment to Birdie Golf. This will increase Hybrid's debt-to-equity ratio from .50 to 1.00. Birdie Golf will also be able to use a $25 million tax-loss carryforward in 2008 and 2009 from Hybrid Golf's previous operations. The total value of Hybrid Golf is expected to be $900 million in five years, and the company will have $300 million in debt at that time.

Stock in Birdie Golf currently sells for $94 per share, and the company has 18 million shares of stock outstanding. Hybrid Golf has 8 million shares of stock outstanding. Both companies can borrow at an 8 percent interest rate. The risk-free rate is 6 percent, and the expected return on the market is 13 percent. Bryce believes the current cost of capital for Birdie Golf is 11 percent. The beta for Hybrid Golf stock at its current capital structure is 1.30.

Bryce has asked you to analyze the financial aspects of the potential merger. Specifically, he has asked you to answer the following questions.

1. Suppose Hybrid shareholders will agree to a merger price of $68.75 per share. Should Birdie proceed with the merger?
2. What is the highest price per share that Birdie should be willing to pay for Hybrid?
3. Suppose Birdie is unwilling to pay cash for the merger, but will consider a stock exchange. What exchange ratio would make the merger terms equivalent to the original merger price of $68.75 per share?
4. What is the highest exchange ratio Birdie would be willing to pay and still undertake the merger?

CHAPTER 20

International Corporate Finance

OPENING CASE

Relatively few large companies operate in a single country, and companies based in the United States are no exception. In 2005, multinational companies based in the United States received a significant tax break with the passage of the American Jobs Creation Act. The act allowed multinational companies to return or "repatriate" profits earned overseas prior to 2003 back to the United States at a tax rate of only 5.25 percent. Previously, the tax rate on repatriated profits were as high as 35 percent, which encouraged companies to invest profits from foreign operations in other countries, thereby avoiding the tax. The goal of the act was to encourage companies to move resources from foreign operations to the United States. Economists estimated the total amount repatriated could reach as much as $300 billion. Pharm giant Pfizer, for example, was expected to repatriate as much as $38 billion, and Johnson & Johnson said it would bring home $11 billion. Of course, taxes are only one of the intricacies involved in global operations. In this chapter, we will explore the roles played by currencies and exchange rates, along with a number of other key topics in international finance.

Corporations with significant foreign operations are often called *international corporations* or *multinationals*. Such corporations must consider many financial factors that do not directly affect purely domestic firms. These include foreign exchange rates, differing interest rates from country to country, complex accounting methods for foreign operations, foreign tax rates, and foreign government intervention.

The basic principles of corporate finance still apply to international corporations; like domestic companies, these firms seek to invest in projects that create more value for the shareholders than they cost and to arrange financing that raises cash at the lowest possible cost. In other words, the net present value principle holds for both foreign and domestic operations, although it is usually more complicated to apply the NPV rule to foreign investments.

One of the most significant complications of international finance is foreign exchange. The foreign exchange markets provide important information and opportunities for an international corporation when it undertakes capital budgeting and financing decisions. As we will discuss, international exchange rates, interest rates, and inflation rates are closely related. We will spend much of this chapter exploring the connection between these financial variables.

We won't have much to say here about the role of cultural and social differences in international business. Neither will we be discussing the implications of differing political and economic systems. These factors are of great importance to international businesses, but it would take another book to do them justice. Consequently, we will focus only on some purely financial considerations in international finance and some key aspects of foreign exchange markets.

20.1 TERMINOLOGY

A common buzzword for the student of business finance is *globalization*. The first step in learning about the globalization of financial markets is to conquer the new vocabulary. As with any specialty, international finance is rich in jargon. Accordingly, we get started on the subject with a highly eclectic vocabulary exercise.

The terms that follow are presented alphabetically, and they are not all of equal importance. We choose these particular ones because they appear frequently in the financial press or because they illustrate the colorful nature of the language of international finance.

See www.adr.com for more.

1. An **American Depositary Receipt (ADR)** is a security issued in the United States that represents shares of a foreign stock, allowing that stock to be traded in the United States. Foreign companies use ADRs, which are issued in U.S. dollars, to expand the pool of potential U.S. investors. ADRs are available in two forms for a large and growing number of foreign companies: company sponsored, which are listed on an exchange, and unsponsored, which usually are held by the investment bank that makes a market in the ADR. Both forms are available to individual investors, but only company-sponsored issues are quoted daily in newspapers.
2. The **cross-rate** is the implicit exchange rate between two currencies (usually non-U.S.) when both are quoted in some third currency, usually the U.S. dollar.
3. A **Eurobond** is a bond issued in multiple countries, but denominated in a single currency, usually the issuer's home currency. Such bonds have become an important way to raise capital for many international companies and governments. Eurobonds are issued outside the restrictions that apply to domestic offerings and are syndicated and traded mostly from London. Trading can and does take place anywhere there is a buyer and a seller.

4. **Eurocurrency** is money deposited in a financial center outside of the country whose currency is involved. For instance, Eurodollars–the most widely used Eurocurrency–are U.S. dollars deposited in banks outside the U.S. banking system.
5. **Foreign bonds**, unlike Eurobonds, are issued in a single country and are usually denominated in that country's currency. Often, the country in which these bonds are issued will draw distinctions between them and bonds issued by domestic issuers, including different tax laws, restrictions on the amount issued, and tougher disclosure rules.

   Foreign bonds often are nicknamed for the country where they are issued: Yankee bonds (United States), Samurai bonds (Japan), Rembrandt bonds (the Netherlands), Bulldog bonds (Britain). Partly because of tougher regulations and disclosure requirements, the foreign bond market hasn't grown in past years with the vigor of the Eurobond market.
6. **Gilts**, technically, are British and Irish government securities, although the term also includes issues of local British authorities and some overseas public sector offerings.
7. The **London Interbank Offer Rate (LIBOR)** is the rate that most international banks charge one another for loans of Eurodollars overnight in the London market. LIBOR is a cornerstone in the pricing of money market issues and other short-term debt issues by both government and corporate borrowers. Interest rates are frequently quoted as some spread over LIBOR, and they then float with the LIBOR rate.
8. There are two basic kinds of **swaps**: interest rate and currency. An interest rate swap occurs when two parties exchange a floating-rate payment for a fixed-rate payment or vice versa. Currency swaps are agreements to deliver one currency in exchange for another. Often, both types of swaps are used in the same transaction when debt denominated in different currencies is swapped.

For current LIBOR rates, see www.bloomberg.com.

20.2 FOREIGN EXCHANGE MARKETS AND EXCHANGE RATES

The **foreign exchange market** is undoubtedly the world's largest financial market. It is the market where one country's currency is traded for another's. Most of the trading takes place in a few currencies: the U.S. dollar ($), the British pound sterling (£), the Japanese yen (¥), and the euro (€). Table 20.1 lists some of the more common currencies and their symbols.

The foreign exchange market is an over-the-counter market, so there is no single location where traders get together. Instead, market participants are located in the major commercial and investment banks around the world. They communicate using computer terminals, telephones, and other telecommunications devices. For example, one communications network for foreign transactions is maintained by the Society for Worldwide Interbank Financial Telecommunications (SWIFT), a Belgian not-for-profit cooperative. Using data transmission lines, a bank in New York can send messages to a bank in London via SWIFT regional processing centers.

The many different types of participants in the foreign exchange market include the following:

1. Importers who pay for goods using foreign currencies.
2. Exporters who receive foreign currency and may want to convert to the domestic currency.
3. Portfolio managers who buy or sell foreign stocks and bonds.
4. Foreign exchange brokers who match buy and sell orders.

Visit SWIFT at www.swift.com.

TABLE 20.1
International Currency Symbols

COUNTRY	CURRENCY	SYMBOL
Australia	Dollar	A$
Canada	Dollar	Can$
Denmark	Krone	DKr
EMU	Euro	€
India	Rupee	Rs
Iran	Rial	Rl
Japan	Yen	¥
Kuwait	Dinar	KD
Mexico	Peso	Ps
Norway	Krone	NKr
Saudi Arabia	Riyal	SR
Singapore	Dollar	S$
South Africa	Rand	R
Sweden	Krona	SKr
Switzerland	Franc	SF
United Kingdom	Pound	£
United States	Dollar	$

5. Traders who "make a market" in foreign currencies.
6. Speculators who try to profit from changes in exchange rates.

Exchange Rates

An **exchange rate** is simply the price of one country's currency expressed in terms of another country's currency. In practice, almost all trading of currencies takes place in terms of the U.S. dollar. For example, both the Swiss franc and the Japanese yen are traded with their prices quoted in U.S. dollars. Exchange rates are constantly changing.

EXCHANGE RATE QUOTATIONS Figure 20.1 reproduces exchange rate quotations as they appeared in *The Wall Street Journal* in 2005. The first two columns (labeled "U.S. $ equivalent") give the number of dollars it takes to buy one unit of foreign currency. Because this is the price in dollars of a foreign currency, it is called a *direct* or *American quote* (remember that "Americans are direct"). For example, the Australian dollar is quoted at .7659, which means that you can buy one Australian dollar with U.S. $.7659.

Get up-to-the-minute exchange rates at www.xe.com and www.exchangerate.com.

The third and fourth columns show the *indirect,* or *European, exchange rate* (even though the currency may not be European). This is the amount of foreign currency per U.S. dollar. The Australian dollar is quoted here at 1.3057, so you can get 1.3057 Australian dollars for one U.S. dollar. Naturally, this second exchange rate is just the reciprocal of the first one (possibly with a little rounding error), 1/.7659 = 1.3057.

You can also find exchange rates on a number of Web sites. Suppose you have just returned from your dream vacation to Jamaica and feel rich since you have 10,000 Jamaican dollars left over. You now need to convert these to U.S. dollars. How much will you have? We went to www.xe.com and used the currency converter on the site to find out. This is what we found:

xe.com Universal Currency Converter® Results

Live mid-market rates as of 2005.05.14 17:51:51 UTC.

10,000.00 JMD Jamaica Dollars	=	**162.537 USD** United States Dollars
1 JMD = 0.0162537 USD		1 USD = 61.5245 JMD

Another Conversion? · Bookmark Us

Key Currency Cross Rates

Late New York Trading Thursday, May 12, 2005

	Dollar	Euro	Pound	SFranc	Peso	Yen	CdnDlr
Canada	1.2514	1.5900	2.3351	1.0303	.11374	.01172	...
Japan	106.77	135.66	199.23	87.903	9.704	...	85.319
Mexico	11.0023	13.9795	20.530	9.0582	...	.10305	8.7919
Switzerland	1.2146	1.5433	2.2665	...	.11040	.01138	.9706
U.K.	.53590	.6809	...	.4412	.04871	.00502	.42824
Euro	.78700	...	1.4686	.64796	.07153	.00737	.62892
U.S.	...	1.2706	1.8660	.82330	.09089	.00937	.79910

Source: Reuters

Exchange Rates

May 12, 2005

The foreign exchange mid-range rates below apply to trading among banks in amounts of $1 million and more, as quoted at 4 p.m. Eastern time by Reuters and other sources. Retail transactions provide fewer units of foreign currency per dollar.

	U.S. $ EQUIVALENT		CURRENCY PER U.S. $	
Country	**Thu**	**Wed**	**Thu**	**Wed**
Argentina (Peso)-y	.3457	.3453	2.8927	2.8960
Australia (Dollar)	.7659	.7746	1.3057	1.2910
Bahrain (Dinar)	2.6524	2.6524	.3770	.3770
Brazil (Real)	.4053	.4073	2.4673	2.4552
Canada (Dollar)	.7991	.8014	1.2514	1.2478
1-month forward	.7995	.8018	1.2508	1.2472
3-months forward	.8004	.8026	1.2494	1.2460
6-months forward	.8022	.8045	1.2466	1.2430
Chile (Peso)	.001736	.001737	576.04	575.71
China (Renminbi)	.1208	.1208	8.2764	8.2765
Colombia (Peso)	.0004274	.0004275	2339.73	2339.18
Czech. Rep. (Koruna)				
Commercial rate	.04241	.04280	23.579	23.365
Denmark (Krone)	.1707	.1720	5.8582	5.8140
Ecuador (US Dollar)	1.0000	1.0000	1.0000	1.0000
Egypt (Pound)-y	.1724	.1724	5.7991	5.7995
Hong Kong (Dollar)	.1282	.1282	7.8003	7.8003
Hungary (Forint)	.005076	.005128	197.01	195.01
India (Rupee)	.02305	.02316	43.384	43.178
Indonesia (Rupiah)	.0001056	.0001057	9470	9461
Israel (Shekel)	.2288	.2287	4.3706	4.3725
Japan (Yen)	.009366	.009454	106.77	105.78
1-month forward	.009391	.009479	106.48	105.50
3-months forward	.009443	.009533	105.90	104.90
6-months forward	.009530	.009620	104.93	103.95
Jordan (Dinar)	1.4115	1.4115	.7085	.7085
Kuwait (Dinar)	3.4247	3.4238	.2920	.2921
Lebanon (Pound)	.0006616	.0006614	1511.49	1511.94
Malaysia (Ringgit)-b	.2632	.2632	3.7994	3.7994
Malta (Lira)	2.9598	2.9829	.3379	.3352
Mexico (Peso)				
Floating rate	.0909	.0908	11.0023	11.0096
New Zealand (Dollar)	.7192	.7297	1.3904	1.3704
Norway (Krone)	.1569	.1584	6.3735	6.3131
Pakistan (Rupee)	.01680	.01680	59.524	59.524
Peru (new Sol)	.3073	.3073	3.2541	3.2541
Philippines (Peso)	.01842	.01845	54.289	54.201
Poland (Zloty)	.3051	.3084	3.2776	3.2425
Russia (Ruble)-a	.03585	.03590	27.894	27.855
Saudi Arabia (Riyal)	.2667	.2666	3.7495	3.7509
Singapore (Dollar)	.6043	.6081	1.6548	1.6445
Slovak Rep. (Koruna)	.03267	.03299	30.609	30.312
South Africa (Rand)	.1593	.1613	6.2775	6.1996
South Korea (Won)	.0010008	.0010025	999.20	997.51
Sweden (Krona)	.1377	.1387	7.2622	7.2098
Switzerland (Franc)	.8233	.8293	1.2146	1.2058
1-month forward	.8250	.8309	1.2121	1.2035
3-months forward	.8286	.8346	1.2069	1.1982
6-months forward	.8347	.8407	1.1980	1.1895
Taiwan (Dollar)	.03194	.03216	31.309	31.095
Thailand (Baht)	.02532	.02538	39.495	39.401
Turkey (New Lira)-d	.7326	.7307	1.3650	1.3685
U.K. (Pound)	1.8660	1.8716	.5359	.5343
1-month forward	1.8632	1.8689	.5367	.5351
3-months forward	1.8587	1.8641	.5380	.5365
6-months forward	1.8539	1.8592	.5394	.5379
United Arab (Dirham)	.2723	.2723	3.6724	3.6724
Uruguay (Peso)				
Financial	.04090	.04090	24.450	24.450
Venezuela (Bolivar)	.000466	.000466	2145.92	2145.92
SDR	1.5027	1.5106	.6655	.6620
Euro	1.2706	1.2804	.7870	.7810

Special Drawing Rights (SDR) are based on exchange rates for the U.S., British, and Japanese currencies. Source: International Monetary Fund.

a-Russian Central Bank rate. b-Government rate. d-Rebased as of Jan. 1, 2005. y-Floating rate.

FIGURE 20.1

Exchange Rate Quotations

Source: Reprinted by permission of *The Wall Street Journal*, © 2005 Dow Jones & Company, Inc., May 13, 2005. All Rights Reserved Worldwide.

Looks like you left Jamaica just before you ran out of money.

EXAMPLE 20.1 A Yen for Euros

Suppose you have $1,000. Based on the rates in Figure 20.1, how many Japanese yen can you get? Alternatively, if a Porsche costs € 100,000 (recall that € is the symbol for the euro), how many dollars will you need to buy it?

The exchange rate in terms of yen per dollar (third column) is 106.77. Your $1,000 will thus get you:

$1,000 × 106.77 yen per $1 = 106,770 yen

Because the exchange rate in terms of dollars per euro (first column) is 1.2706, you will need:

€100,000 × $1.2706 per € = $127,060

CROSS-RATES AND TRIANGLE ARBITRAGE Using the U.S. dollar as the common denominator in quoting exchange rates greatly reduces the number of possible cross-currency quotes. For example, with five major currencies, there would potentially be

10 exchange rates instead of just 4.[1] Also, the fact that the dollar is used throughout cuts down on inconsistencies in the exchange rate quotations.

Earlier, we defined the cross-rate as the exchange rate for a non-U.S. currency expressed in terms of another non-U.S. currency. For example, suppose we observe the following for the euro (€) and the Swiss franc (SF):

€ per $1 = 1.00
SF per $1 = 2.00

Suppose the cross-rate is quoted as:

€ per SF = .40

What do you think?

The cross-rate here is inconsistent with the exchange rates. To see this, suppose you have $100. If you convert this to Swiss francs, you will receive:

$100 × SF 2 per $1 = SF 200

If you convert this to euros at the cross-rate, you will have:

SF 200 × €.4 per SF 1 = €80

However, if you just convert your dollars to euros without going through Swiss francs, you will have:

$100 × €1 per $1 = €100

What we see is that the euro has two prices, €1 per $1 and €.80 per $1, with the price we pay depending on how we get the euros.

To make money, we want to buy low and sell high. The important thing to note is that euros are cheaper if you buy them with dollars because you get 1 euro instead of just .8. You should proceed as follows:

1. Buy 100 euros for $100.
2. Use the 100 euros to buy Swiss francs at the cross-rate. Because it takes .4 euros to buy a Swiss franc, you will receive €100/.4 = SF 250.
3. Use the SF 250 to buy dollars. Because the exchange rate is SF 2 per dollar, you receive SF 250/2 = $125, for a round-trip profit of $25.
4. Repeat steps 1 through 3.

This particular activity is called *triangle arbitrage* because the arbitrage involves moving through three different exchange rates:

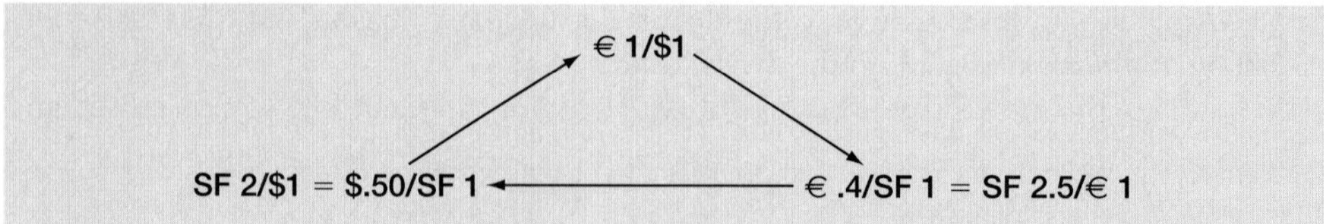

To prevent such opportunities, it is not difficult to see that because a dollar will buy you either 1 euro or 2 Swiss francs, the cross-rate must be:

(€1/$1)/(SF 2/$1) = €1/SF 2

[1]There are four exchange rates instead of five because one exchange rate would involve the exchange of a currency for itself. More generally, it might seem that there should be 25 exchange rates with five currencies. There are 25 different combinations, but, of these, 5 involve the exchange of a currency for itself. Of the remaining 20, half are redundant because they are just the reciprocals of another exchange rate. Of the remaining 10, 6 can be eliminated by using a common denominator.

That is, the cross-rate must be one euro per two Swiss francs. If it were anything else, there would be a triangle arbitrage opportunity.

EXAMPLE 20.2 Shedding Some Pounds

Suppose the exchange rates for the British pound and Swiss franc are:

Pounds per \$1 = .60
SF per \$1 = 2.00

The cross-rate is three francs per pound. Is this consistent? Explain how to go about making some money.

The cross-rate should be SF 2.00/£.60 = SF 3.33 per pound. You can buy a pound for SF 3 in one market, and you can sell a pound for SF 3.33 in another. So we want to first get some francs, then use the francs to buy some pounds, and then sell the pounds. Assuming you have \$100, you could:

1. Exchange dollars for francs: \$100 × 2 = SF 200.
2. Exchange francs for pounds: SF 200/3 = £66.67.
3. Exchange pounds for dollars: £66.67/.60 = \$111.12.

This would result in an \$11.12 round-trip profit.

For international news and events, visit www.ft.com.

TYPES OF TRANSACTIONS There are two basic types of trades in the foreign exchange market: spot trades and forward trades. A **spot trade** is an agreement to exchange currency "on the spot," which actually means that the transaction will be completed or settled within two business days. The exchange rate on a spot trade is called the **spot exchange rate**. Implicitly, all of the exchange rates and transactions we have discussed so far have referred to the spot market.

A **forward trade** is an agreement to exchange currency at some time in the future. The exchange rate that will be used is agreed upon today and is called the **forward exchange rate**. A forward trade will normally be settled sometime in the next 12 months.

If you look back at Figure 20.1, you will see forward exchange rates quoted for some of the major currencies. For example, the spot exchange rate for the Swiss franc is SF 1 = \$.8233. The 180-day (6-month) forward exchange rate is SF 1 = \$.8347. This means that you can buy a Swiss franc today for \$.8233 or you can agree to take delivery of a Swiss franc in 180 days and pay \$.8347 at that time.

Notice that the Swiss franc is more expensive in the forward market (\$.8347 versus \$.8233). Because the Swiss franc is more expensive in the future than it is today, it is said to be selling at a *premium* relative to the dollar. For the same reason, the dollar is said to be selling at a *discount* relative to the Swiss franc.

Why does the forward market exist? One answer is that it allows businesses and individuals to lock in a future exchange rate today, thereby eliminating any risk from unfavorable shifts in the exchange rate.

EXAMPLE 20.3 Looking Forward

Suppose you are expecting to receive a million British pounds in six months, and you agree to a forward trade to exchange your pounds for dollars. Based on Figure 20.1, how many dollars will you get in six months? Is the pound selling at a discount or a premium relative to the dollar?

(continued)

In Figure 20.1, the spot exchange rate and the 180-day forward rate in terms of dollars per pound are \$1.8660 = £1 and \$1.8539 = £1, respectively. If you expect £1 million in 180 days, then you will get £1 million × \$1.8539 per pound = \$1.8539 million. Because it is cheaper to buy a pound in the forward market than in the spot market (\$1.8539 versus \$1.8660), the pound is said to be selling at a discount relative to the dollar.

As we mentioned earlier, it is standard practice around the world (with a few exceptions) to quote exchange rates in terms of the U.S. dollar. This means that rates are quoted as the amount of currency per U.S. dollar. For the remainder of this chapter, we will stick with this form. Things can get extremely confusing if you forget this. Thus, when we say things like "the exchange rate is expected to rise," it is important to remember that we are talking about the exchange rate quoted as units of foreign currency per dollar.

20.3 PURCHASING POWER PARITY

Now that we have discussed what exchange rate quotations mean, we can address an obvious question: What determines the level of the spot exchange rate? In addition, because we know that exchange rates change through time, we can ask the related question, What determines the rate of change in exchange rates? At least part of the answer in both cases goes by the name of **purchasing power parity (PPP)**, the idea that the exchange rate adjusts to keep purchasing power constant among currencies. As we discuss next, there are two forms of PPP, *absolute* and *relative*.

Absolute Purchasing Power Parity

The basic idea behind *absolute purchasing power parity* is that a commodity costs the same regardless of what currency is used to purchase it or where it is selling. This is a very straightforward concept. If a beer costs £2 in London, and the exchange rate is £.60 per dollar, then a beer costs £2/.60 = \$3.33 in New York. In other words, absolute PPP says that \$1 will buy you the same number of, say, cheeseburgers anywhere in the world.

More formally, let S_0 be the spot exchange rate between the British pound and the U.S. dollar today (Time 0), and remember that we are quoting exchange rates as the amount of foreign currency per dollar. Let P_{US} and P_{UK} be the current U.S. and British prices, respectively, on a particular commodity, say, apples. Absolute PPP simply says that:

$$P_{UK} = S_0 \times P_{US}$$

This tells us that the British price for something is equal to the U.S. price for that same something multiplied by the exchange rate.

The rationale behind PPP is similar to that behind triangle arbitrage. If PPP did not hold, arbitrage would be possible (in principle) if apples were moved from one country to another. For example, suppose apples are selling in New York for \$4 per bushel, whereas in London the price is £2.40 per bushel. Absolute PPP implies that:

$$\begin{aligned} P_{UK} &= S_0 \times P_{US} \\ £2.40 &= S_0 \times \$4 \\ S_0 &= £2.40/\$4 = £.60 \end{aligned}$$

That is, the implied spot exchange rate is £.60 per dollar. Equivalently, a pound is worth \$1/£.60 = \$1.67.

Suppose that, instead, the actual exchange rate is £.50. Starting with \$4, a trader could buy a bushel of apples in New York, ship it to London, and sell it there for £2.40. Our trader could then convert the £2.40 into dollars at the prevailing exchange rate, S_0 = £.50, yielding a total of £2.40/.50 = \$4.80. The round-trip gain would be 80 cents.

Because of this profit potential, forces are set in motion to change the exchange rate and/or the price of apples. In our example, apples would begin moving from New York to London. The reduced supply of apples in New York would raise the price of apples there, and the increased supply in Britain would lower the price of apples in London.

In addition to moving apples around, apple traders would be busily converting pounds back into dollars to buy more apples. This activity would increase the supply of pounds and simultaneously increase the demand for dollars. We would expect the value of a pound to fall. This means that the dollar would be getting more valuable, so it would take more pounds to buy one dollar. Because the exchange rate is quoted as pounds per dollar, we would expect the exchange rate to rise from £.50.

For absolute PPP to hold absolutely, several things must be true:

1. The transactions costs of trading apples–shipping, insurance, spoilage, and so on–must be zero.
2. There must be no barriers to trading apples–no tariffs, taxes, or other political barriers.
3. Finally, an apple in New York must be identical to an apple in London. It won't do for you to send red apples to London if the English eat only green apples.

Given the fact that the transactions costs are not zero and that the other conditions are rarely met exactly, it is not surprising that absolute PPP is really applicable only to traded goods, and then only to very uniform ones.

For this reason, absolute PPP does not imply that a Mercedes costs the same as a Ford or that a nuclear power plant in France costs the same as one in New York. In the case of the cars, they are not identical. In the case of the power plants, even if they were identical, they are expensive and would be very difficult to ship. On the other hand, we would be very surprised to see a significant violation of absolute PPP for gold.

As an example of a violation of absolute PPP, in late 2003, the euro was going for about $1.30. Porsche's new, and very desirable, Carrera GT sold for about $440,000 in the United States. This converted to a euro price of €338,462 before tax and €392,615 after tax. The price of the car in Germany was €452,690, which means that if German residents could ship the car for less than €60,000 they would be better off buying it in the United States.

Violations of PPP are actually sought out by corporations. For example, in the middle of 2004, Alcoa announced that it would build a $1 billion aluminum smelter plant on the Caribbean island of Trinidad. At the same time, the company was breaking ground on another $1 billion plant in Iceland and looking into other locations including China, Brunei, Bahrain, Brazil, and Canada. In all cases, low energy costs were the attraction (aluminum smelting is very energy-intensive). Meanwhile, the company had several plants in the Pacific Northwest that were closed because higher electricity prices in this region made the plants unprofitable. A nearby *The Real World* box explores a famous example of PPP violations.

Relative Purchasing Power Parity

As a practical matter, a relative version of purchasing power parity has evolved. *Relative purchasing power parity* does not tell us what determines the absolute level of the exchange rate. Instead, it tells us what determines the *change* in the exchange rate over time.

THE BASIC IDEA Suppose the British pound–U.S. dollar exchange rate is currently S_0 = £.50. Further suppose that the inflation rate in Britain is predicted to be 10 percent over the coming year, and (for the moment) the inflation rate in the United States is predicted to be zero. What do you think the exchange rate will be in a year?

THE REAL WORLD

McPRICING

As we discussed in the chapter, the idea of absolute purchasing power parity (PPP) does not seem to hold in practice. One of the more famous violations of absolute PPP is the Big Mac index constructed by *The Economist.* To construct the index, prices for a Big Mac in different countries are gathered from McDonald's. Below you will find the December 2004 Big Mac index from www.economist.com (we will leave it to you to find the most recent index).

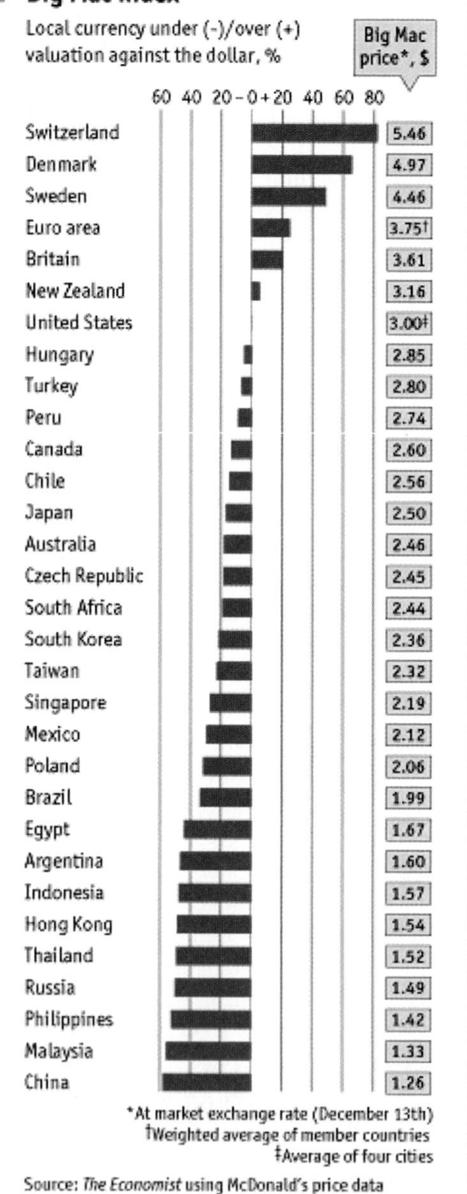

As you can see from the index, absolute PPP does not seem to hold, at least for the Big Mac. In fact, in only 4 of the 29 currencies surveyed by *The Economist* is the exchange rate within 10 percent of that predicted by absolute PPP. The biggest disparity is in Switzerland, where the currency is apparently overvalued by 80 percent. And 12 of the 29 currencies are "incorrectly" priced by more than 40 percent. Why?

There are several reasons. First, a Big Mac is not really transportable. Yes, you can load a ship with Big Macs and send them to Denmark where the currency is supposedly overvalued by more than 60 percent. But do you really think people would buy your Big Macs? Probably not. Even though it is relatively easy to transport a Big Mac, it would be relatively expensive and the hamburger would suffer in quality along the way.

Also, if you look, the price of the Big Mac is the average of the prices from New York, Chicago, San Francisco, and Atlanta. The reason is that the Big Mac does not sell for the same price in different areas of the United States, where presumably they are all purchased with the dollar. The cost of living and competition are only a few of the factors that affect the price of a Big Mac in the United States. Since Big Macs are not priced the same in the same country and currency, would we expect absolute PPP to hold across currencies?

Finally, differing tastes can also account for the apparent discrepancy. In the United States, hamburgers and fast food have become staples of the American diet. In other countries, hamburgers have not become as entrenched. We would expect the price of the Big Mac to be lower in the United States since there is much more competition.

Having examined the Big Mac prices, we should say that absolute PPP should hold more closely for more readily transportable items. For instance, there are many companies with stock listed on both the NYSE and the stock exchange of another country. If you examine the share prices on the two exchanges you will find that the price of the stock is almost exactly what absolute PPP would predict. The reason is that a share of stock in a particular company is (usually) the same wherever you buy it and whatever currency is used.

If you think about it, you see that a dollar currently costs .50 pounds in Britain. With 10 percent inflation, we expect prices in Britain to generally rise by 10 percent. So we expect that the price of a dollar will go up by 10 percent, and the exchange rate should rise to £.50 × 1.1 = £.55.

If the inflation rate in the United States is not zero, then we need to worry about the *relative* inflation rates in the two countries. For example, suppose the U.S. inflation rate is predicted to be 4 percent. Relative to prices in the United States, prices in Britain are rising at a rate of 10 percent − 4 percent = 6 percent per year. So we expect the price of the dollar to rise by 6 percent, and the predicted exchange rate is £.50 × 1.06 = £.53.

THE RESULT In general, relative PPP says that the change in the exchange rate is determined by the difference in the inflation rates of the two countries. To be more specific, we will use the following notation:

$\mathbf{S_0}$ = **Current (Time 0) spot exchange rate (foreign currency per dollar)**
$\mathbf{E(S_t)}$ = **Expected exchange rate in *t* periods**
$\mathbf{h_{US}}$ = **Inflation rate in the United States**
$\mathbf{h_{FC}}$ = **Foreign country inflation rate**

Based on our discussion just preceding, relative PPP says that the expected percentage change in the exchange rate over the next year, $[E(S_1) - S_0]/S_0$, is:

$$[E(S_1) - S_0]/S_0 = h_{FC} - h_{US} \tag{20.1}$$

In words, relative PPP simply says that the expected percentage change in the exchange rate is equal to the difference in inflation rates. If we rearrange this slightly, we get:

$$E(S_1) = S_0 \times [1 + (h_{FC} - h_{US})] \tag{20.2}$$

This result makes a certain amount of sense, but care must be used in quoting the exchange rate.

In our example involving Britain and the United States, relative PPP tells us that the exchange rate will rise by $h_{FC} - h_{US}$ = 10 percent − 4 percent = 6 percent per year. Assuming the difference in inflation rates doesn't change, the expected exchange rate in two years, $E(S_2)$, will therefore be:

$$\begin{aligned} E(S_2) &= E(S_1) \times (1 + .06) \\ &= .53 \times 1.06 \\ &= .562 \end{aligned}$$

Notice that we could have written this as:

$$\begin{aligned} E(S_2) &= .53 \times 1.06 \\ &= .50 \times (1.06 \times 1.06) \\ &= .50 \times 1.06^2 \end{aligned}$$

In general, relative PPP says that the expected exchange rate at some time in the future, $E(S_t)$, is:

$$E(S_t) = S_0 \times [1 + (h_{FC} - h_{US})]^T \tag{20.3}$$

As we will see, this is a very useful relationship.

Because we don't really expect absolute PPP to hold for most goods, we will focus on relative PPP in our following discussion. Henceforth, when we refer to PPP without further qualification, we mean relative PPP.

EXAMPLE 20.4 It's All Relative

Suppose the Japanese exchange rate is currently 105 yen per dollar. The inflation rate in Japan over the next three years will run, say, 2 percent per year, whereas the U.S. inflation rate will be 6 percent. Based on relative PPP, what will the exchange rate be in three years?

Because the U.S. inflation rate is higher, we expect that a dollar will become less valuable. The exchange rate change will be 2 percent − 6 percent = −4 percent per year. Over three years, the exchange rate will fall to:

$$\begin{aligned} E(S_3) &= S_0 \times [1 + (h_{FC} - h_{US})]^3 \\ &= 105 \times [1 + (-.04)]^3 \\ &= 92.90 \end{aligned}$$

CURRENCY APPRECIATION AND DEPRECIATION We frequently hear things like "the dollar strengthened (or weakened) in financial markets today" or "the dollar is expected to appreciate (or depreciate) relative to the pound." When we say that the dollar strengthens or appreciates, we mean that the value of a dollar rises, so it takes more foreign currency to buy a dollar.

What happens to the exchange rates as currencies fluctuate in value depends on how exchange rates are quoted. Because we are quoting them as units of foreign currency per dollar, the exchange rate moves in the same direction as the value of the dollar: It rises as the dollar strengthens, and it falls as the dollar weakens.

Relative PPP tells us that the exchange rate will rise if the U.S. inflation rate is lower than the foreign country's. This happens because the foreign currency depreciates in value and therefore weakens relative to the dollar.

20.4 INTEREST RATE PARITY, UNBIASED FORWARD RATES, AND THE INTERNATIONAL FISHER EFFECT

The next issue we need to address is the relationship between spot exchange rates, forward exchange rates, and interest rates. To get started, we need some additional notation:

F_T = **Forward exchange rate for settlement at time** T
R_{US} = **U.S. nominal risk-free interest rate**
R_{FC} = **Foreign country nominal risk-free interest rate**

As before, we will use S_0 to stand for the spot exchange rate. You can take the U.S. nominal risk-free rate, R_{US}, to be the T-bill rate.

Covered Interest Arbitrage

Suppose we observe the following information about U.S. and Swiss currencies in the market:

$$\begin{aligned} S_0 &= \text{SF } 2.00 \\ F_1 &= \text{SF } 1.90 \\ R_{US} &= 10\% \\ R_S &= 5\% \end{aligned}$$

For exchange rates and even pictures of non-U.S. currencies, see www.travlang.com/money.

where R_S is the nominal risk-free rate in Switzerland. The period is one year, so F_1 is the 360-day forward rate.

Do you see an arbitrage opportunity here? There is one. Suppose you have $1 to invest, and you want a riskless investment. One option you have is to invest the $1 in a riskless U.S. investment such as a 360-day T-bill. If you do this, then, in one period, your \$1 will be worth:

$$\textbf{\$ value in 1 period} = \$1 \times (1 + R_{US}) \\ = \$1.10$$

Alternatively, you can invest in the Swiss risk-free investment. To do this, you need to convert your \$1 to Swiss francs and simultaneously execute a forward trade to convert francs back to dollars in one year. The necessary steps would be as follows:

1. Convert your \$1 to \$1 × S_0 = SF 2.00.
2. At the same time, enter into a forward agreement to convert Swiss francs back to dollars in one year. Because the forward rate is SF 1.90, you will get \$1 for every SF 1.90 that you have in one year.
3. Invest your SF 2.00 in Switzerland at R_S. In one year, you will have:

$$\textbf{SF value in 1 year} = \text{SF } 2.00 \times (1 + R_S) \\ = \text{SF } 2.00 \times 1.05 \\ = \text{SF } 2.10$$

4. Convert your SF 2.10 back to dollars at the agreed-upon rate of SF 1.90 = \$1. You end up with:

$$\textbf{\$ value in 1 year} = \text{SF } 2.10/1.90 \\ = \$1.1053$$

Notice that the value in one year resulting from this strategy can be written as:

$$\textbf{\$ value in 1 year} = \$1 \times S_0 \times (1 + R_S)/F_1 \\ = \$1 \times 2 \times 1.05/1.90 \\ = \$1.1053$$

The return on this investment is apparently 10.53 percent. This is higher than the 10 percent we get from investing in the United States. Because both investments are risk-free, there is an arbitrage opportunity.

To exploit the difference in interest rates, you need to borrow, say, \$5 million at the lower U.S. rate and invest it at the higher Swiss rate. What is the round-trip profit from doing this? To find out, we can work through the steps outlined previously:

1. Convert the \$5 million at SF 2 = \$1 to get SF 10 million.
2. Agree to exchange Swiss francs for dollars in one year at SF 1.90 to the dollar.
3. Invest the SF 10 million for one year at R_S = 5 percent. You end up with SF 10.5 million.
4. Convert the SF 10.5 million back to dollars to fulfill the forward contract. You receive SF 10.5 million/1.90 = \$5,526,316.
5. Repay the loan with interest. You owe \$5 million plus 10 percent interest, for a total of \$5.5 million. You have \$5,526,316, so your round-trip profit is a risk-free \$26,316.

The activity that we have illustrated here goes by the name of *covered interest arbitrage*. The term *covered* refers to the fact that we are covered in the event of a change in the exchange rate because we lock in the forward exchange rate today.

Interest Rate Parity

If we assume that significant covered interest arbitrage opportunities do not exist, then there must be some relationship between spot exchange rates, forward exchange rates, and relative interest rates. To see what this relationship is, note that, in general, Strategy 1 from the preceding discussion, investing in a riskless U.S. investment, gives us $1 + R_{US}$ for every dollar we invest. Strategy 2, investing in a foreign risk-free investment, gives us $S_0 \times (1 + R_{FC})/F_1$ for every dollar we invest. Because these have to be equal to prevent arbitrage, it must be the case that:

$$1 + R_{US} = S_0 \times (1 + R_{FC})/F_1$$

Rearranging this a bit gets us the famous **interest rate parity (IRP)** condition:

$$F_1/S_0 = (1 + R_{FC})/(1 + R_{US}) \tag{20.4}$$

There is a very useful approximation for IRP that illustrates very clearly what is going on and is not difficult to remember. If we define the percentage forward premium or discount as $(F_1 - S_0)/S_0$, then IRP says that this percentage premium or discount is *approximately* equal to the difference in interest rates:

$$(F_1 - S_0)/S_0 = R_{FC} - R_{US} \tag{20.5}$$

Very loosely, what IRP says is that any difference in interest rates between two countries for some period is just offset by the change in the relative value of the currencies, thereby eliminating any arbitrage possibilities. Notice that we could also write:

$$F_1 = S_0 \times [1 + (R_{FC} - R_{US})] \tag{20.6}$$

In general, if we have T periods instead of just one, the IRP approximation is written as:

$$F_t = S_0 \times [1 + (R_{FC} - R_{US})]^T \tag{20.7}$$

EXAMPLE 20.5 Parity Check

Suppose the exchange rate for Japanese yen, S_0, is currently ¥120 = $1. If the interest rate in the United States is R_{US} = 10 percent and the interest rate in Japan is R_J = 5 percent, then what must the forward rate be to prevent covered interest arbitrage?

From IRP, we have:

$$\begin{aligned} F_1 &= S_0 \times [1 + (R_J - R_{US})] \\ &= ¥120 \times [1 + (.05 - .10)] \\ &= ¥120 \times .95 \\ &= ¥114 \end{aligned}$$

Notice that the yen will sell at a premium relative to the dollar (why?).

Forward Rates and Future Spot Rates

In addition to PPP and IRP, there is one more basic relationship we need to discuss. What is the connection between the forward rate and the expected future spot rate? The **unbiased forward rates (UFR)** condition says that the forward rate, F_1, is equal to the *expected* future spot rate, $E(S_1)$:

$$F_1 = E(S_1)$$

With T periods, UFR would be written as:

$$F_t = E(S_t)$$

How are the international markets doing? Find out at cbs.marketwatch.com.

Loosely, the UFR condition says that, on average, the forward exchange rate is equal to the future spot exchange rate.

If we ignore risk, then the UFR condition should hold. Suppose the forward rate for the Japanese yen is consistently lower than the future spot rate by, say, 10 yen. This means that anyone who wanted to convert dollars to yen in the future would consistently get more yen by not agreeing to a forward exchange. The forward rate would have to rise to get anyone interested in a forward exchange.

Similarly, if the forward rate were consistently higher than the future spot rate, then anyone who wanted to convert yen to dollars would get more dollars per yen by not agreeing to a forward trade. The forward exchange rate would have to fall to attract such traders.

For these reasons, the forward and actual future spot rates should be equal to each other on average. What the future spot rate will actually be is uncertain, of course. The UFR condition may not hold if traders are willing to pay a premium to avoid this uncertainty. If the condition does hold, then the 180-day forward rate that we see today should be an unbiased predictor of what the exchange rate will actually be in 180 days.

Putting It All Together

We have developed three relationships, PPP, IRP, and UFR, that describe the interaction between key financial variables such as interest rates, exchange rates, and inflation rates. We now explore the implications of these relationships as a group.

UNCOVERED INTEREST PARITY To start, it is useful to collect our international financial market relationships in one place:

$$\text{PPP: } E(S_1) = S_0 \times [1 + (h_{FC} - h_{US})]$$
$$\text{IRP: } F_1 = S_0 \times [1 + (R_{FC} - R_{US})]$$
$$\text{UFR: } F_1 = E(S_1)$$

We begin by combining UFR and IRP. Because we know that $F_1 = E(S_1)$ from the UFR condition, we can substitute $E(S_1)$ for F_1 in IRP. The result is:

$$\text{UIP: } E(S_1) = S_0 \times [1 + (R_{FC} - R_{US})] \quad (20.8)$$

This important relationship is called **uncovered interest parity (UIP)**, and it will play a key role in our international capital budgeting discussion that follows. With T periods, UIP becomes:

$$E(S_t) = S_0 \times [1 + (R_{FC} - R_{US})]^T \quad (20.9)$$

THE INTERNATIONAL FISHER EFFECT Next, we compare PPP and UIP. Both of them have $E(S_1)$ on the left-hand side, so their right-hand sides must be equal. We thus have that:

$$S_0 \times [1 + (h_{FC} - h_{US})] = S_0 \times [1 + (R_{FC} - R_{US})]$$
$$h_{FC} - h_{US} = R_{FC} - R_{US}$$

This tells us that the difference in returns between the United States and a foreign country is just equal to the difference in inflation rates. Rearranging this slightly gives us the **international Fisher effect (IFE)**:

$$\text{IFE: } R_{US} - h_{US} = R_{FC} - h_{FC} \quad (20.10)$$

The IFE says that *real* rates are equal across countries.[2]

The conclusion that real returns are equal across countries is really basic economics. If real returns were higher in, say, Brazil than in the United States, money would flow out of U.S. financial markets and into Brazilian markets. Asset prices in Brazil would rise and their returns would fall. At the same time, asset prices in the United States would fall and their returns would rise. This process acts to equalize real returns.

[2]Notice that our result here is in terms of the approximate real rate, $R - h$ (see Chapter 5), because we used approximations for PPP and IRP. For the exact result, see Problem 17 at the end of the chapter.

Having said all this, we need to note a couple of things. First of all, we really haven't explicitly dealt with risk in our discussion. We might reach a different conclusion about real returns once we do, particularly if people in different countries have different tastes and attitudes toward risk. Second, there are many barriers to the movement of money and capital around the world. Real returns might be different in two different countries for long periods of time if money can't move freely between them.

Despite these problems, we expect that capital markets will become increasingly internationalized. As this occurs, any differences in real rates that do exist will probably diminish. The laws of economics have very little respect for national boundaries.

20.5 INTERNATIONAL CAPITAL BUDGETING

Kihlstrom Equipment, a U.S.-based international company, is evaluating an overseas investment. Kihlstrom's exports of drill bits have increased to such a degree that it is considering building a distribution center in France. The project will cost €2 million to launch. The cash flows are expected to be €.9 million a year for the next three years.

The current spot exchange rate for euros is €.5. Recall that this is euros per dollar, so a euro is worth $\$1/.5 = \$2$. The risk-free rate in the United States is 5 percent, and the risk-free rate in "euroland" is 7 percent. Note that the exchange rate and the two interest rates are observed in financial markets, not estimated.[3] Kihlstrom's required return on dollar investments of this sort is 10 percent.

Should Kihlstrom take this investment? As always, the answer depends on the NPV, but how do we calculate the net present value of this project in U.S. dollars? There are two basic ways to go about doing this:

1. *The home currency approach.* Convert all the euro cash flows into dollars, and then discount at 10 percent to find the NPV in dollars. Notice that for this approach, we have to come up with the future exchange rates to convert the future projected euro cash flows into dollars.
2. *The foreign currency approach.* Determine the required return on euro investments, and then discount the euro cash flows to find the NPV in euros. Then convert this euro NPV to a dollar NPV. This approach requires us to somehow convert the 10 percent dollar required return to the equivalent euro required return.

The difference between these two approaches is primarily a matter of when we convert from euros to dollars. In the first case, we convert before estimating the NPV. In the second case, we convert after estimating NPV.

It might appear that the second approach is superior because for it we only have to come up with one number, the euro discount rate. Furthermore, because the first approach requires us to forecast future exchange rates, it probably seems that there is greater room for error with this approach. As we illustrate next, however, based on our previous results, the two approaches are really the same.

Method 1: The Home Currency Approach

To convert the project future cash flows into dollars, we will invoke the uncovered interest parity, or UIP, relation to come up with the projected exchange rates. Based on our earlier discussion, the expected exchange rate at time T, $E(S_t)$, is:

$$E(S_t) = S_0 \times [1 + (R_€ - R_{US})]^T$$

[3]For example, the interest rates might be the short-term Eurodollar and euro deposit rates offered by large money center banks.

where $R_€$ stands for the nominal risk-free rate in euroland. Because $R_€$ is 7 percent, R_{US} is 5 percent, and the current exchange rate (S_0) is €.5:

$$\begin{aligned} \mathbf{E}(\boldsymbol{S_t}) &= .5 \times [1 + (.07 - .05)]^T \\ &= .5 \times \mathbf{1.02}^T \end{aligned}$$

The projected exchange rates for the drill bit project are thus:

YEAR	EXPECTED EXCHANGE RATE
1	€.5 × 1.02^1 = €.5100
2	€.5 × 1.02^2 = €.5202
3	€.5 × 1.02^3 = €.5306

Using these exchange rates, along with the current exchange rate, we can convert all of the euro cash flows to dollars (note that all of the cash flows in this example are in millions):

YEAR	(1) CASH FLOW IN €MIL	(2) EXPECTED EXCHANGE RATE	(3) CASH FLOW IN $MIL (1)/(2)
0	−€2.0	€.5000	−$4.00
1	.9	.5100	1.76
2	.9	.5202	1.73
3	.9	.5306	1.70

To finish off, we calculate the NPV in the ordinary way:

$$\begin{aligned} \mathbf{NPV_\$} &= \mathbf{-\$4 + \$1.76/1.10 + \$1.73/1.10^2 + \$1.70/1.10^3} \\ &= \mathbf{\$.3\ million} \end{aligned}$$

So the project appears to be profitable.

Method 2: The Foreign Currency Approach

Kihlstrom requires a nominal return of 10 percent on the dollar-denominated cash flows. We need to convert this to a rate suitable for euro-denominated cash flows. Based on the international Fisher effect, we know that the difference in the nominal rates is:

$$\begin{aligned} \boldsymbol{R_€ - R_{US}} &= \boldsymbol{h_€ - h_{US}} \\ &= 7\% - 5\% = 2\% \end{aligned}$$

The appropriate discount rate for estimating the euro cash flows from the drill bit project is approximately equal to 10 percent plus an extra 2 percent to compensate for the greater euro inflation rate.

If we calculate the NPV of the euro cash flows at this rate, we get:

$$\begin{aligned} \mathbf{NPV_€} &= \mathbf{-€2 + €.9/1.12 + €.9/1.12^2 + €.9/1.12^3} \\ &= \mathbf{€.16\ million} \end{aligned}$$

The NPV of this project is €.16 million. Taking this project makes us €.16 million richer today. What is this in dollars? Because the exchange rate today is €.5, the dollar NPV of the project is:

$$\mathbf{NPV_\$ = NPV_€/\boldsymbol{S_0} = €.16/.5 = \$.3\ million}$$

This is the same dollar NPV that we previously calculated.

The important thing to recognize from our example is that the two capital budgeting procedures are actually the same and will always give the same answer.[4] In this second approach, the fact that we are implicitly forecasting exchange rates is simply hidden. Even so, the foreign currency approach is computationally a little easier.

Unremitted Cash Flows

The previous example assumed that all aftertax cash flows from the foreign investment could be remitted to (paid out to) the parent firm. Actually, substantial differences can exist between the cash flows generated by a foreign project and the amount that can actually be remitted, or "repatriated," to the parent firm.

A foreign subsidiary can remit funds to a parent in many forms, including the following:

1. Dividends
2. Management fees for central services
3. Royalties on the use of trade names and patents

However cash flows are repatriated, international firms must pay special attention to remittances, because there may be current and future controls on remittances. Many governments are sensitive to the charge of being exploited by foreign national firms. In such cases, governments are tempted to limit the ability of international firms to remit cash flows. Funds that cannot currently be remitted are sometimes said to be *blocked.*

20.6 EXCHANGE RATE RISK

Exchange rate risk is the natural consequence of international operations in a world where relative currency values move up and down. Managing exchange rate risk is an important part of international finance. As we discuss next, there are three different types of exchange rate risk, or exposure: short-run exposure, long-run exposure, and translation exposure.

Short-Run Exposure

The day-to-day fluctuations in exchange rates create short-run risks for international firms. Most such firms have contractual agreements to buy and sell goods in the near future at set prices. When different currencies are involved, such transactions have an extra element of risk.

For example, imagine that you are importing imitation pasta from Italy and reselling it in the United States under the Impasta brand name. Your largest customer has ordered 10,000 cases of Impasta. You place the order with your supplier today, but you won't pay until the goods arrive in 60 days. Your selling price is $6 per case. Your cost is 8.4 euros per case, and the exchange rate is currently €1.50, so it takes 1.50 euros to buy $1.

At the current exchange rate, your cost in dollars of filling the order is €8.4/1.5 = $5.60 per case, so your pretax profit on the order is 10,000 × ($6 − 5.60) = $4,000. However, the exchange rate in 60 days will probably be different, so your profit will depend on what the future exchange rate turns out to be.

[4]Actually, there will be a slight difference because we are using the approximate relationships. If we calculate the required return as 1.10 × (1 + .02) − 1 = 12.2%, then we get exactly the same NPV. See Problem 17 for more detail.

For example, if the rate goes to €1.6, your cost is €8.4/1.6 = $5.25 per case. Your profit goes to $7,500. If the exchange rate goes to, say, €1.4, then your cost is €8.4/1.4 = $6, and your profit is zero.

The short-run exposure in our example can be reduced or eliminated in several ways. The most obvious way is by entering into a forward exchange agreement to lock in an exchange rate. For example, suppose the 60-day forward rate is €1.58. What will be your profit if you hedge? What profit should you expect if you don't?

If you hedge, you lock in an exchange rate of €1.58. Your cost in dollars will thus be €8.4/1.58 = $5.32 per case, so your profit will be 10,000 × ($6 − 5.32) = $6,800. If you don't hedge, then, assuming that the forward rate is an unbiased predictor (in other words, assuming the UFR condition holds), you should expect that the exchange rate will actually be €1.58 in 60 days. You should expect to make $6,800.

Alternatively, if this strategy is not feasible, you could simply borrow the dollars today, convert them into euros, and invest the euros for 60 days to earn some interest. Based on IRP, this amounts to entering into a forward contract.

Long-Run Exposure

In the long run, the value of a foreign operation can fluctuate because of unanticipated changes in relative economic conditions. For example, imagine that we own a labor-intensive assembly operation located in another country to take advantage of lower wages. Through time, unexpected changes in economic conditions can raise the foreign wage levels to the point where the cost advantage is eliminated or even becomes negative.

The impact of changes in exchange rate levels can be substantial. For example, during 2003 and the early part of 2004, the U.S. dollar continued to weaken against other currencies. This meant foreign manufacturers took home less for each dollar's worth of sales they made, which can lead to big profit swings. Volkswagen estimated that it lost €1.2 billion ($1.5 billion) due to currency swings in 2003. And Peugeot Citroën of France estimated it might lose as much as €600 million ($744 million) in 2004.

Hedging long-run exposure is more difficult than hedging short-term risks. For one thing, organized forward markets don't exist for such long-term needs. Instead, the primary option that firms have is to try to match up foreign currency inflows and outflows. The same thing goes for matching foreign currency–denominated assets and liabilities. For example, a firm that sells in a foreign country might try to concentrate its raw material purchases and labor expense in that country. That way, the dollar values of its revenues and costs will move up and down together. Probably the best examples of this type of hedging are the so-called transplant auto manufacturers such as BMW, Honda, Mercedes, and Toyota, which now build a substantial portion of the cars they sell in the United States at plants located in the United States, thereby obtaining some degree of immunization against exchange rate movements.

For example, BMW produces 160,000 cars in South Carolina and exports about 100,000 of them. The costs of manufacturing the cars are paid mostly in dollars, and, when BMW exports the cars to Europe, it receives euros. When the dollar weakens, these vehicles become more profitable for BMW. At the same time, BMW exports about 217,000 cars to the United States each year. The costs of manufacturing these imported cars are mostly in euros, so they become less profitable when the dollar weakens. Taken together, these gains and losses tend to offset each other and provide BMW with a natural hedge.

Similarly, a firm can reduce its long-run exchange rate risk by borrowing in the foreign country. Fluctuations in the value of the foreign subsidiary's assets will then be at least partially offset by changes in the value of the liabilities.

Translation Exposure

When a U.S. company calculates its accounting net income and EPS for some period, it must "translate" everything into dollars. This can create some problems for the accountants when there are significant foreign operations. In particular, two issues arise:

1. What is the appropriate exchange rate to use for translating each balance sheet account?
2. How should balance sheet accounting gains and losses from foreign currency translation be handled?

To illustrate the accounting problem, suppose we started a small foreign subsidiary in Lilliputia a year ago. The local currency is the gulliver, abbreviated GL. At the beginning of the year, the exchange rate was GL 2 = $1, and the balance sheet in gullivers looked like this:

Assets	GL 1,000	Liabilities	GL 500
		Equity	500

At 2 gullivers to the dollar, the beginning balance sheet in dollars was as follows:

Assets	$500	Liabilities	$250
		Equity	250

Lilliputia is a quiet place, and nothing at all actually happened during the year. As a result, net income was zero (before consideration of exchange rate changes). However, the exchange rate did change to 4 gullivers = $1 purely because the Lilliputian inflation rate is much higher than the U.S. inflation rate.

Because nothing happened, the accounting ending balance sheet in gullivers is the same as the beginning one. However, if we convert it to dollars at the new exchange rate, we get:

Assets	$250	Liabilities	$125
		Equity	125

Notice that the value of the equity has gone down by $125, even though net income was exactly zero. Despite the fact that absolutely nothing really happened, there is a $125 accounting loss. How to handle this $125 loss has been a controversial accounting question.

One obvious and consistent way to handle this loss is simply to report the loss on the parent's income statement. During periods of volatile exchange rates, this kind of treatment can dramatically impact an international company's reported EPS. This is a purely accounting phenomenon, but, even so, such fluctuations are disliked by some financial managers.

The current approach to handling translation gains and losses is based on rules set out in the Financial Accounting Standards Board (FASB) *Statement of Financial Accounting Standards No. 52* (FASB 52), issued in December 1981. For the most part, FASB 52 requires that all assets and liabilities be translated from the subsidiary's currency into the parent's currency using the exchange rate that currently prevails.

Any translation gains and losses that occur are accumulated in a special account within the shareholders' equity section of the balance sheet. This account might be labeled something like "unrealized foreign exchange gains (losses)." The amounts involved can be substantial, at least from an accounting standpoint. For example, IBM's December 31, 2004, fiscal year-end balance sheet shows a gain from equity in the amount of

$3.06 billion for translation adjustments related to assets and liabilities of non-U.S. subsidiaries. These gains and losses are not reported on the income statement. As a result, the impact of translation gains and losses will not be recognized explicitly in net income until the underlying assets and liabilities are sold or otherwise liquidated.

Managing Exchange Rate Risk

For a large multinational firm, the management of exchange rate risk is complicated by the fact that there can be many different currencies involved in many different subsidiaries. It is very likely that a change in some exchange rate will benefit some subsidiaries and hurt others. The net effect on the overall firm depends on its net exposure.

For example, suppose a firm has two divisions. Division A buys goods in the United States for dollars and sells them in Britain for pounds. Division B buys goods in Britain for pounds and sells them in the United States for dollars. If these two divisions are of roughly equal size in terms of their inflows and outflows, then the overall firm obviously has little exchange rate risk.

In our example, the firm's net position in pounds (the amount coming in less the amount going out) is small, so the exchange rate risk is small. However, if one division, acting on its own, were to start hedging its exchange rate risk, then the overall firm's exchange rate risk would go up. The moral of the story is that multinational firms have to be conscious of the overall position that the firm has in a foreign currency. For this reason, management of exchange rate risk is probably best handled on a centralized basis.

20.7 POLITICAL RISK

One final element of risk in international investing is **political risk**. Political risk refers to changes in value that arise as a consequence of political actions. This is not a problem faced exclusively by international firms. For example, changes in U.S. tax laws and regulations may benefit some U.S. firms and hurt others, so political risk exists nationally as well as internationally.

Some countries do have more political risk than others, however. When firms have operations in these riskier countries, the extra political risk may lead the firms to require higher returns on overseas investments to compensate for the possibility that funds may be blocked, critical operations interrupted, and contracts abrogated. In the most extreme case, the possibility of outright confiscation may be a concern in countries with relatively unstable political environments.

Political risk also depends on the nature of the business; some businesses are less likely to be confiscated because they are not particularly valuable in the hands of a different owner. An assembly operation supplying subcomponents that only the parent company uses would not be an attractive "takeover" target, for example. Similarly, a manufacturing operation that requires the use of specialized components from the parent is of little value without the parent company's cooperation.

A great site for evaluating the political risk of a country is www.cia.gov/cia/publications/factbook.

Natural resource developments, such as copper mining or oil drilling, are just the opposite. Once the operation is in place, much of the value is in the commodity. The political risk for such investments is much higher for this reason. Also, the issue of exploitation is more pronounced with such investments, again increasing the political risk.

Political risk can be hedged in several ways, particularly when confiscation or nationalization is a concern. The use of local financing, perhaps from the government of the foreign country in question, reduces the possible loss because the company can refuse to pay on the debt in the event of unfavorable political activities. Based on our discussion in this section, structuring the operation in such a way that it requires significant parent company involvement to function is another way to reduce political risk.

SUMMARY AND CONCLUSIONS

The international firm has a more complicated life than the purely domestic firm. Management must understand the connection between interest rates, foreign currency exchange rates, and inflation, and it must become aware of a large number of different financial market regulations and tax systems. This chapter is intended to be a concise introduction to some of the financial issues that come up in international investing.

Our coverage has been necessarily brief. The main topics we discussed are the following:

1. Some basic vocabulary. We briefly defined some exotic terms such as *LIBOR* and *Eurocurrency*.
2. The basic mechanics of exchange rate quotations. We discussed the spot and forward markets and how exchange rates are interpreted.
3. The fundamental relationships between international financial variables:
   a. Absolute and relative purchasing power parity, PPP
   b. Interest rate parity, IRP
   c. Unbiased forward rates, UFR

   Absolute purchasing power parity states that \$1 should have the same purchasing power in each country. This means that an orange costs the same whether you buy it in New York or in Tokyo.

   Relative purchasing power parity means that the expected percentage change in exchange rates between the currencies of two countries is equal to the difference in their inflation rates.

   Interest rate parity implies that the percentage difference between the forward exchange rate and the spot exchange rate is equal to the interest rate differential. We showed how covered interest arbitrage forces this relationship to hold.

   The unbiased forward rates condition indicates that the current forward rate is a good predictor of the future spot exchange rate.
4. International capital budgeting. We showed that the basic foreign exchange relationships imply two other conditions:
   a. Uncovered interest parity
   b. The international Fisher effect

   By invoking these two conditions, we learned how to estimate NPVs in foreign currencies and how to convert foreign currencies into dollars to estimate NPV in the usual way.
5. Exchange rate and political risk. We described the various types of exchange rate risk and discussed some commonly used approaches to managing the effect of fluctuating exchange rates on the cash flows and value of the international firm. We also discussed political risk and some ways of managing exposure to it.

CONCEPT QUESTIONS

1. **Spot and Forward Rates** Suppose the exchange rate for the Swiss franc is quoted as SF 1.50 in the spot market and SF 1.53 in the 90-day forward market.
   a. Is the dollar selling at a premium or a discount relative to the franc?
   b. Does the financial market expect the franc to strengthen relative to the dollar? Explain.
   c. What do you suspect is true about relative economic conditions in the United States and Switzerland?
2. **Purchasing Power Parity** Suppose the rate of inflation in Mexico will run about 3 percent higher than the U.S. inflation rate over the next several years. All other things being the same, what will happen to the Mexican peso versus dollar exchange rate? What relationship are you relying on in answering?

3. **Exchange Rates** The exchange rate for the Australian dollar is currently A$1.40. This exchange rate is expected to rise by 10 percent over the next year.
   a. Is the Australian dollar expected to get stronger or weaker?
   b. What do you think about the relative inflation rates in the United States and Australia?
   c. What do you think about the relative nominal interest rates in the United States and Australia? Relative real rates?
4. **Yankee Bonds** Which of the following most accurately describes a Yankee bond?
   a. A bond issued by General Motors in Japan with the interest payable in U.S. dollars
   b. A bond issued by General Motors in Japan with the interest payable in yen
   c. A bond issued by Toyota in the United States with the interest payable in yen
   d. A bond issued by Toyota in the United States with the interest payable in dollars
   e. A bond issued by Toyota worldwide with the interest payable in dollars
5. **Exchange Rates** Are exchange rate changes necessarily good or bad for a particular company?
6. **International Risks** At one point, Duracell International confirmed that it was planning to open battery manufacturing plants in China and India. Manufacturing in these countries allows Duracell to avoid import duties of between 30 and 35 percent that have made alkaline batteries prohibitively expensive for some consumers. What additional advantages might Duracell see in this proposal? What are some of the risks to Duracell?
7. **Multinational Corporations** Given that many multinationals based in many countries have much greater sales outside their domestic markets than within them, what is the particular relevance of their domestic currency?
8. **Exchange Rate Movements** Are the following statements true or false? Explain why.
   a. If the general price index in Great Britain rises faster than that in the United States, we would expect the pound to appreciate relative to the dollar.
   b. Suppose you are a German machine tool exporter, and you invoice all of your sales in foreign currency. Further suppose that the euroland monetary authorities begin to undertake an expansionary monetary policy. If it is certain that the easy money policy will result in higher inflation rates in euroland relative to those in other countries, then you should use the forward markets to protect yourself against future losses resulting from the deterioration in the value of the euro.
   c. If you could accurately estimate differences in the relative inflation rates of two countries over a long period of time, while other market participants were unable to do so, you could successfully speculate in spot currency markets.
9. **Exchange Rate Movements** Some countries encourage movements in their exchange rate relative to those of some other country as a short-term means of addressing foreign trade imbalances. For each of the following scenarios, evaluate the impact the announcement would have on an American importer and an American exporter doing business with the foreign country.
   a. Officials in the administration of the United States government announce that they are comfortable with a rising euro relative to the dollar.
   b. British monetary authorities announce that they feel the pound has been driven too low by currency speculators relative to the dollar.
   c. The Brazilian government announces that it will print billions of new cruzeiros and inject them into the economy in an effort to reduce the country's unemployment rate.
10. **International Capital Market Relationships** We discussed five international capital market relationships: relative PPP, IRP, UFR, UIP, and the international Fisher effect. Which of these

would you expect to hold most closely? Which do you think would be most likely to be violated?

11. **Exchange Rate Risk** If you are an exporter who must make payments in foreign currency three months after receiving each shipment and you predict that the domestic currency will appreciate in value over this period, is there any value in hedging your currency exposure?
12. **International Capital Budgeting** Suppose it is your task to evaluate two different investments in new subsidiaries for your company, one in your own country and the other in a foreign country. You calculate the cash flows of both projects to be identical after exchange rate differences. Under what circumstances might you choose to invest in the foreign subsidiary? Give an example of a country where certain factors might influence you to alter this decision and invest at home.
13. **International Capital Budgeting** An investment in a foreign subsidiary is estimated to have a positive NPV, after the discount rate used in the calculations is adjusted for political risk and any advantages from diversification. Does this mean the project is acceptable? Why or why not?
14. **International Borrowing** If a U.S. firm raises funds for a foreign subsidiary, what are the disadvantages to borrowing in the United States? How would you overcome them?
15. **International Investment** If financial markets are perfectly competitive and the Eurodollar rate is above that offered in the U.S. loan market, you would immediately want to borrow money in the United States and invest it in Eurodollars. True or false? Explain.
16. **Eurobonds** What distinguishes a Eurobond from a foreign bond? Which particular feature makes the Eurobond more popular than the foreign bond?

QUESTIONS AND PROBLEMS

Basic
(Questions 1–14)

1. **Using Exchange Rates** Take a look back at Figure 20.1 to answer the following questions:
   a. If you have $100, how many euros can you get?
   b. How much is one euro worth?
   c. If you have five million euros, how many dollars do you have?
   d. Which is worth more, a New Zealand dollar or a Singapore dollar?
   e. Which is worth more, a Mexican peso or a Chilean peso?
   f. How many Mexican pesos can you get for a euro? What do you call this rate?
   g. Per unit, what is the most valuable currency of those listed? The least valuable?

2. **Using the Cross-Rate** Use the information in Figure 20.1 to answer the following questions:
   a. Which would you rather have, $100 or £100? Why?
   b. Which would you rather have, 100 Swiss francs (SF) or £100? Why?
   c. What is the cross-rate for Swiss francs in terms of British pounds? For British pounds in terms of Swiss francs?

3. **Forward Exchange Rates** Use the information in Figure 20.1 to answer the following questions:
   a. What is the six-month forward rate for the Japanese yen in yen per U.S. dollar? Is the yen selling at a premium or a discount? Explain.
   b. What is the three-month forward rate for British pounds in U.S. dollars per pound? Is the dollar selling at a premium or a discount? Explain.
   c. What do you think will happen to the value of the dollar relative to the yen and the pound, based on the information in the figure? Explain.

4. **Using Spot and Forward Exchange Rates** Suppose the spot exchange rate for the Canadian dollar is Can$1.26 and the six-month forward rate is Can$1.22.
   a. Which is worth more, a U.S. dollar or a Canadian dollar?
   b. Assuming absolute PPP holds, what is the cost in the United States of an Elkhead beer if the price in Canada is Can$2.19? Why might the beer actually sell at a different price in the United States?
   c. Is the U.S. dollar selling at a premium or a discount relative to the Canadian dollar?
   d. Which currency is expected to appreciate in value?
   e. Which country do you think has higher interest rates—the United States or Canada? Explain.
5. **Cross-Rates and Arbitrage** Suppose the Japanese yen exchange rate is ¥115 = $1, and the British pound exchange rate is £1 = $1.70.
   a. What is the cross-rate in terms of yen per pound?
   b. Suppose the cross-rate is ¥185 = £1. Is there an arbitrage opportunity here? If there is, explain how to take advantage of the mispricing.
6. **Interest Rate Parity** Use Figure 20.1 to answer the following questions. Suppose interest rate parity holds, and the current six-month risk-free rate in the United States is 3.8 percent. What must the six-month risk-free rate be in Great Britain? In Japan? In Switzerland?
7. **Interest Rates and Arbitrage** The treasurer of a major U.S. firm has $30 million to invest for three months. The annual interest rate in the United States is .45 percent per month. The interest rate in Great Britain is .6 percent per month. The spot exchange rate is £.56, and the three-month forward rate is £.59. Ignoring transactions costs, in which country would the treasurer want to invest the company's funds? Why?
8. **Inflation and Exchange Rates** Suppose the current exchange rate for the Polish zloty is Z 3.84. The expected exchange rate in three years is Z 3.92. What is the difference in the annual inflation rates for the United States and Poland over this period? Assume that the anticipated rate is constant for both countries. What relationship are you relying on in answering?
9. **Exchange Rate Risk** Suppose your company imports computer motherboards from Singapore. The exchange rate is given in Figure 20.1. You have just placed an order for 30,000 motherboards at a cost to you of 168.5 Singapore dollars each. You will pay for the shipment when it arrives in 90 days. You can sell the motherboards for $145 each. Calculate your profit if the exchange rate goes up or down by 10 percent over the next 90 days. What is the break-even exchange rate? What percentage rise or fall does this represent in terms of the Singapore dollar versus the U.S. dollar? 
10. **Exchange Rates and Arbitrage** Suppose the spot and six-month forward rates on the Norwegian krone are Kr 6.43 and Kr 6.56, respectively. The annual risk-free rate in the United States is 5 percent, and the annual risk-free rate in Norway is 8 percent.
    a. Is there an arbitrage opportunity here? If so, how would you exploit it?
    b. What must the six-month forward rate be to prevent arbitrage?
11. **The International Fisher Effect** You observe that the inflation rate in the United States is 3.5 percent per year and that T-bills currently yield 3.9 percent annually. What do you estimate the inflation rate to be in:
    a. Australia, if short-term Australian government securities yield 5 percent per year?
    b. Canada, if short-term Canadian government securities yield 7 percent per year?
    c. Taiwan, if short-term Taiwanese government securities yield 10 percent per year?
12. **Spot versus Forward Rates** Suppose the spot and three-month forward rates for the yen are ¥131.30 and ¥129.76, respectively.
    a. Is the yen expected to get stronger or weaker?

b. What would you estimate is the difference between the inflation rates of the United States and Japan?

13. **Expected Spot Rates** Suppose the spot exchange rate for the Hungarian forint is HUF 215. Interest rates in the United States are 3.5 percent per year. They are 8.6 percent in Hungary. What do you predict the exchange rate will be in one year? In two years? In five years? What relationship are you using?

14. **Forward Rates** The spot rate of foreign exchange between the United States and the United Kingdom is $1.50/£. If the interest rate in the United States is 13 percent and it is 8 percent in the United Kingdom, what would you expect the one-year forward rate to be if no immediate arbitrage opportunities existed?

Intermediate
(Questions 15–16)

15. **Capital Budgeting** Lakonishok Equipment has an investment opportunity in Europe. The project costs €12 million and is expected to produce cash flows of €2.7 million in year 1, €3.5 million in year 2, and €3.3 million in year 3. The current spot exchange rate is $1.22/€ and the current risk-free rate in the United States is 4.8 percent, compared to that in euroland of 4.1 percent. The appropriate discount rate for the project is estimated to be 13 percent, the U.S. cost of capital for the company. In addition, the subsidiary can be sold at the end of three years for an estimated €7.4 million. What is the NPV of the project?

16. **Capital Budgeting** You are evaluating a proposed expansion of an existing subsidiary located in Switzerland. The cost of the expansion would be SF 27.0 million. The cash flows from the project would be SF 7.5 million per year for the next five years. The dollar required return is 13 percent per year, and the current exchange rate is SF 1.72. The going rate on Eurodollars is 8 percent per year. It is 7 percent per year on Euroswiss.

a. What do you project will happen to exchange rates over the next four years?

b. Based on your answer in (a), convert the projected franc flows into dollar flows and calculate the NPV.

c. What is the required return on franc flows? Based on your answer, calculate the NPV in francs and then convert to dollars.

Challenge
(Question 17)

17. **Using the Exact International Fisher Effect** From our discussion of the Fisher effect in Chapter 5, we know that the actual relationship between a nominal rate, R, a real rate, r, and an inflation rate, h, can be written as:

$$1 + r = (1 + R)/(1 + h)$$

This is the *domestic* Fisher effect.

a. What is the nonapproximate form of the international Fisher effect?

b. Based on your answer in (a), what is the exact form for UIP? (Hint: Recall the exact form of IRP and use UFR.)

c. What is the exact form for relative PPP? (Hint: Combine your previous two answers.)

d. Recalculate the NPV for the Kihlstrom drill bit project (discussed in Section 20.5) using the exact forms for the UIP and the international Fisher effect. Verify that you get precisely the same answer either way.

S&P PROBLEM

www.mhhe.com/edumarketinsight

1. **American Depositary Receipts** Nestlé S. A. has American Depositary Receipts listed on the over-the-counter market. Many ADRs listed on U.S. exchanges are for fractional shares. In the case of Nestlé, 4 ADRs are equal to one registered share of stock. Find the information for Nestlé using the ticker symbol "3NSRGY."

a. Click on the "Mthly. Adj. Prices" link and find Nestlé's closing price for April 2005. Assume the exchange rate on that day was $/SFr 1.231 and Nestlé shares traded for SFr 14.65. Is there an arbitrage opportunity available? If so, how would you take advantage of it?

b. What exchange rate is necessary to eliminate the arbitrage opportunity available in (a)?

c. Dividend payments made to ADR shareholders are in U.S. dollars. Suppose you own 90 Nestlé ADRs. Assume the current exchange rate is the rate you calculated in (b). Nestlé declares a dividend of SFr 1.15. What U.S. dollar dividend payment will you receive?

WHAT'S ON THE WEB?

1. **Purchasing Power Parity** One of the more famous examples of a violation of absolute purchasing power parity is the Big Mac index calculated by *The Economist*. This index calculates the dollar price of a McDonald's Big Mac in different countries. You can find the Big Mac index by going to www.economist.com, following the "Markets & Data" link and then the "Big Mac index" link. Using the most recent index, which country has the most expensive Big Macs? Which country has the cheapest Big Macs? Why is the price of a Big Mac not the same in every country?
2. **Inflation and Exchange Rates** Go to www.marketvector.com and follow the "Exchange Rates" link. Select the "Australian Dollar" link. Is the U.S. dollar expected to appreciate or depreciate compared to the Australian dollar over the next six months? What is the difference in the annual inflation rates for the United States and Australia over this period? Assume that the anticipated rate is constant for both countries. What relationship are you relying on in answering?
3. **Interest Rate Parity** Go to the *Financial Times* site at www.ft.com, click on the "Markets" link and then the "Currencies" link. Find the current exchange rate between the U.S. dollar and the euro. Next, follow the "Currencies home" link and the "Money rates" link to find the U.S. dollar LIBOR and the euro LIBOR interest rates. What must the one-year forward rate be to prevent arbitrage? What principle are you relying on in your answer?

CLOSING CASE

EAST COAST YACHTS GOES INTERNATIONAL

Larissa Warren, the owner of East Coast Yachts, has been in discussions with a yacht dealer in Monaco about selling the company's yachts in Europe. Jarek Jachowicz, the dealer, wants to add East Coast Yachts to his current retail line. Jarek has told Larissa that he feels the retail sales will be approximately €5 million per month. All sales will be made in euros, and Jarek will retain 5 percent of the retail sales as commission, which will be paid in euros. Since the yachts will be customized to order, the first sales will take place in one month. Jarek will pay East Coast Yachts for the order 90 days after it is filled. This payment schedule will continue for the length of the contract between the two companies.

Larissa is confident the company can handle the extra volume with its existing facilities, but she is unsure about any potential financial risks of selling its yachts in Europe. In her discussion with Jarek, she found that the current exchange rate is $1.20/€. At this exchange rate, the company would spend 70 percent of the sales income on production costs. This number does not reflect the sales commission to be paid to Jarek.

Larissa has decided to ask Dan Ervin, the company's financial analyst, to prepare an analysis of the proposed international sales. Specifically, she asks Dan to answer the following questions:

1. What are the pros and cons of the international sales plan? What additional risks will the company face?
2. What happens to the company's profits if the dollar strengthens? What if the dollar weakens?
3. Ignoring taxes, what are East Coast Yacht's projected gains or losses from this proposed arrangement at the current exchange rate of \$1.20/€? What happens to profits if the exchange rate changes to \$1.30/€? At what exchange rate will the company break even?
4. How could the company hedge its exchange rate risk? What are the implications for this approach?
5. Taking all factors into account, should the company pursue international sales further? Why or why not?

APPENDIX

A

Mathematical Tables

Table A.1
Present Value of \$1 to Be Received after T Periods $= 1/(1 + r)^T$

Table A.2
Present Value of an Annuity of \$1 per Period for T Periods $= [1 - 1/(1 + r)^T]/r$

Table A.3
Future Value of \$1 at the End of T Periods $= (1 + r)^T$

Table A.4
Future Value of an Annuity of \$1 per Period for T Periods $= [(1 + r)^T - 1]/r$

Table A.5
Future Value of \$1 with a Continuously Compounded Rate r for T Periods: Values of e^{rT}

Table A.6
Present Value of \$1 with a Continuous Discount Rate r for T Periods: Values of e^{-rT}

TABLE A.1

Present Value of $1 to Be Received after T Periods = $1/(1 + r)^T$

	Interest Rate								
PERIOD	1%	2%	3%	4%	5%	6%	7%	8%	9%
1	.9901	.9804	.9709	.9615	.9524	.9434	.9346	.9259	.9174
2	.9803	.9612	.9426	.9246	.9070	.8900	.8734	.8573	.8417
3	.9706	.9423	.9151	.8890	.8638	.8396	.8163	.7938	.7722
4	.9610	.9238	.8885	.8548	.8227	.7921	.7629	.7350	.7084
5	.9515	.9057	.8626	.8219	.7835	.7473	.7130	.6806	.6499
6	.9420	.8880	.8375	.7903	.7462	.7050	.6663	.6302	.5963
7	.9327	.8706	.8131	.7599	.7107	.6651	.6227	.5835	.5470
8	.9235	.8535	.7894	.7307	.6768	.6274	.5820	.5403	.5019
9	.9143	.8368	.7664	.7026	.6446	.5919	.5439	.5002	.4604
10	.9053	.8203	.7441	.6756	.6139	.5584	.5083	.4632	.4224
11	.8963	.8043	.7224	.6496	.5847	.5268	.4751	.4289	.3875
12	.8874	.7885	.7014	.6246	.5568	.4970	.4440	.3971	.3555
13	.8787	.7730	.6810	.6006	.5303	.4688	.4150	.3677	.3262
14	.8700	.7579	.6611	.5775	.5051	.4423	.3878	.3405	.2992
15	.8613	.7430	.6419	.5553	.4810	.4173	.3624	.3152	.2745
16	.8528	.7284	.6232	.5339	.4581	.3936	.3387	.2919	.2519
17	.8444	.7142	.6050	.5134	.4363	.3714	.3166	.2703	.2311
18	.8360	.7002	.5874	.4936	.4155	.3503	.2959	.2502	.2120
19	.8277	.6864	.5703	.4746	.3957	.3305	.2765	.2317	.1945
20	.8195	.6730	.5537	.4564	.3769	.3118	.2584	.2145	.1784
21	.8114	.6598	.5375	.4388	.3589	.2942	.2415	.1987	.1637
22	.8034	.6468	.5219	.4220	.3418	.2775	.2257	.1839	.1502
23	.7954	.6342	.5067	.4057	.3256	.2618	.2109	.1703	.1378
24	.7876	.6217	.4919	.3901	.3101	.2470	.1971	.1577	.1264
25	.7798	.6095	.4776	.3751	.2953	.2330	.1842	.1460	.1160
30	.7419	.5521	.4120	.3083	.2314	.1741	.1314	.0994	.0754
40	.6717	.4529	.3066	.2083	.1420	.0972	.0668	.0460	.0318
50	.6080	.3715	.2281	.1407	.0872	.0543	.0339	.0213	.0134

PERIOD	10%	12%	14%	15%	16%	18%	20%	24%	28%	32%	36%
1	.9091	.8929	.8772	.8696	.8621	.8475	.8333	.8065	.7813	.7576	.7353
2	.8264	.7972	.7695	.7561	.7432	.7182	.6944	.6504	.6104	.5739	.5407
3	.7513	.7118	.6750	.6575	.6407	.6086	.5787	.5245	.4768	.4348	.3975
4	.6830	.6355	.5921	.5718	.5523	.5158	.4823	.4230	.3725	.3294	.2923
5	.6209	.5674	.5194	.4972	.4761	.4371	.4019	.3411	.2910	.2495	.2149
6	.5645	.5066	.4556	.4323	.4104	.3704	.3349	.2751	.2274	.1890	.1580
7	.5132	.4523	.3996	.3759	.3538	.3139	.2791	.2218	.1776	.1432	.1162
8	.4665	.4039	.3506	.3269	.3050	.2660	.2326	.1789	.1388	.1085	.0854
9	.4241	.3606	.3075	.2843	.2630	.2255	.1938	.1443	.1084	.0822	.0628
10	.3855	.3220	.2697	.2472	.2267	.1911	.1615	.1164	.0847	.0623	.0462
11	.3505	.2875	.2366	.2149	.1954	.1619	.1346	.0938	.0662	.0472	.0340
12	.3186	.2567	.2076	.1869	.1685	.1372	.1122	.0757	.0517	.0357	.0250
13	.2897	.2292	.1821	.1625	.1452	.1163	.0935	.0610	.0404	.0271	.0184
14	.2633	.2046	.1597	.1413	.1252	.0985	.0779	.0492	.0316	.0205	.0135
15	.2394	.1827	.1401	.1229	.1079	.0835	.0649	.0397	.0247	.0155	.0099
16	.2176	.1631	.1229	.1069	.0930	.0708	.0541	.0320	.0193	.0118	.0073
17	.1978	.1456	.1078	.0929	.0802	.0600	.0451	.0258	.0150	.0089	.0054
18	.1799	.1300	.0946	.0808	.0691	.0508	.0376	.0208	.0118	.0068	.0039
19	.1635	.1161	.0829	.0703	.0596	.0431	.0313	.0168	.0092	.0051	.0029
20	.1486	.1037	.0728	.0611	.0514	.0365	.0261	.0135	.0072	.0039	.0021
21	.1351	.0926	.0638	.0531	.0443	.0309	.0217	.0109	.0056	.0029	.0016
22	.1228	.0826	.0560	.0462	.0382	.0262	.0181	.0088	.0044	.0022	.0012
23	.1117	.0738	.0491	.0402	.0329	.0222	.0151	.0071	.0034	.0017	.0008
24	.1015	.0659	.0431	.0349	.0284	.0188	.0126	.0057	.0027	.0013	.0006
25	.0923	.0588	.0378	.0304	.0245	.0160	.0105	.0046	.0021	.0010	.0005
30	.0573	.0334	.0196	.0151	.0116	.0070	.0042	.0016	.0006	.0002	.0001
40	.0221	.0107	.0053	.0037	.0026	.0013	.0007	.0002	.0001	*	*
50	.0085	.0035	.0014	.0009	.0006	.0003	.0001	*	*	*	*

*The factor is zero to four decimal places.

TABLE A.2

Present Value of an Annuity of $1 per Period for T Periods = $[1 - 1/(1 + r)^T]/r$

NUMBER OF PERIODS	Interest Rate 1%	2%	3%	4%	5%	6%	7%	8%	9%
1	.9901	.9804	.9709	.9615	.9524	.9434	.9346	.9259	.9174
2	1.9704	1.9416	1.9135	1.8861	1.8594	1.8334	1.8080	1.7833	1.7591
3	2.9410	2.8839	2.8286	2.7751	2.7232	2.6730	2.6243	2.5771	2.5313
4	3.9020	3.8077	3.7171	3.6299	3.5460	3.4651	3.3872	3.3121	3.2397
5	4.8534	4.7135	4.5797	4.4518	4.3295	4.2124	4.1002	3.9927	3.8897
6	5.7955	5.6014	5.4172	5.2421	5.0757	4.9173	4.7665	4.6229	4.4859
7	6.7282	6.4720	6.2303	6.0021	5.7864	5.5824	5.3893	5.2064	5.0330
8	7.6517	7.3255	7.0197	6.7327	6.4632	6.2098	5.9713	5.7466	5.5348
9	8.5660	8.1622	7.7861	7.4353	7.1078	6.8017	6.5152	6.2469	5.9952
10	9.4713	8.9826	8.5302	8.1109	7.7217	7.3601	7.0236	6.7101	6.4177
11	10.3676	9.7868	9.2526	8.7605	8.3064	7.8869	7.4987	7.1390	6.8052
12	11.2551	10.5753	9.9540	9.3851	8.8633	8.3838	7.9427	7.5361	7.1607
13	12.1337	11.3484	10.6350	9.9856	9.3936	8.8527	8.3577	7.9038	7.4869
14	13.0037	12.1062	11.2961	10.5631	9.8986	9.2950	8.7455	8.2442	7.7862
15	13.8651	12.8493	11.9379	11.1184	10.3797	9.7122	9.1079	8.5595	8.0607
16	14.7179	13.5777	12.5611	11.6523	10.8378	10.1059	9.4466	8.8514	8.3126
17	15.5623	14.2919	13.1661	12.1657	11.2741	10.4773	9.7632	9.1216	8.5436
18	16.3983	14.9920	13.7535	12.6593	11.6896	10.8276	10.0591	9.3719	8.7556
19	17.2260	15.6785	14.3238	13.1339	12.0853	11.1581	10.3356	9.6036	8.9501
20	18.0456	16.3514	14.8775	13.5903	12.4622	11.4699	10.5940	9.8181	9.1285
21	18.8570	17.0112	15.4150	14.0292	12.8212	11.7641	10.8355	10.0168	9.2922
22	19.6604	17.6580	15.9369	14.4511	13.1630	12.0416	11.0612	10.2007	9.4424
23	20.4558	18.2922	16.4436	14.8568	13.4886	12.3034	11.2722	10.3741	9.5802
24	21.2434	18.9139	16.9355	15.2470	13.7986	12.5504	11.4693	10.5288	9.7066
25	22.0232	19.5235	17.4131	15.6221	14.0939	12.7834	11.6536	10.6748	9.8226
30	25.8077	22.3965	19.6004	17.2920	15.3725	13.7648	12.4090	11.2578	10.2737
40	32.8347	27.3555	23.1148	19.7928	17.1591	15.0463	13.3317	11.9246	10.7574
50	39.1961	31.4236	25.7298	21.4822	18.2559	15.7619	13.8007	12.2335	10.9617

NUMBER OF PERIODS	10%	12%	14%	15%	16%	18%	20%	24%	28%	32%
1	.9091	.8929	.8772	.8696	.8621	.8475	.8333	.8065	.7813	.7576
2	1.7355	1.6901	1.6467	1.6257	1.6052	1.5656	1.5278	1.4568	1.3916	1.3315
3	2.4869	2.4018	2.3216	2.2832	2.2459	2.1743	2.1065	1.9813	1.8684	1.7663
4	3.1699	3.0373	2.9137	2.8550	2.7982	2.6901	2.5887	2.4043	2.2410	2.0957
5	3.7908	3.6048	3.4331	3.3522	3.2743	3.1272	2.9906	2.7454	2.5320	2.3452
6	4.3553	4.1114	3.8887	3.7845	3.6847	3.4976	3.3255	3.0205	2.7594	2.5342
7	4.8684	4.5638	4.2883	4.1604	4.0386	3.8115	3.6046	3.2423	2.9370	2.6775
8	5.3349	4.9676	4.6389	4.4873	4.3436	4.0776	3.8372	3.4212	3.0758	2.7860
9	5.7590	5.3282	4.9464	4.7716	4.6065	4.3030	4.0310	3.5655	3.1842	2.8681
10	6.1446	5.6502	5.2161	5.0188	4.8332	4.4941	4.1925	3.6819	3.2689	2.9304
11	6.4951	5.9377	5.4527	5.2337	5.0286	4.6560	4.3271	3.7757	3.3351	2.9776
12	6.8137	6.1944	5.6603	5.4206	5.1971	4.7932	4.4392	3.8514	3.3868	3.0133
13	7.1034	6.4235	5.8424	5.5831	5.3423	4.9095	4.5327	3.9124	3.4272	3.0404
14	7.3667	6.6282	6.0021	5.7245	5.4675	5.0081	4.6106	3.9616	3.4587	3.0609
15	7.6061	6.8109	6.1422	5.8474	5.5755	5.0916	4.6755	4.0013	3.4834	3.0764
16	7.8237	6.9740	6.2651	5.9542	5.6685	5.1624	4.7296	4.0333	3.5026	3.0882
17	8.0216	7.1196	6.3729	6.0472	5.7487	5.2223	4.7746	4.0591	3.5177	3.0971
18	8.2014	7.2497	6.4674	6.1280	5.8178	5.2732	4.8122	4.0799	3.5294	3.1039
19	8.3649	7.3658	6.5504	6.1982	5.8775	5.3162	4.8435	4.0967	3.5386	3.1090
20	8.5136	7.4694	6.6231	6.2593	5.9288	5.3527	4.8696	4.1103	3.5458	3.1129
21	8.6487	7.5620	6.6870	6.3125	5.9731	5.3837	4.8913	4.1212	3.5514	3.1158
22	8.7715	7.6446	6.7429	6.3587	6.0113	5.4099	4.9094	4.1300	3.5558	3.1180
23	8.8832	7.7184	6.7921	6.3988	6.0442	5.4321	4.9245	4.1371	3.5592	3.1197
24	8.9847	7.7843	6.8351	6.4338	6.0726	5.4509	4.9371	4.1428	3.5619	3.1210
25	9.0770	7.8431	6.8729	6.4641	6.0971	5.4669	4.9476	4.1474	3.5640	3.1220
30	9.4269	8.0552	7.0027	6.5660	6.1772	5.5168	4.9789	4.1601	3.5693	3.1242
40	9.7791	8.2438	7.1050	6.6418	6.2335	5.5482	4.9966	4.1659	3.5712	3.1250
50	9.9148	8.3045	7.1327	6.6605	6.2463	5.5541	4.9995	4.1666	3.5714	3.1250

TABLE A.3

Future Value of $1 at the End of T Periods $= (1 + r)^T$

PERIOD	Interest Rate								
	1%	2%	3%	4%	5%	6%	7%	8%	9%
1	1.0100	1.0200	1.0300	1.0400	1.0500	1.0600	1.0700	1.0800	1.0900
2	1.0201	1.0404	1.0609	1.0816	1.1025	1.1236	1.1449	1.1664	1.1881
3	1.0303	1.0612	1.0927	1.1249	1.1576	1.1910	1.2250	1.2597	1.2950
4	1.0406	1.0824	1.1255	1.1699	1.2155	1.2625	1.3108	1.3605	1.4116
5	1.0510	1.1041	1.1593	1.2167	1.2763	1.3382	1.4026	1.4693	1.5386
6	1.0615	1.1262	1.1941	1.2653	1.3401	1.4185	1.5007	1.5869	1.6771
7	1.0721	1.1487	1.2299	1.3159	1.4071	1.5036	1.6058	1.7138	1.8280
8	1.0829	1.1717	1.2668	1.3686	1.4775	1.5938	1.7182	1.8509	1.9926
9	1.0937	1.1951	1.3048	1.4233	1.5513	1.6895	1.8385	1.9990	2.1719
10	1.1046	1.2190	1.3439	1.4802	1.6289	1.7908	1.9672	2.1589	2.3674
11	1.1157	1.2434	1.3842	1.5395	1.7103	1.8983	2.1049	2.3316	2.5804
12	1.1268	1.2682	1.4258	1.6010	1.7959	2.0122	2.2522	2.5182	2.8127
13	1.1381	1.2936	1.4685	1.6651	1.8856	2.1329	2.4098	2.7196	3.0658
14	1.1495	1.3195	1.5126	1.7317	1.9799	2.2609	2.5785	2.9372	3.3417
15	1.1610	1.3459	1.5580	1.8009	2.0789	2.3966	2.7590	3.1722	3.6425
16	1.1726	1.3728	1.6047	1.8730	2.1829	2.5404	2.9522	3.4259	3.9703
17	1.1843	1.4002	1.6528	1.9479	2.2920	2.6928	3.1588	3.7000	4.3276
18	1.1961	1.4282	1.7024	2.0258	2.4066	2.8543	3.3799	3.9960	4.7171
19	1.2081	1.4568	1.7535	2.1068	2.5270	3.0256	3.6165	4.3157	5.1417
20	1.2202	1.4859	1.8061	2.1911	2.6533	3.2071	3.8697	4.6610	5.6044
21	1.2324	1.5157	1.8603	2.2788	2.7860	3.3996	4.1406	5.0338	6.1088
22	1.2447	1.5460	1.9161	2.3699	2.9253	3.6035	4.4304	5.4365	6.6586
23	1.2572	1.5769	1.9736	2.4647	3.0715	3.8197	4.7405	5.8715	7.2579
24	1.2697	1.6084	2.0328	2.5633	3.2251	4.0489	5.0724	6.3412	7.9111
25	1.2824	1.6406	2.0938	2.6658	3.3864	4.2919	5.4274	6.8485	8.6231
30	1.3478	1.8114	2.4273	3.2434	4.3219	5.7435	7.6123	10.063	13.268
40	1.4889	2.2080	3.2620	4.8010	7.0400	10.286	14.974	21.725	31.409
50	1.6446	2.6916	4.3839	7.1067	11.467	18.420	29.457	46.902	74.358
60	1.8167	3.2810	5.8916	10.520	18.679	32.988	57.946	101.26	176.03

PERIOD	10%	12%	14%	15%	16%	18%	20%	24%	28%	32%	36%
1	1.1000	1.1200	1.1400	1.1500	1.1600	1.1800	1.2000	1.2400	1.2800	1.3200	1.3600
2	1.2100	1.2544	1.2996	1.3225	1.3456	1.3924	1.4400	1.5376	1.6384	1.7424	1.8496
3	1.3310	1.4049	1.4815	1.5209	1.5609	1.6430	1.7280	1.9066	2.0972	2.3000	2.5155
4	1.4641	1.5735	1.6890	1.7490	1.8106	1.9388	2.0736	2.3642	2.6844	3.0360	3.4210
5	1.6105	1.7623	1.9254	2.0114	2.1003	2.2878	2.4883	2.9316	3.4360	4.0075	4.6526
6	1.7716	1.9738	2.1950	2.3131	2.4364	2.6996	2.9860	3.6352	4.3980	5.2899	6.3275
7	1.9487	2.2107	2.5023	2.6600	2.8262	3.1855	3.5832	4.5077	5.6295	6.9826	8.6054
8	2.1436	2.4760	2.8526	3.0590	3.2784	3.7589	4.2998	5.5895	7.2058	9.2170	11.703
9	2.3579	2.7731	3.2519	3.5179	3.8030	4.4355	5.1598	6.9310	9.2234	12.166	15.917
10	2.5937	3.1058	3.7072	4.0456	4.4114	5.2338	6.1917	8.5944	11.806	16.060	21.647
11	2.8531	3.4785	4.2262	4.6524	5.1173	6.1759	7.4301	10.657	15.112	21.199	29.439
12	3.1384	3.8960	4.8179	5.3503	5.9360	7.2876	8.9161	13.215	19.343	27.983	40.037
13	3.4523	4.3635	5.4924	6.1528	6.8858	8.5994	10.699	16.386	24.759	36.937	54.451
14	3.7975	4.8871	6.2613	7.0757	7.9875	10.147	12.839	20.319	31.691	48.757	74.053
15	4.1772	5.4736	7.1379	8.1371	9.2655	11.974	15.407	25.196	40.565	64.359	100.71
16	4.5950	6.1304	8.1372	9.3576	10.748	14.129	18.488	31.243	51.923	84.954	136.97
17	5.0545	6.8660	9.2765	10.761	12.468	16.672	22.186	38.741	66.461	112.14	186.28
18	5.5599	7.6900	10.575	12.375	14.463	19.673	26.623	48.039	86.071	148.02	253.34
19	6.1159	8.6128	12.056	14.232	16.777	23.214	31.948	59.568	108.89	195.39	344.54
20	6.7275	9.6463	13.743	16.367	19.461	27.393	38.338	73.864	139.38	257.92	468.57
21	7.4002	10.804	15.668	18.822	22.574	32.324	46.005	91.592	178.41	340.45	637.26
22	8.1403	12.100	17.861	21.645	26.186	38.142	55.206	113.57	228.36	449.39	866.67
23	8.9543	13.552	20.362	24.891	30.376	45.008	66.247	140.83	292.30	593.20	1178.7
24	9.8497	15.179	23.212	28.625	35.236	53.109	79.497	174.63	374.14	783.02	1603.0
25	10.835	17.000	26.462	32.919	40.874	62.669	95.396	216.54	478.90	1033.6	2180.1
30	17.449	29.960	50.950	66.212	85.850	143.37	237.38	634.82	1645.5	4142.1	10143.
40	45.259	93.051	188.88	267.86	378.72	750.38	1469.8	5455.9	19427.	66521.	*
50	117.39	289.00	700.23	1083.7	1670.7	3927.4	9100.4	46890.	*	*	*
60	304.48	897.60	2595.9	4384.0	7370.2	20555.	56348.	*	*	*	*

*FVIV > 99,999.

TABLE A.4

Future Value of an Annuity of $1 per Period for T Periods = $[(1 + r)^T - 1]/r$

NUMBER OF PERIODS	Interest Rate 1%	2%	3%	4%	5%	6%	7%	8%	9%
1	1.0000	1.0000	1.0000	1.0000	1.0000	1.0000	1.0000	1.0000	1.0000
2	2.0100	2.0200	2.0300	2.0400	2.0500	2.0600	2.0700	2.0800	2.0900
3	3.0301	3.0604	3.0909	3.1216	3.1525	3.1836	3.2149	3.2464	3.2781
4	4.0604	4.1216	4.1836	4.2465	4.3101	4.3746	4.4399	4.5061	4.5731
5	5.1010	5.2040	5.3091	5.4163	5.5256	5.6371	5.7507	5.8666	5.9847
6	6.1520	6.3081	6.4684	6.6330	6.8019	6.9753	7.1533	7.3359	7.5233
7	7.2135	7.4343	7.6625	7.8983	8.1420	8.3938	8.6540	8.9228	9.2004
8	8.2857	8.5830	8.8932	9.2142	9.5491	9.8975	10.260	10.637	11.028
9	9.3685	9.7546	10.159	10.583	11.027	11.491	11.978	12.488	13.021
10	10.462	10.950	11.464	12.006	12.578	13.181	13.816	14.487	15.193
11	11.567	12.169	12.808	13.486	14.207	14.972	15.784	16.645	17.560
12	12.683	13.412	14.192	15.026	15.917	16.870	17.888	18.977	20.141
13	13.809	14.680	15.618	16.627	17.713	18.882	20.141	21.495	22.953
14	14.947	15.974	17.086	18.292	19.599	21.015	22.550	24.215	26.019
15	16.097	17.293	18.599	20.024	21.579	23.276	25.129	27.152	29.361
16	17.258	18.639	20.157	21.825	23.657	25.673	27.888	30.324	33.003
17	18.430	20.012	21.762	23.698	25.840	28.213	30.840	33.750	36.974
18	19.615	21.412	23.414	25.645	28.132	30.906	33.999	37.450	41.301
19	20.811	22.841	25.117	27.671	30.539	33.760	37.379	41.446	46.018
20	22.019	24.297	26.870	29.778	33.066	36.786	40.995	45.762	51.160
21	23.239	25.783	28.676	31.969	35.719	39.993	44.865	50.423	56.765
22	24.472	27.299	30.537	34.248	38.505	43.392	49.006	55.457	62.873
23	25.716	28.845	32.453	36.618	41.430	46.996	53.436	60.893	69.532
24	26.973	30.422	34.426	39.083	44.502	50.816	58.177	66.765	76.790
25	28.243	32.030	36.459	41.646	47.727	54.865	63.249	73.106	84.701
30	34.785	40.568	47.575	56.085	66.439	79.058	94.461	113.28	136.31
40	48.886	60.402	75.401	95.026	120.80	154.76	199.64	259.06	337.88
50	64.463	84.579	112.80	152.67	209.35	290.34	406.53	573.77	815.08
60	81.670	114.05	163.05	237.99	353.58	533.13	813.52	1253.2	1944.8

NUMBER OF PERIODS	10%	12%	14%	15%	16%	18%	20%	24%	28%	32%	36%
1	1.0000	1.0000	1.0000	1.0000	1.0000	1.0000	1.0000	1.0000	1.0000	1.0000	1.0000
2	2.1000	2.1200	2.1400	2.1500	2.1600	2.1800	2.2000	2.2400	2.2800	2.3200	2.3600
3	3.3100	3.3744	3.4396	3.4725	3.5056	3.5724	3.6400	3.7776	3.9184	4.0624	4.2096
4	3.6410	4.7793	4.9211	4.9934	5.0665	5.2154	5.3680	5.6842	6.0156	6.3624	6.7251
5	6.1051	6.3528	6.6101	6.7424	6.8771	7.1542	7.4416	8.0484	8.6999	9.3983	10.146
6	7.7156	8.1152	8.5355	8.7537	8.9775	9.4420	9.9299	10.980	12.136	13.406	14.799
7	9.4872	10.089	10.730	11.067	11.414	12.142	12.916	14.615	16.534	18.696	21.126
8	11.436	12.300	13.233	13.727	14.240	15.327	16.499	19.123	22.163	25.678	29.732
9	13.579	14.776	16.085	16.786	17.519	19.086	20.799	24.712	29.369	34.895	41.435
10	15.937	17.549	19.337	20.304	21.321	23.521	25.959	31.643	38.593	47.062	57.352
11	18.531	20.655	23.045	24.349	25.733	28.755	32.150	40.238	50.398	63.122	78.998
12	21.384	24.133	27.271	29.002	30.850	34.931	39.581	50.895	65.510	84.320	108.44
13	24.523	28.029	32.089	34.352	36.786	42.219	48.497	64.110	84.853	112.30	148.47
14	27.975	32.393	37.581	40.505	43.672	50.818	59.196	80.496	109.61	149.24	202.93
15	31.772	37.280	43.842	47.580	51.660	60.965	72.035	100.82	141.30	198.00	276.98
16	35.950	42.753	50.980	55.717	60.925	72.939	87.442	126.01	181.87	262.36	377.69
17	40.545	48.884	59.118	65.075	71.673	87.068	105.93	157.25	233.79	347.31	514.66
18	45.599	55.750	68.394	75.836	84.141	103.74	128.12	195.99	300.25	459.45	700.94
19	51.159	64.440	78.969	88.212	98.603	123.41	154.74	244.03	385.32	607.47	954.28
20	57.275	72.052	91.025	102.44	115.38	146.63	186.69	303.60	494.21	802.86	1298.8
21	64.002	81.699	104.77	118.81	134.84	174.02	225.03	377.46	633.59	1060.8	1767.4
22	71.403	92.503	120.44	137.63	157.41	206.34	271.03	469.06	812.00	1401.2	2404.7
23	79.543	104.60	138.30	159.28	183.60	244.49	326.24	582.63	1040.4	1850.6	3271.3
24	88.497	118.16	158.66	184.17	213.98	289.49	392.48	723.46	1332.7	2443.8	4450.0
25	98.347	133.33	181.87	212.79	249.21	342.60	471.98	898.09	1706.8	3226.8	6053.0
30	164.49	241.33	356.79	434.75	530.31	790.95	1181.9	2640.9	5873.2	12941.	28172.3
40	442.59	767.09	1342.0	1779.1	2360.8	4163.2	7343.9	22729.	69377.	*	*
50	1163.9	2400.0	4994.5	7217.7	10436.	21813.	45497.	*	*	*	*
60	3034.8	7471.6	18535.	29220.	46058.	*	*	*	*	*	*

*FVIFA > 99,999.

TABLE A.5

Future Value of $1 with a Continuously Compounded Rate r for T Periods: Values of e^{rT}

PERIOD	Continuously Compounded Rate (r)													
(T)	1%	2%	3%	4%	5%	6%	7%	8%	9%	10%	11%	12%	13%	14%
1	1.0101	1.0202	1.0305	1.0408	1.0513	1.0618	1.0725	1.0833	1.0942	1.1052	1.1163	1.1275	1.1388	1.1503
2	1.0202	1.0408	1.0618	1.0833	1.1052	1.1275	1.1503	1.1735	1.1972	1.2214	1.2461	1.2712	1.2969	1.3231
3	1.0305	1.0618	1.0942	1.1275	1.1618	1.1972	1.2337	1.2712	1.3100	1.3499	1.3910	1.4333	1.4770	1.5220
4	1.0408	1.0833	1.1275	1.1735	1.2214	1.2712	1.3231	1.3771	1.4333	1.4918	1.5527	1.6161	1.6820	1.7507
5	1.0513	1.1052	1.1618	1.2214	1.2840	1.3499	1.4191	1.4918	1.5683	1.6487	1.7333	1.8221	1.9155	2.0138
6	1.0618	1.1275	1.1972	1.2712	1.3499	1.4333	1.5220	1.6161	1.7160	1.8221	1.9348	2.0544	2.1815	2.3164
7	1.0725	1.1503	1.2337	1.3231	1.4191	1.5220	1.6323	1.7507	1.8776	2.0138	2.1598	2.3164	2.4843	2.6645
8	1.0833	1.1735	1.2712	1.3771	1.4918	1.6161	1.7507	1.8965	2.0544	2.2255	2.4109	2.6117	2.8292	3.0649
9	1.0942	1.1972	1.3100	1.4333	1.5683	1.7160	1.8776	2.0544	2.2479	2.4596	2.6912	2.9447	3.2220	3.5254
10	1.1052	1.2214	1.3499	1.4918	1.6487	1.8221	2.0138	2.2255	2.4596	2.7183	3.0042	3.3201	3.6693	4.0552
11	1.1163	1.2461	1.3910	1.5527	1.7333	1.9348	2.1598	2.4109	2.6912	3.0042	3.3535	3.7434	4.1787	4.6646
12	1.1275	1.2712	1.4333	1.6161	1.8221	2.0544	2.3164	2.6117	2.9447	3.3201	3.7434	4.2207	4.7588	5.3656
13	1.1388	1.2969	1.4770	1.6820	1.9155	2.1815	2.4843	2.8292	3.2220	3.6693	4.1787	4.7588	5.4195	6.1719
14	1.1503	1.3231	1.5220	1.7507	2.0138	2.3164	2.6645	3.0649	3.5254	4.0552	4.6646	5.3656	6.1719	7.0993
15	1.1618	1.3499	1.5683	1.8221	2.1170	2.4596	2.8577	3.3201	3.8574	4.4817	5.2070	6.0496	7.0287	8.1662
16	1.1735	1.3771	1.6161	1.8965	2.2255	2.6117	3.0649	3.5966	4.2207	4.9530	5.8124	6.8210	8.0045	9.3933
17	1.1853	1.4049	1.6653	1.9739	2.3396	2.7732	3.2871	3.8962	4.6182	5.4739	6.4883	7.6906	9.1157	10.8049
18	1.1972	1.4333	1.7160	2.0544	2.4596	2.9447	3.5254	4.2207	5.0531	6.0496	7.2427	8.6711	10.3812	12.4286
19	1.2092	1.4623	1.7683	2.1383	2.5857	3.1268	3.7810	4.5722	5.5290	6.6859	8.0849	9.7767	11.8224	14.2963
20	1.2214	1.4918	1.8221	2.2255	2.7183	3.3201	4.0552	4.9530	6.0496	7.3891	9.0250	11.0232	13.4637	16.4446
21	1.2337	1.5220	1.8776	2.3164	2.8577	3.5254	4.3492	5.3656	6.6194	8.1662	10.0744	12.4286	15.3329	18.9158
22	1.2461	1.5527	1.9348	2.4109	3.0042	3.7434	4.6646	5.8124	7.2427	9.0250	11.2459	14.0132	17.4615	21.7584
23	1.2586	1.5841	1.9937	2.5093	3.1582	3.9749	5.0028	6.2965	7.9248	9.9742	12.5535	15.7998	19.8857	25.0281
24	1.2712	1.6161	2.0544	2.6117	3.3201	4.2207	5.3656	6.8210	8.6711	11.0232	14.0132	17.8143	22.6464	28.7892
25	1.2840	1.6487	2.1170	2.7183	3.4903	4.4817	5.7546	7.3891	9.4877	12.1825	15.6426	20.0855	25.7903	33.1155
30	1.3499	1.8221	2.4596	3.3204	4.4817	6.0496	8.1662	11.0232	14.8797	20.0855	27.1126	36.5982	49.4024	66.6863
35	1.4191	2.0138	2.8577	4.0552	5.7546	8.1662	11.5883	16.4446	23.3361	33.1155	46.9931	66.6863	94.6324	134.2898
40	1.4918	2.2255	3.3201	4.9530	7.3891	11.0232	16.4446	24.5235	36.5982	54.5982	81.4509	121.5104	181.2722	270.4264
45	1.5683	2.4596	3.8574	6.0496	9.4877	14.8797	23.3361	36.5982	57.3975	90.0171	141.1750	221.4064	347.2344	544.5719
50	1.6487	2.7183	4.4817	7.3891	12.1825	20.0855	33.1155	54.5982	90.0171	148.4132	244.6919	403.4288	665.1416	1096.633
55	1.7333	3.0042	5.2070	9.0250	15.6426	27.1126	46.9931	81.4509	141.1750	244.6919	424.1130	735.0952	1274.106	2208.348
60	1.8221	3.3201	6.0496	11.0232	20.0855	36.5982	66.6863	121.5104	221.4064	403.4288	735.0952	1339.431	2440.602	4447.067

PERIOD (T)	Continuously Compounded Rate (r) 15%	16%	17%	18%	19%	20%	21%	22%	23%	24%	25%	26%	27%	28%
1	1.1618	1.1735	1.1853	1.1972	1.2092	1.2214	1.2337	1.2461	1.2586	1.2712	1.2840	1.2969	1.3100	1.3231
2	1.3499	1.3771	1.4049	1.4333	1.4623	1.4918	1.5220	1.5527	1.5841	1.6161	1.6487	1.6820	1.7160	1.7507
3	1.5683	1.6161	1.6653	1.7160	1.7683	1.8221	1.8776	1.9348	1.9937	2.0544	2.1170	2.1815	2.2479	2.3164
4	1.8221	1.8965	1.9739	2.0544	2.1383	2.2255	2.3164	2.4109	2.5093	2.6117	2.7183	2.8292	2.9447	3.0649
5	2.1170	2.2255	2.3396	2.4596	2.5857	2.7183	2.8577	3.0042	3.1582	3.3201	3.4903	3.6693	3.8574	4.0552
6	2.4596	2.6117	2.7732	2.9447	3.1268	3.3201	3.5254	3.7434	3.9749	4.2207	4.4817	4.7588	5.0351	5.3656
7	2.8577	3.0649	3.2871	3.5254	3.7810	4.0552	4.3492	4.6646	5.0028	5.3656	5.7546	6.1719	6.6194	7.0993
8	3.3201	3.5966	3.8962	4.2207	4.5722	4.9530	5.3656	5.8124	6.2965	6.8210	7.3891	8.0045	8.6711	9.3933
9	3.8574	4.2207	4.6182	5.0531	5.5290	6.0496	6.6194	7.2427	7.9248	8.6711	9.4877	10.3812	11.3589	12.4286
10	4.4817	4.9530	5.4739	6.0496	6.6859	7.3891	8.1662	9.0250	9.9742	11.0232	12.1825	13.4637	14.8797	16.4446
11	5.2070	5.8124	6.4883	7.2427	8.0849	9.0250	10.0744	11.2459	12.5535	14.0132	15.6426	17.4615	19.4919	21.7584
12	6.0496	6.8210	7.6906	8.6711	9.7767	11.0232	12.4286	14.0132	15.7998	17.8143	20.0855	22.6464	25.5337	28.7892
13	7.0287	8.0045	9.1157	10.3812	11.8224	13.4637	15.3329	17.4615	19.8857	22.6464	25.7903	29.3708	33.4483	38.0918
14	8.1662	9.3933	10.8049	12.4286	14.2963	16.4446	18.9158	21.7584	25.0281	28.7892	33.1155	38.0918	43.8160	50.4004
15	9.4877	11.0232	12.0871	14.8797	17.2878	20.0855	23.3361	27.1126	31.5004	36.5982	42.5211	49.4024	57.3975	66.6863
16	11.0232	12.9358	15.1803	17.8143	20.9052	24.5325	28.7892	33.7844	39.6464	46.5255	54.5982	64.0715	75.1886	88.2347
17	12.8071	15.1803	17.9933	21.3276	25.2797	29.9641	35.5166	42.0980	49.8990	59.1455	70.1054	83.0963	98.4944	116.7459
18	14.8797	17.8143	21.3276	25.5337	30.5694	36.5982	43.8160	52.4573	62.8028	75.1886	90.0171	107.7701	129.0242	154.4700
19	17.2878	20.9052	25.2797	30.5694	36.9661	44.7012	54.0549	65.3659	79.0436	95.5835	115.5843	139.7702	169.0171	204.3839
20	20.0855	24.5325	29.9641	36.5982	44.7012	54.5982	66.6863	81.4509	99.4843	121.5104	148.4132	181.2722	221.4064	270.4264
21	23.3361	28.7892	35.5166	43.8160	54.0549	66.6863	82.2695	101.4940	125.2110	154.4700	190.5663	235.0974	290.0345	357.8092
22	27.1126	33.7844	42.0980	52.4573	65.3659	81.4509	101.4940	126.4694	157.5905	196.3699	244.6919	304.9049	379.9349	473.4281
23	31.5004	39.6464	49.8990	62.8028	79.0436	99.4843	125.2110	157.5905	198.3434	249.6350	314.1907	395.4404	497.7013	626.4068
24	36.5982	46.5255	59.1455	75.1886	95.5835	121.5104	154.4700	196.3699	249.6350	317.3483	403.4288	512.8585	651.9709	828.8175
25	42.5211	54.5982	70.1054	90.0171	115.5843	148.4132	190.5663	244.6919	314.1907	403.4288	518.0128	665.1416	854.0588	1096.633
30	90.0171	121.5104	164.0219	221.4064	298.8674	403.4288	544.5719	735.0952	992.2747	1339.431	1808.042	2440.602	3294.468	4447.067
35	190.5663	270.4264	383.7533	544.5719	772.7843	1096.633	1556.197	2208.348	3133.795	4447.067	6310.688	8955.293	12708.17	18033.74
40	403.4288	601.8450	897.8473	1339.431	1998.196	2980.958	4447.067	6634.244	9897.129	14764.78	22026.47	32859.63	49020.80	73130.44
45	854.0588	1339.431	2100.646	3294.468	5166.754	8103.084	12708.17	19930.37	31257.04	49020.80	76879.92	120571.7	189094.1	296558.6
50	1808.042	2980.958	4914.769	8103.084	13359.73	22026.47	36315.50	59874.14	98715.77	162754.8	268337.3	442413.4	729416.4	1202604.
55	3827.626	6634.244	11498.82	19930.37	34544.37	59874.14	103777.0	179871.9	311763.4	540364.9	936589.2	1623346.	2813669.	4876801.
60	8103.084	14764.78	26903.19	49020.80	89321.72	162754.8	296558.6	540364.9	984609.1	1794075.	3269017.	5956538.	10853520.	19776403.

TABLE A.6

Present Value of $1 with a Continuous Discount Rate r for T Periods: Values of e^{-rT}

PERIOD (T)	Continuous Discount Rate (r)																
	1%	2%	3%	4%	5%	6%	7%	8%	9%	10%	11%	12%	13%	14%	15%	16%	17%
1	.9900	.9802	.9704	.9608	.9512	.9418	.9324	.9231	.9139	.9048	.8958	.8869	.8781	.8694	.8607	.8521	.8437
2	.9802	.9608	.9418	.9231	.9048	.8869	.8694	.8521	.8353	.8187	.8025	.7866	.7711	.7558	.7408	.7261	.7118
3	.9704	.9418	.9139	.8869	.8607	.8353	.8106	.7866	.7634	.7408	.7189	.6977	.6771	.6570	.6376	.6188	.6005
4	.9608	.9231	.8869	.8521	.8187	.7866	.7558	.7261	.6977	.6703	.6440	.6188	.5945	.5712	.5488	.5273	.5066
5	.9512	.9048	.8607	.8187	.7788	.7408	.7047	.6703	.6376	.6065	.5769	.5488	.5220	.4966	.4724	.4493	.4274
6	.9418	.8869	.8353	.7866	.7408	.6977	.6570	.6188	.5827	.5488	.5169	.4868	.4584	.4317	.4066	.3829	.3606
7	.9324	.8694	.8106	.7558	.7047	.6570	.6126	.5712	.5326	.4966	.4630	.4317	.4025	.3753	.3499	.3263	.3042
8	.9231	.8521	.7866	.7261	.6703	.6188	.5712	.5273	.4868	.4493	.4148	.3829	.3535	.3263	.3012	.2780	.2576
9	.9139	.8353	.7634	.6977	.6376	.5827	.5326	.4868	.4449	.4066	.3716	.3396	.3104	.2837	.2592	.2369	.2165
10	.9048	.8187	.7408	.6703	.6065	.5488	.4966	.4493	.4066	.3679	.3329	.3012	.2725	.2466	.2231	.2019	.1827
11	.8958	.8025	.7189	.6440	.5769	.5169	.4630	.4148	.3716	.3329	.2982	.2671	.2393	.2144	.1920	.1720	.1541
12	.8869	.7866	.6977	.6188	.5488	.4868	.4317	.3829	.3396	.3012	.2671	.2369	.2101	.1864	.1653	.1466	.1300
13	.8781	.7711	.6771	.5945	.5220	.4584	.4025	.3535	.3104	.2725	.2393	.2101	.1845	.1620	.1423	.1249	.1097
14	.8694	.7558	.6570	.5712	.4966	.4317	.3753	.3263	.2837	.2466	.2144	.1864	.1620	.1409	.1225	.1065	.0926
15	.8607	.7408	.6376	.5488	.4724	.4066	.3499	.3012	.2592	.2231	.1920	.1653	.1423	.1225	.1054	.0907	.0781
16	.8521	.7261	.6188	.5273	.4493	.3829	.3263	.2780	.2369	.2019	.1720	.1466	.1249	.1065	.0907	.0773	.0659
17	.8437	.7118	.6005	.5066	.4274	.3606	.3042	.2567	.2165	.1827	.1541	.1300	.1097	.0926	.0781	.0659	.0556
18	.8353	.6977	.5827	.4868	.4066	.3396	.2837	.2369	.1979	.1653	.1381	.1153	.0963	.0805	.0672	.0561	.0469
19	.8270	.6839	.5655	.4677	.3867	.3198	.2645	.2187	.1809	.1496	.1237	.1023	.0846	.0699	.0578	.0478	.0396
20	.8187	.6703	.5488	.4493	.3679	.3012	.2466	.2019	.1653	.1353	.1108	.0907	.0743	.0608	.0498	.0408	.0334
21	.8106	.6570	.5326	.4317	.3499	.2837	.2299	.1864	.1511	.1225	.0993	.0805	.0652	.0529	.0429	.0347	.0282
22	.8025	.6440	.5169	.4148	.3329	.2671	.2144	.1720	.1381	.1108	.0889	.0714	.0573	.0460	.0369	.0296	.0238
23	.7945	.6313	.5016	.3985	.3166	.2516	.1999	.1588	.1262	.1003	.0797	.0633	.0503	.0400	.0317	.0252	.0200
24	.7866	.6188	.4868	.3829	.3012	.2369	.1864	.1466	.1153	.0907	.0714	.0561	.0442	.0347	.0273	.0215	.0169
25	.7788	.6065	.4724	.3679	.2865	.2231	.1738	.1353	.1054	.0821	.0639	.0498	.0388	.0302	.0235	.0183	.0143
30	.7408	.5488	.4066	.3012	.2231	.1653	.1225	.0907	.0672	.0498	.0369	.0273	.0202	.0150	.0111	.0082	.0061
35	.7047	.4966	.3499	.2466	.1738	.1225	.0863	.0608	.0429	.0302	.0213	.0150	.0106	.0074	.0052	.0037	.0026
40	.6703	.4493	.3012	.2019	.1353	.0907	.0608	.0408	.0273	.0183	.0123	.0082	.0055	.0037	.0025	.0017	.0011
45	.6376	.4066	.2592	.1653	.1054	.0672	.0429	.0273	.0174	.0111	.0071	.0045	.0029	.0018	.0012	.0007	.0005
50	.6065	.3679	.2231	.1353	.0821	.0498	.0302	.0183	.0111	.0067	.0041	.0025	.0015	.0009	.0006	.0003	.0002
55	.5769	.3329	.1920	.1108	.0639	.0369	.0213	.0123	.0071	.0041	.0024	.0014	.0008	.0005	.0003	.0002	.0001
60	.5488	.3012	.1653	.0907	.0498	.0273	.0150	.0082	.0045	.0025	.0014	.0007	.0004	.0002	.0001	.0001	.0000

PERIOD (T)	Continuous Discount Rate (r)																	
	18%	19%	20%	21%	22%	23%	24%	25%	26%	27%	28%	29%	30%	31%	32%	33%	34%	35%
1	.8353	.8270	.8187	.8106	.8025	.7945	.7866	.7788	.7711	.7634	.7558	.7483	.7408	.7334	.7261	.7189	.7118	.7047
2	.6977	.6839	.6703	.6570	.6440	.6313	.6188	.6065	.5945	.5827	.5712	.5599	.5488	.5379	.5273	.5169	.5066	.4966
3	.5827	.5655	.5488	.5326	.5169	.5016	.4868	.4724	.4584	.4449	.4317	.4190	.4066	.3946	.3829	.3716	.3606	.3499
4	.4868	.4677	.4493	.4317	.4148	.3985	.3829	.3679	.3535	.3396	.3263	.3135	.3012	.2894	.2780	.2671	.2567	.2466
5	.4066	.3867	.3679	.3499	.3329	.3166	.3012	.2865	.2725	.2592	.2466	.2346	.2231	.2122	.2019	.1920	.1827	.1738
6	.3396	.3198	.3012	.2837	.2671	.2516	.2369	.2231	.2101	.1979	.1864	.1755	.1653	.1557	.1466	.1381	.1300	.1225
7	.2837	.2645	.2466	.2299	.2144	.1999	.1864	.1738	.1620	.1511	.1409	.1313	.1225	.1142	.1065	.0993	.0926	.0863
8	.2369	.2187	.2019	.1864	.1720	.1588	.1466	.1353	.1249	.1153	.1065	.0983	.0907	.0837	.0773	.0714	.0659	.0608
9	.1979	.1809	.1653	.1511	.1381	.1262	.1153	.1054	.0963	.0880	.0805	.0735	.0672	.0614	.0561	.0513	.0469	.0429
10	.1653	.1496	.1353	.1225	.1108	.1003	.0907	.0821	.0743	.0672	.0608	.0550	.0498	.0450	.0408	.0369	.0334	.0302
11	.1381	.1237	.1108	.0993	.0889	.0797	.0714	.0639	.0573	.0513	.0460	.0412	.0369	.0330	.0296	.0265	.0238	.0213
12	.1154	.1023	.0907	.0805	.0714	.0633	.0561	.0498	.0442	.0392	.0347	.0308	.0273	.0242	.0215	.0191	.0169	.0150
13	.0963	.0846	.0743	.0652	.0573	.0503	.0442	.0388	.0340	.0299	.0263	.0231	.0202	.0178	.0156	.0137	.0120	.0106
14	.0805	.0699	.0608	.0529	.0460	.0400	.0347	.0302	.0263	.0228	.0198	.0172	.0150	.0130	.0113	.0099	.0086	.0074
15	.0672	.0578	.0498	.0429	.0369	.0317	.0273	.0235	.0202	.0174	.0150	.0129	.0111	.0096	.0082	.0071	.0061	.0052
16	.0561	.0478	.0408	.0347	.0296	.0252	.0215	.0183	.0156	.0133	.0113	.0097	.0082	.0070	.0060	.0051	.0043	.0037
17	.0469	.0396	.0334	.0282	.0238	.0200	.0169	.0143	.0120	.0102	.0086	.0072	.0061	.0051	.0043	.0037	.0031	.0026
18	.0392	.0327	.0273	.0228	.0191	.0159	.0133	.0111	.0093	.0078	.0065	.0054	.0045	.0038	.0032	.0026	.0022	.0018
19	.0327	.0271	.0224	.0185	.0153	.0127	.0105	.0087	.0072	.0059	.0049	.0040	.0033	.0028	.0023	.0019	.0016	.0013
20	.0273	.0224	.0183	.0150	.0123	.0101	.0082	.0067	.0055	.0045	.0037	.0030	.0025	.0020	.0017	.0014	.0011	.0009
21	.0228	.0185	.0150	.0122	.0099	.0080	.0065	.0052	.0043	.0034	.0028	.0023	.0018	.0015	.0012	.0010	.0008	.0006
22	.0191	.0153	.0123	.0099	.0079	.0063	.0051	.0041	.0033	.0026	.0021	.0017	.0014	.0011	.0009	.0007	.0006	.0005
23	.0159	.0127	.0101	.0080	.0063	.0050	.0040	.0032	.0025	.0020	.0016	.0013	.0010	.0008	.0006	.0005	.0004	.0003
24	.0133	.0105	.0082	.0065	.0051	.0040	.0032	.0025	.0019	.0015	.0012	.0009	.0007	.0006	.0005	.0004	.0003	.0002
25	.0111	.0087	.0067	.0052	.0041	.0032	.0025	.0019	.0015	.0012	.0009	.0007	.0006	.0004	.0003	.0003	.0002	.0002
30	.0045	.0033	.0025	.0018	.0014	.0010	.0007	.0006	.0004	.0003	.0002	.0002	.0001	.0001	.0001	.0001	.0000	.0000
35	.0018	.0013	.0009	.0006	.0005	.0003	.0002	.0002	.0001	.0001	.0001	.0000	.0000	.0000	.0000	.0000	.0000	.0000
40	.0007	.0005	.0003	.0002	.0002	.0001	.0001	.0000	.0000	.0000	.0000	.0000	.0000	.0000	.0000	.0000	.0000	.0000
45	.0003	.0002	.0001	.0001	.0001	.0000	.0000	.0000	.0000	.0000	.0000	.0000	.0000	.0000	.0000	.0000	.0000	.0000
50	.0001	.0001	.0000	.0000	.0000	.0000	.0000	.0000	.0000	.0000	.0000	.0000	.0000	.0000	.0000	.0000	.0000	.0000
55	.0001	.0000	.0000	.0000	.0000	.0000	.0000	.0000	.0000	.0000	.0000	.0000	.0000	.0000	.0000	.0000	.0000	.0000
60	.0000	.0000	.0000	.0000	.0000	.0000	.0000	.0000	.0000	.0000	.0000	.0000	.0000	.0000	.0000	.0000	.0000	.0000

APPENDIX B

Solutions to Selected End-of-Chapter Problems

CHAPTER 2

2. Net income = $126,100
Add. to RE = $78,100

4. Average tax rate = 32.86%
Marginal tax rate = 39%

6. $1,425,000

8. $40,000

10. $400,000

13. Net income = $195,000
OCF = $395,000

15. $6,092

20. $15,000

CHAPTER 3

2. Equity multiplier = 2.40
Return on equity = 20.88%
Net income = $108,576

4. $16,866

6. 16.62%

8. $388

10. **a.** 5.85%

12. Profit margin = −8.93%
Net income = −$23,903

15. $6,178

19. 17.65%

CHAPTER 4

2. **a.** $1,628.89
b. $1,967.15
c. $2,653.30

4. 7.63%; 10.66%; 9.97%; 8.12%

6. 10.24 years; 20.49 years

8. $62,827.67

10. **a.** $1,822.12
b. $1,349.86
c. $1,648.72
d. $1,750.67

12. X = $28,431.29
Y = $25,976.86

14. $187,500; 7.69%

16. 7.94%; 7.35%; 15.55%; 23.27%

18. EAR = 176.68%

20. APR = 1,733.33%
EAR = 313,916,515%

25. G: 11.20%
H: 12.06%

30. $1,232.56

35. 10%: $30,722.84
5%: $38,608.68
15%: $25,093.84

40. $18,758,930

45. $112,518

50. $1,361.82

CHAPTER 5

2. **a.** $1,000
b. $828.41
c. $1,231.15

4. 9.16%

6. 6.60%

8. 8.52%

10. Current yield = 5.77%
YTM = 4.93%

15. 7.10%

17. $881.25

CHAPTER 6

2. 11.46%

4. $42.35

6. $3.96

8. 7.30%

13. $31.18

18. $91.67

24. $2.49

29. **a.** $15.75
b. New price = $31.18

CHAPTER 7

2. 3.57 years; 5.95 years; Never

4. 4.76 years

6. 44.44%

8. A: 47.15%
B: 36.19%

10. Alpha: 2.60
Beta: 1.52

13. **a.** Fishing: 24.30%
Submarine: 21.46%
b. 19.92%
c. Fishing: $96,688
Submarine: $190,630

20. **a.** Dry: 2.00 years
Solvent: 1.00 years
b. Dry: $627,348
Solvent: $277,611
c. Dry: 39.79%
Solvent: 49.20%
d. 34.45%

CHAPTER 8

2. NPV = $2,404

4. Year 0: −$3,000,000
Year 1: $1,251,000
Year 2: $1,251,000
Year 3: $1,687,500
NPV = $143,320

6. 23.85%

8. $1,927,464

10. Techron I EAC: −$84,274
Techron II EAC: −$83,794

16. $22,770,000

21. NPV = −$11,232

25. NPV = −$590,131

CHAPTER 9

2. Best-case NPV = $3,109,608
Worst-case NPV = −$1,848,883

4. 20,532

6. Go now NPV = $12,500,000
Test market NPV = $12,130,435

8. Go now NPV = $17,850,000
Test market NPV = $18,043,478

10. 3,518

14. Payback = 2.95 years
NPV = $9,103,637
IRR = 28.24%

22. $66.00

CHAPTER 10

2. R_D = 1.69%
R_C = 9.64%

4. **a.** $44.00
b. 3.93%
c. .90%

6. Government bonds: 2.62%
Corporate bonds: 3.01%

8. **a.** Large stocks: 3.24%
T-bills: 6.55%

b. Large stocks: 24.11%
T-bills: 1.24%

10. **a.** 4.41%
b. 3.70%

12. 98.55%

14. 1.37%

16. 7.48%

20. 12.40%

25. 4.62%

CHAPTER 11

2. 14.06%

4. X: $6,400
Y: $3,600

6. A: E(R) = 8.10%
σ = 1.92%
B: E(R) = 15.70%
σ = 14.89%

8. 14.50%

10. E(R) = 13.29%
σ = 17.81%

12. 1.1

14. 1.67

16. 4.33%

18. Slope of SML = .0846

20. 3.07%

28. E(R) = 16.20%
σ = 38.36%

31. **a.** E(R) = 10.60%
b. E(R) = 13.75%

CHAPTER 12

2. Pretax R_D = 7.37%
Aftertax R_D = 4.79%

4. BV of debt = $100,000,000
MV of debt = $68,000,000
Aftertax R_D = 5.48%

6. 13.69%

8. **a.** E/V = .2603
D/V = .7397
b. S/V = .7978
B/V = .2022

10. **a.** 7.50%
b. 13.78%

12. **a.** B/V = .2672
S/V = .7328
b. 14.09%

14. $43,385,321

CHAPTER 14

2. **a.** $1.46; $3.64; $4.73
b. $1.13; $4.77; $6.59

4 **a.** Plan I: $1.33
Plan II: $0.83
b. Plan I: $4.67
Plan II: $9.17
c. $250,000

6. **a.** I: $7.59
II: $8.06
All-equity: $7.14
b. I: $4.55
II: $4.83
All-equity: $4.29
c. $7,700

8. **a.** $800
b. $960

10. $4,550,000

12. **a.** 18.30%
b. 15.19%
c. 20.40%; 16.20%; 12.00%

14. V_U = $280,682
V_L = $301,682

17. V_L = $187,000

21. **a.** 0.50
b. 16.00%
c. 16.00%

CHAPTER 15

4. $650,000

7. **a.** Low-volatility: $600
High-volatility: $450
b. Low-volatility: $100
High-volatility: $150
d. $600

CHAPTER 16

2. **a.** Shares issued = 1,000
b. Shares issued = 2,500

4. a. \$39.00
b. \$56.52
c. \$45.61
d. \$113.75
e. 250,000; 172,500; 213,750; 85,714

6. Shares outstanding = 4,885
Price = \$35.00

8. Shares outstanding = 392,000
Capital surplus = \$2,448,000

10. New borrowing = \$576
Capital outlays = \$1,296

12. a. \$720,000
b. \$0

14. a. \$95.00
b. \$100,000
c. 20,000

18. a. \$1,412,000
b. \$138.00
c. \$1,412,000
d. 76.67 shares

CHAPTER 17

4. a. \$13.96
b. \$2.31

6. \$7.70

8. \$70.98

10. Call = \$5.90
Put = \$2.38

12. Call delta = .6436
Put delta = −.3565

14. \$164,883

21. Equity = \$2,051.70
Debt = \$8,448.30

25. a. \$11,876,514
b. \$10,123,486
c. 10.86%
d. \$12,481,437
e. 10.72%

CHAPTER 18

2. Cash = \$6,450
Current assets = \$10,150

4. a. I; I
b. I; N
c. D; D
d. D; D
e. D; N
f. I; I

6. Operating cycle = 92.75 days
Cash cycle = 42.48 days

8. a. \$189.00; \$213.00; \$235.50; \$186.30
b. \$162.00; \$189.00; \$213.00; \$235.50
c. \$171.00; \$197.00; \$220.50; \$219.10

10. a. \$106,667
b. \$117,143
c. \$136,929; \$160,021; \$183,200

13. a. 7.90%
b. \$580,667

CHAPTER 19

2. Pooling assets = \$540,000
Purchase assets = \$860,000

4. Goodwill = \$1,600

6. Goodwill = \$4,150

8. a. EPS = \$4.88; P/E = 16.15

10. a. \$300
b. \$34.20
c. \$2,700
d. \$37.06
e. \$4,588

15. a. £22.22
b. .6429

CHAPTER 20

2. SF/£ = .4412; £/SF = 2.2665

4. a. C\$/\$ = .7937
b. \$1.74

6. Great Britain = 4.45%
Japan = 2.08%
Switzerland = 2.43%

8. .69%

10. a. Kr/\$ = 6.5257
b. Kr/\$ = 6.5257

15. \$914,619

NAME INDEX

A

Agrawal, Anup, 475

B

Banz, R. W., 408n
Becher, David A., 416
Beltran, Carlos, 89, 101
Berens, J. L., 471
Berra, Yogi, 78
Blume, Marshal, 314n
Bowie, David, 150
Boyle, Barbara, 228
Brav, A., 509
Briloff, Abraham, 58
Brown, James, 150
Buffett, Warren, 131, 512

C

Chan, Louis K. C., 407–408
Cuny, C. L., 471
Cutler, David M., 457

D

Dell, Michael, 14
DiMaggio, Joe, 164
Dirksen, Everett, 460n

E

Ebbers, Bernie, 18
Elizabeth I, Queen of England, 462
Ellison, Larry, 14, 20
Elton, E. J., 343

F

Fama, Eugene F., 409n, 410, 411, 505–506
Fiorina, Carleton "Carly," 1, 14–15
Fisher, Irving, 155–156
Franklin, Benjamin, 93
French, Kenneth R., 409n, 410, 505–506

G

Gaye, Marvin, 150
Gibson, Mel, 14, 20
Graham, John R., 226, 227, 277, 283, 477, 509
Gruber, M. J., 343
Grullon, Gustave, 495

H

Hall, Brian J., 416
Harvey, Campbell R., 226, 227, 277, 283, 477, 509
Hull, John C., 539n

I

Ibbotson, Roger, 96–97, 301–305, 308, 309, 351
Ikenberry, D., 415n

J

Jamail, Joe, 457
Jegadeesh, Narasimhan, 407–408
Jensen, M. C., 466n

K

Keim, Donald, 408, 408n
Keynes, John Maynard, 462
Kilts, James, 614
Kothari, S. P., 409n

L

Lakonishok, Josef, 407–408, 415n
Lang, L., 468n
Liebman, Jeffrey B., 416
Lintner, John, 506–507
Litwak, Mark, 227n
Loughran, Tim, 409

M

Malkiel, B. G., 398n
Mark, Reuben, 14
Meckling, W., 466n
Michaely, Roni, 495, 509
Miller, Merton, 392, 431–447, 461, 491–494, 496, 498, 501
Minuit, Peter, 97
Modigliani, F., 431–447, 461, 491–494, 496, 498, 501
Monroe, Marilyn, 164

N

Nagarajan, Nandu, 475

P

Pastor, Lubos, 403
Porter, Michael, 605n

R

Reinganum, M. R., 408n
Ritter, Jay, 413–414
Roberts, Brian, 185

S

Shah, K., 465
Shanken, J., 409
Shleifer, Andrei, 394–395, 404–405
Siegel, Jeremy J., 157
Sinquefield, Rex, 96–97, 301–305, 308, 309, 351
Sloan, R. G., 409n
Smith, Adam, 466
Smith, Frederick, 458
Stambaugh, Robert F., 403
Stulz, R., 468n
Summers, Lawrence H., 457
Szewcyzk, Samuel H., 401–402

T

Thornton, Billy Bob, 271
Trump, Donald, 480
Tsetsekos, George P., 401–402
Tufano, Peter, 392n

V

Varitek, Jason, 89
Vermaelen, T., 415n
Vick, Michael, 89
Victoria, Queen of England, 462

W

Walkling, R., 468n
Warner, Jerold B., 416n, 417
Watts, Ross L., 416n, 417
Winfrey, Oprah, 14, 20
Woods, Tiger, 14, 20
Wruck, Karen H., 416n, 417

Z

Zantout, Zaher Z., 401–402

COMPANY INDEX

A

aaiPharma, 298
ABN AMRO, 137
Accenture Ltd., 371
Acme Metals, 350
Adelphia Communications, 34
Adobe Systems, 523
Adolph Coors, 185
Air Products & Chemical, 380
Albemarle Corp., 380
Alcoa, 344
Alitalia, 455
Allied Waste Industries, 476
Allstate, 45, 523, 616
Alpha Wireless, 192
Amazon.com, 179, 322, 330, 341, 348–349, 369, 569–571, 574
Amerada Hess, 382
American Airlines, 422
American Eagle Outfitters, 570
American Electric Power, 42
American Express, 362
America Online (AOL), 274
AmeriCash Advance, 105
AmeriServe Food Distributors, 147
Ameritrade, 614
Amgen, 182, 453
Anadarko, 382
Apache, 382
Apple Computer, 8, 193
Atlantic Southeast Airlines, 455
AT&T, 338, 344, 616
Automatic Data Processing, 371
AutoZone, 167
Avon Products, 594

B

Barnes & Noble, 569–571
Bayerische Moterenwerke (BMW) AG, 11, 643
Bear Stearns, 182
Bell Atlantic, 599
BellSouth, 137, 146, 600, 616
Beltran, Carlos, 89, 101
Berkshire Hathaway, 131, 149, 512
Best Buy, 480
Biogen Idec, 424
Bizfilings, 20
BJ Services Company, 594
Black & Decker, 85
BMW, 11, 643
Boeing, 400
Boston Red Sox, 89
Burger King, 147, 285, 405
Burlington Resources, 382

C

Cabot Corp., 380
Cambrex Corp., 380
Caterpillar, 86, 182, 344
Charmin Paper Company, 604–605
ChevronTexaco, 226, 341, 382
Chicago and Eastern Railroad, 137
Chrysler Corporation, 548
Cigna, 565
Cingular, 600
Cisco Systems, 182, 322, 341
Citigroup, 400
Clear Channel Communications, 22
CNN Money, 350
Coca-Cola Company, 42, 85, 137, 165, 399, 400
Colgate-Palmolive, 14, 507
Comcast, 15, 185
Compaq Computers, 1, 14–15
Compare Generiks, 350
Computer Associates, 45, 58, 371
Computer Sciences, 371
Congoleum, 481
Conoco, 616
ConocoPhillips, 201, 341, 382
Continental Airlines, 85, 480–481
Cooper Tire and Rubber Company, 42
Countrywide Financial, 149
Coventry Health, 146
Cytec Industries, 380

D

DaimlerChrysler, 53, 365
Deere & Company, 341
Dell Computer Corporation, 14, 86, 193, 512
Delta Air Lines, 58, 422, 455, 456–457
Detwiler, Mitchell & Co., 513
Disney, 15, 86, 137, 271, 286–287, 330
Dornier GmBH, 11
Dow Chemical Company, 85, 362, 385
Dow Corning, 481
DreamWorks, 271
Duke Energy, 319
Du Pont Corporation, 56–59, 86, 362, 616
Dutch West India Company, 97
Dynegy, 34

E

Eastman Chemical, 379–383
Eastman Kodak, 146–147, 344, 379

eBay, 179
Edison International, 453
Elan, 424
Electronic Data Systems, 371
Elizabeth Arden, 129
Enron, 412, 456
E*Trade Financial, 614
Euro Disney, 286–287
ExxonMobil, 28, 226, 322, 341, 382

F

Federal Express, 45, 458
Federal Mogul, 481
Fiat SpA, 11, 274
Fidelity Magellan, 311
Financial Accounting Standards Board (FASB), 247, 602–603, 644
First Data Corp., 371
Fiserv Inc., 371
Fitch, 146–147, 426
Ford Motor Company, 46, 185, 330, 399, 633

G

Gap, 570
Gateway, 85, 165
General Dynamics, 42
General Electric (GE), 34, 65, 330, 370, 459, 500
General Mills, 350
General Motors Acceptance Corporation (GMAC), 119–120
General Motors (GM), 46, 53, 57–58, 119–120, 182, 186, 203, 274, 338, 395, 399, 453, 463–464, 467
Georgia Pacific, 165, 453
Getty Oil, 457
Gillette, 614
Global Crossing, 412
Goldman, Sachs and Co., 10
Google, 179, 185
Graftech International, 584
GTE, 599

H

Halliburton, 481
Harley-Davidson, 42, 193–195, 201
Hawaiian Electric Industries, 42
HCA, Inc., 426
Hewlett-Packard (HP), 1, 14–15, 376
H.J. Heinz, 42, 59, 60
Home Depot, 344, 362
Honda, 643
Honeywell, 362

I

IBM, 182, 191–193, 330, 338, 376, 400, 524–525, 644–645
Idaho Power and Light Company, 365
Intel Corporation, 17, 193, 344, 528–529
International Paper Co., 149
Iron Maiden, 150

J

J. M. Smucker, 350
Johns-Manville, 481
Johnson & Johnson, 65, 201, 476, 625

K

Kellogg, 453
Kerr-McGee, 382
Kindred Healthcare, 350
Kohl's, 570
KT&G, 500

L

Landry's Seafood Restaurants, 42
Lastminute, 18
LG Philips LCD, 240
Limited Brands, 426
Lindt, 512
Lion Bioscience, 18
Lockheed Corporation, 548
Lycos, 350

M

McGraw-Hill, 167
Manpower, Inc., 51
Manville, 481
Marathon, 382
Matsushita Electric, 500
Maytag, 58
McDonald's, 79, 179, 214–215, 285, 330, 400, 405, 570, 634, 651
Mercedes-Benz, 633, 643
Merck, 344, 453
Merrill Lynch, 149, 188
Microsoft, 17, 73–74, 193, 319, 369, 371, 400, 487, 500, 512, 548, 565
Millipore Corp., 380
Monsanto Co., 380
Moody's, 145–147, 149, 165
MTS, Inc., 480
Murphy, 382

N

National Payday, 105
Navistar International, 165
Neiman-Marcus, 61–62
Nestlé S. A., 650–651
Nextel, 596, 599, 607
Northwest Airlines, 455

O

Occidental, 382
Ontario Lottery, 104
Oracle Corp., 14, 20, 371
Owens Corning, 481

P

Pacific Corp., 365
Pacific Gas and Electric, 426
Pall Corp., 380

Palm Computing, 406, 616
palmOne, 406
Panasonic, 500
Pennzoil, 457
Peugeot Citroën, 643
Peugeot SA, 11
Pfizer, 400, 625
Philip Morris, 369
Porsche, 633
PPG Industries, 380
Procter & Gamble, 174, 362, 400, 500, 507, 523, 604–605, 614
Psychex, Inc., 371

R

Ramp, 298
Republic National Bank, 137
Reynolds American, 167
Risk Management Association (RMA), 62–64
RJR Nabisco, 600
Robert Morris Associates, 62–64
Rolls-Royce PLC, 11
Royal Dutch Petroleum, 405–407

S

St. Louis Federal Reserve Board, 165, 319
Saks, 570
Samsung Electronics, 240
SBC Communications, 600, 616
Sears, 79, 330, 369, 401, 616
Sharper Image, 42
Shell Transport, 405–407
Shell UK Ltd., 11
Siemens AG, 18
Sirius Satellite Radio, 192
Smartforce PLC, 192
Society for Worldwide Interbank Financial Telecommunications (SWIFT), 627–628
Sony Corporation, 287
Southern California Edison, 142, 143, 145, 453
SouthTrust, 599
Southwest Airlines, 85, 129
Sprint, 596, 599
Sprint Nextel, 596, 599, 604, 607
SPX Corp., 27
Standard & Poor's (S&P), 145–147, 149, 426
Starbucks, 182, 193
SunGard Data, 371
Superior Oil, 385
Symantec Corp., 371
Syndicated Food Service, 350

T

Target, 61–62
Tele Norte Leste Participacoes SA (Telemar), 500
Terrace Food Group, 350
Texaco, 457
3Com, 406, 616
3M Company, 380
Time Warner, 42, 274
Tower Records, 480
Toyota Motors, 203, 643
Toys "R" Us Inc., 330
Trump Hotels and Casinos, 480
Tyco, 34

U

Unilever NV, 11
United Airlines, 422, 455, 456–457
United States Steel, 45
Unocal, 382
US Airways, 455, 456–457

V

Verizon Communications, 330, 599, 600, 616
Verizon Wireless, 600
Viacom, 22, 37
Virgin Megastores, 480
Vodaphone, 600
Volvo AB, 11

W

Wachovia, 599
Wal-Mart, 51, 61–62, 176, 189–190, 201, 480, 512
Walt Disney Company, 15, 86, 137, 271, 286–287, 330
Wendy's, 405
Whole Foods Markets, 365
WorldCom, 18, 412, 456

X

Xerox, 182, 412
XM Satellite Radio, 176

Y

Yahoo!, 193, 350

SUBJECT INDEX

Note: Key terms are set in **bold** type.

A

Abandonment option, 285–287
Abnormal returns (ARs), 401–403
Absolute priority rule (APR), 479
Absolute purchasing power parity, 632–633, 634
Accelerated depreciation, 183, 245–246
Accounting choices
  for depreciation, 245–254
  for inventory accounting, 183, 412–413
  for merger and acquisition accounting, 601–603
Accounting equation, 24
Accounting liquidity, 24, 49–51, 56
Accounting profit
  cash flows versus, 6
  as goal of financial management, 11–12
Accounting rate of return, in practice of capital budgeting, 226–228
Accounts payable
  payables turnover, 53, 573
  payment of, 581
Accounts payable period, 568–569, 570, 573
Accounts receivable, 24
  average collection period (ACP), 53, 56, 568–570, 572
  days' sales in receivables, 53, 56, 568–570, 572
  receivables turnover, 53, 56, 572
Accounts receivable financing, 584–585
Accounts receivable period, 53, 56, 568–570, 572
Acid-test ratio, 50–51, 56
Acquisitions. *See also* Mergers and acquisitions
  of assets, 599
  classification of, 599
  of stock, 598–599
Additions to net working capital, 31
Agency costs
  of debt, 457–459, 468
  of dividend payments, 502–503
  of equity, 466–468
  nature of, 13–14
Agency problem
  defined, 13
  management goals and, 13–15
Agreement of merger, 607
Allocated costs, incremental cash flows and, 242–243
American Depository Receipt (ADR), 626
American Jobs Creation Act, 625
American options, 524, 534, 536
American quotes, 628
American Stock Exchange (AMEX)
  as auction market, 17
  dividend payouts and, 505–506
Amortization, of goodwill, 602–603
Announcements, impact of, 340–341
Annual percentage rate (APR), 102
Annuity, 110–116
  annuity due, 113–114
  defined, 110
  delayed, 112–113
  equating present value of two annuities, 114–115
  growing, 115–116
  infrequent, 114
  present value of, 110–116, 133–135
Annuity due, 104, 113–114
Annuity factor, 111–112
Annuity in arrears, 113–114
Anomalies, 405–411
Arbitrage
  covered interest arbitrage, 636–637
  debt versus equity financing and, 439
  defined, 395
  efficient capital markets and, 395, 405–407
  limits to, 405–407
  triangle, 630–631
Arithmetic average return
  defined, 312
  geometric average return versus, 314–315
Arrearage, dividend, 186–187
Articles of incorporation, 9
Asked price, 152, 191–193
Aspirant group, 62
Asset-backed bonds, 150
Asset beta, 374–375
Asset management ratios, 52–54, 56
  capital intensity, 56, 69
  days' sales in inventory, 52–53, 56
  days' sales in receivables, 53, 56, 568–570, 572
  inventory turnover, 52, 56, 572
  receivables turnover, 53, 56, 572
  total asset turnover, 53–54, 56, 76
Asset-specific risk. *See* Unsystematic risk
Asset write-ups, 606–607
Auction markets
  for corporate securities, 16–17, 187
  dealer markets versus, 17
  defined, 16
  listings and, 17, 18
Average, 305–308
Average accounting return method, 209–211
  analyzing, 211
  investment rule for, 209–210
  NPV method versus, 211
  steps in, 210–211
Average collection period (ACP), 53, 56, 568–570, 572

Average return, 305–308
calculating, 307–308
risk-free returns and, 308–310
stock, 308–310, 312–315
Average tax rate, 28–29

B

Balance sheet, 23–25
accounting liquidity and, 24, 49–51, 56
common-size, 46–48
debt versus equity and, 24
defined, 23
graphic conceptualization of, 3
model of firm based on, 2–3
percentage of sales approach to, 68–70
pro forma, 66–71
sample, 23
value versus cost and, 24–25
Balance sheet identity, 566–567
Balloon payments, 144
Bankruptcy costs, 456–460
agency costs in, 457–459
direct, 456
indirect, 456–457
leverage and, 461–464
pie model of capital structure and, 463–464
Bankruptcy process, 478–481
agreement to avoid bankruptcy, 481
financial management and, 480–481
legal bankruptcy, 478
Bankruptcy Reform Act (1978), 478–480
Beachhead, 604–605
Bearer form, 143
Bear hug, 614
Behavioral finance, 404–405, 408, 501–502
Bellwether bond, 153
Benchmarking, 59–65
defined, 59
peer group analysis in, 61–66
time-trend analysis in, 60
Beta, 368–375
defined, 349
determinants of, 372–375
divergence in betas, 350
estimation of, 368–372
expected return and, 351–352
formula for, 349
of industry, 371–372
nature of, 346–348
portfolio, 353
project evaluation and, 367–368, 375–376
real-world betas, 369–370
of security, 368–369, 374–375
stability of, 370–371
Bid price, 152, 191–193
Big Board. *See* New York Stock Exchange (NYSE)
Big Mac Index, 634
Black-Scholes option pricing model, 523, 537, 539–543
Blanket inventory lien, 585
Blanket mortgages, 143
Blume's formula, 314–315
Board of directors. *See* Directors
Bond(s), 131–161
coupon, 132, 143
defined, 141
features of, 132, 139–145, 149–150, 460–461
foreign, 626, 627
holding period returns and, 301–305, 310
indenture, 142–145
as interest-only loans, 132
in international corporate finance, 144
markets, 16, 150–154
maturity of, 132, 135–137, 141
as options, 545, 546–547
ratings, 145–147, 149, 426
types of, 143, 147–150, 627. *See also* Treasury bonds
yields on, 156–160
Bond valuation, 132–139, 150–160
interest rate risk in, 135–137, 154–159
market prices in, 16, 150–154
yield to maturity in, 137–139, 156–160
Book value
defined, 24–25
market value versus, 25
Book value per share, 55
Book-value-to-stock-price ratio, 408–409
Bop analysis, 275–278
Bowie bonds, 150
Break-even analysis, 278–280
Brokers, 187–188
types of, 188–190
Bubbles, 390, 404, 409–411
Bubble theory, 409–411
Budgets and budgeting. *See* Capital budgeting; Cash budget
Bulldog bonds, 627
Business failure, 478

C

Call option(s), 523, 524–525
defined, 524
firm expressed in terms of, 544–545, 547
option pricing formula, 536–543
put-call parity and, 530–532, 547–548
selling, 527–528
valuation of
bounding value of, 532–533
factors determining value, 533–536
variability of underlying asset, 535–536
value at expiration, 524–525
Call premium, 144
Call protected, 144
Call provision, 144–145
Canada, "chewable pill," 613
Capital asset pricing model (CAPM)
characteristics of, 353
expected return on stock, 366
formula for, 351–352
relationship between risk and expected return, 351–354
security market line and, 352–354, 398
Capital budgeting
for acquisition decisions, 274
average accounting return method in, 209–211

Capital budgeting—*Cont.*
beta and, 368–375
break-even analysis in, 278–280
cost of capital and, 366–368
decision trees in, 272–274
defined, 2
discounted payback period method in, 209, 226–228
dividend payments and, 499
example of, 243–249
firm versus project and, 375–376
foreign currency approach to, 640, 641–642
home currency approach to, 640–641
incremental cash flows and, 241–243
inflation and, 249–254
internal rate of return in, 212–224
international, 640–642
investments of unequal lives, 254–258
Monte Carlo simulation in, 280–283
net present value in, 203–206, 208, 211, 550–552
options and, 550–552
payback period method, 206–209, 226–228
practice of, 226–228
profitability index (PI) and, 224–226
real options versus, 284–288
for replacement decisions, 256–258
scenario analysis in, 277–278, 283
sensitivity analysis in, 275–278, 283
unremitted cash flows, 642
Capital gains, 299–301
capital gains effect in mergers and acquisitions, 600–601
in common stock valuation, 168–169
computing, 299–301
defined, 299
Capital gains yield, 174
Capital intensity ratio, 56, 69
Capital losses, 298–299
Capital markets, 15
Capital rationing, profitability index and, 225
Capital spending, 31
Capital structure
components of, 3–4
debt versus equity in, 431–440, 471–473
defined, 2
establishment of, 473–478
financial distress costs and, 477
limits to debt in, 455–482
maximizing firm value and, 11–12, 427–429
MM Propositions in, 431–440, 443–447, 469–470
organization charts, 4, 571
pecking-order theory and, 468–471
pie model of, 427, 439–442, 463–464
static trade-off theory of, 462, 470–471
taxes and, 440–447, 469–470, 477
trade-off theory of, 462, 470–471
value of the firm and, 3, 464
Carrying costs, 575, 576
Carrying value, 24–25
Cash
for acquisitions, 610, 611–612
defined, 567
sources of, 567
uses of, 567
Cash budget, 580–582
cash balance and, 582
cash outflows in, 581–582
defined, 580
sales and cash collections in, 580–581
Cash collections, in cash budget, 580–581
Cash coverage, 52, 56
Cash cycle, 568–574
accounts payable period and, 568–569, 570, 573
applications of, 570
calculating, 572
defined, 569, 573
interpreting, 573–574
operating cycle and, 569
payables turnover and, 53, 573
Cash flow. *See also* Discounted cash flow valuation
accounting income versus, 241
accounting profit versus, 6
calculating, 30–33
categories of, 30–33
defined, 30
dividends and, 468, 498–500
dividends set equal to, 490–491
dividends set greater than, 491
financing, 30–33
from financing activities, 35–36
between firm and financial markets, 5
firm expressed as put options and, 546–547
identification of, 5–6
incremental, determining, 241–243, 607–608
from investing activities, 34
manipulating, 34
net working capital versus, 30
operating, 32, 252–254
from operations, 30, 33, 252–254
outflows in equivalent annual cost method, 254–258
paid to creditors, 32
in payback period method, 207
in project evaluation, 247
risk of, 7
statement of cash flows, 30, 33–36
to stockholders, 32
taxes and, 441–442
timing of, 6–7
unremitted, in international finance, 642
Cash ratio, 51, 56
Cash reserves, 579
Change in net working capital, 30
Changes in fixed assets, 30–31
Chapter 11 bankruptcy, 479–481
Chicago Board Options Exchange (CBOE), 523, 524
Clean price, 154
Cleanup period, 583
Clienteles, 504–505
Closely held corporation, 9
CoCo bonds, 149
Coinsurance effect, 550
Collateral, 143
Collateral trust bonds, 143
Commercial paper, 585
Commission brokers, 188, 189

Committed lines of credit, 583
Common-size statements
balance sheets, 46–48
defined, 46
income statements, 48
Common stock. *See also* Stock markets; Stock valuation
acquisition of, 598–599
classes of, 185, 615
defined, 183
executive stock options, 14, 497
features of, 183–186
as options, 544–545, 546, 547
shareholder rights, 183–185, 613
in stock acquisitions, 610–612
Compensating balances, 583–584
Complementary resources, in mergers and acquisitions, 605
Completed contracts accounting method, 183
Compounding
compounding periods and, 101–107
continuous, 106–107
defined, 93
frequency of, 103
of growth, 176
in multiperiod case, 93–97, 105–107
power of, 96–97
Compound interest, 93
Compound value
defined, 90
in one-period case, 90–93
Conglomerate acquisition, 599
Conglomerates, financial statement analysis and, 65
Conservatism, efficient capital markets and, 404–405, 411–412
Consolidation, 598
Consolidation of debt, 461
Consols, 107–108
Constant dividend growth, 170
Continuation, serial correlation and, 399
Continuous compounding, 106–107
Contribution margin, 279
Control of firm, 14–15
Conventional factoring, 584–585
Convertible bonds, 149
Corporate charter, 612
Corporate finance. *See also* Capital budgeting; Capital structure; Financial markets; Financial statements; Financing decisions
agency problem in, 13–15
balance sheet model of firm and, 2–3
business organization in, 7–11
capital structure in, 3–4
financial manager in, 4–7
financial markets and, 15–18
goal of financial management, 11–13
implications of efficient market hypothesis for, 412–417
international. *See* International corporate finance
management goals and, 13–15
stockholder interests in, 14–15
Corporation, 9–11. *See also* Corporate finance; Debt securities; Equity securities
advantages of, 9
agency problem and, 13–15
articles of incorporation, 9
corporate tax rates, 28, 29
defined, 9
disadvantages of, 10
goal of financial management, 12–13
international. *See* International corporate finance
other forms of business organization versus, 9–11
Correlation, 323, 324–327
serial, 399, 400
in weak form efficiency, 399–401
Correlation coefficients, 399
Cost of debt capital, 376–378, 380–381
Cost of equity capital, 366–368, 379–380
Cost reduction, in mergers and acquisitions, 605
Countertender offer, 615
Coupon, 132, 135, 143
Coupon rate, 132
Covariance, 323, 324–327
Covered-call strategy, 531
Covered interest arbitrage, 636–637
Crashes, 409–411
Creditors
cash flow paid to, 32
defined, 3
Credit risk, in bond pricing, 159–160
Crossover bonds, 146
Cross-rates, 626, 629–631
"Crowd," 190
Crown jewel, 614
Cumulative abnormal returns (CARs), 401–403
Cumulative dividends, 186–187
Cumulative probability, 541–543
Cumulative voting, 184
Current assets, 24
defined, 2, 566, 575
financing of, 574, 576–580
in practice, 580
size of, 574–576
Current liabilities
defined, 2, 566
in practice, 580
Current ratio, 49–50, 56

D

Dart throwing, market efficiency and, 398
Dates convention, 110
Days' sales in inventory, 52–53, 56
Days' sales in receivables, 53, 56, 568–570, 572
Dealer markets, 15
auction markets versus, 17
defined, 16, 187–188
Debenture(s), 141, 143–144
Debt-asset ratio, 473–474
Debt beta, 374
Debt capacity, 462
Debt-equity ratio, 51, 56
capital structure and, 473–478
growth and, 471–473
in Japan, 461
MM Propositions and, 431–440
Debt securities. *See also* Leverage
agency costs of, 457–459, 468
cash flow from financing activities, 35–36

Debt securities—*Cont.*
cost of capital, 376–378, 380–381
defined, 2, 15
direct bankruptcy costs and, 456
equity securities versus, 24, 139–141, 431–440, 471–473
financing with, 438–439
long-term, 2, 141–142. *See also* Bond(s); Bond valuation
in option valuation, 538
preferred stock as type of, 187
primary markets and, 16
reducing costs of, 460–461
sale of new, 32
secondary markets and, 16–17, 150–154
short-term, 141, 577, 582–585. *See also* Note(s)
types of, 141. *See also* Bond(s); Note(s)
unused debt capacity, 606
Debt service, 24, 31
Decision trees, 272–274
Declaration date, dividend, 488–489
Default risk premium, 159–160
Deferred call provision, 144
Deferred taxes, 27
Delisting, 613–614
Delta, in option valuation, 538, 543
Depreciation
accelerated, 183, 245–246
classes of assets for, 249
defined, 27
in project evaluation, 245–247, 248–254
Depreciation tax shield, 254
Differential dividend growth, 171–172
Dilution, dividends versus stock repurchase and, 497
Direct bankruptcy costs, 456
Directors
dividends and, 186–187
election of, 183–185
information in market prices and, 416–417
interests in corporation, 9
Direct quotes, 628
Dirty price, 154
Discount bond, 134
Discounted cash flow valuation, 89–119
compounding periods, 101–107
multiperiod case, 93–101
one-period case, 90–93
simplifications in, 107–116
annuities, 110–116
perpetuities, 107–110, 176, 178–179
value of firm and, 117–118
Discounted payback period method, 209, 226–228
Discounting
defined, 97
in multiperiod case, 97–100
nominal versus real, 250–252
in one-period case, 90–93
Discount price, 631
Discount rate, 90. *See also* Interest rate(s)
in capital budgeting, 375–376
in internal rate of return (IRR), 212–213
in mergers and acquisitions, 608
in net present value analysis, 204–206
on risky project, 205
Distribution, 488
Diversifiable risk. *See* Unsystematic risk
Diversification, 342–345
effect of, 343
from mergers and acquisitions, 609
options and, 549–550
principle of, 343–344
systematic risk and, 345
unsystematic risk and, 344–345
Diversification effect
described, 329–330
efficient set and, 331–332
Divestiture, 615–616
Dividend(s), 76, 487–514
capital gains versus, 168–169
cash availability and, 498–500
cash dividend payment method, 488–490
cash flow and, 468, 498–500
characteristics of, 186
clientele effect and, 504–505
in common stock valuation, 168–175
constant growth, 170
differential growth, 171–172
dividend-discount model, 172–175
growth opportunities versus, 178
zero growth, 170
corporate dividend policy and, 505–510
defined, 186, 488
dollar returns and, 298–299
factors favoring high dividend, 501–504
irrelevance of dividend policy, 490–494
payment of, 109–110, 186
procedures for paying, 488–489
pros and cons of paying, 508–509
smoothing, 506–507
stock, 412–413, 488, 510–512
stock repurchase versus, 494–497, 499–500
survey evidence on, 509–510
taxes and, 498–501
types of, 488
Dividend payout ratio, 68, 488, 505
Dividend per share, 488
Dividend reinvestment plans (DRIPs), 520
Dividend yield, 174, 299, 488
Dollar returns, 298–299
Double taxation, 10
Dow Jones Industrial Average (DJIA), 344
Dual class capitalization, 615
Du Pont identity, 56–59, 76
applications of, 57–59, 60
described, 56–57
expanded, 58–59, 60

E

Earnings before interest and taxes (EBIT), 26, 253, 442–444, 471–473
Earnings per share (EPS), 55
earnings surprises and, 407–408
growth from mergers and acquisitions, 608–609
growth opportunities versus, 178–179
leverage and, 429–431
translation exposure, 644–645

Economies of scale, in mergers and acquisitions, 605
Economies of vertical integration, in mergers and acquisitions, 605
Effective annual rate (EAR), 103–105
Efficient frontier, 333
Efficient market hypothesis (EMH), 183, 391, 393–411
  behavioral challenge to, 404–405
  common misperceptions, 398–399
  efficient capital markets, defined, 393
  empirical challenges to, 405–411
  evidence on, 399–404
  foundations of, 394–395
  implications for corporate finance, 412–417
  implications for investors, 393–394
  speculation and, 415–416
  summary on, 417–418
  types of efficiency, 395–398, 399–404
Efficient set, 331–336
  defined, 335
  for many securities, 335–336
  two-asset case, 331–335
Electronic communications networks (ECNs), 191–193
End-of-the-year convention, 111
Equity beta, 374–375
Equity bond, preferred stock as type of, 187
Equity carve-out, 616
Equity markets, exchanges, 16–17
Equity multiplier, 51, 56
Equity securities. *See also* Common stock; Preferred stock
  agency costs of, 466–468
  auction markets for, 16–17
  cash flow from financing activities, 35–36
  cost of capital, 366–368, 379–380
  debt securities versus, 24, 139–141, 431–440, 471–473
  defined, 15
  equity shares, defined, 2
  financing with, 436–437
  primary markets and, 16
  secondary markets and, 16
Equivalent annual cost method, 254–258
Erosion, incremental cash flows and, 242
Eurobonds, 626, 627
Eurocurrency, 627
European options, 524, 534n, 536
European quotes, 628
Event studies, 401–403
  abnormal returns and, 401–403
  defined, 401
Exchange offers, signaling and, 465–466
Exchange rate(s), 628–632
  cross-rates, 629–631
  defined, 628
  quotations, 628–629
  triangle arbitrage, 629–631
  types of transactions, 631–632
Exchange rate risk, 642–645
  defined, 642
  long-run exposure, 643
  managing, 645
  short-run exposure, 642–643
  translation exposure, 644–645
Ex-dividend date, 488–489
Exercise (strike) price, 524, 527, 533–534
Exercising the option, 524
Expansion option, 284–285
Expected return
  calculating, 339–340
  on individual security, 323–324, 351–354
  on market, 351
  on portfolio, 327–328
  taxes and, 444–445
Expiration date, option, 524, 534
External financing needed (EFN), 71–78
  calculating, 69–70
  growth and, 71–74
Extra cash dividends, 488

F

Face value, 132
Factoring, 584–585
Fair price provision, 614
"Fallen angels," 146–147
Feasible set, 332–333
Field warehouse financing, 585
FIFO (first in–first out) inventory accounting, 183, 412
Fifteen-year class of depreciable assets, 249
Financial distress costs, 457. *See also* Bankruptcy costs
  capital structure and, 477
  integrating tax effects and, 461–464
  reducing costs of debt, 460–461
  signaling and, 464–466
Financial leverage
  firm value and, 429–433
  nature of, 374–375
Financial management
  bankruptcy process and, 480–481
  financial managers and, 4–7, 571
  goal of, 11–13, 427–429
Financial managers, 4–7
  in short-term finance, 571
  types of, 4–5
Financial markets, 15–18
  cash flows between firm and, 5
  primary, 16, 187
  secondary, 16–17, 150–154, 187
  types of, 15–18
Financial policy, 76
Financial ratios, 48–56
  asset management or turnover measures, 52–54, 56
  defined, 48
  long-term solvency measures, 51–52, 56
  market value measures, 55, 56
  profitability measures, 54–55, 56
  short-term solvency or liquidity measures, 49–51, 56
  sources of financial information, 62–65
Financial slack, 471
Financial statements, 22–36
  balance sheet. *See* Balance sheet
  income statement. *See* Income statement
  pro forma, 66–71
  statement of cash flows, 30, 33–36
  taxes and, 28–29
Financial statements analysis, 45–79. *See also* Balance sheet; Income statement; Statement of cash flows

Financial statements analysis—*Cont.*
common-size statements, 46–49
Du Pont identity, 56–60, 76
external financing and growth and, 69–78
in long-term financial planning, 66–71, 78
ratio analysis, 48–56
asset management or turnover measures, 52–54, 56
long-term solvency measures, 51–52, 56
market value measures, 55, 56
profitability measures, 54–55, 56
short-term solvency or liquidity measures, 49–51, 56
standardizing statements for, 46–49
using information from, 59–66
benchmarking, 59–65
problems of, 65–66
Financial structure. *See* Capital structure
Financing decisions, 390–418
cash flow from financing activities, 35–36
creating financing opportunities, 391–392
debt versus equity securities in, 139–141, 431–440
efficient capital markets and, 393–411
First in–first out (FIFO) inventory accounting, 183, 412
Fisher effect, 155–156
5B bonds, 146
Five-year class of depreciable assets, 249
Fixed assets, 24
changes in, 30–31
defined, 2
investments in, 607
Fixed costs
defined, 27, 275
in sensitivity analysis, 275
Flat-rate tax, 29
Flexibility, dividends versus stock repurchase and, 497
Flip-in provision, 613
Floating-rate bonds, 148–149
Floor brokers, 188
Floor planning, 585
Floor traders, 189
Foreign bonds, 627
Foreign currency approach to capital budgeting, 640, 641–642
Foreign exchange market, 627–632
defined, 627
participants in, 627–628
Forms of business organization, 7–11
corporation, 9–15
partnership, 8–10, 12–13
sole proprietorship, 7–10, 12–13
Forward exchange rate, 631, 636–637, 639
Forward trade, 631
Fractional coupon period, 154n
Free cash flow, 33, 468
Frequency distributions, 305–308
Future value
defined, 90
in multiperiod case, 93–97
in one-period case, 90–93

G

Generally accepted accounting principles (GAAP)
balance sheet and, 24–25
cash flow and, 34
income statement and, 26–27
General partnership, 8
Geometric average return
arithmetic average return versus, 314–315
calculating, 313–314
defined, 312
Geometric series, 107–108
Gilts, 144, 627
Globalization, 626. *See also* International corporate finance
Going-private transactions, 467, 500, 600, 613–614
Golden handcuff, 614
Golden parachute, 614
Goodwill, 601, 602–603
Government securities. *See* Municipal notes and bonds; Treasury bills (T-bills); Treasury bonds; Treasury notes
Growing annuity, 115–116
Growing perpetuity, 108–110, 176, 178–179
Growth
compound growth calculation, 176
debt-equity ratio and, 471–473
determinants of, 76–77
dividend, in stock valuation, 169–175
dividend growth model, 179–181
external financing and, 71–74
financial policy and, 74–75
internal growth rate, 74–75, 77–78
long-term financial planning and, 66–71
net present value of growth opportunity (NPVGO), 176–181
opportunities for, in stock valuation, 175–179
rates of, 176
sustainable growth rate, 75–76, 77–78, 173
value versus, 408–409

H

Half-year convention, for depreciation, 249
Hedges, 328, 579
Hockey stick diagram, 525
Holding period, 168
Holding period returns, 301–310
Home currency approach to capital budgeting, 640–641
Homemade dividends, 492–493
Homemade leverage strategy, 431–433
Homogeneous expectations, 345–346, 350–351
Horizontal acquisition, 599
Hybrid securities, 141

I

Income
cash flow versus, 241
dividend policy and desire for, 501
in project evaluation, 245–246
smoothing, 26–27
Income bonds, 149
Income statement, 25–27
common-size, 48
defined, 25–26
noncash items on, 27
percentage of sales approach to, 67–68
pro forma, 66–71
sample, 26
time and costs on, 27

Indenture, 142–145
components of, 142–145
as deed of trust, 142–143
defined, 142
Independent deviations from rationality, efficient capital markets and, 394–395, 404–405
Independent projects
defined, 214
internal rate of return (IRR) and, 214–219
profitability index and, 224
Indirect bankruptcy costs, 456–457
Indirect quotes, 628
Indivisibilities, 226
Industry
beta of, 371–372
capital structure variations by, 475–476
peer group analysis and, 61–66
INET, 191–193
Inflation
bond pricing and, 154–156
capital budgeting and, 249–254
historic rates of, 305, 309
inflation-linked bonds and, 149, 154, 157–158
inflation premium, 158–159
Inflation premium, 157
Information content effect, 503–504
Initial public offerings (IPOs), 413, 616
Innovation, impact of, 340–341, 392
Insider trading, 404
Insolvency. *See also* Financial distress costs
accounting, 478
technical, 478
Intangible assets, 24
Interest expense, in project evaluation, 249
Interest on interest. *See also* Compounding; Compound interest
concept of, 93, 94, 102
Interest rate(s). *See also* Discount rate
in bond valuation, 135–137, 154–159
covered interest arbitrage, 636–637
effective annual (EAR), 103–105
floating, 148–149
nominal, 154–156
option valuation and, 536
real, 154–156
stated annual (SAIR), 102, 103–105
term structure of, 156–160
uncovered interest parity (UIP), 639
Interest rate parity, 637–638
Interest rate risk, 135–137, 156–159
Interest rate risk premium, 158–159
Internal financing, pecking-order theory and, 470
Internal growth rate, 74–75, 77–78
Internal rate of return (IRR), 212–224
advantages of, 223–224
comparing incremental IRR to discount rate, 222–223
defined, 212
investing versus financing decisions and, 216
investment rule for, 212–213
IRR rule, 212–213
modified, 217–218
multiple rates of return and, 216–219
mutually exclusive projects and, 214–215, 219–223
NPV versus, 215, 217, 219–221, 223–224, 226–228
in practice of capital budgeting, 226–228
problems with, 214–223
International corporate finance, 625–646
bonds in, 144, 626, 627
capital budgeting in, 640–642
corporate form of organization and, 10–11
exchange rate risk in, 642–645
foreign exchange markets and exchange rates in, 627–632
forward rates and, 631, 636–637, 639
interest rate parity and, 637–638
international Fisher effect (IFE) and, 639–640
political risk in, 645
purchasing power parity and, 632–636
terminology of, 626–627
International corporations, 626
International Fisher effect (IFE), 639–640
Internet stock bubble, 410–411
Intrinsic value of options, 532–536
Inventory, 24
accounting for, 183, 412–413
blanket lien, 585
days' sales in, 52–53, 56
Inventory loans, 585
Inventory period, 568, 570, 572
Inventory turnover, 52, 56, 572
Investments. *See also* Capital budgeting
cash flow from, 34
dividend policy and, 494
dividends versus stock repurchase and, 497, 499–500
in project evaluation, 244–245
selfish strategies and bankruptcy, 457–460
IRR rule, 212–213
ISDEX, 390

J

Japan, debt-equity ratios in, 461
Joint stock companies, 10–11
Joint venture, 600
Junior debt, 144
Junk bonds, 146–147

L

Large-company common stocks, holding period returns on, 301, 302, 303, 306–307, 308, 309
Large stock dividends, 510, 511
Last in–first out (LIFO) inventory accounting, 183, 412
Letters of credit, 584
Level coupon bond, 132
Leverage
bankruptcy costs and, 461–464
debt versus equity and, 431–440
financial, 374–375, 429–433
homemade leverage strategy, 431–433
MM Propositions and, 431–440, 444–445
operating, 372–374
taxes and, 431–445
Leveraged buyouts (LBOs), 467, 500, 600, 613–614
Liabilities, defined, 24
LIFO (last in–first out) inventory accounting, 183, 412

Limited liability company (LLC), 10–11
Limited liability instrument, call options as, 525
Limited partnership, 8
Limit orders, 193
Liquidating dividend, 488
Liquidation
  bankruptcy, 478–480
  defined, 478
Liquidity, 24
Liquidity measures, 49–51, 56
  cash ratio, 51, 56
  current ratio, 49–50, 56
  quick (acid-test) ratio, 50–51, 56
Liquidity premium, 160
Listings, exchange, 17, 18
Loan guarantees, 548–549
Lockup, 614
London Interbank Offer Rate (LIBOR), 627
London Stock Exchange, 17, 18
Long-lived assets, 2
Long run, defined, 27
Long-term assets, 577
Long-term debt, 2, 141–142. *See also* Bond(s); Bond valuation
  holding period returns on, 301, 302, 303, 309
  types of, 142
Long-term planning
  caveats concerning, 78
  for growth, 77–78
  percentage of sales approach to, 67–70
  pro forma statements in, 66–71
  scenarios in, 70–71
  simple model for, 66–67
Long-term solvency measures, 51–52, 56
  cash coverage, 52, 56
  debt-equity ratio, 51, 56, 431–440, 471–478
  equity multiplier, 51, 56
  times interest earned, 51–52, 56
  total debt ratio, 51, 56
Lotteries, 104, 111

M

MACRS (Modified Accelerated Cost Recovery System), 245–246
"Make-whole" call, 144–145
Making a market, 17
Management buyouts (MBOs), 500, 600, 613–614
Management by exception, 60
Marginal tax rate, 28–29
Market capitalization, efficient capital markets and, 408, 409
Market equilibrium, 345–351
Marketing, acquisitions and, 604
Market makers, 188, 190
Market portfolio, 346–349
Market power, in mergers and acquisitions, 605
Market prices
  in bond valuation, 16, 150–154
  information in, 416–417
  market efficiency and fluctuations in, 398
  option prices and, 534–535
  taxes and taxation and, 445–446
Market risk. *See* Systematic risk
Market-to-book ratio, 55, 56
Market value
  book value versus, 25
  defined, 25
  in mergers and acquisitions, 607
Market value measures, 55, 56
  market-to-book ratio, 55, 56
  price-earnings (PE) ratio, 55, 56, 181–183
Maturity
  bond, 132, 135–137, 141
  interest rate risk and, 135–137
Maturity hedging, 579
Mean, 305–308
Members, New York Stock Exchange (NYSE), 188–189
Merger. *See also* Mergers and acquisitions
  advantages and disadvantages of, 598
  alternatives to, 600
  defined, 597–598
Mergers and acquisitions, 596–615
  accounting for, 601–603
  benefits of, 603–608
  cost of, 609–612
    cash acquisition, 610
    cash versus common stock, 611–612
    stock acquisition, 610–611
  defensive tactics in, 600, 612–615
  dividend payments and, 499
  evidence on, 615
  financial side effects of, 608–609
  impact of, 416
  legal forms of acquisitions, 597–600
  options and, 549–550
  problems in, 597
  taxes and, 600–601, 606–607, 611
Microcaps, 192
Milking the property, 459
MIPS (monthly income preferred securities), 187
MM Proposition I, 431–440
  described, 431–433
  no-tax environment and, 433–440, 469–470
  taxes and, 443–447
MM Proposition II, 434–440, 443–447
Modified Accelerated Cost Recovery System (MACRS), 245–246
Modified internal rate of return, 217–218
Money markets
  core of, 16
  defined, 15
Monte Carlo simulation, 280–283
  defined, 280
  steps in, 280–283
Mortgage securities, 143, 150
Multinational corporations. *See* International corporate finance
Municipal notes and bonds, 147–148, 160
Mutual funds
  performance of, 403
  semistrong efficiency and, 403
  trading activity of, 512
Mutually exclusive projects
  agency costs and, 457–458
  defined, 215
  internal rate of return and, 214–215, 219–223
  profitability index and, 224–225

N

Nanocaps, 192
NASDAQ, 17, 187, 190–193, 390
  delisting by, 513
  described, 190–191
  dividend payouts and, 505–506
  New York Stock Exchange versus, 190
  participants, 191–193
  reporting by, 193
  separate markets within, 190–191
National Association of Securities Dealers Automated Quotations. *See* NASDAQ
Negative capital gains, 298–299
Negative coupon bonds, 131, 149
Negative covenant, 145
Net cash inflow, 582
Net operating losses (NOL), in mergers and acquisitions, 606
Net present value (NPV). *See also* Present value
  algebraic formula for, 101
  attributes of, 205–206
  calculating, 91–93
  in capital budgeting, 203–206, 208, 211, 550–552
  comparing NPVs, 222–223
  concept of, 91–92
  decision trees and, 272–274
  dividend smoothing and, 506–507
  of firm, 117–118
  indifference position for dividends, 491–492
  internal rate of return versus, 215, 217, 219–221, 223–224, 226–228
  investments of unequal lives and, 254–258
  of merger, 609–610
  in Monte Carlo simulation, 283
  in multiperiod case, 93–101
  nominal versus real, 250–252
  NPV rule, 204–206, 217
  in one-period case, 90–93
  other methods versus, 208, 211, 215, 217
  in practice of capital budgeting, 226–228
  in project evaluation, 247
  reasons for using, 204–206
  scenario analysis and, 277–278
  sensitivity analysis and, 275–278, 283
  uncertainty and, 92
Net present value (per share) of growth opportunity (NPVGO), 176–181
Net profit, in break-even analysis, 278–279
Net working capital
  additions to, 31
  cash flow versus, 30
  change in, 30
  defined, 2, 30, 244, 566–567
  in project evaluation, 248
  tracing, 566–567
"New economy," 274
News, impact of, 340–341
New York Stock Exchange (NYSE), 188–190, 301
  as auction market, 16–17, 187
  bonds on, 150–151
  classes of stock and, 185
  dividend payouts and, 505–506
  floor activity and, 189–190
  listings on, 17, 18
  members of, 188–189
  NASDAQ versus, 190
  operations of, 189
  reporting by, 193–195
Nominal cash flow, 249–252
Nominal interest rates, 154–156
Noncash items, 27
Noncumulative dividends, 186–187
Nondiversifiable risk. *See* Systematic risk
Nonmarketed claims, 464
NoNo bonds, 149
Normal distribution, 311–312
North American Industry Classification System (NAICS), 62–65
Note(s), 141, 143–144
  municipal, 147–148, 160
  Treasury, 147, 152–154, 159
NPV rule, 204–206, 217

O

Odd lots, 512
Omnibus Budget Reconciliation Act (1993), 28
Open market purchases, 494–497
Operating cash flow, 30–33
  alternative definitions of, 252–254
  bottom-up approach to, 253
  defined, 32
  tax shield approach to, 254
  top-down approach to, 253–254
Operating cycle, 568–574
  accounts receivable period in, 53, 56, 568–570, 572
  applications of, 570
  calculating, 573
  cash cycle and, 569
  defined, 568, 572
  inventory period in, 568, 570, 572
  organization chart and, 571
Operating leverage, 372–374
Opportunity costs
  incremental cash flows and, 245
  in net present value analysis, 204–206
  in project evaluation, 245
Opportunity set, 332–333
Option(s), 523–555
  American, 524, 534, 536
  bonds as, 545, 546–549
  call. *See* Call option(s)
  combinations of, 529–532
  corporate decisions and, 549–552
  defined, 524
  European, 524, 534, 536
  option pricing formula, 536–543
  put. *See* Put option(s)
  quotes on, 528–529
  real, 284–288, 552–554
  selling, 527–528
  stock, 14, 497
  stocks as, 544–545, 546, 547
  terminology used with, 524
  valuing, 523, 532–536, 537, 539–543
Order costs, 575

Order flow, 189
Ordinary annuity, 113–114
Organization charts, 4, 571
OTC. *See* Over-the-counter (OTC) markets
Out-of-sample tests, 412
Out-of-the-money options, 524–525
Over-the-Counter Bulletin Board (OTCBB), 192
Over-the-counter (OTC) markets
  for bonds, 150–154
  defined, 16
  examples of, 17
  for stocks, 17, 187, 190–193
Overvalued firm, 469

P

Pacific Stock Exchange, 17
"Pac-man" defense, 615
Partnership
  corporation versus, 9–10
  defined, 8
  factors in using, 8
  goal of financial management, 12–13
  types of, 8
Par value, 132
Par value bond, 132
Payables turnover, 53, 573
Payback period method, 206–209
  investment rule for, 206–207
  management perspective on, 208
  NPV method versus, 208
  in practice of capital budgeting, 206–209, 226–228
  problems with, 207–208
Payback rule, 206–207
Payment date, dividend, 488–489
Payoff of call options, 525
Pecking-order theory, 468–471
  described, 468–470
  implications of, 470–471
  rules of pecking order, 470
Peer group analysis, 61–66
Penny stocks, 192
Percentage-of-completion accounting method, 183
Percentage of sales approach, 67–70
Percentage returns, 299–301
Period costs, 27
Perks, 466–467
Perpetuity, 107–110
  defined, 107–108
  delayed, 112–113
  growing, 108–110, 176, 178–179
Phantom interest, 148
Pie model, of capital structure, 427, 439–442, 463–464
Pink Sheets, 192
Planning
  floor, 585
  long-term, 66–71, 77–78
  short-term, 586
Plowback ratio, 68
Poison pill, 612, 613
Poison put, 614
Political risk, 645
Pooling of interests accounting method, 602
Portfolio beta, 353
Portfolio risk, 327–331, 336–337, 342–345
Positive covenant, 145
Post, exchange floor, 17
Preemptive right, 185–186
Preferred stock. *See also* Stock markets
  defined, 186
  features of, 186–187
Premium bond, 134
Premium price, 631
Prepackaged bankruptcies, 480
Present value. *See also* Net present value
  of annuity, 110–116, 133–135
  in bond valuation, 133–135
  in break-even analysis, 279–280
  of common stocks, 168–172
  defined, 90
  of firm, 117–118
  in multiperiod case, 97–100
  in one-period case, 90–93
  of perpetuity, 107–110
  of tax shield, 442
Present value factor, 97–99
Price-earnings (PE) ratio, 55, 56, 181–183
Primary markets
  debt, 16
  equity, 187
Principal value, 143
Principle of diversification, 343–344
Private placements, 16, 142
Product costs, defined, 27
Profitability index (PI)
  application of, 224–226
  calculating, 224
  defined, 224
  in practice of capital budgeting, 226–228
Profitability measures, 54–55, 56
  profit margin, 54, 56, 76, 77
  return on assets (ROA), 54, 56–59, 429–431
  return on equity (ROE), 54–55, 56–59, 76–77, 173–175
Profit margin, 54, 56, 76, 77
Profit maximization
  debt and, 471
  as goal of financial management, 11–12, 427–429
Profit repatriation, 625
Pro forma financial statements
  defined, 66
  in long-term financial planning, 66–71
Project net income, 253
Property valuation, weighted average cost of capital (WACC) in, 382
Protective covenant, 145, 460–461
Protective puts, 529–530
Proxy, 185
Proxy contests, 15, 185, 600
Proxy fights, 15, 185
Proxy voting, 185
Public issues, of long-term debt, 142

Public limited companies, 10–11
Purchase accounting method, 601–602
Purchasing power parity (PPP), 632–636
absolute, 632–633, 634
currency appreciation and depreciation, 636
defined, 632
relative, 633–636
Put bonds, 149
Put-call parity, 530–532, 547–548
Put option(s), 526–527
defined, 526
firm expressed in terms of, 546–547
put-call parity and, 530–532, 547–548
selling, 527–528
valuation of, 536
value at expiration, 526–527

Q

Quick (acid-test) ratio, 50–51, 56
QUIPS (quarterly income preferred securities), 187

R

Ratio analysis, 48–56
asset management or turnover measures, 52–54, 56
long-term solvency measures, 51–52, 56
market value measures, 55, 56
profitability measures, 54–55, 56
short-term solvency or liquidity measures, 49–51, 56
Rationality, efficient capital markets and, 394–395, 404–405
Real cash flow, 250–252
Real interest rates, 154–156
Real options, 284–288, 552–554
defined, 284
option to abandon, 285–287
option to expand, 284–285
timing options, 287–288
Receivables turnover, 53, 56, 572
Record date, dividend, 488–489
Registered form, **143**
Registrar, 143
Registration statements, 16
Regular cash dividends, 488
Relative interest rates, 579
Relative purchasing power parity, 633–636
Rembrandt bonds, 627
Reorganization
bankruptcy, 479–480
defined, 478
Repayment, long-term debt, 144
Replacement decisions
equivalent annual cost and, 256–258
general decision to replace, 256–258
Representativeness, efficient capital markets and, 404, 411
Reserves, cash, 579
Restructurings, 615–616
Retained earnings, in dividend-discount model, 172–175
Retention ratio, 68
defined, 173
in dividend-discount model, 173
Return(s), 298–310. *See also* Capital asset pricing model (CAPM)
average stock, 308–310, 312–315
dollar, 298–299
expected, 323–324, 327–328, 339–340, 351–354
historic, 306–307
holding period, 301–310
individual security, 323–327
leverage and, 429–431
percentage, 299–301
portfolio, 327–331
relationship between risk and, 351–354
risk-free, 308–310
to shareholders, 429–431
statistics concerning, 305–308
systematic components of, 342
unexpected, 339–340
unsystematic components of, 342
Return on assets (ROA), 54, 56
in Du Pont identity, 56–59
leverage and, 429–431
Return on book, 54–55, 56
Return on book equity, 54–55, 56
Return on equity (ROE), 54–55, 56
determinants of growth and, 76–77
in dividend-discount model, 173–175
in Du Pont identity, 56–59, 76
leverage and, 429–431
Return on the retained earnings, in dividend-discount model, 172–175
Revenues
acquisitions and, 604–605
cyclicality of, 372
in sensitivity analysis, 275
Reversal, serial correlation and, 399
Reverse splits, 512–513
Revolving credit arrangement, 583
Rights
shareholder, 183–186, 613
share rights plans (SRPs), 612–613
Risk. *See also* Beta; Capital asset pricing model (CAPM)
of cash flows, 7
exchange rate, 642–645
firm versus project, 375–376
individual security, 323–327, 351–354
interest rate, 135–137, 156–159
in option valuation, 538–539
political, 645
portfolio, 327–331, 336–337, 342–345
relationship between return and, 351–354
riskless borrowing and lending, 336–339
systematic, 341–342, 345
unsystematic, 341–342, 344–345
when investors hold portfolio, 346–349
Risk-free returns, 308–310
Risk-neutral investors, 538–539
Risk premium, 309
default risk premium, 159–160
interest rate risk premium, 158–159
Rounding errors, 46
Round lots, 512
Round trip trades, 34

S

Sales
  in cash budget, 580–581
  days' sales in inventory, 52–53, 56
  days' sales in receivables, 53, 56, 568–570, 572
  percentage of sales approach, 67–70
Salvage value, in project evaluation, 247
Samurai bonds, 627
Sarbanes-Oxley Act (Sarbox; 2002), 18, 192
Scale problem, internal rate of return and, 219–221
Scenario analysis, 70–71, 277–278, 283
"Scorched earth" strategy, 614
Seasoned equity offerings (SEOs), 413–415
Secondary markets
  debt, 16–17, 150–154
  equity, 187
Secured loans, 584–585
Securitized bonds, 150
Security beta, 368–369, 374–375
Security market line, 352–354, 398
Selling, general, and administrative expense, 27
Semistrong form efficiency
  described, 396–398, 418
  evidence for, 401–403, 414–415
    event studies, 401–403
    mutual fund performance and, 403
Senior debt, 144
Seniority, bond, 144
Sensitivity analysis, 275–278, 283
Serial correlation, 399, 400
Seven-year class of depreciable assets, 249
Shareholder(s)
  defined, 3
  interests in corporation, 9, 14–15
  maximizing value of stock of, 12–13, 15, 427–429, 615
Shareholder rights, common stock, 183–185, 613
Shareholders' equity
  defined, 2, 23
  maximizing value of, 12–13, 15, 427–429
Share rights plans (SRPs), 612–613
Shark repellent, 614
Sharpe ratio, 311
Shirking, 466–467
Shortage costs, 575, 576
Short run, 27
Short-term debt, 141, 577, 582–585. *See also* Note(s)
  other sources of, 585
  secured loans, 584–585
  unsecured loans, 583–584
Short-term finance, 565–587
  cash cycle in, 53, 568–574
  cash in, 566–567
  defined, 566
  managers dealing with, 571
  net working capital in. *See* Net working capital
  operating cycle in, 568–574
Short-term planning, 586
Signaling
  dividends and, 503–504, 508
  nature of, 464–466
Simulation. *See* Monte Carlo simulation
Sinking fund, 144, 187
Small-company common stocks, holding period returns on, 301, 302, 303, 308, 309
Small stock dividends, 510–511
Smoothing dividends, 506–507
Smoothing income, 26–27
Sole proprietorship
  corporation versus, 9–10
  defined, 7
  factors in using, 7–8
  goal of financial management, 12–13
Solvency measures
  long-term, 51–52
  short-term, 49–51, 56
Specialists, 17, 188
Specialist's post, 189–190
Specific risk. *See* Unsystematic risk
Speculation, efficient market hypothesis (EMH) and, 415–416
Spin-off, 616
Split ratings, 146
Split-up, 616
Spot exchange rate, 631
Spot trades, 631
Spreadsheet techniques
  calculating annuity present values, 112
  calculating bond prices and yields, 140
  calculating IRR, 214
  calculating NPV, 206
  calculating present values, 102
Staggered elections, 184–185
Stakeholders, 15
Standard deviation
  defined, 310
  individual security, 310–312, 323
  portfolio, 329
Standard Industrial Classification (SIC) codes, 61–62, 63–64
Standardized normal distribution, 541
Standard & Poor's 500 Index, 45, 182, 301, 330–331, 346, 565
Standstill agreements, 612
Stated annual interest rate (SAIR), 102, 103–105
Stated value, of preferred shares, 186
Statement of cash flows, 30, 33–36
Static trade-off theory of capital structure, 462, 470–471
Stock dividends, 412–413, 488, 510–512
  defined, 510
  examples of, 510–511
  value of, 511–512
Stockholder disinterest, market efficiency and, 398–399
Stockholders' books, 247
Stockholders' equity, defined, 24
Stock markets, 187–195
  dealers and brokers in, 188–189
  listed markets, 188–190, 193–195
  over-the-counter, 17, 187, 190–193
  reporting in, 193–195
  types of, 187–188
Stock options, 14, 497
Stockouts, 248, 575
Stock repurchase, 494–497, 499–500, 612
Stock splits, 412–413, 488
  defined, 510
  example of, 511

reverse, 512–513
value of, 511–512
Stock valuation, 167–195
common stock features and, 183–186
dividend-discount model of, 172–175
dividend growth model in, 179–181
dividends versus capital gains in, 168–169
growth opportunities of firm in, 175–179
net present value of growth opportunity (NPVGO) and, 176–181
preferred stock features and, 186–187
present value of common stocks and, 168–172
price-earnings (PE) ratio in, 55, 56, 181–183
types of stock and, 169–172
Straight-line depreciation, 183
Straight voting, 184, 185
Strategic alliance, 600
Strike (exercise) price, 524, 527, 533–534
Strong form efficiency
described, 396–398, 418
evidence for, 403–404, 414–415
Subordinated debt, 144
Sunk costs, 241
SuperDOT system, 188
Supermajority amendment, 612
Surplus funds, 606
Surprise, impact of, 340–341
Sustainable growth rate, 75–76, 77–78, 173
Swaps, 627
Sweepstakes, 104
Synergy
acquisitions and, 603–604, 607
incremental cash flows and, 242
options and, 549–550
Synthetic T-bills, 532
Systematic risk, 341–342, 345

T

Takeovers, 15. *See also* Mergers and acquisitions
defensive tactics, 600, 612–615
jargon of, 614–615
nature of, 599–600
political risk and, 645
Tangible fixed assets, 24
Targeted repurchase, 495, 612
Tax(es), 28–29
average versus marginal tax rates, 28–29
capital structure and, 440–447, 469–470, 477
corporate tax rates, 28, 29
corporations and, 10
deferred, 27
depreciation tax shield, 254
dividends versus stock repurchase and, 497, 501
in financing decisions, 391
integrating financial distress costs and, 461–464
leverage and, 431–445
in mergers and acquisitions, 600–601, 606–607, 611
on municipal notes and bonds, 147–148, 160
personal, 498–501
in project evaluation, 245–249
Taxability premium, 160
Tax books, 247
Tax Reform Act (1986), 28, 248–249
Tax shield, 254, 442, 446, 606
Tender offer, 495, 598–599, 615
Ten-year class of depreciable assets, 249
Terms of bond, 143
Term structure of interest rates, 156–160
Texas Comptroller of Public Accounts, 382
Texas State Court, 457
Three-year class of depreciable assets, 249
Times interest earned, 51–52, 56
Time-trend analysis, 60
Timing
of cash flows, 6–7
efficient market hypothesis and, 413–415
internal rate of return and, 221–223
pecking-order theory and, 468–471
as real option, 287–288
TIPS (Treasury Inflation Protection Securities), 149, 154, 157–158
Tokyo Stock Exchange, 17
Top management. *See also* Financial managers
agency problem and, 13–15
control of firm and, 14–15
inefficient, in mergers and acquisitions, 608
information in market prices and, 416–417
interests in corporation, 9
managerial compensation and, 14, 497
shareholder interests and, 9, 14–15
stock options for, 14, 497
takeovers and, 614
TOPrS (trust-originated preferred securities; toppers), 187
Total asset turnover, 53–54, 56, 76
Total bond value, 133–135
Total cash flow of the firm, 33, 35–36
Total debt ratio, 51, 56
Trade credit, 585
Trade-off theory of capital structure, 462, 470–471
Trading range, 512
Transactions Report and Compliance Engine (TRACE), 151–154
Translation exposure, 644–645
Transparency, 150–151
Treasury bills (T-bills)
holding period returns on, 301, 302, 303, 306–307, 309–310
risk-free returns and, 308–310
Treasury bonds, 147–149, 152–154, 157–158, 159, 165
holding period returns on, 301, 302, 306–307, 309
Treasury notes, 147, 152–154, 159
Treasury yield curve, 159
Triangle arbitrage, 630–631
Trust deeds, 143
Trust receipt, 585
Turnover measures. *See* Asset management ratios
Twenty-year class of depreciable assets, 249

U

Unbiased forward rates (UFR), 636–637
Uncommitted lines of credit, 583
Uncovered interest parity (UIP), 639
Underinvestment, 458–459
Underwriting, 16

Unequal lives, equivalent annual cost method for, 254–258
Unfunded debt, 141
Unique risk. *See* Unsystematic risk
United States securities. *See* Treasury bills (T-bills); Treasury bonds; Treasury notes
U.S. Securities and Exchange Commission (SEC), 16, 18, 404
Unsecured loans, 583–584
Unsystematic risk
  diversification and, 344–345
  nature of, 341–342

V

Valuation
  bond. *See* Bond valuation
  discounted cash flow. *See* Discounted cash flow valuation
  option, 532–536
    Black-Scholes option pricing model, 523, 537, 539–543
    call option, 532–536
    put option, 536
  stock. *See* Stock valuation
  value of the firm, 117–118
    expressed in terms of call options, 544–545
    expressed in terms of put options, 546–547
Value additivity, 205
Value Line Investment Survey, 350
Value of the firm, 3, 117–118, 464
Variable costs
  defined, 27, 275
  in sensitivity analysis, 275
Variance
  defined, 310
  individual security, 310–311, 323–324
  portfolio, 328–329, 332, 333
Vertical acquisition, 599
Vertical integration, 605

W

Wall Street Journal
  bond quotes in, 151–154
  stock quotes in, 193–195
Warrants, 131, 149
Weak form efficiency
  described, 396, 418
  evidence for, 399–401
Weighted average cost of capital (WACC), 365, 377–378
  calculating, 381–383
  debt capital, 376–378, 380–381
  equity capital, 366–368, 379–380
  example of, 379–380
  government use of, 382
  in property valuation, 382
  taxes and, 445, 461–462
What-if analysis, 275–278
White knight, 614
Whitemail, 614
Working capital. *See also* Short-term finance
  investments in, 607
  in project evaluation, 245
Workout, 481
Write-up effect, 601

Y

Yankee bonds, 627
Yield
  bond, 137–139, 156–160
  capital gains, 174
  dividend, 174, 299, 488
Yield to maturity (YTM), 132–135, 137–139, 156–160

Z

Zero coupon bonds, 148
Zero dividend growth, 170